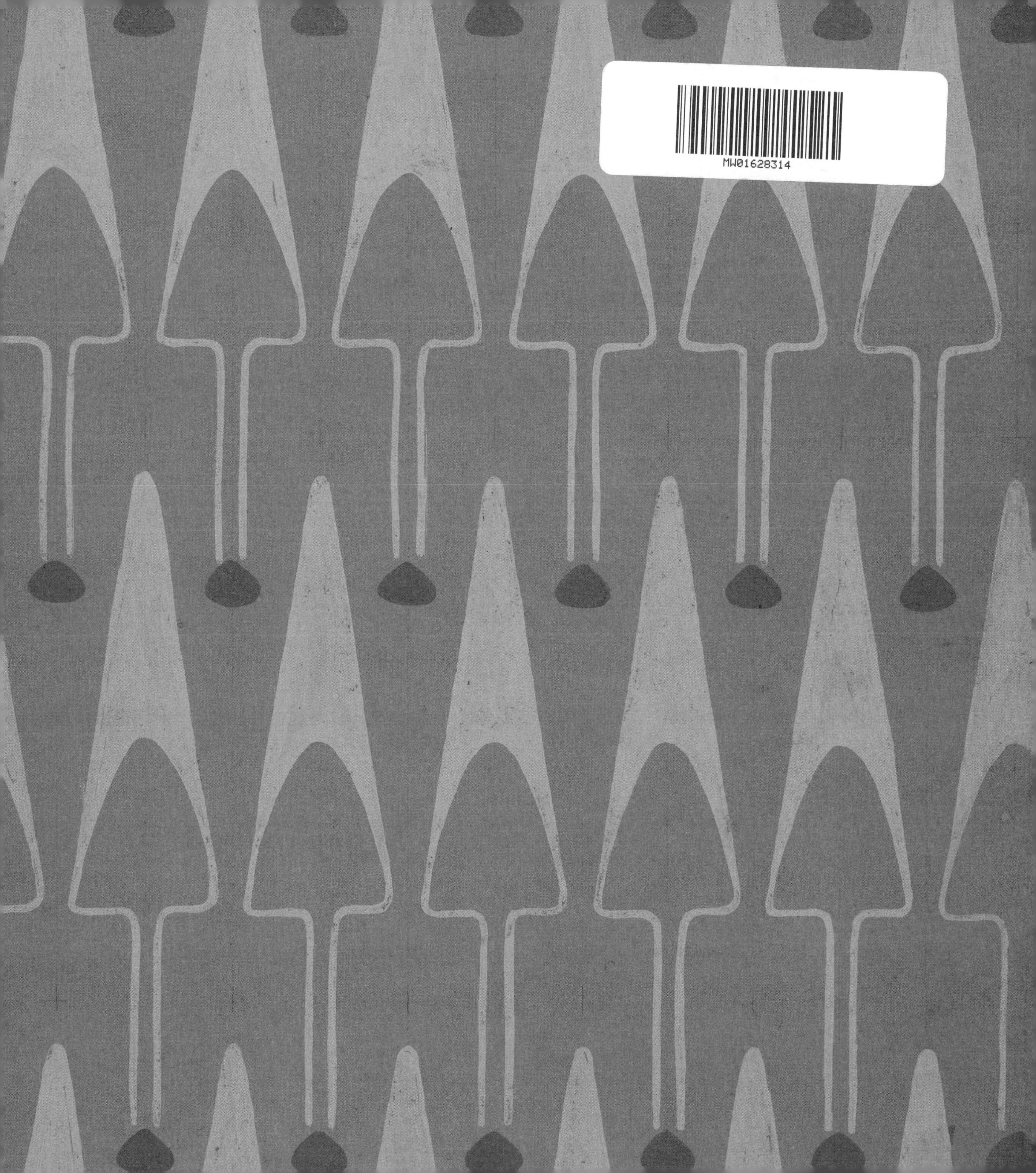
MW01628314

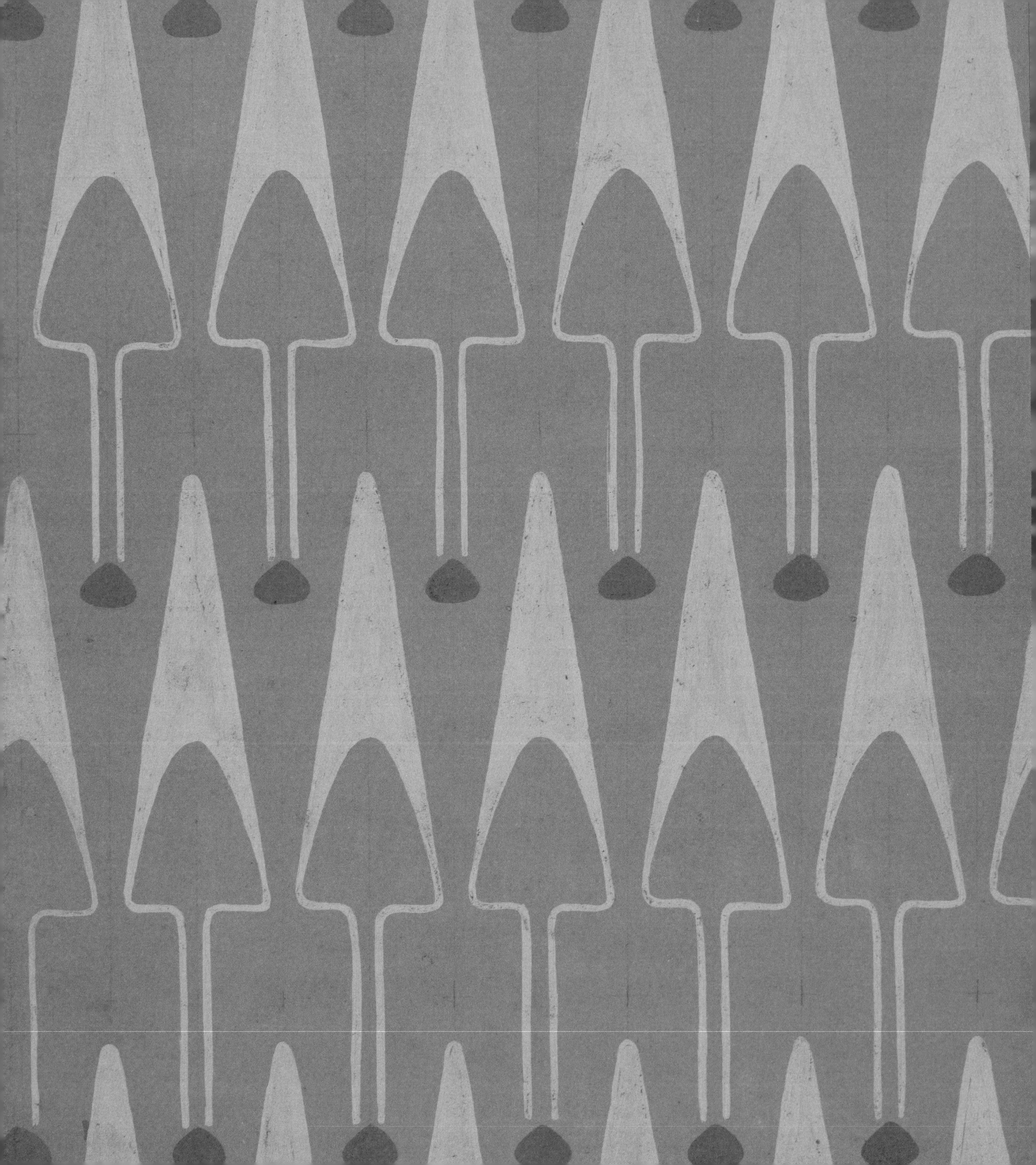

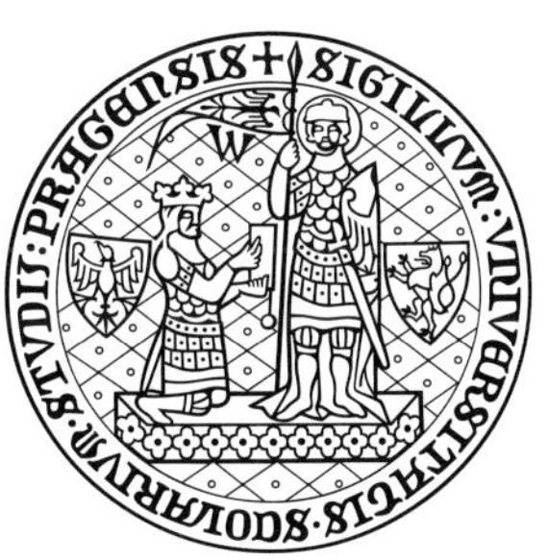

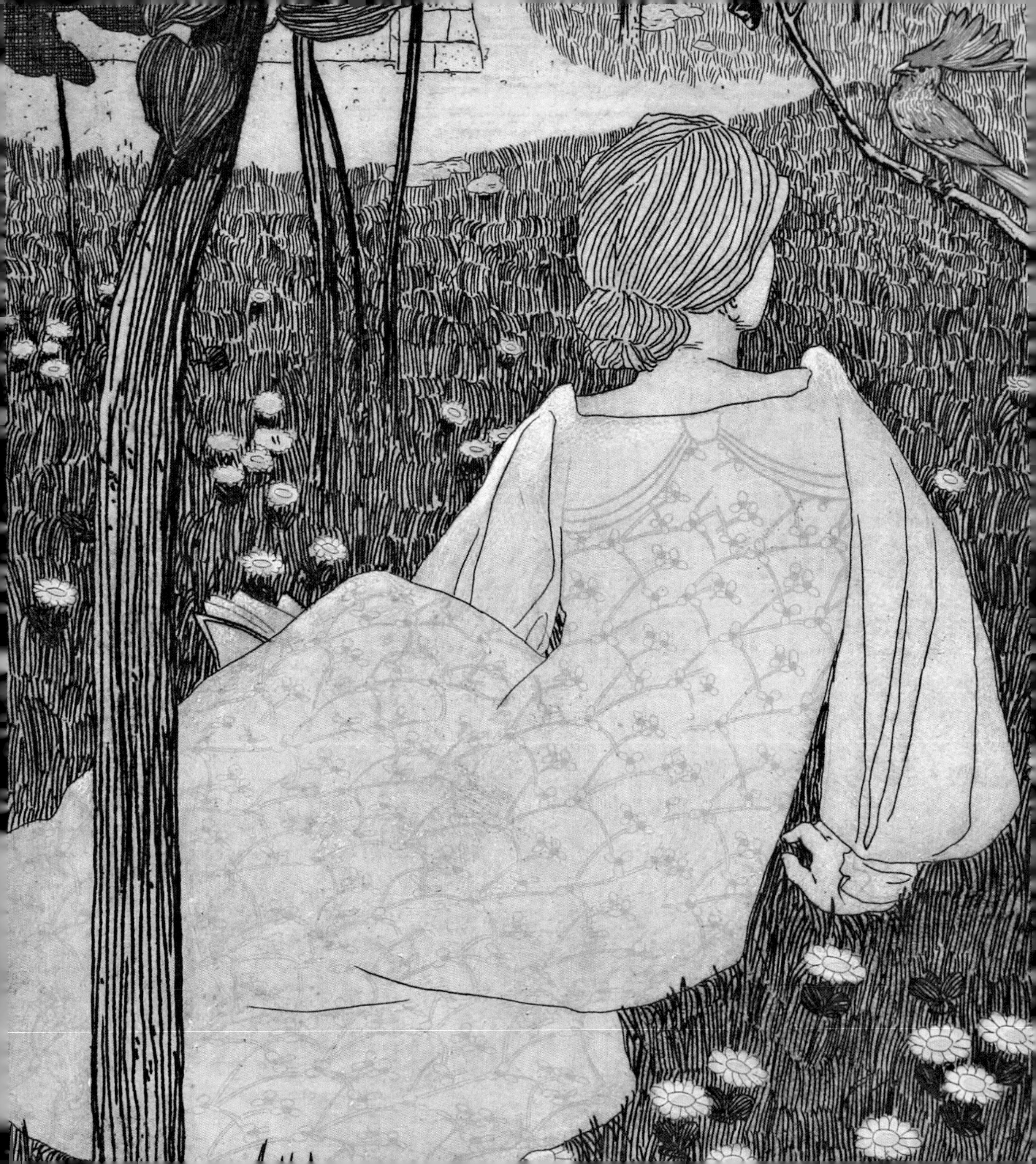

PETR WITTLICH

CZECH SECESSION

ART AND ARCHITECTURE 1890–1914

CHARLES UNIVERSITY
KAROLINUM PRESS

ISBN 978-80-246-5133-0

CONTENTS

For Jana

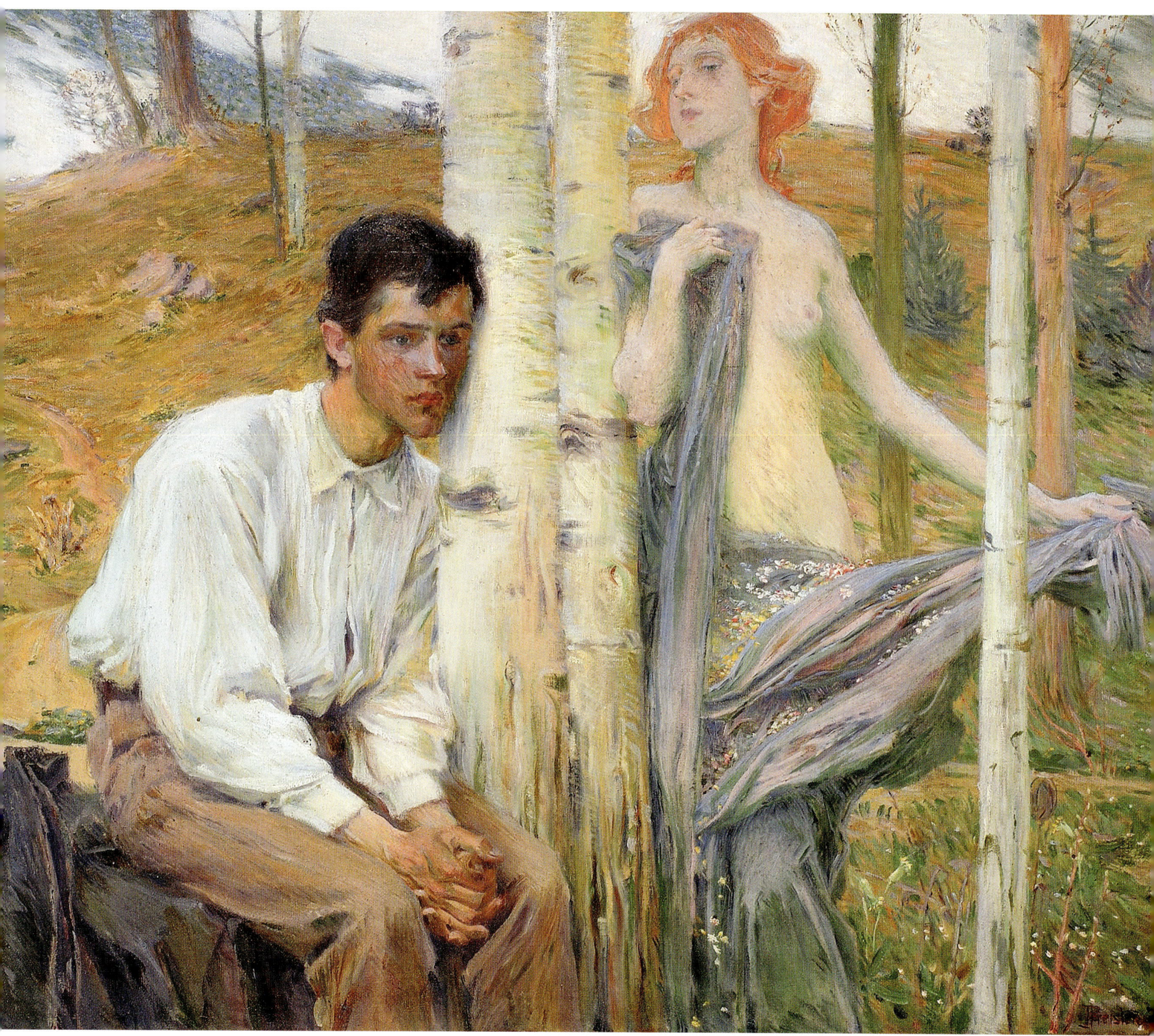

1 Jan Preisler, *Spring*, centre of the triptych, 1900, oil, 112 × 186 cm, detail

What birds plunge through is not that intimate space
in which you feel all forms intensified.
(There, in the Open, you'd be denied yourself
and vanish on and on without return.)

Space reaches out from us and translates each thing
to accomplish a tree's essence
cast inner space around it, out of that space
that has its life in you. Surround it with restraint.
In itself it has no bounds. Only in the spell
of your renouncing does it rise as Tree.

Rainer Maria Rilke
(translated by Edward Snow)

SECESSION

The late 19th and early 20th century heralded a remarkable flourishing in Czech art. A large and dynamic generation of painters, sculptors, architects, and decorative artists reached maturity in the 1890s, and by the end of the decade they had created new work that had fundamentally transformed the Czech scene and laid the foundations for all subsequent Czech modern art.

In the spring of 1898, Spolek výtvarných umělců Mánes (the Mánes Association of Fine Artists, known as SVU Mánes), which had become the nucleus of this generation, opened its first exhibition at the Topič Salon in Prague. There, the association's chairman, sculptor Stanislav Sucharda, delivered a collectively drafted speech in which he announced that the exhibition was "a decisive corporate showcasing of our young generation of artists, whose allegiance is to the banner of modern art."[1]

Modernity had become the watchword for new thinking on art and its manifestations. It meant above all a disdain for the prevailing eclecticism and false idealism "in thought, in form and in colour." The young rejected historicism, the guiding principle for the art of earlier generations, and demanded originality. They sought to release art from the influence of established models and the narrative burden imposed by the general public. At the time, their manifesto was heresy:

> Many still believe that the mere question of colour, or the mere resolving of a decorative task, is insufficient for artistic gratification, and on the other hand that intellectual content without adequate artistic expression can pass muster and suffices for the qualification of an artwork. What is generally forgotten is that, just as there are ideas that we could call literary, and ideas that are musical, there are also ideas that are painterly, and their justification is in no way lesser. Many an impression that is absolutely inexpressible in words can still be captured by brush on canvas, or sung in mysterious melodies, and who can say that this impression or that idea is less valuable?

This programme, emphasising the specific character of the discovery and embrace of reality in art, held up the study of nature as a counterweight to convention. Nature was again proclaimed to be "the eternal and most reliable teacher for any true art," offering an opportunity for a new revival and pointing the way out of the current impasse.

> [Nature] removes the moralist's or the philosopher's spectacles from the painter's eye and permits the candid expression of his individuality and his mastering of the material. From nature springs the new art's creativity, opposed to all uniformity of thought and expression, to Mannerism and secondary and banal conclusions that facilitate a deficiency of artistic quality.

This combination of the notion of modernity and the focus on nature became the guiding principle for the young generation. These artists' emphatic opposition to traditionalism also had another label. Recalling the first SVU Mánes exhibition, Miloš Jiránek, who had become a prominent spokesman for his generation, wrote, "Barely nine months have passed since the first one. We all welcomed it then as an event that, in our narrow confines, was frankly epochal, and we greeted it as a bold act, and declared it a *secession*."[2]

The original meaning of *secession* was concerned not with art, but morality. For educated people schooled in classical history and culture, it was chiefly associated with the *secessio plebis*, the story of what was perhaps the first ever general strike, when the people of Rome, dissatisfied with patrician rule, relocated to the Sacred Mount and refused to return to the city until their demands were met. In the latter half of the 19th century, the word was popularised by one of the most widely discussed events at the time, the American Civil War, when the southern states that had broken away from the Union were referred to in newspaper jargon as "the secession." On this basis, in the 1890s the word *secession* was also applied to new groups of young artists who, following the example of the Salon des Indépendants in France, demanded the right to hold public exhibitions of unconventional art.

It was thus that the Munich Secession was founded in April 1892. As one of the leading centres of art in the 19th century, Munich had in place all the preconditions for a conflict between old and new. The magazine *Jugend* (Youth), first published in 1896, would then stimulate new art throughout Central Europe. In 1897 another Secession was established in the Austro-Hungarian capital, Vienna, and a year later it was followed by the Berlin Secession, where there had been turmoil since the beginning of the decade as the new artistic sentiment came into conflict with the German emperor's despotism. Incidentally, the premature closing of Edvard Munch's exhibition in Berlin in 1892 illustrates that the dates on which these various societies were founded did not mark the inception of the secession movement as such in the individual cities, but merely reflected the point in history at which the young generation was ready and willing (both in terms of its art and its world view) to become organised and enter into public cultural life as a separate entity. The same is true of the most prominent organisation of young Czech artists, SVU Mánes, formed from a student society originally founded in 1887.[3] SVU Mánes became substantially more active in the mid-1890s. In 1896 it gained its own critical tribune in the form of the magazine *Volné směry* (Free Currents), and from 1898 onwards its systematic exhibition activities transformed the fundamental orientation of Czech national culture.

Although these movements were from the start quite diverse in their artistic orientation, the word *secession* became a common bond, expressing their general demand for artistic self-determination and freedom.[4] In each and every case, the founding of a secession was prompted by dissatisfaction with contemporary exhibition practice. Generally, there would be annual exhibitions held by traditional art societies, museum associations, and similar organisations, where the most varied and often quite incompatible works would be assembled, regardless of their artistic quality, in quantities that

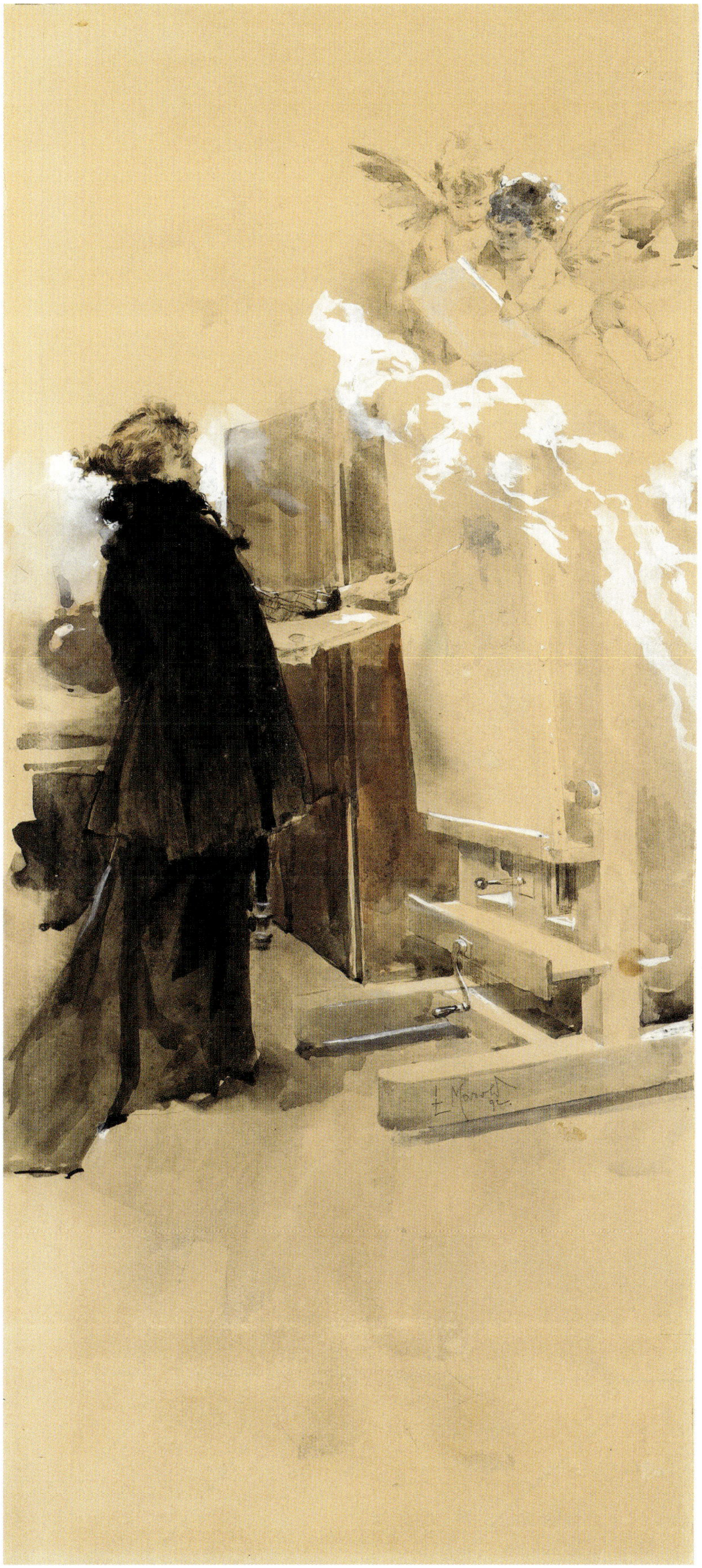

2 Luděk Marold, *Painter*, 1892, watercolour, 46 × 20.2 cm

could only be accommodated by hanging paintings in several rows, one above the other. This offered no opportunity to view the paintings from an appropriate distance, nor did it respect the need for proper lighting. These shortcomings were particularly apparent at the annual exhibitions that one such art society, Krasoumná jednota (the Fine Arts' Union), held at the Rudolfinum in Prague. For active Czech artists, such exhibitions were the only way they could present their work to the public, for the organisation of individual exhibitions was practically unknown at this time and was, in

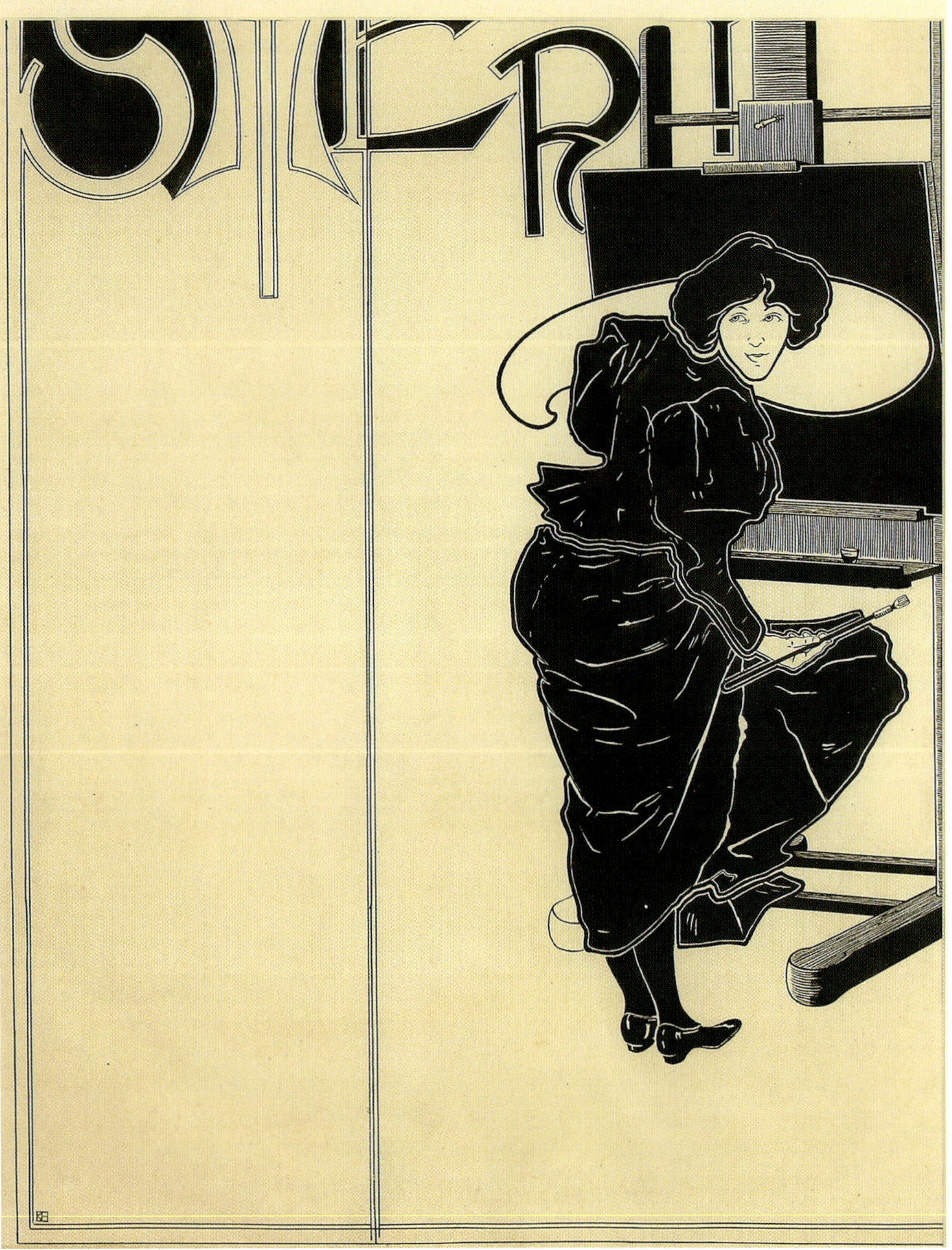

3 Karel Hlaváček, Design for the cover of *Volné směry*, 1897, Indian ink, 62 × 46.7 cm

fact, only introduced by the secession movements. Behind this practice – which was exacerbated by conservative juries who, in the young artists' opinion, were incompetent to judge on matters of art – lay far graver problems for fine art at the end of the 19th century. At the core of this dissatisfaction was the question of the importance of art for society, and its proper appreciation. However, for this fundamental question of the value of art, it was first necessary to win public recognition, and this gave rise to new *secessiones plebis*.

The original ethical meaning of *secession* was vividly present in pronouncements by the young generation's spokesmen. In 1899 Miloš Jiránek welcomed an exhibition by a revived art association, Jednota umělců výtvarných (the Union of Creative Artists), as a secession from the culturally stagnant and ossified Umělecká beseda (the Art Society). Jiránek embraced Jednota as a potential ally for SVU Mánes in the struggle for new art, but he also extended the requirements for new artistic value to Jednota's output, on which point he was entirely uncompromising. There appeared here another meaning of *secession*, which overlapped with its original ethical sense. Jiránek polemicised against the ornamentation of Jednota's exhibition rooms:

> Mr Novák has had the staircase decorated in the "modern way," in the dreadful "Secession" style, which has recently been rampaging all over Prague … and even in the furnishings of the exhibition room … the Wiener Secession reigns again. Have not even the experts in our country grasped the emptiness of this ersatz style?[5]

Jiránek, who had already divined the impact of French Impressionism and whose criteria placed him on the side of contemporary naturalism in painting, disliked the Vienna Secession's stylisation and was just as vehemently opposed to Alphonse Mucha and Parisian Art Nouveau.[6] In general, he rejected all of the prominent ornamental stylisation that had begun to be associated with the term *secession*, which he considered a passing fad, a new uniformity of artistic expression and thinking, against which SVU Mánes protested in the name of authenticity and artistic quality. Yet, as he demonstrated in other writings, he was not unappreciative of the decorative values of art.[7] Jiránek's assault was testimony to his indignation, as one of the original Secession artists, at the institutionalisation and commercialisation of such new endeavours. Nor was he alone in this, as we see from a similar reaction to the same exhibition penned by the young Stanislav Kostka Neumann, who in 1895 had initiated the literary *Almanach Secese* (The Secession Almanac), which also devoted considerable attention to fine art.[8]

In this way, the original notion of *secession* became increasingly empty, until, in Karel Boromejský Mádl's review of the seventh SVU Mánes exhibition in 1903, it was merely "an empty, hollow-sounding word that in Prague has no sense or meaning." And Mádl, who had from the start sympathised with the young artists, recalled how Mánes's members had declared at their 1898 exhibition that "they did not want to express the mere negation of everything that currently existed, to pursue ephemeral watchwords and relay every foreign nonsense to our land."[9]

There was also a political reason for rejecting the word *secession* – one that had considerable weight in the Austro-Hungarian Empire in the years before the First World War. The Secession was the name of the most active art society in Vienna, which, thanks to architects trained by Otto Wagner, also had a pronounced stylistic foundation. Politically, Wagner was by no means as opposed to official power as were the German societies, or, for that matter, their Czech counterparts. The Vienna Secession soon became quite acceptable for the state's official representation.[10] In the eyes of Czech critics, it remained "foreign," a product of Vienna – although, in truth, relations in the art world were much more open, with especially strong interaction between the two countries in the field of architecture. However, for ideological reasons, Czech theorists and artists sought to demonstrate the specifically national quality of Czech art, which was also one of the reasons why Czechs rejected the word *secession*, which continued to be chiefly associated with Viennese ornamentalism. Mádl tried to replace *secession* – which, in its broader and looser meaning, referred more to the moral content of the new art than to a particular formal stylistic system – with the term *modernity*. Here too he appealed to Sucharda's speech for SVU Mánes, which gave no thought to any particular style for young art.

This non-stylistic concept of modernity – which for Jiránek resulted ultimately in Czech Impressionism, and for Mádl became a fixation with emotionality – could not, of course, be a comprehensive theory of the new art. But it did create a certain normative opinion, such that even the decorative stylist Karel Vítězslav Mašek could claim in a 1903 article, entitled "The Study of Ornament," that, against learned styles, including "the Secession," it was necessary to uphold the principle of the study and individual appraisal of nature, so that "for each author, ornament is individual."[11] The SVU Mánes concept of modernity from 1898 could only serve as a starting point, especially with regard to its criticism of deeply rooted eclecticism, which was ultimately also adapted to the Secession's formulas. The association's emphasis on individuality and originality was concerned with naturalistic art, and it did not extend to the very essence of the problem for modern art: the question of the new art's general validity. This of necessity raised the issue of style. The requirement for naturalness and authenticity would continue to operate as a filter, revealing all the impurities created by the profaning and commercialising of what had, until recently, been revolutionary slogans. Nor was Mádl's *modernity* exempt from this. Writing about the Third German Decorative Arts Exhibition in Dresden in 1906, Jiránek put it in the same basket as the profaned *secession*:

> Numerous exhibits by manufacturing companies demonstrate how the authentic modern taste now prevails in mass production and retail; what is presented to us here, although it does not yet particularly excel, is at least very far removed from the run-of-the-mill products, labelled Secession or Modern, that so appal us in the shops.[12]

However, the new art very much needed some grand generalisation that would reflect its ambitions. The moral high ground originally associated with the terms *secession* or *modern* extended to the idea of a new style that should be superior to all eclecticism. František Xaver Šalda succinctly expressed the ethos of this idea in his 1903 essay "The New Beauty: Its Genesis and Character," one of the Czech movement's key programmatic declarations. In it, Šalda highlighted style as the supreme

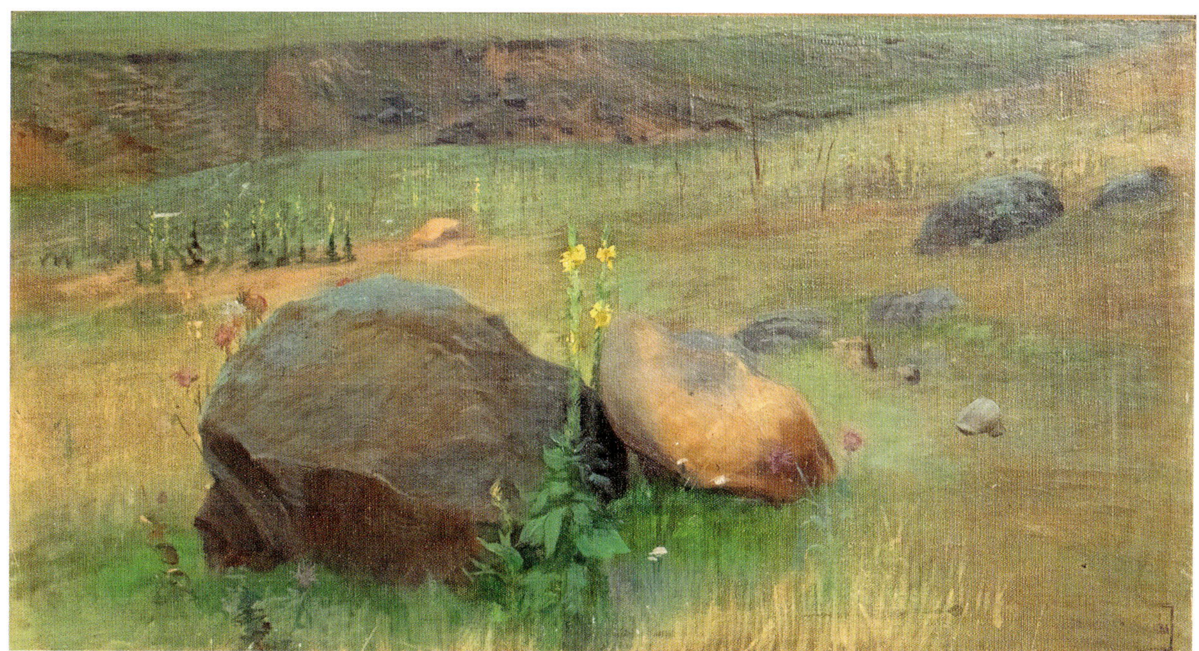

cultural value, a unity of art and life that was an expression of necessity and in no way "speculation for cheap applause."[13] Henceforward, the two earlier terms would be mere labels for style in the superficial sense of the word, as descriptive, established conventions that had nothing to do with any truly creative artistic content, but rather designated work that was similar to the earlier imitating of the Renaissance or the Baroque. From the start, Jiránek and Šalda rejected the now-prevalent tendency to describe a particular artwork as "secession" simply by virtue of some outward formal aspect that has become associated with the term.

This new concept of style was no mere theoretical abstraction, for it logically arose from the more advanced phase of Secession art, which in style began to become aware of its synthetic problem. If we view the artistic output of that era from the perspective of art history, we see that there had been hints of this problem everywhere, and right from the start, although reflected in different ways, and that it had shaped the main characteristics of turn-of-the-century art. Šalda had already defined the question of style as "a constant relation and regard to the whole," as an awareness of the higher unity of art and life from which the criteria for artistic creation are derived. In his essay "The Ethics of the Current Revival of Applied Art" from 1903, devoted to understanding one of the most important issues in the Secession movement – the new unity of fine art and applied art – Šalda expressed quite clearly his understanding of how this new style must be seen:

> From derivative forms amassed through fantasy or convention, we return to forms that are *fundamental, simple and effective*; from trickery and deceit to fidelity and substance; from false ornament to structure and skeleton; from the secondary to the principal and primary. All of the arts are gradually freeing themselves from

4 Jan Preisler, *Landscape with Boulders and Mullein*, 1898, oil, 25 × 46 cm

> their isolation and introspection, and sensing more and more keenly that their foundation and root is *ornamental and symbolic*, and their purpose is to work for the adorning of life, to work on the whole and to serve the whole: *style* as the supreme cultural value, the unity of art and life, is becoming the object of our hopes.[14]

What he expressed were the original principles of the Secession and modernism as viewed in the current situation in art, and he was concerned not only with negation but, above all, with constructing a new artistic and cultural stylistic whole. The interest here was focused on the essential characteristics, from which it followed that a precondition for a new unity was a fundamental *reduction* of the existing state of affairs. This reduction did not entail the mere pruning and depleting of the artistic register, but a more radical purging that would yield the building blocks for this new construction, now understood as a matter of the essential structural relationships. The 19th century had seen an inflation of values in fine art. The artists we now encounter in books on the history of art are only a narrow selection, carefully chosen for their universal artistic quality. Were we to look at the art of this time through contemporaneous eyes, we would see an entirely different picture. We would be overwhelmed by the thousands of canvases and sculptures that appeared at official exhibitions modelled on the Salon in Paris. The hyperproduction of art that was so typical of the latter half of the 19th century was unquestionably a direct consequence of how capitalist market economics had also extended to this part of society. This false democratisation, which in ideological terms was mass consumption for the petite bourgeoisie, resulted in the labyrinth of aesthetic norms known as *eclecticism*. The system of supply and demand resulted in a constant avalanche that released more and more examples from the history of art – understood as a vast storehouse or inexhaustible mine – to be freely imitated. By the end of the century, everything was permitted under late capitalism's aesthetic norms, but this liberalism did not bring satiation. In artistic circles, where the response was the most sensitive, it produced instead an acute crisis, for by now it was evident that what was being lost was what was essential in art: the very heart of creativity. There were new demands for eclecticism's liberalism to be applied not just to the past, to imitations of venerable models, but also to the quest for a contemporary expression; that is, to turn licensed manufacturing into free artistic creation. However, this inevitably resulted in conflicts between the principles of conservative taste, which constantly demanded guarantees of value that could be verified by comparisons with earlier models, and the willingness and courage to create new art, to take uncertain and untested paths with no clear destination.

The Secession mentality arose wherever artists subjected late capitalism's mercenary concept of art to scrutiny. This was not too difficult, for they could see its unfortunate consequences in everyday life. The next step was for them to realise that this syncretism, this mining of history's deposits, was merely a vicious circle, and that, after the main seams and veins had been exhausted (the most recent of them in Bohemia had been the Baroque Revival of the early 1890s), this process could no longer continue at its usual brisk pace. Now it was necessary to proceed in the opposite direction, by rejecting this unprincipled blend of eclectic styles, themes, and expressive devices. The alternative to this marketplace of vanity was, above all, nature – if possible, untainted by human civilisation. Only in nature – or in pure emotion; that is, in love – could the individual, now beyond the reach of society's conventions and wilfully existing as a psychological unit, find externalisation.

This emotional naturalism was a characteristic element in the young generation's programme, and it was reflected primarily by painters and sculptors, in line with their disciplines' expressive potential. However, from the start, architects also exhibited with SVU Mánes, albeit to a lesser extent than in the Vienna Secession, for instance. Architects brought additional requirements, which at first chiefly concerned decoration – in particular, the quest for a new system of ornament. This, the Secession movement's second characteristic preoccupation, was largely prompted by decorative printmaking, which soon found broad public application, and by the full range of arts and crafts, of which ceramics and stuccowork especially took new inspiration from their close association with architecture. In fact, it extended to all disciplines involved in furnishing the contemporary interior, which became the common denominator in their cohesive stylistic development. We can therefore distinguish in the Secession's reduction a certain polarity between naturalistic and decorative tendencies, and out of their interaction the Secession's own style was born. Of course, this only concerned the physioplastic aspect of the new art's aesthetics. There was also the ideoplastic aspect, where Symbolist tendencies reigned.

Symbolism was the third important component of fin de siècle art. It first became known in Bohemia through literature, chiefly among the authors associated with the periodical *Moderní revue* (The Modern Review), which was launched in 1894. *Moderní revue* included information on French and Belgian Symbolist and Decadent writers and artists, which was certainly of interest to the painters and sculptors of SVU Mánes, who wanted to renounce all notion of fine art as illustration – something that eclecticism and literature had made more pervasive. However, the Mánes artists' adherence to naturalism meant that they did not entirely share the literati's enthusiasm for Symbolism, which did not always take the question of artistic value into account.[15]

The conditions for Symbolism to flourish had also been established in Czech art by some artists from the preceding generation, especially Hanuš Schwaiger and Maxmilián Pirner, with their late Romanticism. František Bílek, always an isolated figure in SVU Mánes, offered a distinctive revaluation of such inspiration, but nor should we overlook the early work of Jan Preisler and Maxmilián Švabinský, who combined late Romanticism with the legacy of the English Pre-Raphaelites.

Even the "official" Mánes programme, as set out in the speech introducing the association's first exhibition, did not in fact preclude an open relationship with authentic Symbolism. The most original French Symbolists, such as Mallarmé and Gauguin, would surely not have objected to the speech's words about the uniqueness of the "painterly idea," for it was a formulation that was related to Mallarmé's well-known device of the poem-dream, whose content can only be suggested.[16]

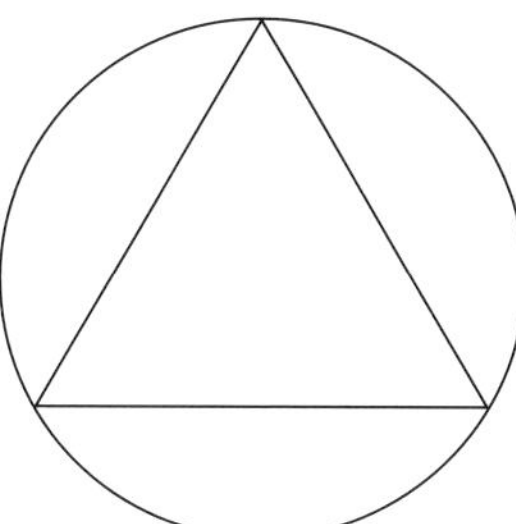

Taking all these aspects into consideration, the system for the Secession's reduction of eclectic syncretism can be visualised as a triangle within a circle, where the triangle's

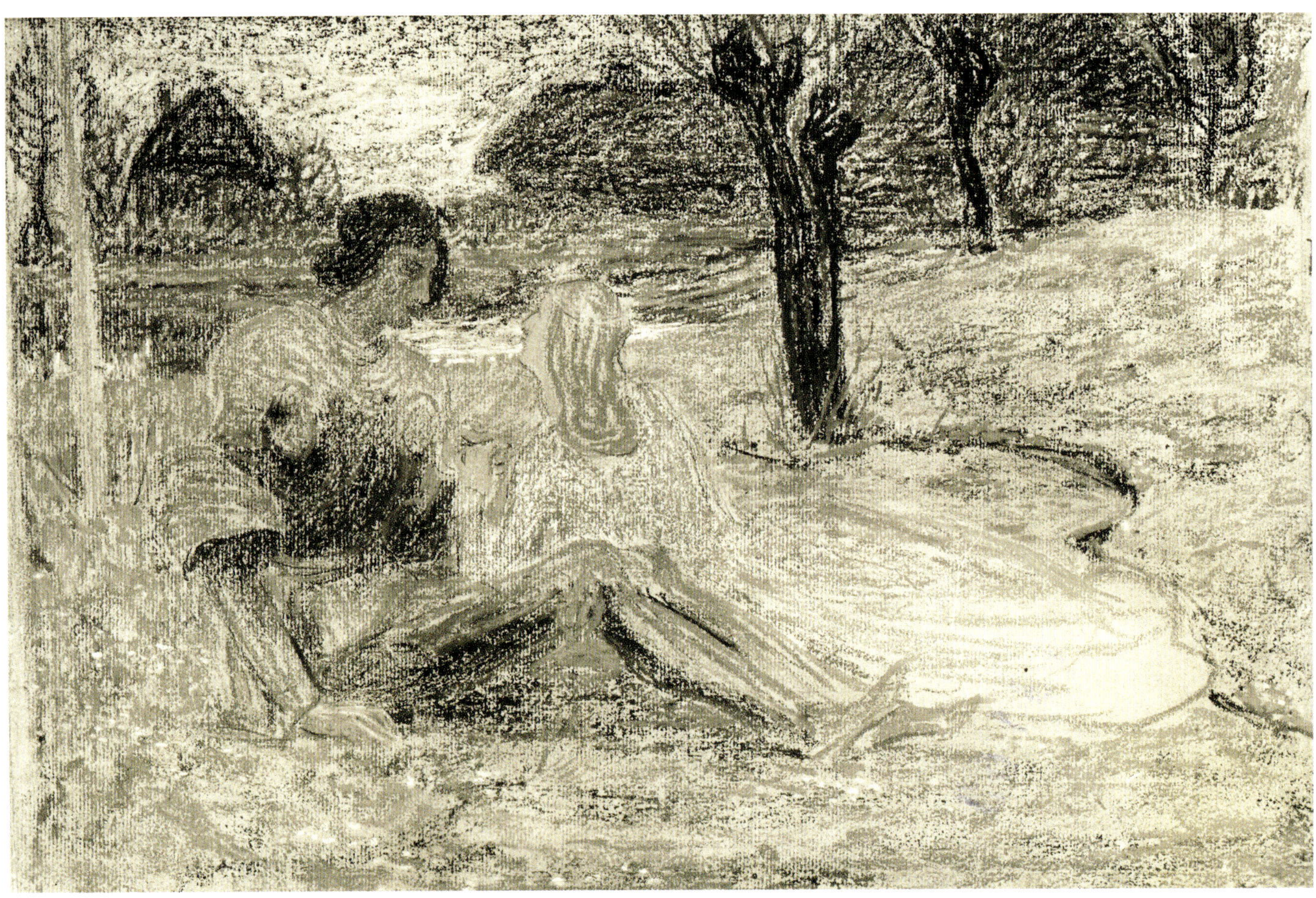

three corners are the aforementioned key tendencies – namely, naturalism, Symbolism, and ornamental decorativism.

Crucially, each of these tendencies covered a particular field out of which the theory and practice of the new art could emerge. Naturalism highlighted the relationship with objective nature through the sense of sight, while Symbolism emphasised fantasy and the imagination, and ornamental decorativism stressed the syntactical foundation of formal artistic expression. These tendencies complemented one another to create a new unity of vision, imagination, and expression. Although they may have been relatively independent, or even have lent themselves to extreme emphasis in contemporary artistic programmes that were aligned with the specific interests of certain individuals or groups, in reality they created a meaningful whole for the new art and its conceptual and expressive structure. The Secession was anti-traditionalist in the sense that it rejected the verbose entropy of art under eclecticism. It was a purge, a return to the essential functions of art, and this process of reduction laid the groundwork for a new art, one that would again be able to contribute to the core problem of how we approach and shape reality.

5 Jan Preisler, *Knight and Fairy*, 1901, pastel, 29 × 41 cm

We can view the new art that emerged at the turn of the century as the basis of all modern art, which over the course of the 20th century sought to fundamentally transform art's statutes in conjunction with the revolutionary rebuilding of the modern world. The graph outlined above also characterises the first, Secession, phase in this complex process of historical evolution, when the most pressing need was for a critical appraisal of the current situation, to highlight the elementary points. This mentality was reflected in the marked expansion of art criticism, with an individual and social impact that went beyond anything previously achieved in the history of Czech critical thinking on art.

Despite the divergent interests that are evident in the critical conflicts and programmes of the period, the new art's chief contribution was in fact its inner unity, although at the time this was seen as problematic and often only intuited. This unity, an inkling of which found its way into the consciousness of contemporary artists through the notion of style, was the point where their efforts converged, and it was a constant requirement for all artistic endeavour. It was understood as an ideal that contemporary art was only beginning to approach and was working to bring about. This convergence of interests then created a natural dialectical pole for Secession art, whose fundamental inner contradiction made it truly animated and capable of evolving.

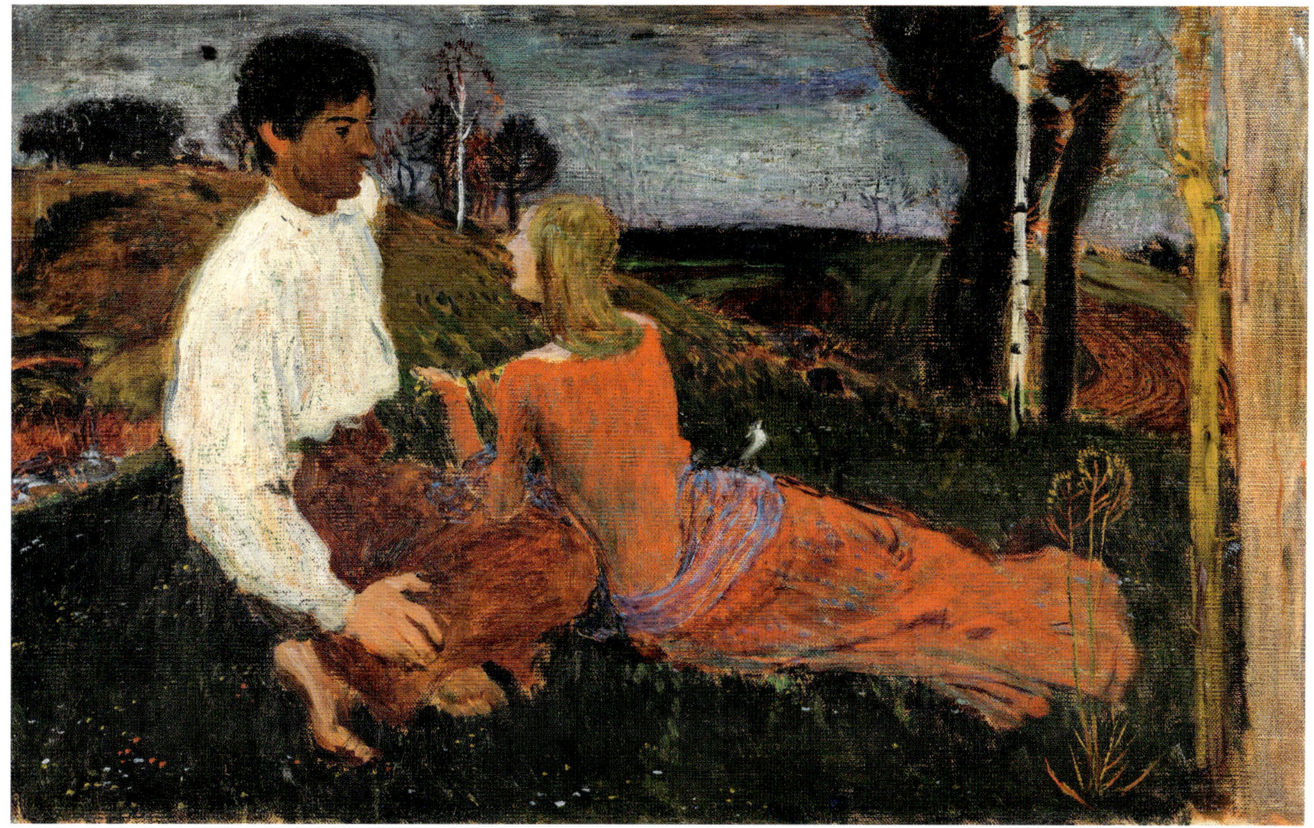

6 Jan Preisler, Sketch for *Painting from a Larger Cycle*, 1902, oil, 40 × 62 cm

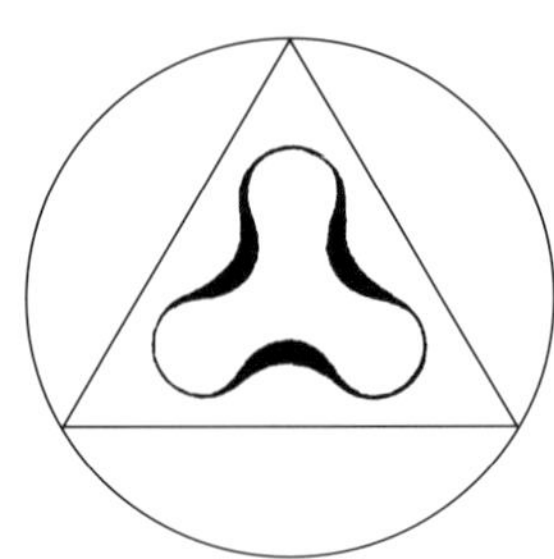

In this context, the Secession's typical ornamental line, its chief morphological characteristic, takes on a deeper meaning. Its endless repetition, the way it was developed in long loops and curves that narrowed and broadened, is a visual symbol for this sought-after inner unity. We can insert it in our triangle to indicate the constant exchange between the three main points generated by contemporary criticism and visual thinking. Secession ornament was then an expression of contemporary intentionality, directed towards a new totality of art. It was not yet the very style of this art, at least not in the higher sense of the word as defined by F. X. Šalda and other prominent spokesmen of the epoch.

The Secession line acquired its stylistic character in relation to space. Its typical broadening and narrowing meant that it ceased to be a line in the strict sense of the word and became a two-dimensional element, which in its optical interaction with a sheet of paper in a graphic design resulted in an ambivalent alternating of positive and negative forms. It was not therefore sufficient for a line simply to be drawn ornamentally over an abstract plane, as was the case with certain pseudo-Renaissance façades and interior decoration; instead, it should be integrated with the plane and animate it in a deeper sense. Henry van de Velde's construction of the stylised Secession interior was based on this principle. This way of connecting a line with a plane created a rhythm, an important stylistic category that was reflected in architecture – for instance, in the gradation of materials – and in paintings in the order of the decorative planes and how they related to one another.

Style was connected with the overall structuring of an artwork's form, but it was also a quality that bound art to life. It was not merely a matter of artistic skill, but of emotion too. For Secession artists, style was a way of addressing life and the world. Accordingly, it is not difficult to recognise a Secession artwork from its outward appearance, but it is far harder to understand and explain its inner motivation as a necessary and historically unique combination of form and content. For the artists of this epoch, an interest in style was not something external or modish; instead, it constituted the very essence of their artistic endeavours, often where we cannot at first sight discern any prominent stylisation or any of the ornamental clichés commonly labelled "Secession." In the broader but nevertheless entirely original sense, Slavíček's "Impressionist" landscape paintings are also in the Secession style. Besides his spontaneous sketches, we can also include here his decorative and carefully composed canvases, whether as individual works or as part of a series. The remarkable unity of form and content that came to the fore in the Secession's dynamic and dramatic inception was without question one of its most important advances.

The dominance of style in the background of Secession art resulted in the illustrating of general ideas and motifs that anchored this new art and set out its distinctive iconography. A typical theme was the depiction of the act of painting itself. The starting point here was traditional allegorical personification, which we find, for instance, in a drawing by Mikoláš Aleš from the 1890s showing a pretty girl, her long hair loose, kneeling on a cloud and painting on an easel. A rainbow arching in the background hints at the connection between the natural order of colours and their artificial, artistic order on the painter's palette. Aleš's drawing lent this traditional idea an intimate lyricism, but at heart it remained within the confines of the idealised images that had been commonplace in art since the Renaissance.

In 1892 Luděk Marold painted an illusionistic watercolour of a young woman at her easel, where only an amorphous little cloud and a pair of putti reveal that this too is an allegory of painting. Everything else here is contemporary: the impersonal sphere of the abstract allegorical space has become an artist's studio in typical disarray. Marold's painting of this bohemian scene does not represent a generalised ideal of beauty, but a modern woman with an unmistakably Parisian appearance and dress sense. In 1897 Marold's de-allegorisation of this traditional theme was taken a step further in Karel Hlaváček's ink drawing for the cover of *Volné směry*, where the female subject, now in a painter's smock, turns towards the viewer, breaking with what Marold had retained of the traditional notion of ideality as the last vestige of the imaginary. The attributes have been immortalised, but even more symptomatic is the Secession stylisation of the whole. Traditional painting has been given a realist and programmatic role. Style was then also the surpassing of the naturalism of Marold's treatment and a return to universality, but never again would it have the fanciful character that Aleš's drawing still possessed. Allegory had been lost and all that remained was the link between the realistic, naturalistic vision and the new "poster" stylisation. Another similar example from this time is Alphonse Mucha's design for a poster advertising his own decorative drawing classes. The negation of the old allegory would go so far that, for Antonín Slavíček's posthumous exhibition, Vladimír Županský produced a poster based on a photograph of the painter working *en plein air*. The universality of Marold's naturalism here serves the cult of the individual, yet the essential equilibrium between the uniqueness of the painter's appearance and the decorative arrangement of the picture plane has been preserved.

On this basis, by combining realistic painting's sharp perception with ornamental abstraction, the unique with the universal, Secession art could also cultivate its dominant ideas. Like the two instances above, initially these also seemed extreme and exaggerated when compared with traditionalism's "classic" mediocrity.

At its inception then, Secession art offset extreme naturalism with an extreme Symbolist detachment from the phenomenal world of ordinary visual experience, and it turned to "inner vision" to give fantasy free rein. Here too, however, this was not a question of caprice. It created, even more effectively than "poster" stylisation, a distance between "reality" and the imaginary that brought forth this art's chimeras and utopias, but also created a need to bridge this seeming chasm.

A typical Symbolist motif in Czech art from the late 1890s was the individual gazing into the depths of space. Karel Hlaváček's 1897 drawing for a collection of his poems called *Late before Morning* shows a male nude, probably the poet himself, reclining in a natural setting as he gazes at the large moon rising on the horizon; Arnošt Hofbauer's drawing for the cover for the third volume of *Volné směry* in 1898 depicted a naked boy kneeling at the foot of a statue of Pan and marvelling at the spirals of the Milky Way, while Vojtěch Preissig's etching *Meditation* from 1899 is a variation on the

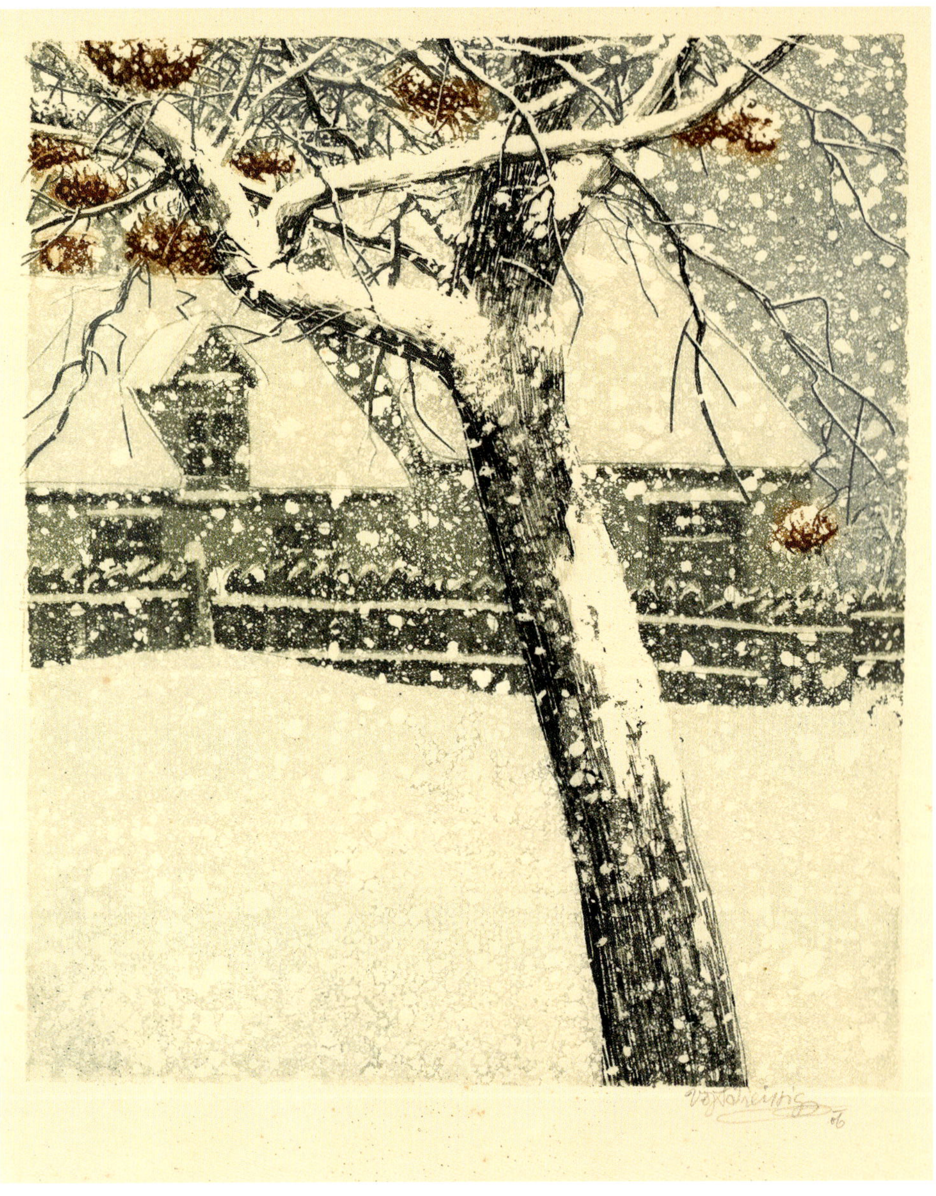

same theme, with a young woman sitting in a garden at night and looking dreamily at the starry sky. Beside her a young tree grows, symbolising new life.[17] We find many similarly motivated images in František Bílek's work. The drawing that opens his tract *On the Number* (1899) expresses not just the traumatic tone of the concept but also its ideation, through the apparition of a large open book containing the order of the universe. All these examples testify to the existence of certain fundamental collective ideas, which, although interpreted individually, were symptomatic of contemporary culture and the young generation. From our perspective, it is again not the extremity of these approaches, whether individual or collective, that is important, but what they have in common. It was only in an inner synthesis of these innovations that the most

7 Vojtěch Preissig, *Winter Motif II*, 1906, coloured etching with aquatint, 42.1 × 31.8 cm

important part of the Secession's creative endeavours unfolded, producing what was most fruitful for future developments.

This creative work can be very illuminatingly mapped in examples of stylistic integration from the oeuvre of the finest artists, such as Jan Preisler, who is in many respects a model for the entire Secession movement. In 1898 Preisler painted a small landscape study that testifies to his preoccupation at this time with naturalistic painting, which had become attractive thanks to the influence of Vojtěch Hynais's school. In the same year, Preisler was also working on the problem of colour, initially in the spirit of the new colour illusionism. The study shows part of a meadow in the mountains, with two rocks of different sizes between which two mulleins grow. This modest landscape study takes on a deeper meaning in Preisler's oeuvre if we compare it with his paintings from three years later, when he was again drawn to the idea he had developed in his unfinished cycle of 1898, *The Adventurous Knight*. A pastel from 1901 shows a landscape with a knight-errant sitting with a female figure, who is probably a poetic personification of the knight's soul. In the following year, Preisler's creative process then led from this Symbolist fairy tale to one of his most important works, *Painting from a Larger Cycle*. Here the fantastical vision became something much more realistic, while losing nothing of its poetic charm. In it, a country boy again encounters a girl who is not entirely corporeal but unquestionably belongs to the landscape in which their silent encounter plays out.

The sequence of these three works is interesting, and it indicates that a certain creative process was underway in the painter's imagination, in which he integrated what he could see in nature with what he could imagine and what he could ultimately masterfully express in art. We cannot claim with any certainty that Preisler's earlier landscape study inspired *Painting from a Larger Cycle* or indeed the pastel of the knight. Yet even if this were not so, the fact remains that originally, when he had no intention of producing a figure painting, he was preoccupied with a configuration of forms in nature from which such a painting could then arise just as naturally as a mother giving birth.

Viewed from the perspective of art history, Preisler's creative process integrated naturalism with Symbolism, and thanks to his experience of decorative work he could apply this seemingly contradictory combination to a large and definitive painting. This somewhat arid description does not, of course, capture the depth and richness of Preisler's creative act, sanctified by his pure poetic intuition, but it does indicate the character and breadth of the Secession's stylistic synthesis, allowing valuable work to be created. In many respects, especially concerning the use of colour to unite the effect of lines and space, we can consider Preisler's *Painting from a Larger Cycle* the first truly modern Czech painting.

The importance of the Secession's stylistic synthesis for the future development of modern thinking on art also stands out if we compare three works by Vojtěch Preissig. As a leading printmaker and decorative artist from the 1890s' generation, Preissig was very much concerned with these questions, and what he learned from working on them would then take the Secession's decorative stylistic synthesis further still, making it the basis for a solution that extended beyond the historical confines of this synthesis and deepened it by introducing additional, even more complex requirements.

Preissig's coloured etching *Winter Motif*, much praised by Miloš Jiránek, dates from 1906. It is one of the finest examples of Preissig's technical mastery and mature artistry, precisely in the sense of the Secession's stylistic synthesis. The motif is realistic, and, in its freshness, almost Impressionist, yet it is deftly and decoratively composed, and there is also a Symbolist element in the paraphrasing of the tree of life, which is depicted linearly against the planar village houses in the background. The restrained colours quietly and melodiously accompany the picture's harmonious formal composition and complete its emotional effect.

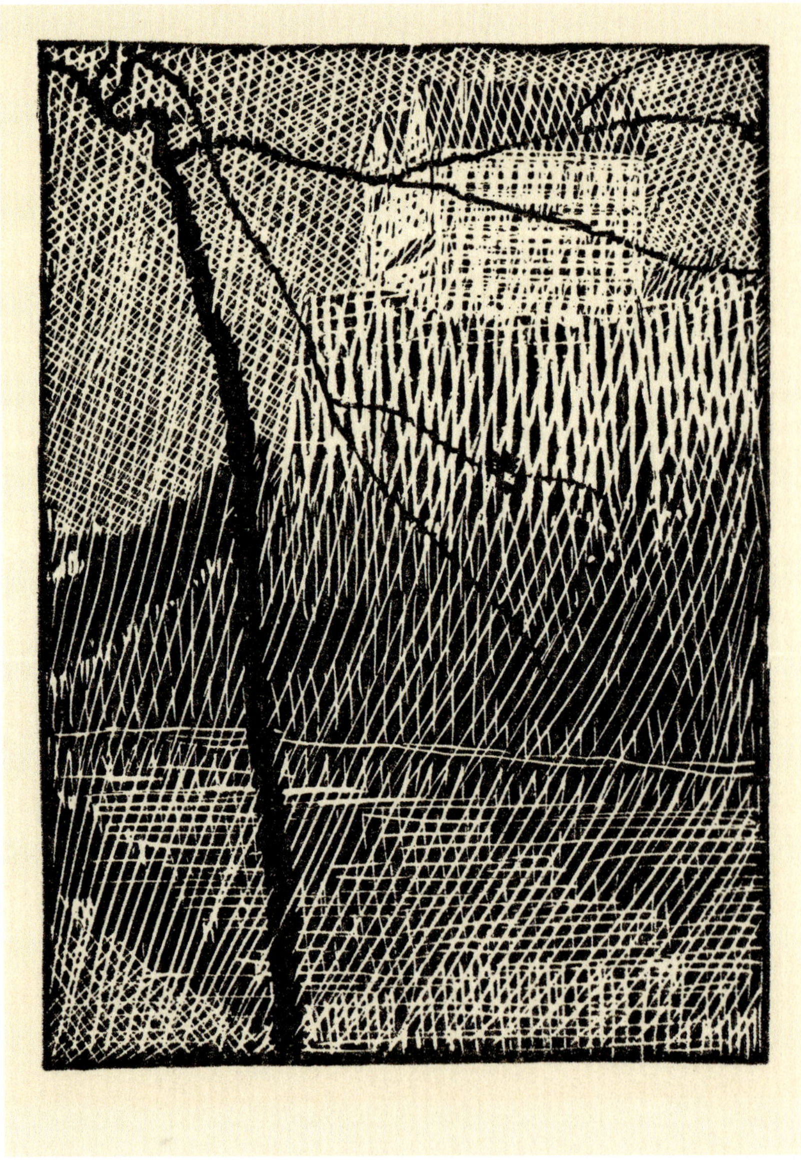

8 Vojtěch Preissig, *Plumlov*, woodcut from Petr Bezruč's *Silesian Songs*, 1909, 10.3 × 7.2 cm

Although nothing more perfect can be imagined (in the artistic sense) in the context of the Secession, rather than contenting himself with what he had achieved, Preissig first problematised and then accentuated this quality. The woodcut *Plumlov* was one of his illustrations for a 1909 bibliophile edition of Petr Bezruč's *Silesian Songs*. The motif is similar: a confrontation between the linearity of the bare tree in the foreground and the architecture in the background. This time, however, it is a castle on a hill, and this difference, drawing on the dramatic subtext of Bezruč's poems, introduces a disquiet that is manifested visually. The entire picture plane is covered with bold hatching that dematerialises these objects and turns them into a vision in which the image's contrasts are in equilibrium. From an art historical perspective, Preissig's *Plumlov* dates from the revival of expressive tendencies in Czech art. What is crucial here, however, is that the new drama that has replaced the tranquil idyll of *Winter Motif* has also increased the formal potential of the artistic image. Yet the fundamental stylistic quality, Šalda's "constant relation and regard to the whole," has not been lost, but adapted to more far-reaching content.

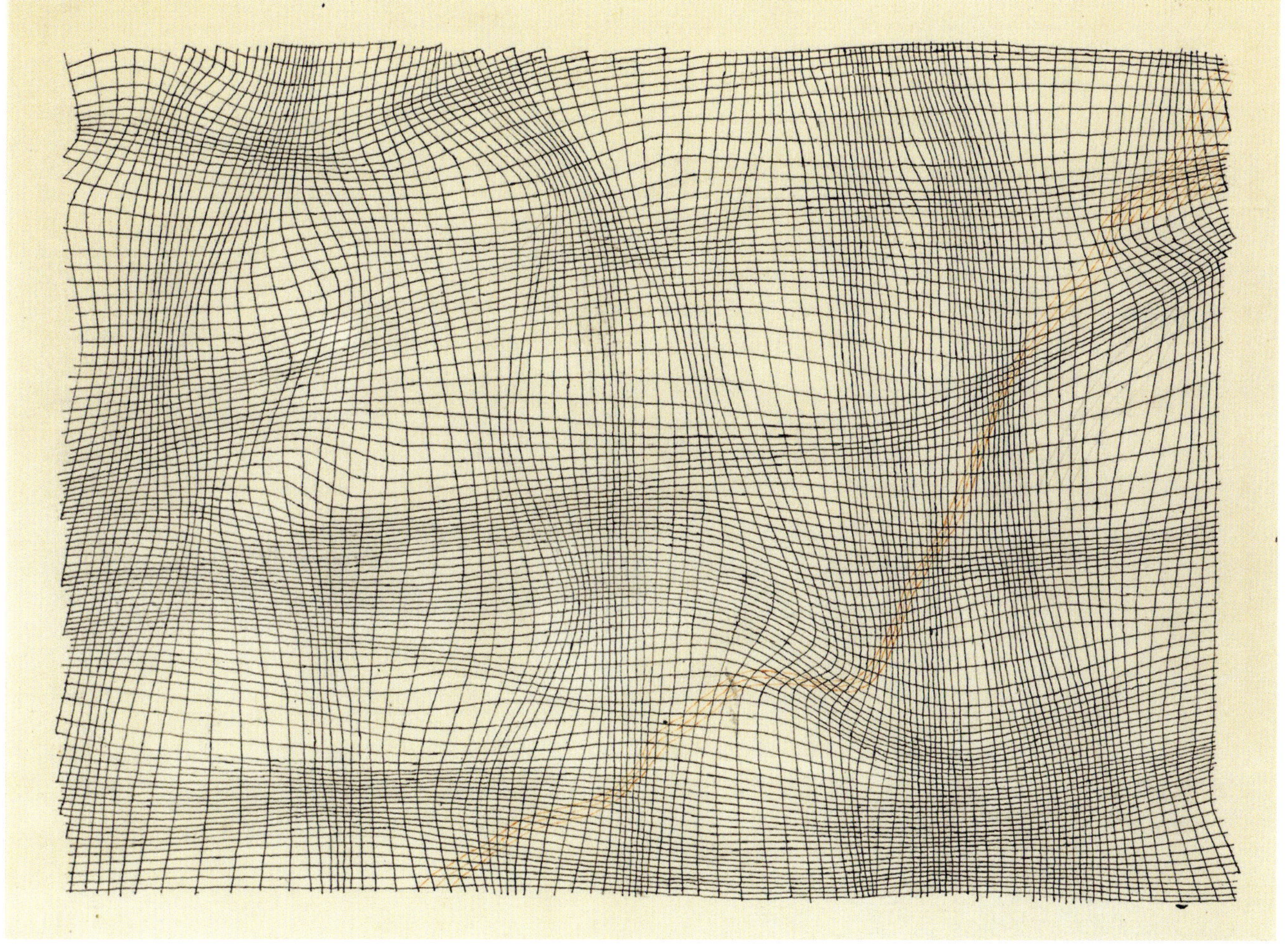

9 Vojtěch Preissig, *Geometrical Drawing*, after 1920, black and red Indian ink, 18.7 × 26 cm

The third work in our comparison is from the 1920s, by which time developments had moved beyond the Secession, which was now generally considered unsuited to the needs of contemporary art. It is one of the drawings that Preissig created as purely private works. These were not intended for the public, but they evidently had considerable significance for the artist himself. The mesh of lines drawn in ink does not depict any subject. Although "abstract," it is quite different from abstract art of the period, which was mostly concerned with the diktat of right angles and straight lines. Preissig's geometrical mesh differs, above all, in its elasticity, resembling perhaps the contours of a plastic map of the earth's surface, between whose uplands and valleys a line curves like a road or river.[18]

All three of these works by Preissig share the same fundamental compositional principle, in which space meets line to together create the image as a whole. This new unity, which in *Winter Motif* still has the character of a decorative equilibrium between these elements, gradually becomes a higher value in which the two components fully interpermeate. This escalation of the expressive devices also involves the activation of their content – for a picture ceases to be merely a report on the world, or an adaptation of the world, and becomes a record of its active experiencing and co-creating, not as the enforcing of a stylistic formula but as a sensibility that sees the internal relations of things and can express them in a sensitive graphic depiction of a web of psychophysical energies, in the force field of their tension and relaxation. A drawing can then be understood not as a static symbol but as a means of recording the dialectically variable processes underway in all of nature, as a way of identifying the artist's psyche with these processes and expressing a new and nondescriptive experience of the unity of the world. In this respect, Preissig's later drawing still belongs to the legacy of fin de siècle art. It is merely its distilled essence, combining the original elements of the Secession mentality – its cult of nature facilitated by the sense of sight; its fondness for Symbolist motifs and themes; its formal, technical artistic ability – to create a cohesive symbol that is the simplest, most elementary exemplar of the unity of art and life proclaimed by the Secession style.

Through its initial act of rejection, the Secession created a great opportunity for a new concept of art. The fruitfulness of its negation lay precisely in this perspective, and the Secession's reductive approaches created the necessary conditions to bring about this new concept. However, the fulfilling of these conditions remained more the work of individuals. This did not happen in the more general form that artists desired, for the society in which they had to work was rather less progressive than their concept. It is only now that we can recapitulate their endeavours and verify the values that have persisted to the present day.

For these reasons, the term *Secession*, as it is used in this book, differs from how it is often used today:

1. *Secession* refers not merely to a trend from the turn of the century, but to all new art of that era, chiefly in terms of its critique of the eclecticism that preceded it. We therefore understand the Secession in the original sense of the word, as an art movement.

2. The process of the Secession's negation involved a fundamental reduction of eclecticism through the movement's three main programmes, which we have labelled naturalistic Impressionism, Symbolism, and ornamental decorativism. This reduction was directed at restructuring the entire system of art, at the levels corresponding to the individual fundamental capacities of its creation (i.e., how it related to "external" nature, mental imagery, and symbolic communication).
3. At the time, these three tendencies were manifested separately, as different programmes, but in reality they led to demands for their integration, expressed in the notion of style. It is common for a single Secession work to reflect all three elements, with their typical characteristics.
4. The Secession culminated in style as an objective quality and a new unity of art and life, and this was its legacy for the subsequent development of art.

To trace the significance of the Secession for the present day, its place in the logic of artistic development, it is not enough to consider only the founding generation of the 1890s. We also have to map the early work of the subsequent generation that emerged in the first decade of the 20th century. Its members were also some of the first to appraise Secession art, and this younger generation's response to it initiated the tradition of Czech modern art that is the connection between us and fin de siècle creativity.

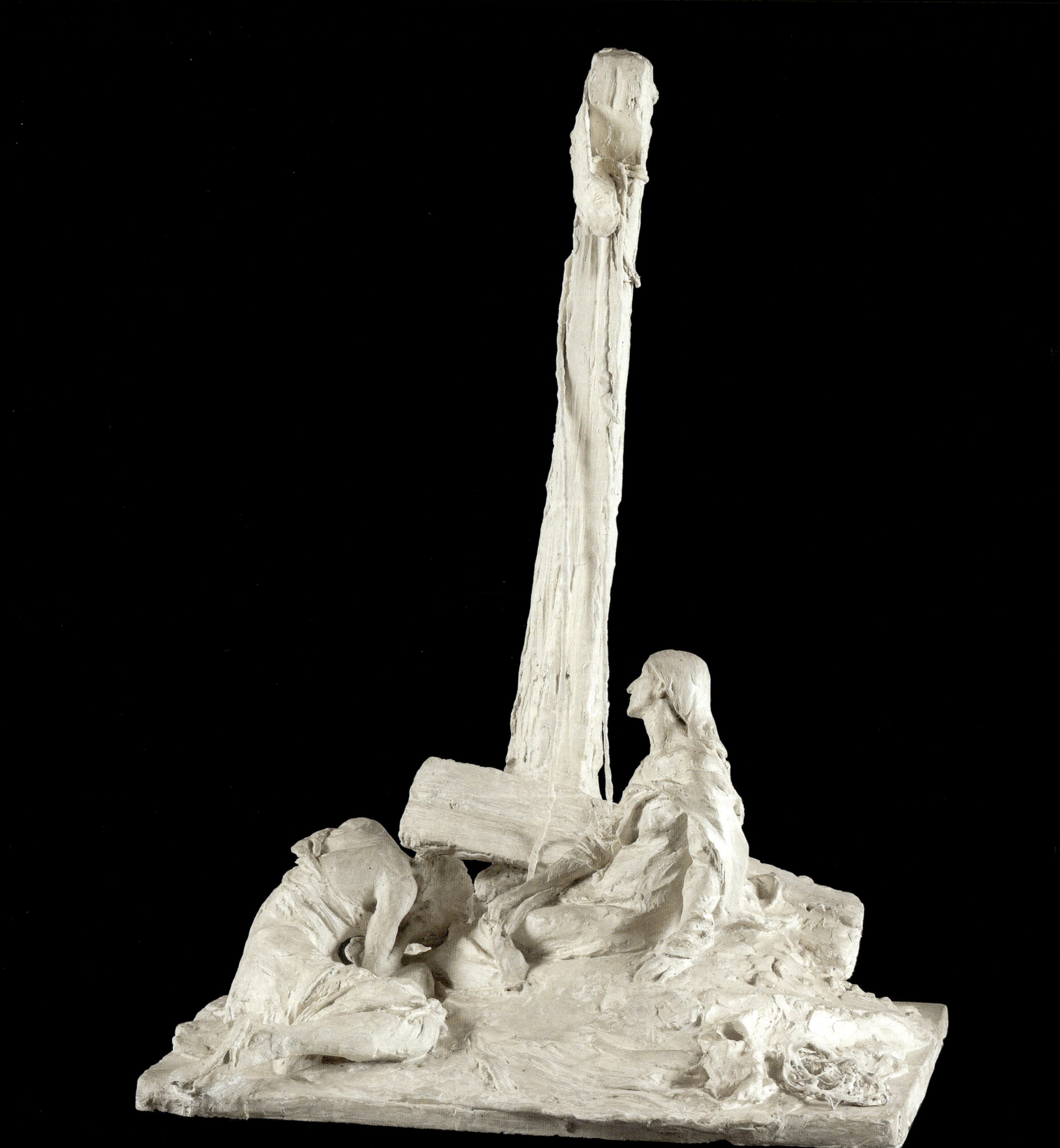

SIGNALS

The Czech Secession began its ascent in the mid-1890s, but this collective phase had already been heralded by a series of individual manifestations. In the eclecticism of the latter half of the 19th century, these initially seemed to have been created by chance, or as the work of somewhat eccentric individuals standing outside the main current of contemporary art, who in retrospect prove to have anticipated future developments. One of these outsiders from this earlier period was Hanuš Schwaiger, to whom the Secession generation enthusiastically devoted a triple issue of *Volné směry* in 1900, and when, two years later, he became a professor at the Academy of Fine Arts in Prague, many of the younger artists, especially Miloš Jiránek and Antonín Slavíček, befriended him. Their interest in him remained undiminished, and was reflected in a large album of reproductions published by Česká grafická unie, and especially by a book that Jiránek wrote on Schwaiger, first published in 1908 and then in SVU Mánes's Zlatoroh edition of 1912. By this time, Schwaiger could no longer influence his young friends as a teacher, but he remained for them the exemplar of an artist who had gone his own way right from the start. In his monograph, Jiránek described Schwaiger as "one of those rare artists, where the man is always greater still than the painter, whose art is merely the necessary expression of an entire world view. No one was less influenced by those around him; no one followed his tastes more freely."[19] Schwaiger was born in 1854 in Jindřichův Hradec, in a mixed Czech and German family. His interest in art made him the black sheep of the family, and the petite bourgeoisie's acquisitiveness and narrow intellectual outlook would become his driving force. He studied painting in Vienna, where his teachers included Hans Makart, who evidently impressed him with his lofty aristocratic manner. Professor Makart was intrigued by his idiosyncratic student, and in 1879 he bought *The Pied Piper*, a set of six pen drawings that Schwaiger exhibited at the academy's annual exhibition. Thanks to Makart, Schwaiger's first patrons were prominent art collectors from the ranks of the Austrian nobility. In the first half of the 1880s, he chiefly worked for Count Hans Wilczek, whose personal taste was one of the most typical examples of contemporary historicism. At this time, Schwaiger also reworked his late Romanticism into the desired archaic style of the German Renaissance, and this imaginative fixation on the lost world of the past would remain one of the chief characteristics of his oeuvre.

However, Schwaiger's view of the past in his paintings diverged substantially from how it was usually illustrated at the time. His subject matter did not belong to the popular repertoire of the legendary deeds of historical heroes and monarchs. *The Anabaptists* (1889), Schwaiger's most important painting from this period, depicts the anarchic religious sect's occupation of the city of Münster in the 16th century. Beneath this late Romantic fantasy, the bizarre appearance of the figures, combining religious fervour

10 František Bílek, *Golgotha*, 1892, plaster, 85 cm

with utopian fanaticism in a naturalistic depiction of social upheaval, already anticipates much of the world view that would erupt at the end of the 19th century. Here, at odds with the ideological ordering of history, a previously unknown or overlooked force has exploded with devastating violence in a doomed popular uprising. In contrast to the refinement of royal history, Schwaiger's apparitions seem like caricatures, indicating that, in his conception, this "other" force of history is anarchic and individualistic, yet his depiction is artistically appealing in its naturalism, its expressiveness, and in the attention Schwaiger devotes to the undercurrent of life that has continued to flow just as powerfully across the eras.

Schwaiger's late Romantic paintings were not then merely an accomplished variation on what taste demanded at this time, for they embodied a world view and an artistic programme that went far beyond contemporary historicism, breaking with its escapism. Although Schwaiger worked with legends, fairy tales, and stories from literature, which appealed to contemporary viewers educated primarily through reading, he was able to present new ideas and a fresh and purely artistic imagination. He brought his own contribution to the ideology of the time, demanding to shape viewers' opinions: he offered his services, but proudly insisted that they be duly appreciated.

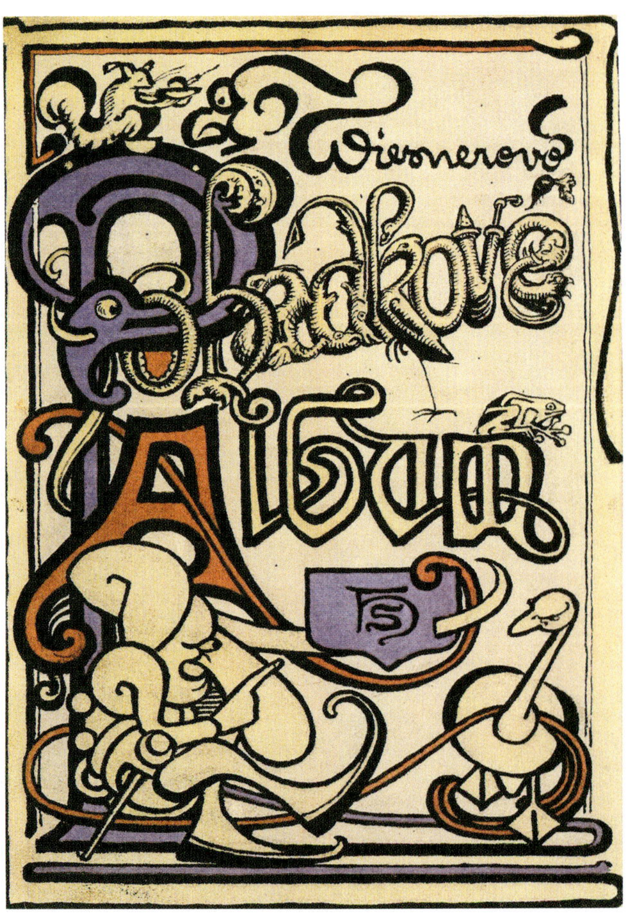

11 Hanuš Schwaiger, Cover for *Wiesner's Fairy Tale Album*, 1885, Indian ink and tempera, 24.5 × 17.3 cm

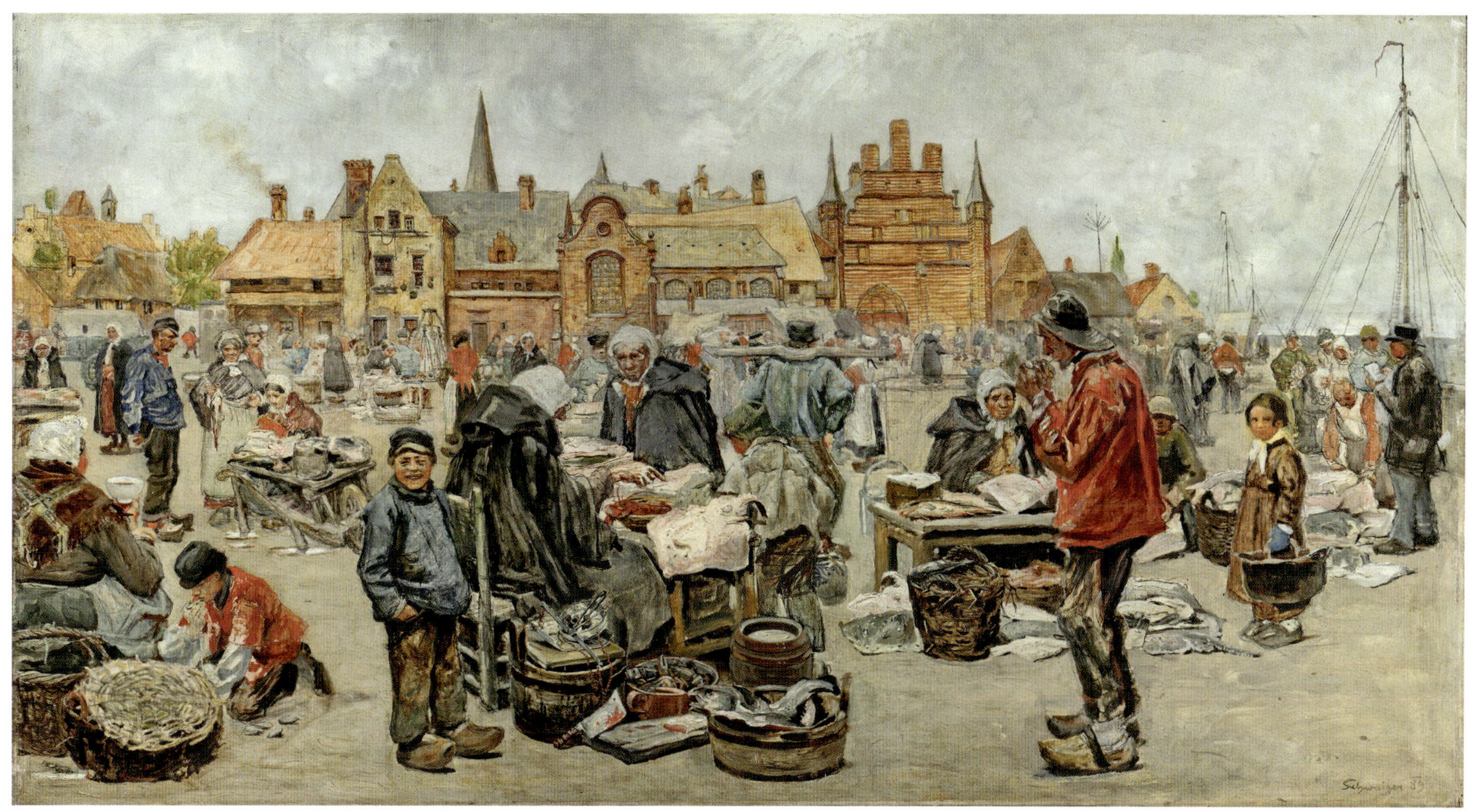

This was symbolised by Schwaiger's figure of *The Pied Piper*, with whom he began his independent work and to whom he would return several more times. The Pied Piper comes from far away; his piping has remarkable powers, and he rids the townspeople of the evil afflicting them, but when they trick him, he takes his revenge by leading their children away.

This conceptual anticipation, in which it is as if Schwaiger had prescribed the Secession movement's motifs twenty years earlier, is accompanied in some of his variations on the Pied Piper by a formal anticipation. Among the watercolours he produced for Count Wilczek are paintings whose simplification to lines and spaces, and whose use of colour as the dominant emotional chord, directly prefigured the Secession's visual style. For Schwaiger and his successors, the attempt to visualise the Pied Piper's mysterious music unquestionably played an important role.

The cover for *Wiesner's Fairy Tale Album*, which Schwaiger designed in 1885, similarly seems an entirely original forerunner of Secession art. It can be considered one of the first attempts to reform the Czech book with a modern, uniform, and nondescriptive treatment. The world of grotesque fairy-tale figures, mostly animals, that form part of the lettering, reflects a reduction to the simplest artistic means in the service of a new integration of lettering and image. The ornamental flourishes that connect these elements into a rhythmic whole already have the Secession's character, in its most interesting and as yet unschematised form.

12 Hanuš Schwaiger, *Fish Market in Bruges I*, 1889, oil and tempera, 76 × 116 cm

The cover dates from Schwaiger's time in Prague, where he stayed at the publisher's invitation. Alois Wiesner also owned the Ruch gallery in Prague, which in early 1887 hosted the first comprehensive exhibition of Schwaiger's work. It was enthusiastically received by artists, and Schwaiger's considerable influence on the younger Czech generation probably dated from this time. For Schwaiger, this period marked something of a watershed in his life and work, bringing a fundamental change of scene. In 1888 he visited the Netherlands for the first time, to better know the people and the country of his beloved Dutch Old Masters. Upon returning, he moved to the Moravian Slovakia region, where he spent almost the whole following decade in a rented gamekeeper's lodge on the slopes of Hostýnské vrchy. Here the focus of Schwaiger's art changed. While he was still in Prague, the naturalistic aspect of his work had become unusually prominent, and although he never renounced his initial late Romanticism in repeated scenes from fairy tales, his grotesque visions were henceforward based more on what he saw than what he could imagine. However, what was most remarkable in this shift in Schwaiger's concept for his paintings – one that essentially corresponded to developments in contemporary painting as a whole, when, at the turn of the 1890s, naturalism became generally established as the "modern" way of painting – was that it was in no way detrimental to his integrity as an artist, and even less to the technical quality of his paintings. In the case of Schwaiger, the grotesque fantasy of his late Romantic fairy-tale images was consistent with his scenes of grinding poverty or depictions of the landscape's natural charms. In this strange interaction between seemingly contradictory elements, Schwaiger perhaps belonged even more to the spirit of the Secession than in the formal stylistic qualities of his work from the first half of the 1880s.

The inner unity between the two main stages in Schwaiger's life and work is most apparent in his view of Holland, where the Old World and Old Masters are organically combined with the present day. However, this unity is also found in works from Schwaiger's own country, largely because both elements, the fantastical and the naturalistic, had a common denominator. The integrity of his art came from the correspondence between the appearance of the common people and their legends. Both aspects converge in Schwaiger's sustained interest in nature. Nature is the permanent backdrop to country life, both in the hard physical labour that shapes the costumes and physiques of Schwaiger's country folk, and in the fairy-tale mythology of natural forces personified by the mountain spirit Krakonoš, Little Longnose, water sprites, will-o'-the-wisps, elves, and giants, but also by knights, princesses, and numerous other characters. In Schwaiger's world view, fairy tales and reality were complementary, and this was what so attracted Jiránek and his peers to the artist in the first decade of the 20th century. It was more an ethical than a moral value, overarching all the individual formulas for painting. These formulas were in fact derived from this ethos in quite a remarkable way, and they reshaped the conventional world of contemporary art into original hallmarks of the new mentality.

At the start of the 1890s, this courage to embrace the new also extended to a discipline far more resistant to innovation than painting. Czech architecture of the latter half of the 19th century had mainly belonged to the Neo-Renaissance style. The

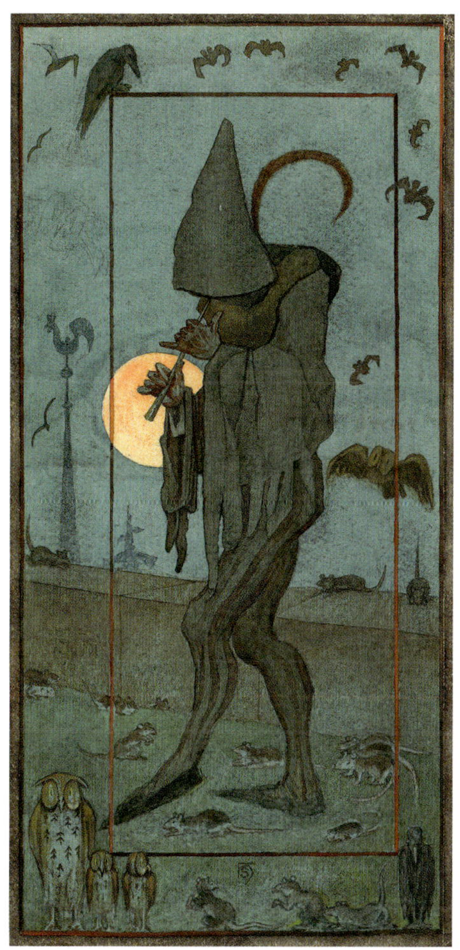

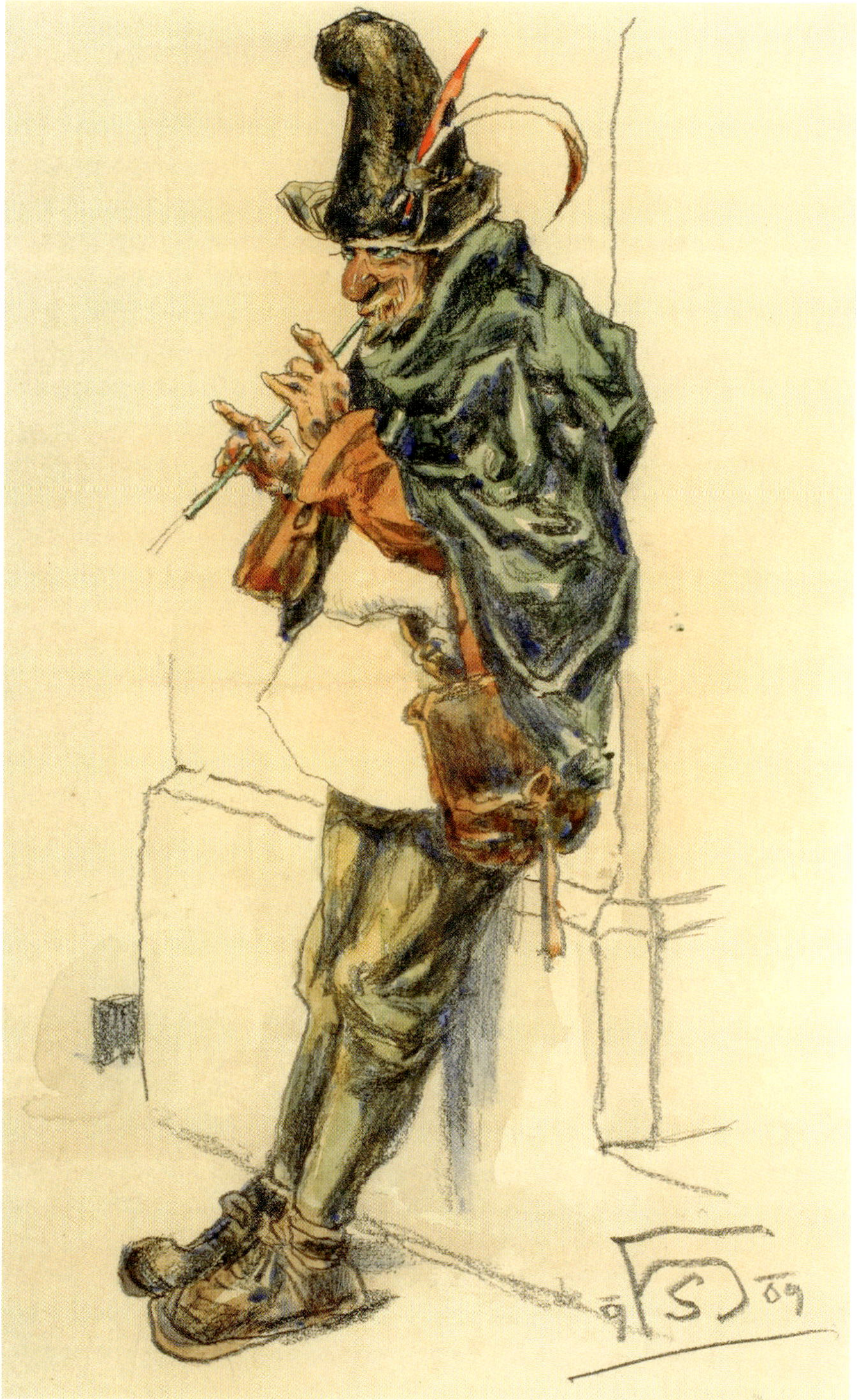

13 Hanuš Schwaiger, *The Pied Piper*, 1882, watercolour, 51 × 25 cm

14 Hanuš Schwaiger, *The Pied Piper*, 1909, pencil and watercolour, 33 × 21.5 cm

revival of Renaissance forms, promoted and practised by Gottfried Semper since the 1840s, was a Europe-wide phenomenon, but it acquired a particular significance in Bohemia, where it was considered representative of a burgeoning Czech national art. The greatest manifestation of this was the building of the National Theatre in Prague. Its architect, Josef Zítek, based his design on his intimate knowledge of High Renaissance forms, which he combined with Czech motifs, especially in the elongated cupola that crowned the building. The project was beset with difficulties right from the start, and following a devastating fire shortly after the theatre opened in 1881, Zítek resigned. He was succeeded by his former pupil, Josef Schulz, who would later take Zítek's concept of the Renaissance Revival in a different direction. Schulz built the National Museum around 1890, and its ornamentation shaped Czech decorative art for the entire decade. In it, he relaxed Zítek's harmonious restraint in favour of a monumentality that was treated much more illusively and grandly. This made the building somewhat more academic in style. Unlike the National Theatre, the National Museum, standing at the top of Wenceslas Square, was at the very centre of the rapidly expanding capital city. Seeking to give it an appropriately metropolitan grandeur, which was something Schulz had noted in similar buildings abroad, he went beyond the original requirements for faithfulness to historical models and introduced a certain Mannerist aspect, which would henceforward also characterise his other buildings in Prague, including the Museum of Decorative Arts, built in 1897–1901.

This relaxation of the classical canon was highly influential for the architecture of the 1890s, and it ushered in the late phase of architectural historicism in this country, with an eclecticism that paved the way for other endeavours. It soon began to encroach on the Neo-Renaissance and Neo-Baroque monopoly, and this only accelerated the illusionistic dismantling of historicism.

At a time when there was mounting pressure from clients and architects for an appropriately national grandeur, something that was now felt much more individualistically than before, an extensive exhibition was held in Prague that greatly influenced the contemporary mentality. This was the 1891 General Land Centennial Exhibition (*Všeobecná zemská jubilejní výstava*).

This showcasing of the Czech Lands' economic and cultural achievements in the 19th century was inspired by the world expositions that, ever since the Great Exhibition in London in 1851, had been held at ever-shorter intervals in the principal metropolises of Europe and America. These were the most extensive manifestations of contemporary nationalism, but they were also an opportunity to celebrate the 19th century's technological progress. Attractions at the Prague exhibition included František Křižík's colourful illuminated fountain, powered by electricity, and the Aeronautical School, which offered balloon flights. No less remarkable, however, was the Industrial or Central Palace, built at the centre of the large new exhibition grounds in Holešovice.

Visitors were astonished by its sheer size, measuring 208 metres in length and covering an area of 12,870 square metres. This scale was achieved thanks to a new building technique pioneered in the large halls built for the Great Exhibition in London and the 1889 Exposition Universelle in Paris. Instead of solid masonry, they used iron arches for the basic construction, and filled the large spaces between them with glass. Although the main material for this "engineered" architecture – iron – was entirely modern, this new way of building halls with iron arches was also inspired by Gothic rib vaulting.

The exhibition palace in Prague consisted of a stable central part created by eight main supporting arches rising 25 metres above the floor, with a span of 38 metres. At each of the four corners, the arches rested on a masonry pylon with elaborate ornamentation. Above this relatively massive part rose a delicate-looking clock tower, topped with the crown of Saint Wenceslas. The tower's spiral staircase could be seen from all sides, and it added a light touch to this immense building. Wings extended on either side of the palace's entrance; the original plan was that they would be removed once the exhibition had ended, reducing the size of the exhibition space.

The building's architect was Bedřich Münzberger, and the design for the construction of the central part was the work of František Prášil, chief engineer at the Prague Bridgeworks, part of the First Bohemian-Moravian Machine Works, which supplied the 500-tonne structure. Münzberger was the nephew of the first architect to work systematically on the Czech Renaissance Revival, Ignác Ullmann, and during the previous decade Münzberger had built Karlín Town Hall and an extension to the Náprstek Museum in the Neo-Renaissance style, as well as designing Palacký Bridge. For the Centennial Exhibition, Münzberger had originally envisaged a traditional masonry building, but with the executive committee's blessing he revised his plans, desiring "to characterise the present day in the choice of building material, and then by using an iron structure greater space could be achieved and thereby the easier and more advantageous placing of the exhibits."[20] The imperative of practicality and modernity would henceforward characterise Czech modern architecture, and the "engineering" building technique using iron and glass was the most striking example of such attempts. Even at the time of the exhibition, it was not just this new technique's practical merits that were appreciated, but also its new aesthetics: "the iron palace surprised everyone with its lightness, elegance and boldness."[21] Its glass and iron construction, offering entirely new lighting conditions for the exhibits, was also admired.

> What is most remarkable is the glasswork. This is the first time that this kind of decoration has been used in a building of this kind, and with patterns that are in keeping with the structure. It is cathedral glass, of Czech manufacture.

The new architectural, spatial, and decorative qualities of Münzberger and Prášil's building were sure to have initially been associated with the celebratory atmosphere of the exhibition grounds, and it would probably not have occurred to a contemporary viewer to compare it with the monumental architecture of grand public buildings. However, the exhibition palace continued to adorn the grounds, which would subsequently host a number of other large exhibitions, including the Czech-Slav Ethnographic Exhibition (*Národopisná výstava českoslovanská*) in 1895 and the Architecture and Engineering Exhibition (*Výstava architektury a inženýrství*) in 1898, which were especially popular with the younger generation. For these visitors, the palace's lightness and spaciousness seemed to be another of the remarkable experiences on offer,

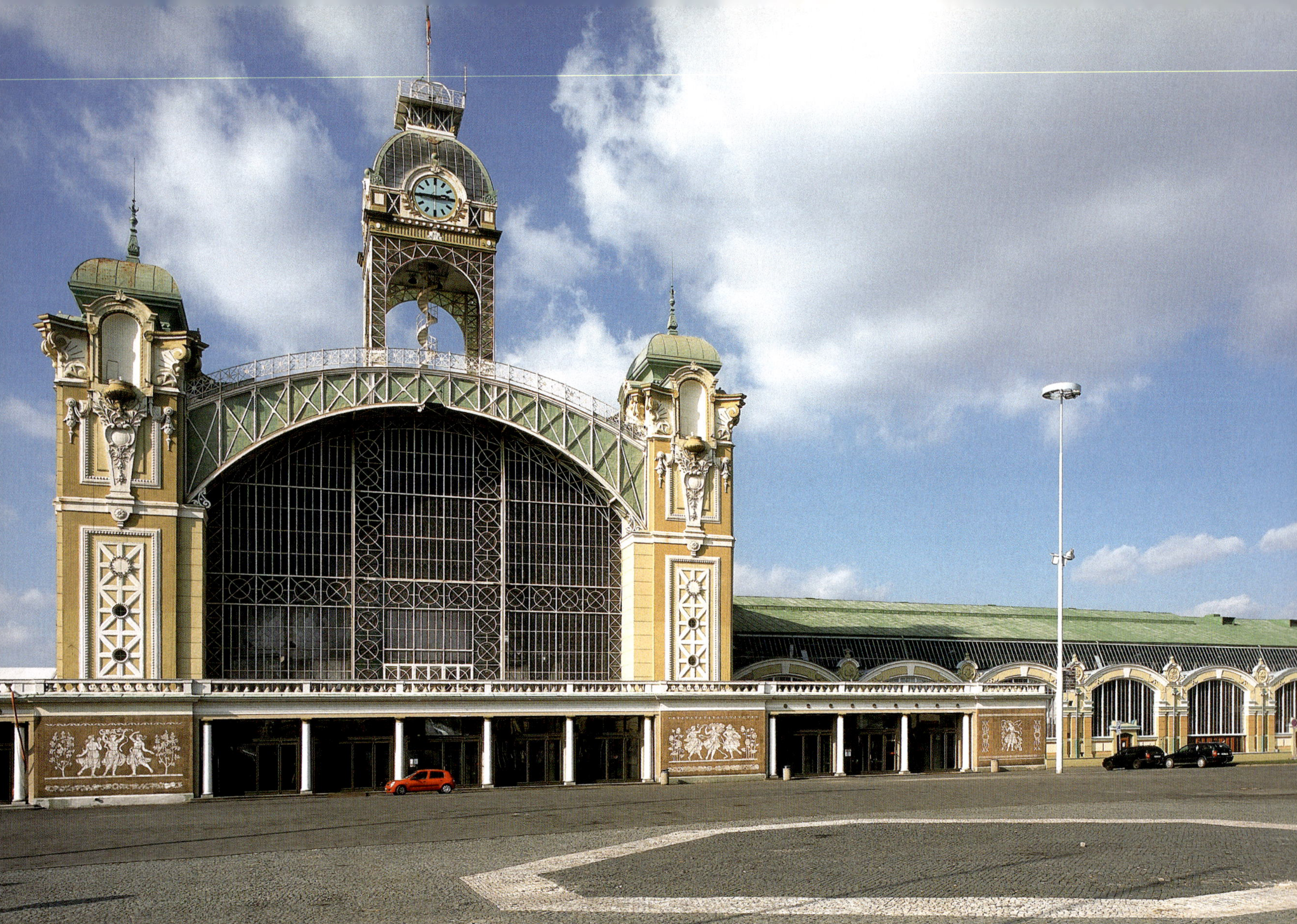

and it perhaps shaped their aesthetics far more than much of the "official" architecture erected during Prague's building boom in the late 19th century.

The Centennial Exhibition showcased economic and technical progress in the Czech Lands, but culture was not overlooked, for it also included an extensive retrospective of Czech art up to the present day. Here it was contemporary art that drew the most visitors, at least if we can judge from a vivid account by K. B. Mádl that was published in a book commemorating the exhibition. Following the death of Miroslav Tyrš, Mádl had become the most agile Czech art critic, and he enthusiastically mapped contemporary developments in Czech painting and sculpture.[22]

In the painting section, Jakub Schikaneder's *Murder in the House* and Emanuel Dítě's *The Building of the Hunger Wall in Prague under Charles IV* attracted particular attention. Both were typical examples of what interested contemporary painters and the general public. Dítě, who had started working on his painting while studying in Munich in the

15 Bedřich Münzberger and František Prášil, Industrial Palace in Prague, 1891

early 1880s, drew on the popular historical genre, to which he added a contemporary note in line with the social commentary that had begun to appear in Central European painting during that decade. Schikaneder, who came from the realist genre, further accentuated this same tendency in his contemporary social drama. The title of his painting confused viewers, who thought this melancholy scene of a dead woman lying in a small courtyard depicted a suicide. Mádl considered this another of the painting's merits, because the viewer could not be satisfied by the title alone and had to examine and evaluate the painting itself.

However, what Mádl most admired was a collection of Vojtěch Hynais's work, including a sketch for his famous curtain for the National Theatre. Although in 1883, when the curtain was created, its commissioners had been somewhat doubtful, it had soon become the first great victory of a taste that was explicitly guided by contemporary Parisian art. The cosmopolitan and effortless elegance of Hynais's allegorical figures, and especially the new colour tones for the curtain, whose pinks and greys were inspired by Italian late Baroque colourism, reflected a concept of painting that, to artists in Prague, trained in traditional draughtsmanship and locally defined colours, seemed all but unattainable.

While there were several promising painters, in sculpture it was a different matter. Here too there was an undisputed master who easily surpassed all others, but Mádl's assessment of the works exhibited by Josef Václav Myslbek sounded more like confirmation of something that was "classic," in the sense of its being so perfect that nothing could better it.

Myslbek exhibited *Saint Joseph with the Infant Jesus* and *Crucifix*, two sculptures that had already won him much international acclaim. Mádl too praised them as works before which "everything that was thought here to be the pinnacle of the plastic arts now retreats." In the statue of the seated Saint Joseph, he admired above all the "perfectly beautiful head," and he considered the body of the martyred Christ to be one of the very finest European sculptures of the Crucifixion. Compared with Myslbek, the remaining selection of Czech sculpture seemed impoverished. Although Mádl enthusiastically welcomed Ludvík Wurzel's *The Victim of Faith* as a promise of further flourishing, his pronouncement that "the exhibition could not have brought us anything more welcome than that the arch-sculptor Myslbek has found an epigone of talent so brilliant that the master can be proud of his pupil" reveals that his assessment remained circumscribed by eclecticism. This mentality, this respect for an exemplar that could only be imitated, was not only a weakness in Mádl's art criticism, for it was also an aspect of the aesthetic inertia that would later be challenged by the Secession.

Against this backdrop, a year after the Centennial Exhibition a scandal broke that seemed symptomatic of the looming crisis. It concerned sculpture, and the protagonist was František Bílek, just twenty years old at the time and one of the most prominent artists of the 1890s' generation. Bílek had begun studying at the academy in Prague in 1887, arriving at the time of a major reorganisation when, following the retirement of the conservative Antonín Lhota, teaching was entrusted to Julius Mařák and Maxmilián Pirner, both newly appointed. Bílek soon proved to be a superb draughtsman, but his original intention to become a painter foundered owing to his partial colour blindness. His professors advised him to switch to sculpture, and he was taught by Josef Mauder. The results were so good that Bílek exhibited his busts of the academy's rector Mařák and his daughter at the Centennial Exhibition, and he then received a grant from Vojtěch Lanna that allowed him to travel to Paris at the beginning of 1891.

While in Paris, away from Prague's art scene, Bílek came to reject all the earlier criteria. His French was too poor for him to fit into his new surroundings, nor was he sociable enough to do so. A sensitive young man, he was profoundly homesick – and for *home* in the most intimate sense of the word. It seems that even before this, back in Prague, Bílek had never lost his shyness. Some attributed this to his rural origins, but those who knew him better thought it reflected a profound moral distrust.[23]

In Paris, Bílek studied not at the official École des Beaux-Arts but at the private Académie Colarossi, where he only attended modelling courses during his first year in the city. It seems that his teacher, Jean-Antoine Injalbert, praised his work without correcting it in any way. Much more appealing than his studies were the collections in the city's museums, especially the casts of old French medieval religious sculptures that were on display at the Palais du Trocadéro, where Bílek found art that had been created on a different basis from the customary academic study of posed models, and its ideoplasticity corresponded to an unusual degree to his own interests, which since childhood had been powerfully shaped by old religious traditions.

Unfortunately, we have no record of Bílek's response to the contemporary art he must have seen in Paris. A drawing of him by the Polish painter Stanisław Wyspiański is the only indication that he was not quite as isolated as his own account of his time in the city would suggest.[24] Bílek's circumstances in Paris – like his visit to Chartres Cathedral, where he would have seen the western portal's famous "column statues," whose elongated forms were later reflected in his own elongation of the figure – may have served merely as the inspiration for him to crystallise his ideas on sculpture, above all with regard to its content.

In 1892 Bílek created two sculptures in Paris that would come to characterise all his subsequent work, and by chance they also anticipated a turning point for Czech sculpture in the 1890s. The first was *Golgotha – The Mountain of Skulls*, showing the Virgin Mary and John the Evangelist grieving at the foot of a roughly hewn cross whose crossbeam has been removed. If the subject was a common one, its rendition was unusual. Bílek gave the sculpture expressive naturalistic and Neo-Baroque elements. The overall scene was naturalistic, as was the unconventional use of real materials, such as the ropes dangling from the cross and the crown of thorns woven from wire. Also naturalistic was the rendition of the Virgin Mary, but the stylisation of the figures, especially John the Evangelist, who is bent double with grief, is Neo-Baroque. Despite its novelty, *Golgotha* still drew on the customary compositional methods for French sculpture at the time. However, Bílek's next sculpture was entirely nonconformist. *Tilling Is the Punishment for Our Trespass* shows a nude and emaciated Christ exhaustedly "tilling" the hard ground, which is made of tablets carved with small and illegible inscriptions. Before him, incomparably smaller in scale, are tiny figures who similarly wrestle with the weight of the tablets bearing the Ten Commandments. These figures represent the sin of mankind that is redeemed by Christ.

In *Tilling*, Bílek accentuated his naturalism to the point where it became explicitly expressive, and the Neo-Baroque element of his style renounced all remaining compositional elegance and is most reminiscent of Matthias Braun's hermits from Bethlehem Wood, near the village of Kuks. The motif of a large central figure and small secondary figures created a new effect that would frequently be adopted by others, especially to contrast the moral greatness of an individual with the triviality of humanity's usual concerns. Stanislav Sucharda used this effect in his designs for the Jan Hus Memorial in Prague, as did František Kupka in his illustrations for Josef Svatopluk Machar's poems.

Despite their differences, the two sculptures are in a sense complementary. The absence of Christ's body gives *Golgotha* its particularly traumatic aspect and tension, bringing forth the vision of *Tilling*. In *Golgotha*, grief is expressed visually through the greater stylisation of the sculpture, in which typical Baroque Revival devices – such as John the Evangelist's bare foot extending over the sculpture's plinth – are deployed to a more profound end. Bílek explained this motif as the result of the *S curve* that shapes the sculpture's mass, which he understood as "a symbol of life."[25] Bílek's *Gol-*

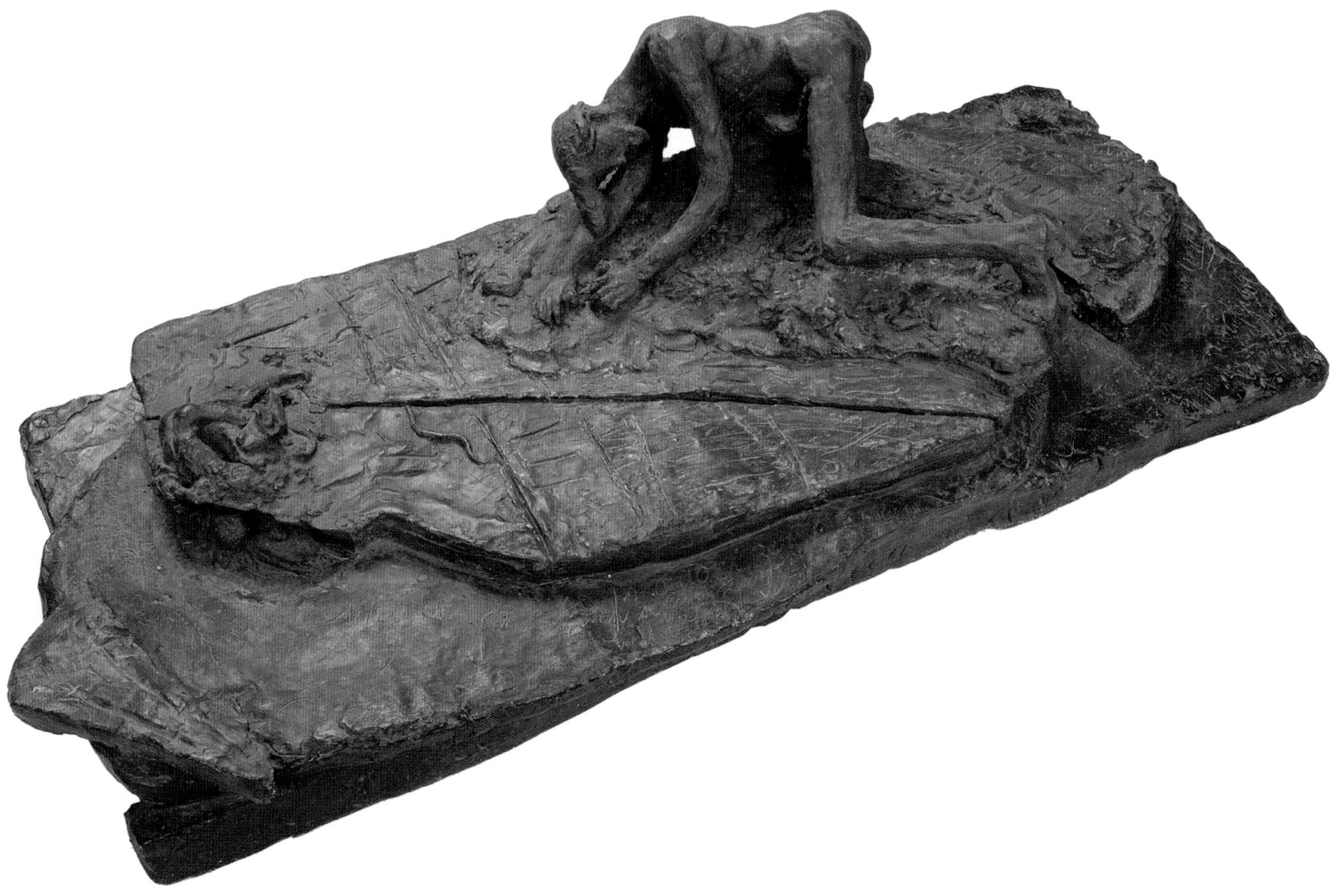

16 František Bílek, *Tilling Is the Punishment for Our Trespass*, 1892, patinated plaster, 30 cm

gotha therefore established the rationale for the Secession's typical approach. The contrast between the stylised *Golgotha* and the expressive *Tilling* not only reflects the inner conflict that informed Bílek's overall concept, based on the disparity between the urgency of desire and the impossibility of its satisfaction, but also anticipates the essential semantic structure of typical Secession art.

Bílek submitted these two sculptures to the grant committee, where their unconventionality created a scandal. The committee's members, schooled as they were in the prevailing Neo-Renaissance taste, were outraged by their rawness and their subjectivist interpretation of traditional scenes. The debacle culminated in strong condemnation from Josef Václav Myslbek.[26] Bílek's grant was withdrawn, and at the end of 1892 he returned to Bohemia, defeated. He retreated to his birthplace, Chýnov, where he would remain for several years as he slowly recovered from this devastating wound.

In 1892 this affair was probably generally considered to be Bílek's personal failure, but it was in fact the first volley in a bitter conflict between two fundamentally opposed concepts of art. The highly personal form that this confrontation took in Bílek's case resulted in a psychological complex that, for the rest of the 1890s, would compel him to reject almost desperately the small-mindedness of Czech culture and instead to embrace extremes that would ultimately bring new advances in art.

Yet the ground had already been prepared for much of what was so surprising in Bílek's sculpture, and this was also why it would prove all the more influential by the

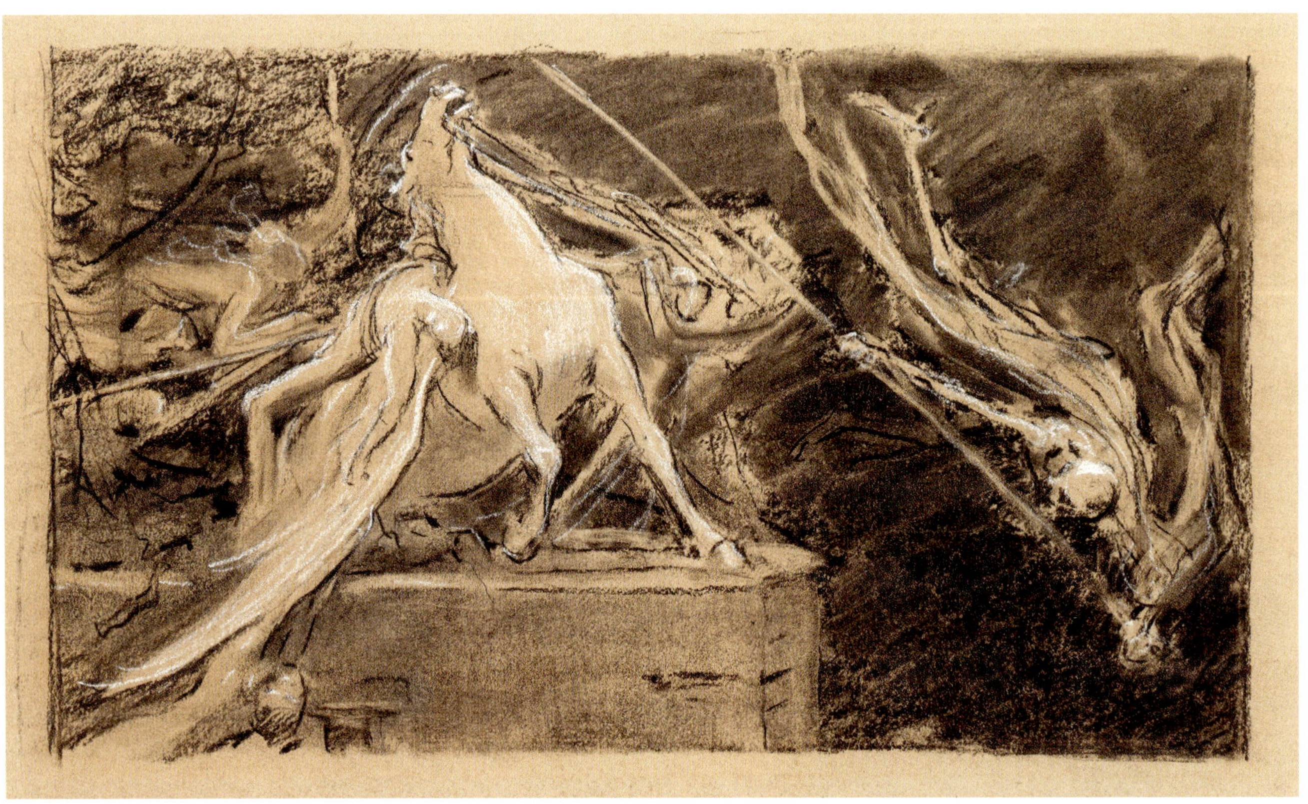

17 Maxmilián Pirner, Sketch from the cycle *Pegasus*, 1889–91, black and white chalk, 24.2 × 30.6 cm

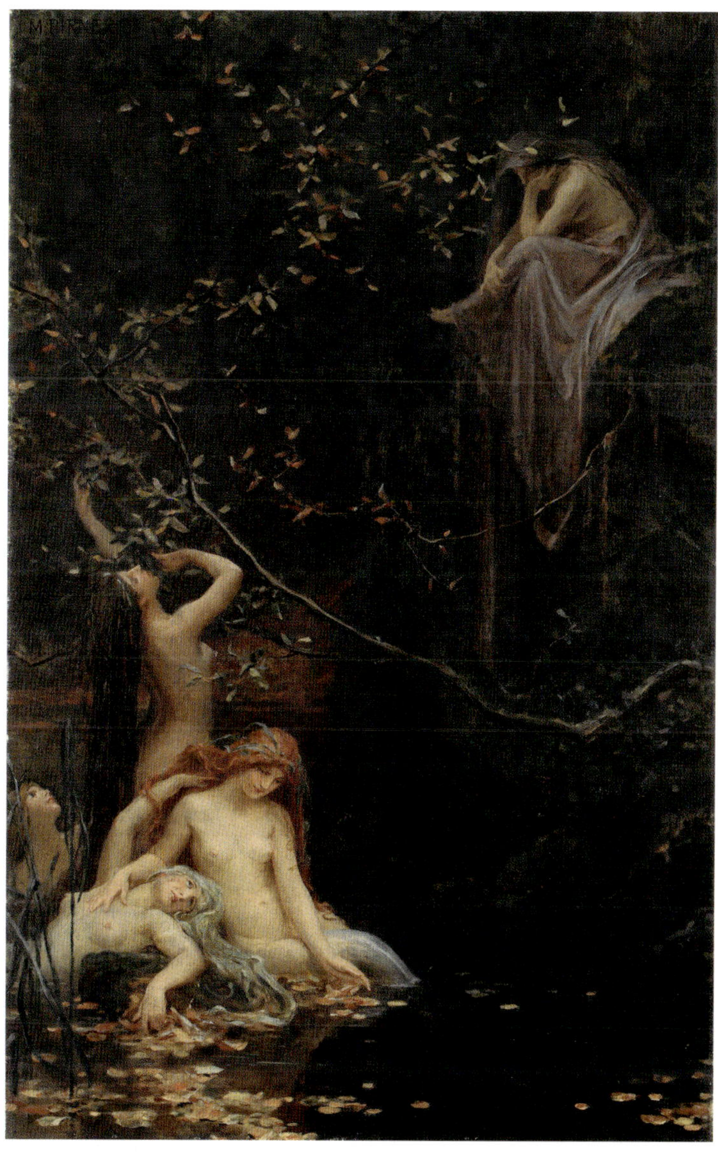

end of the decade. Behind Bílek's art lay the work of his first teacher at the Academy of Fine Arts in Prague, Maxmilián Pirner.

In 1887, as part of the academy's reorganisation, Pirner, who had himself been taught there by Josef Matyáš Trenkwald, was made the head of the genre school. This appointment was evidently on account of his extensive *Demon Love* cycle, which was exhibited at the Ruch gallery in Prague in the same year. The keynote of the entire cycle was of course a romantic one. If Pirner's earlier work had been characterised by his ironic take on older chivalric romanticism in *The Ballad of the Knight* (1876), and his nod to the contemporary wave of social realism in the *Mother* triptych from the 1880s, as soon as he joined the academy's leadership his true interest became apparent: a longing to paint grand ideas. He may have been influenced by the poet Jaroslav Vrchlický,

18 Maxmilián Pirner, *Fairies by the Brook*, 1895, oil, 99 × 61 cm

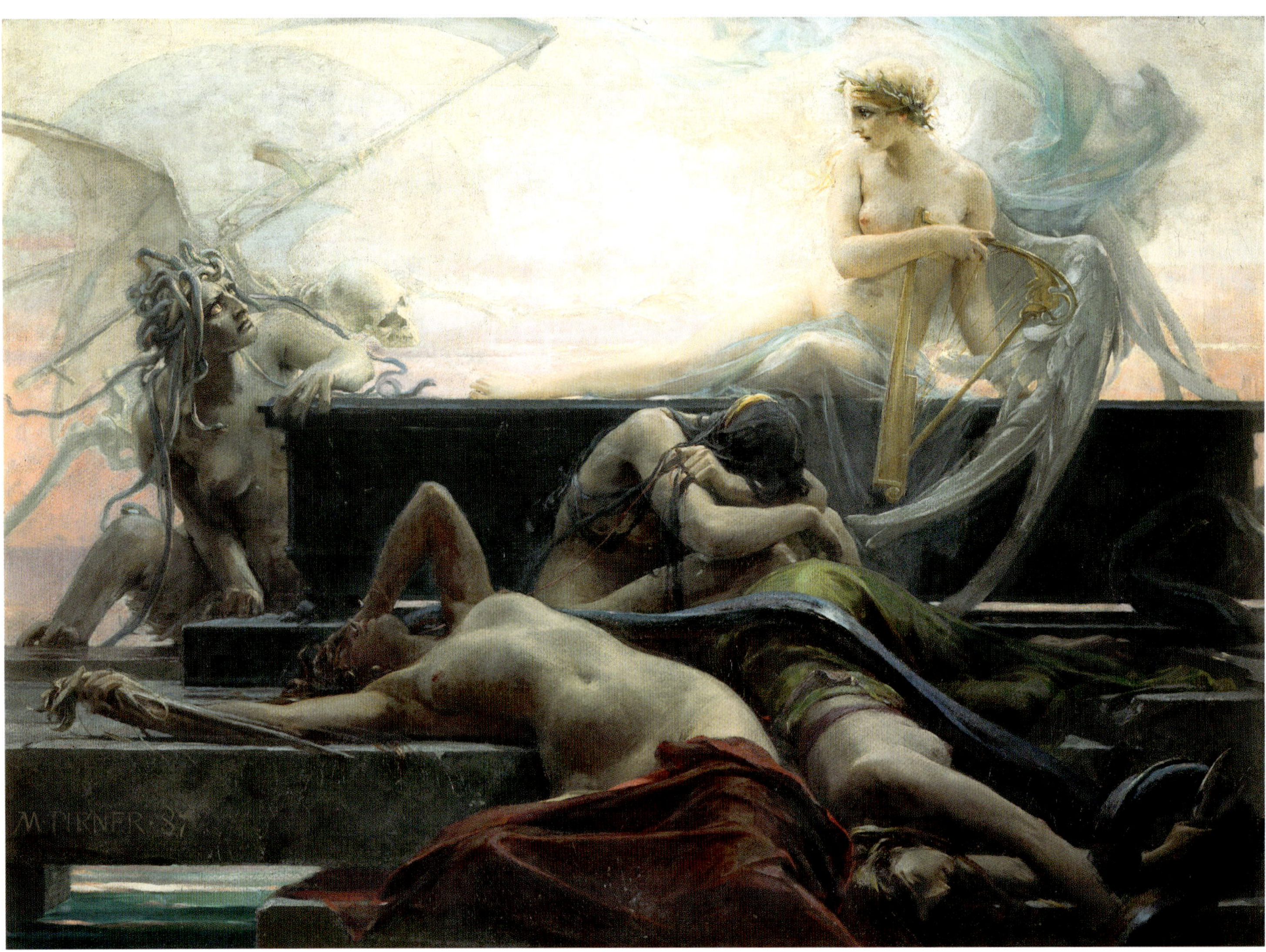

for the two were friends and Pirner illustrated Vrchlický's poems. Pirner adopted the Parnassian concept of an all-encompassing poetry that transcended national and social divides, as he announced in his painting *Finis* from 1887, which was later exhibited at the Centennial Exhibition. Its subject was the confrontation of the two fundamental forces in the world, Life and Death, personified by the radiant winged Poetry, who holds a harp, and the Medusa-headed demon Quietus, who is accompanied by a skeleton. In contemporary terminology, the idea behind the painting was a philosophical one. However, its universality was distinguished by the effective arrangement of Pirner's treatment, accentuated by the three swooning nudes in the foreground, representing humanity languishing under the dark dominion of Quietus.

Some of Pirner's paintings from the turn of the 1890s are filled with large allegorical figures, suggesting that these paintings were intended for official display. They include

19 Maxmilián Pirner, *Finis*, 1887, oil, 100 × 130 cm

Moira, and a sweeping triptych whose wings again juxtapose Thought, Love, and Life with Madness, Hatred, and Death. The central part depicts a dramatic scene: a poet soars up to the heights on the winged horse Pegasus, where Genius awaits him with a laurel wreath, but just as the poet reaches his goal, demons cast him back down to earth, where we see a naked woman lying lifelessly, an old man sitting with a plough, and a winged child with a golden apple. In their formal aspects, the paintings on either side reveal Pirner's attempt to approximate contemporary French allegorical painting, while the central painting's dynamism and contrasts of light recall Baroque altar paintings.

These works had a somewhat peculiar status in contemporary Czech painting, which by now generally favoured naturalism. It was not their subject matter that was unique, but rather the consistency of their standpoint and Pirner's attempt to place late Romantic idealism at the same level as salon painting. They were evidently not too well received by the general public, as is also indicated by the tentativeness of Mádl's otherwise appreciative remarks on Pirner's *Finis* in his account of the Centennial Exhibition's art section. This was probably also why Pirner gradually abandoned this way of conveying his ideas and ultimately ceased exhibiting altogether.

This meant he could devote all the more attention to his pupils, not only teaching them to draw flawlessly but also influencing the content of their work, especially in his first decade at the academy. Pirner's late Romanticism was not merely seeking to produce an effect; it also had an intellectual core, for which Pirner was substantially drawing on tradition. This is evident in a number of paintings that remained hidden in the depths of his studio, such as one showing an androgynous winged ephebe gazing upwards as he ascends from a turbid stream of half-human figures. This was a late Romantic allegory of the old Platonic myth of the immortality of the human soul, winged insofar as it approaches the eternal forms, an idea that had been one of the most influential in ideoplastic European art since the Renaissance. Among the younger artists, Bílek was one of the most devoted disseminators of this classical idea, which he originally discovered in the Bible and the work of William Blake, and also in the imagery of Pirner's paintings. Bílek's attentiveness to Pirner's motifs can be seen in the way he repeats his teacher, especially in his drawings and sculptural reliefs. In the first works Bílek produced to overcome his profound personal crisis following the debacle with the grant committee, we again find the figure of an artist astride the winged Pegasus and figures with outstretched arms (*From the Struggle for Existence*, 1893; *Time's Wrath, Our Dowry*, 1895). It is not just the individual motifs that are repeated, but the overall tragic tone of the allegory, which for Pirner ended in downfall and for the young Bílek was further amplified by his early disillusionment.

Yet Pirner's oeuvre also included more lyrical works, based on his childhood enchantment with Moritz von Schwind, and his lesser-known partiality to Josef Mánes, which he shared with others of his generation, such as Josef Tulka, Mikoláš Aleš, and Josef Mauder. This side of his work, based on a romantic attachment to nature, which he animated with chimerical visions of fairies, was also popular with the younger generation, and in the work of Jan Preisler and Max Švabinský it again took on new and more contemporary forms.

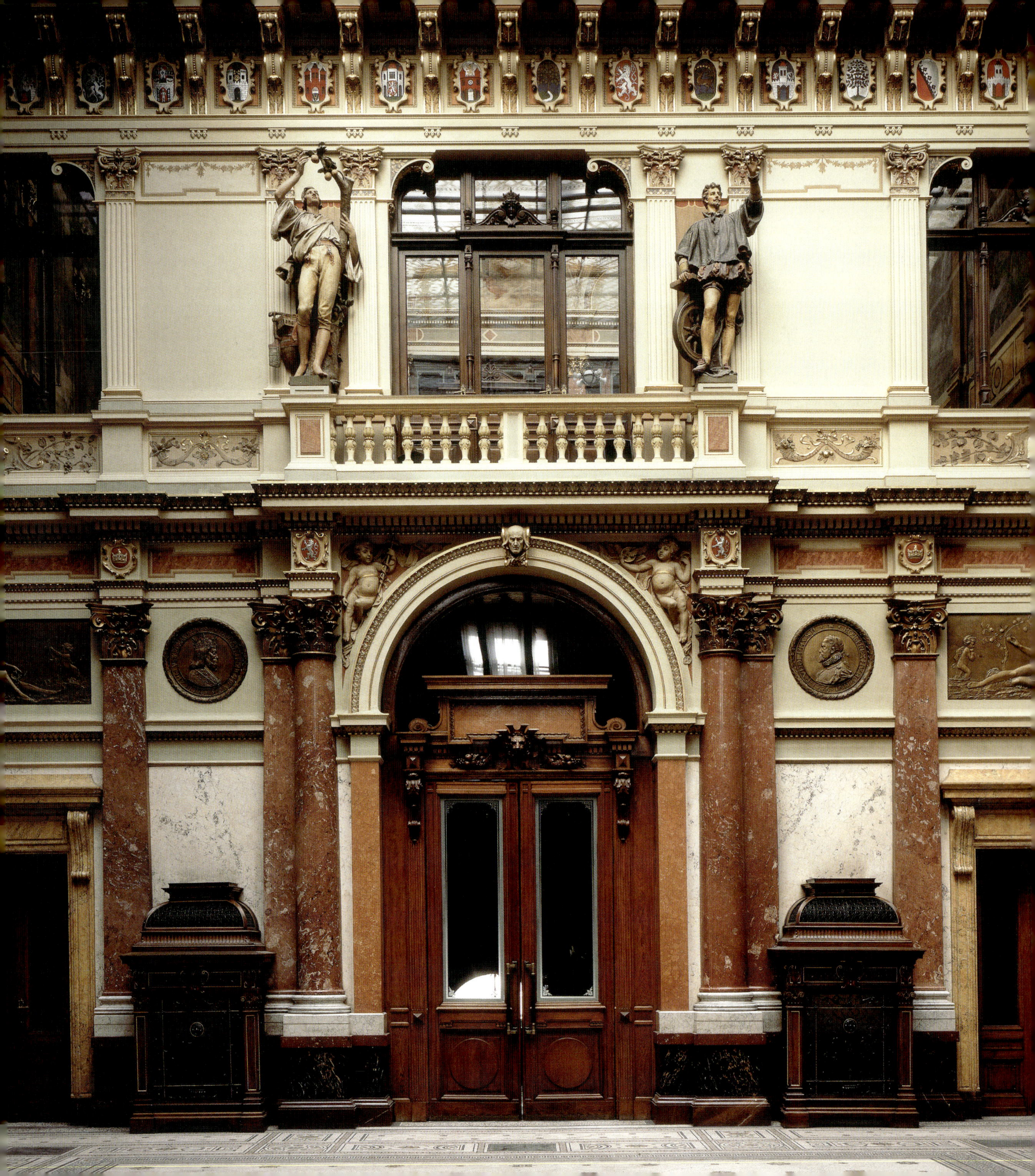

THE END OF THE CENTURY

The art milieu of the 1890s was still essentially influenced by the historicism that had defined 19th-century culture. However, historicism too had evolved. Its main phases can be divided into an initial period of Romantic historicism, when a distinctively patriotic enthusiasm generated colourful ideas about the nation's heroic past, followed by the "scientific" historicism period, when the positivist mentality of the latter half of the century led to the archaeological study of historic sites and their often somewhat insensitive purist restoration. Examples from the glossary of historical styles were sought ever more systematically for new works. However, by the end of the 19th century we find the third phase of historicism, when it was as though certain aspects of the initial Romanticism had returned, but now on the basis of the experience gained during the second period by art conservators, restorers, and the publishers of historical models and monographs.

One consequence of this meticulousness was the oversaturation we see in artworks from the 1890s, where the focus on fine detail is frequently more important than the whole. This level of detail makes little sense for a complex whole inspired by classical examples – Josef Zítek's buildings, for instance – and another kind of integrity was sought, although one that, for the time being, was still dictated by stylistic compendiums and examples.

There was a turn away from monumentality in favour of the intimate and picturesque, still of course within the bounds of social convention. This was not a personal, confidential intimacy, but one mediated by the salon. Some aristocratic art lovers commissioned works that introduced late Romantic elements: in 1892 Hanuš Schwaiger created a large sgraffito depicting Saint George and the dragon for the courtyard of Count Sylva-Taroucca's charming chateau in Průhonice.

Still more typical of the twilight of historicism were several small buildings such as the Hanau Pavilion, built for the 1891 Centennial Exhibition to promote the Principality of Hanau's ironworks and foundries. This somewhat whimsical little building, assembled from pseudo-Renaissance casts, reflects the shift in focus from the Italian Renaissance to the Northern Renaissance and Mannerism that can be considered symptomatic of historicism's decline. It is notable that both the pavilion and Schwaiger's sgraffito sought to integrate architecture and nature, albeit in the form of a landscape park or orchard. Nature was becoming irresistible to the artistic imagination. Another sign of this was the reopening of the landscape painting school at the reorganised Academy of Fine Arts. It was headed by Julius Mařák, who had painted series of spectacular views of historic sites in the Kingdom of Bohemia for the National Theatre and National Museum. What most interested him was painting in the depths of forests, where he could give full voice to his late Romantic soul in scenes animated only by forest fauna.

20 Osvald Polívka, Provincial Bank in Prague, 1895–96, interior

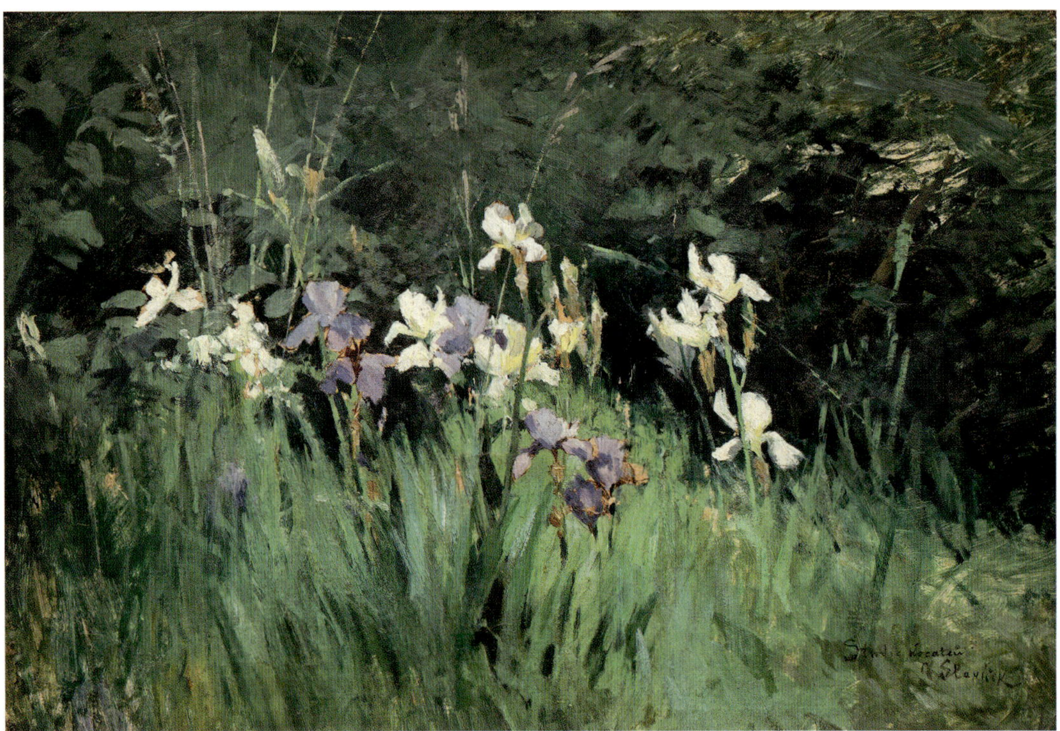

He brilliantly sketched these in charcoal, as well as depicting them in etched copper plates that marked a new development in Czech printmaking. Mařák devoted much of his time to his students, and the "Mařák school" would greatly influence the course of Czech painting. His first students included Antonín Slavíček, Václav Březina, Josef Holub, and Jan Minařík, who in 1889–90 were joined by František Kaván, Bohuslav Dvořák, Ferdinand Engelmüller, and others. Of these, only Engelmüller would later remain faithful to late Romanticism. As students, they would go on excursions around Prague, where initially they were all captivated by the sunlit forest scenes that so excited their teacher. The colours of their paintings were subdued, and landscape painting still retained the ornamental function that had defined it throughout the 19th century.

Antonín Slavíček, the most talented of these students, was also influenced by Antonín Chittussi, another noted landscape painter from the previous generation. Slavíček and František Kaván together pioneered new motifs. They were drawn to open landscapes, panoramas viewed through trees, usually still bare in early spring, that created compositionally effective verticals. The contrast between the sweeping horizon and the trellis of trees would anticipate later Secession landscapes.

These young landscape painters began to emphasise other motifs too. Initially they were captivated simply by their picturesqueness, but by returning to them they gave them a special significance, and these motifs came to symbolise a new relationship with nature. Mařák's students also found picturesque sites by the stream running through the little village of Okoř, where they would regularly stay in the 1890s. Flowing water gave their paintings a new animation.

21 Antonín Slavíček, Study of *Irises*, 1892–93, oil, 44.5 × 64 cm

In this way, landscape painting began to look beyond its usual compositional schemata. This was accompanied by a change of colour, which gradually moved away from local tones. One such painting is Slavíček's *Irises*, dated to 1892–93. It was fashionable in the choice of flower and the new application of colour to a foundation that was still, in the style of salon paintings, entirely dark green. The painting is considered a turning point in Slavíček's early work.[27]

While in landscape painting the first stirrings of this new mentality were marked by a youthful bashfulness, in figure painting it was much more assertive. In 1893 Vojtěch Hynais became a professor at the academy in Prague. This had long been anticipated, for Hynais's paintings for the National Theatre had been well received in the city. Having spent many years in Paris, Hynais was known as an expert on contemporary French painting, and he introduced a new concept for Czech painting based on adopting and adapting contemporary French inspiration. His new colleagues viewed this somewhat ironically, with Pirner dubbing him "Monsieur Yné," but Hynais would soon ignite his students' enthusiasm with innovations that made him the academy's most influential teacher in the latter half of the 1890s.

Vojtěch Hynais crowned his arrival with a large painting that he completed in 1894. The subject was a traditional one, drawing on ancient Greek mythology and the classical repertoire of representative figure painting. However, the subject of *The Judgement of Paris* allowed him to concentrate on the new form and the key question of colour and light. Naked bodies in nature, lit by the sun, had become a motif that tormented young painters with the problem of reflected colour. There was a popular anecdote about how sculptors at the academy refused to work with Hynais's models because they were covered with "green blotches." In fact, the history of Czech Impressionism began with Hynais's *The Judgement of Paris* and his studies for it.

Yet there was also much in Hynais's oeuvre that was traditional. This, however, was not at odds with contemporary naturalistic interests, for it was principally based on Italian Baroque painting and its luministic effects. The response to French Impressionism that we see, for instance, in Hynais's vividly painted views of his studio in Paris, and in his portraits and decorative work, was channelled and viewed through this prism. In the 1890s Hynais developed his feel for visual reality, with its foundation in the Baroque Revival, to a degree that recalled period photography. Nevertheless, with his excellent sense of colour, his increasing naturalism still remained very much painting. We can, however, see some of the more curious aspects of this situation in the decorative panels with allegorical cherubs hovering in the sky that Hynais painted for the dome of the National Museum's pantheon in the late 1890s.

The popularity of Hynais's art with the younger generation can be understood as largely due to its raising of new questions precisely when this next group of artists was starting out, and it did so on a basis that was easily understood and traditional in its themes. Although from a logical standpoint Hynais's combination of naturalism and allegory was questionable, it was a development that extricated painting from routine "literary" convention and focused attention more on how painting related to visual reality than to narrative. It therefore opened an opportunity for painters to work largely without grand speculative subject matter, yet it did not preclude the possibility that painters could contribute to the interpretation of major "literary" themes. This mutual exchange and enrichment established the conditions for culture to be understood as something that was multifaceted and, above all, created. Hynais therefore introduced a new value in form and content that young artists felt was the "French spirit," and it resonated with what was most precious to them: a sense of freedom and the opening of new possibilities for creative art. This was what Hynais set in motion. At a propitious moment in history, his painting became identified with the younger generation's main psychological motivation, and in the end it mattered little that much of it was also superficial elegance and epigonism. Besides, in the still nebulous ideas of young painters there was also a great deal of naivety and a willingness to create new legends. One of the most pervasive legends was the cult of French art and the myth of Paris as art's "city of light."

The foundations of this myth had been laid earlier, in fact ever since the mid-19th century, when Czech artists had first discovered modern French art and found in it a way out of the contemporary crisis. Under the Austro-Hungarian Empire and its regimenting of the development of Czech national consciousness, there were also compelling political reasons for this. These were only confirmed by the artists' own experience, and they became more and more convinced that it was Paris that decided the destiny of art. Artists from the National Theatre generation had a pressing sense that it was not enough to dogmatically pursue the ideal of a Czech national art, but that achieving this ideal required a sound knowledge of current issues in world art. They wanted to represent their revived nation on the European stage, and in this regard many of them did achieve considerable official acclaim. For these artists, awards from the Salon in Paris were more important than exhibitions in Germany. A French prize was seen as an acknowledgement of the artistic qualities of a work, a guarantee of its contemporariness.

This longing for recognition in France was typical not just of artists working in Paris, such as Václav Brožík and Vojtěch Hynais, but also of artists who had remained in Bohemia and whose oeuvre seemed entirely Czech. This was also the case with Josef Václav Myslbek, the most important Czech sculptor of the latter half of the century. If we read his extensive correspondence with his friends Hynais and Brožík, we find a constant interest in the current output of famous French academicians, as well as impatient requests for photographs of their works and for Hynais and Brožík to investigate exhibition opportunities.[28] Ever since his memorable visit to Paris in 1878, Myslbek had continued to take a keen interest in French art, and this was reflected in his own work. His sculptures made in 1882–84 for the attic of Prague's poorhouse leave little doubt over the French source of his inspiration, especially in terms of how he modelled the naked body and rich drapery of his *Supporters*. These sculptures created an exemplar for decorative sculpture, directly setting out the types that would be used extensively in the 1890s.

However, Myslbek was guided above all by his powerful individualism, leading to the deeper integration of this new inspiration with his own approach, seasoned as it

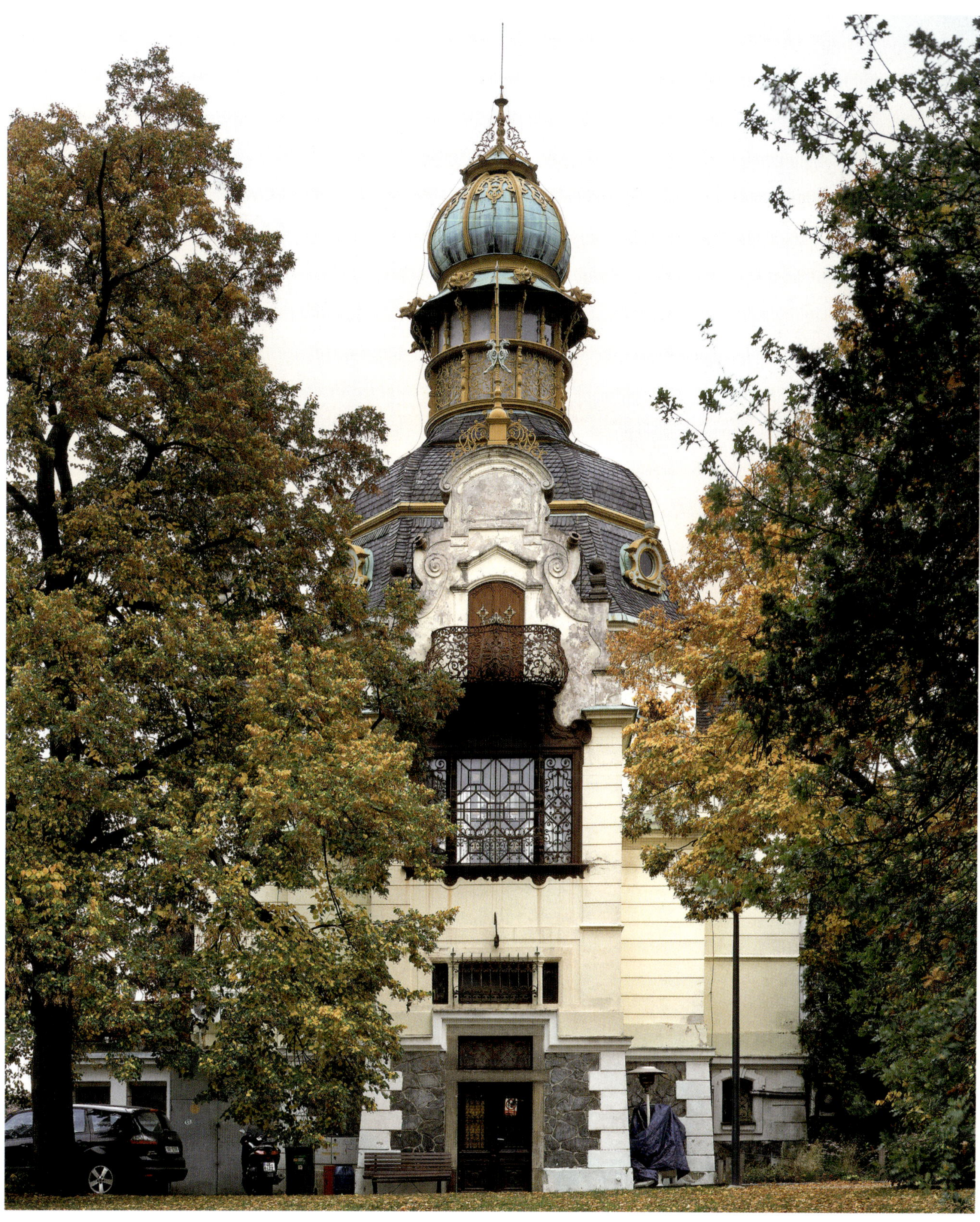

22 Hanau Pavilion in Prague, 1891

was by the firm structuring of form in the Czech Empire style. His admiration for the French masters mostly resulted in a greater sensuality in the modelling and the skilful working of the richly developed drapery. It was a challenge that, with his unusually high demands, he even sought to surpass.[29]

In the largely classical orientation of Myslbek's work, there are many instances where his interest in contemporary art suddenly came to the fore but was ultimately reabsorbed into his creative process. The most striking example of this oscillation concerns the designs he produced in 1892–94 for his statue *Music*. The subject was his own choice, for he considered music the supreme art. In his notes, he wrote "music–soul–spring–flower," and this is reflected in the models that have been preserved, which indicate the unusual breadth of Myslbek's creative struggle. Initially he had two ideas for the statue. The first was inspired by literature, and at its core was the idea of a young woman as a personification of Music, with a tree as the first musical instrument. Strings were to be stretched on this mythical tree to symbolise the union of art and nature, and its trunk was to be inscribed with the names of the most important composers, whether Czech or other nationalities. His second idea was to combine this allegorical figure with a specific string instrument, the Old Bohemian harp, where a "kiss of consecration" would express the emotion of the scene. The models with a tree, drawing on motifs from Julius Zeyer's poems, occupy a special place in Myslbek's oeuvre. The delicacy achieved by the bold linear extending of these statues' substance into space marks the extreme limit of Myslbek's lyricism, and his second sketch for the first concept, now including drapery, can be considered the prototype of later Czech Secession sculpture. It seems that here Myslbek sought to overcome the contradiction between music and fine art, which he succinctly formulated, in his notes for *Music*, as the contradiction between the "ethereal invisibility" of music, accessible to everyone "in God and joy," and the obscurity of "tangible" fine art.[30] Ultimately, however, he would stoically abandon this attempt in favour of his second concept, a variation on which signalled the basic form for the sculpture that Myslbek would only complete twenty years later.

The background to the contradiction opened by the creative process for *Music* was more far reaching than the mere quest for an appropriate form. By ultimately retaining the statue's monumentality, Myslbek remained within the "classic" concept of the specificity of fine art that had been defined for 19th-century thinking by Hegel's *Aesthetics*.[31] The models with a tree belonged more to the legacy of Romanticism that, in Myslbek's work, often broke through the carapace of ascetic rigour, and what was most interesting about them was that they updated the Romantic legacy to a point where its pathos was impersonally and yet intimately subdued. These are characteristics that we then frequently encounter among Myslbek's pupils.

However, in the first half of the 1890s not everything had already been decided, even for Myslbek. This is demonstrated by how he further developed the theme of music. In the autumn of 1894, seeking to satisfy the request for the drapery of his approved "monumental" model to be lighter, Myslbek suddenly radically changed his concept for the sculpture. He made a model of *Swansong*, a prone female nude listening to a dying swan as it sings, and he did everything possible to be permitted to execute this entirely new concept, but in vain.

Swansong, where late Romanticism crossed over into Symbolism, marked the high point of Myslbek's attempts to channel contemporary French sculpture. This extreme position in his oeuvre was perhaps a consequence of his acquaintance with Hynais, but the female figure lying limp with arms outstretched was also one of Pirner's motifs, and the overall concept was again rooted in poetry, influenced by Myslbek's friendship with Zeyer.[32] However, *Swansong* would remain merely an intermezzo. In the same year, 1894, Myslbek won the commission for a statue of Saint Wenceslas in Wenceslas Square, after a close contest with Bohuslav Schnirch, and henceforward these tendencies would be thoroughly suppressed. Although Myslbek would not entirely lose touch with the ideals of the younger generation of sculptors, he would break with them in the latter half of the 1890s, often at the cost of bitter personal conflict. This was related to the emergence of talented young artists, of whom Stanislav Sucharda was the most prominent of Myslbek's pupils from the School of Decorative Arts in Prague. Sucharda came from an established family of woodcarvers and stonemasons in East Bohemia, whose ascent was contemporaneous with the rise of Czech nationalism. Sucharda made his name with *Lullaby*, a high relief from 1892. With its ethnographic detail and the Neo-Renaissance compactness of the figural composition, precisely modelled in a lunette, it was very much of its time. Here too the subject was music, but in an intimate, familial form, and this assured the sculpture's popularity with a broad sweep of viewers. The figures of this relief are still rather small, and the sculptor is struggling with his inclination towards descriptiveness, but the overall design points to an artist who would find application in decorative sculpture. The real bow that Sucharda used in a marble replica of *Lullaby* from 1897 creates a somewhat peculiar effect.

The wave of intimacy that swept through all branches of the Czech visual arts in the early 1890s proved to be truly symptomatic. It also extended to major undertakings such as the construction of the new Provincial Bank (*Zemská banka*) building on Na Příkopě in Prague in 1894–95. Its architect, Osvald Polívka, had already worked with an older architect, Antonín Wiehl, on the Prague City Savings Bank (*Pražská městská spořitelna*), built in 1892–94.

The relationship between these two buildings is highly instructive for the development of late historicism in Czech architecture. The Savings Bank was still conceived in the spirit of the Renaissance, symmetrically enclosing the building's mass and carefully balancing the verticals and horizontals. The Provincial Bank had an entirely different proportional canon; it was vertically oriented, and it violated the relationship between the constructional elements and the ornamentation. In this relaxation of the building's tectonics there was a characteristic shift towards the picturesque, which was also reflected in the unusual colourfulness of the entire façade.

For his building, Polívka freely adopted motifs that belonged more to the Northern Renaissance, such as the lunettes beneath the pronounced cornice and the tall attic storey. In this, he was evidently still inspired by Wiehl, who had pioneered the so-called Czech Renaissance in the apartment blocks he built in Prague and in his own house on

Wenceslas Square, erected in 1894–96. This latter building likewise had a more prominent vertical concept, which Wiehl further emphasised with an asymmetrically placed two-storey oriel. In both buildings, this new proportionality was also a consequence of their high plinths, where a mezzanine was used as a functional element, a device that remained popular later.

Wiehl was noteworthy as a late historicist architect. Some of his temporary buildings for the Centennial Exhibition, made of wood and reflecting the inspiration of vernacular architecture, had a contemporary "modern" character. However, his apartment buildings with extensive sgraffiti or painted ornamentation on the upper floors, usually based on designs by Mikoláš Aleš, looked more traditional. In contrast, Polívka's Provincial Bank had Mannerist features and an elegance that was typical of the time in which it was built. Its construction offered many opportunities for young artists who for the most part had already worked on the Savings Bank. Although they had yet to find any more clearly defined common style, these projects required them to work on

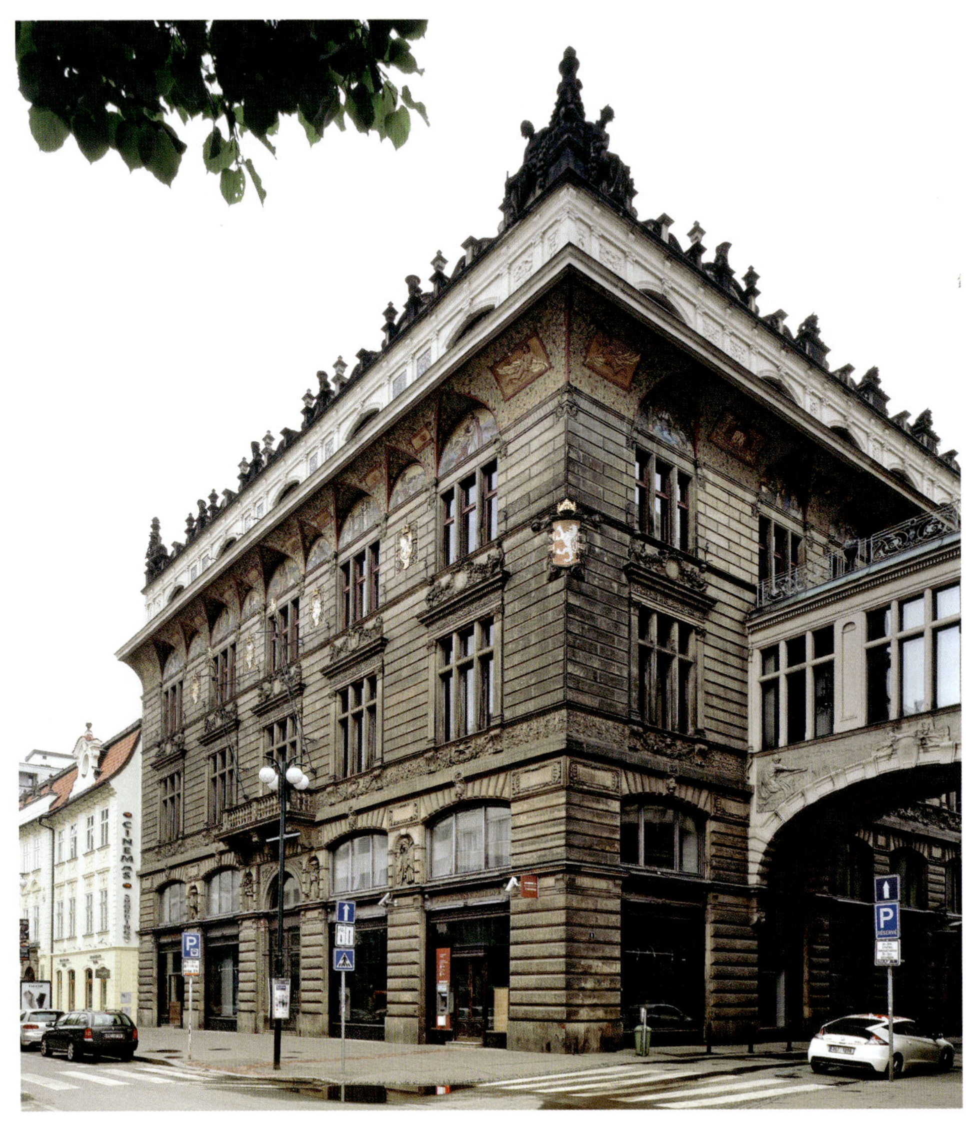

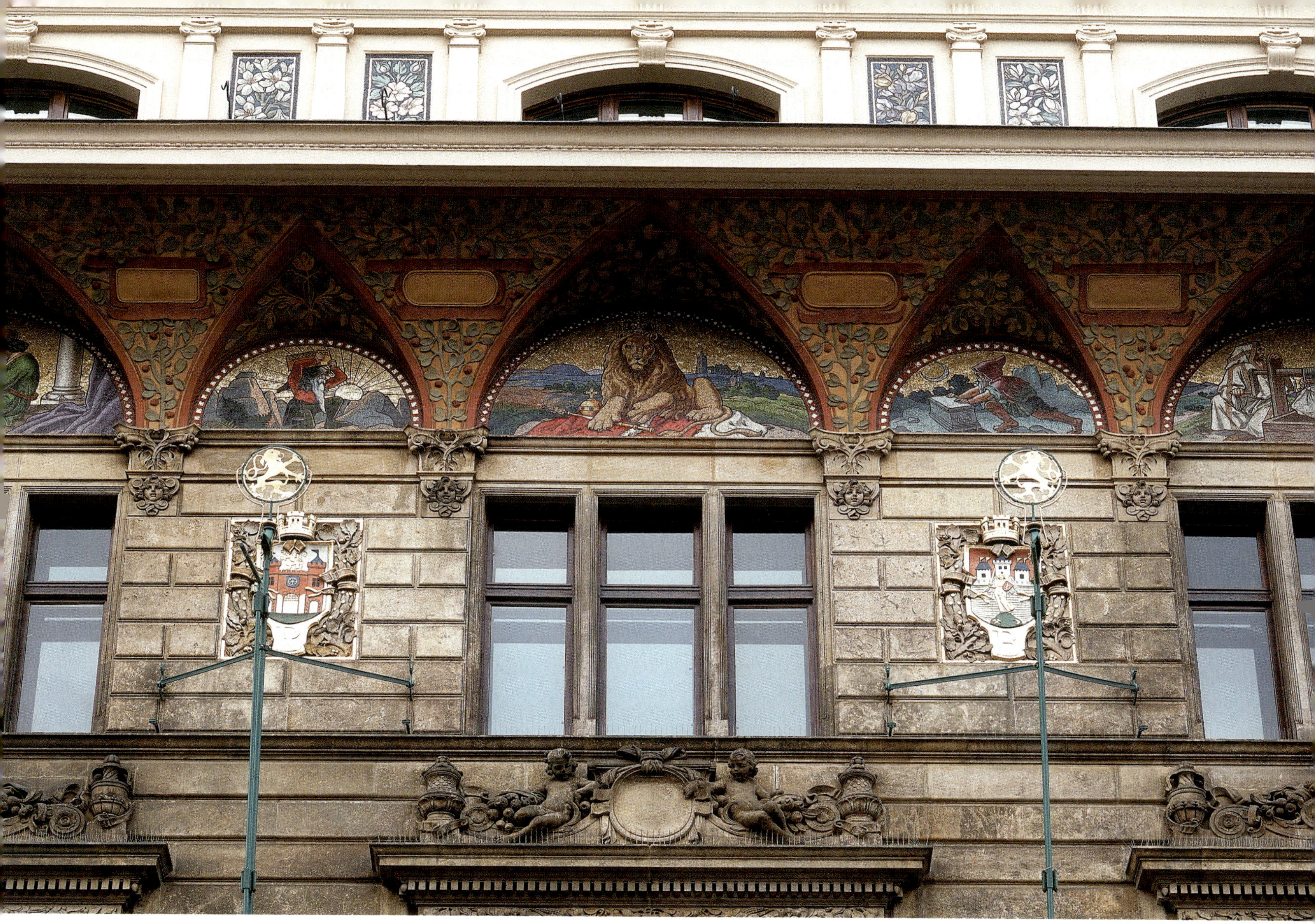

assignments of an explicitly decorative character, and it was this that prompted them to seek a common visual language.

The Provincial Bank's ornamentation was a consequence both of its purpose and of contemporary artistic concerns. The façade, with sculptures by Stanislav Sucharda and Celda Klouček, is dominated by its lunettes with mosaics after cartoons by Mikoláš Aleš. Above them, on the attic, are narrow floral panels designed by Anna Boudová; they were the most progressive Secession-style decorative motif on the façade. Inside, there is a grand staircase, built from costly stone, leading to a hall with statues representing the regions of Bohemia, installed beneath the high ceiling. In their ethnographic naturalism, these statues by Bohuslav Schnirch, Stanislav Sucharda, Antonín Procházka, and František Hergesel are almost like a museum exhibit. Karel Vítězslav Mašek's and Karel Klusáček's paintings on the staircase, like Emil Holárek's cycle of paintings in the conference room, display this same descriptive naturalism. Klusáček tried to visu-

23–24 Osvald Polívka, Provincial Bank in Prague, 1895–96, façade and detail

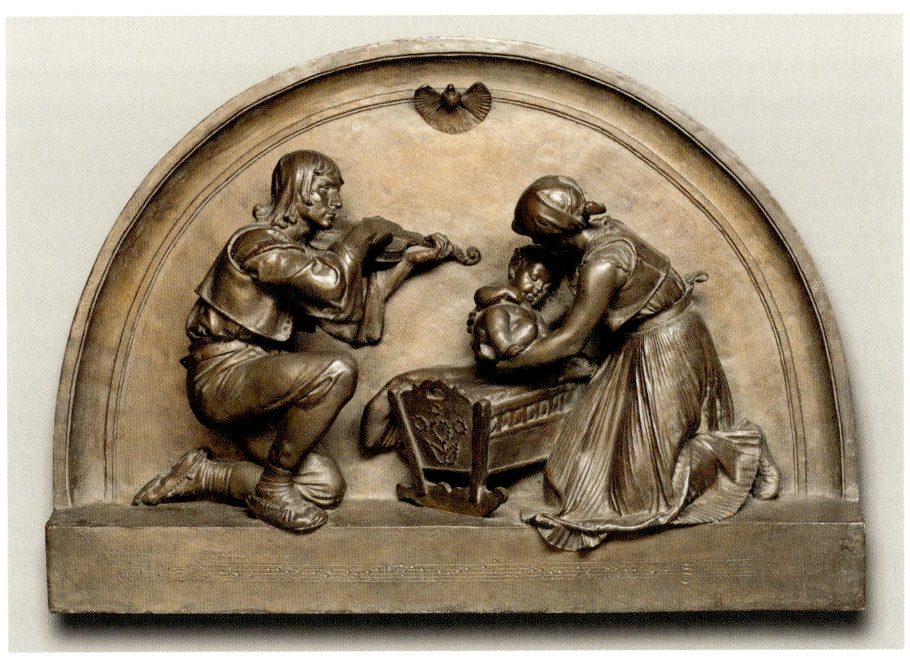

ally join up the picture space behind the architectural elements, creating panoramas that surpassed the usual fragmentary character of ornamentation and reflected the contemporary penchant for tableaux vivants.

The most noteworthy artworks in the Provincial Bank are situated in the relatively narrow space just behind the entrance doors, where Maxmilián Švabinský, a graduate of the academy, created two wall paintings facing one another: *Saint Wenceslas Blessing Labour* and *Labour, the Fount of Prosperity*. Their execution was interesting. The compositions reflected their Neo-Renaissance architectural framing, with allegorical figures symmetrically assembled in the way of old "conversations" around the central symbols of the saint, seated on a throne, and the garlanded fountain. What was remarkable, however, was the freshness of their rendering, with a vivacity that did not hesitate to include realistic figures in these idealised narratives. Švabinský demonstrated his ability to use colour to balance the natural and idealised elements, creating effective decorative works.

In their lightness, where they seem to be floating on the flowering lawn, the kneeling girls in the Saint Wenceslas painting recall some of Puvis de Chavannes's figures. The colour of the saint's attire abandons all pseudo-historical realism, and its mysterious luminescence elevates this likeness of the nation's patron saint to the level of myth. Yet these paintings also had naturalistic contemporary elements, such as the figure of a Czech farmer, or the little girl dressed in white. This was all combined to create a distinctive whole with an entirely new expressive quality.

The Secession character of Švabinský's paintings for the Provincial Bank was by virtue of how they combined the ideal and the real with a new treatment of colour, whose intensity gave them an unusually lyrical tone. This was a particular kind of colourfulness,

25 Stanislav Sucharda, *Lullaby*, 1892, replica 1897, marble, 60 × 85 cm

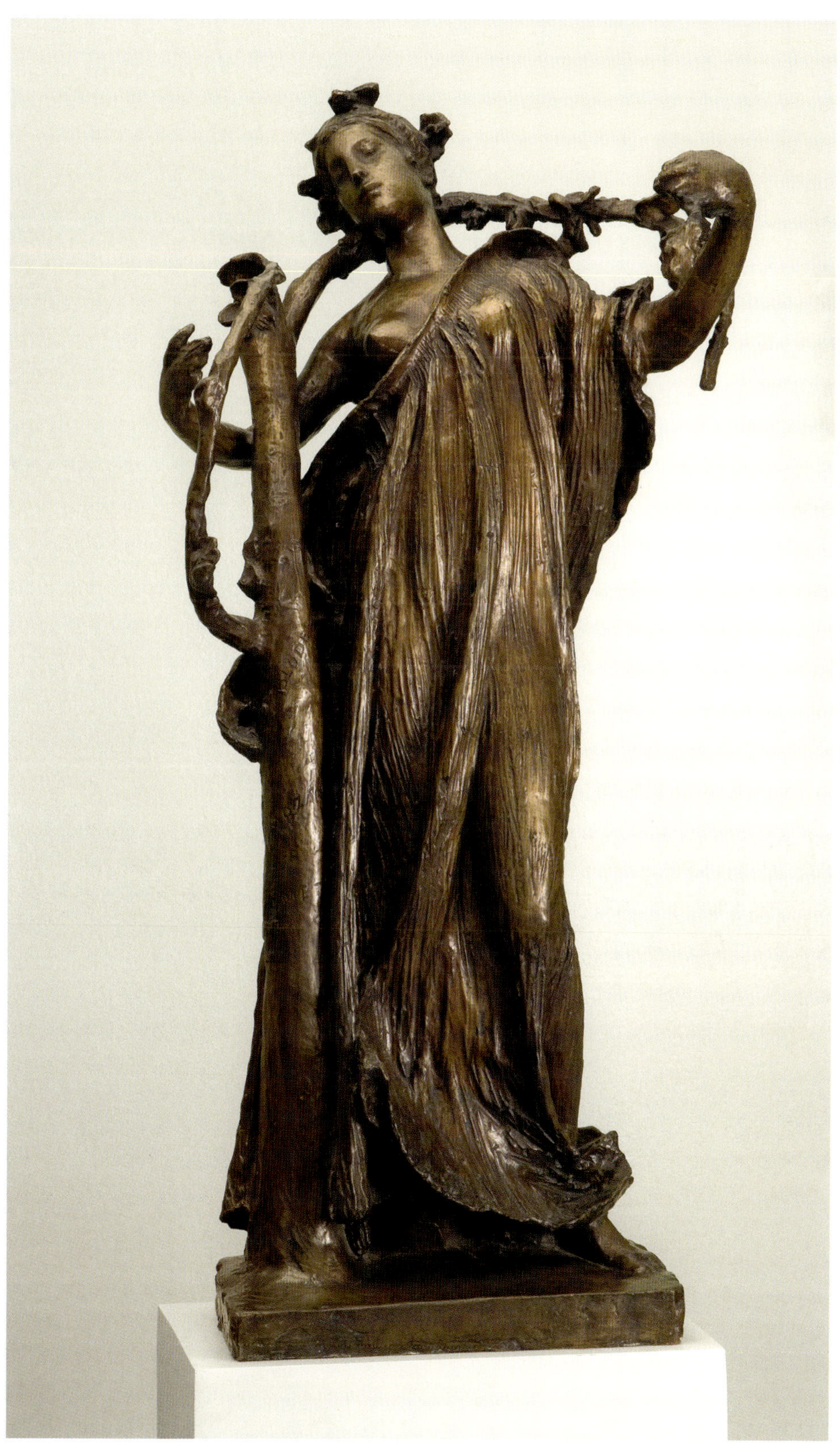

26 Josef Václav Myslbek, *Music*, second sketch, 1892–94, bronze, 108 cm

both in the range of hues (there is here the characteristic pairing of dark green with white to create a harmony enlivened by other colours, principally shades of yellow) and in their decorative distribution over the picture plane. This combination of colour modulations, with particular dominant chords, and the decorative formula for the composition was clearly the most important innovation in Švabinský's paintings. It was accentuated by the shallow picture space, and the characteristic way in which the white brushstrokes of the garb of the kneeling girls in the group with Saint Wenceslas seem not three- but two-dimensional against the dark green background, thereby lightening the composition, which otherwise is still arranged in a Renaissance pyramid.[33] These paintings marked the beginning of a new way of thinking in Czech decorative painting.

For painting, this posed the problem of the higher totality of a composition. Detail was not an unknown element in the contemporary art equation, for it had already been discovered by naturalism in the 1880s. Focusing on an individual item with a photographic precision was initially a simpler and more successful approach. However, the more thorough naturalism became in its descriptiveness, the more urgently it raised the question of its own integrative qualities. Here the Neo-Renaissance could no longer provide an entirely satisfactory response, for its compositional method was in essence additive. Artistic sentiment required a more complete concept of the picture plane, and to a considerable extent this need also prompted interest in the Baroque. Accordingly, in the 1890s the Baroque Revival became a kind of stylistic counterweight to the Renaissance Revival, and for a time it attracted the attention of a number of young artists. It was surely no accident that contemporary art theory examined the polarity of the Renaissance and the Baroque, and made their principles for the treatment of form the basic modes for understanding the entire history of art.[34] The legacy of 19th-century historicism had been projected into two basic concepts of art, but in practice the Baroque Revival began to overpower the Renaissance Revival with its facility for grand expressive qualities, its exaltation of colour and modelling, and its dynamism of form, which, when compared with the static nature of the Neo-Renaissance, seemed to contemporaries to be more appropriate to the accelerating tempo of life.

The Baroque Revival found fertile soil in Prague thanks to the city's wonderful stock of Baroque sights, whose cult was ignited in the 1890s by the progressive redevelopment of the city's old quarters. It was taken up in Czech architecture from the first half of the decade. Václav Roštlapil, who had been taught by Theophil Hansen, one of the pioneers of this trend in Europe, built the Academy of Count Jan Petr Straka (*Strakova akademie*) in Prague in 1893–95. The building demonstrated the advantage that the Neo-Baroque had in the city in terms of seamlessly integrating a large new building into its historical surroundings.

Another devotee of the new trend was Friedrich Ohmann, who had started teaching at Prague's School of Decorative Arts in 1889. His buildings in this style demonstrate how the Baroque Revival was taken up in Prague, and how its effect was further intensified. If the palace that Ohmann built for the industrialist Matyáš Valter was still "strictly" historicist, his large building for the Assicurazioni Generali

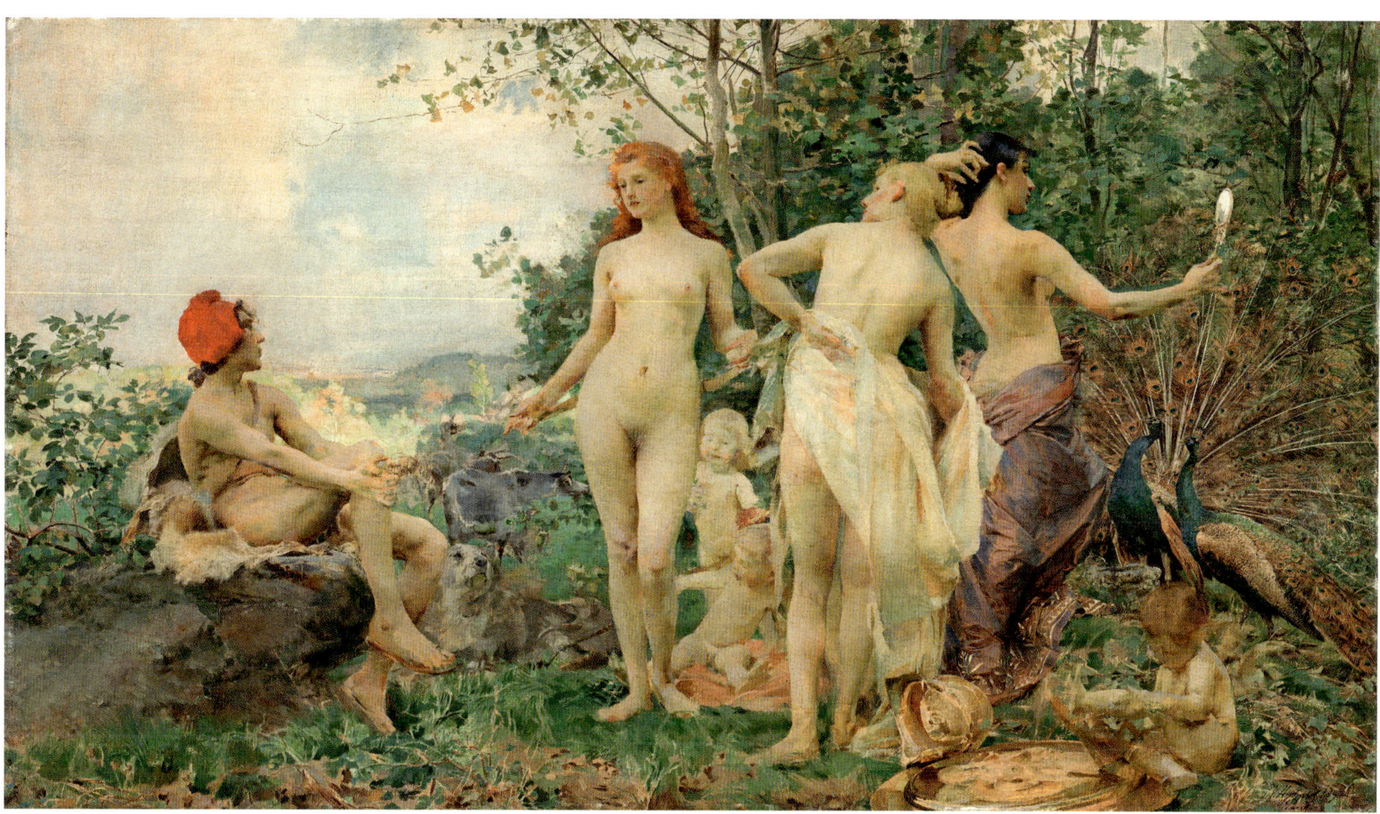

insurance company – which Ohmann designed with Osvald Polívka and constructed on Wenceslas Square in 1895 – made free use of Baroque motifs and applied them to a building whose mass could not deny its 19th-century origin. In the Théâtre Variété, built in Prague's Karlín district in 1896–98, the historicist morphology was merely a springboard for the architect's fantasy to pursue a vision of dazzling splendour.

With its emotionality, the Neo-Baroque also appealed to sculptors and painters, and its grandeur was a necessary counterbalance to their naturalism. For Stanislav Sucharda, the Neo-Baroque not only brought new commissions for decorative sculpture, but was also a way of overcoming his original tendency towards a smallness of form. One of his first significant low reliefs, a medal with a portrait of Baroque architect Kilian Ignaz Dientzenhofer (1897), clearly shows in its subject and form where Sucharda had learned to wield this "grand" form. It was here that the foundations were laid for his enthusiastic, if somewhat one-sided, understanding of the oeuvre of Auguste Rodin.

Of the paintings commissioned for Neo-Baroque architecture, Jan Preisler's ceiling painting for Dientzenhofer's church in Přeštice merits special attention. Preisler painted it in 1898, evidently at the instigation of Friedrich Ohmann, who was responsible for the church's restoration. It was the young painter's first major commission, and his treatment of this large fresco was masterful. The composition of his ethereal *The Assumption of the Blessed Virgin Mary* follows the Baroque's illusionistic models, but

27 Vojtěch Hynais, Study for *The Judgement of Paris*, 1892, oil, 58 × 100 cm

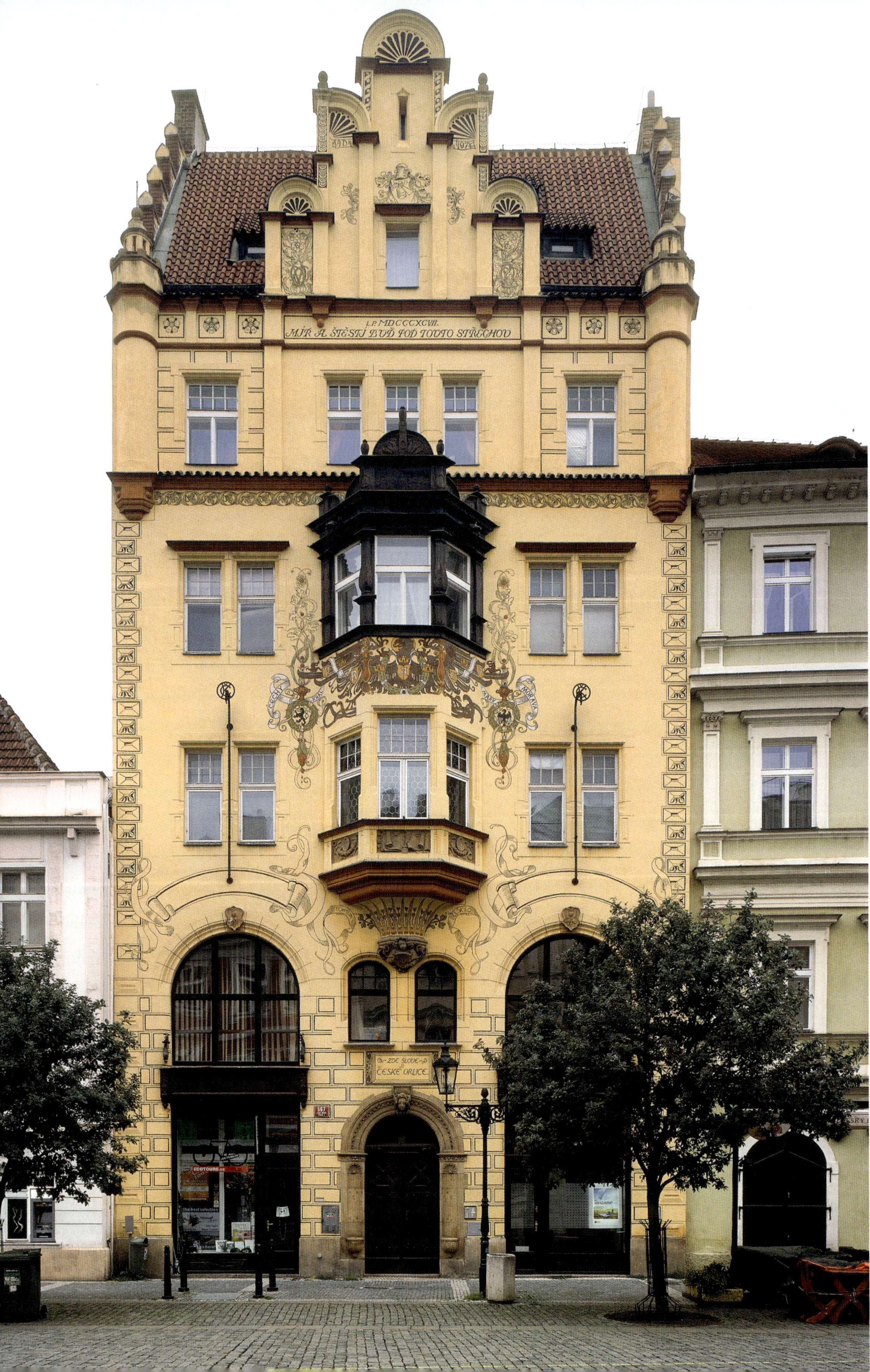
L.P. MDCCCXCVII.
MÍR A ŠTĚSTÍ BUĎ POD TOUTO STŘECHOU
ZDE SLOVE U ČESKÉ ORLICE.

what was new was Preisler's use of colour, with harmonies of greens and reds that were typical of the Secession. As with Švabinský's paintings for the Provincial Bank, colour comprised the artist's original contribution, and it was the most progressive element here. With Preisler, the combination of colour and light played a greater role, and this can be attributed to the influence not only of the Baroque, but principally of Vojtěch Hynais, the painter against whom Preisler measured himself. This Luminism was reflected once more in 1901, in Preisler's wall painting for the Hotel Central, whose architect, at least initially, was again Friedrich Ohmann. Although the Baroque Revival was soon overshadowed by the Secession, it greatly influenced the artists of the 1890s' generation and formed one of the poles between which their new concept crystallised. It seems that it was forever associated with emotional and sensual exaltation, as both these paintings by Preisler would suggest.

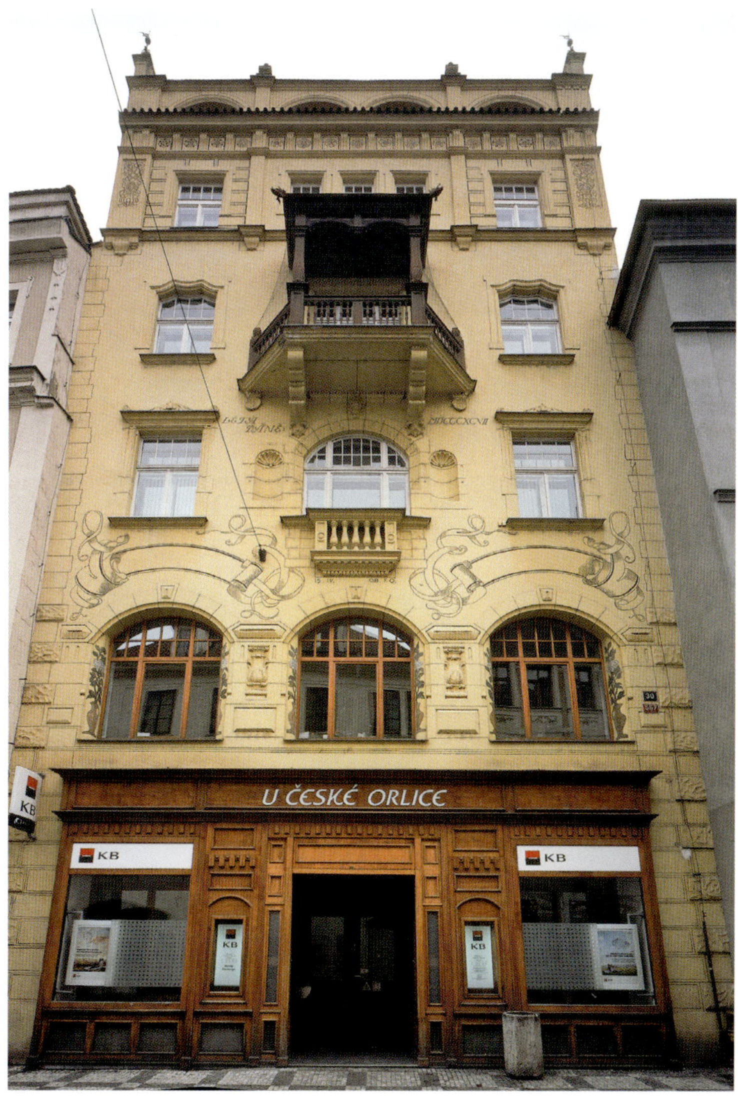

28–29 Friedrich Ohmann, House at the Bohemian Eagle in Prague, 1897, Ovocný trh and Celetná façades

In Prague, Ohmann gained a reputation for being "temperamental, haphazardly eclectic, moody and immensely volatile, but an artistic soul through and through."[35] This also included a liking for novelty. Ohmann's Café Corso, built on Na Příkopě in 1897–98, is often presented as the first Secession building in Prague.

Today, we only know the Café Corso from photographs, but it is quite clear that it is inaccurate to describe it as Secession architecture. The only Secession elements in its façade were the main cornice, which extended from the building in Secession-style "awnings," and a certain two-dimensionality, offset by Viktor Oliva's paintings. The Corso's tall attic was most probably a response to the building opposite, the Provincial Bank, and the two allegorical winged figures holding an inscription panel on the façade were an allusion to late Romanticism. The interior, with wooden panelling on the walls, was probably more in keeping with the Secession style. The Corso seemed new largely on account of its stylistic diversity, and it can be considered typical of this transitional period, when the "crisis of style" had also become pronounced in Prague. The syncretism of contemporary architecture is best illustrated by the fact that, besides Neo-Baroque projects, Ohmann also designed buildings in Prague in the style of the late Middle Ages, such as the Štorch House on the Old Town Square and the House at the Bohemian Eagle on Ovocný trh, both from 1897. This latter building came closest to the Secession in its integration of the ornament into the façade, and in several other motifs too: its carved wooden oriel would become a popular architectural ele-

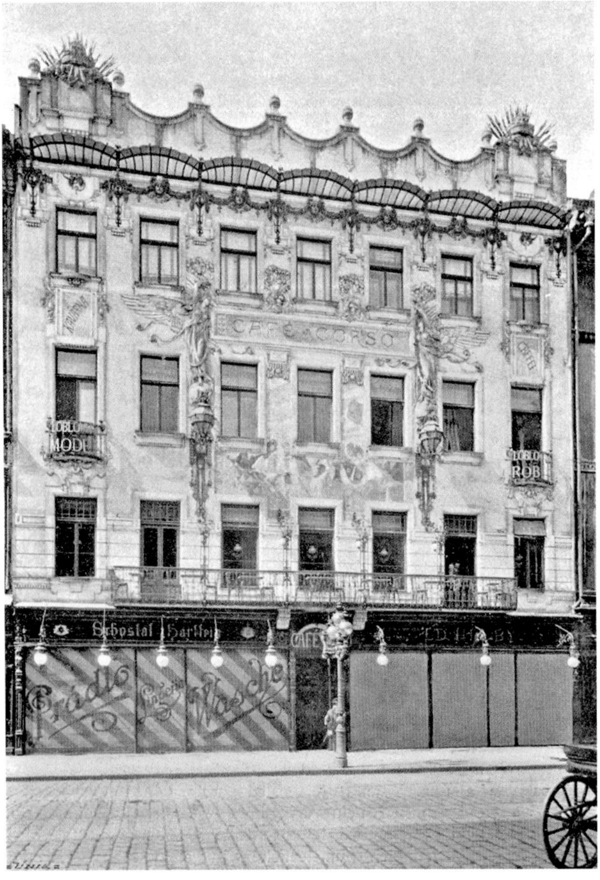

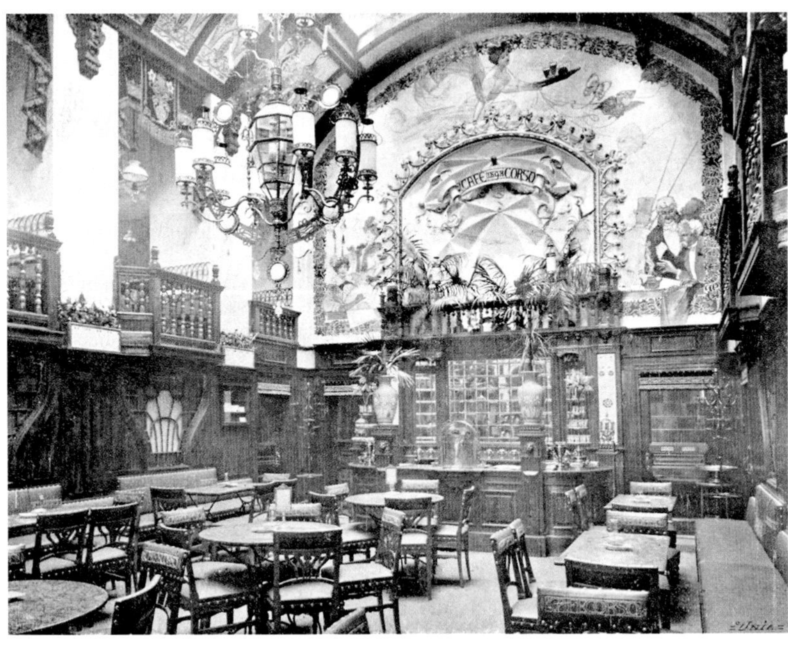

30–31 Friedrich Ohmann, Café Corso in Prague, 1898, exterior and interior

ment during the first wave of the Secession. Although the buildings Ohmann designed before returning to Vienna helped to stir the stagnant waters of Czech architecture, they did not fundamentally resolve a problem whose urgency became fully apparent at the Architecture and Engineering Exhibition in 1898. This important exhibition demonstrated how architecture's historicist eclecticism had proved to be a blind alley, and it prompted discussion that would lead to calls for a new, modern, architecture.

The exchange of opinions in the second volume of *Volné směry* largely revolved around the requirement that this new architecture not merely adopt whatever was currently labelled "modern" in Europe, but that it be specifically Czech.[36] The greatest fears were of the influence of Otto Wagner's school at Vienna's Academy of Fine Arts, which was producing its first typical practical and written work, with Wagner's stations for Vienna's Stadtbahn attracting particular attention.

This discussion from 1898 can be said to mark the end of the transitional period of the 1890s. Although it did not identify any specific way out, it had the merit of explicitly stating a problem that had increasingly preoccupied artists and the general public ever since the Centennial Exhibition. Its resolution was hastened by various external circumstances and practical needs, such as the extensive redevelopment of Prague's old quarters, which freed up space for whole new streets and blocks. This required architecture to prove its technical and artistic worth. There was a general sense that this was the key moment for the future not just of architecture, but of all visual culture. The need for a turning point was felt both by older generations schooled in the historical styles and by the younger generation. When discussing the merits of individual styles, young architects typically defended the seemingly entirely passé Gothic, and they stressed that, regardless of the desire for Czech art to be a national art, it could not shut itself off from the rest of the world.

Yet the argument for this new art to be a "national" art was so compelling that even the younger generation's spokesmen always felt obliged to repeat that they too had no desire to imitate the example of other countries, including Otto Wagner. This posed a peculiar dilemma in which both old and new styles were disputed. The only way out, and the only corrective for art, seemed to be to seek the source of style in nature. This was one of the consequences of the development of the earlier naturalism, though it was not blind to Czech artists' new appreciation of nature. Such an appreciation had long nurtured English and French modern art, which was becoming better and more fully known in the Czech Lands as it was discovered by local artists, mainly through periodicals.

The situation was in many respects a provocative one. If the younger generation reproached its elders for imitating long-dead values, and the older generation found an effective riposte in accusations of plagiarising foreign "modernity," the only untainted value was the originality of individual work. This demand for authenticity, strangely contrasting with the contemporary inclination towards a uniform formulation and the call for a new and universal style, became entrenched in artistic thinking and was one of the main sources of the pronounced individuality of fin de siècle artists.

In consequence, artists became more sensitive to any criticism of their work. This did not only concern written criticism; it also applied to relations between pupil and

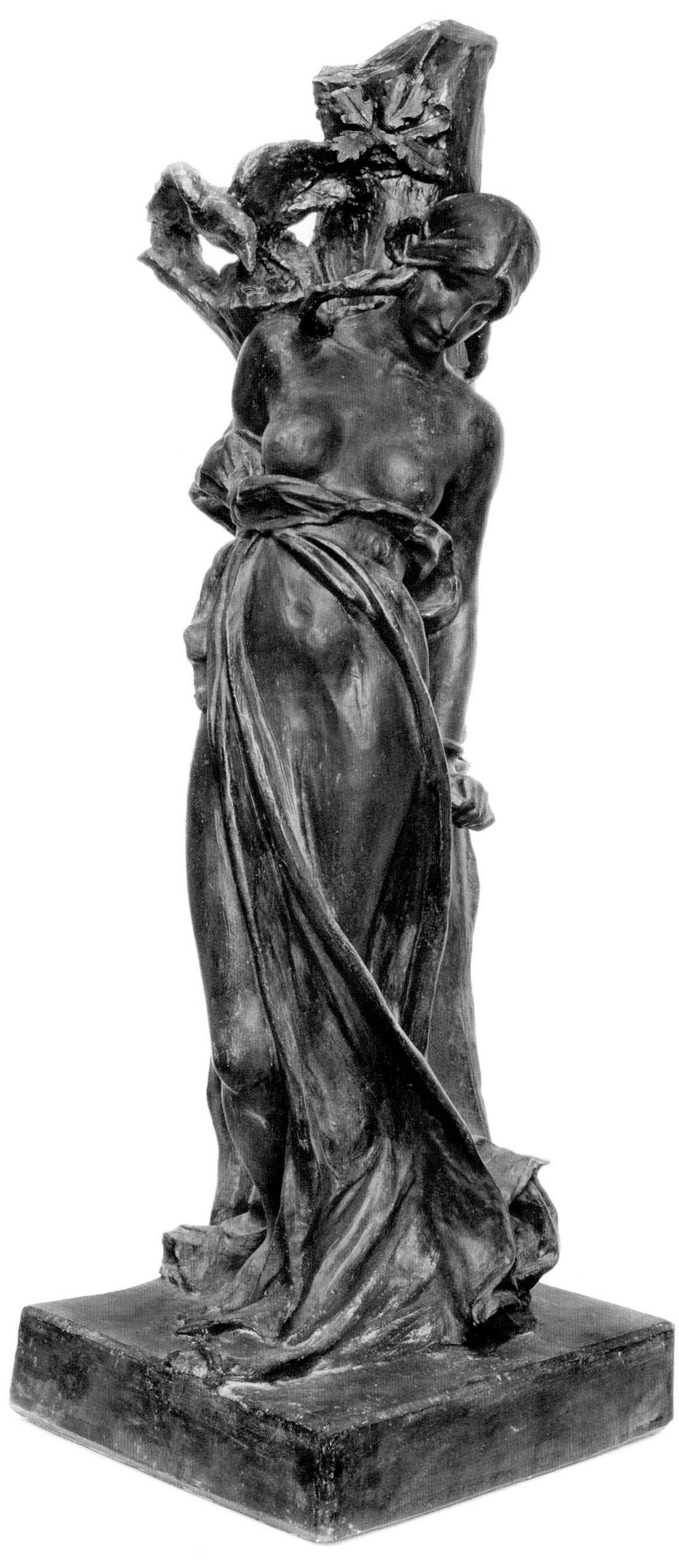

32 Quido Kocián, *Šárka*, 1897, patinated plaster, 132 cm

teacher. If the teacher was authoritarian, there was a danger of conflict. One typical example concerned *Šárka*, a statue by one of Myslbek's pupils, Quido Kocián. In 1897 Myslbek completed *Ctirad and Šárka*, the last of his monumental statues of figures from Czech legends for Palacký Bridge. It was based on a model from two years earlier. At the same time, Kocián was finishing his own statue of Šárka, which depicted only the principal figure. It was said (perhaps by K. B. Mádl) that in this work the pupil had surpassed his teacher, and this resulted in a rift that was only healed after several years.

Importantly, this was not merely a matter of personal relationships, for there was a more general background to the case. When *Volné směry* later reviewed Mádl's monograph on Myslbek, there was again mention of his sculptures for Palacký Bridge. Their definitive versions were presented as an example of Myslbek's failure to match the high standard of his original competition sketches from 1881, which, in "the bloom of their formulation and spirit," were "heroic visions of the creative mind." These were the words of Stanislav Sucharda, and they reflected the views of a generation that was distancing itself from "the anxious striving for correctness and formal perfection" that, in their opinion, encumbered Myslbek's later work.[37] Kocián's *Šárka* unquestionably came closer to the emotional immediacy of Myslbek's sketches than their cooler final renditions. The pupil's statue was understood as one that brought sculpture back to the Romantic principle that a work of art can never be completed, to a concept that emphasised powerful emotion and direct experience, and understood an artwork to be more a means than an end. Here lay more profound aesthetic differences and differences of opinion, and these were related to the younger generation's nascent world view.

There was, of course, nothing unusual in the fact that young artists would base their work on the forms they had encountered at art school and in their milieu. In their programme declaration from 1898, the SVU Mánes artists had said, "Our modernity is not the mere negation of everything that currently exists, it is not the pursuit of grandiloquent ephemeral watchwords,"[38] and they included works by their teachers in the first volume of *Volné směry*. In their attempt to be "a mere step forwards in the natural evolution of our art," they took on the themes their elders had worked with and tried to stamp their own conception onto them. However, this created friction between the generations, for the old repertoire could not merely be passively adopted. Alternatively, there were returns to the past, as in Kocián's *Šárka*, when the conclusions drawn from older assumptions were other than the ones official art had arrived at in the 1890s. In this period, when the younger generation still lacked a stylistic form of its own, we find in its works characteristics that are generally labelled "decadent," and in terms of art they are more Mannerist in the way they filled old forms with new content.

Wagner's stations for the Vienna Stadtbahn were admired for their "metropolitan refinement" and the way simple means could create an effect that easily surpassed all the lavish ornamentation of the older architectural styles. This natural and almost playful lightness of touch seems to have been the aesthetic ideal for young architects, who initially tried to work it into the old stylistic repertoires, as we can see in several of Jan

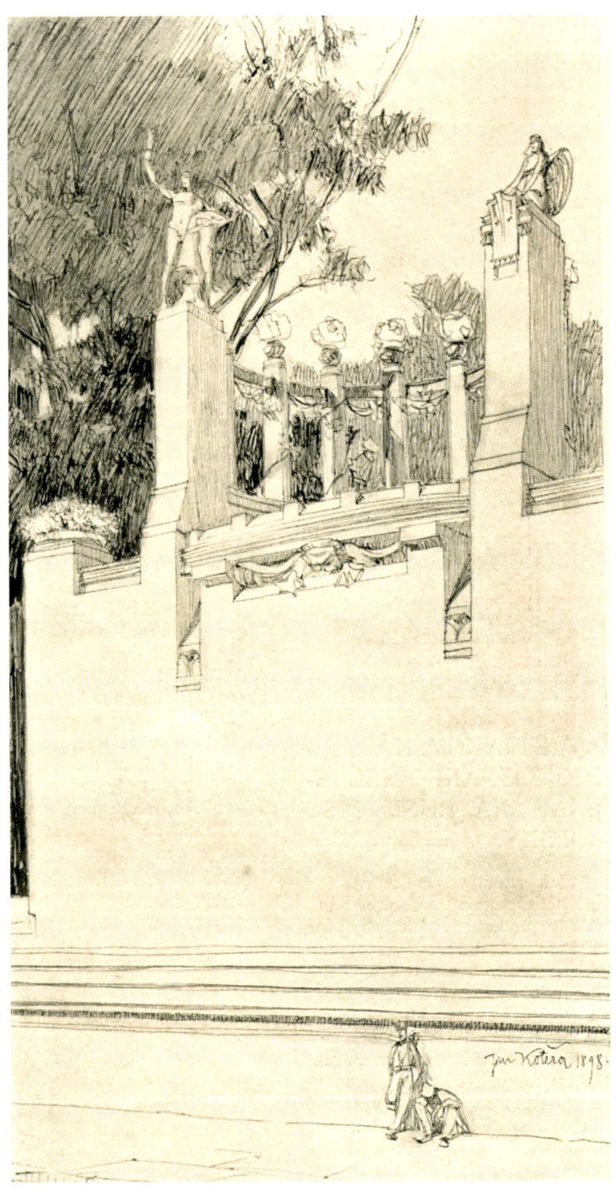

Kotěra's sketches towards the end of his schooling in 1894–97, when he was taught in Vienna by Otto Wagner himself. Kotěra was in Wagner's studio in the years when the founding of the Vienna Secession was under preparation, and his drawings and student work illustrate just how rapidly the creative climate was changing. If Kotěra's designs for a church and a royal spa, for which he won the Füger gold medal in 1896, were still in the spirit of late historicism, his drawings from the following year have a new energy. There is a fantastic sense of freedom that is unafraid to hypertrophy historic forms and confront them with real life in the staffage. This contrast produces a peculiar harmony that ultimately breaches the inviolability of late historicism, making way for new forms that better correspond to life's demands.

33 Jan Kotěra, *View from the Park*, 1898, reproduced in *Volné směry* 3 (1899)

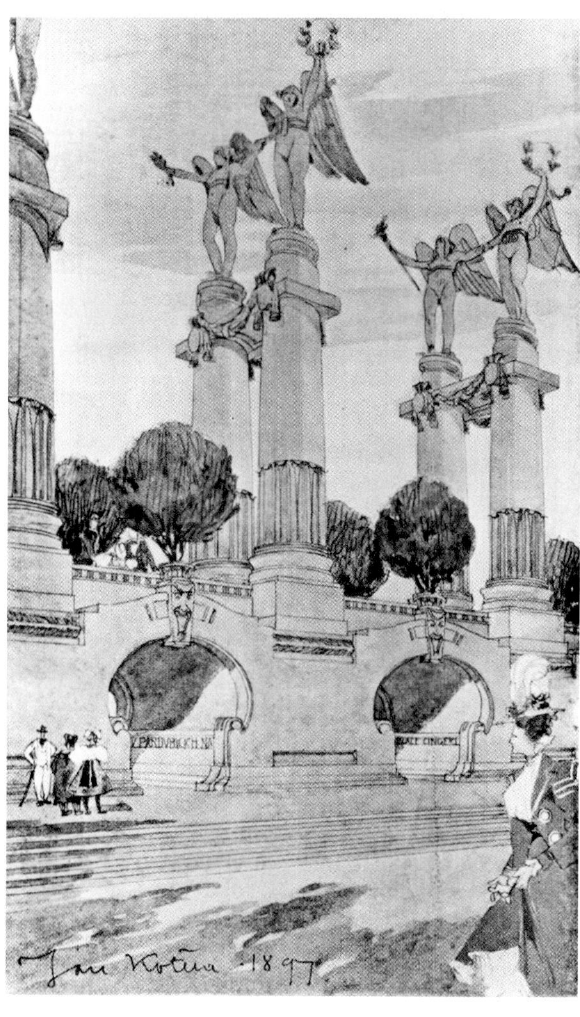

It was these qualities that so captivated Kotěra's peers. The author of a review of the Architecture and Engineering Exhibition for *Volné směry* wrote,

> On one side historicism, on the other modernity, if possible its absolute negation – and some have found a kind of *juste milieu* to save art's patriotism. If I am not deceived in the quality of the youngest talents emerging, and should Jan Kotěra settle in Prague, all the clashes and skirmishes to date will become a great battle – and you may be assured, modernity will triumph. It is only a question of whether this will be with the language of forms currently spoken in this country, or whether more original expression will be found. It will have powerful allies: beautiful talents and the vigour of youth – and in the background of this battle, in the manner of the tableaux vivants popular here, there will be a didactic group expressing history's lesson that all progress depends on evolution, a group that is trying to overcome tradition and ossified formalism, that honours the old but thirsts for the new, and to be its own.[39]

It was not easy to find a productive way out of the world of late historicism. It had, after all, exhausted almost everything from the history of art, without touching

34 Jan Kotěra, *Gallery by the Sea*, 1897, reproduced in *Volné směry* 3 (1899)

on the deeper purpose of art. Most young Czech artists were convinced that this was the fault of the narrowness of their homeland, as František Bílek expressed in his woodcarving *An Allegory of the Great Fall of the Czechs* (1898), showing a figure who has collapsed before the ruins of some giant idol. However, the emotion this sculpture produced was supranational, and when exhibited in Vienna it caught the attention of the critic William Ritter, who in the magazine *Art et Décoration* compared it to Rodin.

Even those young Czech artists who set off into the world to discover an art milieu that was more free and more expansive ran up against this same barrier: eclecticism was in crisis there too, and the purpose of art had been exhausted. From František Kupka's time in Vienna came *The Riddle of Life*, a drawing now known only in reproduction. In this allegory, two female nudes are sitting on old tomes, one blowing bubbles and the other holding aloft a pair of masks. They are accompanied by a sphinx and a whirling circle of human figures that point to the predestination that is the lot of humanity and of art. All these attributes of the old allegory of Vanitas would be repeated frequently in the 1890s. Solving the riddle of life as an opportunity for the fruitful opening of the old system of art was of course a task facing not just Kupka but all of his generation.

What was important was that all these impassioned debates about modernity were followed by concrete action. Friedrich Ohmann's response to the aforementioned

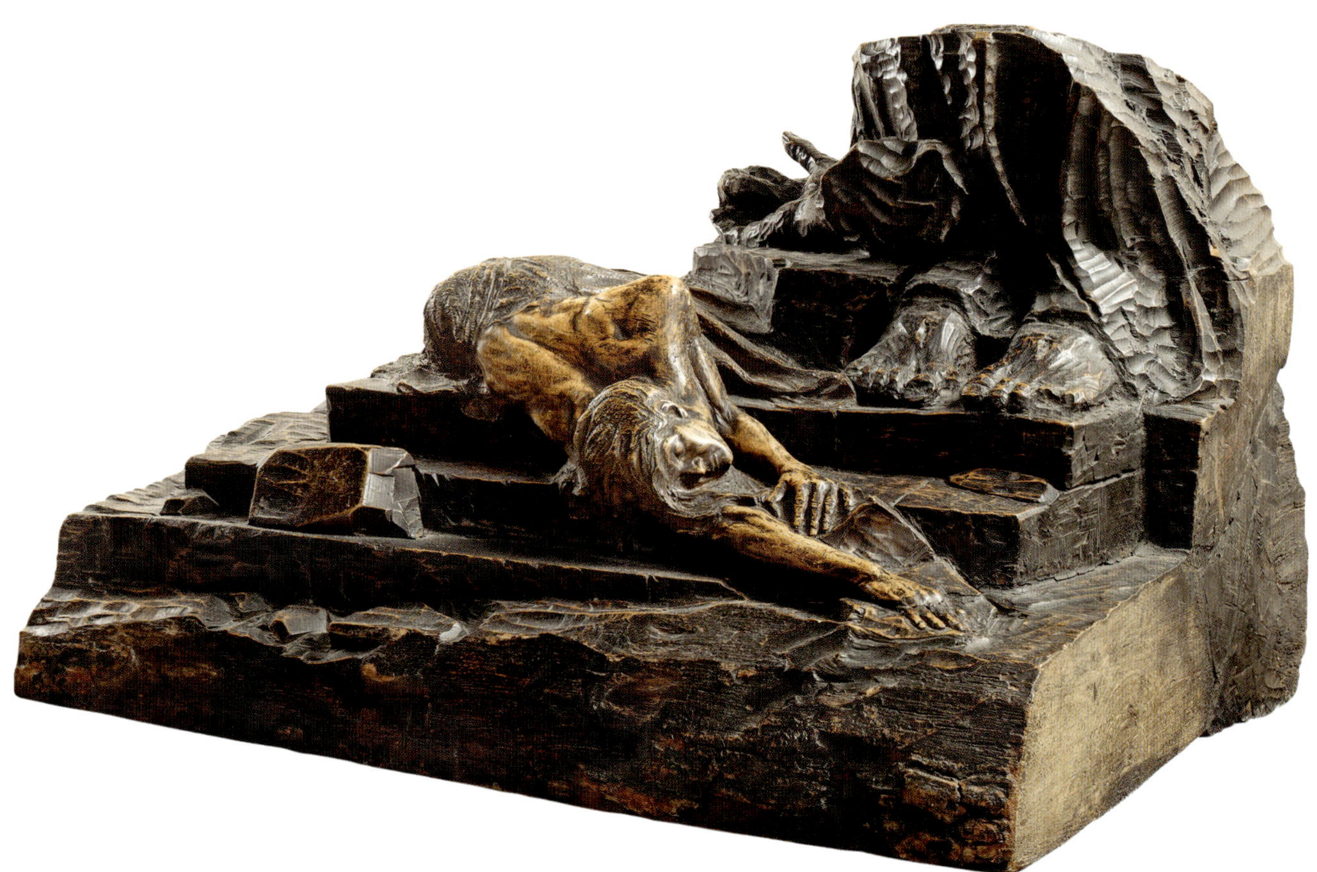

35 František Bílek, *An Allegory of the Great Fall of the Czechs*, 1898, wood, 52 cm

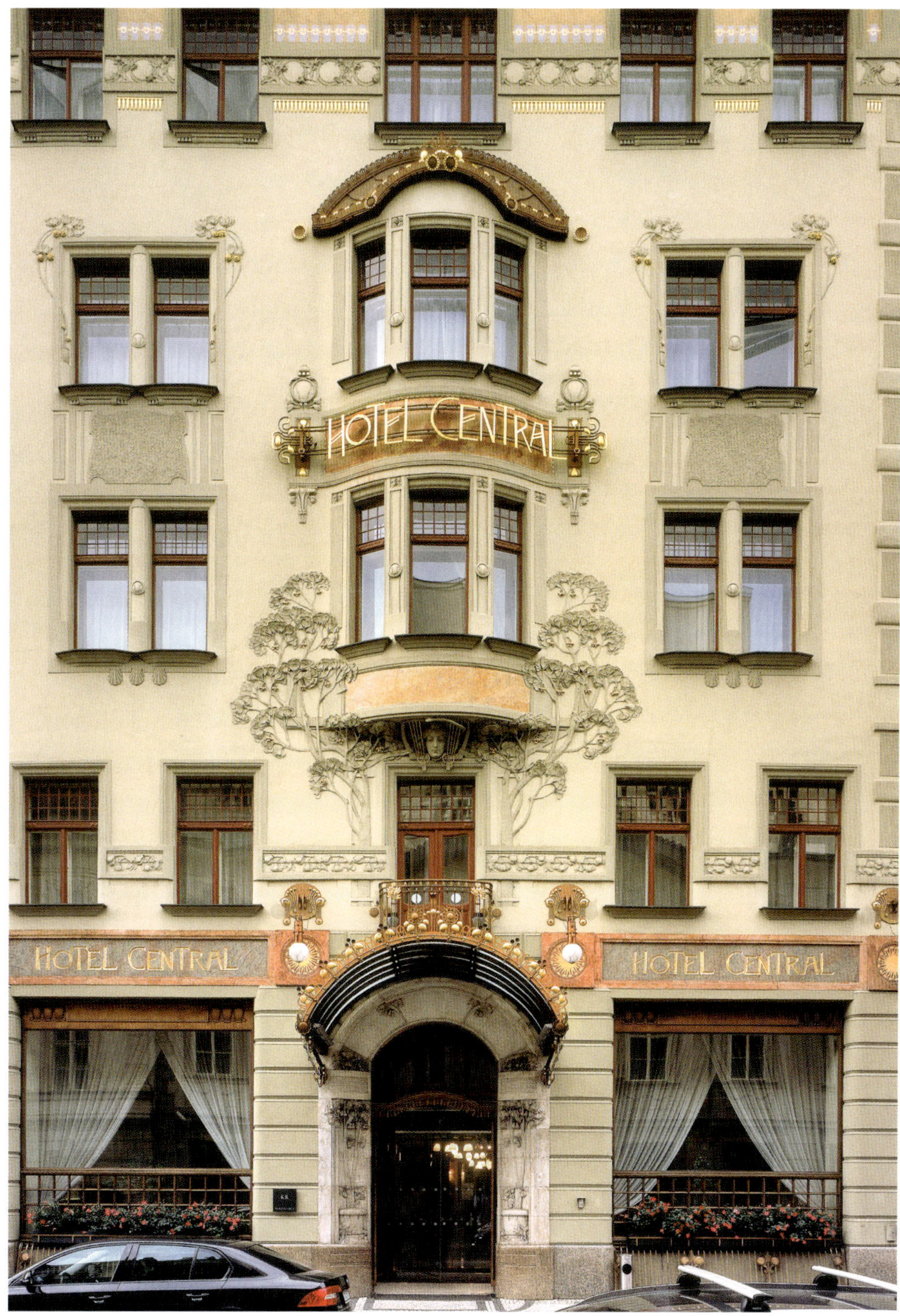

discussion about modernity in architecture came in the form of two designs for the façade of Hotel Central in Prague. Especially in his second design from 1898, he used his by now typically naturalistic botanical motif of a bush spreading over the façade, here with a Symbolist mascaron and a modern typeface. Also extraordinary were the façade's colours, accentuated by the gilding. The hotel's construction was overseen by two of his pupils from the School of Decorative Arts, Alois Dryák and Bedřich Bendelmayer, and on completion in 1901 the hotel was warmly welcomed as "the latest example of the Secession style in Prague."[40]

36 Bedřich Ohmann, Hotel Central in Prague, 1898–1902, detail of the façade

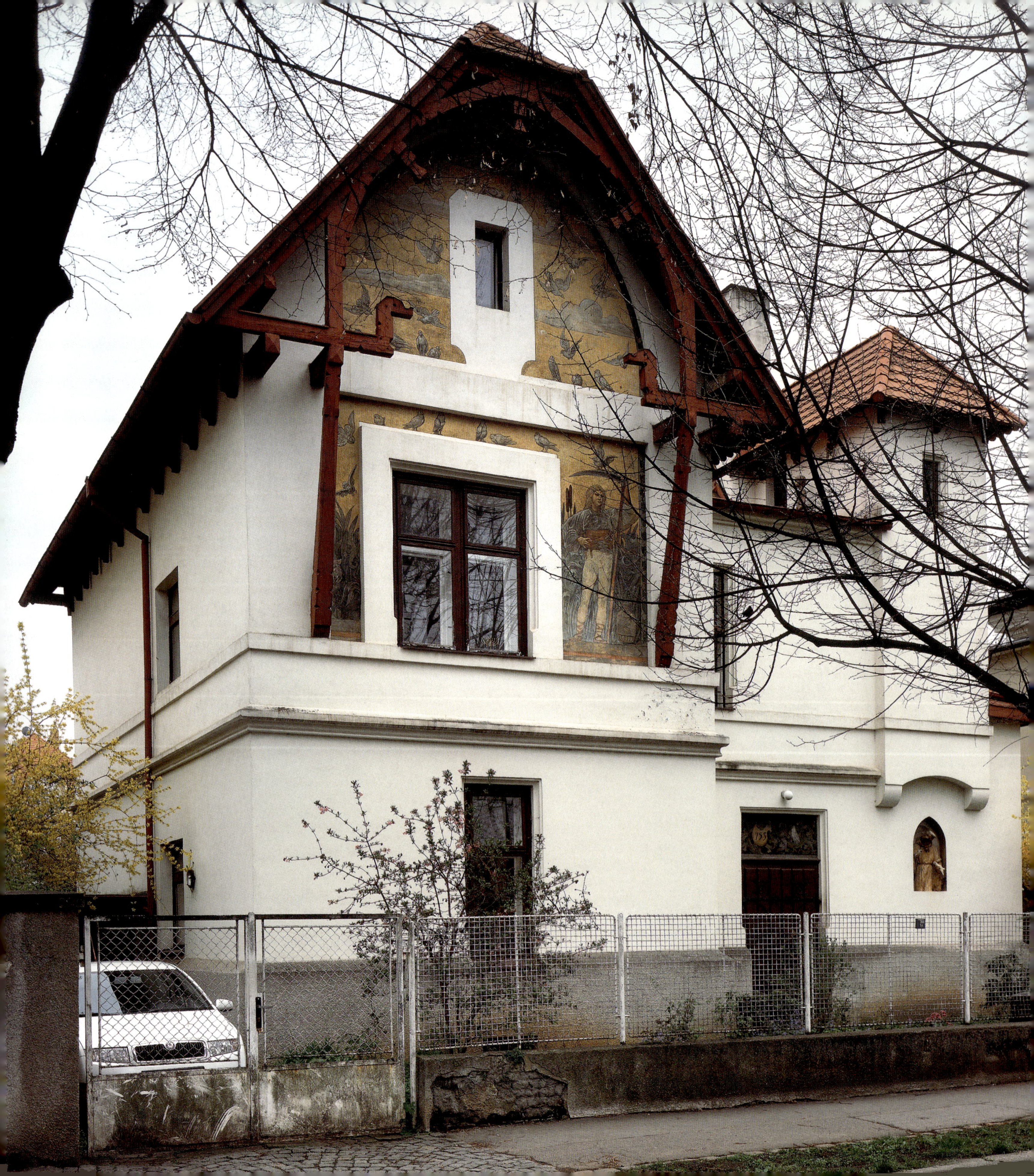

GO TO THE PEOPLE

The artists of the 1890s' generation had grown up in an environment in which the ideals of the National Revival had become widespread. The rebuilding of the National Theatre, after it had been destroyed by fire, was something that affected all strata of Czech society, and it highlighted the popular character of the nationalist movement. These artists mostly came from poorer rural backgrounds, and nationalist ideology – embodied by František Palacký and expounded principally in literature that emphasised the nation's former greatness – was the first sweeping idea that moulded them intellectually. The social crisis of the 1880s had of course eroded the historical idealism under whose guise the Czech bourgeoisie had sought to represent the national struggle, and naturalism had been applied in art to offer a more realistic view of society. However, naturalistic aesthetics had first and foremost to take on board the ideals of the National Revival, which carried such weight in Czech society. That part of the new naturalism that focused on depicting rural life became a chapter in itself.

The great attention devoted to the countryside in the 1890s is explicable by the mere fact that it was where there was the greatest clash between the contradictions within this ideology. Romanticism had already elaborated the idea of the rural population as the guardians of the national character, the life force of the national culture, which in Czech art had found a brilliant interpreter in the person of Josef Mánes. Of course, this new wave of naturalism was not based on Mánes's Neo-Renaissance "ideal art," which Miroslav Tyrš's aesthetics had accorded classic status. Its starting point was the visual reality of country life, frequently picturesque but often harsh, and interest in it was prompted by Otto Seitz's school in Munich, where young Czech painters, frustrated by the conservatism of the academy in Prague, went to study in the 1880s.

Of these painters, Joža Uprka soon stood out. Uprka came from the remote Moravian Slovakia region, and he was guided by his desire to become the painter of his people. Right from the beginning, his art was exclusively concerned with depictions of life in the region's villages, which at the time still retained all their folklore and traditions. On returning from Munich in 1890, Uprka wished to continue his studies under Maxmilián Pirner, but this, his final attempt to become part of Prague's art scene, resulted only in him making the acquaintance of Hanuš Schwaiger. Schwaiger was similarly out of step with prevailing tastes and was exploring new possibilities for naturalism in painting in his depictions of genre figures from Prague. He travelled to Moravian Slovakia with Uprka, where both initially found new inspiration in the region's picturesque customs and colourful characters.

Uprka's schooling in Munich had cultivated his need to express himself in large genre compositions that initially still favoured anecdote and descriptiveness. Such was his first larger painting, *Trial at the Horse Fair* from 1890, but it was not well received by

37 Jan Koula, House in Prague (Koula Villa), 1896

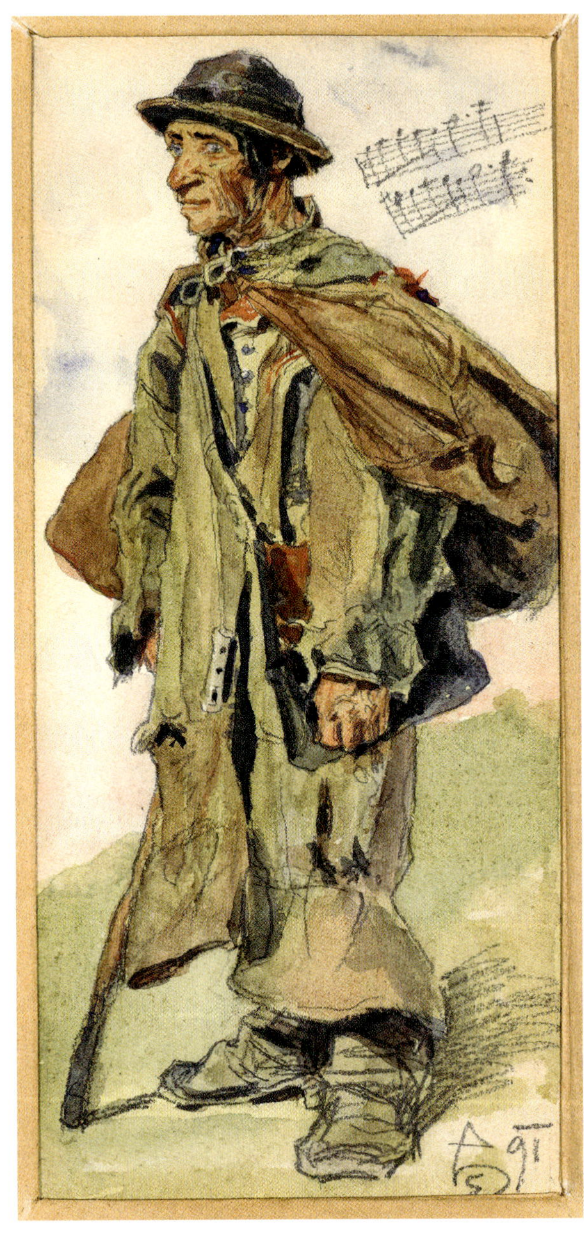

Czech critics. His acquaintance with Schwaiger introduced him to a different approach. Schwaiger's modest watercolours and paintings on wood, which in the early 1890s depicted figures not from the fertile lowlands but from mountainous Moravian Wallachia, had the force of a vision in which the exoticism of the folk costumes did not mask the reality of rural life, where people toiled simply to survive. Schwaiger cannot of course be considered a rigorous social critic. His paintings came out of his passion for the medium, and their high standard drew more on what he had learned from the Dutch Old Masters. However, in their content they were the opposite of the ideal, heroic concept that Josef Mánes had stamped on his ethnographic studies. This

38 Hanuš Schwaiger, *Pluhař the Rag-and-Bone Man*, 1891, pencil and watercolour, 18.8 × 8.5 cm

created a tension that was a particular problem for ethnographic painters in the 1890s. Their task was to find a way to combine both approaches in their paintings: to work with the truth of the painter's experience, but also with the beauty of an idealised image that reflected the irrepressible optimism that folk costumes represented.

Most of the so-called regionalists from the 1890s were unable to respond to this challenge in a way that went beyond the usual academic compromise. Joža Uprka brought new possibilities for painting that were not confined to the narrow interests of folklorists. In 1893 he visited Paris, and although his time there did not change his subject matter in any way, it significantly influenced his technique. His discovery of Luminism in Paris resulted in a brightening of his palette and an atmospheric modulation of colour. Abandoning his customary greys emphasised the decorativeness of the solid colours from which a painting was composed. Uprka triumphed with this approach, producing the first versions of his *Pilgrimage to St. Anthony's* (1893), which would become his best-known subject. It allowed him to work with the glorious colours of Moravian Slovakia's folk costumes in full sunlight.

Joža Uprka's large exhibition in Paris in 1897 was a cultural event welcomed by all critics, whether for nationalistic or aesthetic reasons. Young painters from SVU Mánes devoted an entire issue of *Volné směry* to Uprka, and their review of his exhibition

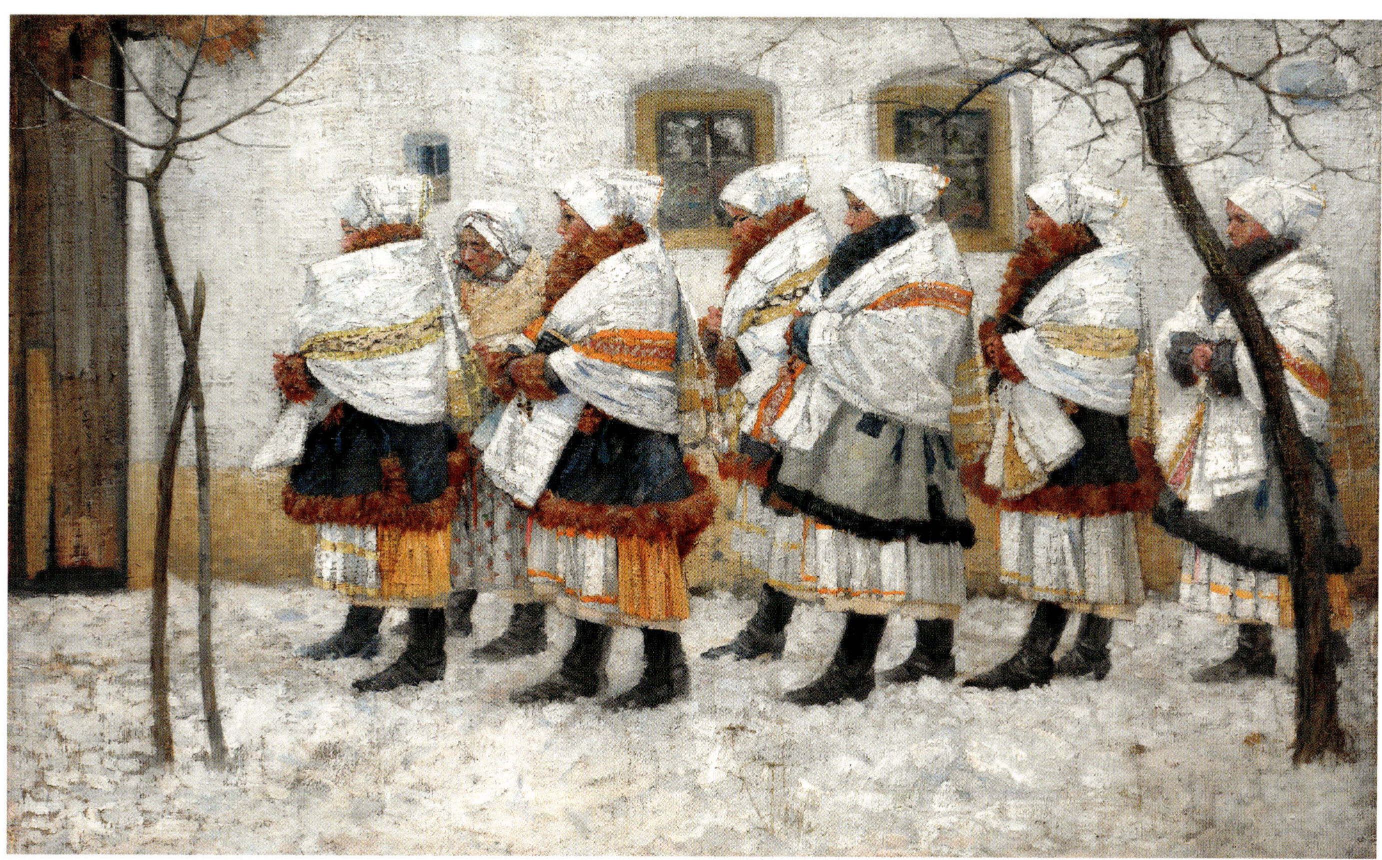

39 Joža Uprka, *Shawls from Velká*, 1896, oil, 80 × 130 cm

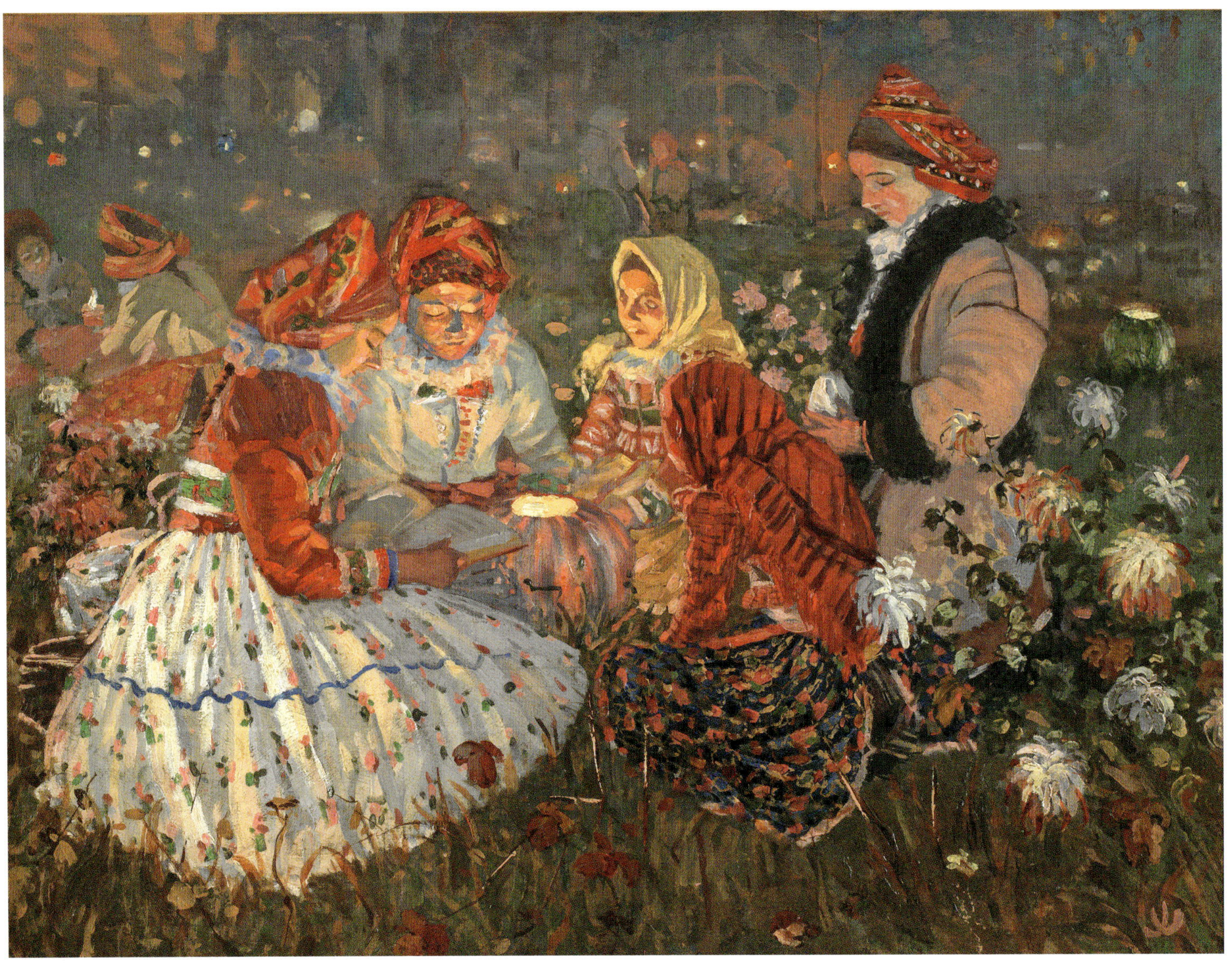

40 Joža Uprka, *All Souls' Day*, 1897, oil, 79.5 × 102 cm

was particularly appreciative of his ability to present a popular theme in a modern way.[41]

Uprka gradually made the social commentary that was still present in *The Stone Breaker* (1895) subordinate to the idea of life in Moravian Slovakia as the embodiment of an optimistic union of man and nature, reviving a romantic myth that was ultimately more attuned to the younger generation's world view than descriptive naturalism was. By extending this myth to the common people, he created an effective counterpoint to melancholy and more pessimistic treatments of the same fundamental idea. Contemporary thinking, still attracted to the contrast between dream and reality, saw here an opportunity to realise its need for ideality in a way that was realistic while also serving nationalist ends.

It was this aspect that made the ethnographic genre one of the most prominent in the 1890s, resulting in it being used not just in its original small formats, but also in major projects such as public buildings that celebrated the "revived nation." In particular, new buildings for financial institutions, whose clientele came largely from the masses, invariably included series of decorative wall paintings with scenes from country life. The Prague City Savings Bank and the Provincial Bank both had paintings by Karel Vítězslav Mašek, whose travels in Moravian Slovakia in 1895 had provided him with their subject matter. However, Mašek's oil paintings (*Reaper* was reproduced in *Volné směry*) were criticised on the grounds that he viewed country people from a city dweller's perspective.[42] This was evidently the consequence of a certain decorative stylisation that was, however, essential for Mašek's needs. This stylisation also contrasted with the naturalistic treatment represented, for instance, by Jaroslav Špillar, whose work sometimes included a moral reproach, such as in the case of *From the Times of Serfdom* (1899).

Uprka made Moravian Slovakia the archetypal region for the new ethnographic genre that was one of the main currents in Czech painting of the mid-1890s. The region attracted young painters, including Antonín Hudeček, who worked on the new genre in Moravian Slovakia before finding his true talent in landscape painting. Although there were other tempting options for this new genre, in the imagination of contemporary artists Moravian Slovakia would remain one of the prototypes of paradise lost.[43]

The different structure of society in Bohemia meant that folklorics had a far more limited foundation, and here the naturalistic generation had no talent comparable with Uprka. Of Bohemia's regions, the area around Pilsen and the historical Chodsko region were represented in this movement thanks to Augustin Němejc, the painter of an ornamental cycle for the new Museum of Decorative Arts in Pilsen (1900). Bohemian ethnography was also more influenced by the older tradition of local history, as was the case with the painter Ludvík Kuba, a noted collector of Bohemian, Russian, and Lusatian folk songs and the author of scholarly treatises.[44]

Nevertheless, in Prague itself there lived an artist from the older generation who was in fact the most important figure in this trend of painting the lives of the common people. This was Mikoláš Aleš. The younger generation regarded him warmly, electing Aleš honorary president of SVU Mánes. A special evening was held to celebrate his birthday, and in order to promote public appreciation of Aleš's oeuvre, the young artists from Mánes published his collected works, at considerable financial risk. They also rescued Aleš's *Motherland* cycle of cartoons from their undignified storage in the passageway of a Prague apartment block. *Volné směry* reproduced Aleš's youthful sketches of his bold visions for historical cycles. Their monumental and harmonious line was seen as an original continuation of the legacy of Josef Mánes, and it significantly shaped the Czech Secession's thinking on art. Aleš's popularity with young artists, and the new conditions for working in the 1890s, were substantially responsible for the relaunching of his art following his earlier crises, and in a form that, in the history of Czech art, would forever be associated with his name.

It was symptomatic of this new phase in the 1890s that Aleš worked in two complementary fields: illustration, where the high point was his collection of Czech folk songs and nursery rhymes, and monumental decorative work, where he drew cartoons to be reproduced on the façades of public and private buildings. In his pen drawings illustrating Czech folk songs and nursery rhymes, Aleš, who had always improvised brilliantly, was a virtuoso. In his simple black-and-white drawings, he unerringly conjured up stereotypical characters and scenes from rural life, capturing them with a familiarity only accessible to an eye and a heart that had always retained a childlike innocence. Although this small-scale and poorly paid work seemed to be only casual employment, evidence perhaps that the painter had given up struggling against the vicissitudes of fate, it in fact created a treasure trove of images that came as a purgative after all the

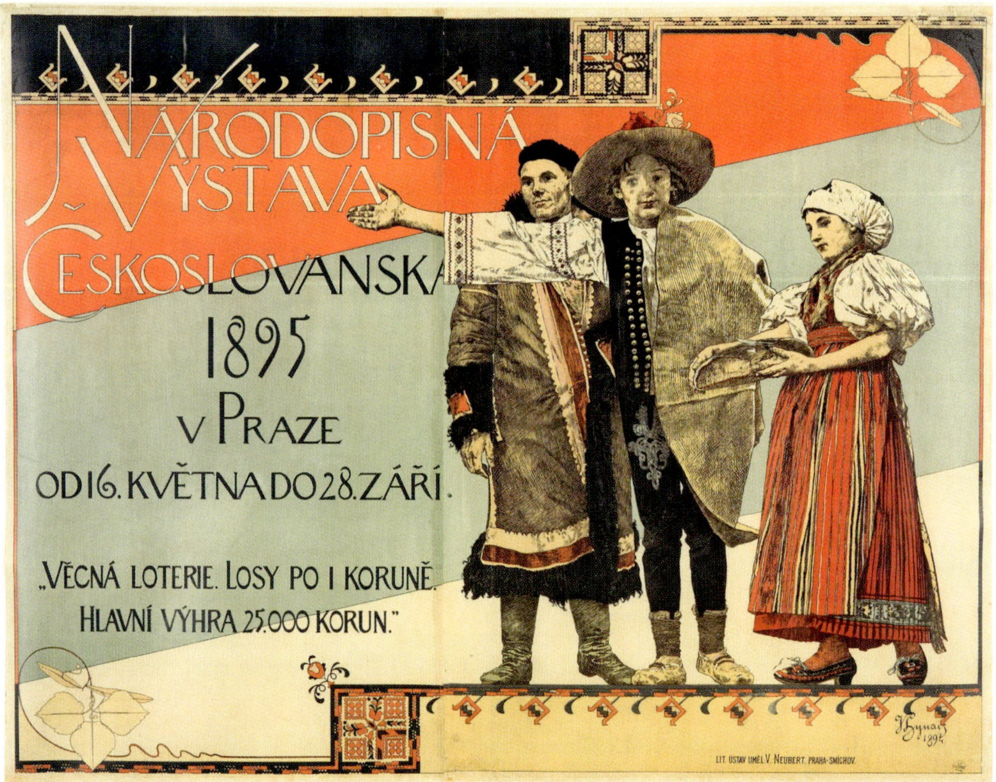

41 Vojtěch Hynais, Poster for the Czech-Slav Ethnographic Exhibition in Prague, 1894, colour lithograph, 104 × 134 cm

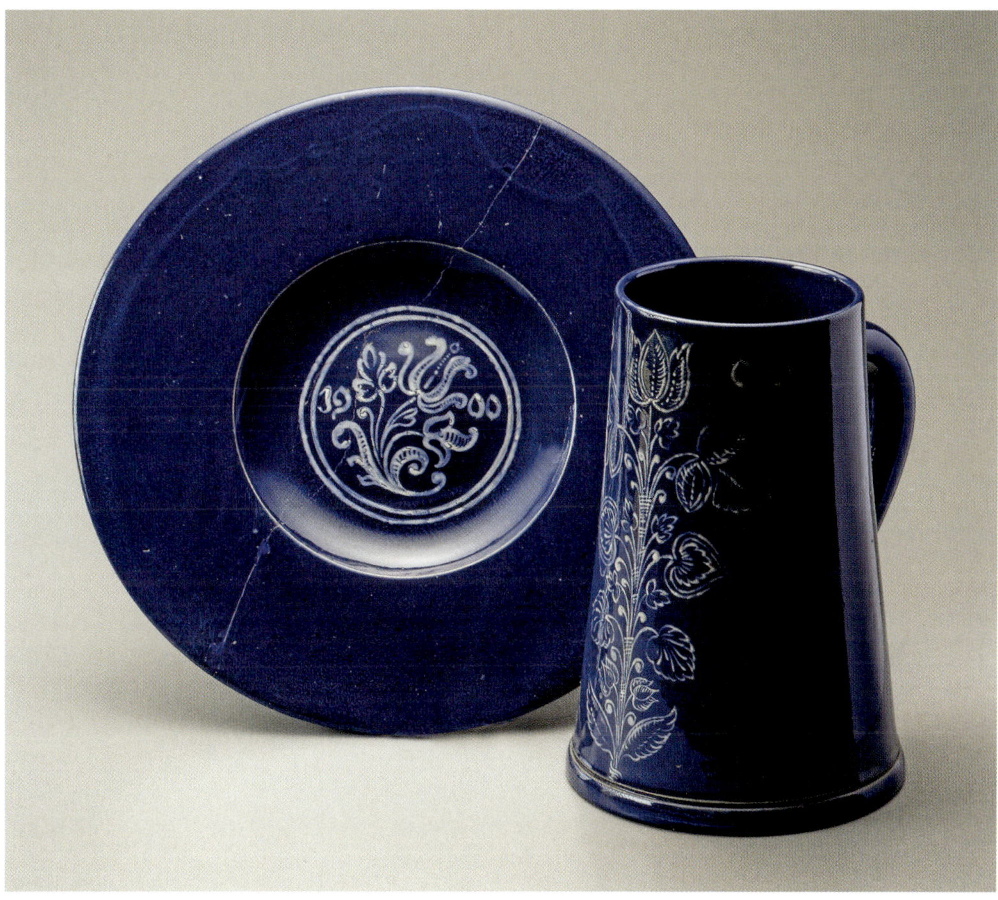

imported naturalisms of contemporary ethnographic art. Young artists soon realised that they possessed a quality that was purely national, or, more precisely, that they fully reflected the idea of the Czech national character.

Young artists' enthusiasm for Aleš stemmed from the perception that here was a living example of how injustice and misunderstanding had almost suffocated an artist's talent. The Secession was first and foremost opposed to the narrow-mindedness of Czech art. In the case of Aleš, these moral imperatives were accompanied by an interest in the distinctiveness of his art, which merited fresh attention. The sketch-like nature of Aleš's drawings was now seen as an example not just of his skill, but also of the "openness" of his style, which relied more on a flow of images linked by free association than on any closed and codified system of forms. One example of this was Aleš's set of illustrations of the months of the year, where his rich and lyrical imagination produced a panorama of the yearly cycle in freely yet logically arranged scenes that were combined with text to form a continuous wave.

Aleš created his illustrations by applying a principle that was not far removed from the later collage technique. Here too fragments of external visual reality were combined with fantastical elements and various symbols (for instance, the signs of the

42 Jan Koula, Stein and plate, 1900, glazed earthenware, 19.8 cm and 26 cm

horoscope), such that it is only in its entirety that this pictorial poem can fully express the powerful sentiments communicated by all these devices. This breaking down of the traditional visual unity of a painting was something Aleš introduced in the 1890s, and it unleashed viewers' imagination, allowing them to take part in creating a painting that acquired ever broader contexts with each new association they made.

Aleš then applied the principle he had devised for drawing illustrations to monumental decorative works, where the lyricism of his pen drawings was joined by an epic quality. He was now working on something that had excited him from the very start: a celebration of the heroes of the Czech nation. *Jan Kozina Sladký*, his 1894 watercolour of the leader of a 17th-century peasant uprising, demonstrates how he approached this task. At the centre is the figure of the hero himself, framed by emblems that place him in his geographical and historical contexts, but also reflect a certain timelessness. Aleš's

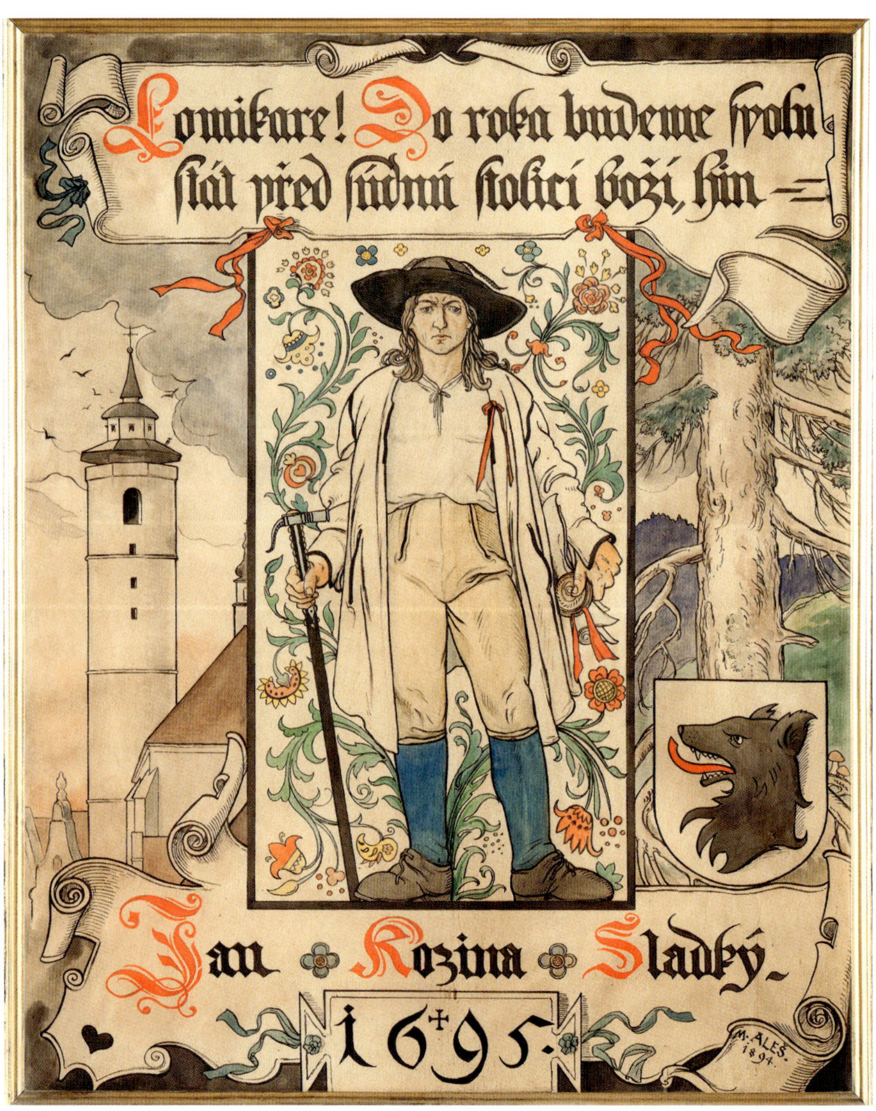

43 Mikoláš Aleš, *Jan Kozina Sladký*, 1894, watercolour, 124 × 100 cm

execution makes good use of the interplay of line and space to create the requisite decorative form. In the 1890s, Aleš could finally work on large wall spaces, something he had longed to do as a young man. These were not, of course, the walls of grand interiors such as the pantheon at the National Museum, which remained the preserve of more renowned artists. For the most part, Aleš worked on the façades of privately owned buildings, producing full-size cartoons that were then painted on the buildings or applied in the form of sgraffiti by more or less capable assistants, including members of the Mánes generation such as Arnošt Hofbauer, who by the end of the decade would be known for his decorative Secession work.

Initially these commissions were rather modest – for example, the sgraffiti of 1889–91 for Masarykova vinárna, a wine bar in Prague. But thanks to Antonín Wiehl, the most active proponent of painted façades as part of his "Czech Renaissance Revival," they soon became popular and would remain so until the start of the new century. In Prague, Aleš designed some of the paintings for Wiehl's own house (1896); he added tradesmen and country folk to the large façade of the Rott House (1896); for the Štorch House, designed by Ohmann, he drew a large figure of Saint Wenceslas on horseback (1896); and for Stanislav Sucharda's villa he sketched the figure of Božetěch, Abbot of Sázava (1896), who, according to legend, was the first Czech artist.[45] Aleš also produced a large number of sgraffiti for Pilsen, and thanks to Julius Zeyer's friends he was commissioned to design the ornamentation of the interior of a church in the town of Vodňany (1895–96).

Aleš's monumental decorative work played its part in the evolution of Czech art in the 1890s. It was surely no coincidence that onlookers from abroad described him as the Czech Walter Crane.[46] Aleš's style, combining figure and ornament to create grand two-dimensional decoration, probably played much the same role in Bohemia as the Arts and Crafts movement in England. In his combining of monumental fine art with decorative work, in his reduction of form to line and space, and in his understanding of art as serving to elevate popular taste, Aleš paved the way for the Secession.

The Czech-Slav Ethnographic Exhibition, held in Prague in 1895, was a unique opportunity for the more extensive application of Aleš's art. Preparations for this major exhibition had been underway for several years, the culmination of a wider ethnographic campaign that in many respects was a political demonstration of Czech nationalism. The exhibition poster was drawn by Vojtěch Hynais; unlike his allegorical poster for the General Land Centennial Exhibition, here were figures in folk costume, arranged in a composition that also pointed to a new decorative appreciation of the ethnographic motif.

Aleš produced numerous works for the exhibition, from cheap leaflets to paintings of *King Ottokar II* and a *Hussite Warrior* for a pub operated by a certain Mr. Myška. For Leopold František Šmíd's music hall he created *Piper*, *Pilsen Woman*, and *Fiddler from Moravian Silesia*. Although these were only temporary works, Aleš was very pleased with their reception at the exhibition.

The Ethnographic Exhibition was a manifestation of naturalistic taste. It attempted to present rural life in all of Bohemia and Moravia as faithfully as possible, with the aid of carefully designed settings. Vernacular architecture was an important element in these tableaux vivants. The exhibition's centrepiece was a village built in a circle, with examples of vernacular architecture all the way from the Domažlice district in the west to the River Orava in the east.

Vernacular architecture had attracted attention ever since the Centennial Exhibition, where Antonín Wiehl had built his "Czech cottage." For political reasons, it had become the exhibition's top attraction, and this was the genesis of the idea for the Ethnographic Exhibition. Wiehl had also used elements of vernacular architecture in his large wooden gate at the entrance to the 1891 exhibition grounds. Here Wiehl had in fact set out two approaches to vernacular architecture: as the subject of ethnographic studies, and as something that could be applied in new commissions. Other proponents of cultivating the "national spirit" in architecture operated with the same duality. Prominent among them was Jan Koula. Besides publishing scholarly works on the national heritage,[47] Koula was also the architect of a number of buildings that worked with this legacy. His own house, built in 1896 in Bubeneč, then on the outskirts of Prague, was particularly significant. In time, a small artists' colony would take shape around Koula's house and Stanislav Sucharda's first villa, recalling similar residential colonies in Germany.[48]

Although inspired by vernacular architecture, Koula's villa is very restrained. There is a simplicity of form, and Koula did not adhere to the decorative details that at the time were still largely considered the essence of a distinctively national architecture. His concept for the villa focused on the relationship between the building's mass and its roofing, the counterpoint between the plastered wall and the line of the roof, which is borne by a relatively simple structure of wooden beams that is typical of Secession architecture. This reveals how, besides vernacular architecture, Koula was also familiar with English garden houses, which at the time were the subject of much interest in Central Europe. Koula's house was a distinctively national response to an international concern with healthier and more aesthetic housing for city dwellers. With its happy synthesis of national vernacular architecture and international thinking, Koula's house was the first example of Czech modern architecture.

Koula, who was already attempting to create a new Gesamtkunstwerk, also designed the furnishings for his buildings' interiors. Although his furniture was influenced by vernacular designs, it still owed much to his original Neo-Renaissance approach. An interesting example of Koula's efforts to elevate and apply traditional techniques was his collaboration with a ceramics cooperative in Bechyně, experimenting with a new artistic appreciation of traditional ceramics. Here we can again sense a distant echo of the English workshops that sought to revive the former significance of old handicrafts and move away from mundane industrial output in favour of authentic aesthetic quality. This created an awareness of the effectiveness of simple forms, a lesson that would also be useful for the subsequent development of Czech Secession ceramics.

Besides Koula, Jan Kastner, the professor of the woodcarving studio at the School of Decorative Arts in Prague, also worked on "vernacular" furniture. He presented his designs at the Architecture and Engineering Exhibition in 1898, where he earned praise from young modernists. His designs had relatively simple forms based on traditional wardrobes, shelves, and chests, and Kastner's ornamentation included figure carvings of farmers and their wives.

Koula's and Kastner's work shows how architects and decorative designers made good use of the Ethnographic Exhibition, finding inspiration in its decorative motifs but also realising that folk art could be reworked in a modern way. This prompted a quest for a new style, for there was now a national and popular foundation that could support Czech endeavours both socially and artistically. It also opened up an opportunity to draw on progressive tendencies in other countries, offering a broader outlook to offset a certain one-sidedness in the requisite "tribal orientation." Prague's artists took a predominantly rationalist attitude, for it was they who had discovered folk art for the "high" culture to which they belonged by virtue of their schooling and work to date. Among them, however, was an architect who had grown up in close contact with the living tradition of vernacular architecture and had become not just an acknowledged expert on it but its direct heir, with a progressiveness that potentiated its contribution to modern architecture. Besides the large circular village, the Ethnographic Exhibition also featured a smaller "village" from Moravian Wallachia, built on the sloping ground below the Industrial Palace to reflect the region's terrain. There were cottages furnished in a "protestant" and "rebel" style,[49] farm buildings, a pub called The Last Groschen, an oast house, a sawmill, a bell tower, and a shepherd's hut. These wooden buildings were made in Vsetín and assembled at Prague's exhibition grounds under the supervision of Dušan Jurkovič, a young trainee architect at a practice in Vsetín. Jurkovič was originally from Slovakia, where his family was one of the most active in the nationalist movement, having produced a number of prominent figures in Slovak political and cultural life.

Like Koula, Jurkovič had been much impressed by the Slovak Gate that carpenters, supervised by Blažej Bulla, a graduate of the Prague Polytechnic, had built in 1887 for an exhibition of folk embroidery in Turčianský Svatý Martin in Slovakia. This marked the start of Jurkovič's enchantment with the artistic richness of wooden vernacular architecture, and he became an expert on its construction, ornament, and social function. He demonstrated his knowledge at the Ethnographic Exhibition, where he also designed a large house for an extended family to showcase the collective housing that was typical of the Slovak village of Čičmany. This house led to his first larger commissions. In 1897 he began building a tourist complex on Pustevny, a mountain pass on the slopes of Radhošť, where he could fully develop his ideas about drawing on the vernacular tradition. He lived on Pustevny with the workmen to oversee construction, adapting it to the local climate and style. First, he built Maměnka, a chalet in which he wanted to create a new type of Slavic summer retreat.[50] Jurkovič based it on specific examples of large family houses and manors, adapting them to meet the needs of a modern hotel. The wooden structure stands on a stone foundation wall, and the picturesque effect is magnified by Maměnka's richly carved gallery and broad eaves. The roof has many gables that are adorned with complicated oblique or fan-shaped latticework, and there are dormer windows, chimneys, cupolas, and a tower that admits

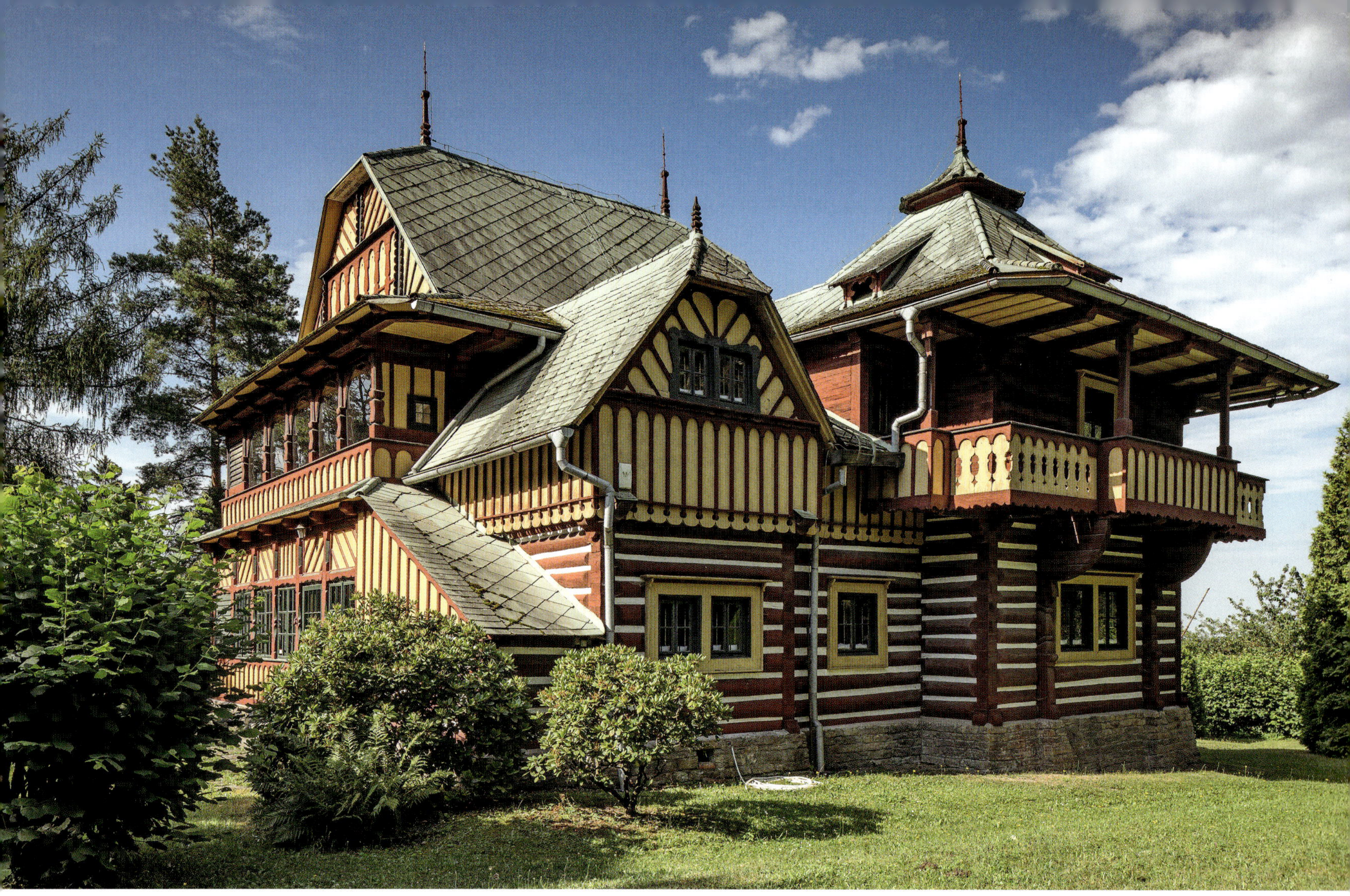

light to the staircase. All of these were faithfully executed according to vernacular examples, down to the very last detail. Yet the building as a whole is not merely a compilation of ethnographic elements, for it has its own architectural rhythm. For the interior, and in the furnishings of the rooms with their beam ceilings, Jurkovič took inspiration from traditional furniture. Ornamental painting throughout the building further enhanced the cheerful effect.

Due to the success of Maměnka, plans for the site were extended, and eventually Jurkovič would build an entire tourist resort on Pustevny. To the original lodge, erected earlier in the style of a Swiss chalet, he added a new dining hall, where the need for a large room made it impossible to adhere strictly to traditional models. Although Jurkovič based his design on the floor plan of a vernacular church, he abandoned excessive ethnographic faithfulness in favour of a freer approach, extending his previously wholly ethnographic orientation to include original architectural work. Here he again made use of the picturesque contrast between stone and wood, and there are also several Secession motifs.[51] The dining hall's exterior is grander and more cogent

44 Dušan Jurkovič, Villa in Rezek, 1900

than the playful Maměnka, although Jurkovič's penchant for decorativeness remained evident principally in the interior, lit by large windows. Here the rich carving turned the wooden panelling and the furniture into a play of curves and coloured spaces of such intensity that the interior was later described as Impressionist. Jurkovič invited two painters he had met at the Ethnographic Exhibition to work on the interior. One of them, Karel Štapfer, covered the walls in a variety of folk ornamental designs, and in the widest part of the dining hall he painted four large Slovak brigands, based on cartoons by Mikoláš Aleš.

At Pustevny, Jurkovič added a skittle alley, a summer gym, a bell tower, and a carved information panel, and together they created the first group of permanent buildings in which young architecture found creative expression for the new way of combining art with nature.

For his work on Radhošť, Jurkovič earned the epithet "the poet of wood," which followed him to his next commission, this time in Brno, where in 1899 he applied what he had learned to the interior of a boarding house for a girl's school run by a patriotic Czech women's society called Vesna. However, the main focus of his work now shifted to a spa town, Luhačovice, where he had been commissioned to plan its redesign.

The Czech joint-stock company that had bought the spa wanted to rebuild it in a distinctively "Slavic" style that would distinguish it from other spas. The company's director, František Veselý, was an agile proponent of this idea, and accordingly he engaged Jurkovič, who in the autumn of 1901 set to work on a series of remodelling projects planned for the first phase of construction. However, nothing was to be rushed, and Jurkovič began by visiting noted spas in Austria and Germany so that he could ensure that Luhačovice would differ from them, but also to give him a better understanding of the needs of a fairly sizeable spa.

The most important structure in the first phase of building the new Luhačovice was the Jan Building. Jurkovič had to base his work on the original layout of an older Neo-classical building, but he entirely remodelled it and connected it to another spa building that was already standing there. This larger structure now had a prominent entrance in the form of an avant-corps roofed with a carved gable. It is, however, the only more markedly ethnographic motif in the building, which is otherwise quite modern in the working of the half-timbered upper floor built on top of the original brickwork, the dormer windows, and other elements. The building's profile was enlivened by a staircase tower whose wooden frame was filled with green glass bricks, a material that introduced a new and modern note in Jurkovič's repertoire. This motif also aptly symbolised the spa building's purpose, with the green colour recalling water. In the evening, the tower was lit from inside by electric light, making it an attractive feature in the liveliest part of the spa.

Particularly noteworthy in the Jan Building was the articulation of the façade in conjunction with the flawless decorative use of polychromy. The colours ranged from the glossy purple of the fireclay plinth to the dominant orange and white of the walls, with details picked out in blue, olive, and yellow. The end result was cheerful and harmonious, and it greatly helped in making the building's relatively large mass seem

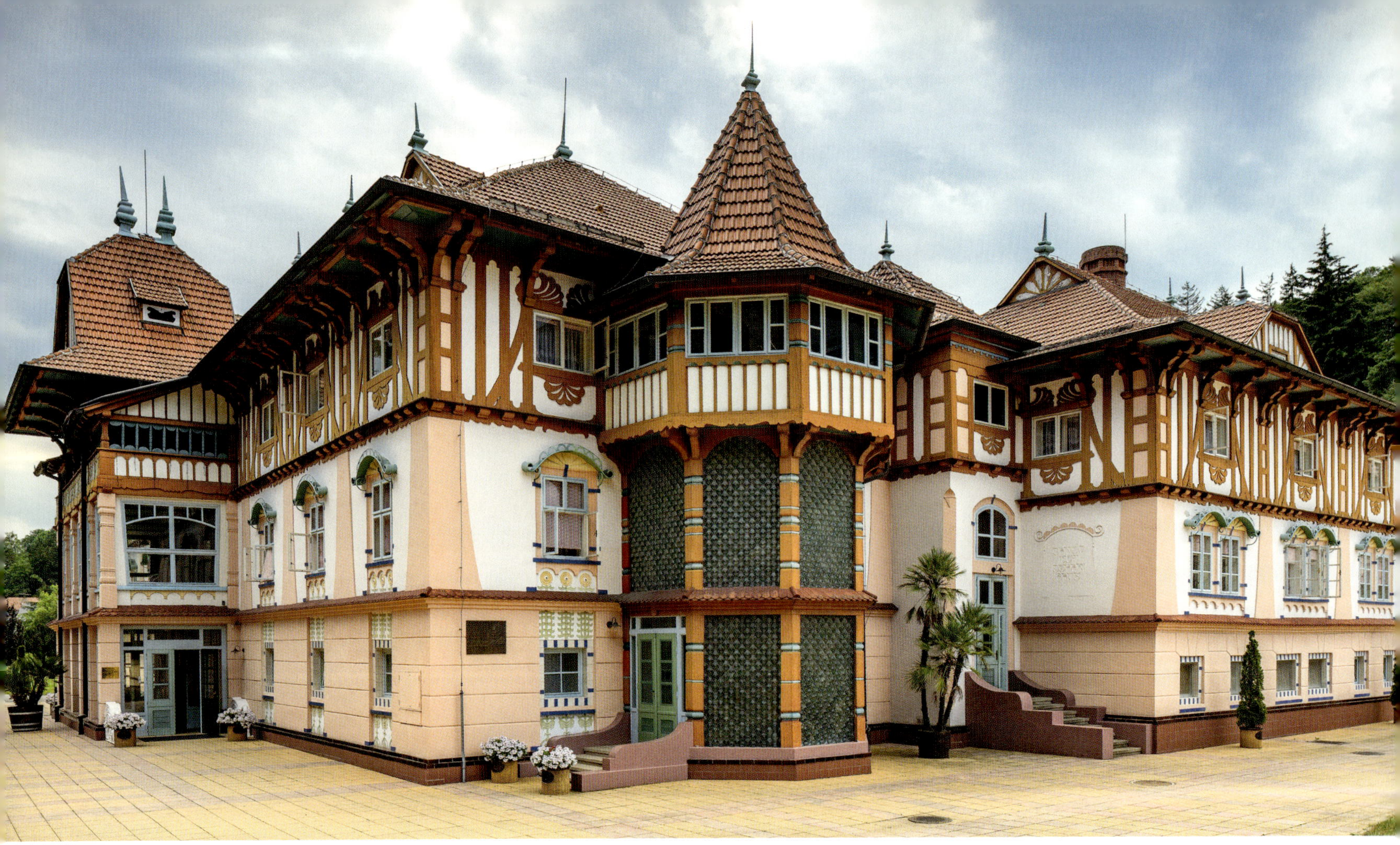

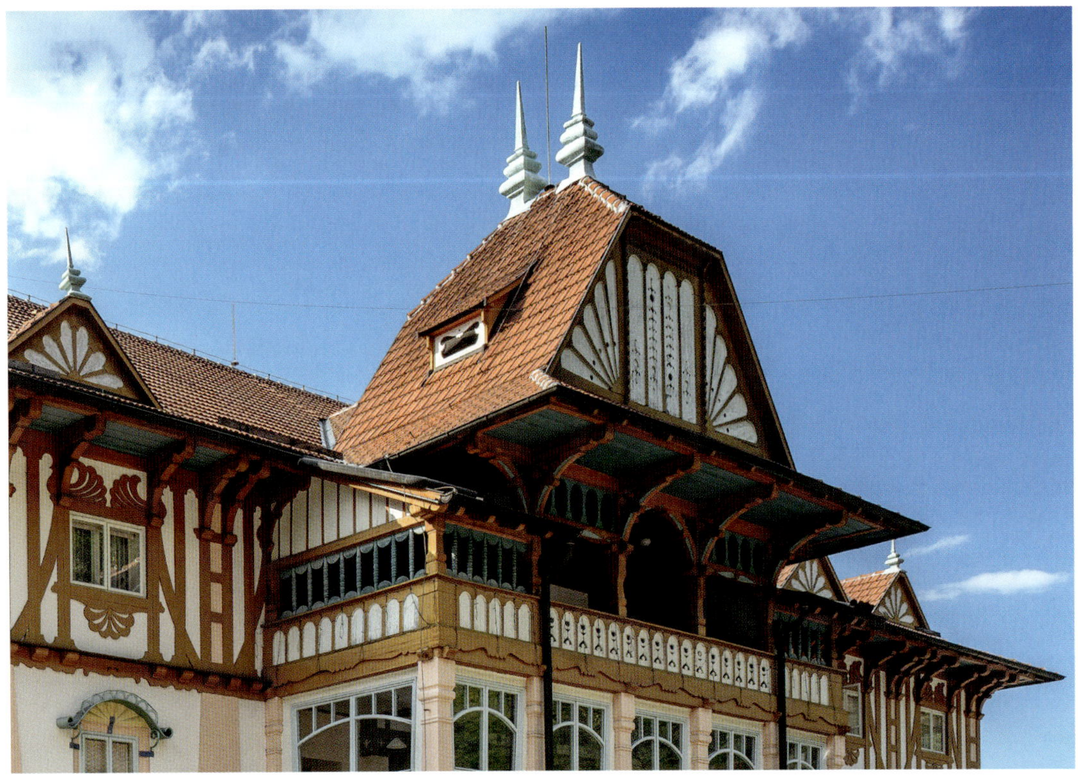

45–46 Dušan Jurkovič,
Jan Building in Luhačovice, 1902

more intimate, as well as enhancing the spa's summertime ambience. The decorative aspect of the Jan Building amplified its Secession motifs, such as the stylised swans by the entrance and the floral designs around the windows, as well as the rhythmic curves of the half-timbered upper floor. Even more symptomatic of Jurkovič's modernity was how he balanced the decorative and functional elements. The internal organisation of the Jan Building, and its furnishings, courtyard, and passageways, were entirely in line with the requirements of a modern facility. Besides his favoured material, wood, Jurkovič also used concrete here.

Jurkovič's other buildings in Luhačovice from 1902–3 demonstrate how his ideas developed as he took on these varied tasks. Villa Jestřábí is more compact, as befits its location on the edge of the spa against a backdrop of wooded slopes, and this compactness is further emphasised by the tall plinths made of rubble at the corners of the building and the relatively simple articulation of its half-timbered upper floor. The villa's polychromy is also more restrained. Chaloupka is an example of a smaller spa building, and it was much praised by the writer Alois Mrštík.[52] Jurkovič's buildings in Luhačovice were erected at a rapid pace, driven by the desire to start operating the spa at full capacity as soon as possible. For this reason, besides expensive remodelling, light wooden structures were favoured, such as the restaurant pavilion, the lido by the hydropathic institute, and the inhalation pavilion, where there was neither time nor money for lavish ornamentation. However, it was thanks to this that Jurkovič's designs for these buildings were the most architecturally progressive, and their simplicity and functional ingenuity in no way detracted from their elegance. The restaurant pavilion, lit from above, had a system of a load-bearing frame and panels that recalled Japanese architecture, which was reflected in its geometrical structure and subdued ornamentation. This best demonstrated how far Jurkovič had come since building the dining hall on Pustevny just a few years earlier. Formerly, ornamental details had dominated, but now the emphasis was on a spatial concept that integrated the architecture internally. The same was true of the modest inhalation pavilion, whose white timber frame was filled with cork panels. The art historian František Žákavec thought that the unusual slanting of the building's walls (to make better use of the steam from the inhalation apparatus) anticipated Cubist architecture.[53]

However, many other designs for Luhačovice remained on paper. They included the large Polenka Café with its novel floor plan, and especially Jurkovič's designs for the central spa building, the colonnade, the Slovak House, and the overall layout of the spa's centre. Although Jurkovič's work in Luhačovice was much praised in progressive intellectual circles,[54] the joint-stock company wasted the opportunity to create a spa that would be a unique, coherent, and harmonious set of buildings based on Jurkovič's concept. By commissioning generally less talented architects to design other buildings, they fragmented an idea that had promised to create one of the prime examples of contemporary modern architecture in Europe. Koula's villa in Prague and Jurkovič's work for Radhošť and Luhačovice demonstrated the fertile inspiration that both architects had found in the vernacular heritage. Their results were distinguished above all by how they worked creatively with this heritage and took from it new struc-

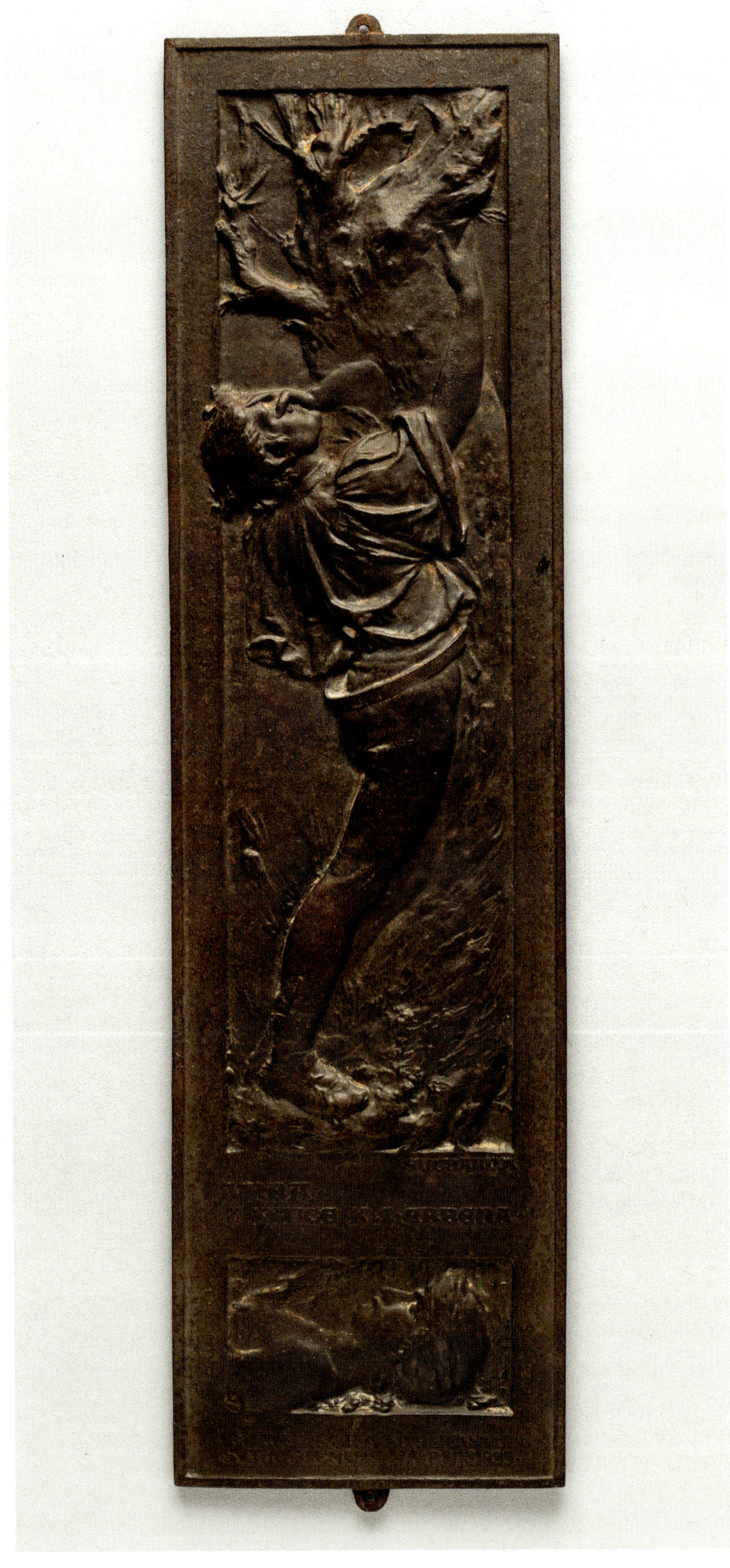

47 Stanislav Sucharda, *Willow*, 1897, bronze, 60.5 × 16.5 cm

tural elements for modern architecture. The essence was a respect for building with wood, which, according to Czech ethnographic theories at the time, was typical of "Old Slavic" architecture. Ornamentation was derived from this basic constructional element, and its motifs completed the concept. In this way, the preconditions for the development of a modern Czech architecture took shape. Increasing familiarity with similar tendencies in other countries both extended and reinforced this foundation.

While architects were quick to discern the most progressive elements in the contemporary enthusiasm for folk art, the situation in other disciplines was more complicated. There was the distracting influence of the older descriptive naturalism, and there were certain ideological demands that exploited the interest in folk art for nationalist ends. In painting, the success of the Ethnographic Exhibition led to endless reproductions of stereotypical ornament, the genre known as anecdotal painting, and a sentimental attachment to pseudo-folk art. Similarly, in sculpture, the years after 1895 saw a flood of statuettes of Jeníček and Mařenka (Hansel and Gretel) as "patriotic" adornments for bourgeois households.

The more artistically valuable part of this output was produced by Myslbek's pupils, such as František Stránecký or František Hošek, who died while still young. Hošek's *Farewell* (1895), a high relief depicting a young tinker parting from his mother, was praised for its "Mánesian" classic qualities.

In sculpture, the ethnographic genre also flourished in monumental decorative works, especially those produced for new public buildings. Here too, however, it was mostly combined with naturalism to create an effect much like a museum exhibit, as with the figures representing the regions of Bohemia in the hall of the Provincial Bank. The genre was applied most successfully by Stanislav Sucharda, whose *Thrift* – an allegorical statue of a young man for the façade of the Prague City Savings Bank – anticipated Preisler's archetypal adolescent Janík, derived from the same contemporary ideas.

In his 1892 relief *Lullaby*, Sucharda had in fact initiated the application of ethnography in sculpture, and he was also the first to go beyond its sentimentality. In 1897 he created *Willow*, a relatively large plaquette inspired by a poem by Karel Jaromír Erben that was based on a folktale. Although Neo-Baroque in style, especially in the male figure, the lower part of the plaquette has the softly modelled head of a woman with her eyes closed, which introduced into Czech sculpture a key Symbolist motif – sleep.[55]

The ballads in Erben's *A Bouquet of Czech Folktales* offered a way out of the blind alley of the fashion for ethnography. Behind its subject matter lay humanity's ancient experience of the fundamental archetypal situations of the human psyche, offering metaphors for our deeper and more ambivalent relationship with nature and natural processes. At the end of the century, artists sensed in this aspect of Erben's work an opportunity for more profound content in the new art. The cult around Erben was especially fruitful now that the sources from which the power of his poetry was drawn seemed, at least superficially, to have been exhausted.

Sucharda also worked with Erben's *Treasure* (1898), but with less success than in *Willow*, for here he was too carried away with the emotional drama. By now, however,

Erben was well-established in Czech art. In sculpture, this interest in the writer led to a competition to design a monument to him in his birthplace, Miletín. Particularly interesting was Ladislav Šaloun's entry, featuring a bust of Erben on a plinth surrounded by fairy-tale figures, including a water sprite that was typical of the new fondness for the grotesque. This took the picturesque aspect of ethnography to another level, offering greater room for the artist's fantasy. Sculpture illustrates how, by the end of the 1890s, it had become essential to move beyond descriptive naturalism if art was to develop further. One way was to increase its psychologically motivated expressiveness, for which Erben's *Bouquet* offered the most cogent themes. Nevertheless, sculpture could not draw on literature alone, and it was reluctant to abandon the innovation that empirical naturalism had brought. The only thing to be done was to accentuate the

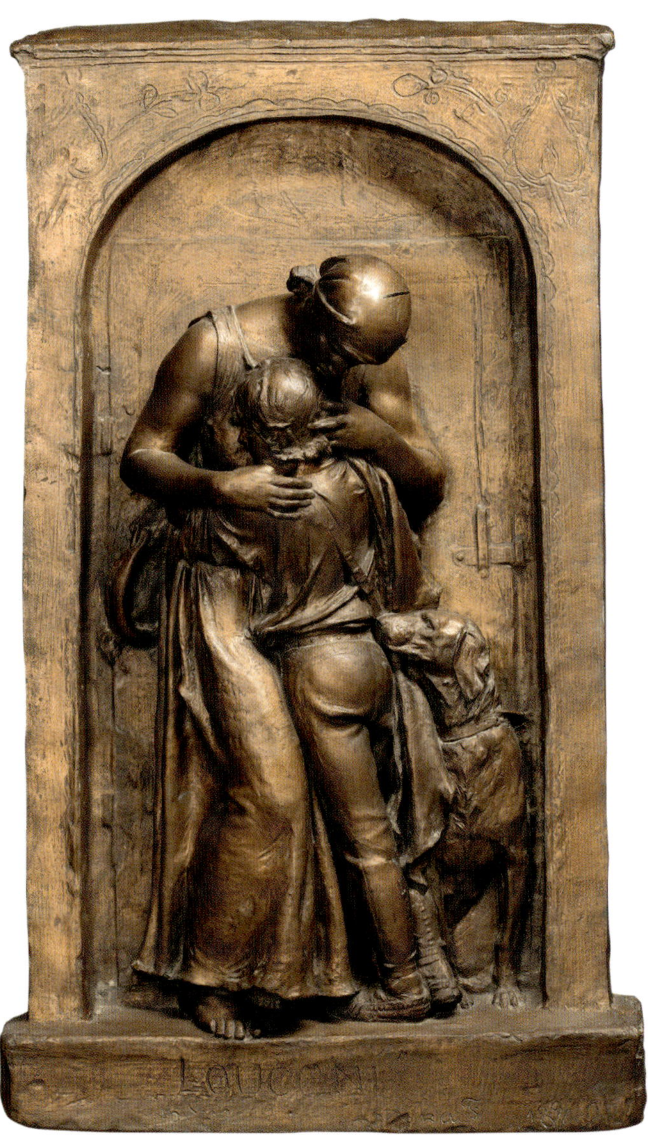

48 František Hošek, *Farewell*, 1895, bronze, 120 × 68 cm

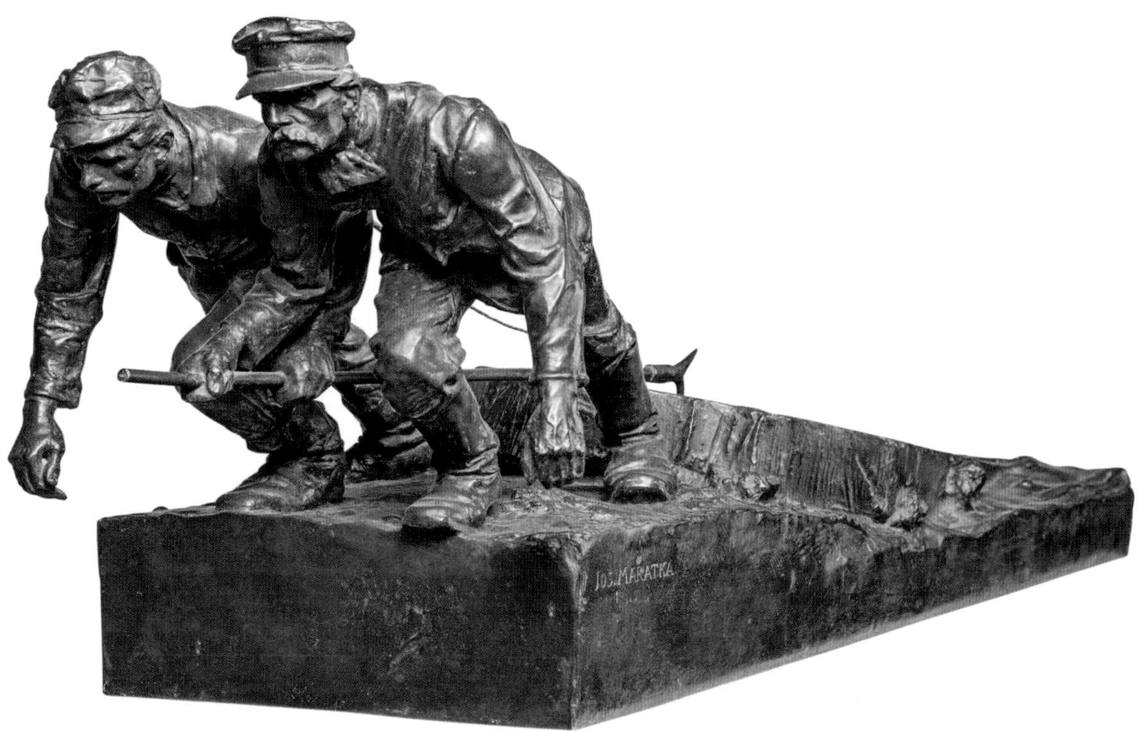

"potency of the eye" in the name of originality. This began quite modestly. Early in the decade, František Hergesel's sculptural group *Ploughing in the Giant Mountains* (1891) had attracted critics' attention for its social commentary on human toil. However, Hergesel's depiction of people hitched to a plough like draught animals and struggling against the land was a motif that invited better execution. Perhaps František Bílek was responding to it in his *Tilling with the Cross* (1895), which turned naturalism into its reverse. Josef Mařatka used the same motif in his naturalistic *Icemen* (1900), a sculpture in which he defied his teacher, Myslbek, in favour of the direct study of a model taken from the street.[56] Besides its meticulous faithfulness – for which he was castigated by a young critic called Stanislav Kostka Neumann[57] – Mařatka's sculpture also captured mankind's age-old struggle with its burden, which established a certain symbolic significance. While Mařatka could not yet achieve a convincing unity of form and content, Ladislav Šaloun was more successful. In *Man of Toil* (1900) he transposed the entire problem to a single figure, which was sculpturally a more effective solution. Here too, however, there was a certain disparity between the descriptive naturalism of the modelling and the conceptual content, which besides its social aspect also had a Symbolist note as a naturalistic interpretation of the myth of Sisyphus.

This differentiation came as the artists' world view was extending beyond the bourgeois ideology associated with ethnography's popularity. Their work shifted the focus to a dramatic concern with the hero's fate and an interest in contemporary social conflicts. Both of these were consequences of 1890s' ethnography and resulted in its reappraisal for the needs of the new art.

49 Josef Mařatka, *Icemen*, 1900, bronze, 40 cm

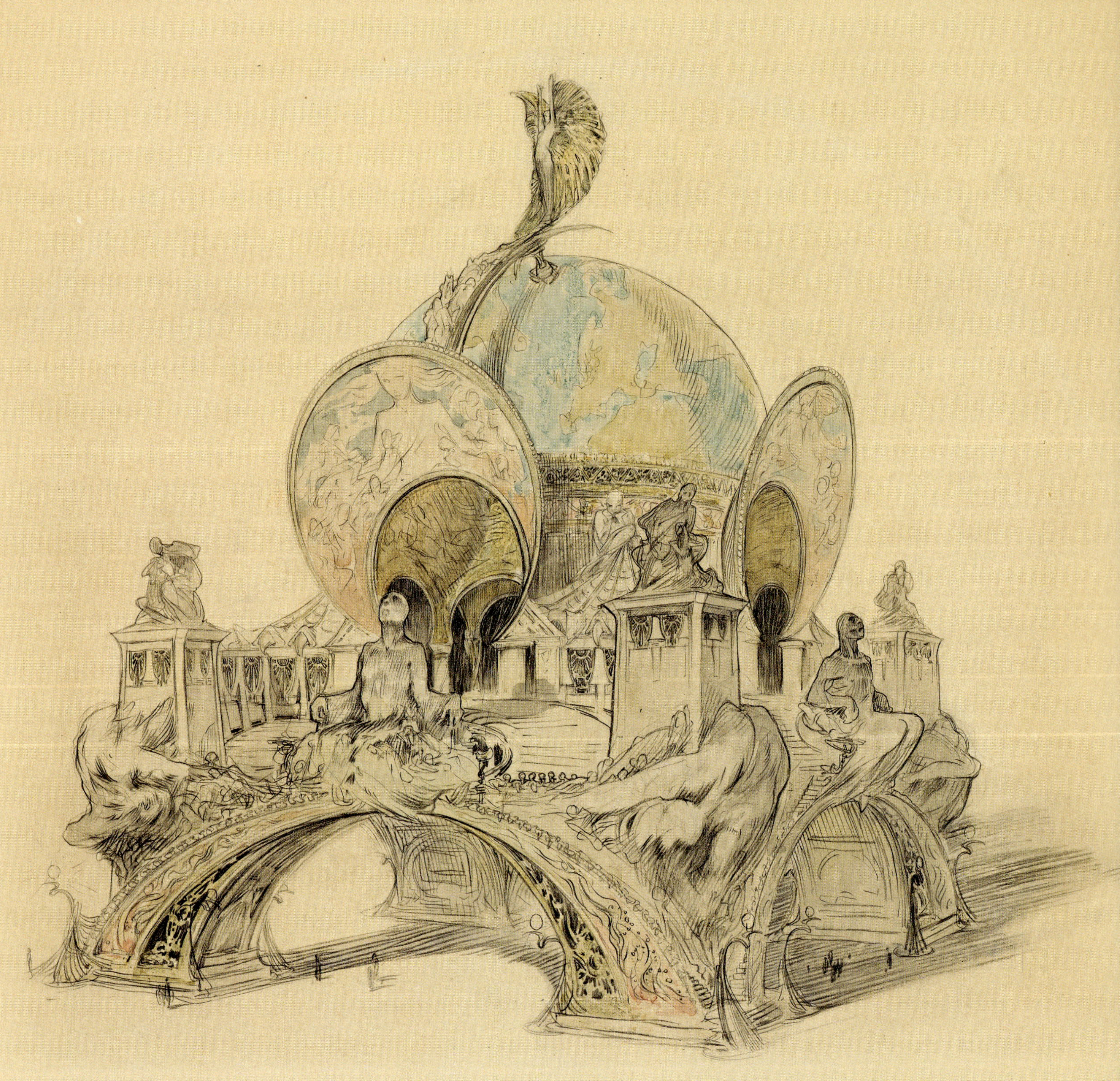

INTO THE WIDER WORLD

> And then so much was said and written about national art, about drawing on old traditions, recommendations to use ethnographic motifs, that in the end young people's independent spirit rebelled against this kind of moral coercion. National motifs and their superficial differences were not enough for us; in fact, they repelled us, for we sensed in them mitigating circumstances, almost a ploy to win praise for poorer work and lighten the responsibility of art. The folk art they put before us as our model seemed to us to be something that was closed, finished, over and done with; all subsequent developments had distanced us from it. And first and foremost, we wanted to master everything being done abroad, to be in step with the rest of Europe…

These words were written by Miloš Jiránek, looking back at his generation's early years a decade later.[58] His opinion was shared by everyone who was repulsed by the indiscriminateness of the bourgeois comedy of ethnography, the patriotic fervour of "national festivals," folk costumes sown in Prague by bespoke tailors, and decorations painted on the joists of luxurious apartment buildings. It seemed to them that freedom lay wherever art was fully part of the present, and that was where they sought their models and idols. This role fell to Luděk Marold.

Marold's life and work were stormy and precipitous. An illegitimate orphan whose studies were supported by his aunt, he was accepted at the Academy of Fine Arts in 1881, where he soon found himself in conflict with its conservative management. Like many others, he left Prague for Munich, where at the city's academy he became an enthusiastic member of Škréta, an association of Czech artists named after the Czech Baroque painter Karel Škréta; it was the predecessor of SVU Mánes. For Škréta's magazines *Paleta* (The Palette) and *Špachtle* (The Spatula), Marold contributed his first realistic studies of life in the German metropolis. In an outline of his autobiography that he later sent to Jan Neruda, he ironically remarked that he had done nothing in Munich but study the city's beer. On returning to Prague, however, he dazzled the art world with his painting *The Egg Market* (1888) and the astonishing veracity with which it depicted the atmosphere of this part of Prague's Old Town and the colourful characters who worked there. Marold's talent was indisputable. The plan was to recruit him to teach at the School of Decorative Arts in Prague, and to this end he was awarded a grant to study decorative painting in Paris under Pierre-Victor Galland. Once there, however, Marold felt that the study of ornament and the laborious process of mechanically enlarging it on walls was a form of martyrdom. What appealed to him was capturing the immediacy of life as it pulsed around him

50 Alphonse Mucha, Second design for the Pavilion of Man at the Exposition Universelle in Paris, 1897, pencil and watercolour, 50.1 × 64.9 cm

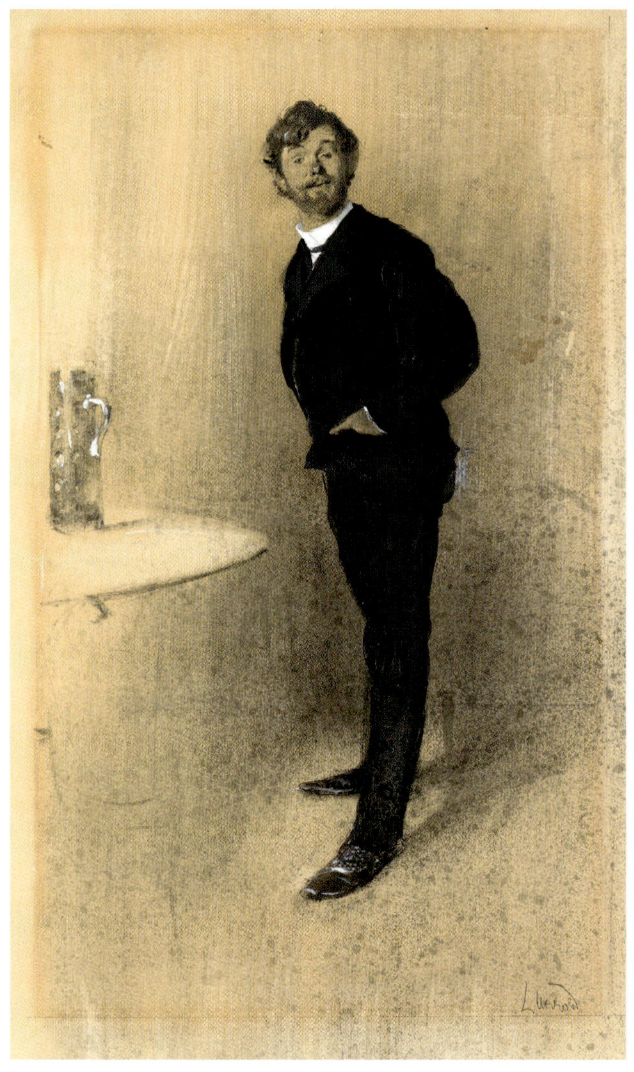

on the city's embankments and boulevards. He ceased attending Galland's school and his grant was soon withdrawn, leaving him in dire need. Vojtěch Hynais came to his aid, offering him his studio and securing Marold his first commission, the cover for some nondescript catalogue that nevertheless proved to be a turning point. Publishers of illustrated magazines and books in Paris were quick to recognise Marold's talent for illustration, and they began showering him with commissions that over the next six months would make his name. Marold became a new star in the artistic firmament.

Such was Marold's reputation when he returned to Prague in 1897, perhaps for good. The city's young artists were much taken with his affability and fascinated by his life story, which had all the ingredients of the biography of a true Secession artist, although Marold had reservations about the movement's decorative Symbolist aspects and even feared that SVU Mánes members considered him insufficiently modern.

51 Luděk Marold, *The Painter Viktor Oliva*, c. 1890, charcoal, pencil, and gouache, 49.5 × 31.6 cm

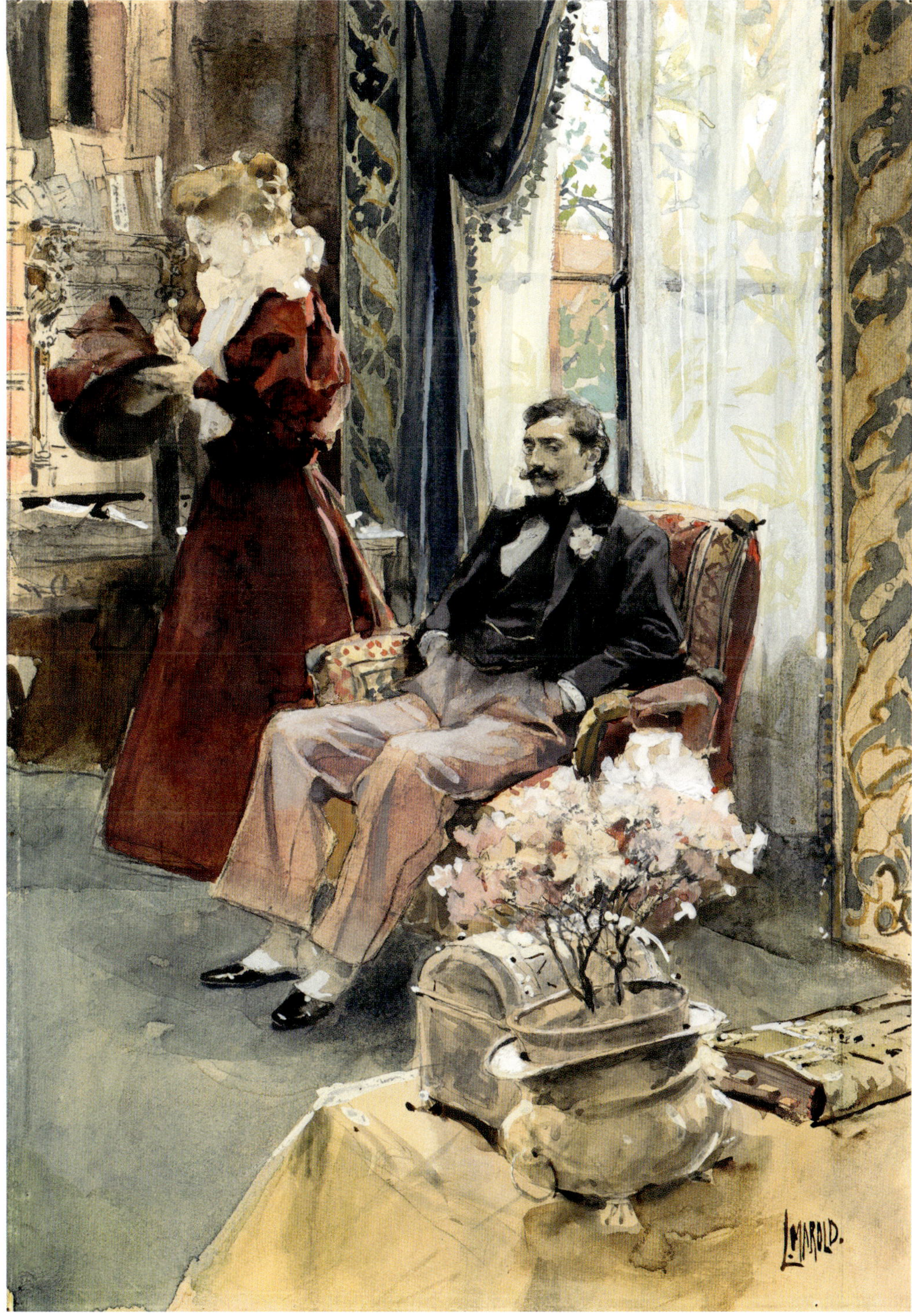

52 Luděk Marold, *A Poor Excuse*, after 1890, watercolour and gouache, 43.8 × 28.5 cm

Marold's much-admired independence and freethinking, the way he had defied the authorities and pursued his own interests, was coupled with what his work represented in the context of contemporary Czech art. While the Munich academy's customary naturalism was stifled by its descriptiveness, Marold elevated this aspect to a form that had great lightness and charm. His technical skill and his unconventional way of combining different techniques were incredible: in a single painting he might use pencil, chalk, pen, watercolour, and gouache with the sole aim of capturing a particular moment, creating a compelling illusion of reality for the viewer. He used these means to capture scenes from ordinary life that were seen with an extraordinary sharpness and observed with a photographer's alertness and acuteness, yet they were also full

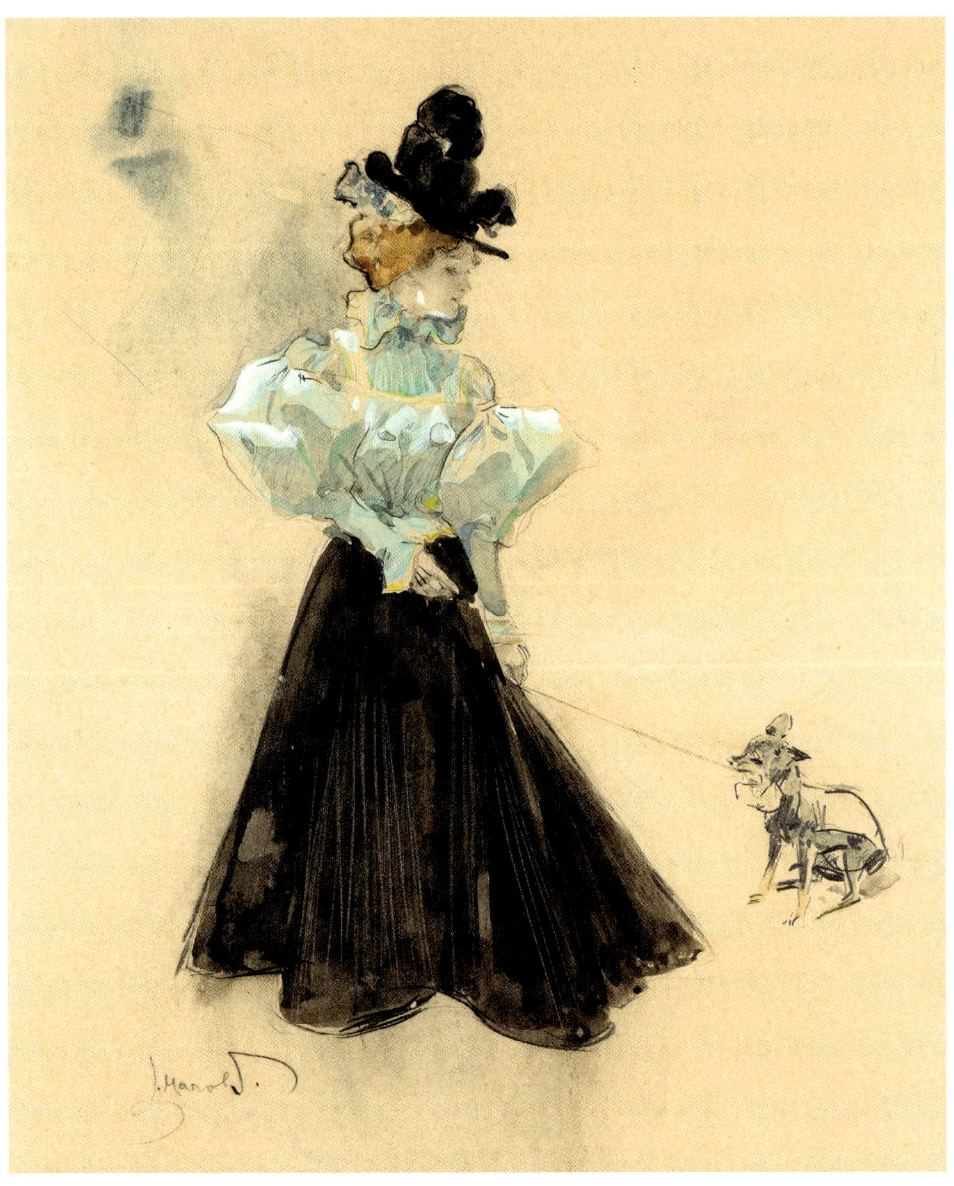

53 Luděk Marold, *Lady with a Little Dog*, after 1890, Indian ink and watercolour, 37 × 28.5 cm

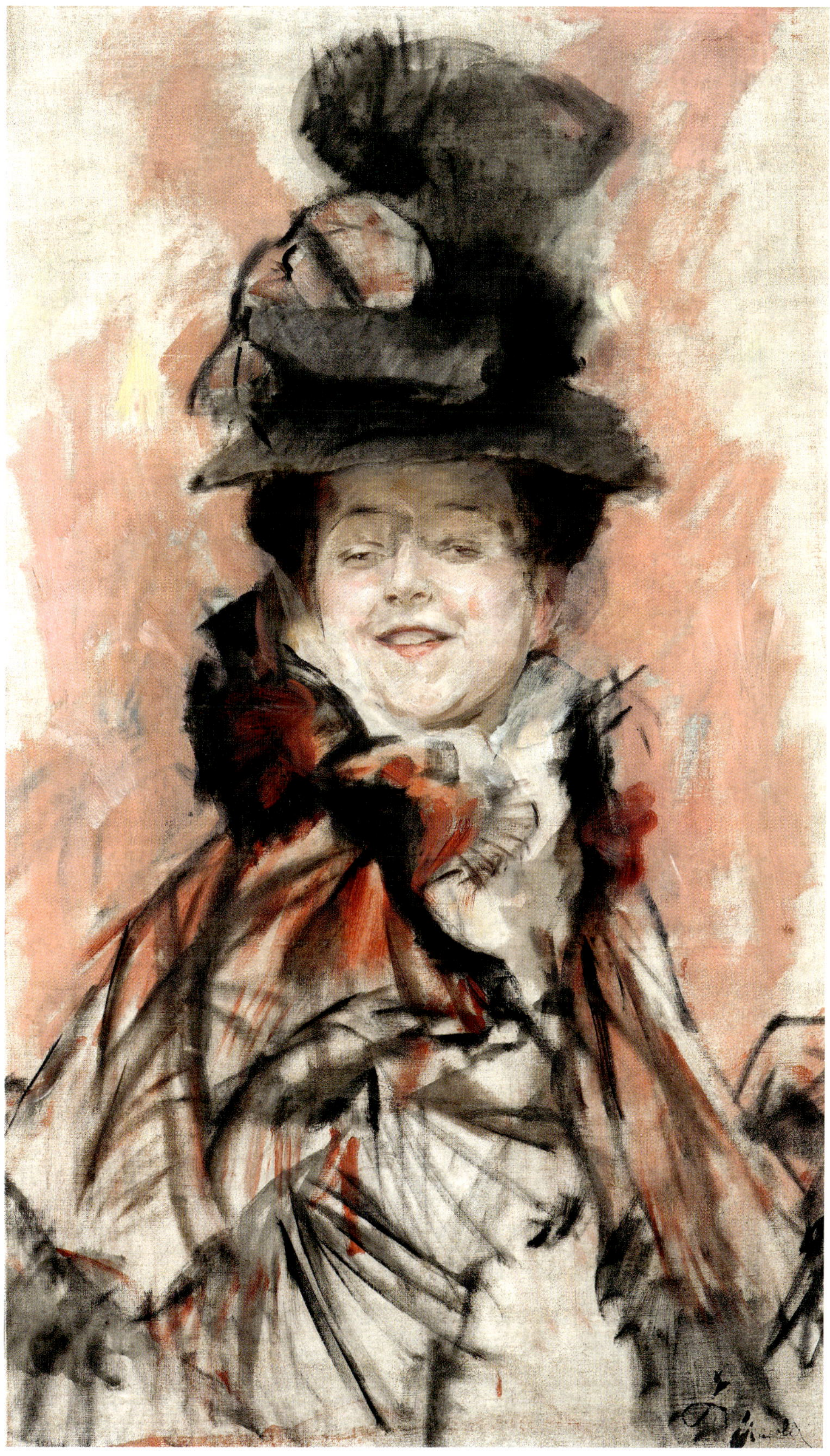

54 Luděk Marold, Study for a portrait of Anna Červená, 1897, oil, 52.8 × 46.5 cm

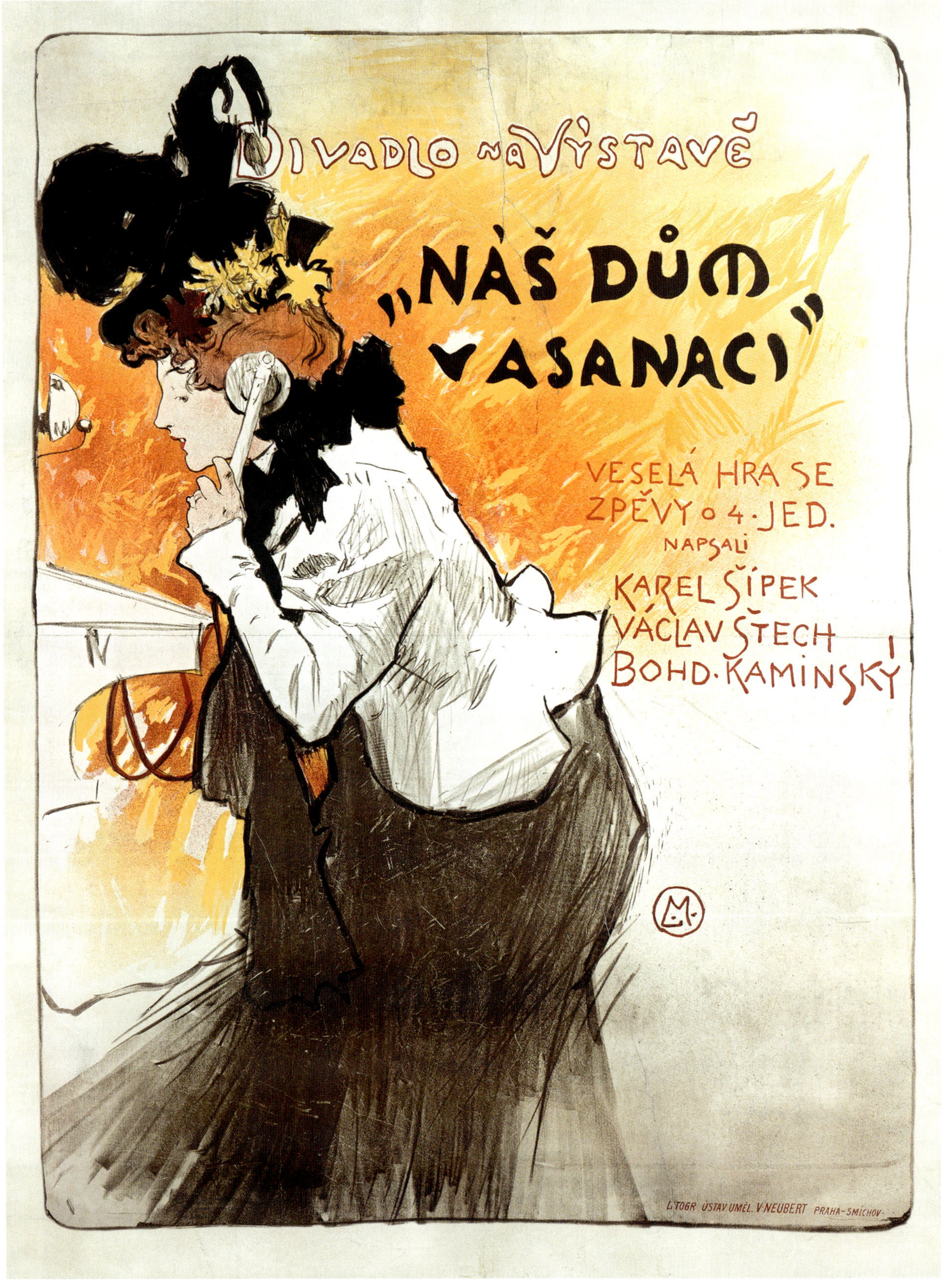

55 Luděk Marold, Poster for *Our Apartment is Under Renovation* at the Exhibition Theatre, 1898, colour lithograph, 124 × 92 cm

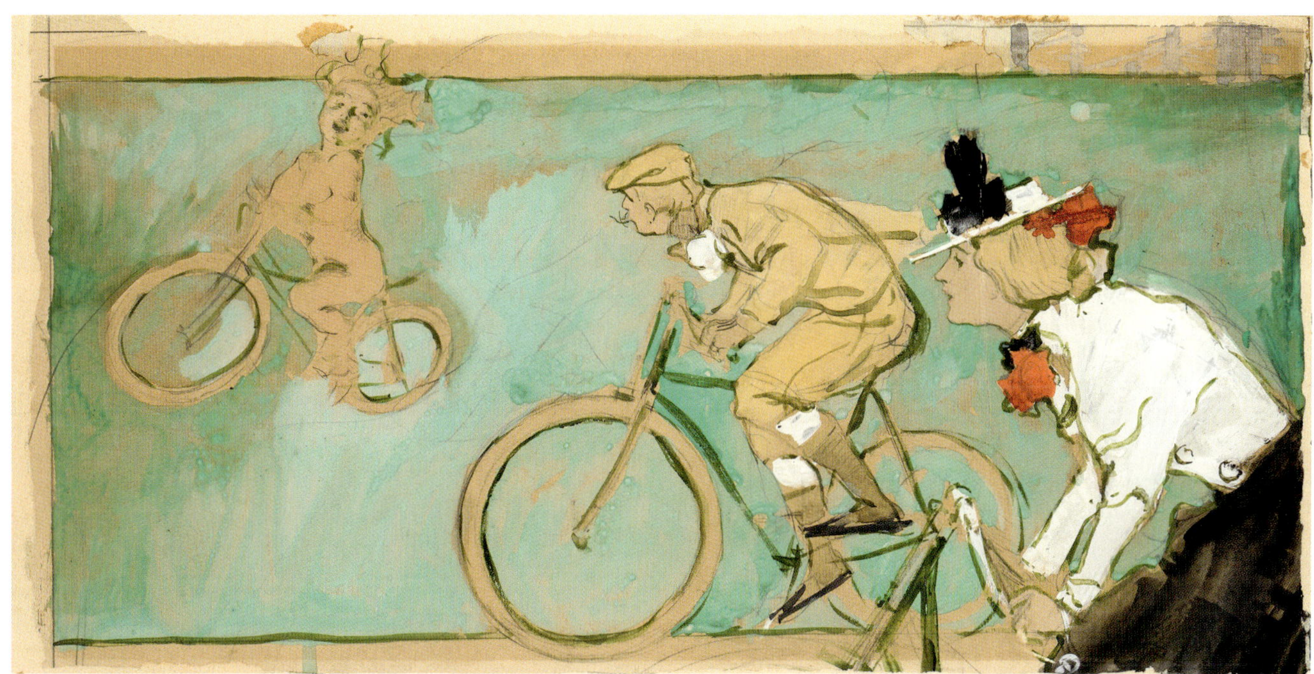

of psychological understanding. To his contemporaries, it seemed that they could hear Marold's figures speaking, and even knew what they were talking about. His art was truly at one with the mentality and vision of the social stratum that comprised his audience at the time.

As K. B. Mádl noted, women were central to Marold's world:

> Marold does not philosophise about his women, he does not preach to them, he does not quarrel with them about the purpose of life. … Not one of them is cold or dead, everywhere life sparkles and glitters within them. The artist has left them in intoxicating possession of everything they boast. The comeliness of the limbs, the warm elasticity of the flesh, the svelte fullness of the arms and legs, the undulation of the lines, the heady scent of the body, the beautiful suppleness of its motion and pose. … They are dressed in the latest fashion, with a desired fullness or a deliberate simplicity, and they are as one with what they wear. Every exaggeration and extravagance of their toilet becomes natural and picturesque. They are full of finesse, full of life. … An emotional warmth, a feline playfulness, an obscure sadness and a momentary carelessness emanate from these petite daughters of our days, before the right word can find its way to their dainty lips.[59]

Other figures and anecdotes would revolve around a woman walking on a gleaming wet street or conversing in the intimacy of her boudoir. Artistic ideality was fully projected into the everyday world. This was how Marold was known to readers of magazines in Paris and *Fliegende Blätter* (Flying Pages) in Berlin, and Prague's popular illustrated magazines *Světozor* (Seeing the World) and *Zlatá Praha* (Golden Prague).

56 Luděk Marold, Poster design, after 1895, gouache, 23.7 × 46.5 cm

Besides this, Marold also painted oil paintings, especially portraits. He admired Rembrandt and longed to work solely on painting, but he was fully occupied with illustrating. Then there was a third Marold, clearly the best: the Marold of spontaneous sketches, improvised works that recalled Toulouse-Lautrec.

Among this latter group of works, which usually only concerned Marold's close personal relationships, there is a colour lithograph poster for *Our Apartment is Under Renovation*, a musical comedy at a theatre that was part of the Architecture and Engineering Exhibition in Prague in 1898. There is a masterful conciseness here, an immediacy that revealed that Marold had a great natural feel for the decorative, and that his naturalism had much potential for further renditions.

For the same exhibition, Marold created his tour de force, a panorama of the Battle of Lipany. Panoramas of famous historical events were a popular attraction at all large exhibitions in the 1890s. Each exhibition wanted a panorama more remarkable than the last, resulting in a kind of evolution that also indicated how viewers' and painters' perspective on art was changing. The Centennial Exhibition had the historical realism of *The Battle with the Swedes on Charles Bridge*, painted by the brothers Karel and Adolf Liebscher together with Vojtěch Bartoněk. The installation was designed like a peep show to achieve the greatest degree of illusion, even incorporating a three-dimensional foreground that merged more or less imperceptibly with the painting. The Ethnographic Exhibition had Mikoláš Aleš's *The Slaughter of the Saxons*, which remains one of the largest paintings in Europe. Marold's panorama was a return to visual illusion, and in the spirit of the new plein-air sentiment he added to the illusion by creating a painting that curved round in a circle, anticipating the circarama cinema. Here too a foreground with replicas of historical weapons enhanced the realism of Marold's tableau vivant. The landscape painter Václav Jansa and other assistants worked with Marold on this massive painting, while the decoration was the work of Karel Štapfer.

We know from contemporary accounts that the panorama made a great impression, although Marold himself was dissatisfied with it. He may perhaps have realised that, despite wanting to devote himself to "pure" painting, he had again been drawn back to illustration, and this had now become onerous to him. However, in its broader historical context, Marold's *The Battle of Lipany* is a noteworthy full stop to the era of historical painting that had been so typical of the 19th century. The form Marold gave his panorama showed how this theme now fell outside the domain of fine art, and modern demands for factual accuracy would have to be satisfied by another kind of art. Yet this also paradoxically underlined Marold's modernity, subverting the established conventions in culture. Then quite suddenly, Marold fell ill and died of typhus. His death was felt to be a national catastrophe, but it was a wound that was surprisingly quick to heal. Marold's commentary on contemporary life had come at just the right time to boost the self-confidence of Czech artists, and by updating the older naturalism he had taken it to new heights. The new sensualism at the heart of Marold's approach did not disappear from Czech art but became one of the measures of its modernity. There was also a need to extend this new quality from illustration to painting itself, thereby achieving a higher level of abstraction. Marold had anticipated this in printmaking, as his exhibition poster showed, but any further progress ran up against his deep-seated distaste (perhaps because he had had to struggle to survive) for any more thorough tackling of the decorative arrangement of a painting and the Symbolist accentuation of its significance. Other painters would have to take on this task.

In Paris in the mid-1890s, at the same time that Marold was becoming known for his illustration, a new artistic phenomenon emerged. A German art dealer called Siegfried Bing opened a gallery called L'Art Nouveau, and this would soon designate a new decorative style that, under the influence of Belgian architects in particular, quickly

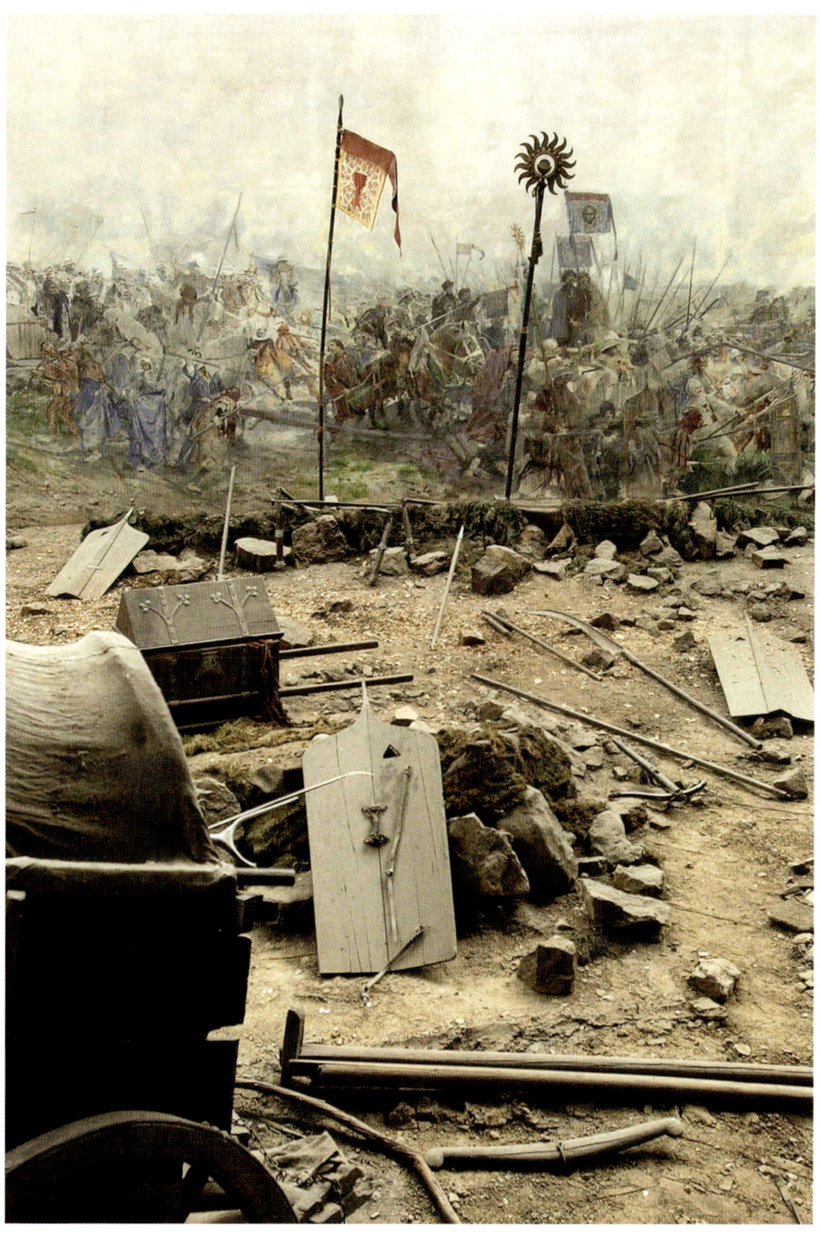

57 Luděk Marold, *The Battle of Lipany*, 1898, detail

acquired a precise set of forms. An artist from Moravia called Alphonse Mucha had much to do with creating and disseminating the new style.

Following his unsuccessful application to the academy in Prague, Mucha had worked in Viennese workshops creating set designs for the theatre before, thanks to his patron, he moved to Munich to study at the city's academy, where he associated with Czech students such as Joža Uprka, Luděk Marold, Augustin Němejc, and others. By the autumn of 1887 Mucha was in Paris, but he would have to wait seven more years before his great opportunity came. In the meantime he earned a living from irregular illustration and printmaking work, but he also became thoroughly acquainted with a café in rue de la Grande-Chaumière, where the poorest but most progressive artists in Paris congregated. Gauguin, Paul Sérusier, and other members of Les Nabis, as well as Polish, Hungarian, and Dutch Symbolists, all frequented this establishment, where their wide-ranging discussions gave shape to a new Post-Impressionist vision of art.

In 1893 Mucha and Gauguin even worked for a time in the former's studio, after Gauguin had returned from his first journey to Tahiti and found himself penniless. However, Mucha felt that, as a professional artist, he had the edge over the amateur, and he was more influenced by Gauguin's ideas than his paintings, which he thought too primitive. He also adopted the ideas of other Symbolists. The essence of Jean Moréas's "Symbolist Manifesto," to "dress the Idea in a sensible form," was a precept he tried to understand in his own way.

Around 1890, Symbolism became a phenomenon in contemporary Parisian art and literature. It was not a monolithic movement with a rigid programme, and the Symbolists were united only by their opposition to the prevailing materialist view of the world. They stressed the importance of fantasy and were willing to take this to extremes in a new kind of mysticism that was often paradoxically associated with a "scientifically" motivated philosophy of nature. Mucha was evidently taken with the philosophical side of Symbolism, which looked to primitive religions and cultures in a quest for the very essence of the world. Theosophy became fashionable as a new intellectual religion based on the old antagonism between spirit and matter, and it proclaimed that beyond the external, physical world lay the spiritual world, far more complicated and fundamental, which artists too must access if their work was to preach any more profound mystery. The unusual influence these idealist teachings had in artistic circles can largely be explained by the fact that they left plenty of room for free imagination. They also drew on certain Neoplatonic ideas that had played an important role in the development of European art ever since the Renaissance.[60] Mucha too believed in the importance of this new Idea, but as an artist he was mostly concerned with finding the means to communicate this great unknown. He could not but notice that two more pronounced wings were taking shape within the diversity of Symbolism. One wing, represented by Sâr Péladan, the founder of the Salon de la Rose + Croix, considered art merely a prerequisite for the depiction of imaginary content, while the other, best represented by Mallarmé and Gauguin, held that "the mysterious centre of thought" could only be revealed through the medium of a new and simpler art form. Mucha, of course, did not want to belong to any particular "tendency." He admired Pierre Puvis

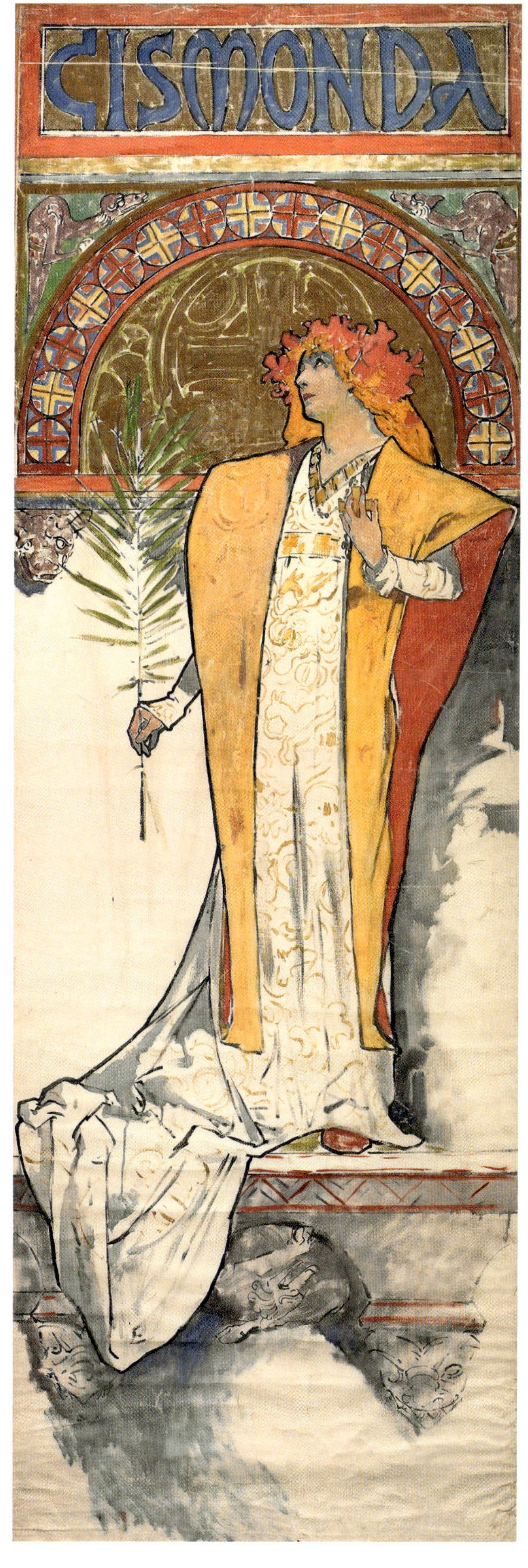

58 Alphonse Mucha, Poster design for *Gismonda*, 1894, tempera, 198 × 67 cm

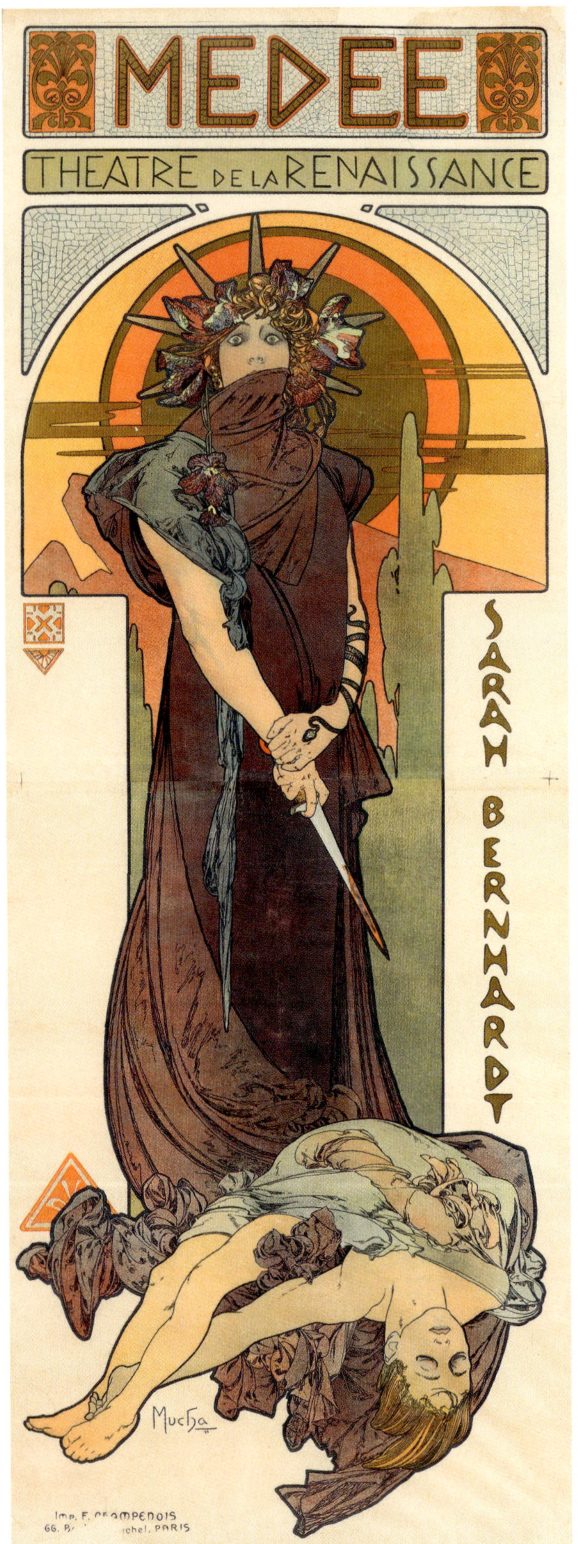

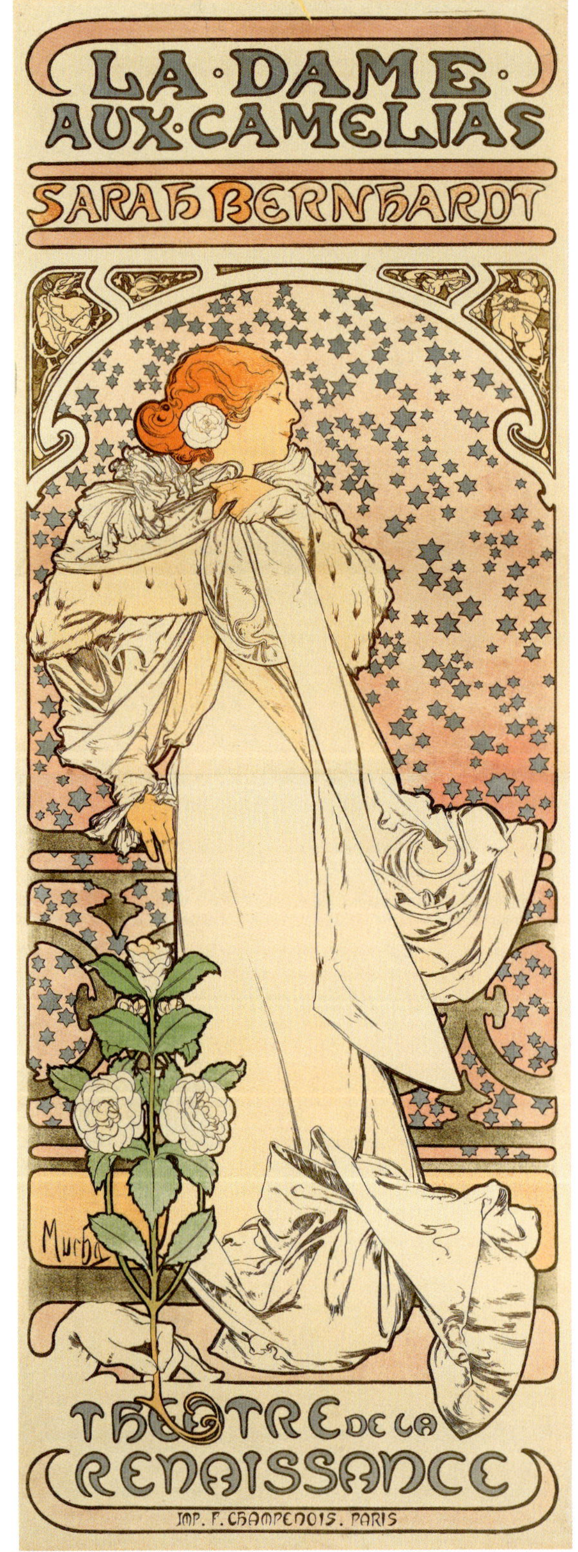

59 Alphonse Mucha, Poster for *Médée*, 1898, colour lithograph, 205 × 74 cm

60 Alphonse Mucha, Poster for *La Dame aux camélias*, 1896, colour lithograph, 210 × 77 cm

de Chavannes for his large decorative murals, where both aspects were somehow in harmony.

Art Nouveau came from the intersection between these two wings of Symbolism. In his illustrations for Xavier Marmier's *Contes des grand'mères*, Mucha displayed his feel for the mystery expressed in fairy tales, while in *The Death of Frederick Barbarossa*, one of his illustrations for Charles Seignobos's *Scènes et épisodes de l'histoire d'Allemagne*, he captured a Wagnerian fatefulness. Here Mucha was displaying elements of the new style that show he was following the same path as pioneers of Art Nouveau such as Eugène Grasset and Carlos Schwabe. However, Mucha still had no essential set of motifs from which he could develop truly original work. It was chance that helped him to create his core imagery. At the end of 1894 he hurriedly drew his first poster for the actress Sarah Bernhardt, depicting her in the lead role of Victorien Sardou's *Gismonda*. It was an instant success. The poster's narrow format and especially its muted colours differentiated it from routine poster design. The figure of Bernhardt, standing upright in ceremonial "Byzantine" garb and holding a palm leaf, was welcomed as the idealisation of the actress, whose cult in Paris was then at its apex. She was considered the embodiment of "eternal womanhood," which shone through the masks of her various roles like some atheist divinity. Following this success, Mucha signed a contract with Bernhardt that resulted in a series of posters over the next few years that will forever be part of the history of this modern art form. He developed a full expressive range to suit the mood of the individual plays, ranging from the tender harmony of colours in *La Dame aux camélias* to the drama of *Médée*. The common denominator in these contrasting works was a vision that embraced all these aspects. In 1897 Mucha drew an idealised portrait of the "divine Sarah" for *La Plume*, a literary and artistic review, depicting in precise lines her head viewed en face and surrounded by an ornamental nimbus. Her expression is ambiguous: there is a touch of sadness, but with the abstract quality of the line it loses any immediate significance, and this transforms the customary emotionality of the face into what is almost a kind of mediumism. In this way, Symbolism found appropriate expression through purely decorative devices.

Mucha did not come up with his distinctive style in his very first poster. In 1895 he was still experimenting with various options, and it was not until the following year that the floodgates opened and Paris was awash with the decidedly uniform style of Mucha's commercial art. Besides posters, he also designed decorative panels – series of colour lithographs that variously depicted the four seasons, flowers, the times of day, the stars, and precious stones. He also produced magazine and catalogue covers, calendars, postcards, and soap packaging. There were constant variations on the theme of a beautiful woman with a languid expression, usually seated and framed by a richly ornamented horseshoe-shaped nimbus. This arrangement, using Mucha's typical motifs such as long hair or tendrils, created a complicated ornamental pattern in which certain lines were used to lead the viewer's eye into the labyrinth. Here too a Symbolist idea lay in the background, even if these images served mundane ends. Orthodox Symbolists accordingly considered Art Nouveau a vulgarisation of their ideas, but they were powerless to suppress the public's appetite for such work.

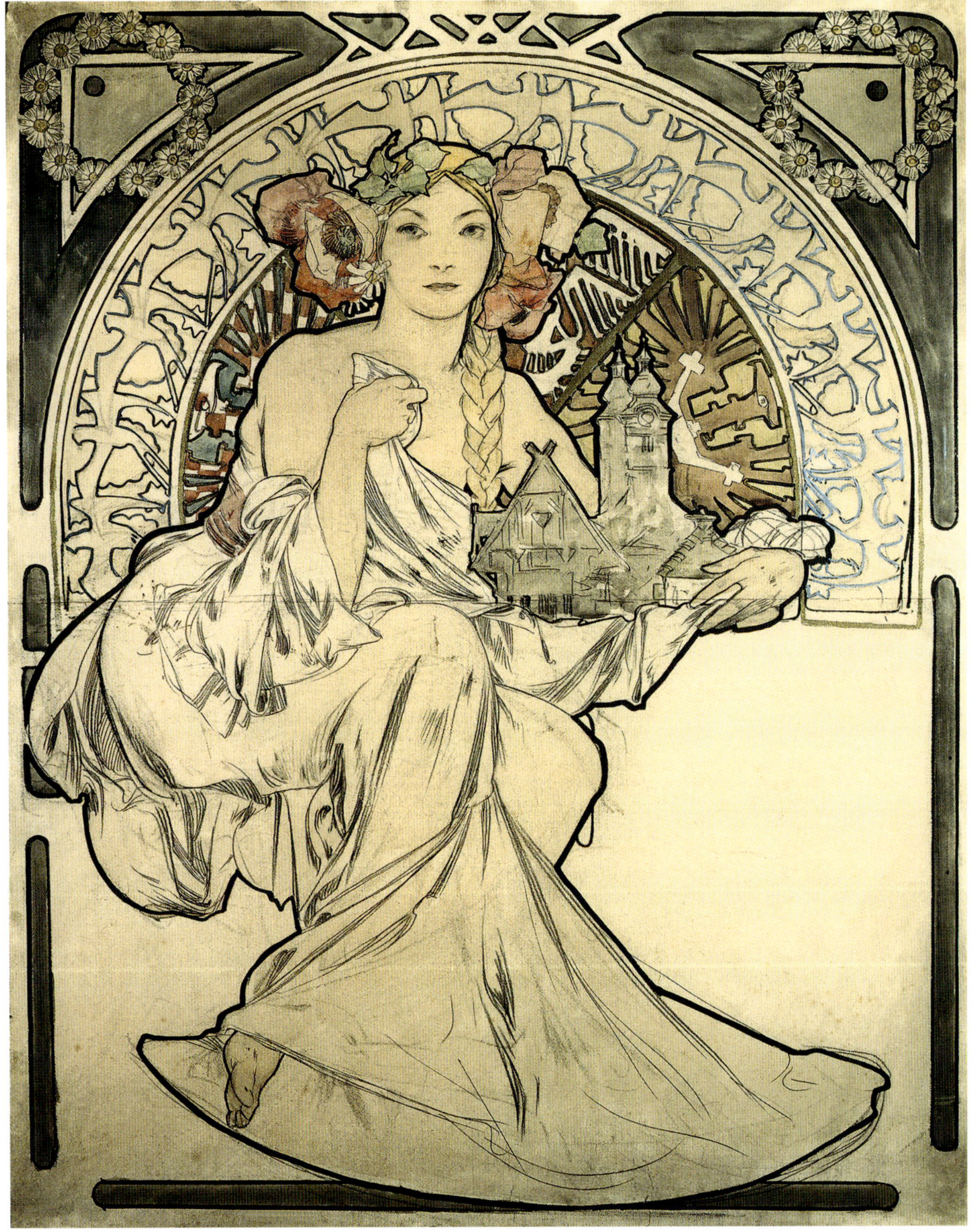

61 Alphonse Mucha, Poster design for the Architecture and Engineering Exhibition, 1897, charcoal and watercolour, 108.5 × 85 cm

Mucha did not confine himself to printmaking but extended his formula to utilitarian items as well as adornments for special occasions. He designed the furnishings and ornament for the interior of Georges Fouquet's jewellery shop in Paris, converting his two-dimensional design into a three-dimensional realisation. He also designed a variety of jewellery for Fouquet; his bracelet for Sarah Bernhardt, an enamelled gold snake with chains connecting it to a richly ornamented ring, is one of the most beautiful examples of Art Nouveau work. Behind the artist's idea again lay the Symbolist femme fatale, seen here in the Orientalist splendour of the biblical Salome. Mucha's labyrinthine ornament was also ideal for carpets, but it found its most significant application in a discipline that the entire movement, starting with William Morris (whose ideas on the revival of decorative art were enthusiastically relayed to Mucha by the composer Frederick Delius), considered fundamental: book illustration. One such example of a Mucha Gesamtkunstwerk was a Symbolist variation on an old legend from Provence that its author, Robert de Flers, titled *Ilsée, princesse de Tripoli*. One of the merits of this richly decorative work was that it viewed the book as a typographic whole and successfully combined figurative illustrations with ornamental fields, lines, titles, and endpapers. The book was also published in an abbreviated form in Prague, where it again became a much-admired example of the new book art. An 1897 exhibition that had opened at the La Plume gallery in Paris before travelling to Germany and then to Prague showcased Mucha's accomplishments. This was the first manifestation of the full Art Nouveau decorative style in Prague, which previously had only been familiar with the German Jugendstil and was still undecided on the merits of the Vienna Secession. There is no question that Mucha's success reinforced the determination of Czech artists to concentrate on stylised graphic work. In the same year, Jan Preisler used Art Nouveau's ornamental line to illustrate Jaroslav Kvapil's *Princess Dandelion* and Karel Mašek's *Fairy Tales Ending Badly*, albeit in a modest scope that could not compete with Mucha and indeed had no ambition to do so.

Although swamped by work in Paris, Mucha never lost interest in what was happening back home. He entered a sketch for a competition to design a poster for the Architecture and Engineering Exhibition. His design was an allegory of architecture as a young woman, with a wreath of poppies around her head, who is sitting and holding as her attributes a wooden cottage and a Baroque church. The choice of buildings was typical of contemporary interests and reflected what was considered the Czech architectural tradition. With its artistic freshness, the poster design is one of Mucha's finest works from this time, a welcome change from his often excessively decorative work in Paris. It was much appreciated for these qualities by the young artists of SVU Mánes, but Mucha's sketch did not win the competition, with the jury preferring Karel Vítězslav Mašek's poster. Although artistically it was undeniably weaker, the delicate stylisation of Mašek's figures was evidently more in line with the approach to the new ornamentalism that still prevailed in Prague. Mucha had treated his sketch as a painting, and in doing so he pointed the way to the artistic freeing of the poster that subsequently became firmly entrenched in SVU Mánes and quickly dispelled any earlier uncertainty. Mucha was disappointed by the competition's outcome, and when Mašek

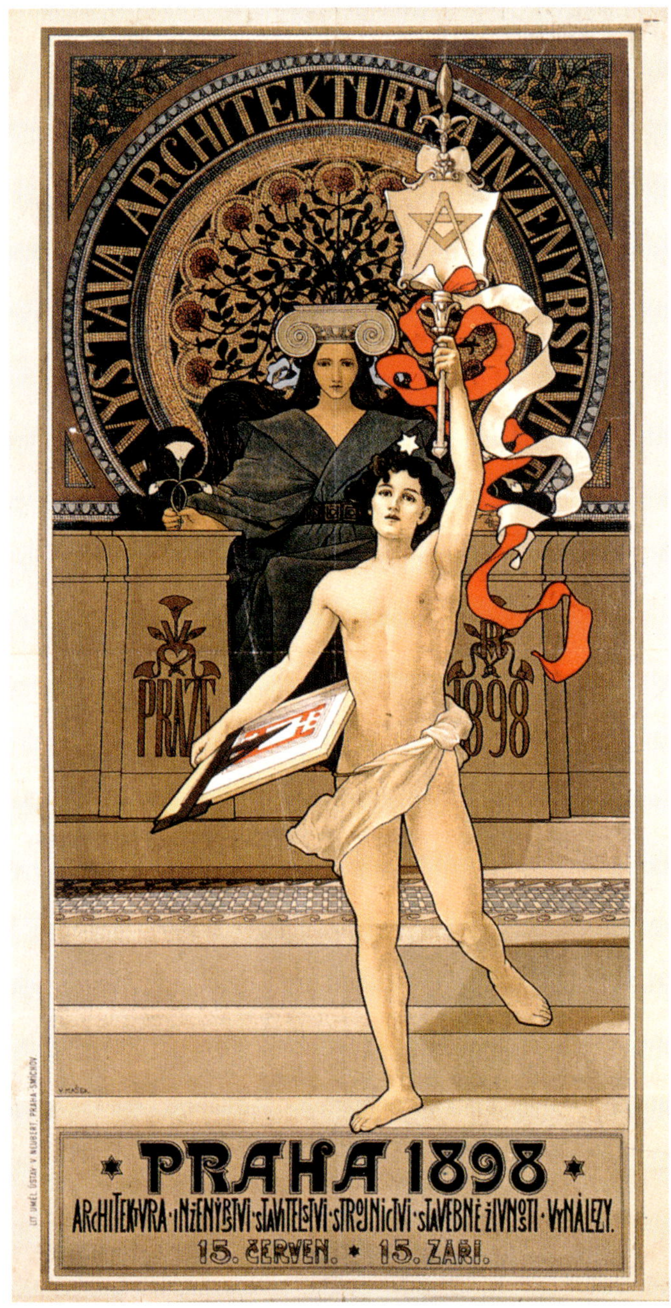

was also appointed professor of ornamental drawing at the School of Decorative Arts, the question of Prague was settled for Mucha, at least for a time.

However, Mucha's work was a revelation for the school's graduates, demonstrating entirely new possibilities. In printmaking he was unparalleled, and when the young Vojtěch Preissig travelled on Luděk Marold's recommendation to Paris in 1898, he made his way to Mucha. At the School of Decorative Arts, Preissig had attended

62 Karel Vítězslav Mašek, Poster for the Architecture and Engineering Exhibition, 1898, colour lithograph, 128 × 68 cm

Friedrich Ohmann's classes for the study of ornament, especially of course historical ornament, but some of his watercolours of flowers from this time show that he had already created a foundation for the stylisation of natural form that his subsequent schooling in Paris could easily draw on in the process of developing a more refined stylistic idiom. In the same year that Preissig arrived in Paris, Mucha started teaching at the city's newly opened Académie Carmen, where one of his colleagues was James McNeill Whistler. Although most of the teaching work fell to Mucha,[61] the presence of two such different individuals must have been very stimulating for their students. Whistler, a famous veteran of the modern movement, represented the advances that had been made in both French and English art, and he was a first-class colourist. His *Nocturnes*, colourful fantasies evoking musical motifs in painting, were admired throughout Europe, as were his subtle psychological portraits in white and shades of grey. In his studio, he had posters by Mucha, whose draughtsmanship he admired. Whistler was himself one of the pioneers of the new decorative style, having created his Peacock Room in London as early as the 1870s. His influences included old Chinese and Japanese art, of which he was an enthusiastic collector and proponent.

Although at the Académie Carmen there was a common foundation in the new decorative treatment of pictorial form, a certain contradiction emerged between its application in drawing and in painting. Mucha had rashly signed exploitative contracts with printers in Paris, and perhaps under the influence of this contradiction he began to feel that his work was becoming stereotypical, that his ornamental stylistic formula was obstructing his art. He consoled himself with the thought that he was working "for the people," and he became an active member of the Société internationale de l'art populaire, founded by Jean Lahor. However, the latter's teachings on "social art," drawing on William Morris's utopian socialism, did not entirely reassure Mucha, for they were based on the assumption that people must be edified through art. They therefore contained the idea of the prototype of the self-sufficient artwork as the essential starting point for all concrete work towards transforming the human habitat.

Lahor's society, whose members included other prominent figures in Art Nouveau in Paris and Brussels, was a typical example of the hopes invested in the new decorative movement, which soon spread from artists' studios to take possession of the city's exterior. There was a certain theatricality in the way this new movement was promoted, and it was no accident that its creators focused on the world's fair that would again be held in Paris in 1900. The very year of the Exposition Universelle marked the start of the new century, and artists wanted to usher it in not just with a retrospective, but above all by demonstrating the inventiveness of the new art. The Austrian government commissioned Mucha to design the ornament for the Bosnia and Herzegovina pavilion. Politically this was a smart move, with the intention of presenting the occupied country in the best possible light. However, Mucha approached the wall paintings as an apology to the Slavic people. He divided the paintings into three bands encircling the pavilion's interior, which could also be read vertically. The lowest, narrower, band had flowers symbolising nature, giving birth to the mythical foundation of the South Slavic tribes

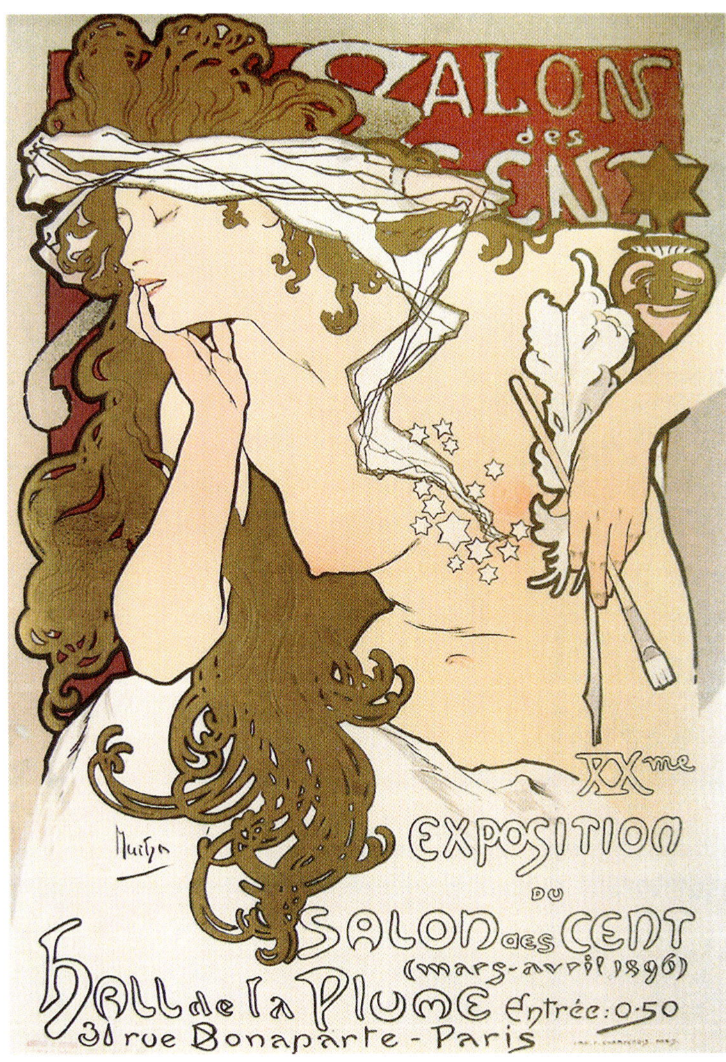

in the band above, and at the top, again in a narrower band, were scenes from history, finished by a floral border. The conceptual framework for the pavilion's walls was then a cyclical understanding of the fundamental relationships between humanity and the world. The idea that historical events were contingent on ancient myths was a typical component of the Secession world view. The pavilion also had statues by Mucha, for no art form would be neglected in this new Gesamtkunstwerk.

The Bosnia and Herzegovina pavilion revived an aspect of Mucha's work that had hitherto been sidelined by Art Nouveau's idealised themes. Earlier it had lived in Mucha's illustrations, and its depiction now in these large wall paintings proved that it held further possibilities that were as yet untapped. It is little wonder that Mucha, whose decorative work had recently lost something of its spontaneity in favour of virtuosic over-ornamentation, sensed that he could work with his earlier interests and experiences to attain the requisite artistic depth. The results of his mediumistic sym-

63 Alphonse Mucha, *Salon des Cent*, 1896, colour lithograph, 63.6 × 43.2 cm

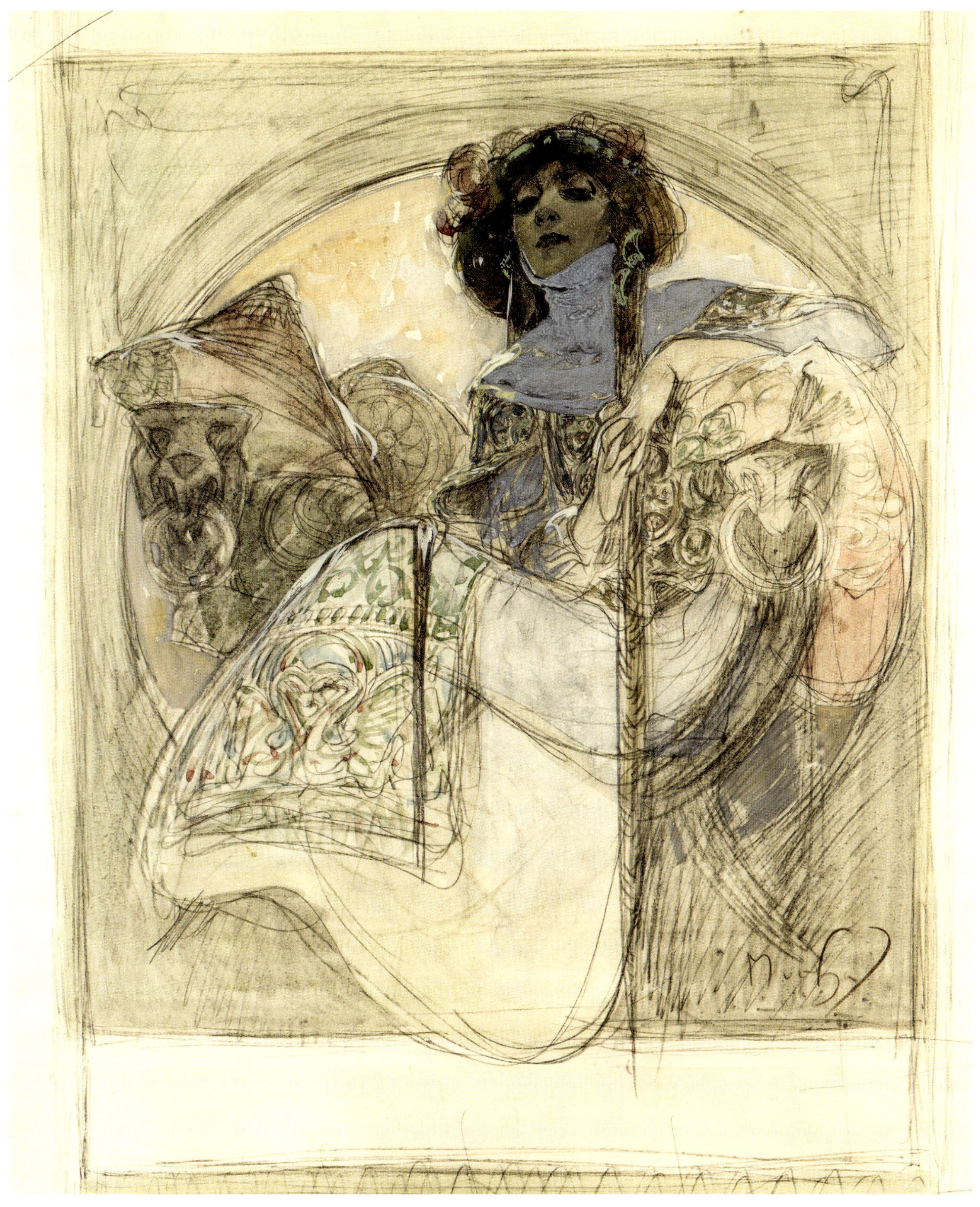

64 Alphonse Mucha, *Woman Sitting in an Armchair*, before 1900, pencil and watercolour, 49.5 × 44 cm

bolism, guided by the experiments with extrasensory perception that he conducted with Camille Flammarion and Albert de Rochas, would no longer suffice. With the greater demands that Art Nouveau's success had brought, and his own ambitions (which went well beyond his art), the "philosophy of history" again emerged as a question asked of any attempt to flesh out the Art Nouveau world view.

Symbolism was evidently a constant challenge for Mucha, who had first learned of it in the free-ranging debates in rue de la Grande-Chaumière. He sought to emulate it, for his talents pointed him not just to posters in the "salon of the street," but also to what he admired in Puvis de Chavannes, and earlier, as a child, to what had impressed him in Baroque sacred art and architecture: the ornamenting of large spaces that were significant not just for their art, but above all for the ideas they embodied. When Mucha saw that, beyond the popularity and success he had now achieved, there were stricter, harsher criteria, it brought about a personal crisis. There were various ways he could proceed. In *Le Pater* (1899), Mucha's literary and visual interpretation of The Lord's Prayer, he took Art Nouveau graphic ornament to its high point, and in his stylebook *Documents décoratifs* (1902) he summed up all its finesses and applications. He used floral motifs to explain how the Art Nouveau ornamental artist obtained the building blocks for his ornamentation, by carefully studying a plant's appearance in nature, its characteristic properties, proportions, and growth structure. By rendering these shapes as contrasting forms that were positive and negative, depending on the proportion of black and white, the artist could create a rhythmical, linearly repeating floral motif, and drawing this motif as a pattern would produce a continuous ornamental line whose suppleness and dynamism retained the requisite vitality and became a symbol of the internal cycle of nature's entelechy. Psychologically, the idea of the endlessness of life in nature, masterfully expressed in Mucha's art, reflected teachings on the transmigration of the soul and life after death. Dead things also had to play their part in this fundamental Idea, through the biologising of their morphology and the fantastical transubstantiation of their matter. Mucha's *Documents décoratifs* became a textbook for the projection in art of a world view that sought to understand the world and the entire universe as permeated by a single creative force, and it saw in the new decorative style a means for this permeation, transforming everything into its homogenous essence.

The idea at the core of this teaching, which in decorative designs influenced the ordinary world of everyday life, was to be manifested in a gigantic three-dimensional construction that Mucha had sketched as a design for the 1900 Exposition Universelle. This was the Pavilion of Man, intended as a permanent structure whose exhibits and, above all, whose very form would be a monument to the immortality of the human soul. Around the massive dome, borne on arches, were some kind of battlements upon which sat the figures of great thinkers, behind each of whom was a large egg-shaped nimbus painted with frescos. Had Mucha's fantasy been built, it would have surpassed not just Hector Guimard's metro stations but all the other picturesque examples of Art Nouveau architecture from the turn of the century.

Mucha's design for the Pavilion of Man was the culmination of his cosmopolitan Art Nouveau. It also demonstrated his increasing philosophical ambitions, which resulted in the numerous Masonic and Rosicrucian symbols of *Le Pater*. When his plans for the Pavilion of Man came to nothing, Mucha turned to more concrete objectives. His work on the Bosnia and Herzegovina pavilion, together with the theories propagated by Lahor, pointed the way ahead, and ultimately Mucha realised that his opportunity to make a unique contribution lay in his fatherland. This was the genesis of his idea for *The Slav Epic*, a cycle of paintings that was inspired by the artist's own ethnic origins, signalling his mission to exhalt the nation's heritage. This plan too, guiding all Mucha's later work, was, however, the logical outcome of his personal understanding of Symbolism.

From the time of Mucha's creative crisis, which evidently became more acute after he had finished working on the Exposition Universelle, there is a set of drawings executed in charcoal and chalk on dark-toned paper. Their articulation is unusually free, as is their subject matter. These dreamy mythical images and scenes from daily life were not intended as the basis for any superficially attractive decorative work, for these are dark visions reflecting the other side of life, primitive and volatile: the mysterious and inexplicable, and depression, even despair. It was this darkness that probably decided their fate, and they would remain isolated, private works in Mucha's oeuvre, even though here he came closest to the new expressivity that was in the

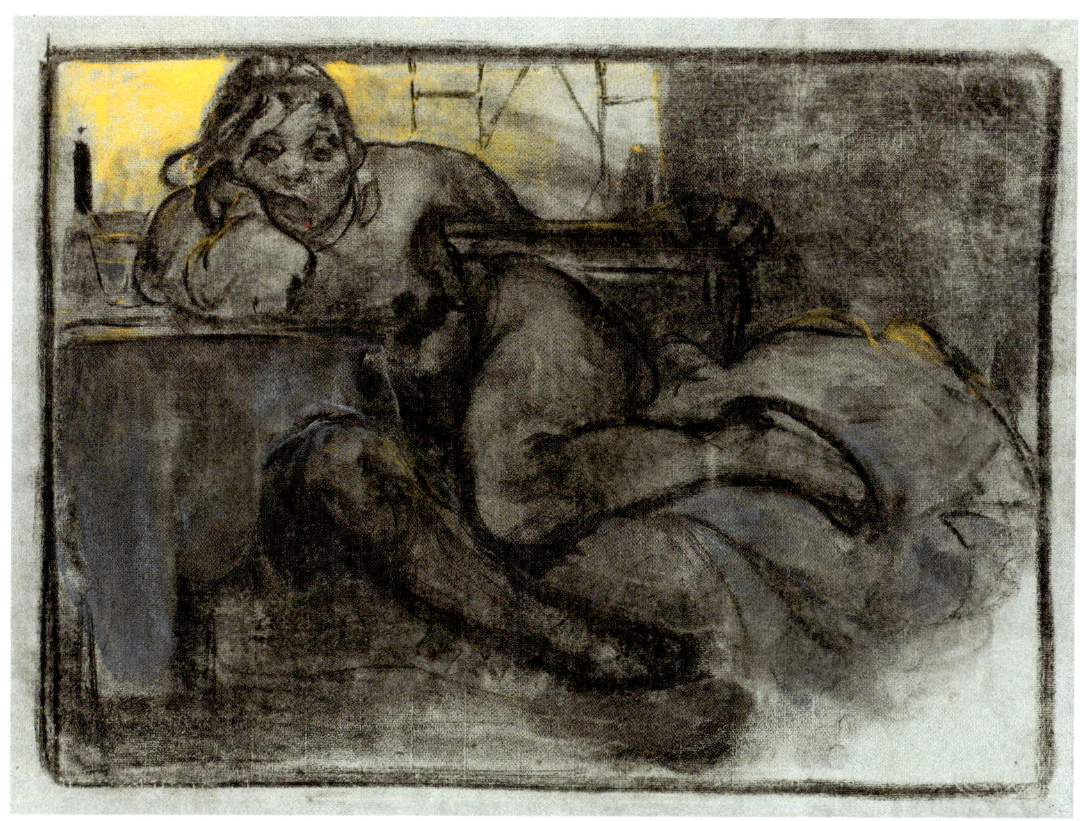

65 Alphonse Mucha, *Absinthe*, after 1900, charcoal and coloured chalks, 48 × 62 cm

vanguard of modern art at the dawn of the new age. Around 1900 Mucha found himself in a truly paradoxical situation. He was both victor and victim: he had been the first Czech artist to immerse himself fully in Art Nouveau, and his decorative style had become synonymous with it, but he himself stubbornly refused this label, convinced that he was working wholly according to his own lights. Ultimately, he was also the first to discover the pitfalls of his own creation. In this context, the response from the younger generation of Czech Secession artists to Mucha is interesting. At the time that Mucha ruled this field, they were just starting out. When Mucha had had his exhibition in Prague in 1897, their sympathies had evidently mostly been with him, but their opinions soon became more heterogeneous. At the extreme end of this disenchantment is a passage from Miloš Jiránek's famous review of an exhibition by Jednota umělců výtvarných, published in *Radikální listy* (Radical Pages) in 1899:

> Another cold draughtsman and a considerable Mannerist who is going out of fashion just as astonishingly quickly as he came into it: Mucha, from Paris. Is anyone still impressed by the dolls he keeps turning out? Let no one be fooled by his success, which beyond our borders is still growing; these are only the rings that spread far and wide when you throw a stone into water: the rings are still expanding, but the stone is sinking to the bottom.[62]

This unusually barbed criticism could be considered mere personal animosity were it not for the fact that Jiránek was held in such esteem by the majority of SVU Mánes artists. He was attacking Mucha's weakest side, his by now often hackneyed and affected ornamentalism. Had the aforementioned charcoal drawings not remained entirely private works, Jiránek would certainly have written about them. His criticism perhaps reflected how Paris itself was turning away from Symbolism and Art Nouveau in the closing years of the century, and in their place would soon hail Cézanne. Nor can we overlook Jiránek's enthusiasm at this time for Marold, who, although he was Mucha's most intimate friend, was considered by Prague's young radicals to be the enemy of all styles and a painter of "the most sensitive tremors of life." Yet Marold and Mucha were both in the same situation: their customary work was no longer enough for them, and both longed, however nebulously, for "pure" painting. Mucha's solution was to go to America and devote himself to painting. Jiránek's peers were approximately a decade younger than Marold and Mucha. They were therefore the next in line, and would have had a quite different outlook from the artists who, after a naturalistic period in Munich in the 1880s, had made their way to Paris on their own initiative. Mucha and Marold had both come from this common foundation, to which each was responding in his own way. However, the younger generation that was now familiar with their mature work considered them to be opposites and tried to find its way between them. This laid the groundwork for Czech synthetism, whose structural preconditions had already crystallised in the work of the older artists.

Nor could a third painter who had studied in Munich in the 1880s before heading to Paris withstand modernist criticism. After returning to Prague, Karel Vítězslav Mašek had captivated the art world with his bold Luminism (*Spring*, 1888) and his Symbolist subjects, among which *Libuše* (c. 1893) is remarkable for its decorative use of pointillism. However, Mašek's exhibition at the Topič Salon in 1897, crowned with a massive moralistic painting called *At the Crossroads*, disappointed expectations. Karel Hlaváček wrote, "And now it suffices to recall that a painter with such an extraordinary and interesting intuition for colour has painted these large canvases hung up all around, utterly worthless, sterile, empty and repellent!" Mašek, the author of numerous decorative works, especially for churches, would never exhibit his work again.[63]

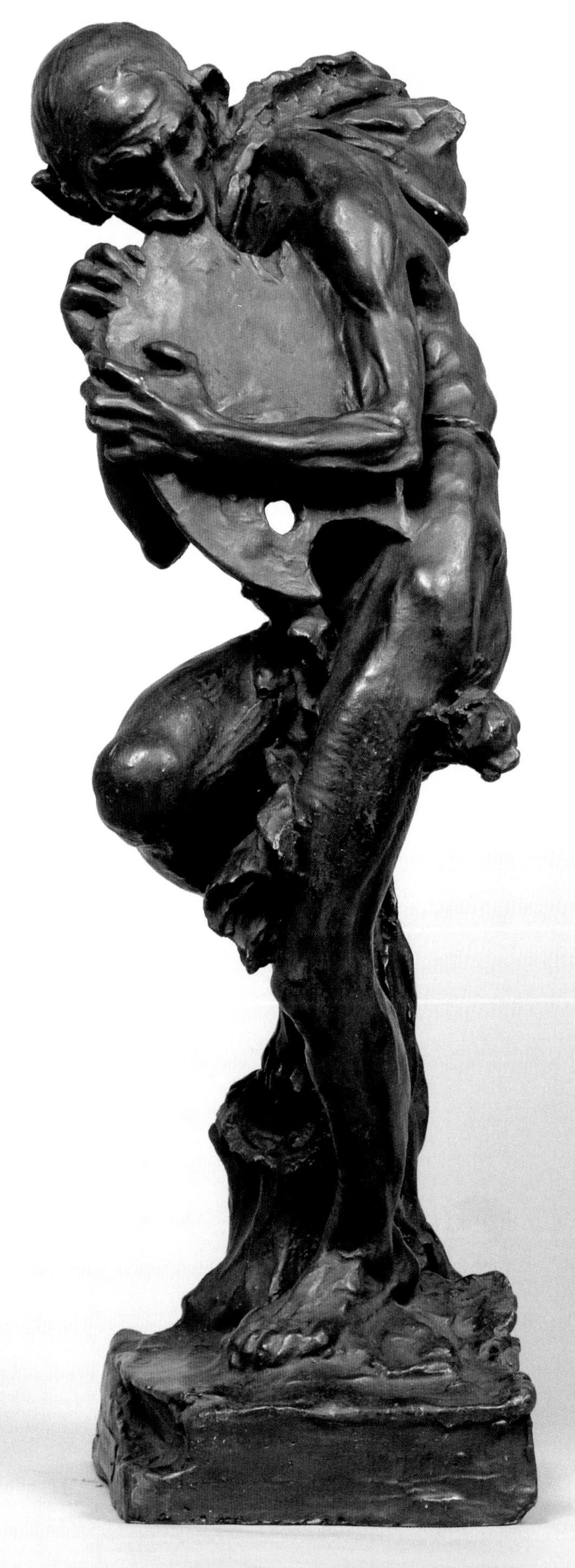

DEFIANCE

Marold and Mucha's success in Paris was in sharp contrast to the limited opportunities for modern art back home. The official patrons of Czech art – the most prominent of whom, the architect Josef Hlávka, President of the Czech Academy of Sciences and Arts, had made his fortune from building in Vienna – had been aesthetically moulded by the Renaissance Revival. In the 1890s, prompted by the international reputation of painters from the National Theatre generation, these patrons extended their favour to work that was more aligned with the Baroque Revival. Nevertheless, there were still only a few names to whom Zdenka Braunerová, a wealthy patron of art and an accomplished painter and illustrator in her own right, could turn with her impassioned appeals on behalf of the talented young artists she so enthusiastically promoted. The Czech bourgeoisie was relatively powerless and only valued that which could directly facilitate its social ascent, while the petite bourgeoisie had no genuine interest in culture. It was against this complacency that the young generation's criticism was directed, and new periodicals were the principal channel for this criticism.

Moderní revue was launched in 1894. Its publisher, Arnošt Procházka, was an admirer of Symbolist and Decadent literature, ranging from Joris-Karl Huysmans to Stanisław Przybyszewski. For Procházka, decadence was not degeneracy but an artist's challenge to society's hypocritical conventions, and he called for artists to ruthlessly uncover the darker sides of public and private life. He believed that most of these problems were to do with relations between men and women, which he liked to discuss in mythological comparisons. He was impressed by the cynicism with which French Naturalist authors unmasked commonplace morality, and the openness with which they wrote about sex. Of course, Procházka too was unaware of the true reasons for the moral crisis of late bourgeois society. He was fascinated by the Decadent notion of the femme fatale as the personification of "the natural fount of all evil."

It was from this perspective that Procházka selected examples of literature and art for *Moderní revue*. Most suitable for him were printmakers whose fantasy cycles allowed him to add lyrical commentaries on their work. In this way, Procházka wrote essays on Félix Vallotton, Odilon Redon, James Ensor, Aubrey Beardsley, and Henry de Groux, and he also reproduced the work of Félicien Rops and Edvard Munch. *Moderní revue* introduced Czech readers to many influential artists from the turn of the century, and for this Procházka was appreciated, even though his overall concept would quite soon come under fire. Young artists did not entirely accept Procházka's rejection of Impressionism, nor his pronounced liking for fantastic symbolism. Besides the magazine, Procházka also published books. The very first volumes he released, which included Otokar Březina's *Mysterious Distances* in 1895, demonstrated the originality of this new series' content and typography. Partly for financial reasons, Procházka's books

66 Quido Kocián, *The Artist's Lot*, 1900, patinated plaster, 64 cm

were tall, slender booklets with simple titles. However, it was precisely the modest neatness of their covers and design that seemed so new, as the idea of the beautiful book was still associated with the excessively ornate luxury of heavy bindings. The simple elegance and affordability of Procházka's books were the calling cards of a new cultural standpoint that was especially appreciated by their intended readers among the Czech intelligentsia.

Besides the simple lettering of their titles, the covers of *Moderní revue* books soon began to include graphic elements that were related to the ascent of Secession ornament. In 1896 a young member of Procházka's circle, S. K. Neumann, produced one of the first such designs for the cover of his collection of poems, *Apostrophes Proud and Passionate*. Neumann's artistic dabblings were part of a still common trend for writers to draw, the most notable example in the 19th-century being Victor Hugo. This practice, still unburdened by any demands for professionalism, was a means to develop an author's imagination, and it permitted a free exchange between word and image on a common and broader cultural basis. Although Neumann soon broke with the *Moderní revue* circle, he continued drawing for his own magazine, *Nový kult* (The New Cult), where he produced many abstract ornamental designs in the spirit of Henry van de Velde. In the poet Karel Hlaváček, *Moderní revue* then acquired its first "in-house" artist and another representative of this dual disposition.

Hlaváček mostly produced illustrations for the third volume of *Moderní revue*. The greater part of his art dates from the period between the autumn of 1896, when he returned from military service with tuberculosis, and the summer of 1898, when he died of the disease. He did not leave behind an extensive oeuvre. Besides his illustrations for Procházka's poetry collection *A Prostibulum of the Soul*, there are graphic works for magazines, where his greatest successes were the header for *Żyćie* (Life), a Secession magazine published in Krakow, the covers and frontispieces of his own collections *Late before Morning* and *A Vindictive Cantilena*, some of his final prints, and especially his small drawings. These are not the coherent cycles of a professional draughtsman or printmaker, and for this reason they are considered a mere fragment

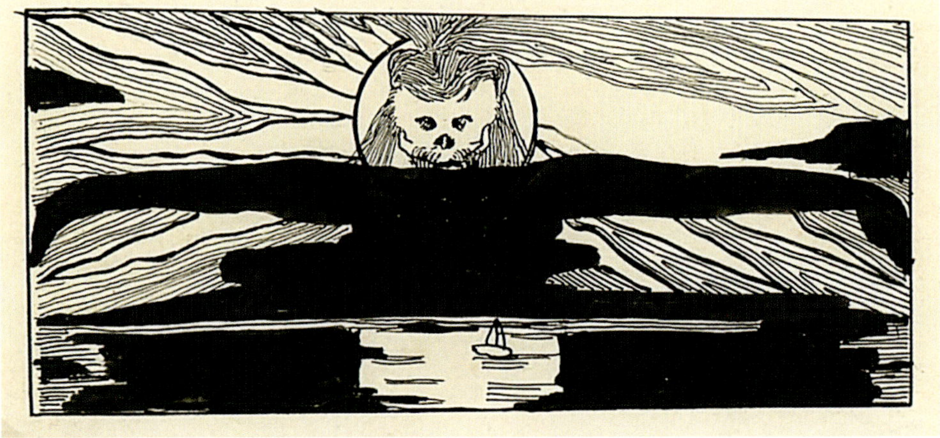

67 Karel Hlaváček, *Head of a Demon*, 1897, Indian ink, 7.3 × 16 cm

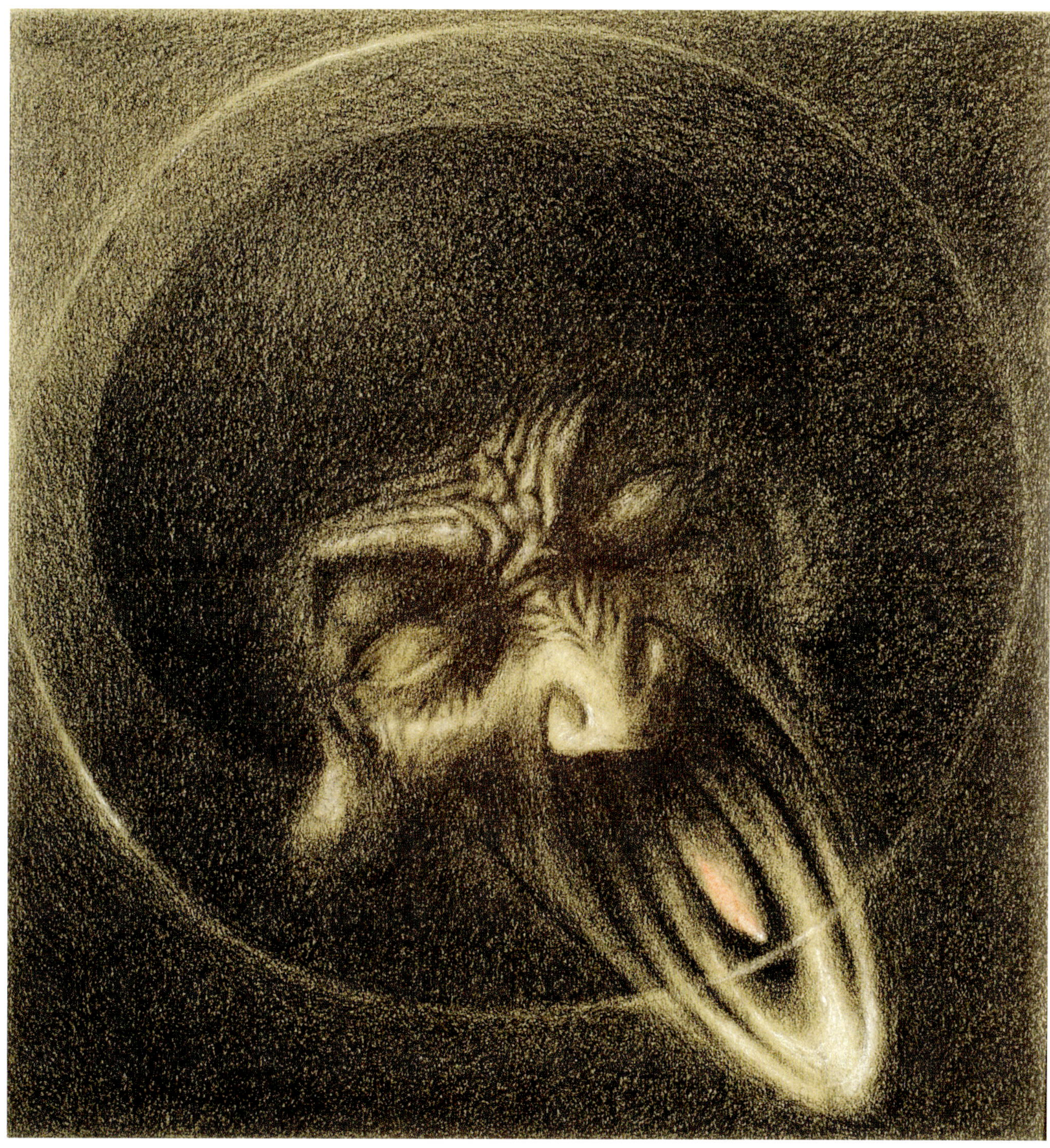

68 Karel Hlaváček, *Expellee*, 1897, charcoal, 26.3 × 24.3 cm

of Hlaváček's personal ambitions. This assessment, which was also extended to his poetry, was only revised recently.[64]

Hlaváček's tragic fate and his entire concept of the destiny of art gave greater weight to the Decadent circle around *Moderní revue*. His life and his thinking on art were full of contradictions. Although he came from an impoverished proletarian background, he upheld the most refined values, and while his exaltation, a state of excitement that verged on oblivion, still had certain elements of the Baroque Revival, what was more fundamental in his poems and his art was that, behind the extremity of his experience, with its motifs of fear and futility, lay the Secession's typically melancholy landscape, seemingly modest in the monotony of its props but receding into an unfathomable distance (as in the case of the etching *On the Outskirts of Prague*, 1898).

Compared with poetry, what appealed to Hlaváček in art was that he had to capture an idea at once, in the full intensity of its visual potency. This was something he probably took from Odilon Redon, whose influence on Hlaváček was the most fruitful. Although Hlaváček perhaps intuited that Secession ornament permitted the dimension of time to be incorporated into an image, the drawings he produced of this kind have a certain torpor. He evidently understood ornamentalism as the legitimising of ideas whose origin was private and often extreme. These were ignited by the question of eroticism, a topic fervently discussed in the *Moderní revue* circle.

Hlaváček was also an uncompromising and caustic art critic. In place of the traditional allegorical apparatus, he promoted the modern symbol, which he understood in much the same way that Freud did in psychoanalysis at this time: as a manifestation of the individual subconscious as it vents, in dreams and fantasies, its trauma, which is predominantly of sexual origin. In this respect Hlaváček gave his imagination free rein, resulting in a series of novel forms that are not easily described or interpreted. They could also be adapted in ways that were an outlet for Hlaváček's acrimony – for instance, in his caricature of an intellectual as a flea with bat's ears (*Metamorphosis*, 1897), or his self-portrait beside a skull, both wearing pince-nez, and so on.

More important for the question of whether Hlaváček was a dilettante, however, are examples of how he obsessively returned to particular symbols. While his conscious emphasis on the uniqueness of the imagination would support the thesis of the fragmentary nature of his art, this obsessive repetition reveals that within his modest oeuvre, and especially in his prints, there are certain motifs that establish the distinctiveness of Hlaváček's visions. A motif that appears again and again in his drawings is the moon. On his cover for the original manuscript of *Late before Morning*, a large moon rises over a rock formation, where a female nude toys with a large snake. In the more ornamental published version, a naked man – the poet – reclines in a meadow, gazing at the rising moon. More original, however, is the associating of the moon with woman, as in *Apparition* (1897), where the moon's outline forms a kind of nimbus behind the head of a woman, whose face is hidden by her long black hair and of whose body only the arms can be seen, suggesting that this female apparition is emerging from the moon itself. In its conciseness, *Apparition* recalls Mucha's variations on the vampire, which clearly shared the same idea of the conjunction of woman and moon as a personifica-

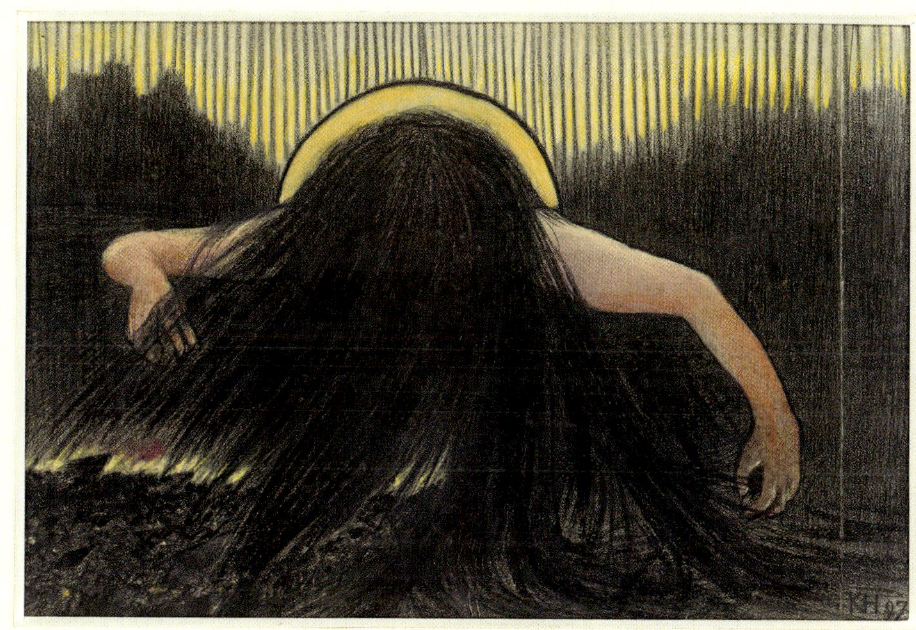

tion of some dark, demonic, and bewitching power. In Hlaváček's *Vignette for a Book*, from the same year, the motif becomes ornamental and the sitting nude's hair fans out to form a black circle, recalling an octopus's tentacles or Medusa's snakes. The moon appears in many more of Hlaváček's drawings, such as *Pilgrim*, reproduced in *Moderní revue*, where it touches the ground and is both path and magic circle, or in endpaper designs where the moon assumes plant or animal form.

The moon motif illustrates how thoroughly Symbolist lyricism imbued all of Hlaváček's work, and in his drawings it organically linked the main ideas with their visual form. Yet Hlaváček's advocacy of the symbol over the allegory was not a departure from tradition, for in older art the circle had routinely been used to depict dream-like visions, incorporated of course into an image's realistic or allegorical scenery.[65] Hlaváček's updating of this old device was directed, however, at its totalisation, its dominance of the picture space, and this had its foundations in a world view that dissolved the boundaries between the outer, physical world and the inner, psychological one in favour of the psychological phenomenon.

Hlaváček's fantasticism was in this regard much more far reaching than its often grotesque manifestations would suggest, for it marked the first more emphatic reappraisal of late Romantic fantasy. If we compare Schwaiger's elves and other fairy-tale creatures with Hlaváček's demons, there is a clear shift from socially acceptable picturesqueness to a much more personal expression that touches on various social taboos. This frankness was unquestionably also one of the obstacles to the recognition of Hlaváček's art, which opened up new possibilities for fantastical symbolic expression and inaugurated the exploration of dreams and visions in Czech art. In this,

69 Karel Hlaváček, *Apparition*, 1897, pastel, 32.6 × 48 cm

Hlaváček was greatly stimulated by contemporary Decadent literature, which led him to express the psychological turmoil of his visions and his hectic experiencing of reality in a concept that understood society's evils as an objective manifestation of some kind of metaphysical original evil. Through philosophical symbols, the contemporary literary cult of Satanism magnified the sense that beneath the surface of "banal" reality lay the apocalypse, destroying the individual's essential psychological ties to the world. There were many other examples that document how the extent of the crisis of the creative individual in late capitalism was symptomatic of contemporary society. A common phenomenon was a clash with social and, above all, cultural conventions, often escalating into personal conflicts and scandals. The creative individual, whose fundamental needs for self-realisation were in jeopardy, ran up against a barrier that was known to be morally questionable yet remained insurmountable. The rejection of this social humiliation became a fundamental negation. A counterbalance was sought in the Decadent "breakthrough" to what was taboo, and also in other externalisations that were mostly ideative. Within this alternative, this overcoming of depression and the creating of a new conceptual model, a new art formed at the turn of the century as its symbolic realisation.

The case of František Bílek and his development as an artist in the 1890s was one of the most extreme examples of this situation. The shock he had suffered in 1892 brought about a profound personal crisis from which he only recovered in the latter half of the decade, this time with indisputably positive results. Bílek's ideas about the role of the artist were based on a notion that had already been widespread among the previous generation: the artist should be the nation's teacher, guiding the people to moral elevation. The circumstances of Bílek's origins, his psychological type, and the situation in which he had found himself in Paris meant that he took on this mission with a sincerity that was almost messianic in its intensity. He sought a remedy to the decadence of bourgeois society, which he saw all around him, in its idealised opposite, which for him was religion. In the 1890s he tried to become actively engaged with the literary movement Katolická moderna (Catholic Modernism), and in 1897 he published an enthusiastic proclamation called "The Artist's Confiteor" in its magazine, *Nový život* (New Life). He also spoke at the movement's congress and published his speech as a booklet. Typically, however, for most of the audience his opinions were quite incomprehensible, and they were even condemned as errant and an expression of pride. Nor would Bílek's views later reflect any of the church's teachings, and his religious mythology, which he developed into an idiosyncratic system, was essentially his own fantastical artistic ideology.

At the heart of Bílek's ideas in the 1890s was the suffering Christ, understood as the son of man, symbolising humanity's tragic struggle for a higher existence. In his art, this Gnostic interpretation stemmed from the naturalistic and Neo-Baroque foundation that was typical of Bílek's early work. In the autumn of 1896 Bílek sketched in charcoal the head and entire body of *The Crucified*, which already demonstrated his characteristic arrangement of the arms at right angles to the body. Its execution, however, first in clay models and ultimately as a large woodcarving, was only completed in 1899. In

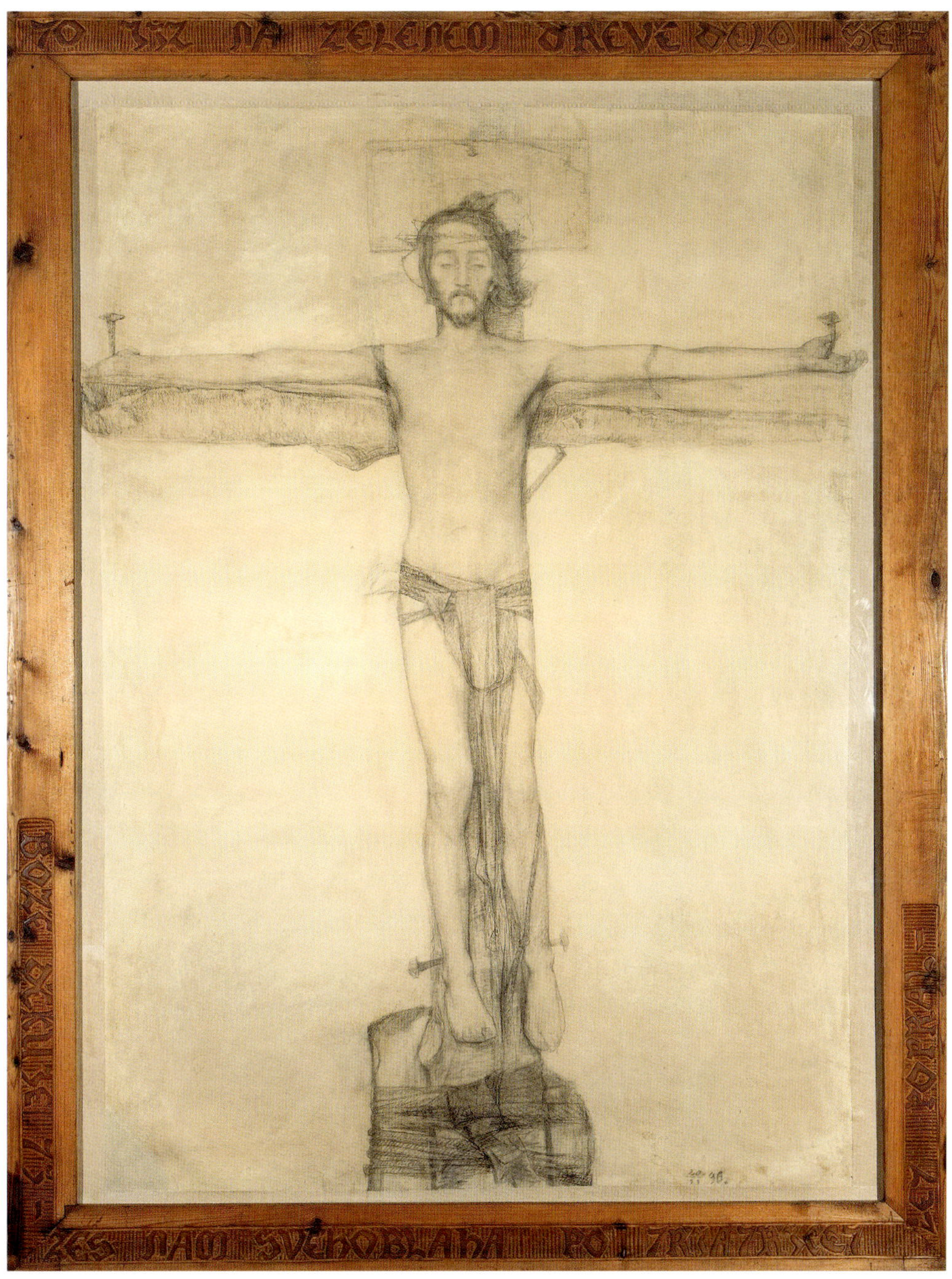

the interim, Bílek clarified his ideas on the work's content, as can be traced in his correspondence with the poet Julius Zeyer.[66] Initially, in keeping with his turbulent psyche, he had approached the sculpture as a drastic and illusionistic depiction of Christ's suffering that would assail the viewer. Zeyer, however, wanted the facial expression to be less that of a mortal and more that of a god, which could be achieved by using light to lessen the mass. This meant going beyond expressive naturalism to approximate the

70 František Bílek, *The Crucified*, 1896, charcoal, 200 × 142 cm

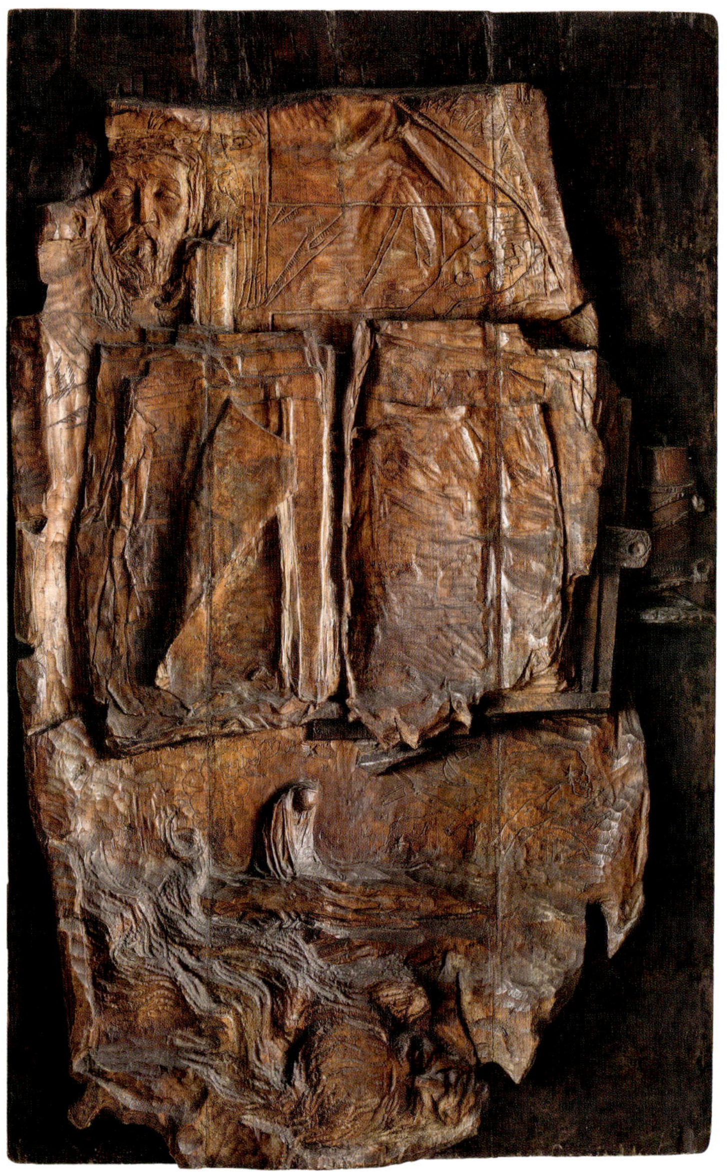

sculpture to the linearity of Bílek's initial drawing from 1896, which is interesting for its element of Anglicanism. Bílek's *The Crucified* was the first large authentically Secession sculpture, and in this sense it created a counterpoint to Myslbek's *Crucifix*, which had dominated at the Centennial Exhibition. For Bílek, it marked a maturing of his artistic talents and an understanding of an artwork as a fundamentally symbolic undertaking.

During the three years that Bílek spent working on *The Crucified* he also created a number of other works that extended his world view and his concept of art. In 1897 he began working with ceramics, drawing on the local tradition in his birthplace, Chýnov. His dark graphite vases, ornamented with floral forms and his distinctive lettering, were remarkably original.

71 František Bílek, *The Meaning of the Word Madonna*, 1897, wood, 153 × 93.5 cm

At this time, he was chiefly concerned with how to express religious content in his art. For the symbolism of light, which played such an important role in the genesis of *The Crucified*, he looked to the Bible for support, for like all heretics he considered it the sole authoritative source of higher knowledge. For his relief *The Meaning of the Word Madonna*, originally commissioned by Zdenka Braunerová, he used the text of the gospels as the basis for a meditation on light and darkness. Light became a Neoplatonic emanation of the fundamental creative energy that lies beyond matter, beyond the world, which here is "made by a wastrel – obscuring the light with clouds, his darkness, that he may sleep more easily."[67] To convey this idea, Bílek created an arrangement of fragments of an open book, figural images, candles, stars, and many other engravings and small inscriptions. This was highly unusual for sculpture at the time, but he managed to maintain a visual unity in all these details by using light to gradate the planes of the relief. As his symbolism became more clearly defined, Bílek also found his characteristic material for these sculptural visions. For him, woodcarving was not just an affordable medium, but it also had a philosophical basis. The contemporary trend for reviving Romantic ideas of nature as the original objectifying basis of human existence was adopted by Bílek for his sculptures, in which he associated the human figure with a tree, an Old Testament symbol for life growing towards the light.

However, Bílek first presented this idea in its entirety in his drawings. A large cartoon called *Mother!* from 1899 depicts a fantastical scene – a moonlit nocturnal landscape, in which part of a mighty tree trunk has split off and taken the form of a luminous human face with somnambulistically closed eyes. High above it, a star shines faintly, and it seems that the spirit of the tree wishes to ascend to the star. The drawing is mounted in a carved frame, where there are stars, a figure with traumatically outstretched arms, and a meandering line that symbolises a path. The mysterious metamorphosis of physical nature into cosmic spiritual essence is conducted through a process of anthropomorphosis. In Bílek's images, man is part of the fundamental cosmic law that imbues and unifies all material and spiritual reality. A large charcoal drawing from the following year, entitled *Places of Harmony and Reconciliation*, presents this idea more didactically: after "the cruel struggle of life," the two pilgrims or bards have come to an alley of tall trees that turn into figures, whose raised arms form a vault in which a luminous hand appears, full of "Mercy and Truth." Bílek also used this symbolic union of man and cosmic nature in the form of a tree in his portraits, as in the likenesses of his parents he carved in wood for his "Cottage," the studio he built in Chýnov.

Bílek's work from the late 1890s was made after he had parted ways with Katolická moderna, and it came out of his quest for a Symbolist conception based on certain old religious symbols. With his unorthodox position, stressing the importance of his own vision, Bílek recalled the early 19th-century English poet and draughtsman William Blake; Zdenka Braunerová was one of those who drew this comparison.[68] Bílek paid little heed to contemporary artistic style, which he thought a mere profanation of the true problem, and he polemicised against ornamental Secession art. He created his own version of *The Lord's Prayer*, in which, unlike Mucha, he renounced all ornament.

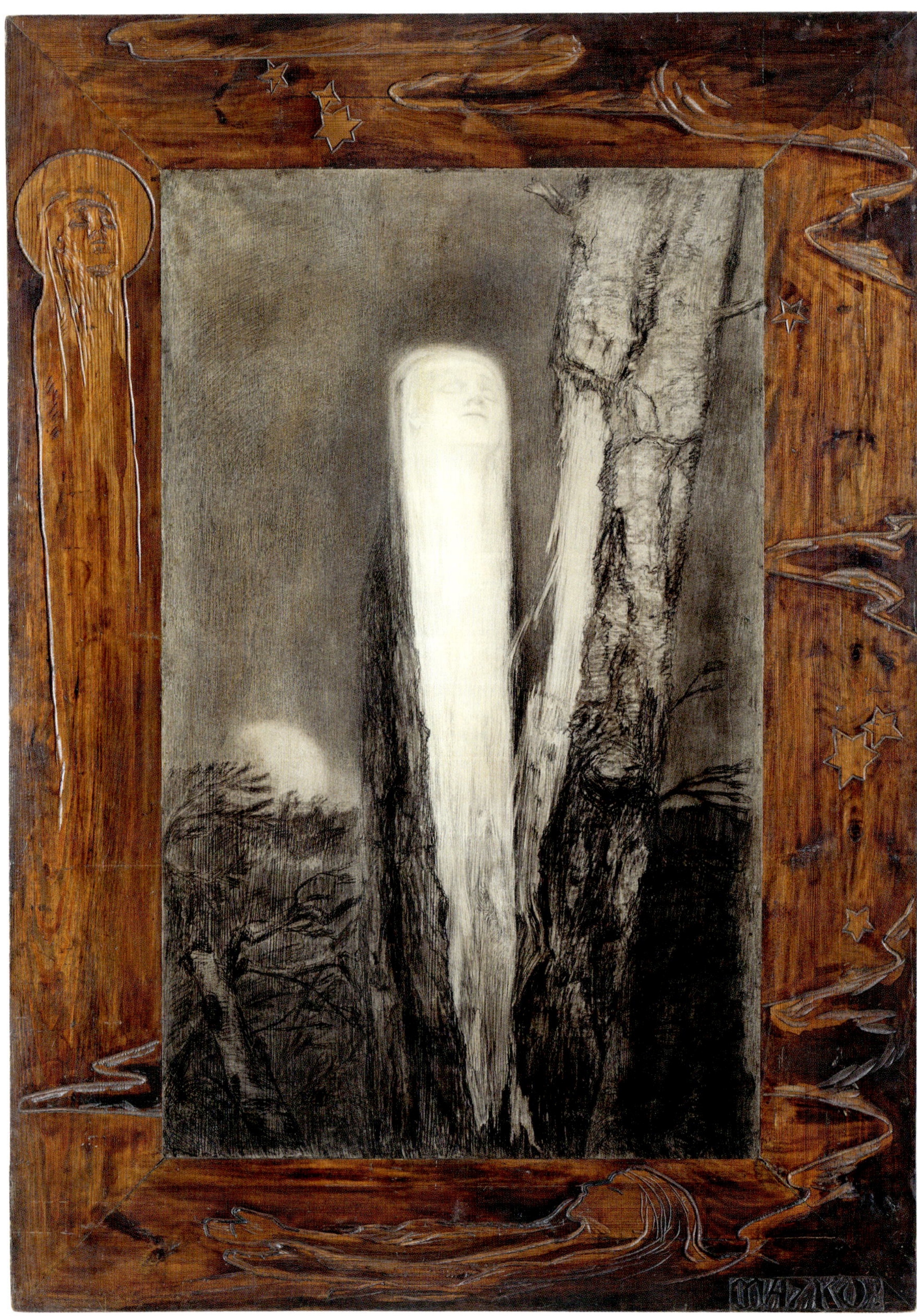

72 František Bílek, *Mother!*, 1899, charcoal, 139 × 83 cm

Yet in his drawings we can find the Secession's lines, although they are closer to Blake's "springs of life" (from which the original English modern movement grew) than to routine stylised ornament of Parisian or Viennese provenience.

Bílek's need to create a more comprehensive belief system was reflected in a set of twenty-six drawings from 1899, collected in a tract with the title *The Reckoning and Reading in Letters of the Body of Man*. The notions depicted here included the fundamental idea of humanity's identification with the cosmos, which, mirroring evolutionist theories, was seen as a constant cycle of growth playing out in all realms and levels of life and leading to culmination followed by disintegration and new germination. This dynamic linear concept was based on the Gnostic and Orphic belief that the natural world offered an opportunity to release the soul from matter, but this was constantly thwarted by man's "naturalness." Another typical idea from Bílek's tract was his Pythagorean speculation with mystical numbers, which separated the symbolic body of cosmic man from the supreme unity after the final seven.

Bílek took much inspiration for his Symbolist vision from like-minded poets. Among them was Julius Zeyer, his closest confidant in the latter half of the 1890s, whose tact and constant exhortations for artistic freedom did much to ease Bílek's mental distress. Bílek's sensitive portrait of Zeyer from 1897 conveys his poetic imagination and his typically melancholy features. When the poet suddenly died at the beginning of 1901, Bílek produced a model for a monument based on his cartoon *Mother!* It depicts the poet escaping from storm-tossed waves, where a female figure reaches out her

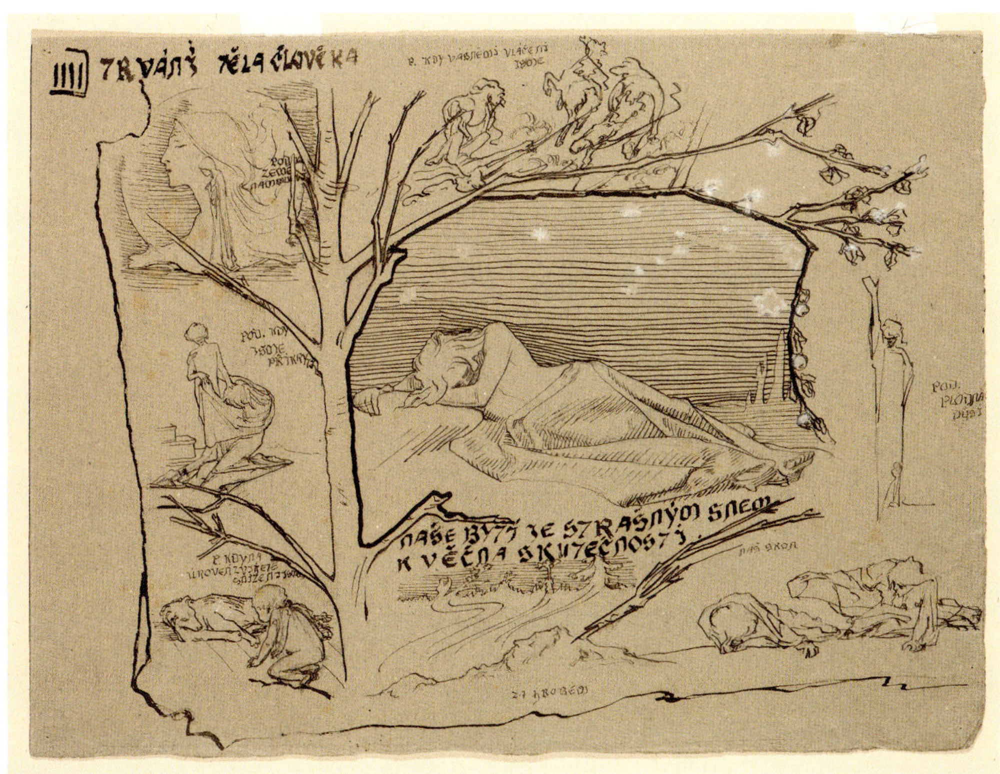

73 František Bílek, Page from the tract *The Reckoning and Reading in Letters of the Body of Man*, 1899, pencil, ink, Indian ink, and white chalk, 34.1 × 45.6 cm

arms to him. Here Bílek boldly defied all the prevailing conventions for contemporary monument art. This innovation came out of purely personal inspiration, and it would soon yield further results. In 1900 a competition was announced for a monument to Jan Hus in Prague, which was won by Ladislav Šaloun with a design that favoured a tableau vivant over the usual allegorical monuments. Šaloun showed the martyr wearing a heretic's cap as he stands at the stake, on a plinth made of Romanesque columns representing "the orders of the Roman Church, fossilised for centuries." On one side of him are Hussite troops – "Warriors of God" – and on the other, a small band of exiles after the Protestant defeat at the Battle of White Mountain. Šaloun's figures were naturalistic and Neo-Baroque, and much influenced by theatrical staging. Stanislav Sucharda submitted a somewhat more accomplished design – *You Sprouted Forth above the Mud*. For the architectural part of the monument, he was assisted by Jan Kotěra, who also submitted his own design – *You Went Cleanly, Leaving a Furrow*. All these entries featured the gigantic figure of the solitary Hus accompanied by a small staffage on the plinth. Sucharda showed Hus as a condemned man, bare-headed and with his hands by his sides, but whose scale reflects the immensity of his moral superiority, while Kotěra's Hus is resigned as he walks with one hand pressed to his chest.[69]

The extraordinary interest the competition generated among young sculptors was understandable not just because it offered an opportunity to work on a large monument, but also on account of its subject matter. The tragic figure of Jan Hus, a key figure in Czech history, seemed to them to be the supreme moral prototype of the Secession artist. Their idealism and their critical views on society found in Hus a symbol that connected the legacy of the past to the present day. It was also characteristic that their designs expressed a reproach. They saw Hus as a solitary giant, a historical projection of the problem of modern individualism. For this reason, the relation between the main figure and the staffage remained unresolved in their designs, where the different scales violated the memorial's unity and monumentality.

Although Bílek did not enter the competition, he also worked on the theme of Hus. While the designs for the competition seemed to draw inspiration from Bílek's tilling motif, a different concept lay at the heart of his own Hus, carved in wood in 1901. He titled the statue *A Tree Which Struck by Lightning Burned for the Ages*, and expressed this idea in his portrayal of the martyr. Bent like a bow, Hus grows from the stony soil like a mighty tree trunk, his face turned up to the heavens, his eyes closed in ecstasy, and his hair swirling like a flame. The symbolism of light that Bílek had developed in earlier works has an emotional charge here that emphasises not Hus's passive devotion but his passionate conviction of the power of truth, which is based on the cosmic order. Bílek presents Hus as the supreme representation of his mythological conception of man's status in the impersonal, universal world, and although Bílek's treatment must have seemed extreme, it drew inner strength from its resolute optimism. By taking the monument out of what was essentially the funerary realm and turning it into a panegyric appeal, it created a striking alternative.

Secession artists needed a bedrock upon which they could define the positive values of their world view. The epoch of naturalism had opened their eyes not just

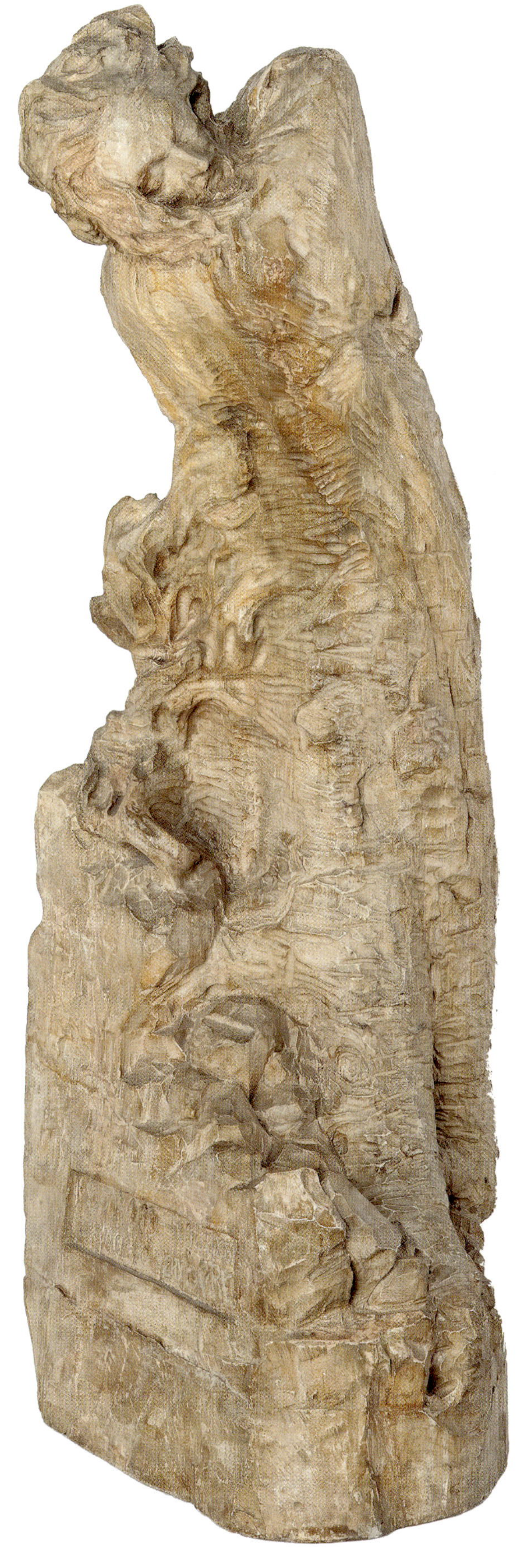

74 František Bílek, *Jan Hus*, 1901, plaster, 89 cm

to visual reality but also to social reality, which they largely rejected. However, naturalism could only hold up a mirror to the dispiriting aspects of "everyday" life, and young artists needed to find a counterweight to this combination of visual "truth" and moral ugliness. They sought it in "beauty," in ideas that necessitated moving away from naturalism in favour of more stylised and abstract forms. It was typical of the artistic mentality of the 1890s to think in terms of sharp contrasts that were paradoxically complementary. This also resulted in the strange coexistence of naturalistic and idealistic conceptions and formal considerations; any contradictoriness was offset by a sense of their ambivalent reversibility. Just as demonic and angelic apparitions lived side by side in Decadent lyricism, their opposition resolved in the contemporary type of the femme fatale, at this time art too was full of the antagonism between either the raw transcription of reality or its abandonment in favour of purely imaginary ideas. This antagonism had already been introduced during the artists' schooling, when nude drawing classes resulted in constant contrasts between the seen and the imagined.

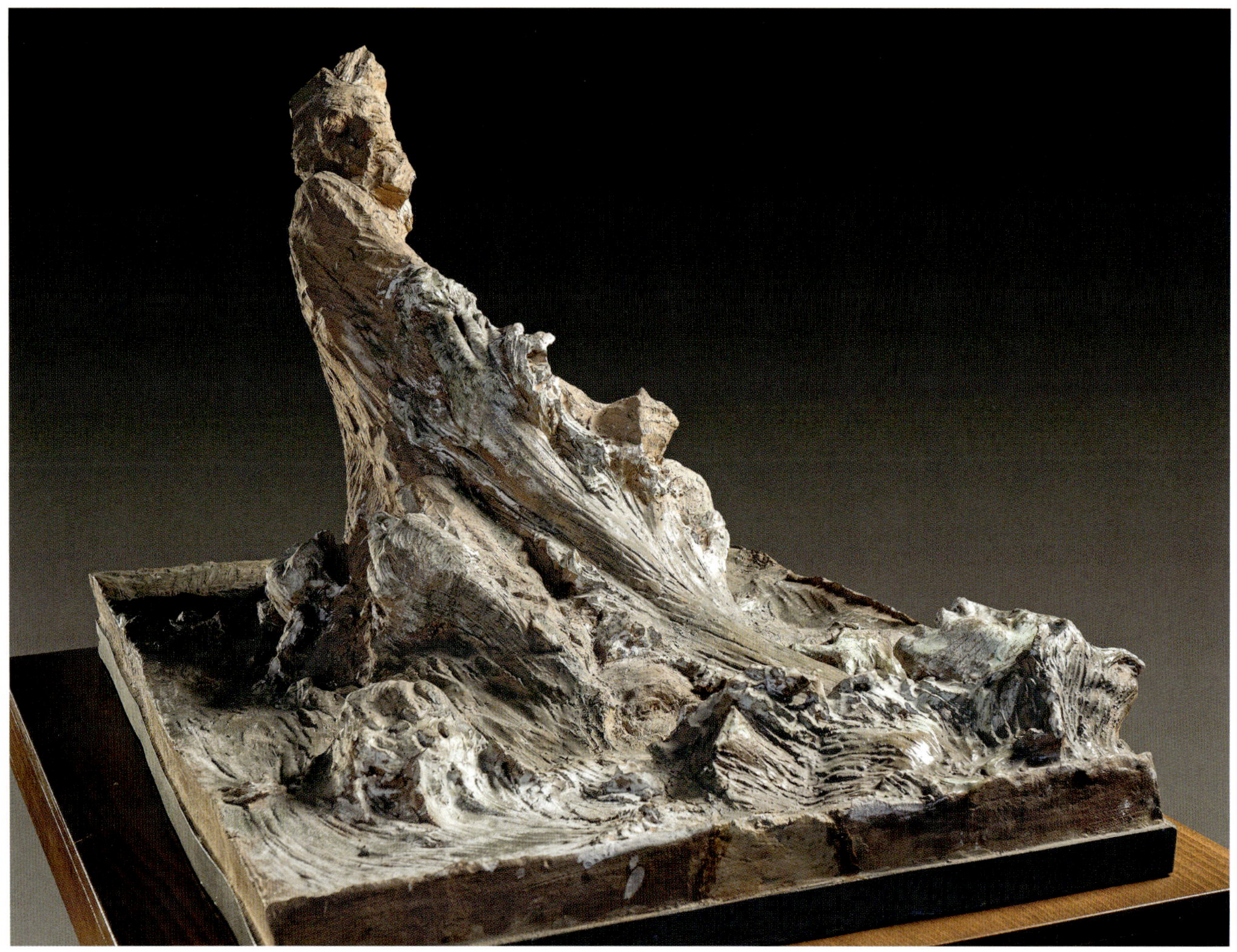

75 František Bílek, Sketch for a monument to Julius Zeyer, 1901, terracotta, 50 cm

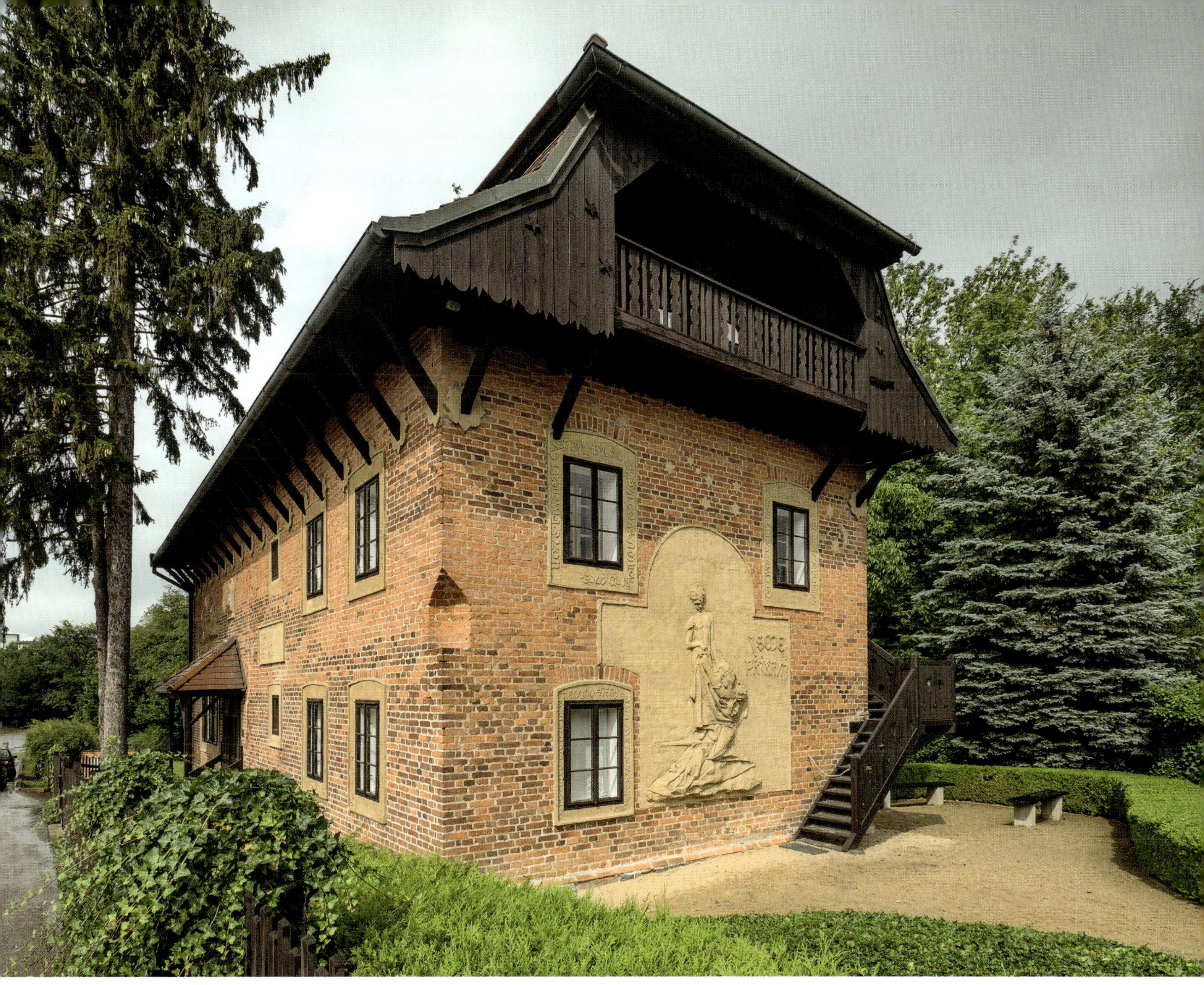

More important, however, was how this practice shaped an artist's view of reality. In this sense, it created a peculiar dynamic in artistic expression, and it remained for art to find a solution to this contradictory situation.

It seems that the generation that emerged in the late 1890s sensed that in this at first sight chaotic situation, there were certain values that would allow them to develop their individuality. For these artists, chaos was not just a crisis but also an embryonic state in which new projects could be defined. For this reason, we often find in these artists and their spokesmen a distrust of any attempts to resolve this situation in

76 František Bílek's house ("The Cottage") in Chýnov

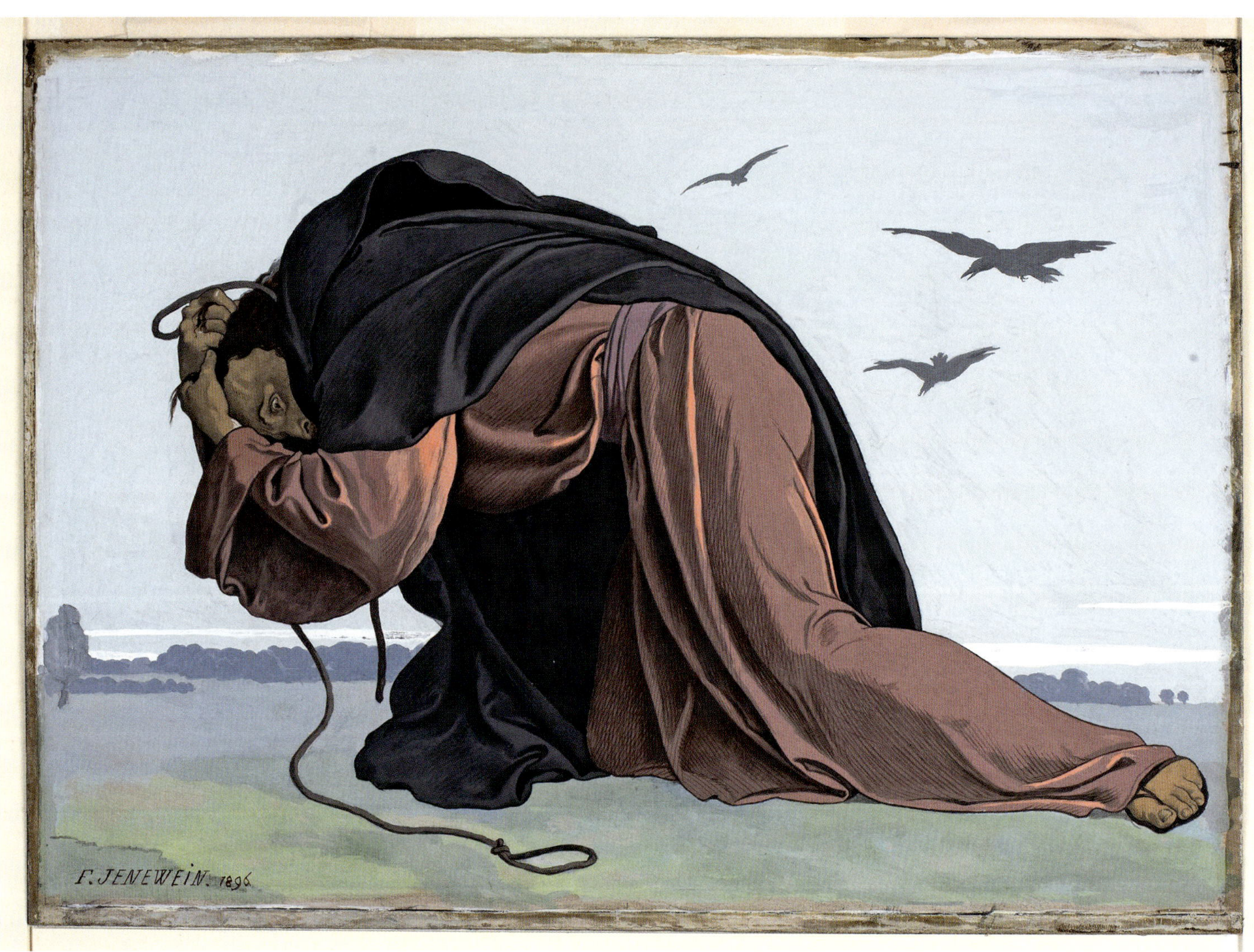

too forceful or one-sided a manner. This distrust was accompanied by a rejection of external influences and authorities, and a constant emphasis on the need for independence and originality. This led to reservations over a number of artists from the older generation, still influenced by late Romanticism, who around 1900 became part of the new Secession formula. One such controversial artist was Felix Jenewein. In 1901, when he exhibited his six-part cycle *The Plague*, which became his best-known work, K. B. Mádl wrote,

> Since his second exhibition twelve years ago, Jenewein has enjoyed high esteem: we admire the tragic greatness of his art, and yet almost all the works he has created since then he has drawn and painted for his own sake. What is the reason for this? There can be no doubt that Jenewein's art is unflattering; it is free of all platitudes and lacks popular appeal. Its profound authenticity terrifies the philistines, and in

77 Felix Jenewein, *Judas*, 1896, gouache, 36.4 × 51.3 cm

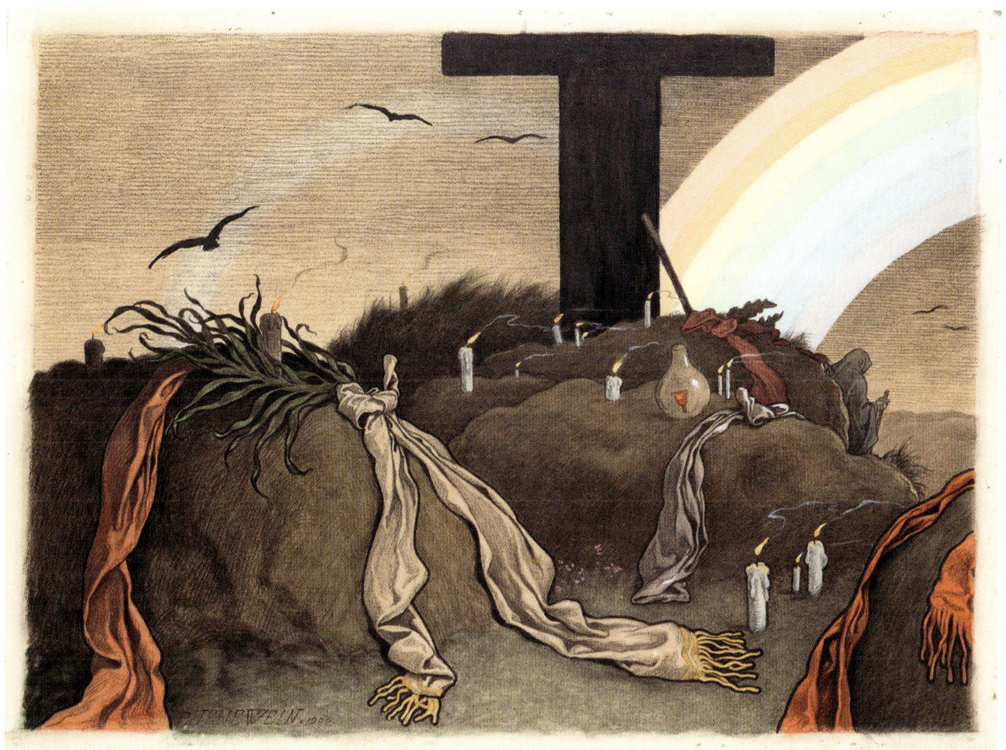

its immense tragedy and stormy pathos it is unwilling to conform to bourgeois superficiality; with its spartan form and ascetic colours, it does not seek to measure itself against the soft comfort of our salons.[70]

Jenewein was truly too sombre for ordinary decorative work. He had struggled in the 1880s, earning a modest living as an illustrator, and his art from this time had conveyed his criticism of society through illusive naturalism (for instance, in his anti-war cycle *The Death Toll*). In the following decade he turned to religious themes (*The Lamentations of Jeremiah*, 1892; the *Judas* triptych, 1896), in which he resumed the linearity of his early work, but now its naive lyricism gave way to a grand monumentalism that focused on the expressiveness of the large, almost sculptural figures that filled the foreground. Colour remained an auxiliary element. Jenewein's mature compositions were evidently influenced by his experience of working on church windows, which were popular at this time.

The Plague marked a move away from conventional religious themes. In his allegory of the medieval epidemic, Jenewein wished to create a "universal" ballad about the apocalypse of the human race. Here, however, he ran up against the demands of young critics. Arnošt Procházka especially condemned the lack of philosophical and psychological depth in Jenewein's work, and while he did not deny its decorative value, he disliked its stiffness, which bore the stamp more of the older Nazarene movement than of modern painting. A comparison with a younger artist, František Bílek, corroborated Procházka's verdict:

78 Felix Jenewein, Final image in the cycle *The Plague*, 1900, Indian ink, charcoal, and watercolour, 46 × 62 cm

> In addition to his new forms, Bílek has managed to illuminate old abstractions with a new religious spirit, molten and white-hot, and despite this religiousness (or precisely because of it) to elevate them anew to vertiginous heights as a symbol of universal and endless and inevitable suffering; to make of them, perhaps even against his will and beyond what he had intended, cosmic visions that surpass the bounds of any particular religion. It is this immense breadth and prodigious flowering of the soul that Jenewein has failed to achieve; he does not appear to be especially religiously or even mystically inclined; he stays close to the ground and within the received traditions – he composes beautiful decorations, but he does not pour his living soul into them.[71]

In many respects, the formal aspects of Jenewein's monumental decorativism recall Ferdinand Hodler, but Jenewein lacks Hodler's focus on Secession themes. His content is more a pseudo-religious paraphrasing of the four last things of man; it is at heart Neo-Baroque, and this is in conflict with its Secession-style linearity. Although Mádl's article was favourable, at its conclusion he wondered why Jenewein had had so little success with his art, attributing this to "the harshness with which he expresses himself" and "the lugubriousness of his drawings and paintings."

Although young critics may have promoted mutually contradictory tendencies, they were relatively united in their opposition to the persistence of old allegorising in the new art. Nor was Maxmilián Pirner spared such reproaches. Miloš Jiránek wrote of Pirner's paintings at an exhibition by Jednota umělců výtvarných in 1899,

> The relatively large exhibition by Max Pirner is a rare event for Prague. Long promised and long postponed, I think it has come too late in the day. By now we all feel that such philosophising does not belong in painting, and we have largely become unaccustomed to laboured allegories and symbolising with the aid of attributes. … Pirner's "Gulliver" best demonstrates what it looks like when a draughtsman with such a cold style forces himself to do caricature.[72]

This last sentence was in reference to one of the linearly drawn paintings that Pirner produced around the year 1900 as an attempt at contemporary art. Pirner was evidently favourably disposed towards the Secession, partly due to the profile of his oeuvre to date, but also because the Vienna Secession, of which he was a member, had devoted an issue of its magazine *Ver Sacrum* to him. Moreover, in 1898 Pirner had created a grand coloured window for St. Bartholomew's Church in Pilsen, and the linearity of this technique had also steered him towards the Secession's morphology, which he applied in large drawings with ornamental frames whose subjects were either humorous (*Alma Mater*, 1903) or highly sarcastic. They include his *Pan and Psyche* from 1899. In a three-piece ornamental frame "decorated" with animal attributes of Art (Pegasus, a unicorn, a swan, and an eagle), this drawing presents a scene in which the massive figure of Pan, lying on the ground with a sly smile as he cradles the petite Psyche in his bosom, is fussily measured, described, and studied by numerous diminutive figures in top hats who swarm over him. This was evidently a satire on academicism and the public's "common-sense" incomprehension of true art. In other drawings of this kind, Pirner takes an ironic view of another blind alley in contemporary art,

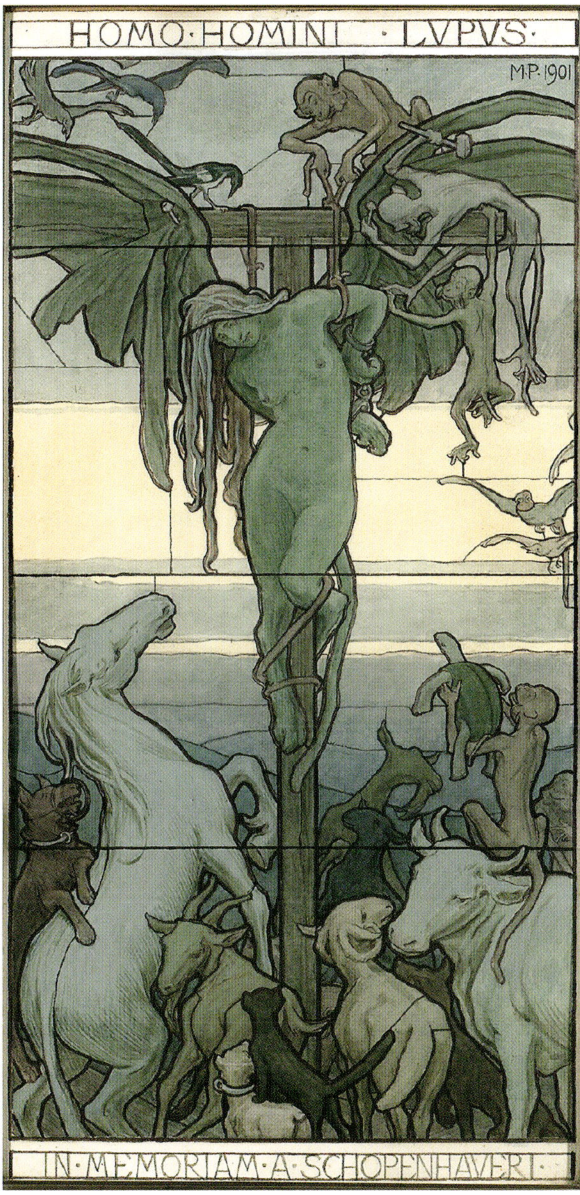

naturalism, which is symbolised by a camera and a marionette. Jiránek, ever quick to respond, defended naturalism with caustic criticism that seems to have played a large part in encouraging Pirner's definitive retreat into the privacy of his studio.

Eccentric by nature, Pirner later became famously solitary and misanthropic. He found support for his pessimism in philosophy, as reflected in his large watercolour *Homo Homini Lupus* (1901), dedicated to the memory of Arthur Schopenhauer. It shows a female nude, symbolising Truth and Beauty, who has been crucified by monkeys before an audience of farm animals. Pirner's increasing distaste for public life and the prevailing programmes in art ultimately extended to the Secession itself,

79 Maxmilián Pirner, *Homo Homini Lupus*, 1901, watercolour, 96 × 47.4 cm

as indicated by his drawing *Conjuror* from 1904. Framed by emblems from classical antiquity, it depicts a grotesque scene of a magician with an empty skull who offers his heart, suspended on red blood vessels drawn in the style of the Secession's famous ornamental "macaroni," to a nude who represents Art.

The rather forced tone of Pirner's new works suggests that these were merely the commentary of someone who was already too isolated. His art remained within the confines of late Romanticism, which saw an impassable divide between fantasy and reality. However, this boundary was not recognised by the young generation, and for this reason their approach was never essentially an escape into fantasy but more a constant struggle to balance it with reality.

This tendency, the result of a compelling need to confront the ideal with the real, gave young art its unusual psychological sensitivity. Its very diverse motivations met at the psychological level and insisted on their expression in art, for only this could sublimate the emotional agitation provoked by a situation that was essentially neurotic.

In sculpture, a new concept that emphasised sketching in clay was well suited to express this ceaseless struggle. Here the base material's three-dimensionality and substance could accommodate the contemporary need to go beyond naturalism while retaining its sensitivity. The striking developments in Czech sculpture from the turn of the century were unquestionably due in part to the fact that its basic technique matched contemporary requirements for its content. Emotion acquired a particular urgency in sculptural sketches. Here too, of course, these developments were pioneered by artists whose reasons for this new expressiveness came directly from their own lives. Quido Kocián, whose *Šárka* from 1897 had brought him into conflict with Myslbek, expressed his sense of being an outlaw in both art and life in a sculpture from 1901 called *The Artist's Lot*. It can be seen as a satire on Myslbek's *Music*. Whereas the latter work has an idealised and harmonious lyricism, here an emaciated artist wearing only an augur's cap twists in a Neo-Baroque convulsion as he clutches at his instrument, a palette. In contrast with *Music*, he does not give this instrument the "kiss of consecration" but gnaws at it with closed eyes, as though sucking from it some intoxicating potion. This dramatic vision turns the sculpture's mass into an ecstasy of form, a rapture in which the material is torn asunder, flickering like a flame. Kocián's polychrome relief *Forbidden Love* was another confrontation between the naturalistic framework and his ballad on a theme from folklore, while his first sketches for a memorial to the 6th Light Infantry Battalion for Vysokov in the Náchod district had an unconventional emphasis on its skull attribute – at the time Kocián was drawing heavily on the legacy of the Czech radical Baroque, taking from it the theme of Vanity. Although Kocián was venting his personal deprivation here, these sculptures won him prizes from various foundations. A scholarship to Rome resulted in his sculptural group *Dead Abel* (1901), an allegory of how he had been wronged by Myslbek, which ultimately led to their famous reconciliation. Abel's body sags as he lies surrounded by bleating sheep. This gave the sculptor a foundation for his typically linear treatment of the nude, and it lent the dead body a new expressiveness, which is also reflected in the Neo-Baroque way one leg is extended beyond the plinth, and similarly in how

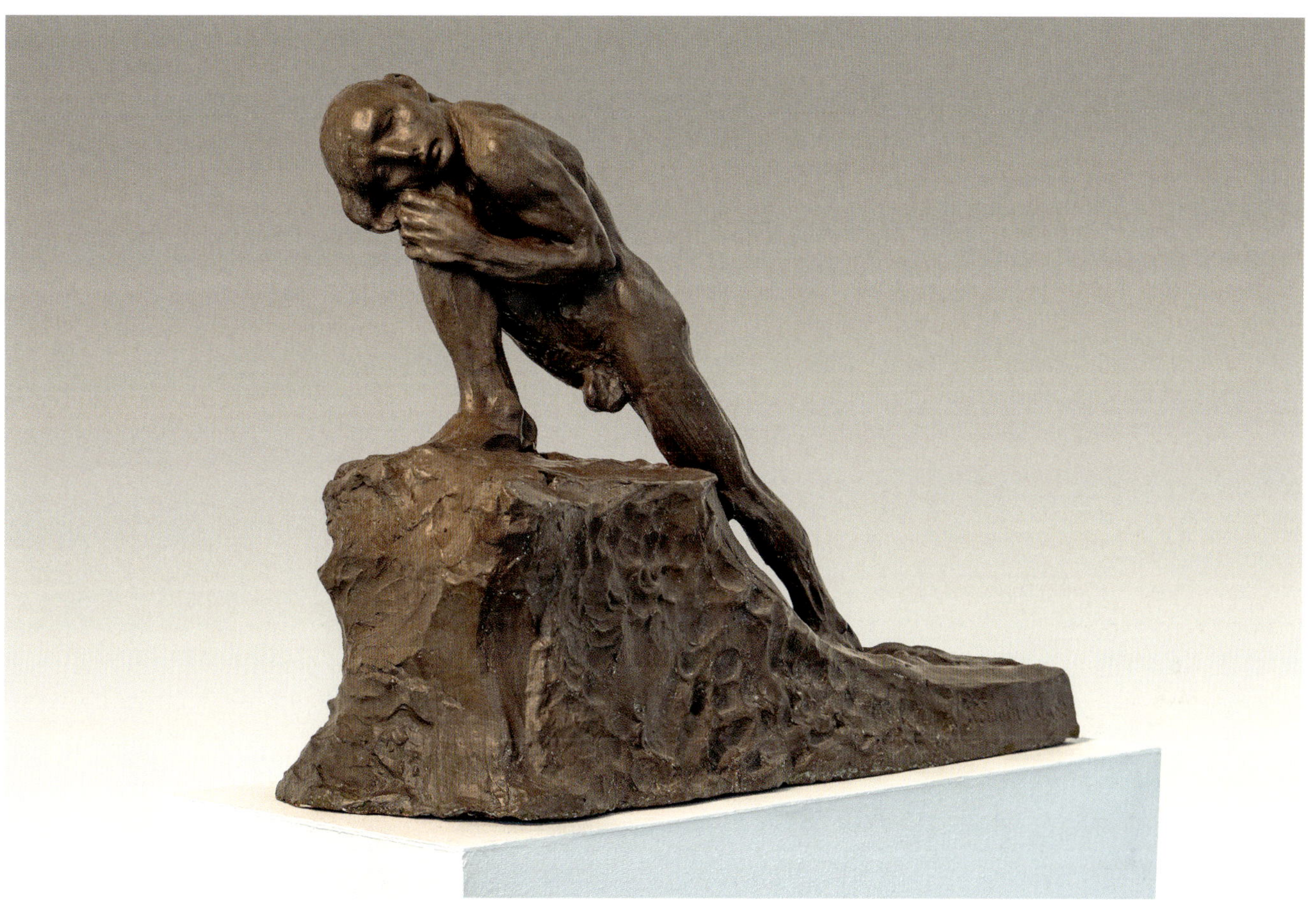

Abel's head is propped up: this is not the head of a dead man, but of one who is asleep. This aspect was important, for Kocián had succeeded in applying Neo-Baroque and naturalistic expression to a deeper symbolic meaning, thereby creating a new kind of Symbolist sculpture that was both profound and rawly emotional.

Although Kocián drew on Bílek's sculptures from the 1890s, his work did not embody any more comprehensive belief system. His art remained critical, as demonstrated by another sculpture from Rome, *Life Is Struggle!* (1902), with two nudes locked in combat as they roll the earth's globe down an inclined plane. More substantial than this caricatured moralising, however, was *Sick Soul* (1903), where in the traumatic diagonal described by the adolescent nude, and in the crudely worked base, Kocián expressed much of the contemporary sense of a constant wrestling with the tormenting mystery of life.

The problem of artistic externalisation was at the heart of the Secession generation's endeavours. Their rejection of established convention fruitfully unearthed the emotional and sensual sources of artistic work, but this rejection could not in itself constitute a new culture. Yet to create the forms and content of this culture it was essential to keep feeding the flame of defiance, which consumed depleted schemata

80 Quido Kocián, *Sick Soul*, 1903, patinated plaster, 52 cm

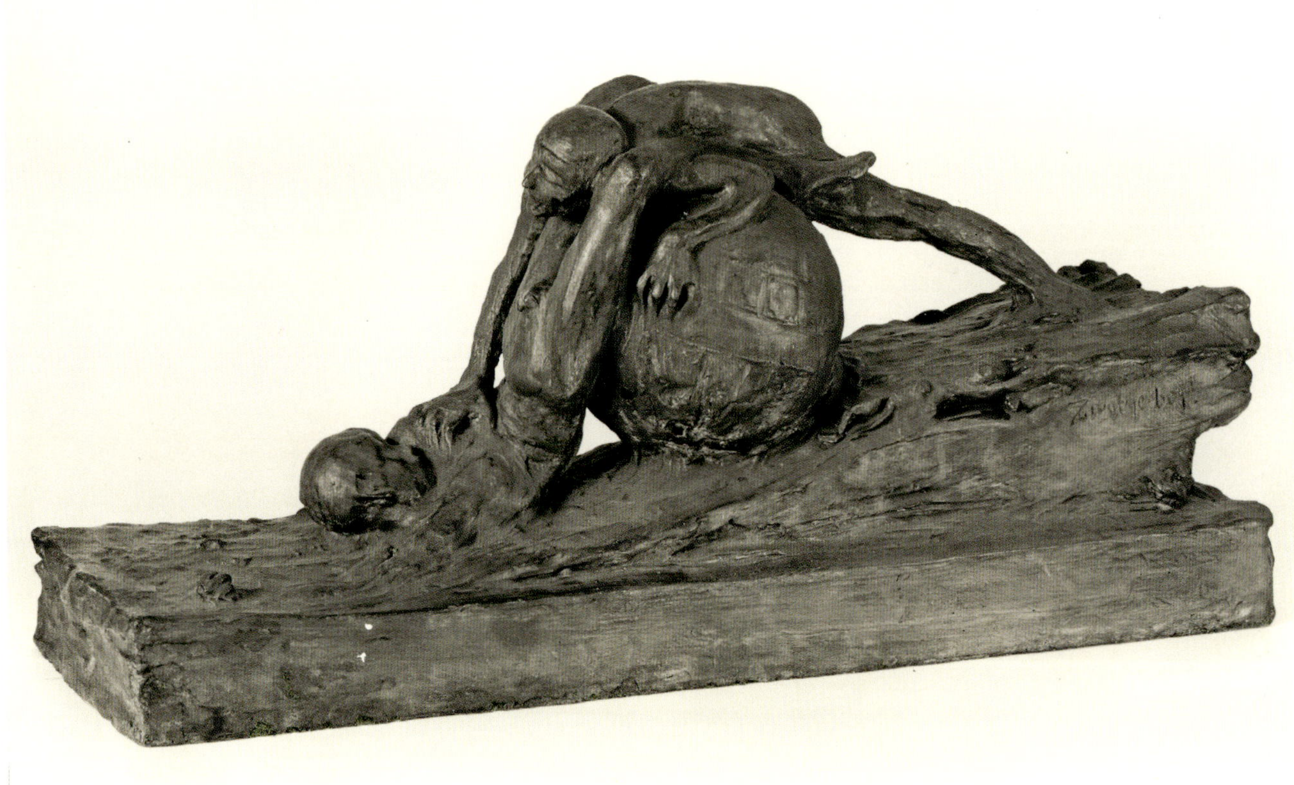

and freed the way for a new conception. This concerned not just purely artistic matters, but the new art's standpoint on public and private life.

František Kupka's development as an artist is a good illustration of the many facets and consequences of the younger generation's negation. As an ambitious young painter, Kupka first left Prague for Vienna, hoping to find acclaim there, but despite his technical accomplishments he was unsuccessful. Nevertheless, while in Vienna – this was in the era before the Secession – he learned of new ideas in philosophy and religion, subjects that already interested him, and he soon exchanged his academic ambitions for those of a painter-philosopher.[73] In 1895 he exhibited a large painting at the Künstlerbund, whose present whereabouts are unknown. He tried to answer the sceptical question posed by its title, *Quam ad causam sumus?*, with the "Sphinx of Life," allegorical nudes, and other attributes, but this too was poorly received in the city, where Klimt and his group had yet to emerge. In search of greater understanding, Kupka then moved to Paris, where in 1897 he painted *The Book Lover*, renouncing his earlier philosophising in favour of "practical" life.

In these dramatic reversals, Kupka's true disposition began to come to the fore. The realism or naturalism of Marold's paintings of daily life would not suffice, for Kupka could well see that beneath the surface of the everyday there were deeper forces shaping social reality. In 1899 he painted *Money*, where a female nude is seduced by an

81 Quido Kocián, *Life Is Struggle!*, 1902, patinated plaster, 38 cm

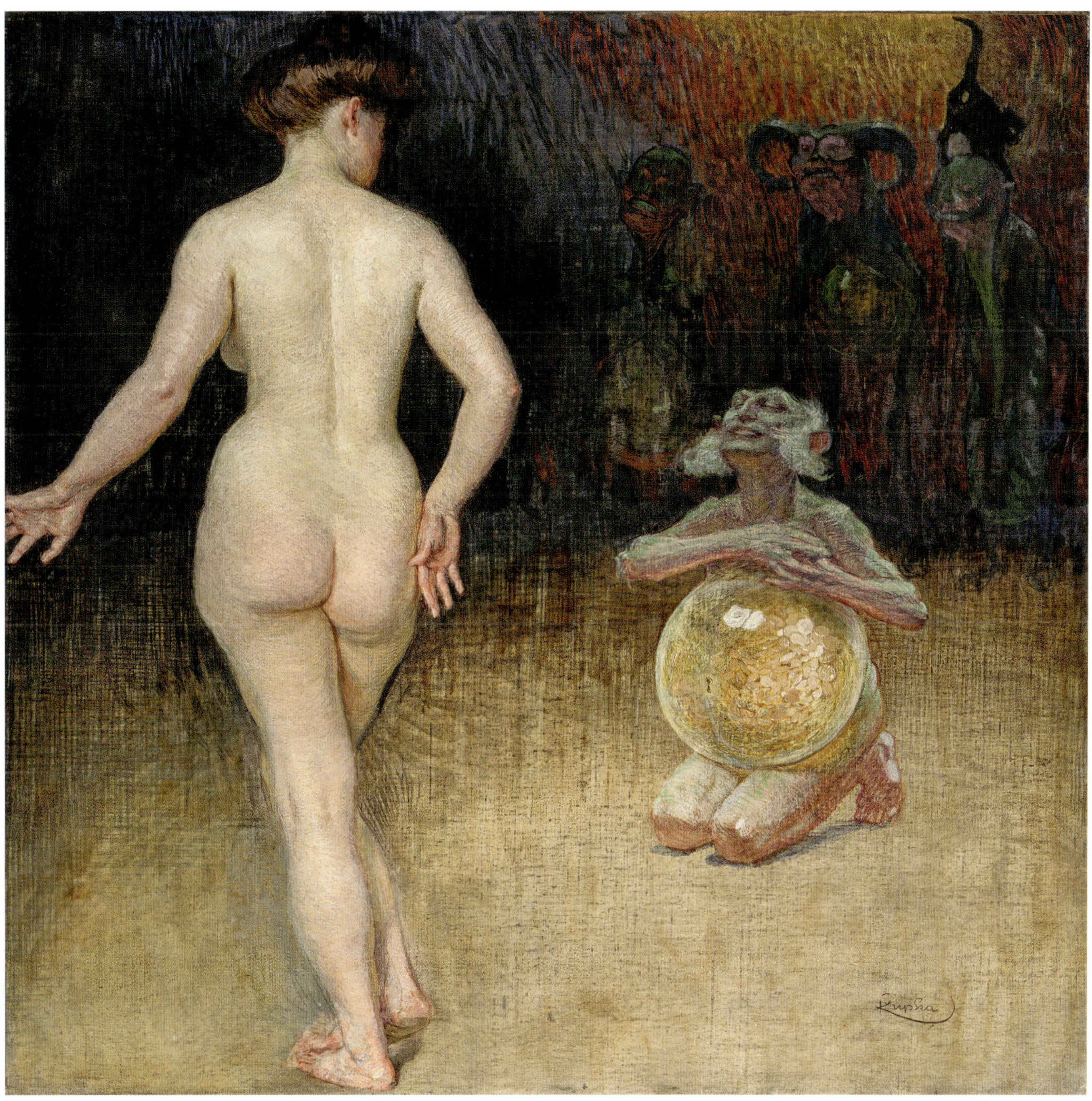

82 František Kupka, *Money*, 1899, oil, 81 × 81 cm

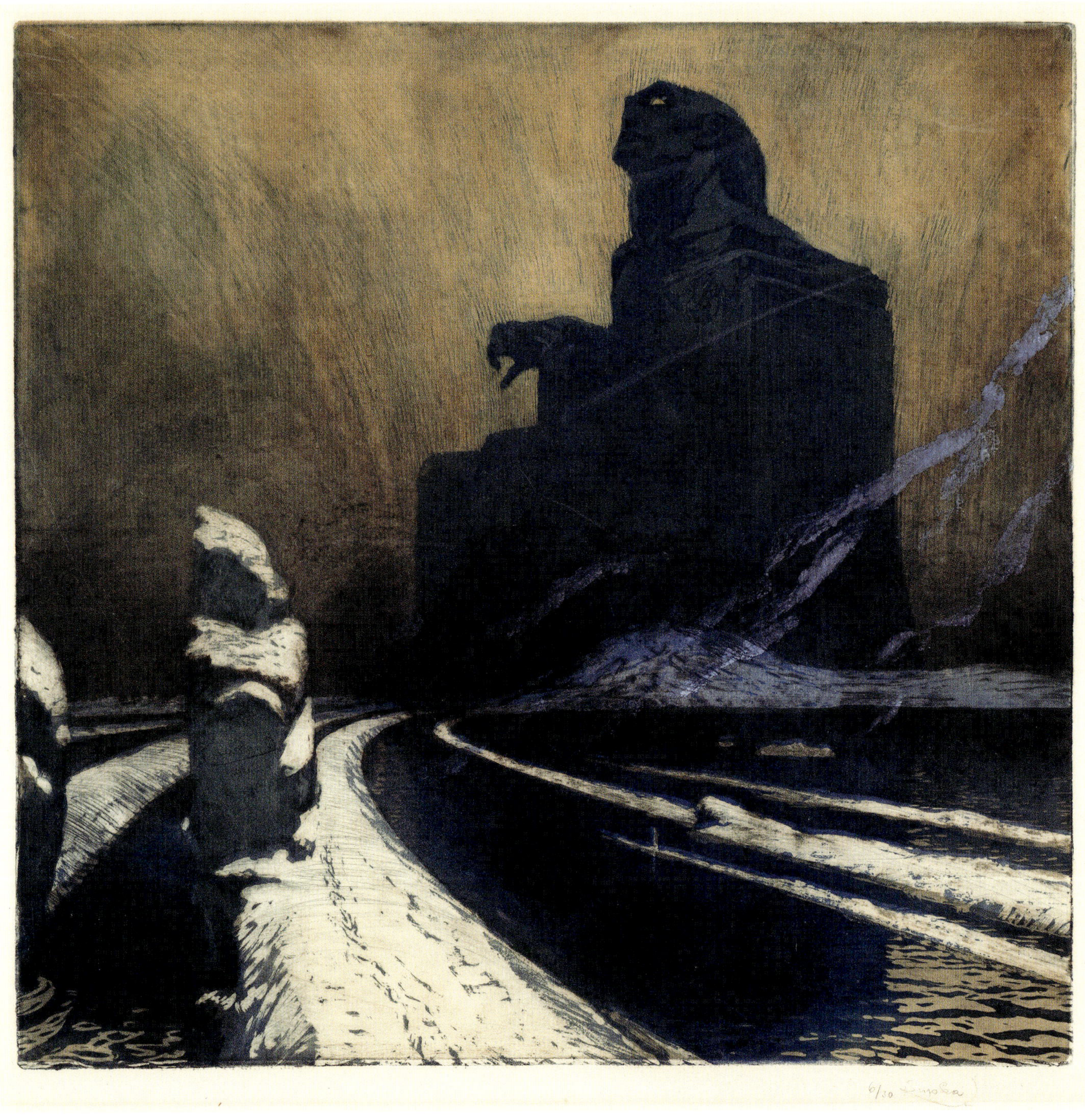

83 František Kupka, *Defiance – The Black Idol*, 1900–1903, coloured aquatint, 34.7 × 34.7 cm

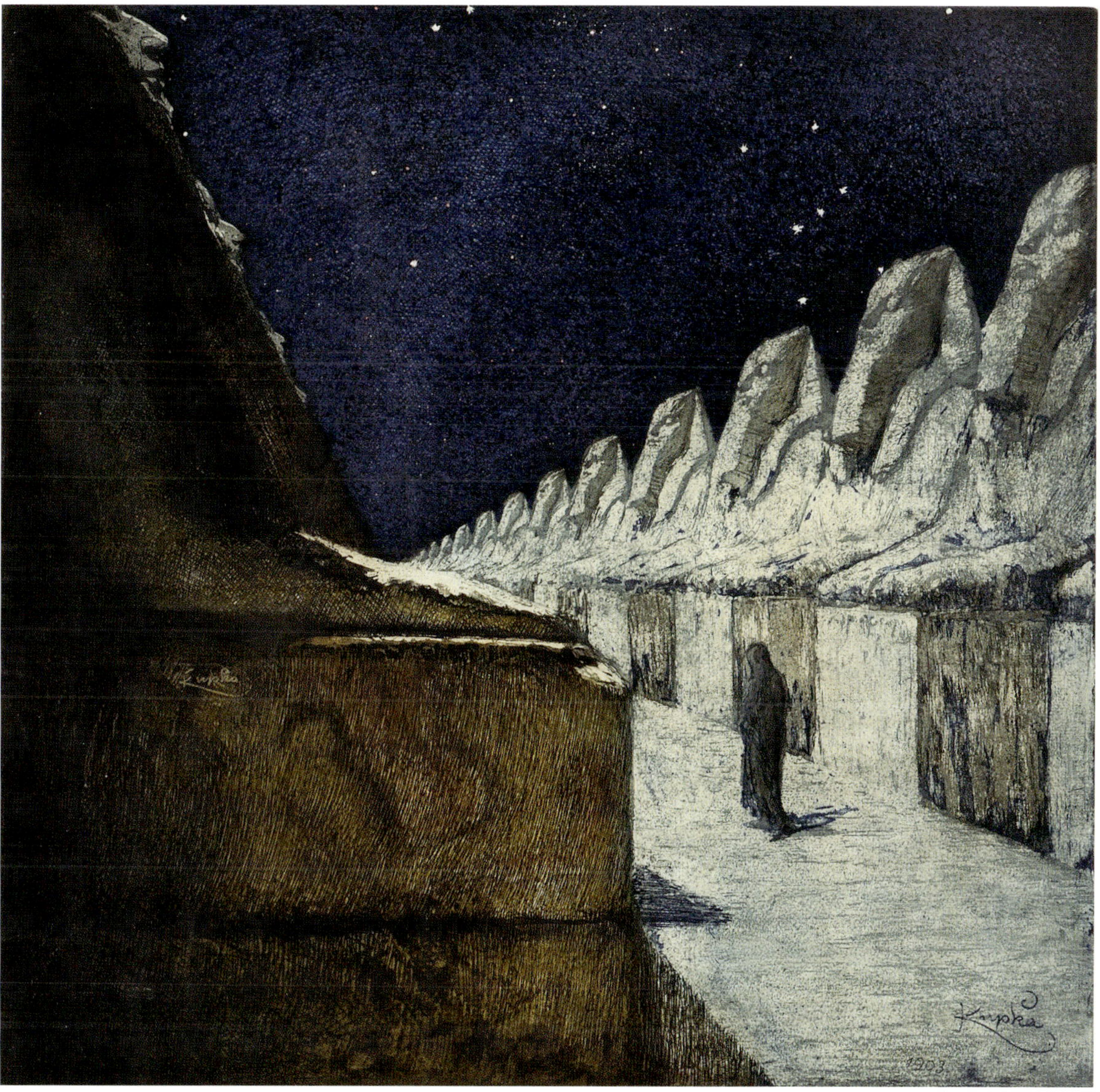

old man, gold coins gleaming in his round belly, while animalistic demons lurk in the background. Stylistically, it is still a combination of naturalism and literary Symbolism. Kupka gave a drawing of the painting to the poet Josef Svatopluk Machar, whose scathing criticism of bourgeois society was Kupka's model. More socially critical works followed, culminating in Kupka's print cycles *Money* (1901–2), *Religion* (1902–4), and *Peace* (1902–4) for the anarchist-leaning magazine *L'Assiette au Beurre* (The Butter Plate). In these series, Kupka pitilessly attacked bourgeois social, intellectual, and political hypocrisy, and declared his allegiance to the forces opposing international capitalism, militaristic imperialism, religious superstition, and other forms of trickery. These works were also much praised by spokesmen for the workers' movement, and they were shown at exhibitions in Czech towns and cities. Although based on the tradition of

84 František Kupka, *The Way of Silence*, 1900–1903, aquatint coloured with gouache and watercolour, 34.8 × 34.5 cm

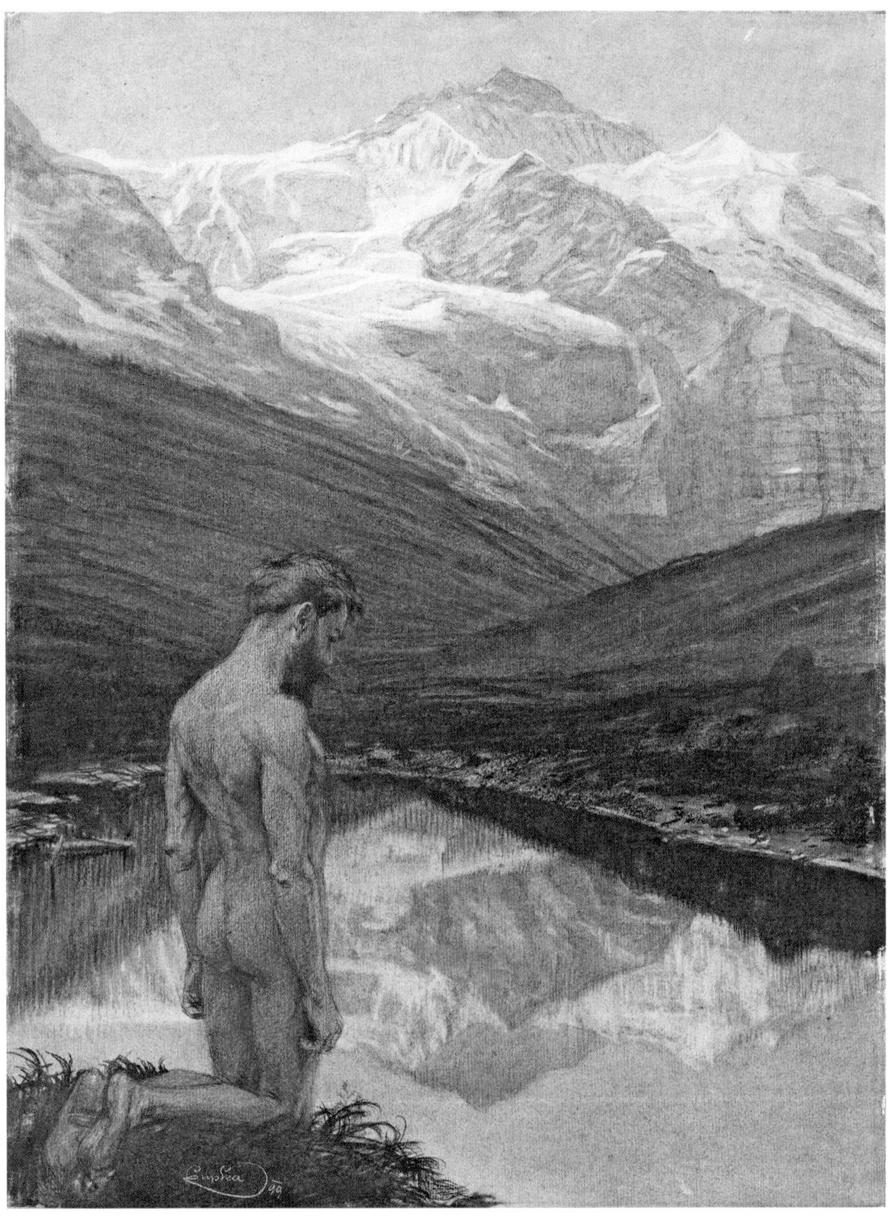

French political drawings, they also had Czech antecedents, such as Hanuš Schwaiger's drawing *The Pursuit of Happiness* (1895) for Gerlach's *Allegorien und Embleme*, in which a well-nourished capitalist is confronted by the struggling masses. Kupka's activities were taken up by another Czech artist in France, Václav Hradecký (the author of the cycle *La Bête Victorieuse*, published in *L'Assiette au Beurre* in 1903), who worked with symbolic contrasts of light and shadow.

In unveiling the brutal mechanisms of bourgeois social and international politics, Kupka's position was that of an anarchist for whom individual freedom was paramount, and it would shatter the conspiracy of dark forces. Kupka always generalised

85 František Kupka, *Meditation*, 1899, charcoal and chalk, 60 × 24.3 cm

the enemy, as, for instance, in his drawing *Vous devriez bien nous la foutre!*, from the cycle *Peace*. A man in a red blouse, whose features resemble Kupka's own, addresses an assembly of caricatured European monarchs who are seated on cannons. Behind these puppets, however, are the true "Molochs" of Capital and Violence, drawn as animals standing in a circle that separates the brave protagonist from the panorama of smoking factory chimneys in the background.

The honourable thing, then, was for an individual to reveal the ills that blight social reality. However, the strength to do so could only be found in virgin nature, the very opposite of society's turmoil. In *Meditation* (1899), Kupka, naked, kneels by the shore of a lake that reflects the summit of a high mountain covered with snow and ice. Kupka further developed the metaphysical background to his critique in the prints that were to comprise the cycle *Voices of Silence* (1900–1903), where the individual becomes a pilgrim wandering through fantastical scenery. In a print titled *Defiance* (also *Revolt*), or *The Black Idol*, the individual is a tiny figure, surrounded by dark, dead water, who stands on a long jetty leading to a massive statue of a demon looming against an empty sky. Here Kupka was in part inspired by Poe's poem "Dream-Land," but he used his own devices to create an effective sense of fear in the face of an unknown fate. In *The Way of Silence*, the pilgrim walks along a silent alley of Egyptian sphinxes, magically lit by stars shining in the night sky. The third aquatint is a view of a tranquil body of water covered with lotus leaves, above which two rings of light hover. In one ring there is a human embryo, whose umbilical cord is connected to a radiant body in the other ring. This vision is called *The Beginning of Life*. The order of these three square-format prints is uncertain, but it seems they were meant to form a triptych in which Kupka returned to his philosophical ambitions, albeit now in a much more suggestive and artistic form. He drew here on French Symbolism and theosophical speculations about man's place in the cosmos, which remained influential even after artists had begun moving away from literary Symbolism.

Kupka's work from his first decade in Paris demonstrates how the Secession artist's mentality was still drawn to mutual opposites. Artistically, this was the opposition of naturalism and Symbolism, which were only gradually finding common ground through the application of the Secession's stylistic criteria. In his print cycles, Kupka often used the dynamism of curviform lines, but they did not become directly ornamental. This dynamism became more a formal symbol of the transition between two seemingly incompatible poles: thought and true form, or the visible and the invisible. Ideologically, however, the concern was still with seeking a better alternative. Against the demonic world of the brutal "struggle for life" was an idealised, sometimes even utopian notion of redemption. Resistance to social ills could often become the illusion of escaping to higher, "eternal," values. However, the idealistic aspects of this position were mostly not in vain, for they helped to structure an ideological conflict whose critical revelations made room for original art, for the creation of new and genuine artistic value.

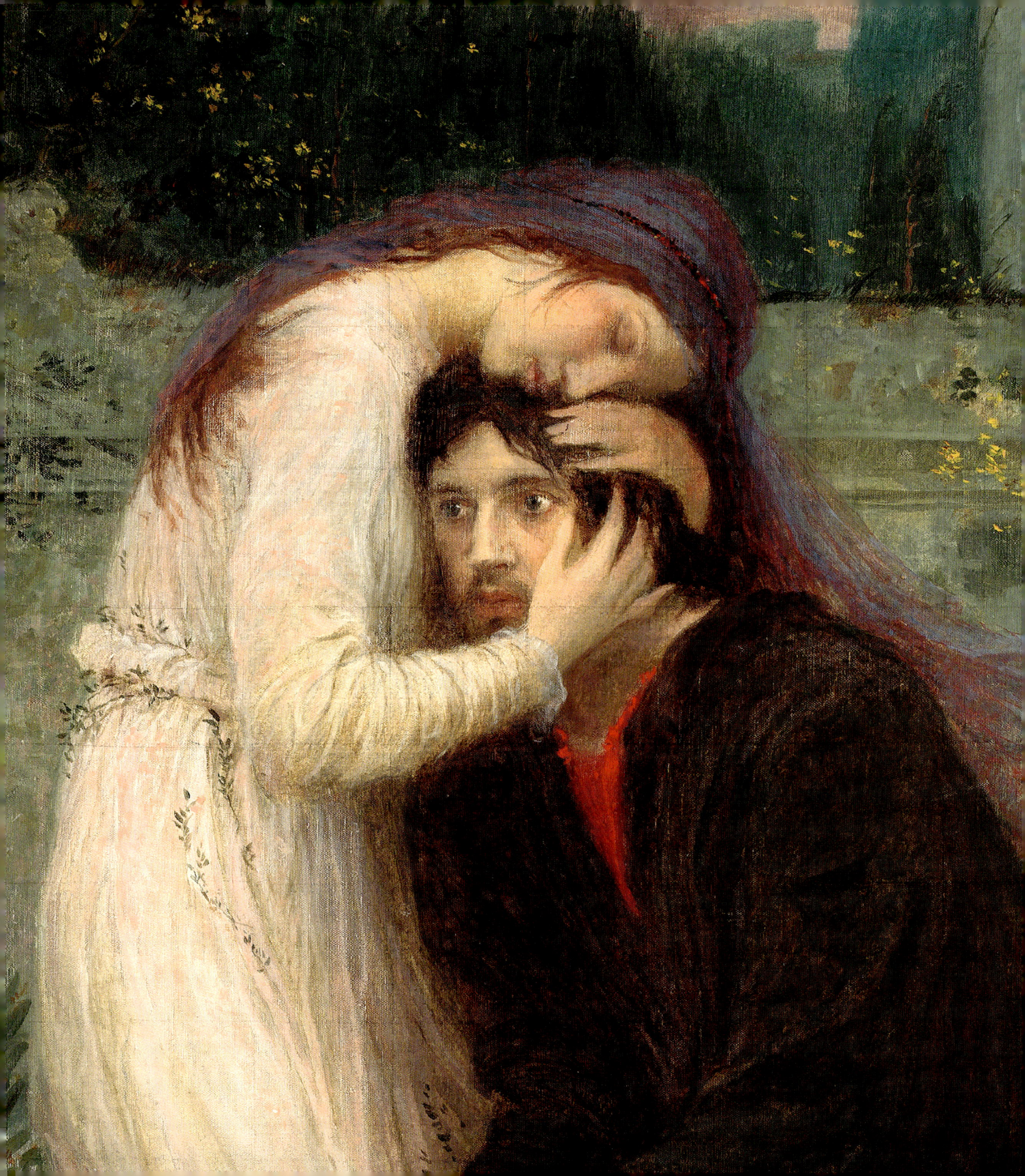

PAINTERS OF THE SOUL

The call for a new art, which had become an agenda for the latter half of the 1890s, had deeper roots in the younger generation's outlook. This found its most intimate interpretation in painting, and initially in drawing too, which was the most suitable technique for expressing new and unconventional ideas. There was a strong cult of drawing in the late 19th century, and young artists received first-class training at Prague's art schools, for Pirner, Hynais, Ženíšek, and the other professors were all eminent draughtsman and their pupils could further develop their professors' talent. We also find these young artists' first mature and distinctive creations in their drawings.

At the inception of the new figure painting were two artists who had studied at different schools but whose work in 1895, when this history began, was surprisingly complementary. If Maxmilián Švabinský's paintings for the Provincial Bank and Jan Preisler's paintings for the church in Přeštice had demonstrated an obligatory respect for local requirements, their private work revealed their personal interests. For Preisler, there was a sudden turning point in 1895–96, when besides his conventional lunette for the gate to a stadium hosting the Sokol movement's third rally, influenced entirely by František Ženíšek, he also created works whose orientation was wholly different. With Švabinský, the transition was more gradual, for here the foundation had been laid by Pirner. Although the triptych *Wine – Woman – Song* still belonged to late Romanticism, the tone here was markedly different. Pirner had extensive contacts with publishers in Vienna, and he evidently arranged for both young graduates to contribute to Gerlach's *Allegorien und Embleme*, an assortment of prints with allegorical themes by celebrated artists who included the president of the Vienna Secession, Gustav Klimt. Švabinský painted his triptych for this edition, and Preisler drew allegories of Music and Song that were also late Romantic in style.

Also from 1895, however, was Preisler's charcoal drawing *The Kiss*, which he reworked in oils shortly afterwards. Here Preisler went beyond late Romanticism and into the realm of Symbolism. The difference lay principally in how he progressed from drawing based on a posing model to a more direct expression of poetic fantasy. To what extent Preisler's first Symbolist painting was original remains an open question. There is no argument that a familiarity with examples from other countries must have played a large role in his sudden reorientation; the young painter had probably seen such work in periodicals. Yet it is significant that he found in them inspiration for his own art. The poetic world of Preisler's *The Kiss* was of a provenience much more remote than the usual journeys undertaken by students of modest means, for it was indebted to French and Belgian Symbolism; nor did it deny certain influences from England. The painting was a manifestation of a dramatic departure from naturalism, and even if we cannot rule out a literary background, the painting is of such high qual-

86 Maxmilián Švabinský, *Communion of Souls*, 1896, oil, 65.5 × 45.5 cm, detail

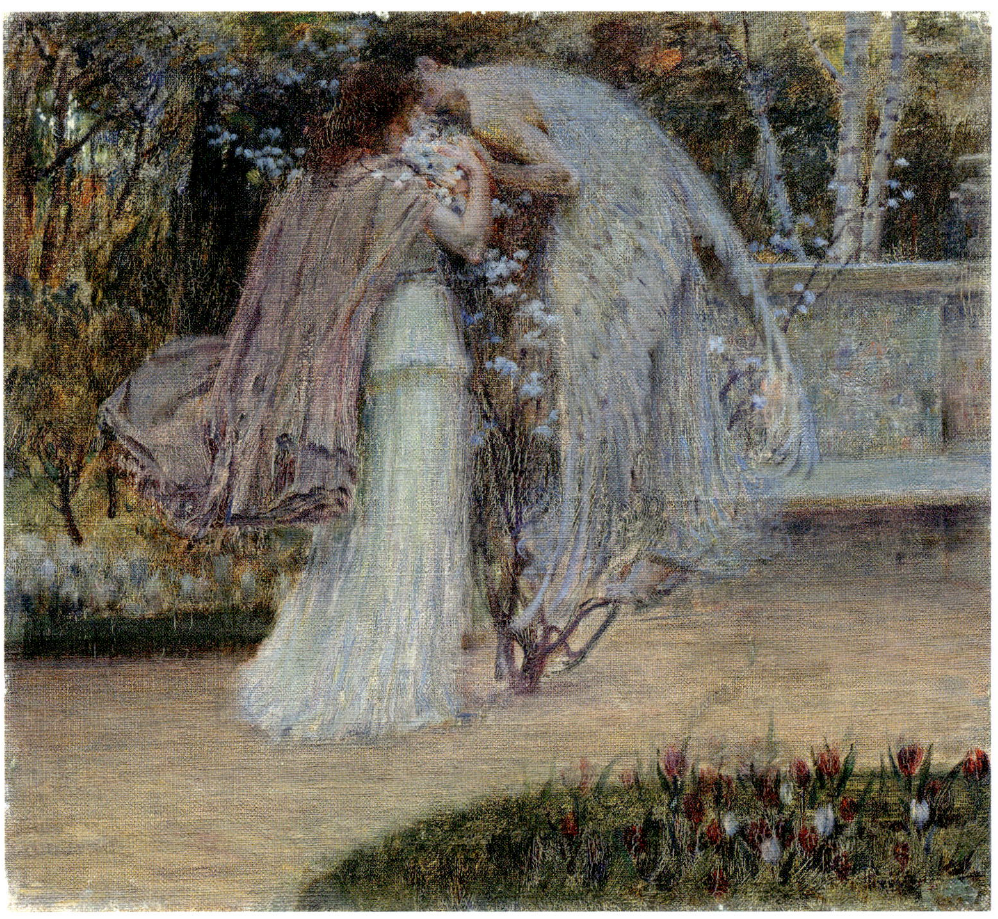

ity that the question of its originality is secondary. The theme of an idealised female figure in a garden at dusk, filled with the intoxicating scent of flowers (conveyed by the unusually flaming colours of this painting, albeit covered with sfumato), would remain one of the most popular images for the new painting, for it was a fitting basis for the new aesthetics of man's harmony with nature, understood as a setting that permitted an undisturbed and spontaneous expressing of individuality. However, this emotionality was hidden behind a mask of poetic illusion. The break with allegorical convention was not then complete, but the main role had now been entrusted to the magic of a colourful vision, and this opened up a new path.

In 1895 Švabinský similarly worked with the theme of an idealised figure in nature. His pen drawing *Summer – Poplars near Kroměříž* features a nude in the summer sun in a real, if idealised, landscape. These elements indicate how the essence of Švabinský's approach had changed, and this was again reflected in the triptych *Desire – Bliss – Pleasure* (1896), whose hedonism had a much more realistic basis than the dreamlike vision that Preisler spun from halftones.

However, Švabinský's *Communion of Souls*, which he depicted in various techniques in 1896, blazed with the poetic idealism of the time. His painting, created in the passion

87 Jan Preisler, *The Kiss*, 1895–96, oil, 32 × 35 cm

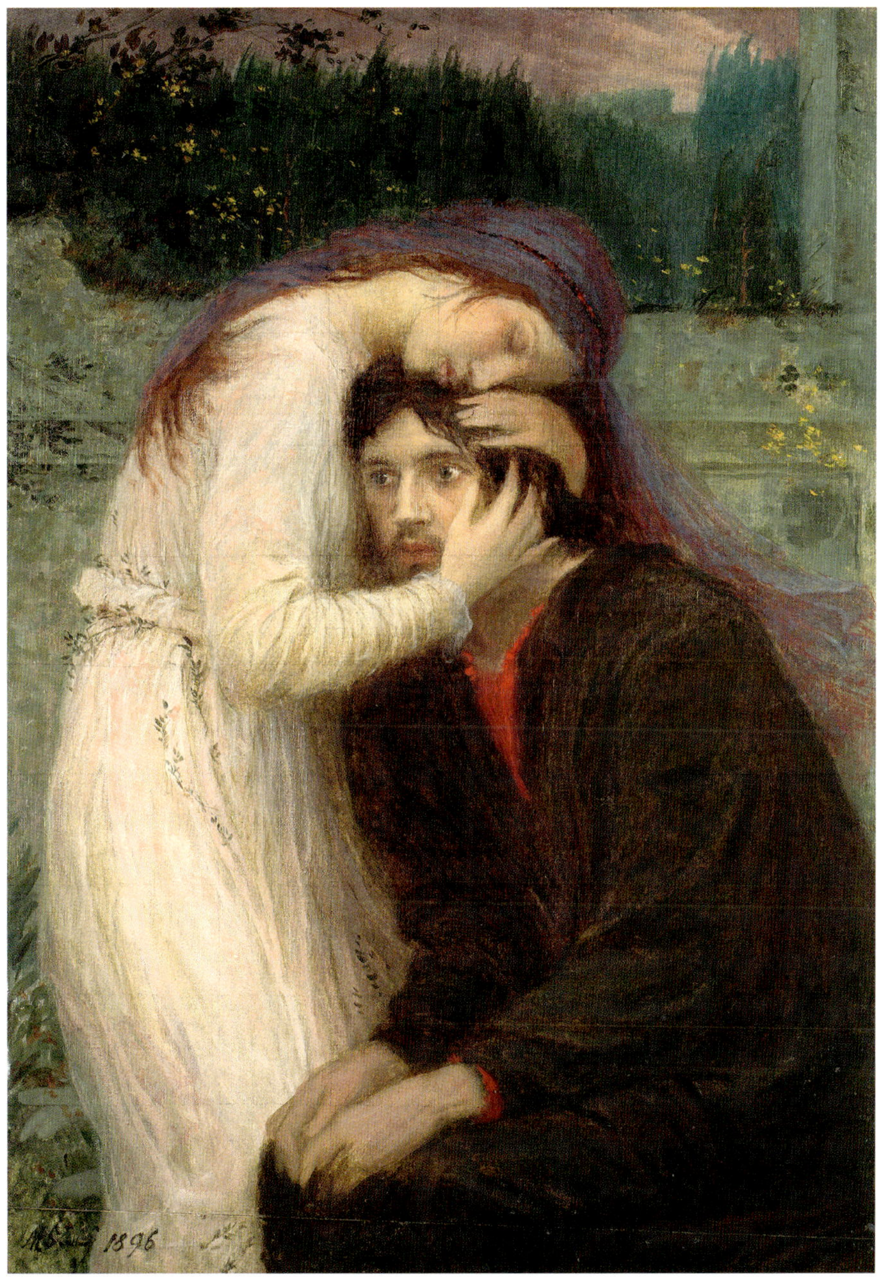

of young love, introduced another important motif in the new painting: a figure sitting motionless in a romantic landscape, dreaming with open eyes. Such depictions of melancholy as the supreme creative disposition had already appeared in the 18th century, and they were significantly developed by the Romantics. In the late 19th century they were revived, and melancholy became a key symbol. Švabinský's painting still had much of late Romanticism, especially the unreal apparition of the Muse, dressed in white, who cradles the dreaming young artist's head in her arms. The landscape is

88 Maxmilián Švabinský, *Communion of Souls*, 1896, oil, 65.5 × 45.5 cm

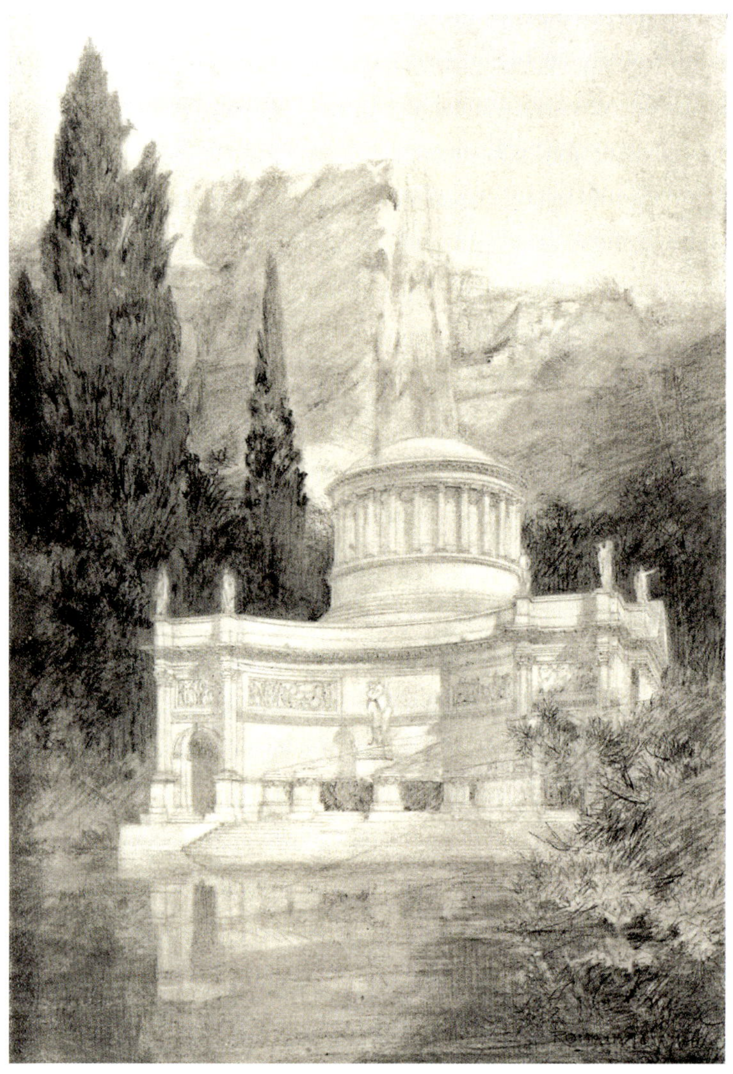

also still idealised. It is a southern one, with dark cypresses whose forms, resembling flickering flames in the strong wind, combine sorrow and ecstasy. Another young artist, Ferdinand Engelmüller, painted similar landscapes, and we can also find the late Romantic cult of the idealised southern landscape in Jan Kotěra's contemporaneous drawings made in Italy in 1898 (for example, *The Temple of Amor and Psyche – A Roman Fantasy*). These were admired for their delicacy, and K. B. Mádl wrote that they could be considered more the studies of a landscape artist who loved picturesque views of architecture than the drawings of an architect, who in the classic country of his art should instead go equipped with a ruler, a compass, and a scale.[74]

The exoticism of all these incunabula of the new painting was substantially influenced by examples from other countries. Interestingly, they all had a quite markedly English quality, viewed of course through the medium of French and Belgian Symbolism. This included the combining of pseudo-classical ideality with an emotionality that

89 Jan Kotěra, *The Temple of Amor and Psyche – A Roman Fantasy*, 1898, reproduced in *Volné směry* 3 (1899)

was so typical of the English Pre-Raphaelites, and also the treatment of colour, which in oil paintings seemed more to imitate matte chalk pastels. Such was the basis of Švabinský's *Communion of Souls*, and even later, when all these inspirations had been absorbed, Švabinský made no secret of his partiality for the English painters. His study of lovers in the drawing *Joy-Joy* from 1899 was directly taken from the right part of Dante Gabriel Rossetti's 1855 triptych *Paolo and Francesca da Rimini*. With Preisler, these connections were still more pronounced, as can be seen in his delicate three-part charcoal drawing *Wind and Breeze* from 1896, where the idealised figures have much of Edward Burne-Jones's typology and linearity. Preisler in fact wrote Burne-Jones's obituary for the second volume of *Volné směry*, where he rated him one of the greatest artists.[75]

Of the French painters, there was above all Edmond Aman-Jean. Czechs were familiar with his work from exhibitions in Munich and Vienna; they frequently quoted from it and continued to follow him in later years. Besides Aman-Jean, also Henri Martin, Henri Le Sidaner, and other "painters of the soul" had developed Symbolism in French painting in the early 1890s, where the English example was largely released from its graphic linearity and transposed to a more painterly rendition that reflected a typically French emphasis on poetic nuance as interpreted by Verlaine. In the 1880s Aman-Jean had worked as Puvis de Chavannes's assistant on his famous painting *The Sacred Grove*, which was more or less the model for the idealised landscapes with static figures that we find in the young Czech painters' early work.

This combination of English ideality and French sensuality created a backdrop against which the specific qualities of the new Czech modern school began to emerge. In 1897 Preisler painted *Autumn* for Gerlach's *Allegorien und Embleme*. The painting's very subject was eye-catching. In the central part of the triptych is a woman standing

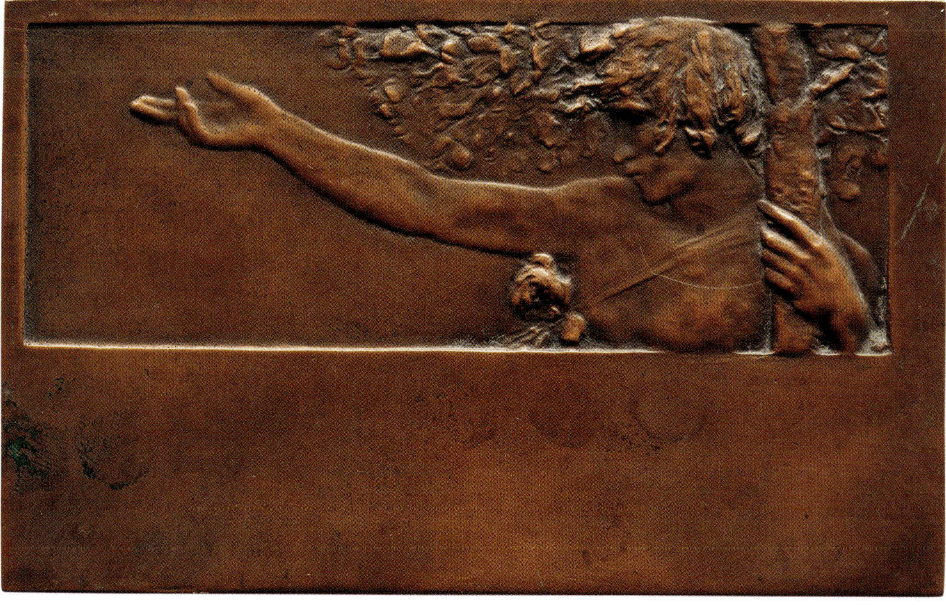

90 Stanislav Sucharda, *Nameplate*, 1896, bronze, 6.2 × 9.4 cm

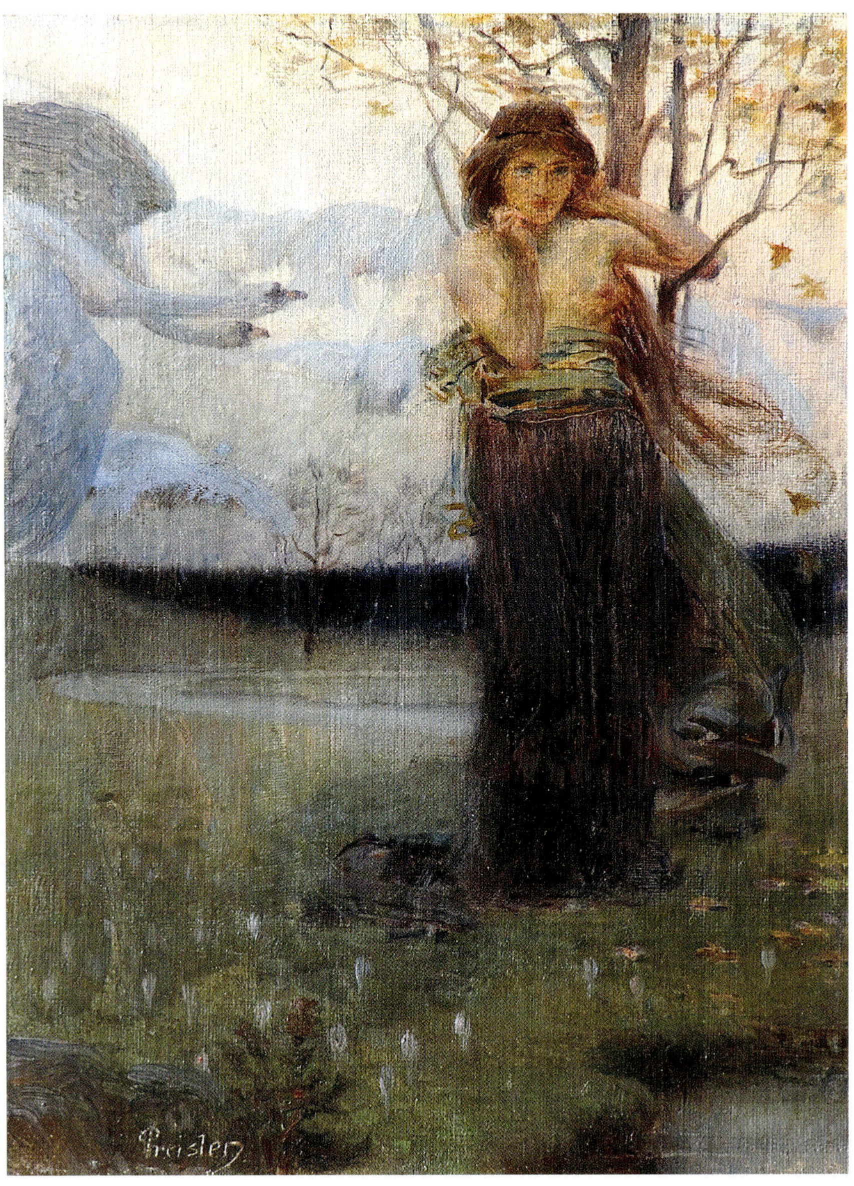

in a melancholy pose in a meadow full of autumn crocuses. The wind blows at her gown, and there are swans in flight whose wings and necks describe graceful curves. The meadow extends into the distance, where birch trees are outlined against a dark forest on the horizon. The female figure is standing in front of a few young trees, and the linearity of their branches and slender trunks introduces a certain stylisation in the painting. The sad but limpid harmony of late autumn, which so appealed to contemporary poets, was expressed in a painting that, in its sensuous charm, symbolised the younger generation's sentiments. It is interesting that this correspondence between the painting and the mentality of a generation was established by the painter going beyond the late Romantic or stylistically Neo-Baroque "painterly" treatment of the

91 Jan Preisler, *Autumn*, 1897, oil, 31 × 22 cm

subject of man and nature, to condense it into a more pleasing and succinct symbol that now took on a Secession stylisation. There is an equilibrium here between humanity, represented by the woman, and nature, represented by the trees, and the painting thus ceases to be a landscape painting with a staffage and becomes a monumental work. The intimacy of the new sentiment had become a new world view. This stylisation of a Romantic theme prompted a broad response – for instance, in the first of Stanislav Sucharda's celebrated plaquettes, which he modelled in 1896. Originally created as an invitation to an evening organised by SVU Mánes to celebrate Mikoláš Aleš's birthday, it was subsequently titled *Nameplate*, perhaps on account of its small format, but perhaps also symbolically. It depicts a male figure, reflecting the more active side of contemporary symbolism.[76]

Preisler's great decorative sense, which he so notably applied in *Autumn*, consisted above all in how he organically combined new inspiration from abroad with his sensitive treatment of scenes from his homeland. Preisler had already demonstrated this ability in 1896, in a large triptych drawn in charcoal for which he had won a prize from the magazine *Světozor*. He titled it *Easter*. It shows a young swineherd sitting enraptured in an early spring landscape. Its derivation was in fact Neo-Baroque, but Preisler's depiction of the landscape with the sitting boy, astonished by his inner visions, belonged equally to the Secession. At the same time, as was often stressed, this stylised landscape was taken from a real landscape in the vicinity of Popovice, near Králův Dvůr, Preisler's birthplace and childhood home. Here the style came not just from a model, but above all from a certain emotional consistency that also sought the imaginary paradise of "sacred groves" in the real paradise of lost childhood.

Although in the latter half of the 1890s young Czech figure painting began from a position of intense idealism and still displayed numerous aspects of late Romanticism, this quite quickly gave way to greater realism. Ideality persisted as an essential abstract and generalising element, but explicitly imaginary figures were gradually abandoned. While Preisler's *Spring Evening* from 1898 may have had an Icarus-like winged nude lying in a birch grove at dusk, the painting's atmosphere was created more by the colours of nature, where the idealised figure served only to channel literary associations.

Švabinský had already indicated the direction he would take with *Communion of Souls*, where the artist's own face was at the centre of the painting. In 1897 he painted *Circular Portrait*, depicting his fiancée, Ela Vejrychová. Three years later it would win him an honorary diploma at the Exposition Universelle in Paris. It is one of the Czech Secession's most cogent paintings, principally in the way it presents new content. The painting was based on the newly established theme of man and nature, but it discreetly transformed them into what looked like a conventional portrait. The young woman is sitting in an arbour of vine leaves, but this bacchanalian note is countered by the almost photographic treatment of form. She herself has this same inner polarity: the sense of melancholy in her pose is combined with a fresh corporeality, while her unflinching gaze is testimony to her strong will. The colours also have this polarity in the harmonious interplay of violet and green. The overall impression is one of nostalgia, as was typical at the time, but beneath the tranquillity of the forms a powerful emotional life

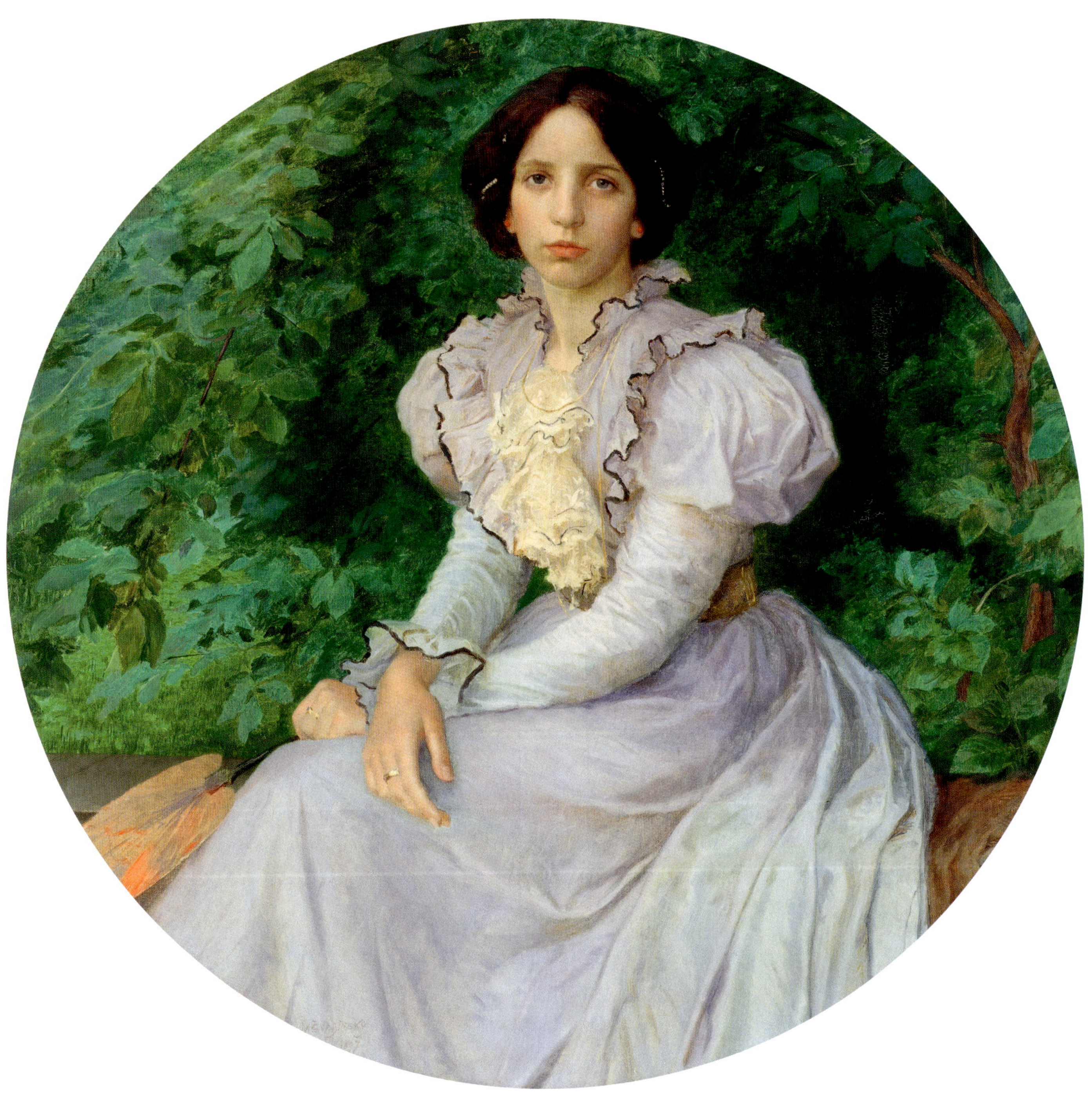

92 Maxmilián Švabinský, *Circular Portrait*, 1897, oil, 105.5 cm

stirs. The significance of *Circular Portrait* went beyond the portrait genre, for it demonstrated that poetry could be seen not just in imaginary forms, but also in real ones.

These examples of figure painting confirm just how much importance was attached to landscape as the framework for a new externalisation. Švabinský and Preisler were also sensitive landscape painters, and their lightness of expression can be largely credited to professional landscape painting, which had opened the eyes of figure painters and subsequently the general public to a new way of seeing landscape. The flourishing of landscape painting in the 1890s was primarily due to how the overall concept for the genre was changing. While pictures of landscapes on the walls of bourgeois households had previously been mostly small and intimate, the painters of the National Theatre generation had included landscape in their grand conceptual programmes. In the 1890s, landscape painting belonged to neither one nor the other tendency, although the degree of personal involvement on the part of both painters and consumers was substantially larger. Landscape painting's ambitions were in fact greater, for now it sought to encompass contemporary man in his entirety. This demanding enterprise required a fairly broad basis from which the new landscape painting could grow. Old concepts such as views from close up or from afar were in some way reconciled, and there was a move towards a perspective that sought to overcome the traditional distance between viewer and landscape dictated by the convention of the frame and the relationship between foreground and background. These paintings' formats accordingly became larger and larger, and by the end of the 1890s they had assumed dimensions that had previously been highly unusual for the genre.

Landscape painting was also influenced by photography, and this explains the seemingly chilly correctness and muted colours that characterised a number of paintings from the mid-1890s. These paintings were also related to the idea of "metropolitan refinement" that we have already encountered in architecture and sculpture. One such painting was *Meadow with Trees* from 1895 by Václav Radimský, who had studied in Munich and Vienna. However, beneath this mask, the picturesque remained alluring. In Radimský's case this became apparent when he subsequently joined Claude Monet's circle in France. There, in Giverny, Radimský painted according to what he had learned from Monet's late work. Although these paintings made him for a time the most progressive Czech landscape painter, it is interesting that his impact on Czech painting was not so great as to be truly groundbreaking. He may have encouraged Slavíček to liberate his brushwork and colour, but most probably because Radimský was not in direct contact with the group of Mařák's pupils who represented the core of the new Czech landscape painting, or because the influence of Monet was too apparent and soon resulted in the ostentatious use of the new luminous colours, Radimský ultimately remained a peripheral figure in Czech painting. Although Mařák's pupils liked to cite the realism of Antonín Chittussi's paintings, in reality the original Romantic element played a major role. Initially they were interested not so much in the analytical French Impressionists as in painters from Central Europe or Scotland, or the American painter Alexander Harrison. Like them, these painters emphasised an emotional relationship with landscape that drew on Romanticism's attachment to nature.

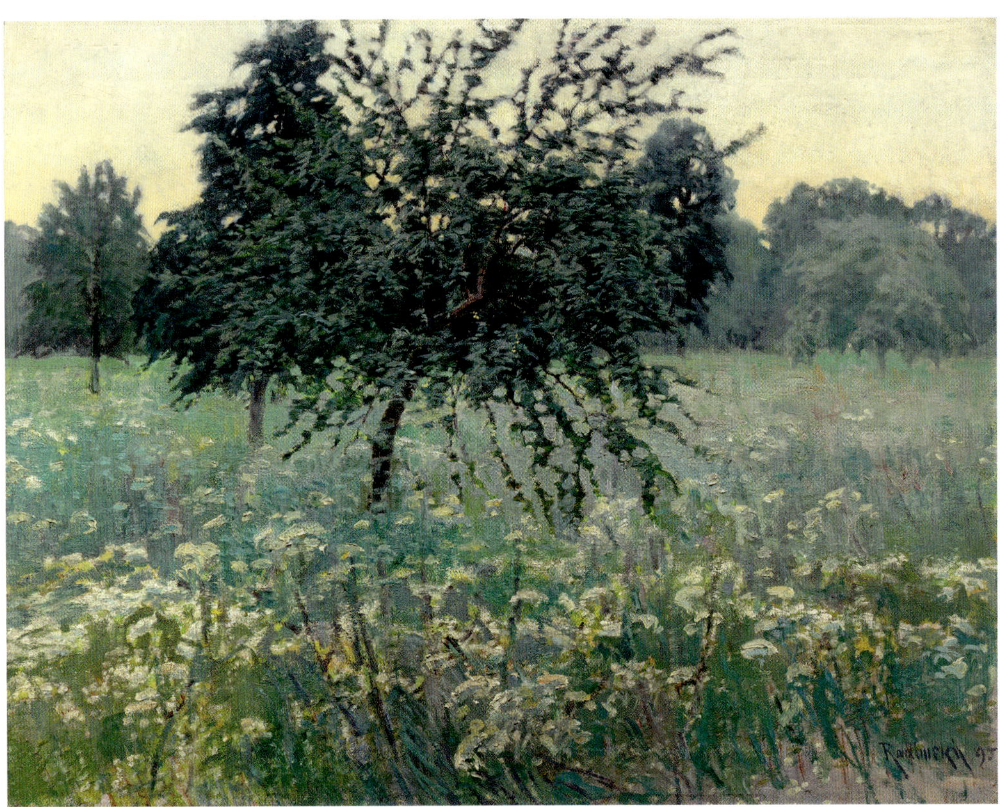

Plein-air painting now dominated, and the landscape artist would no longer go to nature merely for a picturesque motif, but for an entire painting. Here too the essence consisted in sensing nature's moods and trying to find a correspondence between the artist's state of mind and the configuration of forms and colours in a landscape. The very word "mood" became a favourite with painters and art critics alike, and in the first issue of *Volné směry* Jaroslav Kvapil noted Jan Neruda's lament that the young were "all moods and no thought."[77] What the older generation saw as a shortcoming, the younger generation considered something that encapsulated the content they gave their paintings, and an inalienable expression of their world view. K. B. Mádl used the word to explain the artist's creative method not just when looking at landscapes, but also when looking at architecture. In his account of Kotěra's Italian drawings, Mádl wrote, "They come out of a particular mood. He is not concerned with a false reconstruction of old architecture … he is simply relating his architectural dreams and fantasies for a specific site, or a site he is searching for, and its surroundings." In 1899 one of the most capable contemporary theoreticians, Alois Riegl, published an essay called "Mood as the Content of Modern Art" in the journal *Die Graphischen Künste* (The Graphic Arts), which was also read by Czech modernists. In his essay, Riegl used the example of contemporary landscape painting to illustrate a broadly based concept of mood as something fundamental to the modern world view, which sought a new harmony between emancipated, rational knowledge and the faith that knowledge had

93 Václav Radimský, *Meadow with Trees*, 1895, oil, 65 × 81 cm

marginalised but which remained indestructible. This harmony was based on the idea of man as the final link in the evolution of the universe.[78]

Riegl's speculative account reveals the hopes that were invested in the new emotionality and its ability to take possession of the world through a visual image. This was a response that opposed the positivistic understanding of the world simply as a conglomeration of material facts to be employed in logical reasoning, and in the name of the new art it sought to restore the lost equilibrium between thought and emotion – at first, primarily to the benefit of emotion, which had been neglected.

As a fleeting state of mind, mood belonged to the art of nuances and halftones that contemporary Symbolism celebrated. Its changeability was a manifestation of the constant flow of emotions and impressions, and contemporary modern artists wanted to reflect this. The same idea reigned in literature, and the first volumes of *Volné směry*, which had large literature sections, reveal young painting's broader cultural framework. In the poems and short stories published in *Volné směry*, we often encounter a troubled protagonist, poisoned by civilisation's toxicity, who seeks to soothe his emotional turmoil in nature, in the experience of its ever-changing echo. The subjectivity of this position was compensated by the expansive range of new sensations and impressions that substantially enriched this epoch's visual vocabulary. This represented a break with classical idealism, which kept art within the confines of traditional allegories and "ideas," and it held out an opportunity for a new externalisation on an incomparably broader and more diverse basis.

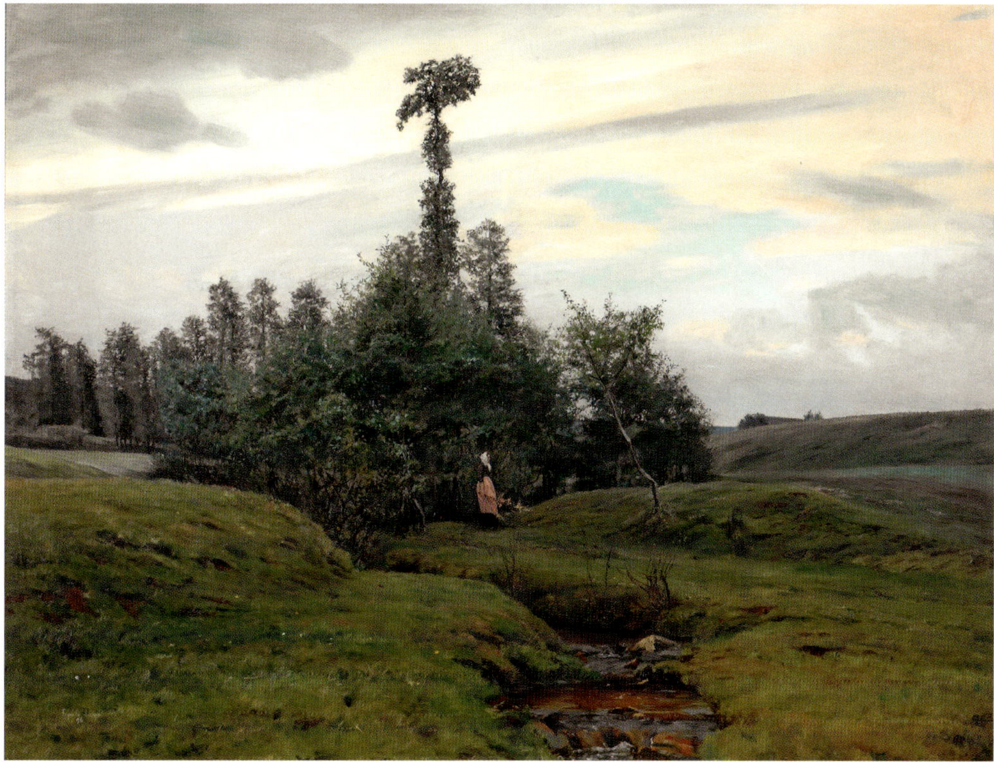

94 František Kaván, *Flowing*, 1896, oil, 102 × 132 cm

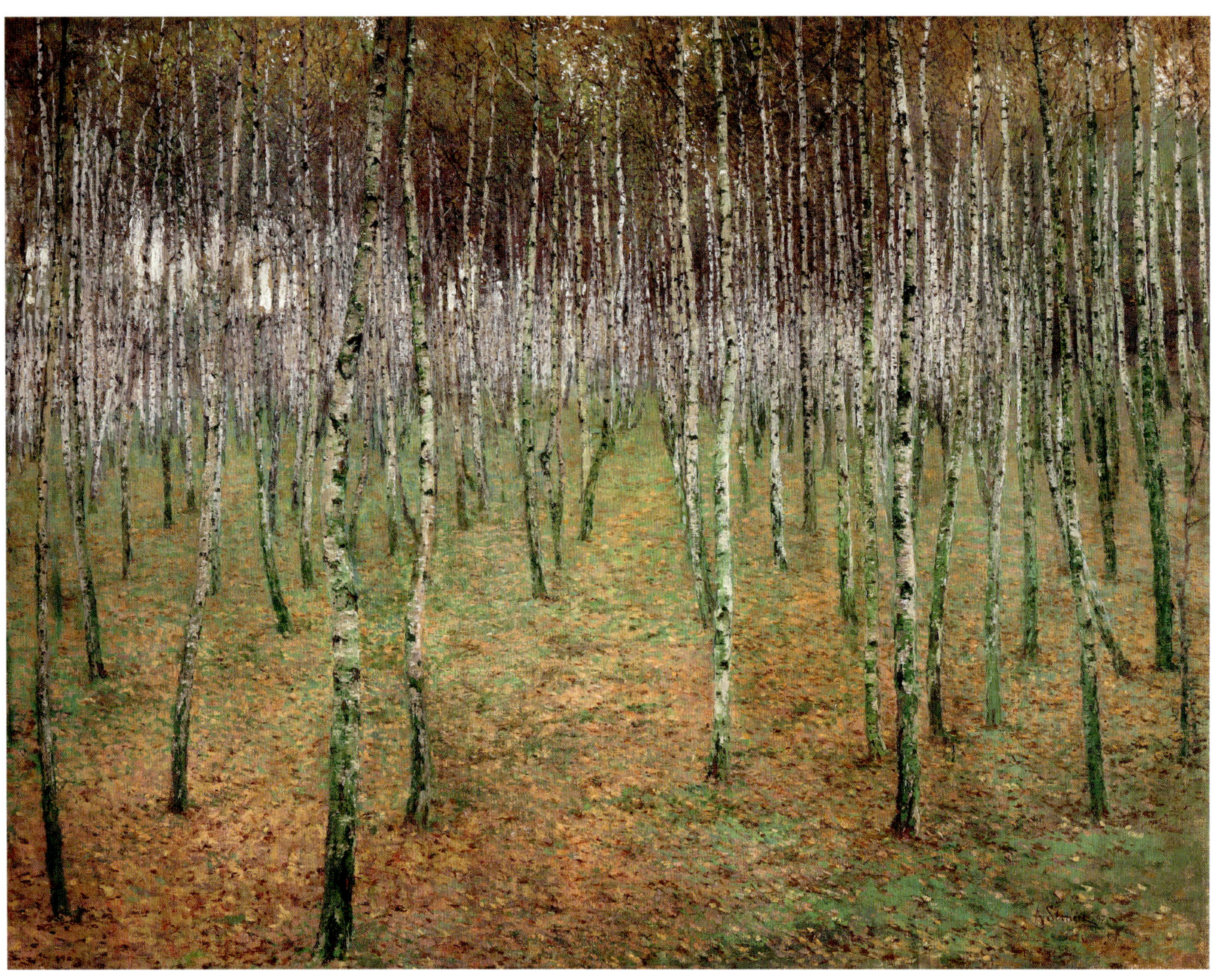

95 Antonín Slavíček, *Birch Mood*, 1897, oil, 91.5 × 114.5 cm

This parting with the old world was accompanied by a melancholy that was both typical of the contemporary mentality and an expression of a naive and "pure" sensibility. It was apparent in young artists' frequent personal crises, which were especially prevalent in the 1890s, a decade that fostered a predilection for extremes. Yet this predilection was still overlaid by the requirement for appropriate social behaviour, which only magnified the general sense of moral and social crisis. This tended to afflict the most talented young artists: Antonín Slavíček briefly retreated to an abbey in Rajhrad; Otakar Lebeda took his own life. This period was full of such incidents, and they affected artists working in all disciplines. Contemporary art should therefore be understood as a certain form of mental hygiene, an escape valve to release accumulated pressures that largely originated outside art itself. This was all supported by the thesis of a painting as a mirror of "moods," and the identification of artistic expression with an artist's state of mind. Yet this thesis also complicated such an understanding, because in return it subjugated art to emotional subjectivism. This dual role of "mood" in the art of the 1890s would later have to be corrected. However, its direct outcome was the emergence of art that was unparalleled in the urgency of its intimacy.

The turbulent psyches of young landscape painters were drawn to nature in states that eluded any static depiction. The transitional seasons, spring and autumn, and the transitional times of day, morning and evening, were subjects that had a deeper meaning. Autumn retained nature's colourful profusion while evoking the melancholy of life coming to an end, which made it a favourite theme in the period immediately after the midpoint of the 1890s, when this new generation's character was becoming more clearly defined. This preoccupation could be explained not just in terms of the need for psychological release, but also as a reflection of how art had to respond to the exaggerated forms and colours of the Baroque Revival, the most recent form of eclectic historicism, which called for a modulation that was essential in developing the Secession's stylistic concept.

In 1897 Antonín Slavíček painted two such paintings, the most eloquent works from this phase, in the chateau park in Veltrusy and at Hvězda in Prague. While for *Autumn in the Mist* Slavíček still used a cart as staffage in the alley of trees to create an impression of the inexorable passing of time, *Birch Mood* required no such inventory, although this substantially complicated Slavíček's task. The trunks of the birch trees themselves create the rhythm of the picture plane, and this seemingly simple view of a birch wood already has the Secession's stylistic character, as is evident in the way this kind of frontal view of a forest became a motif to which landscape painters would constantly return in large-format works throughout the Secession era.[79] The apparent monotony of the motif places great demands on a decorative sense of form and a feel for colour, which has to resonate within the nuances of a limited range with no dramatic effects. We can see in Slavíček a similar progression from late Romanticism to the Secession that we find in the figure painters Preisler and Švabinský.

It is important to recognise that the works we are now happy to label "Secession" were not created simply by relaying motifs the artists had seen and appropriated elsewhere. This new quality arose organically from their creators' need for expression,

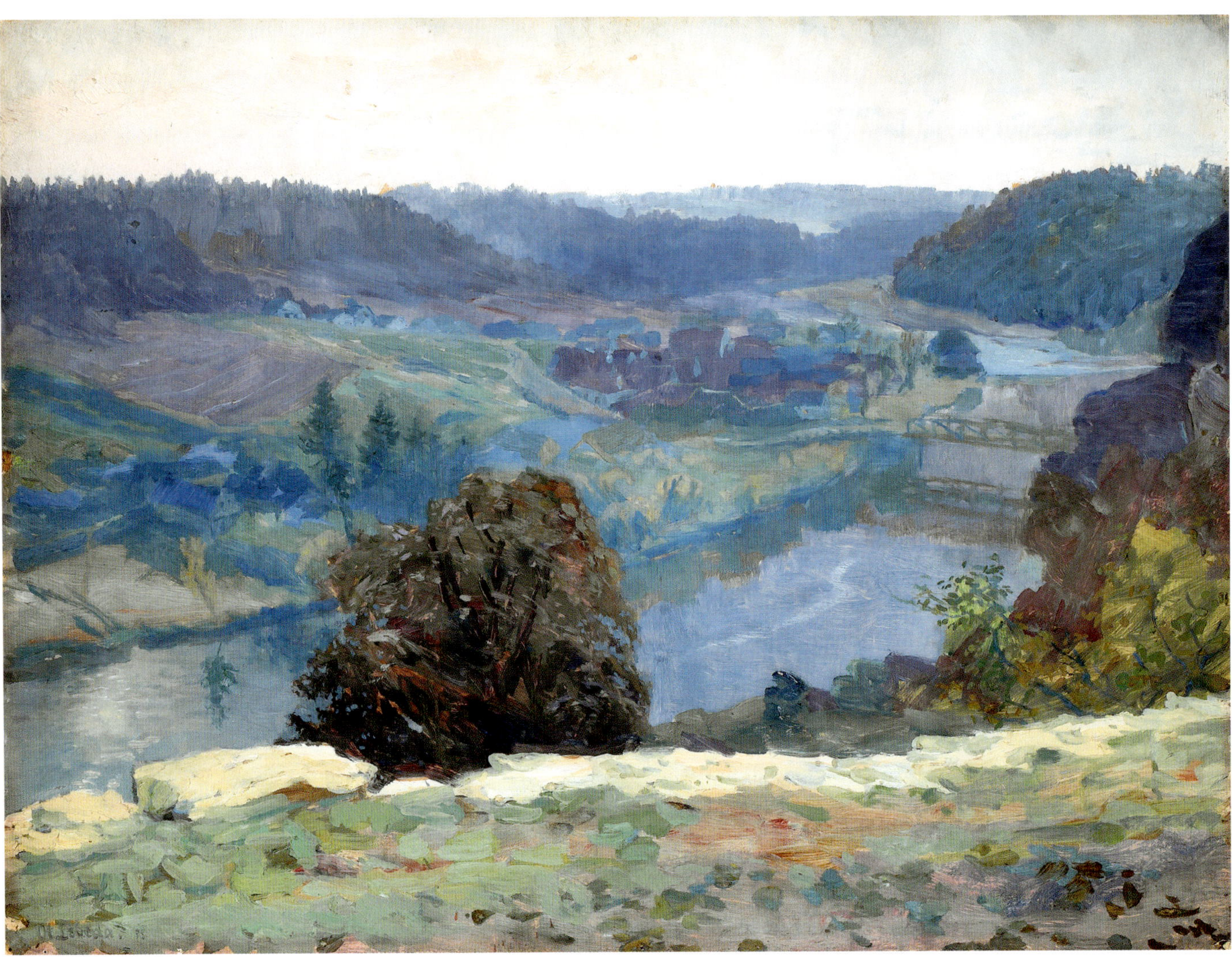

the outcome of an artistic maturing in which each found a unique but also a common vocabulary. In this context, we should expand on what was said earlier about the contemporary artistic neurosis. Artistic emotionality was far from being a final or mature state of mind: it was more a fever that accompanied the inception of the new art, a kind of puberty. Maturity only came with the mastering of this inner turmoil, and this mastering, expressed in artistic terms, also led to the emergence of the new style. Any subsequent Neo-Baroque and late Romantic relapses were merely points at which, for whatever reason, artists lost control of their emotionality and could not use their energy productively. A new artistic spirit that truly belonged to the modern age took shape between the extremes of tempestuousness and ennui.

Slavíček's companions from Mařák's school achieved similar results in their work from the 1890s, although not often with the same assurance. Following a period of realistic views of the panorama of the Iron Mountains (*The Air of Home*, 1895), František

96 Otakar Lebeda, *Above the River Lužnice*, 1899, oil, 50.5 × 66 cm

Kaván turned to more intimate and languidly painted scenes from the edges of forests. His *Flowing* from 1896 was based on the contemporary lyrical view of nature, which fostered a greater sensitivity to this atmospheric landscape, to the discreet decorative stylisation of the clusters of trees, and to the Symbolist motif announced in the painting's title and contained in the stream welling from the ground. Kaván also wrote "decadent" poems, and he was especially influenced by Karel Hlaváček from the *Moderní revue* circle, to the extent that he painted a number of landscapes paraphrasing Symbolist poems. He was criticised by Julius Mařák for his interest in such themes, which led Kaván to quit his school at the beginning of 1896.[80]

In the autumn of the previous year, one of the most promising younger landscape painters, Otakar Lebeda, had accompanied Kaván to the ponds around the town of Třeboň in Southern Bohemia. Lebeda's resulting sombre and melancholy works were criticised as "decadent and black painting." He worked alongside first Kaván and then Slavíček, but created his own style that was primarily derived from his particular psychological disposition. Lebeda travelled widely, driven by an inner restlessness, and his oeuvre has few sunlit paintings and many melancholy ones. Initially their colours were dark, but later they became aggressively bold. His brushwork similarly become more emphatic, and in his final years he composed his paintings from numerous brief brushstrokes, or broadly fashioned a likeness of a landscape using a brush soaked in thick and heavy paint.

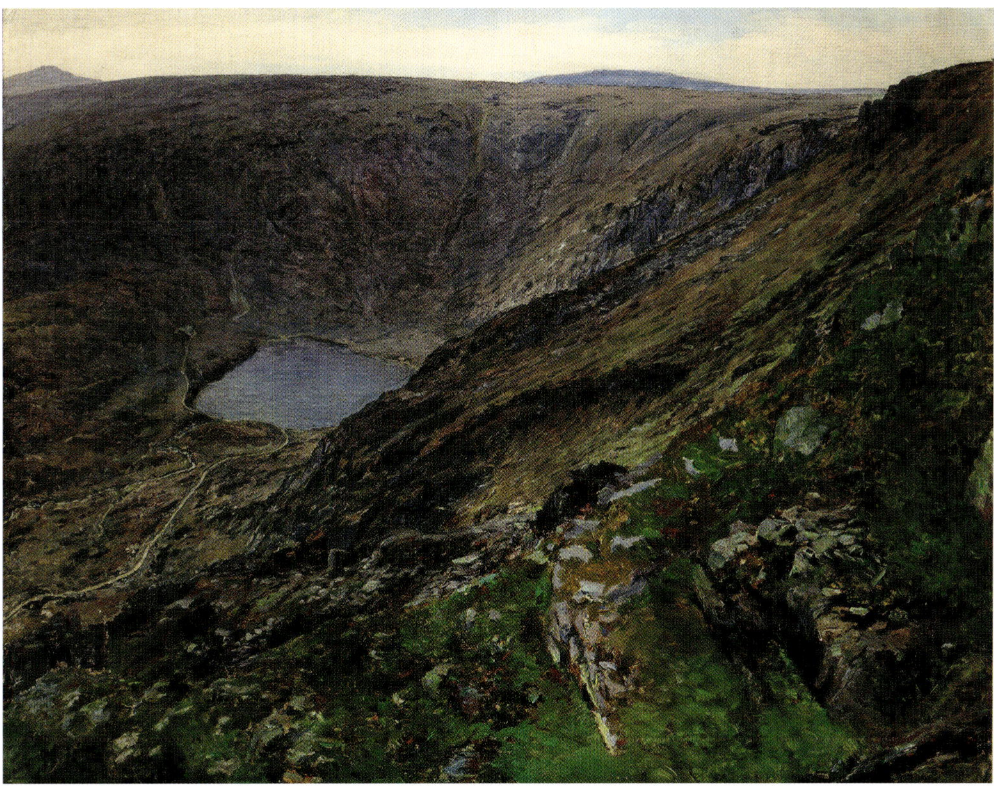

97 Otakar Lebeda, *Tarn*, 1896, oil, 78 × 98 cm

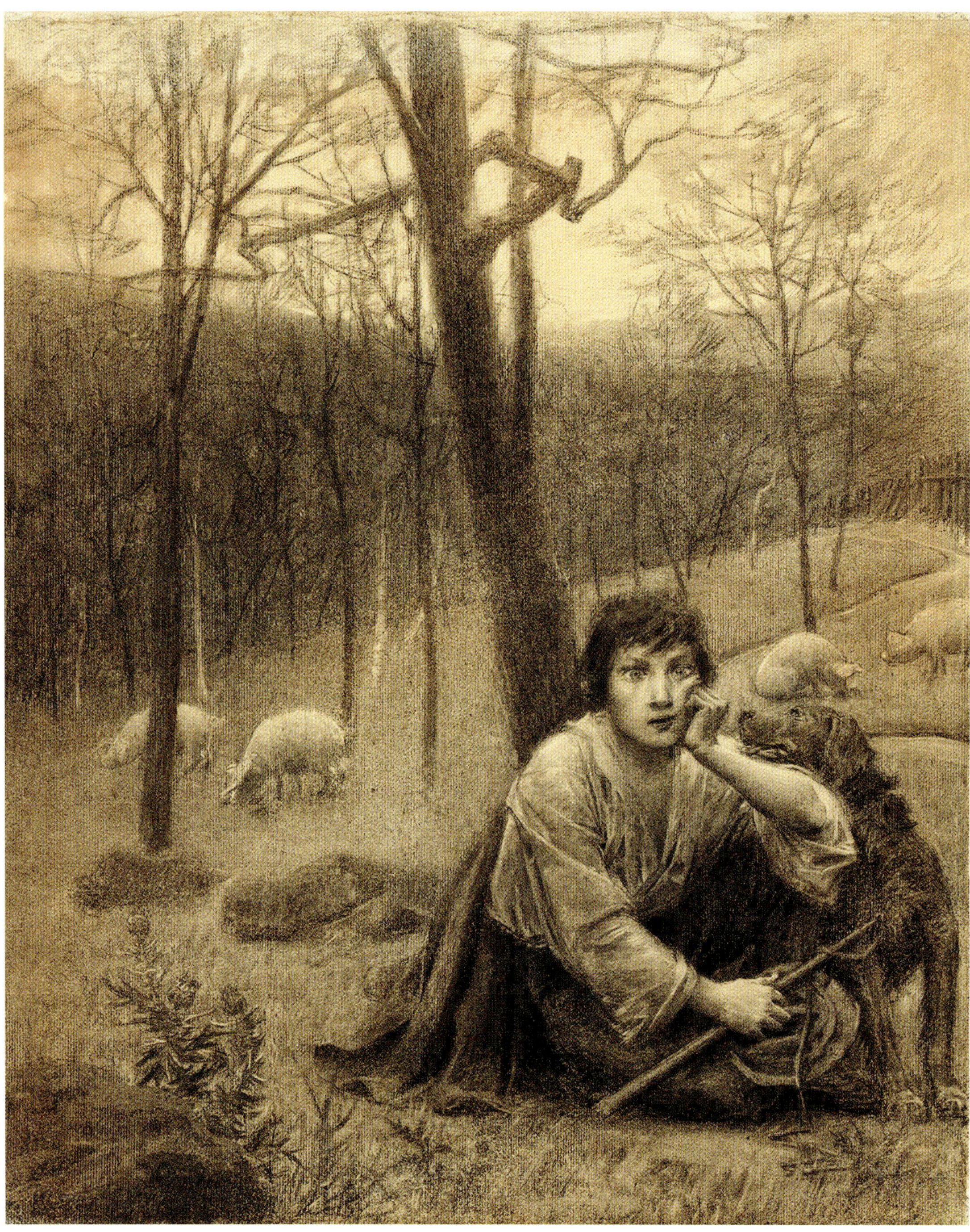

98 Jan Preisler, *Easter*, centre of the triptych, 1897, charcoal, 55 × 43 cm

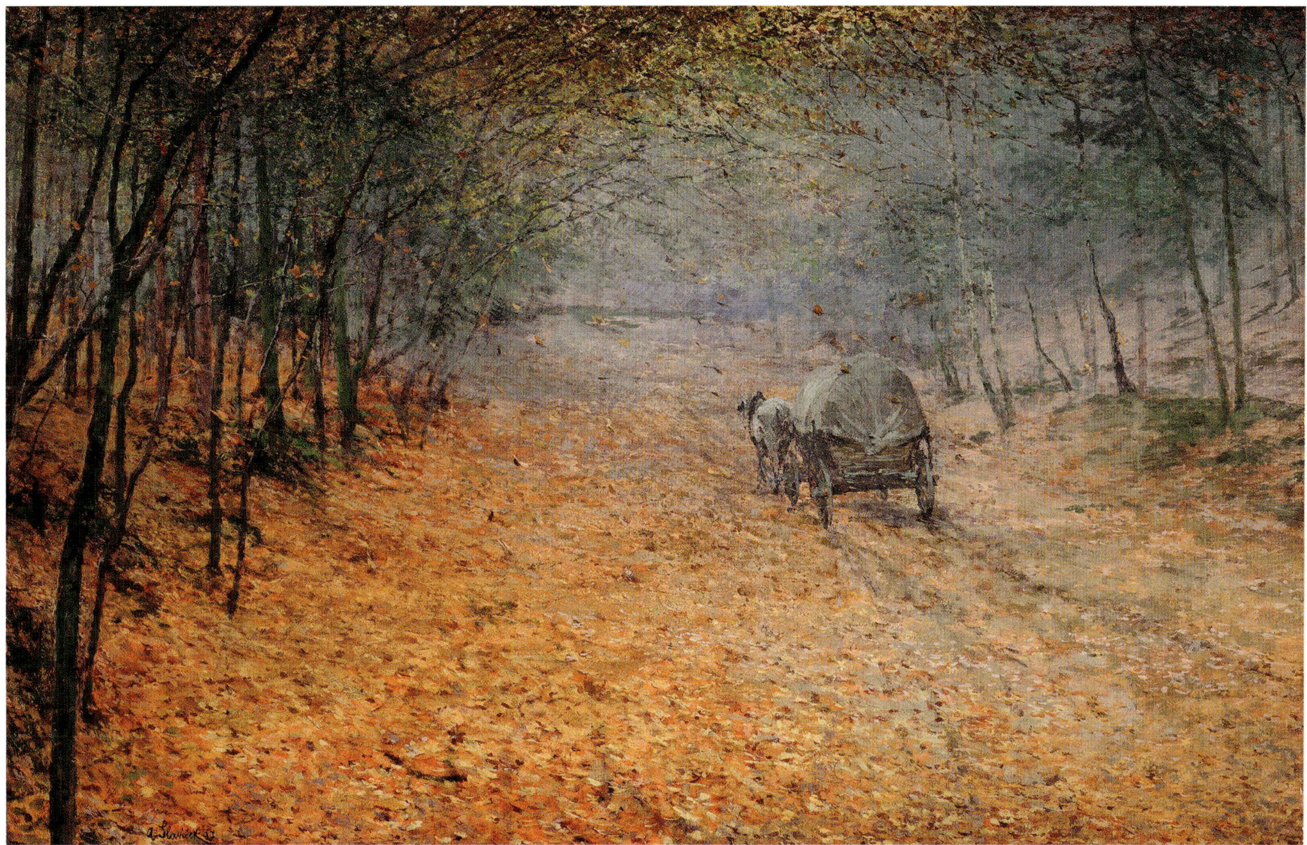

With his fondness for painting scenes from the Giant Mountains (*Tarn*, 1896), Lebeda cultivated a habit of viewing a landscape from above, and this would remain typical of his work. When Mařák's school vacationed in Okoř, Lebeda would leave the group to go and paint alone. Depictions of landscapes became a way of reflecting his emotional state. In the last two years of his life, Lebeda's paintings documented his struggle with his incipient mental illness. After the nostalgia and pastel colours of his hazy views of a bridge over a river flowing tranquilly in the early evening (*Above the River Lužnice*, 1899) – painted in Bechyně, where his thoughts may have been with his late friend, the sculptor František Hošek[81] – Lebeda turned ever more urgently to the reality he saw in the dramatic union of man and earth. His final paintings were an attempt to demolish the contemporary artistic neurosis, but at the cost of an extreme and self-destructive act.

The way out of the crisis of the new emotionality had to be sought in a more sublimated way. For this reason, Lebeda's artistic legacy seemed to his contemporaries to be incomplete, although its other artistic contexts were much more complicated. The need to confront the imagination with reality was also prompted by Hynais's *The Judgement of Paris*, which was finally put on public display in 1898, at an exhibition organised by Krasoumná jednota. For its treatment of coloured light and shadow, the

99 Antonín Slavíček, *Autumn in the Mist*, 1897, Syntonos paint, 68 × 101.5 cm

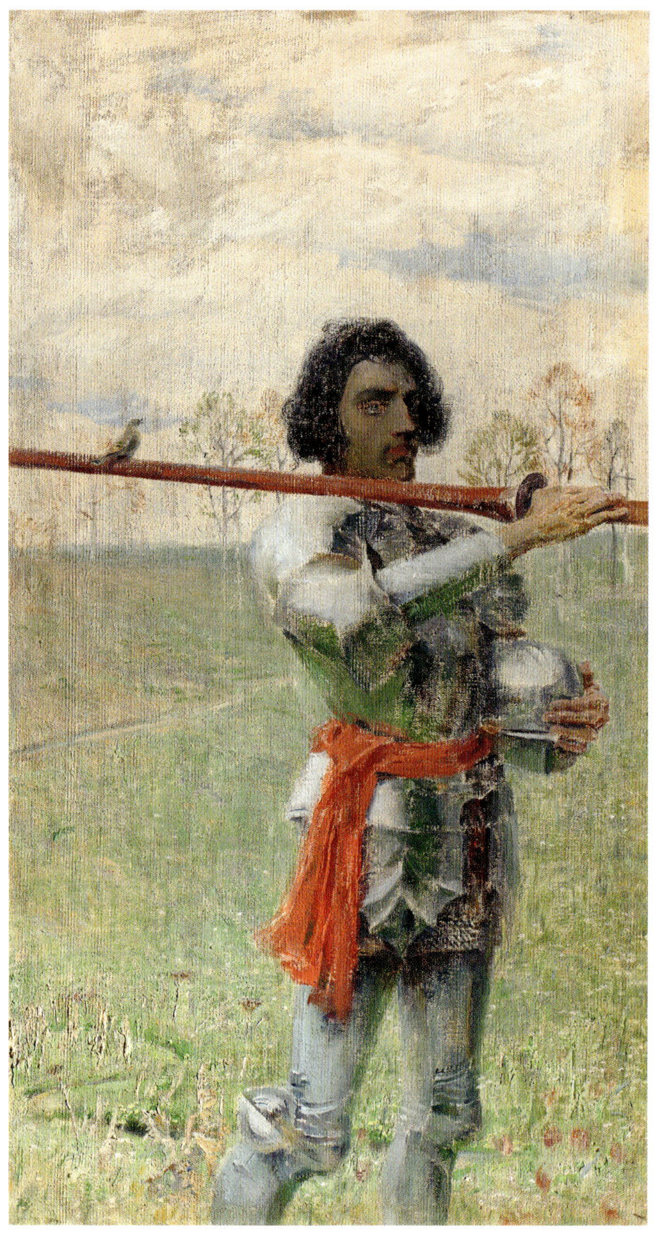

painting was considered the last word in modern art. We can see from Jan Preisler's work from this time how much he admired Hynais's painting, and under its influence he modulated his earlier imaginative Symbolism. Preisler's palette became brighter, and he now painted fresh landscape studies that included *The Thaw*, the first idea for his later painting *Spring*, while in his cycle *The Adventurous Knight* he attempted to create a larger work.

A sketch has been preserved that reveals the cycle's structure. Unlike the conventional triptychs that were still so popular, the rhythm of the paintings here is different.

100 Jan Preisler, Study for the cycle *The Adventurous Knight*, 1898, oil, 87.5 × 46 cm

The two main paintings at the centre present a contrast: in the painting on the left, naked wild women try to seduce the knight, while the painting on the right shows a calmer scene, with a view of the horizon and the knight sitting melancholically, while behind him is a seated female figure who perhaps personifies his soul, or desire. These central paintings are symmetrically framed by a painting of the knight-errant and allegorical figures, although between them are narrow sections of "mood" landscape painting. The horizon in these paintings is at the same height, suggesting that, like literature and music, the cycle was meant to be read from left to right.

While the sketch is stylistically uniform, in the surviving larger-format studies a certain disparity emerges. Hynais's Luminism was applied to a theme that contemporary art had taken from late Romanticism, but the green reflections on the knight-errant's armour and face seem highly incongruous, and this was probably why Preisler ultimately abandoned the cycle. If Preisler's attempt to combine an imaginary scene with a naturalistic form was unsuccessful here, the problem was one that continued to weigh on the painter's mind in his subsequent work. Both elements had equal value: the imaginary for its capacity for figurative generalisation and freedom of imagination, and the naturalistic for its sensuality of form. What was lacking was a connection between them that would bring both into a higher and unified synthesis. *The Adventurous Knight* cycle provided Preisler with several stimuli. There was the motif of seduction, which in numerous variations became a key theme in his oeuvre. His work on the cycle also revealed the internal opposition between expressive and compositional elements that were either dynamic or static, and this was one of the fundamental syntactical problems not just for Preisler but for all nascent Secession art. Another way to read the cycle is as a diptych, with three paintings on either side. The left side is more mobile and dramatic, while the right is calmer and more static. The left side also owes more to the effects of Hynais's Luminism, and stylistically it is therefore closer to the Baroque Revival, while in the right side we sense a new decorative arrangement of the picture plane that is more aligned with Preisler's mature work. The diptych aspect also corresponds to the intimate mood of this work, inviting solitary contemplation of the story.[82]

Preisler's arrangement sought to overcome the conventional triptych to approximate Symbolist literature, which treated narrative as a free-flowing sequence of poetic events without the customary moralistic conclusion. This sequence was in fact endless, or constantly recurring, as was human life itself. This idea guided Preisler's illustrations for Zeyer's poem *The Song of the Sorrow of the Good Young Man Roman Vasilich*, printed at the end of the third volume of *Volné směry* in 1901. The very title of *Painting from a Larger Cycle*, also created at this time, demonstrates how the understanding of the cycle had gradually changed. Ultimately, the cycle as the 19th century had understood it (as a rigidly structured sequence of images depicting the key events in the hero's life, or as an exhaustive account of all the modalities of a particular concept, as in the classic cycle of the four seasons) was abandoned. Now the cycle was life in its entirety, and the artist attempted to capture its endless changeability in a poetic image, a symbol that had no exact meanings or associations.

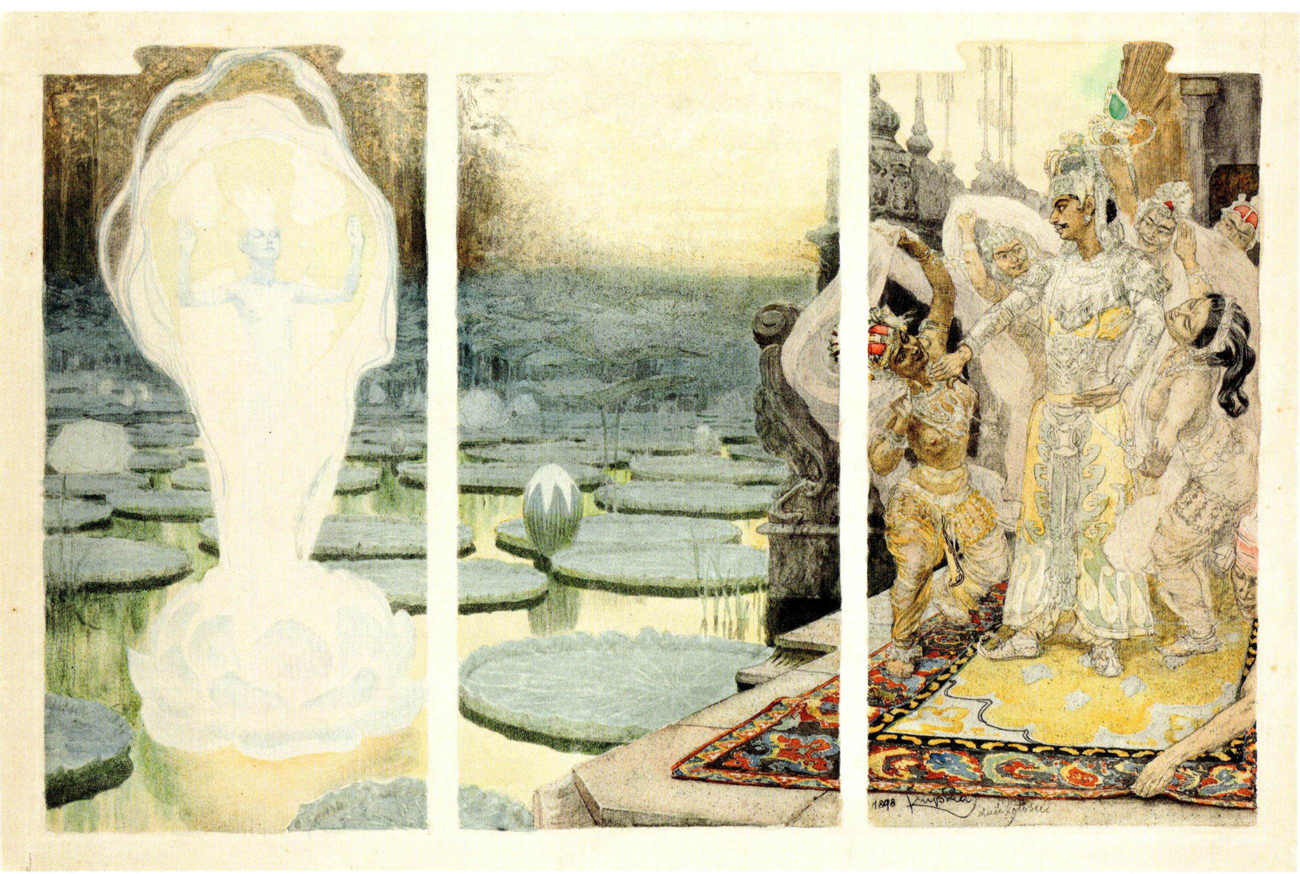

This then raised the essential question of finding a form for the psyche's endless dynamism. The whole Secession was in fact directed towards this end, and solutions were sought in accentuating the tension between form and content, in the paradox of the static nature of a painting and the dynamism of its semantic context, and in the demand that viewers engage their empathy and imagination to let the immobile mask of a painting resonate. This was what Preisler was seeking: not illustration, but a grand and monumental form. The new decorative stasis in the right half of his cycle *The Adventurous Knight* had already appeared in *Remembrance* (1898), where Preisler illustrated his own melancholy poem. In it, a meadow with birch trees creates a decorative unity with the heads of a man and a woman who are characteristically viewed en face and in profile. The drawing is executed in the mature Secession style. Preisler's success was unquestionably due to his sensitive balancing of naturalistic, Symbolist, and decorative elements. Just how animated this question was can be seen in *The Lotus Soul*, a watercolour by František Kupka from the same year (1898). By now, Kupka had been in Paris for three years, where he had achieved recognition as an illustrator, which was the most viable way of earning a living. The watercolour's subject was taken from the interest in exoticism and Indian philosophy that Symbolism had stimulated. The format was a standard triptych, but, as with Preisler, the contrast between the wings –

101 František Kupka, *The Lotus Soul*, 1898, watercolour, 38.5 × 57.7 cm

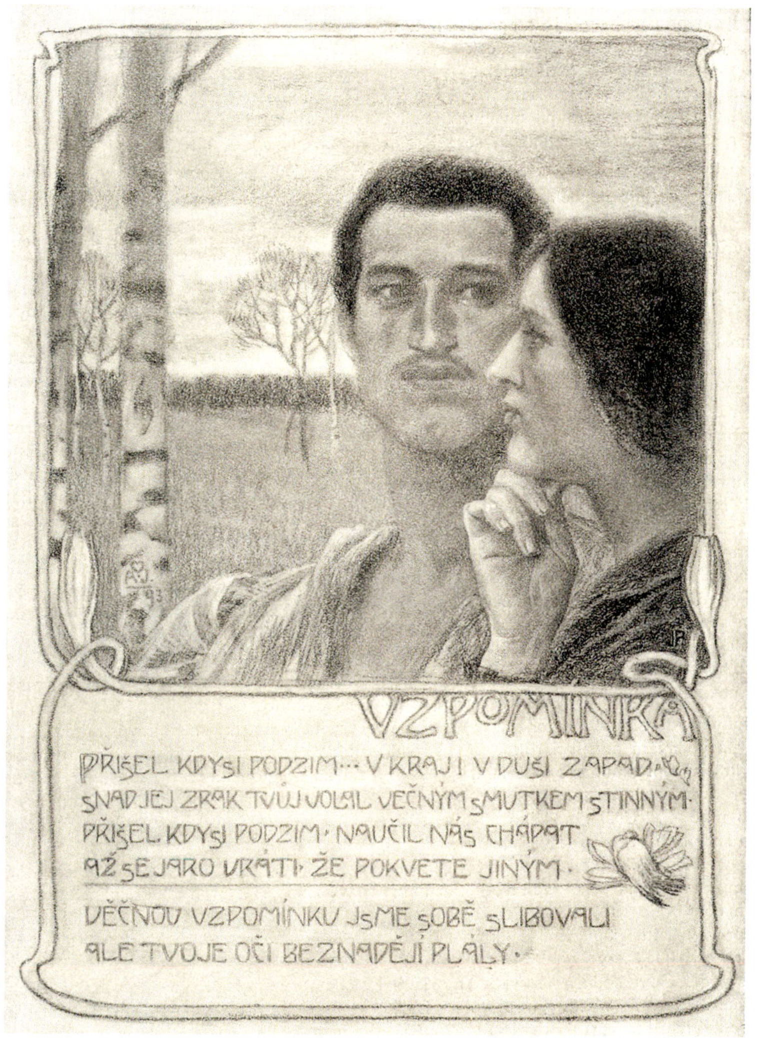

one expressing worldly sensuality and the other pure spirituality – gave it more the character of a diptych. This was achieved by excluding from the narrative the central section, a view of a body of water covered with waterlilies, vanishing into the mist. Another interesting correspondence is that both painters worked with the motif of seduction, although in Kupka's watercolour it is treated more epically. The contrast between the wings is also much sharper with Kupka than with Preisler, both in the content, where two entirely disparate worlds are presented, and in the form, where the academic composition of the seduction scene is juxtaposed with the luminous lotus soul, depicted in the Parisian Art Nouveau style. The transition between them is achieved by the mood landscape in the central section, which is quite indispensable to the composition. This "empty" interval expresses the hero's inner desire: in his melancholy, it is the bridge between him and his ideal. The triptych reflects the old division of man into mind, body, and soul, viewed in wholly contemporary terms.

102 Jan Preisler, *Remembrance*, 1898, charcoal, 60 × 45 cm

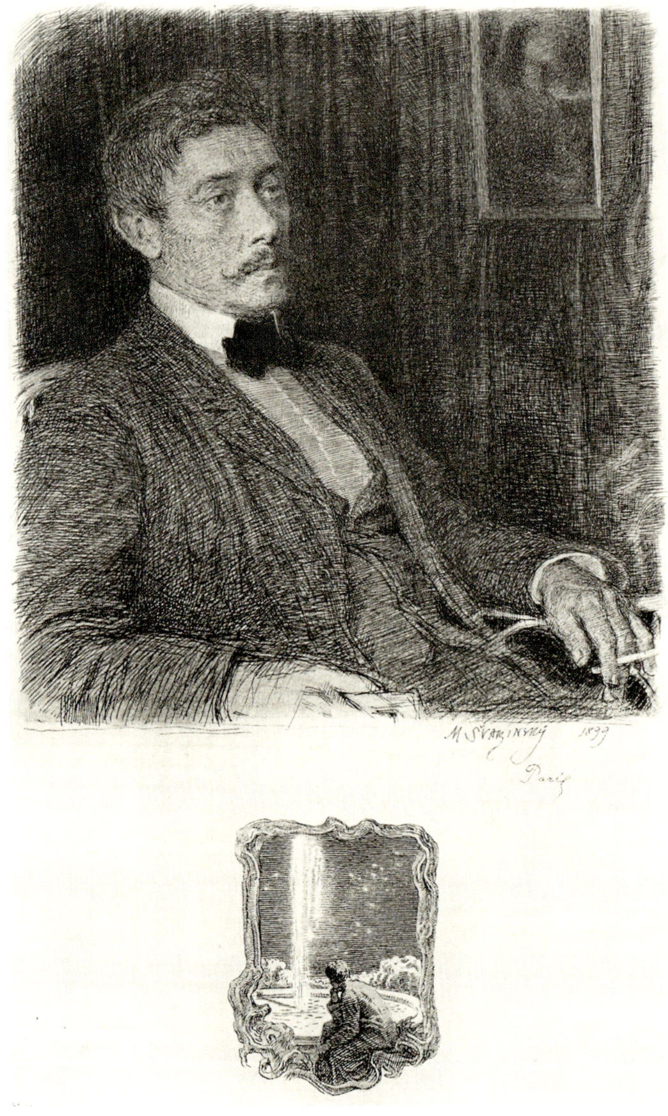

However, *The Lotus Soul* seems more an illustration than a painting. Any social cachet the watercolour may have earned Kupka did not have any great significance for him, as he emphasised in his large painting *The Book Lover* (1896–98), an ironic view of literary absorption that underlined the insistency of life, both in the scene itself and in its luminous and naturalistic rendition. This discrepancy between Kupka the painter and Kupka the illustrator shows how he had yet to achieve a stylistic balance. Perhaps he was bothered by his almost excessively flawless draughtsmanship, but the main reason surely lay deeper still, in the controversy that was the essence of the man and his art and would ultimately lead Kupka to a radical rejection of all "conventional" painting.

Although Symbolism's influence had now receded in France,[83] Symbolist works and authors would continue to attract Czech artists. This was apparent in Maxmilián

103 Maxmilián Švabinský, *Maurice Maeterlinck*, 1899, Indian ink, 25.8 × 22.7 cm

Švabinský's portrait of the Belgian poet and playwright Maurice Maeterlinck, which he evidently drew while studying in Paris. The duality between the realistic portrait of the daydreaming poet and the idealised depiction of his vision, framed in a small vignette, made this pen drawing typical of its time. Maeterlinck similarly underpinned the stylised, ethereal visions of his "neomysticism" with his own psychological experience, and he based the dramatic effect of his best works on the impossibility of achieving the ideal of a purer, higher life. It was for this quality that F. X. Šalda had praised Maeterlinck's play *Aglavaine and Sélysette* in 1897 as his finest work yet, comparing him to Gerhart Hauptmann:

> Both plays express modern man's powerful and urgent desire for a life that is purer, higher, greater, more intense and more joyous, but both also express man's weakness, how unready he is for this third realm of the Soul, his fear and dread, the horror of this interim period and the anguish of trial and error.[84]

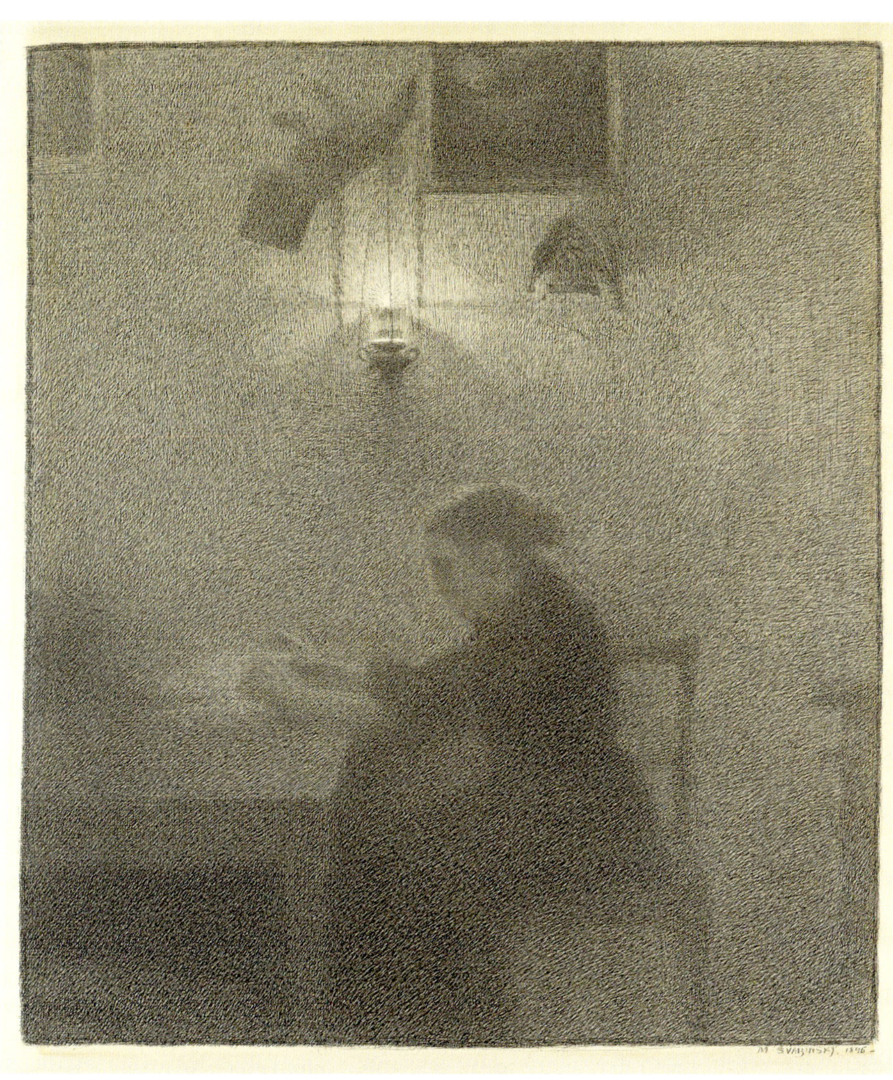

104 Maxmilián Švabinský, *Old Pavlína Stripping Feathers*, 1896, Indian ink, 57.6 × 45.5 cm

This again demonstrates how the key development in the late 1890s was the conflict between naturalism and idealism, and the seeking of its synthetic resolution. It was important that both tendencies could assume various forms, some of which were more amenable to the new need for synthesis and others not at all. When the young artists of SVU Mánes refused to exhibit paintings by Vojtěch Bartoněk, whose *Conscripts* from the late 1880s had been celebrated for the bravura of its naturalism, and declared the painter a failure,[85] they distanced themselves from any naturalism that was merely descriptive. On the other hand, however, their enthusiasm for Emil Holárek (whose cycle of drawings *Catechism* they had reproduced in the second volume of *Volné směry*) also soon flagged, for he had remained a mere imitator of late Romanticism. Only an artistic take on naturalism following the example of Hynais, and a deeper form of idealism that encompassed Symbolist introspection and psychological concerns, could comprise a more suitable foundation for their quest for a modern art of their own making.

The combining of naturalism's sensuousness and attention to an empirically convincing real form with Symbolism's themes of "cosmic" melancholy brought a convergence of form and content, and ultimately a state in which typical psychological contents could resonate with natural phenomena, as in "mood" landscapes. Reality itself could be understood as something mysterious, in which the life of the human soul could be seen. Švabinský's masterful pen drawings, such as *Old Pavlína Stripping Feathers* from 1896, used black and white to create a mysterious sfumato, in which a scene from everyday life took on a poetic magic that transformed reality into a dreamlike state. It is interesting that in such transitional paintings, between naturalism and Symbolism, Czech artists found themselves alongside progressive artists who were truly influential. Švabinský's pen drawing can be compared to certain drawings by Georges Seurat, such as his portrait of his friend and fellow artist Edmond Aman-Jean (1883), although the latter remained much more accessible to Czech painters.

The young artists' emotionalism, a consequence of complicated social factors, found the first framework for its externalisation in a melancholy that sought solace in nature, and for this reason landscape painting also attracted figure painters, some of whom switched entirely to landscapes.

Antonín Hudeček had initially been taught by Pirner and Václav Brožík (the latter only taught rarely), before seeking enlightenment at the academies in Vienna and Munich, but it was not until he attended the landscape school in Okoř in the summer of 1897 that he found his way in painting. Hudeček had yet to abandon his original figure painting, and his sketchbooks from these years include a number of idealised themes. However, coming from the countryside himself, he found in landscape a subject that lent his ideas greater realism. In this respect, the evolution of his painting *November* (1897–98) was typical. In his sketchbook it was a vision of a female figure in a birch grove that recalled Preisler, while the finished painting showed a girl dressed in ordinary clothes amidst the autumn leaves, with the painter's original idea indicated only in the way she holds out her hands. Hudeček soon became known alongside the more robust Slavíček as a lyrical poet of nature's moods, as K. B. Mádl remarked in one of his reviews of the exhibitions that SVU Mánes held:

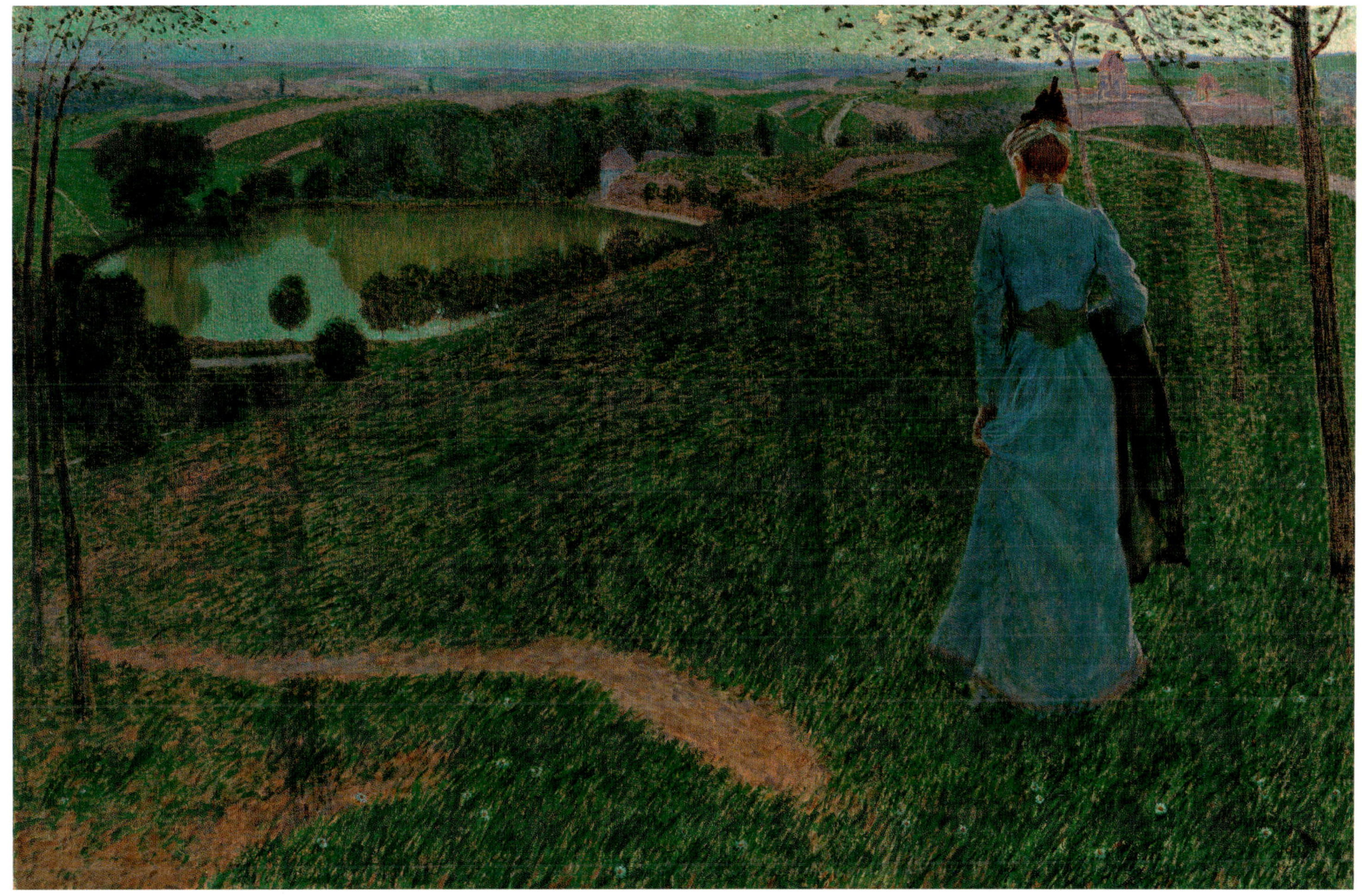

Only three years ago many of us shrugged our shoulders at Hudeček; now there is no need to argue that Antonín Hudeček is an intimate poet, a landscapist bard of whispered elegies who can capture with humble and straightforward means the magic of dusk, its almost mystical charm, in the simplest motifs of some overlooked spot by a pond. In his modest tones the landscape's quiet and contemplative soul slumbers, something of which a poet can sing only in the subtlest of verses.[86]

Hudeček's devices were not, of course, quite as simple as his paintings would seem to suggest, and herein lay his contribution to the development of Czech art. Hudeček adopted a method that drew loosely on French pointillism, covering the picture plane with brief brushstrokes to create a rich mosaic of diffused halftones. This resulted in a certain two-dimensionality and precluded expressive effects, but it also brought a new quality in the uniformity of the thin layer of paint. On this basis, the individual elements of a painting could create a whole that resonated with a single mood, conveyed by the colours and luminosity, and varying according to the time of day depicted. *Sunset* (1899), with its simple depiction of a reaper returning home at dusk beside a pond, is

105 Antonín Hudeček, *Stillness at Dusk*, 1900, oil, 120 × 180.5 cm

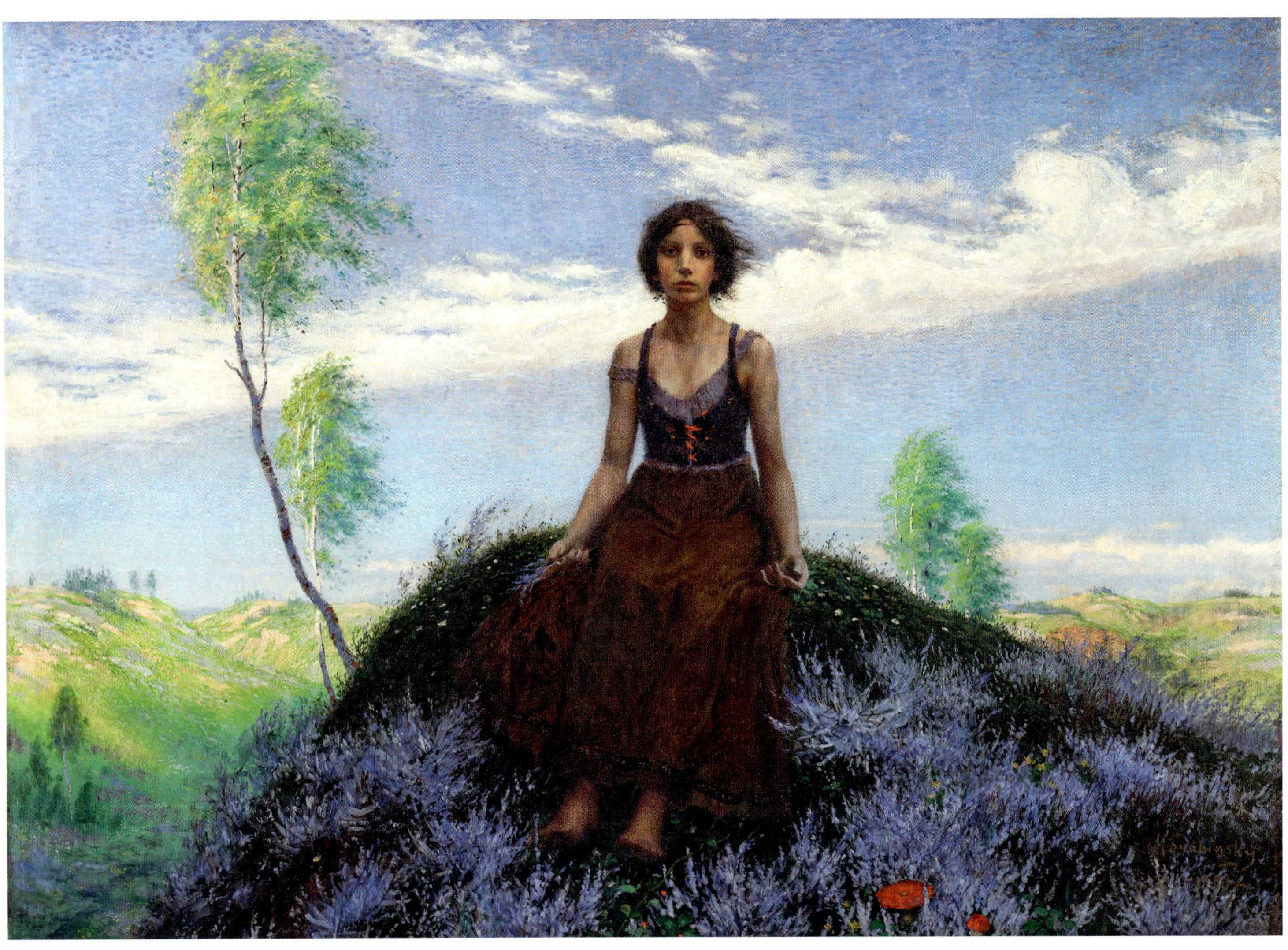

106 Maxmilián Švabinský, *A Poor Land*, 1900, oil, 179 × 246 cm

an example of the flawless combining of figure and landscape in a way that belongs neither to landscape painting nor to figure painting in the traditional sense. Moodier landscapes also bore the stamp of this modernity, and among them *Stillness at Dusk* from 1900 exemplified the new painting. The scene, looking down on a pond as it gleams in the twilight, recalls Lebeda's motifs, but the figure of the woman, standing with her back to us and decoratively framed by slender trees, adds a sense of balance to the painting that expresses the harmony of evening, suffused with a melancholy tranquillity. The sensitive, decorative treatment of composition and colour allowed Hudeček to achieve an equilibrium between the naturalistic and Symbolist elements, and in this sense the painting brought the turbulent late 1890s to a close.

In the same year, Maxmilián Švabinský painted his large canvas *A Poor Land*. This too was a synthesis of the new combining of figure and landscape that opened up modern art to young painters. In Švabinský's painting, however, the figure is central, and there is a simplicity in how she directly faces the viewer. The surrounding landscape is hilly, an idealised view of the open, windswept places the painter knew intimately from holidays in the Bohemian-Moravian Highlands. It is bathed in golden sunlight, but the hillock in the foreground is in shadow and glowing with purple heather, which introduces a contrast in the painting to soften the brightness of the sky and the landscape. The figure's portrayal creates another contrast with the painting's idealised mood. A comparison of Švabinský's *A Poor Land* with Hudeček's *Stillness at Dusk* reveals a certain polarity in what Czech painting had achieved by the end of the century. The starting point for both paintings is the same, but each tackles it differently. Hudeček's painting emphasises an immersion in nature, a way of sensing its mood through a process of introspection. In the tranquillity of dusk, Hudeček's figure gazes into the water's mirror, and in the poetic vocabulary of the time the water's depth symbolised both the earth's mystery and the human unconscious. Švabinský's landscape, however, has brought forth the painting's figure as its fruit, and it addresses the viewer directly. Hudeček's landscape allures; Švabinský's invites. Yet despite their differences, the two paintings are complementary, representing two interrelated aspects of the contemporary psyche.

These two works also show how young Czech painting had matured within just a few years, and how it had come to represent the younger generation's sentiments, rooted in the melancholia of the late 1890s that was symptomatic of young artists' longing for something they lacked in quotidian reality. This keen sense of the discrepancy between what was and what could be remained their stimulus as they strenuously looked for a new programme for their art, one with new values.

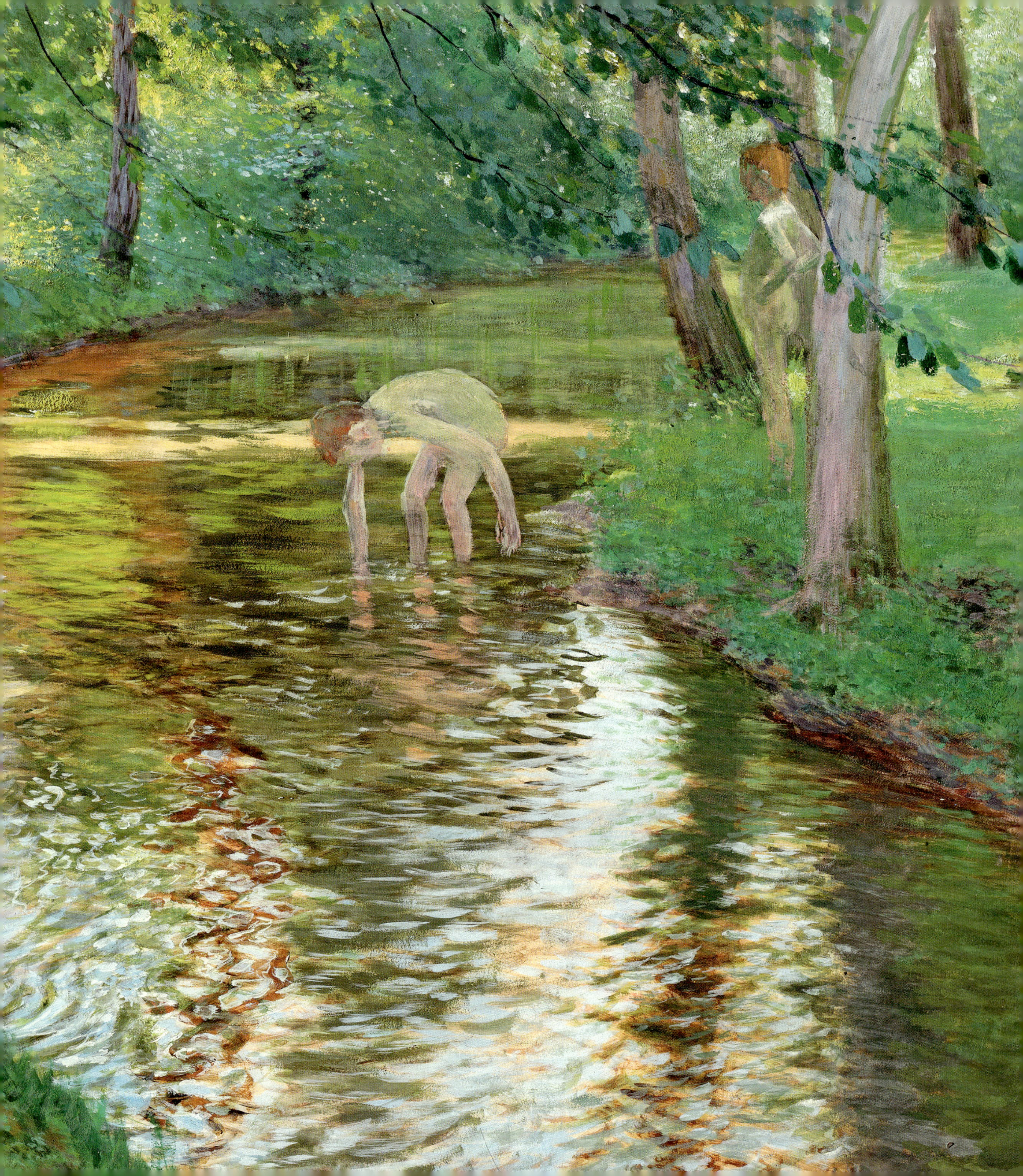

SPRING

> In vain do I search my memory for an impression similar to the one I took away on Saturday from this small exhibition at the Topič Salon, and all that remains is the certainty that the group of works exhibited by the Mánes artists gave me a delight and pleasure whose like I had yet to experience at an exhibition in Prague. It seems to me as though all corners of the exhibition space were filled with a balmy and pleasant atmosphere, as though it were bathed in a soft yet powerful warm light. I feel as if I had suddenly found myself – in the midst of a foul, muddy and rainy winter – in a radiant land, where the sun warmly kisses the earth until it becomes wet and weeps, where an invisible stream of sap rises into the young buds, and young, pale, fresh greenery colours the tips of thickets and trees. Spring breathes through the landscape …[87]

So the critic K. B. Mádl greeted the first exhibition by SVU Mánes in February 1898. In this "lyrical" way, he articulated the impression the young generation's first public collective exhibition had made, and his enthusiastic account pointed to a new chapter that had now opened in the history of Czech art. Painters and sculptors from Mánes made a careful selection of their work from the previous two or three years and succeeded in assembling a collection that generally surprised visitors with its quality and principally with the somewhat uniform tone of its content, distinguished by its poetic treatment of the advances that naturalism had made.

The young artists of SVU Mánes were conscious of their revivalist mission. It was reflected in Arnošt Hofbauer's exhibition poster, in which a young woman, an allegory of Art, has disturbed the inertia of the fat deity of Mammon and Worldliness. This largely traditional idea was conveyed through figures with a new Secession-styled naturalism. Hofbauer's poster for the second SVU Mánes exhibition, in the autumn of the same year, shows a man drowning in stormy seas who reaches for a lifebelt thrown from a schooner with billowing sails and the Mánes logo on its bow. The poster's stylisation was informed by Japanese woodcuts, and its colours – a simple harmony of reddish-brown, blueish-green, and white – were a typical calling card for the new Secession taste. Hofbauer's posters well illustrate the catholicity of the young art's interests, its critical view of society's morals, and its attempt to combine decorative ornamental elements with naturalistic and symbolic ones. The posters' message was continued in the content of the two exhibitions, with paintings that sought to achieve their effect principally through their immediacy. This was something that came out of the ideological basis the young artists had collectively created. The ten years of the student society's existence had come to fruition.

The two exhibitions were dominated by landscape paintings by Antonín Slavíček, Antonín Hudeček, Otakar Lebeda, Ludvík Kuba, and František Kaván, with other

107 Antonín Hudeček, *Stream*, 1898, Syntonos paint, 70 × 104 cm, detail

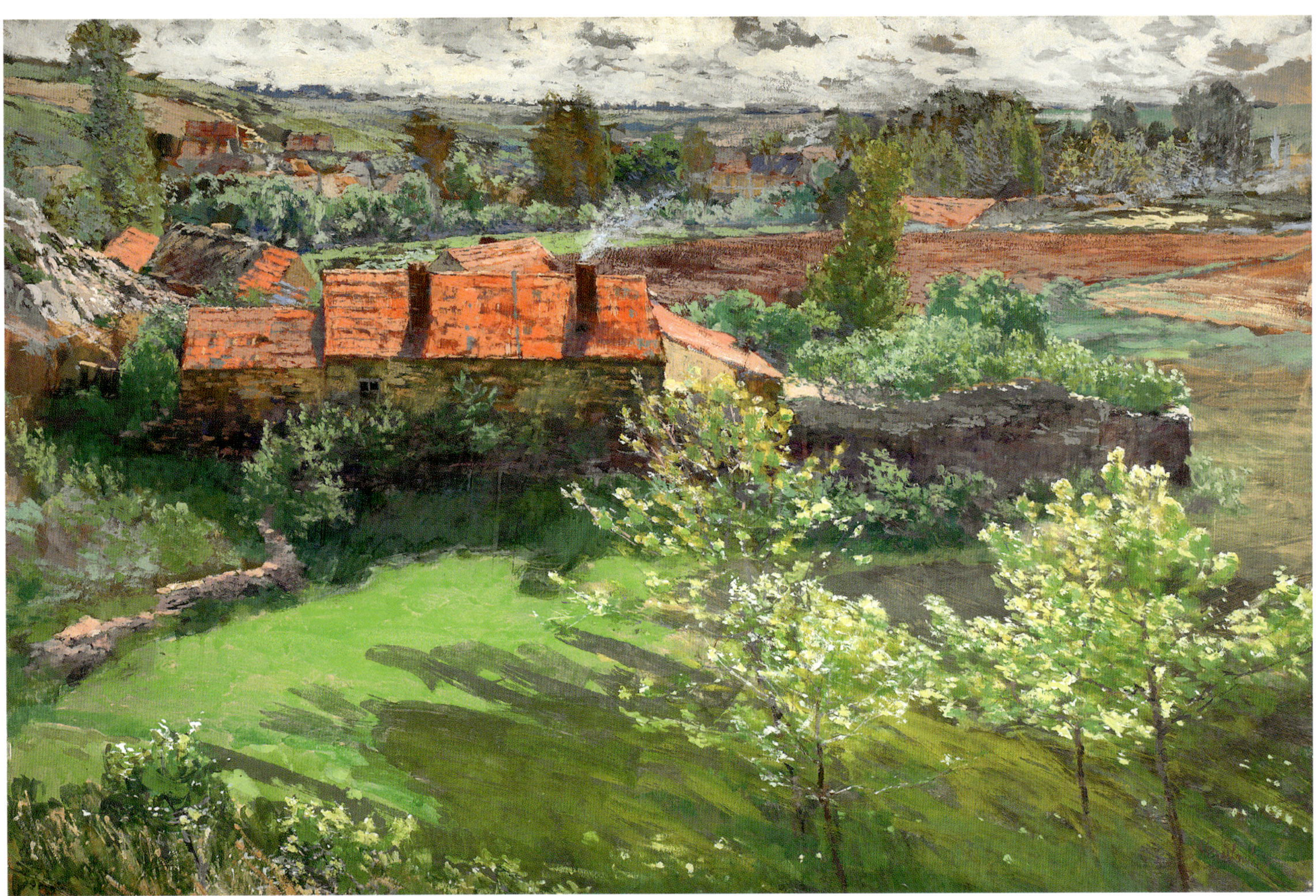

landscape scenes by Zdenka Braunerová, Josef Jelínek, Adolf Wiesner, Josef Holub, Alois Kalvoda, and Bohuslav Dvořák. This reflected the young art's fundamental world view, suppressing detail in favour of the whole. In his review, Mádl wrote that many figure painters "paint man as if they were painting a landscape." Landscape painting forged the path to a new poetism that sought, through visual "mood," to combine subjective emotion with the more objective mirror of nature. Within this general framework of the new externalisation, landscape painting also created an expressive structural opposition by selecting from the rich panorama of the natural year its two most affecting seasons – spring and autumn. In terms of their content, these two seasons were understood as fundamental symbols of the emotional experiencing of the world in its totality. The creating of this polarity, which had an unusual significance as the framework for an entire new ideology in art, had its own internal logic. In the latter half of the 1890s, when the young art was maturing, we can trace in the frequency of landscape scenes a certain shift from autumn to spring. Autumnal melancholy, so beloved of the contemporary mentality, was the foundation from which the spring

108 Antonín Slavíček, *June Day*, 1898, tempera, 71 × 105.5 cm blossom of the new art gradually emerged. This may also have been related to how the young generation was coalescing and maturing both personally and artistically, and gaining through group endeavours a more optimistic perspective on society and morality. The emotional crises prompted by contemporary individualism did not cease, but the young art's increasing popularity with the public was unquestionably a stimulus for further cultural activity.

This shift was most marked among the most promising young talents. During a vacation in Okoř in 1898, Antonín Slavíček painted *June Day*, a tempera that is rightly considered significant in the artist's own development and in the evolution of contemporary Czech painting as a whole.[88] In their unaffected "Impressionism," the slender trees lit by strong sunlight in the foreground introduce an unusually integrative treatment of the landscape purely through the painting's temperament. In this happy combination of light and bright colours, Slavíček, perhaps for the first time, fully achieved an exuberant and dynamic interplay between the forces of nature and a new openness and freshness of the painter's eye and mind. In this way, the painting expresses a state of euphoria, an unusually intense experience of an excess of the life force as it spills over from nature into man, who basks in the glory of the scenery. The energetic brushstrokes of *June Day* would remain a typical expressive device for Slavíček, and in the new century he would develop this further to produce his finest works.

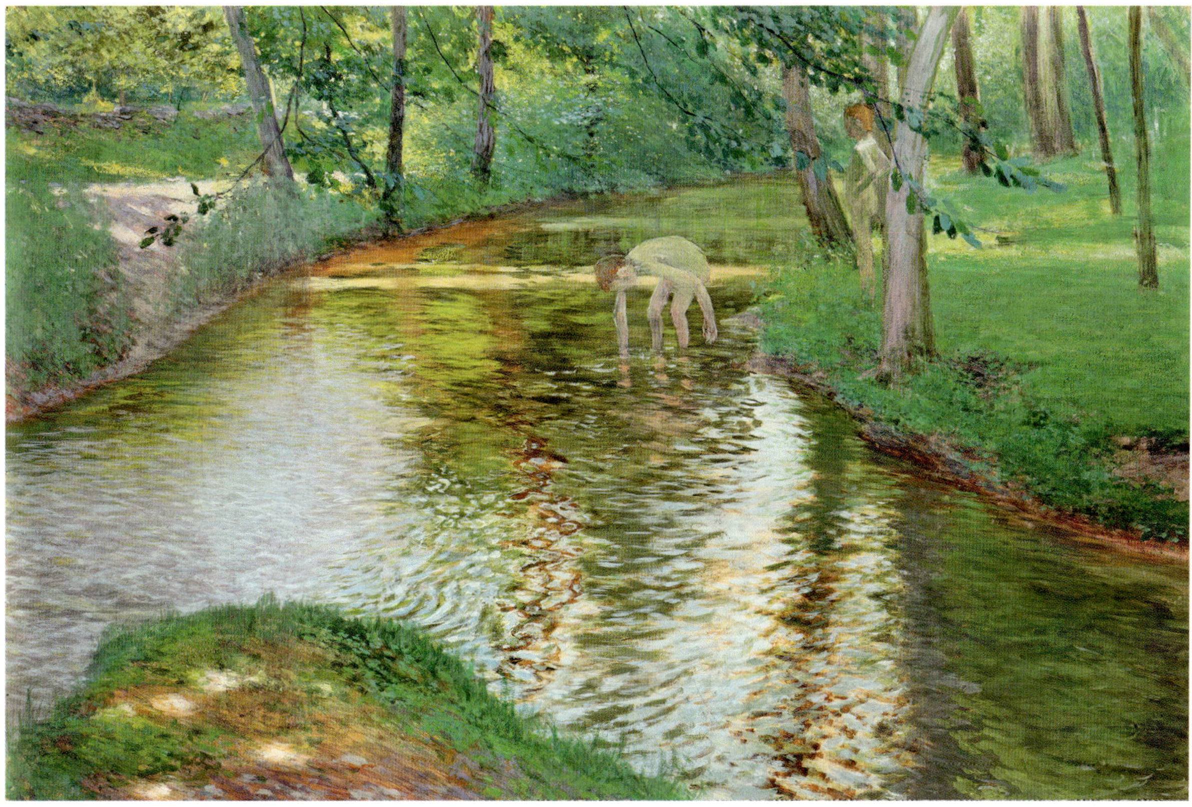

109 Antonín Hudeček, *Stream*, 1898, Syntonos paint, 70 × 104 cm

In Antonín Hudeček too, although he was by nature a far more intimate lyricist, the expressive polarity of the new art was fully manifest. His melancholy and tranquil late-afternoon landscapes found their counterparts in scenes from the stream in Okoř, where the main element is the water flowing merrily, reflecting the sunlight in its ripples to create a sparkling mosaic. Here too, Czech art is natural and all-embracing in its youthful vigour. Hudeček's scenes of naked children wading in the stream in no way violate the principle of plausibility, yet they are also symbolic. The motifs of flowing water, the verdant banks of the stream, the trees, and the naked young bodies form a thematic group whose meaning becomes fully evident in the context of similarly motivated contemporary literature, in which a stream is compared to a journey, and its course from source to river and then to the sea is an allegory for the progress of a human life.[89] Paintings of children bathing in the clear water of a stream suffused with sunlight were also "modern" symbols of humanity's state of innocence in paradise. This second semantic layer in Hudeček's Okoř paintings was also expressed in the way that, beneath their Impressionist surface, these works are very carefully and subtly decora-

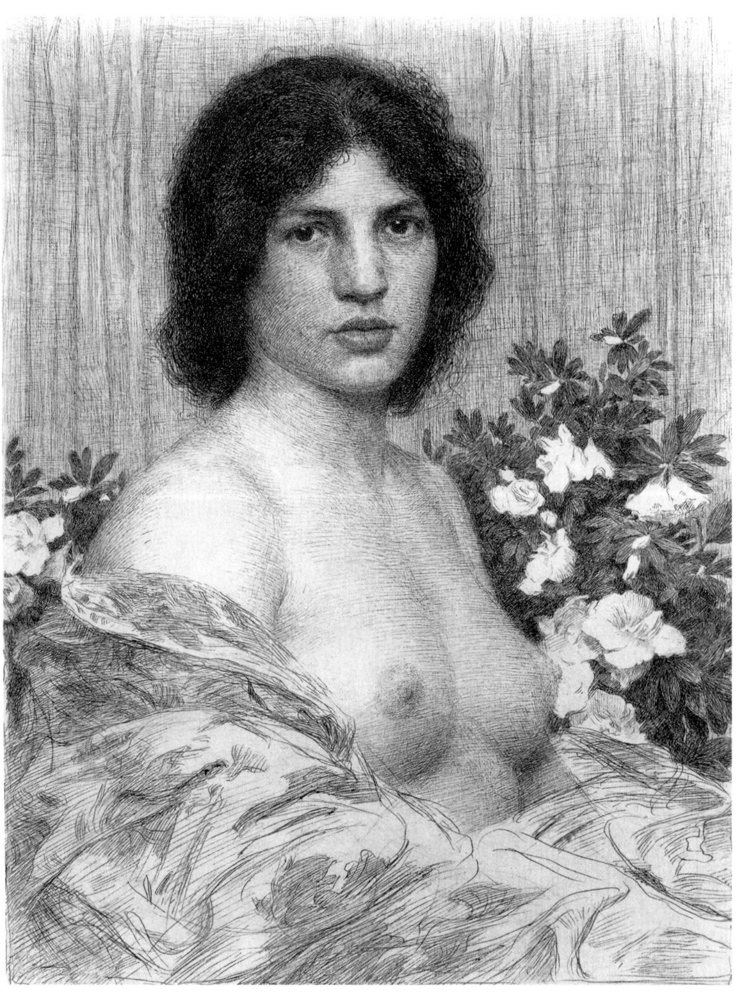

110 Maxmilián Švabinský, *Youth*, 1897, Indian ink, 43 × 31.5 cm

tive, which is particularly apparent in their basic composition. Hudeček was by now following the typical synthetic tendency in Secession art that sought to achieve an unconventional combination of highly diverse naturalistic, decorative, and symbolic elements.

At the initial SVU Mánes exhibitions, figure painters were somewhat overshadowed. However, they too could demonstrate new values in their work. Max Švabinský attracted critics' attention with his pen drawings, where his portraits and more general themes (*Youth*, 1897) were firmly based on visual reality while simultaneously softening it poetically. However, the greatest praise (including from painters themselves) was for Josef Schusser, one of Hynais's pupils, who surprised viewers with his bold application of Luminism to intimate scenes from ordinary life. His *Lady with a Red Parasol* (1898) was exciting for the effect produced by a bold splash of colour in an otherwise smoothly painted picture. Schusser's *May Evening* from the previous year was devoted

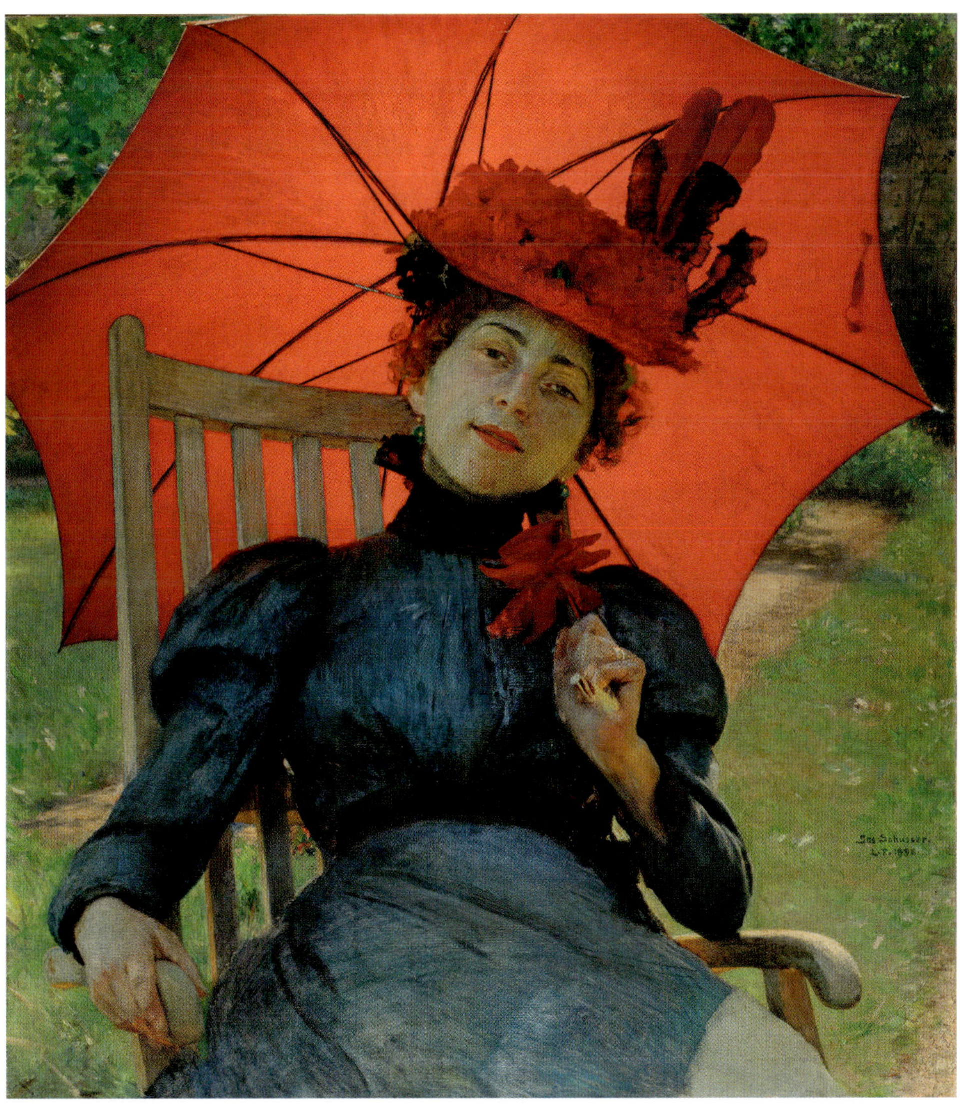

111 Josef Schusser, *Lady with a Red Parasol*, 1898, oil, 95 × 82.5 cm

to a moody evocation of a young woman in a flower garden at dusk, an idea that was immensely popular in contemporary poetry. His *Evening in the Pasture* was considered a masterpiece at the time. The figure of the girl lit by the yellowish light of the setting sun as she tends her goats was a much-admired solution to what was by then the number one problem in painting: how to depict a figure *en plein air*.

In 1898 it seemed to many that Schusser's paintings expressed a programme that, in figure painting in particular, had had to shed numerous encumbrances and radically break with the established way of looking at the nature of a painting. *Volné směry* expressed this new position in its introduction to its reports from exhibitions by Franz Stassen, Vasily Vereshchagin, and Václav Brožík that were held prior to the young artists' own exhibition. The main idea in the introduction was to point to the specific artistic self-sufficiency of painting as such, to abandon the established way of evaluating paintings according to their themes, and to emphasise the importance of form as that which the painter himself contributes, in which "he triumphantly overcomes the obstacles to painting placed by nature."[90] The rejection of the "literary" conception became an essential part of the new Mánes aesthetic, and it meant that all traditional allegorical practices that had tried to express general themes by means of attributes were from now on considered an undignified attempt to simplify the artist's task. In this way, the leading group in SVU Mánes gradually parted ways with those who, like Emil Holárek or Karel Ladislav Klusáček, persisted with the old approach and merely adapted it to late Romanticism.

However, unlike the relative unity in landscape painting, the situation in figure painting was more complicated. Besides the main current, which tried to combine the figure with a natural setting in the most authentic and spontaneous way by means of reflected colours, there was another current that had a no less valid claim to modernity. It was based on the requirements for decorative painting, and it cultivated a new Secession ornamentalism in paintings that found full application in architecture. An original example of the genre was Arnošt Hofbauer's *Decorative Panneau* (1898), which even Mádl, who was much taken with lyrical Impressionism, commended for opening up a promising perspective. Here too, of course, the rejection of allegory played a substantial role. Mádl wrote,

> *Decorative Panneau* could not have been named otherwise, for it represents neither Psyche nor Eros, nor Poetry nor anything else; it is the youthful freshness of the girl's body, kneeling in profile, the tender and deeply felt drawing; the harmony of the lines and shimmering colours, applied, spread and spattered in the given or chosen space. They are vivid and enticing, and the eye is happy to rest on their play without reason coolly ruminating on whether this is mythology or allegory.[91]

Young painters found common ground for both these currents by formulating the task as one of mastering nature through painting technique. This notion was symptomatic of the time – one of the leading contemporary art theoreticians, Alois Riegl, described the human artistic instinct as a matter of competing with nature.[92] The goal, of course, was not a lifeless imitation of nature, but an attempt to express through a direct, clear relationship with nature the experience of it and therefore an appreciation

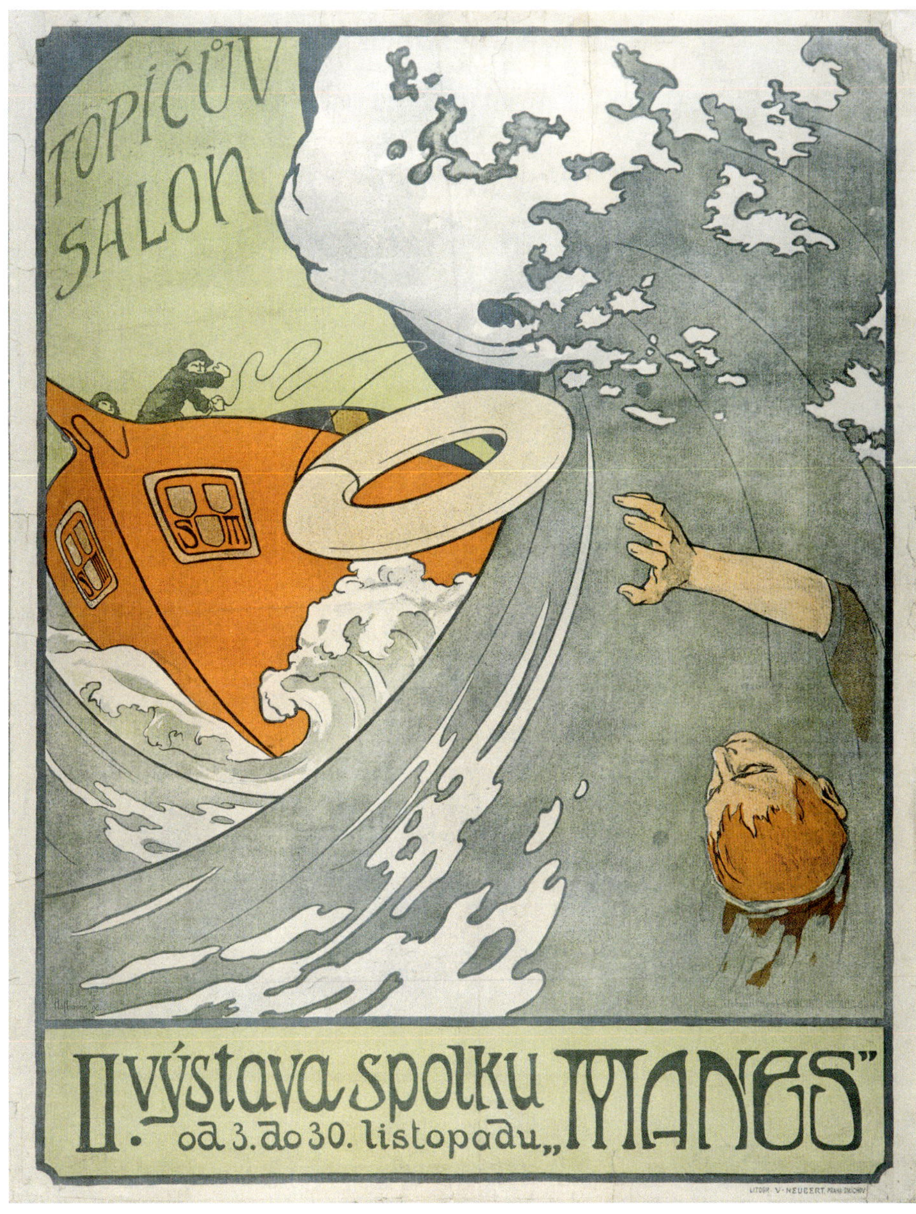

of it. The principle emphasising the importance of nature for form in art now became a higher valorisation of naturalism.

Theoretical justification for this position was sought in the writings of John Ruskin, excerpts from whose books were published in *Volné směry* in 1898–99. The significance of these excerpts was primarily that they presented the first more comprehensive theory that Czech modernism was willing to accept. Ruskin's account includes a vivid comparison between two primitive, "barbarous" works: an abstractly schematic angel from an illuminated manuscript of the insular English school, and a sculpture of *The Serpent Beguiling Eve* from St. Ambrogio's Church in Milan. For Ruskin, the angel is the

112 Arnošt Hofbauer, Poster for the second SVU Mánes exhibition, 1898, colour lithograph, 110 × 84 cm

embodiment of a dead barbarism, because the draughtsman does not look at nature but merely draws an imagined arrangement of symmetric geometrical forms. It seems that Aristotle's principles of the beautiful – order, symmetry, and the definite – are similarly hopeless. However, the Milanese sculpture, crude as it may be, contains the elements of life in their first form, and it opens up the entire rich subsequent development of European art. Reality, not correctness nor formal beauty, was its creator's ideal. The primitive asymmetrical serpent is an expression of its heart, its malice and insinuation, and Eve is rendered in a way that shows how

> she is pleased at being flattered, and yet in a state of uncomfortable hesitation. And some look of listening, of complacency, and of embarrassment he has verily got: – note the eyes slightly askance, the lips compressed, and the right hand nervously grasping the left arm: nothing can be declared impossible to the people who could begin thus – the world is open to them.[93]

Ruskin's elevating of this early medieval sculpture, as an example of the foundations of a concept of art, promoted an organic treatment of form that was also typical of the Czech Secession. Form – which the authors of the introduction to the Stassen, Vereshchagin, and Brožík exhibitions in *Volné směry* so emphasised as the new art's supreme interest, and which they sharply contrasted with the "literary" conception – was not yet the later notion of "pure" form. It was chiefly a matter of the artistic expression of a new appreciation for the connection between the perception of visual reality and its emotional experiencing on the part of the artist and the viewer.

This fundamental premise for the new aesthetic also comprised the core of the critical norm applied to the contemporary ornamental style. Critics from *Volné směry* rejected as "pseudo-Secession" all ornamentalism – whether from Munich, Vienna, or Paris – that was adopted as formal cliché, but they praised any ornamental decorative work that was "created," meaning that it respected the situation so vividly described in Ruskin's comparison.

Arnošt Hofbauer's work satisfied these requirements, for his stylisation was an artistic reappraisal of a "motif" taken from reality while having an unconventional philosophical reach. His posters for the initial Mánes exhibitions, which did not yet entirely reject any "tendency," were joined in 1899 by a poster for *Obrázková revue* (The Illustrated Review) showing a young intellectual standing beneath the flying buttresses of a Gothic cathedral. In the same year, Hofbauer created his finest poster, for a recital by Hana Kvapilová, in which he renounced any conspicuously "Secession" lines. His lithograph, printed in yellow, red, blue, and grey, introduced a more intimate note in the "salon of the street" that was becoming ever more popular with the general public. Hofbauer's idea of portraying the actress in a large oval mirror was interesting, for the resulting double portrait created an intimacy that brought the viewer closer to the picture, while wittily expressing Kvapilová's dual existence as a real person and as the heroine of the imaginary tales from her recitation. This unity of reality and fiction therefore had a conceptual core, and it was also a noteworthy modernisation of the Romantic motif of the double. In the confrontation of the head viewed simultaneously in profile and en face, Hofbauer also anticipated an issue that

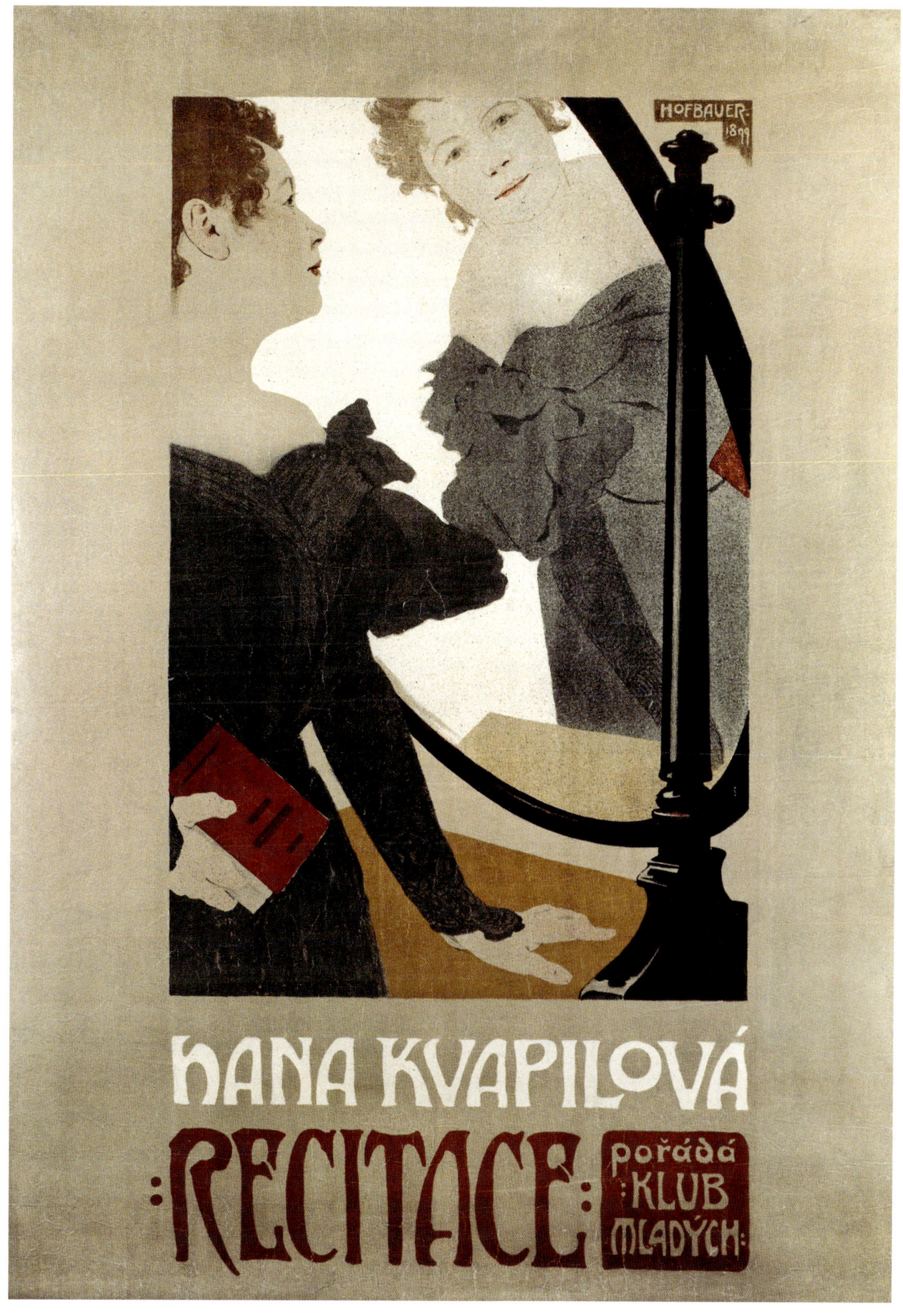

113 Arnošt Hofbauer, Poster for a recital by Hana Kvapilová, 1899, colour lithograph, 110 × 81 cm

would later play an important role in Cubism. Hofbauer's work illustrates how decorative art also had to respect contemporary naturalism, which could theoretically be included under the problem of perception. The requirement to "see well" the natural motif, which constantly recurred in the contemporary vocabulary of painting,[94] was closely associated with the requirement to "do well" the painting. At its heart was not merely the imitating of nature, but the correct combination of sensory and conceptual qualities and the need to express an equilibrium between sensation and idea on the basis of a visual percept. These concerns, which in painting were generally resolved practically, were addressed in the 1890s by an emerging discipline that would eventually become Gestalt psychology. It too stressed the importance of integrative perception, and demonstrated through experiment that the entirety of a percept could not be deduced simply from its parts, and that in the process of perception there were certain fundamental qualities of form derived from the very structure of the human psyche.[95] In the field of theory, this opened an issue that in painting too led from pronounced naturalism to a concern with the formative elements of artistic vision.

The question of "correct seeing" was what separated young art from late 19th-century salon painting, which in the latter half of the century had cultivated a flawless illusionistic technique. In this, photography played a large role as both aid and corrective, facilitating great veracity in scenes that were taken not just from the present day but also from history, mythology, classical antiquity, and religion. For salon painting, the ideal was to present as convincingly as possible even the most bizarre subjects elicited by the previous century's narrative literary spirit. By the close of the 19th century, young artists could see that the technical wizardry of this illusionistic pseudo-realism was a fiction that helped to confirm a false, and so only seemingly uniform, image of the world stemming from late bourgeois ideology. Initially they too had been dazzled by the French academic masters' technical bravura, but they soon realised that behind the wonderful façade lay nothing of any great value, and that even the admired illusionistic effects were merely a formula, a matter of technical skill. A critical reappraisal of this seeming abundance could only take the path of reducing it to the fundamental questions – above all, the question of the authenticity of artistic depictions of reality. Truth, now understood not just as a flawless description but also as a constitutive value, was the first "integrative" quality to emerge in the practising of the new art, which demonstrated that this new value was not merely a constituent of idea and effect, but their intersecting. This value was difficult to capture in programme declarations, because the antithetical character of such expression led to the excessive suppression of one aspect in favour of the other, in the interests of greater clarity. It is therefore essential to view the practice of the new art (and to read the critiques its practitioners wrote) from a global perspective, for only the whole can accurately convey the true historical tendency.

Seeking a vivid symbol for the new Secession world view, fine art renounced salon painting's illustrative technique. Its attempt at a new solution was then most illuminating not so much in depictions of contemporary life and nature (although they do demonstrate its resolve to extricate itself from false illusionism) as in images with ideal-

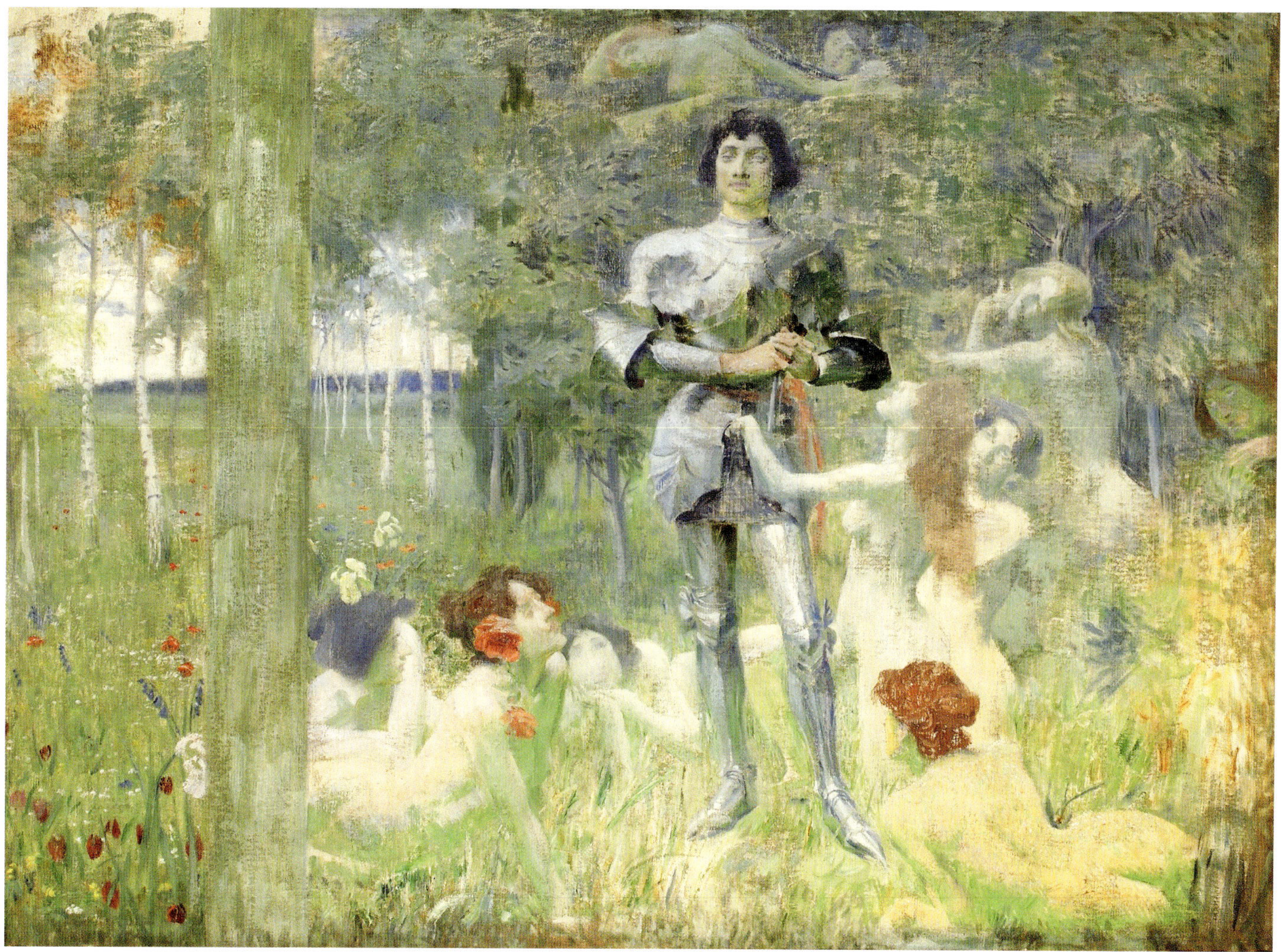

ised subject matter. Figure painting of this kind was still a field in which art achieved its greatest abstraction.

The difficulties figure painting faced are also evident from the fact that the most important Czech figure painter, Jan Preisler, made no great impression at the first SVU Mánes exhibitions, and in the early volumes of *Volné směry* he appeared more as a superb draughtsman. Yet in private, Preisler was working intensively on the question of painting. His work on *The Adventurous Knight* cycle in 1898 was an important stage in his development.

The direction that Preisler took becomes most apparent if we compare his cycle to *The Knight of Flowers*, an 1894 painting by the French artist Georges Antoine Rochegrosse.[96] Where or how Preisler encountered Rochegrosse's painting remains unknown, but the similarity of the motif in the latter's canvas and the left central part of Preisler's polyptych is so striking that there can be no doubt that he was directly influenced by the French work. Rochegrosse recorded the idea behind the

114 Jan Preisler, *The Adventurous Knight*, 1898, oil, 87 × 115 cm

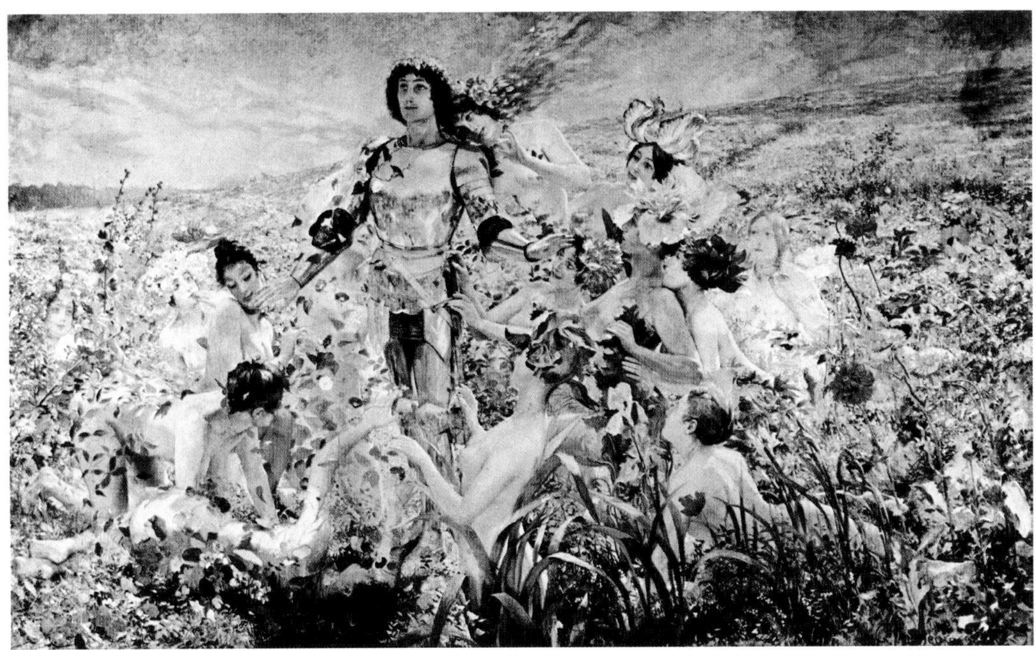

painting on its frame: "The Predestined One, dressed in symbolic Silver Armour, goes towards the Idea, heedless of the calls of life."[97] He depicted the knight bare-headed and gazing upwards, as he walks through a meadow full of flowers that all around him turn into beautiful naked women who vainly try to tempt him away from his path. In terms of technique, it is interesting that Rochegrosse presents this romantic scene in a landscape bathed in sunlight and painted as though *en plein air*. The knight's gleaming armour becomes a mirror that reflects the whole meadow. The absurd contrast between the idealised main figure and the entirely realistic landscape is softened by the female figures, who add an amusing and theatrical note to the scene.

Preisler's interest in Rochegrosse's painting must have been due in part to the demands made by young Czech criticism. With its study of the naked body in a natural setting, Hynais's much-admired *The Judgement of Paris* had tackled a similar problem. Preisler too was seeking to satisfy the requirements of Luminism, but he placed his knight in the shadows at the edge of a forest, and so avoided replicating the effect of the French painting. Preisler's painting is also more static, and it therefore makes greater use of its decorative compositional elements. Nevertheless, Preisler too had not yet entirely overcome the dualism between ideality and reality that we see in Rochegrosse's use of salon technique for his painting's pseudo-Symbolist content.

Looking at Preisler's large study for the knight's *Temptation* (now in the Gallery of West Bohemia in Pilsen), we can see how he tried to use colour to unify the picture plane by imbuing the local tones with a luminous value to create an impression of mistiness. In this way, the painting satisfied Luminist demands while also seeming to return to late Romanticism and Pirner. Rochegrosse's theatrical definiteness has become more of a Romantic visualisation. It now has Preisler's authentic lyricism, but the veil

115 Georges Antoine Rochegrosse, *The Knight of Flowers*, 1894, oil, 235 × 375 cm

of greys obscures its intensity. In 1899 Preisler was still wrestling with these problems when he painted the themes of Spring and Autumn for the spandrels of Josef Fanta's interior at the Exposition Universelle in Paris. In the figures of the ploughman and the female nude in Spring, and the mother with her children in Autumn, he emphasised the significance of tonal value to try to connect the figures with their landscape setting. However, these paintings proved to him that this use of tonal values was unsuited to the needs of the new decorative painting; in fact, they returned it to academicism. For this reason, Preisler would later make no reference to these paintings.

It was only in 1900, when Jan Preisler presented his large triptych *Spring* at the third SVU Mánes exhibition, that he would achieve true success and come to the forefront of Czech Secession figure painting.

Spring shows how Preisler had freed his imagination from any dependency on specific models. His earlier painting of the knight had much that was at odds with the new world view, for its original meaning was an extreme idealism, the ideal juxtaposed with

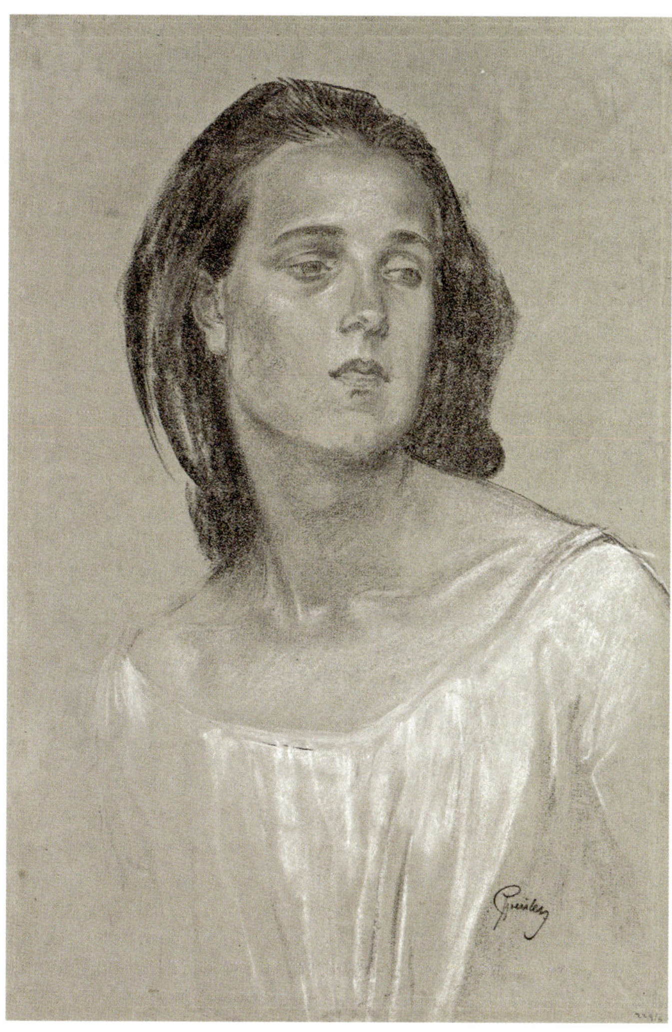

116 Jan Preisler, Drawing for *Spring*, 1900, charcoal and white chalk, 43.3 × 28 cm

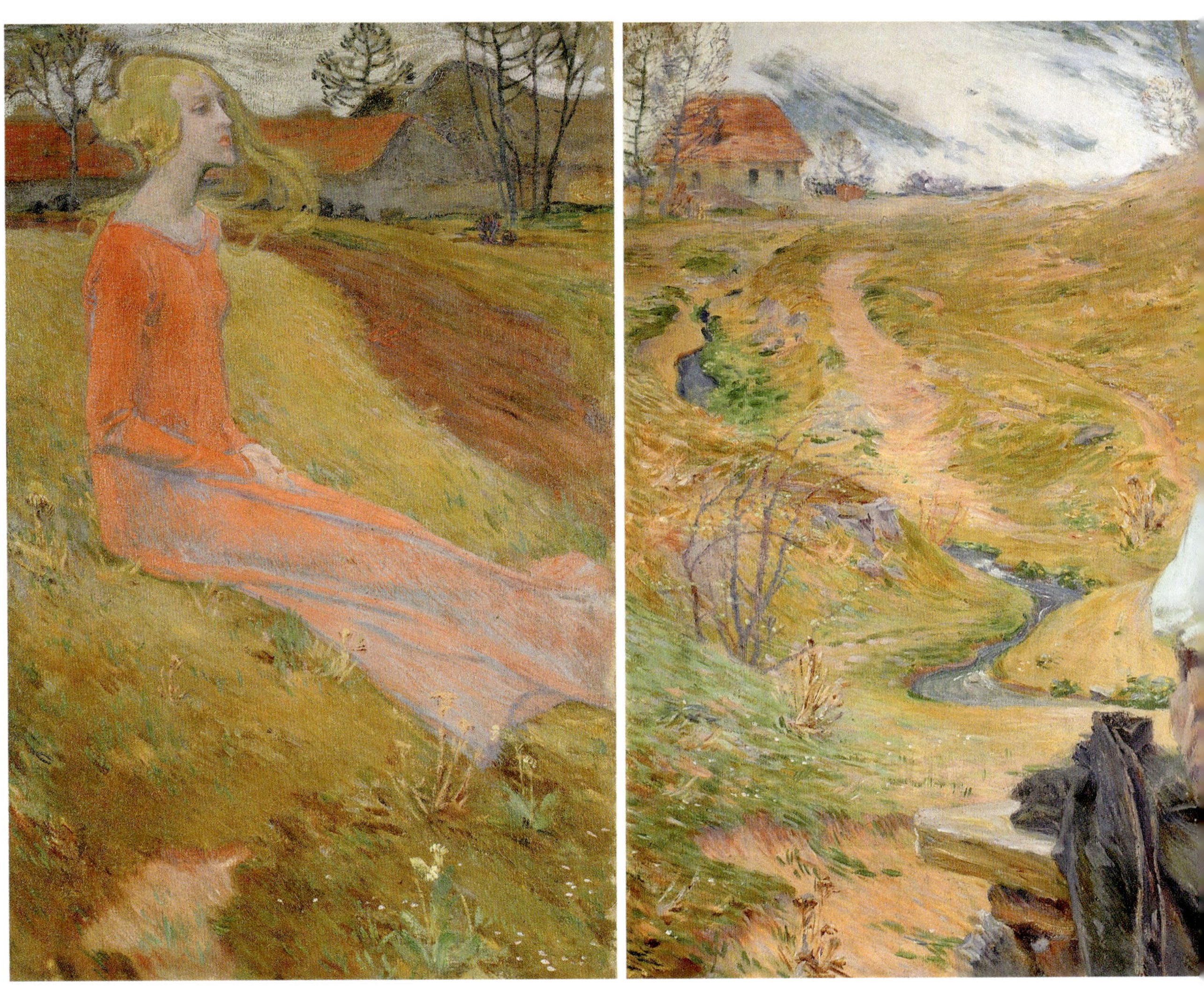

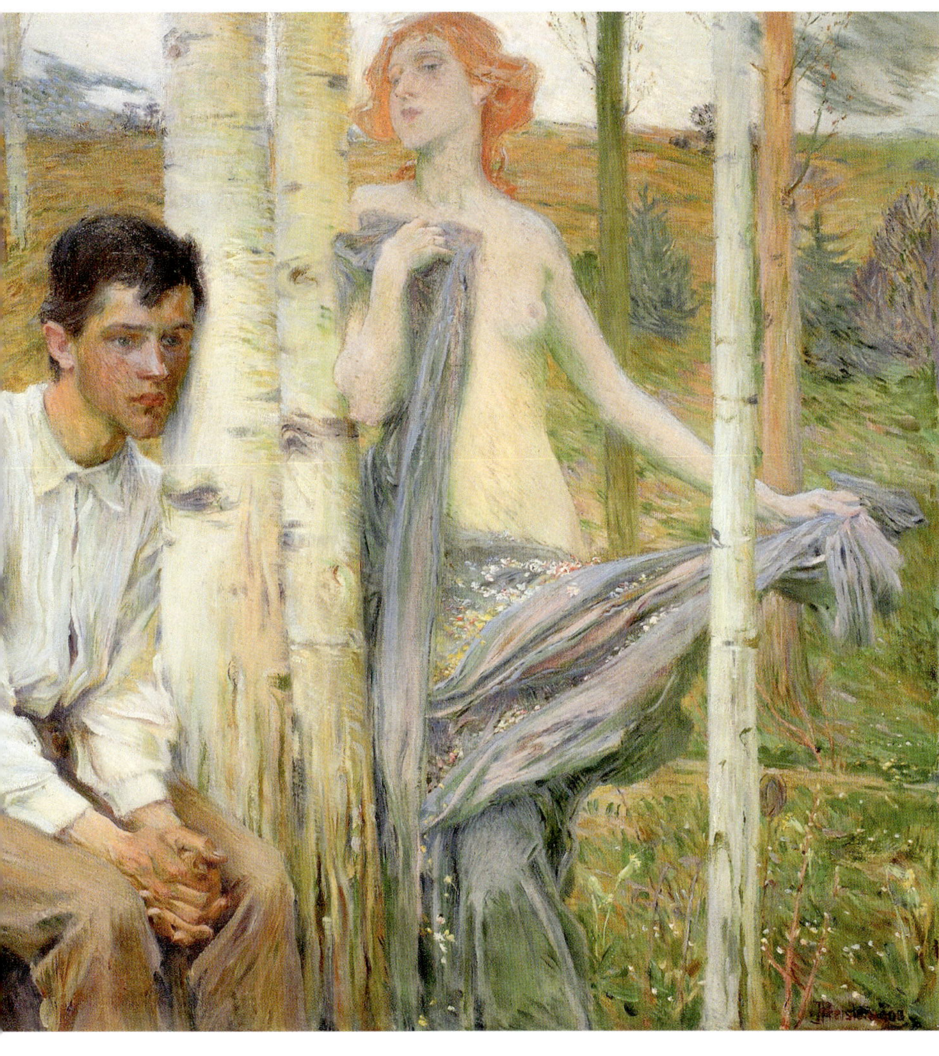

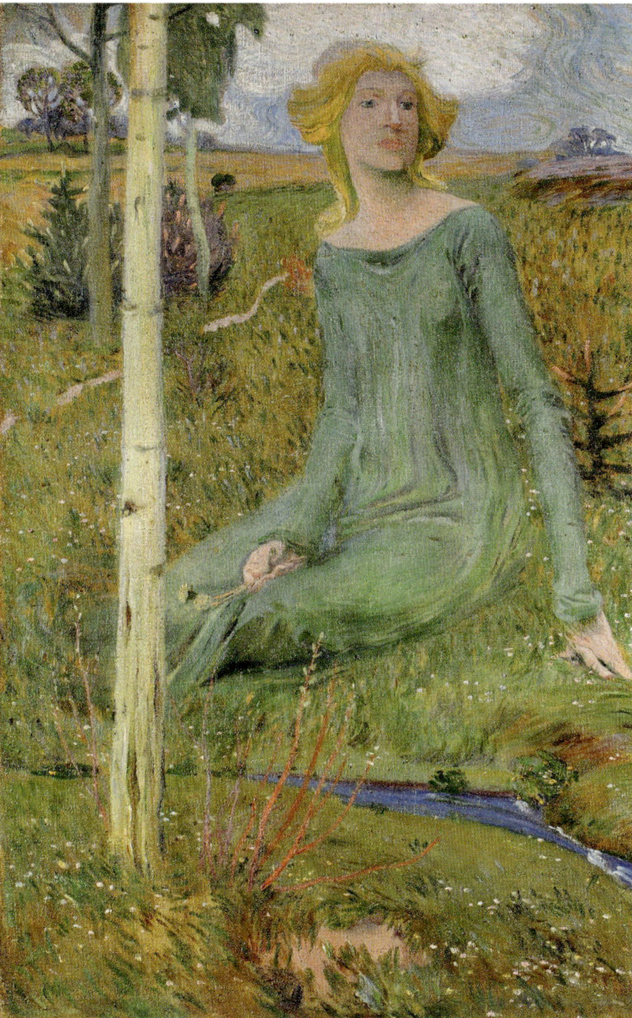

117 Jan Preisler, *Spring*, 1900, oil, 112 × 70 cm, 112 × 186 cm, 112 × 70 cm

real life, while the new, young lyricism did not shrink from life but tried to understand it in all its depth, which it expressed in the theme of the human figure in landscape. In *Spring*, Preisler's hero has accordingly removed his gleaming armour to become a country boy sitting among the birch trees in a springtime landscape, devoid now of snow but yet to bloom. The painting also expresses the inner harmony between man and the forces of nature as they awaken, yet this new song of youth is not spirited but elegiac. As always with Preisler, the essential concept is cyclical, mixing joy and sorrow. Traditional paintings of this kind presented ideality as a permanent utopia existing beyond the ordinary world, but now this heavenly ideal is understood simply as a beautiful moment occurring in the cycle of nature and human life, and only once for each person.

To understand the melancholy sense of reconciliation in this painting, which at the same time is full of all the colours of life, it should be recalled that, before *Spring*, Preisler had produced his most significant work as an illustrator in his drawings for Julius Zeyer's *The Song of the Sorrow of the Good Young Man Roman Vasilich* (1899). For Zeyer's sad tale of a hero who follows a chimera that turns into a demon of self-negation, Preisler reworked Secession stylisation in an original and distinctive way. This involved an unusual combination of linear graphic stylistic qualities and qualities that were explicitly painterly, and this interweaving of two essentially very different artistic principles was particularly well suited to Zeyer's poem, whose content did not otherwise lend itself to illustration. The common denominator of the "modern" sentiment here was psychomachia, a conflict within the soul stemming from an ambiguous desire for fulfilment. Artistically then, this attempt to find an equilibrium between different ways of depicting form – accomplished in such a way that neither became subordinate to the other, but instead their ambivalent collaboration allowed both to play their part in the resulting image – became an original vehicle for complicated psychological content.

The structure of the *Spring* triptych also illustrates how Preisler had systematically developed his thinking in this respect. In his analysis, Antonín Matějček would later point to the difference between the central part of the triptych and the wings, where in the centre we can still see something of the aesthetics developed principally in contemporary landscape painting, while for the female figures sitting in the landscape on either side Preisler "went a step further in the use of colour to structure space, and consciously switched from an Impressionistic analysis of light and colour to a synthesis of colour."[98] The central figures follow the formula for green reflections on the skin tones that Hynais's pupils had popularised in Czech painting, but here too the reflections are rendered more as hatching than as a solid tonal value. In the wings of the triptych, it is expressly a matter of using solid colours to construct form in complementary colours. In this way, Preisler excludes all illusionistic effects from his painting and creates a new decorative pictorial composition in which colour and line operate independently. The central figures are dominated by linear brushstrokes, while in the wings this treatment is applied in more compact areas.

Preisler's *Spring* was then not just a succinct symbol of its time, a testimony to the emotional disposition of Czech modernism and a sensitive expression of its outlook, but artistically it also represented a significant step towards a modern Czech concept of painting. It satisfied the fundamental requirement for the content to be not only dependent on the theme, but also communicated through artistic means. In this respect it also went beyond the transitional phase of the new lyricism that still sought to satisfy this condition through faithfulness to the natural appearance. This new understanding of the expressive qualities of pure colour went hand in hand with compositional principles that revealed their genetic origin. The source of these new approaches was not the usual way of painting individual pictures, but was developed from decorative painting, a discipline that had in the 19th century been pushed into the background by the great success of salon painting. Although in the latter half of the 19th century decorative painting had generally been reduced to the mere adornment of eclectic architecture or the disseminating of the sterile ideas of contemporary nationalism and pietism, the discipline nevertheless boasted an artist so exceptional that he must have captured Preisler's attention. Halfway through its 1899–1900 volume, *Volné směry* printed examples of the work of Puvis de Chavannes, together with a translation of an article by Georges Rodenbach, perhaps to mark the French painter's recent death. The reproductions included *The Poor Fisherman*, *Winter*, and several large murals. Rodenbach wrote that Puvis had resuscitated decorative painting with a new style that combined realism and Symbolism. This synthesis took shape outside the usual salon duels, for since 1870, when Puvis had been mocked at the Salon, he had labelled his paintings "decorative panneaux," to avoid any unnecessary confrontation with militant academic illusionism. By the end of the century, however, it was clear that with his fundamental respect for the space of a wall, Puvis had created in painting not just a counterbalance to clamorous naturalism, but also a distinctive aesthetic that could be developed further – which is exactly what Paul Gauguin did.[99]

Preisler intuited the significance of Puvis's legacy and drew his own conclusions, for it was not until many years later that he would have an opportunity to see Gauguin's art. Puvis was much more influential for his orientation than the German painters Hans von Marées, Ludwig von Hofmann, and Heinrich Vogeler, with whom Preisler also had much in common. He would certainly have felt an unusual affinity with the subtle melancholy of Puvis's *The Poor Fisherman*, which was framed by a large and tranquil expanse of realistic natural scenery – although within Preisler there also burned a restless flame that found kinship with much more decadent artists, such as the Belgian painter Fernand Khnopff, whose work, about which Czech critics had considerable reservations, Preisler had seen in Vienna. In this, however, Khnopff's contacts with English artists, especially Edward Burne-Jones, also played a part. For Preisler, this logically completed the circle of new European decorative painting.

Another reason for Preisler to favour the new decorative aesthetic of solid colours was that *Spring* had been commissioned by the architect Jan Kotěra for an interior he was furnishing in Prague. This was the first fruit of their collaboration, which in subsequent years would yield several more first-class examples of the incorporation of painting into Secession architecture.

The development of young Secession architecture was one of the most important elements of Czech culture at the turn of the century. The Secession's curvilinear style was first adopted in printmaking, but it was architecture that gave full weight to these new ideas. While in printmaking the inspiration for the new stylistic idiom was *Jugend* magazine from Munich and Alphonse Mucha's Parisian Art Nouveau, the springboard for Czech Secession architecture was Vienna.

Prague's citizens could see the first indications of Secession architecture at the Architecture and Engineering Exhibition in 1898, where Alois Dryák, one of Friedrich Ohmann's pupils, worked on the ornamentation for the central hall of the Industrial Palace. The decoration was white, with colour applications and hermae extending over the hall's breadth, and along the sides were candelabras shaped like stylised little trees. Dryák's architectural base for Stanislav Sucharda's design for the František Palacký Monument from the same year, with its broad exedra flanked by pylons, was similarly in what was by now the typical Secession style.

In 1898 a young architect arrived in Prague to replace Ohmann at the School of Decorative Arts. With his great energy and single-mindedness, Jan Kotěra soon proved his organisational ability and creativity, and he gave Secession architecture a clear direction. Previously he had studied in Otto Wagner's architecture school at the Academy of Fine Arts in Vienna (1894–97). Among his fellow pupils were Joseph Maria Olbrich and Josef Hoffmann, who at the turn of the century would, with Wagner, create from the Vienna Secession a bold chapter in the early years of modern architecture.

From Wagner's teaching, Kotěra adopted the principles that he explained in his article "On the New Art," published in the fourth volume of *Volné směry*. The main idea was to emphasise that the primary and most important aspect of architectural creation was not what the layman most appreciated in architecture – that is, its ornament – but what all embellishment as expressive form stemmed from – that is, a building's purpose and technical construction, which are what shape it:

> Architectural creation therefore has two functions: first and foremost, the constructive creation of space, and then embellishment. It follows that the part common to individual works, the creating of space and structure, must be the reason for the new movement, and it cannot be the shape and form of the ornament; the former is truth itself, the latter is the expressing of truth.[100]

This theoretical proposition had a great influence on the question of what was known as the new stylisation. The practice of late eclecticism was based on how it entirely separated the functional and artistic aspects of a building. An erudite eclectic architect was willing and able to apply various historicist styles to the same ground plan, governed at most by ideas about the suitability of individual historical styles for particular purposes. What was most important was what the client wanted. Architects were routinely taught in this spirit, especially at technical colleges.

The discussion on modernism had begun before Kotěra published his article, and it stressed the need for locally specific architecture. This was not only a response to nationalist demands: since the passing of the Redevelopment Act in 1893, new construction to replace the parts of Old Prague that had been demolished had met with severe criticism, especially from conservationists. There were also demands for architects to be given greater creative freedom. Nevertheless, all calls for a new style were, for the time being, mainly concerned with finding new decorative forms. An awareness of the full extent and radicalness of the question of the new style only came with Kotěra's article, based on the ideas of Otto Wagner, whose key text on modern architecture would later be published in Czech.

Kotěra's ideas ushered in all subsequent thinking on the development of Czech modern architecture. Later, of course, from the perspective of rigorous Functionalism, Kotěra could be criticised for not fully applying his most progressive ideas, and for failing in practice to overcome the old dualism.[101] But such criticism usually loses sight of the fact that Kotěra's theory was that of the Secession Gesamtkunstwerk, in which it was largely a question of a harmonious balance between a building's purpose and its artistic quality, and the concept of function at this time was understood more broadly than it would be later by Functionalist extremism. It is also evident that Kotěra too developed as he sought to apply his ideas on style with greater thoroughness.

Shortly after arriving in Prague, Kotěra presented his new concept for an apartment building. In 1899 he designed the Peterka House, which he built on Wenceslas Square in the following year. Its layout, with both public and private premises, was expressed through its triaxial composition, with a broader central part, slightly convex on the upper floors, and narrower sections on either side that each ended in triple gables on the façade. It is interesting that in its dividing up of form, this arrangement had much in common with Preisler's *Spring*. The equilibrium between function and ornament that Kotěra demonstrated in this, his first larger project, was reflected in the dimensions of the windows (the generous display window on the ground floor was unusual for Prague) and especially in the ratio of empty space to linear ornament. New elements were the discreet colours of the façade and certain characteristic details – for instance, the windows lacked sculpted surrounds. The building's verticality, emphasised by the tall stone plinth on the ground floor and the continuous articulation of the upper stories, lightened the building's mass and greatly enhanced the powerfully lyrical impression created by the façade. Inside the building, Kotěra designed the rooms in a uniform style. Their discreet stuccowork with botanical motifs did not detract from their lightness, and this gave prominence to the elegant forms of the doors, wrought ironwork, light fittings, and other details.

The Peterka House was a successful example of a modern Secession Gesamtkunstwerk. However, it was a surprisingly long time before Kotěra had a further opportunity to demonstrate his unquestionable talent in another large project. This was partly for personal and collective reasons, but also because Friedrich Ohmann and his pupils (Alois Dryák, Jiří Justich, Bedřich Bendelmayer, Rudolf Němec, and others) had already established another concept that had been adopted in Prague largely because it offered greater continuity. They were principally interested in the artistic, ornamental side of architecture, and Ohmann and his pupils began using a new repertoire of forms inspired by botanical nature to replace the prevailing eclectic and historicist articulation. However, their approach to this new ornament was still based on a Neo-Baroque treatment of form. In this, they drew on the recent popularity of the Baroque Revival, and on their conviction (which had only been reinforced by discussions on Prague's

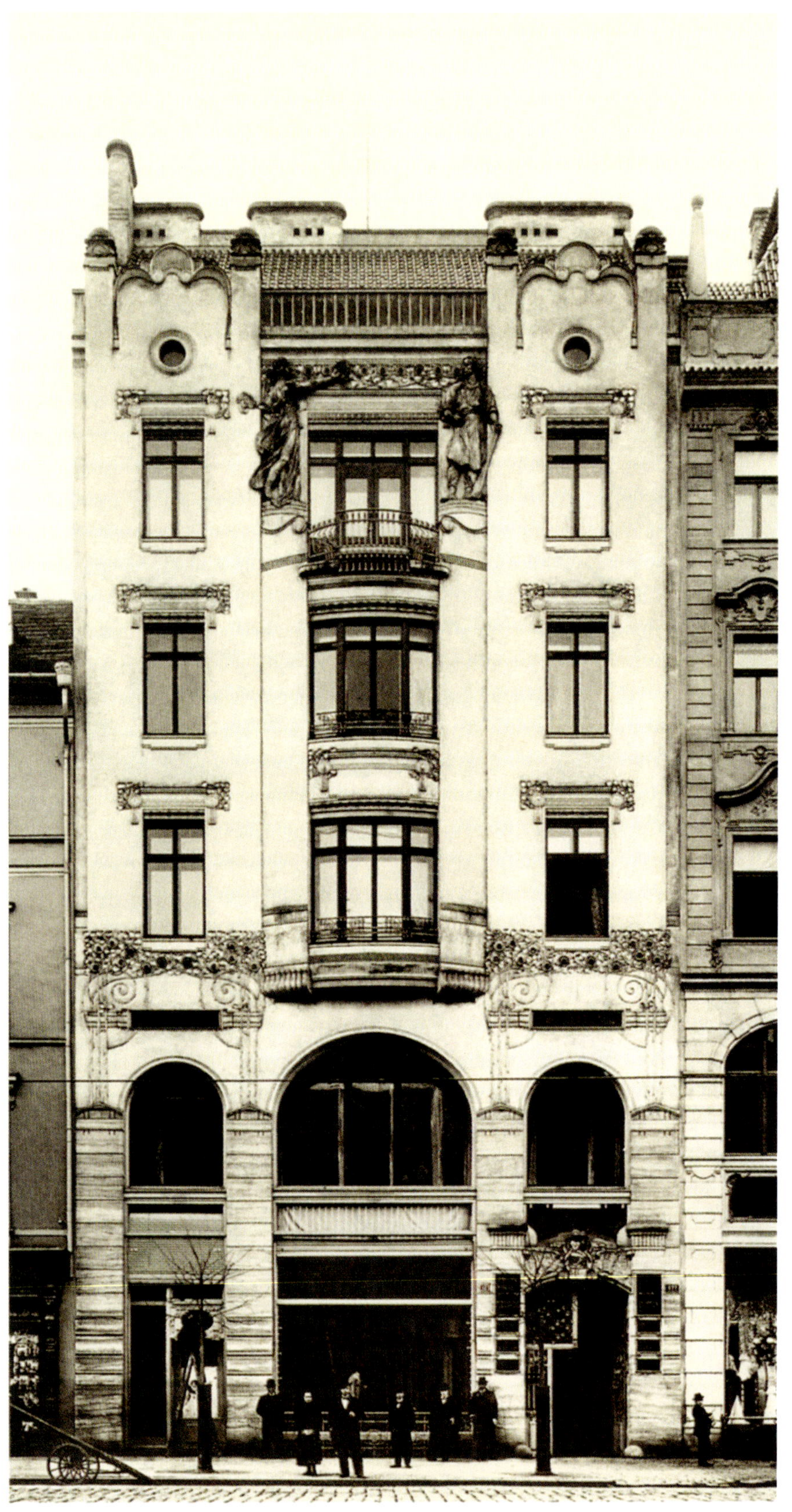

118 Jan Kotěra, Peterka House in Prague, 1899–1900

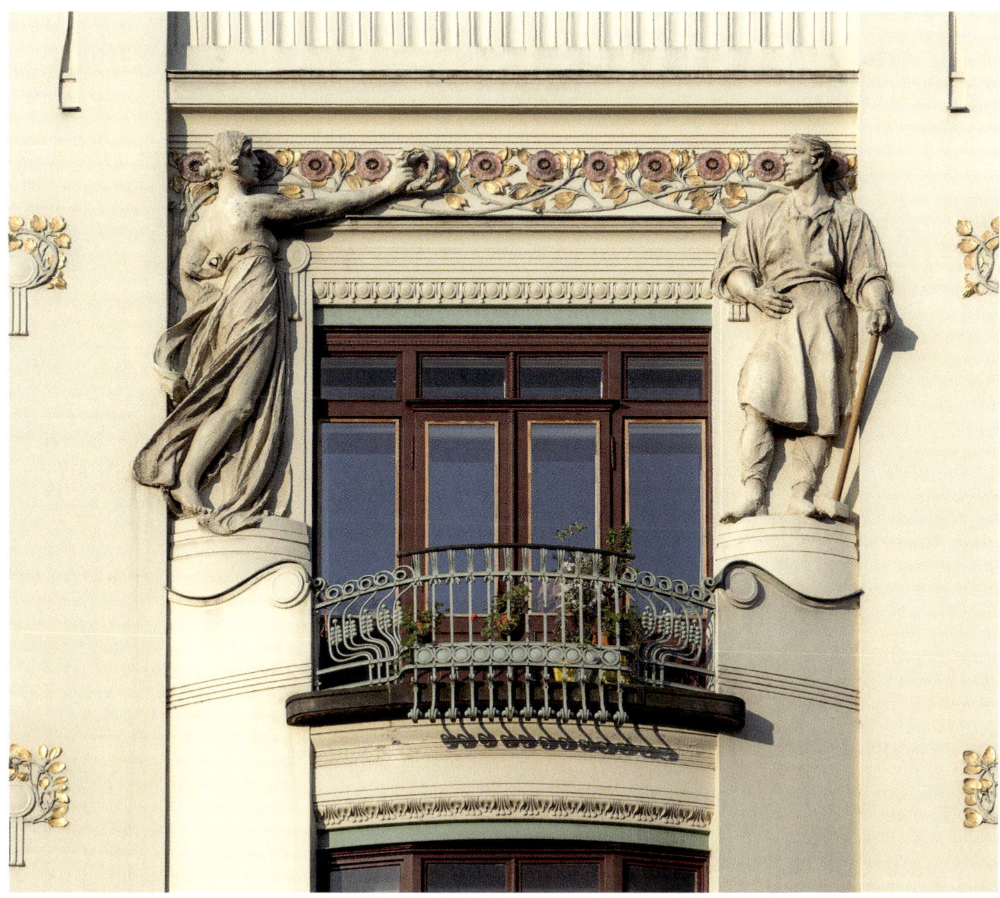

redevelopment) that the "domestic" Baroque was the foundation of the city's exteriors, and new architecture should therefore be in harmony with it. Ohmann also influenced the ideas of the SVU Mánes generation with his unrealised design for the area around the Church of the Holy Trinity in Spálená in Prague's New Town, which was published in the June 1898 issue of *Volné směry*. His sketch combines pseudo-Secession curves with new Baroque Revival construction that was unquestionably sensitive from a conservationist perspective. From the start, there was then a conflict within Czech Secession architecture that would later only escalate.

This conflict would become fully apparent when the Secession began to be considered acceptable for major public contracts. At the turn of the century, however, Kotěra himself preferred more modest and intimate forms of architecture, for which he found suitable customers among admirers of the new art, mostly from the intelligentsia. His designs for houses came to symbolise the Secession's intimacy and a sense of the closeness between people in smaller groupings, typically the family. Kotěra paid great attention to the layout of the rooms, combining economy with comfort and new hygiene requirements. In his houses, sited in gardens and thereby reflecting this architecture's affinity with the motif of the human figure in nature that dominated Secession painting,

119 Jan Kotěra, Peterka House in Prague, 1899–1900, detail

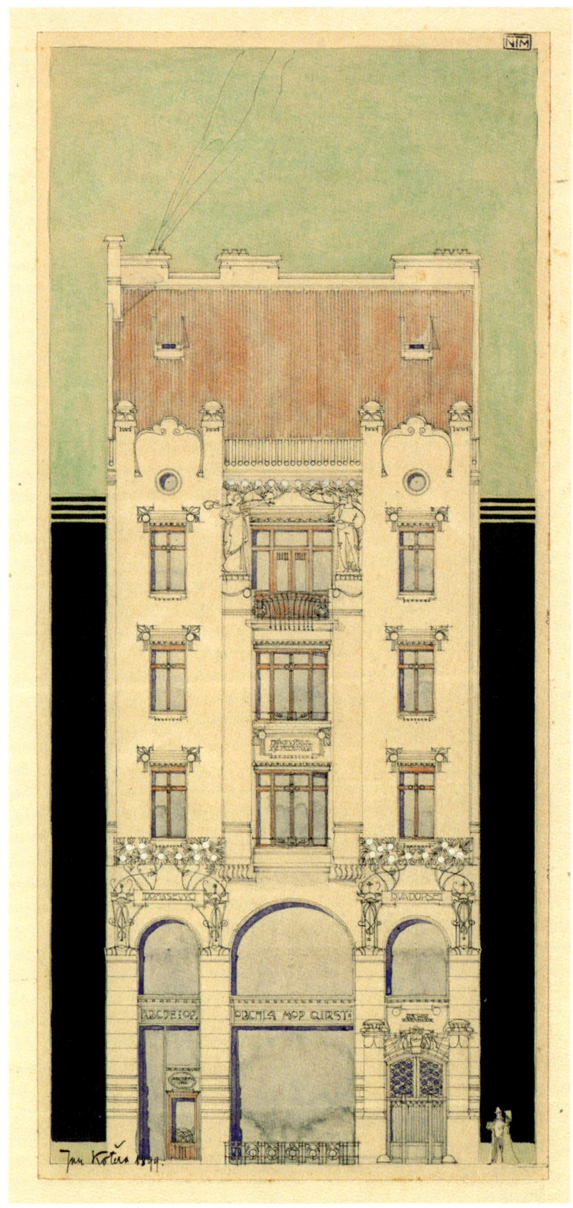

Kotěra sought a synthesis of forms derived from ethnographic inspiration and those informed by popular examples of English houses. Ethnographic forms were dominant in the Trmal Villa in Strašnice (1902), while the English influence guided the remodelling of the Mácha Villa in Bechyně from the same year. Common to both houses was Kotěra's attempt to open up the North European house's originally closed layout to its surroundings, by means of balconies, bay windows, and loggia at the entrances. In his proposal of 1900 for the reconstruction of St. George's Church in Doubravka, now part of Pilsen, Kotěra approached religious architecture much as he did an intimate villa, with only the ornamentation of the tower reflecting the building's purpose.

120 Jan Kotěra, Drawing for the Peterka House in Prague, 1899, watercolour, 41 × 18 cm

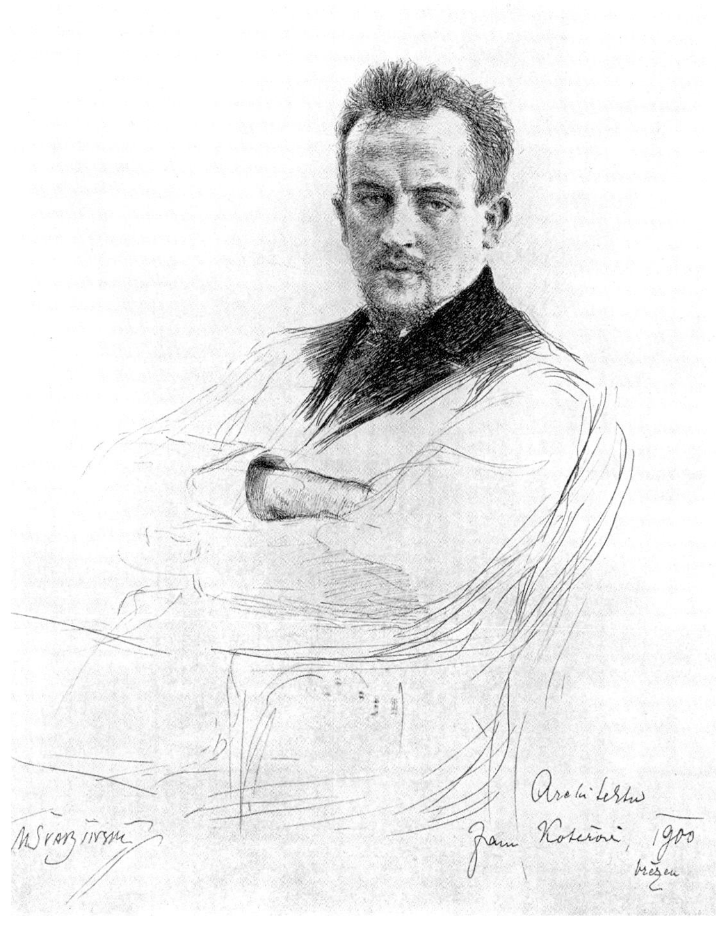

Designs for tombs were similarly private works, and here Kotěra displayed great inventiveness and contributed significantly to the high standard of funerary art. It was a field that was especially attractive for the Secession, offering an opportunity to work with melancholy subject matter. Kotěra's Elbogen Tomb in the New Jewish Cemetery in Strašnice in Prague (1901) was surprising in its lack of ornamentation, making use instead of the expressive qualities of polished stone. Its composition is a typical three-part arrangement, evoking the gates of death. Kotěra's sketch anticipated the effect of cypresses standing in front of the pylons on either side of the slab at the rear, adding an emotional quality to their monumentality. Secession curves only featured in the wrought ironwork. The adjacent Robitschko Tomb (1901–2) is more picturesque, and besides the wrought ironwork the sculpted ornamental capitals of the small pillars also stand out. In their plasticity, the tomb's architectural elements assume an almost sculptural character, and they symbolically and fantastically combine the botanical with the human on an abstract ornamental foundation. A comparison between these two tombs also reveals how Kotěra was seeking an expressive form, which was symptomatic of how he was developing as an artist.

121 Maxmilián Švabinský, *Jan Kotěra*, 1900, Indian ink, 33 × 25.5 cm

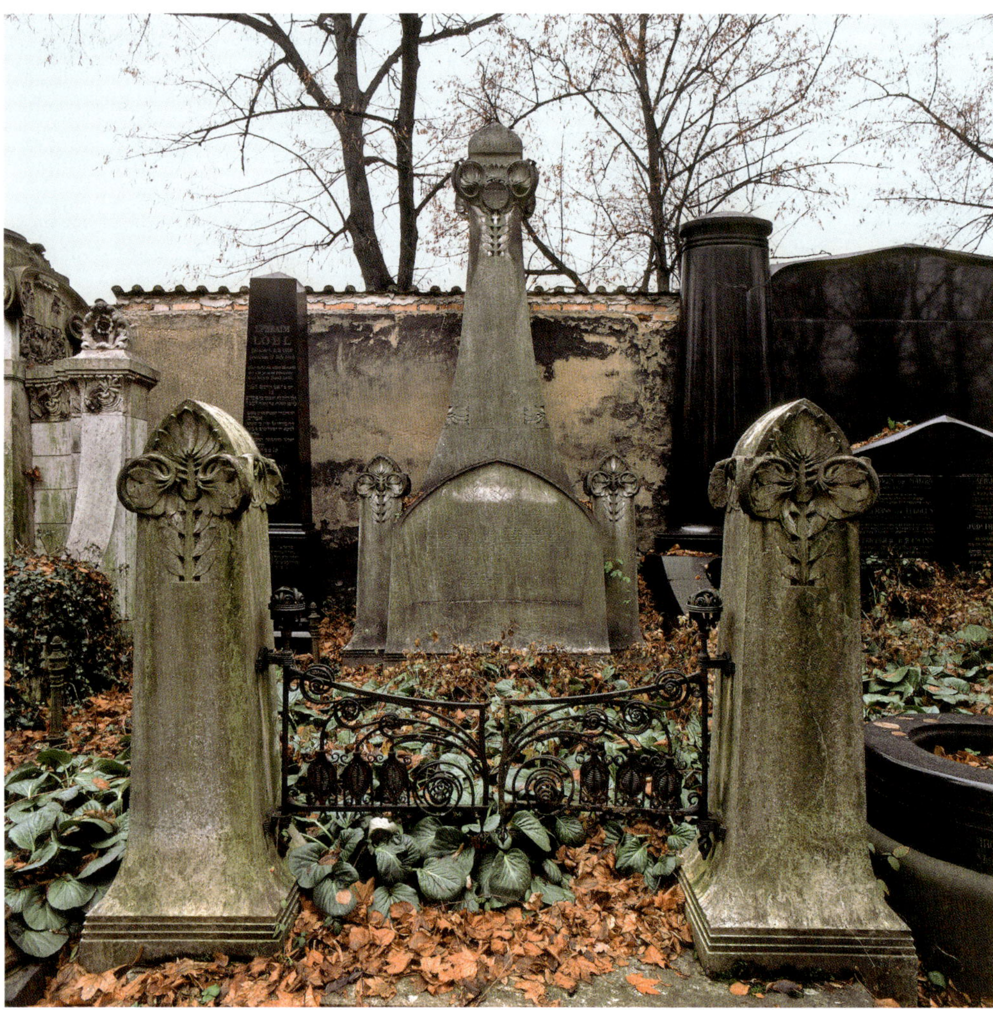

Kotěra's position as professor of decorative architecture at the School of Decorative Arts in Prague placed him at the very centre of the quest for a new style. The school had been founded in the mid-1880s and had initially followed the usual eclectic historicism, but since the mid-1890s it had acquired a new authority in connection with the theoretical ferment that was now emerging in the decorative arts. The reformist thinking that had spread from England to the continent was gradually permeating, and it soon led to the conviction that the applied arts had much to say about the new modern style. Marked interest in this issue was prompted in 1896, when two of the schools' professors, Josef Václav Myslbek and František Ženíšek, switched to the Academy of Fine Arts, which was where they truly belonged, and the school could henceforward concentrate on the programme for which it had originally been intended. Another factor was that, at the start of the following year, preparations began for the 1900 Exposition Universelle in Paris, where the school planned to display the results of its work in its own exhibition space in the Austrian pavilion. The pavilion would also

122 Jan Kotěra, Robitschko Tomb in the New Jewish Cemetery in Prague, 1901–2

have another room that would be furnished at the expense of the Prague Chamber of Trade and Commerce, under the artistic guidance of two teachers from the Prague Polytechnic, Josef Fanta and Jan Koula, and this only intensified the competition to innovate.

Looking at the material available today on the two interiors that represented the Czech decorative arts at the Exposition Universelle,[102] we have to conclude that they were more assemblages of artistically quite diverse exhibits than true stylistic wholes. Ohmann designed the layout of the exhibition space for the School of Decorative Arts, but not even his skill could entirely overcome the fact that individual showpieces were seen as the very essence of the exhibition. Fanta's approach was seemingly more progressive, for he designed the exhibition space as "the study of a member of the Czech intelligentsia," but he too achieved nothing more than the sum of the parts contributed by individual artists.

Fanta's concept was based on the contrast between the more intimately furnished lower part, decorated according to his design, and the philosophical framework for the upper part, where beneath a heavy-looking joist ceiling the walls were covered

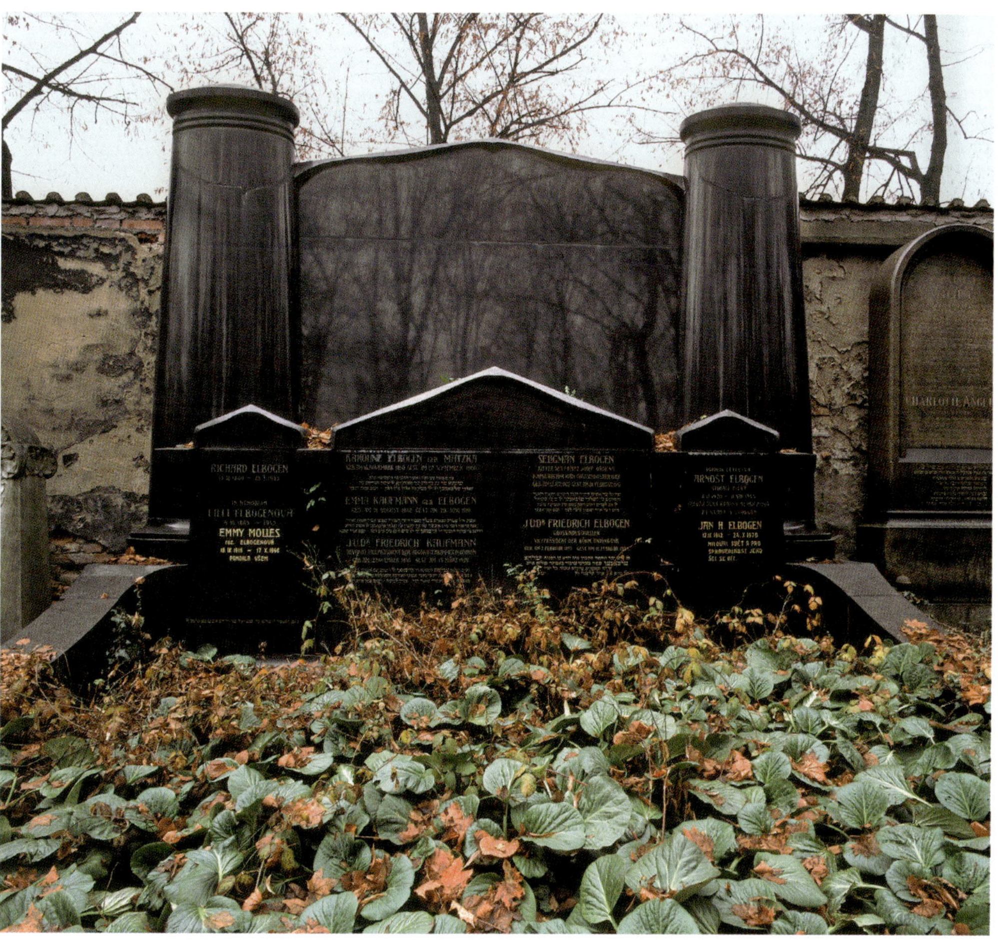

123 Jan Kotěra, Elbogen Tomb in the New Jewish Cemetery in Prague, 1901–2

with mythological and allegorical scenes painted by František Urban, Jan Preisler, and Karel Špillar. Jan Koula designed the entrance hall for this exhibition space in keeping with the contemporary popularity of folk-art motifs. In terms of style, the most interesting part of the interior of the Chamber of Trade and Commerce was Fanta and Koula's furniture, featuring relatively simple and geometrical bodies with restrained ornamentation. Like his chair and his desk with its tall upper part, Fanta's maplewood cabinet, decorated with bronze plaquettes and terracotta by Ludvík Wurzel, made no secret of the inspiration of traditional furniture that had, in fact, only lost its conventional articulation. The effect produced by Koula's dresser is similarly due more to its ornamentation than to any particular originality in the design for its construction. Developmentally, the thinking represented in Fanta and Koula's work could be aligned with some early examples from the modern movement, such as those created in England some twenty or thirty years earlier. While Fanta and Koula's pioneering role in their own country should be acknowledged, given how late in the day it came, their work very soon began to seem outmoded.

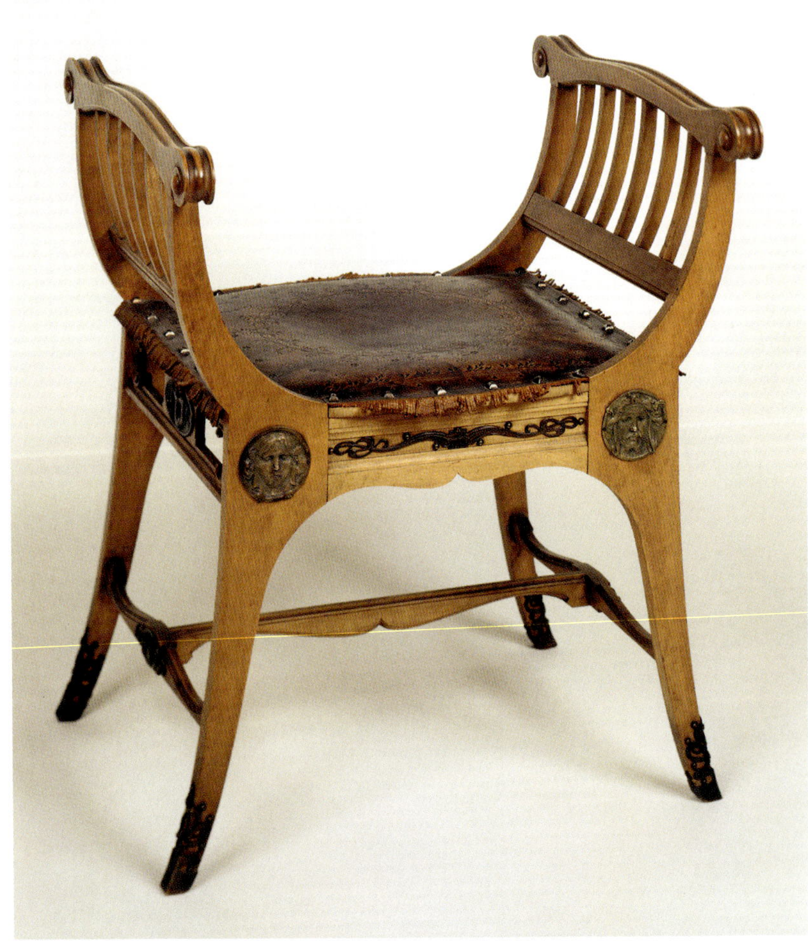

124 Josef Fanta, Chair, 1899, wood and metal, 68 cm

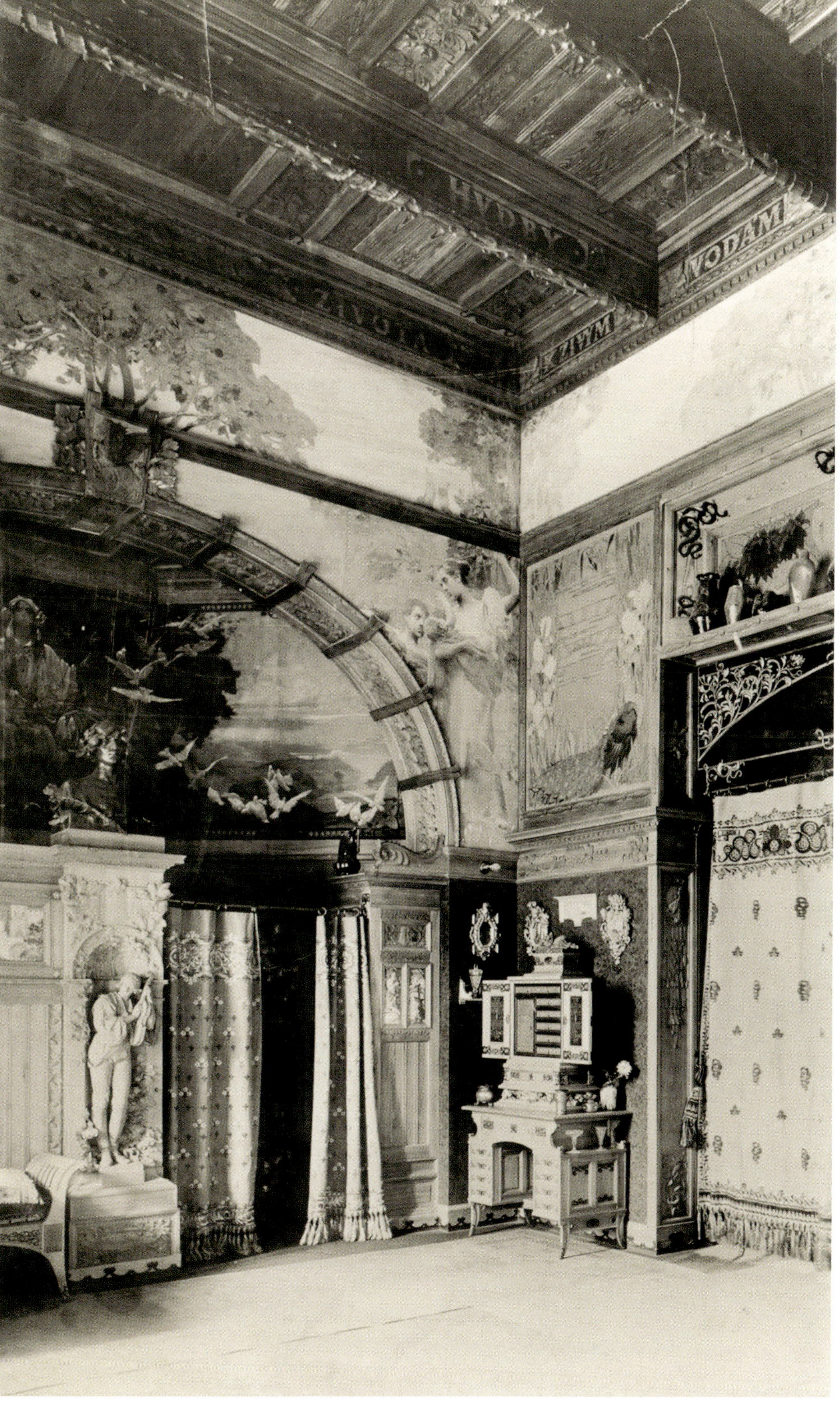

125 Josef Fanta, Interior for the Chamber of Trade and Commerce at the Exposition Universelle in Paris, 1900

The interior created by the School of Decorative Arts was possibly even more fragmented, but it did include a number of works that were stylistically much closer to the contemporary international standard. Besides the school's professors, its recent graduates also exhibited their work, which promised a more dynamic treatment of the question of style, and it indicated the direction that subsequent developments would take. Although the school did not quite find a common language, its professors had now proved themselves to be creative and stimulating individuals.

Jan Kastner, the head of the woodcarving school, showed his most demanding work here, the large polychrome Czech Altar (now installed in St. Bartholomew's Cathedral in Pilsen), featuring the Virgin, the kneeling figure of Saint Wenceslas, and

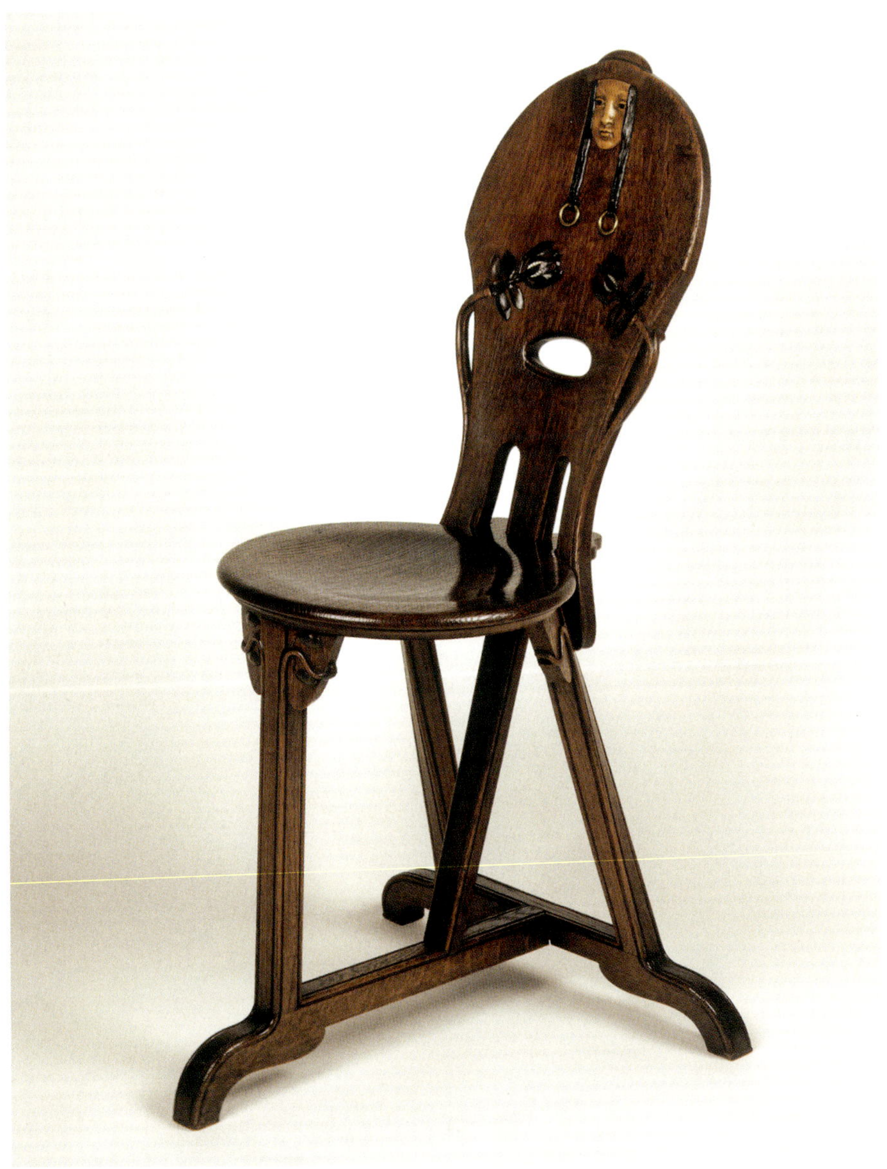

126 Josef Kastner, Folding chair, 1899, wood, mother-of-pearl, and metal, 92 cm

Saint Ludmila. He brought to it his knowledge of late medieval woodcarving, which he modernised through an unusual combination of naturalistic modelling and the hieratic gestures of the figures. Also by Kastner was another smaller altar with simple ornamentation, fitted with a triptych by Felix Jenewein. A corner cabinet and an original folding three-legged chair, whose back was decorated with the carved head of a Native American and a mother-of-pearl inlay, were Kastner's contributions to contemporary attempts to break with traditional furniture designs.

Celda Klouček, the professor of the "school for modelling, predominantly ornamental," created the installation's other dominant feature – a richly shaped limestone portal that highlighted the broad architectural collaborations that Klouček had introduced in his school. In addition, Klouček's studio produced a large group of ceramic vases that were some of the installation's most noteworthy exhibits. The influence of his decorative sculpture was also apparent in works by the metalworking professor Emanuel Novák and his pupils, for whom Klouček often created designs. If there was any more marked collective tendency in the work of the School of Decorative Arts,

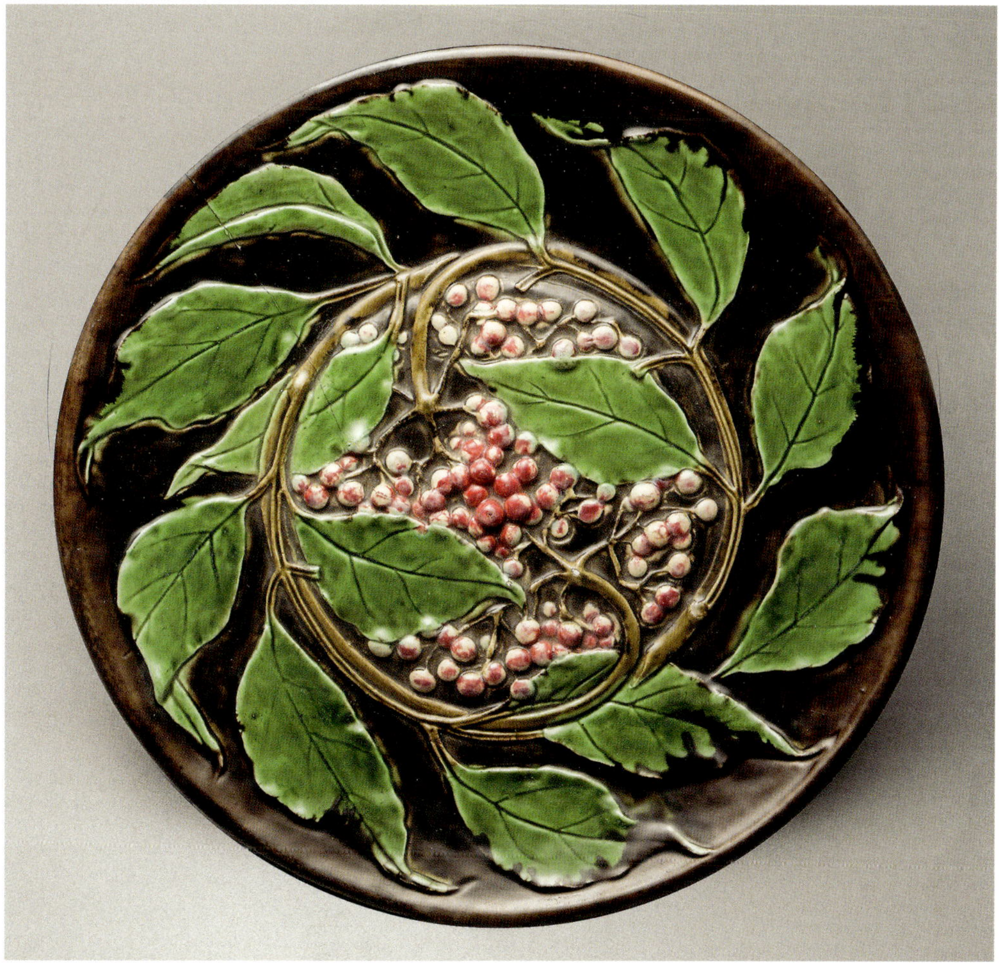

127 Celda Klouček, Bowl decorated with leaves and fruit, 1895 (made 1899), glazed chamotte, 31 cm

it was initiated by Klouček, who emerges as an insufficiently appreciated figure in the development of Czech decorative art at the turn of the century.

Before being recruited by František Schmoranz, the first director of the School of Decorative Arts, Klouček had worked for the decorative sculptor Otto Lessing in Berlin and studied at the Arts and Crafts School in Vienna. He had then spent almost six years teaching at the School of Applied Arts in Frankfurt. His ideas about art were primarily shaped by his study of late Italian Renaissance decorative art, as is evident from an album of drawings and sketches he published in Prague in 1893, under the title *Designs for the Decorative Arts*. They show Klouček to be an eminent draughtsman who even had traces of Josef Mánes's lyricism. Here he relied chiefly on his spontaneous and virtuosic Mannerist draughtsmanship, or what was known at the time (for art historians had yet to rehabilitate the term *Mannerism*) as the "informal" Renaissance. To this was added the fashionable influence of the Baroque, whose combination of virtuosity and naturalism was well suited to Klouček. In 1890 he used a greater degree of applied sculptural decoration for the Mortgage Bank (*Hypoteční banka*) in Prague, and this would form the basis of his subsequent great influence on the ornamentation of Secession architecture.

Klouček turned away from historicism in 1895, when examinations at the School of Decorative Arts began emphasising direct naturalistic inspiration. The first examples of a new thematic concept in decoration were concurrent with the breakthrough we also see in young painting, and it was applied in ceramics, a discipline that allowed experimentation with new ideas. Naturalism shaped Klouček's reliefs and friezes for the Provincial Bank (1895) and, more prominently, albeit still remaining within Klouček's Neo-Baroque formula, his stuccowork for the Straka Academy (1896). Klouček then developed his thinking on Secession ornament largely by working on buildings whose relatively unassertive architects welcomed his contribution. They included the Vohanka House in Prague (1898) and the City Museum in Pilsen (1900), where Klouček collaborated with the architect Josef Škorpil. Klouček also enjoyed working with businesses, as for their buildings he could devise the entire façade and the ornamentation of the interiors. This resulted in Celda Klouček's best-known work, his ornate stone façade for Matěj Blecha's Prague Credit Bank (*Pražská úvěrní banka*), from 1902. Besides his decorative reliefs, the figure of Mercury on top of the attic also demonstrated Klouček's talent as a sculptor.

These buildings saw the maturing of Klouček's Secessionist decorative system. Its significance lay not just in its undisputed artistic qualities, but also because, thanks to Klouček's many pupils, it rapidly became widespread, in many ways becoming synonymous with the Secession in the eyes of the general public. Its initial forms were markedly naturalistic, and this was reflected in the depth of the plastic relief. Instead of the usual acanthus, Klouček favoured indigenous plants: peonies, guelder roses, bay trees, common mallows, primroses, and elderberries formed a new repertoire whose colours were suitable for ceramics. Their stalks, stems, leaves, flowers, and berries were arranged so that the ornament would appear natural while satisfying the requirement for the rhythmic decorative structuring of the architecture.

In this process, the ceramic vase offered a basic circular form on which the new ornament could be fully developed. The cult of the ceramic vase in contemporary decorative art was most probably due to how it naturally combined the new form with motifs suggested by the vase's substance. Symbolists emphasised the substance, meditating on the relationship between the empty space inside the vase and the material sheathing it. They saw in the vase a symbol of the new art, which drew its ideas from the depths of the unconscious.[103] A set of dark graphite vases that František Bílek began producing in 1896 was explicitly motivated by the material, based on the moral symbolism of the natural elements: the vase was made of clay, that is the earth, which was scorched by fire, the artist's imagination, into a form holding water, an essential nutrient, from which flowers can grow into the air and towards the sun. The flower, a contemporary symbol for art itself, was then not just the object of the artist's attention, but also a means through which artists could express themselves and bring about their externalisation. This is also why we see a typical progression in vase decoration from an initial marked naturalism to ever greater stylisation and ultimately the creation of new ornament.

Around the year 1900, Anna Boudová-Suchardová, who typically painted flowers and decorative floral patterns, made a set of Secession vases. Besides vases and bowls

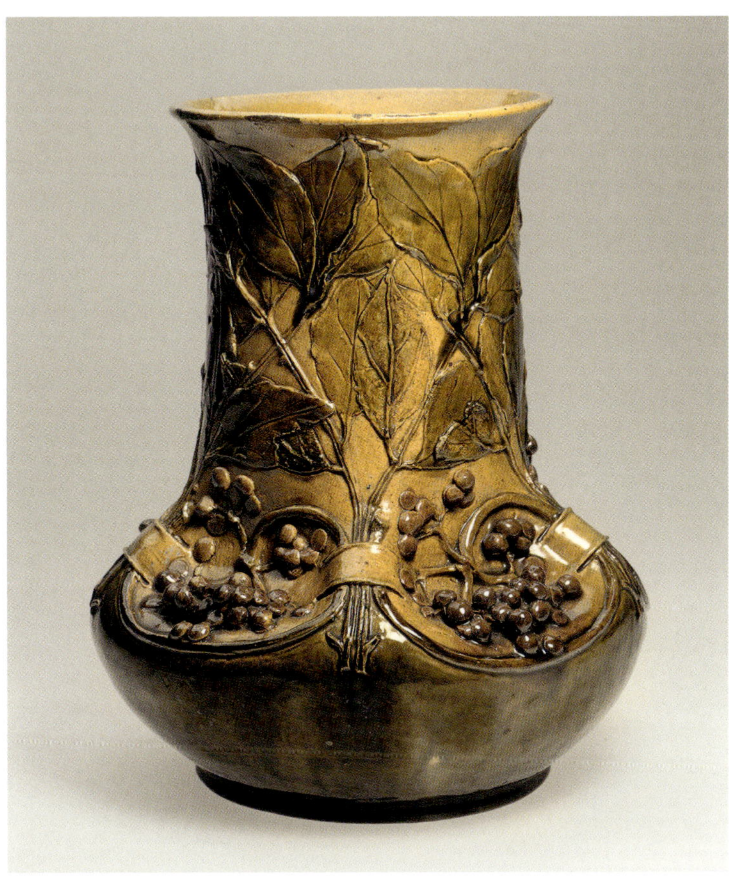

128 Václav Mařan, Vase, 1899, glazed earthenware, 22.5 cm

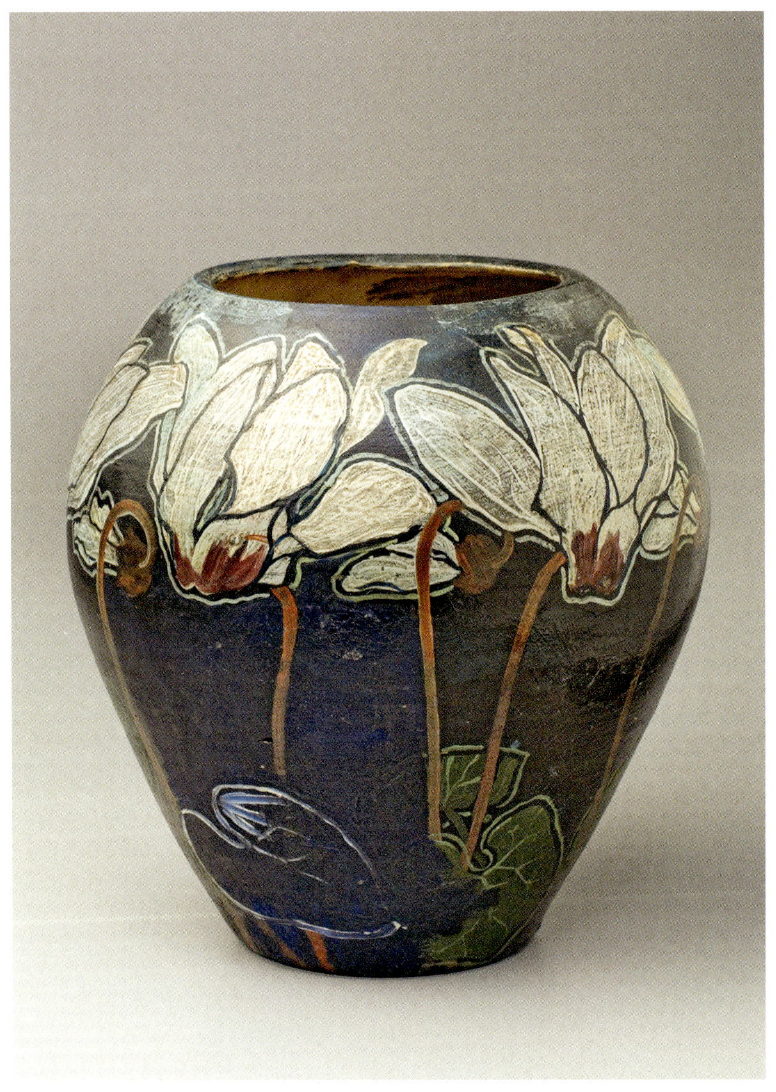

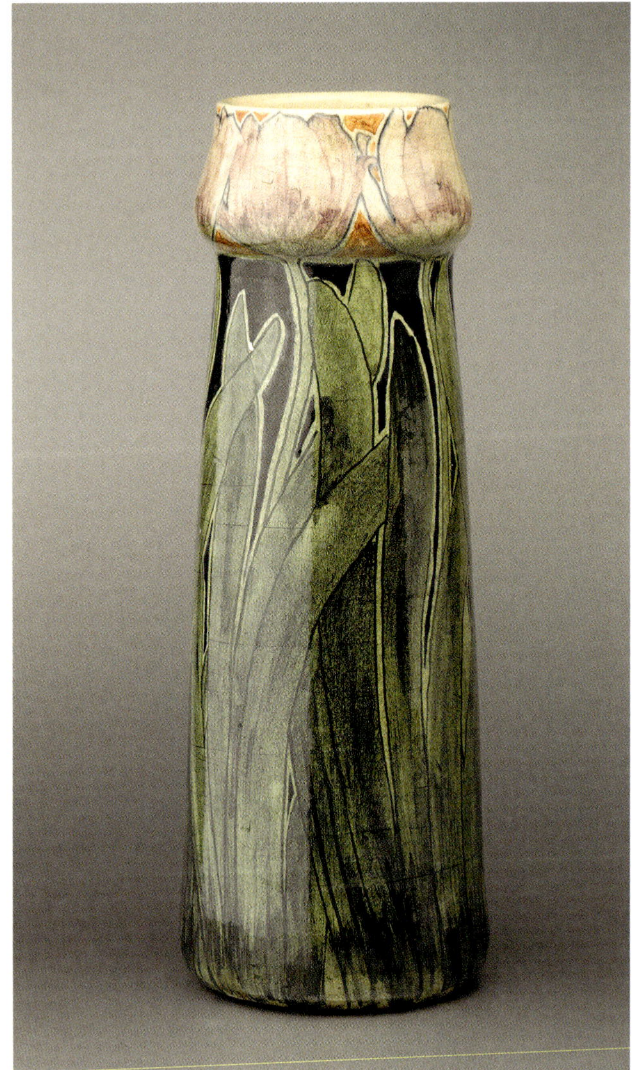

129–130 Anna Boudová-Suchardová, Two vases, c. 1900, glazed earthenware, 23 cm, 38.5 cm

with relatively simple shapes, which she painted with Japanese-style floral ornament in violet and green and with markedly linear stylisation, she also made quite different vases that had "natural" monochrome glazes and even featured sculpted female mascarons. Like Bílek's vases, hers were original and distinctive works.

Vases by Celda Klouček and his pupils (Václav Mařan, Rudolf Hameršmíd, Václav Šidlík, František Soukup, Karel Pavlík, Robert Hájek, and others) retained more of the school's common style, but it is in them that the development of Czech ornament can best be traced. Vases from the early period are naturalistic in their modelling; their shapes frequently reference prehistoric specimens, and their colouring does not disdain explicitly painterly effects. Other than a few fantastical examples, vases from the finest period, between 1899 and 1904, have very simple forms. Both tall, slender, conical vases and short, squat ones were popular. The decoration is very flat and stylised, sometimes engraved, and it extends symmetrically from a central axis. However, there are also interesting examples of discreet asymmetrical stylisation that again emphasise the two-dimensionality of the decorative elements. The glaze is monochrome, most often green or yellow, but also pale blue or rose. The school's later ceramic vases

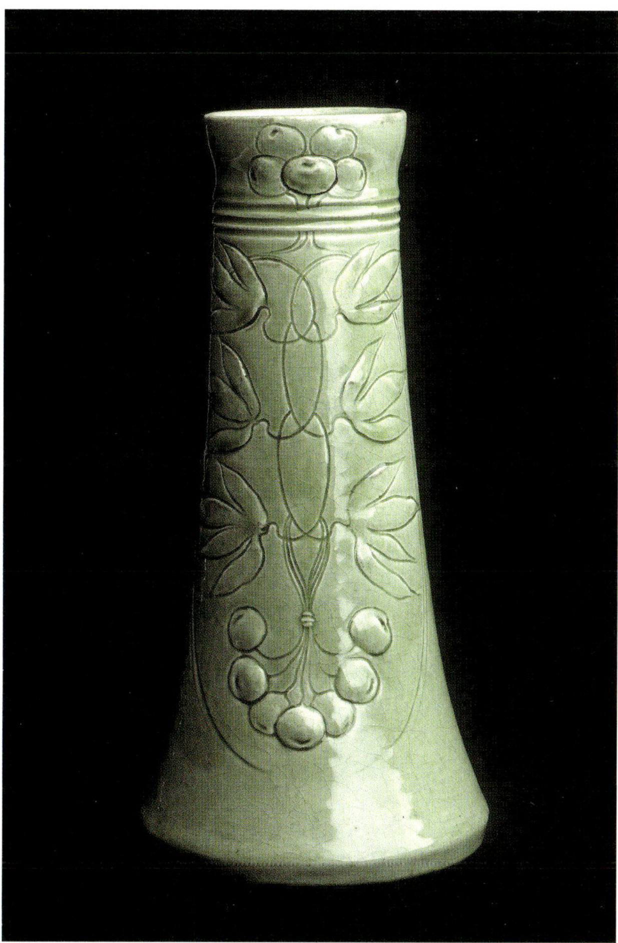

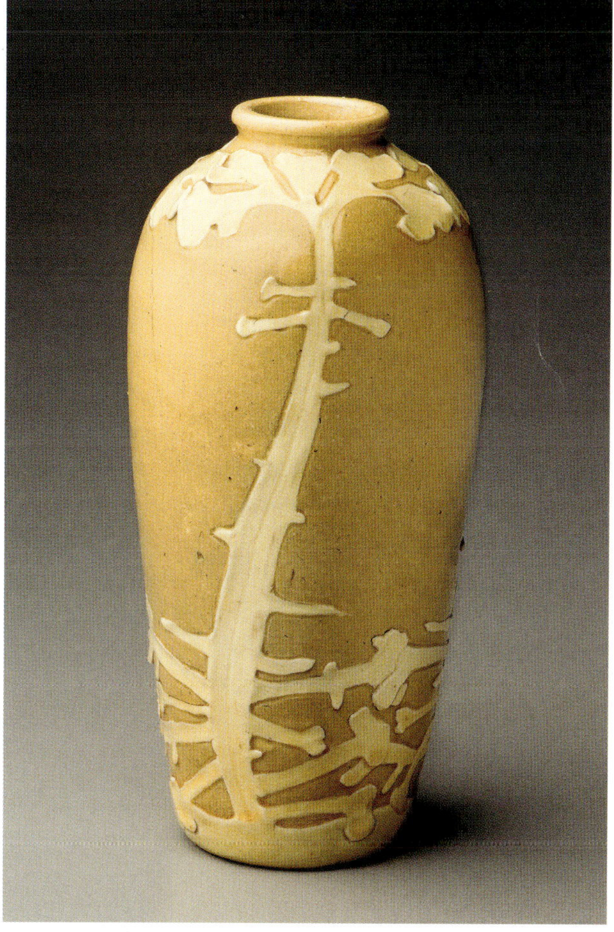

131–132 Rudolf Hameršmíd and Celda Klouček, Two vases, 1904, 1899, glazed earthenware, 22.5 cm, 27 cm

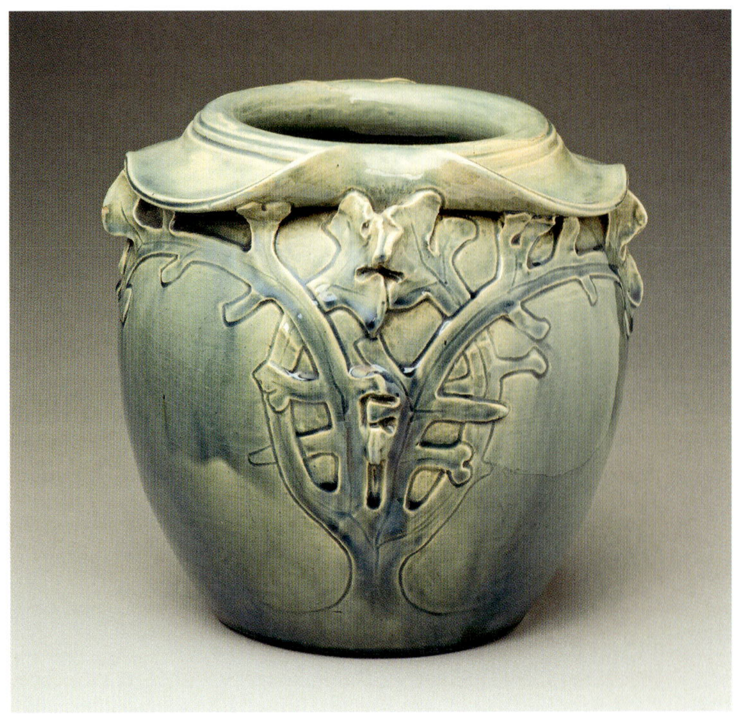

are usually tall and slender, and decorated with symmetrically stylised sprigs of plants whose fruits or flowers form handles along the sides. They are mostly white, with little details picked out in various colours.

A similar stylistic evolution can be mapped in Klouček and his pupils' stuccowork for Secession architecture. The naturalistic foundation and the vivid plastic treatment of botanical and figural motifs are never lost, but the rhythm of the ornament is guided even more here by the requirement for grand form. This is particularly apparent in Klouček's overdoors, friezes, and panels, featuring symmetrical botanical curves on either side of a central motif, typically a female mascaron. Here we again find the fundamental theme in Secession painting: the combination of the human figure and nature. It is another manifestation of the world view common to all Secession art. Unlike the Renaissance Revival's idealised mascarons, Klouček's heads embody much of the new emotionality, and it gives them a much more extensive expressive range.

In the decorative arts, the abstraction of natural form was the key developmental problem for the Secession. Its successful solution would guarantee the Secession's overall outcome, for it was becoming ever more apparent that natural form alone was insufficient to counter the exhausted eclectic morphology: what was needed was a higher and more elaborate artistic system. In contemporary thinking on art, these questions were centred around the concept of ornament. This was also why professors of ornamental drawing had a special status at applied art schools during this time. In 1903 the ornamental drawing professor at the School of Decorative Arts in Prague, Karel Vítězslav Mašek, put forward his views on the study of ornament in the periodi-

133 František Soukup, Vase, 1904, glazed earthenware, 18 cm

cal *Dílo* (Artwork).[104] According to Mašek, the foundation of ornament in the modern age is not imitating traditional systems of ornament, but nature. This is because ornament is just one part of art as a whole, and any results achieved and progress made are decided solely by respecting nature as the foundation of all individual creation. Like any other artist, the ornamental artist draws on nature, but while a painter depicts a human face or a landscape, the ornamental artist "draws on all of nature," selecting from its wealth of forms whatever is closest to the artist's individuality. Ornament is then "the ideal use of a particular part of nature." Ideality is based on the ornamental artist's ability to distinguish the beautiful from the ugly, the good from the bad. The significance of ornament is that it is the best means of connecting art with the people, and in this way it can lead to a revival of art. When studying ornament, a pupil should, if possible, be guided individually, for only then will such study satisfy its purpose.

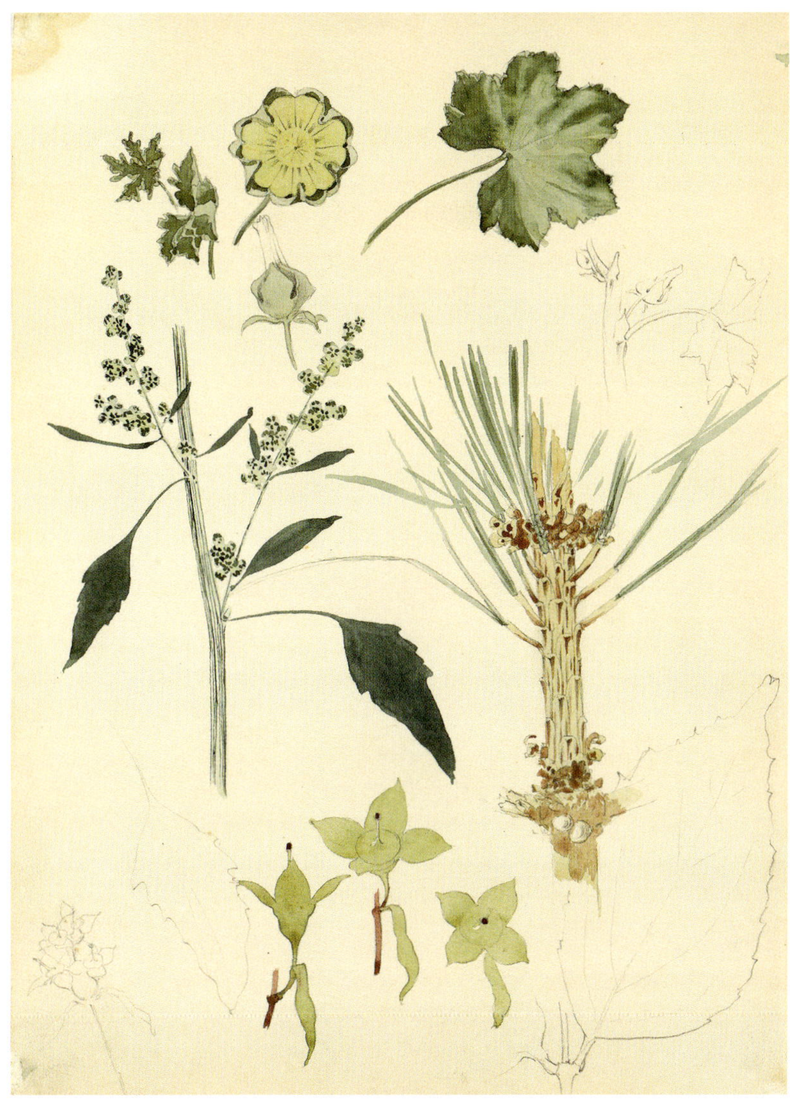

134 Karel Vítězslav Mašek, Study of plants, c. 1900, watercolour, 30.3 × 21.5 cm

Mašek's theory was appealing in its sensitivity to the artist's individuality (previously the decorative arts had been subject to rigid templates), but it did not specifically formulate the fundamental problem of the relationship between the natural phenomenon and the ornamental pattern. More illuminating than this theory were examples of studies by Mašek's pupils, reproduced in an appendix to the article in *Dílo*. They showed, usually on a single page, a meticulously naturalistic depiction of a natural object next to a study of its form in terms of its symmetry and the graphical processing of its individual parts (as in Jakub Obrovský's study of a twig and a pine cone). The ornamental motif could then be adapted to the needs of the material in which the resulting decorative object was to be rendered. These studies demonstrated how the naturalistic concept brought new inspiration to the study of ornament, stimulating students' imagination. They showed that there was a smooth transition from a photographic or naturalistic way of viewing a natural object to its abstraction in geometrical ornament. This removed the boundary between perception and idea, allowing a wealth of artistic forms to create the root system for the Secession style.

It is interesting, however, that in his article Mašek sought to excuse, on the grounds of his pupils' youth, the "generally modern impression" made by their work, which he tried to avoid describing as *Secession*. Here too there was a need to distance creativity from the formula that, under the label of *Secession*, was rapidly becoming widespread in commercial art and architectural ornamentation, where the decorative problem was vulgarised to the point of cliché. In contrast with the routine linear stylisation of a subject based solely on its contours, the drawings by Mašek's pupils at the School of Decorative Arts revealed, especially in their floral ornaments, an attempt to capture the growth structure in two-dimensional and symmetrical graphic designs. These works were the furthest from the popular "macaroni." In some respects, they drew on folk ornament and prepared the ground for the treatment of ornament in the Secession's late period.

The original forms of curvilinear Secession stylisation, as promoted by Mucha and elaborated by Klouček, were immediately taken up and rapidly disseminated primarily through the vocational education system. The School of Decorative Arts in Prague was part of a network of vocational schools that included a ceramics school in Bechyně, a sculpture school in Hořice, a metalworking school in Turnov, a woodworking school in Chrudim, a metalsmithing school in Hradec Králové, and other institutions that were happy to propagate the Secession formula in their teaching and output, as well as in courses for the general public. It was thanks to their intensive design and popularisation work that, after 1900, *Secession* swiftly became synonymous with the modern decorative style and was seen as almost a benchmark for contemporary art.

The success of the naturalistic Secession was unquestionably due to the fact that, unlike the diverse forms of historicism, it offered a new unity that could be seen as an artistic gain for the modern age, without being too remote from some of the customary ways of shaping and seeing an object. Even in Mucha's most ornamental designs, it is clear that a pattern is created by lines of various thicknesses, with the main body of the ornamental field – usually a female figure – having the thickest outline. Although

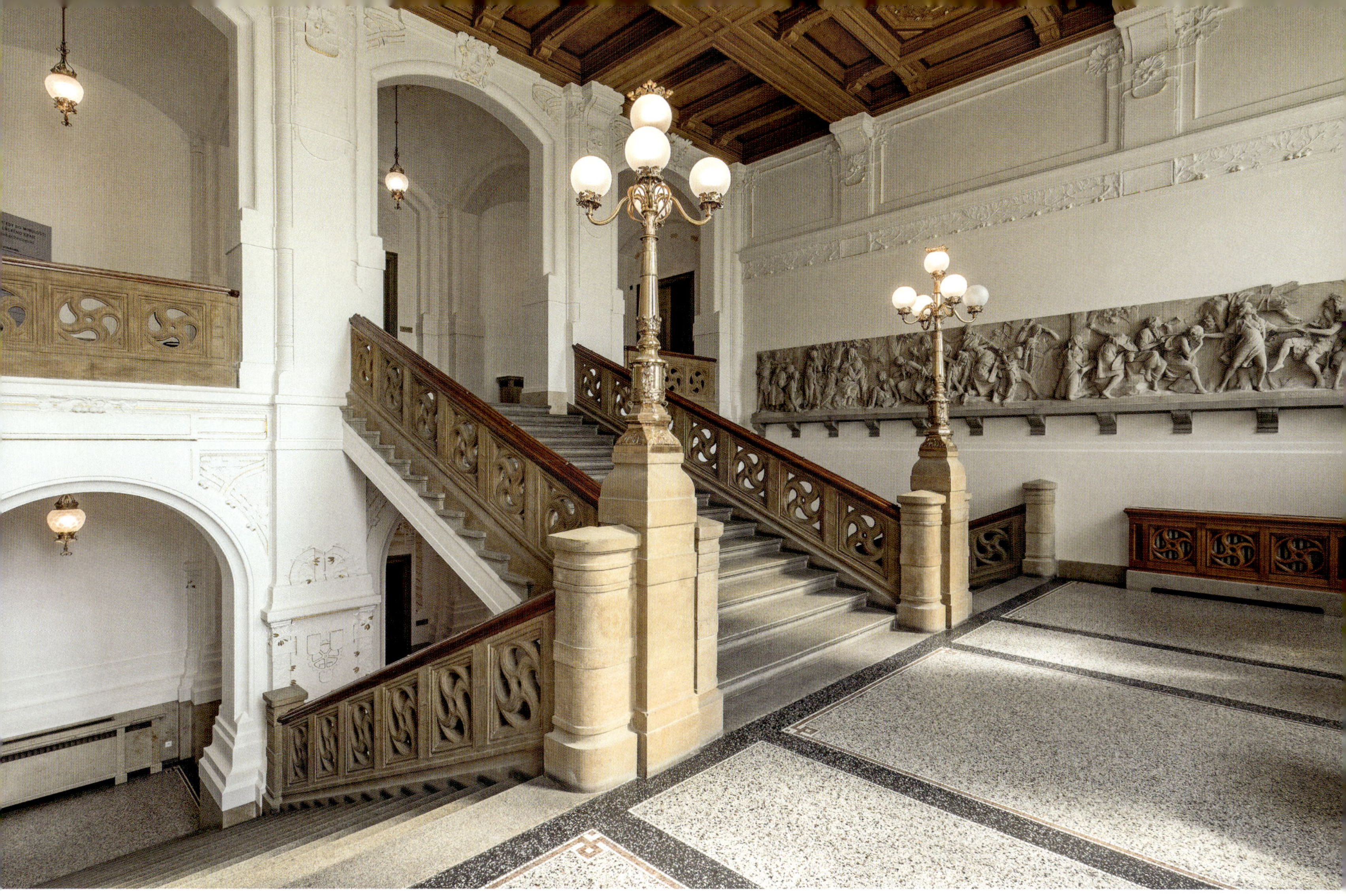

two-dimensional, this treatment of form is in fact highly plastic; it is only that the body's shadow has shrunk into the line, and the more massive the original body was, the thicker the line. In Klouček's decorative sculpture, which was a counterpart to Mucha and a template for the Czech Secession, the treatment of the relief follows a similar principle. Ultimately, it always retains the distinction between the body and the background, although the tendency is for the relief to spread over the entire surface, turning it into a rhythmical whole.

This stylistic layer of Secession art continued to respect the traditional separation of figure and background, but it also opened up a way of overcoming this separation in a new and total vision, in which body and space interpermeate to express an original and dynamic experiencing of the world. It was symptomatic, however, that Klouček was not an architect but a decorative sculptor, and he approached architecture in much the same way a printmaker approaches a sheet of paper: he was interested in the façade, not in the three-dimensional structure. The very technique of applied stucco meant that he built his art outwards from the ideal plane of the façade and

135 Celda Klouček and Josef Škorpil, Staircase of the Museum of Decorative Arts in Pilsen, 1900

towards the viewer, and he took little interest in what lay behind the plane. He composed his ornamentation from individual motifs that he repeated, with variations, on a façade. His most successful motif was a new treatment of the mascaron, in which he achieved a high degree of unity between the content and the formal elements. Here he created, on a purely ornamental foundation, an attractive composition and a vivid symbol of the new emotional experiencing of the world. The frontal view of a woman's face, her expression vaguely languid, surrounded on either side by tendrils or other botanical elements, permitted a refined play between the basic symmetrical form and the asymmetrical naturalistic details. In this sensuous visual event, the motif of the symmetrical mirroring of form had a deeper meaning, even if only intuited by Klouček. Later psychological interpretations of such arrangements showed how they were also deeper symbols of the process of individuation, in which an artwork is a symbol of a complex understanding of the human psyche: the symmetrical mirroring of the right and left sides expresses an attempt to balance conscious and unconscious elements. The distinctive expression of Klouček's masks, where dreaminess merges with the real and the ideal, only supports such an interpretation.[105]

It was therefore primarily through such symbols, unusually attractive as they were for the contemporary mindset, that the Secession became established. Klouček's mascaron motif was repeated innumerable times, not just on the façades and interiors of Secession buildings, but also in more modest sculptures. It also became a heraldic motif in Secession jewellery, where it took the most refined forms, leading to the creation of a new kind of amulet. In Czech metalworking, the Secession reform was initiated by Professor Emanuel Novák at the School of Decorative Arts, and it was further developed by his talented pupils František Anýž, who founded a notable busi-

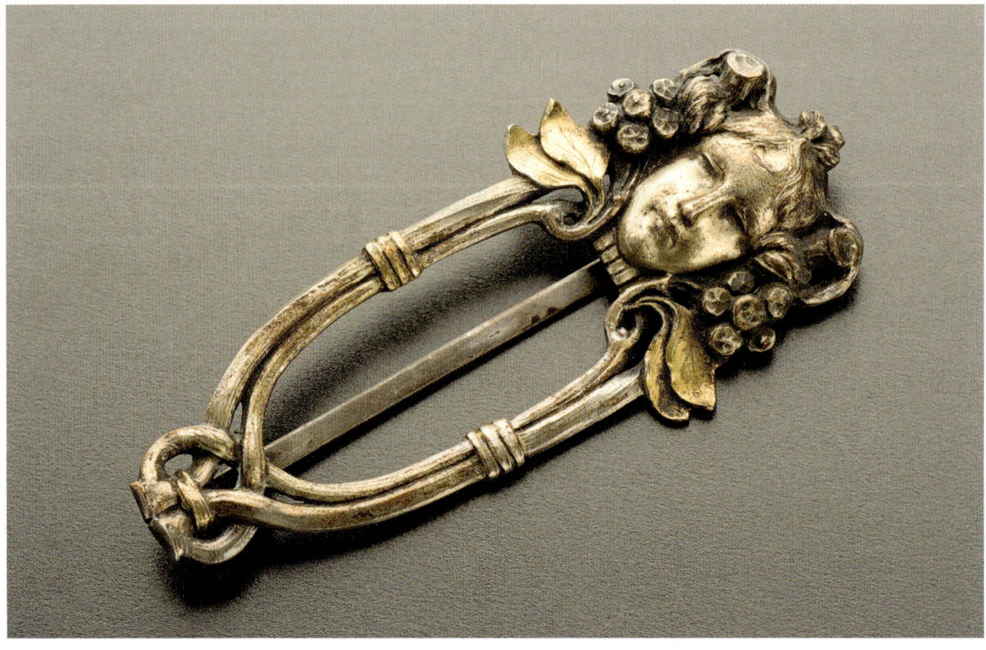

136 Emanuel Novák, Clasp, 1900, silver, 8 cm

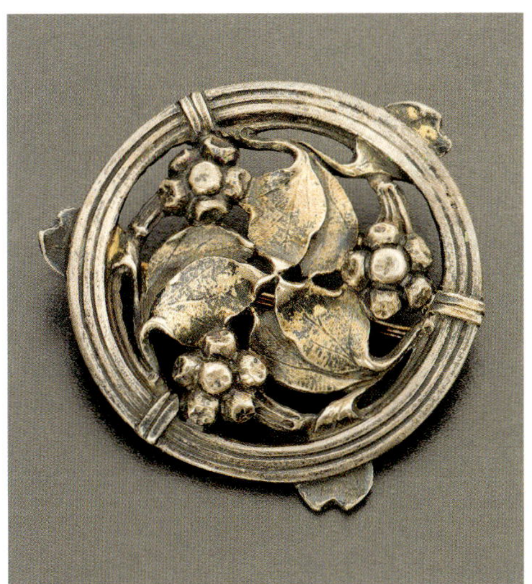
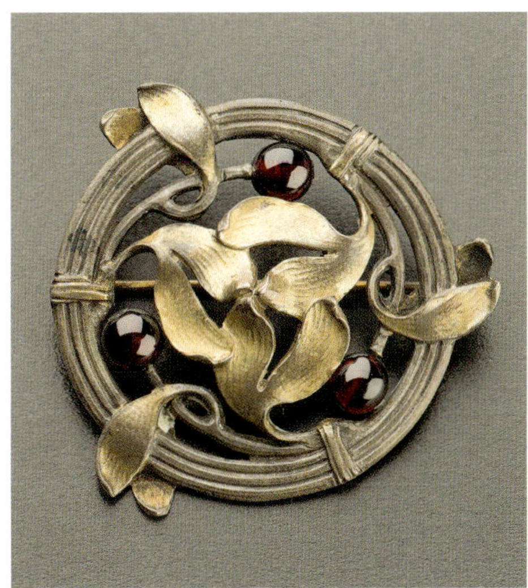
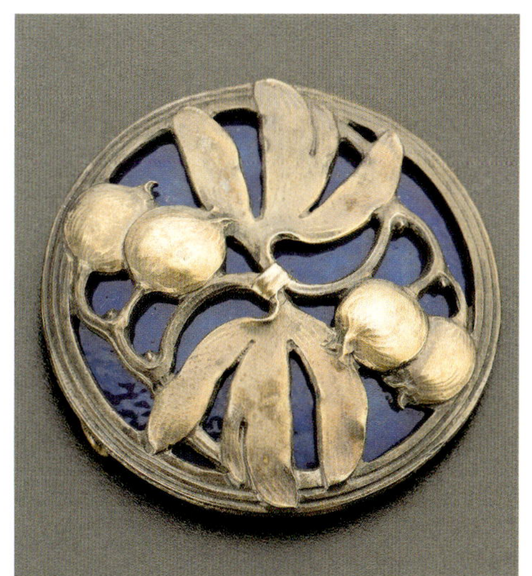

ness in Prague, and Josef Ladislav Němec, who spent three years in Paris perfecting his craft and became the driving force behind a new vocational school for goldsmithing in Prague. If around the year 1900 a respect for the sculptural body had still been central to Czech Secession decorative art, and the result of work was, above all, the individual artefact (as demonstrated by the contributions of Czech artists to the 1900 Exposition Universelle), the process of a new stylistic integration had already begun, and its more advanced phases would soon follow. The work of some of the younger Secession artists indicated what these would be. In Vojtěch Preissig's gouaches with wallpaper designs from this time, the problem of the ornamental elaboration of a floral motif has gone beyond the earlier preference for a figure described against a passive background. The motif has not lost its individuality, but instead of simple repetition it is executed as part of a much more complex relationship between the individual forms. Here, serial repetition works with various diagonals, and overlapping is not aimed at producing an illusive effect but is a tool purely for the artistic development of the pictorial structure. A characteristic aspect is that the two-dimensional motifs still have a spatial arrangement, but there is a certain ambivalence here, as the background is also an active agent in these relations. Preissig's pattern offers then a way of overcoming the old dualism between subject and space. Without entirely abandoning the contrast between the natural and the ideal, so popular in the Secession, he brings these elements into a state of active mutual exchange. It was probably no accident that this advanced solution first appeared in wallpaper, a pattern that has no individual meaning but serves to visually unify a space. The question of greater unity gradually became more pressing in all branches of the decorative arts. In this respect, a differentiation began to appear in the so far relatively united ranks of the creators of the new art, and it would become more conspicuous. This was apparent in preparations for another collective effort for the next world's fair, which was to be held in 1904 in St. Louis in the United States. This time, the ministry responsible directly appointed Jan Kotěra to design the exhibition

137–139 Emanuel Novák, Three brooches, 1900, silver and brass, 3.5 cm

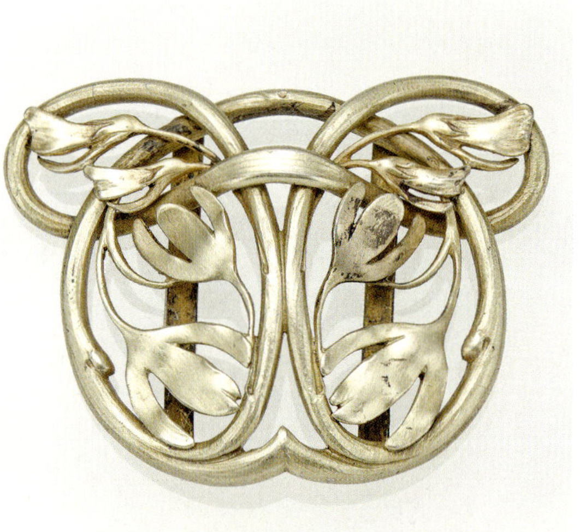
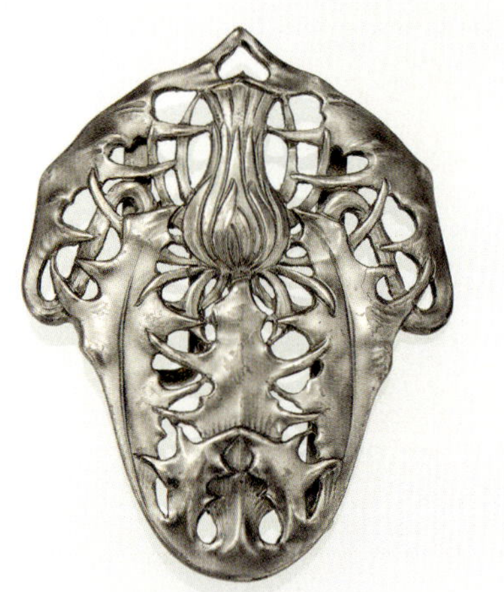
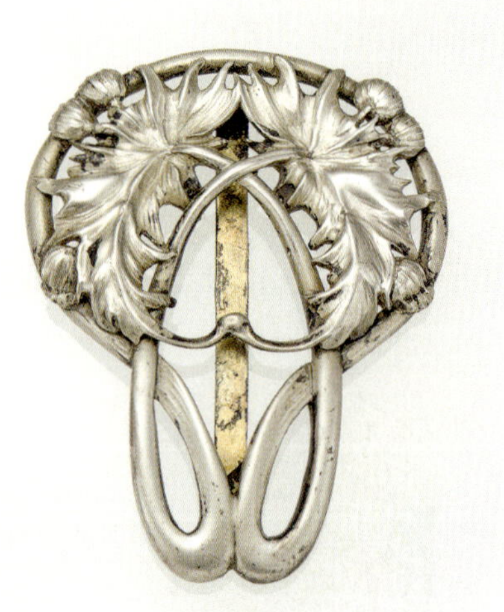

space for the School of Decorative Arts, with the recommendation that the exhibition be planned, in the spirit of recent Austrian Secession exhibitions, as "three-dimensional art." Czech artists protested against this – not for reasons of nationality, but because the appointing of Kotěra made it clear that the overall concept for the exhibition space would play the main role, rather than the exhibits themselves.[106]

Kotěra designed the interior for the Louisiana Purchase Exposition as the hall of a villa with overhead lighting. It was built of oak, lightly treated with ammonia, with beams bearing a gable roof covered with an embroidered awning. The exhibits were mounted in the wooden panelling on the walls, while the wall at the entrance had a fireplace made of black marble decorated with a large relief by Stanislav Sucharda on the theme of Prague and the River Vltava. The dominant colours were grey and yellow, which complemented the colours of the natural materials.

Works from the individual schools were only used as decorative elements, and this emphasised the uniform concept for the exhibition space, whose architectural and ornamental details were the work of Kotěra's pupils Emanuel Pelant, Richard Novák, and Jan Zázvorka. The interior's architecture was devoid of the usual "Secession" curves and was dominated instead by straight lines, which underlined the significance of the structure's linearity and the flatness of the panels. Pelant's ornaments were markedly geometrical, with a return to the motif of spirals at the end of long and only slightly curved lines.

It was with this visual vocabulary that tendencies diverging from the original naturalistic starting point first became more pronounced. The conditions for the creating of this vocabulary were primarily established in Kotěra's studio at the School of Decorative Arts. The drafting of the new vocabulary, which initially mainly concerned interior architecture, can be traced in Kotěra's collection of reproductions called *My Own and My Pupils' Work*, published in German in 1902 by Anton Schroll in Vienna. Kotěra's book shows how the concept for furnishing an interior had progressed from indi-

140–142 Josef Ladislav Němec, Three brooches, after 1900, metal

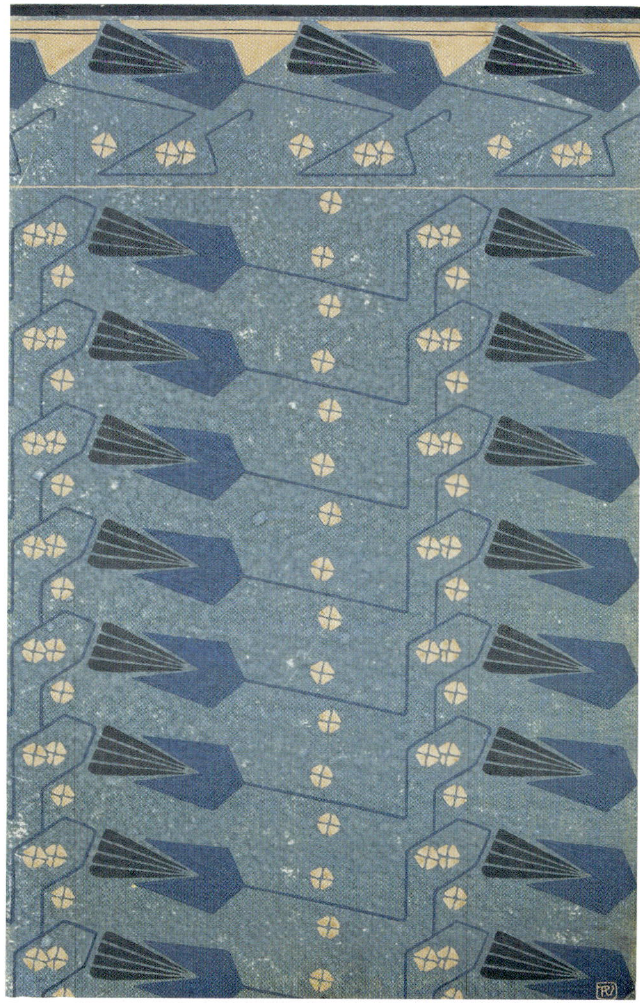

vidual items to entire suites. Sometimes these were rather clumsy wall units, combining multiple functions (cabinet, bookcase, sofa, and table) in a single piece of furniture. This somewhat misbegotten idea was swiftly adopted by furniture manufacturers for "modern" interiors, and it was rightly criticised, but nevertheless it was evidence of attempts to create a new and unified interior.

Kotěra's model for this period, in which geometrism became more prominent (although it had been there from the start in the symmetry of Secession ornament), was perhaps the glass punch bowl that he also exhibited in St. Louis. Interestingly, it was produced in two versions, one of which was more decorative and worked with motifs of grapes and vine leaves, while the other had a much simpler form and was unornamented. Kotěra based his design on the roundness of the bowl, but he broke up its surface into planes. The transparency of the glass further lightens the bowl and highlights the formal concept. In its material, and even more in its very artistry, Kotěra's punch bowl was a prototype for a different concept from Klouček's vases.

143–144 Vojtěch Preissig, Wallpaper designs, after 1900, gouache, 49 × 32 cm

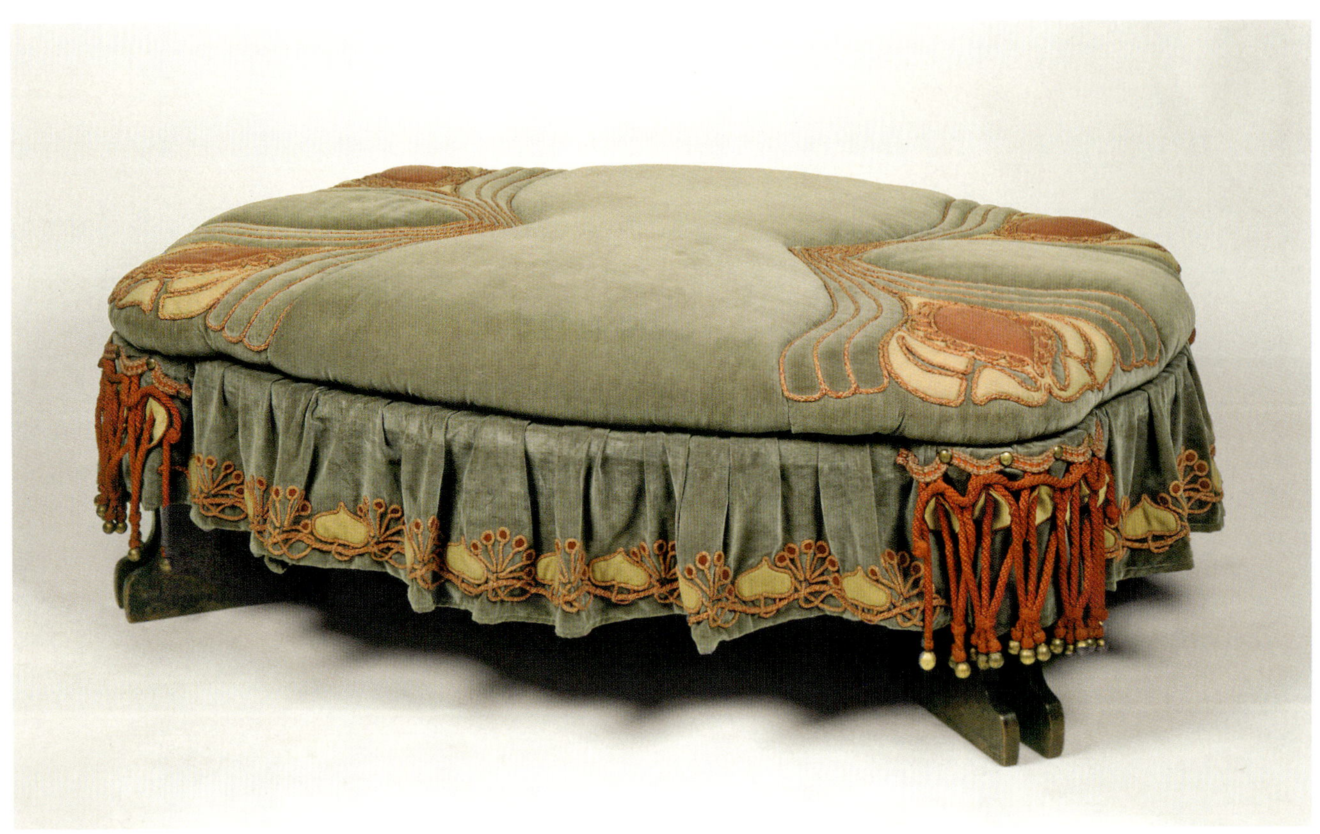

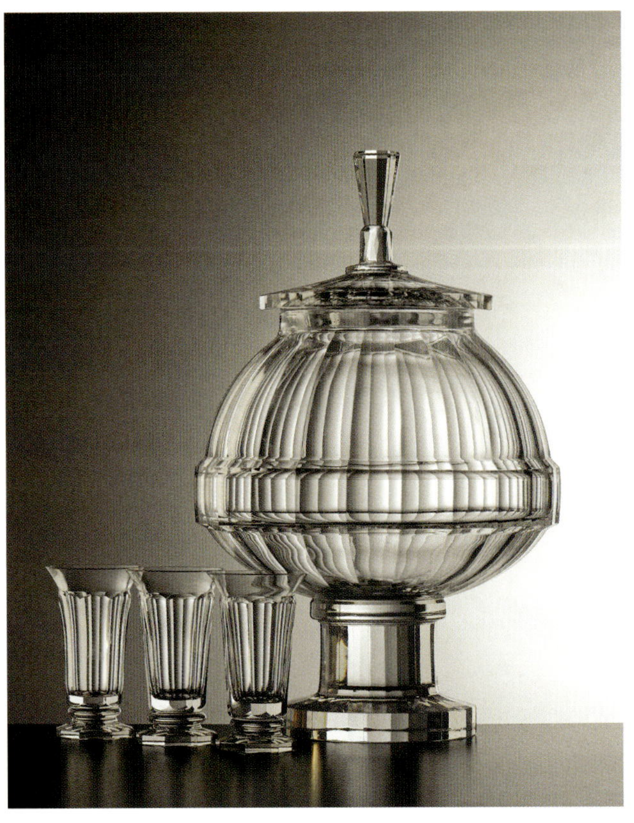

145 Jan Kotěra, Divan, 1899, textiles, 49 cm

146 Jan Kotěra, Bowl, 1903 (1910 version), lead glass, 41 cm

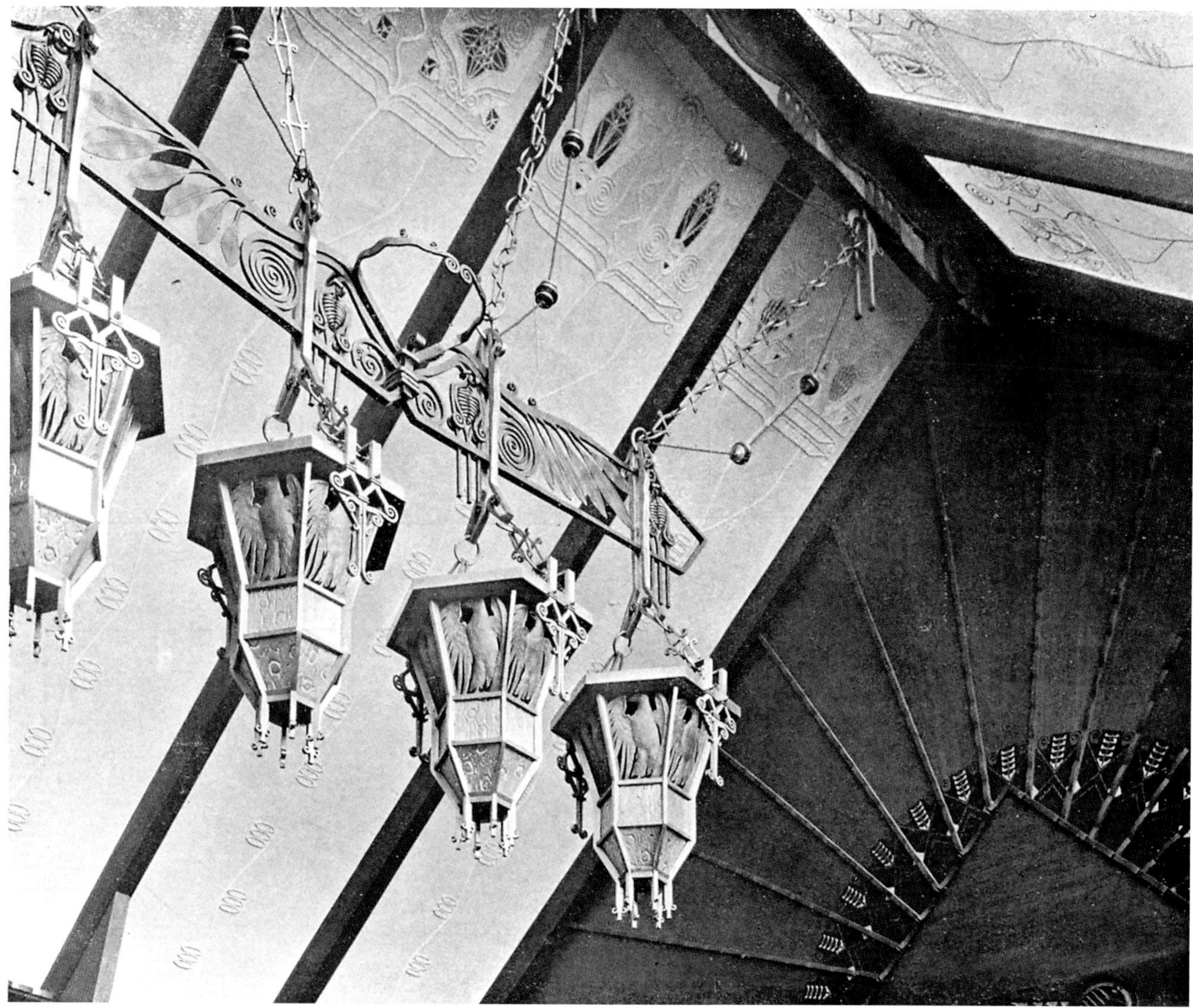

Of course, there was also progress of a sort in Klouček's school, where the vases for St. Louis by Rudolf Hameršmíd, Eman Stehlík, and Václav Mach stylised the botanical ornament into flat bands that became concave at the ends, and ornamental panels also worked with the idea of a sunken relief. Emanuel Novák's metalworking school applied ornamental bands to jewellery, and in handbeaten pieces the relief was flattened to the very minimum. However, such examples were more a matter of adapting to changing stylistic norms than truly forging a new path. The increasing demands for stylistic abstraction required a way of thinking based not on individual details but on the overall vision. Here Kotěra could rely on his architectural erudition and, of course, on what he had learned from his familiarity with contemporary European art. He was probably the only one who properly understood that the task was far from complete and that the advances made so far were only the first steps on this journey.

147 Jan Kotěra, Interior for the School of Decorative Arts at the Louisiana Purchase Exposition, 1904, detail with chandelier

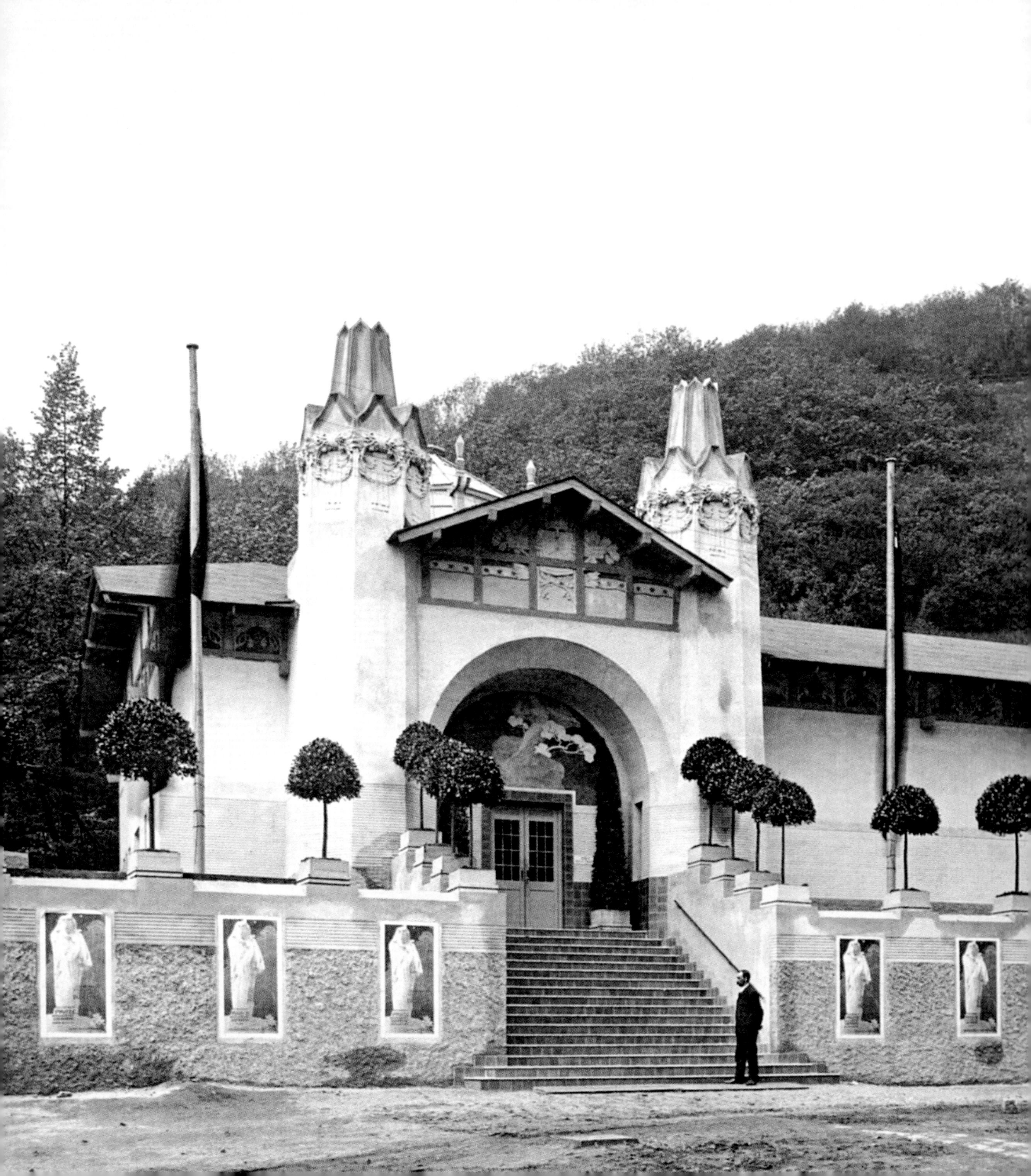

FAIRY TALES

In the spring of 1902, SVU Mánes's new exhibition pavilion was swiftly erected by the entrance to the Kinský Garden in Prague, to house an exhibition of the work of Auguste Rodin. The exhibition was seen as a welcome manifestation of Franco-Czech relations, and the municipality had accordingly been happy to grant planning permission. SVU Mánes took advantage of this opportunity to acquire a building in which it could continue to expand its cultural activities through regular exhibitions of Czech and foreign art.

The pavilion, designed by Jan Kotěra, greeted visitors with the popular motif of a gate between two slender pylons, while its ornamentation, with Karel Špillar's stucco wreaths and floral motifs over the entrance, magnified the architecture's poetic effect. Inside the pavilion, an octagonal entrance area beneath a glazed cupola led to smaller and larger exhibition rooms. For admirers of the new art, this modest and originally only temporary building became something of a bastion, a metaphor that was well established in the contemporary imagination. This is illustrated by Kotěra's drawing for "The Tale of the Red Knight" from the same year, where the architectural motif for the entrance to the proud castle is the same, although instead of the pavilion's broad and welcoming staircase there is a narrow bridge guarded by two large statues.

Comparing the drawing with the pavilion reveals how the contemporary artistic mentality was happy to dwell not just on nature but also on idealised fantasies that were seemingly very remote from naturalistic inspiration. There was also, of course, the persistence of the literary orientation that had been typical of the previous century, but the main reason for this interest in the world of fantasy was the need to acquire more general symbols for the new art.

For Christmas 1902, *Volné směry* published a triple issue entitled *Snow*. Although aimed at children, it captured many of the interests of the artistic imagination. There were short fairy tales illustrated by Hugo Böttinger, Vítěslav Stretti, František Kupka, Tavík František Šimon, Mikoláš Aleš, Ladislav Šaloun, Artuš Scheiner, Stanislav Sucharda, and Jan Kotěra, and besides traditional folk tales there were also new stories, mostly written by Václav Tille. They included moral fables on the difference between truth and falsehood, or between true art and false art, but the most affecting stories were those that updated the old romantic legend of the hero's quest for his ideal, which appears before him in a dark forest in the form of either a beautiful girl with golden hair or a magnificent and radiant palace, which the hero then loses due to trickery or his own weakness. Under the liberal aesthetics of the time, the illustrations for the stories were quite diverse, ranging from illusionism (Böttinger) to stylisation (Scheiner). Particularly interesting were illustrations by sculptors: Stanislav Sucharda's plaquettes

148 Jan Kotěra, SVU Mánes exhibition pavilion in Prague, 1902

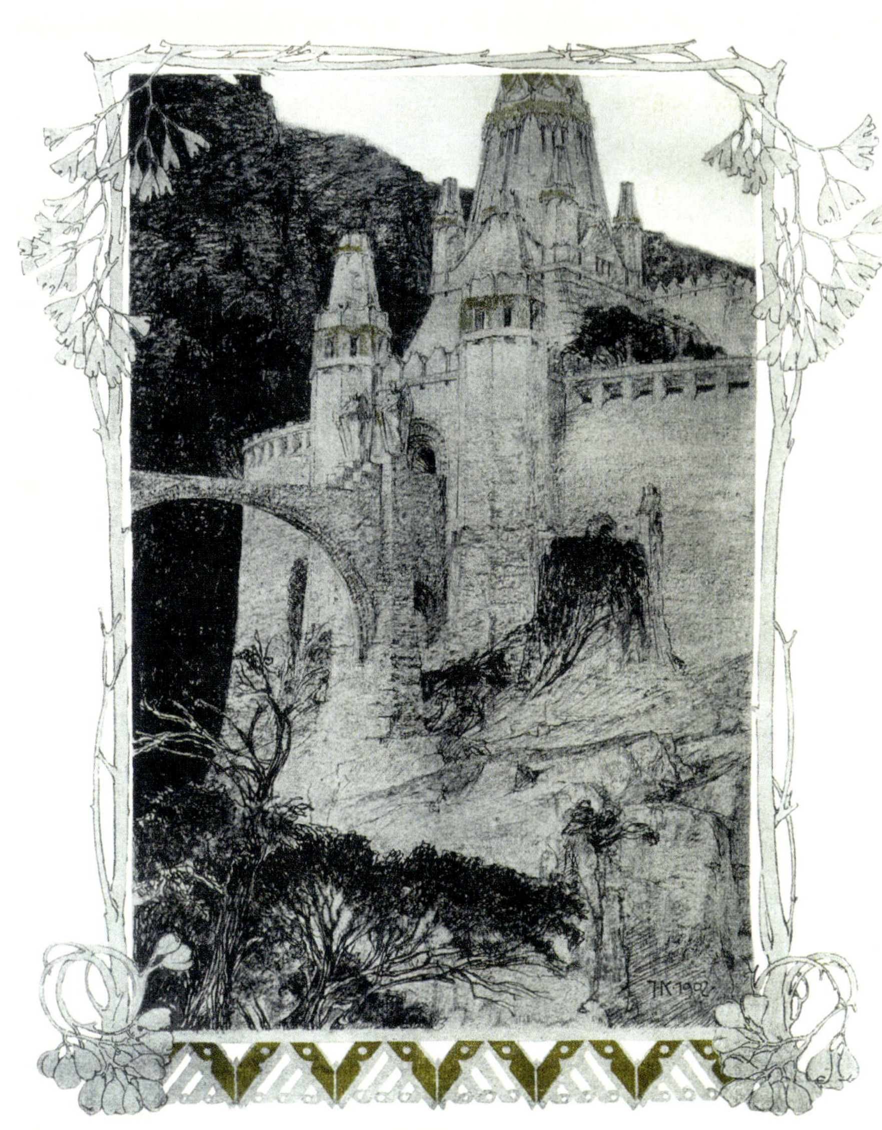

for Tille's "The Tale of the Beautiful Maiden Liliana" were given ornamental frames drawn by Anna Boudová.

The Czech Secession's interest in fairy tales and fantasy was far from exhausted by this collective enterprise. It was in fact one of the most typical characteristics of the new iconography, and it created an effective counterpoint to contemporary naturalism. It seems that the second high point of naturalism in the late 1890s was followed by a counterwave of imagination in Czech art, which sought to offset naturalism with the increasingly stylistic abstraction of decorative art. It also reflected motivations that were deeply rooted in the contradictoriness of the Secession mentality. In his review of the seventh Mánes exhibition in 1903, K. B. Mádl even asked,

149 Jan Kotěra, Illustration for "The Tale of the Red Knight," published in *Volné směry* 7 (1903)

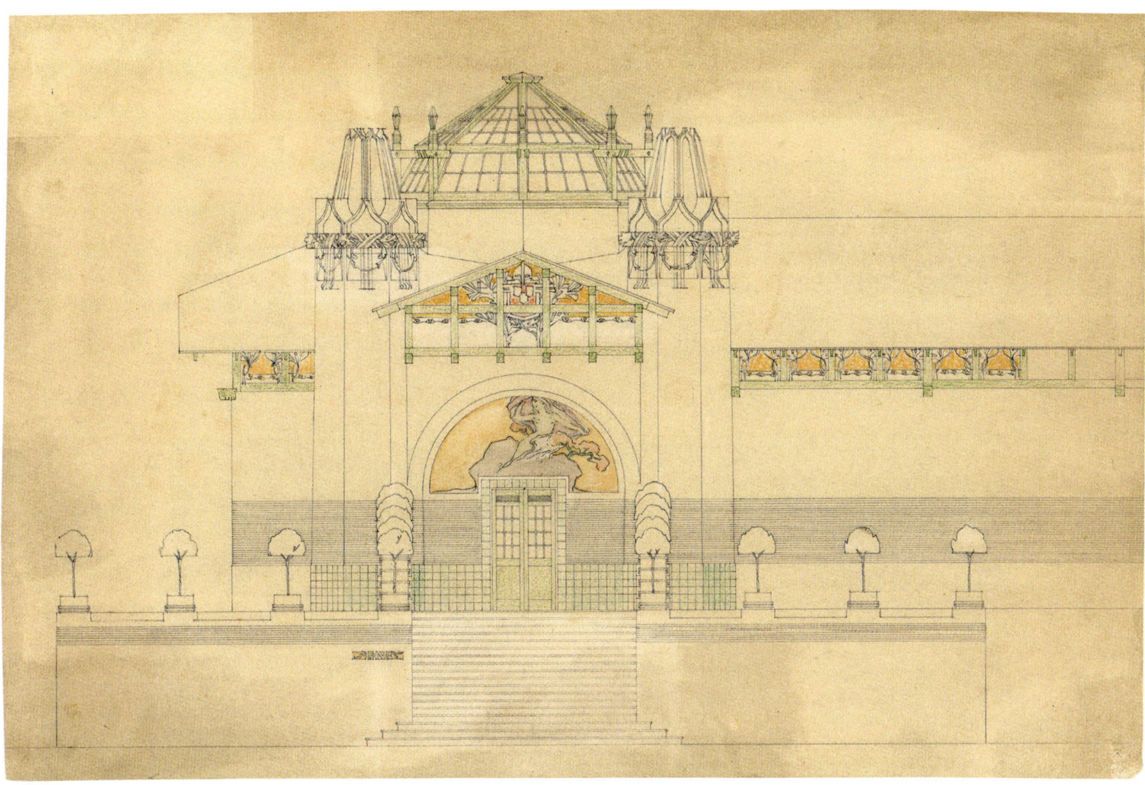

> Are we again living in a time of fairy tales? Is our material life so trivial and repellent that we retreat from it into the realm of mysterious and magical visions? It truly seems that artists have reason to avoid quotidian reality as far as possible, as though they have become weary of it and are revolted by it. … As if we had become jaded with realist and naturalistic art and were obliged to surpass it.[107]

Yet the theme of fairy tales was not merely a means of escaping harsh reality, for it also served the deeper needs of the new artistic externalisation. It all depended on how the theme was understood, as Mádl pointed out in his review, criticising Karel Špillar's idealised figures for their vacuity, and contrasting his elegant but superficial decorativeness with Jan Preisler's art. Of the latter, he wrote,

> His face is one of the most interesting of all our young people. The face of a melancholy idealist, whose eye, as if plucked from a dream, wanders uncertainly and restlessly over all of the everyday manifestations of the comedy of life, failing to comprehend it, and when he does understand it he immediately looks away, as if offended and most assuredly pained by it. He turns inward, to his thoughts and dreams. But here there is no merriment; laughter does not sparkle; joy does not swell. Nevertheless, for Preisler the pain and sorrow of his dreams is sweeter than the harshness, banality and superficial splendour of reality, for he cannot see it otherwise. These pains and woes are his; there is no doubt that the world has these sorrows and melancholy reflections on its conscience, but the artist caresses

150 Jan Kotěra, Drawing of the SVU Mánes exhibition pavilion, 1902, coloured Indian inks, 32 × 47 cm

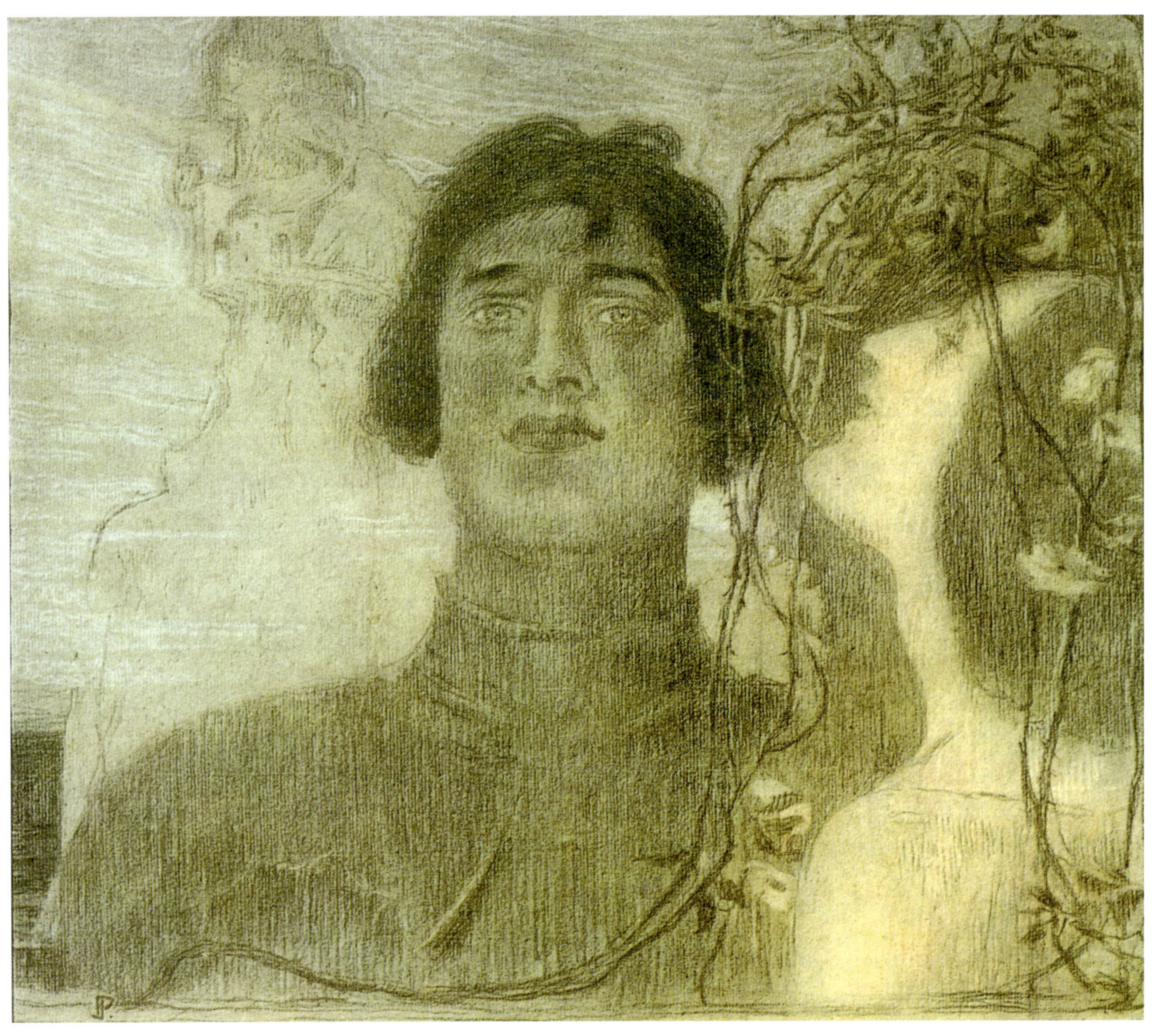

151 Jan Preisler, *Knight-Errant*, 1901, charcoal and white chalk, 36.3 × 40.6 cm

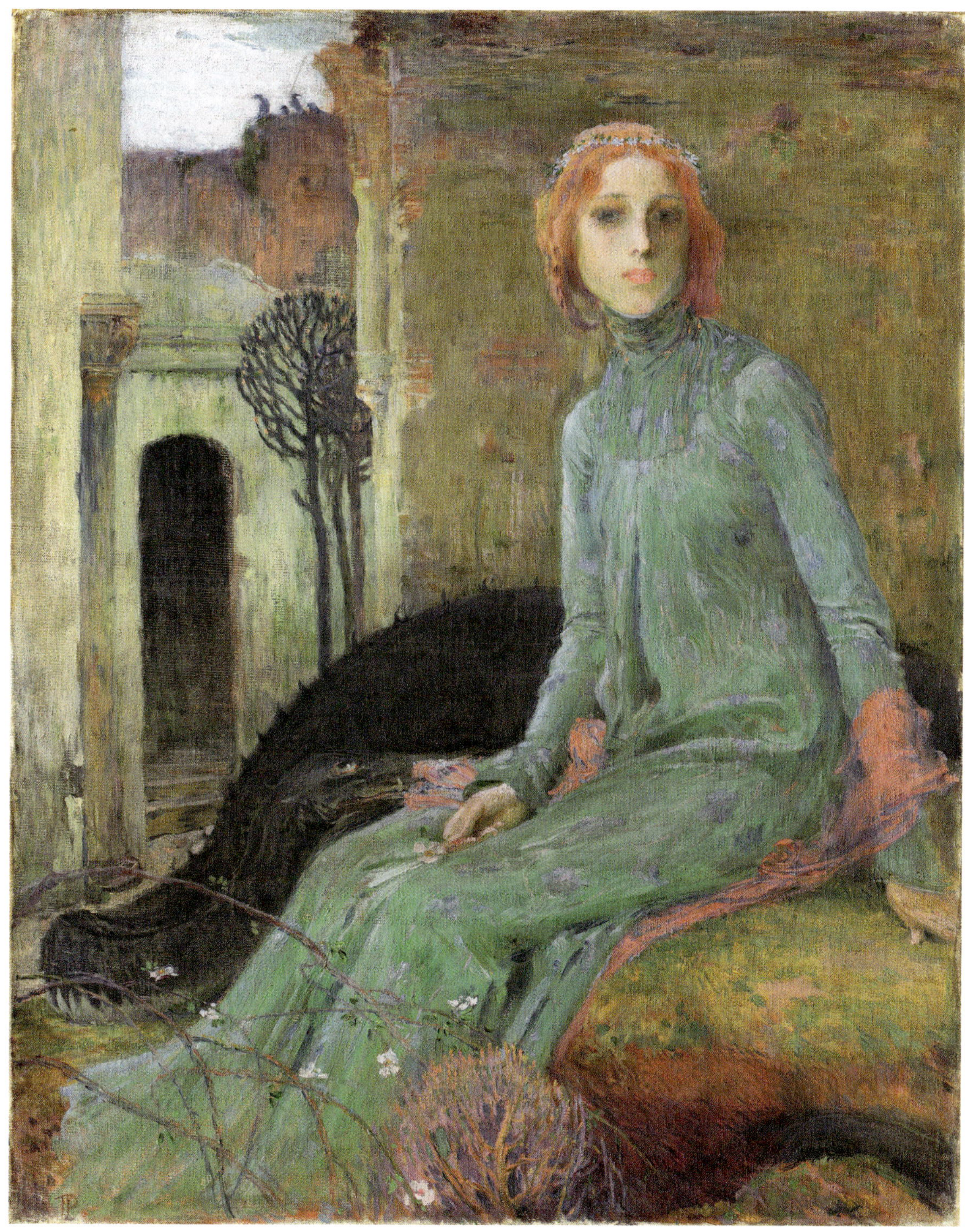

152 Jan Preisler, *Fairy Tale*, 1902, oil, 101.5 × 79 cm

and cossets them, for they are his and his alone, and he seeks for them a mould in which he could cast them in a form that would suit and satisfy him alone. This also makes Preisler's art in essence one of the most subjective we have. I do not think he has found this mould; indeed, everything persuades me that he shall perhaps long be seeking it, and this, his struggle with mysterious powers for an expressive form, also has the aspect of bitter pain and sour melancholy, for in it the blood drips red. Jan Preisler works heart and soul, with everything in him, and such work is always painful.

In the first issue of the sixth volume of *Volné směry* (autumn 1901), dedicated to the memory of Jan Neruda, Preisler had returned once again to the theme of the knight-errant. The drawing is confined to a bust of the hero, viewed en face, as he listens (with Preisler's typically sorrowful expression) to the voice of a white apparition addressing him from a rosebush, while in the background a fantastical castle rises from a steep cliff. In this delicate drawing, created with light vertical strokes of graphite crayon, the knight's face is striking for its seeming immobility, as if masking an unusual emotional tension. Preisler drew several similar faces at this time, evidently captivated by the expressive possibilities of the contrast between outward calm and inner turmoil, and they comprise a series ranging from joy to sorrow, which is accomplished by discretely accentuating individual details. Although these faces recall Klouček's mascarons, they express the psychological content far more delicately. Here this is projected into a fairy-tale scene, where behind the fantasy there is a subtle psychomachia that operates through the artistic devices of illustration and directs the resulting emotional ferment. Preisler does not speak here merely for himself but expresses the sentiments of his entire generation, which gives this scene a profound and transcendent significance.

At this time, Preisler also began painting *Fairy Tale*, which he developed in several variations. In it, he took the figure of the young woman from the right wing of his *Spring* triptych and placed her in the ruins of an abandoned castle, like a princess. He also added a dragon, which, rather than presenting any threat to the young woman, gazes at her as though besotted with this pale and melancholy creature. The painting's expressive intensity comes principally from its colours. The copper green of the princess's gown creates numerous harmonies with the reddish-yellow tones of her surroundings and the dull black of the dragon, the castle's mysterious entrance, and the bare tree that grows beside it. Also noteworthy is how the paints have been applied in translucent glazes that overlap in a complicated manner to create an unusual colouristic richness. The immaterial lightness of the glazes helps to give the painting its oneiric quality, its dreaminess and lyrical charm.

The connection between *Fairy Tale* and *Spring* was no accident. Mirroring again appears as a characteristic principle in Secession art. The world of reality, expressed by the figure of a young woman sitting in an open landscape, is harmoniously complemented by the world of the imagination embodied by the princess – and this ambivalence of ideas, linked by the figure's identical pose, again testifies to how Secession artists intuitively sought a synthesis of the conscious and unconscious elements of the human psyche. We find this dual deploying of a single motif relatively frequently

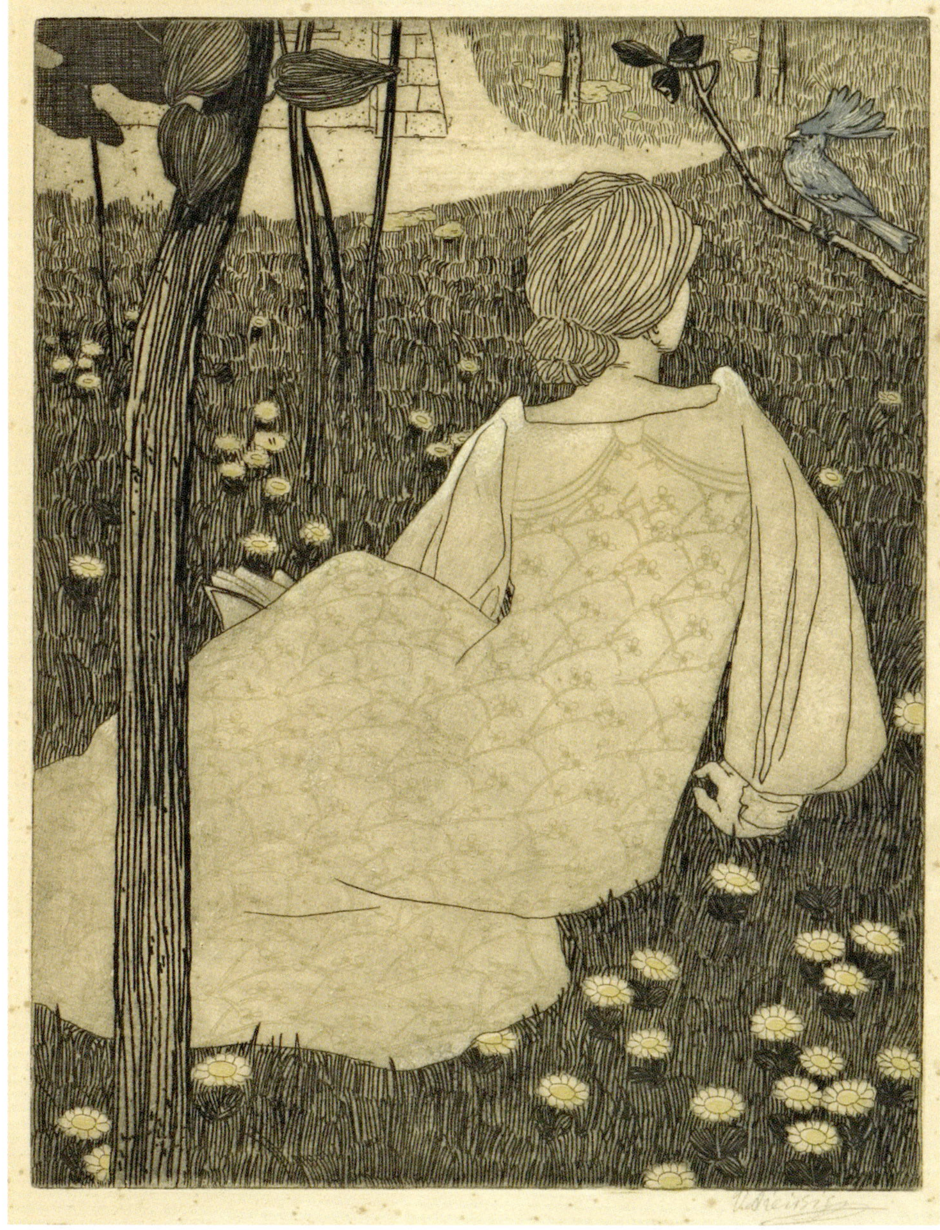

in Czech art from this time. Vojtěch Preissig, who by the turn of the century had become a leading Czech printmaker, also worked with realistic and fantastical fairy-tale renditions of the then-popular motif of a seated young woman. An example of a realistic depiction is his coloured etching *Young Woman in Nature*, dated 1899, while a fantastical depiction is the subject of a larger coloured etching, *Bluebird*, whose stylised decorativeness necessitated a certain modification of the theme.

Bluebird was from 1900, and this progression, in which an originally naturalistic idea was projected into the realm of the imagination and stylistic decorativeness, seems

153 Vojtěch Preissig, *Bluebird*, 1900, coloured etching, 49.5 × 37.5 cm

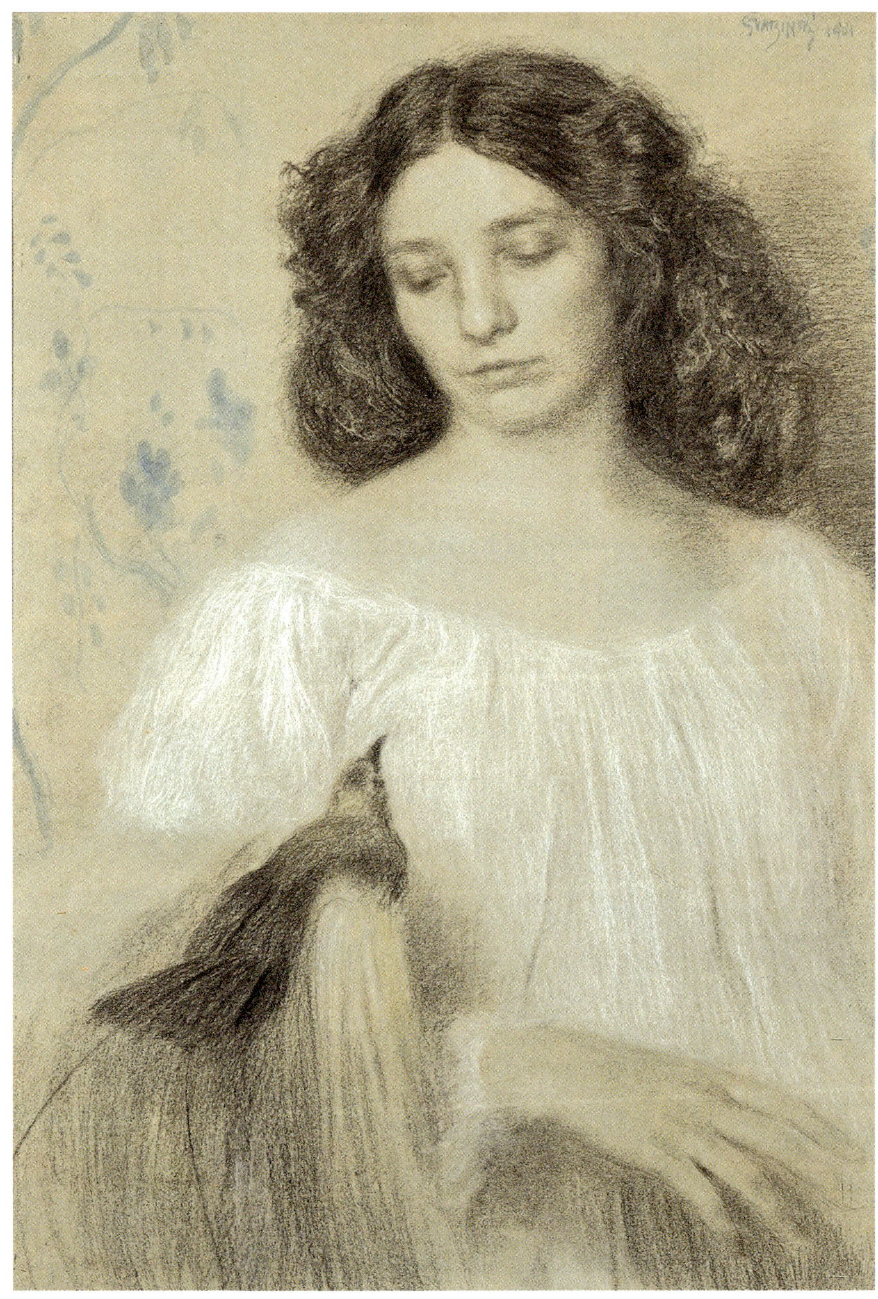

also to have been a response to the ascent of Secession decorativism, which, through its "stylised" interiors for exhibitions, offered an effective visualisation of a further externalising framework in the sense of a "higher," artistic, form of nature. The new decorative art had from the start presented a complicated problem. Although it had itself largely invoked nature as the mould from which it took its forms, in practice this often resulted in an aestheticism that, reinforced by echoes of Decadence's distaste for the everyday and its inclination to seek out what was rare and extraordinary, rather

154 Maxmilián Švabinský, *Paradisaea Apoda*, 1901, charcoal, coloured chalks, and watercolour, 72 × 50 cm

contradicted the original imitating of nature and began emphasising the uniqueness of the human soul and its needs. This also led to the later emergence of Constructivist tendencies. In the context of the Secession, this shift resulted in greater demands for a homogenous stylistic totality.

This made all the more important the role of artists who, like Preisler and Preissig, had always sought to retain the new style's multiplicity and its fruitful ties to the original world view. One of the key aspects of such efforts was the capacity to identify and cultivate symbols that strengthened the new culture by reactivating, through an artist's own ideas on art, the fundamental world view presented in Secession painting. The Secession found one such symbol in the cult of nature, which initially tended to be seen only in terms of its manifestations, and this moreover through the prism of ideological mediation. However, nature and its material attributes could only be mere symbols for human sentiments and opinions. They helped to create what was most essential – a new model of the human psyche.

Only an authentic understanding of these relationships could produce art that spontaneously and even obsessively found the requisite symbols and reproduced them not by merely imitating them, but through their natural and creative evocation. If the figure of a princess (like the earlier figure of an ordinary young woman) meant, at its core, a personification of art that was now perhaps more rarefied, more "sacred," and if placing her in a natural setting, usually next to a symbolic tree of life, expressed the fundamental relationship between art and reality, there were then further symbols that amplified these meanings. One such symbol was the combination of this idealised figure with the animal aspect of nature, usually represented by a bird: for Preissig, a bluebird; in Švabinský's drawing *Paradisaea Apoda* from 1901, a greater bird of paradise; in Bohumil Kafka's plaquette *Science (Meditation)* from 1908, an owl. Swans and peacocks, the Secession's "heraldic" birds, also belong here to some extent. A symbolic bird has also settled on the dreamlike figure who accompanies Preisler's adolescent boy in *Painting from a Larger Cycle* (1902). The appearance of animal symbols in the Czech Secession's repertoire, which had from the start mostly comprised botanical symbols, is symptomatic of how the new art's symbolic system was gradually becoming more elaborate. The greater use of avian symbolism indicates that Czech art was focusing on matters of the psyche. Here too it was about expressing the relationship between the conscious and the unconscious, hidden behind the veil of contemporary ideas. In this relationship, however, the unconscious, dreamlike aspect was manifestly becoming more attractive, and even if it had yet to exceed the bounds of the metaphor that had been adopted, its presence in an image provided the main impetus for its poeticising.

Another characteristic of this process of symbolisation was its individuality. Although the tendency was a collective one, this in no way detracted from the originality of the individual artists, who added their personal notes to the collective archetype according to their dispositions. Švabinský's approach was more sensual, as is reflected in the plastic and painterly style of his work. It is also quite evident that his version took its example from Whistler's treatment of the female type. Preissig was decorative, and he

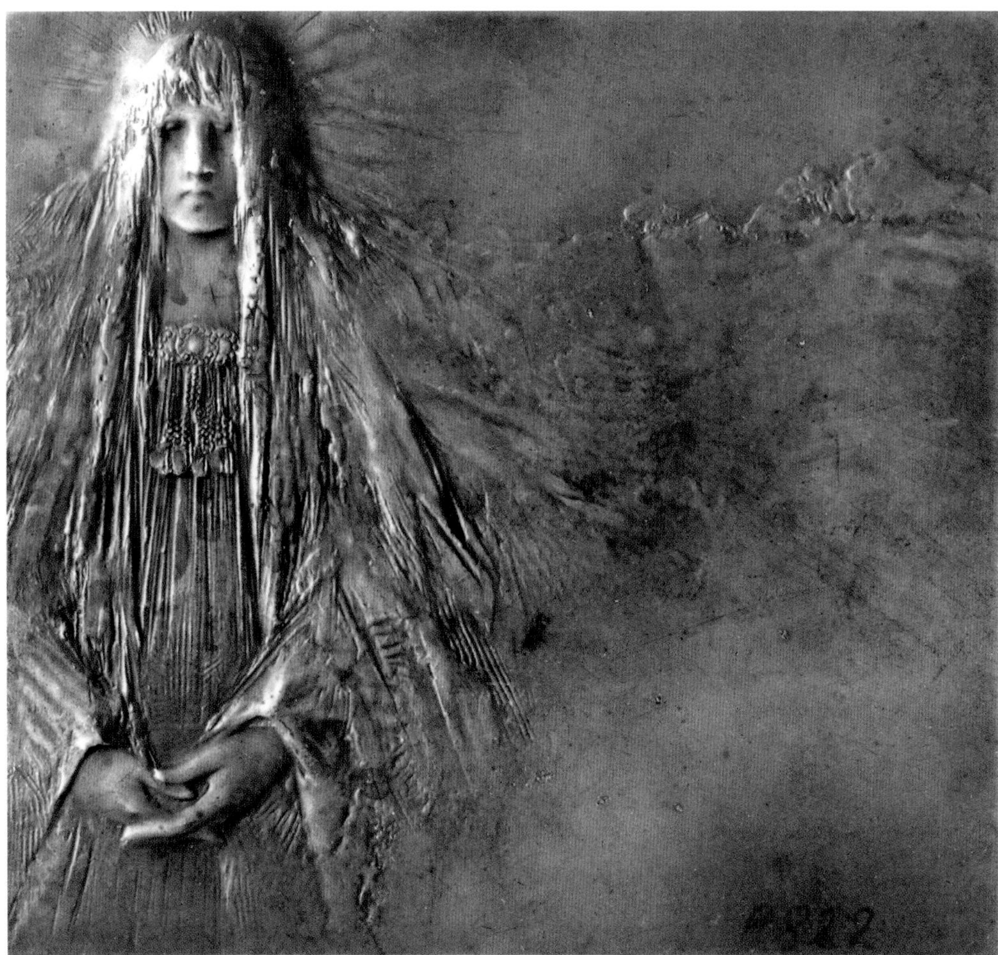

combined his simplicity with the refinement of his technique; this corresponded to his experimental approach to art. Kafka used the effect produced by light on a low relief, and here he was influenced, of course, by his teacher at the School of Decorative Arts, Stanislav Sucharda.

In 1909 Sucharda's plaquettes for "The Tale of the Beautiful Maiden Liliana" were reproduced in a cycle that encompassed perhaps all the Secession's thematic interests. Besides its allusions to folk art, the original version had been dominated by a vision in which a radiant Secession palace appears before Liliana as she works her magic; in its style it recalled Kotěra's design for a palace as part of the stage set for Dvořák's *Rusalka* (1901). The introductory plaquette again presents the princess type. The figure, in low relief, is modelled as if bathed in light, representing nature. This was a notable innovation in the development of this symbol, for Sucharda had moved from narrative attributes to devices that found symbolic accentuation directly in the original naturalistic qualities. For Sucharda, light never had the ideological significance it held for Bílek, for instance, but it did have a specific meaning. Sucharda also wanted to enhance the

155 Stanislav Sucharda, Plaquette from a series for "The Tale of the Beautiful Maiden Liliana," 1902–9, bronze, 9.9 × 10.4 cm

aesthetic effect of Secession imagery, and in this sense he saw new possibilities in the synesthetic qualities of modelling that worked with the effect of light.

The development of contemporary relief work that resulted in the plaquette as a popular small-format version found in Sucharda its exemplar. Plaquettes were a sensitive expression of the new stylistic volition. As with printmaking, important questions concerning the concept and constructing of space were addressed in low relief plaquettes, which led to the gradual negating of the prevailing three-dimensional understanding of space. The increasing integration of a plastic figure with the plane of a relief proceeded by breaking down a figural or even a landscape motif into decorative planes. Light played an important role in this process, as an element that unified the

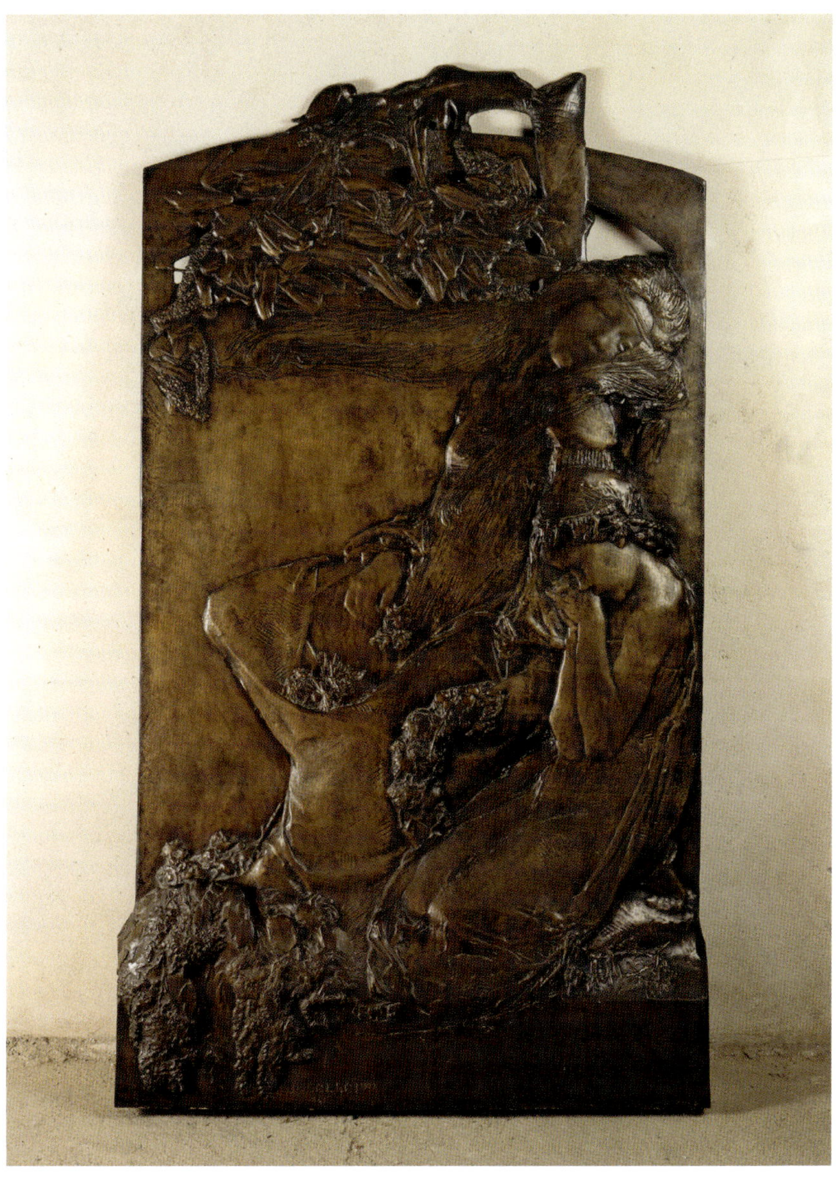

156 Bohumil Kafka, *Grave Relief*, 1903, bronze, 172 × 96 cm

entire relief and let its individual components resonate. Sucharda was able to use light in a very refined way, to pick out the highest parts of even a very low relief plaquette. Light and shadow, animating entire surfaces and expressive lines in the modelling, were in fact a substitute for the emotional impact of colour, and in his plaquettes Sucharda created images that were not lacking in this quality.

In his original plaquettes for "The Tale of the Beautiful Maiden Liliana," Sucharda was attempting an effect only rarely found in sculpture. Rather than relying solely on atmospheric light, he created the illusion that a plaquette had its own light source. A radiance emanates from the figure of the princess and the palace, and this is also an allusion to their unearthly origin: these are psychological phantasms. The significance of the plaquettes' narrative consists in this interplay between real and imagined light. Sucharda was then taking on a problem typical of the Secession, which always sought to combine the real and the unreal in a new unity.

This way of expressing the fundamental problem was, of course, too exclusive in terms of the general stylistic needs. The contre-jour effect seemed excessively painterly and could not be repeated, which is why it did not appear in the final version of the plaquettes. Nevertheless, it introduced a particular concept that could also be elaborated through the far more formal devices of decorative abstraction. Sucharda and his pupils explored these approaches in his modelling studio at Prague's School

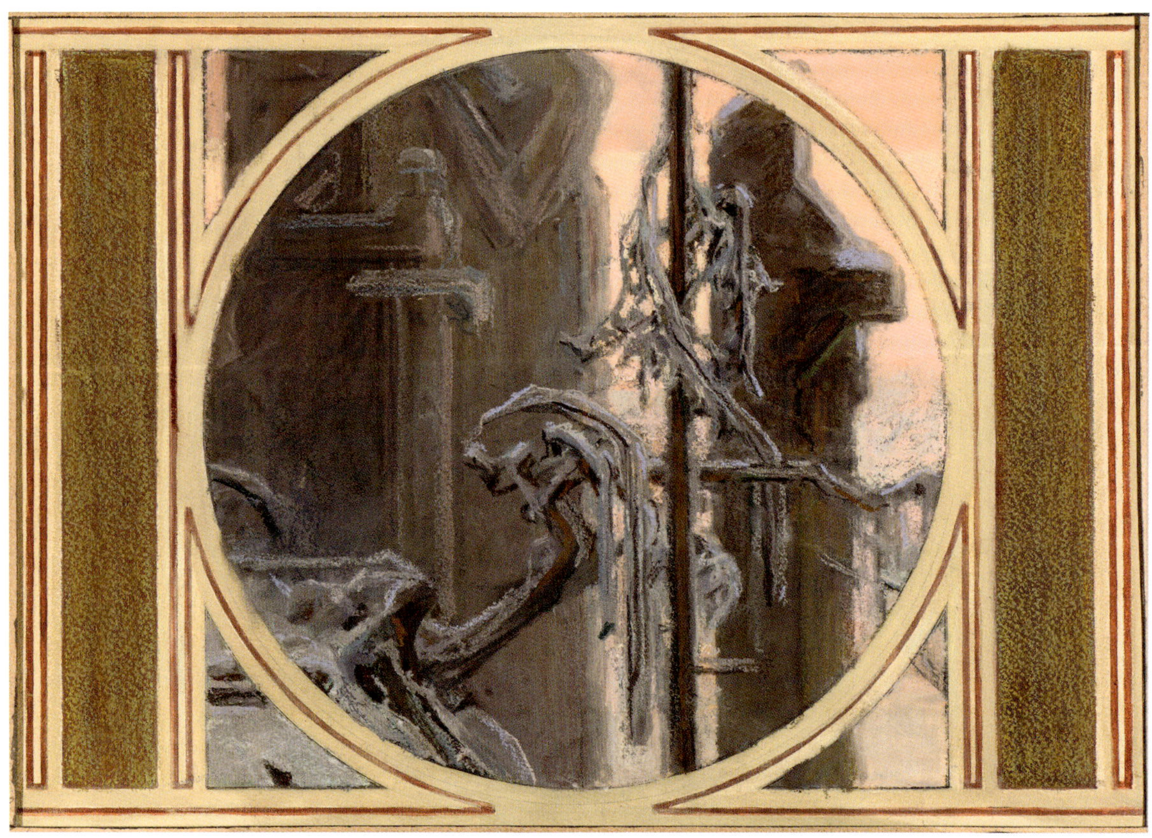

157 Maxmilián Pirner, Epilogue from the series *Hans Heiling*, after 1900, pastel, 51 × 71 cm

of Decorative Arts, and Bohumil Kafka's *Grave Relief* from 1903 was the sum of what they had learned.

In the work he produced while studying under Sucharda, Kafka tried to extract the maximum from the new decorative possibilities. There was still an echo of the ethnographic genre (such as the relief *Harvest*, 1902), and Kafka produced several portraits, but more important than the theme was a new sensitivity expressed through the subtle nuances of the artfully applied plastic planes. In Kafka's reliefs, the painterly silhouette of the figures corresponds to the engraved line drawing, curling into Secession curves, and it also reflects the decorativeness of the lettering. The drapery is flattened and animated by the use of hatching, which creates a tension between the

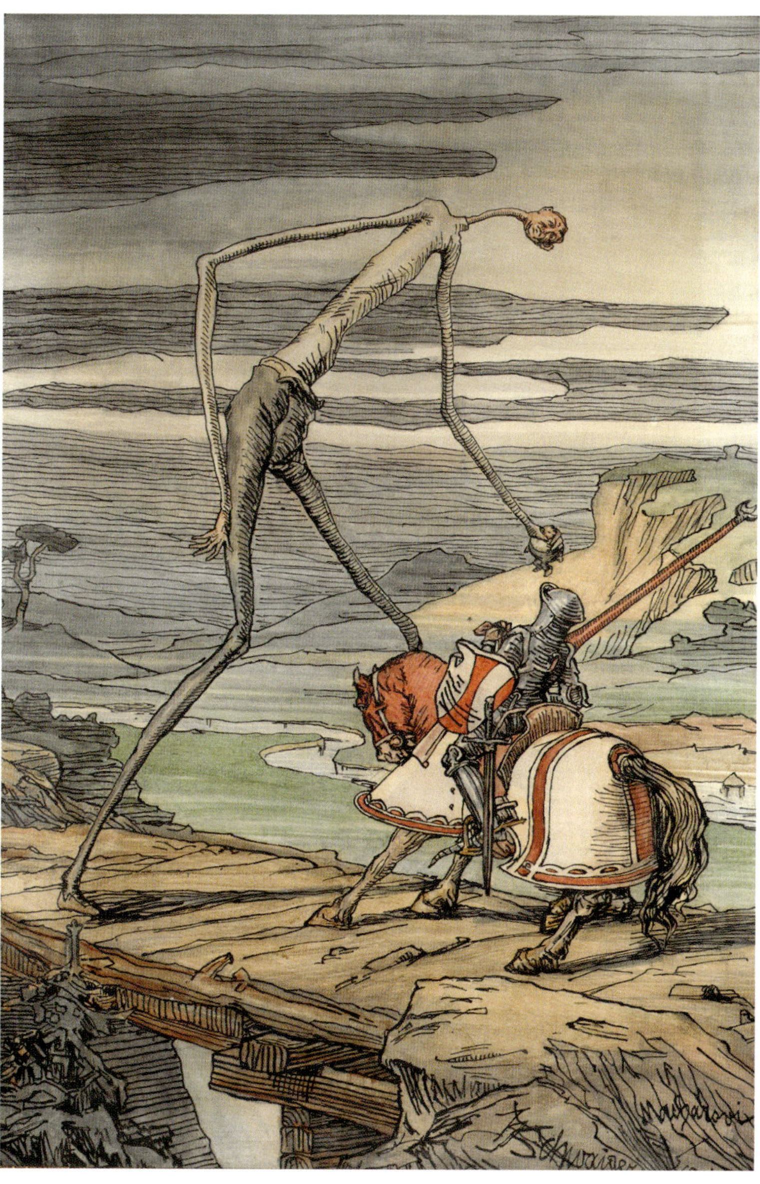

158 Hanuš Schwaiger, *Long, Broad and Quickeye*, 1900, Indian ink and watercolour, 105 × 70 cm

rhythmically harmonious two-dimensional forms. Individual surfaces are treated differently, with roughened surfaces used next to smoothly rounded ones, over which the light pours. Through these devices the naivety of the subject matter becomes merely the basis for decorative work that is itself a contemporary symbol.

Kafka's *Grave Relief* is one of the most typical examples of Czech Secession sculpture, primarily by virtue of how the decorative structuring and stylised forms are carefully balanced with the sensual immediacy of the effect produced by light. This latter element is also in harmony with the emotionality of the theme, which features the popular motif of young women melancholically dreaming in the lap of nature. The unity of the intellectual, sensual, and emotional aspects is manifested in a way that allows emotionality to dominate while not being overly insistent. The theme itself contains the idea of remembering, yet here painful recollection is presented as a sense of the cycle of life as it passes. In the relief there is also an affecting contrast between the sensory richness of its forms and the knowledge that they too arise and pass away. The new sculptural technique therefore allowed a decorative object to symbolise an outlook that attempted to see the tragedy of life through the prism of organic beauty.

The harmony achieved between elements that were essentially very disparate was of course a fragile creation that was subject to all kinds of internal pressures. The art that produced this harmony was seen as something out of the ordinary, exceptional, and the fairy-tale aspect of its themes was also a protective mimesis against the coarseness of a world that would soon demolish what had been erected. Secession artists took it upon themselves to forge a new link between art and life, and they naturally saw this as the necessity of bringing art into life to refine it, both aesthetically and ethically. However, they were well aware of the immense superiority of life and its unbridled manifestations over any artistic regulation. They projected this into their art as the struggle between the light and dark principles of life itself, and this intuition of the fundamental contradictoriness of existence was symbolised and presented in all manner of ways.

In art then, as in a fairy tale, the princess went forth from her castle to encounter in nature – in life – numerous fantastical creatures that represented the positive or negative forces in the fight between good and evil. In this respect, the Secession artists' imagination was powerfully influenced not just by literature, but also by theatre. Many of these artists were involved with theatre, designing sets and costumes, and fairy tales formed a substantial part of this work. Also related to theatre's influence was the immense popularity of puppetry, which was even more the domain of artists.[108] The projecting of fundamental artistic issues into fairy tales already had a classic representative in Czech art in the person of Hanuš Schwaiger. This was quite apparent in publications from the turn of the century that disseminated Schwaiger's work, such as a triple issue of *Volné směry* from the beginning of 1900. Schwaiger was popular chiefly for the picturesque humour of his depictions of folk tales and stories. *The Happy Shepherd* (1894), *Long, Broad and Quickeye* (1894), and *The Extracting of the Mandrake* (1894) were more in the spirit of illustrations, without Schwaiger's earlier naturalistic physiognomies. It was probably this that perpetuated Schwaiger's influence among the

159 Ladislav Šaloun, *Krakonoš*, 1902–6, sandstone, Smetanovy sady in Hořice

younger generation. Nor had they lost sight of Maxmilián Pirner, who took fairy tales much more seriously. At the beginning of the century, he worked on a second edition of a folk ballad about Hans Heiling that had captivated him during his childhood in Loket, the town from which the story originated. Hans Heiling was the son of a man and a forest fairy, and Pirner told the tale of his tragic encounter with the demonic forces of nature in a cycle of large pastels that combined late Romantic drama with the new stylisation. Artistically, the most interesting of these pastels is the epilogue, expressing the idea of the indestructibility of human desire, which has returned to the world in a botanical metamorphosis. The Secession generation's fairy-tale fantasies seemed to vacillate between these two approaches. Although attracted to Pirner's tragic tone, they were distrustful of his late Romantic scenery, and ultimately Schwaiger's grotesqueness seemed more attuned to their mentality.

Similar to Schwaiger's work was Ladislav Šaloun's *Krakonoš* (1903–6), a large sculpture that he made following the success of his illustrations for a fairy tale about the

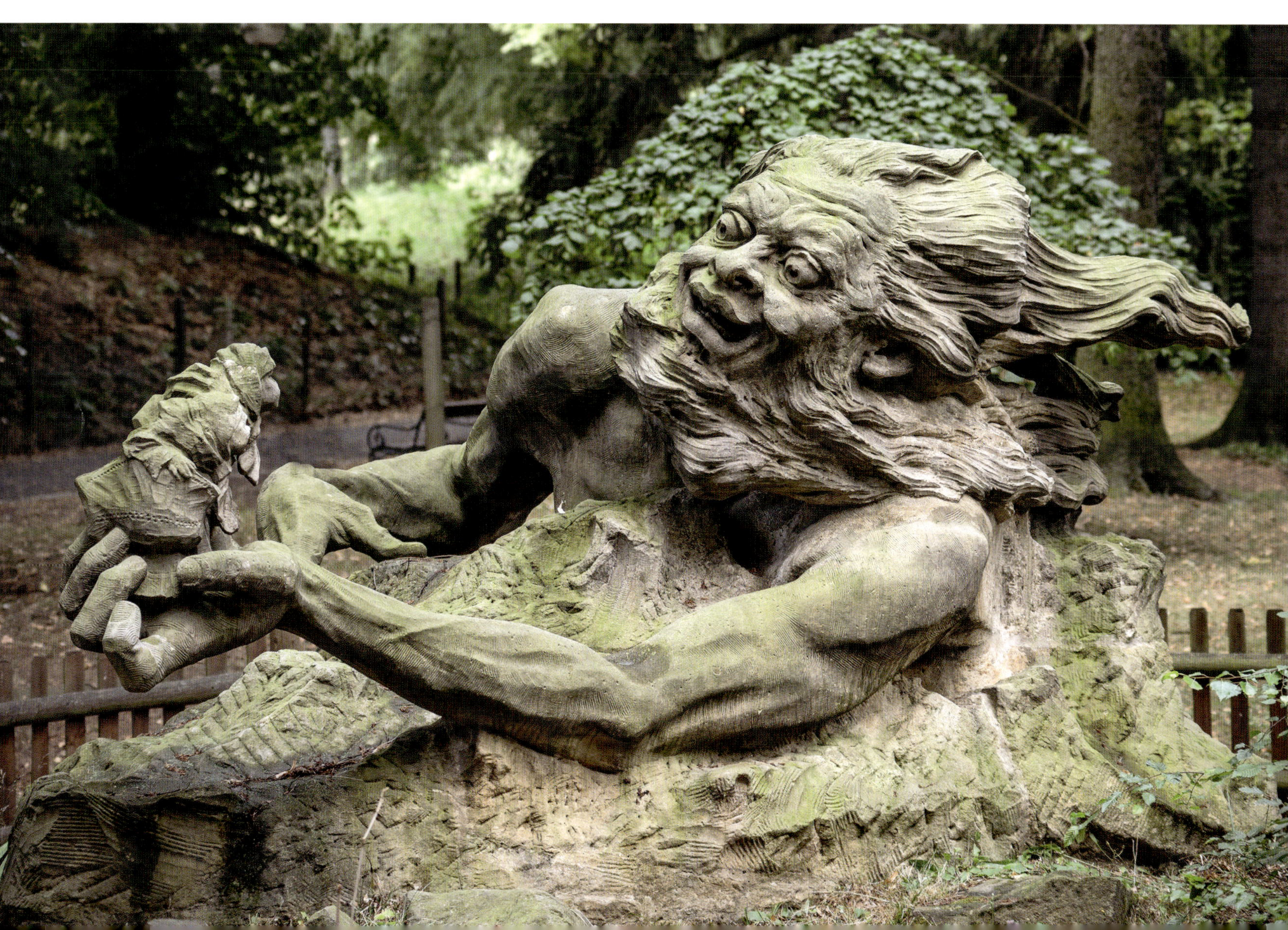

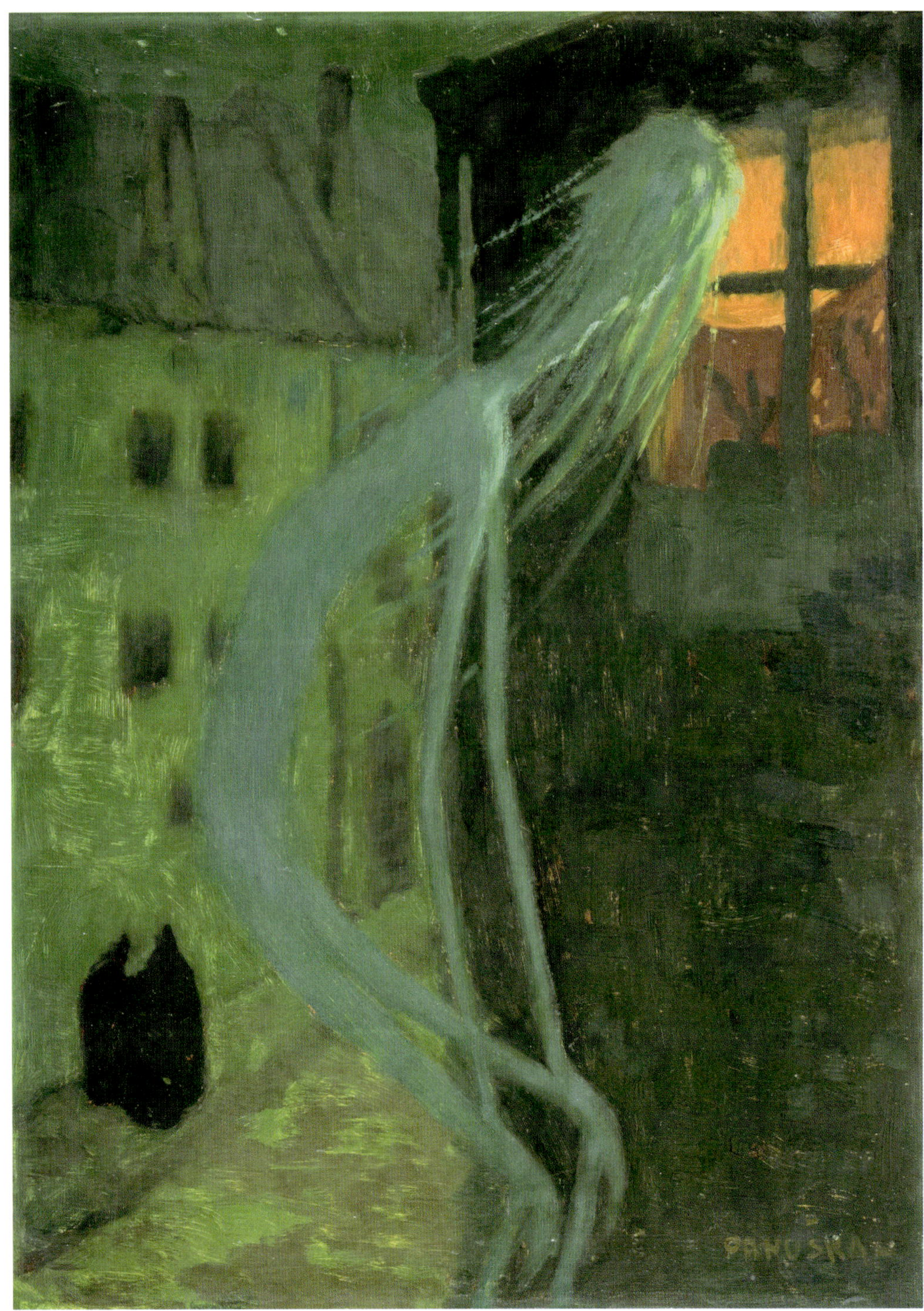

160 Jaroslav Panuška, *Ghost of a Mother*, c. 1900, oil, 68 × 48 cm

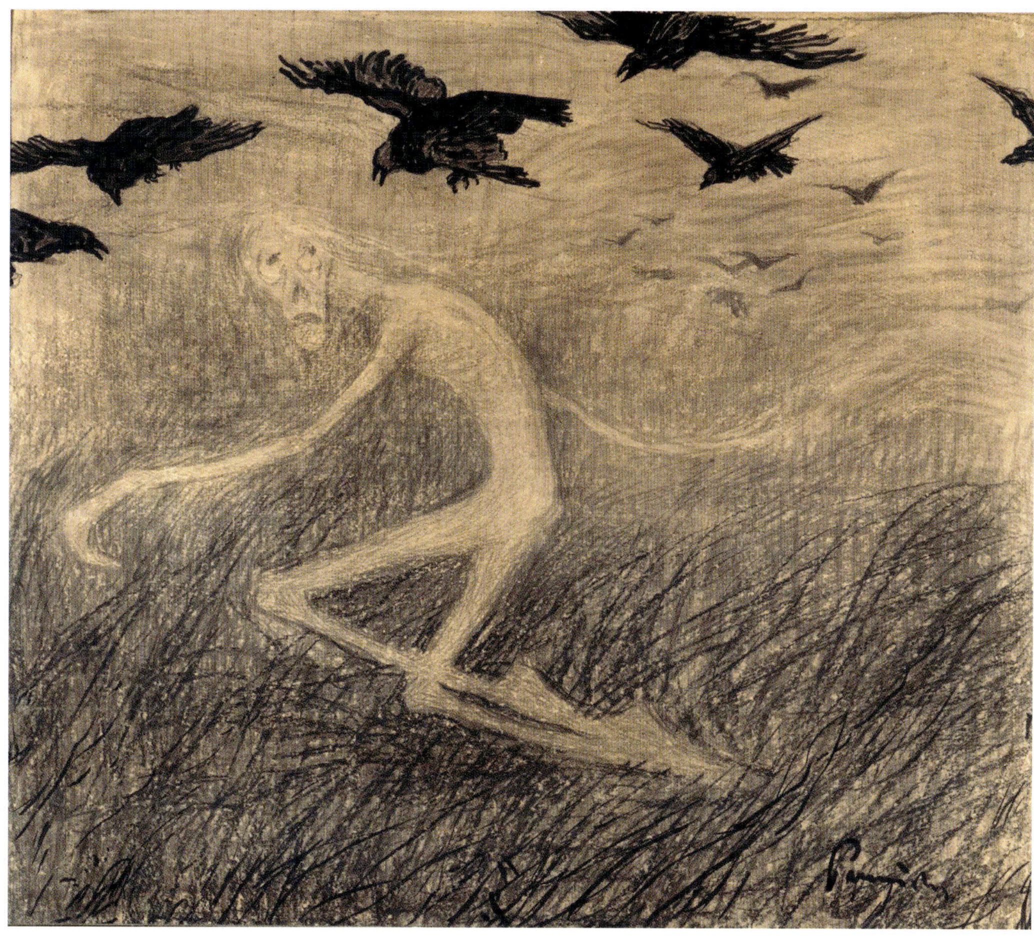

mountain spirit in Václav Tille's anthology *Snow*. The sculpture, which stands in a park in Hořice, shows the giant's monstrous head emerging from the bracken and staring with bulging eyes at the two children kneeling in his outstretched palms. Rather than depicting man in harmony with nature, Šaloun stressed the latter's supremacy. The contrasts in the scales of the figures, and between the naked personification of nature and the details of the children's garb, seem comic, but they also have a deeper meaning. This projection was part of a broader view, as demonstrated by the similarly contrasting scales in Šaloun's entirely sober designs for his Jan Hus Memorial. It is as though here too there was a concept that contrasted man with a higher and transcendental power, a concept in which nature was no longer a tranquil garden but a capricious being, demonically toying with human gullibility. In *Krakonoš*, Šaloun adapted his expressive devices to reflect this idea. The sculpture has a linear dynamism in the motif of the giant's long arms and the details of his flowing locks, expressively wavy lines in which the giant's head and eyes appear as eddies. In this turbulent dynamism of form, the diminutive figures of the children are a frozen, naturalistic, and alien element. This also reflects a certain evolution in depictions of Krakonoš. Behind his bizarre form there

161 Jaroslav Panuška, *Revenant Pursued by Ravens*, 1898, charcoal, 65 × 72 cm

now lay a vitalist conception that still drew much from the older Romantic reservoir, but it was animated by the contemporary interest in Spiritism and the occult, a field in which Šaloun was an enthusiastic amateur.

The motif of Krakonoš's exaggeratedly long arms, as though the demonism hidden in nature were reaching out to man, also appears in fairy-tale fantasies by other Czech Secession artists. As with the typology of Krakonoš's head, which recalls Schwaiger's water sprite, we find it in the work of the painter Jaroslav Panuška from the turn of the century. For him too the world of macabre folk tales was a wellspring of images through which he could express his sense that behind nature's welcoming, sunny aspect lay a moonlit realm where dreamlike and fairy-tale beings became forces that were independent of humanity and even hostile to it. Panuška painted them as apparitions that assail the wandering hero in a fairy tale, or visit the sleeper in terrifying dreams in the form of spiders or bizarre, elongated, and zoomorphic *Moths* and *Vampires* (c. 1903). Like Schwaiger, Panuška illustrated *Long, Broad and Quickeye*, and he also drew Gulliver in Lilliput. He had a predilection for prehistoric scenes, pagan rituals, and primitive landscapes from the dawn of humanity, and in his best work of this kind he was able to evoke a sense of menace while hardly ever exceeding the acceptable bounds of grotesqueness. The element of caricature in his *Revenant Pursued by Ravens* or his sinister roosting *Birds* metaphorically conveyed his conviction of the fragility of the human psyche and our inability to escape the forces of destiny. While Panuška's sarcasm was not as pointed as in fantastical works by contemporaries, such as James Ensor from Belgium or Alfred Kubin from Austria, his charcoals in particular are no less sensitive in their transcription of psychological phenomena. In his technique and fairy-tale scenery there is always in Panuška's work a lyrical softening of expression that was, in fact, characteristic of the Czech Secession as a whole. In his charcoals, the expressive immediacy of his spectres' physiognomies, where the human face becomes the crazed or carrion-eating mask of a demon, is only used indirectly. Such is the case in Panuška's *Illustration for a Fairy Tale* (c. 1902), where, behind a fantastical vessel rocking on the ocean waves, two glowing discs appear, the eyes of some cosmic giant disturbed by this human presence. The idea Šaloun expressed in *Krakonoš* has therefore returned in Panuška's pastel, although Panuška has moved away from Schwaiger's humour towards a concept that more closely recalls Pirner. While in Schwaiger's work the meeting of giant and man is always played out in a realistic setting and on firm ground, with his younger heirs, such as Šaloun and Panuška, this "objective" background to such encounters disappears and we find ourselves in the giant's hands, or alternately the vessel of our destiny is bobbing in a natural element, of which the giant is ultimately only a menacing personification. It is not without interest that this element is deep water. Here too this was a sublimated symbol of a deeper contemporary theme that the Secession unearthed in its attempt to capture the plight of modern man. Themes from folk fantasies opened up the unconscious, which asserted itself through comprehensible and acceptable symbols.

However, the Secession's discovery of nature's non-human essence in fairy tales immediately prompted a very human need to master these wild and even demonic natural forces, and this brought various magicians onto the stage of this symbolic fairy-tale fantasy. Panuška's *Warlock* (reproduced in the December 1898 issue of *Volné směry*) shows a figure with a staff seated on the circular terrace of a castle and surrounded by the black apparitions he has summoned. Panuška was again drawing on Schwaiger, yet the latter's *Enchanter* (1883) was more a satire on superstition, and one moreover with contemporary political relevance. Panuška's scene is veiled in twilight, creating a certain frisson. Although the motif of a magic circle protecting the warlock and allowing him to control the forces of darkness is used here to illustrate a particular story, it seems that something of the motif's symbolism found its way into seemingly quite different works. The finest vignettes in Jan Preissig's illustrations (1901–3) for Jan Karafiát's *Fireflies* have a circular format. The edition was significant as the first Czech book to feature a consistent and uniform concept for all elements of the Secession's new treatment of this medium as Gesamtkunstwerk. From its illustrations to its headers, lines, vignettes, title page, endpapers, and binding, Preissig's *Fireflies* manifested this stylistic concept for book design, and unlike Mucha's sumptuous books it adhered to the principle of sensitively balancing the typographic and artistic elements. The content of the book, which projects human ethical and moral standards into the world of nature, was also expressed through its form. Preissig based his fireflies on the contrast between their human clothing and their insectean eyes and legs. The anthropomorphising of natural form was in itself a kind of magic circle, with a graphically flawless stylisation of the natural world to indicate how the artist had mastered it.

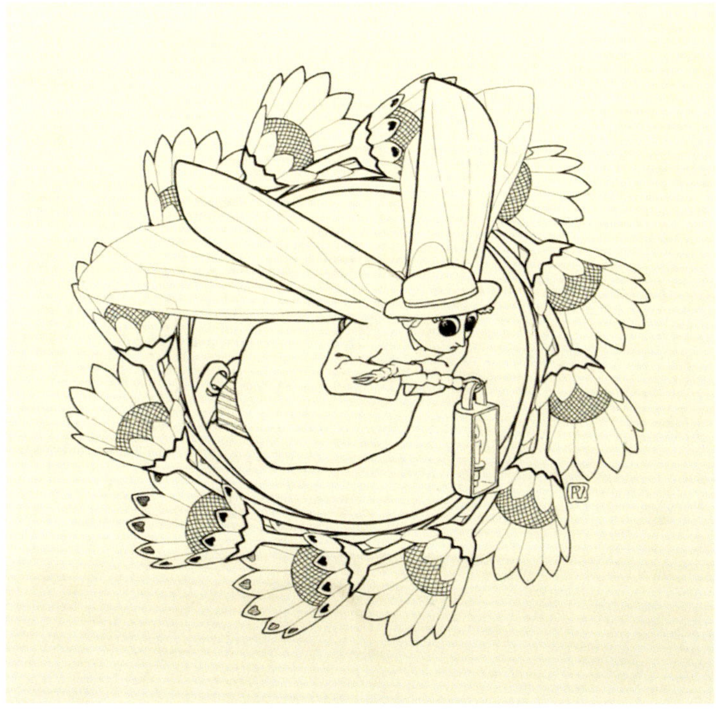

162 Vojtěch Preissig, Drawing for the cover of Jan Karafiát's *Fireflies*, 1901–3, Indian ink, 57 × 42 cm

While stylistic endeavours led to elementary formal symbols, figurative art sought a conceptual combination of form and content. František Bílek's woodcut *The Poet's Vision* (c. 1902–3) was based on the conclusions he had reached in his *Studies of Creative Motion* (1900). The figure of the initiate in his long gown resembles a tree trunk as he raises his arms in veneration of the mystery of the natural cosmos. Meanwhile, a cat, symbolising the forces of darkness, creeps towards the doves surrounding the saint, but this is merely an allusion to temptation in this sacred grove filled with symbolic stars. Unlike *Warlock*, we find here another kind of authority on the hidden forces of nature, one that can use these forces' dynamism to serve the loftier and more noble goal of cosmic harmony. For this reason, Bílek treated the woodcut as a negative,

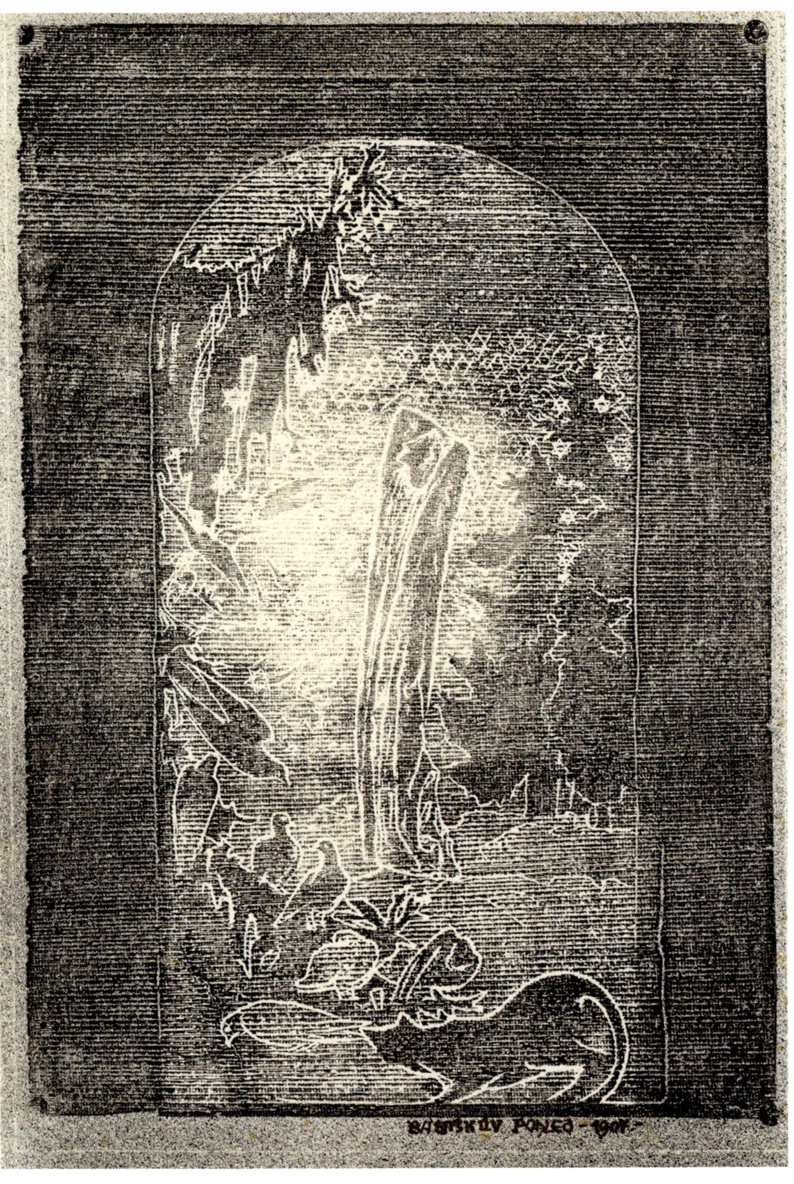

163 František Bílek, *The Poet's Vision*, 1902–3, linocut, 29 × 14.2 cm

where the white lines, which in the figure of the saint are largely vertical, stand out against the coarse black horizontal structure of the wood. In the composition of this scene there is then a certain hierarchy of symbols, expressing the idea of spiritual progress that so appealed to Bílek.

The contrast between black and white natural magic rapidly became a conceptual framework for that part of Secession fantasy that began to focus on the need to add a symbol of the artist as creator to the widespread symbol of art as a young woman or princess. Printmaking allowed these general symbols to be presented in distinctive conceptual and stylistic forms. This was more complicated in painting or sculpture, which made greater demands on realism, but these disciplines could also lend the experiential depth and urgency of plastic form to something that in printmaking was merely an idea.

In 1901 Bílek made his first sketches for one of his finest sculptures, *The Blind*, which he later replicated many times. The sculpture expressed a series of questions that was typical of Symbolism: "Who are we, what do we want, where are we going?" It presents the human world as a man and woman, wandering and blind, whose sole support is their solidarity and intuition. The man is the more active of the two, raising his head and extending one arm upwards, while the woman clutches a lyre, an instrument of prophecy and invocation. In its pronounced diagonal line, the sculpture reflects the trauma of spiritual longing. *The Blind* was not meant as a solitary work: together with the sculptures *I Know* and *Cleaving to the Tree of the Brethren* it formed Bílek's cycle *Life*, representing the progression from an initial statement of contemporary humanity's ruination to a knowledge of spiritual truth, and then to a vision of a new and active sense of fellowship built on firm foundations. This ordering of plastic images in cycles did not merely bridge the divide between graphical and plastic expression and replicate graphic art's capacity to group symbols together, for above all it satisfied the need to move beyond mere allegory. For Bílek and other Secession artists, deploying symbols in cycles was not simply a relic of the concept of art as illustration or an attempt to overcome art's seeming inability to generate anything resembling a literary narrative. Instead, it was a positive development that effectively broke with classical aesthetics' traditional concept of the artistic image as an enduring symbol in a semantic code. The Secession's way of working in cycles was more an artistic expression of the creative process, a way of answering the question raised by the initial querying of the value of the world of appearances. A symbol could no longer be merely adopted: now it had to be created, and art became a process of creating new values.

Secession artists also sought personal paradigms for this situation. At this critical moment in their development, Czech artists found one such paradigm in Auguste Rodin. The Mánes artists were enthralled by the pavilion on Place d'Alma where the French sculptor exhibited his life's work as part of the 1900 Exposition Universelle. Personal contacts were swiftly forged, resulting in a monographic edition of *Volné směry* in 1901, followed by Rodin's memorable exhibition in Prague in 1902.

Rodin's appeal for Czech modernism is evidenced in Vladimír Županský's exhibition poster and Švabinský's charcoal *Rodin's Inspiration,* which SVU Mánes presented to its guest as a gift. Županský's poster, printed in greyish-green, purple, and gold, features Rodin's *Monument to Balzac* against a backdrop of stylised curves that represent the whirling cosmos. In Švabinský's drawing, a nude young woman and a naked, winged adolescent fly through the starry skies above Rodin, who is depicted in a pose of creative concentration that recalls Michelangelo.

"The Mother Tongue of Genius," a speech that F. X. Šalda delivered at the opening of the exhibition, also underlined Rodin's quite extraordinary importance for the new art. Rodin excelled not just as "a great restorer and reviver" of sculpture itself, which had formerly seemed to be merely "the dead and rigid language of old, powerful, bygone times," but as the prototype of an artist who was able to give voice to "the artistic mother tongue of the time, fervid, unconventional and truthful, the very artery of the present day's intellectual ebb and flow." The capacity of Rodin's art to address its time and express its most essential tendencies stemmed not merely from a sense of the peculiarities of the age, but from much more substantial and fundamental sources of creativity. Šalda stressed Rodin's creative introspection, the inner psychological roots of his work:

> there has been no sculptor, and in recent times few artists, who have taken you so deep, down to the dark wells of creative chaos, and who have drawn from them so originally and directly, who have raised their hands, with the holy water they took, to your fevered lips that you might drink, who have let you look so deeply into the mystery of creation … Rodin's art is all at first hand.

Central to Šalda's admiration was his view of Rodin as the supreme embodiment of original creativity, which, while deep in introspective concentration, also captures values that are universal and impersonal:

> In his sculpture, like no other artwork of these modern times, resonate the primary forces of life and destiny, their oldest and most profound elements, the fundamental tones on which they are rhythmically extended. … Here everything that was most essential, most eternal and strongest in life and death was articulated, expressed with a line as intoxicating and fevered as pain and pleasure, as sensitive, tremulous and tractable as the nervous fluid, as glorious and expansive as the very law of existence, inception and demise.[109]

Šalda was speaking not just for himself but for the whole avant-garde at this time. His great influence, which was further amplified when he became editor-in-chief of *Volné směry* for the next few years, resulted chiefly from his ability to express artists' conceptual needs and bring his broad knowledge and eloquence to bear on the significance and meaning of their work. In this respect, his account of Rodin as an ideal artist brought together a number of fundamental ideas about art's purpose and essence that were current among artists, whether these were an echo of other, mostly literary, contemporary ideals or the outcome of their own processes of externalisation. Here the Secession world view had many elements that recalled a mythological model of the world. The very development of Secession art, rejecting historicist eclecticism as bankrupt and seeking to create a new stylistic alternative, pointed to the myth of paradise lost, which was indeed the fundamental conceptual framework for the

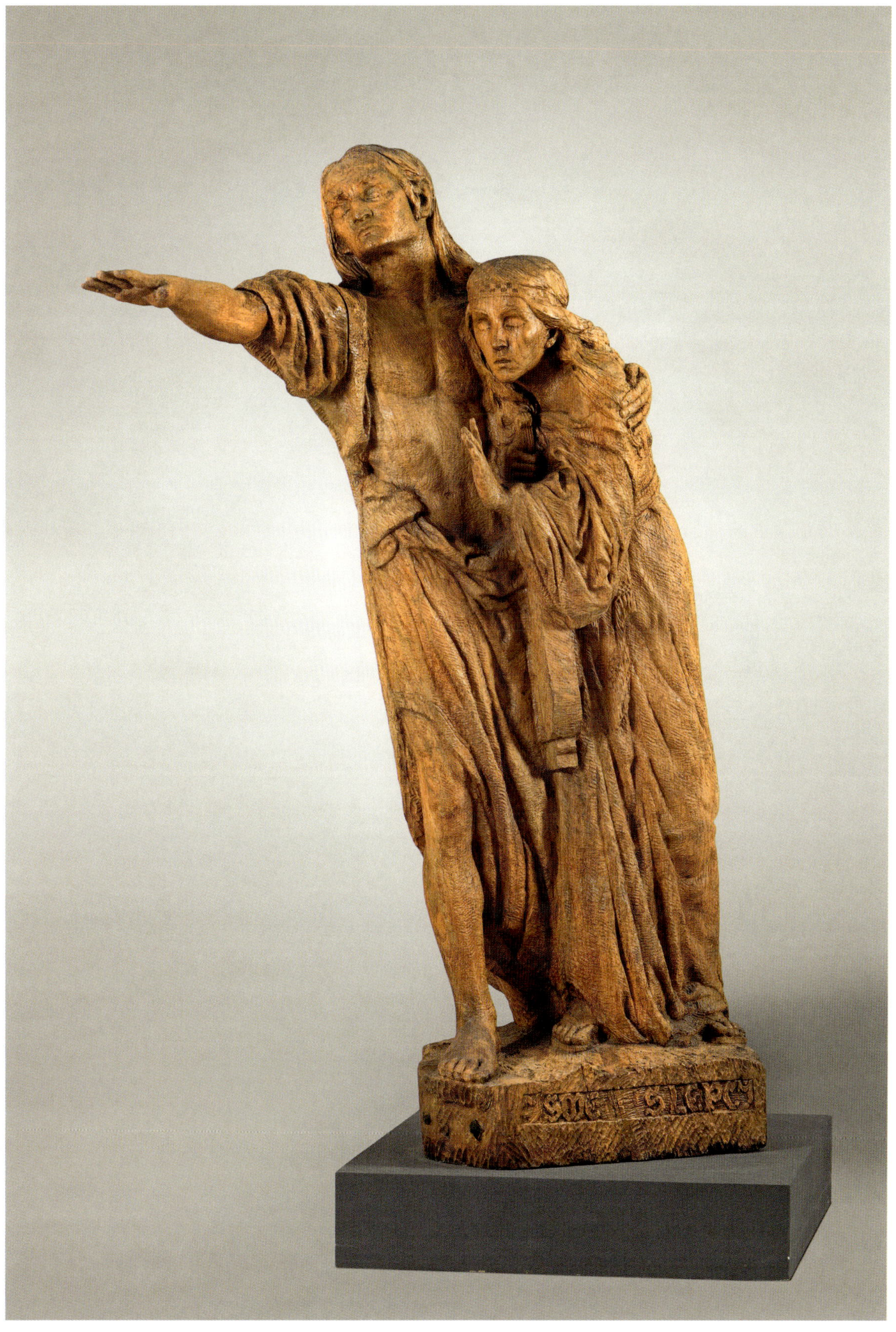

164 František Bílek, *The Blind*, 1902 (made 1926), wood, 216 cm

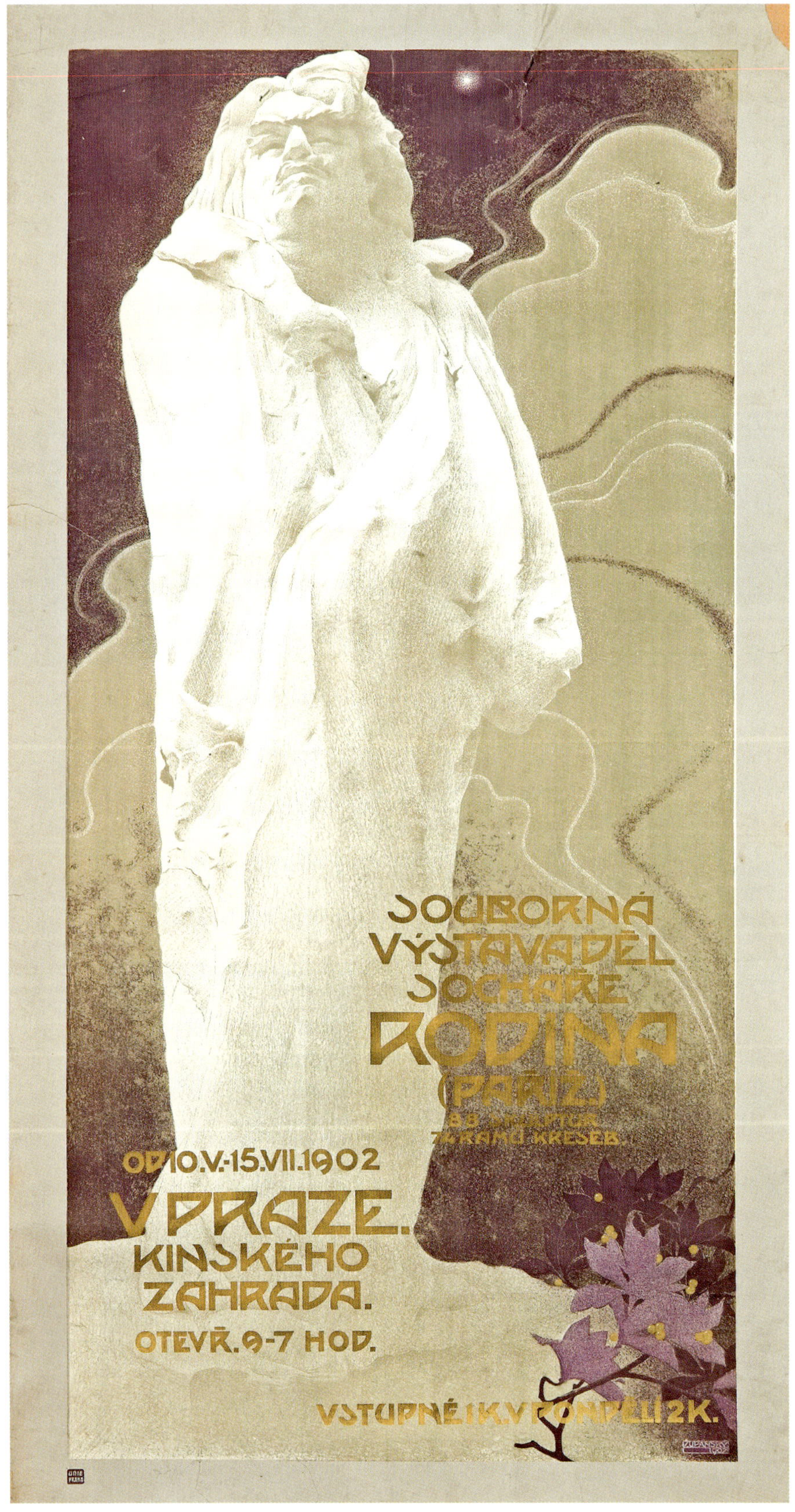

165 Vladimír Županský, Poster for the Rodin exhibition in Prague, 1902, colour lithograph, 158 × 84 cm

Secession's ideas. The core of the Secession was not the pessimism and decadence that had characterised its early years in the 1890s, combined with the rejection and negation of the old world of "bankrupt" artistic values, but a desire for new art. The Secession's attempt to create a new style was in fact an attempt to recreate the art world, and the key means for this fundamental regeneration was the idea of a return to the original, authentic sources of artistic creation; in this sense, the Secession's spokesmen also talked of a new unity of art and life. Initially, these sources were sought in nature, but it became ever more apparent that it was principally a matter of how the creative individual conceived of nature, and this shifted the focus to the psychological aspect.

Šalda's speech at the opening of the Rodin exhibition was a bold manifesto for this shift of focus, which is why there was so much talk of the artist's psychological mother tongue, of his ability to draw artistic symbols from the mysterious depths of his own soul and his sense of the tragedy of life. Here the artist was someone who created out of the primordial chaos a new world of artistic forms, and his fundamental cosmogonic ethos was also expressed theoretically – for instance, when Rodin was referred to as "an element of nature," or even "a cosmic force."[110] Rodin's exceptional status, and Czech modernism's veneration of him, came from a recognition of his role as some kind of new cosmocrator, whose model of the world was an ideal archetype of the creative situation, and thus of every artwork too. His art came to symbolise ideas about the fundamental unity of the biological, psychological, and ideational aspects that were incorporated into a view of the elementary components of art, a way of thinking about mass, line, light, and space. Genius in art was no longer nourished by nature's mere appearance but by its interconnections and processes, which were explicitly cosmic in character. This was why both Županský and Švabinský associated Rodin with a vision of the depths of the universe.

Compared with fairy-tale creatures, Rodin and his *Monument to Balzac* were an unusually vital symbol. As mere imitation would not suffice, a principle was sought for new art, and this resulted in a true deepening of the process of symbolisation. Šalda ended his speech with a clarion call:

> And revivers can only be understood by those they have revived, and only the revived can respond to them. The artistic mother tongue of genius can only be answered in the mother tongue: *they must themselves* seek its resonant voice within their own depths.

His words did not fall on deaf ears, as demonstrated by the creative process that Jan Preisler developed in 1903–4 for a motif whose extraordinary appeal for Secession artists we have already witnessed in numerous instances. These are his paintings from his *Black Lake* period, a group of works that is generally considered one of the most characteristic symbols not just of Preisler's art but of the whole Czech Secession.

In the spring of 1902 Preisler and Antonín Hudeček were in Italy, where they first saw the sea, depicting it in a number of small sketches. The following year, Preisler summarised his impressions in the romantic *Island of Monte Christo*, which recalled Capri in its white chalk cliffs and their harmony with black and blue-grey. These colours

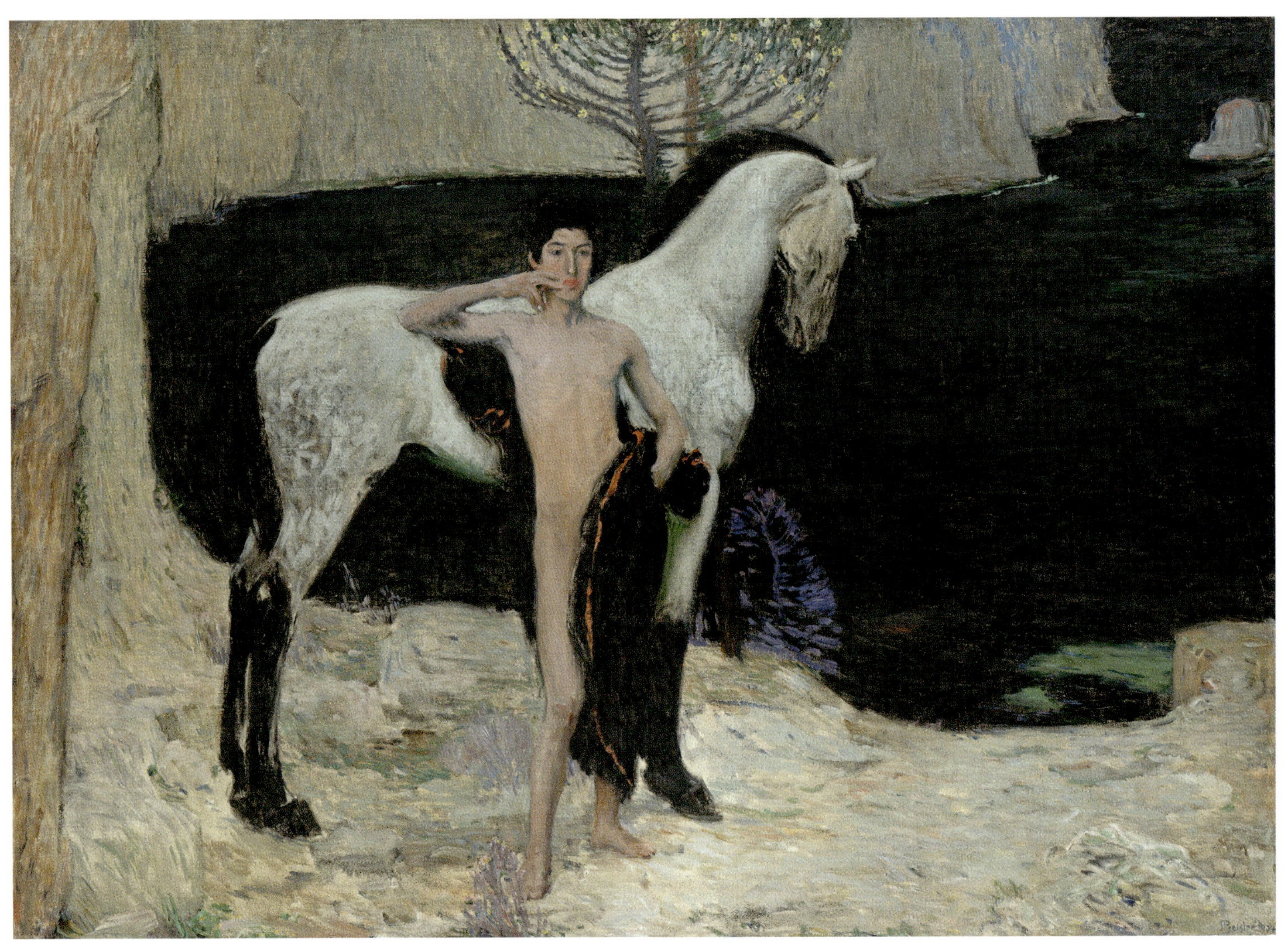

166 Jan Preisler, *Black Lake*, 1904, oil, 111 × 153 cm

were the foundation of the limited range he would then use in paintings devoted to "assorted sorrows, infidelity and melancholia,"[111] showing lovers standing on the white shores of lakes with forbiddingly deep, black water. In their attire, and in the entire mood of these paintings, reality and dream have fused inseparably. The tension in these works, accentuated by the refined play of subtle accents of purple, yellow, red, and green over large expanses of white and black, produces an unusual intensity of poetic feeling. These modest paintings, prompted by Preisler's private compulsions, displayed the greater interest in psychological introspection that Šalda had proclaimed. The depth of poetic space in the new paintings was further magnified by the attention devoted to the element of water. It is as if further images rise up from its depths quite spontaneously, an aspect that was most notably expressed in the painting *Adolescent by a Lake*, whose relaxation of form suggests that this was truly a private work. It shows a chasm with a naked boy sitting by a small tree, only summarily sketched, as he gazes at the dark surface of the lake before him. However, this theme is only a means of establishing the inner narrative, which is chiefly played out in the relations between the solid colours. Preisler's usual linear brushstrokes have receded, while the expanses of dark and muted greens, greys, and blues have lost their sharp definition and become luminous coloured fluids, whose dim glow creates a captivatingly poetic and dreamlike mood. In this painting, Preisler anticipated the development of modern lyrical painting all the way to Josef Šíma.

In the motif of the black lake, Preisler reached into the depths of his imagination. The motif's fecundity is apparent in another series of paintings featuring figural symbols, which laid the iconographic foundation for Preisler's by now entirely mature art. These are the figures of a woman and rider who have come to the lake, either alone or together, and are fascinated by the stillness of its surface. In a variant from 1904, the rider has dismounted and is gazing at a naked water fairy, sitting on a rock in the lake as she braids her red hair. A progression can be seen in this group of paintings, from the intimate lyricism of *Adolescent by a Lake* to ever-larger canvases that fix the original creative impulse and address the viewer. This is then manifested in the crystallisation of these paintings' iconography and their precise decorative composition: various arrangements of the symbols of lake, tree, white horse, and adolescent nude from 1904 that ranged from regular paintings to large wall decorations, until the original symbol had been exhausted by the fulfilment of this contemporary objective.

In these large paintings, Preisler would later value above all his instinctive achievement of an artwork's essential unity in both their linear and colour composition:

> For instance, the painting with a youth and a white horse in front of a black lake, which could be called melancholia or some such. The theme is already there in the black tones that were most intense in the black colour of the youth's drapery, some kind of centre of the painting. This colour, in various nuances from the darkest tones to greys and greens, then imbues the entire painting, ultimately becoming the light greys and almost white tones of the horse the youth is leaning against. So it isn't a black or grey painting, but a colour one. I couldn't do it any more logically today.[112]

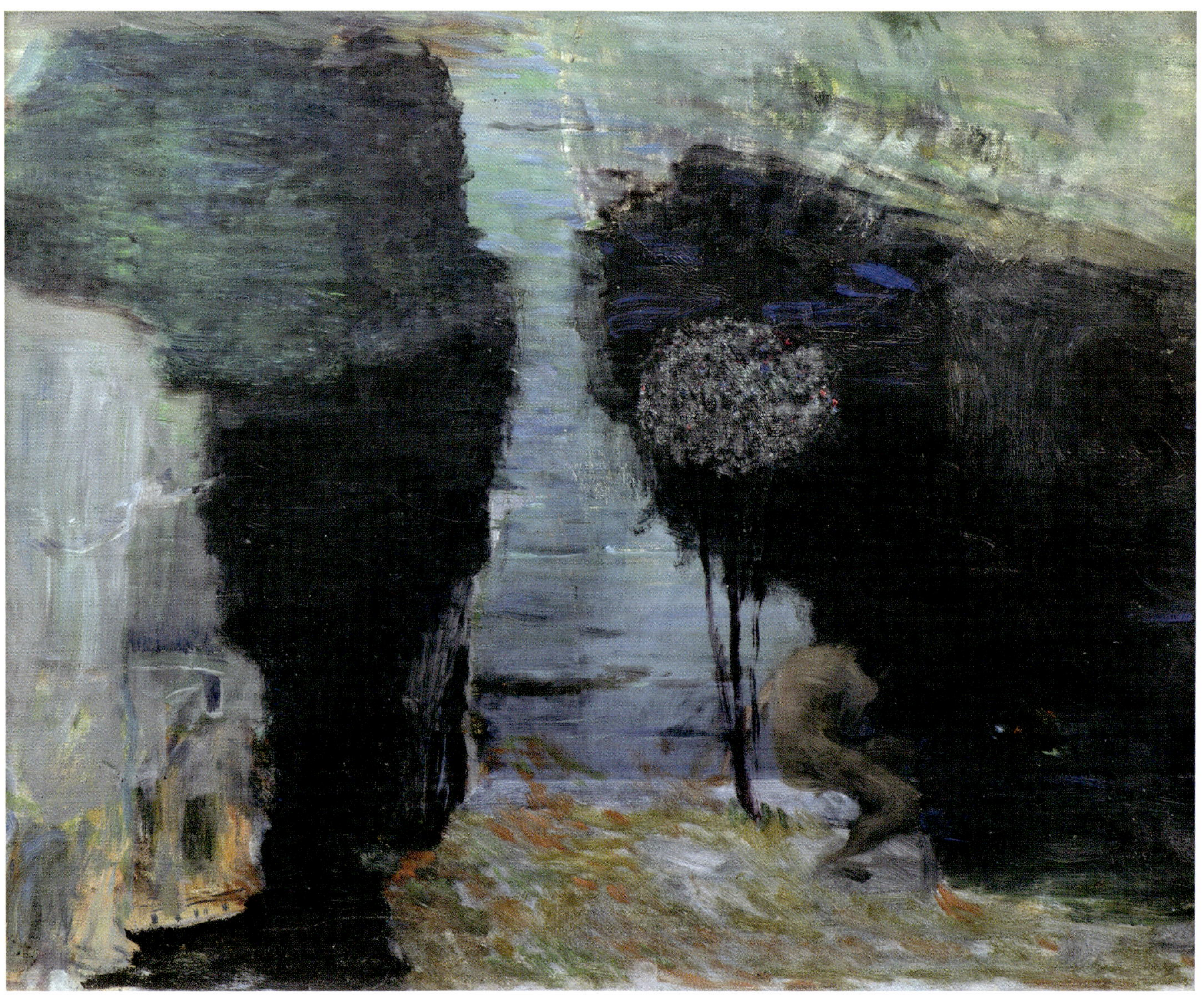

167 Jan Preisler, *Adolescent by a Lake*, 1903, oil, 44 × 53 cm

The unity of which Preisler speaks in reference to the painting's colours was also achieved in its motifs and symbolism. The white horse is traditionally associated with water (classical mythology, for instance, has Neptune's horses), and its combination with the adolescent was a manifesto for the essential character of the new art. Henceforward the rider would become Preisler's dominant theme, replacing his earlier knight, as can be seen in his *Composition with a White Horse* (1905–6), which brought together some of the key motifs in Preisler's "cycle of life."

Of all Czech artists, Preisler achieved the most organic combination of fairy-tale themes with the requirements for fantastical symbolisation that had a more profound content. In this respect, his contribution lay not just in how remarkably symptomatic his symbols were of the time and of the Secession's ideals, but especially in how he broke with persistent ideas about the uniqueness of a painting, or the need to confine a series to particular themes and concepts. Instead, Preisler painted free variations, which earned him the title of "our greatest subjectivist." Contemporary critics particularly appreciated the fragile sensitivity of Preisler's types. For the 16th SVU Mánes exhibition, K. B. Mádl wrote,

> Jan Preisler dreams. Wrapped in wistful melancholy, he muses on worlds that are voiceless, still, in which silence is more expressive than the human voice. Once he saw wooded hills and plains in flower, awakened by the breath of the first spring, where people, young people from fairy tales, sit and muse on premonitions that they themselves cannot explain, in which the mystery of growth is hidden. In their youthful beauty and immaculate fragility, it is as if they are standing before the gates of life, which they unconsciously fear. Nowhere are there any grand gestures; nowhere is there any advancement, only a constant passive pose, a kind of unresisting surrender. If they love, then their love is a communion without heat or commotion, more a poignant sorrow for which they have no explanation. Nor are they individuals: they have shed any distinctiveness they might have had, they have ascended to a type of people who breathe melancholy, who live in spring but not in joy, always only in the fear that soon will come something cruel, coarse and crushing.[113]

However, Mádl's account, although sensitive to the effect of individual paintings and to the painter's personality, only captured the more static aspect of Preisler's artistic disposition. Just as Preisler's art intertwined dreams and reality, so his individual paintings were an integral part of an entire oeuvre that sensed motion behind their static individuality – motion that was not just subjectively psychological but also developmentally historical. Preisler tried to realise all these elements equally, in accordance with the Secession's synthetism. This is why in his work an intuitive introspection of a subjective origin went hand in hand with an attempt to apply this introspection through large decorative painting.

This interest was a characteristic limit for some of the discoveries that Secession art had made. The new art had unquestionably opened the way to exploring the phenomena of the psychological unconscious in art, something that had been strictly taboo under academicism's moral inhibitions and formal norms. Some of Secession

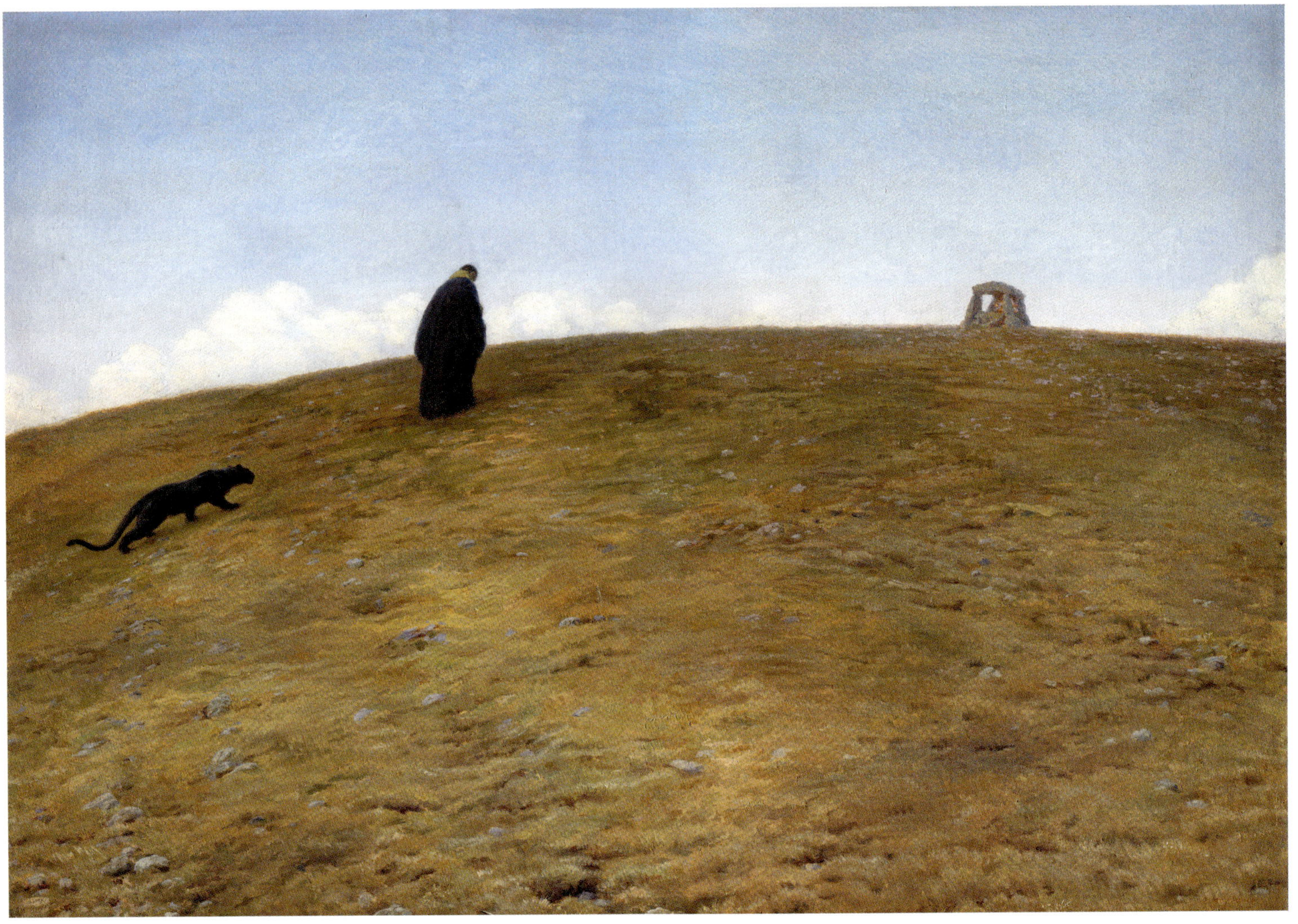

168 Arnošt Hofbauer, *Pilgrim*, 1904, oil, 111 × 114.5 cm

art's finest achievements were based on this principle, as was the case with Preisler. At the same time, the new art never wholly freed itself from the need to express its revelations indirectly. A typical example of this limitation is Arnošt Hofbauer's painting *Pilgrim* from 1904, which seems quite alien in the context of his oeuvre.[114] With its more naturalistic scenery, *Pilgrim* differed from Hofbauer's earlier decorative work and also from the cold fairy-tale mountain of his painting *Before Sunrise* (1902). Nevertheless, his depiction of a pilgrim making his way uphill to a pagan dolmen, unaware that behind him creeps a black panther, symbolising animal sensuality, is an entirely authentic expression of the new concept of the psychological foundation of art, as manifested by the Rodin exhibition. Of course, Hofbauer went no further than the symbolic figuration of this concept. With him, its use in variations – which for Preisler would have comprised an entire "cycle" – resulted only in a series of vividly painted sketches of tigers and other wild animals.

Secession artists used the theme of fairy tales as an attractive means of artistic externalisation, and it revealed to them its hidden possibilities. Besides the theme's psychological and symbolic content, it also lived on in less introspective forms, especially as a popular way of presenting the Secession's amusing commentary on life. The innocent ideality of fairy tales won an audience through an approach in which entertainment and moral lessons found a strong ally in decorativism. The fairy-tale theme comprised a specific enclave in Czech book illustration (especially for children's books), poster art, and set design. Artists who were particularly successful here included František Kysela, Artuš Scheiner, and Josef Wenig.

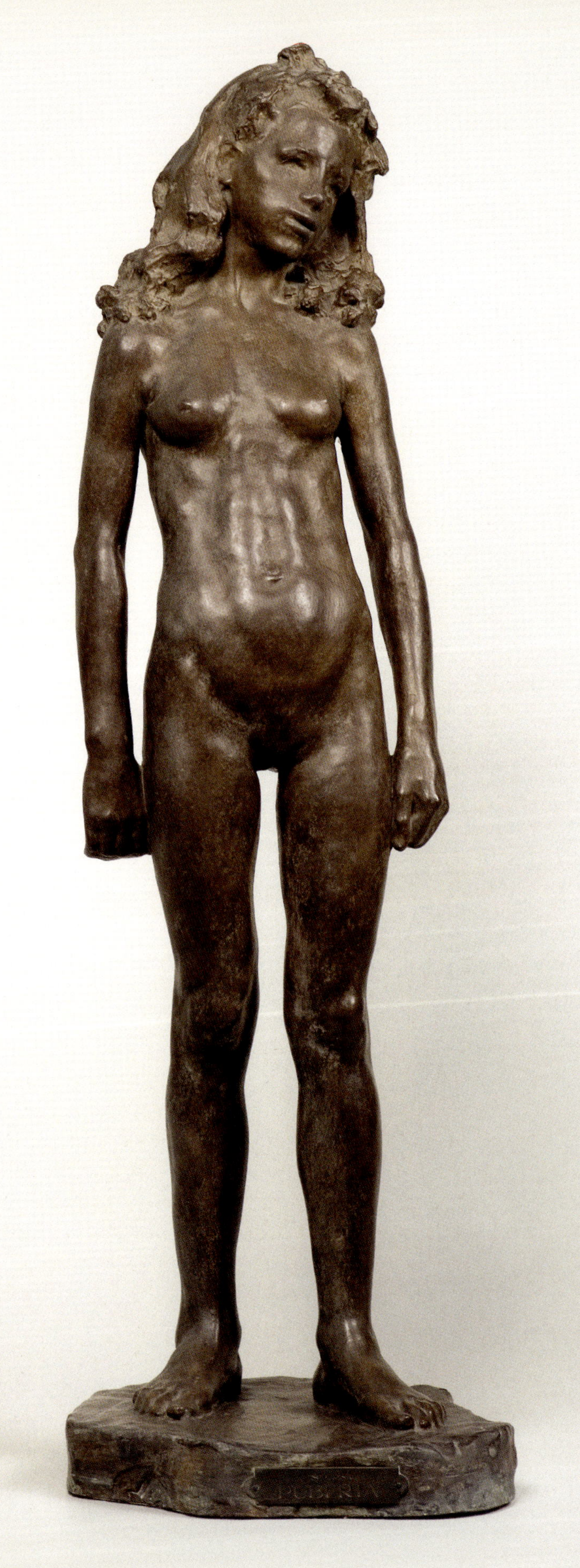

SENSES

In 1902 in Paris, František Kupka finished a painting that was invested with many of his artistic ambitions, as his letters to the poet Josef Machar reveal. This was a creation "that should set the pace for art,"[115] and he named it, somewhat ambivalently, *Ballad-Joys*. Kupka's remarks were more definite:

> I want to express, quite artfully and with simple means, the feelings I used to have when I'd be sitting on the seashore all alone, and as I have plenty of studies of this sort of thing, I set to work. There are two women, fairly hideous, on horseback, trotting along the seashore and revelling in the warm reflection of the setting sun, while the whole seashore and the clouds are tuned to the note of some unknown joys, and in the clouds it's as if a thousand sprites were dancing and jumping for joy. ... We all long for some kind of joy – a pure, immaterial sense of well-being, and I want this piece to produce similar feelings in everyone who sees it.

Kupka executed the painting with a sophisticated technique that allowed him to capture the specific effect of light on colour. This aspect was important, for it united the otherwise very disparate components of a painting that combined both a naturalistic and a Symbolist view of the subject. This problem had also characterised Kupka's earlier work, but here it was more acute. While the painting's setting was taken from the coast by Trégastel, where Kupka holidayed, it was simultaneously transposed to a mythological level, as the meeting of land and sea. Crucial to the composition are the lines made by the outgoing tide, where the seaweed, bands of wet sand, and foaming waves produce typical Secession-style curves receding into the distance. Their serpentine form is a cryptic symbol for the elementary, vital force pervading the entire natural cosmos. This dual root of Kupka's imagery is yet more evident in the staffage. The naked women, depicted with pitiless naturalism, were both figures from Kupka's private life, but their horses are prehistoric breeds. The painting had a second title, *Epona's Ballad*, after the Gallo-Roman goddess who was the protectress of horses, and in this sense the painting also reflects Kupka's extensive research on archaeology and mythology, something that was often expressed in his work and would culminate just a few years later in his illustrations for Élisée Reclus's *Man and Earth*.

The women are of contrasting types, as are their mounts. The difference between the pyknic, fair-haired Danish woman, sitting astride a heavy, dapple-grey horse, and the athletic, dark-haired Gabrielle, crouching on a whinnying pony, recalls psychologists' attempts to determine the fundamental differences between cyclothymic and schizothymic types, or between introverts and extroverts. An enthusiastic dilettante in the natural sciences, Kupka thought out his paintings in detail, and he may have included much of what he had learned in this painting.[116]

More important than all the speculative ideas worked into the painting, however, was what made it an aesthetically effective whole and expressed the main theme, the

169 Jan Štursa, *Puberty*, 1905, patinated plaster, 86 cm

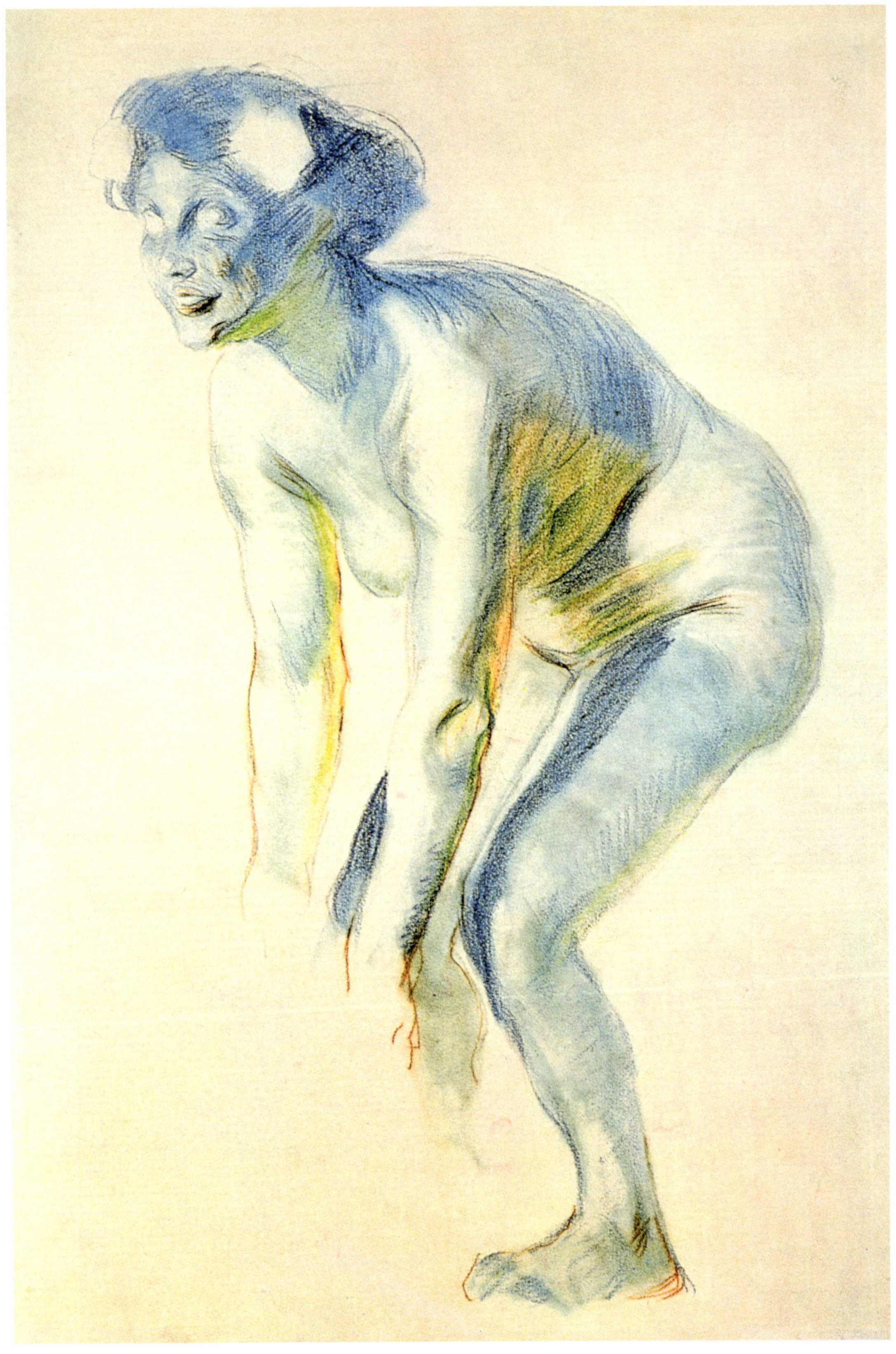

170 František Kupka, Study of a nude for *Ballad-Joys*, 1901–2, coloured pencils, 44.1 × 28.3 cm

metaphysical joy that Kupka referred to in his letters. This was the sunlight, which affected everything in the painting, and it was understood as the bearer of the fundamental cosmic energy so essential for life and its joys. Surviving studies of the figure of Gabrielle also indicate the significance that Kupka attached to the light. Besides drawings of her face, which are masterful examples of contemporary mimetic symbolism, the studies are mostly of her energetic stance. They became an entire series, in which Kupka moved from his customary outline to an unusual dematerialisation of form by means of coloured light. In this process, colour loses its entirely local quality: the nude is executed in blue chalk, with white and yellow reflections. It seems that, independently of any speculative content, in this breaking away from the model there lay a remarkable innovation that opened the way to Kupka's later development, although there would still be several years of hard work before he began consciously applying the results of this innovation. It is not without interest that Kupka is thought to have made the first sketches for his *Moving Blues* in 1902.[117] The motif of curves, familiar from *Ballad-Joys* and continued in the ideoplastic *Rhythm of History* (c. 1905) and the series *Bathers* (1906), became in the 1920s an abstract symbol in a painting that, from a morphological perspective, was the "most Secession" of Kupka's later abstract work.

Given the situation around 1902, it is significant that Kupka had found a new basis for his art that went beyond the coexistence of naturalism and Symbolism. In this

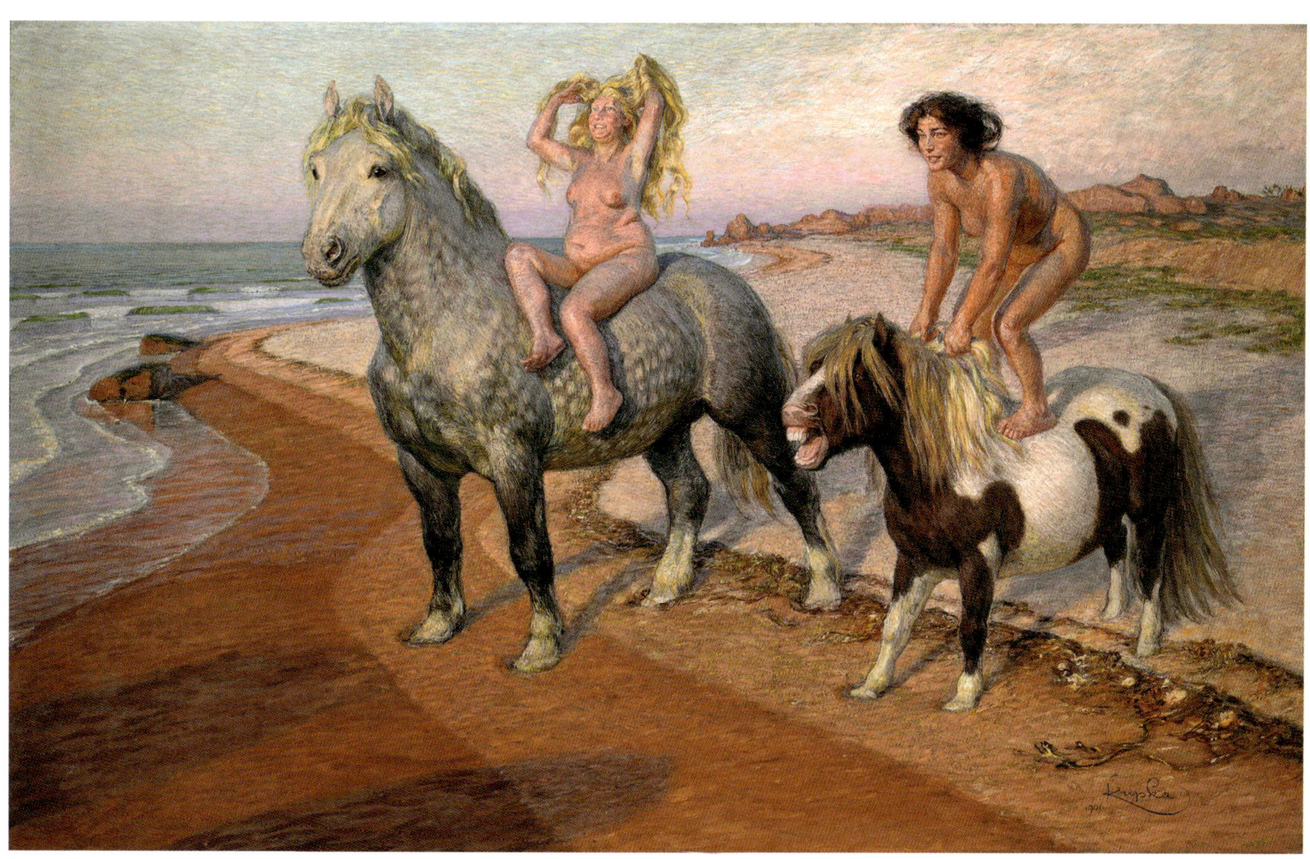

171 František Kupka, *Ballad-Joys*, 1902, oil, 83.5 × 126.5 cm

respect, his quest was not just a personal matter but part of the fundamental changes that French art was undergoing shortly after 1900. At this time, the Symbolist chapter that had typified the 1890s had come to a close, and attention now turned more to the artistic essence of an artwork and its ability to extract a synthetic quality from nature. One manifestation of this change of direction was Maurice Denis's *Homage to Cézanne*, painted in 1901, which showed members of Les Nabis and the Symbolist painter Odilon Redon gathered around a still life by Cézanne. Czech artists, greatly influenced by what was happening in French art, would only decipher this painting's full import later, but the logic of this step towards a modern synthesis was reflected in numerous aspects of contemporary practice.

For Czech artists, the naturalistic foundation they had established in the 1890s still remained the most fruitful stimulus. It was also the most versatile, for both the Symbolist and the ornamental decorative aspects of Secession art were built on this foundation. As they both quite quickly became a matter of convention, usually simplified to thematic or morphologically "stylistic" formulas, the "connection with nature" remained the true buttress of the new art. Here too, however, there were ever greater demands for artistic quality, and in this context approaches were sought that would more profoundly valorise the naturalistic tendency.

Josef Mařatka's Secession sculpture is one example of this development. When a Hlávka scholarship allowed him to go to Paris in 1900, Mařatka entirely abandoned Myslbek's monumentalism in favour of modelling Impressionistic figures from daily life. *Parisian Bricklayer*, *Coalman on the Seine*, *Little Girl with a Loaf of Bread*, and other sculptures belonged to the naturalistic genre. Then, however, Mařatka visited an exhibition by Rodin in Paris, and he was fortunate enough to be taken into Rodin's studio as his pupil and assistant. It is interesting that a gentle correction, with Rodin urging him "chantez plus!," was all that was needed for Mařatka to shed all illustrative description and grasp, entirely spontaneously, the essence of the elder artist's concept of sculpture. As instructed, Mařatka began by working on studies of hands and feet, where he learned to exaggerate form for the purposes of expression. Later, he switched to maquettes of fluid female nudes and torsos, which, like Rodin, he drew according to a freely moving, naked model. There seems nothing new in this method of working from the detail to the whole, but, crucially, this was not concerned with acquiring the usual study material, for Rodin considered each fragment of the body, or its torso, to be an independent artistic whole, and this fragmentariness had a more conceptual significance – it was a way of yoking human corporeality to the absolute. A series of raised hands that Rodin produced in the 1880s went entirely beyond anatomical studies and led explicitly to a psychophysical symbolism. At this time, Rodin associated such a hand with the theme of Fate. Mařatka took his master's lead and developed Rodin's ideas in his own way, especially in contrasting variations of basic motifs. Besides dramatic sketches of expressive stumps, he also produced weary hands whose drooping lines and compactness expressed the other pole of the Secession's sense of life's tragedy. This was also reflected in the different chirognomic typology of the hands, the distinction between the shorter fingers of an intuitive hand and the

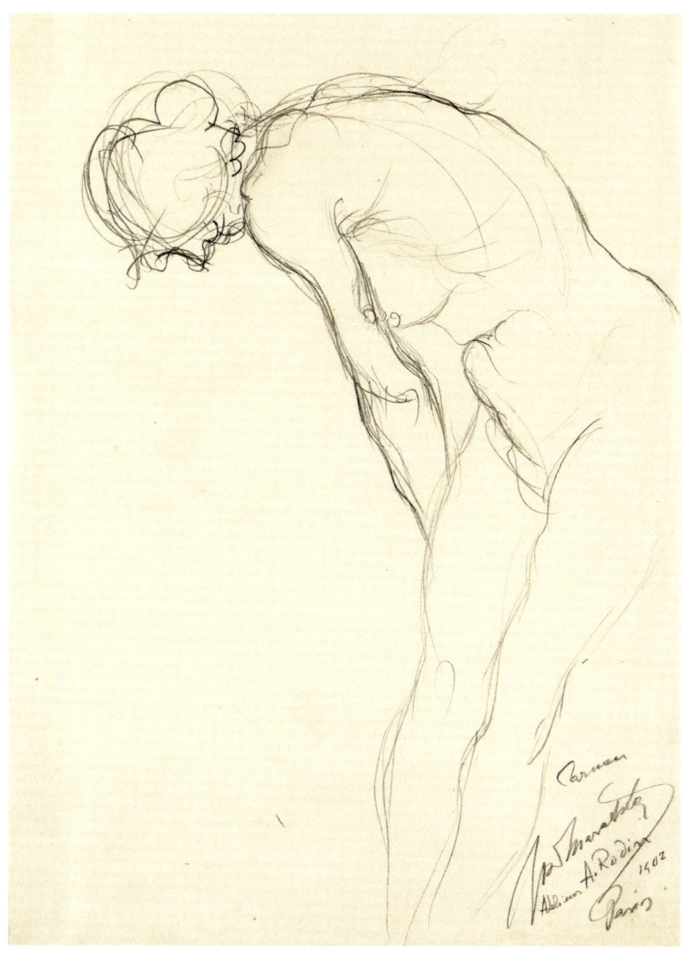

longer fingers of a sensitive one. These typological aspects of physical expressiveness and the human psyche best demonstrate how naturalism was acquiring a deeper meaning for Mařatka. This created the conditions for a kind of Symbolism that was different from literary or fantastical Symbolism, while losing nothing of an artwork's sensuous fullness and artistry. In his sketches of female nudes, Mařatka made full use of what he had learned from his studies of hands and feet. These sketches, mostly from 1902–3, were a truly unique innovation in Czech sculpture. Mařatka was able to shed all his ingrained prejudices about composition, and transform the nude into a free and unrestrained expression of matter animated by the sculptor's sensitivity. In this, he was greatly aided by drawing, which, following Rodin's example, was an impulsive record of the natural and expressive motion of a freely moving model. As these were not static poses arranged specifically for a sculpture but entirely informal sketches, the sculptor became unusually sensitive to a fluid expressivity, and the creative process acquired a broad foundation that connected sculpture with reality. Content came out of experience, and although the basis of this approach was naturalistic, it in no way detracted from the creative freedom of the artist, whose role it was to capture an

172 Josef Mařatka, Sketch of a nude, 1902, pencil, 31 × 20 cm

expressive motif in the flowing current of life and extract from it the essence for how to proceed. In this respect, intuition was not something artificial, but rather the outcome of a wealth of experience.

In his maquettes, Mařatka first relaxed the contrapposto stance to give the nude a freer ponderation and turn the body into a flowing play of irregularly rhythmical curves. In some maquettes the torso's mass forces itself upwards, twisting like a flame, but for the most part the upper half of the body is bent downwards, creating dynamic curves. This motion acquired a symbolic meaning in *Ariadne Abandoned* (c. 1903). The motif of the body arching down to the rock created a composition that was especially interesting in the way the centre of the sculpture remained empty. While Rodin still let the light filter through a thin, translucent layer of marble, Mařatka chose to perforate the mass. This was perhaps the most radical formal concept that could be achieved at the time. It intuited the modern "inner" space of a sculpture and corresponded exactly to the Secession's key mythological ideas about revival as a return to the very

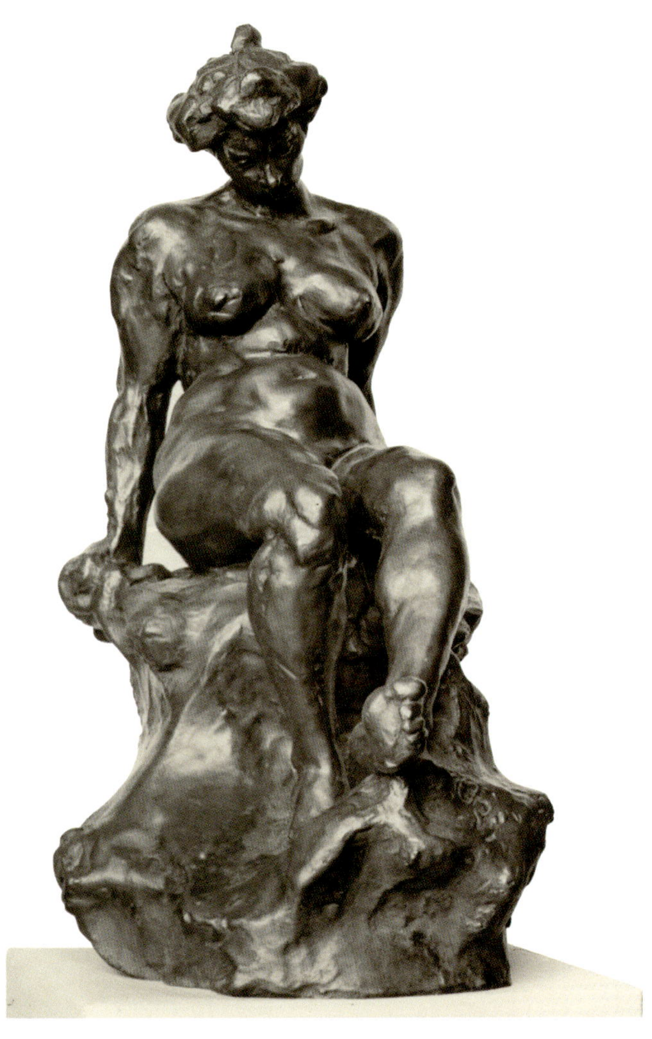

173 Josef Mařatka, *Fat Woman*, 1903, bronze, 34.2 cm

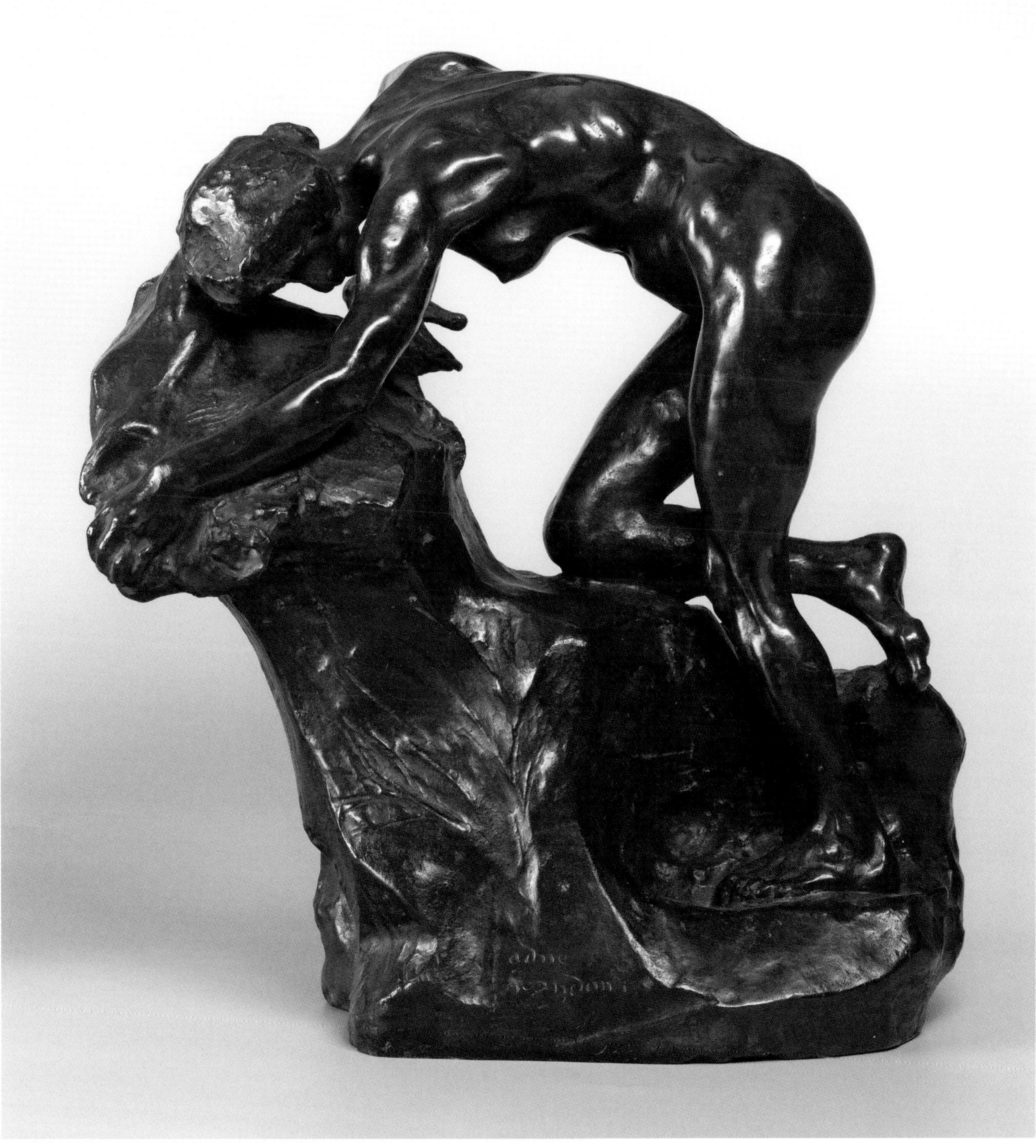

174 Josef Mařatka, *Ariadne Abandoned*, 1903, bronze, 30.5 cm

beginning. With this loss of the sculpture's centre of mass, Mařatka's Ariadne was as far removed as possible from the traditional, classical conception of sculpture. Yet this was not merely negation, but also a searching for new possibilities. In this way, *Ariadne Abandoned* recalls Kupka's watercolour *The Lotus Soul*, where the triptych's "empty" central section is the focal point for all the painting's emotional tension. The difference is that Kupka had to use a fantastical narrative to produce this authentic Secession motif, whereas for Mařatka, entirely ordinary means sufficed. The transformation that Mařatka had undergone in less than three years would of course be unthinkable without the direct influence of Rodin, who was a powerful stimulus for the young sculptor's artistic maturing.

The intuitive foundation for the concave volume in *Ariadne Abandoned* is also evident from Mařatka's ongoing exploration of antithetical possibilities when working on his nudes – as, for example, in his two studies for *Fat Woman*. In both of these, the mass of the sculpture dominates – not in the classic, static way, but with an expressive exaggeration. One of the studies is an immaculate analysis of the type from a psychophysical perspective, while the other – rather a sketch, with the figure leaning back with her hands behind her – is more interesting as a sculpture. It recalls a passage in Mařatka's handwritten notes and memories of Rodin:

> Rodin wanted me to pay more attention to profiles, which must be studied from all sides, so when modelling not to work en face but to study the profiles; that is, to work with outlines. Only in this way can a stable form be achieved (a stable core for the form), which must be first and foremost architectural, that is, constructed.[118]

The effect of this principle can be seen in the aforementioned study, where the core, constructed from stable masses, is extended into space with the aid of the slight asymmetry of the basic volumes, defined by their outlines from various viewpoints. Unlike in *Ariadne Abandoned*, the outlines are not closed but seek to persist in their material essence and triumphantly emanate into the space around them. The deformations that appear in specific parts of the nude indicate that Mařatka was now reflecting something from more recent developments in French sculpture – heretical innovations that the volatile Antoine Bourdelle, for instance, a friend of the young Henri Matisse, was already exploring in Rodin's studio at this time.

As contacts with France expanded, a sense of lagging behind the latest developments was felt all the more keenly. The case of Mařatka demonstrates just how quickly this lost ground could be made up if the conditions were right. Under these circumstances, Mařatka played a significant role in reinforcing the Francophile orientation. The fact that he was in direct contact with the group of sculptors who were pioneering the new advances, still based around Rodin's studio, was symptomatic of how Czech artists were seeking to access the sources of modern art. They needed to find their bearings in the flood of contemporary art, to see its true value and understand its logical progression, and this gave rise to critics such as F. X. Šalda and Miloš Jiránek, who combined their broad cultural overview with a good knowledge of current thinking among leading French and German art critics. Their eloquence allowed them to promote a programme outlining the main objectives and role models. As a painter,

Jiránek was intimately acquainted with Czech artists' technical problems and the scope within which they operated, and he had a significant influence on the orientation of the most active group.

Jiránek first witnessed modern art's great confrontation at the exhibitions that accompanied the Exposition Universelle in Paris in 1900, and he promptly wrote two reports on them for *Volné směry*. These reveal that, even though he was initially dismayed by the diversity and sheer quantity of paintings, which were assembled chiefly in the Grand Palais, he soon clarified his criteria and subjected himself to pitiless self-criticism based on his new awareness of what was happening in painting internationally. In light of this knowledge, many of the existing idols of the orientation of Czech art were toppled, and paradoxically some things that had been thought passé now returned with a new urgency in this quest for the foundations of modern art.

One such burning issue was the French Impressionists. At the exhibition of French art that SVU Mánes held in the autumn of 1902, the Impressionists were quite well represented, but the general thrust of K. B. Mádl's review was that, although they would forever remain "saints in the calendar of art," their relevance was now exhausted. Mádl valued Impressionism as the historic revolution that had freed painting from academicism. The Impressionists had conquered "the naturalness of light, the subtle truthfulness of colour and the characteristic instantaneousness of gesture … they taught us the courage of our own seeing and observing, and in doing so they affixed us, so to speak, to the present and to reality." But their art was one-sided, and it could not

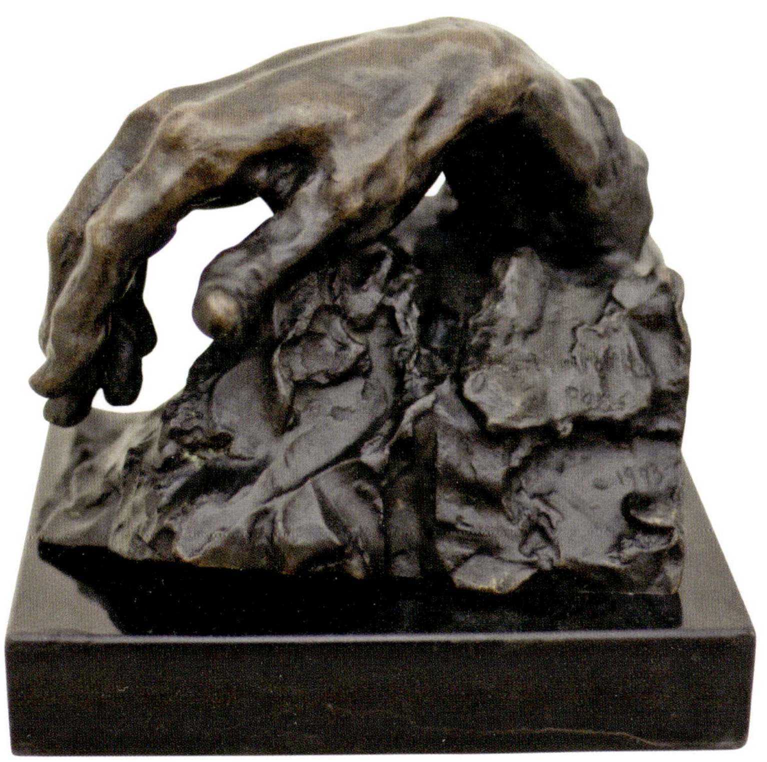

175 Josef Mařatka, Study of a hand, 1903, bronze, 19.5 cm

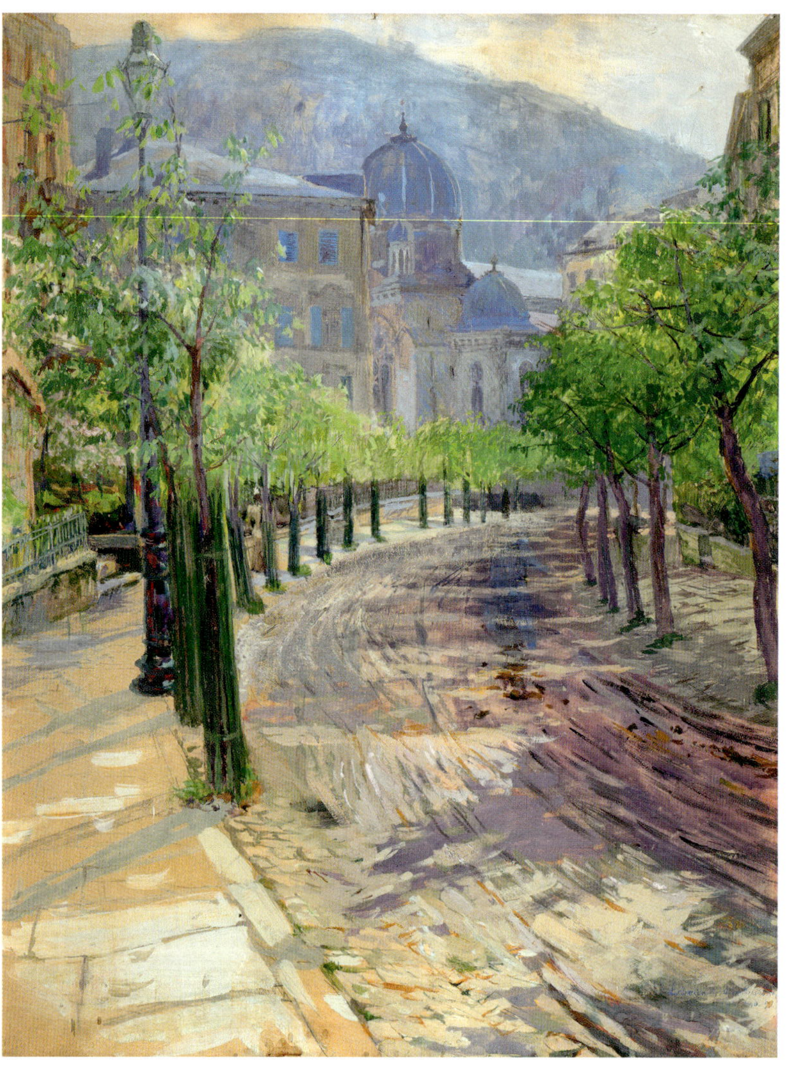

bring forth entirely new creations. Their preoccupation with the optics of light broke down form and destroyed line – not just the academic line but also the line so essential to artistic expression, "extracted from the essence of nature and converted into an individual language." More significant than the Impressionists were their successors, the "Intimists and colourists," who, in contrast with the Impressionists' investigation of light and examination of air, "speak through the quality of colour and the compactness of the lines." Mádl considered Henri Le Sidaner, Edmond Aman-Jean, and Henri Martin to be representative of this more progressive art. These three painters had been known to Czech artists since the mid-1890s, but at their exhibitions in Paris Miloš Jiránek had thought them epigones who lacked the creative courage and drive of true originators. This prepared the ground for differences of opinion that would not only be projected into personal relationships, but would also be important for the development of Czech art.

176 Otakar Lebeda, *Horní Sadová třída in Karlovy Vary*, 1898, tempera, 67 × 50 cm

Mádl's critique of Impressionism reflected the requirements of the Secession's synthetism, and it was not essentially incorrect, but its fatal shortcoming was that it tied its theoretical demands to individuals who could not play any substantial role in the overall development of modern art. Jiránek would later write,

> Initially, it seems to me, we valued in the Impressionists qualities that were quite external and therefore the most prominent: for us, the content of Impressionism was the study of the effects of light, the fleeting moods of the moment; we were impressed by its grand concept of plein air and its technical innovations, and in consequence by the masters who had become virtuosos of this new technique, and in our eyes they overshadowed the combatants who had first fought for it: Bastien-Lepage, Besnard and Harrison obscured from us Manet, Degas, Monet and Renoir. It was a long time before we began to discern the artistic individuality beneath the external uniformity of this common endeavour, but then of course the old and true ones proved their worth: they had one virtue above all, the greatest one, their personal relationship with art.[119]

For Jiránek, the character of a painting was directly related to the psychological type of its painter, and what was required was a creative personality. In the spirit of the authentic Secession's moral pathos, the modern artist was understood in terms that were heroic and dramatic. Jiránek's model was not the pessimistic decadent of the 1890s, but the active combatant in the struggle to establish a new aesthetic and world view. This ideal of direct action was unquestionably connected with the greater activity of SVU Mánes, and of the entire younger generation, but more importantly it established a new norm that covered all aspects of the relationship between art and reality. Whereas Mádl interpreted Impressionism as primarily related to mood, Jiránek spoke of "impressions," and he included here a requirement to express the direct experience of reality in an original and artistic form.

In this respect, Jiránek found an important ally in F. X. Šalda, who in 1903 published a long lecture in *Volné směry* entitled "The New Beauty: Its Genesis and Character." This would become something of a manifesto for their position. Šalda similarly emphasised creative spontaneity and freedom from convention as the essential starting point:

> The new art and new beauty is [*sic*] therefore always passionately devoted to the present, and what is more: it is in fact the sole present, the fullest, realest and most authentic reality there is. … For in this respect man the artist differs substantially and fundamentally from the man of the reproduction, the man of the average and of mediocrity: whereas the average man ekes out a miserable existence from the past and in the past, laboriously and unhappily fastening, joining, binding and stitching his life together according to the external criteria of memory and logic, and so in fact he compiles, based on other people's formulas, impressions that are not even his, mere echoes of other people's impressions, the creative soul alone lives an intensely full and authentic life, unmediated by logic, memory and abstraction, a life that is amplified and heightened, full and at first hand in the singular revelation of the senses.

For Šalda, art is above all original work. The new art does not borrow its means of expression from the past, but "organises the chaos of the present moment in a new law,

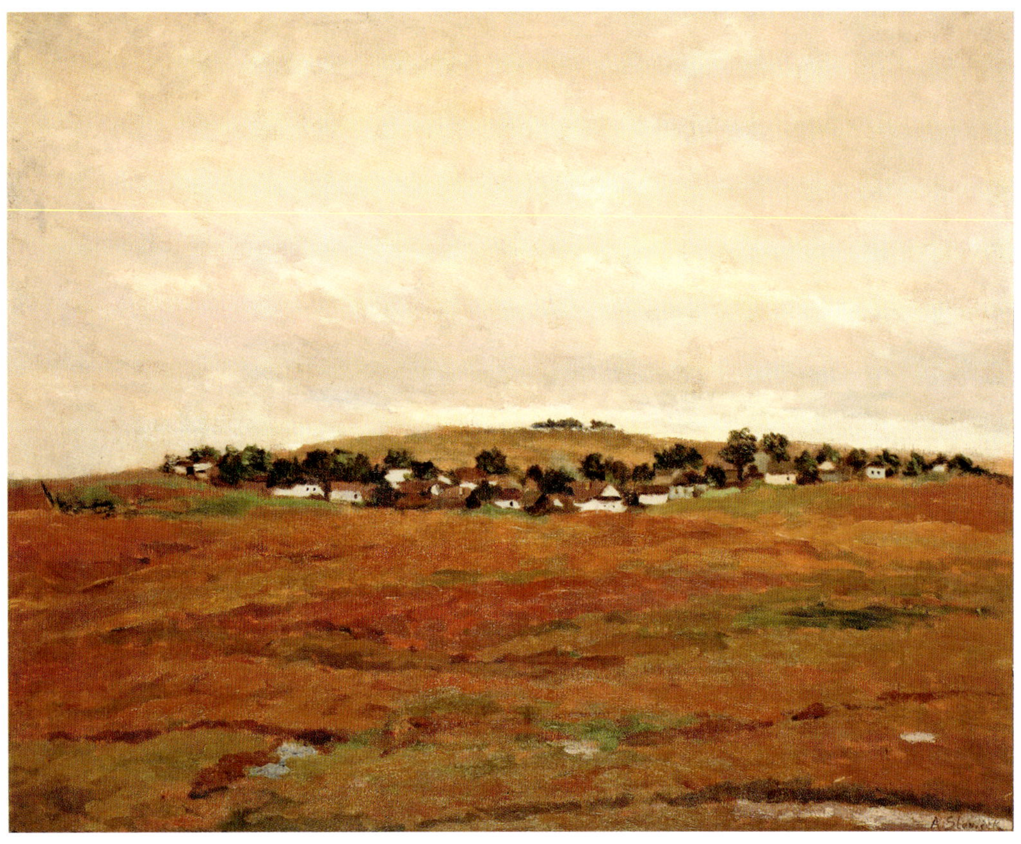

a new expression, a new rhythm." This is why it is only now looking for its style, which is a new higher unity of art and life. Its foundation is "a peculiar mystical sense of reality, a mystical cult of life and the roads to it." The new relation to reality does not set great store by its mere appearance, but rather by its essence and legitimacy. New artworks are therefore the externalisation of this new position on reality and life, which, according to Šalda, is profoundly monistic, convinced of the fundamental unity of all "the forces of life and of the world." For this reason, the new position also rejects exaggerated fantasy, which is at heart dualistic: "We have turned away from fantasy in favour of reality, observation, emotion, intuition, interpretation, in favour of feeling and inferring reality – this explains the genesis of this new aesthetic opinion and sentiment."[120]

Šalda's rejection of fantasy had a significant impact on the contemporary status of Secession art, in which late Romanticism still lived on. It led to the elevating of the empiricist, rationalist position (in his essay, Šalda also admired engineering architecture, offering as an example the great architectural impression produced by a "bare" railway bridge), which was, however, surpassed by emotional experience. Šalda wished to set out a grand scheme for modern art, and in this respect he understood that it was particularly important to indicate its general scope and character. For Šalda, the emotional relationship to reality therefore included not just the act of experiencing it directly, but also the understanding of reality's internal laws, logic, and structure.

177 Antonín Slavíček, *Větrný Jeníkov*, 1904, oil, 111.5 × 135 cm

Emotion was also a means to attain a cosmological capacity. Šalda writes that in the beating of the heart we can see the foundation of all rhythm, and as the essence of things and their beauty is presented to us "in a rhythmic abbreviation," the rhythm of an organism and a thing participate in the common rhythm of the universe. In this, the cosmological keystone of Šalda's aesthetic concept, it is evident that he still owed much to the Secession's fundamental ideas, and he may also have been influenced by contemporary aesthetic "empathy." Šalda's essay was an important symptom of the processes that were already underway in the practice of art, and they prompted a need to express in theory a requirement for some higher artistic synthesis. Šalda was in fact seeking a new basis upon which the question of the Secession could be discussed in the fullness of its breadth and influence.

The revival of this theoretical interest in Impressionism reflected the need to bolster the advances that painters in particular had made by gradually reappraising their naturalistic starting point. Only when this process had reached a certain stage could the lessons of the French Impressionists be fully applied and adapted as appropriate. Some painters had discovered Impressionism relatively early on. In 1893, at the beginning of his studies in Paris, Ludvík Kuba had been inspired by the permanent exhibition of Impressionist painters at Paul Durand-Ruel's gallery on rue Laffitte. However, it was only at Anton Ažbe's multicultural private school in Munich, which Kuba attended between 1896 and 1904, that he acquired the insight needed to organically incorporate the Impressionist vision into his own approach to painting and thereby create his own style. This delay was not due merely to the fact that Kuba's interests had from the start been split between painting and folk music: another reason was that Central European painters had fewer opportunities to develop their art.

This delayed application of Impressionism also meant that art still labelled "Impressionist" was in fact by now quite far removed from the original French Impressionism of the 1870s. The original Impressionism had been analytic – not just in the way a painting was constructed from the spectral colours of refracted sunlight, but also in its relation to its subject. The Impressionist analysis of a natural or man-made object was all-embracing, for it was not confined to the object itself but extended to its entire visual environment. The Impressionists' key innovation was this "simultaneous" way of viewing an object, their ability to instantly and spontaneously grasp life's immediate status while losing nothing of its continuity; it was the depicting of the process of life in a striking "motif," where the analysis of light allowed this motif to be understood as something that was not entirely unique, but was more a constellation of the natural elements' universal matrix of colour and light. The French Impressionists therefore took on the important contemporary issue of civilised man's relationship with nature not only in their themes, but also in their very artistic means. However, painters who had first become acquainted with Impressionism through the work of its Intimist and Romantic followers could not regress a quarter of a century when they belatedly discovered its original form. They understood its technical principles, but they added to Impressionism's analytical objectivism the passionate emotion with which they took hold of visual reality. The overall mental habitus at the turn of the century also played a substantial role in this process, with its fundamental inclination towards dramatic contradictions and their surmounting. This is also why the "Impressionism" of the beginning of the new century had markedly expressive characteristics, and why it was always concerned with the content of painting.

In Czech painting, these aspects first came to the fore in the work of Otakar Lebeda, whose brief but very active career encompassed them entirely. In 1898 Lebeda tried out a modish blue pastel tonality in his paintings from Bechyně, and his scenes from Karlovy Vary brought him to the forefront of the Czech response to Impressionism. The very next year, however, he left landscape painting to one side to concentrate on figure painting. In fact, all he took from Impressionism was its sketch-like quality, which he treated as a way of making a scene unusually vivid. Besides this aspect, a painting of a bullock cart called *On the Way* (1899) also featured a new treatment of paint in thick pastes, following Impressionism's lead. Lebeda's expressiveness unquestionably had its origin in his singular psychological disposition and mental fragility. This can also be read from the aggressive brushstrokes of his forest scenes, and from his final large painting, *Killed by Lightning* (1900–1901), a dramatic depiction of a tragic tale from the Chodsko region. It was these circumstances, underlined by Lebeda's suicide, that resulted in his last painting being considered an unsuccessful diversion, a view shared by his peers. In reality, however, it anticipated the subsequent development of Czech "Impressionism." Lebeda's bold relaxation of form in a figure painting became generally accepted in the wake of the Rodin exhibition, which definitively broke with the persistent norm of descriptive naturalism.

Landscape offered much more fertile ground for Impressionism, for reasons that were both social and psychological. Accordingly, it was landscape painting that produced the most important Czech Impressionist, Antonín Slavíček, whose finest work was based on the counterpoint of autumnal and vernal moods. Slavíček's youthful sensibility was coupled with an athletic disposition that gave his work the semblance of some manly struggle, an aspect that was also due to his strained circumstances, his ambitions and disappointments. In 1901 his hopes of becoming Mařák's successor at the academy in Prague were definitively dashed, and this brought his long Okoř period to an end. Dejected and hoping that a change of scene would restore him, Slavíček went to the village of Hostišov at the invitation of the writer Jan Herben. Here, in 1902, he painted pictures such as *Mountain Village* and *Flowering Meadow (Poppies)* that recapitulated his development thus far in a way that subscribed to the typical Secession concept of landscape painting. In the same year, he showed *Mountain Village* at the Hagenbund's fourth exhibition in Vienna, and its deliberately Secessionist style, recalling Klimt's landscapes, can also perhaps be considered a reflection of Slavíček's distaste for the official arts policy that had deprived him of a much-deserved professorship. Like Klimt, Slavíček used an almost square format and structured his composition in bands based on the golden ratio: between the broad band of the meadow and the narrow band of the sky are cottages with contrasting front and side elevations. However, Slavíček does not stylise the detail itself, and his painting therefore oscillates between the naturalness of the scene and the decorativeness of the composition. This balancing of naturalism and decorative abstraction is one of the principles of Secession style, and around this time we find it not just in painting but in sculpture and architecture too.

The hills around Hostišov brought a number of changes to Slavíček's perspective on landscape, which he was now viewing from a greater distance. Instead of the intimate landscape around Okoř and the water flowing in its brook, here were large open spaces beneath a sky with clouds blown by the wind. Rather than passively accepting the different character of this landscape, Slavíček used it to express his changing ideas. His remarkable *Garden Wall* (c. 1900–1902), where the picture plane consists of nothing but patches of light and colour, shows how he was becoming less and less interested in the traditional "picturesque motif." Here he achieved a new spatial quality in his painting, where the traditional stage setting has disappeared and our gaze, because it is not directed towards the centre, loses its sense of depth and has to take in an unusually broad expanse. This is accomplished by means of the diagonal and gently curving garden wall, and by the diffusion of the light, which in the shaded parts of the painting has the greatest accents along the edges. This gives the scene an unusual vividness, and the painting seems to invite the viewer to step into this landscape and become part of it. However, this is achieved not merely by the luministic effect, but also by the energetic brushstrokes, which offer some manner of emotional identification with reality, and they dynamically guide the viewer's gaze into the living organism of the painting.

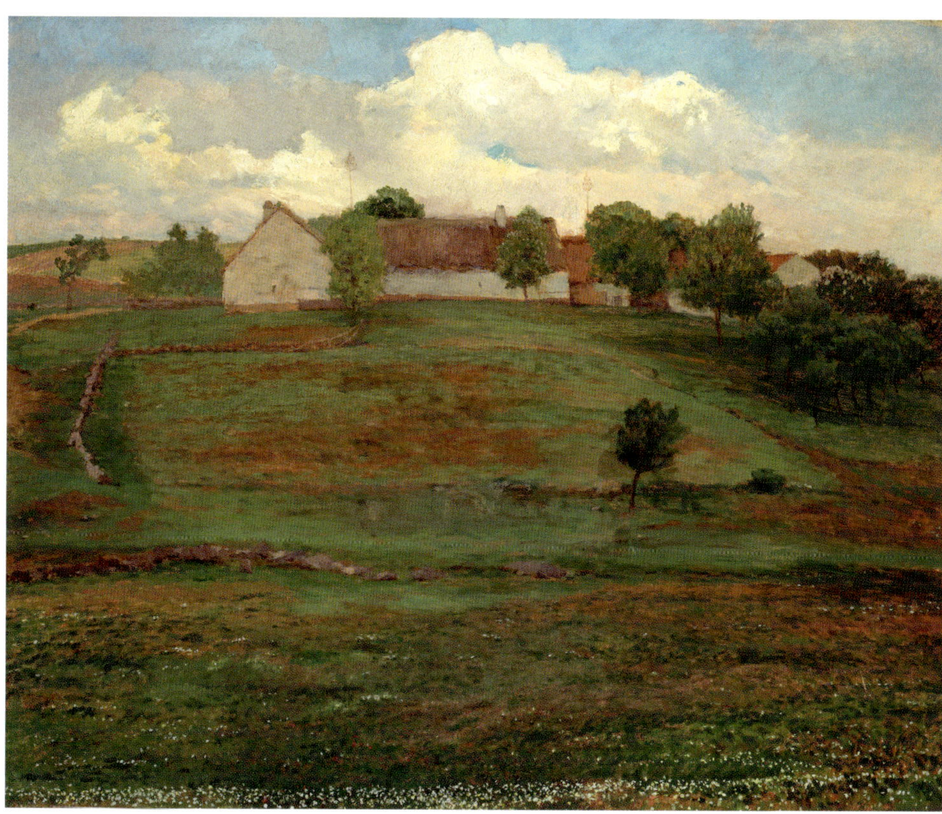

178 Antonín Slavíček, *Mountain Village*, 1902, oil, 114 × 135 cm

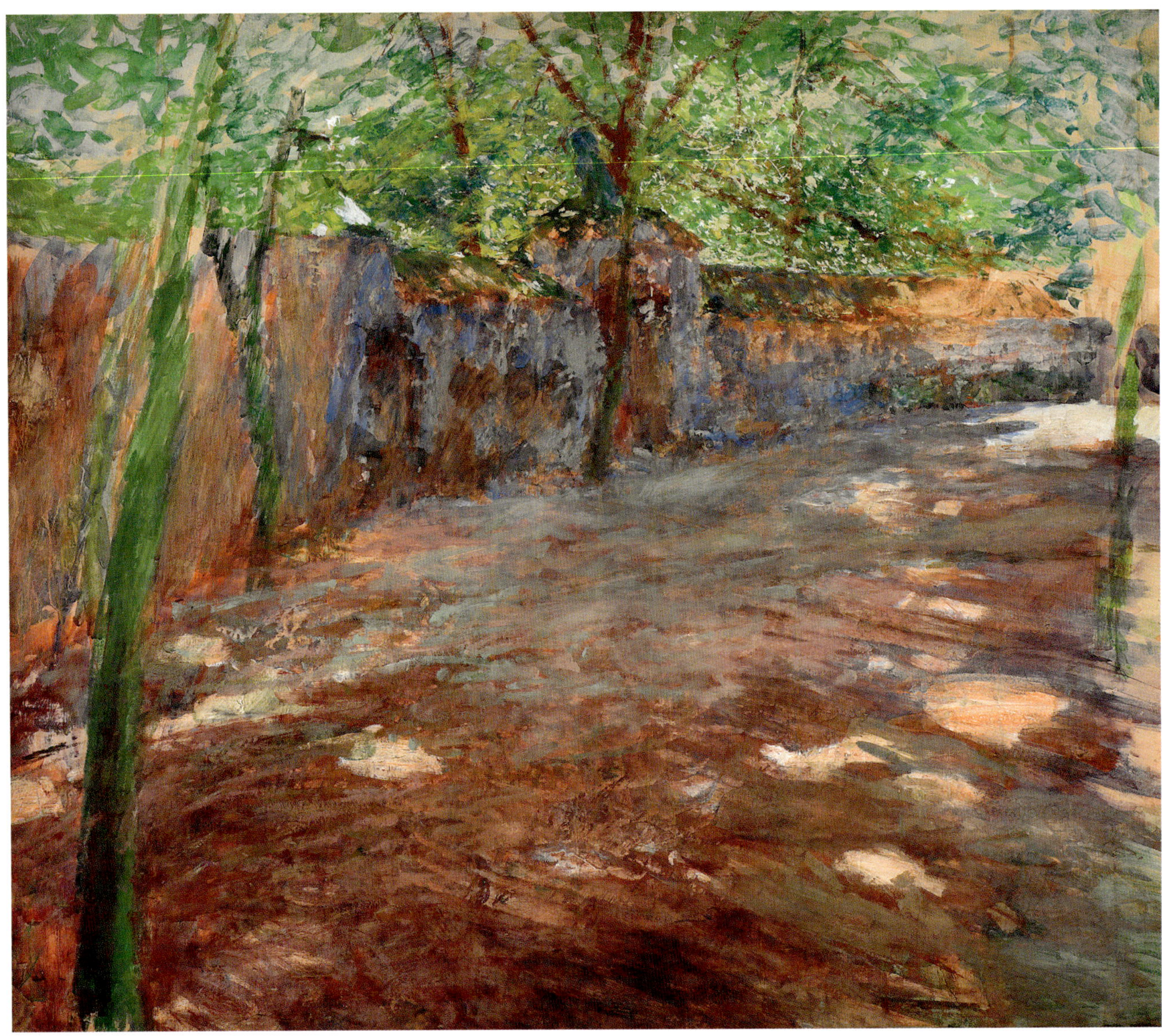

Paintings of this kind were some of the most progressive works in contemporary Czech art, and it is little wonder that Šalda, in his manifesto "The New Beauty: Its Genesis and Character," considered landscape painting to exemplify the new thinking:

> To understand this fundamental change in our tastes and our aesthetic sensibility, and the way the new art has organised and cultivated this change, simply take note of what our forefathers enjoyed in nature's theatres and images, and what we ourselves enjoy today. It was always something small, secluded and forgotten, places that were hidden away, where little of the world's breezes and breath could reach, something removed from the endless rhythm of the universe … today our sensibility loves in nature precisely those places that – if I may be permitted the

179 Antonín Slavíček, *Garden Wall*, c. 1902, tempera, 88.5 × 100 cm

> metaphor – relate most of all to infinity … In painting, this new concept of beauty led to the requirement, first formulated by Impressionism, that a picture, although perhaps limited to a small part of the Earth, should not present it as something sealed and shut off, materially and plastically complete, but rather as flooded with the immensity of the air and the atmosphere, incandescent with luminous cosmic lyricism, shimmering with the vibration of infinity and open to all the affinities of the universe – for solid form to be merely the starting point, the bearer of infinity, not dull, lifeless, stuffed matter but a pretext for capturing the life of the whole atmosphere, a foundation for the subtlest and most fleeting cosmic life.[121]

Šalda's words were echoed in the paintings that Slavíček produced during the summers he spent in Kameničky in the Bohemian-Moravian Highlands in the years 1903–6. He was in no way disconcerted by the sparseness of the landscape there, but instead used the details of the few trees and cottages as natural symbols in the broad panorama of earth and sky, reminders of the presence of the individual human fate amidst the natural elements and their ever-changing conflicts and harmonies. Slavíček's most affecting paintings from Kameničky are those dominated by the long line of the horizon, expressing in its simple melodiousness the endlessness of the relationship between earth and sky. The fragmented "Impressionist" style was unsuited to expressing this expansiveness. Rather than using sunlight to unify a painting, Slavíček looked for its equivalent in local colour. This produced the modality of the original Impressionist division of colour tones, losing nothing of its compositional potential, but with its larger areas and its certain earthiness, local colour was better suited to capturing emotional content. In this way, the original Impressionism was comprehensively surpassed.

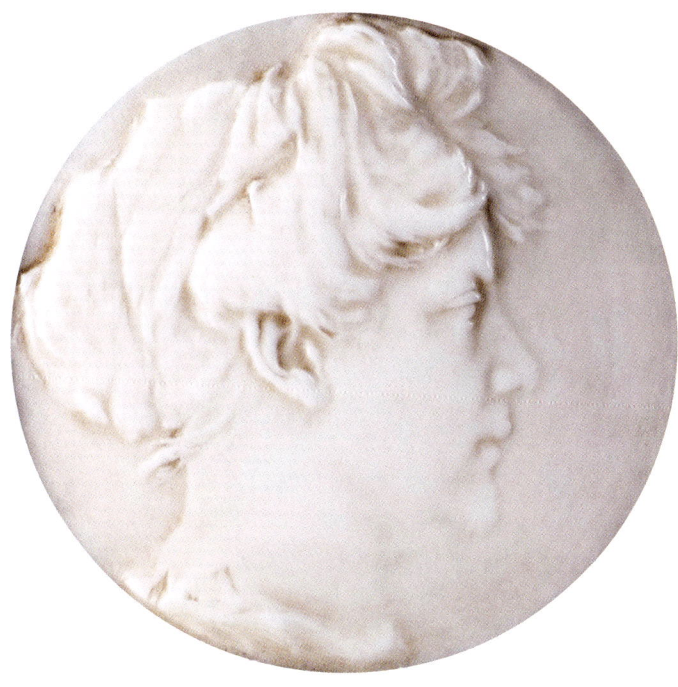

180 Stanislav Sucharda, *Portrait of Mrs. Grohová*, 1905, marble, 8 cm

In the letters that Slavíček wrote from Kameničky, he often emphasised the need for the simplest "straightforward expression" of the powerful impressions produced by the local landscape. The painter should not be a mere tourist who captures the beauties of nature in his sketchbook:

> he must bite into it, digest it, and it must find its way into every corpuscle of his blood; he must be entirely at home there. It is never what there is, but how and what one sees in it. A little thing suddenly becomes large and powerful – it is not the road or the village or the forest – it is just a piece of what is inside, and that is enough. It is a piece of the great sky arching over our brief little lives, over the huts with their smoking chimneys, and the woods around the pastures – a piece of people's lives …[122]

With his call for emotional engagement with a landscape, and seeking common ground between the natural world and human life, Slavíček consummated the naturalistic theme that had emerged in the 1890s, setting the agenda for painting's development with its motif of the figure in landscape. Landscape painting of the kind Slavíček was creating was his solution to this theme; a landscape painting became its painter's emotional testimony, and it shed any last remnants of allegory. The paradox of Hynais's *The Judgement of Paris*, which had so appealed to young painters in the late 1890s, had been resolved: art was no longer a figural allegory, but was identified with the painter's execution, with his treatment and rendering of a real subject. In these developments lay the significance of "Impressionism," for it satisfied the increasing need for the inner unity of art.

Besides Slavíček's emotional imperative, there were other examples of Czech Impressionism based more on realism. These included Miloš Jiránek's paintings, which were principally devoted to a new concept of figure painting. In 1903 Jiránek painted a relatively large canvas called *Showers at a Prague Sokol*, which made unconventional use of an academic nude in a genre scene. It was an important step away from Hynais and towards the present day. At this time, Jiránek became more familiar with the Moravian Slovakia region, as he would become later with Slovakia. With their spirited folk culture, these areas had a similarly magical effect on him as did the doleful Bohemian-Moravian Highlands on Slavíček. Jiránek divided his time between painting and writing, and for this he was criticised, with his detractors claiming that his achievements in both fields fell short, resulting in only sketches and marginal works but no true masterpiece in either medium. In fact, both his paintings and *Impressions and Wanderings*, a collection of short prose pieces that was not published until 1908, reveal Jiránek to be a firm advocate of the Impressionist concept of art, which did away with the idea of the classic chef-d'oeuvre and was instead concerned, in the spirit of Šalda's aesthetics, with recording and observing the universal pulse of the energy of life in the simplest things and situations. Jiránek was equally interested in painting vegetables and floral still lifes, sand miners and cherry pickers, city streets and village squares, all with an eagerness to couple art with life. He was not interested in describing a thing, but in actively taking control of it and emphasising its aesthetic utility. If he was inspired by a folk ballad, he would also reach for more dramatic tones (as in his unfinished cycle about the fabled

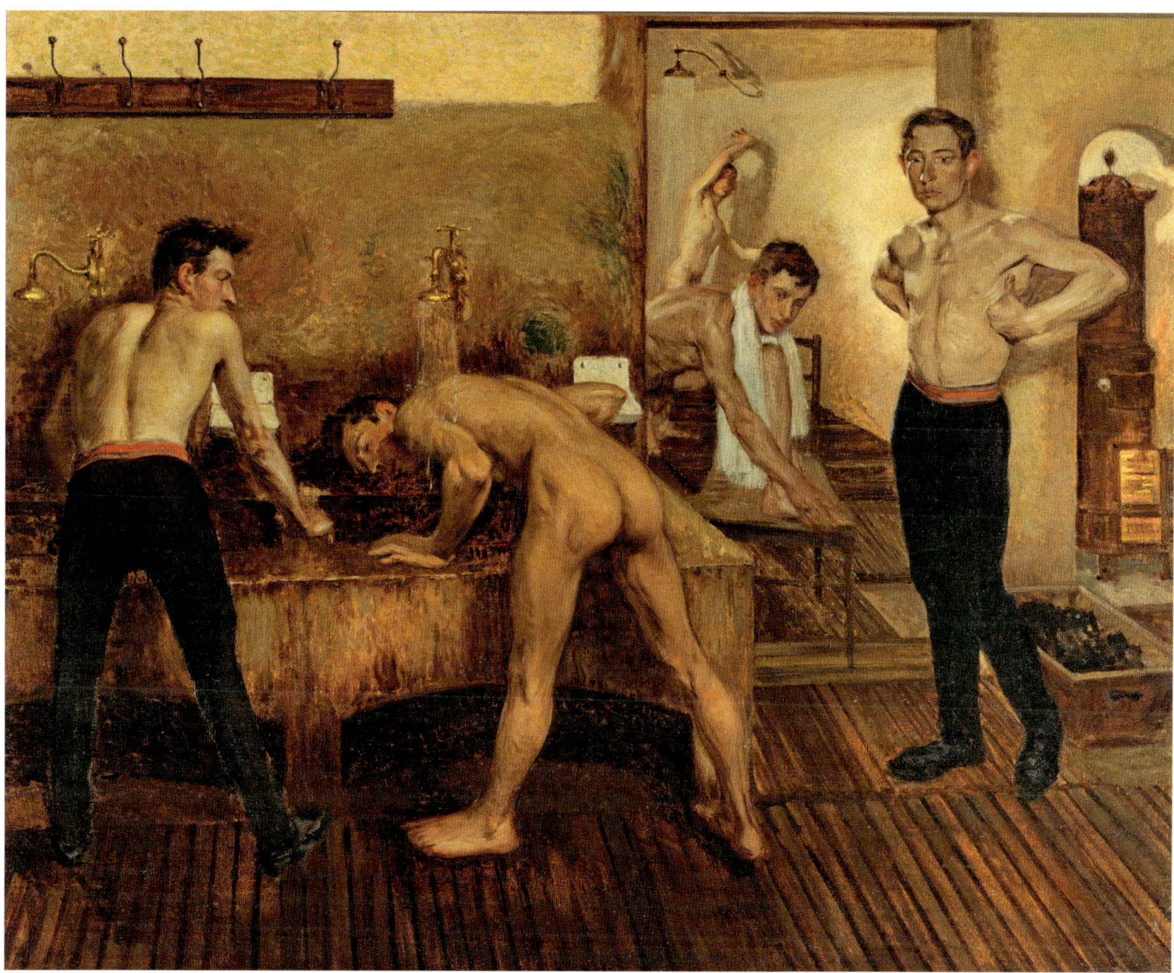

Slovak highwayman Juraj Jánošík), but here too the theme was expressed through real forms. He was fundamentally opposed to schematic decorativism, and he saw Neo-Impressionist speculation as the death of art. He considered artificial fantasy the other mortal sin in modern art, although he did like Schwaiger. What aroused his ire above all was any kind of repetition in art, and he considered dishonest any attempt to make work easier, maintaining that art should always be taken afresh from the artist's original impressions, from an intense sensory and emotional connection with reality.

Jiránek's ideas were influential among Czech artists, especially in the middle of the first decade of the 20th century, when he quite deliberately promoted an Impressionist programme in his writings for *Volné směry*, including a number of pieces on the founders of French modern art. This also contributed to Impressionism becoming, for a time, the main current in Czech art. Its strength was that it fully freed artists from all traditional and contemporary theoretical burdens: all that was required of them was originality, measured against the yardstick of natural and visual reality. Jiránek understood creative work as the constant encounter between the artist's individuality and

181 Miloš Jiránek, *Showers at a Prague Sokol*, 1903, oil, 140 × 169 cm

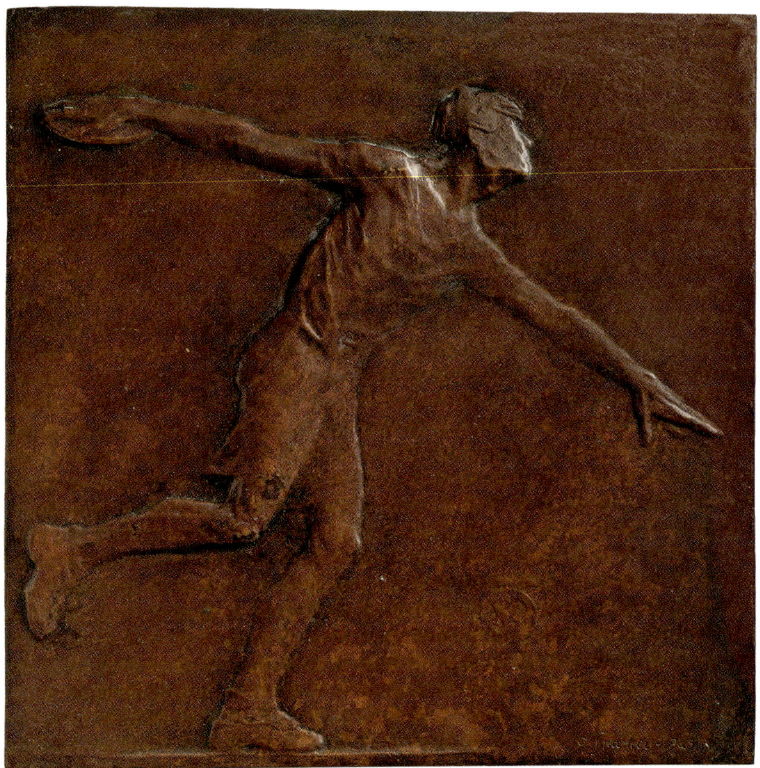

life, whose essence was understood in the sense of Bergson's élan vital. An artwork was the fruit of this encounter, a response to a stimulus that came from life's immense reservoir. An artist should be a sensitive recorder of events that excite the senses and produce an emotional response, and the artist's professionalism consists in the ability to express in art those events that conceal beneath their seeming banality an unusually powerful metaphysical feeling, to extract them from the constant flow of percepts and impressions, as a symbol articulated in form.[123]

After a period of Symbolist and ornamental stylistic experimentation, which often made excessive "philosophical" demands or was open to accusations of plagiarism, Impressionism had a calming effect. It shifted questions to a primary and specifically artistic concern with the depicting of reality, with a concept that gave deeper meaning to normal artistic work. It respected the importance of the artist, whom it placed not in opposition to reality but in harmony with a reality that was understood pantheistically. This made Impressionism more socially adaptable than fantastical Symbolism or ornamentalism, whose exclusivity invited parody.

Impressionism's interest in realism led to a flourishing of the portrait, as a likeness of an individual could now combine the unique with the universal. This concerned not just painting but also sculpture, which found in the plaquette a means of accessing a broader range of clients while employing certain elements from painting. The work of most Czech plaquette makers was Impressionist, ranging from Stanislav Sucharda's delicate relief portraits to plaquettes by Stino Paukert and Josef Šejnost, as well as

182 Otakar Španiel, *Discobolus*, 1907, bronze, 28 × 27.5 cm

Otakar Španiel's first portraits, in which his schooling in France was evident. Španiel also made Impressionist plaquettes with sporting and more intimate themes (*Discobolus*, 1907), while Jaroslav Krepčík worked with animal motifs (*Pelicans*, 1901).

As the principal Impressionist discipline, painting's influence on sculpture was guaranteed not only by Impressionist ideology but also because Rodin was still considered an example of Impressionism, even though this did not entirely correspond to his true profile as an artist.[124] Rodin's themes were entirely Symbolist, and his treatment of light and shadow was not at heart Impressionist. However, the context in which his work was placed in the development of Czech art qualified him as a sensualist, and for this reason he was also labelled an Impressionist.

The cult of the sketch, which Mádl complained about in his review of Mařatka's sculptures at an exhibition SVU Mánes held at the end of 1904, soon took over young Czech sculpture as the hallmark of the "Impressionist" influence. Modelling, which Rodin's example had released from its ties to monumental art, allowed clay to be used to produce all manner of effects. The rapid spread of "Impressionism" here was unquestionably due to the fact that the technical preconditions were already in place, and it remained only to make full use of them. However, Impressionism's limitations also first became apparent in sculpture, as its greater amorphousness seriously jeopardised a sculpture's structural foundation. Such was the experience of Jan Štursa, who, after graduating from the academy, tried out Impressionist modelling for the theme of *Puberty* (1905), although his wax relief *Drowned Cat* (1904) also revealed the perils of formlessness. The effect of light on sculpture had yet to undergo the kind of internal evaluation we see in the case of Antonín Slavíček, but it still yielded a number of striking, mostly smaller, works (Bohumil Kafka, *Moulting Camel*, 1905).

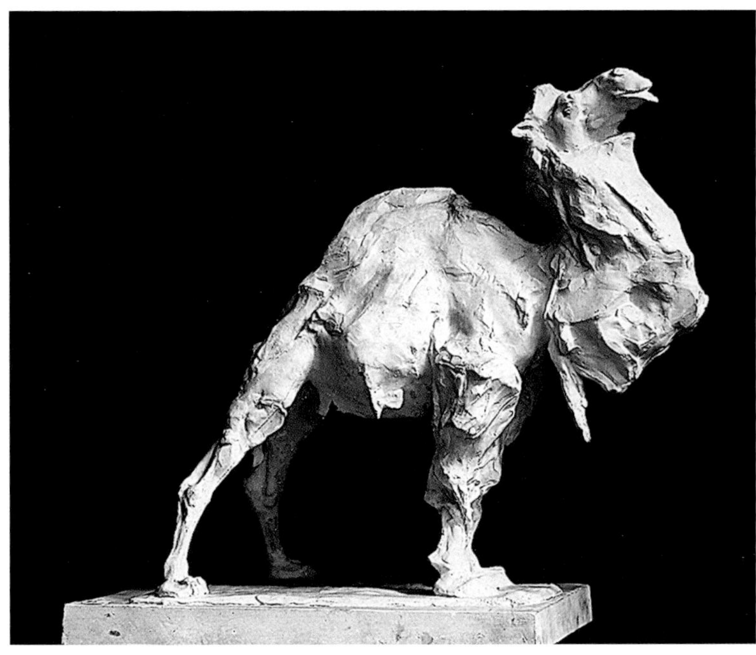

183 Bohumil Kafka, *Moulting Camel*, 1905, plaster, 42 cm

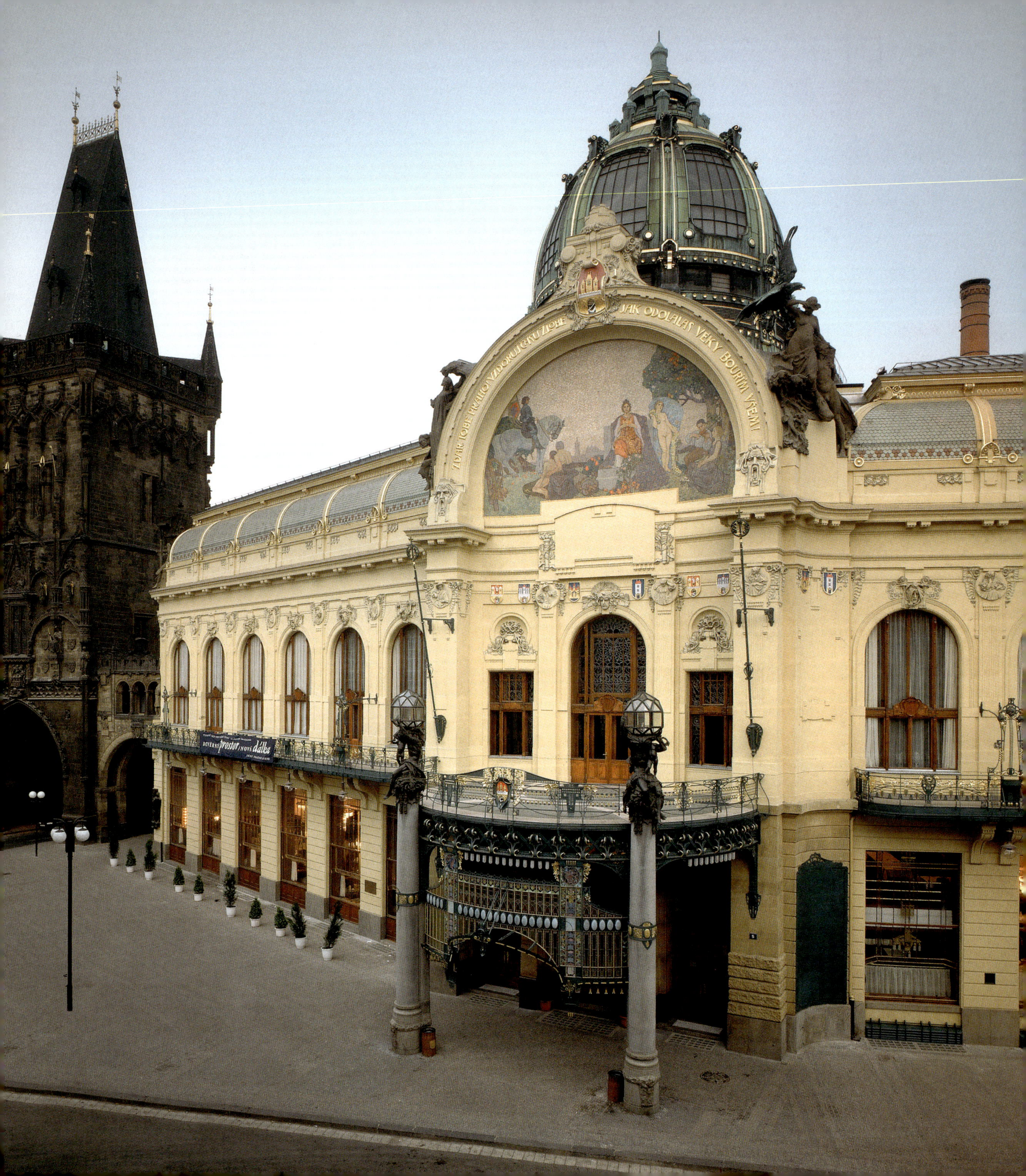
ZDAR TOBĚ PRAHO VZDORUJ ČASU I ZLOBĚ JAK ODOLALAS VĚKY BOUŘÍM VŠEM!

EPOCH

At the beginning of 1904, SVU Mánes held a retrospective exhibition of the work of Joža Uprka. It was a victorious fanfare for "incandescently colourful" Impressionism, which now enraptured even K. B. Mádl:

> You enter, and from all sides and all walls in all the rooms something akin to a wavering, victorious bugle call rings out; from everywhere you are assailed by brilliant jets of colour in which white and fiery red flash like exuberant children choking with laughter … wherever you turn there is the broad, unrestrained, joyous breath of the earth, the aroma of the soil, the harmony of people in their land, the beautiful land of Moravian Slovakia. Wholesome people and wholesome art.[125]

The reason for this enthusiastic reception was that Uprka's paintings seemed to be an entirely modern response to the need for a new conjoining of art with life – one, moreover, that did not break continuity with the older foundations of the national art:

> Joža Uprka is some kind of embodiment of the ideal of the modern painter, the modern artist. Firstly, he lives, observes and works amidst the world whose picturesque content he lays down in artistic form in his paintings. Secondly, he does not permit anyone, any model or any reminiscence to stand between him and his world. If you are looking for art that is direct, here it is: art that bears all the hallmarks of spontaneous improvisation, played out in the piercing impressions experienced in this instant. Thirdly, it is as if his entire execution, all the aspects of his expression, have arisen from the subject, the material, its character and complexion. It suddenly seems that any way of guiding the brush, applying the paint, extending the lines other than Uprka's would be unbefitting for the people of Moravian Slovakia – insipid, or at odds with their rough cheer. And fourthly, the notion of art that Uprka, with what is almost a bold defiance, has erected against all convention, his highly cultivated sensitivity to all the real world's optical impression and effect, the vigorous combinations of forms, colours, light and air and their forceful and admirable capturing and expression, is a supremely logical link in the evolution of all 19th-century art.[126]

Uprka's paintings possessed an essential optimism that accommodated ideological aspirations while appealing to sensitive viewers with their aggressive use of colour. Yet this was only one way of working with the original naturalistic corrective to academic practice. If academic instruction taught painters to make their paintings – prepared and composed according to posing models – ultimately seem illusorily "natural," the naturalistic Impressionist revolution led to a requirement for "immediate" art that dispensed with the model in favour of direct painting. There was, however, another approach that retained the model while emphasising its stiffness, and then extracting

184 Antonín Balšánek and Osvald Polívka, Municipal House in Prague, 1905–11, façade

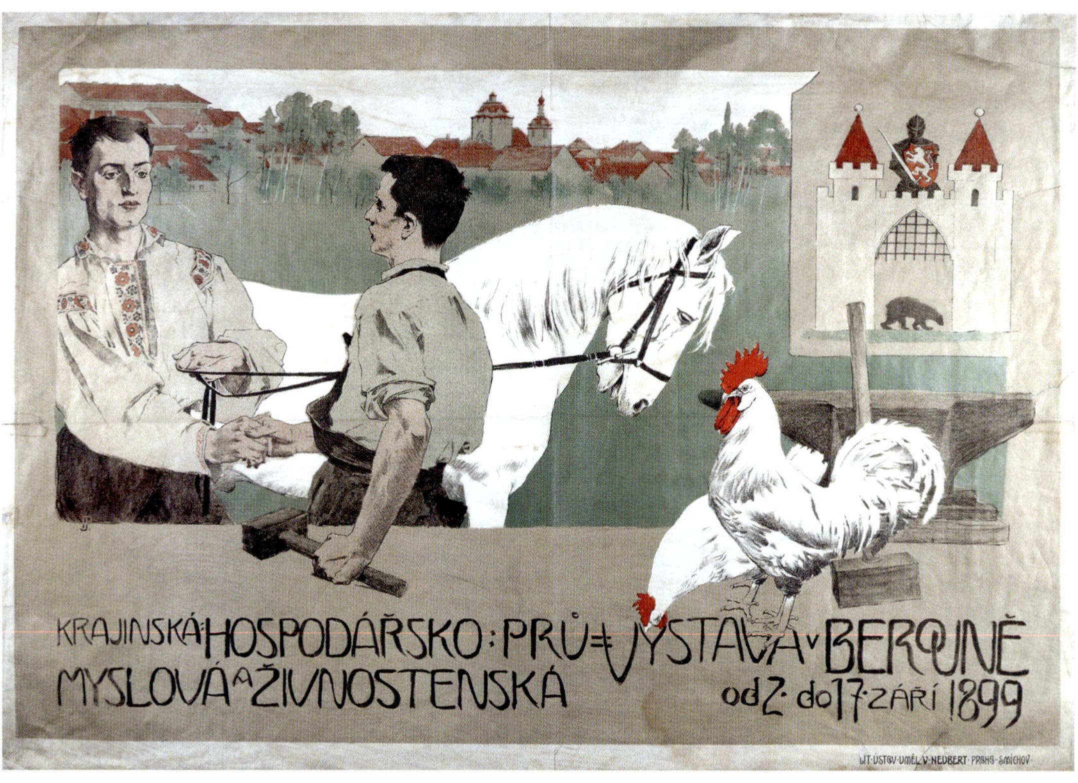

from this stiffness a new decorative monumentality. One such example was Preisler's poster for the Provincial Economic, Industrial and Trade Exhibition in Beroun in 1899. Impressionism and decorativism both rejected the academic falsehood that sought to present what had often been laboriously devised as something entirely natural. Against this academic sleight of hand, which served to illustrate the ideological contents of late bourgeois false consciousness, they held up "bare" art. Late Impressionism led to the cult of connecting the artist with life by means of direct visual and emotional experience, while decorativism represented the more intellectual side of the new art. It recognised that other factors, besides instinctive intuitiveness, were at play in art, and it sought to highlight their expressive potential.

There was therefore a certain polarity within the new art, one that was not purely concerned with art itself but touched more fundamentally on the new art's content and socially formative aspects. At the turn of the century, this differentiation was not yet clearly defined in artists' consciousness. One consequence of the spontaneous ascent of "modernity" was that the first five years of the new century were entirely under its sway, and this applied in all fields of art. Its dominance then created the conditions for artists to crystallise their ideas on further extending what they had already achieved, resulting in a colourful palette of individual approaches that created a rich relief for the movement within the common framework of the Secession epoch.

185 Jan Preisler, Poster for the Provincial Economic, Industrial and Trade Exhibition in Beroun, 1899, colour lithograph, 95 × 130 cm

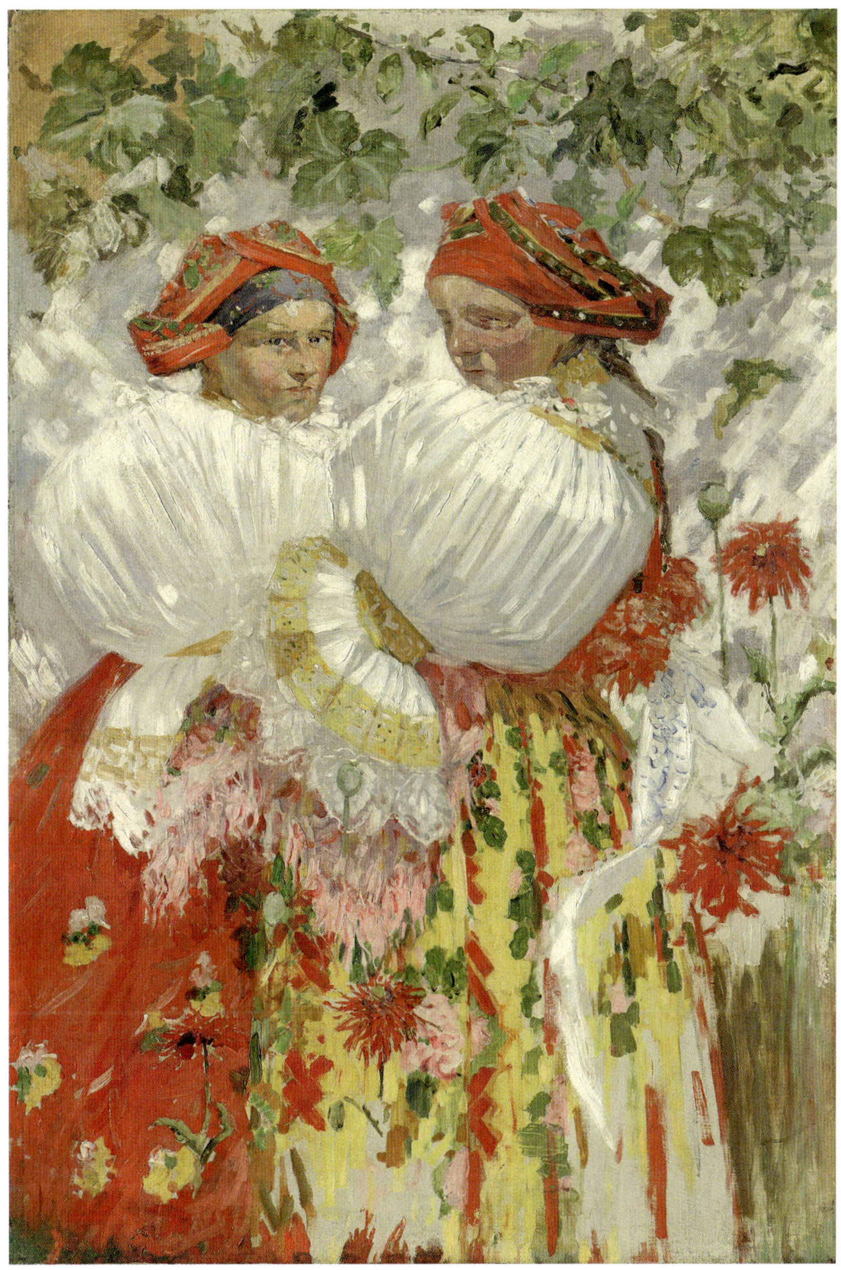

This was also apparent even when the initial collective starting point was reasonably uniform, as in Mařák's landscape school. At the beginning of the new century, František Kaván was living in Železnice in East Bohemia, where he painted a number of masterful winter landscapes (*Showers from Tábor*, 1903) in a distinctive and happy synthesis of realistic foundation and poetic sentiment. In contrast with Kaván's sensitivity, Antonín Slavíček's paintings from his Kameničky period were dramatic and vital. Here he was attempting to create a monumental modern image of the landscape, resulting in a

186 Joža Uprka, *Girls in Flowers*, after 1900, oil, 150 × 100 cm

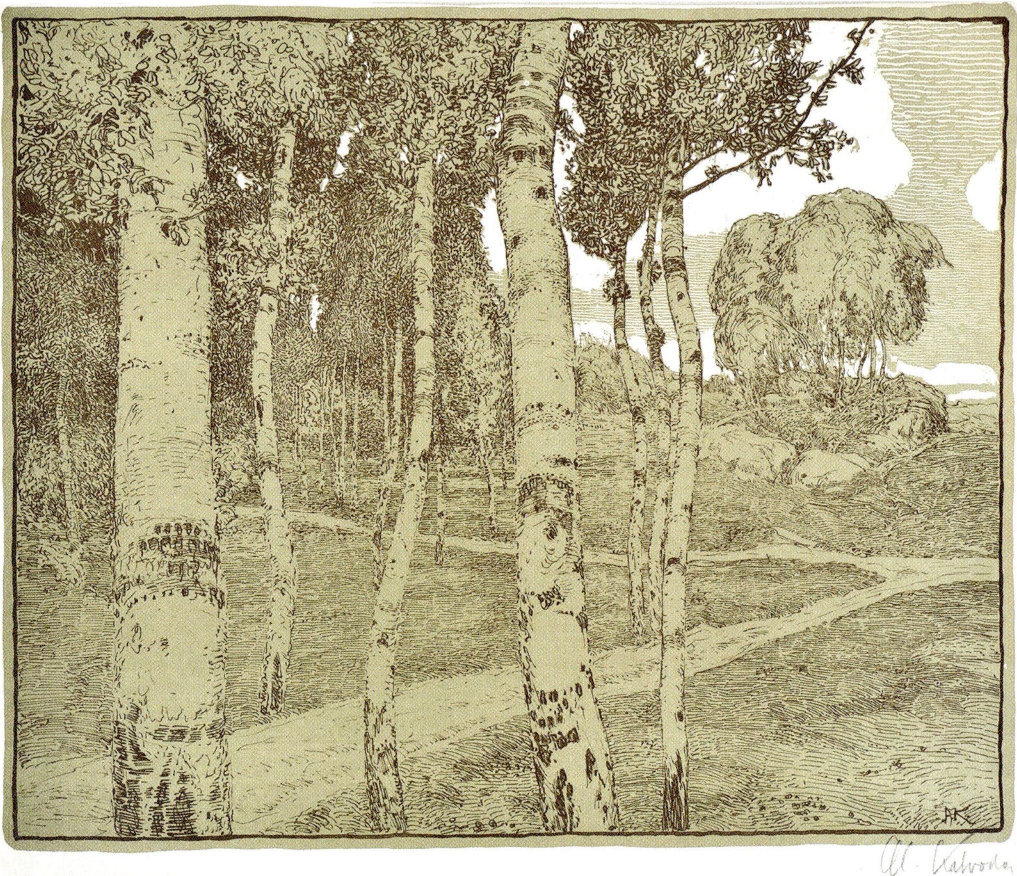

series of large-format paintings based on the motif of *Road in Kameničky* and culminating in the symphonic *In Kameničky* (both 1904), in which Slavíček wished to express all the pathos of the new landscape painting. If in these, the most composed of Slavíček's landscapes, there was a desire for direct expression, then with other landscape artists more decorative tendencies came to the fore – whether in Antonín Hudeček's complicated compositions, Stanislav Lolek's lyrically simpler motifs, or Alois Kalvoda's impressive mood landscapes with birch trees. As in figure painting, here too there were many shades of nuance between the new sensory and emotional spontaneity and decorative stylisation.

In contemporary thinking, landscape painting was perhaps the greatest reservoir of aesthetic experience. As F. X. Šalda wrote to František Kaván,

> I love landscapes enormously; for me they are something eternal, pure, strong, in which the soul can immerse itself and lay itself down as if under the spell of the elements, and eternally. And above yours spread so many presentiments and so much silence and so many immersions.[127]

A landscape painting was not just an opportunity for the individual viewer to "bathe the eyes and heart," but a means of establishing collective ideas. In Kameničky, Slavíček

187 Alois Kalvoda, *Birch Wood*, after 1900, colour lithograph, 32.5 × 39 cm

was attempting to found a painters' colony, perhaps following the example of the Worpswede colony in Germany, which had an impressive exhibition at Mánes in the autumn of 1903. He was joined in Kameničky by Bohuslav Dvořák, who had studied in Mařák's studio, and a young painter called Otakar Nejedlý. For Slavíček, this was not just a matter of compensation for not having been appointed Mařák's successor: he was convinced that the only way for a modern artist to find a truly supportive environment for his work lay in a radical break with the artist's customarily precarious and uncertain standing, in favour of a simple, poor, but "authentic" life in the countryside. Slavíček's correspondence from this time indicates that neither did he consider SVU Mánes an ideal of the new artistic community – for even in Mánes there was too much "aristocracy," too much aesthetic disdain and elitism. In the countryside, however, there was freedom and simplicity, and Slavíček hoped he would "one day become one with it and be in it always."[128]

Slavíček's ideas from his Kameničky period were unquestionably influenced by his high esteem for Uprka, who in the 1890s had refused to make a career in one of the

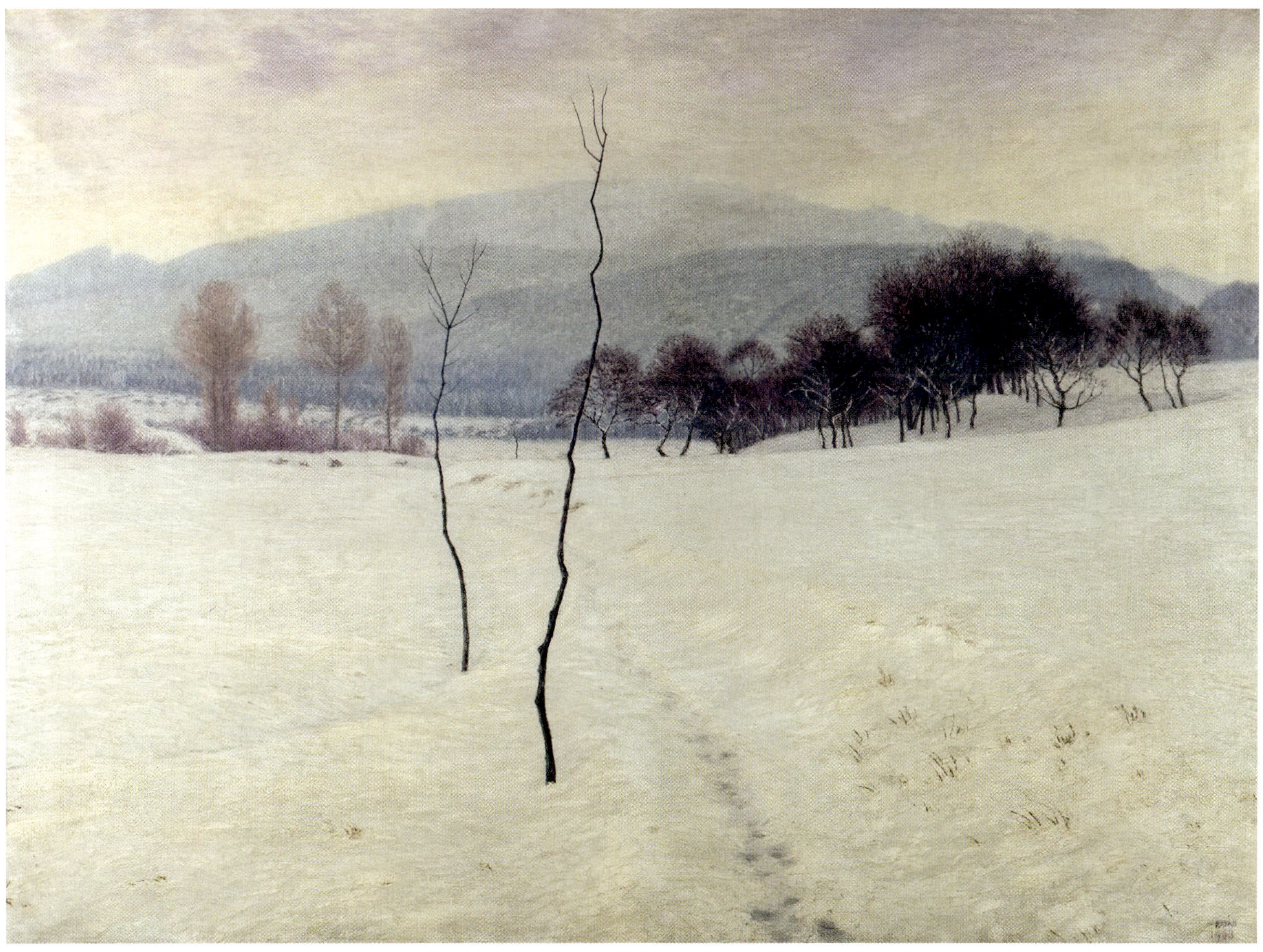

188 František Kaván, *Showers from Tábor*, 1903, oil, 76 × 100 cm

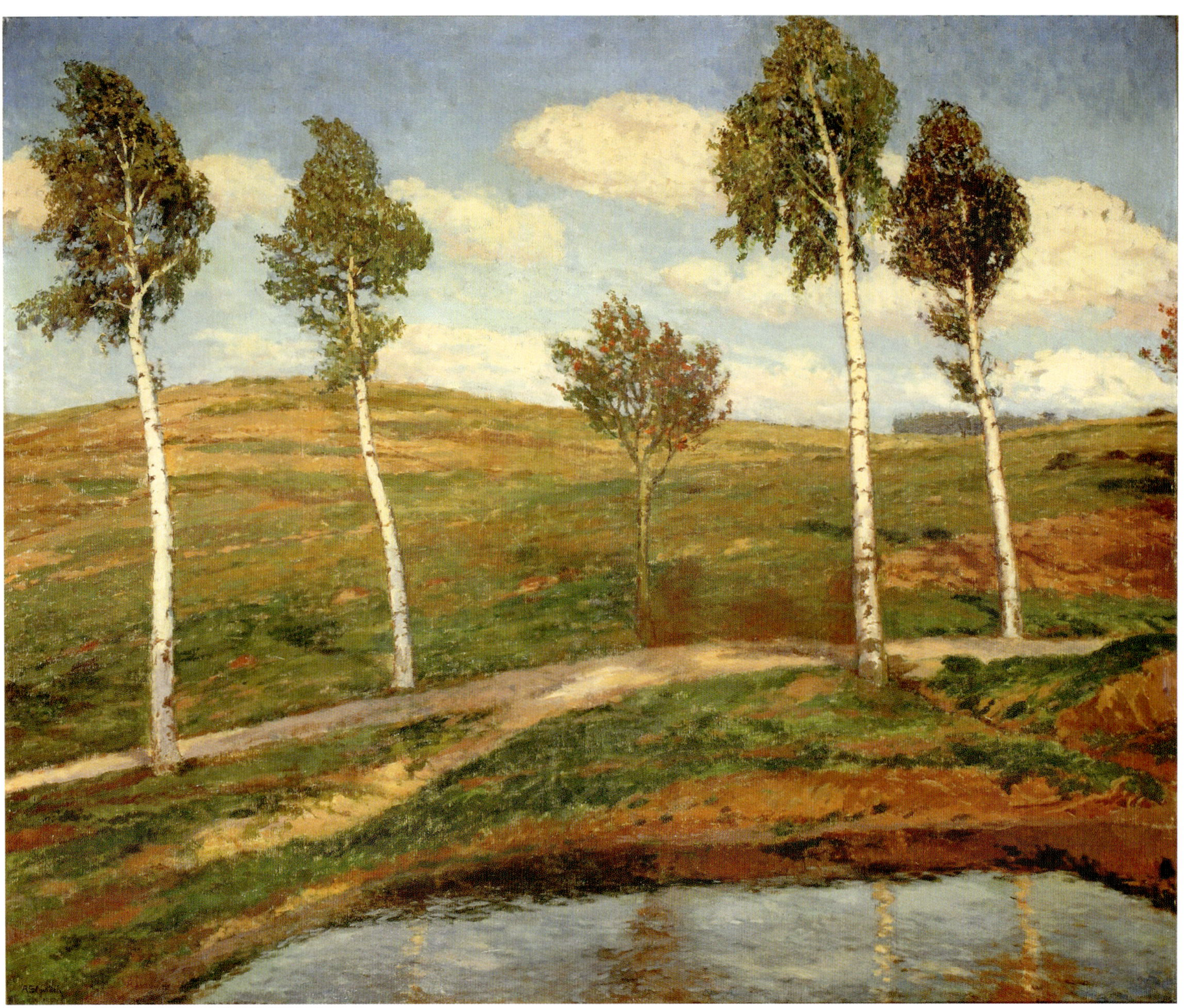

189 Antonín Slavíček, *Road in Kameničky*, 1904, oil, 116 × 136 cm

centres of art and had defiantly triumphed with his regionalism. They were also related to familiar episodes in the history of modern art – to Gauguin's Pont-Aven and Van Gogh's "studio of the south." At the heart of such endeavours was the romantic notion of seeking paradise lost, together with a real need to organise the core of the new art and, above all, find fertile ground to connect it with the world. Nature, as the antithesis of degenerate civilisation, offered new support for these ideas, but it soon became apparent that not even nature could be solely a place of sanctuary. Slavíček was also witness to the harshness of life in Kameničky. After his large paintings, he painted a sketch for *Funeral in Kameničky*, about which he wrote,

> Today in this drab mood there was a poor mountain funeral – a few old women, in red skirts and with their heads covered, accompanied the deceased, who was pulled by a horse. The birches along the road and the grey clusters of clouds – this formed the decoration for this simple scene. – It's nothing, – but it was strange. I cannot even write how it affected me. – In these dog days one perhaps feels more for these poor mountain folk – and perhaps understands all their woes. – But there's nothing sentimental in this. Just that nature in all its adversity perhaps calls forth different impressions, – not cheerful, of course, but powerful.[129]

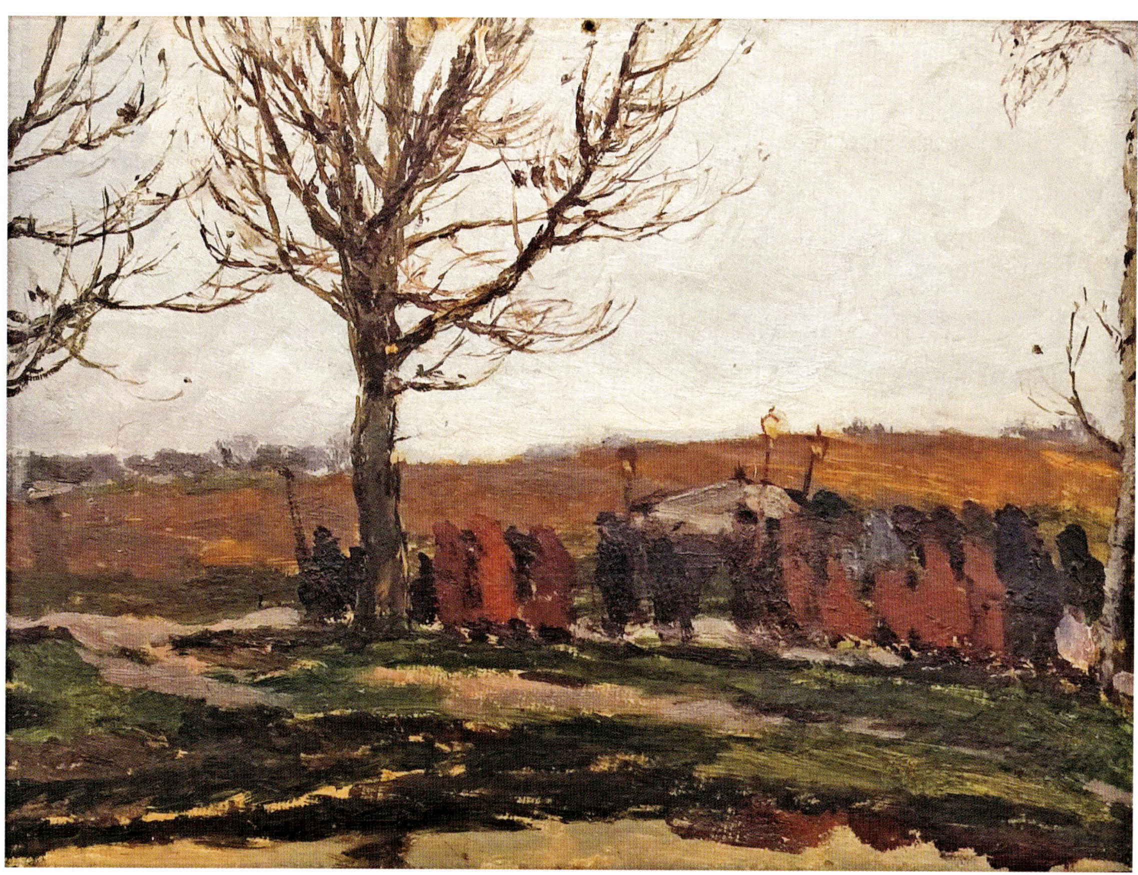

190 Antonín Slavíček, *Funeral in Kameničky*, 1905, oil, 26.5 × 35.5 cm

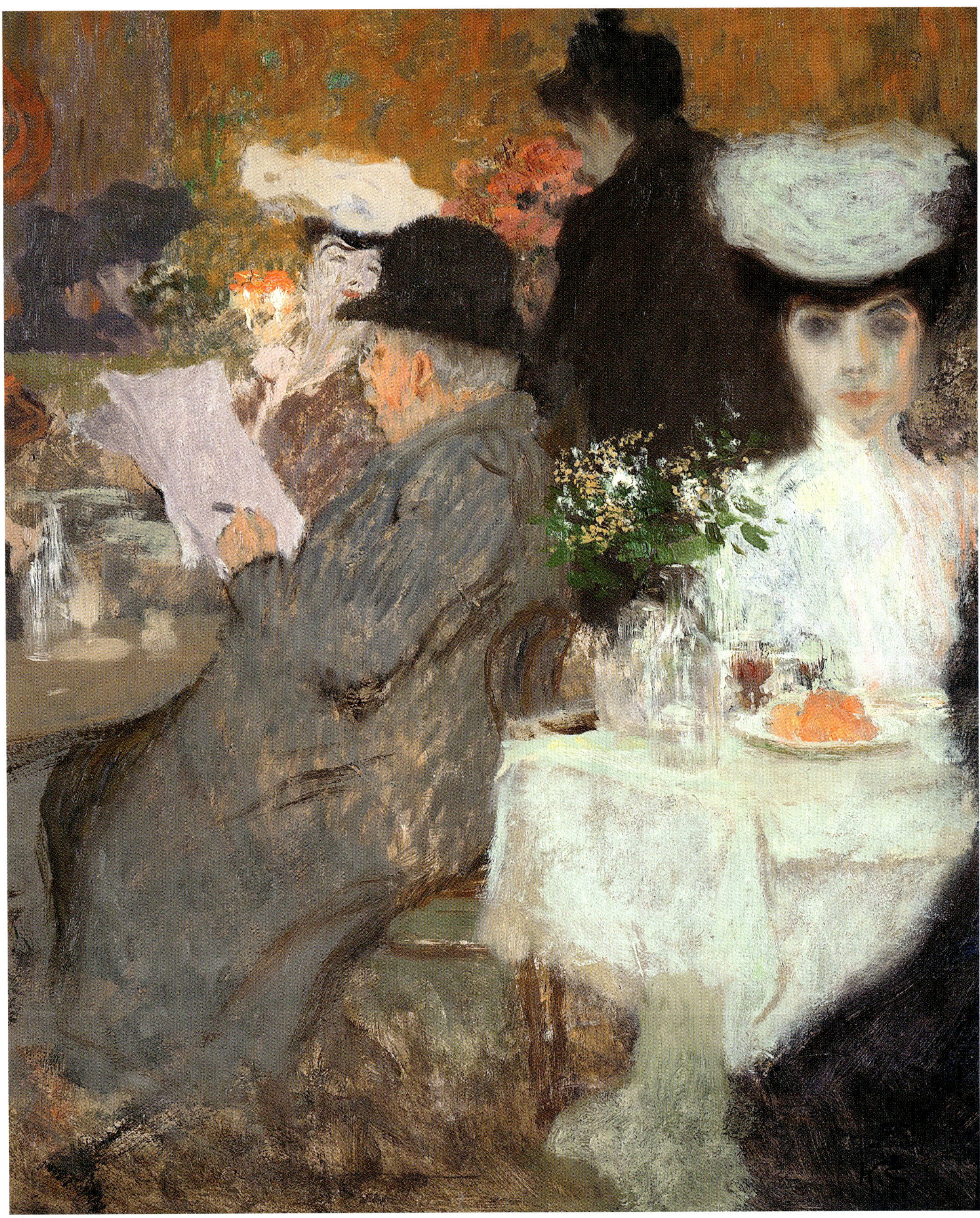

191 Karel Špillar, *In a Café*, 1904, oil, 58 × 47.5 cm

Slavíček was doggedly seeking some overall orientation that would encompass both the social concerns initially prompted by his reading of Karel Václav Rais's novel *Sunset*, and his entirely subjective sensitivity to visual changes in nature's theatre and their reflection. The artist attempts to see reality in its entirety, and to express his experience in art:

> one observes and forgets about everything – seeing neither forms nor lines – only some kind of phantom colours – they bend down closer – they cluster together; at this moment a tree has neither branches nor leaves, only patches of fire – in some kind of – previously unfamiliar ornaments.[130]

Although Slavíček's latter pronouncement is from 1908, the final word demonstrates how influential the fundamental Secession associations were. Slavíček still understood ornament as a painting's overall characteristic and foundation – only this was previously unfamiliar ornament, or, more precisely, ornament that had yet to be read by the artist but which existed in its own right in the book of nature. This idea of ornament was indeed an authentically Secession one, for it did not treat ornament as a "style" to be discovered and imitated, but as a means by which art could grasp the higher totality of the world. The essence of such ornament is objective, but in his paintings the artist treats it as something that presents the mystery of the world, with a profundity extending far beyond the subject who perceives it. Artists knew of this motivation behind Secession ornament. What appeared before the general public, of course, was largely its record in form, for the public was interested in a legible style.

In Secession art, then, this natural transcendentalism was expressed at various levels with the aid of natural forms that were stylised into decorative ornamental systems. The fundamental idea was largely the same, but it was articulated in different ways that resulted in numerous individual approaches within the same organic concept. This was most striking in architectural ornamentation, which soon adopted the original floral concept as a decorative feature. Secession villas had played an important role in promoting the new taste, and their ornamentation was now applied to large new buildings in town and city centres. By chance, hotels and restaurants were especially quick to adopt Secession ornament, perhaps due to their function as places for dining and socialising. These new buildings were still very decorative, but now a coherence was sought between a building's ornamentation and its body. Examples of this stage can be found in two buildings in Prague from 1902. Karel Vítězslav Mašek's villa had a traditional wooden roof, which was used to emphasise the engraved and sculpted decoration (with sculptures by Ludvík Wurzel and Antonín Waigant), while the Hotel Central was designed by Friedrich Ohmann's pupils Alois Dryák and Bedřich Bendelmayer, who took Ohmann's sketch for the façade and gave its forms a markedly Secession look. They maximised the use of floral motifs in their very original design for the lift, which was one of the first examples in Prague of a peculiar symbiosis between organic form and machinery. This paradoxical combination would later be much criticised by adherents of the cult of functionality, but at the time it seemed an extraordinary novelty that displayed an almost surreal imagination. In the hotel's main hall, later destroyed, the architects managed to express the Secession's organic sense in the furniture and in the form and rhythm of the colonnades along the side. Meanwhile, in the ornamentation – especially for the stage, with an allegorical painting by Karel Špillar, and the proscenium, with naturalistic allegorical sculptures by Ladislav Šaloun – the Baroque Revival lived on, albeit overlaid with pseudo-Secession motifs.

The subsequent development of this stylistic integration can be seen in buildings from 1903–4 on Wenceslas Square in Prague, where Bendelmayer's Archduke Stephen Hotel and Dryák's Hotel Merano were later joined to create the Hotel Evropa, and especially in Jan Kotěra's District House (*Okresní dům*) in Hradec Králové. All have asymmetrical façades, indicating that naturalism had now extended to a building's overall structure. It is interesting that this coincided with the ascent of Impressionism in fine art. In Dryák and Bendelmayer's Hotel Evropa, the decoration is applied over almost the entire façade and features a great diversity of details, while Kotěra's District House relies on the contrast between its rustic plinth and the smooth plaster. On the frieze below the cornice there is sculptural decoration by Stanislav Sucharda that is a more refined echo of the heavier plasticity of the plinth, and there are prominent details that drew substantially on Celda Klouček's work. Dryák and Bendelmayer had yet

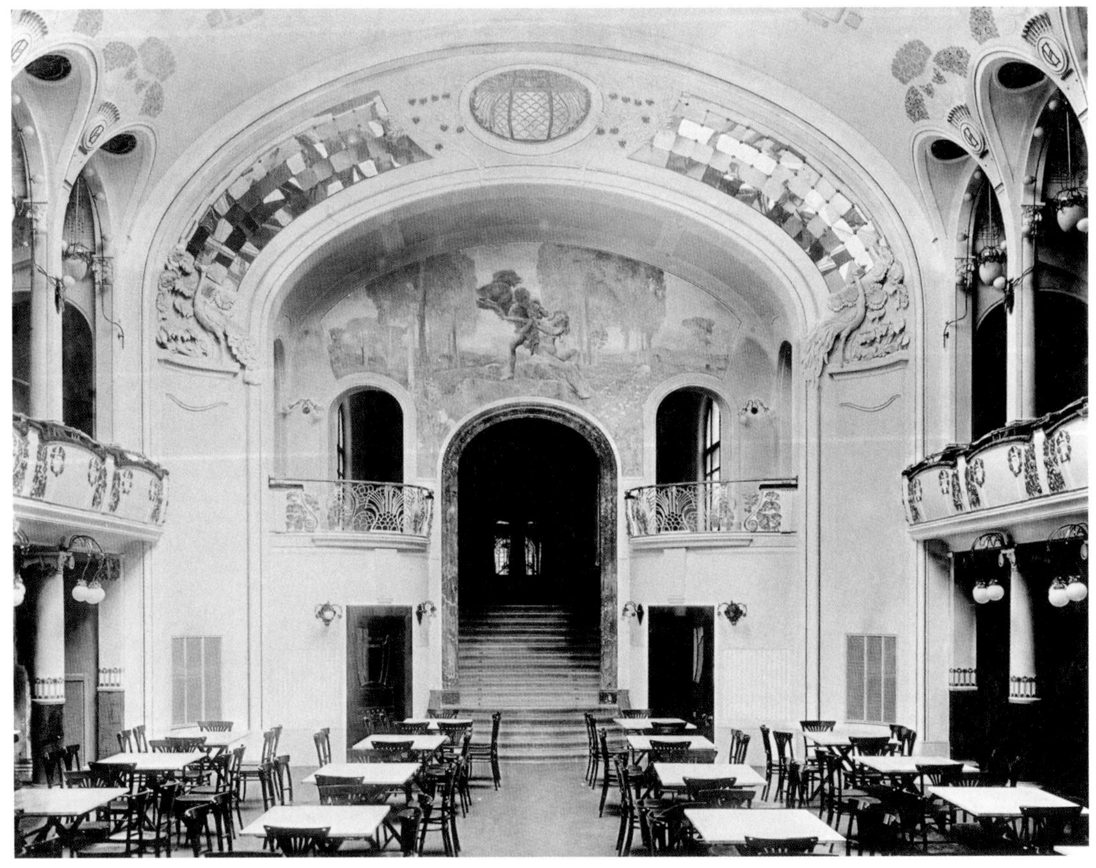

192 Alois Dryák and Bedřich Bendelmayer, Main hall of the Hotel Central in Prague, 1898–1902

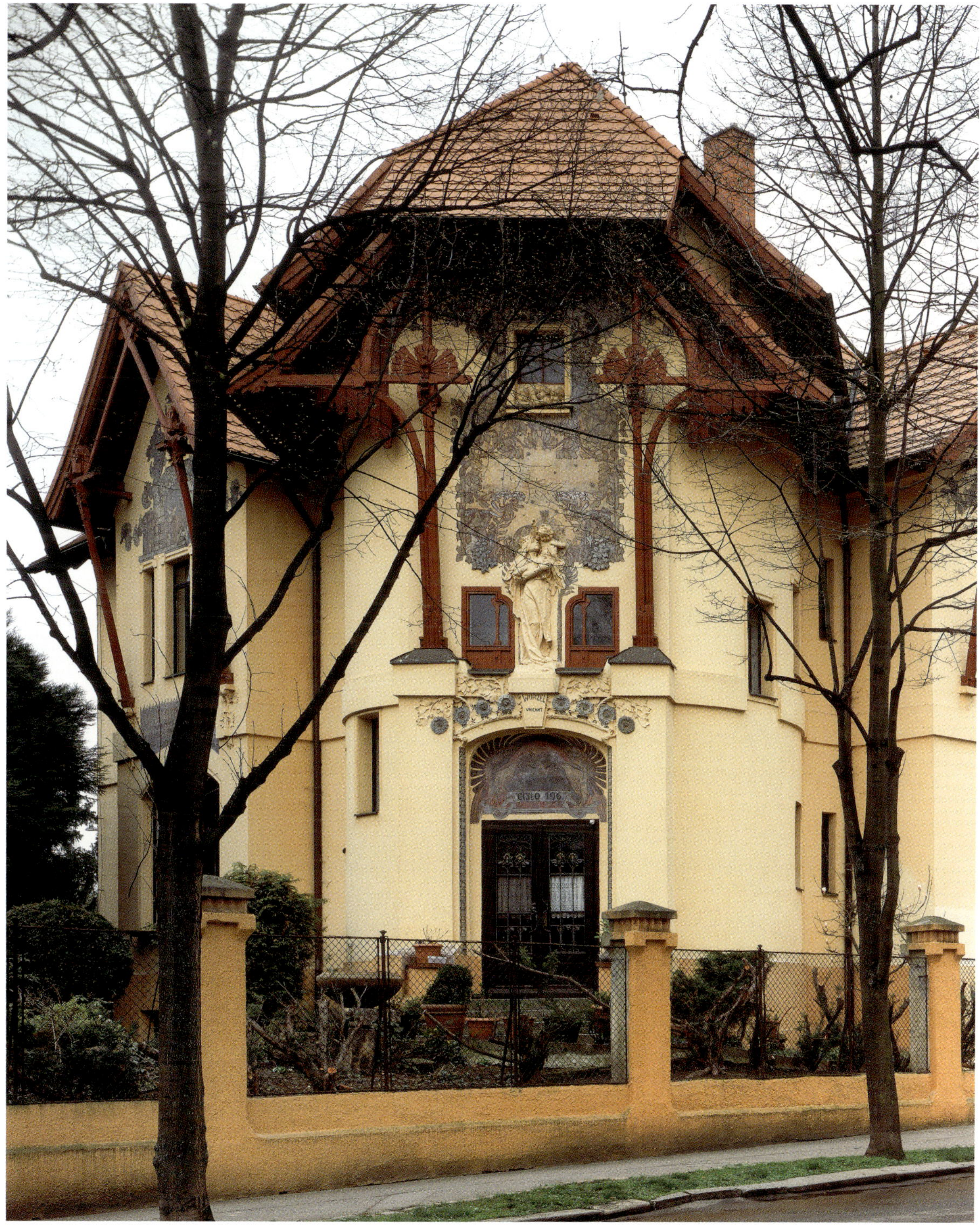

193 Karel Vítězslav Mašek, House in Prague, 1902

to achieve a true unity of architecture and decoration, although they masked this by their use of colour, gilding, and wrought ironwork. While Kotěra did not deploy such striking effects, his building was elaborated far more inventively. The District House's façade features an effective play of architectural devices. It is asymmetrical, and is articulated by the symmetrical main body, with its slightly protruding bay window, and the other part of the building, above a passageway flanked by pylons, which has a recessed balcony on the second floor. This asymmetry is then a consequence of carefully balanced contrasts, and it can also be found in the building's ground plan. The large hall on the ground floor, ending in a stage beneath a semi-dome, is symmetrical within the main body of the building, but its true siting is asymmetrical. Kotěra did not use the relationships between the different parts of the building for their own sake, but for the flawless composition of the building from the perspective of its visual structure, which is then logically reflected in the articulation and character of the ornament. The interplay of the symmetrical and asymmetrical layouts gives the building an unusual spatial activity that is also transmitted to its users.

Kotěra's District House in Hradec Králové was important in the development of Secession architecture. It demonstrated the possibility of overcoming the dualism that had led to a crisis of architectural values in historicism. In Kotěra's District House, the ground plan is in keeping with the composition of the façade, and this achieved the Secession's objective of a new coherence in an architectural work. In this respect, Kotěra was unquestionably the most consistent architect, whereas others of his generation, like the older architects who were also attempting a new Secession style, were often less assured in their solutions to this fundamental question, something they obscured by emphasising often excessively "stylistic" decorative elements.

Shortly after 1900 Secession architecture began to fill and shape the urban exterior, especially in Prague. In numerous apartment buildings Secession ornament now replaced the former historicist ornament. Where once there was acanthus, now Klouček's pupils and imitators produced a great quantity of branches bearing fruit, stylised irises, forsythias, daisies, lilacs, and apple blossom, and the enduring female mascaron motif. Naturalistically modelled stucco ornamentation, occasionally supplemented with sgraffiti, became almost synonymous with Secession architecture, while etched glass and coloured stained-glass windows were used in interiors. Secession ornament was a welcome basis for the plentiful use of wrought ironwork on staircases and balconies, and it also led to decorative wooden walls being fitted on the landings of apartment buildings. The glazed area of façades and interiors increased substantially, and this resulted in a relaxation of their composition, which now had a disquietingly asymmetrical element. The great majority of what was labelled Secession architecture was, of course, content simply to use naturalistic decor for its visual effect on a traditionally designed façade with a superficial tectonicity. The Secession allowed the, by now quite substantial, mass of townhouses to be shaped such that their concept and articulation offered a suitable combination of comfort and grandeur. This also reflected the mentality of their builders, who were usually recruited from the "democratically" minded strata of the bourgeoisie. Typical Secession apartment blocks were mainly erected on plots that had been cleared under Prague's extensive redevelopment programme, whether these were in the Old Town (Bedřich Bendelmayer's apartment building by the Powder Gate, 1904) or on the city's embankments (Josef Fanta's building for the Hlahol choir, 1905). Buildings erected by commercial enterprises usually had a greater proportion of ornamentation, sometimes quite fantastical, which contrasted with their more mundane functions (Jiří Stibral's First Bohemian Reinsurance Bank [*První česká zajišťovací banka*], with sculptural ornamentation by Ladislav Šaloun, 1905).

Construction companies, societies, and institutions owned and operated by the Czech bourgeoisie comprised the main clientele for Secession architecture, and this gave it the characteristics that distinguished it from the official architecture and tastes of the Austro-Hungarian nobility. The ascendant Czech nationalist movement meant that Secession architecture was also used for monumental construction projects.

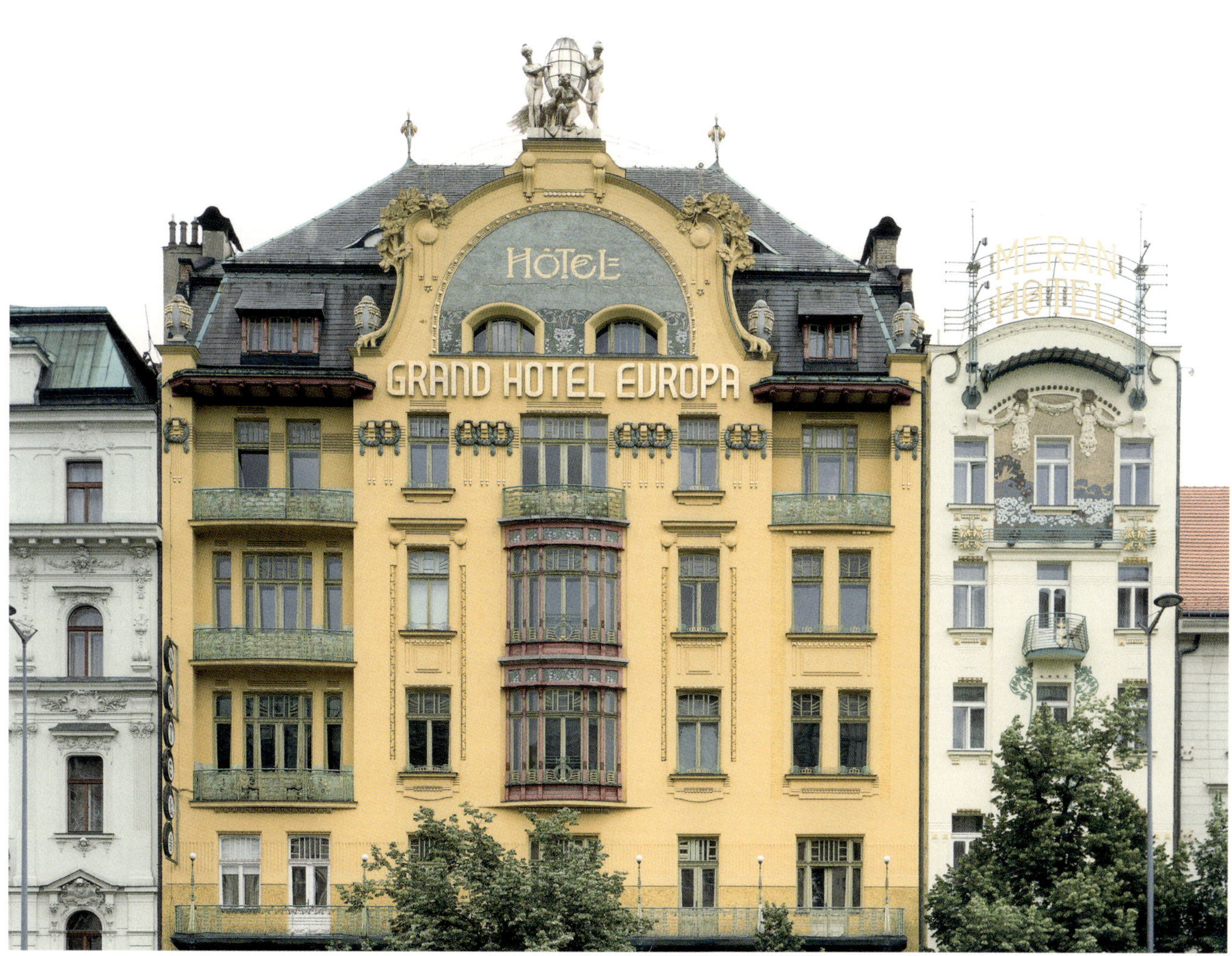

194 Alois Dryák and Bedřich Bendelmayer, Hotel Evropa in Prague, 1903–4

One such enterprise was Prague's Franz Josef Railway Station (now the Main Railway Station), whose dimensions made it one of the city's largest modern buildings. In 1900 Josef Fanta won the competition to design the station, which he built in 1901–9. Fanta's railway station was unusually contemporary in the way it combined its technical function with its role as a public building. The tracks themselves are covered by a double-span glazed roof whose utilitarian form reflects the modern age's industrial technicism. The organic curve of the hangar roof also echoes the Secession's emphasis on dynamism as the common denominator in the work of man, machines, and natural organisms. However, travellers were first greeted by the main building, with wings extending on either side. The large metal canopy over the entrance, with its complicated ornamentation, is a counterpoint to the roof over the tracks, and it introduces the station's stylistic motto. The central pavilion is a typical Secession design, with an open space in the centre ending in a semicircle, and it is entered through a tall portal with a glazed semicircular triumphal arch. On either side are tall pylon towers with prominent sculptures by Stanislav Sucharda and other sculptors. At this time we find the same combination of elements in Kotěra's exhibition pavilion for SVU Mánes, and in his tomb designs. It originated with Otto Wagner in Vienna, but Fanta's treatment gives it a distinctive monumentality by emphasising the plastic segments and their spatial function. The decorative plaster and bare bricks on the façade again signal the station's ornamental and utilitarian aspects.

During the first decade of the new century, the Secession became just as characteristic of Czech society as the Renaissance Revival had been previously. The architecture of these two epochs corresponded to a certain shift in the national mentality. While in the Renaissance Revival, architecture had principally been a manifestation of nationalist ambitions, the Secession no longer produced large buildings of this kind. Yet it comprehensively took over the city, filling entire blocks and avenues, and it gave Prague a specifically Czech character that was no longer just an agenda but was now a matter of fact. In this respect, the Secession created a real environment with its own characteristics. Its ability to do so was rooted in the very essence of Secession art, in which reality and dream, the real and the ideal, everyday life and special occasions constantly complemented and changed one another. This ambivalence was unquestionably a reflection of the liberal and democratic tendencies with which the Secession was associated in ideology and politics.

The Secession's central concept of projecting factual reality into the higher "eternal" totality of the cosmos and nature could also easily be interpreted and applied to promote the key principles and objectives of the Czech National Revival, which challenged the Habsburg Monarchy's status by pointing to the Czech nation's venerable history. Coupling these ideas with the new naturalism gave the Secession social legitimacy and brought about its ultimate success. One example of this tendency is Sucharda's plaquette *Prague and the Vltava* (1902), where the proud allegorical figure of the city is addressed by a personification of the river, representing the life-giving force of the Czech Lands. Interestingly, the panorama of the city in the background includes both historic buildings and modern ones.

195 Jan Kotěra, District House in Hradec Králové, 1903–4, façade

With its decorative ornamental properties, the Secession's line was well suited to a new kind of monumentality. Here, Mikoláš Aleš – whose work the younger generation had always admired as a healthy manifestation of national art – accomplished a great deal. In the late 1870s, while living and working in Suchdol, just to the north of Prague, Aleš had produced brilliant depictions of early Czech history that were recalled in the first few volumes of *Volné směry*. The dynamism of his line in these works was revived in a more decorative form in his panels for Josef Fanta's interior at the 1900 Exposition Universelle. Aleš was the best example of the continuity that emerged, as a deeper connection between the older and younger generations of Czech artists, in instances where art did not limit itself to an adopted style but instead sprang from original sources. His work also demonstrated that historicism's obsolescence was due not to its theme so much as its inability to see history as a living part of the present day. Compared with the refinement of the salon "archaeological school" of the time, Aleš was a primitive folk artist, but it was precisely his naivety that allowed him to see

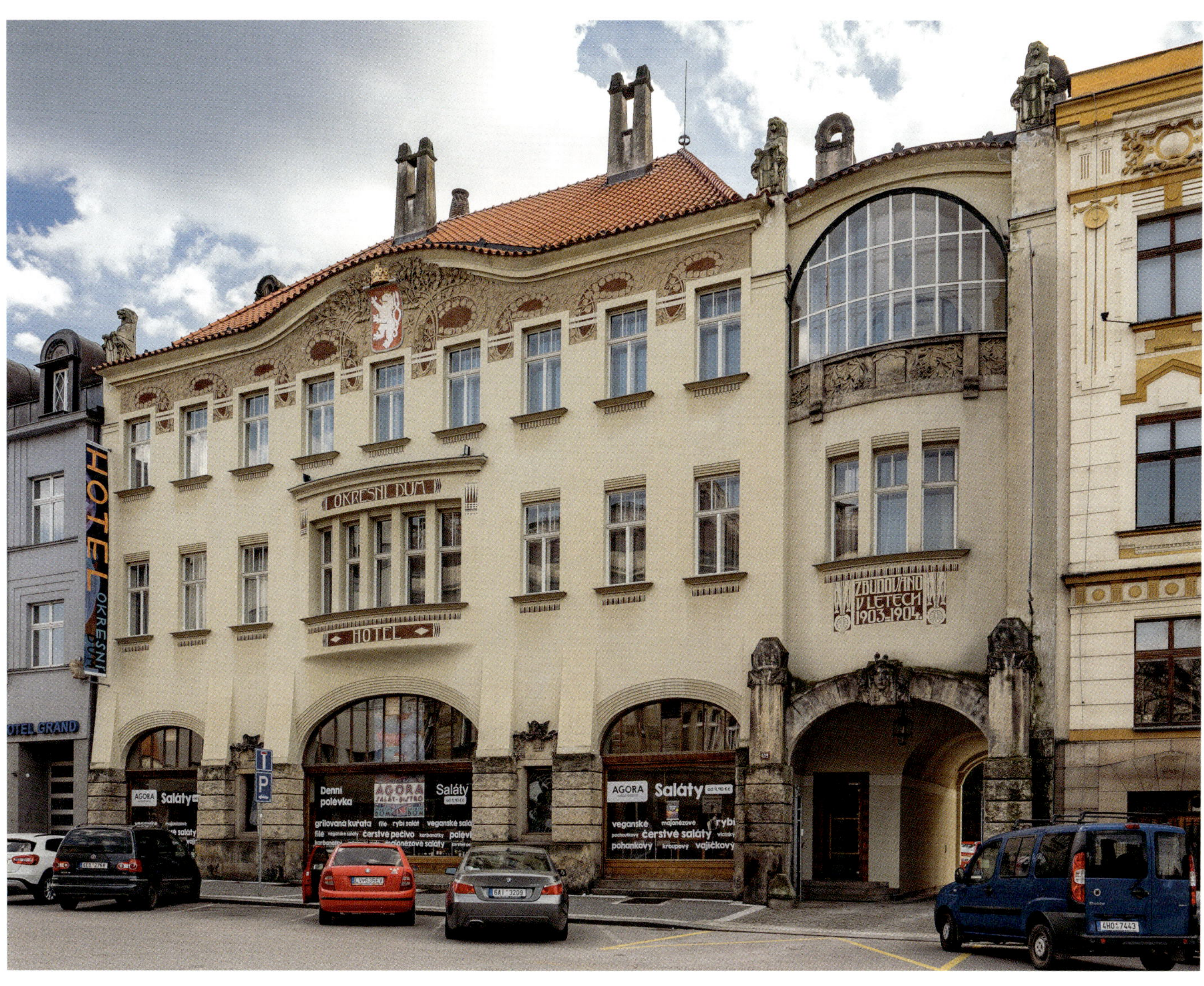

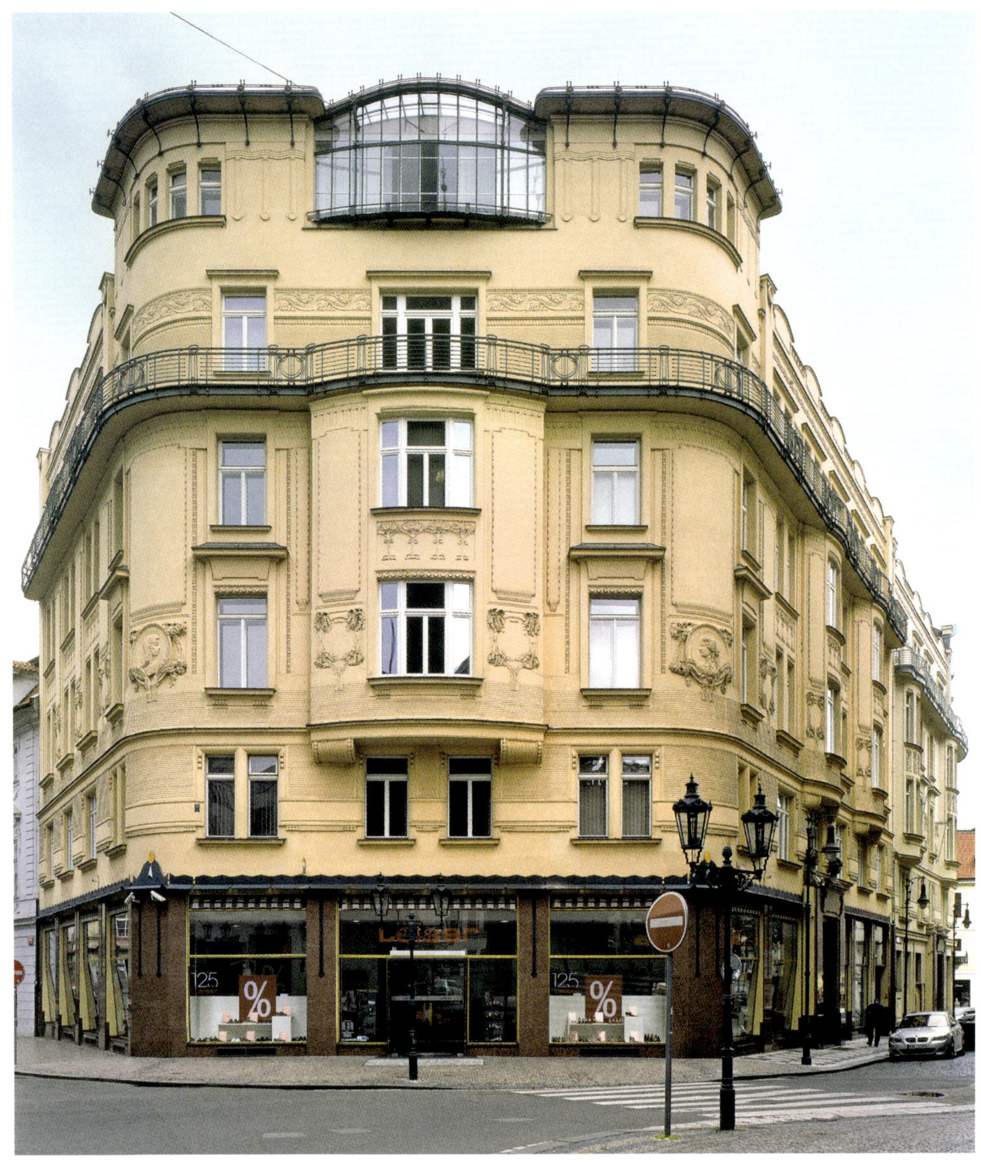

the past as a meaningful whole, and it also gave his art the means for effective modern decoration.

Nor were other prominent artists of the older generation oblivious to the appeal of Secession forms, as is evident from some of the studies of Saint Wenceslas that Josef Václav Myslbek made in 1902–3 for his large monument to the saint. In them, he adopted the motif of stylised long hair, but what Myslbek chiefly shared with young sculptors was the melancholy sensitivity of the youthful hero's expression, and the use of light to produce a lyrical melodiousness of form. The literature on Myslbek has remarked that his sketches recall the youths from Preisler's illustrations for Julius

196 Bedřich Bendelmayer, Apartment building by the Powder Gate in Prague, 1904

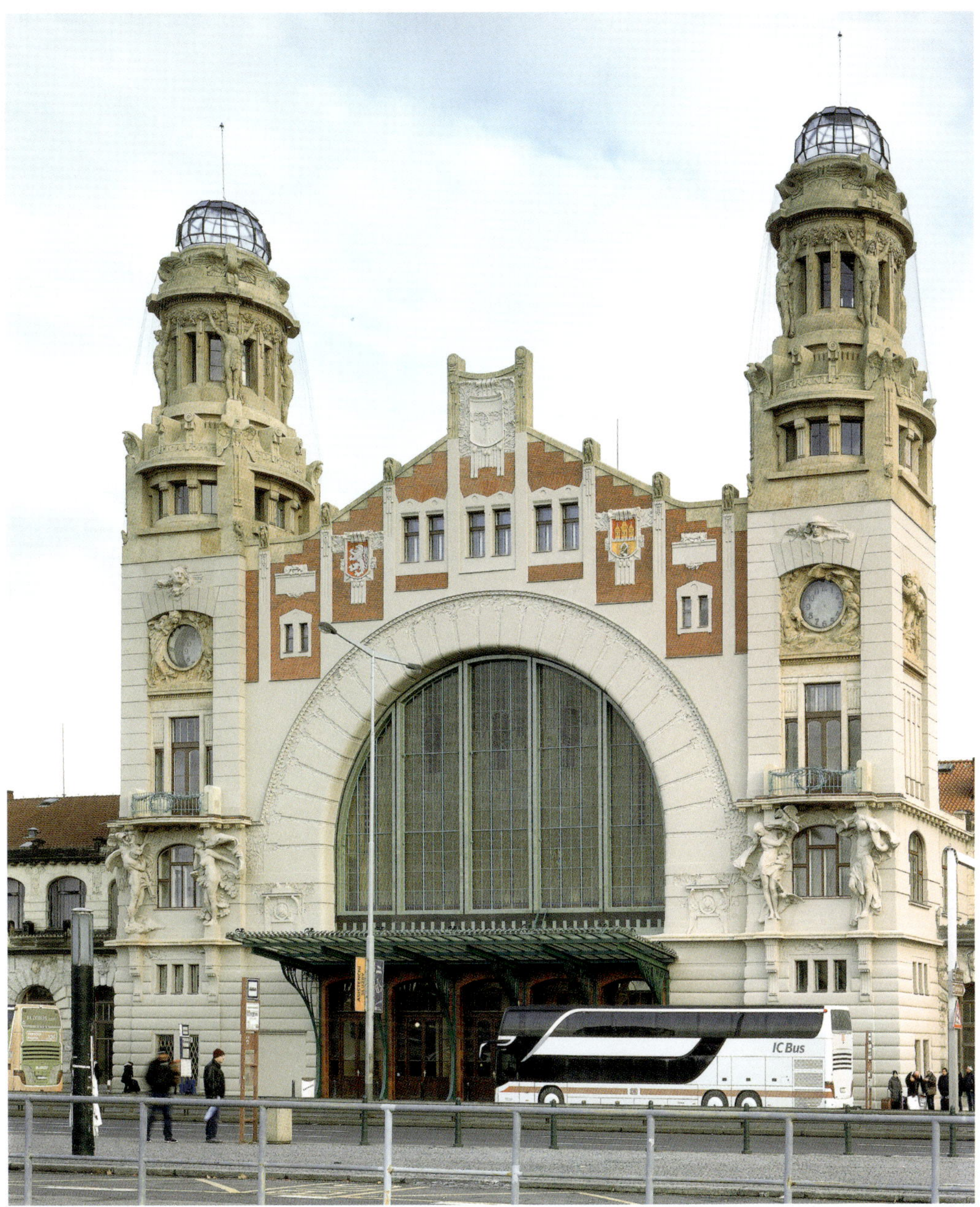

Zeyer, and in both cases it was indeed a matter of producing variations on a delicate equilibrium of basic psychological tendencies conveyed by facial expressions. From the start, Myslbek had worked with more antithetical values, resulting in a simplification that perhaps had a more energetic level of emotion, but in essence the approach of both artists was the same.

Since being appointed professor at the academy in Prague, Myslbek's friend Vojtěch Hynais had been at the centre of the young generation's attention, and it is not surprising that a number of ties with the Secession can be found in his later work. They are most apparent in his painting *Winter*, from 1901, which he added to the allegories of

197 Josef Fanta, Prague Main Railway Station, 1900–1909

the other three seasons he had painted for the National Theatre twenty years earlier. While those paintings had been full of Neo-Baroque spectacle, in *Winter* Hynais accentuated the Luminist aspects. The coloured light of the setting sun is reflected from the blueish snow-covered ground of a birch grove, illuminating a figure, as white as ice, who floats silently through this landscape like a ghost, with black ravens for her companions. In one hand she clutches dried poppy heads, symbolising sleep. The coloured reflections on her gown and skin are meant to indicate the effect of the frost, and this enhances their naturalistic appearance. The red-headed woman and the landscape are realistic, yet at the same time she floats weightlessly, and this renders them unreal. In this way, Hynais took what had comprised the paradoxical unity of *The Judgement of Paris* to its furthest extreme. The coexistence of naturalism, allegorical symbolism, and decorativism in an arrangement of flat and linear bodies makes *Winter* an unusually contemporary painting – yet Hynais's approach was calculated more to intensify the painting's effect than to achieve any true integration. The Secession aspect of *Winter* is refined rather than authentic; it sets out the components from which a new synthesis was to be born, and this makes it more a kind of Secession academicism. *Winter* encapsulates that element of the Secession mentality that did not want

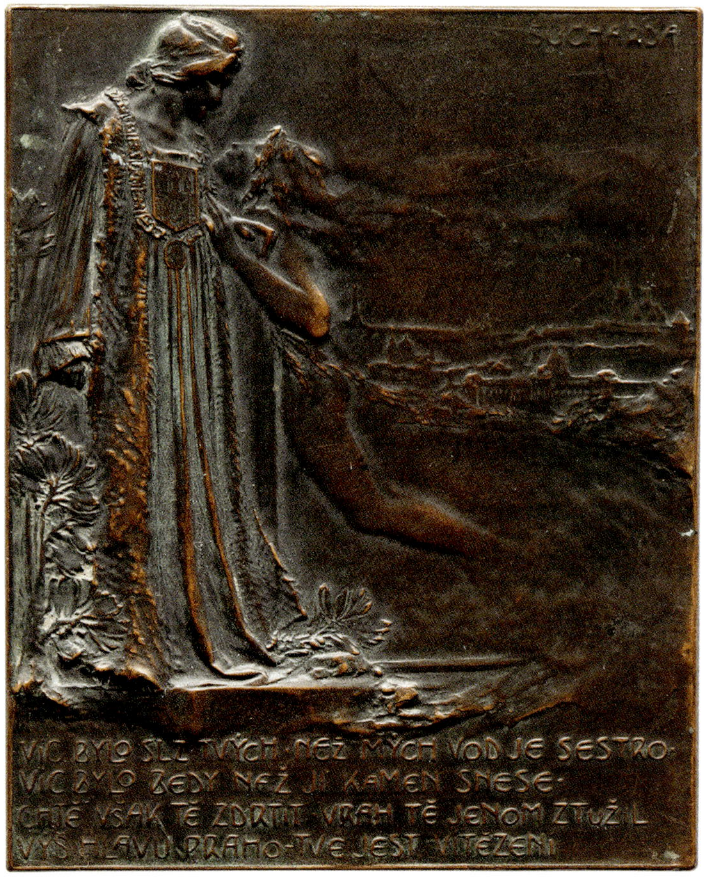

198 Stanislav Sucharda, *Prague and the Vltava*, 1902, bronze, 7.5 × 5.7 cm

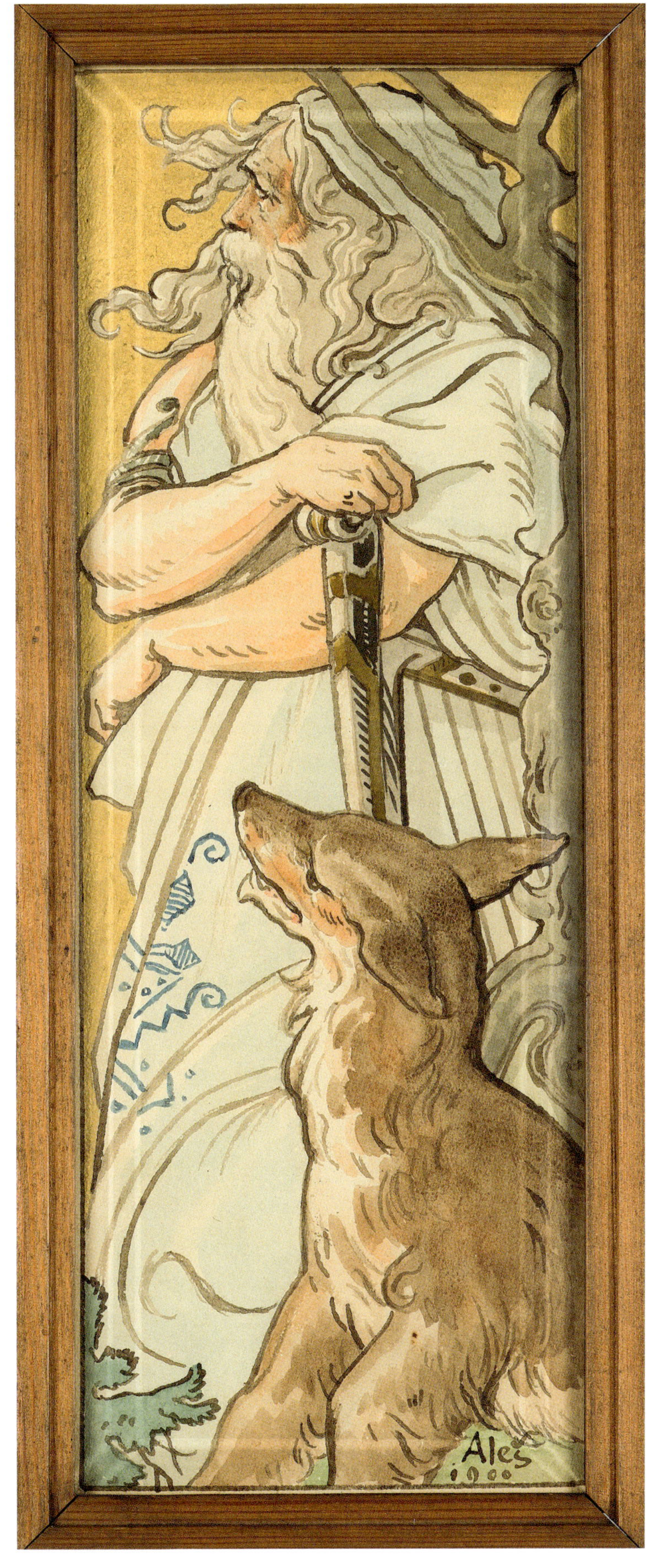

199 Mikoláš Aleš, *Old Bard*, 1900, watercolour, 36 × 13.5 cm

to overcome the opposition of reality and ideal, but instead relished the tantalising encounter between the real and the imaginary.

The Secession's emotionality and its new and appealing artistic devices made it attractive to the public, and also to artists whose original training and orientation had been quite different. This was noticeable not just in fine art but also in architecture, which in the first decade of the 20th century was quick to adapt to the contemporary taste. Some architects who in the 1890s had worked in the spirit of late historicism now favoured Secession architecture, with some even becoming its official representatives. A typical example was Osvald Polívka: while his Prague City Insurance Company (*Pražská městská pojišťovna*) on the Old Town Square (1900) was a combination of the Renaissance and the Baroque, his Novák Department Store (*Dům U Nováků*) on Vodičkova ulice (1902), for which he had been chosen in preference to Kotěra, was in the Secession style. Polívka retained the symmetry of the body of the building and relied chiefly on Secession ornamentation, with its typical combination of metal and coloured glass. The mosaic on the façade was designed by Jan Preisler, and it was the last time he assembled his familiar folkloric motifs around an allegorical nude and a group of dancers. As an architect, Polívka did not in essence exceed the bounds of historicist dualism. This is also why it is symptomatic of his concept of Secession architecture that its functional and ornamental aspects were developed in parallel. In his attempt to achieve a metropolitan elegance, the ornament would be concentrated on an impressive façade, and this tended to produce a rather superficial effect. It was apparent on the façade of the Prague Insurance Company (*Pojišťovna Praha*) on Národní třída (1906–7), to whose plasticity, emphasised by the unusual extending of the main cornice, Ladislav Šaloun contributed significantly. A more positive aspect of Polívka's work (although the architectural avant-garde would soon highlight it as an example of bad modernism)[131] was his feel for colour, which stylistically aligned him more with contemporary poster design. This was also reflected in the breadth of Polívka's Secession architecture. He designed numerous apartment buildings and did much to disseminate the Secession as an expression of Czech urban culture in the years leading up to the First World War. Polívka's most impressive realisation from this period was his addition of a second building to the Provincial Bank on Na Příkopě (1911–12), producing an interesting confrontation with his work from the mid-1890s. It was joined to the earlier building by a covered bridge, and their proximity resulted in greater restraint in Polívka's use of form. Nevertheless, the new building's vertical rhythm and its ornamentation by Klouček and Preisler acknowledged the changes that Czech architecture had undergone in the interim.

In the first decade of the century, the Secession had ceased to be a movement and had become a general cultural phenomenon, and this had various and far-reaching consequences. Initially, there was a sense of cultural homogeneity, which would of course soon be replaced by a marked internal differentiation. The notion of a Secession epoch was principally associated with the initial sense that modernity had now been achieved. The revival of "Impressionism" established a common basis for artistic expression, suppressing the Secession's fantastical Symbolist elements and aligning

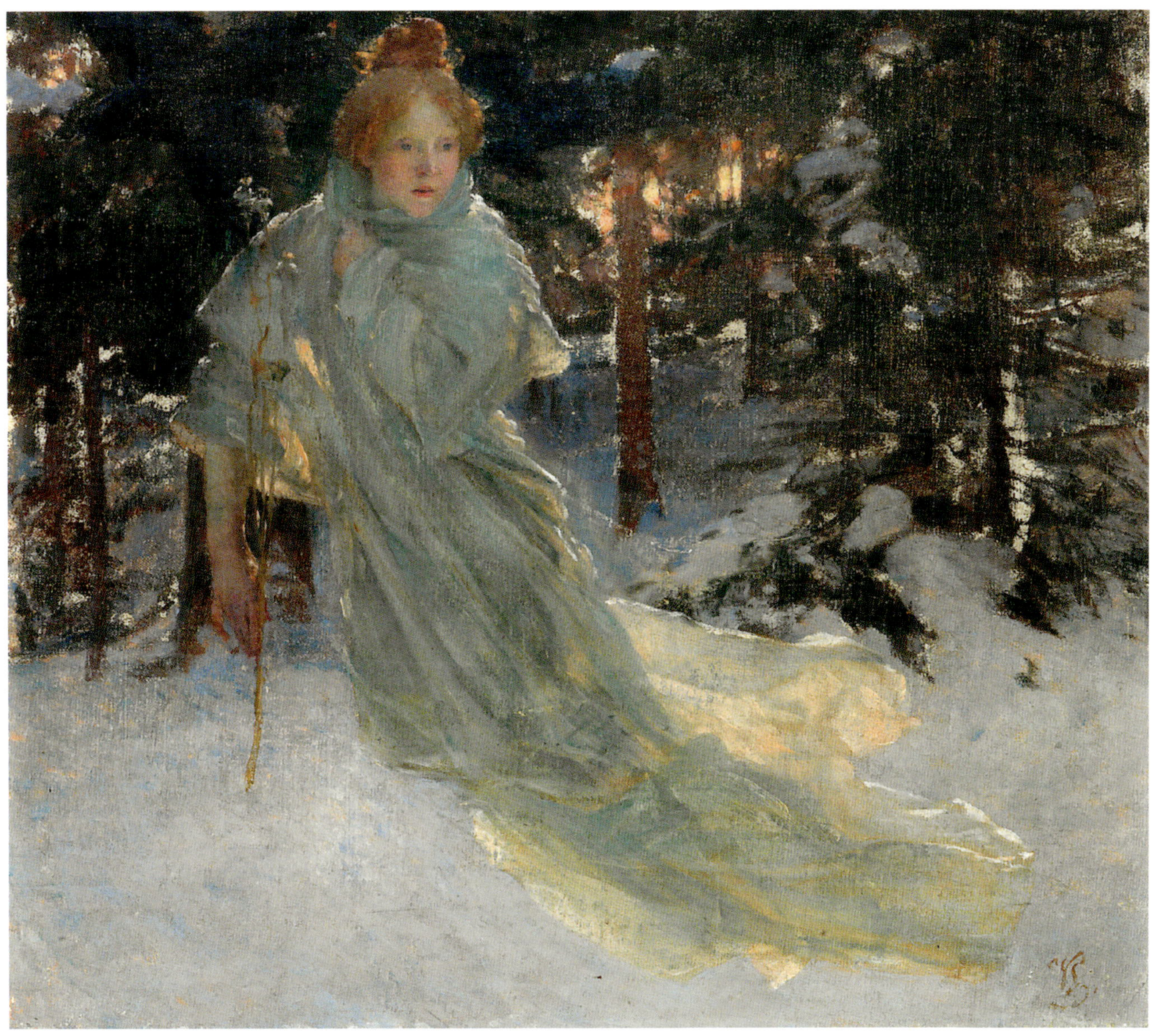

200 Vojtěch Hynais, Study for *Winter*, 1901, oil, 29 × 35 cm

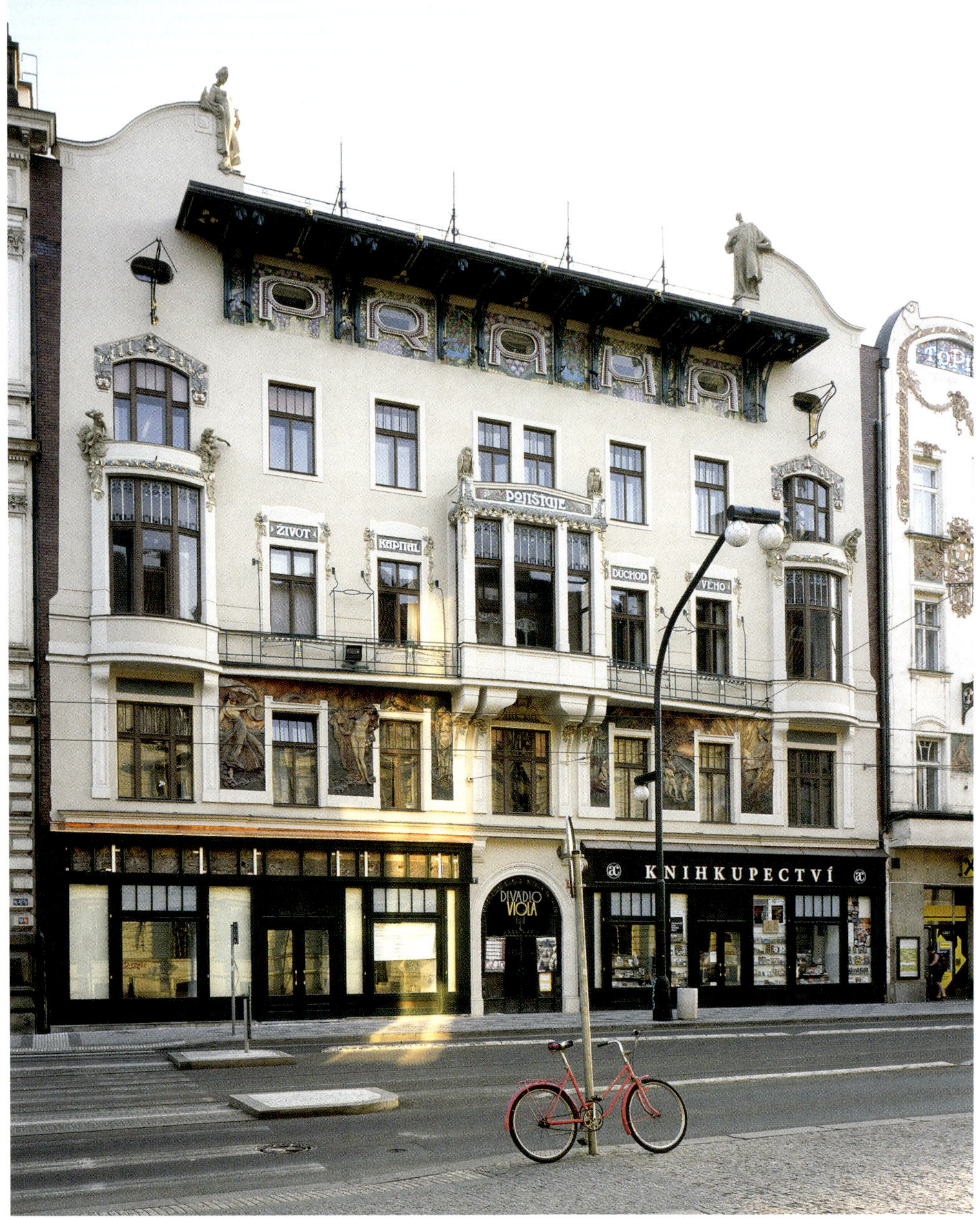

popular graphic ornamentalism more with everyday reality. This closer proximity between art and ordinary life was also due to the fact that Czech artists were now more familiar with the art of countries lying to the west, especially that of France, which had earlier been the preserve of the Decadents. After the 1890s it became quite normal for Czech artists to migrate to Paris, sometimes spending several years there, and this familiarised them not just with the work of those artists they particularly admired, but also with the typical breadth of French cultural life, whose core was in fact realistic. French cultural realism was of a high professional standard, and this dispelled any excessively romantic notions Czech artists may have had, anchoring

201 Osvald Polívka, Prague Insurance Company, 1906–7

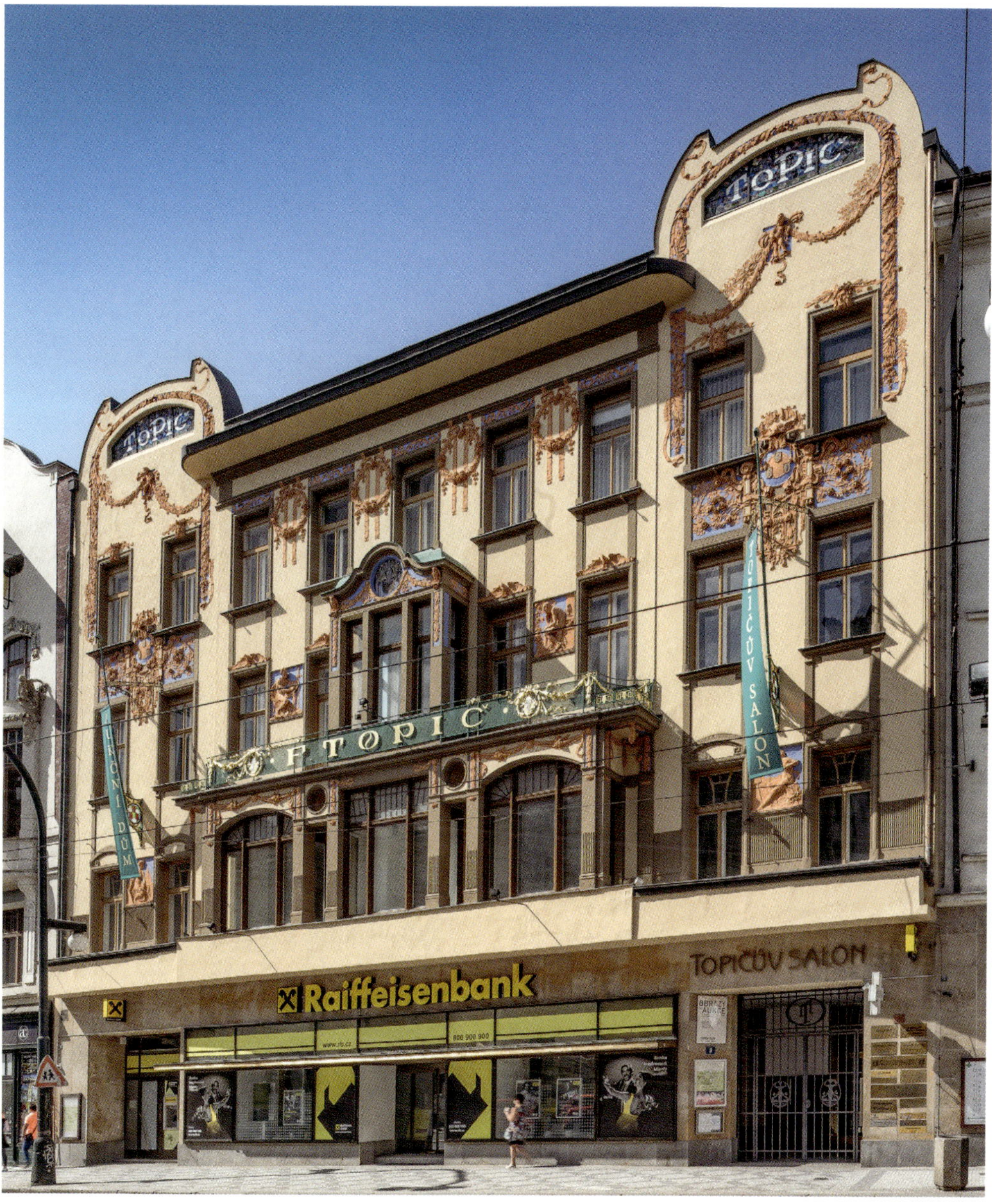

them to demonstrable values. Many Czech artists and printmakers who headed to Paris at the beginning of the century found in France the direction that their life's work would take. Viktor Stretti arrived in Paris in 1901. He already had a picturesque feel for urban folklore (his soft ground etching *Vegetable Market in Prague* from 1901 preceded Slavíček's paintings of Prague's markets), and he developed this further in scenes of bustling Parisian boulevards and colourful French seaside resorts. The same spectacle also attracted Karel Špillar. A figure painter trained in monumental work, he retained these habits in his genre scenes from Parisian exhibitions and beaches on the Atlantic coast. Tavík František Šimon's more successful coloured etchings combined his vision as a painter and as a printmaker. His home in Paris became a hub for many Czech visitors.

202 Osvald Polívka, Topič Building in Prague, 1905–6

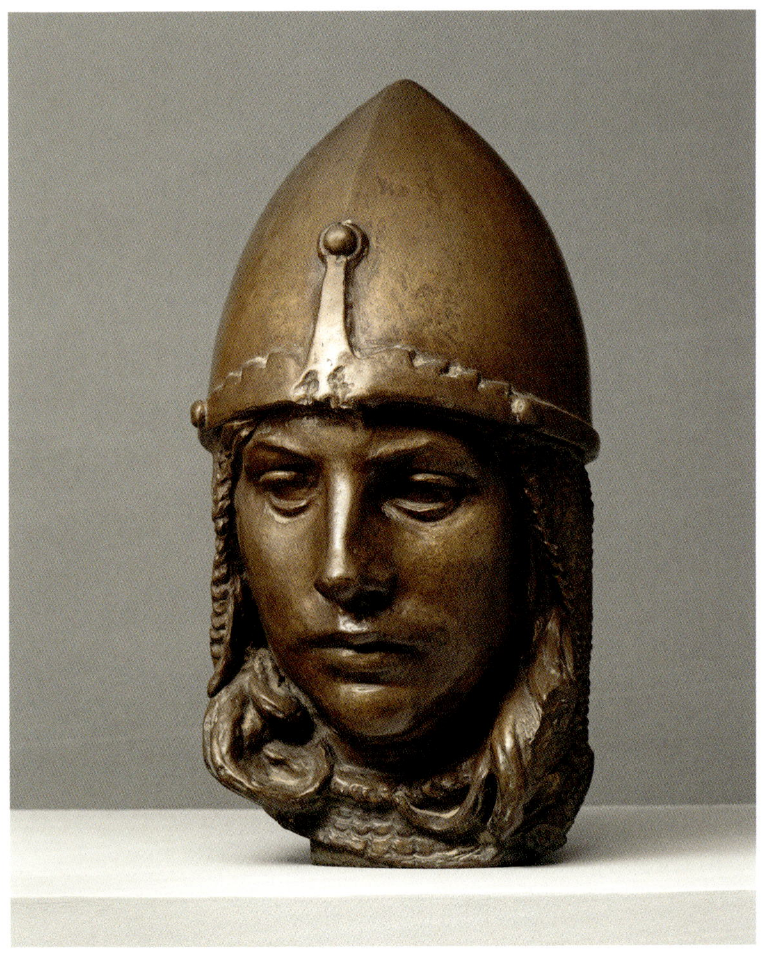

These painters, who ultimately became most successful as printmakers, were not leading figures in Czech art, but their significance in its development was considerable. With their knowledge of French art, they influenced many more famous names and helped to bring about an important shift in focus to seen reality. This was especially due to their coloured prints.

In this way they added a distinctive tone to the Czech cultural milieu, where it blended with all the other layers. Although Impressionism's lessons in realism no longer permitted any late Romantic escapes from reality, a lyrical mood remained irresistible to the contemporary vision of the world. A balance between naturalism and idealism was principally available through the lyrical experience of life's ephemeral charms, its light and shadow. Dreaminess was characteristic mainly of the work of young artists who emerged at the turn of the century; initially they reflected the poetic spirit of these times. Ladislav Kofránek's *To the Theatre* (1903–4) was a frivolous bust in the spirit of lyrical Impressionism, while in another bust, *Dreaming* (1904), he best summed up his sensitivity to both aspects of the Secession psyche. Otakar Nejedlý, a young landscape artist who had painted a village funeral while in Kameničky with Slavíček (*Yel-*

203 Josef Václav Myslbek, Study of the head of Saint Wenceslas, 1902–3, bronze, 42 cm

low Mood, 1904), immersed himself with the same poetic absorption in the mysterious shadows cast by the trees in a park (*Stromovka*, 1905).

There was in Czech Secession painting a master of this approach, a painter, not well known to the public, who had gradually developed his ideas and whose best paintings could rival Seurat's drawings. This was Jakub Schikaneder, whose *Murder in the House* had caused such a stir at the Centennial Exhibition. Formerly František Ženíšek's assistant at the School of Decorative Arts in Prague, Schikaneder was now the professor of decorative drawing there, and his synthetic Czech landscapes were shown at the school's exhibitions in 1900 and 1904. Once an ambitious figure painter, in the mid-1890s he had changed tack and spent the next twenty years painting moonlit and autumnal landscapes, snowy streets in out-of-the-way suburbs lit only by street lamps, silent and gloomy interiors, and deserted seashores. Their common denominator, as K. B. Mádl would later remark in his obituary of the painter, might be the title of one of his paintings: *Solitude*. In these paintings Schikaneder had lost none of his social conscience, but had rather extended it to encompass his entire vision of the world. However, the tragic tone was always alleviated by the coloured veil that shrouded his simple motifs, woven almost like music from richly differentiated shades of blue, brown, and greyish-green. Here, Schikaneder expressed himself not through forceful

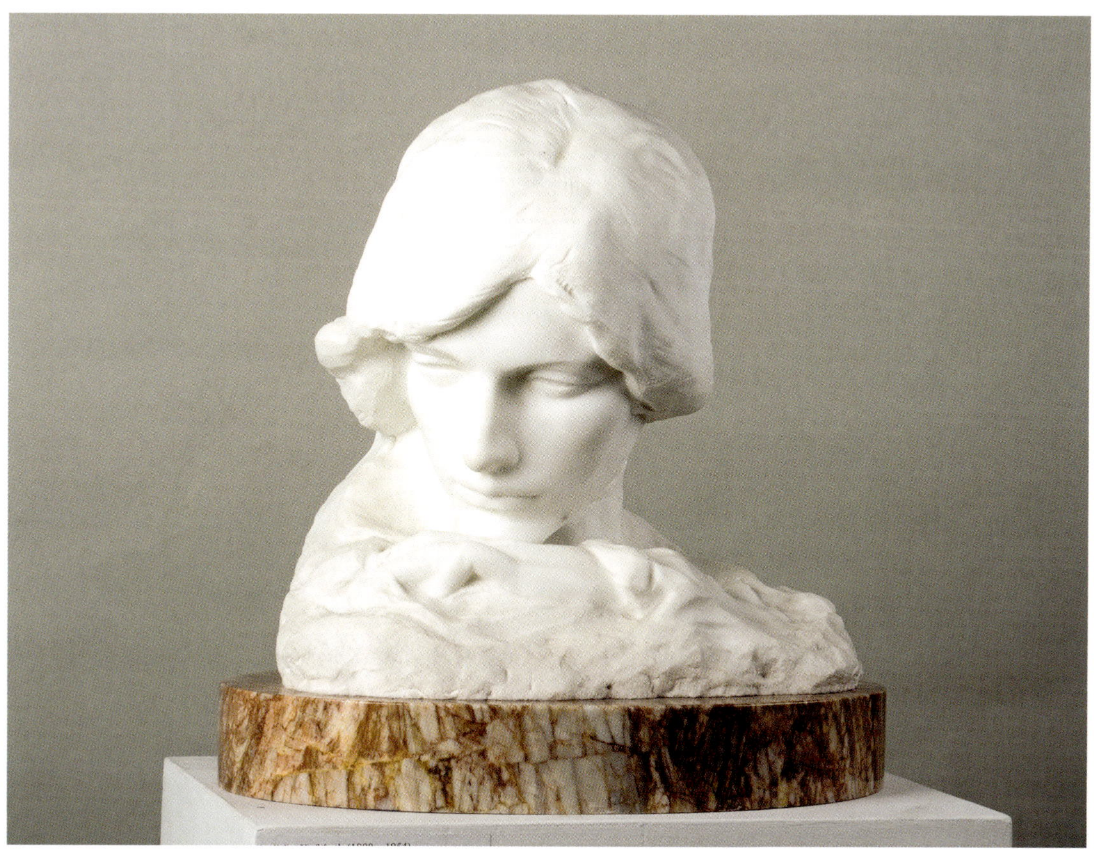

204 Ladislav Kofránek, *Dreaming*, 1904, marble, 31 cm

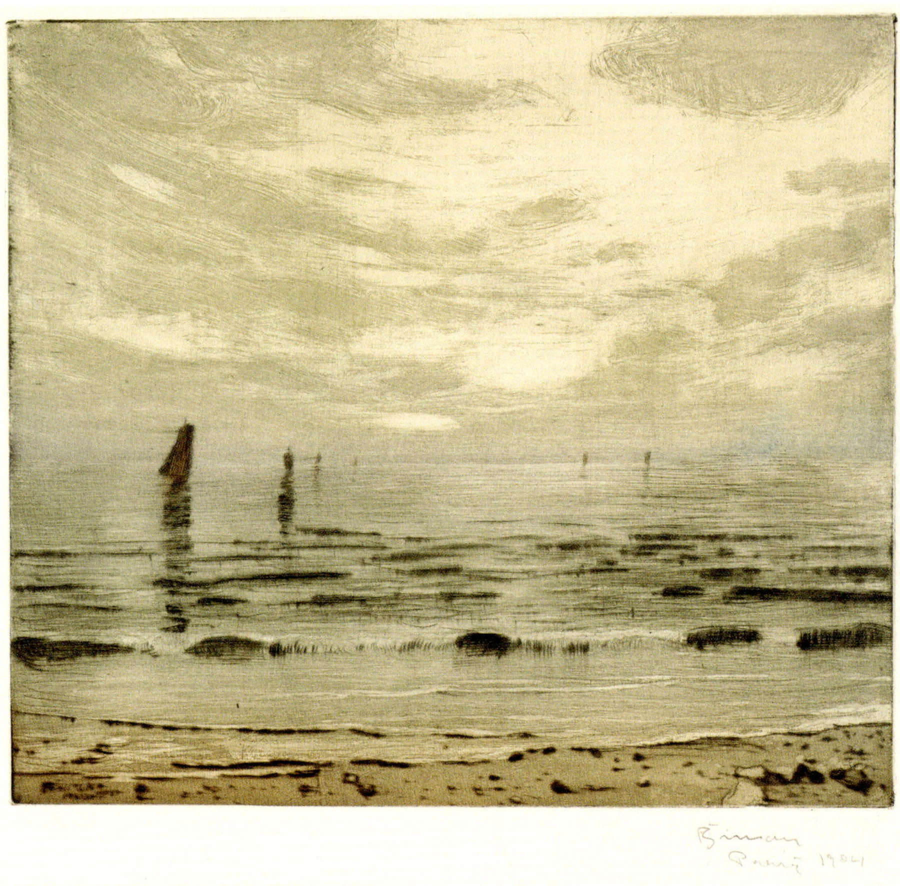

subject matter but with his own artistic devices, serving a profound need for emotional interiorisation.

If Schikaneder's paintings captured a lonely subjectivity, yet one that had not cut all ties with the world, at the opposite pole of the Secession mentality was Max Švabinský's *Large Family Portrait* (1905), illustrating the contemporary sense of collectivity. However, none of the figures in this unconventional group portrait have lost their individuality. The family is a model for the ideal society, which sees the essence of its persistence in a lively exchange of individual values. Even in this seemingly entirely private scene, Švabinský was a figure painter who was concerned with the content, as can been seen in his skilful composition, with its diagonal arrangement of the contrasting ages and interests of those depicted. The cycle of life, which in *Large Family Portrait* is developed through the individual figures, was for Schikaneder consolidated by the unity of his vision, but neither he nor Švabinský lacked a love of life or an awareness of its fleetingness.

Secession Intimism did not always have this dimension. One of its cornerstones was the dazzling charm of the moment, when the colours of a painting would be incandescent with the unity of the seen and the felt. The Impressionist technique

205 Tavík František Šimon, *The Sea*, 1904, coloured etching, 24.6 × 27.4 cm

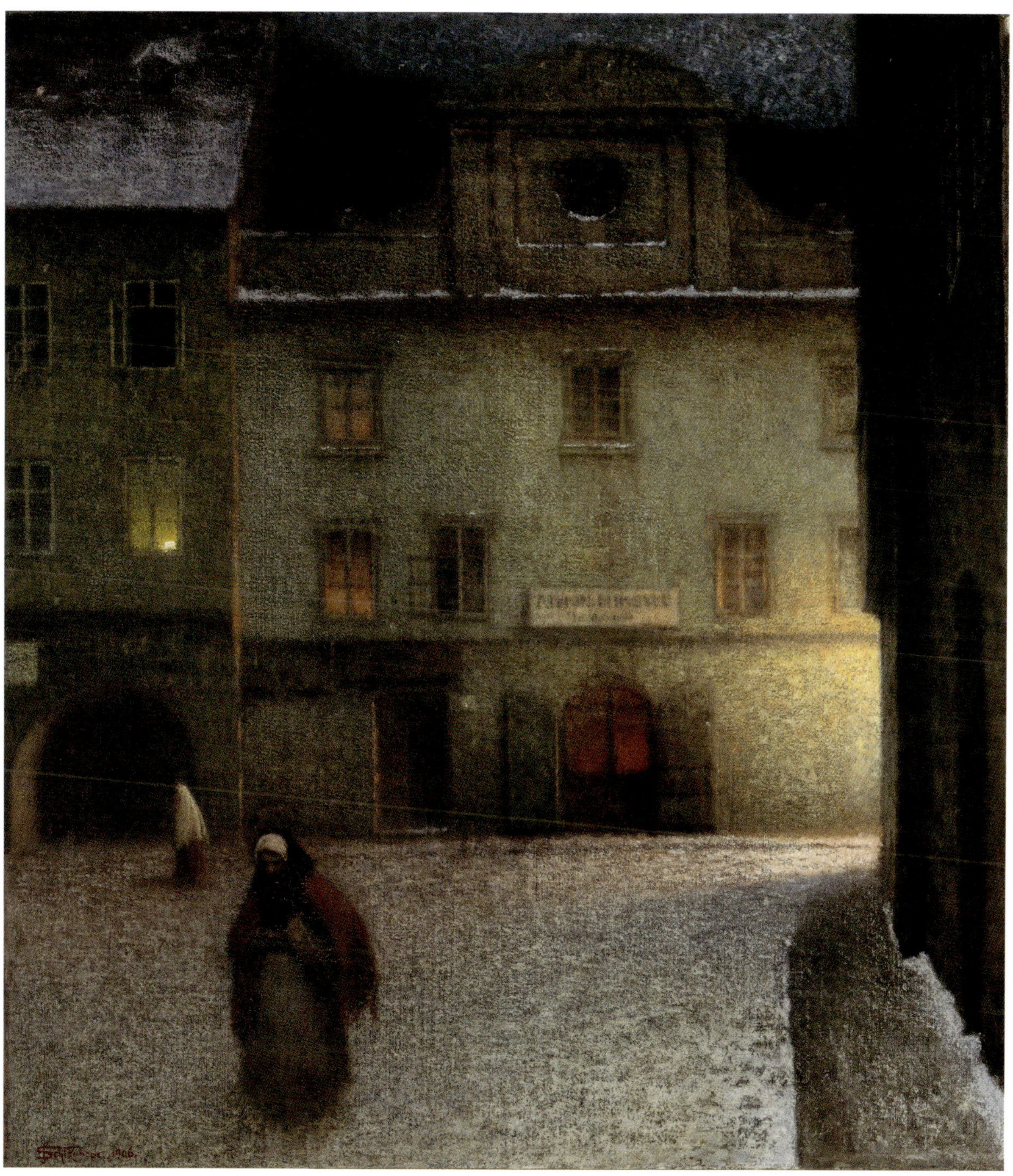

206 Jakub Schikaneder, *Street in the Evening*, 1906, oil, 110 × 95 cm

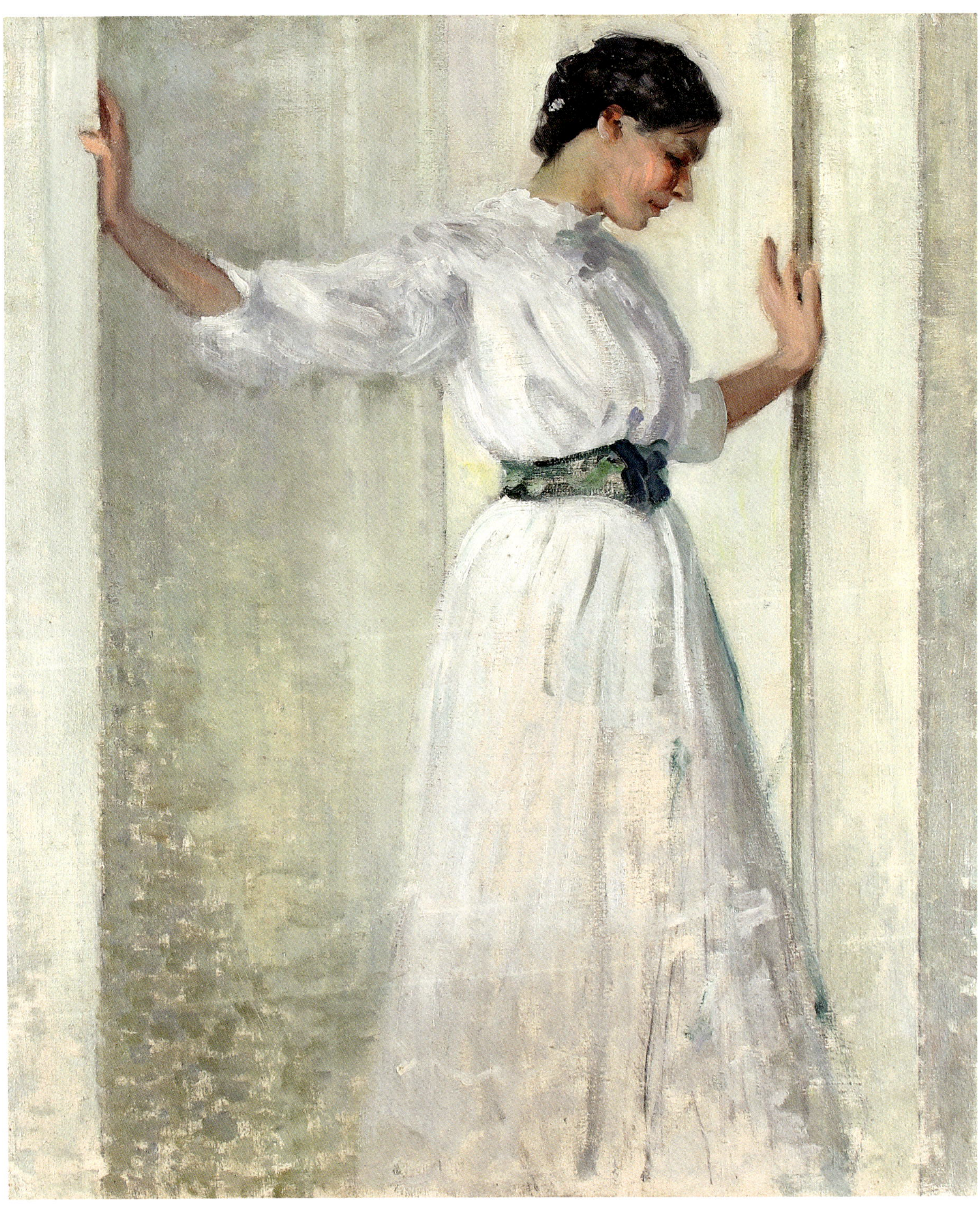

207 Miloš Jiránek, *White Study I*, 1910, oil, 75 × 63 cm

offered various means that Ludvík Kuba, Miloš Jiránek, and many other painters could deploy to depict cheerful scenes of family life. From here, Intimism became a specific tendency, one with which many painters (such as Rudolf Vejrych) worked for decades. Related to this intimate view of humanity was the way painters saw the human environment. Previously, open landscapes and gardens had dominated, but now urban exteriors and interiors were becoming more interesting. This was especially noticeable in the work of Antonín Slavíček. Although since the start of the decade he had produced individual paintings of picturesque sights (*Convent of St. Agnes*, 1901) or city suburbs (*Rainy Evening*, 1902), it was only in autumn 1906 that he began working on large series of paintings devoted to Prague. He now bid farewell to the dream he had nurtured in Kameničky, and in the little streets and squares of his birthplace he found a fresh subject in the constant interplay of old and new (*Mariánské náměstí*, 1906). While Slavíček's landscape syntheses had often had an affecting melancholy, his Prague paintings were filled with a new energy.

In his letters, Slavíček frequently complained about the redevelopment of Old Prague, how its romance and patina were vanishing, yet there was nothing old-fashioned about how he viewed what remained. His paintings pulse with colour, reflect-

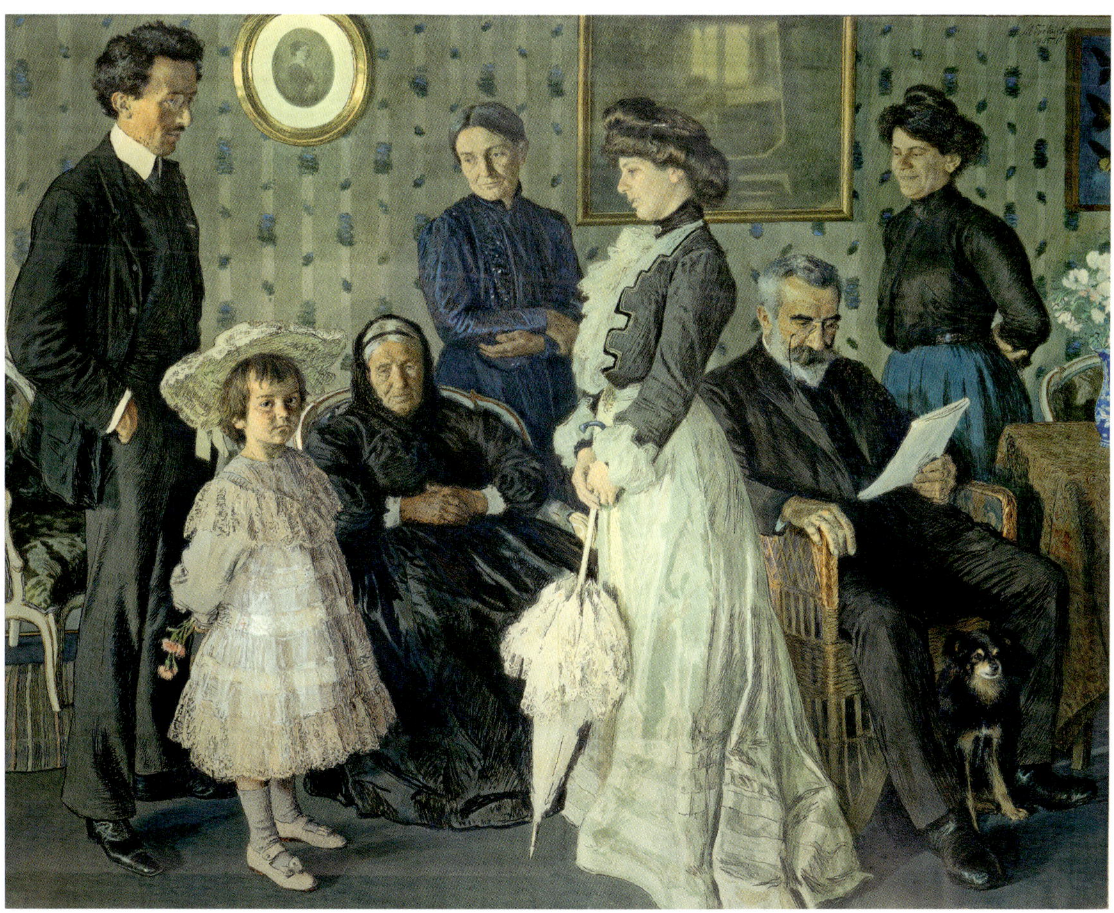

208 Maxmilián Švabinský, *Large Family Portrait*, 1905, Indian ink and watercolour, 182 × 206 cm

ing the indestructibility of life. To capture the singularity of his impressions, Slavíček painted outdoors on small wooden panels, producing a number of sketches that are among the finest Czech paintings from the beginning of the century. He worked these sketches into larger paintings (*Eliška Bridge*, 1906), and he also retained their freshness in his large panoramic views from 1908, when the city council commissioned him to paint *Prague from Ládví*, followed by *Prague from Letná*. Almost four metres wide, the latter painting showed "the city full of bustling activity – a modern city, but with old Gothic spires that are relics from the Middle Ages. I drenched the city in full sunlight, and when I saw it I myself was delighted."[132] He then wanted to paint a third panorama of Prague in the autumn sleet, and it seems there was also to be some kind of landscape cycle of Prague in the changing seasons, in which Impressionism's felicitous moment would again be elevated to a state of permanent ecstasy, a fusion of whirling vital and cosmic energy. This exaltation was to imbue his paintings of Prague as a symbol of "the artery of life and Czech fluidity."[133]

Slavíček's treatment of Prague illustrates how the Secession artist was always seeking some kind of universality, even if the practice of Secession art would seem to suggest that he thrived on entirely personal encounters with the world. Original art of this kind was created with an awareness that the artist's emotions and impressions had a deeper significance, that they were the forms through which the individual could express what was fundamental in the world. Part of this position was a faith in the strength and power of artistic intuition as the main means through which an artist could grasp the world's mysteries. All technique only acquired legitimacy as a way of seizing

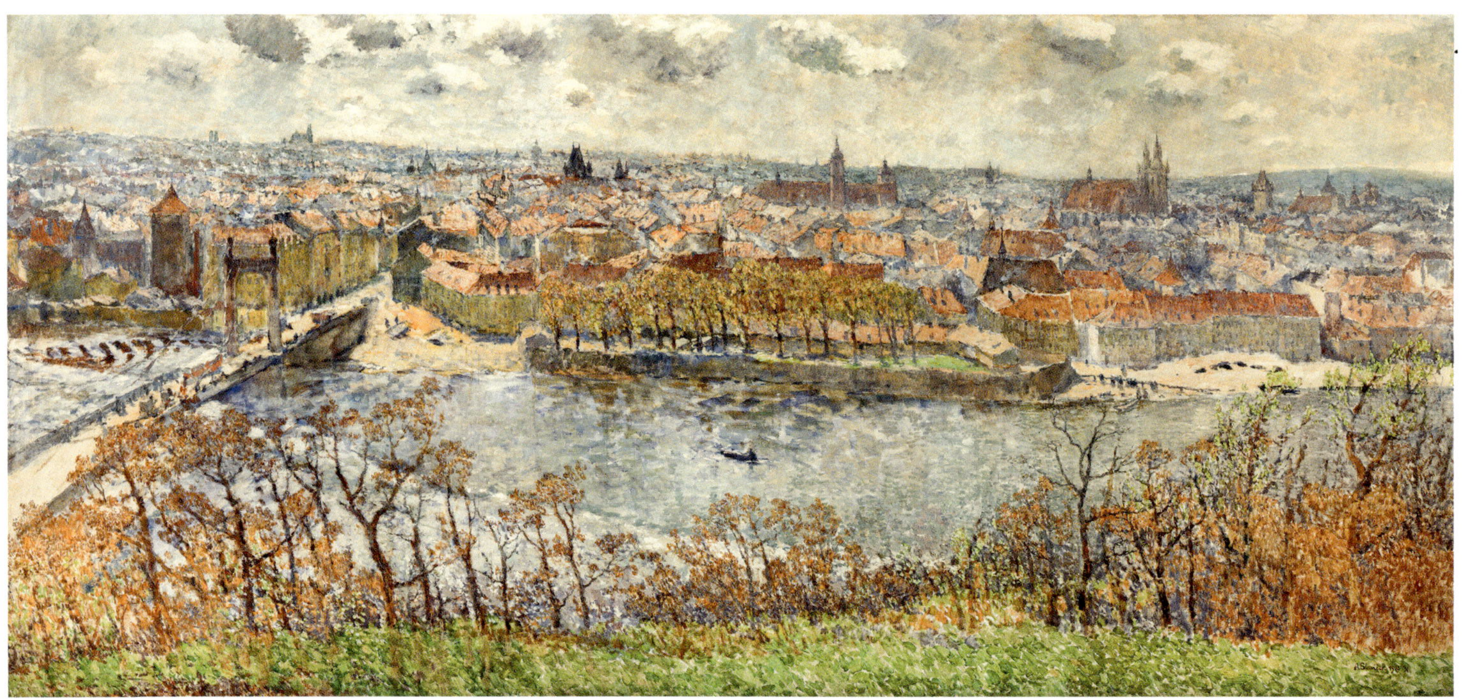

209 Antonín Slavíček, *Prague from Letná*, 1908, tempera, 188 × 390 cm

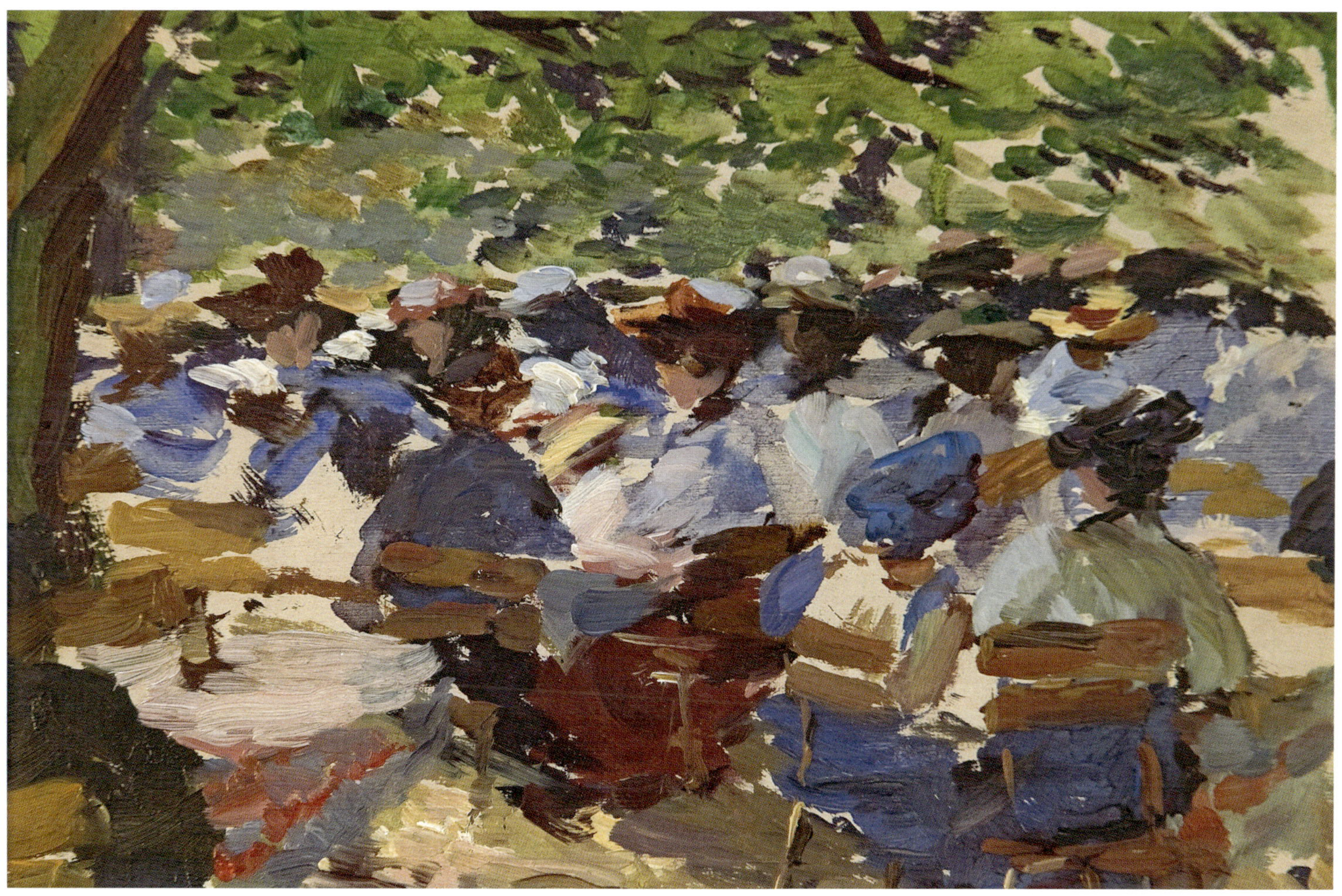

210 Antonín Slavíček, *In Stromovka*, 1907, oil, 18.7 × 24 cm

on what it was in an experience or an idea that would comprise the core of the artist's expression. It is thanks to this aesthetic of emotional engagement that Secession artists often intuitively anticipated forms that were significant in the development of art, or which would only be consciously and theoretically understood much later. The cult of original creativity allowed artistic practice to express what would otherwise have been overlooked or suppressed under a one-sided, ruled-based concept of art. This was why there was so much emphasis on the creative process, and the very relationship between art and society was viewed from this perspective. Slavíček was well aware that his customers would not accept his blue Prague unreservedly: "this Prague in a blue haze looks good, but if I do it the way I like, then the counsellors and aldermen are sure to dislike it ..."[134] He nevertheless painted the picture as he thought best, anticipating that, just as artistic form gradually takes shape in the individual creative process, so society would be slow to acquiesce, but for that reason would ultimately accept a new work all the more firmly.

This was the situation facing all forms of Secession monumental art. In sculpture, the public's tastes were even more inflexible, but here too a new concept came to be established. The popularity of the Rodin exhibition contributed greatly to this, although the decision to install his *The Age of Bronze* in a public park in the city centre had been controversial. Individual patronage was the most viable option, as in funerary sculpture, which produced notable Secession works. Bohumil Kafka's *The Embrace of Love and Death* (1906–7) encapsulated a number of key ideas in Secession sculpture. The basis for the tomb sculpture was a combination of naturalistic modelling and a literary concept in the symbolic form of the angel of death. What was essential here was the sculptural aspect, in which Kafka made effective use of the idea of a concave space creating large hollows beneath the wings of the kneeling angel. He had probably originally come up with this idea simply through observation, as suggested by one of his small sculptures from the previous year inspired by a visit to Onival, a seaside resort in France. In *Woman Styling Her Hair after Bathing*, the model's bathing gown creates a deep concave volume, and Kafka was so taken with this that he used it for his monumental *Embrace*, where it powerfully draws space into the sculpture and emotively conveys its fusion with the dark, archetypal space within. Kafka used light as a symbol, creating a typically Secession structure that works with the contrast between light and shadow, their opposition reconciled by the figure's lyricism.

Introducing artistic innovation while accommodating the public's taste was, of course, more challenging in the supreme form of public sculpture: the monument. This is apparent in the history of the František Palacký Monument, Prague's homage to this historian and statesman, a key figure in the Czech National Revival. In a competition to design the monument, held in 1897, Stanislav Sucharda and Alois Dryák's entry attracted much attention. Unlike more conventional proposals, it presented the idea of a narrative monument that did not commemorate only its subject, but also that which he had discovered and immortalised for the nation. The monument's mass was extended to create a broad exedra with two tall pylons on either side. Sucharda sat Palacký in the centre, beneath the Crown of Saint Wenceslas, and on the pylons he modelled picturesque sculptural groups depicting Paganism and Hussitism, the two most celebrated epochs in Czech history. On the rear of the exedra there was a seated statue of Fama teaching a child, and below her were reliefs of Samo, War, The Departure from Budeč, The Bible, Tomáš of Štítný, and Svatopluk. In 1901 a second round of the competition was held to decide whether Sucharda or Šaloun would be the monument's author. Sucharda won, after which he redesigned his monument. By now he had experience with designing another monument – this one to Jan Hus – which convinced him that he needed to unify what in his first design for the Palacký Monument had still seemed more like a narrative ornament for Dryák's architecture. Relative to the axis of Palacký Bridge, the site was asymmetrical, which necessitated abandoning the monument's symmetry and emphasising the sculptural component. However, Sucharda found the greatest support for his ideas in the revelation of Rodin's work. For a double issue of *Volné směry* in 1901, devoted to Rodin, Sucharda wrote an article that emphasised that the sculptor's objective is "the idea of the whole" and the expressive study of nature. In this spirit, it was essential to suppress all antiquated demands, which, especially in a monument,

> are promoted, when nationalism is well established, by people accustomed to seeing a sculpture executed from the top of the head to the last hobnail on the boot, with the subject's coat and trousers, and with his collar and necktie too, if they

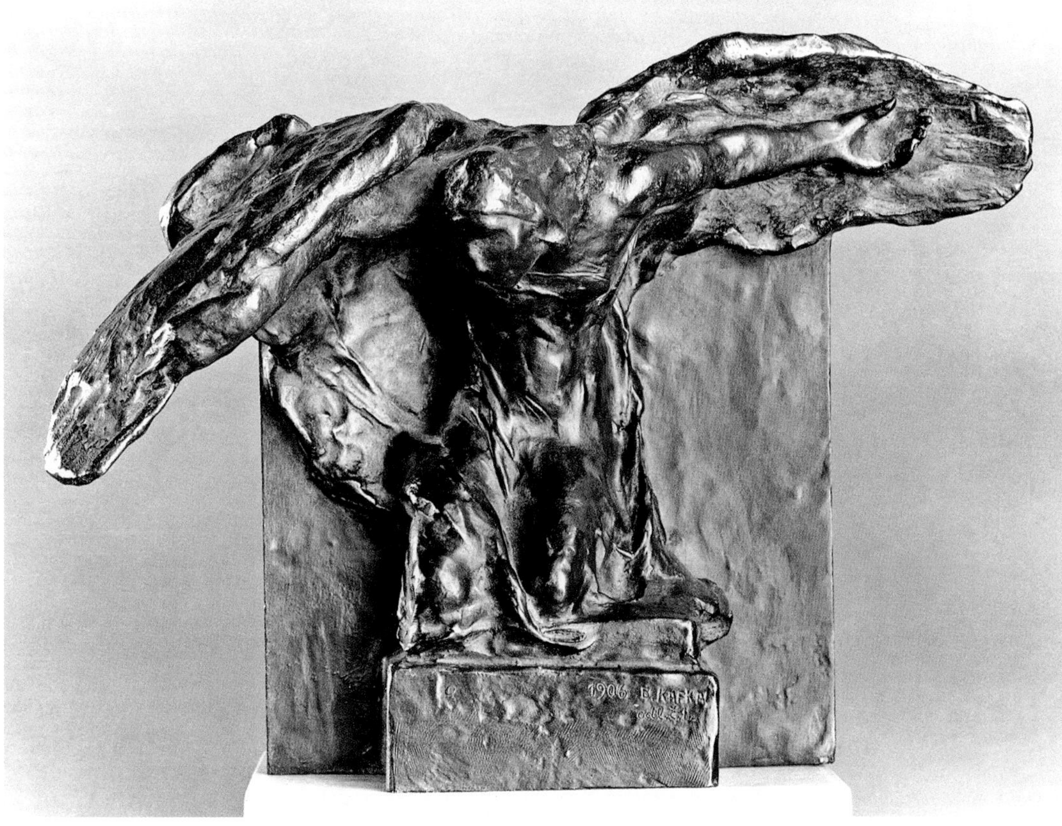

211 Bohumil Kafka, Sketch for *The Embrace of Love and Death*, 1906, bronze, 32.5 cm

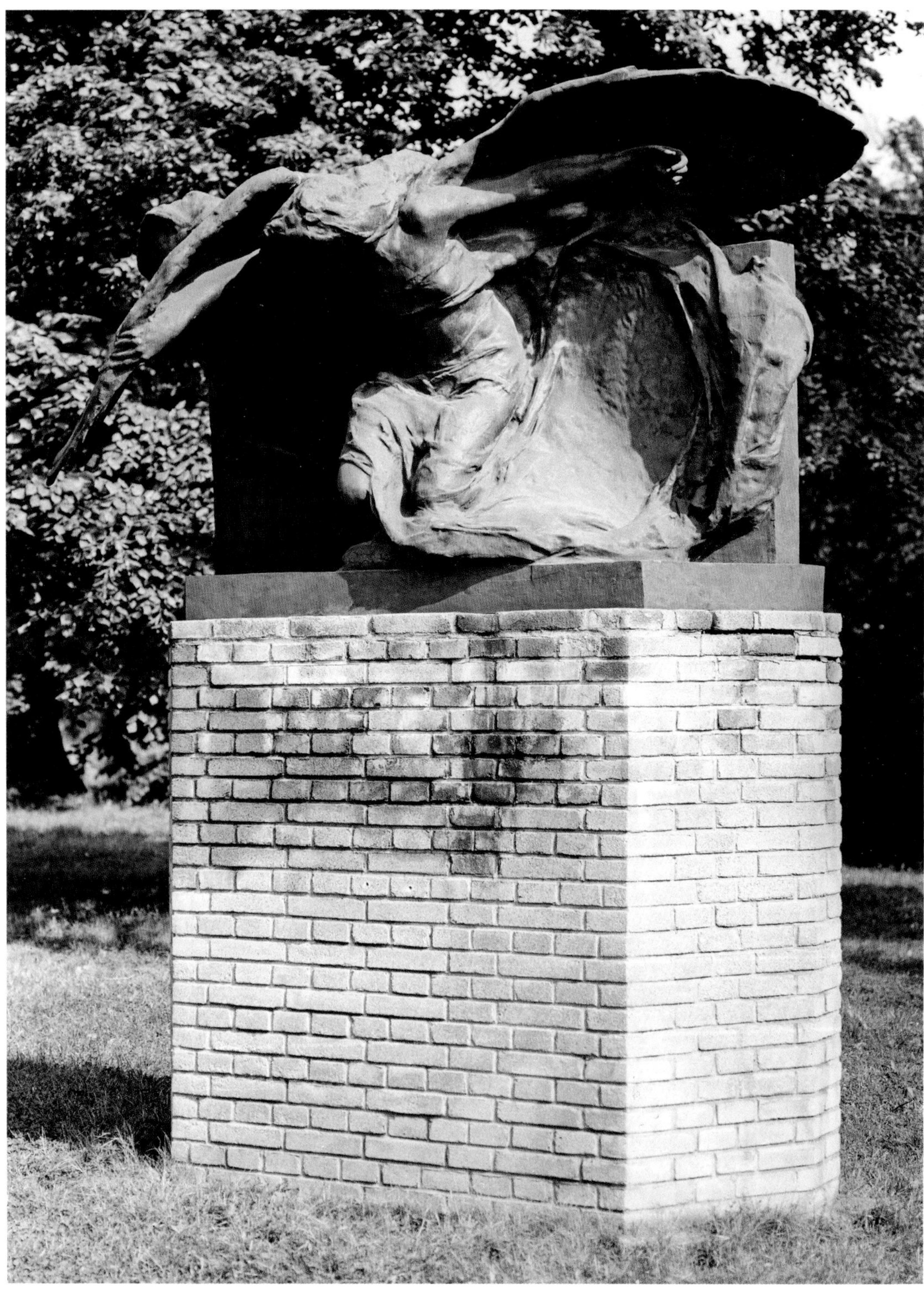

212 Bohumil Kafka, *The Embrace of Love and Death*, 1906–7, bronze, 176 cm

can be found in his estate – and then you will see in this creation a more or less technically accomplished picture of what is external, you will see all that is earthly, all that ends with the death of this man – but that which should be celebrated, the very reason for erecting the memorial … that has been lost entirely.[135]

In his new concept, Sucharda wished instead to present Palacký as the father of the nation. The monument would not be concerned merely with the past, but would embrace "three temporal concepts: the present, which, paying homage to the past, calls forth the future."[136] On either side there were two opposed groups, Oppression and Awakening, connected by the monument's wings to its massive central part. Here, behind Palacký – whose inner vision sees Czech history as a struggle with destiny – an allegorical group spirals up from Fama-History, who tells of the nation's past, to White Mountain (a nude with broken wings), and then to the figure of the Revivalist, who soars up to the top of the monument with its majestic Victory group. Half-size models were made of the sculptures between late 1905 and September 1906. Sucharda's entire workshop was occupied with making the monument, whose rear group of sculptures is nine metres high, and Josef Mařatka assisted Sucharda with the groups at the front. Lastly, the seated figure of Palacký, five metres high, was carved from stone, and in 1912 the monument was finally unveiled.

Sucharda's František Palacký Monument was an ambitious attempt to overcome the crisis in the monument as an art form, something that had been apparent since the late 19th century.[137] Sucharda was familiar with Rodin's *Balzac*, and he tried to approach Palacký in the same spirit: as an evocative medium for the historical, national, and collective forces he represented. Sucharda was concerned with expressing all the pathos of the heroic saga of the nation's history, and linking its victorious outcome with the triumph of a new national art. The dynamism of Sucharda's concept was a great asset, but it was burdened by its romanticism. Above all, two entirely different methods came into conflict here: the idea behind the monument, expressed through an allegorical narrative, had already been defined as its ideological agenda, and what Sucharda had learned from Rodin merely shaped the end result. This is why the Palacký Monument would later be acclaimed for its sculptural details but criticised as a whole – for instance, by F. X. Šalda in his ironic essay "A Plague of Monuments" from 1928. Despite all these difficulties, Sucharda had still succeeded in creating an artistically valuable work that bore the stamp of the present day. Many other monuments made in the Secession's name were less satisfactory. In architecture especially there was a dangerously widespread practice of treating the Secession simply as a set of decorative motifs and forms that could be grafted onto a building's outmoded body. Historical details were merely replaced with natural ornament arranged in a two-dimensional composition, and the Secession became just another "style" on late historicism's palette.

This practice also extended to the most ostentatious new building in Prague from the first decade of the 20th century, the Municipal House (*Obecní dům*), whose construction was initiated by a citizens' association called Měšťanská beseda. In 1903 a competition was held, and the winning projects were by Alois Dryák, Josef Pospíšil, and Antonín Balšánek. A second round was then held, with Osvald Polívka also invited

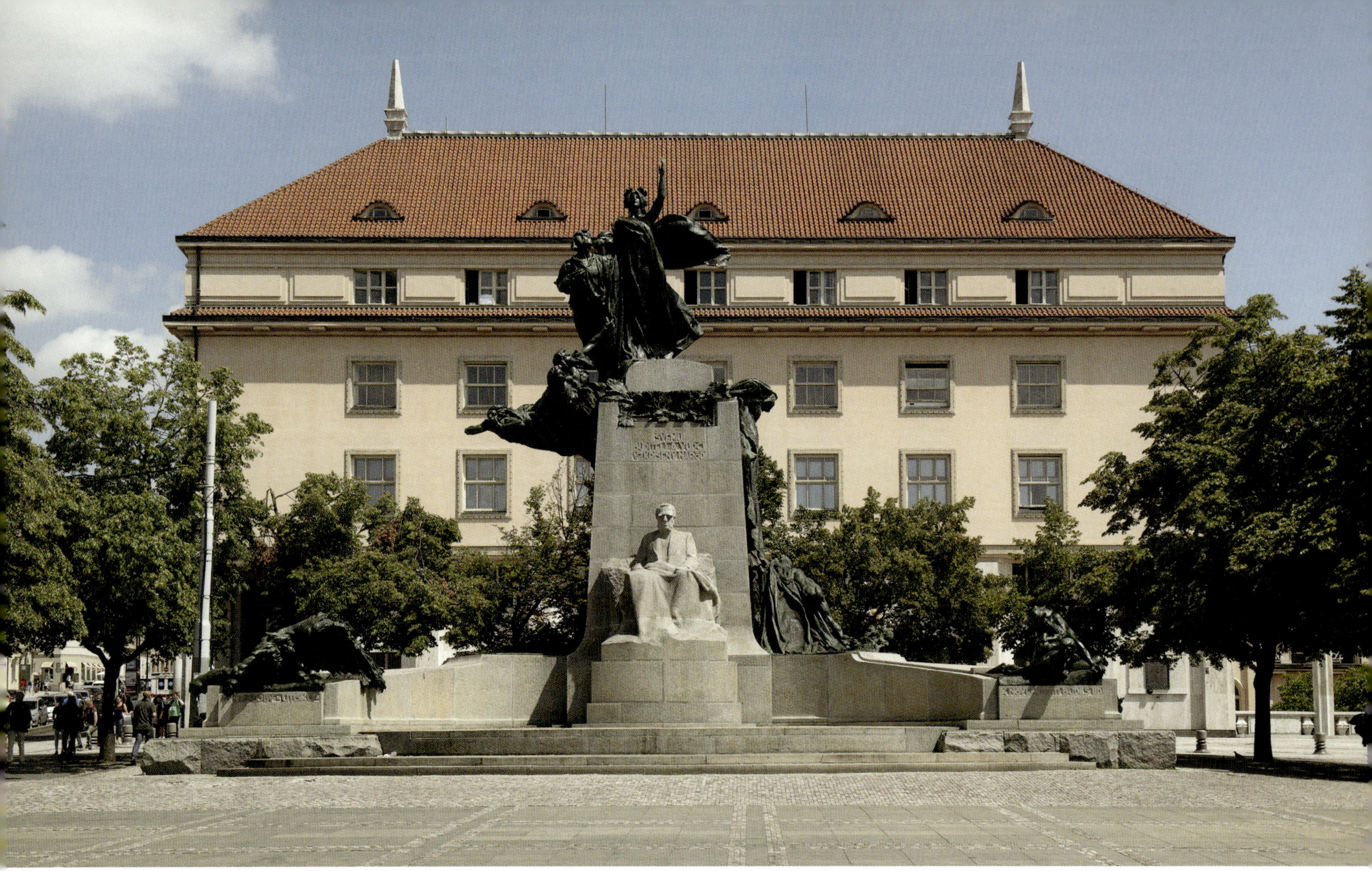

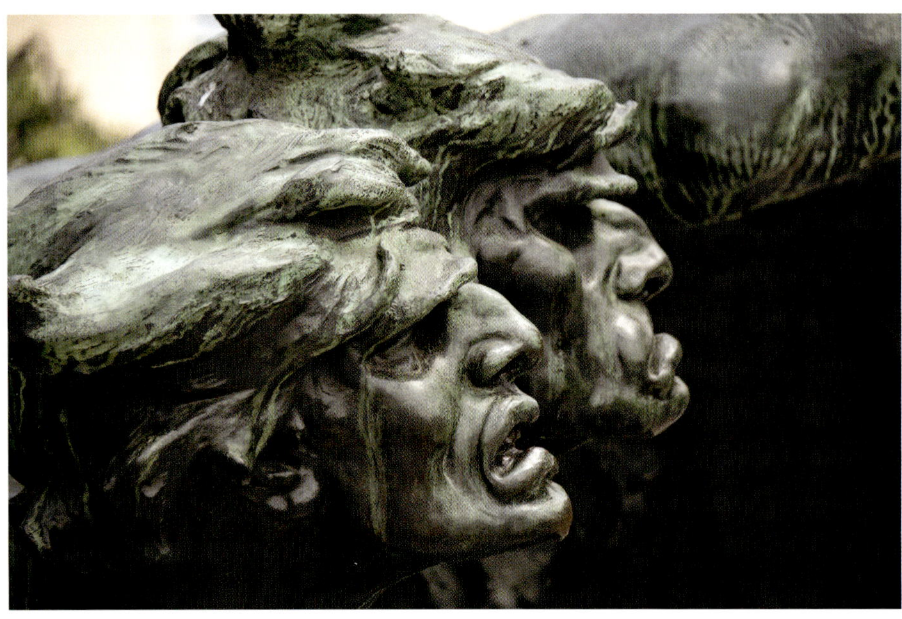

213–215 Stanislav Sucharda, František Palacký Monument in Prague, 1898–1912

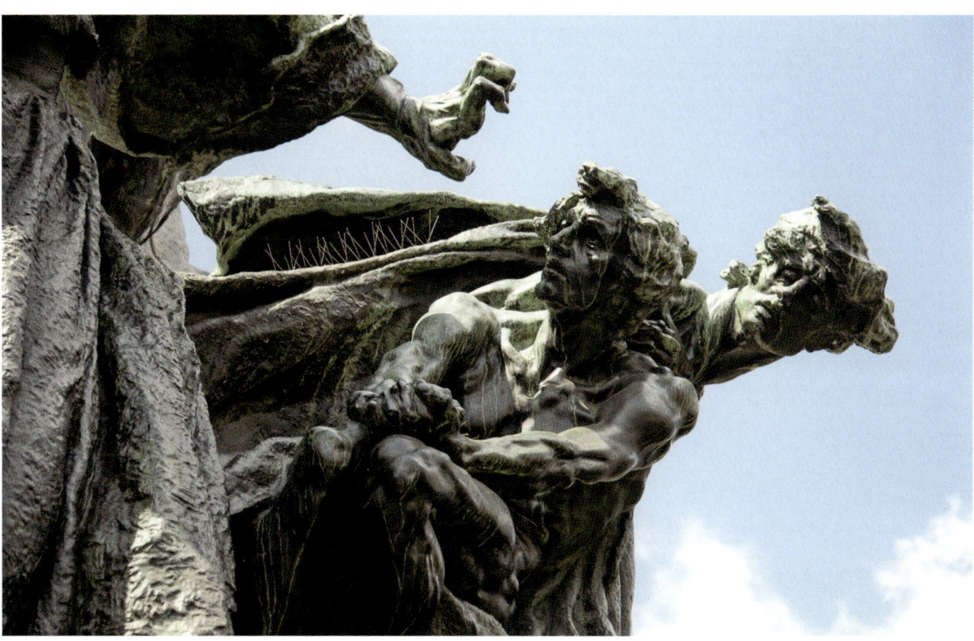

to submit an entry, but it still proved impossible to reach a final verdict. The city council therefore commissioned Balšánek and Polívka to build the Municipal House, and after various delays construction began in 1905 and continued until 1911.

The architects based the Municipal House on Dryák's original design for the ground plan. An axial composition was used for the irregularly shaped site, with the entrance in the central part of the building, signposted by an ornate canopy and topped with a tall dome. On either side of the entrance, wings extended at an oblique angle. At the heart of the Municipal House was its large Smetana Hall, reaching up from floor to ceiling the full height of the building. Around the hall there were a number of reception and exhibition rooms, as well as shops and restaurants.

The contribution made by each architect is still debated today. Antonín Balšánek, who had been taught by Josef Schulz, was a connoisseur of Renaissance and Baroque architecture, which he applied in his designs for the City of Prague Museum and the City Theatre in Pilsen, while his town-planning studies and the Legion Bridge in Prague were more in line with modern requirements. Drawings have been preserved that show he was involved in designing the front façade of the Municipal House and the Smetana Hall. Balšánek exaggerated the motifs used, and to good effect; he did something similar in another of his Secession buildings, the City Theatre in Pardubice (1909). Osvald Polívka evidently played an important role in ultimately giving the Municipal House its Secession character.

The Municipal House represented the city, and this made it a showcase for contemporary Czech painting, sculpture, and applied art. Individual artists worked on the decor for the various halls and reception rooms.

Karel Špillar, the author of the mosaic on the front façade with the theme of the apotheosis of Prague, produced his most important wall paintings for the Smetana Hall, where *Music*, *Dance*, *Poetry*, and *Drama* reflected what he had learned from French examples and from working with Jan Preisler. Špillar had originally been commissioned to produce for the façade a depiction of George of Poděbrady at the diet, with scenes from Smetana's operas for the concert hall. By working instead with lyrical allegories he contributed greatly to the building's Secession character. This prepared visitors for Jan Preisler's large decorative paintings in the Palacký Salon on the theme of the golden age of mankind, in much richer colours. A more realistic counterpart to Preisler's dream were Max Švabinský's *Czech Spring* paintings in the Rieger Salon, with his groups of modern Czech writers, artists, and composers a synthesis of his many years' experience of portraiture. Of the sculptors who worked on the Municipal House, Ladislav Šaloun was particularly successful with his large allegorical sculptural

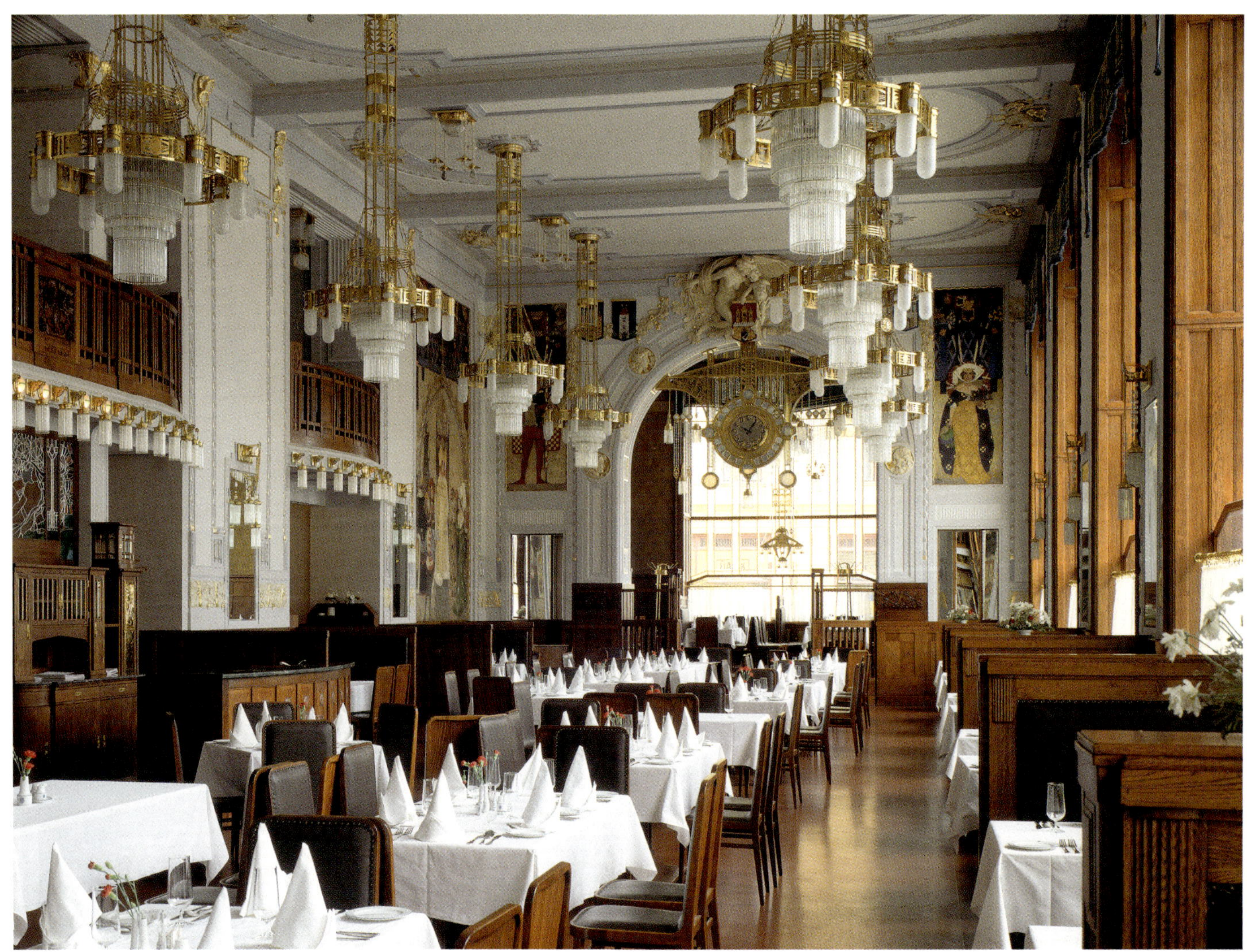

216 Antonín Balšánek and Osvald Polívka, Grand Restaurant of the Municipal House in Prague, 1905–11

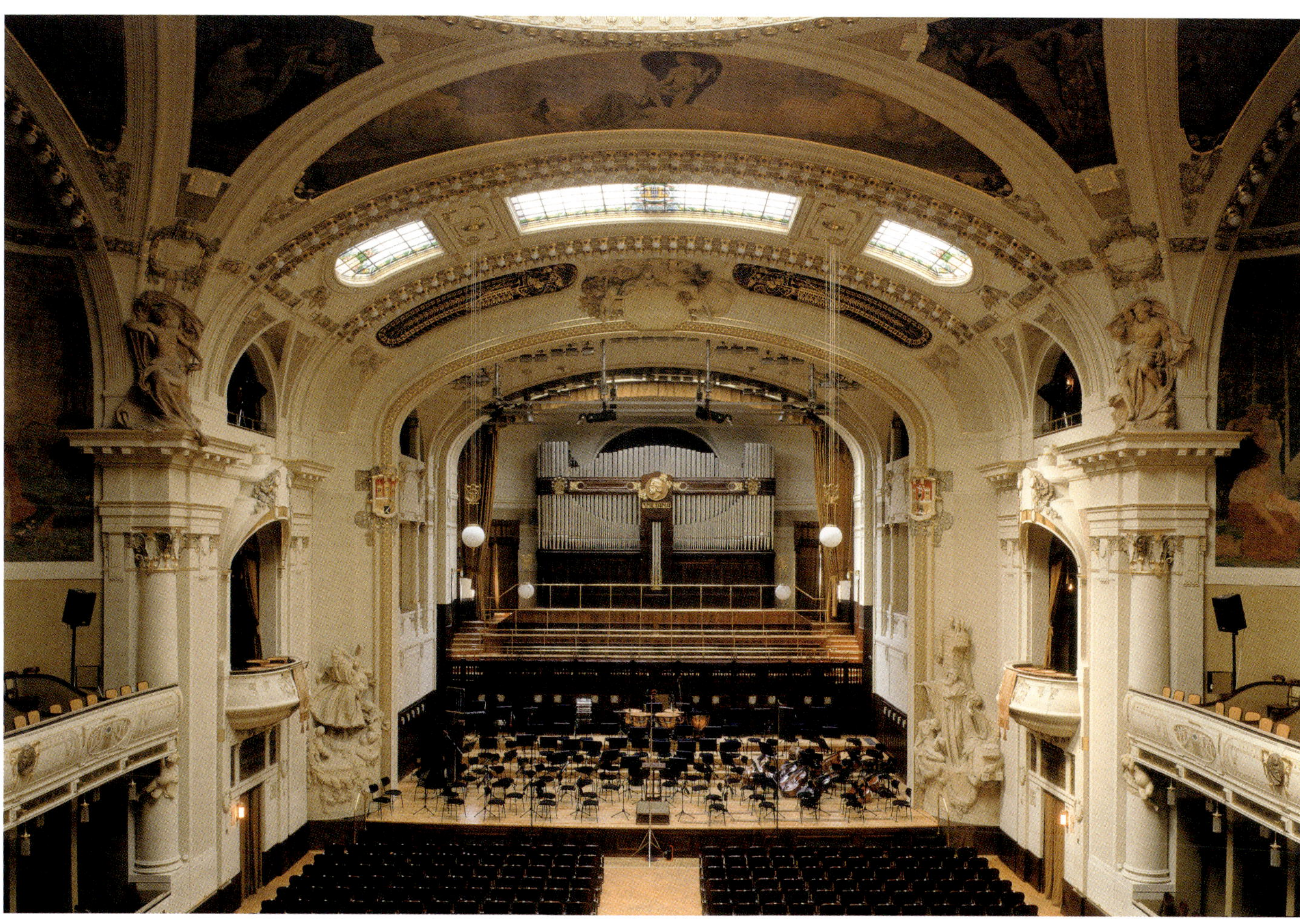

groups, showing the *Humiliation* and *Resurrection of the Nation* on the entrance façade, and *Slav Dances* and *Vyšehrad* on the proscenium of the Smetana Hall.

The paintings for the Mayor's Salon, located at the very centre of the building's front, were entrusted to Alphonse Mucha. He worked on them in 1910, having returned to his homeland after many years in France and the United States. His allegorical and symbolic paintings have a markedly nationalistic subtext. On the pedentives are famous figures from Czech history, representing civic virtues. The impressive ceiling painting shows a ring of people working beneath spreading fruit trees, while a mythical eagle soars overhead.

Mucha's paintings for the Municipal House had provoked much debate even before he began painting them. In 1909, when the commission was being discussed, Prague's art critics had voiced their strong opposition to him, and F. X. Šalda had not hesitated to question the artistic value of Mucha's work.[138] Mucha himself considered these attacks to be prompted by local backwardness and envy, but in fact Czech art had developed very rapidly since the late 19th century, when Mucha's posters had enchanted all who saw them. Especially in the latter half of the first decade of the new century, the differentiation of Czech art had advanced at such a pace that very diverse values were now beginning to appear on the horizon. For Šalda, Mucha lacked

217 Antonín Balšánek and Osvald Polívka, Smetana Hall of the Municipal House in Prague, 1905–11

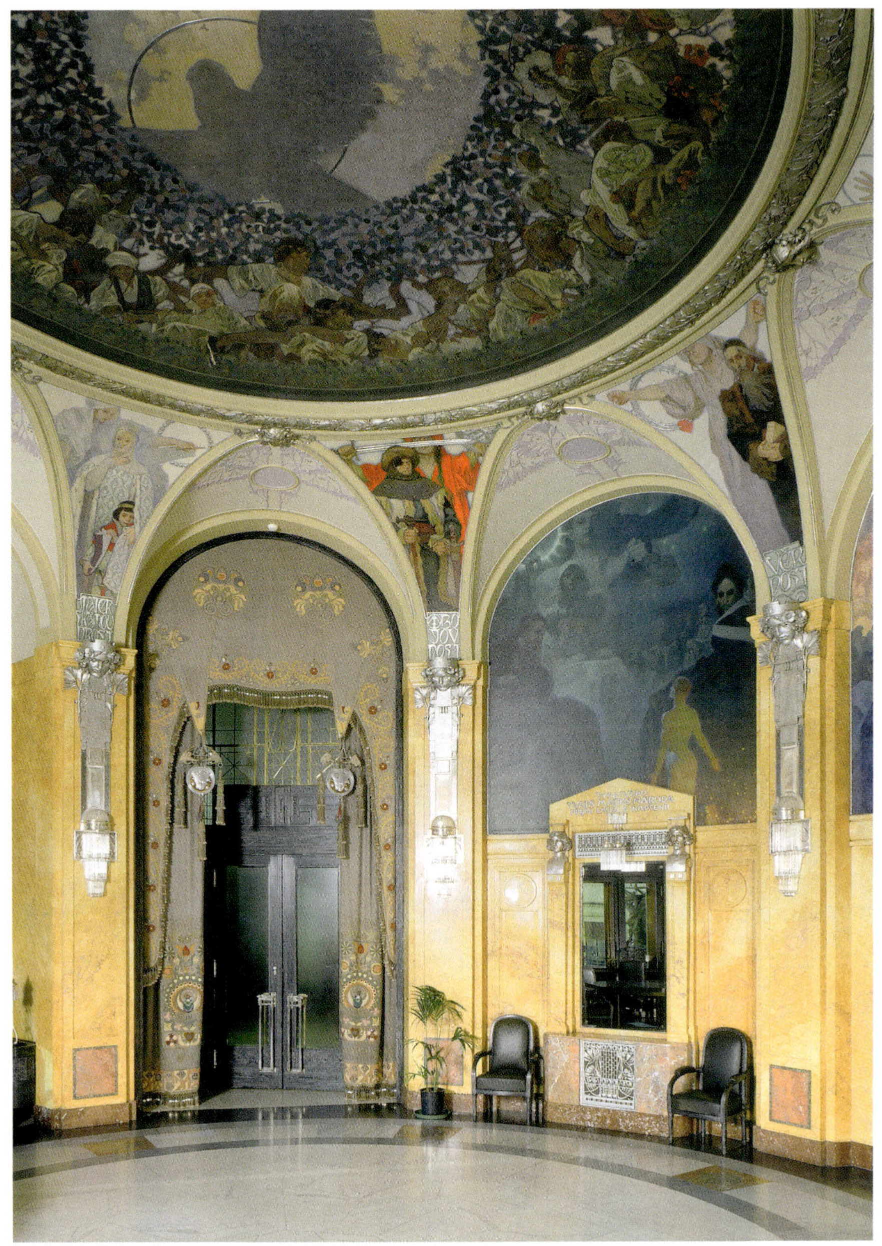

what he considered the most important quality – creativity – and what he saw instead was a virtuous decorativeness whose familiar cosmopolitan form had merely been filled with nationalistic subject matter. The crux of his criticism was that Mucha's art had insufficient inner unity. This opened up a fundamental problem concerning the Secession's overall perspective.

At this time, Mucha was already planning a cycle of large paintings on the history of the Slavs, and he would spend the rest of his life working on it. In 1911–12 he painted

218 Antonín Balšánek and Osvald Polívka, Mayor's Salon of the Municipal House in Prague, 1905–11

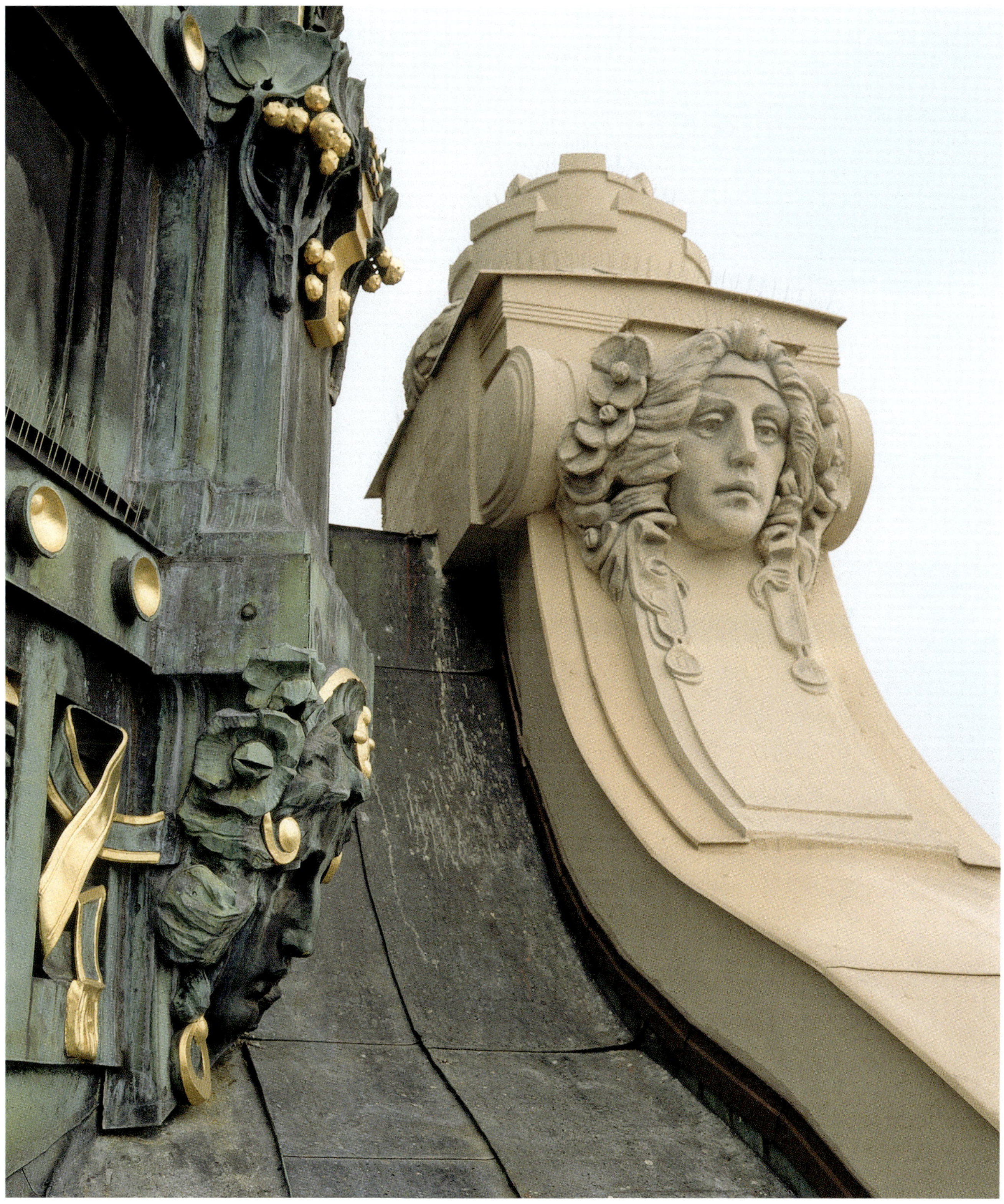

219 Antonín Balšánek and Osvald Polívka, Municipal House in Prague, 1905–11, detail of the dome

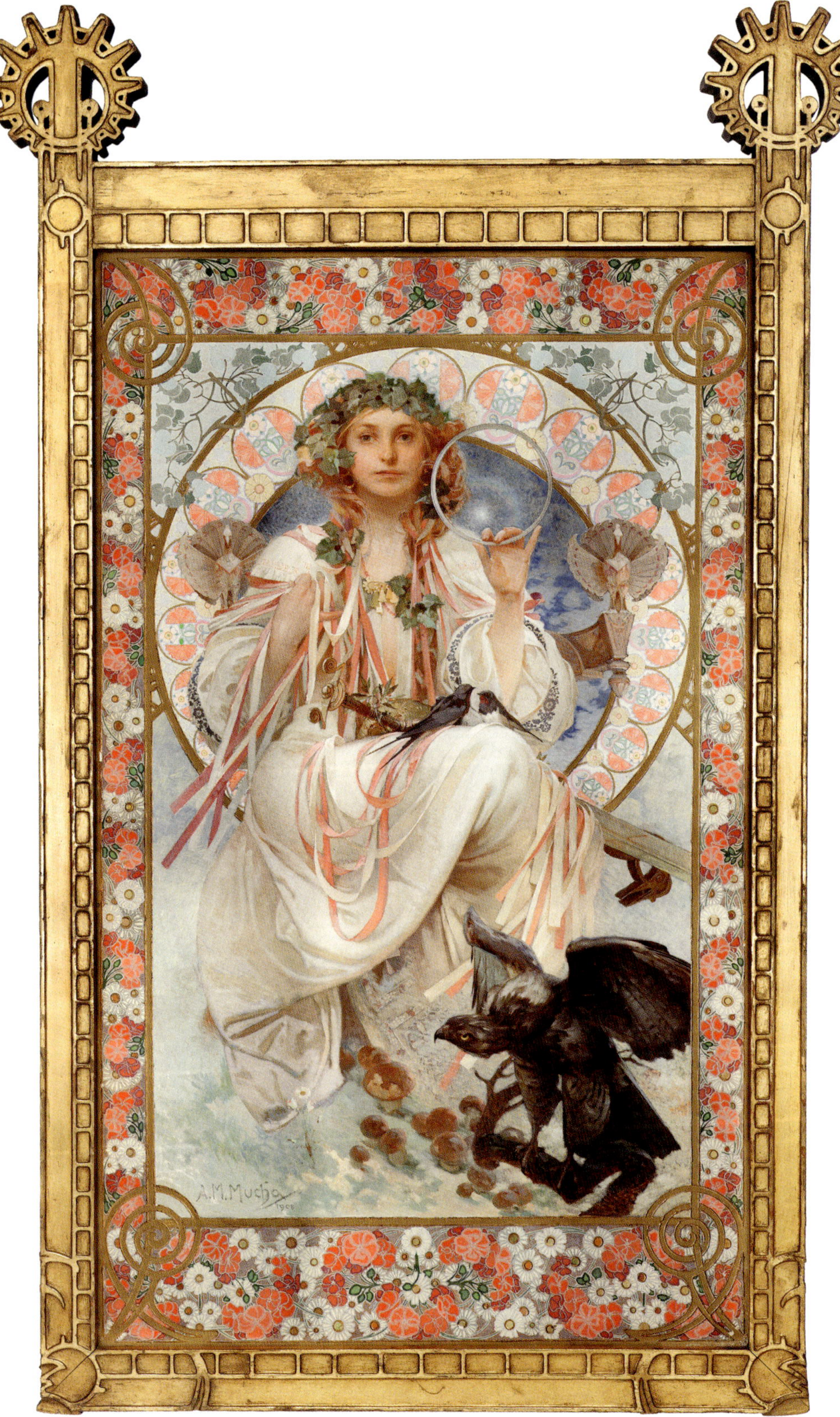

220 Alphonse Mucha, *Slavia*, 1908, oil and tempera, 154 × 92.5 cm

the first three large canvases of his *Slav Epic*, depicting the Slavs in their original homeland, the pagan festival of the Sun, and Methodius bringing the papal bull that made the Slavonic tongue a liturgical language. In these paintings he combined symbols with a decorative immobilising of the narrative, interweaving reality and fantasy by including enlarged figural details in the naturalistic scenery. However, the cycle's subsequent development abandoned this mythical symbolism in favour of an illusionistic consolidation of the picture space. This could logically be explained by the cycle's transition from mythical beginnings to real historical events, but from an artistic perspective the cycle had lost its integrity, and the paintings increasingly became mere illustrations of a distinctive "philosophy of history." Mucha had essentially returned, albeit at a more elevated level, to the illustrated history cycles with which he had started. The disk he frequently gave his figures as an emblem was ultimately only a circle, and he was becoming ever more remote from contemporary developments in art.

The discussion over Mucha in 1909 brought to an end an epoch that had been characterised by the symbolic and decorative reappraisal of the Secession's naturalist foundation. However, this did not mark the end of the Secession as such, because only when naturalism's dominance of contemporary art had been exhausted could the other components of the Secession's reduction be fully developed and play their part in its evolution. These processes had become more pronounced in the latter half of the first decade, when the significance of the symbolic and decorative ornamental components of art was revived on a new synthetic foundation, and the Secession culminated in a dramatic differentiation of opinions that severed its last remaining ties with the 19th century.

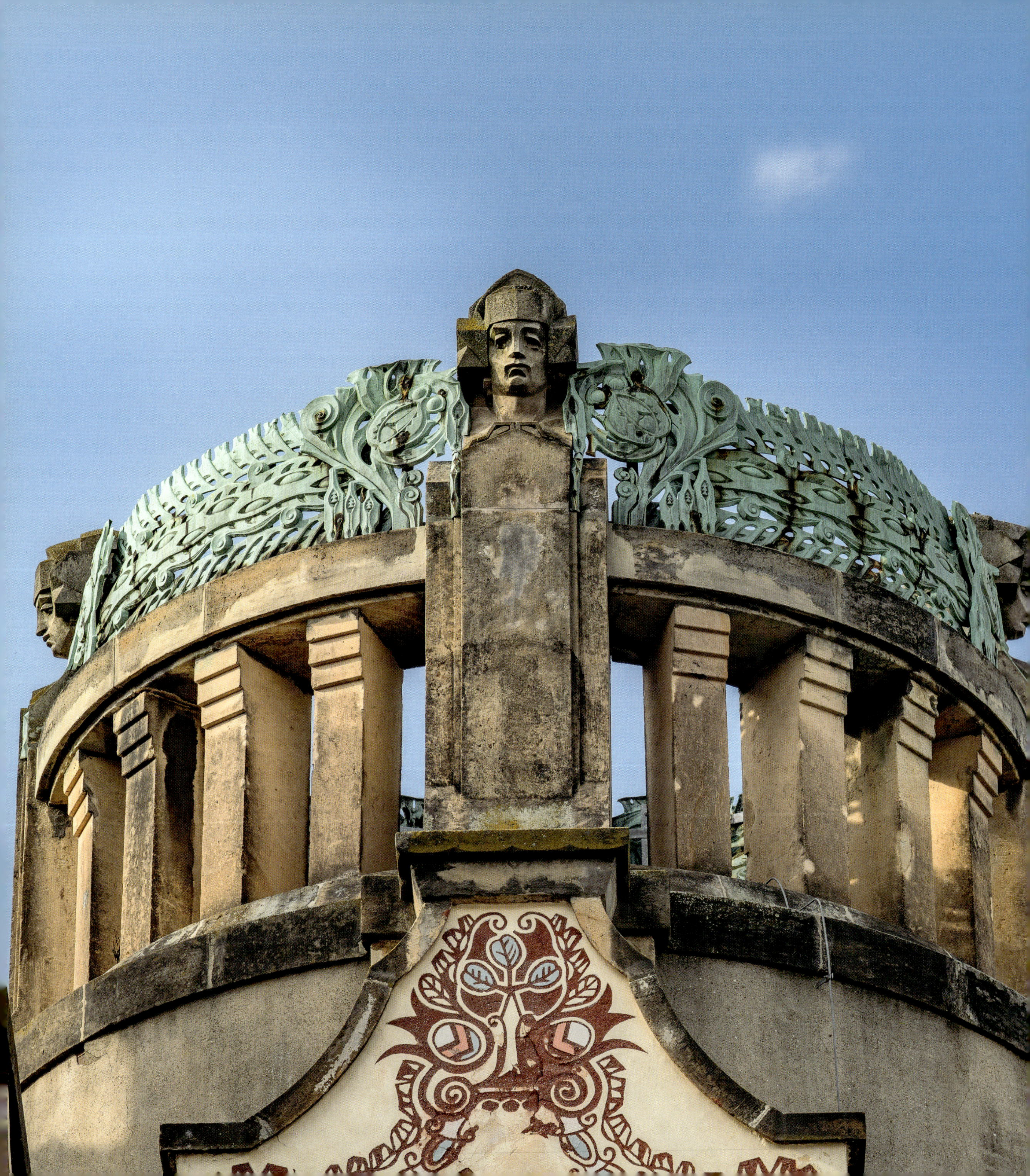

SYNTHESIS

In early 1905 SVU Mánes held an exhibition of the work of Edvard Munch that would initiate a splitting of opinions within the Czech Secession. Munch's work had already appeared on the pages of *Moderní revue*, but then he had been seen more as an illustrator of Decadent literature, especially the Satanism of Stanisław Przybyszewski, whose portrait was included in the Prague exhibition. Now, however, Czech artists had to come to terms with Munch as a painter, and this brought to the surface all the contradictions previously obscured by the Secession's liberal enthusiasm. It was not Munch's subject matter that was surprising, but his treatment of it. The boldness with which he expressed mental states, in pure, vivid colours, produced strong reactions.

K. B. Mádl rejected Munch outright, describing his paintings as "coarse, savage, unruly daubs of paint, combined with forms so shapeless that they are a mockery of their real archetypes." He criticised Munch as a painter who "does not even want to paint, because the entire objective of his art lies beyond the world of picturesque sensuousness, and it cannot be captured by the devices available to the art of painting." According to Mádl, Munch lacked the capacity for a painterly understanding of the existence of life and nature, and had only taken up representative art in error. He did not understand form, and his sense of colour was only open to impressions such as those that prehistoric cave dwellers had grasped. Munch had artificially returned to the fumbling childhood of hand and eye, to the nakedness of prehistoric man. He was conducting the most extreme anarchical opposition to any shade of naturalism. Mádl charged that his

> wild phantasms and neuropathological convulsions are born from a mind wrought with pain, and it is therefore impolite to ridicule him; nevertheless, his excesses cannot be considered a revelation that will reform art. If his art is healthy and strong, then of course everything else is unhealthy and diseased, and if it is displayed to us in the pavilion beneath the Kinský Garden in this conviction, then it would be of paramount importance to turn all our values upside down.[139]

To this, Miloš Jiránek retorted that Munch was by no means as isolated in modern painting as some Czech critics thought, and he listed Van Gogh and Cézanne – "two masters who I believe are entirely unknown in this country" – as examples of a similar position, together with Toulouse-Lautrec and Whistler. For Jiránek, Munch was a painter who

> has cast off all indifferent technical finishing, nor are there any traces of any kind of school, because for him ordinary reality simply cannot suffice. His path is a precarious one, but for him it is propitious and prosperous, for behind each brushstroke you sense that he is always summing up several painterly observations and hinting at multiple perspectives. He is walking the audacious paths of pure subjectivism,

221 Jan Kotěra, National House and theatre in Prostějov, 1905–7, detail of the theatre façade

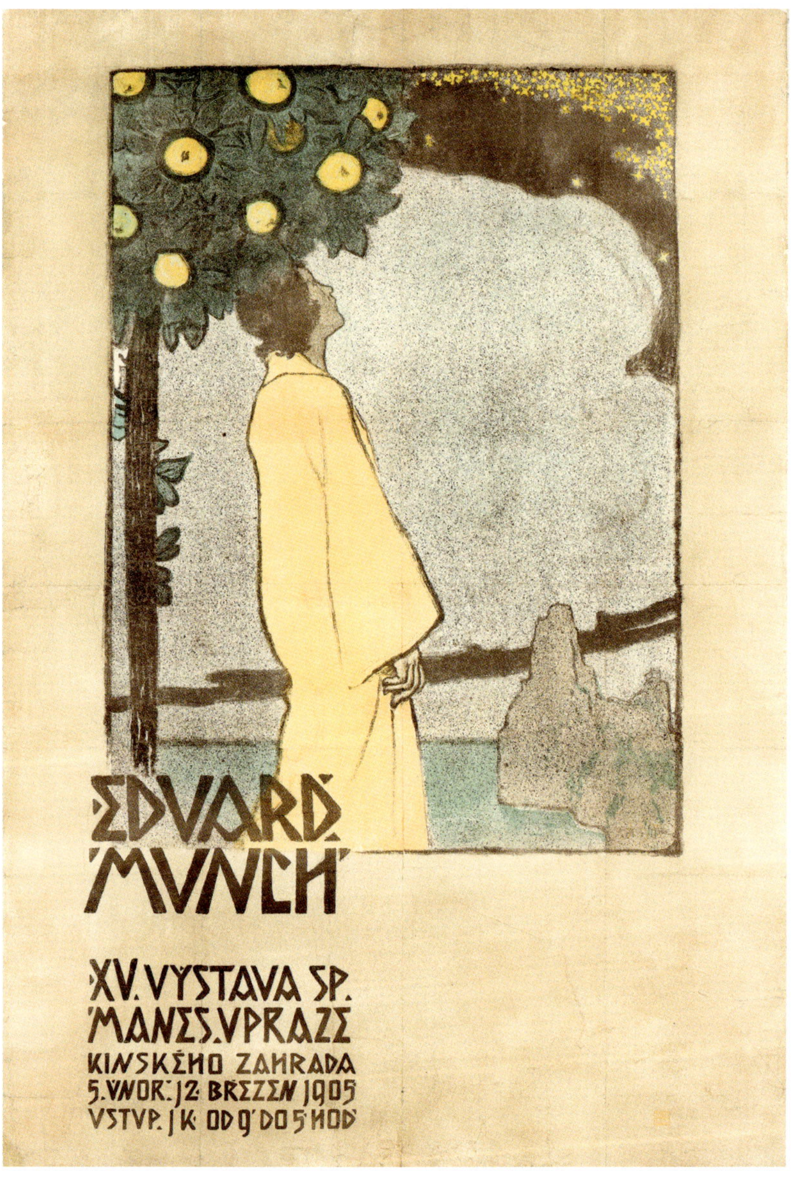

> and is supremely exposed to incomprehension. His new greatness is that he has extended the content of today's art by a whole series of modern-day pains and sorrows, gifts that are cheerless yet familiar and dear to us, for they are the pains and sorrows of all of us modern people.[140]

F. X. Šalda then recapitulated the critical battle waged over Munch. He came out in favour of Jiránek, and declared that Mádl had been unmasked. Šalda wrote that there had had to be a shock such as Munch's painting in order to dispel all the "cleverness, conformist 'progressiveness' and benevolent indifference that can so easily deceive in this country, and which are so easily taken for critical intellect." Munch had tested Czech criticism's sense of the true creative values of modern art, and he

222 Jan Preisler, Poster for the Edvard Munch exhibition in Prague, 1905, colour lithograph, 157.5 × 101 cm

had stripped bare its "bankrupts."[141] Šalda's assault on Mádl was pitiless, in the spirit of the highly personal polemics of the time, but he aptly expressed how the criteria Mádl had brought to bear on Munch not only missed the essence of his art, but also demonstrated how Mádl's "mood" concept was superficial and pointed more to what Secession art had carried over from the 19th century, while being oblivious to what were truly the new problems.

Šalda himself did not hold up Munch as a template for the "progress" of modern art. In his essay "The Dream Violator," he pointed to the markedly individual characteristics of Munch's art, commenting that Munch could only be followed by those with an inner compulsion, who were predestined to do so by everything inside them. For mere imitators, Munch presented a great danger, because like all "dream violators" he tended to obstruct the paths of progress rather than levelling and simplifying them.[142]

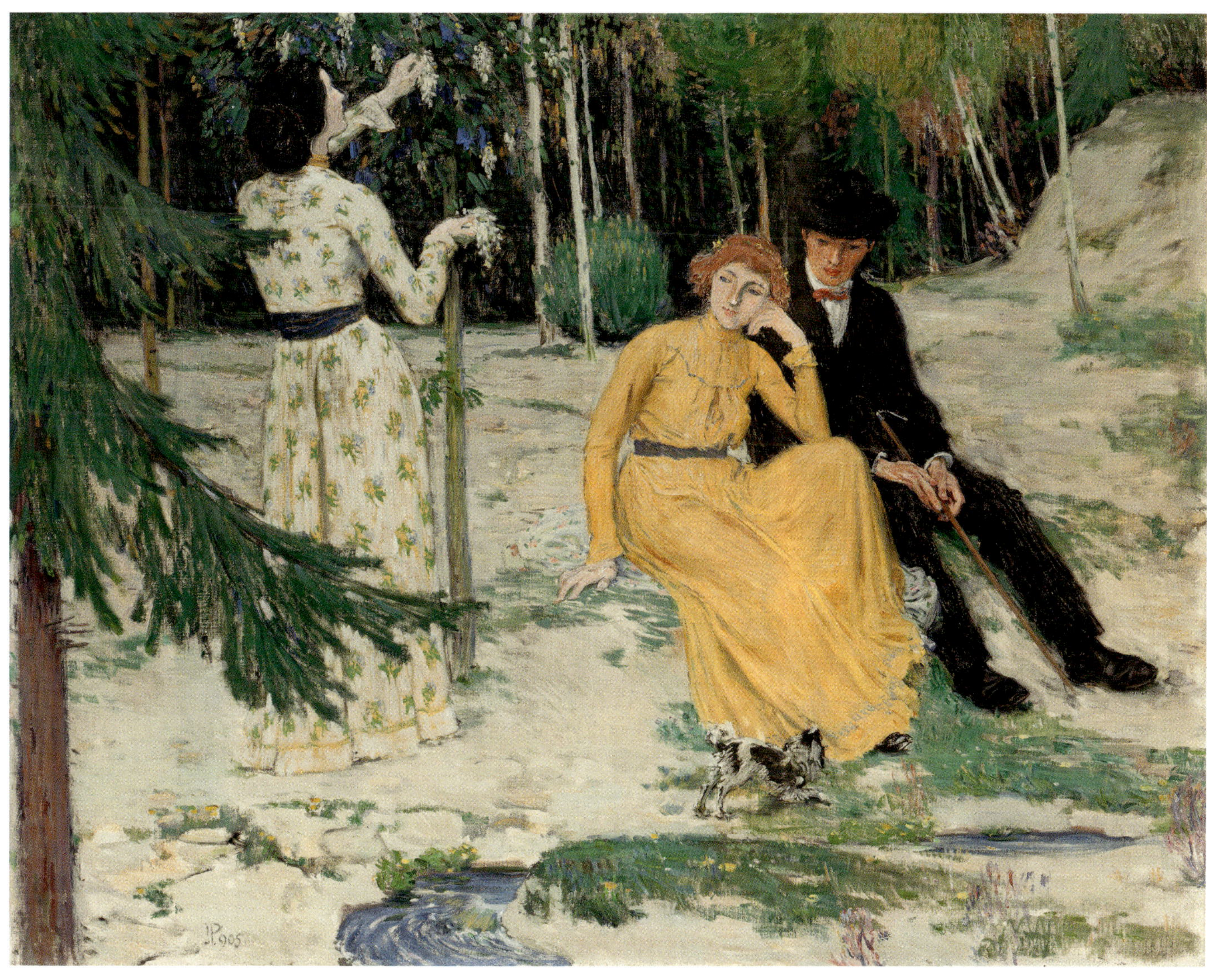

223 Jan Preisler, *Lovers*, 1905, oil, 120 × 150 cm

For artists and critics alike, the Munch exhibition raised difficult questions, for it went to the very heart of Czech art's naturalistic orientation. They were won over by the authenticity with which Munch expressed the modern individual's tragic sense of life. In a letter, Antonín Slavíček wrote:

> There is a superb exhibition by Munch here. It is worth seeing, but not just that – it is worth much more. You lose your taste for many things when you see a man so serious, who in fact paints only the greatest cries of pain and tremors of the soul, too subtle for him to be understood by all. However, in his moments of pain Munch has lost his pleasure in natural beauty – and sometimes he makes fools of people, but with a twisted smile, the kind that pain brings forth in strong characters.[143]

Of the Czech figure painters, Jan Preisler had the greatest affinity with Munch. Besides drawing the poster for the exhibition, he also accompanied the Norwegian painter during his brief stay in Prague. The exhibition's influence is evident in Preisler's greater intensity of colour and the colourful stylisation of his paintings on the theme of *Woman and Rider* from 1905, where there is a more fateful confrontation between man and woman. His series of paintings of *Lovers* (1905–6) also has something of Munch in the intersection between the individual and the universal. Yet it was not the Munch of *The Frieze of Life* cycle and his Decadent and Symbolist period during the 1890s who now interested Preisler, but the present-day Munch. This was the Munch of Jiránek's "third" category, who "after the discipline of the pain and mental torment of which *Life* tells, has returned to reality with remarkably sharper eyes, and what he himself experienced so keenly and painfully he has learned to see in others." These are paintings in which there is life "that has recovered."[144]

In 1906 Preisler painted his large *Spring*, showing two barefoot young women in a meadow by a forest. Its yellow and green colours, which would typify Preisler's work over the next few years, were taken from the rustic jug that is central to the painting's composition. This too was something suggested by Jiránek, who was no longer writing about folk art and architecture as a critic of the former folklorism, but highlighting them as a resource from which even the most modern artist could draw.[145] At this time, Preisler also painted *Still Life from Moravian Slovakia*. It shows a group of traditional jugs standing on a table covered with a tablecloth, and on the wall behind the jugs hangs one of his versions of *Woman and Rider*, a detail that also seems to indicate the greater influence of Jiránek's "Impressionist" aesthetic, which had lost nothing of its expressiveness or sense of artistic value.

Preisler's earlier theme from *Temptation* also underwent a certain transformation. The knight has been replaced by a village youth, and the female personifications who turn to him are more the inviting voices of life, giving the whole a greater sense of tranquillity and reconciliation. These qualities were reinforced by Preisler's work on the ornamentation for Kotěra's architecture. He had already created a decoratively balanced arrangement of figures in nature for the restaurant of the District House in Hradec Králové, and in 1906–7 he developed this inspiration further in a pair of paintings for the vestibule of Kotěra's theatre in Prostějov. Temptation was symmetrised here by the motif of woman and rider, again in a characteristic combination of real

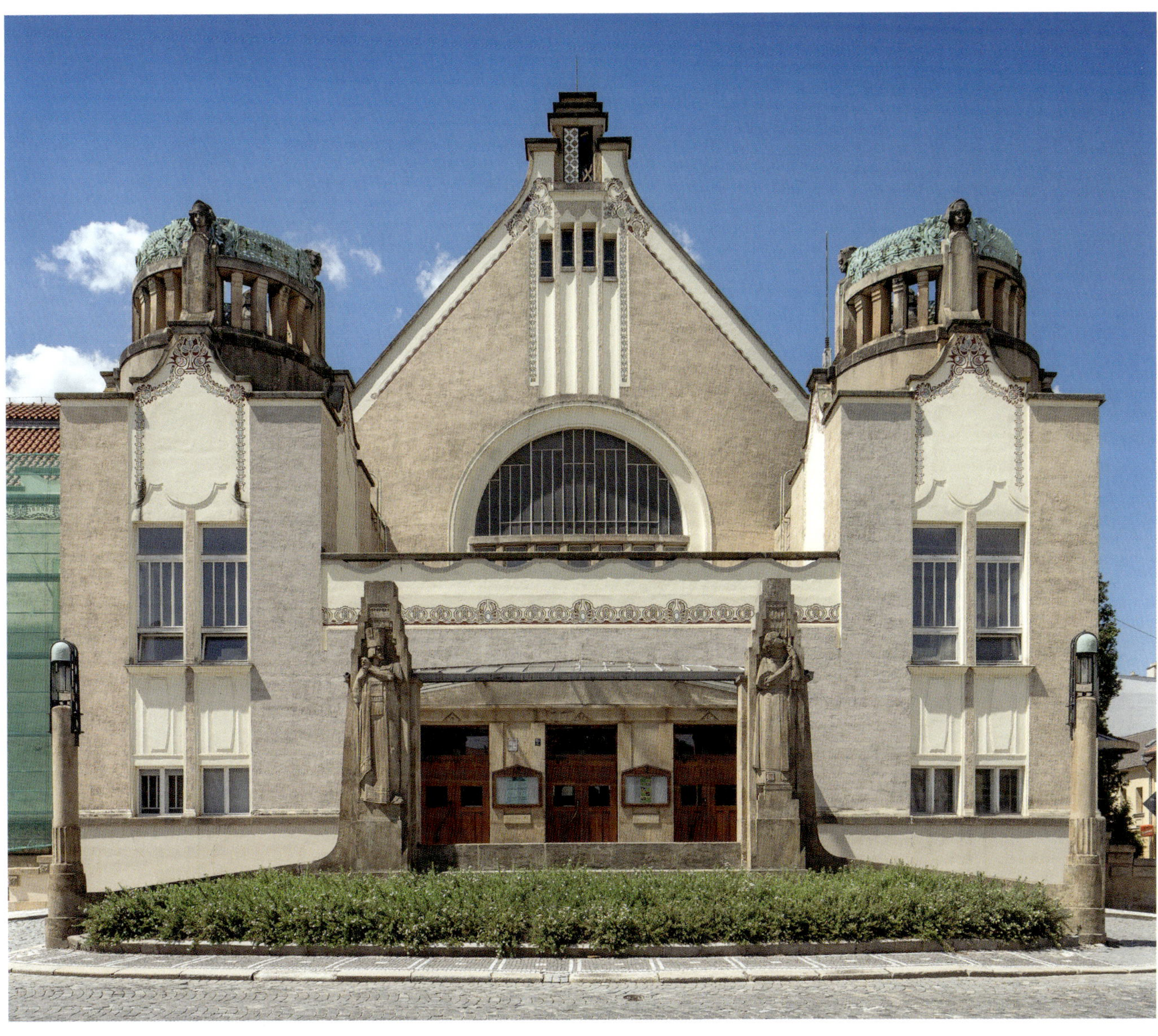

and symbolic abstract elements. Preisler's mythology was therefore incorporated into a more extensive arrangement, while retaining in the paintings the Secession's typical range between real individuality and ideal collectivity in the diagonal developing of the otherwise planar motifs. Artistically, there was also a greater synthesising tendency that united the naturalistic, symbolic, and decorative elements.

Kotěra's National House (*Národní dům*) in Prostějov (1905–7) was his first large free-standing structure. The commission included a theatre and another building housing a restaurant and function rooms. They were arranged in two main elevations, as a block comprising two masses set perpendicular to one another. The theatre has the more resplendent façade. It employs the familiar motif of pylon towers, between which there is a tall triangular gable with a triumphal arch. Comparing Kotěra's National House with other contemporary Secession buildings, we see that here too there was an attempt to balance the National House's utilitarian and ceremonial roles. The

224 Jan Kotěra, National House and theatre in Prostějov, 1905–7

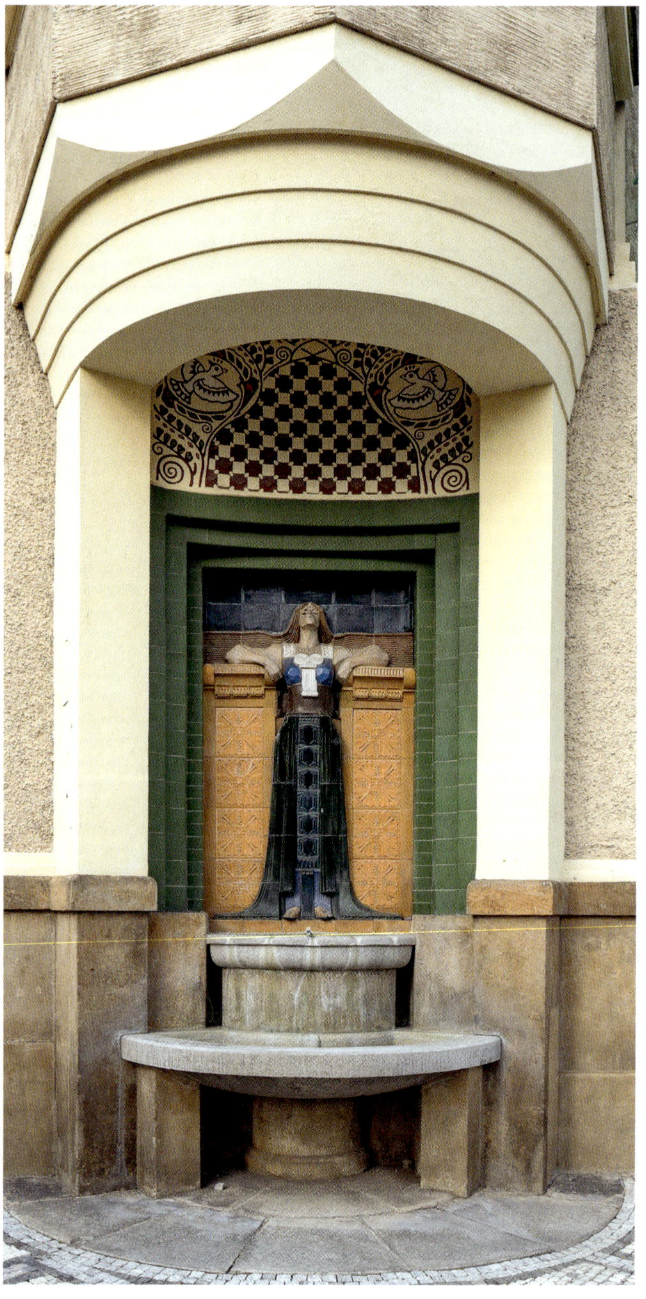

ornamentation was not used for its own sake, but had a number of specific meanings. This is particularly apparent in the theatre's vestibule, where the ornamentation creates the requisite link between Preisler's paintings, completing what they signify. The ornament that Kotěra used in Prostějov was of a different character from Klouček's naturalistic ornament, which had so far been the most popular. While Klouček's work tended to spread over an entire building, Kotěra preferred to create clearly defined areas whose stylisation increased the role of the more abstract geometrical element.

225 Jan Kotěra, Fountain with a sculpture by Stanislav Sucharda at the National House and theatre in Prostějov, 1905–7

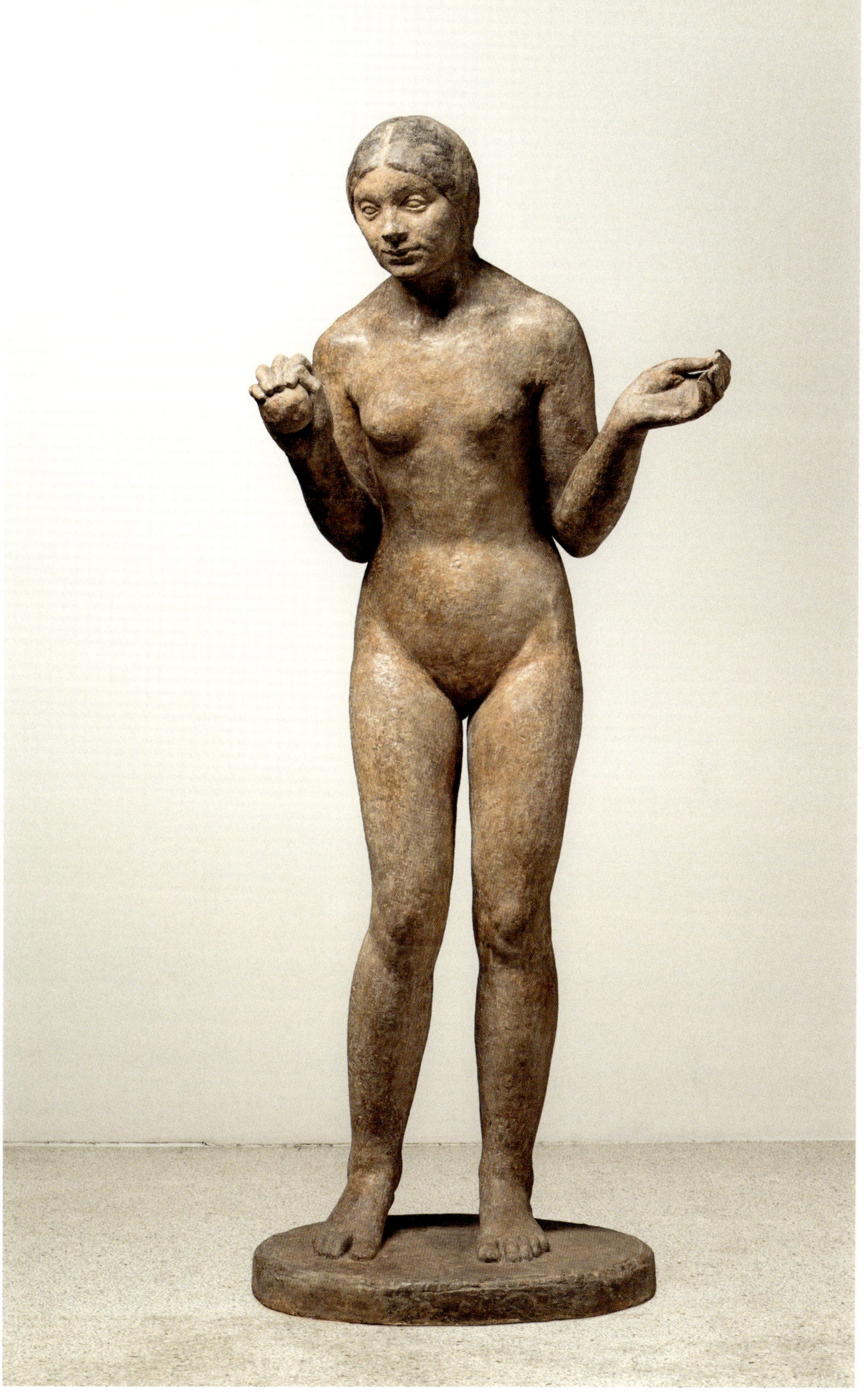

226 Jan Štursa, *Eve*, 1908–9, bronze, 190 cm

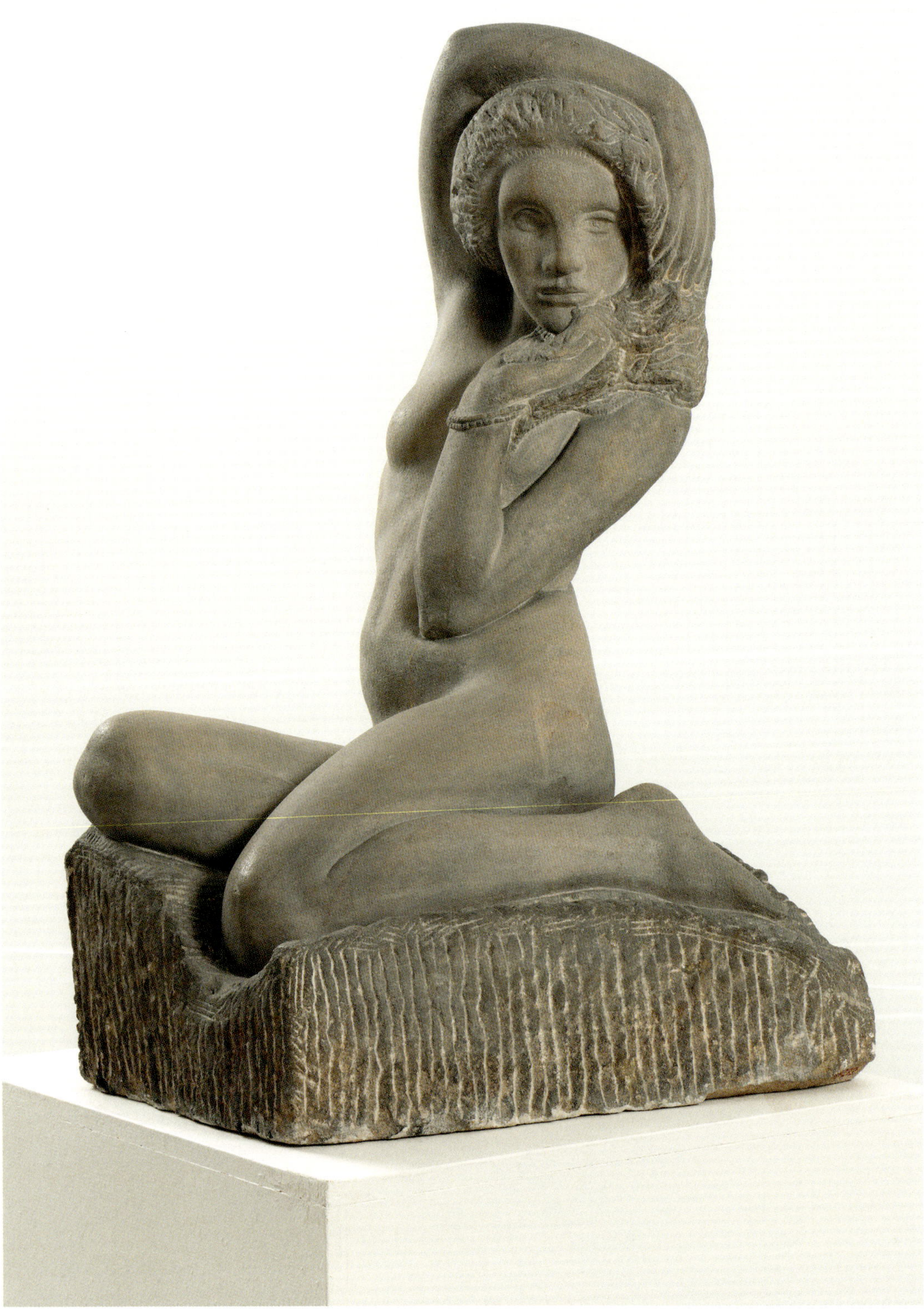

227 Jan Štursa, *Melancholy Girl*, 1906, French limestone, 90 cm

This is apparent in his candelabras for Prostějov, although they are still relatively small and overly complicated. This tendency proved key to future developments; as usual, the groundwork first took shape in the concept for the interior. The reception salon at the National House in Prostějov, decorated with František Kysela's simply stylised paintings and furnished with cuboid furniture, was a direct model for the changes that would ultimately suppress the Secession curve in favour of the right angle. The starting point for the salon was the decoration of the entrance rotunda for the SVU Mánes pavilion in Prague, which Kotěra undertook for the association's exhibition in 1905. Executed in a bold, fiery orange, the rotunda perhaps reflected how Munch's colours assailed the viewer. Straight white borders around the individual blocks added an element of discipline, giving formal definition to the powerful visual emotion produced by the colour.

The effect that Munch's paintings produced similarly consisted in the way he was able to combine the expressiveness of colour with a certain stylisation of form, and how he used a soft line to enclose blocks of colour within larger arrangements. Although these were rather amorphous, when compared with the aggressiveness of the pure colours they had a calming effect, in the manner of some kind of improvised ornaments. This was also apparent in his painting *Dance on the Beach*, which Stanislav Sucharda bought at the exhibition. It seems that Munch's inner tension between expressiveness and stylisation appealed to Czech artists, who were currently preoccupied with the same problem.

This attempt to capture rich emotional content in a pregnant artistic form also characterised Jan Štursa's 1906 sculpture *Melancholy Girl*. A young graduate from Myslbek's studio, Štursa was one of the circle around *Moderní revue*, and his first attempts at Symbolist sculpture were based on literary ideas. Initially they also reflected the influence of František Bílek, as can be seen in the titles Štursa gave his sketches: *The Pure Soul Tames the Passions*, *Thus Sin Always Betrays Us*, and others in a similar vein. Štursa was also influenced by Impressionism, and when modelling in wax he sought to express the fleeting mental states associated with a sense of doom or intimations of transcendence (*Life Passes Swiftly*, 1904, or the unfinished *Nirvana*). Yet Štursa had also studied stonemasonry, and his feel for his specific material and the construction of form was fundamental to his artistic personality. *Melancholy Girl*, carved in limestone, was an accomplished fusion of his talents. Contemporary Czech sculpture generally drew on Rodin's dramatic modelling, but Štursa's sculpture was extraordinary for the definiteness and purity of its form. His peers recognised it as a true symbol of the time, summarising the poetic concept of youth as the central theme in Czech Secession art.

The first sketch for *Melancholy Girl* has been preserved. Štursa drew it over smaller sketches of funerary works, which suggests he was recording an idea that had come to him quite spontaneously. This context, attesting to Štursa's originality, offers a parallel with Munch's way of extracting artistic form from his mournful sense of the crisis of life and death. The sitting girl's face resembles a mask, and her body twists in the shape of a letter *S* as she bends one arm over her head. Here Štursa had found a dynamic three-dimensional ornament that fully captured the absolute significance of the Secession curve. In its ambivalence of flawless form and limitless feeling, in its emotional reach,

Štursa's *Melancholy Girl* was perhaps the most stylish example of Czech Secession sculpture. In his depiction of the melancholy of youth, Štursa intuitively seized on the theme of the Orphic descent into the depths of the psyche, the theme of eternal return that was one of the key elements of the Secession's attempt to create a new myth.

Since the beginning of the Secession movement, the question of art had been framed in terms of the relationship between subjective emotionality and the objective foundation of the world. The solution was first sought in reviving Romantic notions about humanity's participation in nature's cyclical changes and metamorphoses. Naive themes, such as a female figure in a natural setting, were central in this respect, but they were soon exhausted by vulgarisation. Although this resulted in the flourishing of floral "stylistic" decorativism, its success – which ultimately turned the Secession into just another form of bourgeois representation – produced anxiety among artists, who wished to distance themselves from its superficiality. This resulted in new demands to seek the true basis for a synthesis of this world view in a deepening of art itself, attempting to get past the external appearance of things to their inner connections. Rather than being satisfied with the Impressionist charm of the experiential immediacy of the moment, artists wanted their work to access the world's more universal contents and formal structures. Those who had escaped the rigidity of academic teaching and "verified" approaches, and who had immersed themselves in life's changeable current, felt that they could not simply let themselves be carried off in its eddies. Beyond the known world of phenomena loomed the unknown world of abstraction. Impressionism was then merely the starting point for another journey, and those who dared to venture into the unknown had to make their own way. This was also why differentiation was now emerging between artists, who devised various isms and individual projects for these voyages of discovery to a new continent.

Synthetism can be defined as a tendency that sought to proceed by maintaining an equilibrium between subjective experience and objective regularity. It saw this equilibrium not merely as a matter of careful balancing, but as a living process in which the intensity of a painting was proportional to the intensity of life that it expressed. There had always been an expressive tension underlying Preisler's seemingly static figures and their decorative tranquillity. However, the earlier psychological conflicts were now presented in paintings that were assuming greater artistic composure.

There were further possibilities for artistic externalisation, especially where techniques other than painting *alla prima* were becoming more significant in the creative process. One such discipline was printmaking, which involved a whole series of technical processes between an idea and its execution. The coloured etching, the woodcut, and other techniques that were popular at the time obliged artists to seek their final form through complicated registration systems that also permitted all kinds of variations. This resulted in a new experimentation that, unlike Impressionism's emotionality and dependence on natural appearances, underlined the artificiality of the image and led artists to a quite different position vis-à-vis reality. Among Czech printmakers, Vojtěch Preissig stood out in this regard. After several years in Paris's printmaking workshops, in 1903 he returned to Prague, where he set up his own studio and aimed

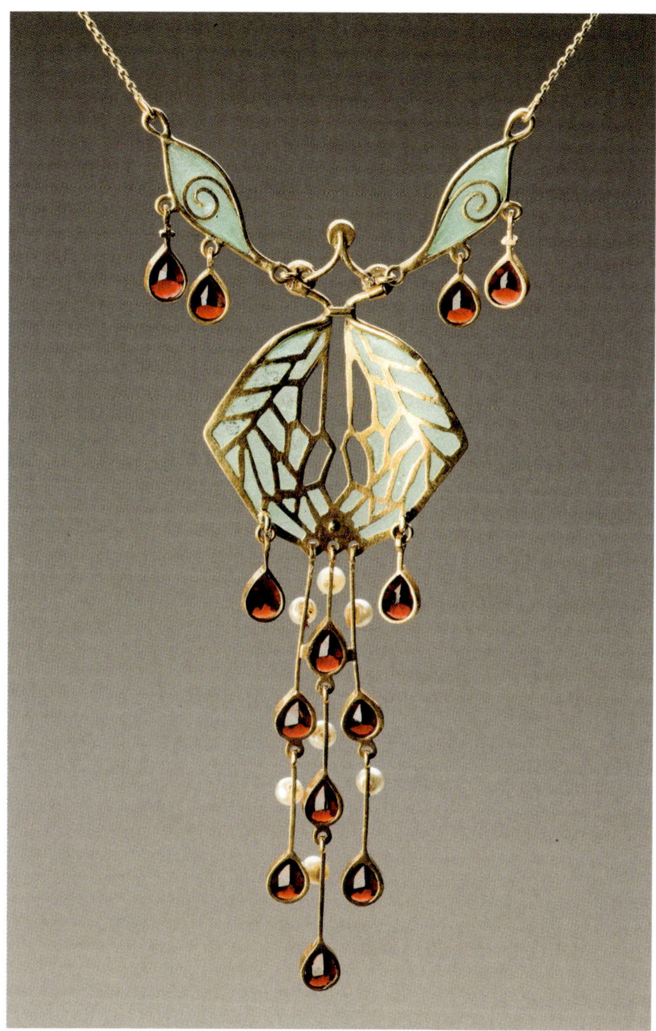

to bring together the best Czech printmaking in his Česká grafika edition. In 1906 he produced a portfolio of his individual loose-leaf prints for a publisher in New York, with a foreword by Miloš Jiránek. These twenty large colour prints revealed Preissig to be not just a technically flawless disseminator of the contemporary style, but also an artist who used printmaking to generate new concepts. Thanks to his reliable feel for the decorative, while in Paris Preissig had swiftly mastered Art Nouveau's stylisation. Compared with Mucha, his work was lyrically more delicate, and more remote from Neo-Baroque dynamism. Fairy-tale motifs such as *Sprite Gathering Stars* were typical of Preissig's fondness for the world of a naive and childlike imagination. Jiránek praised the unforced simplicity of Preissig's landscapes, especially *Winter Motif*. However, the simplicity and primitiveness of Preissig's subject matter was more than offset by the sophistication of his technique. By printing with coloured plates, he achieved effects that were inaccessible to Impressionist painters, especially the colourful radiance produced by the entire surface area of a picture. The emotional modulation of Preis-

228 Josef Ladislav Němec, Necklace, 1907, gold, garnets, and translucent enamel

sig's colours in etchings such as *Evening* (1906), or his more monumental *Mysterious Island* (1904) and *Before the Storm* (1907), was accentuated by the fact that it was accomplished by mechanical rather than manual means. This curious combination of a supremely personal intimacy and the public reproduction of the artist's impressions was again an unusually contemporary symptom of the situation in art.

In 1907 Preissig presented the results of his work at an exhibition at the Topič Salon, for which he designed a poster whose green and violet colours remained faithful to the Secession, but whose floral motif emphasised the need for simplicity and an economy of form. The exhibition was very well received, but it did nothing to improve Preissig's strained financial circumstances. Ultimately his studio was seized by court order, and Preissig could see no way out but to emigrate to the United States, where he remained until the beginning of the 1930s.

The simple elegance of Preissig's exhibition poster was by now typical of the new attempts to synthesise artistic devices. In this respect it evoked a broader synthetic tendency at work in contemporary Czech applied arts, which can also be seen in

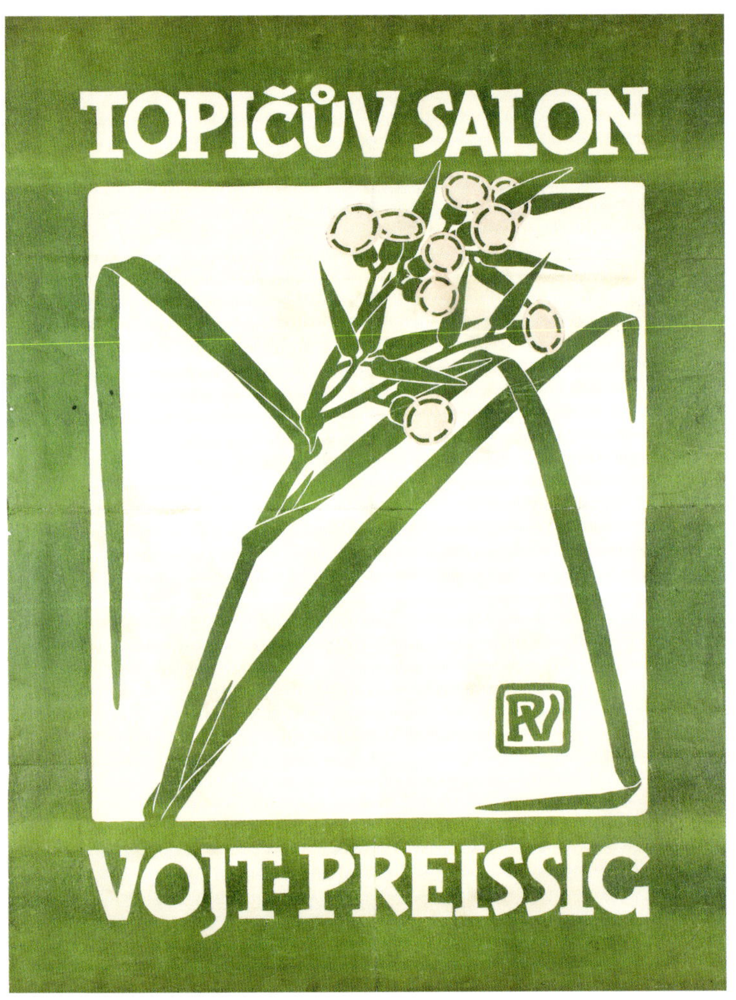

229 Vojtěch Preissig, Exhibition poster, 1907, coloured linocut, 141 × 100 cm

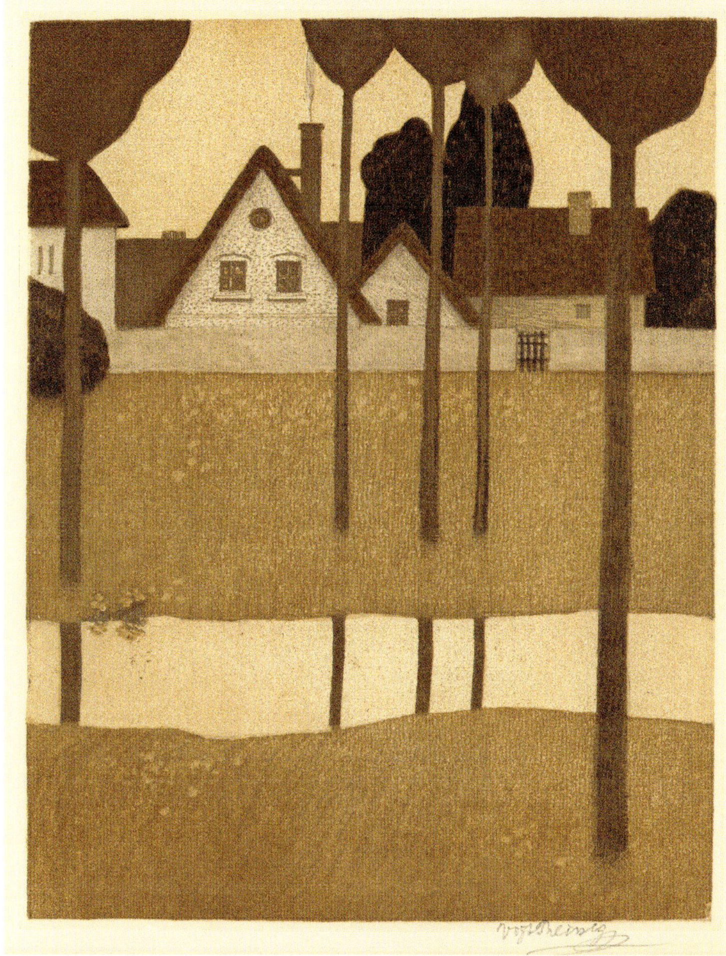

the white glazed ceramic vases that Robert Hájek was making in collaboration with a ceramics cooperative in Bechyně, and in jewellery by Josef Ladislav Němec with similarly simplified yet pregnant forms. This move away from the earlier decorativism, and greater use of the effect produced by refined materials, signalled the cultivation of the Secession's taste while losing nothing of its attachment to natural motifs. The intimacy of Preissig's *Evening* reflected popular contemporary ideas about seeking an emotional harmony between man and nature, but into this Preissig inserted a house, a symbol that gave it a rather different tone from the earlier naturalistic experiencing of nature. Besides the curve, the composition's decorative stylisation deployed a new element, the straight line, and this "linear decor" was indeed becoming a more universal stylistic characteristic at the time. It began appearing chiefly in the new furniture designs with which prominent architects equipped the interiors of their buildings. As usual, initially these designs were for their own private use, where such innovations could be expressed most forcefully, and they served as examples of the changing stylistic formula.

330 Vojtěch Preissig, *Evening*, 1906, coloured etching, 63.5 × 44.5 cm

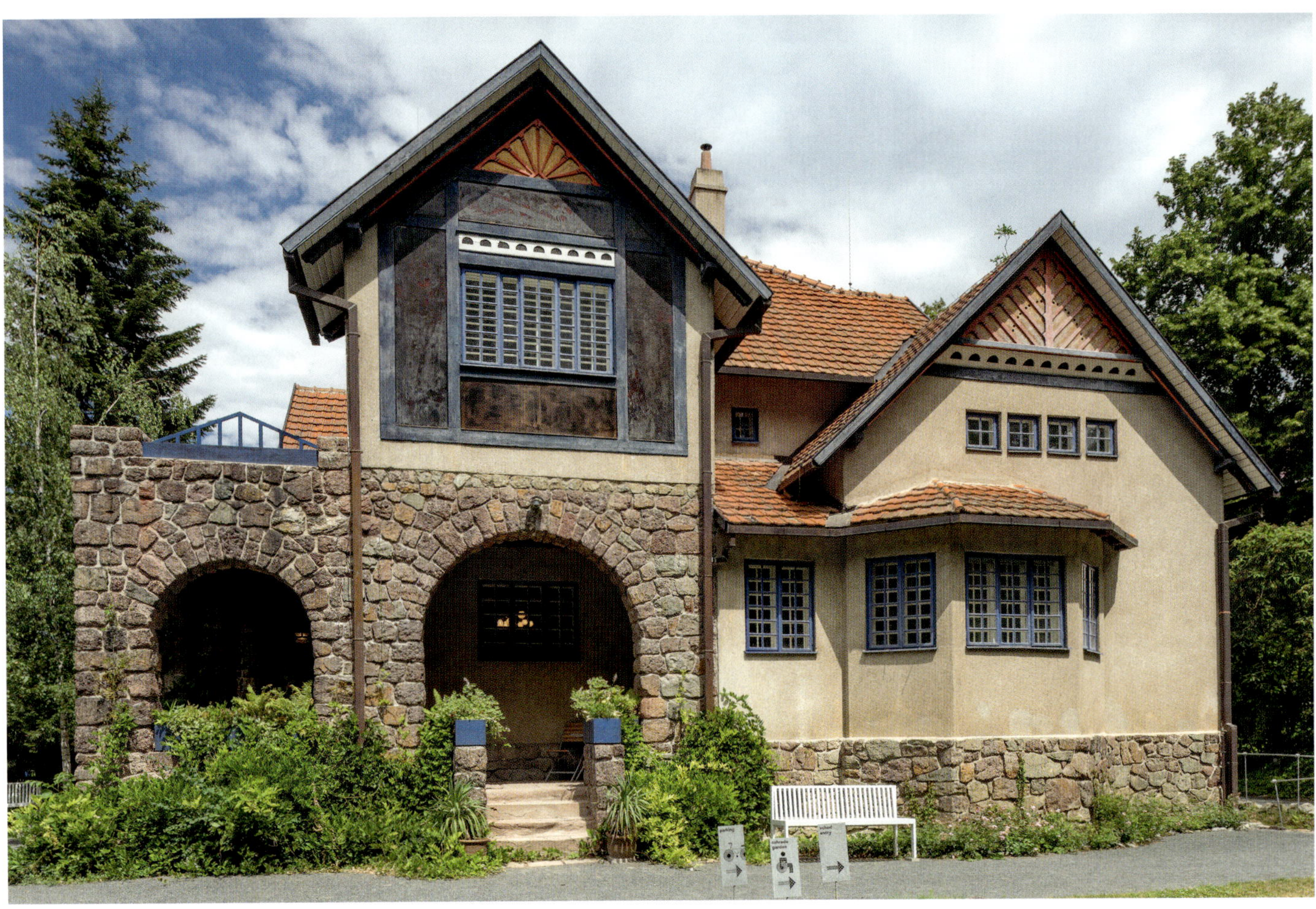

This new use of the straight line in a right-angled composition featured in the furnishings of the villa that Dušan Jurkovič built for himself in 1906 in Žabovřesky, now a suburb of Brno. Before moving in, he held an exhibition of his work there, and later he would reserve one of the rooms to present examples of his furniture designs. The centrepiece of Jurkovič's exhibition was of course the villa itself. It demonstrated how Jurkovič had abandoned his original ethnographic inspiration as far as the decorative motifs were concerned, while retaining many of its more fundamental lessons, especially concerning the constructive understanding of a building. Here the wooden construction was covered with cork panels, a material that was unconventional but affordable and suitable for building; Jurkovič had already used cork in Luhačovice. The construction-set character of Jurkovič's architecture was further underlined in Žabovřesky by the polychromy, where the structural components were in blue and the panels in white and yellow. The bright red roof tiles and the natural colour of the granite foundation walls and terraces completed the cheerful overall impression. Some of the ornamental details, such as the gate carved with peacocks and Adolf Kašpar's design for a glass mosaic on the front gable, depicting a fairy tale about a dragon, testified to the continuity of Secession ideas.

An important element in Jurkovič's architecture was the stylistic unity between interior and exterior, the logical yet lively composition of whose masses stemmed

231 Dušan Jurkovič, House in Žabovřesky in Brno, 1906

from an inventive and ingenious ground plan. Jurkovič had studied English country houses with great interest, and he had taken from them the idea of a central hall and living space as the core of the ground plan and the centre of the occupants' social life. Especially in his designs for family homes, Jurkovič's hall represented the fundamental space around which other rooms were added according to their individual functions. He had already used this kind of large hall in his villa in Rezek (1900), built while he was still directly influenced by wooden vernacular architecture, and he would use it

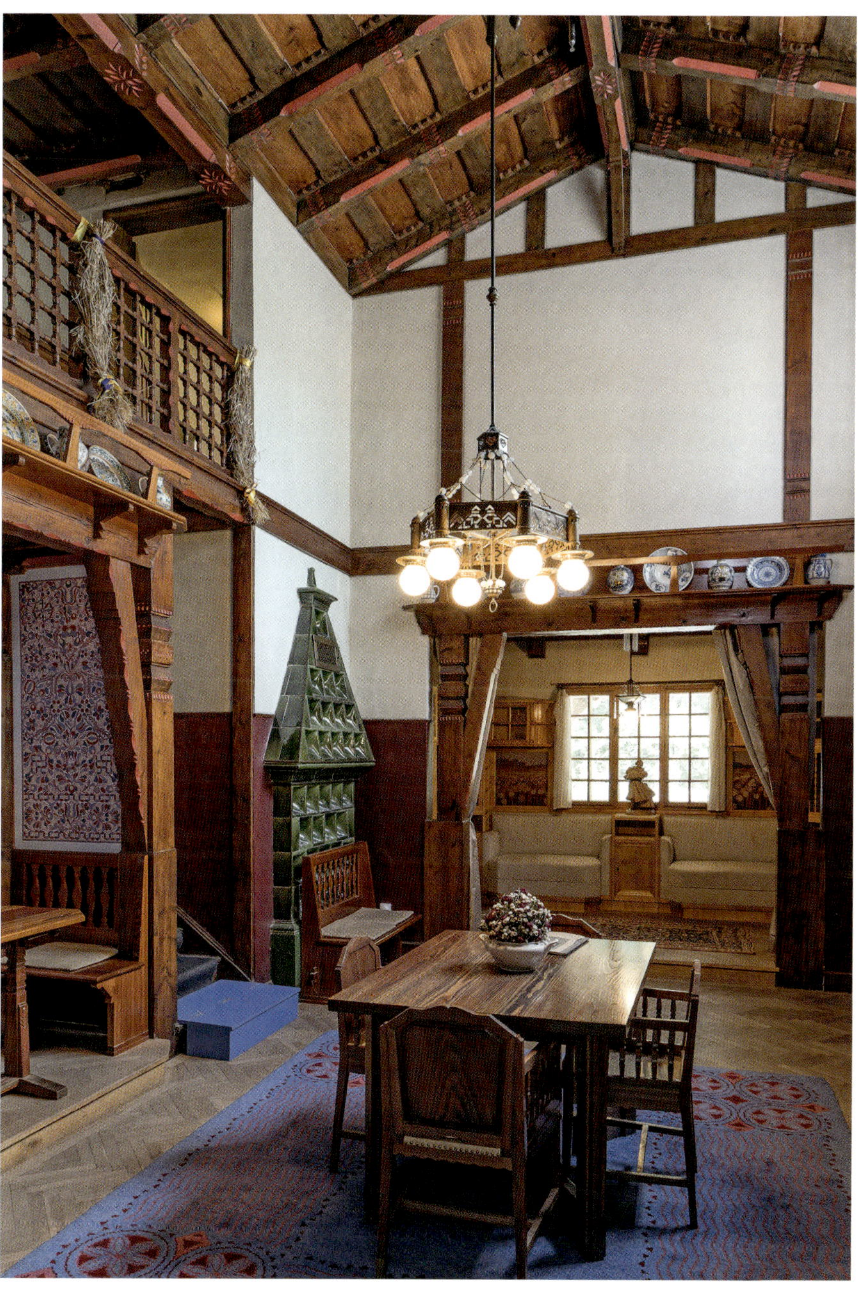

232 Dušan Jurkovič, Hall / Living room in Žabovřesky in Brno, 1906

again in the Náhlovský Villa in Bubeneč (1907), which demonstrated Jurkovič's concept of colour in a simple, modern form, competing with other modern villas in this part of Prague. Jurkovič's English inspiration was mainly channelled through Vienna, where the Secession had already discovered Charles Rennie Mackintosh and the Glasgow School, whose geometrical ornament was more suited to Viennese traditions than Parisian Art Nouveau's curvilinear style. This also introduced new elements of linear decor into the Czech Secession's repertoire. In Vienna, such decor had only been an alternative option for the insular modern movement, but here it became another phase in the denaturalising of the artistic object.

Jurkovič's architecture is still interesting today for its effervescence, a consequence chiefly of his distinctive synthesis of elements belonging to diverse yet complementary aspects of the modern movement. We can best see this syncretism in his public buildings, such as the Community House (*Spolkový dům*) in Skalica (1905). The building's function, which at the time also served the nationalist movement, was reflected in the inspiration it took from folk art.

Here too, however, Jurkovič also applied important elements of his own modern style, in both the organic curvilinearity of the façade and the geometrical linearity of the interior. The Community House's theatre hall is an interesting combination of both qualities, facilitated by Jurkovič's constructivism. The large hall, open all the way up to the rafters, was formed from a system of wooden constructions that created a linear structure. On the walls between them were naturalistic decorative paintings, based on Joža Uprka's work, and the simple geometrical grids of the gallery, which ultimately became the main motif. Jurkovič had not abandoned the idea that the foundation for architecture's renewal lay in the study of folk art as the source of national creativity, which he sought to promote by publishing a collection of photographs with a broad selection of Slovak folk art, under the trilingual title *Práce lidu našeho, Slowakische Voksarbeiten, Les ouvrages populaires des Slovaques*. Nevertheless, examples of his own Viennese-influenced modernism would become more pronounced in his work, albeit with somewhat different motifs (as in his apartment building in Brno, 1908). In his love of folk art, he found an ally in Miloš Jiránek, but the exchange of opinions conducted on the pages of *Styl*[146] – a new magazine for architecture and applied art – showed that, among its leading practitioners, interest in this motivation was waning as they began to emphasise "pure" modern approaches.

This all signalled much more than the mere surpassing of principles inherited from the 1890s. All these changes and shifts in form had a deeper meaning, in the attempt to achieve a stylistic synthesis built on firm foundations. In reality, the overall import of the Secession movement was being decided in these years: as to whether it was able not just to provide a new formula for art, but moreover to accomplish what it had originally set as its objective – to create the conditions for the flourishing of a new culture. This required a pitilessly self-critical review of its efforts thus far and its fundamental models. Out of this need came the cultivation of Czech art criticism, which attained a higher standard by abandoning its earlier apologetic tone in favour of an uncompromising appraisal, whose sole criterion was the artist's creative act.

On this matter, much discussion was prompted by the German critic Julius Meier-Graefe, specifically his treatise *Entwicklungsgeschichte der modernen Kunst* and especially his book *Der Fall Böcklin und die Lehre von den Einheiten*. Meier-Graefe savaged the Swiss Symbolist painter Arnold Böcklin, revered by the German Jugendstil generation and admired by Czech artists,[147] as "an embarrassing misunderstanding of German non-culture," who had achieved superficial effects rather than any true artistic value. Böcklin, by renouncing his laudable early paintings in an attempt to win honour and acclaim (much like Adolph Menzel and other German artists), had become "a poison that may ruin the health and future of modern art." Meier-Graefe, schooled in the French Impressionists, accused Böcklin of a barbaric anachronism: that his "pre-painting" technique, which cared only for the lasting gleam of the paint, was a theatrical pandering to philistines. F. X. Šalda summarised these conclusions in his essay "The Fight for Artistic Culture," published in *Volné směry*, in which he wrote that Böcklin

> seduces and allures souls with passionate artistic dreams who long to soar above the sober gravity of the time, and those who trust him to guide them to artistic freedom he leads into coarseness, violence and uncultured licence. According to Meier-Graefe, he is barring the way to the future, and his influence must be shaken off if there is to be a healthy cultivating of the art of painting in Germany, an art of the pure senses and a well-fermented intellectual charm – an art that is truly a cosmos, a whole and serene world of harmonious inner values.[148]

In this regard, Šalda maintained, the case of Böcklin was not merely a German affair, but a Czech concern too.

The main argument in this dramatic critical reappraisal of Böcklin was a moral and social one.[149] It pointed to "the fissure of anarchic barbarianism" that ran through even more noble souls, such as Nietzsche and Wagner, which, when combined with cheap popularisation, could have grave consequences. Šalda wrote,

> It is not with impunity that they were born in a hypocritical country whose interest in art is fraudulent, a land of spiritual indifference that serves God and the devil alike and is in truth indifferent to everything other than abject, gross selfishness.

Again, he did not only have Germany in mind. Czech art was also at a crossroads: in the wake of society's successful adopting of the Secession, it had become clear that what art fundamentally needed, if it was to truly develop, had by no means been secured. The flourishing of stylised "Secession" naturalism on the façades of Prague's apartment buildings and household items was ultimately a Pyrrhic victory that concealed shortcomings lying much deeper below the surface.

Yet the true Secession had wanted above all to go to the source, to the very essence of art. Its spokesmen saw a buttress for this in the unforced naturalness of French art, whose wealth was for them still far from exhausted. The first issue of the subsequent volume of *Volné směry*, under the leadership of Šalda, Jiránek, Preisler, and Županský, held up against Böcklin the example of Gauguin. It included reproductions of Gauguin's paintings and writings, and a translation of an essay by Maurice Denis, based on his memories of the artist. An interest in the founding figures of modern French art continued in individual issues of *Volné směry* devoted to Manet, Degas,

Monet, Van Gogh, and Cézanne, prompted by their large retrospective exhibitions in Paris. All this culminated in a large exhibition of the French Impressionists, hosted by SVU Mánes in the autumn of 1907 and organised by its new French collaborator, Camille Mauclair.

Within just two years, Czech culture had managed to form a much better idea of the origins of the new painting, whose true form had previously been obscured by painters who had followed these pioneers. With this greater knowledge came a more coherent view of the fundamental developments. This critical view clarified that modern art was not merely a kaleidoscope of individual endeavours, but had its own developmental logic that had led from the original Impressionism to the various forms of Post-Impressionist painting, which sought to complete Impressionism's visual analysis of reality with a new, more comprehensive world view and synthesis.

Among the critics, this awareness was most fully summarised by F. X. Šalda. In his essay "Impressionism: Its Development, Results and Heirs,"[150] he wrote that Impressionism had taught us to quickly see the whole, something that earlier painters had lost in their love of factual detail. It had opened our eyes to the intensity of the moment, and had consummated visual culture, with the painter's entire soul concentrated in the eye. Impressionist painters were able to see as impartially as we can only see in dreams, and seeing became a disembodied function. This was also why the Impressionists did not, in fact, copy reality, but stylised it; of course, this style was purely painterly, accentuating reality's sensual radiance. For these reasons, Impressionism was also the starting point for subsequent developments guided principally by Cézanne, who had grasped the opportunities offered by Impressionism's liberating of colour. He elevated this into a compositional principle, much as the Venetians had once done, but Cézanne's colour values were more dynamic. He taught Gauguin how to develop a painting out of several simple, large, flat coloured elements, and to render it as a harmonious tranquillity. This then set a new goal, which led to the surpassing of naturalism in painting and the creating of grand, harmonious, planar decorative art. The Neo-Impressionist scientification of painting also followed this path. It developed the stylistic and decorative aspects that lay within Impressionism: it de-objectified the painting, showing its geometrical and abstract scheme and diminishing the material component, the weight of the Earth, to emphasise instead its rhythmical and legitimate beauty. Impressionism was the starting point for the struggle for a higher art: "This great and magnificent goal – of creating a new decorative art, a great art, of legitimate beauty and purity – is rising ever more perceptibly on the horizon of contemporary painting: all roads lead to it."

This, Šalda's "developmental logic" of modern art, was explicitly programmatic in character, and it was also applied as such. While staying in Paris in the summer of 1906, Jan Preisler had admired Gauguin's paintings. They inspired him to greater lightness and fullness in his own work: "I have spent years here labouring over something that another did so perfectly there – and as effortlessly as if he were playing,"[151] he lamented. The exhibition of French Impressionists in Prague also loosened Preisler's ties to naturalism, such that in 1908 he could paint his remarkable *Green Landscape*,

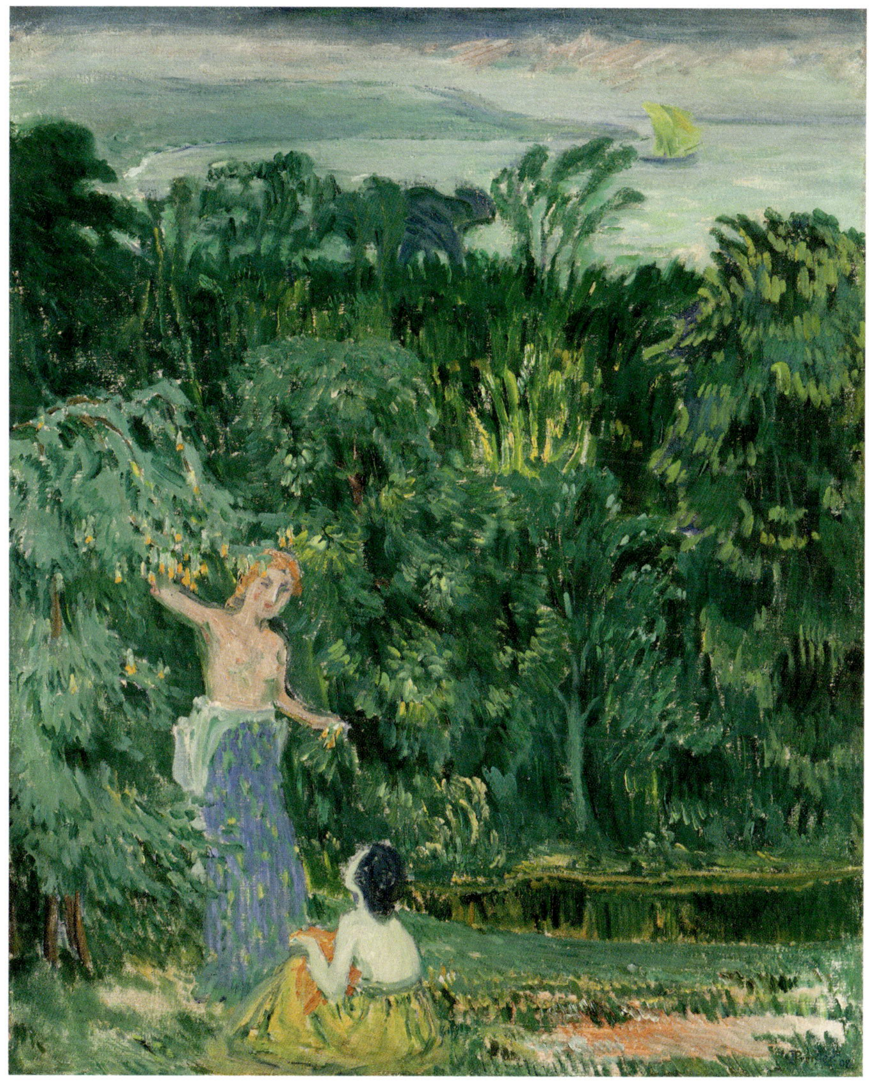

which he himself, although always very self-critical, appreciated for its simplicity, in which colour "justifiably permeates the entire painting."[152]

In its unusually organic interweaving of sensual, symbolic, and decorative elements, *Green Landscape* can be considered the culmination of a key theme in Czech Secession painting: the female figure in landscape. It entirely overcame the initial dualism of the human and the natural, and their new unity was not something merely longed for but truly achieved, and this on the basis of pure painting. The ideal of combining healthy instinct with legitimacy, something Šalda often wrote about at the time, had unquestionably been satisfied here, and moreover in a way whose essence was related to entirely contemporary works by the French Fauvists.[153] In *Green Landscape*, Preisler had caught up with global developments in modern art, and another painting from the same year, *Yellow Landscape*, brought him very close to Henri Matisse. In these

233 Jan Preisler, *Green Landscape*, 1908, oil, 95.5 × 76 cm

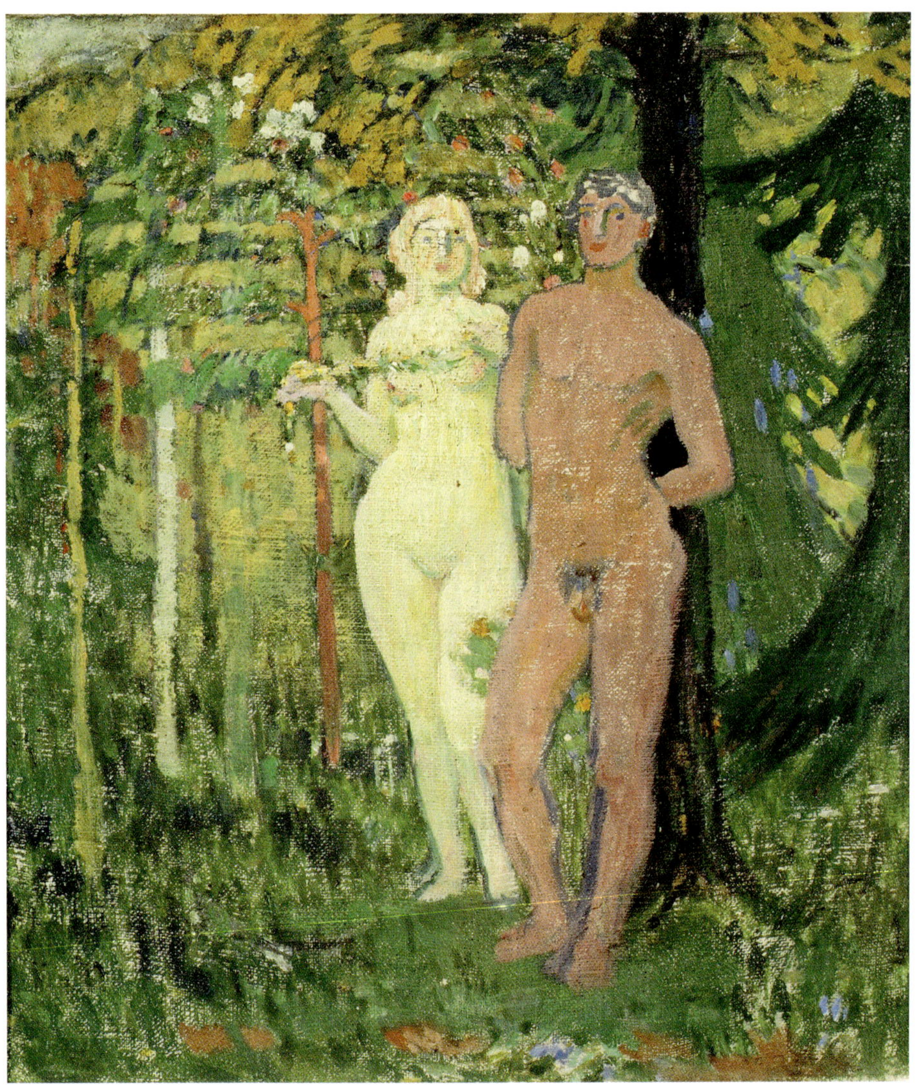

paintings, bearing the stamp of intuition but backed with ten years of intensive work on the problem, talk of a new synthesis acquired real meaning.

As well as the requirement for pure painterliness, Preisler was still influenced by the call for a new decorative art. Besides the French painters, he was also impressed by certain German artists, especially Hans von Marées, who was only now being properly appreciated; *Volné směry* devoted an issue to him. Preisler was also interested in Ludwig von Hofmann, designing the poster for an exhibition of Hofmann's work that SVU Mánes held in 1908. The new painterliness was to be combined with a monumental decorativeness, which architects also requested from Preisler. In 1908 Preisler sought a solution in the theme of *Adam and Eve*. In his first sketch, the large figures of the nudes are shown against the background from *Yellow Landscape*. Preisler had in fact returned to his old theme from *Temptation*, which here he made universal, but despite

234 Jan Preisler, Study for *Adam and Eve*, 1908, oil, 40 × 30 cm

numerous sketches and variations, the end result was not entirely convincing. Although Preisler did not abandon the ideal of monumental decoration – and tried to achieve it in less restrained works (*Leda and the Swan*, 1909) and on the walls of buildings – by 1909, when he showed his work to the public for the last time at the Mánes members' exhibition, he was dissatisfied and experiencing a true crisis in his art. In the end, he was willing to declare all his demanding monumental work a mere necessity compelled by his uncertain existence, but he had in fact devoted immense energy and care to it. However, the situation can be presumed to have been more complicated. Much can be attributed to the influence of the contemporary programmatic theory, which, although it had greatly assisted Preisler with its moral pathos and its overview of the new art, had also generated persuasive slogans, whose emphasis on "developmental logic" made them seem far more infallible than was in fact the case. One example of an understandable error in this kind of construction, and one that had considerable consequences, was the mistake Šalda made in his account of Impressionism's evolution, when he referred to Cézanne as Gauguin's predecessor. Gauguin had indeed learned something from Cézanne's still lifes, but what was much more important was that, at the time Šalda was writing this, Cézanne's later *Bathers* paintings were opening another approach – one that went beyond the stage of planar decoration that to Šalda, however, still seemed to be "the goal on the horizon of contemporary painting."

However, a harmonious synthetism based on sensory painterly qualities was only a phase in the development of modern art, one in which the naturalistic, symbolic, and decorative elements of the Secession's reduction were in happy equilibrium. This equilibrium had its own stylistic value, and it marked the attaining of a foundation upon which further, more progressive attempts at externalisation could be constructed. Under the label of "pure" painting and the concept of some kind of ideal "timelessness," there was a fundamental elementarisation of thinking on art, a thorough purging of its burdensome ties to late 19th-century nationalist ideologies, and the gaining of independent criteria of aesthetic value. Like every equilibrium, however, this too was an unstable state that would soon be disturbed by additional demands.

For the Secessionists of the 1890s' generation, this was evidently the pinnacle of their creativity, when the original Secession can be said to have reached its high point. This applied not just to Preisler but also to some of his prominent contemporaries, especially those who had from the start displayed a well-developed sense for the wholeness of artistic culture. They too attained a pinnacle – in the sense of fulfilling their potential – around 1908. Yet this was a relatively brief period. The dynamics of the time were so powerful that this high point soon brought about a crisis, and any striving to cling to the top was followed by a decline. Preisler's crisis in 1909 and, for instance, Vojtěch Preissig's own crisis – which came at almost the same time and was related to his work on Petr Bezruč's collection of poems, *Silesian Songs* – were in this respect fruitful, even if the results were a long time coming and sometimes could not be fully realised by the artists themselves. Another such case is the late work of Antonín Hudeček, who achieved a synthesis in his paintings of 1910 from Machov, near the Polish border. Like other landscape painters of his generation, he

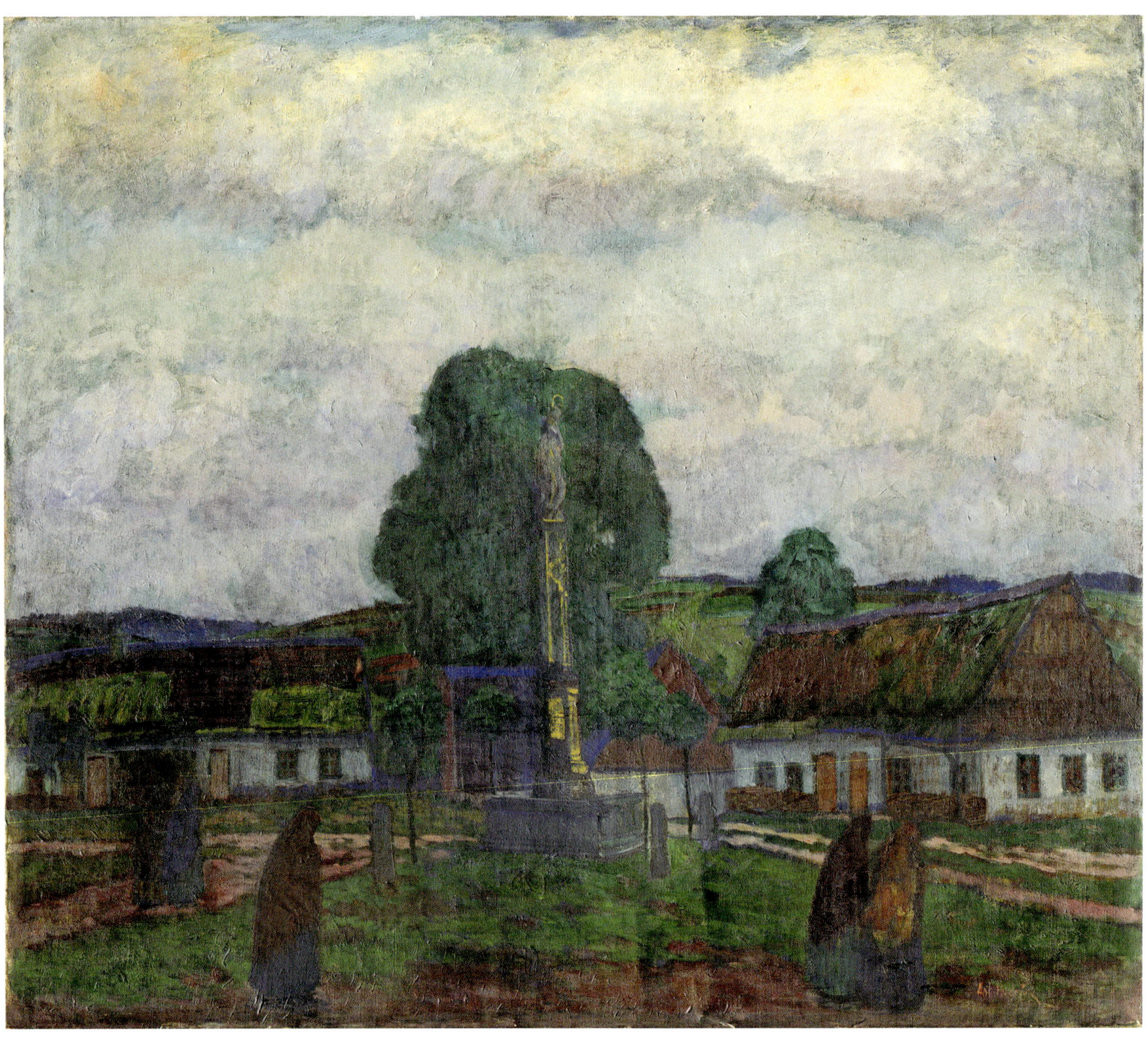

was later most successful when he returned to the sensitivity of his lyrical Impressionist beginnings.

The situation in painting was paralleled by that in architecture, especially in Jan Kotěra's creative profile. Kotěra's critical reception among Czech architects and his consequent difficulties in winning commissions unquestionably led to his emphatic rejection of rampant pseudo-Secession decorativeness. At this time Kotěra was also moving away from his Viennese beginnings and was seeking support in other examples of modern architecture. He was interested in the Dutch architect Hendrik Petrus

235 Antonín Hudeček, *Evening in Machov*, 1910, oil, 118 × 132 cm

Berlage, who had built his Amsterdam Commodities Exchange just as the process of differentiation in architectural modernism was beginning. This simple brick building, with an iron and glass roof and sober ornamentation in white stone, heralded a turning away from the prevailing whimsicality in favour of a logical yet artistic approach. A distaste for cheap decorative materials became characteristic of this change. Stucco and wallpaper gave way to materials that were aesthetic in their solidity and substance. Bare brick permitted not just level surfaces but also new ornament, whose compositional versatility surpassed stucco's naturalism, while losing nothing of its rhythmicality. The Secession's dynamism moved into a more abstract phase, which was also related to how the functions of new construction were expanding.

The first example of this new application of bare brick was Kotěra's Vršovice Waterworks in Prague (1906–7), a combination of low-rise buildings and a dominant tower. If Kotěra's use of unplastered brick here corresponded to the waterworks' function, in his next major commission, the City Museum in Hradec Králové (1906–13), bare brick became the foundation for a monumental concept. As a large free-standing building, the museum was an attractive proposition for Kotěra, offering him great freedom

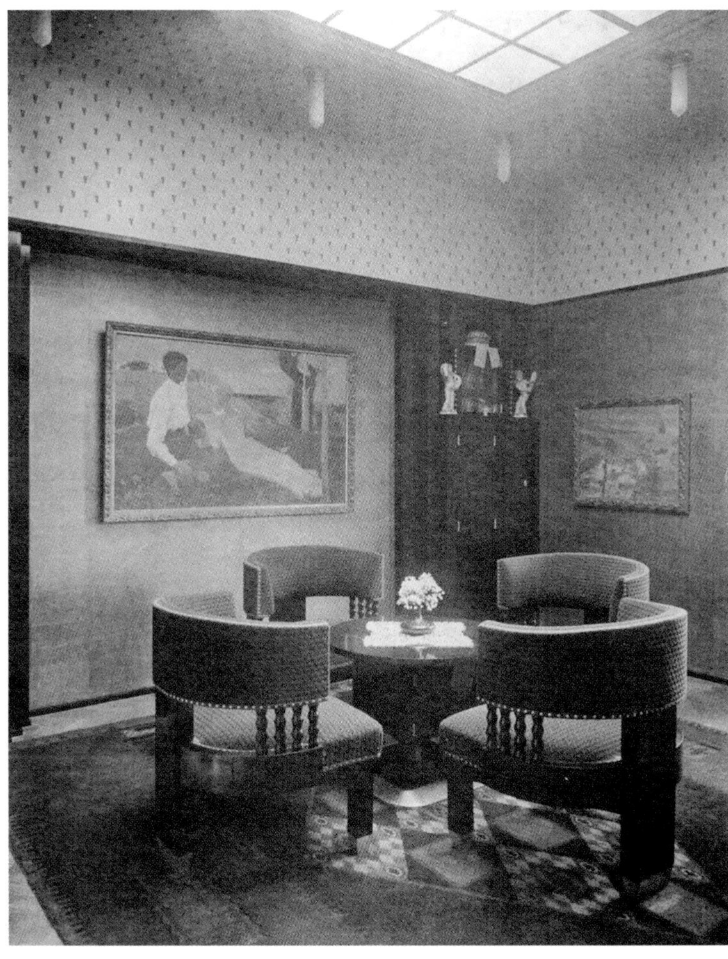

236 Jan Kotěra, Reception room in Kotěra's house in Prague, 1909

when designing its ground plan. He proved himself an artist who respected the logic of his own ideas, for he based the museum's layout on his composition for the SVU Mánes exhibition pavilion in Prague. Here the entrance is in the centre, but again it is introduced by pylons and topped with a cupola. On either side of the entrance are two wings of unequal lengths, housing large halls. Vertically, Kotěra's concept divides the building into the ground floor – which accommodates all the functions of an institution dedicated to culture and learning, including a large lecture theatre and a library with a reading room – and the upper stories, which are home to the exhibition spaces. The culmination of this concept is the vestibule on the first floor, where a rotunda extends all the way up to the cupola. A notable merit of this building is its scale, which, especially in the interiors, very naturally combines spaces of different sizes and purposes to create a whole in which the building's operational and representative functions are in

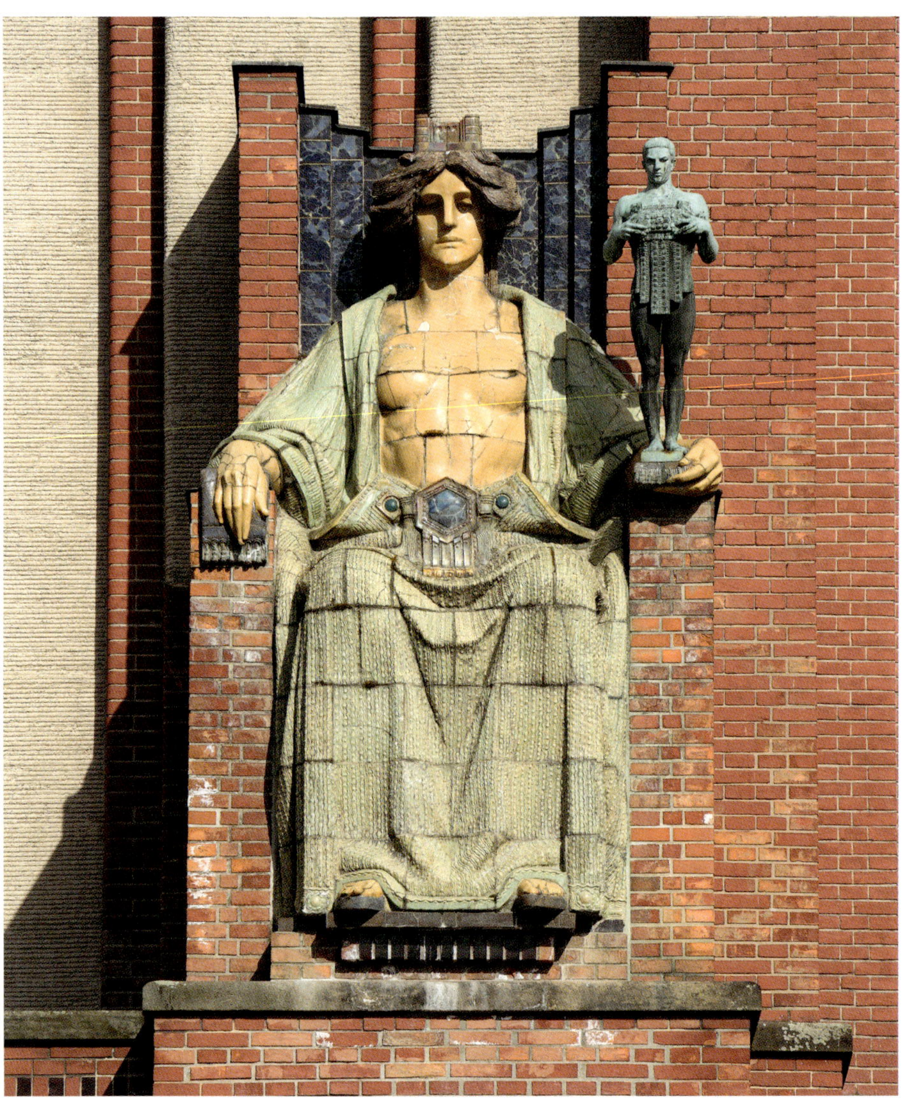

237 Jan Kotěra, History sculpture by Stanislav Sucharda at the City Museum in Hradec Králové, 1909–13

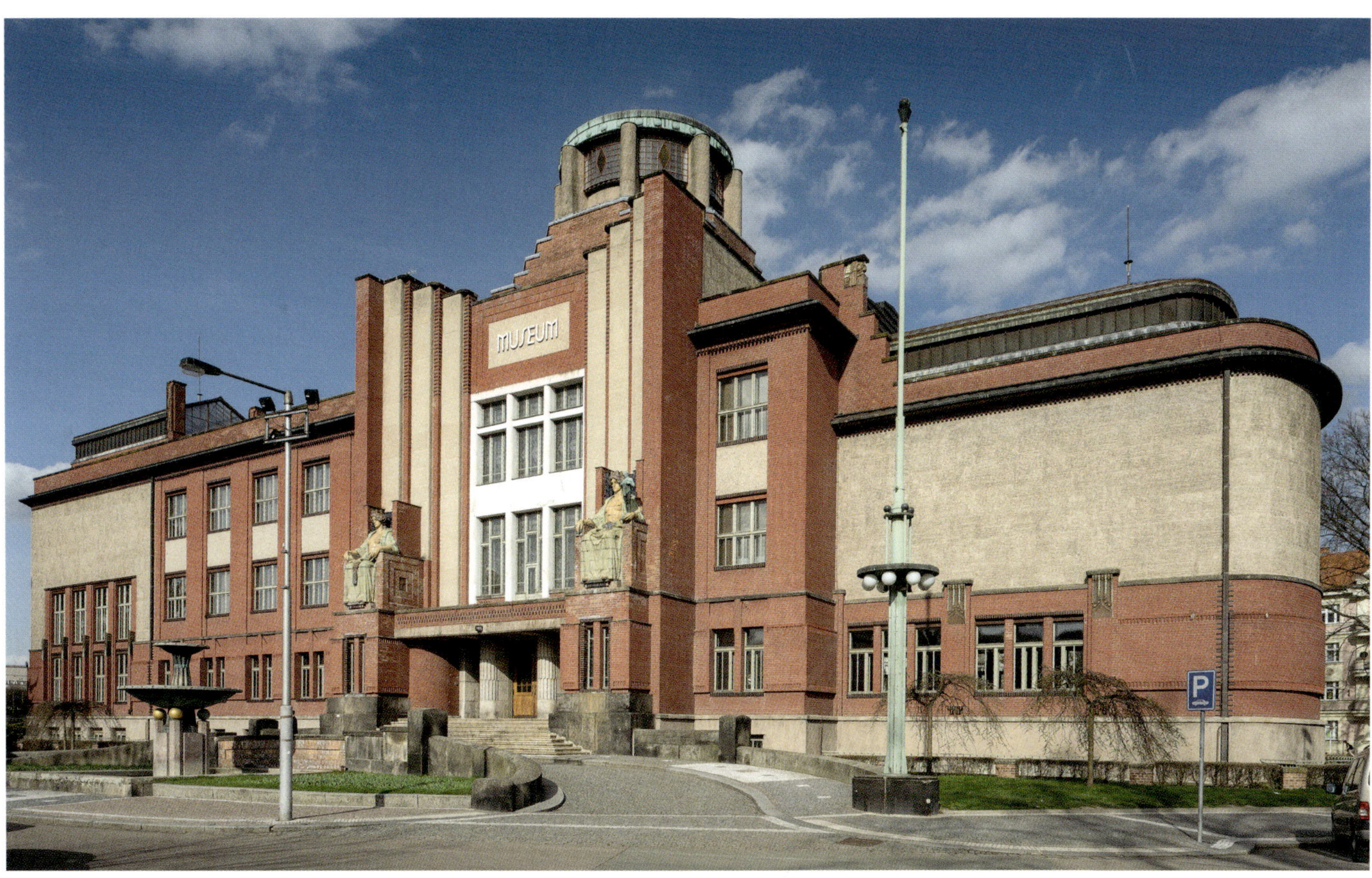

harmony. This reflects the particular synthetic value of Kotěra's building. In the entire canon of Czech modern architecture, there are few buildings that so directly manifest the architect's ability to present, in the very shaping of space, the concept of culture as the intersection of ideals and actions.

If this concept had been clear from the start in the museum's layout, its expression in the body of the building was something Kotěra arrived at gradually. Comparing his first design from 1907 with his definitive version from 1908, we see that the changes he made did not concern the arrangement of the main parts of the building but rather its ornamental details. In 1907 Kotěra had still favoured floral decor and linear dynamics, as can be seen in the concavity of the entrance façade and the curve of the windows on the ground floor. However, in his definitive design he only used geometrical bands, achieving a more uniform connecting of the entrance and the wings. In this way, the architect's dynamic concept extended from the surface of the building to its organism. The building's very substance created its ornament, which was then only emphasised by the use of sculpture in prominent places. Even in this phase of synthetic unification, Kotěra did not deny the Secession foundation of his concept, for in the structuring of the surface he ultimately created another system that worked with opposites, where unplastered brick alternated with bands of plaster that used hatching to produce a rippling effect.

In the latter half of the first decade of the 20th century, Kotěra was attempting to synthesise the elements of sensuousness, function, and symbolism, the distinctive

238 Jan Kotěra, City Museum in Hradec Králové, 1909–13

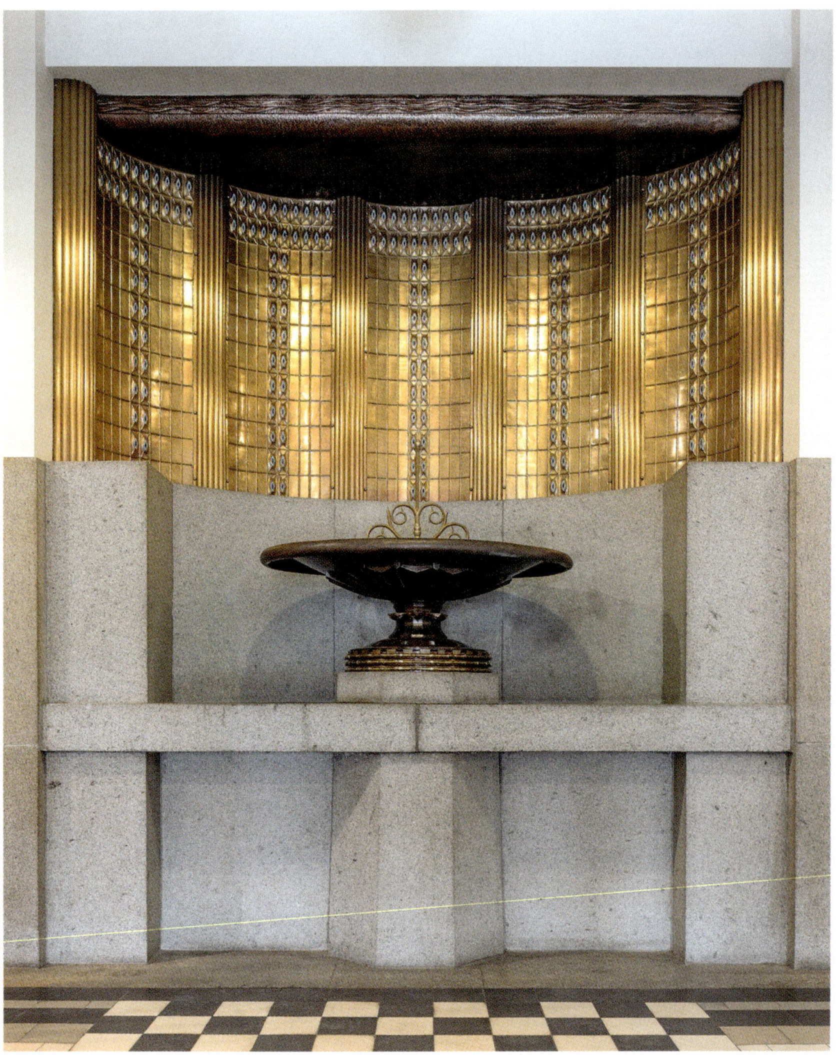

processes of the Secession's reduction in art and culture. The prescience of Kotěra's synthesis was also apparent in some of his buildings for private owners from 1908–9, especially his own villa and another building housing Jan Laichter's publishing company and apartment, both in Prague's Vinohrady district. Their renunciation of what was by now the Secession's commonplace naturalistic ornament seemed almost to be a message from another world. Of course, neither building had lost the decorative element, but in them the process of its development reached a purer stage. They marked the Secession's consummation by taking the fundamental ambivalence of its artistic principle to its logical conclusion. During the naturalistic period, diversity had been achieved by the thematic structuring of a materially homogenous surface, where naturalistic stucco ornament demonstrated the Secession's domination of art. Now, the earlier naturalistic ornament was replaced by the heterogeneity of the materials themselves, which in fact co-created the impression of a certain homogeneity in an

239 Jan Kotěra, Interior of the City Museum in Hradec Králové, 1909–13

unadorned façade. This can be seen in the façade of the Laichter House, which is a less complicated structure than Kotěra's own villa. Brick, stone, and plaster, worked in various ways, together with the glass window panes and the painted window frames, all create an effective decorative system whose relation to the building's construction is expressed by the ornamental brick overdoors. For all its new functionality and purity, architecture was still above all an art form – that is, a means of expression. This new sense of the pure expressive character of the materials themselves not only well suited the Secession's elementarisation, but it also reflected a more profound shift in the underlying concept. The initial idea was becoming something far more realistic

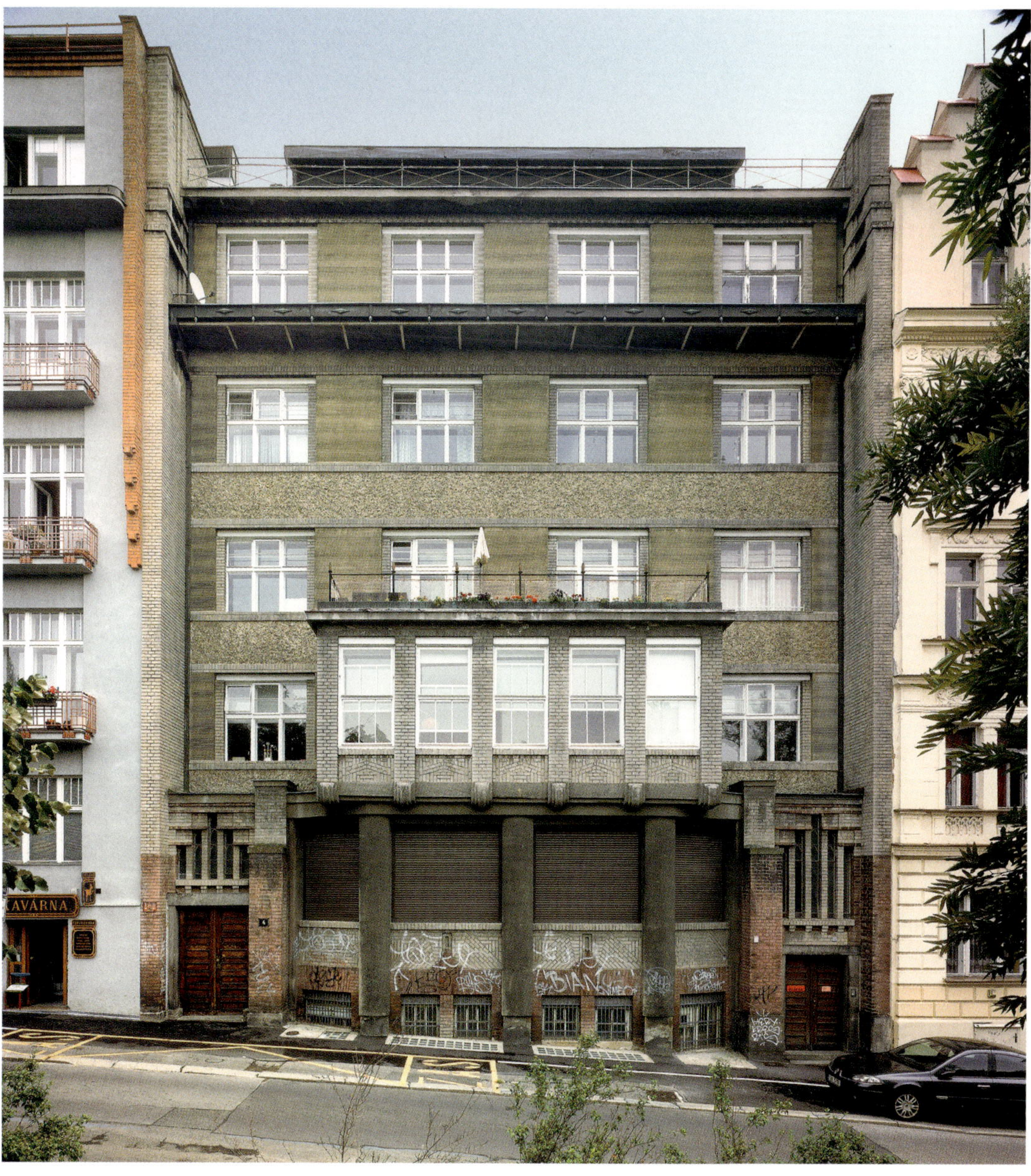

240 Jan Kotěra, Laichter House in Prague, 1908–9

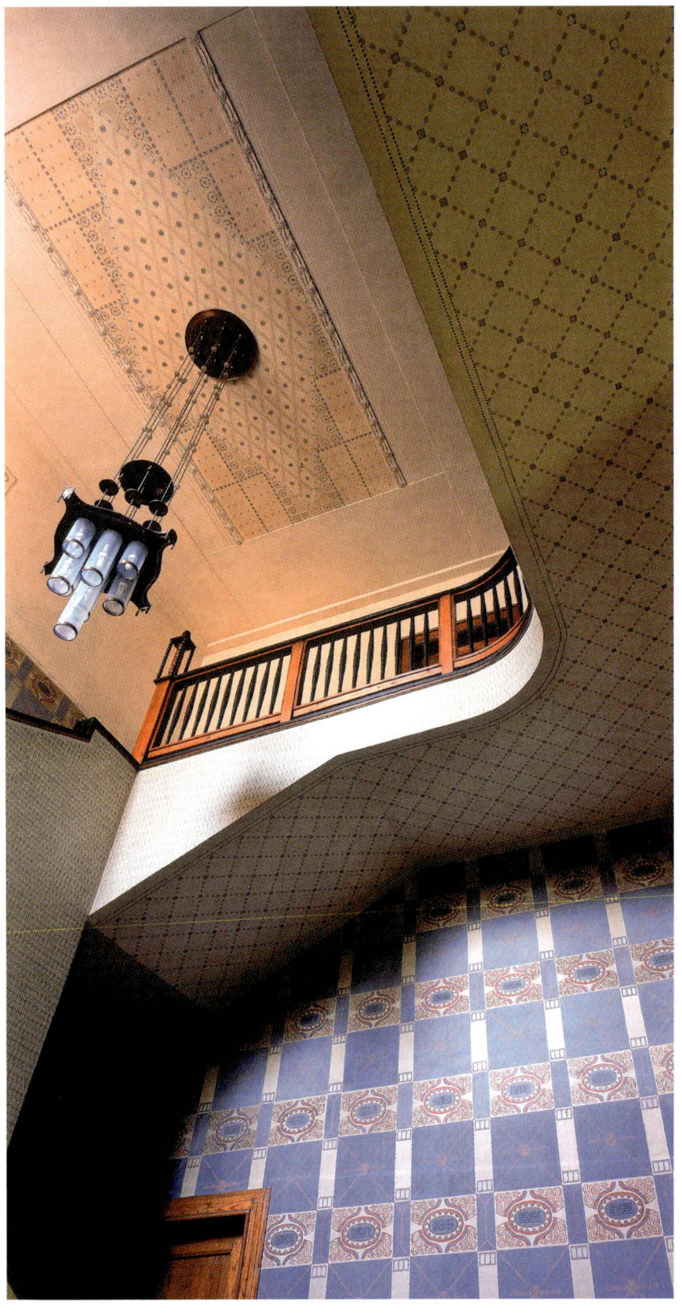

while losing nothing of its universality. This position also significantly influenced thinking on interiors: wall units became less popular, and the plasticity and mass of the individual items in a furniture suite increased. Related to this was a simplification of form in favour of more appropriate geometrical shapes.

Kotěra's response to the changes underway in European architecture was swiftly taken up by his pupils and collaborators, who mostly found in it a springboard for their own development. Otakar Novotný reiterated the inspiration of unplastered brick in

241 Jan Kotěra, Interior of the Laichter House in Prague, 1908–9

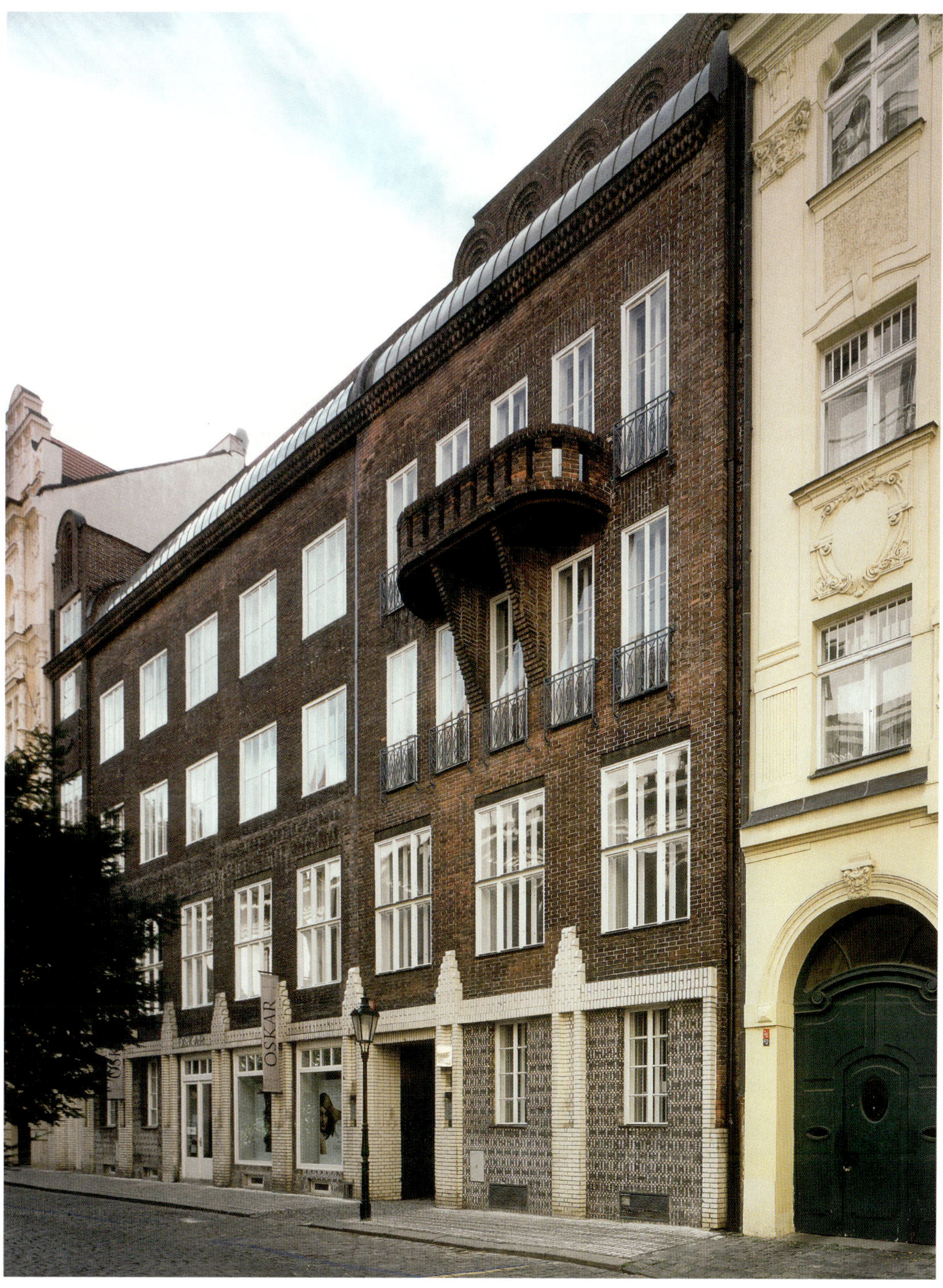

his Štenc House in Prague's Old Town (1909), with a more two-dimensional and lyrical style than Kotěra's pronounced plasticity. He also employed an effective colour combination that worked with the harmony between the red brickwork, the glazed white bricks of the ornamental parts, and the application of sheet copper. Novotný's Štenc House opened the new purist aesthetic to broader tastes, facilitating its incorporation into the repertoire of Czech architecture.

242 Otakar Novotný, Štenc House in Prague, 1909

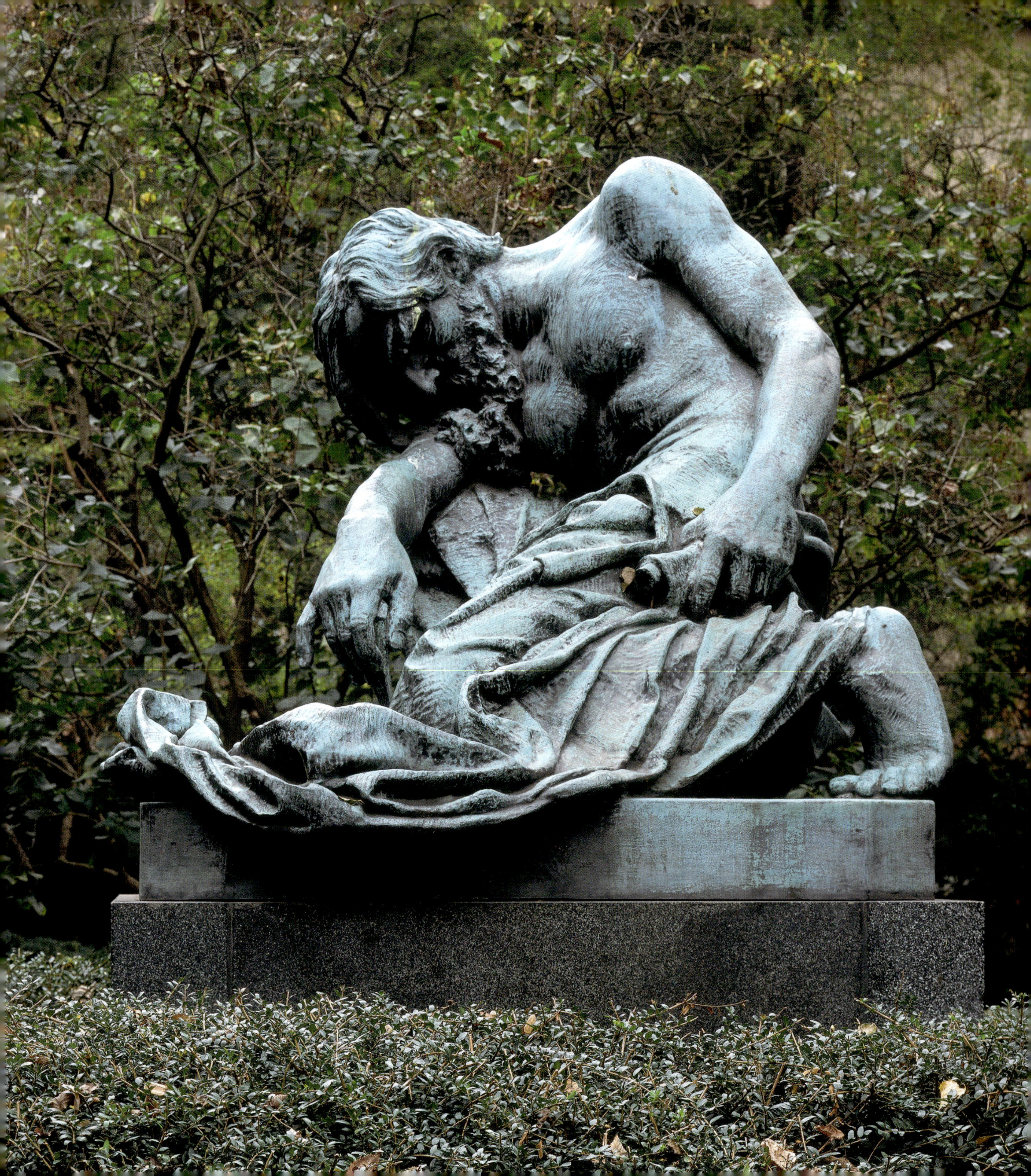

EXPRESSION

The need for synthesis, which in the latter half of the 1900s had emerged as something essential for the development of Czech art, applied across all disciplines. However, it could not be achieved equally in all of them, for it depended on the artists' individual dispositions and on the links forged between the individual disciplines in the earlier process of reduction. The Secession sought its consummation in a new cultural unity, but the centrifugal forces that had allowed the vicious circle of historicism to be broken, promoting in its place originality as a universal model, were still at work in its foundations.

At this time, František Bílek was recapitulating many of his ideas from the mid-1890s onwards in groups of works whose sweeping scope made it impossible for them to be fully realised. Bílek had never placed much value on a single sculpture, which he understood merely as one part of a larger conceptual cycle in which he could capture the breadth and depth of his ideas. His goal was not art itself, but the edification of the beholder. For this reason, these large cycles mainly found tangible form in albums of prints in which Bílek could give free rein to his metaphysical visions, whose magnitude far surpassed what physical matter could offer.

In 1909 he published a book called *Journey*, with a foreword by Miloš Marten. According to the writer, in thirty-eight images Bílek depicted "an epic of man's earthly progress," in which "a burning wave of mystical cosmic desire rises like a column of fire in the darkness of life before plummeting into the abyss of Guilt, Pain and Evil: man wounded by his intimations of the eternal, wandering like a blind man to the wellspring to slake his searing thirst." Bílek envisioned this journey as an alley of colossal statues that would guide the viewer from the Meteor – half man, half fiery boulder – who points to his lips, indicating his immense and tormenting thirst. This is followed by Adam and Eve in the Fall, then the Flood, Sodom, and the Divine Child playing in the ruins, who symbolises new hope for mankind. Next there are Rama, Krishna, Egypt, and Moses as initiates in the journey of true life, although there are still many perils along the way (The Dance around the Golden Calf, The Brutality of War), before we pass Old Testament prophets to the place where the First Disciples, asked what they seek, themselves ask in turn: "Master, where dwellest thou?"

Although Bílek's symbolism was strongly religious, it prompted quite a broad response, for he used imagery that was also current in contemporary secular art. In the first few leafs of the cycle, he initially draws the journey as "straight line and image," a quivering double line that is an image of "the pulse of the arteries" (a projection of the rhythmic impulse within us) and our earthly journey. Here Bílek draws a landscape scene, a valley with a road that winds around trees and water as it stretches into the distance. The symbolic meaning of the word *journey* is therefore associated with

243 František Bílek, *Moses*, 1905, bronze, larger than life-size, Prague

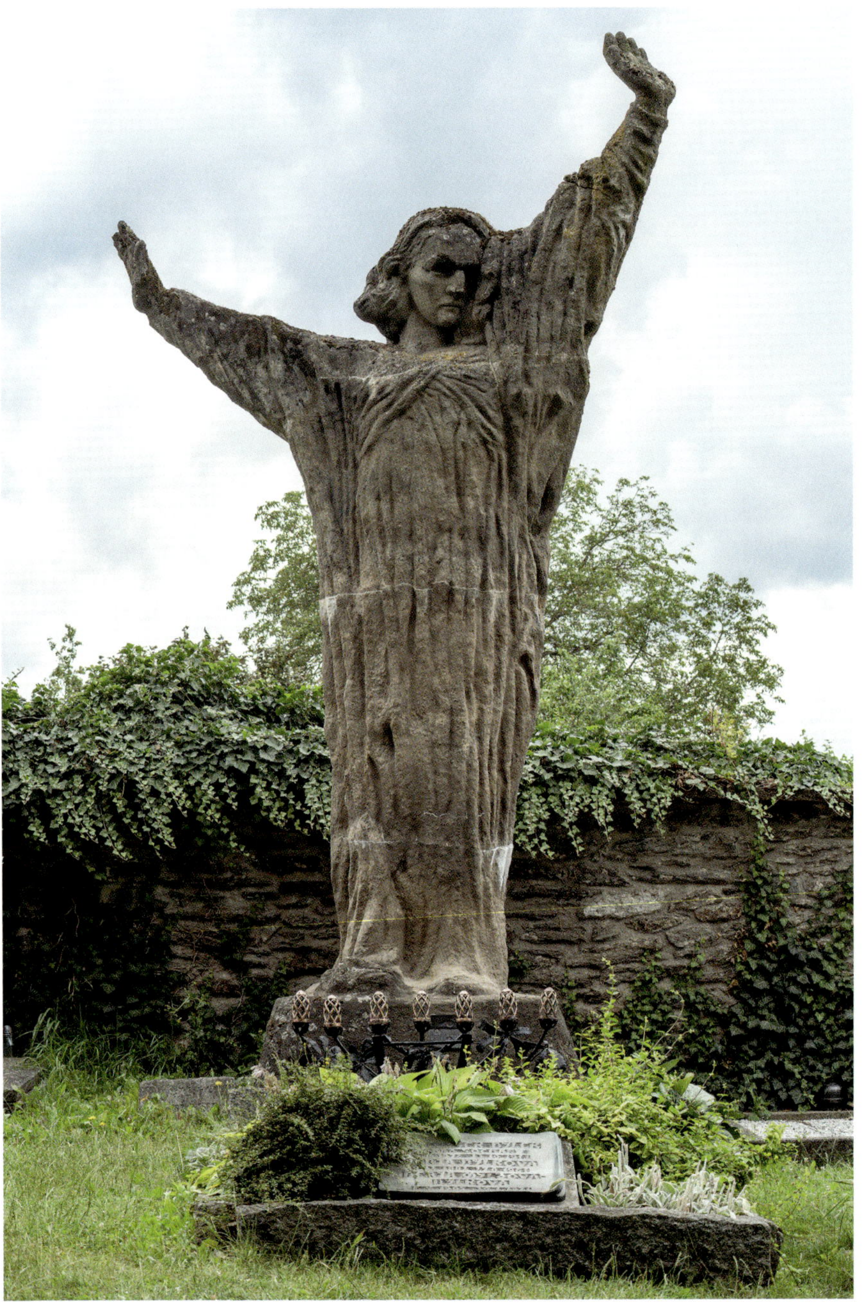

the naturalistic depiction of the landscape and the graphic image of the line, combining the fundamental components in the contemporary system of depiction on the basis of an archetypal theme that is the bearer of meaning. Bílek also synthesises, but his synthesis is directed towards an explication of the content. Bílek was never able to realise his *Journey* project in its entirety, but he did execute some of its stations in various dimensions, and he would also return to them later. He retained a monumental scale in

244 František Bílek, *Prayer over the Graves*, 1905, cement, larger than life-size, Chýnov

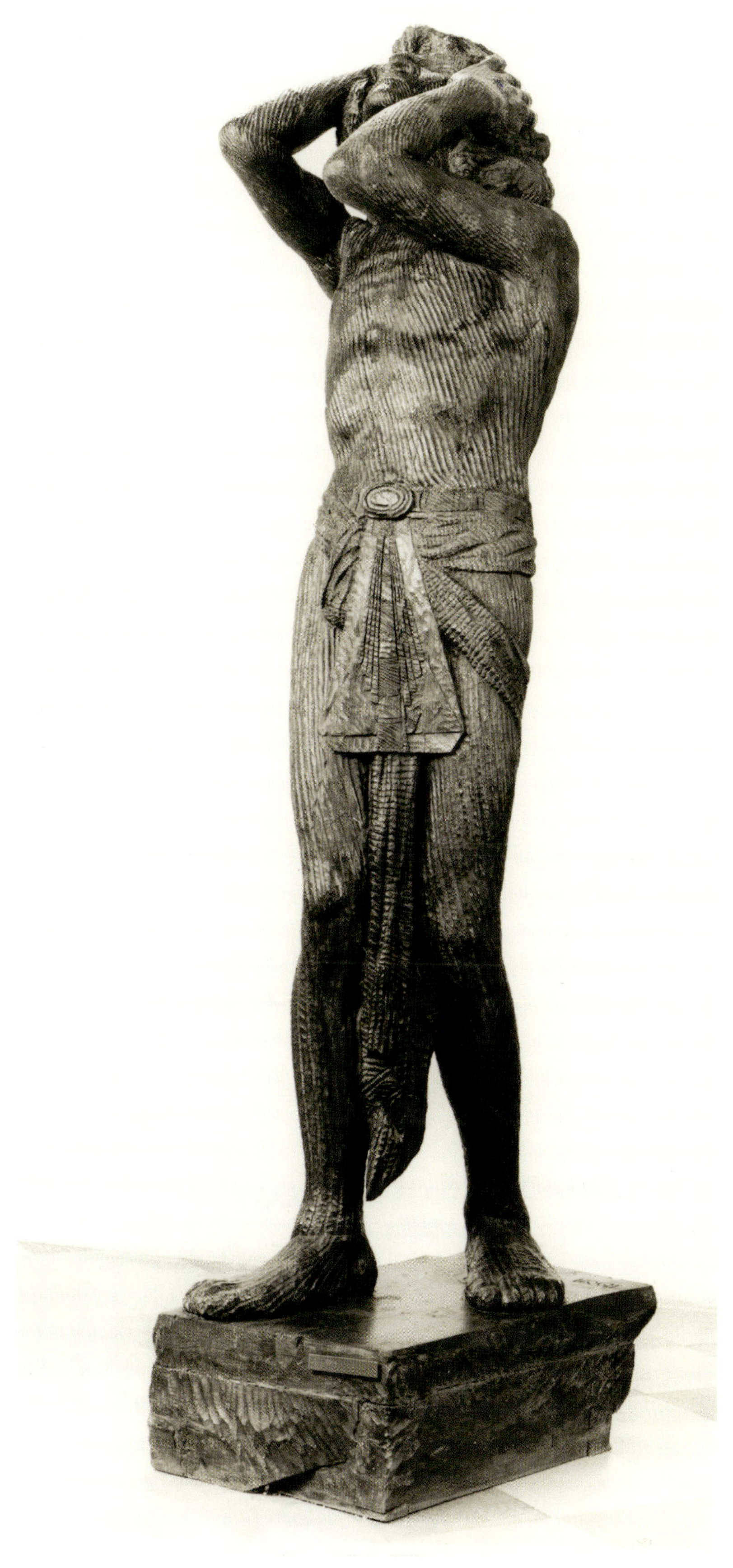

245 František Bílek, *Wonder*, 1907, wood, 307 cm

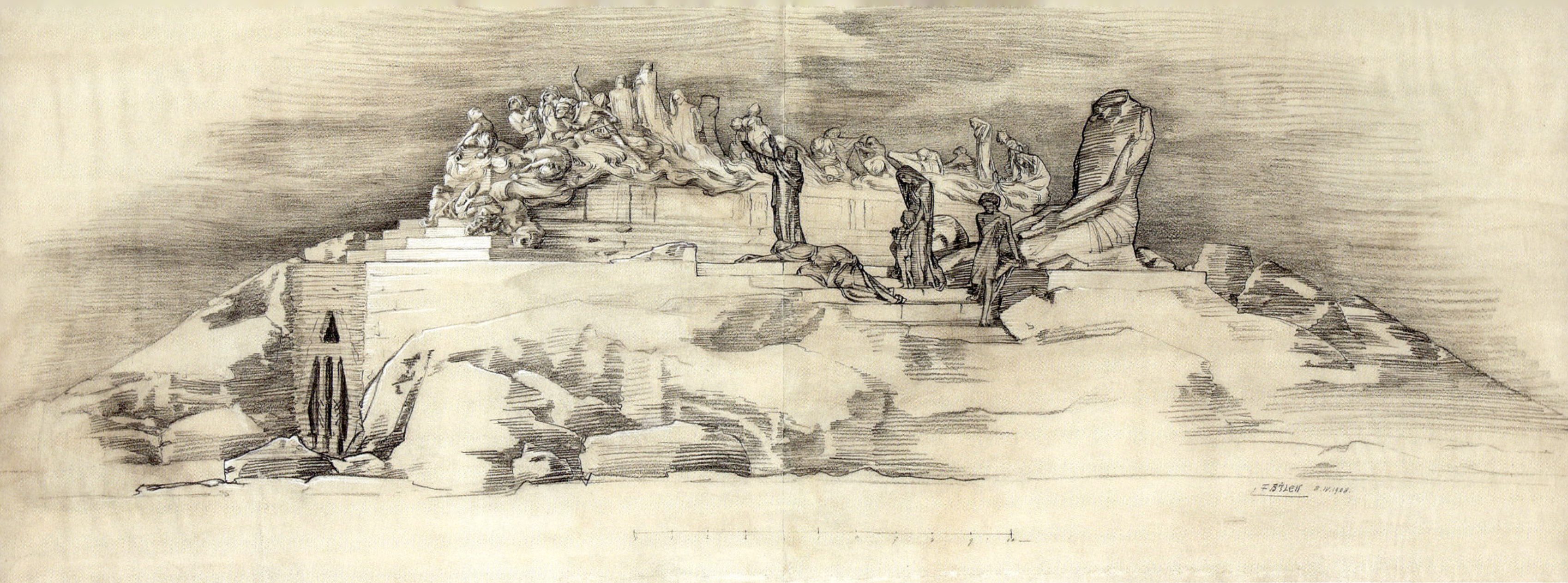

his *Moses* (1905) and his *Prayer over the Graves* in Chýnov (1905); for the latter statue he used the bold gestures of the Psalmist from *Journey*. The sombre figure of Moses, writing Adam's name on a scroll and thus recalling the Fall, is an interesting combination of the naturalistic and still almost Neo-Baroque elements of Secession stylisation. The statue's composition creates a hollow in the kneeling prophet's lap, which gathers the light. This was meant quite literally, as the focal point for the spiritual light or fire that is the source of the new strength for which Moses was traditionally venerated as one of the milestones on mankind's spiritual progress. Here too, contemporary devices have been thoroughly internalised and put in the service of the concept for this work.

The universal character of Bílek's synthetic symbolism was also a consequence of how he applied some of the more general ideas from *Journey* in other works that would draw a more specific response from the national collective. He incorporated a group that he named *The Voice of One Crying in the Wilderness – The Holy Thirst of Those Who Have Longed for Dew from Above* in the National Monument for White Mountain that he designed in 1908. This interchangeability of the universal and the national was one of Bílek's most important contributions to the Czech monument cult, one that had already proved its worth in his depictions of Jan Hus. It released monument design from narrow nationalistic concerns and led once more to a synthetic interweaving of imagery and the developing of abstract capacities.

The National Monument, for which Bílek made a one-tenth scale model, was his response to a proposal by Stanislav Sucharda to erect – in collaboration with a young architect, Josef Gočár – a memorial on White Mountain that would be a national pilgrimage site. Sucharda's memorial would have a monumental staircase leading to a courtyard, in whose centre would be a tomb with a supine figure as an allegory of Bohemia vanquished.[154] Sucharda had already used an allegorical figure of White Mountain, a nude with broken wings, in his František Palacký Monument. Bílek's objections to this concept were above all ideological. For him, it was "unthinkable that our country could ever be in the grave," as he wrote in his notes on the National

246 František Bílek, Design for the National Monument for White Mountain, 1908, chalk, 45 × 90 cm

Monument. In contrast with Sucharda's tragic, pessimistic concept, Bílek's idea was euphoric, presenting the entire history of Bohemia as "a holy sacrifice on a sacred altar." This was a repetition of what had transpired during the competition for the Jan Hus Memorial in Prague, but now these two different approaches to the basic concept for the monument had come into direct conflict. Although neither design was ever built, the confrontation is interesting in the way it reflects a contradiction within the Secession world view.

Bílek's National Monument was to be a "great temple" sunken into the rocky hillock. A staircase leading to the top would pass between the figures of Humility and Purity, the former having been removed and the latter lying in ruins. Here women and girls have come to "honour and mourn" the nation's history. Next there is an old man, who raises his arms in reverence to the main group of figures at the top of the monument, arranged in a great fluid wave with "a single zeal." These figures represent key moments in Czech history: from the original Slav settlers to Cyril and Methodius, Saint Wenceslas, Saint Adalbert, and the building of the Kingdom of Bohemia. At this group's highest point are the Hussites, before a precipitous descent with figures who represent White Mountain. In its very scope, Bílek's vision for the memorial marks the pinnacle of the Czech national monument cult, which began in the mid-19th century with modest memorials to eminent individuals and, since the 1890s, had taken the form of grand narrative works retelling the national myth.

However, Bílek's design was not significant merely for this narrative aspect. In some sketches he confined himself to the most important elements: the figure of the invocator, standing on the steps in front of the main group and gesturing with raised arms to guide the viewer's gaze to the "grand line" of the main group, whose outline creates an impassioned wave. The sketches are an example of the remarkable connecting of the individual figure with the whole, achieved by the unity of form and content. This also touched on something that was important not just for Bílek, but also concerned more general developments in art.

In 1905 Quido Kocián created a large funerary sculpture called *Žalov*, after the final lunette in Mikoláš Aleš's *The Legend of the Homeland*. However, while Aleš's fabled hero had uncomplainingly accepted the end of his life, the death of Kocián's hero was a more "modern" one: his sacrifice was involuntary. Originally, *Žalov* was to be a war memorial. In 1902 Kocián had sketched another war memorial, which he erected in 1906 in Vysokov, a village not far from Náchod, which was the site of a battle during the Austro-Prussian War. It shows a soldier in the uniform of the 6th Light Infantry Battalion, standing on a massive skull embedded in the ground.

As a sculpture, Kocián's *Žalov* is interesting for how the figural group is contrasted with the outsized and broken tombstone. The figures seem only a frame for the tombstone, which becomes the main part of the sculpture. Although its outline suggests that it is made of stone, in its flatness and emptiness the tombstone has been sensitively modelled for bronze. Its surface bears no inscription and seems more a magic mirror, the boundary between the real and the unreal. This impression is magnified by the contrast between the naturalistic rendition of the nudes standing on the rocky ground

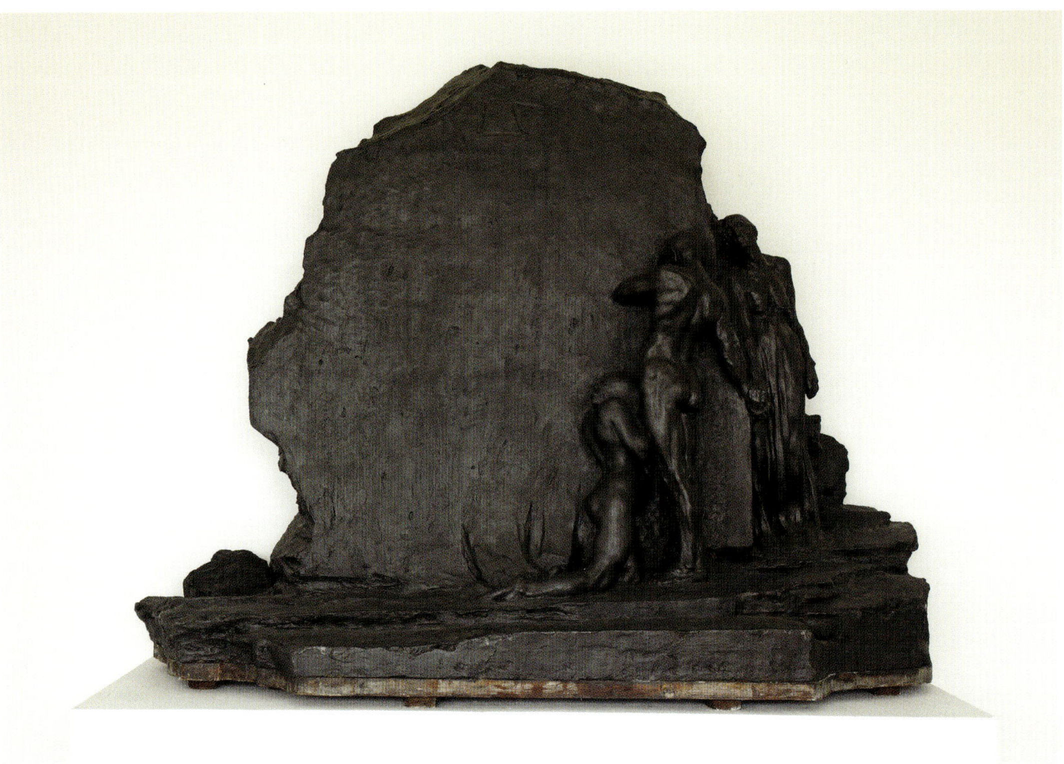

and the outsized tombstone, whose very scale seems unnatural. Yet ultimately it is just a block of stone.

Kocián's *Žalov* and Bílek's sketches for the National Monument have a certain similarity in how the part relates to the whole, the individual figure to the main mass. However, although the problem of form is the same, each sculptor treats the content differently. Bílek's concern is with an exalted example of the collective, in which matter is animated by further figuration, while for Kocián it is about the tragedy of the individual, to whom matter seems indifferent. Yet both operate within the framework of Post-Impressionist aesthetics: it is sufficient to recall what Seurat or Gauguin wrote about the expressive potential of a line ascending above or descending below the horizontal. In Kocián's memorial and Bílek's monument alike, the gestures of the main figures' arms have precisely this expressiveness.

What Kocián and Bílek had in common stemmed from their turbulent psyches, the inner turmoil so typical of fin de siècle artists. Marten noticed this in Bílek, and in his foreword for *Journey* he wrote about its creator's kinship with the anonymous Gothic masters, and how this "primitive beauty of exact scale is crossed in Mr. Bílek's work with some kind of nervous delicacy, with the restless lyricism of plastic nuance, the passionate motion and sickly trembling of Rodin's nudes. But monumentality dominates." Bílek's externalisation is always directed from intuition to lucidity and exemplary effect. With Kocián, a temporary formative quietening of expression is always overwhelmed by an unrelenting emotional eruption that gushes up from some sub-

247 Quido Kocián, *Žalov*, 1905, patinated plaster, 171 cm

conscious emotional complex, and this gives his sculptures their expressive agitation. In 1908 he modelled and carved the figures of *Death* and *Resurrection* for the cemetery gate in Hořice. That same year he had started teaching at the local sculpture school, and Kocián would live and work in Hořice for the rest of his life. In their verticality and linearity, where these figures' poses recall the Belgian sculptor Georges Minne, there is a certain attempt at stylistic abstraction. Yet immediately after these sculptures, the demons that Kocián had previously depicted in fairy-tale themes returned to his work. He was unusually drawn to madness (*Angel with a Broken Wing*, for a tombstone in Žamberk, 1907) and mental confusion (*Idiot*, 1907). His figures are personifications of fateful psychological forces, where, in the hysterical degeneracy of the human race (*The Plague*, 1909), the triumphant principle of evil is presented by *The Devil* (1911).

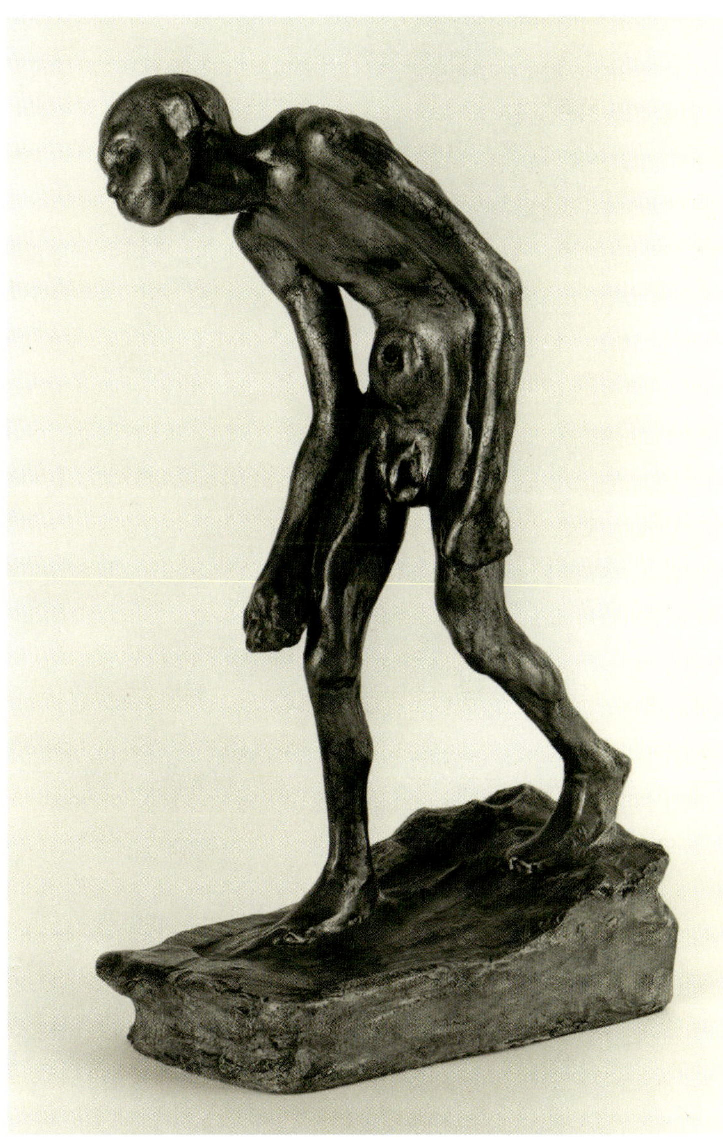

248 Quido Kocián, *Idiot*, 1907, patinated plaster, 37 cm

While Kocián's dramatic sculptures were based on an exhausting struggle between man and the dark forces of depression and disillusion, Bílek sought metaphysical support for his essentially similar trials. In 1907 he carved his largest sculpture, *Wonder*, from the trunk of a beech tree. It depicts a mystic who has glimpsed in a state of ecstasy "the existence of all things in their true light." The figure, dressed in an initiate's loincloth, clutches his head as he gazes into the depths of the universe, marvelling at its immensity and beauty. The light falling on the statue is captured in the broad plastic hatching of its surface, which optically lightens the wood and creates an impression of energy surging upwards. However, Bílek did not intend to install *Wonder* in a natural setting, but at the centre of the room of the initiates (a drawing from 1907) in the antechamber of the idealised temple he outlined in another of his illustrated books, *The Building of the Future Temple within Us* (1908). This change in the siting of Bílek's key ideoplastic works, and the new emphasis he placed on architecture, both belonged to the synthetic tendency of the latter half of the 1900s. The first example of this synthesis in his work was the tomb he built for the biologist František Nekut in the cemetery in Chýnov (1908). It featured a sandstone relief of the Last Supper installed in a columned exedra made of unplastered brick, the same material Bílek had used to build his "Cottage" in Chýnov (1898). Bílek's numerous architectural designs always sought to express a particular concept, and they culminated in the villa he built for himself in Prague in 1910–11. It was guided by his idea of "a field of corn," a bountiful harvest, which he expressed in massive columns loosely based on Ancient Egyptian architecture. It was also symptomatic that this building was the first in Prague to have a flat roof, a detail that reflects Bílek's special status in Czech modernism.

The synthesis that had become an essential programme in the latter half of the decade sought to achieve a dynamic equilibrium between all the essential elements of the Secession's artistic system. Ultimately, the greatest obstacle was not naturalism, which Impressionism had emphasised and even turned into so-called pure art, but the emotional dysfunction of the new artistic personality. The significance and influence of this dysfunction were extraordinary, not just because it was confirmed by the world view presented in the reigning aesthetic theories of empathy, but principally because it was indeed a key mental trait for the entire Secession movement. The resulting discrepancy between the individual experience of the world and the requirement for a new externalisation in the artistic response provided the most powerful impulse in this period, and it sought its resolution in various approaches to the question of expression.

This situation was reflected in a particularly interesting way in sculpture, where the greatest tension arose in connection with the erecting of monuments. By their very nature, these commissions were perhaps the most collective of artworks, in terms of expressing contemporary ideas about depiction. Czech sculptors experienced the modern crisis of the monument all the more dramatically because Czech society – where the process of national emancipation was reaching its climax – demanded monuments from them, and so emphatically that it could almost be called a mania. Yet these sculptors were now intimately familiar with Rodin's work, and it had captivated them. They had discovered in it an oeuvre that was supremely opposed to

249 Ladislav Šaloun, Jan Hus Memorial in Prague, 1900–1915

conventional thinking on monuments and insisted on originality in this discipline – an originality that came out of purely personal creative capacities. The question of a new concept for monuments was therefore entirely open, for not even classically oriented examples could guide it. Myslbek only installed his equestrian statue in Wenceslas Square in 1911, and he added the figures on the plinth later still.

In the latter half of the 1900s large models were produced for both of the monuments in Prague designed by members of the Secession generation. In 1907 Ladislav Šaloun installed a mock-up of his Jan Hus Memorial in the Old Town Square, where it remained for several days. There were substantial differences from the sketch that had won the competition in 1901, but Šaloun still adhered to his idea of placing Hus between two contrasting groups: the victorious Hussites and the Protestant exiles after White Mountain. In response to criticism of his original design, instead of depicting Hus at the stake Šaloun now showed him as a majestic figure – this was the proud sacrifice of a national martyr. The main problem, however, was how to site the memorial in the historic square, and the related question of the coherence between the main figure and the two groups. After several attempts, Šaloun achieved this partly by mounting the sculpture on a tall and broad stone plinth, but above all by the suggestion of motion in the two groups on either side of the immobile and upright figure of Hus. Šaloun's definitive version also expresses this in the relief on the front of the plinth,

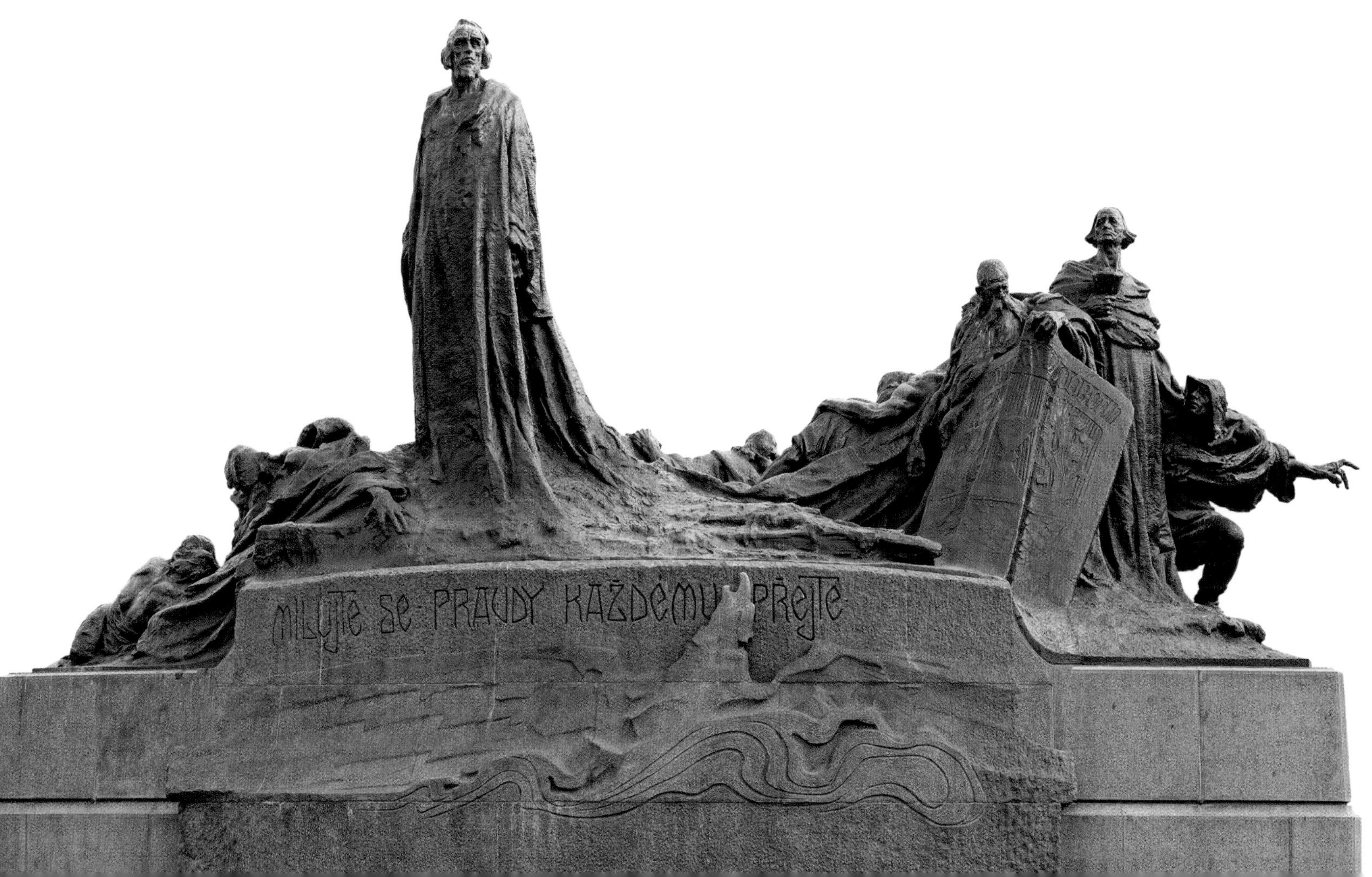

which shows a cliff rising above a stormy sea. In his writings on the memorial, Šaloun described Hus as "the mysterious centre of Czech history," marking its highest ascent and its most precipitous fall.[155]

Šaloun's Jan Hus Memorial was therefore based on powerfully contrasting ideas, which were also reflected in its form. The cataclysm of the nation's history was to be expressed by the contrast between the hieratic stillness of Hus and the maximal releasing of the other figures, and by modelling that dramatically alternates between convex and concave, such that the rapid alternation of the plastic planes unleashes centrifugal and centripetal forces that try to counter the swirling motion. At the rear of the monument another group has been inserted between the Hussites and the exiles – a mother nursing her infant, representing the National Revival – and this creates a smooth gradation of masses: the "wheel of history" is tilted from the figure on the far right, who extends one arm outwards in an appeal to the viewer, down to the sculpture's lowest point both literally and metaphorically, where the exiles turn to face the place where the Protestant nobles were executed in 1621, before it rises again.

When modelling the memorial, Šaloun had tried to learn from Rodin's example. He had large photographs of the latter's *The Burghers of Calais* and *Balzac* in his studio, but the end result seemed somewhat Neo-Baroque. Its excessive exaltation appalled not just conservatives, but also Šalda, who wrote about the model in *Volné směry*:

> Since the time that Šaloun emerged as the competition's winner, our enthusiasm has cooled greatly, and today we stand before his Hus entirely disenchanted. In vain do we seek in it the divine serenity that is the effect produced by Rodin's sculptures, and in vain do we persuade ourselves of the merits of the symbols of national history expressed in the two groups. Perhaps elucidation will give them greater clarity of meaning and the intended contrast. In the definitive design there will perhaps be greater serenity in the lines, and less descriptive historicism. Perhaps...[156]

This clearly reflected the dividing line between synthetism and an emotionality that lacked any stylistic foundation. Although Šaloun tried to accommodate some of the demands for compactness of form when modelling the definitive design, the call for "greater serenity in the lines" was utterly alien to him. Šaloun's place was unquestionably on the Dionysian side of Secession art: he had taken good note of Nietzsche's maxim that true artistic endeavour was impossible without intoxication. This was also reflected in the very idea of motion in the Jan Hus Memorial, rendered as a swirling vortex. This differed from Bílek's elongated, undulating line and Sucharda's use of a spiral to bring opposites together in his Palacký Monument. Josef Mařatka's designs for a monument to the aviator Alberto Santos-Dumont (1904) were more in the spirit of Šaloun's euphoric motion.

In the turbulent masses of the Hus Memorial, the heads of the individual figures played a special role for Šaloun. In the latter half of the 1900s he made a remarkable series of heads that were loosely related to the memorial, and they have a certain cyclical continuity in their content. *Escape from Life*, modelled in the spirit of Rodin, is full of surrender, while *Meditation* and *Concentration*, the eyes closed in the first and staring wildly in the second, have a more linear treatment of matter, and they are energetically worked. The relationships between these sculptures can be best understood in the context of Šaloun's theoretical notes, which he later published in the journal *Dílo*.[157] Šaloun understood art as an intuition of the fundamental cosmic force, for which the artist is a medium. The artist must understand a work internally through the power of emotion, more instinctively than intellectually, and by propagating emotion he also propagates life. His task is the "tremendous emphasising of the main features," and the existence of his work is the existence of wishes and desires. The heads cycle also reflects Šaloun's Symbolist understanding of the theory of empathy, in which the artist dies to the outside world in order to bring forth in secluded concentration an ecstatic stream of intuitive understanding. It is interesting that later, in the second decade of the 20th century, Šaloun would add another head to this series, *Resignation*, where rancour over an unfulfilled dream became another element in his account of the emotional sphere out of which, he maintained, a work of art emerged.

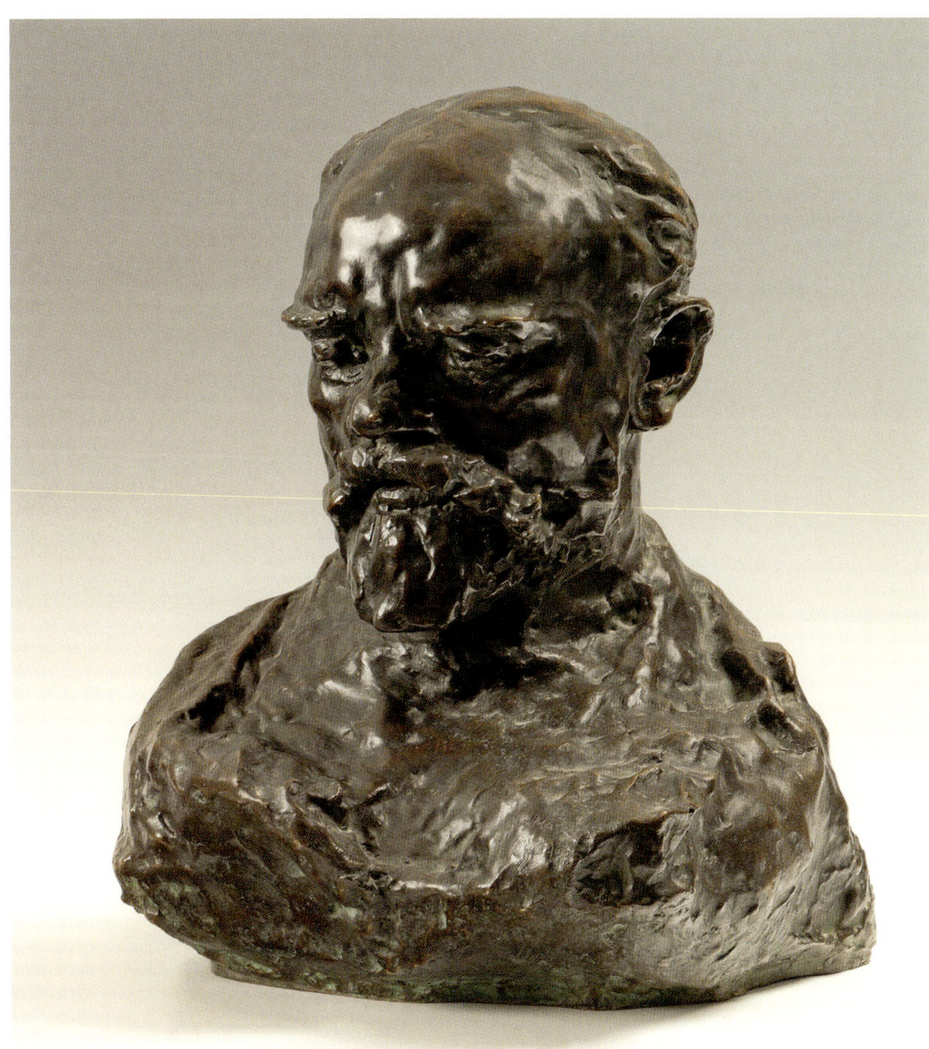

250 Josef Mařatka, Study for *Bust of Antonín Dvořák*, 1906, bronze, 53 cm

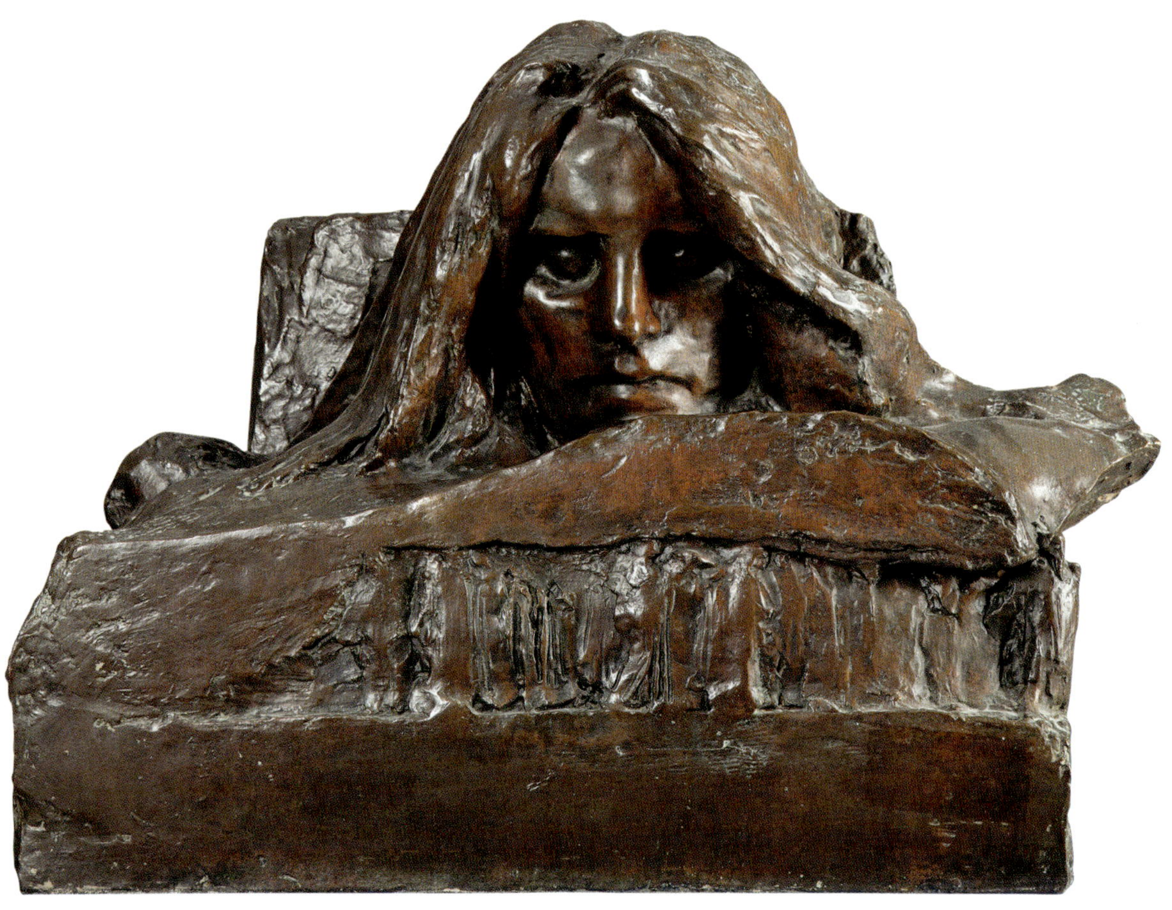

Other Czech sculptors were also working on heads around this time. After returning from several years spent in Rodin's studios in Paris, Josef Mařatka applied what he had learned there to assist Sucharda and Šaloun with their monuments. In 1908 he made his *Bust of Antonín Dvořák*, whom he had known since he was a child, when both had lived in the same building in Prague's New Town. In the bust he sought to depict Dvořák as a Slav musical genius, showing him in a moment of supreme concentration, when the composer, his eyes closed and his features expressively distorted, has surrendered to his emotions. It was only the stamp of Rodin's authority that allowed Mařatka to approach a bust intended for the foyer of the National Theatre in this way: both sculptors shared the idea of "inner vision" that was applied here with a powerful expressiveness. *Tomb Sculpture* by Stanislav Sucharda, where an imaginary funeral procession, depicted in low relief, files beneath the head of the White Mountain figure from the František Palacký Monument, is based on a similar concept, although the tone here is elegiac. The basic theme of emotional intuition that now dominated sculpture had its own expressive scale, which was reflected in how such works were modelled. Its calmer, more intimate aspects were always closer to Impressionism. This was also apparent in Mařatka's remarkable series of studies for *Portrait of Tereza*

251 Stanislav Sucharda, *Tomb Sculpture*, c. 1909, bronze, 40 cm

Koseová (1906–9), where the subject's sensitive face, framed by the wreath of her hair, mirrors her mental states, which in their indeterminacy resonate with an unmistakably contemporary accent. The emotional transparency of matter that Mařatka achieved here recalls Brancusi's contemporaneous development of the same theme, when he had similarly reached an important turning point, after which the accentuating of emotionality would become a new conceptual quality.

At this stage in the development of Czech Secession art, the relationship between impression and expression was a significant alternative to the idea of synthesis. It could be described in terms of the then popular distinction between Dionysian and Apollonian art, but it should be recalled that Nietzsche, the distinction's originator, considered them complementary. The complexity of this relationship also formed the content of contemporary work, as can be seen in the case of individual artists. In 1904 Bohumil Kafka left for Paris, motivated by a desire to understand the perspectives that would transpire from a greater familiarity with French art. He spent several years in the city, working on an important collection of small sculptures, in which it was as if

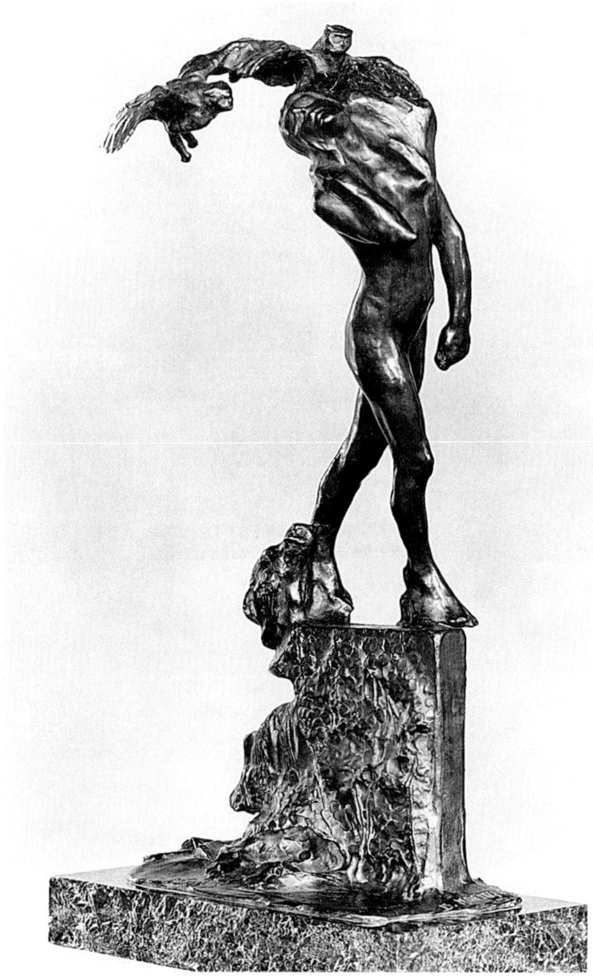

252 Bohumil Kafka, *Sleepwalker*, 1906, bronze, 81.5 cm

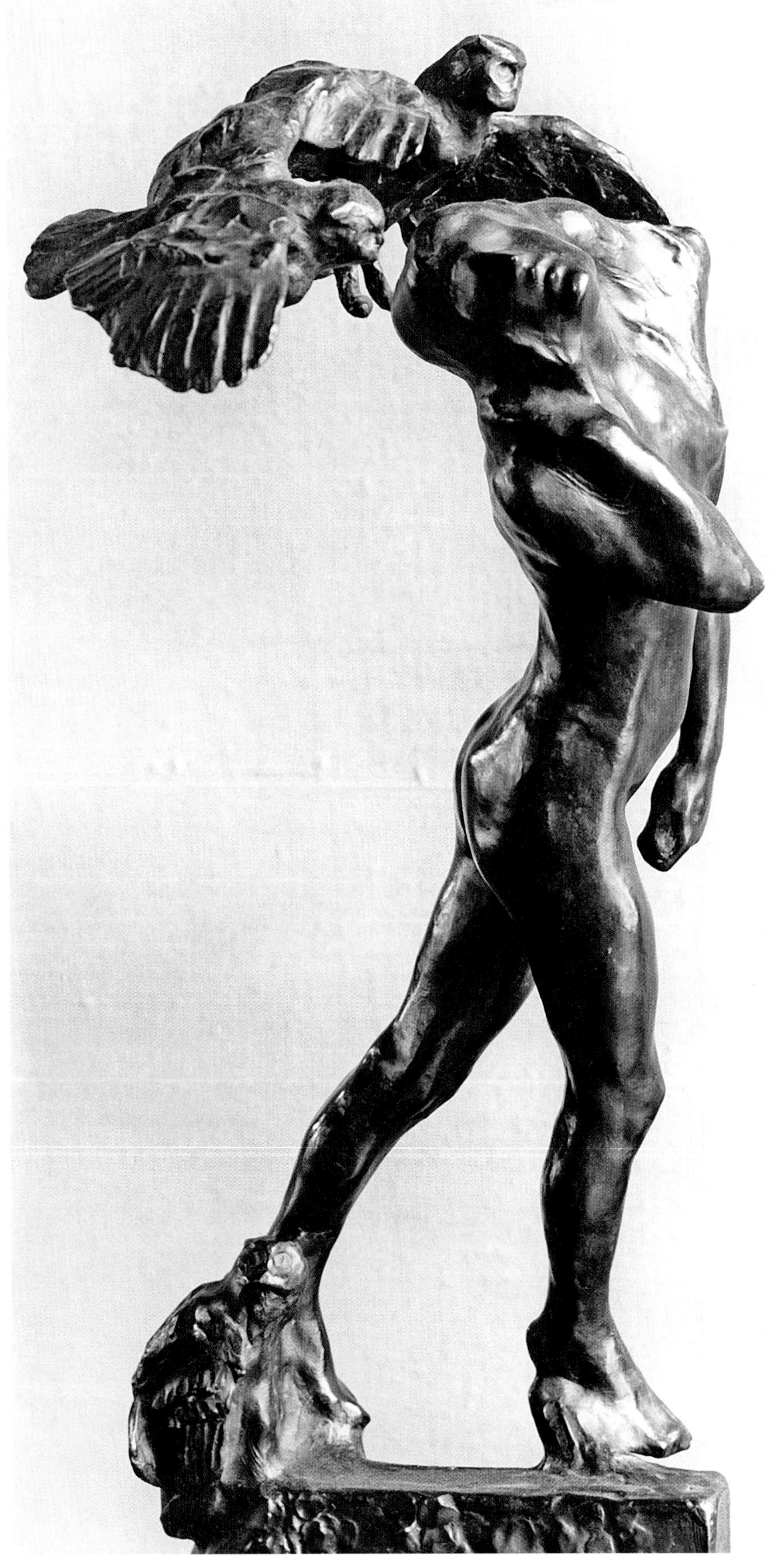

253 Bohumil Kafka, *Sleepwalker*, 1906, bronze, 81.5 cm, detail

he were trying to resolve the contradiction that had resulted from studying under both Sucharda and Myslbek. He was also responding to Rodin's work, to which he now had direct access. Yet differences would soon emerge. In sculptures such as *Visionary*, *Mummy*, *The Head of John the Baptist*, *Bacchanalia*, and *The Mad*, Kafka fully embraced Symbolist themes. Their form, however, was much more nervously agitated, erotically charged, and "primitive" than Rodin's smooth modelling. Initially, it seemed that Kafka had symbolically returned to the expressive naturalism of his *Marquise – The Ruin of Life* from 1902. It was an assault on decorative two-dimensionality, and in *The Mad* Kafka all but ruptured form. This extreme opening of a sculpture was soon joined by a powerful interest in the concave, dark space lying within matter. He experimented with both these options in two seemingly unimportant statuettes inspired by his stay at the French seaside resort of Onival (*Woman Picking Up Her Bathrobe after Bathing* and *Woman Styling Her Hair after Bathing*, both 1905). In 1906 Kafka's work became somewhat calmer, insofar as there was a certain synthesis of both options, especially in the content. It was then that he created *Sleepwalker*. Writing on his drawing for the sculpture, Kafka reminded himself to "give the model a pose that is not standing, so the muscles are not prominent but flowing." His concern was with weightlessness, with negating the fundamental requirement in traditional sculpture and capturing free motion determined by the psychological basis, relaxing the plastic principles. However, the pedestal for *Sleepwalker* is again a plane, covered with delicate natural decor.

The main artistic element in Kafka's approach remained his work with light and its expressive possibilities. Kafka's combining of impression and expression recalls Antonín Slavíček's output at this time, especially his small sketches of Prague. The essential elements of this pressing issue stand out more in sculpture. In the effect of light on matter, the application of which came from the need to express spontaneity and which added to the persuasiveness of rather abstract Symbolist ideas, line was typically the interpreter of the psychological and conceptual component. This line was not a rational one, but a line in the sense of Henry van de Velde's definition, as a force that takes energy from whomever is guiding it. This kind of line of force produces the figure of the naked *Sleepwalker*, bending like a bow, whose corporeality presents the line more as a three-dimensional volume, open or closed according to the side from which it is viewed. This two-sidedness is also facilitated by the work with light, which includes both high gloss and deep shadow. In the sculpture's outline this produces a complicated phenomenon, in which the effect of light gives mass to the line, coupling the visual with the haptic character of the expressive surface. Kafka's great advocate in Paris, Camille Mauclair, expressed something of this in his account of Rodin, quoted in *Volné směry*:

> Sculpture destroys the false idea of linear drawing [which for Mauclair is identified with an unwanted moral tone] to replace it with drawing in planes and volumes, and Rodin reminds us that the limiting of a surface in the air is only an illusion, and he systematically amplifies the planes that silhouette his statues, so as to create the broadest contact between them and the radiant atmosphere that perpetuates them.[158]

The expressive intersecting of mass and space had a profound significance. It meant not just the easing of depression, but was also a quest for freedom and the universal whole. In contemporary thinking it seemed that this could be achieved by returning to nature, to the maternal soil from which an artwork also came. The idea of the whole was therefore directly related to the idea of regeneration, a profound emotional rebirth, and in this sense the expressive tendency was not ultimately hostile to the idea of synthesis but, if anything, extended it. It was not satisfied with decoratively balancing a synthetic equilibrium; instead, it added a complication that created the preconditions to anchor this synthesis more deeply, in those layers of life and art

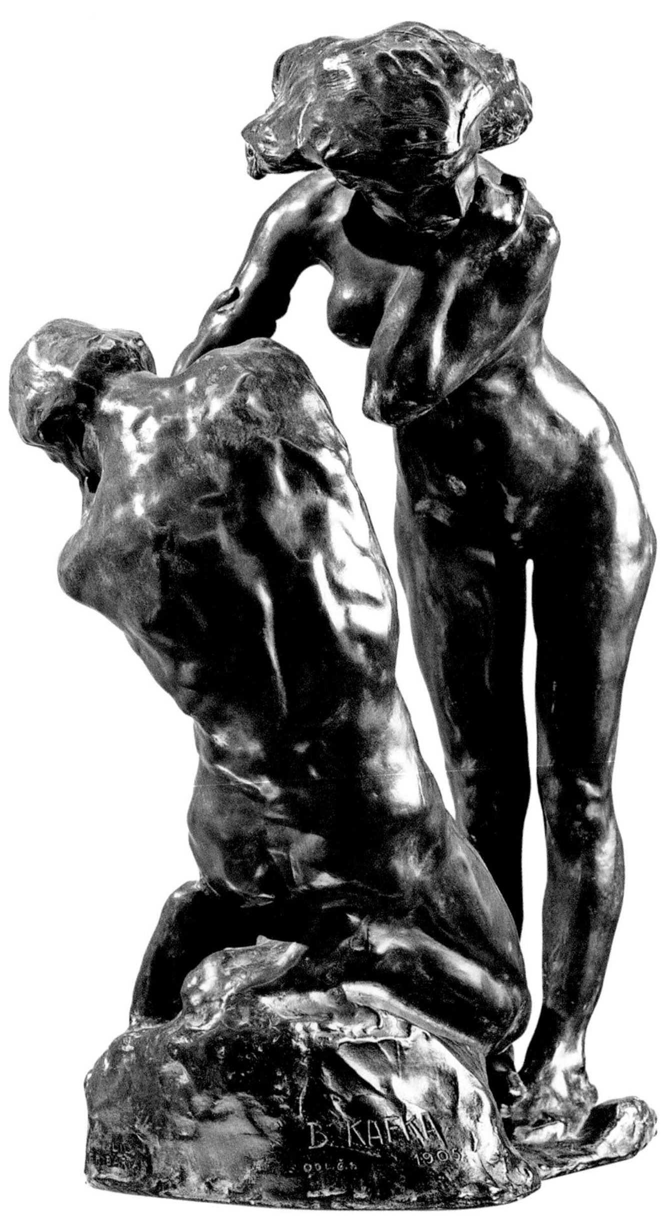

254 Bohumil Kafka, *The Eternal Drama*, 1906, bronze, 59 cm

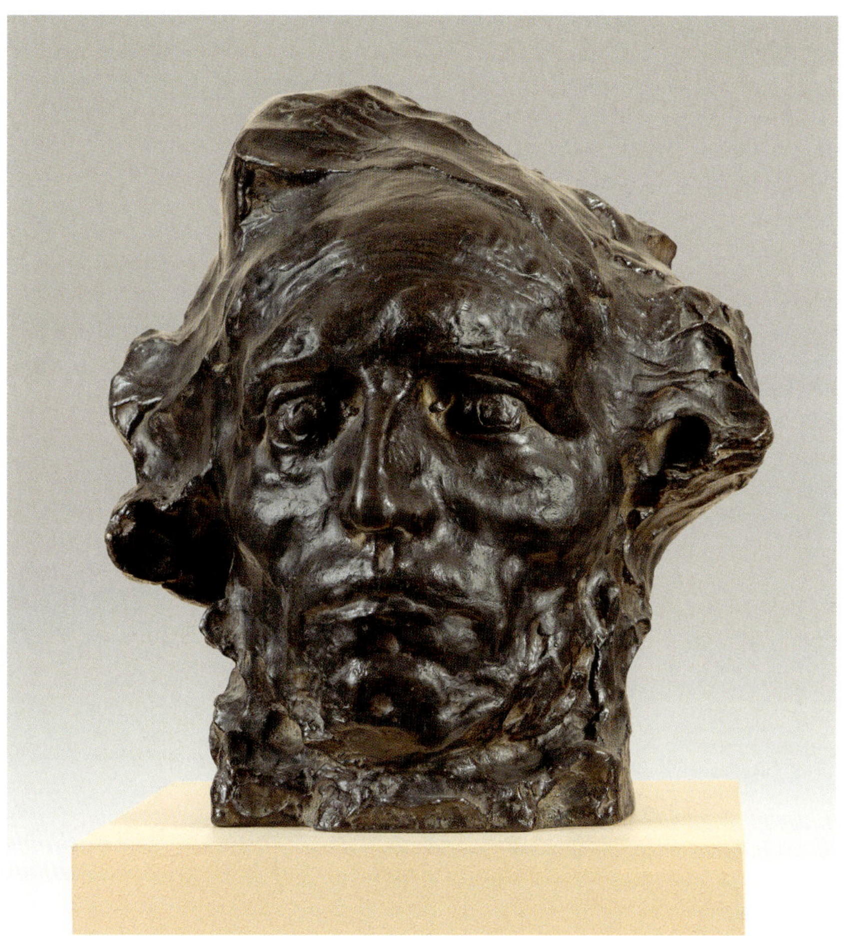

that had passed through the hell of disruption and division and bore the weight of existence no longer deceived by dreams of an ideal paradise.

It is from this perspective that we can understand why Edvard Munch was so enthusiastically received by Czech artists. With Rodin, despite all the drama, there was a fundamental Latin, Romanesque element, leading to peace and reconciliation. Munch's Scandinavian vision was far less merciful to human fate. It openly expressed the perils of the abyss that lured artists at the turn of the century, yet it was not lacking in an acerbic lyricism that brought a brighter note to modern man's constant struggle with himself.

We can also find some of Munch's typical themes among the work of sculptors. Kafka's *The Eternal Drama* (1906) had more in common with Munch than with Rodin, and the new introduction of a linear element in sensual Impressionist modelling can also be attributed to Munch's influence; Šaloun's *Concentration* was a very typical example of this. However, in Czech art we find the main echo of Munch in painting. This was also substantially related to the generational divide that had emerged in the middle of the 1900s. In sculpture, young adepts were won over to the modernist cause thanks especially to Sucharda, who taught at the School of Decorative Arts.

255 Ladislav Šaloun, *Concentration*, after 1905, bronze, 29.5 cm

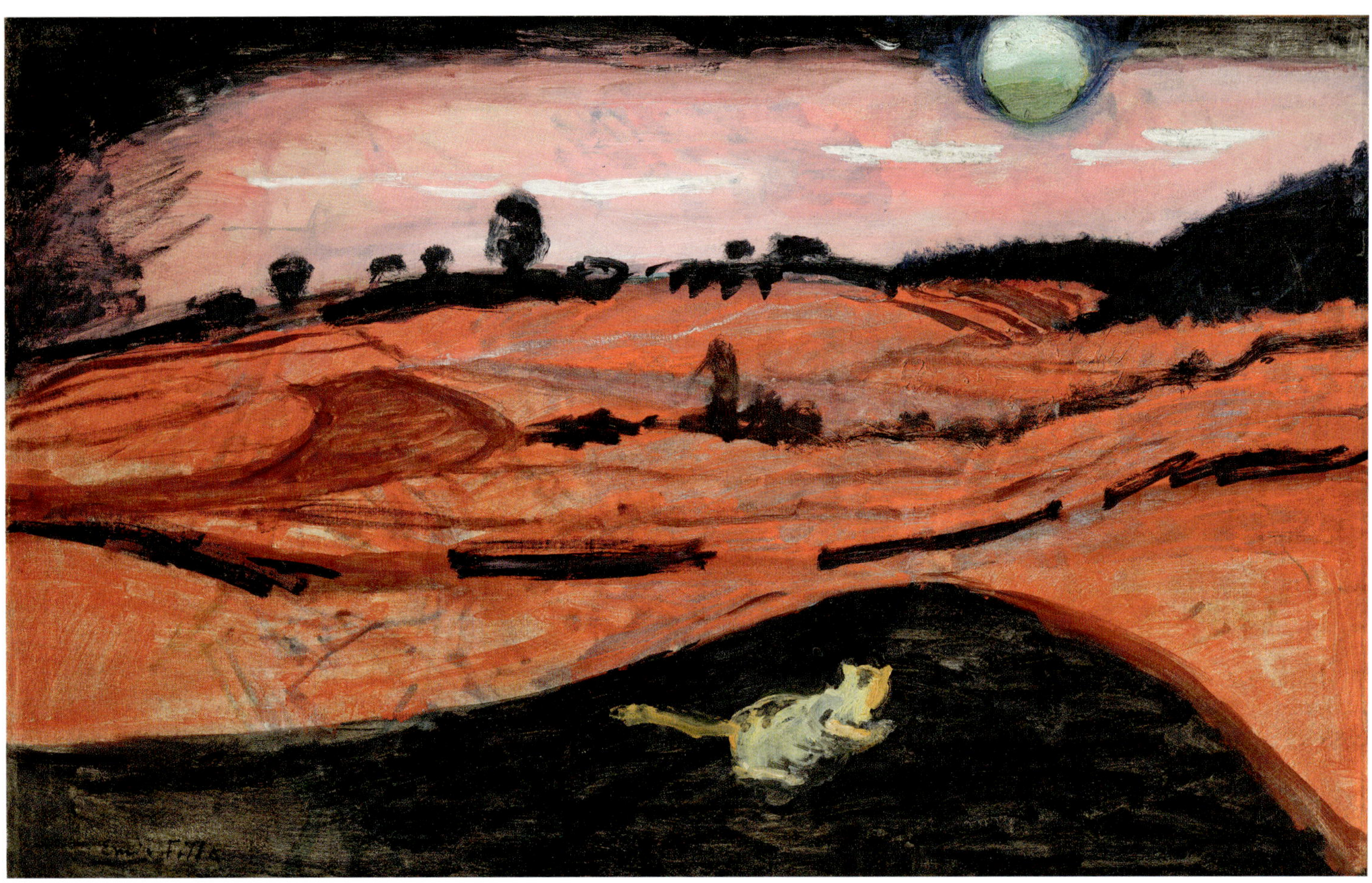

In painting, however, something of a barrier had been erected, for there were no youthful, progressive forces among the professors at the Academy of Fine Arts in Prague. In response, a group calling itself Osma (The Eight) formed among the dissatisfied students and announced its presence at an exhibition in 1907, introducing a new revolutionary spirit in Czech art.

The leading figure in the group was Emil Filla. Later, recalling the Munch exhibition and its impact on the younger generation of painters, he stressed that Munch had made it possible "to express again man's neglected inner state, to present the soul of man as the central agent of every emotion and action, principally that is of artistic endeavour." Filla also asserted that Munch was not expressing "only his own psychoses at the time; these are not expressions of his vexed heart, but universal symbols of the dreams, sufferings, sorrows, and delights of every generation and every individual."[159] Although this formulation also took in Filla's subsequent experiences and opinions, it was symptomatic that, right from the start, young painters understood the new expressiveness associated with Munch as something that transcended the individual, a synthesis of the experience of the individual and the human condition. Impressionism

256 Emil Filla, *Night of Love*, 1907, oil, 73 × 110 cm

had already raised this question, but while it saw the answer in a monistic "cosmic lyricism," in a unity of man and nature facilitated by light, Munch and his followers understood this situation as a crisis.

Filla's paintings from 1907 are a distinctive response to Impressionism. *Night of Love* is one of the most extreme paintings from this period, not just in Czech painting but in European painting as a whole. If the landscape theme is still Impressionist in origin, the painting is a radical reappraisal of Impressionism's content and form. For the content, Filla turned away from bright Impressionist daylight to the eeriness of night, with a moon, reminiscent of Karel Hlaváček's moons, that brings forth animal emotions. These are interpreted in spontaneous and broad brushstrokes, dividing the canvas into bold colours in the manner of poster art. Characteristically, line plays a substantial role in form, and it is treated more as an expressive expanse of colour. Filla followed Munch's symbolic use of shadow, and the shadow in the foreground, animated by the white cat, acts as a springboard for the dynamic absorption of the jarring yet strangely harmonious combination of reds and the pale green moon. Here Filla applied "Munch's abbreviation of an object, necessary and logical in the new pictorial structure," as well as "unique, internally logical harmonies of colours that are appropriate for the chosen material,"[160] in a way that was inspired but did not imitate.

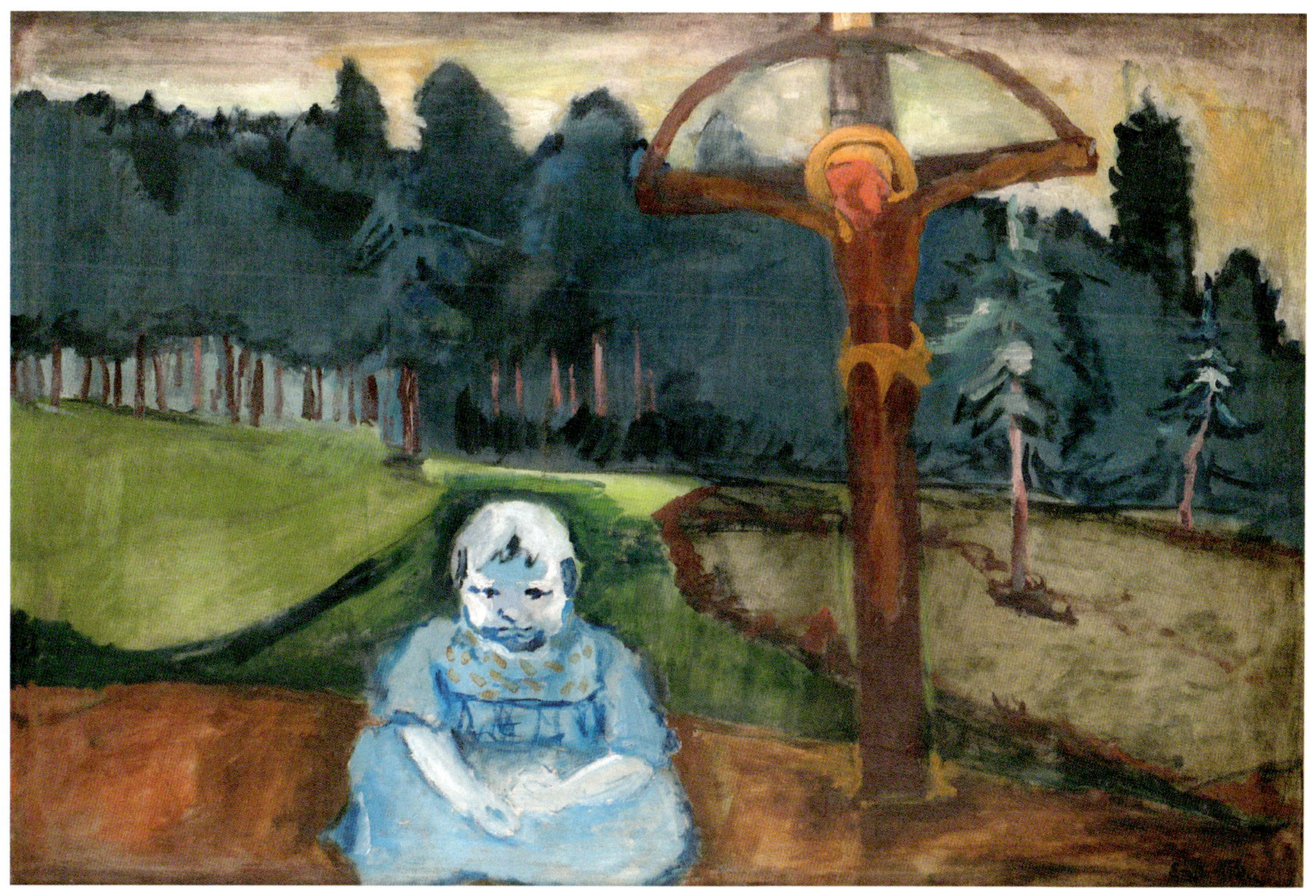

257 Emil Filla, *Child by a Forest*, 1907, oil, 96 × 138 cm

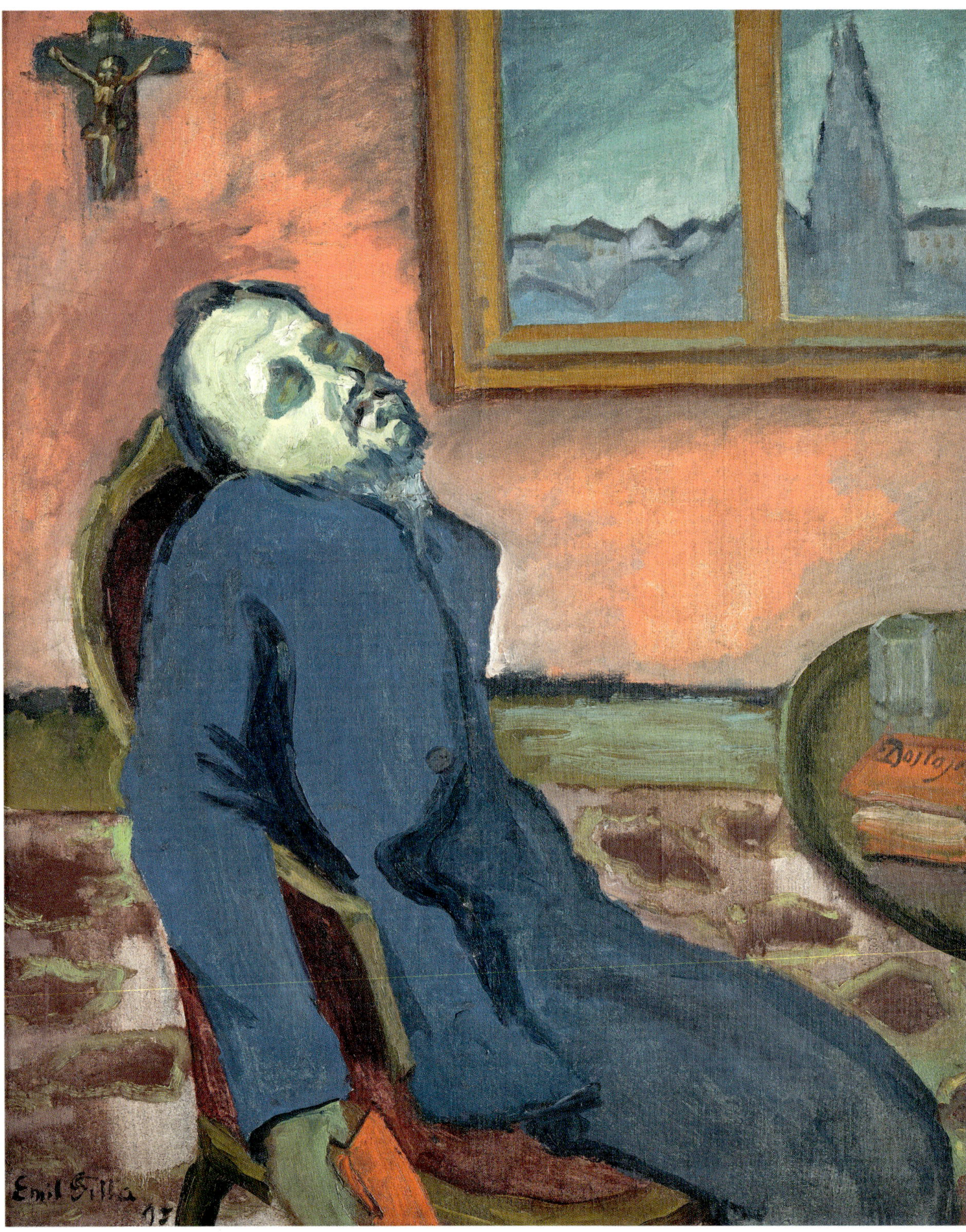

258 Emil Filla, *Reader of Dostoevsky*, 1907, oil, 98.5 × 80 cm

In *Child by a Forest*, Filla's reappraisal of his subject matter was more muted: the Secession's typical theme of a figure in a landscape has a new symbolism. It is interesting that Preisler's modest sketch *Boy by a Forest*, whose colours are similarly unrestrained, is perhaps also from this time, but in the content Filla went further still. In both works, the forest is the old Romantic symbol of a mysterious world. In Preisler's sketch, it is more a grove in the colours of autumn, while the path in Filla's painting leads to a dark and menacing wall of trees. Preisler's boy evokes the melancholy lyricism of puberty, but Filla's pale, ghostlike child, in conjunction with the crucifix, has a more ominous subtext. The emotional unity connecting figure and landscape forebodes tragedy.

Filla's excitement with the psychological resonance of colour culminated in *Reader of Dostoevsky*. The yellow and green modelling of the head of the man sitting in an

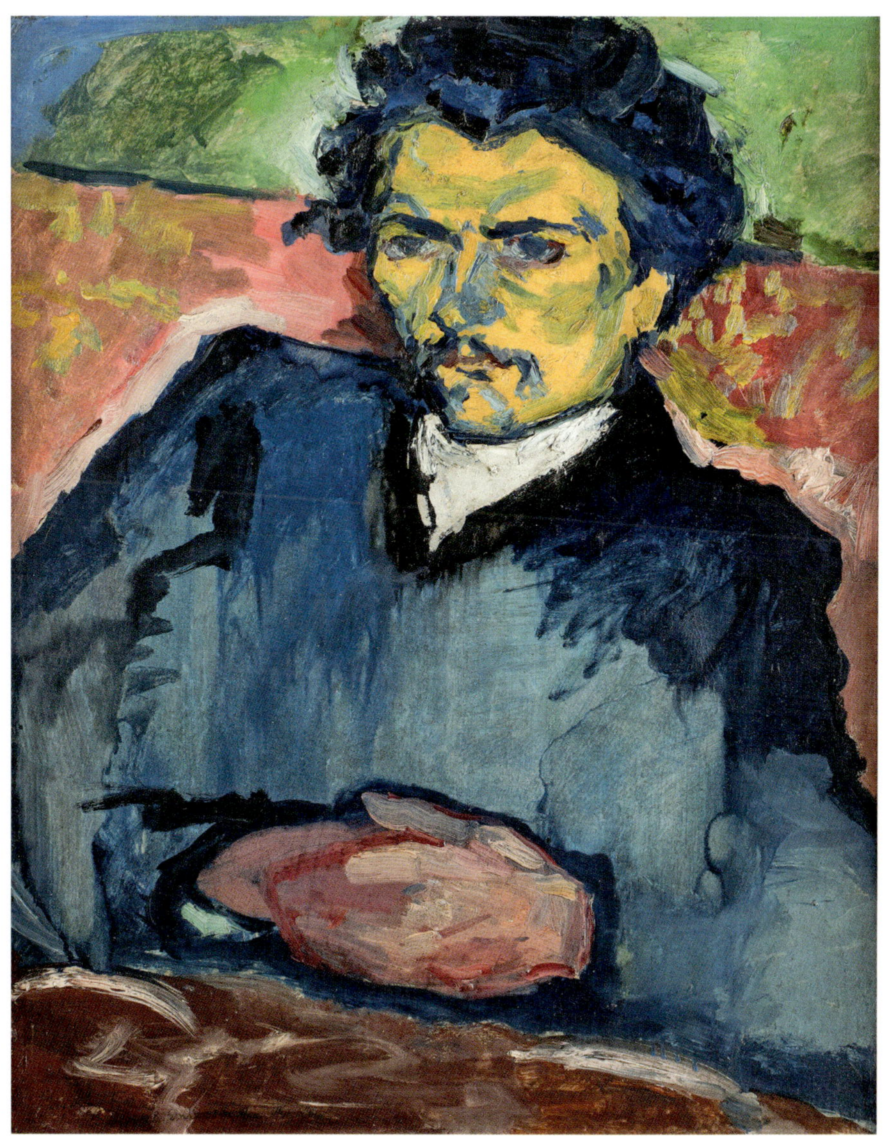

259 Emil Filla, *Portrait of Josef Uher*, 1908, oil, 68.8 × 54.5 cm

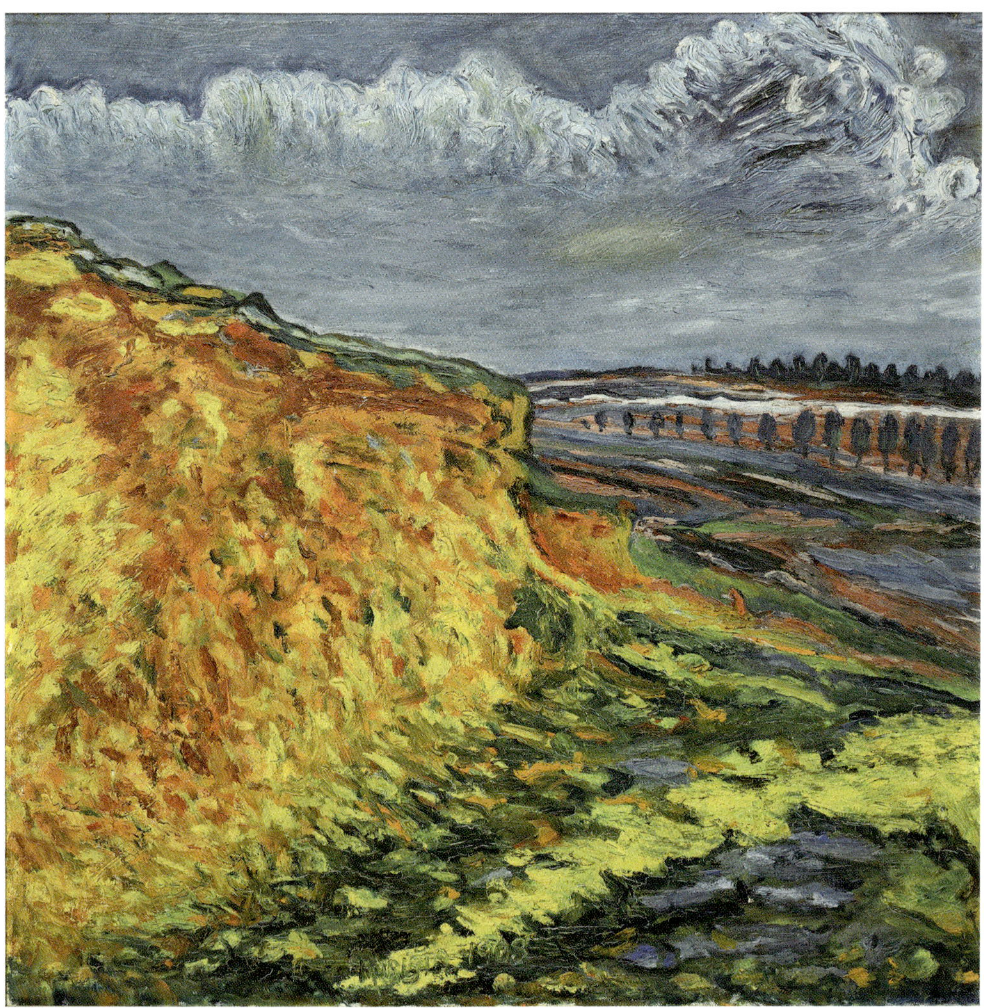

armchair, dejectedly reflecting upon what he has read, is in dissonant harmony with the painting's reds and blueish greens, indicating the psychomachia unfolding in his mind. The diagonal of the reader's body, consumed with inner conflict, connects two contrasting elements: the crucifix on the wall, symbolising the old religion that can offer no solace, and Dostoevsky's writings, which lie on a table next to a glass of water. Here the modern author is presented as an alternative to the old world of humility, above all for his open questioning of the fundamentals of human life and death. For young painters Dostoevsky was the definitive writer, just as Munch was their definitive painter. They looked to "unclassifiable" instances of the new culture to support their increasing aversion to bourgeois mediocrity and those elements of modern art that had now become socially acceptable. Another such "unclassifiable" painter was Vincent van Gogh. *Volné směry* devoted an issue to him in 1908, but the older generation was more interested in the drama of his life than his art. They considered him a "dream violator," a passionate enthusiast who was to be admired for the authenticity of

260 Bohumil Kubišta, *Landscape with Tree Alley*, 1908, oil, 62 × 60 cm

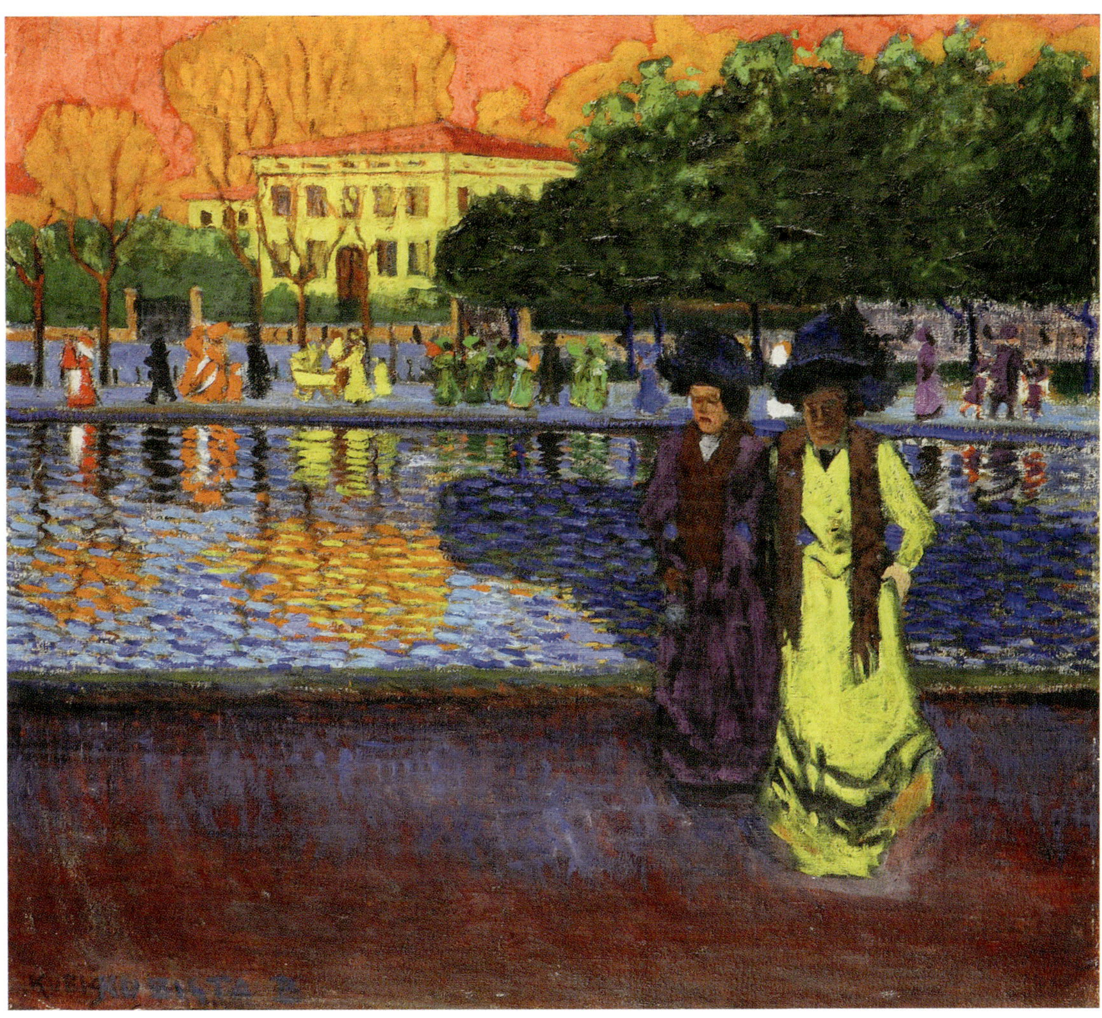

his sacrifice, but whose art was excessive. Younger painters, however, were influenced by his paintings.

In 1907 Bohumil Kubišta painted *Triple Portrait*, an expressive work in which, seconded by his friends and fellow painters Bohumil Feigl and Emil Artur Pittermann, he challenged the viewer to a duel. In 1908 he then painted *Landscape with Tree Alley* and *Interior*, where the inspiration of Van Gogh's expressive line is clear. Their pastose brushwork testifies to his attempt to overcome the usual Impressionist analysis of form by means of pure colour. Kubišta was less introverted than Filla, and his enthusiasm for modern art was prompted by his lofty ambition for Czech art to be in step with the world. Among the younger generation it was he who paid the most attention to contemporary painting in other countries, especially France. He devised a theory to bring together this diverse knowledge, which he applied in the uncompromising critiques he penned for magazines. This is also why, in his own art, he was quick to adopt new sources of inspiration and integrate them into his distinctive style. *Promenade in a*

261 Bohumil Kubišta, *Promenade in a Florence Park*, 1907, oil, 84 × 90 cm

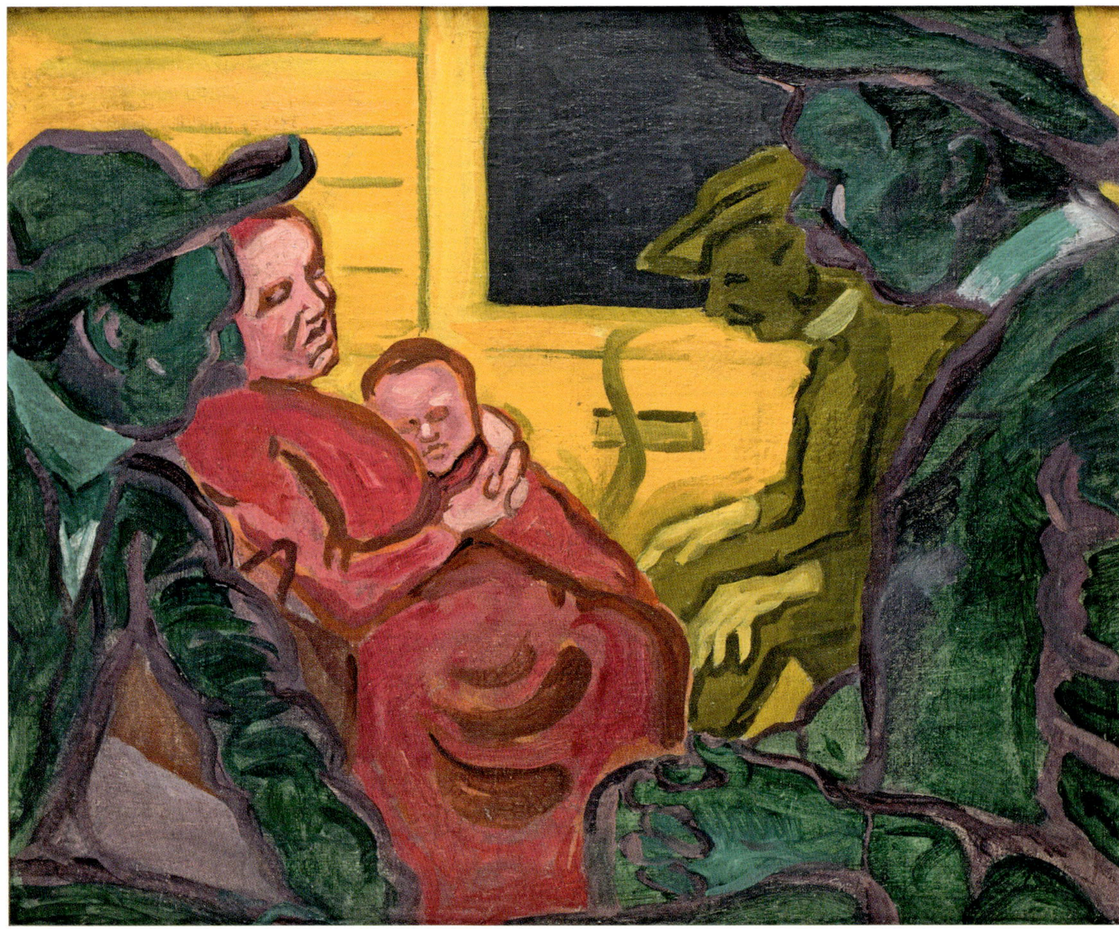

Florence Park from 1907 drew on the year he had spent studying in Florence (1906–7), and it was as if he had returned to the problem of the decorative picture plane, which was now of course tied to an expressive colour scale. Kubišta found a new expressive form in scenes from everyday life, as in his painting *On the Train (Third-Class Passengers)* (1908). His colours – yellow, green, and purple – were again typical of the Secession, but here they were not diffused with luminous values, and this gave them a decorative two-dimensionality and an extraordinary and immediate expressiveness. If the emotion in Filla's work was characterised by a sense of the world's dynamic essence, Kubišta's sensibility was more austere, more disciplined, and more confrontational. *On the Train (Third-Class Passengers)* had a new objectivity that concerned not only its style but also the painter's account of the world. It demonstrated that the new expressive way of painting could surpass Impressionism, not just in its subjective symbolism but also where Impressionism seemed quite unassailable: in collective ideas associated with a conviction about the reality of the world.

In 1907 Antonín Procházka, another Osma painter, was still producing Impressionist work, but he too was captivated by Munch's crowd scenes, which he interpreted with

262 Bohumil Kubišta, *On the Train (Third-Class Passengers)*, 1908, oil, 64 × 76 cm

a certain Baroque accent (*Street* and *Jungmannovo náměstí*, both 1907). Initially, it was as though Procházka were miniaturising the scene. This is how he painted *Circus* (1907), whose colours had a radiant transparency that differentiated it from the heavy pathos of Munch's art. The luminous quality of Impressionist painting has not been expunged but turned upside down: the light does not fall on the subjects but is reflected from the white canvas, turning it into coloured light. This change was in fact far ahead of its time, pointing to the later problems of Orphic Simultaneism, but Procházka evidently could not immediately make full use of it. He sought instead the monumentality that appealed to him in the work of Honoré Daumier, newly appreciated as an example of an artist who was an activist in both art and society. Similarly, Procházka's *Expulsion of the Merchants from the Temple* (1909) takes the Biblical narrative as an allegory of the state of art and society.

The maturing of opinions within Osma is best demonstrated by how the young painters worked on common themes, each artist approaching them as his disposition dictated. One such theme was card players, which Filla, Procházka, and Kubišta painted in 1908 and 1909. Filla's *Red Ace* showed an encounter between a "seeker" in the Dos-

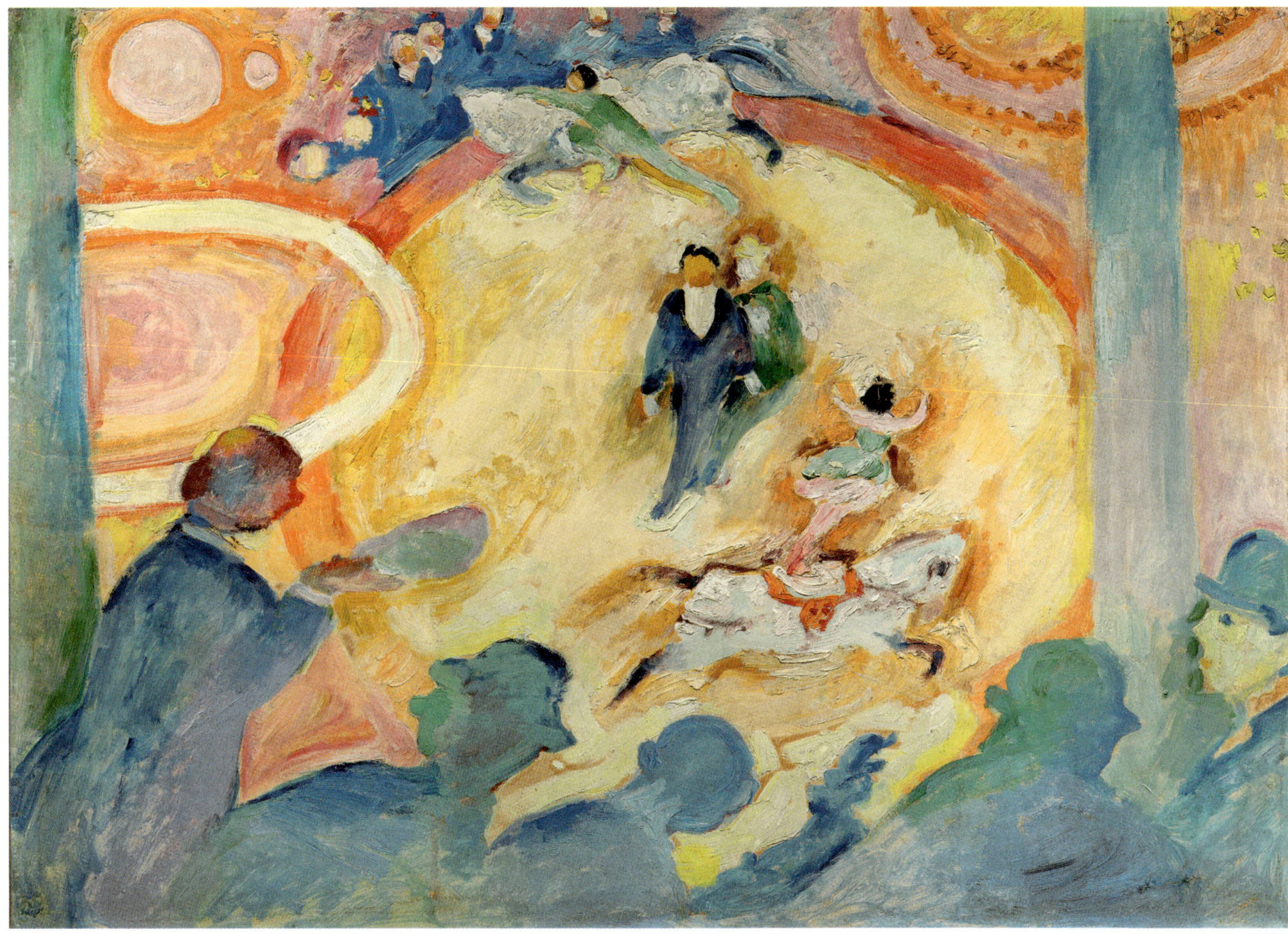

263 Antonín Procházka, *Circus*, 1907, oil, 47.5 × 65 cm

toevsky mould and the wiles of fate, while Kubišta's painting seemed entirely drawn from real life, and Procházka's trio of players were monumental figures. Each painting was wholly associated with its painter's personality, and these works anticipated how their art would subsequently develop. What the paintings shared were those aspects that, in the broader context of the development of Czech art, marked a fundamental reappraisal of what had been achieved so far. In them, Munch's line, in conjunction with expressive coloured space, led to a new conceptuality of the painting – one that had yet to fully abandon the sensory and emotional bedrock of Czech Impressionism. Here, however, the synthesis of formal devices was directed elsewhere than the decorative synthesis that Preisler, for instance, was working on at this time. The primitivism that these young artists embraced overcame the inhibitions that made it impossible for Preisler to draw fully on the chthonic source of creative psychological energy unearthed by the Secession. Of course, the achievements of the 1890s' generation were not in vain, for they had prepared the ground for this descent to the maternal

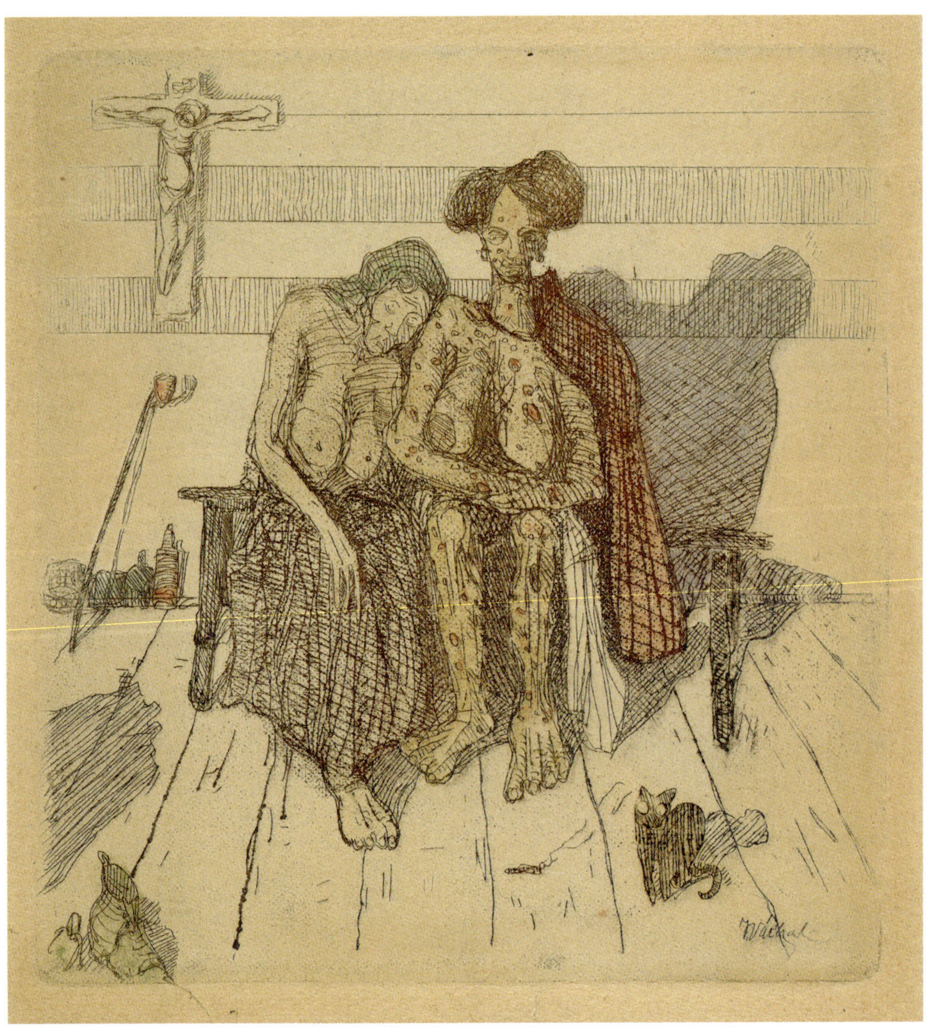

264 Josef Váchal, *Women*, 1906–8, etching, 17.2 × 15.5 cm

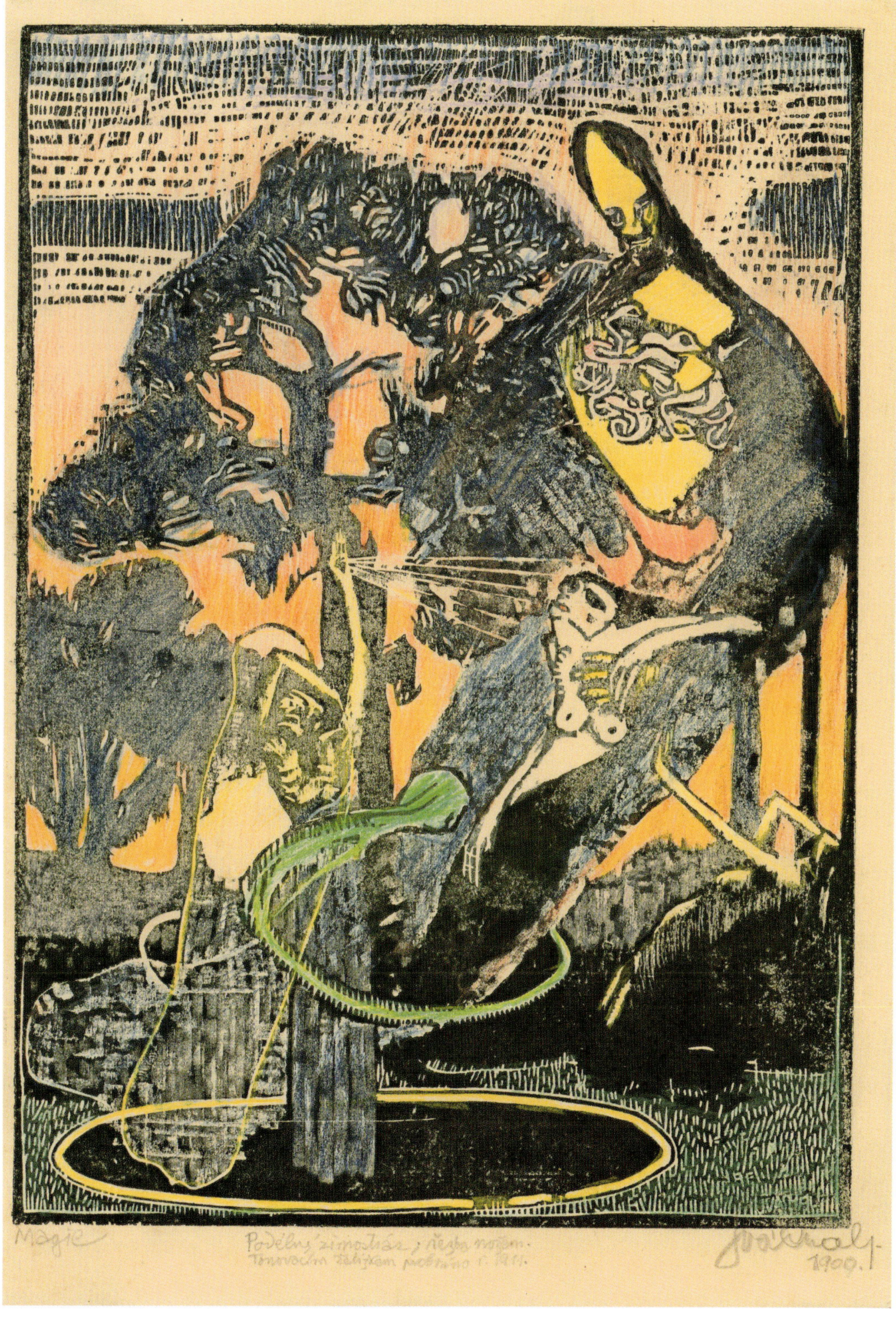

265 Josef Váchal, *Magic*, 1909, coloured woodcut, 52.5 × 38.5 cm

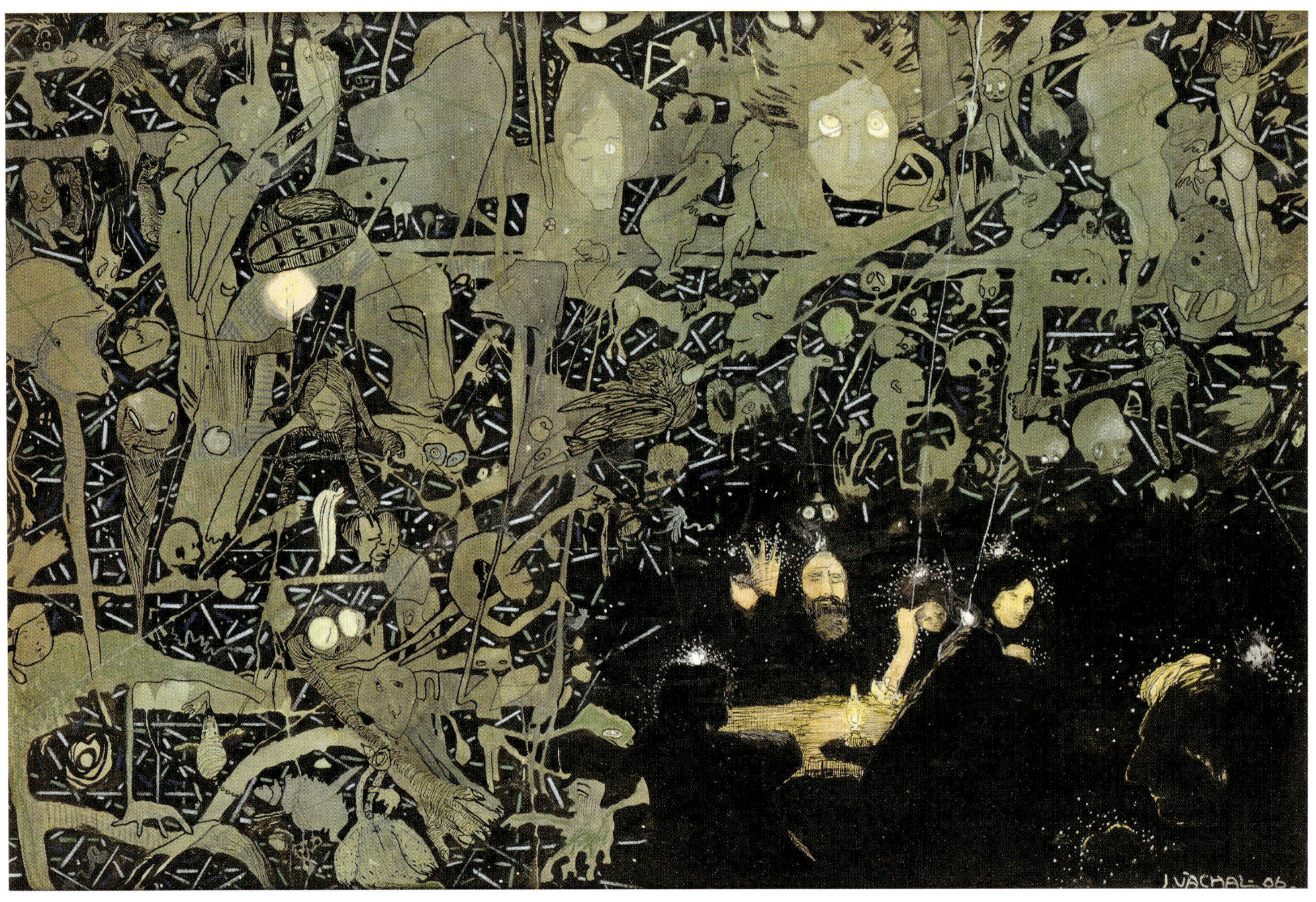

266 Josef Váchal, *The Astral Plane – Spiritist Séance*, 1906, Indian ink and watercolour, 35.7 × 52 cm

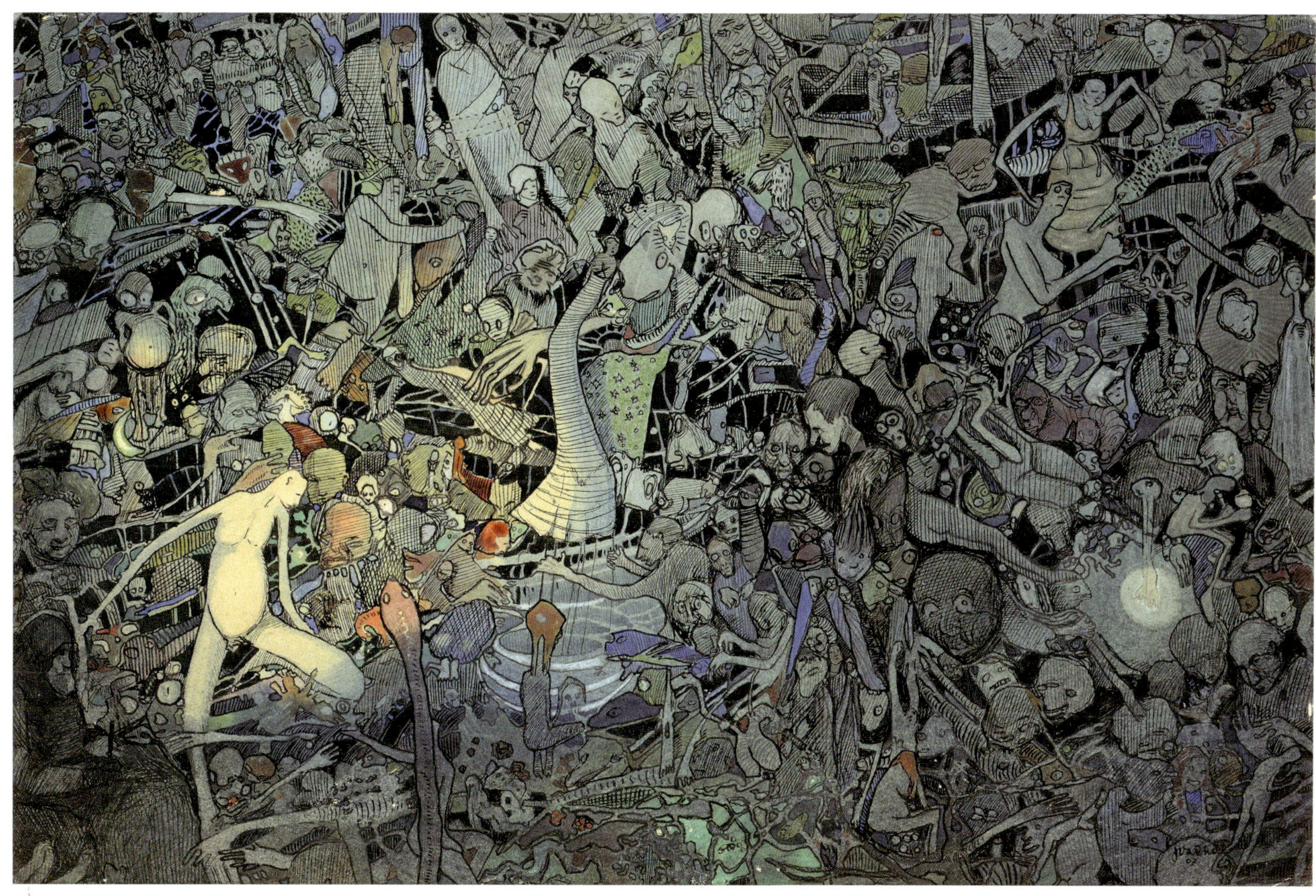

267 Josef Váchal, *The Elemental Plane – The Plane of Passions and Instincts*, 1907, Indian ink and watercolour, 30.6 × 52.5 cm

wellsprings of artistic intuition. Expressionism not only required greater courage in relation to oneself and the public, and more self-sacrifice, but it also involved greater trials and perils. The psychological zone of this art was full of pitfalls. The Osma painters, whose revolt still operated within the rules of the art game, may themselves have felt like card players. Other members of the younger Secession generation, those who stood alone but had the same longing to finish the fight begun ten years previously, often risked much more.

This was the case with Josef Váchal. Like Filla's *Reader of Dostoevsky*, Váchal's etching *Women* (1906–8) draws a connection between human suffering and the Catholic crucifix hung on the wall. However, here the diagonal does not have writings by a modern author, nor does this room have a view of a Gothic spire soaring to the heavens, to recall times when there was no religious division. There is only a black cat sitting on the floor, and on the wall the bizarre shadows cast by this human wreckage. The shadow is a reference to Munch, to the peculiar shadow play of his *Death in the Sickroom*, while the cat is an emissary from the world of demons.

Váchal, whose father was Mikoláš Aleš's cousin, was stigmatised by his illegitimate birth. At the very beginning of the new century he was enthused by the anarchism he discovered in S. K. Neumann's magazine *Nový kult* and the poems of František Gellner.[161] In 1903 he joined the Theosophical Society in Prague, prompted by his father's promotion of Spiritism. In the following year, when he was employed in a library in Bělá pod Bezdězem, Váchal experienced a series of distressing hallucinations that suggested incipient mental illness. However, he decided to become an artist, and his talent, which became apparent after his brief studies in Alois Kalvoda's landscape school, allowed him to vent his psychoses in his art, in this way restoring him to equilibrium.

Although this personal motivation was fundamental for Váchal's art, what is more important is his significance in the Czech Secession as a whole. Váchal's fantastical

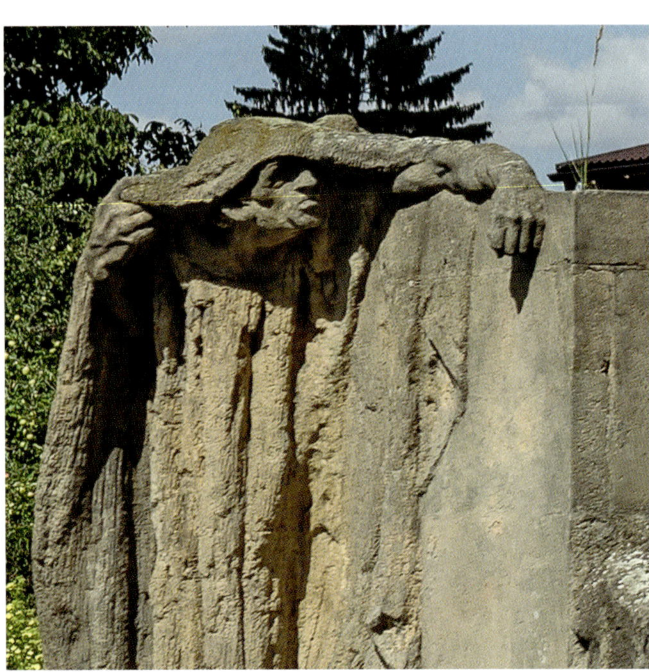

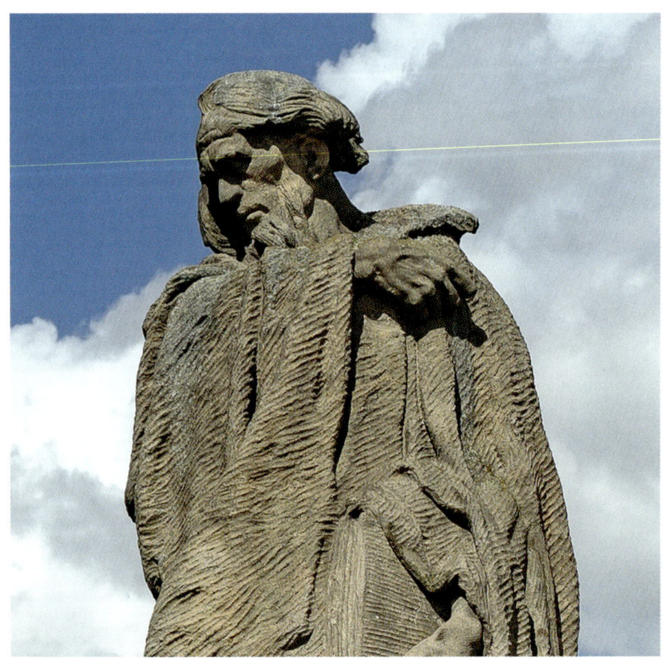

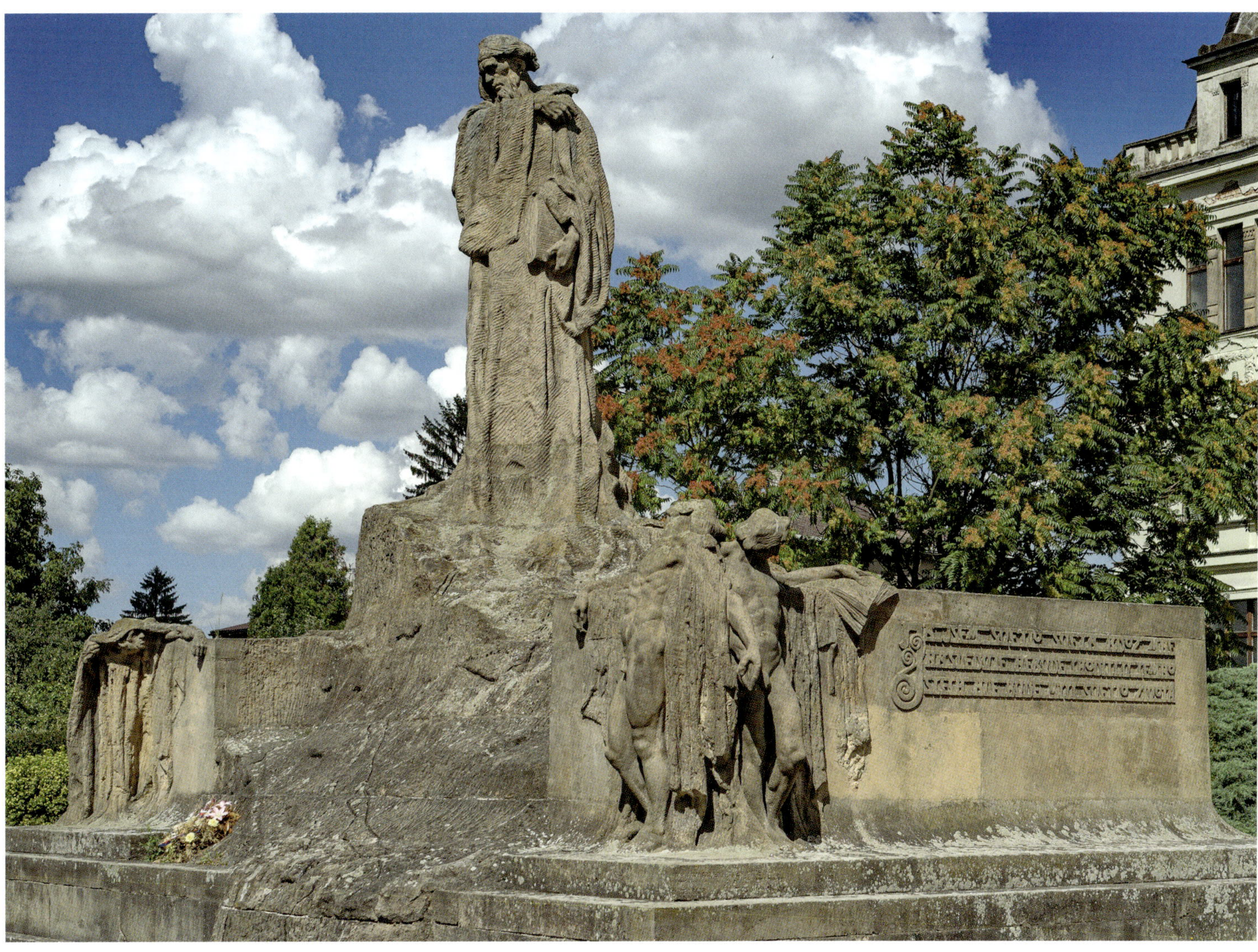

visions were not entirely unrelated to other artists, drawing as they did on the work of Schwaiger, Panuška, and Hlaváček; but, as with the relationship between the Osma painters and the older generation, Váchal escalated both the artistic expression and the content. He mostly worked as a printmaker, and ultimately the simple coloured woodcut allowed to him to express his ideas fully, usually in the form of a series of prints accompanied by his own text.

Váchal's ideas were based on Spiritist thinking that divided the dualistic world into the living and the dead, and he depicted the mediumistic connecting of these two worlds unconventionally in his coloured drawings *The Astral Plane* (1906) and *The Elemental Plane* (1907). He too reflected contemporary ideas about the artist as a medium for unknown forces. While Šaloun, for instance, understood this ability as the source of an artist's power of intuition, Váchal saw here a danger of being possessed by lower

268–270 Ladislav Šaloun, Jan Hus Memorial in Hořice, 1911–13

demons. For this reason, he began working with magic as a means of mastering these treacherous psychological forces. He became a passionate student of old writings and authors, incorporating the curious knowledge he acquired into his pictures and books. His syncretic learning about old religions and magical practices was combined with an interest in historical heretic movements that directly reflected his earlier anarchist leanings. Váchal became familiar with all the religious sects that had flourished in the past and in the turbulent years of the end of the century, but he did not persevere with any of them for very long. His talent for satire and the grotesque, which he used to process all this diverse source material into a distinctive perspective on religious matters, had a strong and earthy sense of humour and a penchant for parodying metaphysical ideas. In this respect, Váchal was an example of the revival of an approach that, in the Middle Ages and the Renaissance, had comprised an "alternative" culture that stood in opposition to official religious dogma.[162] The development of Váchal's art in the latter half of the 1900s can be seen in his coloured woodcut *Magic* (1909). It shows a magician

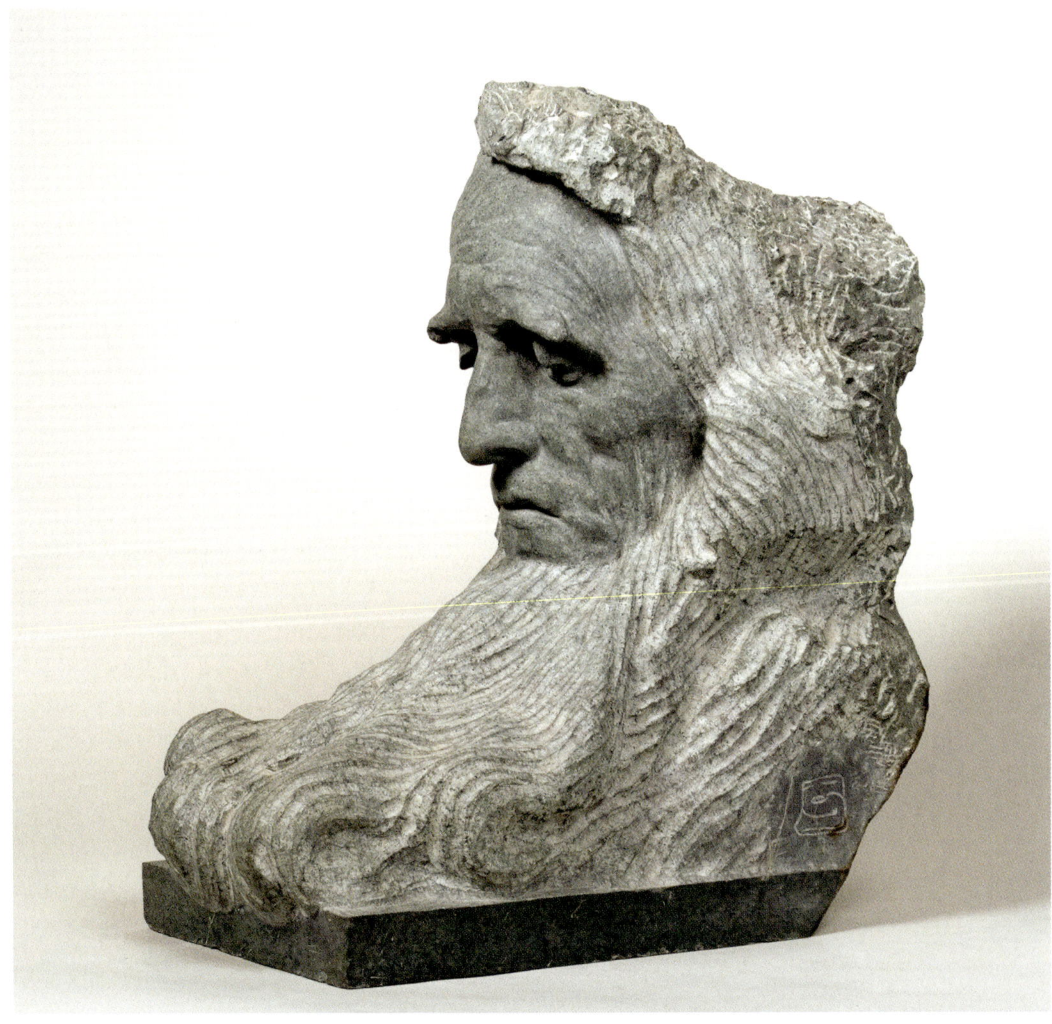

271 Ladislav Šaloun, *Scribe*, 1920, serpentinite, 63 cm

performing an invocation of a hierarchical chain that takes over the mind and body of his chosen subject. The woodcut's primitive execution adds a sense of urgency to its esoteric symbols and narrative. In terms of the contemporary artistic psyche, it manifests an interesting change of perspective: the idea of a passive emotional oneness with the universe, of submitting to the forces of the irrational, has given way to the idea of mastering and wielding such forces. This is a very characteristic depiction of a mentality that was also associated with the processes exploring the problem of artistic expression in the latter half of the decade. The psychological fatigue that had reigned at the end of the 19th century had now been definitively replaced with a new desire to create, prompted by an attitude that was entirely unconventional and cared nothing for official sanction. In this, the process initiated by the Secession was now complete.

If the Secession had been consummated by young artists, something of their attitude was also reflected in the work of older artists. In 1911–13 Ladislav Šaloun erected his second Jan Hus Memorial – this one in Hořice. Its completion in fact preceded the more famous monument to Hus, and in it Šaloun could avoid the difficulties and obstacles that had delayed the Prague memorial. Again, he used the idea of Hus standing between two contrasting groups, but here they concerned a more general moral level, placing him in a different semantic context. The sandstone block, with Hus dressed in a robe and with one foot advanced, is reminiscent of Rodin's *Balzac*. The book he holds characterises him more as a man of learning than a medium for Czech history, but here too the monument was based on more structured relationships. The sandstone memorial has a sculpted cascade of water, echoing the main inscription beneath the statue of Hus: "He opened the rock, and the waters gushed out; they ran in the dry places like a river." As Šaloun continued to associate Hus with "the soul's light and flame," the key concept for the Hořice monument would seem to be the old systematics of natural mythology, based on the correlations between the principal natural elements and how they can be used to describe the whole cycle of the world, with an emphasis on the moral considerations governing it. In its "composition of more balanced forms and lines permitted by the setting," as Šaloun wrote in his account of the monument, it expressed Hus's "moral, cultural and religious" significance in a way that sought a firmer foundation for the revival of the sculptural monument.[163] In 1910 Šaloun produced a sculpture of Rabbi Löw for a new building that is now home to Prague City Hall, and again the main figure's tranquillity expresses his mastery of natural and spiritual forces, based on his profound knowledge of them. Šaloun's later *Scribe* (1920), in which the endlessly flowing symbolic Secession curve was associated with the idea of wisdom and learning, marked the culmination of this line of thinking.

Váchal's black magician and Šaloun's *Scribe* have contrasting meanings, but more importantly they were both symptomatic of a standpoint that stressed the artist's newly activated creative and cognitive powers. In this sense, the need for emotional expression can be said to have logically resulted in a requirement for a new mastery of the sources of the emotion so revealed, and accordingly the structural composition of Czech Secession art, with its greater emotional depth, would soon have to be reinforced at the intellectual level.

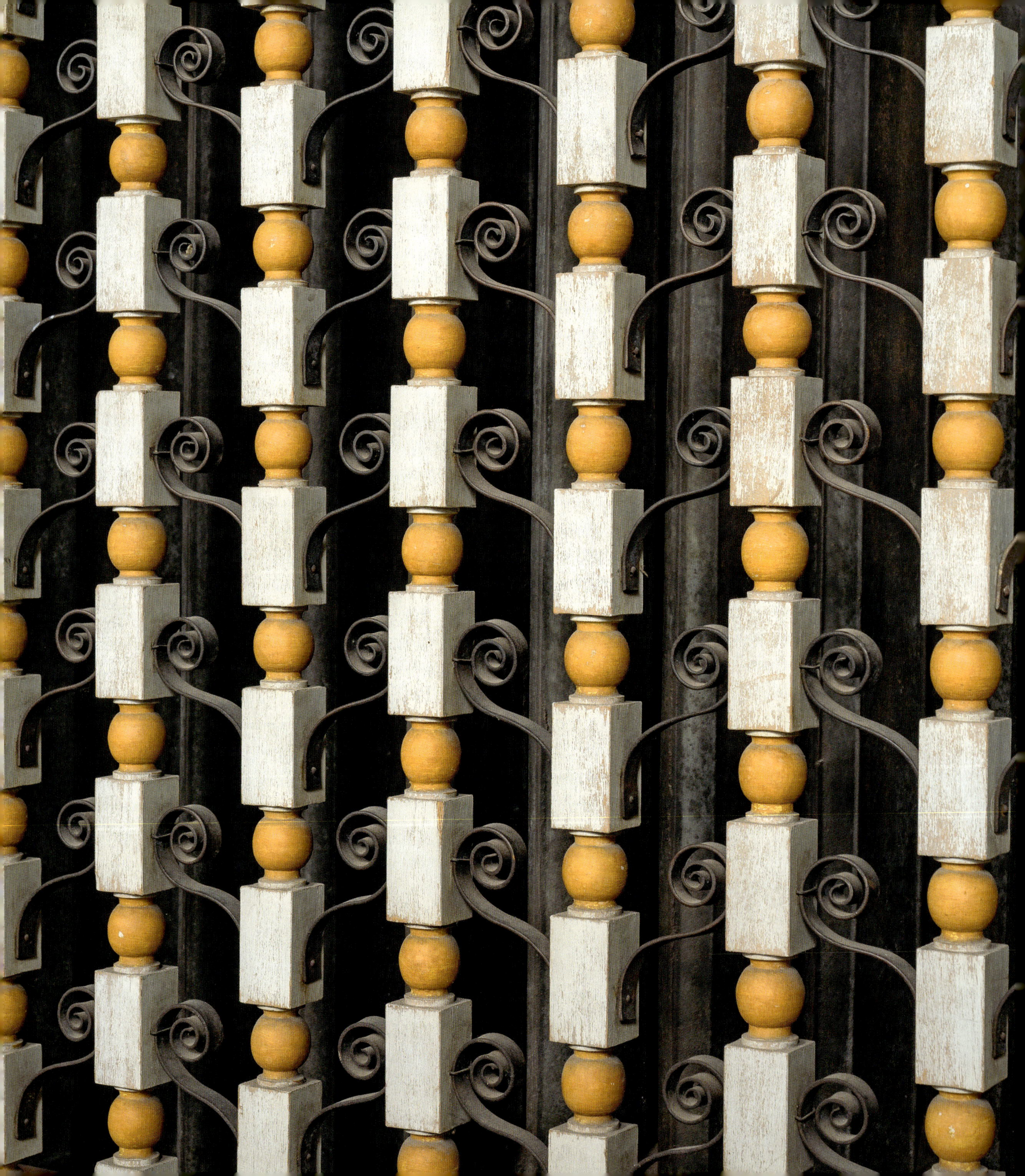

GEOMETRISATION

The changes that were underway in Czech art during the latter half of the 1900s – especially the greater expressiveness and conceptuality of fine art – could not but be reflected in ornament, which to date had been central to the Secession's quest for a new style. Naturalistic ornament, which in this country had chiefly been developed by Celda Klouček and his school, was a successful alternative to historicist ornament. It expressed a general tendency in the Secession, a turning to organic nature as a framework to externalise its world view. The rapid conventionalising of this ornament, which created a misleading impression of the homogeneity of contemporary culture and lifestyle, had principally happened for social reasons. The naturalistic Secession now signalled the ideology of the bourgeois liberal classes, who, resenting the dramatic ascent of monopolistic capitalism, sought an escape from the traumas of real life in the myth of a natural paradise. This was not of course viable, and in this context naturalistic ornament soon lost its artistic value and became merely a badge of social affiliation. In 1910 *Dílo* asserted that Klouček's ornament, "having been misused, became a veil behind which every businessman tried to hide the poverty of his creations, and Klouček's ornament, once so delicate and beautiful but now corrupted and profaned by stuccoists, became a menace to modern architects and artists."[164] The magazine presented examples of the work of Professor Klouček's younger pupils, who were trying "to go with the new currents in modern architecture."

Klouček had himself arrived at a certain limit in naturalism, when in his mascarons he had intuitively expressed the need for a fundamental internalising of the new ornamental style, with a complicated interplay of conscious and unconscious elements that was also apparent in the new rhythmicality of symmetrical and asymmetrical forms. Although this was an important development, with Klouček it was merely a symptom and did not become a more definite idea. Yet only through this fundamental internalising was it possible to develop the original naturalism more thoroughly, for in this way alone could the new ornament's integrating function become a fundamental symbol of modern culture. In Bohemia these questions did not find a thinker and artist as perceptive as Henry van de Velde, for instance, who radically shifted ornament from a description of the phenomenal world to an expression of elemental psychological forces. Nevertheless, in this country too there were attempts to transform the previously static projection of natural forms into a much more dynamic expressive foundation.

One of the manifestations of this change was the introduction of animal motifs rendered in stylised motion, such as Zdenka Braunerová's design of a peacock, the Secession's heraldic bird, on the title page of Miloš Marten's *The Cycle of Pleasure and Death* (1907). Braunerová was originally a landscape painter who had been taught by Antonín Chittussi, and the author of prints of picturesque scenes from Prague, but she now

272 Dušan Jurkovič, Garden Room at the castle in Nové Město nad Metují, 1909, detail

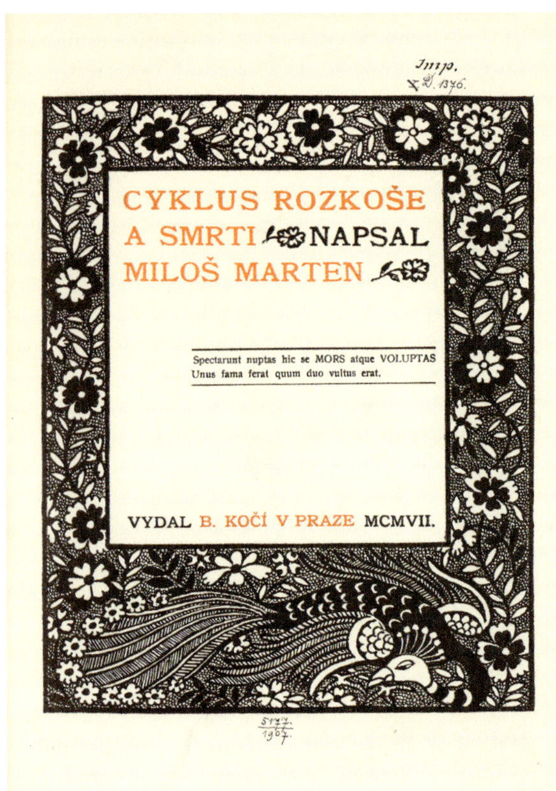

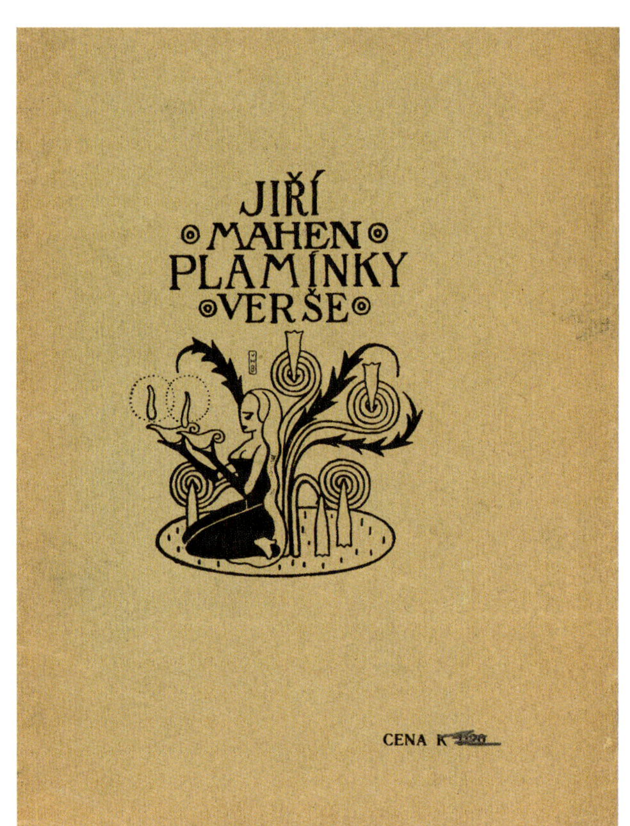

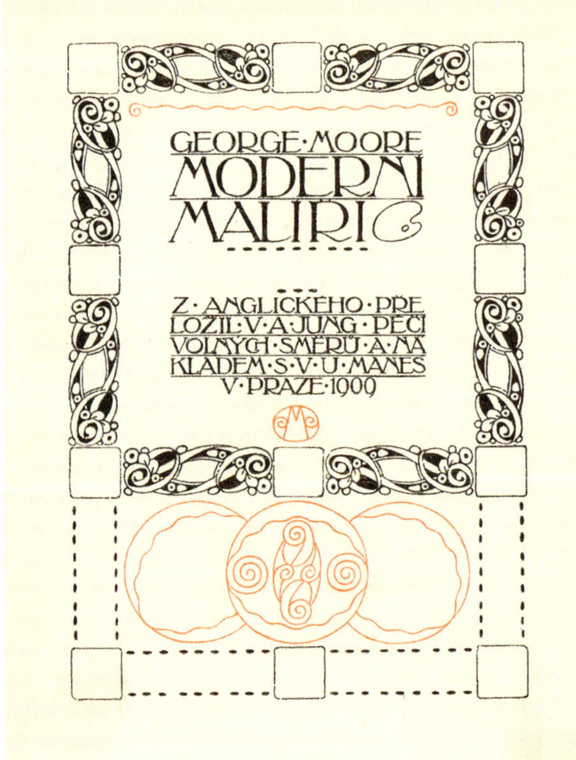

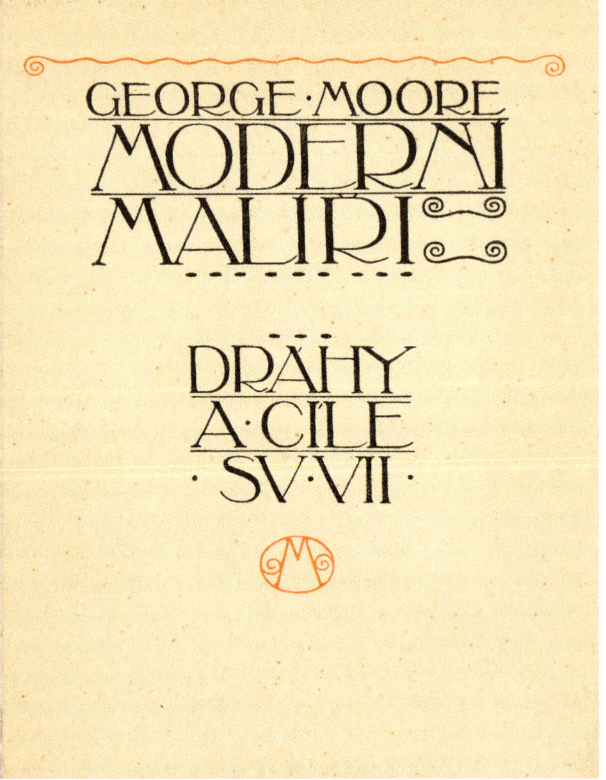

273 Zdenka Braunerová, Title page of Miloš Marten's *The Cycle of Pleasure and Death*, 1907

274 Vratislav H. Brunner, Cover of Jiří Mahen's poetry collection *Little Flames*, 1907

275–276 Vladimír Županský, Title page and cover of George Moore's *Modern Painting*, 1909

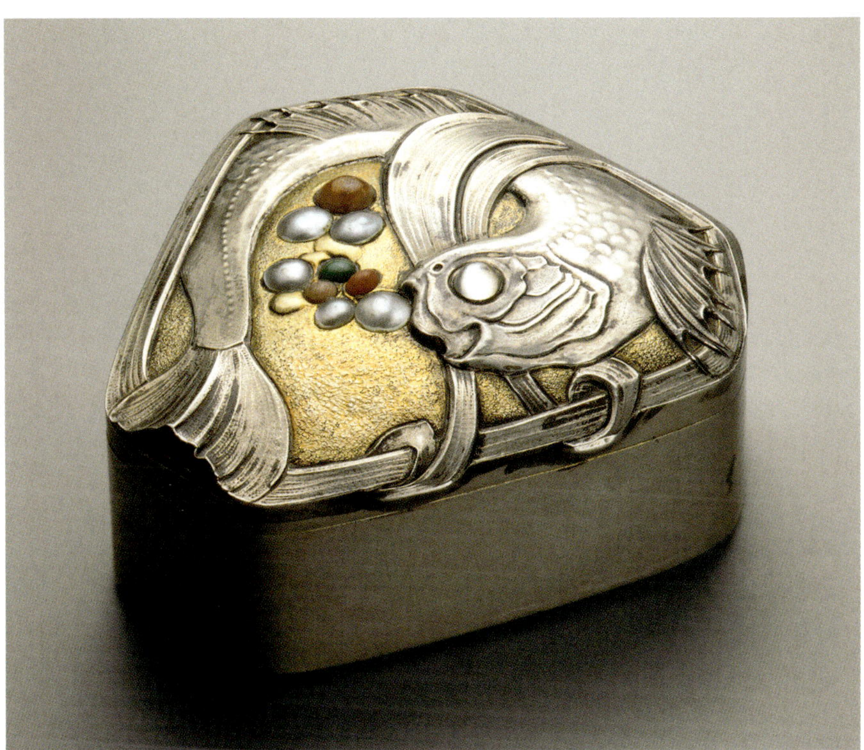

turned to book illustration, primarily working for authors from the *Moderní revue* circle. Her response to their late Symbolism was a synthesising graphic style that turned natural motifs into stylised two-dimensional forms, supplemented with hermetic and other exotic symbols. Karel Ebner's *Box with Fish Motif* (1909) is a similar example of the use of motion to lend dynamism to an ornamental element. The refined material and the colours of the stones help to create a sense of preciousness to balance this artistic object's naturalistic associations. An interest in the individual expressive properties of various materials and an attempt to apply them with an appropriate technique, as was also apparent in the increasing popularity of the woodcut and woodcarving, distinguished this applied art from the predominantly homogenising tendencies of the naturalistic period, expressed in uncoloured stucco and monochrome ceramics.

The emphasis on motion we now find in ornamental work differed from the earlier dynamism of the Secession curve principally in that the rhythmical foundation had changed. Instead of long-drawn-out cadences there were shorter sections expressed with lines, and there was a tendency towards roundness that evoked not a sense of time endlessly passing but the swirling of centrifugal and centripetal forces.

A remarkable aspect of this development was that it was not merely about changing tastes, for it also concerned a malleable process prompted by the complicated interplay of form and content. The aforementioned changes did not just characterise ornament but also fine art that was closely aligned with ornament thanks to its creators' powerful sense of form. These relationships best demonstrated how the question of ornament

277 Karel Ebner, Box with fish motif, 1909, silver, stones, and pearls, 6 cm

had a major impact on the essence of contemporary art, for it was not merely a matter of decoration, but of an overall artistic concept in its syntactic foundations.

These developments are aptly illustrated in Jan Štursa's work. From this perspective, his *Melancholy Girl* (1906) was still related to the "long" periodicity of the Secession curve, but then in 1907 came *Primavera*, in which there is a new rhythm in the articulation of the volumes, which are much more rounded and mobile. It was not a matter of explicit expression (which would be resisted by the chosen material, marble) but of bringing the sculptural structure to life through an inner emotional agitation of a reflexive character. As with Braunerová, this discreet expressiveness was evidently related to the late Symbolist concept of vitalism among the *Moderní revue* circle, with which Štursa was still associated at the time. Štursa then released this dynamic potential in *Hair Washing* (1908), whose basis was now clearly a new circular concept of motion, and he found its true expression in the figure of the belly dancer *Sulamit Rahu*, a kind of modern-day Salome, where this concept is characteristically combined with a primitivist accent (1910–11).

However, in ornament this changing sense of form was recoded in two dimensions. Unlike the plasticity of naturalistic ornament, ornamental synthetism was now expressed by means of a characteristic abstraction over a surface. This trend was significantly influenced by the flourishing of Czech book illustration from the mid-decade onwards, whose first masterpiece was Preissig's work for Jan Karafiát's *Fireflies* (1903). At the beginning of 1905 *Typografia* magazine was launched, as the organ of a society of the same name that did much to elevate artistic standards for the beautiful book. In 1908 the Czech Bibliophile Society was founded, and it began publishing books under its own edition. There was also a growing network of private publishers, such as Josef Florian in Stará Říše in Moravia, Kamila Neumannová in Prague, and many others, who together created a wealth of opportunities, especially for younger adepts of book art.

These young artists then introduced new elements in book ornament. Vratislav H. Brunner's cover for *Little Flames*, a collection of poems by Jiří Mahen published by Časopis pokrokového studentstva in Prague in 1907, shows the stylisation of the Secession line that was typical of this period. The delicate drawing on the cover, which reflects the book's contents, features a bold ornamental motif in the form of disk-shaped spirals of vegetation accompanying a young woman who holds a lamp in either hand. Flowers grow from the centre of each spiral. In the Czech Secession, spirals of this kind had already appeared in the ornamentation of Kotěra's interior for the School of Decorative Arts at the Louisiana Purchase Exposition in 1904. They then became the key ornamental motif for the Secession's synthetic period. Their genetic connection with the naturalistic Secession's original organic curve is quite evident, but they also marked the transferring of its endlessness to a pregnant formula that now had a markedly symbolic quality.

It was precisely because the naturalistic element of the Secession's system of depiction had been the first to be saturated, and most fully, that the need to adapt its ornamental, decorative foundation to the Symbolist element now came to the fore. In this context, a process of symbolic abstraction began, for the Symbolist content was

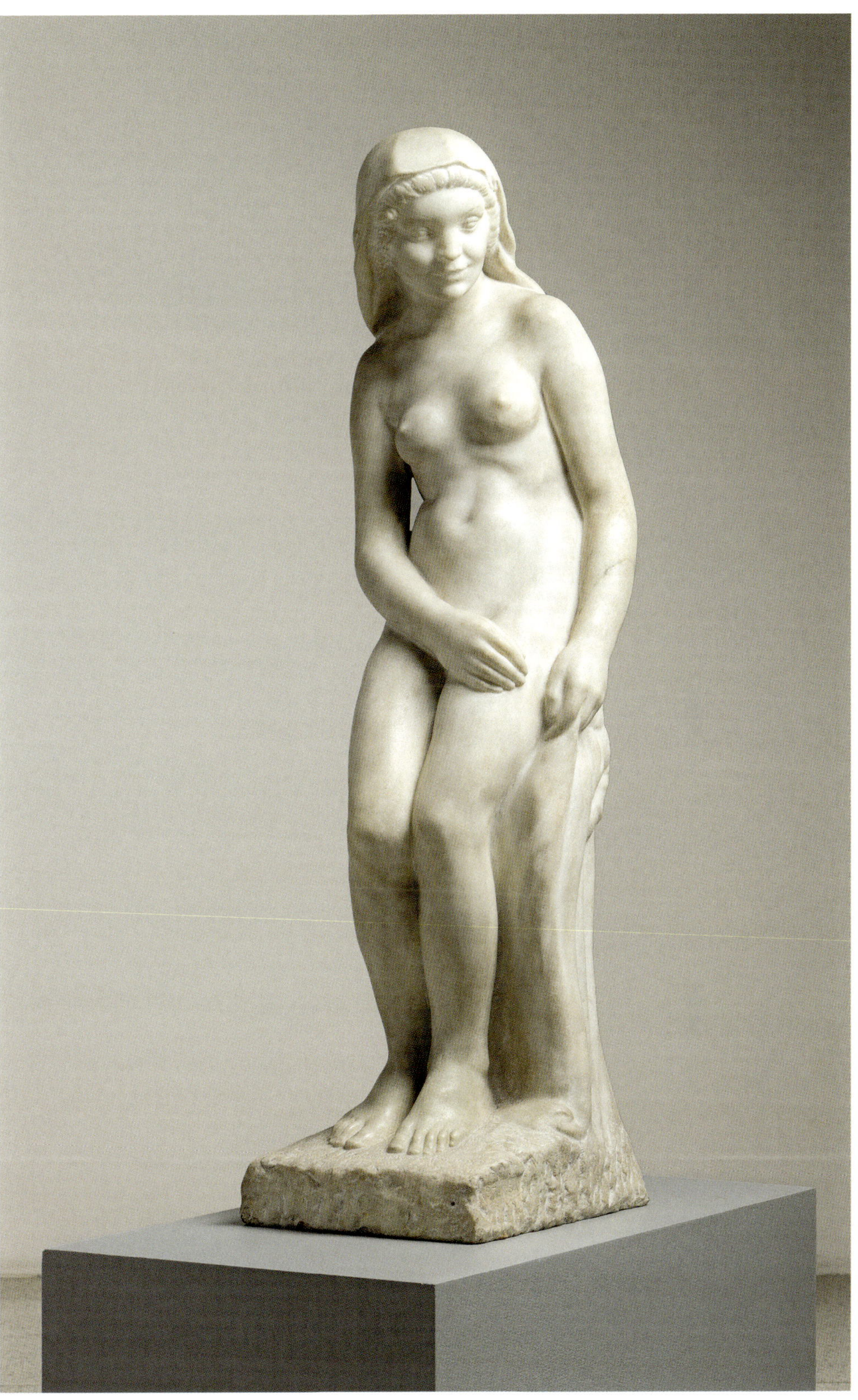

278 Jan Štursa, *Primavera*, 1907, marble, 102 cm

essentially much more universal than the Impressionist and naturalistic experientiality of the world. This also meant that the Secession, which in its defiance of convention had initially stressed the importance of subjective sensory and emotional states in embracing the world through art, now sought more general symbols for its world view, its concept of the fundamental conditions of life. Yet the starting point was still intuition, and the attempt to achieve a style that would reinforce this new outlook was not in opposition to this – on the contrary, the concept came out of intuitive experience. In the context of the maturing of the Secession and the balancing of its individual components, the spiral emerged as an element that could support both form and content. Its elevation to the principal ornamental motif is all the more interesting in that it was not a matter of detached speculation, but came directly from artistic practice, from the essential needs of expression. Secession artists could not have known the significance that experts on mythology would later attach to the spiral as a symbol and ornamental motif that had been widespread in prehistoric and ancient art. It was these experts, perhaps indirectly prompted by the Secession, who would establish that originally it had not been a mere ornamental motif: in primitive societies, the spiral was a cosmological symbol associated with the idea of a labyrinth.[165] In ancient religious thinking, the labyrinth represented the realm of the dead in the underworld, and also a place of initiation through which one must pass to reach adulthood. In the mythologies of prehistoric and ancient peoples, the idea of immortality was tied to the idea of a journey of initiation that led through a dark place where man would either be devoured or emerge victorious. These general and non-discursive ideas were not written down in words but expressed through dance or a graphic record of sacred motion, such as a spiral. The spiral developed from free organic forms to the double and quadruple spiral, the spiral meander, and the right-angled geometrical forms of the Greek meander and its combinations. The Czech Secession's ornament underwent a similar if greatly accelerated evolution. The cover of volume 12 of *Volné směry* (1908) featured a stylised meander labyrinth by another young artist, Jaroslav Benda.

However, it seems that not even Benda's labyrinth can be considered to have been based on the study of cultural anthropology. It was more a question of the very logic of artistic forms, which, under pressure from the contemporary need for externalisation, resulted in the rapid refining of ornament into its graphically most effective form. The tendency towards geometrical purism expressed here became the greatest stimulus for further development and increasingly sharp differentiation within the Secession camp. Yet this differentiation stemmed from a common foundation, with an inner continuity that – in the case of the developing of the Secession's line from the naturalistic curve to the spiral and then the meander – connected the individual forms of the Secession into a larger and meaningful set of developments.

The progress of this evolution became more complicated when other artistic qualities came into play, especially colour. This is evident in a series of coloured woodcuts by Bohumír Jaroněk from 1903 onwards. Jaroněk was a dedicated Moravian regionalist in the mould of Joža Uprka, and he took his landscape motifs chiefly from Štramberk, where there was a tall medieval keep called Trúba. Jaroněk drew on folk art, and

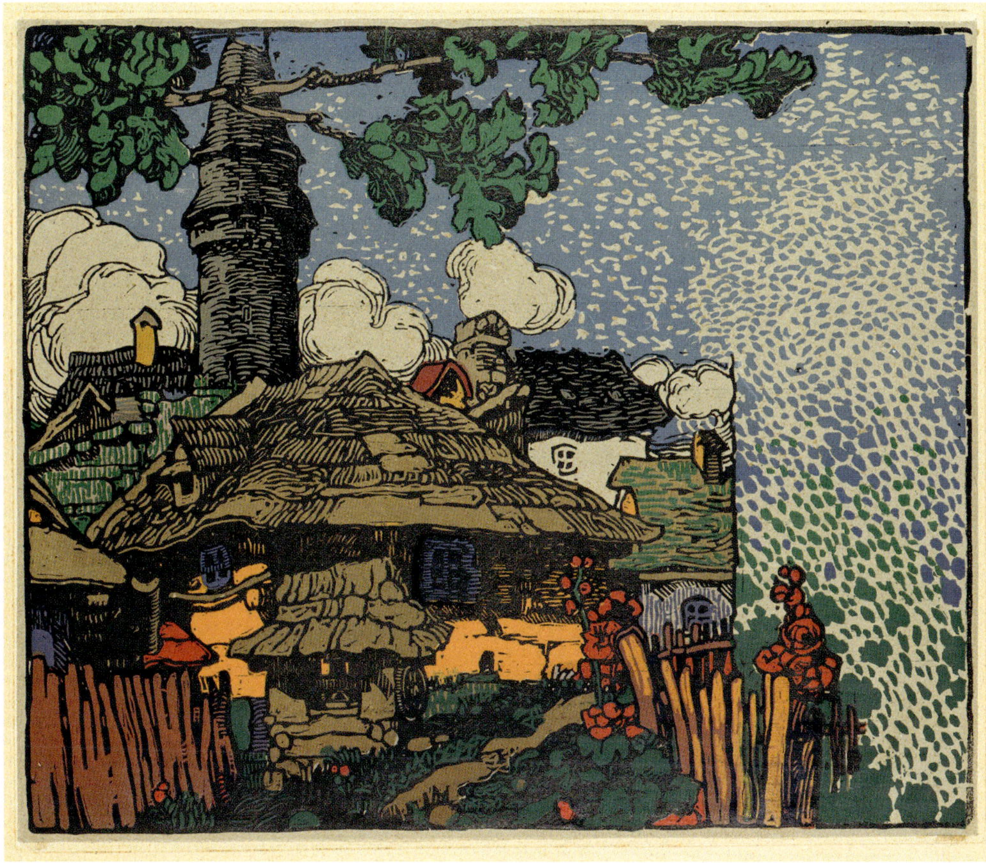

besides cottages from Moravian Wallachia he also liked to depict decorated wooden beehives. Both his drawing and his use of colour were stylised, and Jaroněk made no secret of his interest in similarly oriented Russian artists, such as Nicholas Roerich and others from the Talashkino colony, who were familiar from exhibitions held by SVU Mánes. The art critic and Slavophile William Ritter praised Jaroněk as an artist who combined what he had learned from European modernism with the maternal soil of his ethnic origins.[166] Jaroněk represented another stage in the development of folklorism in art, which was no longer satisfied with ethnographic scenery but wanted to penetrate more deeply below the surface, down to the very roots of the rural mentality. This primitive vitality was expressed in bold colours and a distinctive line. For Jaroněk, expressive emotionality was dominant, and this gave his work considerable variety. As well as remarkable prints that recalled some of Kandinsky's contemporary work, similarly inspired by folklore, he also produced sweet harmonies in colour that would later result in his work being compared with colour printing.

Vladimír Županský's title page for a Czech translation of George Moore's *Modern Painting*, published by SVU Mánes in 1909, has a similar expressive disquiet, nurtured by an excess of feeling and resulting in an exuberant decorativism. Županský had always tended towards the spectacular, and here he created an ornamental frame of a type

279 Bohumír Jaroněk, Motif from Štramberk, c. 1907, coloured woodcut, 44 × 51 cm

that subsequently became widespread in architecture, evidently because it satisfied the new requirements for geometrical stylisation while retaining in its details the floral tendrils that had been so fashionable in the preceding stage. Although Županský's ornament was too Baroque to point the way to future developments, it shared much with contemporary technical drawing; it also recalls how Jan Kotěra drew the ground plans for his villas, adding bubbles representing trees to his geometrical forms (the Marek villa in Holoubkov, 1907–9). The spirals and circles in the lower part of Županský's title page show how variations on these key motifs had become popular in the late Secession.

For decorative artists in this period, the principal problem was how to combine the Secession's botanical forms with a surface defined by right angles. Book illustration could again serve as the model here, but there were also three-dimensional works. A silver box by Jaroslav Maštalíř from 1909 is one of the successful solutions, treating a decorative surface as a three-dimensional polyhedron. It also demonstrates how the new geometrical stylisation related to earlier examples that had been concerned with a similar issue. Maštalíř's box is a variation on early medieval pyxes, and this aspect can be considered a symptom of a more general phenomenon that emerged in the late Secession. In contrast with the naturalistic cult of the present, the past now became more attractive once again, especially those epochs that fell outside classical historicism's focus.

Archaic Greece was particularly appealing to the imagination of late Secession artists; this was one of the consequences of the Secession's externalisation. The Secession had revolted against academic classicism and its veneration of the classical ideal, but it had never lost contact with antiquity, as is evident from the work of Puvis de Chavannes and Rodin. Nor could naturalistic ornamentalism, if it sought any deeper meaning, ignore the ancient vegetation myths – for they alone could provide a conceptual foundation for the new floral ornament. The antiquity thus rediscovered belonged to the mythic imagination, a world inhabited by gods and heroes who personified the forces of nature. It comprised a harmonious whole as ornament in the original sense of the word, a cosmos in which the real was inseparably intertwined with the unreal and whose powerful and resonant motion was embodied by legendary figures that encompassed the archetypes of human behaviour in destinies marked by tragedy. This poetic vision, reflecting the new dramatic élan and the will to externalisation that had arisen from fin de siècle doubt, was the reverse of the initial dejection and sorrow, and in this sense it completed the Secession's conceptual scope. It also entailed the thorough integration of figure and ornament, and for this reason the late Secession offered an additional stylistic option, or rather the illusion of a style, that was used with particular intensity in the period around 1910.

František Kupka's *Red and Blue Prometheus* from 1908 summarises this content in aggressively bold colours, applied next to one another to give the painting a decidedly decorative quality. The powerful and vigorous figure of the Titan, full of his love for life, stands amid lush vegetation. He is intimately connected with the land, from which waves of light seem to spiral upwards. Kupka used the same motif in another

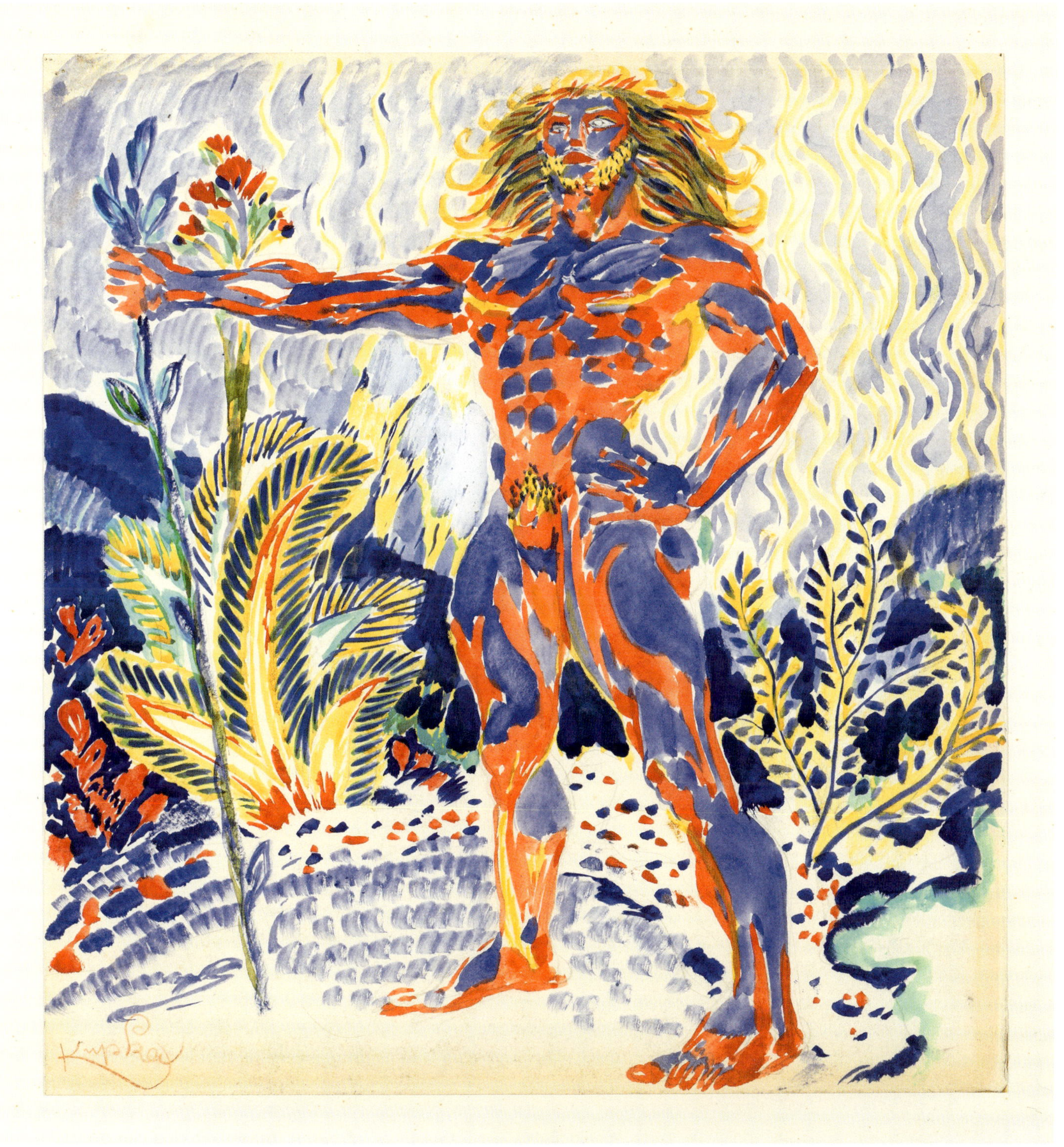

280 František Kupka, *Red and Blue Prometheus*, 1908, watercolour, 32.1 × 29.3 cm

version of this theme (1908–10) rendered in a more muted range of yellows, where Prometheus clutches a glowing ball of light that represents both his gift of fire and the sun god. Prometheus was another projection of the revolutionary ideas familiar from Kupka's anarchist print series, and Kupka returned to the theme in 1911 in his etchings for Aeschylus's *Prometheus Bound*, where he symbolically depicted the Titan's sacrifice and punishment. In the figures of the gods of Strength and Force, sent by Zeus to tame the rebellious giant, and in the scene of Prometheus chained, where characteristic ornamental spirals appear, Kupka most fully captured the stylistic aspect of these classical subjects. Kupka's depictions of Prometheus reflected the great interest in early and primitive cultural forms that had emerged in France since the beginning of the new century, in connection with Neoclassicism. In essence, this was a view that sought to synthetically consummate modern art's assault and demonstrate its progressive, revitalising function by comparing it with these forms, which historically had stood at the dawn of large cultural cycles and consequently had a foundational significance. The idea of a definitive break with the "degeneracy" of 19th-century art had thus triumphed in the artistic mentality. This radicalisation of the Secession's original programme chiefly emphasised the need for a sound basis for new artistic growth. It saw this basis in an adherence to the original foundations of art, to examples from a time when art had still urgently addressed humanity and had served, independently of civilisational ties, as a tool for understanding the world. An interesting element in this programme, which was intended to lead to the legitimation of modern art's victory over academicism, was its attempt to express a continuity with the new art's analytical phase. One of Neoclassicism's spokesmen, Paul Claudel, expressed this with the idea that, in the history of art, classical synthesis had always been preceded by romantic periods that stirred the stagnant waters to create the base substance for a new crystallisation. In this context, the idea of an initial chaos from which a new and orderly world would be born had both mythological and real social roots. This was also reflected in the new concept of the psychological process that Freud's psychoanalysis was forging.

Art critics sought to demonstrate the idea of artistic continuity and cultural legitimacy by reappraising key works of modern art. In Charles Morice's essay "On the Modern Conditions of Beauty," which F. X. Šalda reprinted in *Volné směry* in 1907, Rodin's *Balzac* was interpreted as "the strictest return to the principles of the most synthetic, most idealistic and most traditional (but this word will have to be interpreted) art, through the most honest and most rigorous study of Nature." Morice summed up his account of the statue's origin thus:

> at the close of this unique work, the most modern of sculptors presented to us, as a likeness of the most modern of poets, a figure that was ancient (Greek, primitive, almost Egyptian) and decorative. – This can again verify the admirable definition that Mallarmé educed from the word modern: contemporary to all times.[167]

Czech artists heard a similar reappraisal of Rodin in a lecture that Antoine Bourdelle delivered while visiting Prague on the occasion of his exhibition at SVU Mánes in 1909. Bourdelle's visit had a great influence not just on sculpture but on Czech art as a whole, for the temperamental French sculptor was hailed here as Rodin's successor.

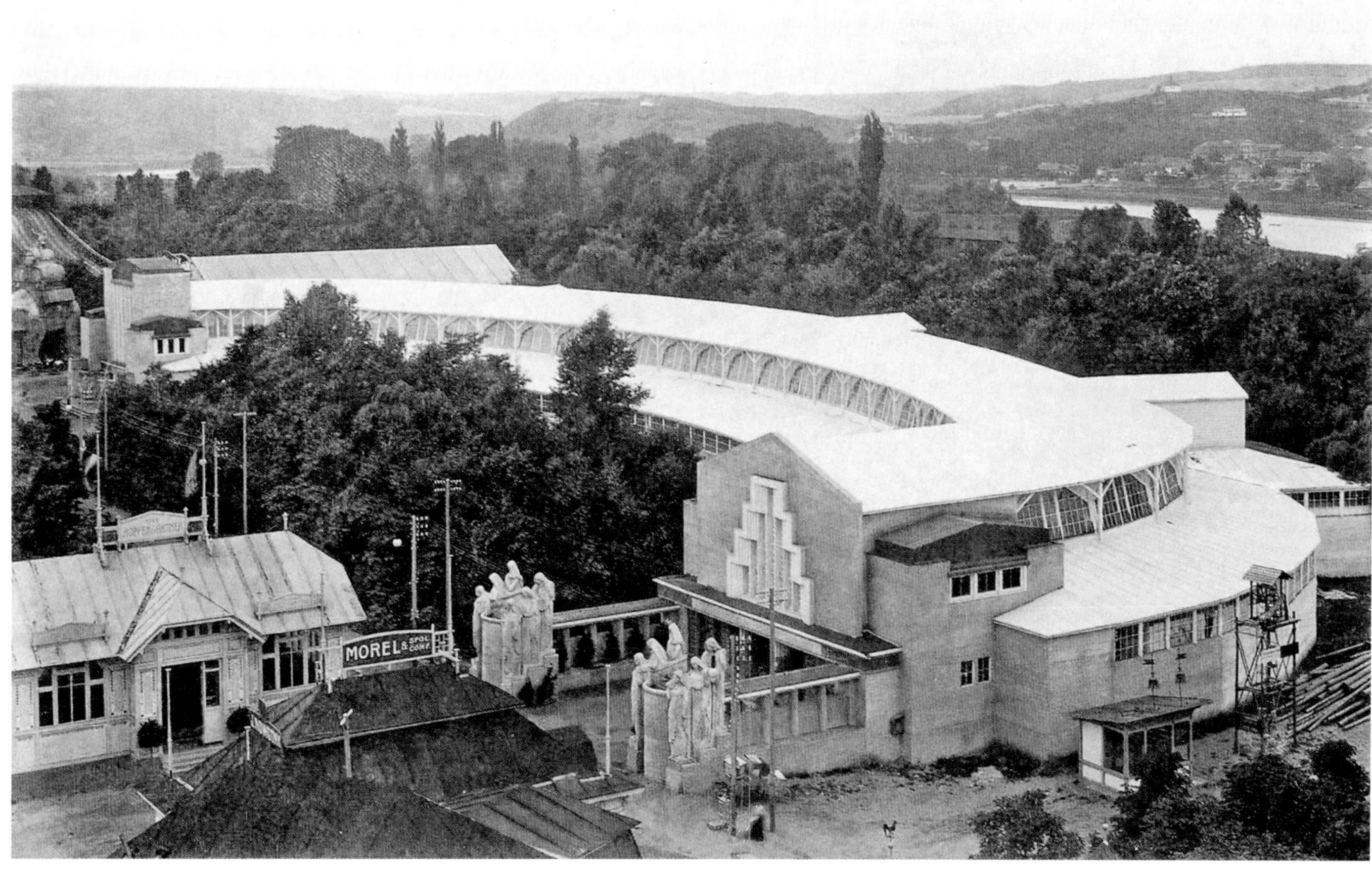

In his lecture, Bourdelle raised as the principal question an evaluation of whether an artwork came from an "orderly mind" or an "adventurous spirit." He criticised Rodin for lacking a decorative system; that the sculptures of his *Gates of Hell* were both in flat relief (and even deepened) and in high relief, and were treated quite plastically. Nevertheless, he found a few lesser-known works by Rodin that could serve as the starting point for a new synthesis, and he followed this by calling on sculptors to pay more attention to questions of form and the beauty of surfaces, profiles, and proportions. Bourdelle himself had more than enough emotion, as was evident from his variations on a portrait of Beethoven, some of which were even Expressionist. Yet his emotionality was of a different kind from Rodin's. It was distinguished by an earthy pathos, and in this respect it set an example for younger sculptors, who were also full of this new expressive drive. For them, emotionality was logically tied to the requirements for structural definiteness and the delimitation of form, which were still understood within the confines of decorative style.

The demiurgic enthusiasm proclaimed by Bourdelle, the apostle of French Neoclassicism, and expressed in the resolutely archaic stylisation of his ancient Greek god-

281 Jan Kotěra and Jan Štursa, Trade and Industry Pavilion at the Anniversary Exhibition of the Chamber of Trade and Commerce in Prague, 1908

desses and heroes (*Heracles the Archer*, 1906–10), was received with understanding in this country. The response to it in art, however, still came up against the Czech Secession's powerfully intimate and lyrical foundation, which applied even when there were attempts to adopt this new and energetic conception. When visiting studios in Prague, Bourdelle himself characterised these attempts as "Assyrian," by which he may have meant that he sensed in them an emotionality that he posited as something oriental, and a structuring that still lacked the natural dynamism and corporeality of ancient Greek sculpture.

The first public declaration of allegiance to Neoclassicism in Czech sculpture came with the decorative larger-than-life figures that Jan Štursa made for the entrance portal to Jan Kotěra's Trade and Industry Pavilion at the Anniversary Exhibition of the Chamber of Trade and Commerce in Prague in 1908. The trios of maidens bearing floral wreaths were stylised in the manner of classical korai, but in their mobile outline they still had much of the gentleness and mildness of Štursa's earlier, intimate marble statues. His large bronze *Eve* (1908–9), holding an apple, was much more stylised. Here it is as though Štursa took note of what Maurice Denis had written about Aristide Maillol, reprinted by F. X. Šalda in *Volné směry* in 1906: that Maillol had a feel for the geometrical perfection of the body, that he was composing an ideal type for the architecture of the senses and working according to Ingres's dictum that beautiful forms are straight planes rounded.[168] Ultimately, however, Štursa was drawn more to Bourdelle's example, a more dynamic stylistic concept that combined a rounded volume with a system of contrasting planes. Štursa's later decorative sculptures feature this typical carving up of volumes into planes (*Day and Night*, 1911), and Štursa's version of Neoclassicism comes from this distinctive combination of flat and rounded sculptural volume.

Jaroslav Horejc began working with this new stylistic idiom towards the end of his studies under Stanislav Sucharda at the School of Decorative Arts. In *Sculpture for a Tomb* from 1908, reproduced in *Styl*,[169] he applied it to the theme of the Crucifixion. Contemporary theory similarly compared early Christian and Byzantine art with classical art from the Aegean, as a form of expression that was common to "early" cultures. Horejc's subsequent *Charon* relief for a bank in Hradec Králové (1909) was an example of decorative form that had renounced all illusionism and naturalism in favour of an "architectural" composition with clearly defined forms. Unlike Sucharda's illusive emphasising of the figure by means of light, in his reliefs Horejc sought to incorporate the figure more thoroughly into the flat, plastic planes. At the time, Sucharda himself was also experimenting with the new stylisation in his *Teaching* medals (1908), but they clearly demonstrated how it remained alien to him. In the even distribution of Horejc's sculpture over the surface, the variety of materials indicated in the masses played a role, as did the figure, which, although decoratively integrated into the system of the relief and treated almost as ornament, retained a certain precedence in the composition. This was unquestionably related to the significance of the Symbolist element, which created a deeper layer of meaning for the new two-dimensionality. This aspect was important in the development of the late Secession. It also featured in the

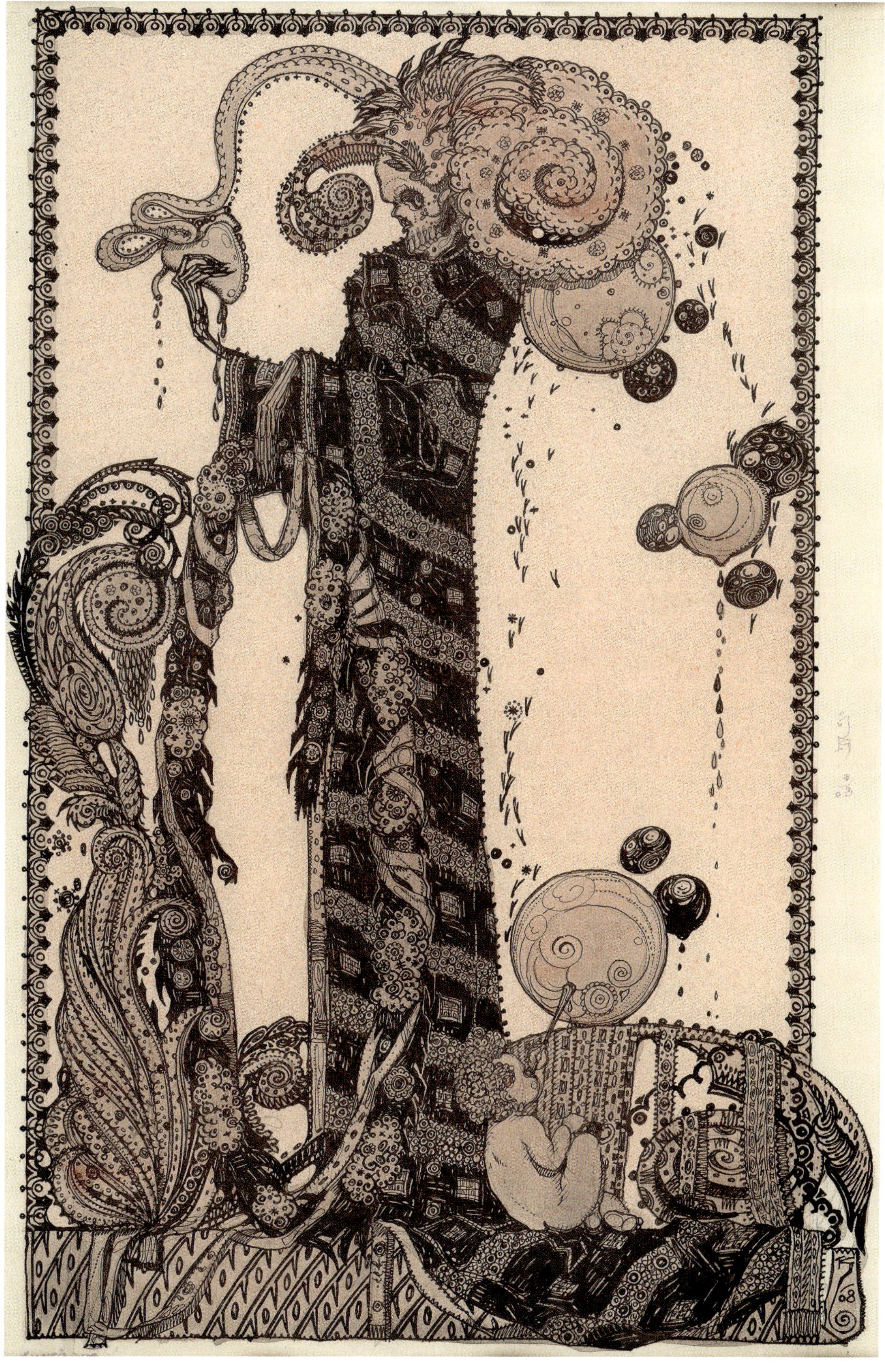

282 Jan Konůpek, *Vanitas*, 1908, Indian ink and watercolour, 59 × 38.5 cm

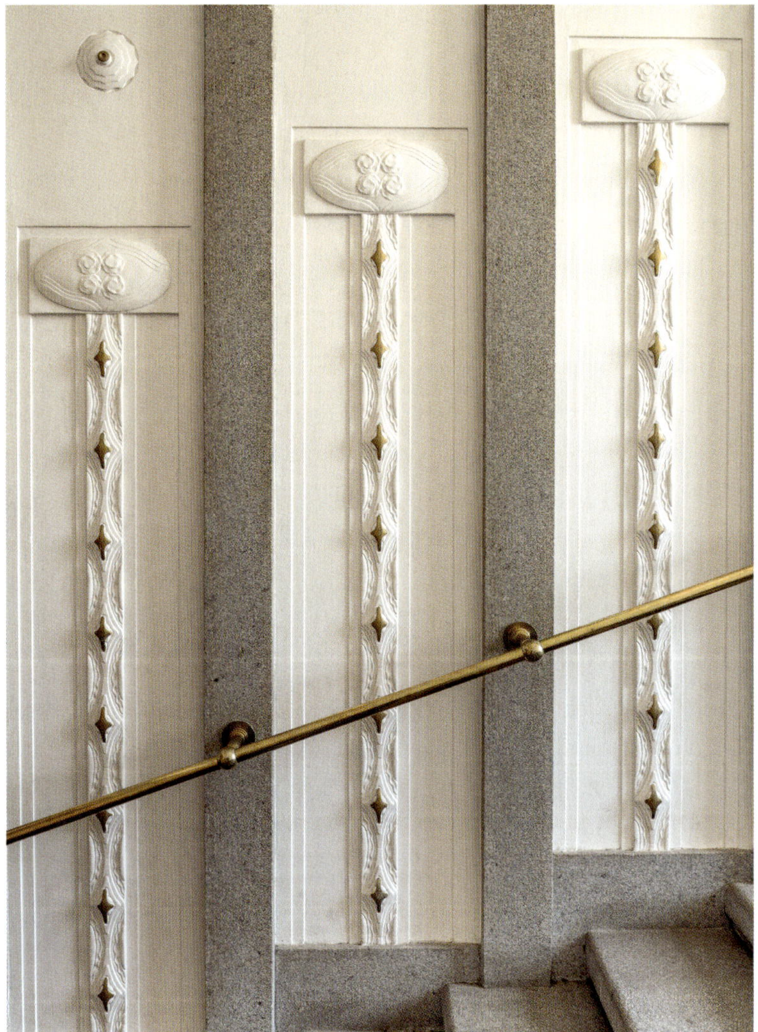

work of Horejc's peers, of whom the printmaker Jan Konůpek was the most fervent advocate of the new ornamentalism.[170] When the new stylisation was then extended to architectural sculpture and printmaking, it emerged that, wherever the ability to add depth to this flatness of form through symbolic content was lacking, the new stylisation was rapidly exhausted and became merely a matter of decorative designs.

From this perspective, the choice of theme was important. Horejc in *Charon* and Konůpek in his drawing *The Underworld* (1908) both explored a mythological image of the boundary between life and death. Konůpek also made several drawings of *Hamlet* (1908), pondering whether to be or not to be. From the same year, there was the watercolour *Vanitas*, where Konůpek used late ornamentalism to produce a depiction, almost Baroque in its extravagance, of the fatal contrast between sensory illusion and its end. It shows a pitiless skeleton cloaked in a marvellous ornamental robe, while a putto sitting at the skeleton's feet blows bubbles in which the familiar spiral motif is

283 Jan Kotěra, Ornamental section on the staircase at the City Museum in Hradec Králové, 1909–13

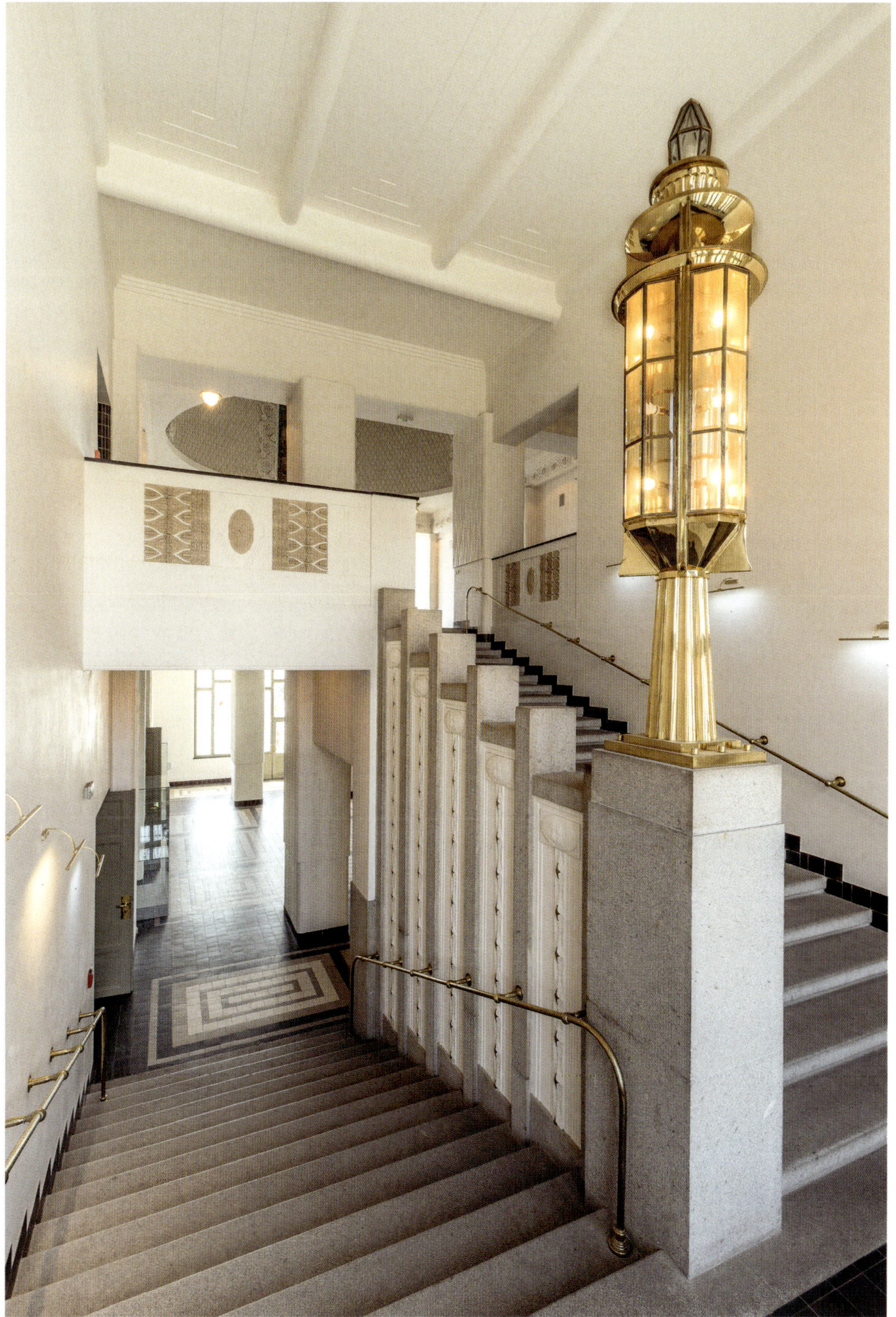

284 Jan Kotěra, Staircase at the City Museum in Hradec Králové, 1909–13

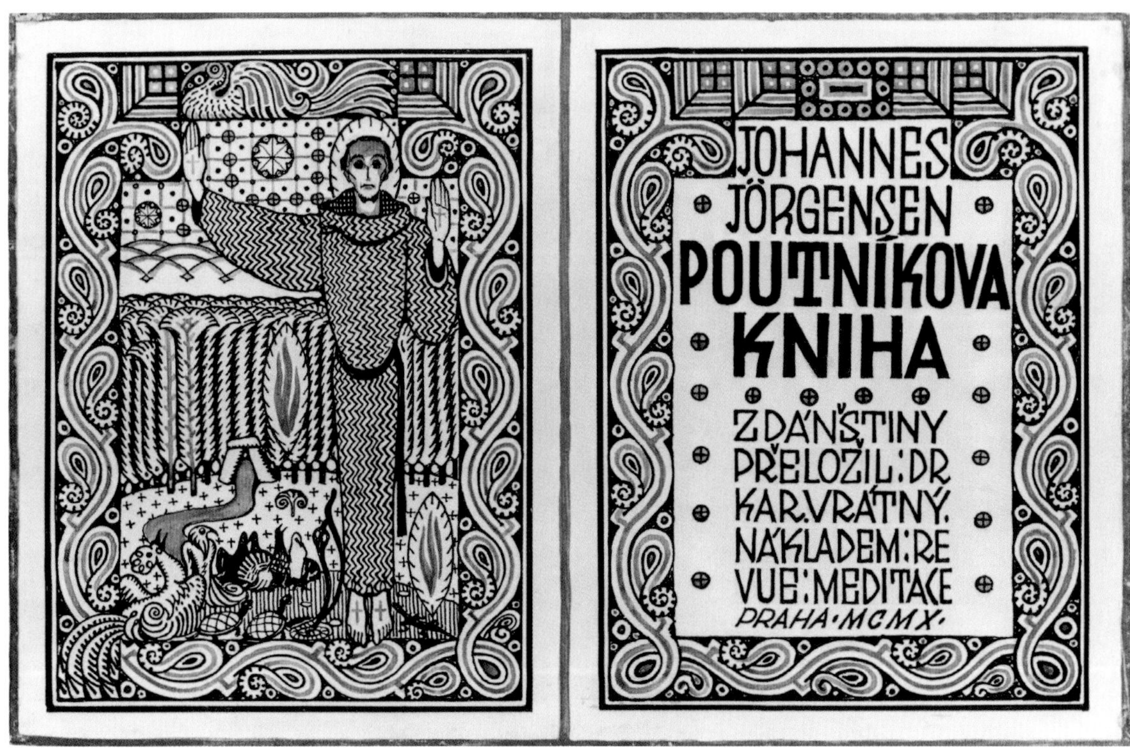

fantastically developed. *Vanitas* seems more like a grotesque caricature of late Secession ornament, yet it was not a true critique of its role and status, for the period in which these works were created still required ornament. Jan Kotěra applied geometrical ornament to his City Museum in Hradec Králové, where he tried to offset its static nature by repeating and rhythmically linking the ornamental sections ascending the staircase. Meanwhile, Konůpek continued to use ornament in his book illustrations: in his title page and frontispiece for Johannes Jörgensen's *Pilgrim Book*, published in Czech translation by the journal *Meditace* (Meditation) in 1910, his earlier curves became calmer and more geometrical, influenced by medieval illuminations. Two key aspects of this development were symptomatic: firstly, there was an ever stronger connection with examples taken from the history of art, and secondly, ornamental sections made increasing use of "frame and filling." Gottfried Semper had defined this format as fundamental for decorative ornament in his epochal treatise *Der Stil*, published in the 1860s, although naturalistic Secession ornament had revolted against this notion in an attempt to achieve a totality of the ornamental space. The Secession's later return to this principle was then a certain form of historicism.

Similar tendencies were also characteristic of the extensive building work that Dušan Jurkovič undertook for Josef Bartoň of Dobenín at his castle in Nové Město nad Metují. The Garden Room from 1909–10 was decorated in the spirit of the late Secession, with stylised trees made of pebbles, and plasterwork with a geometrical chequerboard pattern. For the ceiling decoration and the chandelier, the key orna-

285 Jan Konůpek, Title page and frontispiece of Johannes Jörgensen's *Pilgrim Book*, 1910

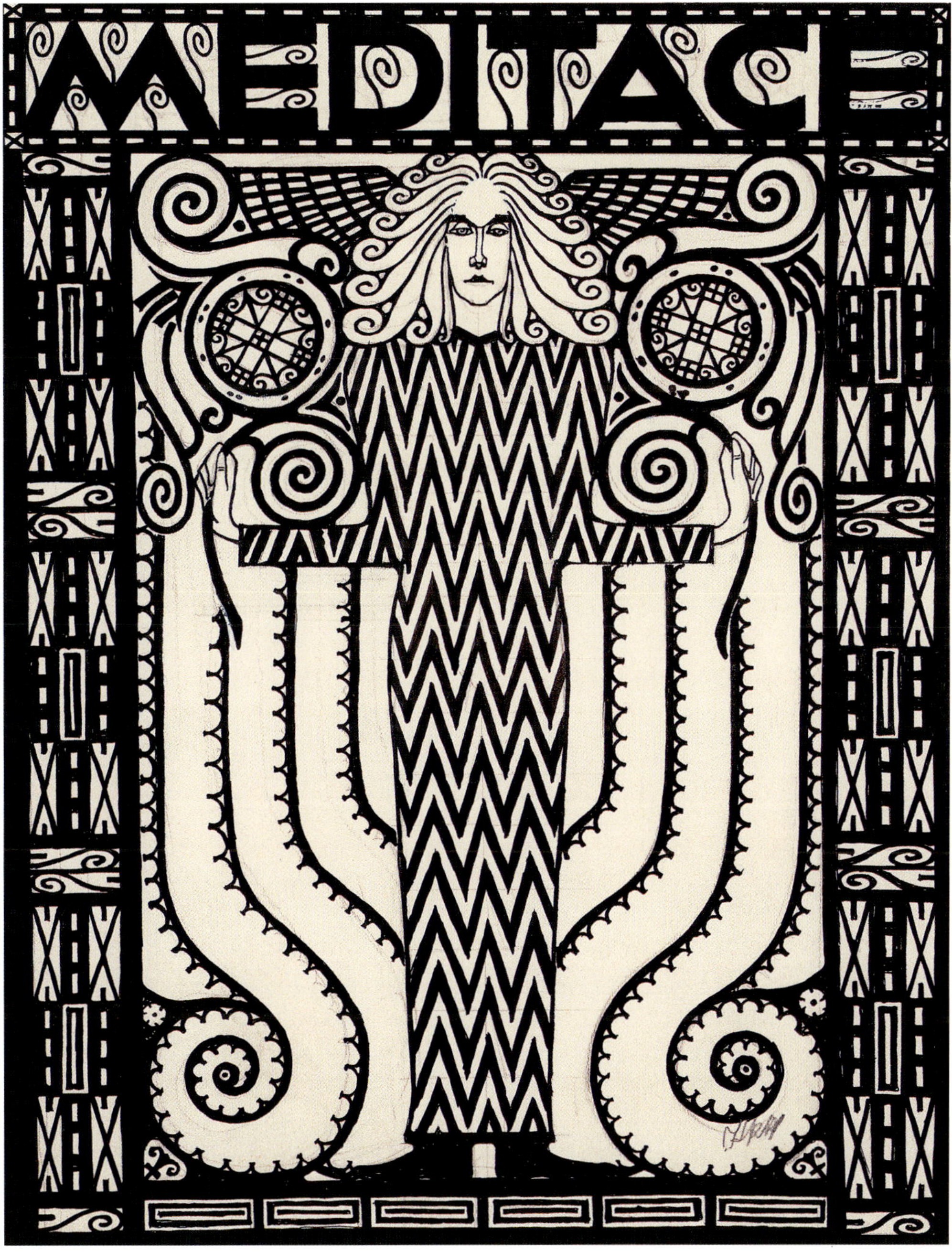

mental motif was again a spiral. The charm of this room, opening onto terraced gardens, lay in the combination of geometrical ornament and lush vegetation, which also featured in the room itself. Ornamental abstraction was complemented by the plants' natural forms, to create a whole that, in the spirit of the late Secession, was now dominated by the human element, incorporating nature into human life and manifesting human dominion through the magical power of ornamental emblems. In Jurkovič's

286 Jan Konůpek, Design for the cover of *Meditace*, 1909, Indian ink, 49.4 × 37.4 cm

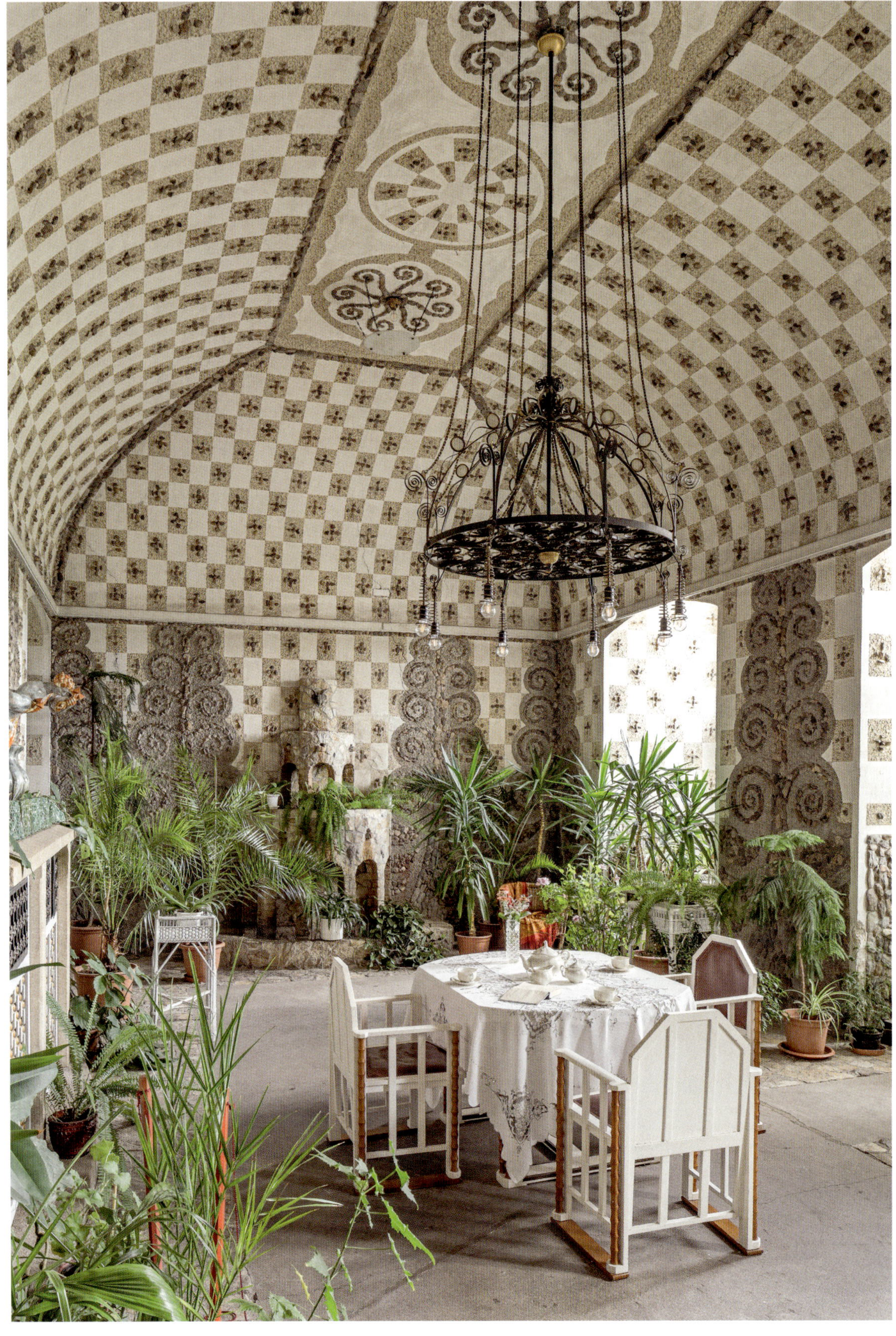

287 Dušan Jurkovič, Garden Room at the castle in Nové Město nad Metují, 1909

other work at the castle, however, especially in the reception rooms, this stylistic unity retreated into the background. The architect respected the requirement for a blend of modernity and antiquity, and this was apparent not just in how he included historical furniture in his interiors, but also in his overall concept for the rooms. The historic setting and the client's wishes also played a part here, but nevertheless Jurkovič's approach can be considered symptomatic of a quite significant change in the concept of style. The requirement for homogeneity that the Secession had once demanded was now relaxed in favour of heterogeneous composition. Thanks to his outstanding feel for architecture, Jurkovič could still, of course, make good use of this enrichment of form, whose fundamental organisation and design were based on a sound functional understanding of the interior. This is why the frequently excessive decorativeness of the individual components and objects did not essentially detract from the feeling of practicality; at most, it added a sense of comfort and luxury. Jurkovič followed developments in Viennese art and architecture, and he was probably aware of the objections that the younger generation and Adolf Loos had raised against the Wiener Werkstätte's stylistic concept in their attempt to undo the negative consequences of the rigorous application of the Secession's principles, which rather than freeing artists frequently prescribed new regulations in the name of style.

Nevertheless, this change of approach opened the back door to historicism. A symbiosis of late historicism and the Secession can be seen in some of Richard Klenka of Vlastimil's buildings in Prague, which would seem to have taken up the legacy of Friedrich Ohmann's "late Gothic" architecture (as in Klenka's apartment building by the Old New Synagogue in Prague's Old Town, 1907). Klenka's picturesque use of Mannerist motifs created a new backdrop for the Old Town's sights. He also worked with František Weyr on a building on Maiselova ulice in the Old Town (1911) that reflected Czech architecture's interest at the time in the Empire and Biedermeier styles, which in the latter half of the first decade were also adopted by several prominent Austrian and German modern architects. Compared with the work of Joseph Maria Olbrich, presented to Czech readers in an article in *Styl*,[171] the details on Weyr's building were much more delicate. The Biedermeier fashion was also reflected in graphic design. František Kysela's poster for the Second Czech Horticultural and Fruit Exhibition (1910) featured typically Biedermeier floral stylisation, complemented by simple graphic elements. In either case, it was a matter of a consistent lyricism of form, marking a departure from Neoclassical pathos. The ornament merely colours the basic arrangement of forms, where the guiding principle is clarity and effectiveness. Weyr's ground plan was in this respect progressive in its use of space and light for the apartments, and in their furnishings; Kysela's form was likewise graphically effective and cleanly articulated. The Biedermeier mood seems to have been chosen so that the ornament would not disrupt the essential layout and would not attract excessive attention or dominate the overall look. In contrast with Romantic late historicism, the internal structure of these instances was then classical, but the balance between ornament and construction did not constitute any true unity. There therefore arose a situation that offered two solutions: either a pleasing form of ornament could be

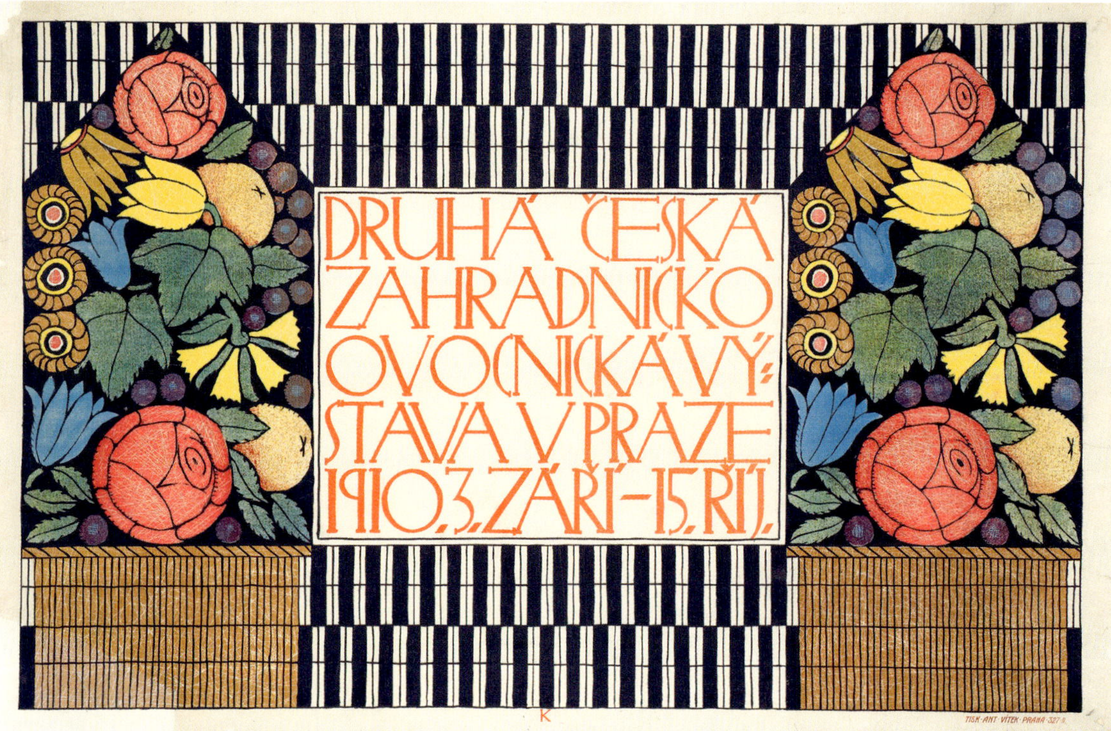

applied to a functional construction, which meant returning to historicism's dualistic principle, or ornament was becoming superfluous and could be omitted by the architect or artist in the name of a new purism.

One of Kotěra's peers, Antonín Engel, chose the latter alternative. In "The Apartment Building," an essay he wrote for *Styl*,[172] he condemned "the loathsome pseudo-magnificence of apartment blocks that serve only to gild metropolitan squalor." These would have to give way to "the sober but authentic appearance of façades as utilitarian objects, with no claim to any greater merit." He valued simple Empire buildings over historicist palaces. He hoped that the current situation could be remedied by emphasising the "hygienic element," which was introducing requirements that were bringing about a revolution in construction. Engel believed that, in consequence, the new architecture was typified by a love for the purity and solidity of its materials, which would in itself lead to simplification and therefore to the more restrained façades he desired. The ideal would be a simple building, free of all unwarranted motifs. The design of its façade would consist in accenting certain elements of its construction, or merely in two-dimensional decoration that would always reflect the tectonics of the materials used. In 1910 Engel designed a building of this sort for a cooperative, a simple apartment block at Břehová 1 in Prague's Old Town, the structuring of whose façade followed tectonic principles. Decoration was still applied in the right-angled sections between the windows, but instead of ornament they featured a variety of surface textures.

288 František Kysela, Poster for the Second Czech Horticultural and Fruit Exhibition, 1910, colour lithograph, 82 × 120 cm

Engel's ideas about the apartment building as one of the most typical aspects of modern architectural work seemed almost proto-Functionalist. This was also reflected in his stressing of the increasing role that the technical component played in a building, and his belief that this component would ultimately be decisive. This standpoint was the logical outcome of the key proposition of Engel's teacher, Otto Wagner, who asserted that modern architecture should satisfy purpose, construction, and poetry,

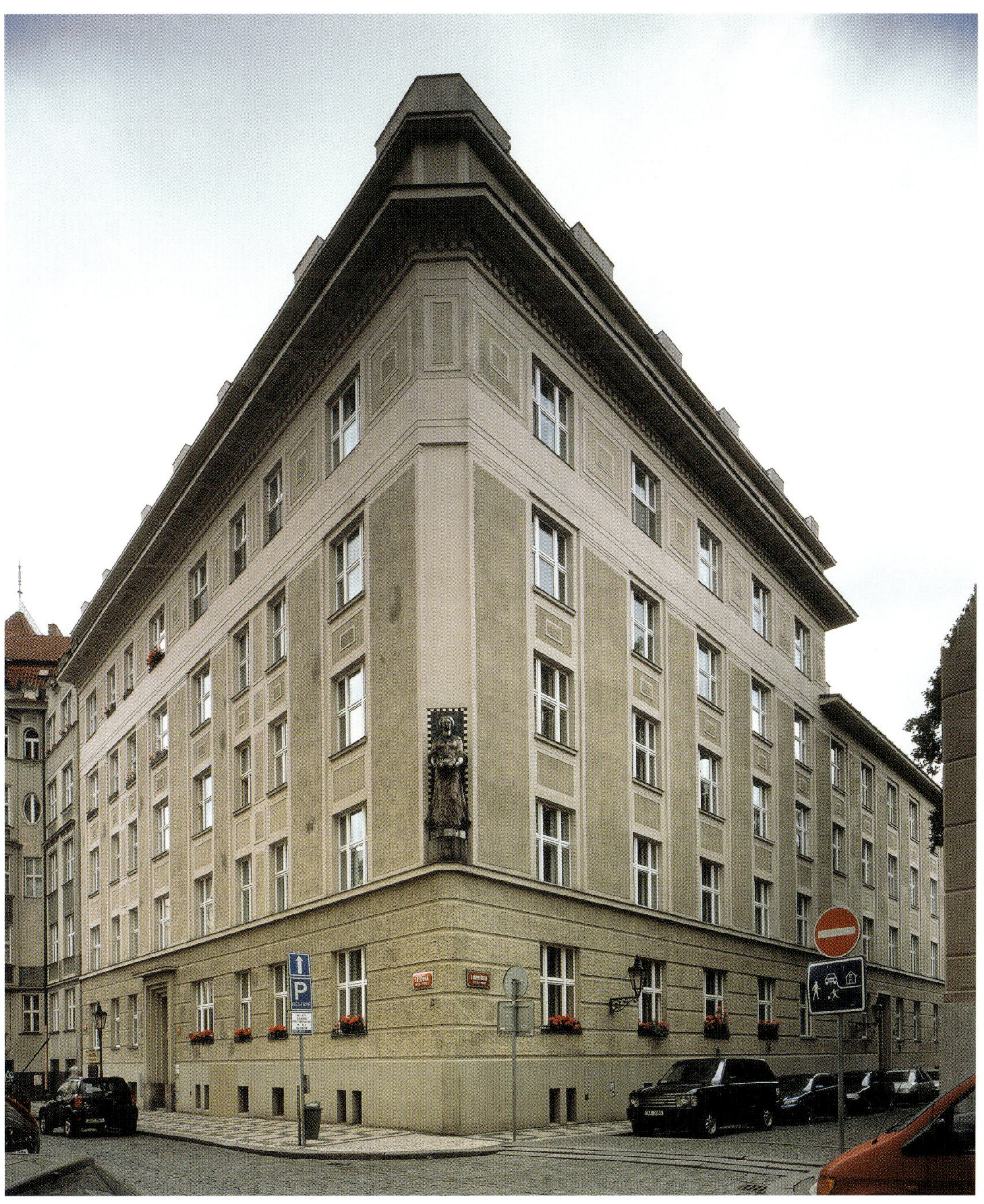

289 Antonín Engel, Apartment building in Prague, 1911

of which the first was the most important. However, the younger architects who had made *Styl* their tribune had certain reservations about this approach.

They were voiced by Pavel Janák in an article from July 1910 called "From Modern Architecture to Architecture," which became something of a manifesto for these changing opinions.[173] Janák began by claiming that there were more and more signs of a new phase in the development of contemporary architecture. Crucially, this would shift the focus from the architect's "instinctively creating hand" to theoretical justification and a more profound grasp of the problems of architecture. In this process, it would be essential to take on board the fundamental propositions that Otto Wagner had set out for modern architecture. Wagner's belief in the primacy of purpose had offered truth and salvation in the darkness of the late 19th century, when purpose had been entirely neglected. However, if poetry were to come after the moral and rational requirements of purpose and construction were satisfied, this ultimately created a situation in which much poetry was added to architecture, but little architectural beauty.

> For poetry in architecture – that is, the superficial element added to the rest of a building – is poetising in architecture, sweetening and enhancing what has been built with poetic details such as masks, flowers and squares (even stylised!) and applied curves, whereas architectural beauty is beauty that is built, perhaps merely the structure of masses, and beauty consisting in the equilibrium between these masses so installed and dramatised.

Contemporary architecture was to elevate poetry to first place, as an expression of architecture's fundamentally artistic essence, for which purpose was merely an opportunity for expression. For this reason, poetry could not be something merely added to architecture to adorn it. The current proposition had led, with

> the inferiority of decorative forms, to a hatred of form, and in the name of demands for purification that were more social than artistic, everything that lacked purpose was increasingly excluded from architecture, ending in the typical two-dimensionality of modern architecture, in parallelepipeds, planes, geometrical patterns and straight lines where it could not be doubted that they *must* be so.

The claim that the façade of a building was a plane was in fact one-sided, as a building's façade *need not* be artistically expressed in a plane. The coming architecture would retreat from this one-sided flatness and would be creation "in which artistic *thinking and abstraction* will take the lead from purpose, now retreating, and will continue the pursuit of *plastic form* and the plastic realisation of architectural ideas." This architecture need not then be declared "modern" architecture, but would become part of everything positive that there had been in architecture since time immemorial.

Janák's essay was important chiefly because it clarified the position on geometrisation, which in architecture especially had become more prominent in the latter half of the decade as a foundation for stylistic abstraction. Young architects, for the most part Kotěra's pupils, worked with the premises that their teacher had taken from Otto Wagner. One of the most important but less comprehensible of these was Wagner's concept of the unity of purpose, construction, and ornamentation. Otakar Novotný tried to maintain his original position, as he wrote in an article called "Interior, Architect and Audience":

All aesthetes consider pure tectonic form to be a framework that is the basis for the ornament and symbolism that give our creations the stamp of art. Yet if an architect proceeds correctly, he works with the whole; for true ornament is not decoration but the final artistic expression of purposefulness.[174]

However, this view, which essentially consisted in the architect's intuitive sense of the ambivalence of tectonics and detail, ceased to be coherent in the context of greater demands for explicit style in modern architecture. Symptomatic of this development was the new practice in leading European architecture studios of swapping sketches for precise technical drawings. In his article, Novotný also made a fundamental distinction between "tectonic" and "organic" composition. He preferred "tectonics,"

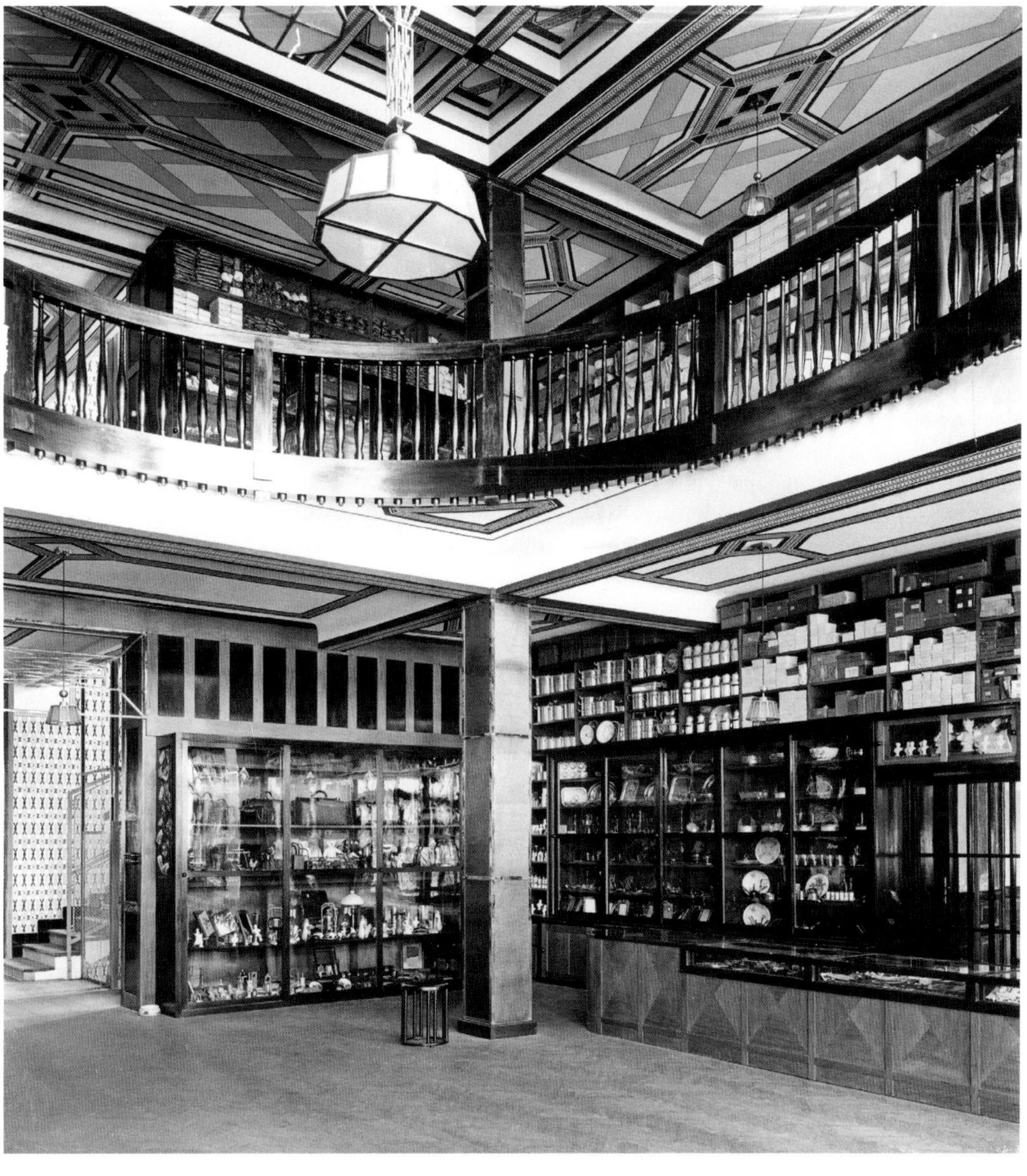

290 Josef Gočár, Interior of the Wenke Department Store in Jaroměř, 1909–10

for these were based on factual forces existing in nature in the laws of gravity and equilibrium, and they were realised in strictly utilitarian forms of construction based on static forces. "Organic" form replaced these factual forces with imaginary ones. It combined naturalism and allegory, yet this "allegory of the higher dynamic states" was not, in fact, of a higher artistic standard than the tectonic "abstract way of creating," which was considered to be merely a matter of craftsmanship. What was originally proclaimed to be a unity collapsed into distinct opposites. Between them, somewhat sophistically, a potential synthesis was then sought, as Novotný wrote elsewhere:

> The geometrisation of natural creations, which is carelessly described as the violating of nature, is not then such a transgression as romantics would believe. Each strictly geometrical element brings as our dowry a simplicity and clarity to the overall concept, and it can of course then be the basis for applying the richest and most complex natural creations. By carefully weighing the contrasts of these two elements, the correct style for the modern garden can be devised – with difficulty, but assuredly.[175]

Another practical attempt to rebalance the elements of architecture was Josef Gočár's Wenke Department Store in Jaroměř (1909–10). Here the requirement for purposefulness was satisfied by the building's very function, and it was reflected in its construction and in the design of the façade, whose simplicity of form distinguished it from other contemporary Czech architecture. However, Gočár did not neglect poetry, which was chiefly present in the ornamental light fittings and the coffered ceiling in the central part of the building. The arrangement of the lighting was in fact a new geometrical expression of the spiral motif, converting it from a curvilinear to a circular form. The lighting's spatial arrangement played an important role in this, with lights at different levels creating an inverted pyramid for the viewer. However, this attempt to move beyond decorative two-dimensionality was still tied to the principle of geometrical ornament.

The passion for geometrical figures was one of the most typical symptoms of the situation at the end of the first decade. In a review of a theoretical work by the Dutch architect Hendrik Petrus Berlage, until recently the idol of Czech architects, readers of *Styl* could learn that the foundation of all construction lay in geometry, which also dictated the fundamental forms of nature. Berlage was convinced that the existence of a particular style was guaranteed by a particular geometrical form that became the fundamental unit for the construction of entire buildings and details alike. For Gothic architecture, which he had studied with great enthusiasm, he held that this form was the equilateral triangle. He also thought that the revival of modern architecture was guaranteed by architects' interest in geometrical ornament. The reviewer objected that Berlage's claim was questionable, for ornament was the end result of a stylistic organism, and ornament without a stylistic present could not predict the geometry of the future.[176] However, the reviewer allowed that the present day pursued "the ornamental effect of bare construction," which made possible further speculation over the geometrical basis of form. In the same year, Bohumil Kubišta, then in Paris, sent F. X. Šalda an essay on Cézanne in which he arranged the number of sentences into rhythmic paragraphs in accordance with the golden ratio, and the key to this construction was the number 129.

Theories developed by architects also found practical application in Czech applied art, where they were an important factor in the development of the Artěl cooperative for young artists. Artěl was founded in 1908. In the same year, Pavel Janák designed the cooperative's kiosk, with a Japanese-style roof, for the Anniversary Exhibition of the Chamber of Trade and Commerce.[177] Next to the kiosk was a flagpole with Artěl's flag, embroidered by Marie Teinitzerová, who would later be celebrated for her carpets and tapestries. The flag featured a simple stylised horse designed by Vratislav H. Brunner, the head of the new cooperative. The kiosk sold gingerbread biscuits with striking designs also by Brunner, as well as boxes with painted lids, strings of coloured beads by Helena Johnová, and comical wooden figures with simple forms that were the work of Brunner and Jaroslav Benda. These, Artěl's first products, had modest materials and dimensions, but their bold and primitivist stylisation, uncomplicated yet highly artistic, attracted attention. In 1909 Artěl began making furniture designed by Janák. It also operated in graphic design, producing logos for retail and publishing, and sold sculpture

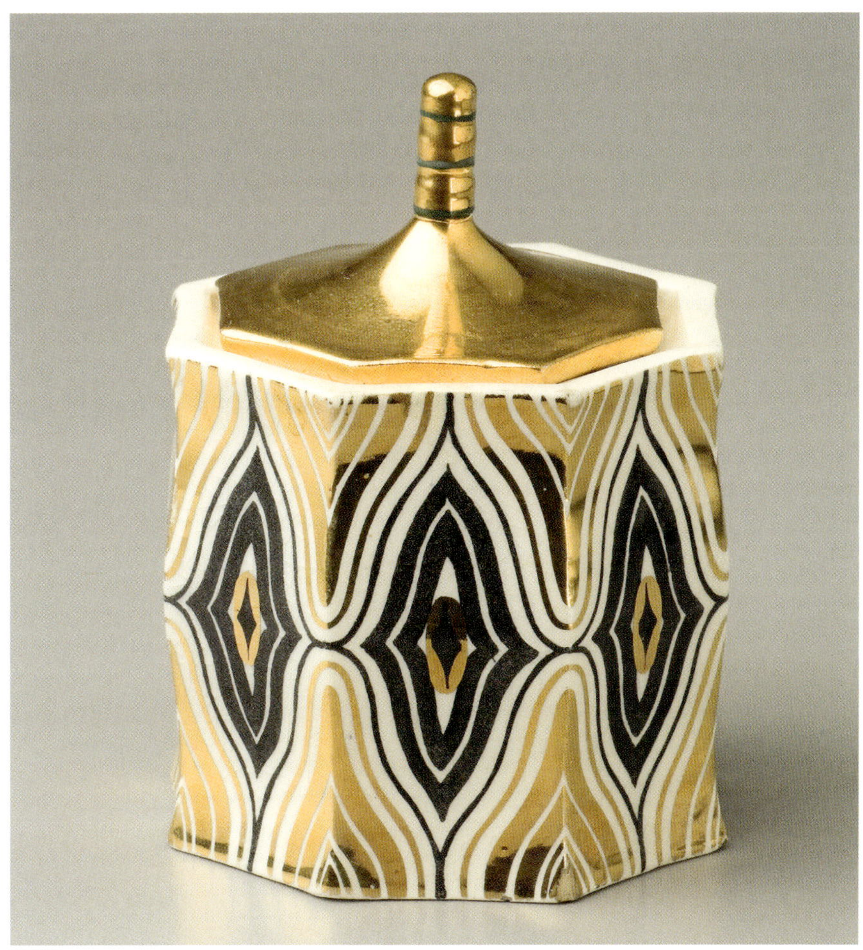

291 Pavel Janák, Box, 1911, glazed earthenware, 12 cm

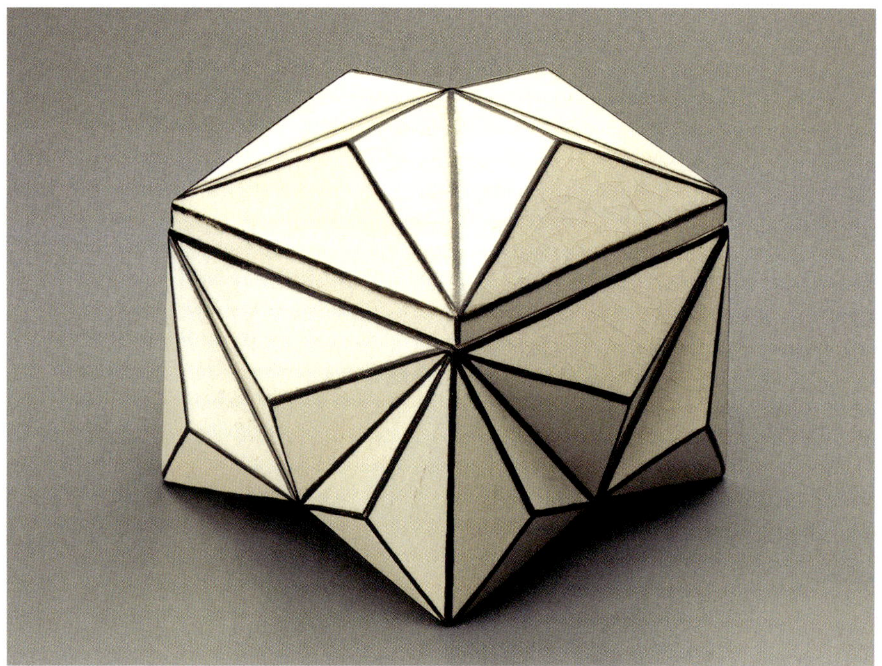

and glass by Jaroslav Horejc, together with new ceramic designs. Artěl was the first Czech collective to specialise in the full breadth of the applied arts, and in this respect it achieved one of the Secession's key objectives: to influence society through artefacts.

Artěl's lively and practical work began to change tastes in the most natural way, leading to the gradual absorption of geometrical ornament into the new purism. In 1908 Jaroslav Benda designed a poster for the *English Etchings* exhibition at SVU Mánes that was executed purely in lettering, a graphic design with no decorative ornament; the "bare structure" of the visual element was itself the ornament. In 1912 Benda took this approach further still in his monumental typography for a poster for Hanuš Schwaiger's posthumous exhibition.

In ceramics too, which had from the start been a very sensitive indicator of the Secession's stylistic development, Artěl's members produced pieces that illustrated this transformation. Vlastislav Hofman's coffee and tea service from 1911, featuring stereometric bodies adorned with only a square grid, reflected the simple elegance that his Viennese namesake had been promoting since the beginning of the decade. A set of ceramics by Pavel Janák from the same year seemed to sum up their creator's theoretical reflections from the pages of *Styl*. Particularly interesting here is a group of boxes with lids. The boxes have hexagonal bases, and their sides have two, three, or four steps and are covered with a diamond-shaped pattern drawn by a zigzag line. Another box is octagonal and is decorated with a rhomboid pattern, executed with an elastic line that produces shapes resembling eyes. These boxes demonstrate the final phase in the development of Czech Secession ornament, and its creative reappraisal that pointed the way ahead. Janák created a unity of decor and form, as required by

292 Pavel Janák, Box, 1911, glazed earthenware, 11.5 cm

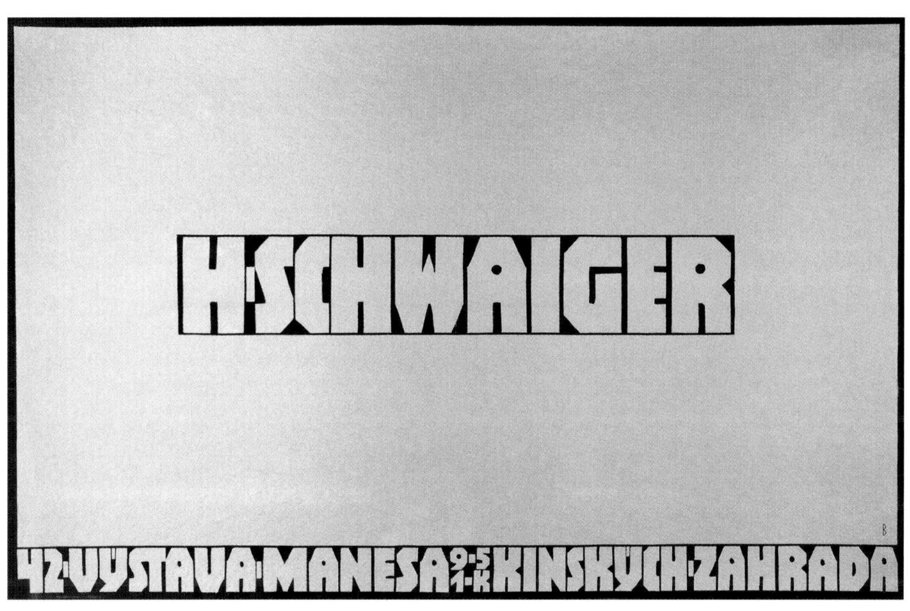

the classic Secession formula of the integrity of purpose, construction, and poetry. When this formula was applied rigorously, a peculiar situation arose that resulted in the superseding of established ideas about ornament. In the traditional concept, decorative ornamental form always intervened between a thing's purpose and use, and this form also labelled and socially "elevated" the object. Historicism had not hesitated to use Rococo ornament on modern machinery, for instance. The authentic Secession had broken with this practice with its insistence on genuine artistic expression; in other words, its demand that ornament be adapted to purpose and use. Then, however, something appeared that had yet to be fully taken into account: the form of the object adorned. This form could no longer be purely functional and utilitarian, just as ornament could no longer be an arbitrary matter of society's current tastes. The common denominator for the new object was then artistic form, which brought together the requirements for construction, purpose, and ornament at a new and previously unfamiliar level. The notion of form thus became a specific expression of the demands of the Secession's synthetism, but it departed from practice to date (which had persisted with the use of non-historicist Secession floral ornament in art and design) by breaking with established ideas about ornament as the embellishment of surfaces and details. Janák's boxes captured the moment at which ornament was truly integrated into form. The box with the elastic "eyes" was an echo of the late Secession's spiral motif, while in the boxes with the zigzag pattern the traditional symbolic function of ornament no longer applied. At the same time, there was, very appropriately, a greater spatial articulation of the object, and its form started being applied as a spatial form, something that Janák had also written about in his manifesto. Janák's ceramics from 1911 included a square box whose surface was articulated by tetrahedrons, and this box pointed quite clearly to the next epoch in the history of Czech art: Cubism.

293 Jaroslav Benda, Poster for Hanuš Schwaiger's posthumous exhibition, 1912, colour linotype, 62 × 95 cm

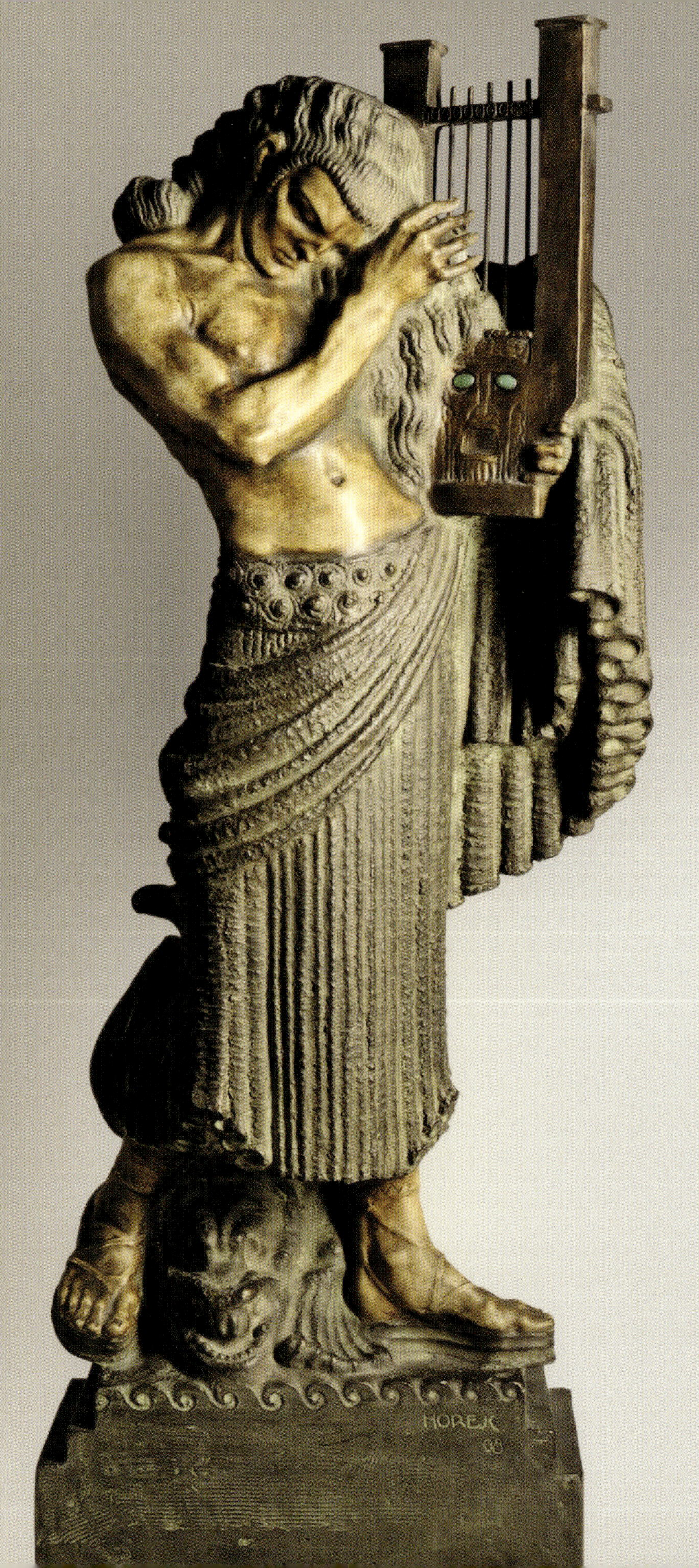
HOREJC
08

THE SECOND SECESSION

In the reaction against naturalism that began to appear halfway through the first decade of the 20th century, the younger generation of artists who had grown up with the naturalistic Secession played the main role. Their unwritten programme was an internalising of the experientiality of the world, an attempt to find more universally valid foundations for modern art. In this regard, they were drawn to Symbolism as a movement that had been largely sidelined by naturalism's predominance. It was not pure Impressionism that met with these young artists' disfavour, but principally the blend of naturalism and idealism that Osma's members saw in their teacher at the Academy, Vlaho Bukovac. However, their interest remained authentically Secessionist in that they were attempting a new and complete capturing of reality in art. In this process, they returned to certain extreme forms of Symbolism that had yet to be adequately explored and could be developed further still.

One example of a spontaneous adopting of this direction was the early work of Jan Zrzavý, who arrived in Prague in the autumn of 1906, aged just sixteen. Thanks to his decorative work in the style of Josef Wenig and Artuš Scheiner, following a year of private study he was accepted by the School of Decorative Arts,[178] where he was to learn naturalistic drawing and painting under the tutelage of his professor, Emanuel Dítě. However, Zrzavý instead immersed himself in the late Romantic literary works of Julius Zeyer, and he would later declare that it was Zeyer who had truly initiated him into art. Besides the contemporary influence of Impressionism, the pictures Zrzavý painted for himself in 1907 demonstrate how he was attempting to combine this romantic vision with a new decorative concept of painting. *Persian Garden* uses a decorative synthetic approach to compose its symbolic trees, path, and mysterious magus in strong lines and blocks of colour, creating a suggestive form of ornamentalism in painting.

In November of the same year, after an unsuccessful attempt to move to Paris, Zrzavý produced a small pastel called *Vale of Sorrow*. Encouraged by Jan Preisler, this led in the following year to his first entirely typical work. It retained the earlier painting's ornamental substructure, but this had been unified and emotionally deepened by the medium of light and its combining with colour.[179] Here too the young painter was influenced by Edvard Munch, albeit indirectly, for Zrzavý only knew Munch from the reproductions published in *Volné směry* at the time of the Norwegian artist's exhibition at SVU Mánes. This was also perhaps why, unlike members of Osma, Zrzavý's response to Munch was not an aggressive use of colour but rather a poetically sombre reflection of a sense of life that was more melancholy than tragic. Zrzavý could also express himself in colour, as in his crucified *Antichrist* (1909), but his authentic note was a lyrical one. In *Nocturne* (1908), the relatively subdued colours of *Vale of Sorrow*

294 Jaroslav Horejc, *Orpheus*, 1908, polychrome plaster and glass, 89.5 cm

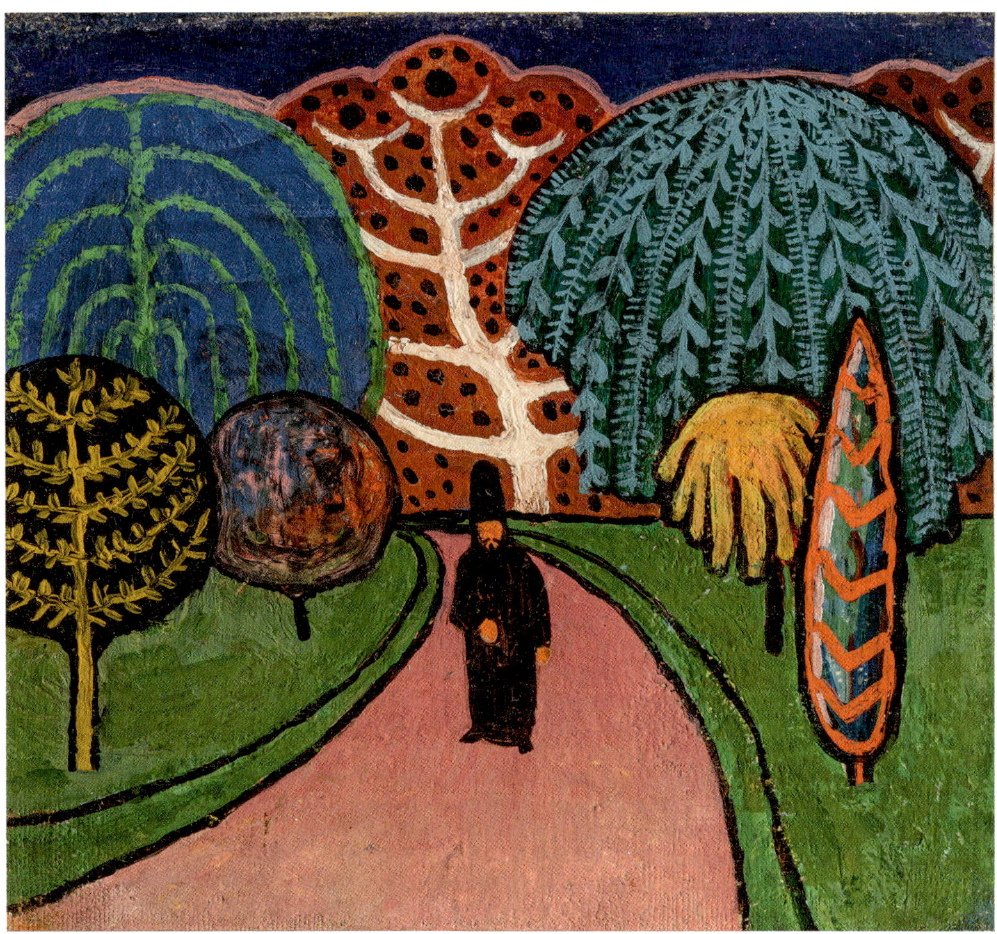

now gleam in the silver moonlight, lending the painting the magic and poetry of the world's "other side" at night. Although the main appeal of Zrzavý's work remained his emotional intensity of colour, this was not merely to do with the usual "mood" of a painting, but with sublimating a position that was present in the symbols he used. His work seemed naive, but it forged a new economy of means and an ability to use elementary symbols to structure a poetic testimony in which he renounced the immediate effects that coarse brushstrokes and dramatically contrasting colours can have on the viewer. He generally created his contrasts cyclically, in the symbolic polarities between individual paintings: he juxtaposed the sensitive melancholy of *Vale of Sorrow* with *Happy Pilgrims* (1908), which represents the light-hearted side of Symbolism. Many more polarities of this kind, reflecting the self in sorrow before slumbering nature or alternatively the stirring of the erotic instinct, the awakening of nature in man, can be found in Zrzavý's work.

The Symbolist aspect of Jan Zrzavý's paintings came from his need for self-expression, but naturally he also sought allies on his journey. In this situation, and as someone who was interested in both literature and Symbolism, Zrzavý was drawn

295 Jan Zrzavý, *Persian Garden*, 1907, oil, 23 × 24.5 cm

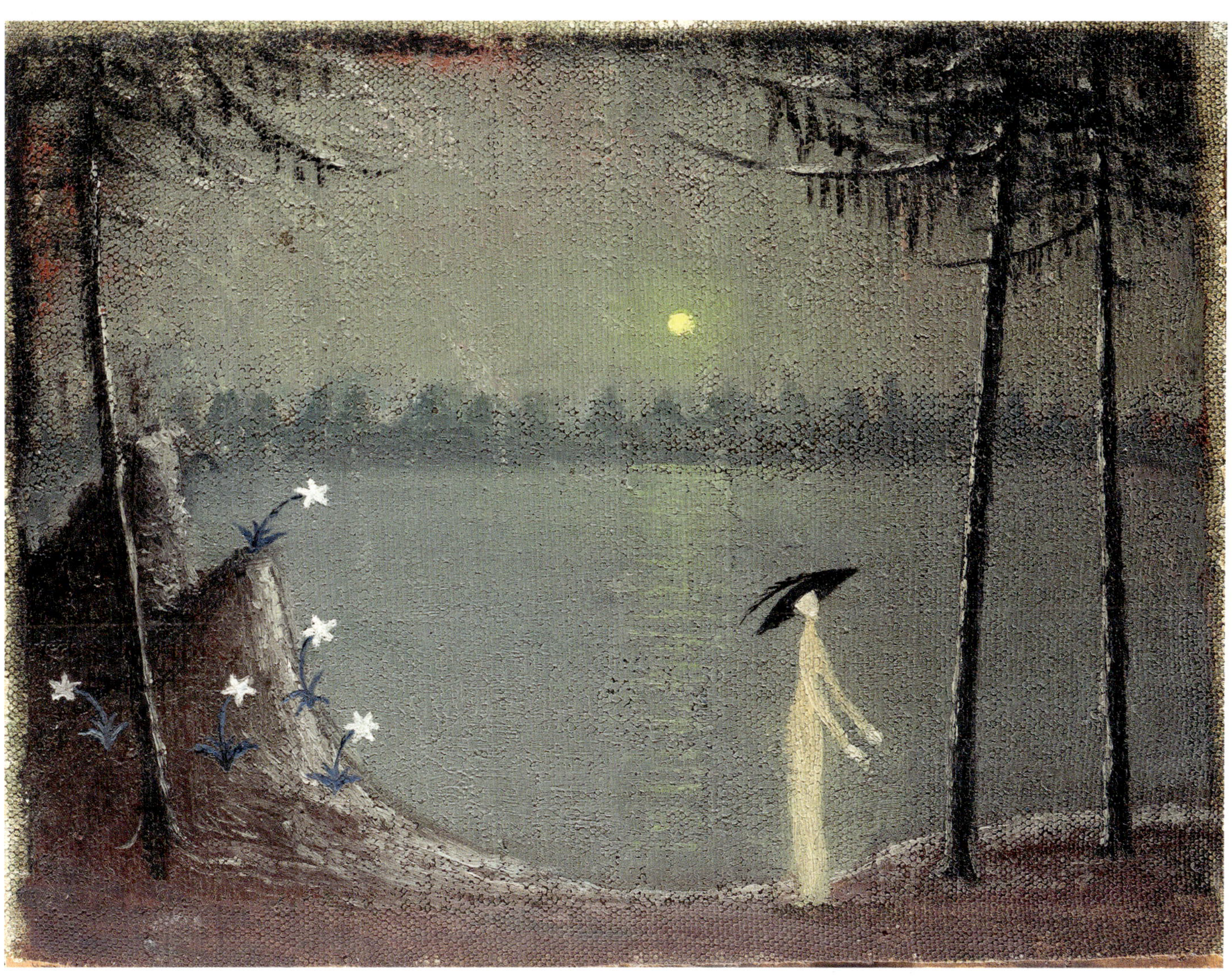

296 Jan Zrzavý, *Nocturne*, 1908, oil, 20 × 25.5 cm

to the circle around *Moderní revue*, which since the mid-1890s had considered itself the Symbolist movement's tribune in Bohemia. It had long lost Karel Hlaváček, who, although censured as a dilettante, had been not just a perceptive critic but also a practitioner of fine art. Following Hlaváček's premature death, other writers in the group turned to art criticism. In 1906 Bedřich Kočí published Arnošt Procházka's *The Path of Beauty*, bringing together the essays Procházka had written on European Symbolist artists since 1898. The volume included accounts of Redon, Ensor, and Beardsley that underlined the Decadent and Symbolist devices in their work. In 1910 Zrzavý presented a drawing of the head of John the Baptist to another member of *Moderní revue*, Jiří Karásek of Lvovice. The subject was one of the Symbolist movement's heraldic symbols, for it was seen as the archetype of man's spiritual transubstantiation.

By now, Zrzavý was in contact with *Moderní revue*'s principal arbiter on art, Miloš Marten, who gave him much the same advice that Karel Vítězslav Mašek had at the School of Decorative Arts: that he should first learn to draw from nature and the Old Masters.[180] Marten was one of the leading contemporary critics, and had written on art since the turn of the century.[181] After Munch's exhibition in Prague, he had self-published an essay he wrote in the artist's defence. In 1907–8 Marten stayed in France, where he met Émile Bernard, a former friend of Paul Gauguin from the Pont-Aven days, and this greatly helped to crystallise Marten's ideas on aesthetics. Bernard – for whom

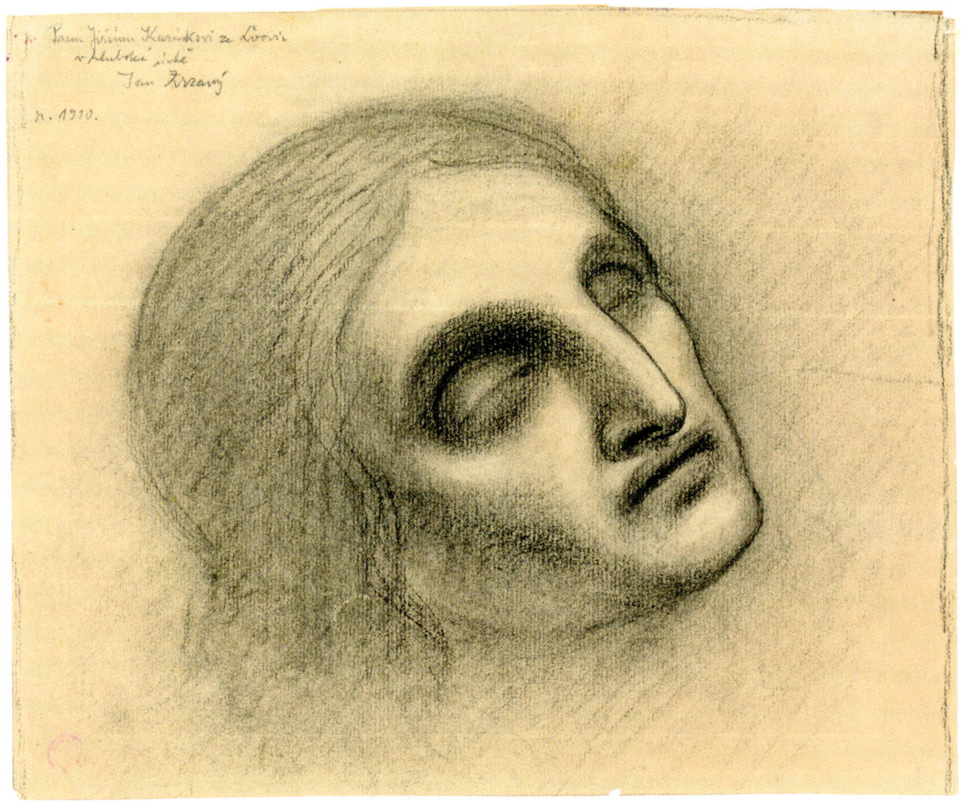

297 Jan Zrzavý, *The Head of John the Baptist*, 1910, charcoal, 22.4 × 26.8 cm

Marten organised an exhibition in Prague in 1909 through SVU Mánes – had become a fervent advocate of Neoclassicism. He had been involved with the reappraisal of Paul Cézanne that had proved to be an important crossroads in the development of modern art at the beginning of the century; he considered Cézanne a crude representation of the ideas leading to the restoration of the eternally valid principles of true art under the cult of Tradition and Ideal. Bernard, and following in his footsteps Marten too, sought a way out of the crisis of subjectivism and naturalistic externality that would lead between the academic School and modernist Anarchy. They resurrected the classical theory of harmony as an "eternal" static equilibrium, and they saw art's objective lying in an ideal Beauty. This was to be promoted through the study in museums of the Old Masters. In one of his letters to Marten, Bernard wrote,

> However, there is a preconception that the Masters are a hazard, and hence the Uncertainty among most artists. They assume or believe that they are insufficiently original to face them without fear. I myself have always considered the Louvre merely an aid for artists, not a book to be copied word for word, and I do not believe there is any need to fear any danger from this side, for *even if someone were to devote himself to outright imitation, he could create nothing pernicious or unclean.*[182]

Yet, as Czech artists could see at Bernard's exhibition in Prague, the end result was evidence only of eclecticism.

Nevertheless, in theoretical terms, Bernard and Marten's programme contained a number of questions that were fundamentally related to the need for a generalisation of modern art's world view. Once naturalism and subjectivism had been abandoned, there logically arose the problem of modern art's position on tradition, and with it the sensitive question of imitation. Capable artists could organically incorporate this element into a new synthesis: one such example of a living relationship with tradition was Zrzavý's admiration for the work of Leonardo da Vinci, which had in fact been prompted by Marten. Importantly, this understanding came from a certain inner affinity, and it stemmed from a common problem in art: the importance of coloured light in a painting. Similarly, in 1910 Bohumil Kubišta was keen to learn from Nicolas Poussin's compositions, copying and analysing in detail his *Landscape with Orpheus and Eurydice* in the Louvre.

Moderní revue, which in these matters increasingly favoured traditionalism, still retained something of its Decadent and Symbolist origins, and this attracted new artists. The printmaker František Kobliha gained access to this relatively closed circle. Although he was from the same generation as the artists who had emerged in the 1890s, unfavourable circumstances meant that he had only been able to develop his talent in the subsequent decade. He began at the turn of the century as a decorative draughtsman in the style of the naturalistic Secession, but his true domain was Symbolism, freely inspired by Romantic and Decadent literature. In the first decade of the new century, Kobliha created in his sensitive drawings a stock of ideas that he would then use for the rest of his life. After experimenting with oil painting, he found in printmaking a technique that was entirely suited to him, and at the end of the decade he created in rapid succession a number of cycles that are among the finest

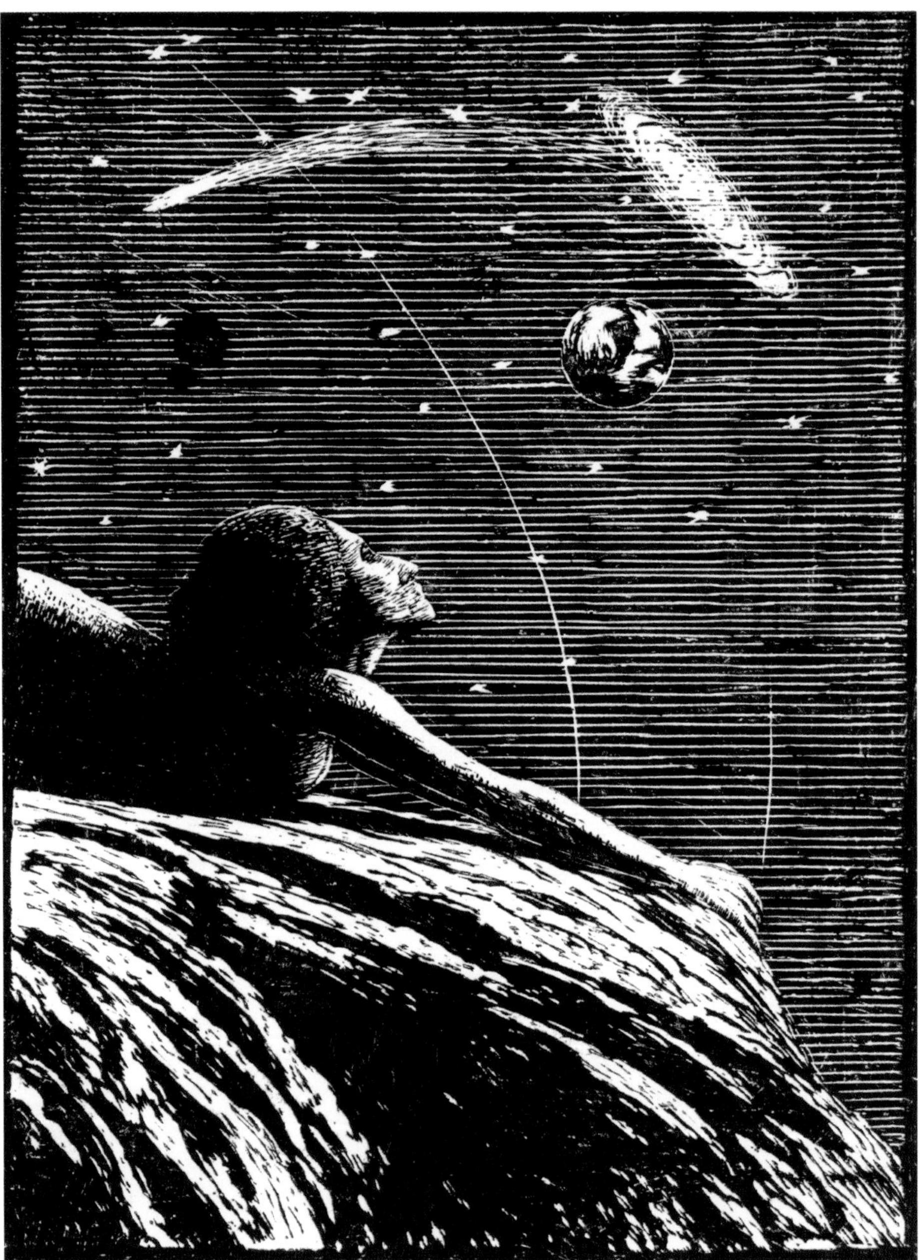

examples of late Czech Symbolism. After his initial *Simple Motifs* (1908), these were chiefly the cycles *Late before Morning* (1909) and *A Vindictive Cantilena* (1910), both based on Karel Hlaváček's poems, as well as *Tristan* (1909–10) and *May* (1911), the latter illustrating Karel Hynek Mácha's famous poem. These cycles also marked the high point of Kobliha's art. The programmatic aspect of his Symbolism was already present in his choice of dark, moonlit nights as his key theme, as opposed to Impressionism's broad daylight.[183] The setting for Kobliha's imagination was a landscape viewed from above as it glimmered mysteriously in the night, a place where visions of phantoms and

298 František Kobliha, *Sphinx*, 1908, woodcut, 20 × 14.2 cm

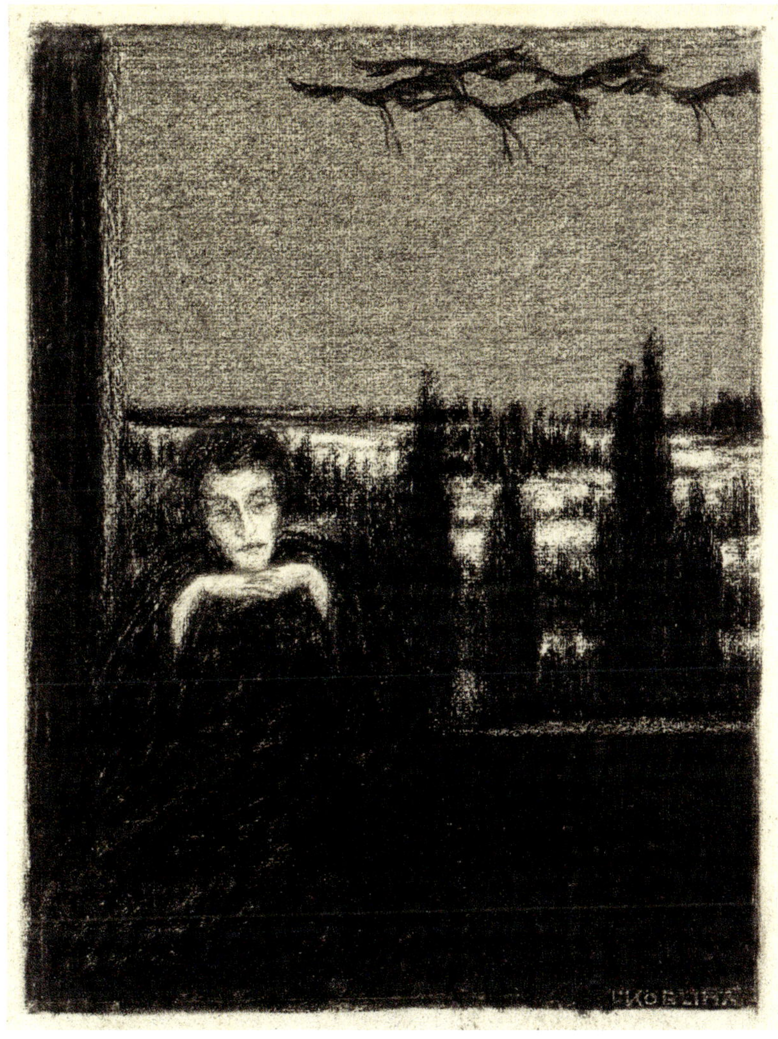

female personifications, dancing or wistfully wandering, appeared before the dreaming poet. The somnambulistic mood of these meticulously executed nocturnes was a state of mind where the silence of the night would reveal everything "that would otherwise remain a secret, unknown," as Kobliha later wrote in his essay on Odilon Redon.[184] This was the characteristic process of Symbolist evocation, calling forth in symbolic images certain fundamental psychological complexes and processes and, by giving voice to them, releasing their pressure. From the surface of this ethereal world, Kobliha's imagination turned to both cosmic distances and the depths of the earth. Examples of the former are his *Sphinx* (1908), who gazes from a rocky promontory at the wonders of the night sky, or a motif taken from Hlaváček of a sleepwalking female nude staring at the moon, or the opening print of *May* showing the poet swooning beneath a starry sky. The latter group of works returns to a motif that Otakar Lebeda had introduced in the 1890s: the figure of a man looking down at a lake that is an

299 František Kobliha, *Reverie*, 1909, charcoal, 32 × 24 cm

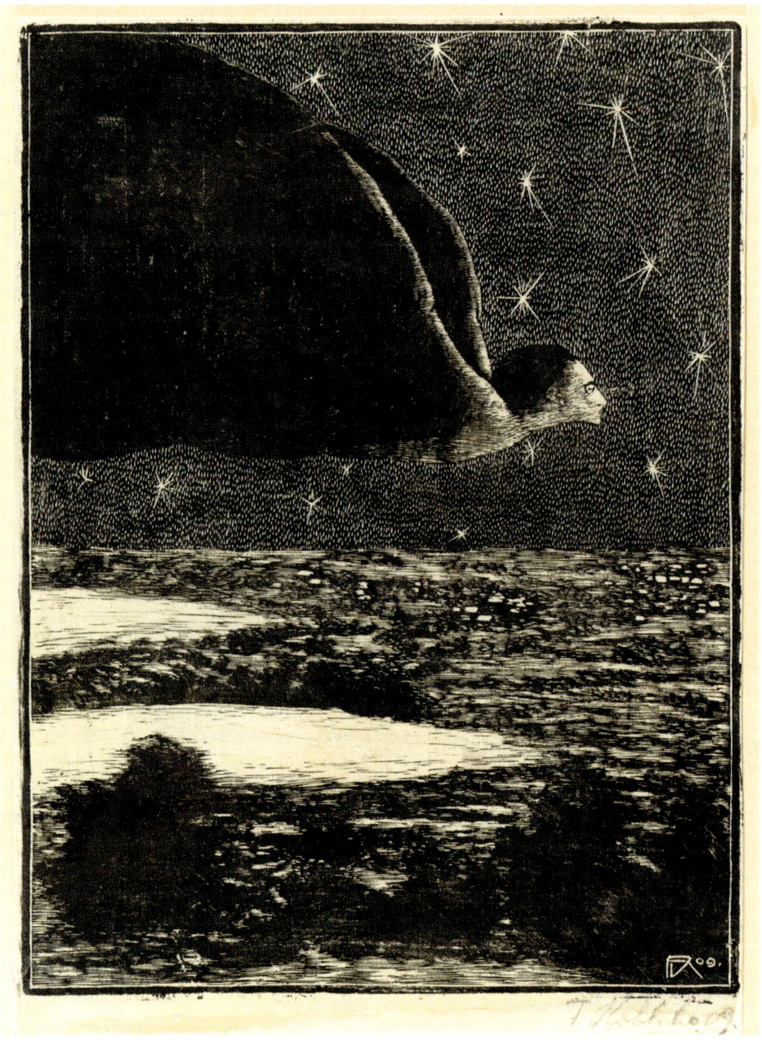

abyss filled with water (*Tristan*; *May*). While Kobliha largely took the theme of cosmic wonder and the power of the moon from the older repertoire of Czech Symbolism, he extended the subaquatic theme. Primarily in *Tristan*, but also in *May*, he evoked a descent into fateful watery depths (the final print of *Tristan*), and in the fantastical vegetation of *Undersea Forests* (1909) and the deep bay in *May* he used lines to produce an impression of energy surging up from the depths. In these prints Kobliha intuitively illustrated the psychological process of sublimation, whose subtext so bewitched him, drawing him to the theme of night and its mysteries. He was able to express what in the 1890s had been reflected in late Romantic and fairy-tale depictions of water sprites, or had been present in realistic landscape paintings. This aspect best demonstrates how Kobliha cannot be considered merely an illustrator of literature, for his work was concerned with a sensitive understanding of deeper relationships. The question of imitation that Bernard and Marten had raised at the level of eclectic traditionalism

300 František Kobliha, *Vampire*, 1909, woodcut, 20.7 × 15.2 cm

found in Kobliha's vivid art another solution that worked with archetypal images and in this way opened up artistic expression to true psychological contents. It is also interesting that the *Tristan* cycle possesses decorative stylistic qualities that make it graphically the most effect work in the sense of the new synthetism.

However, Kobliha's discovery of true symbols was not entirely consummated. A negative factor here was evidently exactly that which Kobliha considered to be acclaim: his acceptance into the *Moderní revue* circle. The majority of prints in the *May* cycle, published by Arnošt Procházka, were less imaginative and more in the spirit of illustrative landscape painting. In 1911 Kobliha produced the frontispiece for Miloš Marten's *Cortigiana*, which combines somnambulism with the Neo-Renaissance that Marten propagated. This situation was still more evident in the *Woman* cycle (1911), where the requirement for more solid form and more vital content gave Kobliha's prints a certain rigidity, together with an element of dilettantism. The delicate poetic dreaminess of Kobliha's sensitive earlier prints was replaced with a transparent eroticism

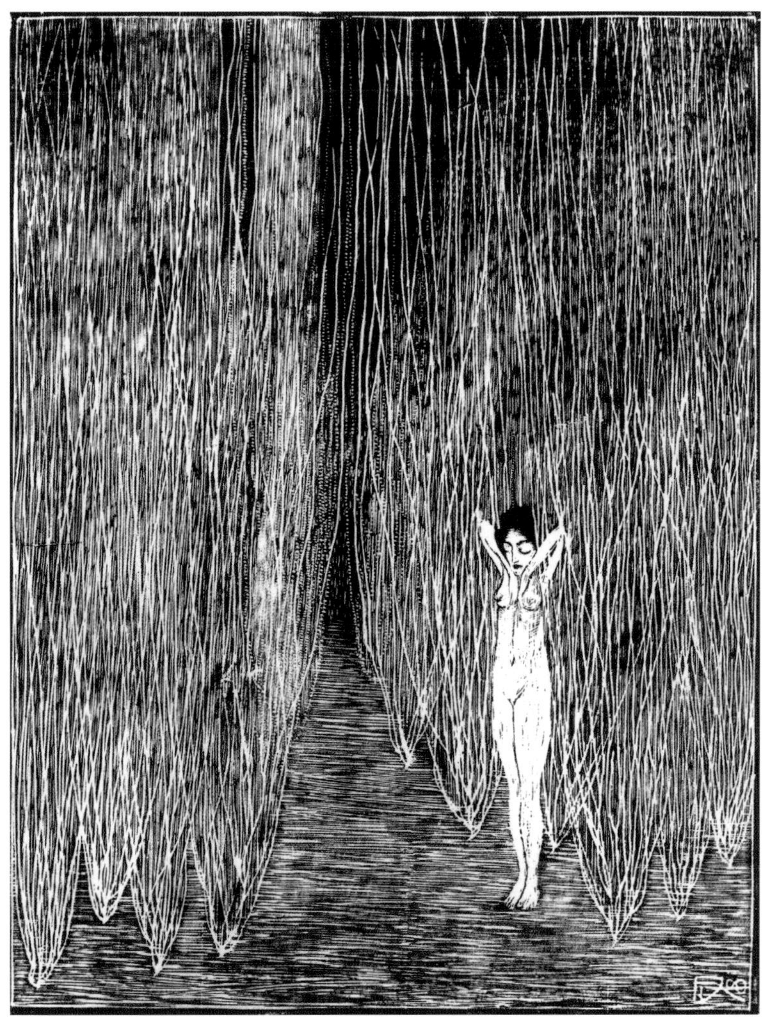

301 František Kobliha, *Undersea Forests*, 1909, woodcut, 20.8 × 15 cm

and a form that tried too hard to please (as in his illustrations for Edvard Bém's *Black and Gold*, 1912). It was probably not unrelated that, in this later period – when Arnošt Procházka, as the most prominent figure in *Moderní revue* (from which even Marten had parted company), was launching conservative and hate-filled attacks on all unconventional work by young artists, accusing them of a primitivist defiling of art – Kobliha was working mainly on book illustration and retreating into a Symbolist reworking of botanical ornamentalism. He only returned to the world of his imagination in 1916, in the *Ballads* and *Fairy Tales and Legends* cycles, but without regaining his original intensity.

Kobliha's true legacy is to be found in his collective symbols, such his *Vampire* from the *Late before Morning* cycle (1909), a reimagining of his frequent motif of a swan in flight as an emblem of poetic symbolism. *Vampire* was also a characteristic combination of the distinctive features of Kobliha's art and the existing scope of Symbolism in Czech art, as expressed primarily in prints and drawings ranging from Hlaváček's Decadent tone to Jan Preisler's lyricism and František Bílek's transcendentalism.

It was perhaps precisely because Kobliha brought together the different traditions in Czech Symbolism, and also on account of his age, that young Symbolist-leaning printmakers and painters chose him as their leader. These artists were contributors to the Catholic review *Meditace*, and the publication's capable editor, the printmaker Emil Pacovský, initiated the founding of a society called Sursum in mid-1910.[185] In October of that same year, Sursum held an exhibition at the Friends of Art Club in Brno, having been unable to find an exhibition space in Prague. In their youthful enthusiasm, Sursum's members – who besides Kobliha and Pacovský included Jan Konůpek, Josef Váchal, and Jan Zrzavý – imagined that it would become a prominent society for literature and art with a broad range of cultural activities. To promote Sursum they sought allies among older and better-known artists, and in this respect František Bílek must have been an especially attractive proposition.

Bílek had by then joined Umělecká beseda. He had recently been the subject of a scandal in *Dílo* magazine, provoked by conservative artists who had been scathing about his statue for Václav Beneš Třebízský's grave in Vyšehrad Cemetery in Prague.[186] The article described *Grief* as "a freak in an agonised theatrical pose" and "an experiment that perhaps sees and seeks its highest potency in the most profound failure"; a drawing of the statue reproduced in the magazine was compared to Carlo Wostry's caricatures. F. X. Šalda countered this attack, defending Bílek's unconventionality and individuality, although he also criticised his inclination towards "some kind of Baroque sentimentality" and called for "a more legitimate plasticity."[187]

This demonstrated how Bílek's work remained controversial and continued to provoke discussion, especially over its artistic merit. Yet Bílek still stressed, and in the content of his work too, his opposition to any limits on intellectual freedom. In 1907 he was visited by students from Southern Bohemia, who wanted him to assist them in erecting a memorial to their fallen comrade. Bílek designed a large sculptural group depicting the forces that youth had to overcome to attain spiritual beauty. In 1910 he carved in maple (the quality of the woodcarving is among Bílek's finest work) a smaller

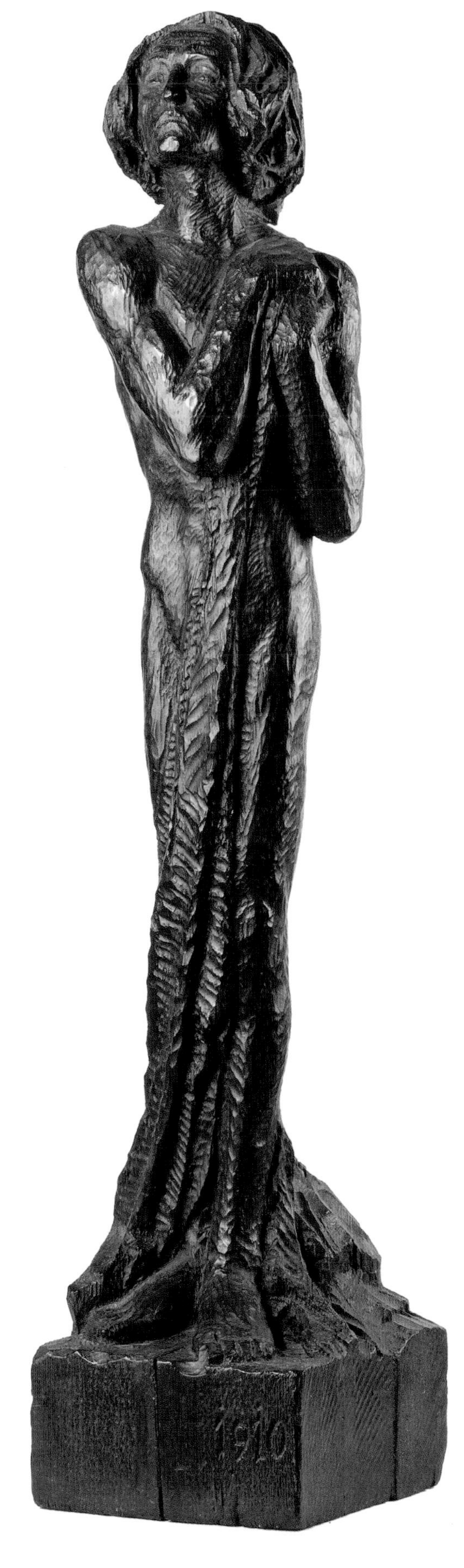

302 František Bílek, *The Beauty of Youth in Its Struggle*, 1910, wood, 80 cm

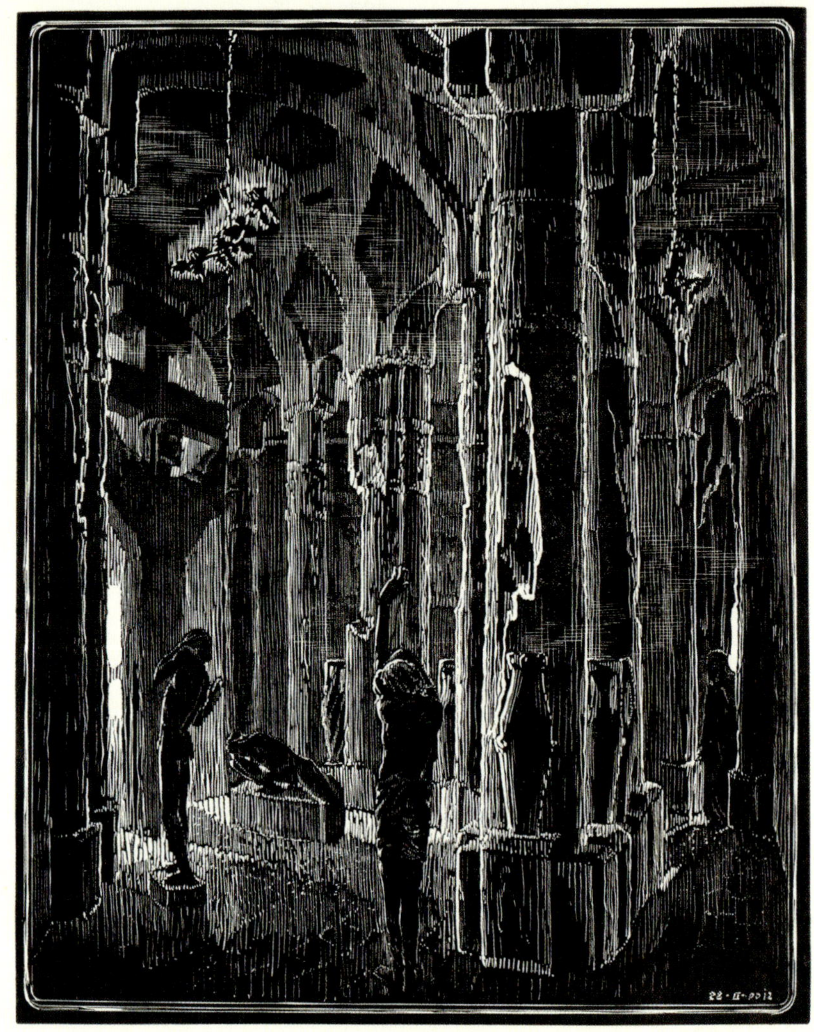

model of the main statue for this grand memorial, which, like many of Bílek's ideas of this sort, was never realised. *The Beauty of Youth in Its Struggle* is a typically elongated figure of an adolescent, his eyes closed as he declares his vocation. The figure's verticality was based on the idea of spiritual growth expressed by means of the human body, which had been central to Bílek's art since the turn of the century. The motion here is less agitated, and the statue lacks Bílek's earlier elements of naturalism. Instead, there is a more subtle plastic penetration of the mass, and the surface is nervously worked. This is evidence of how Bílek was in step with stylistic developments at this time, and it also shows how his endless striving for large monuments, especially in the latter half of the decade, was not without synthetic results. Bílek succeeded in muting the "Baroque sentimentality" that Šalda had criticised, replacing it with a more monumental but still sufficiently animated form. This experience proved its worth in 1912, when Bílek

303 František Bílek, *The Hall of Dread*, 1912, woodcut, 29.5 × 22.7 cm

had an opportunity to realise at least one of his spectacular monuments – a twelve-metre-high statue of Jan Hus for Kolín. The massive stone sculpture, which required an immense amount of work, brought to a close the cycle he had begun with *A Tree Which Burned for the Ages*.[188]

Even more than as a sculptor, Bílek appealed to the young artists of Sursum as a printmaker. In the first decade of the new century his excellent draughtsmanship found a counterpart in the woodcut. Here he was able to use everything the medium offered, and in the virtuoso play of black and white lines carved with a burin he gave his visions an ethereal impression of light, creating imaginary forms. His interest in light, which was one of the Czech Secession's most essential ideas, was developed here with the same richness of shades we see in Impressionist painting, but with an entirely different content: this was the light of Julius Zeyer and Otokar Březina's "inner vision." In his woodcuts, Bílek could express the mysterious atmosphere of half-light (*The Hall of*

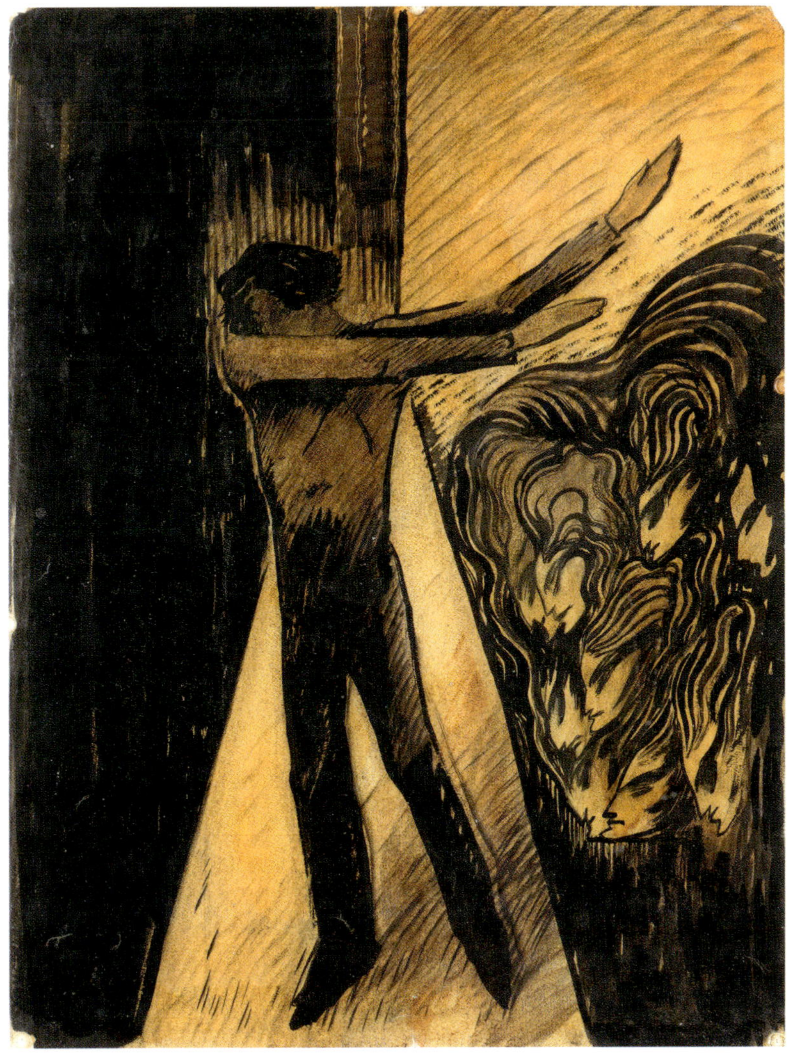

304 Jan Konůpek, *Renunciation*, 1909, varnished ink, 59.5 × 41.1 cm

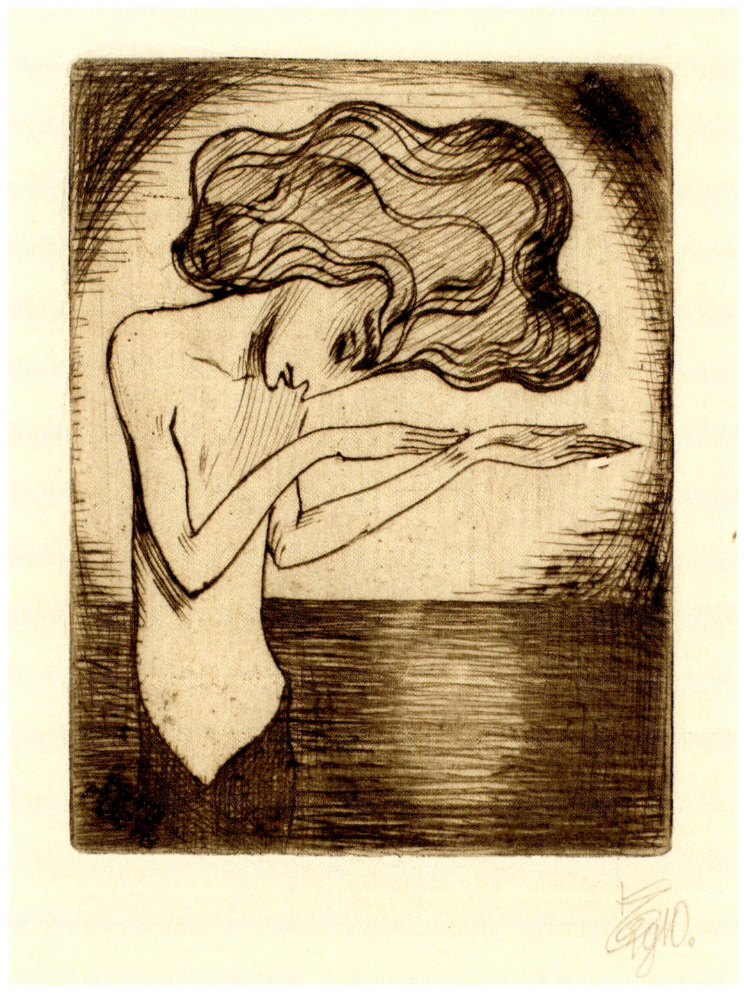

Dread, 1912), or soft moonlight, or bright sunshine, but light was always a symbol, a means of guiding the viewer towards some fundamental idea.

Despite the admiration of its young members and Bílek's interest, he never worked with Sursum. This was not only due to the uncertainty that resulted from Sursum's sudden takeover by writers (mostly rather inferior ones).[189] More important were their philosophical differences: the younger generation had a quite different mentality. These differences become clear if we consider Jan Konůpek's work from this time. Konůpek initially worked on Symbolist themes as a decorative ornamental draughtsman, where the high points were his illustrations for Willem Gerard van Nouhuys's *Egidius and the Stranger* (1909) – in which he divided up linear symbols into square fields – and the cover of *Meditace* (1909), with the hieratic figure of an orant, in which Konůpek used all the varieties of late Secession spiral ornament. The cover also featured a zigzag motif, which for Pavel Janák would play an important role in moving beyond labyrinthine ornamental lines. However, Konůpek was not only an ornamentalist but also a figuralist, as is evident from an earlier competition design for the Chapel of St. John

305 Jan Konůpek, *Resignation – Dream*, 1910, etching, 12 × 9 cm

the Baptist at Prague's St. Vitus Cathedral (1905), where this dualism was reflected in a pair of Gothic stained-glass windows, one with a simple ornamental design and the other with a somewhat illegible apocalyptic scene.

There is a coloured charcoal drawing by Konůpek from 1908 called *Black Flame – Salome*, in which the hieratic orant motif is not rendered ornamentally (although it does retain the archaic frontal stylisation) but in illusively flowing modelling, where the figure's hair swirls upwards like a flame. Konůpek would frequently return to this motif in the years that followed. The figure is labelled Salome, an embodiment of the femme fatale. In the late 19th century, French Symbolist and Decadent artists had paid much attention to Salome's role in the legend of John the Baptist, and had elevated her to a symbol of the world's mystery. For Konůpek too, the old legend became the key to a new crystallisation of the phenomenal world. Besides his surprisingly primitivist woodcut *Baptism in Jordan* (1908), Konůpek was drawn mainly to Salome and her twisted

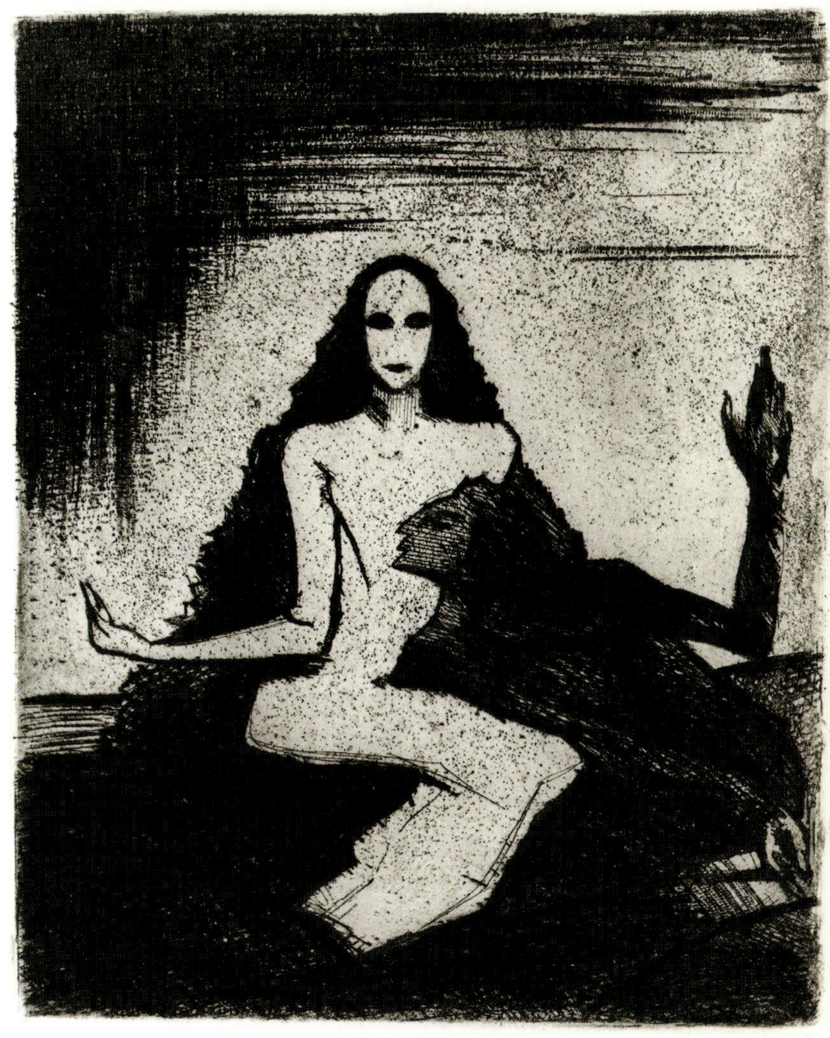

306 Jan Konůpek, *Evocation*, 1911, etching, 24.4 × 19.4 cm

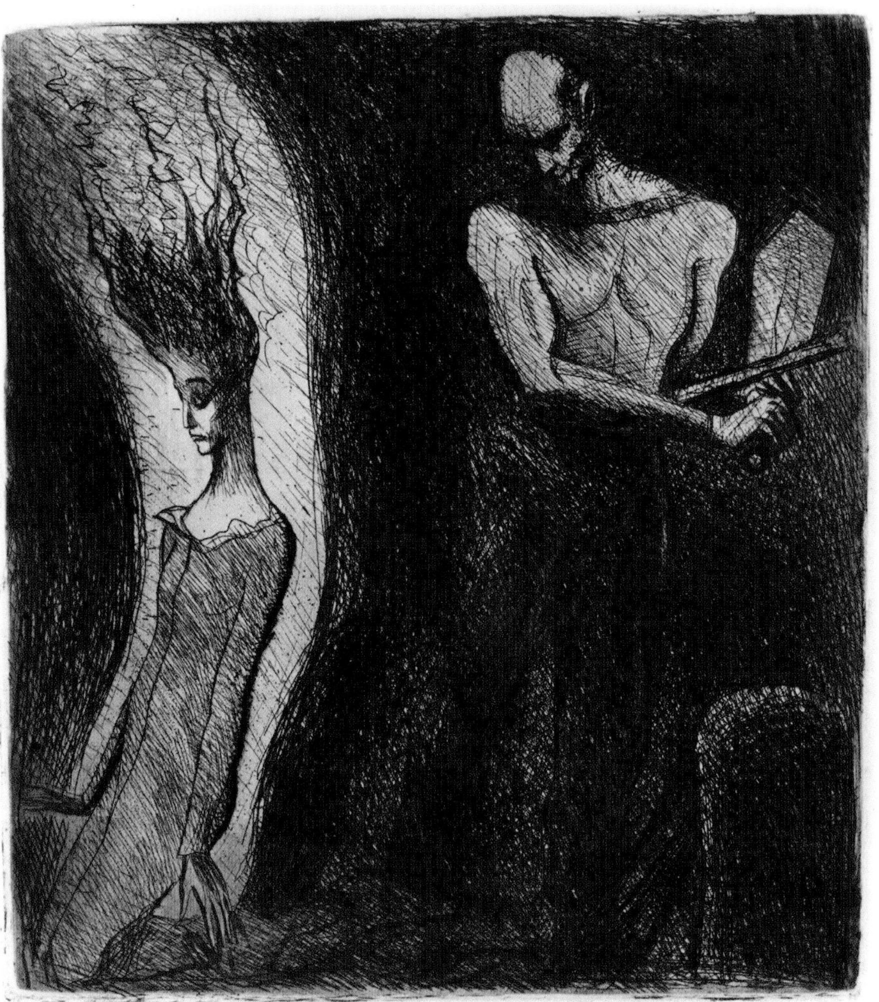

attachment to the prophet, and over the next few years he would resolve a number of fundamental questions while working on this theme. An important difference between Konůpek and Bílek is evident in their very choice of subject. For Bílek, Mystery and Darkness, which he personified according to the Book of Revelation as "a woman arrayed … full of abominations and filthiness of her fornication,"[190] were the very opposite of true knowledge, which consisted in Truth and Radiance. His uncomplicated moralism did not call for any immersion in the mysteries of the psyche. Konůpek also attempted to moralise on the theme of Salome. This was evident whenever he used stylisation in her depiction, as in a subsequent version of *Black Flame* (c. 1910), where the figure is shown in "Egyptian" profile. It was also the antithesis of his etching *Smouldering*, in which an anaemic nude with sunken eyes and an immense mane of hair is consumed by her morbid passion, and the flame that in the "Egyptian" version fills the image like a fountain of light here merely flickers in the palm of her hand. Another etching, *Beheading* (1909), shows Salome kneeling before an executioner as if it were

307 Jan Konůpek, *Beheading*, 1910, etching, 27.2 × 23.5 cm

she and not John the Baptist who should be punished and sacrificed. In *Ecstasy* (1912), the frontal version of Salome with swirling hair has become a terrifying phantom, in which the theme of Vanitas has returned in the motif of the animated skull, although now at a quite different level that entirely negates the former ornamentalism in favour of expressiveness.

It was within this range, when Konůpek also discovered in the etching his most biddable graphic technique, that he matured as an artist. His variations on the theme of Salome may often seem arbitrary, but the play of his imagination followed an inner discipline. It belonged to images that were far more labile, but also more modern, than Bílek's religious visions. Konůpek's antitheses were not based on clearly defined opposites (as was the case with Bílek's light and darkness, for instance), but more on a differentiation of the same initial subject. In *Black Flame*, Konůpek created both its positive and its negative aspects, but the two were connected by the theme of Salome.

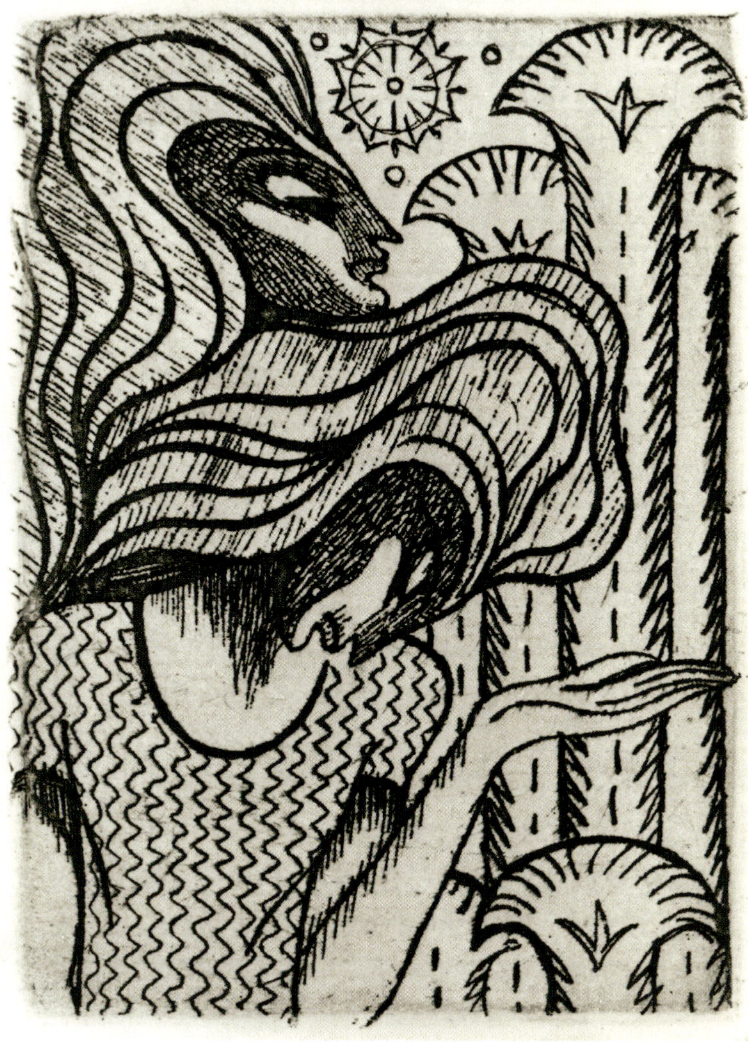

308 Jan Konůpek, *Egypt*, 1911, etching, 9.5 × 6.7 cm

As a female figure, Salome is also a symbol of art and the soul, and in her relationship with John the Baptist there is a certain archetype that the artist was intuitively trying to access. From a psychological standpoint, their relationship embraces contradictory tendencies of the human psyche, in representations of what Jung would later dub *anima* and *animus*. Overall, then, this series of drawings and etchings by Konůpek can be summarised as an attempt to express intuitively, with the aid of a familiar example from mythology, the process of finding psychological equilibrium, in which contradictory tendencies interact in complicated ways but are directed towards some kind of fundamental, ambivalent, and reflexive unity. The final print in this series shows Salome dancing with wild abandon before the severed head of John the Baptist (1912–13). Watching her is a man on a throne, who resembles not so much King Herod as a modern philosopher. The naked dancer and the prophet's head are depicted as equally animal: this is then about identification, a spiritual moment that resonates with the thinker. In this way, the imagery "overcomes" the contradiction between the corporeal and the spiritual, which have now united to create a strong personality.

Konůpek expressed the motif of ambivalent values in his etching *Resignation – Dream* (1910), where the negative femme fatale's hair twists in a spiral to visually link her with the positive idea of the Holy Virgin. This key motif is markedly Secession in origin, but its form is enhanced by a new plasticity that goes beyond the earlier ornamental two-dimensionality. Konůpek's etchings on the theme of Temptation also expressed this psychological ambivalence, although their visualisation of this theme was somewhat more static, making them more in the nature of imaginary parables. Konůpek had come up with a new graphic language, softer than in the times of strict ornamentalism and with a new spontaneity that was related to how he was now working with psychological themes.

While older Symbolists such as Bílek or even Preisler tended to work with clearly defined concepts that had a single dominant idea or mood, younger Symbolists were in this respect much more diverse. They were also more restless, and they constructed their phenomenal world with their characteristic syncretism. However, their recapitulating of old ideas was expressed in a form that not only involved an entirely new artistic execution but also constituted a distinctive deformation and reappraisal of these ideas. One example of this kind of iconoclasm was the increasingly idiosyncratic work of one of Sursum's founding members, Josef Váchal. For Váchal, art was the best way of soothing the anxiety that had plagued him as a young man and still threatened to disrupt his psychological equilibrium. This was the source of the unconventional primitivist expressiveness of his drawings and prints, which for the most part recorded how he overcame this peril. The interest in Spiritism and magic we find in Váchal's work from the latter half of the decade was extended by his discovery of other branches of what is known as the esoteric tradition, and art played an important part in making this miscellany of curious dogmas and teachings somewhat more cohesive. For a time, Váchal even turned to Catholicism, but he soon began fulminating against clericalism and professing all manner of heresy. He contrasted the Christian God with the idea of Satan as a powerful adversary, creating a Satanic altar in his painting *Devil Worshippers*

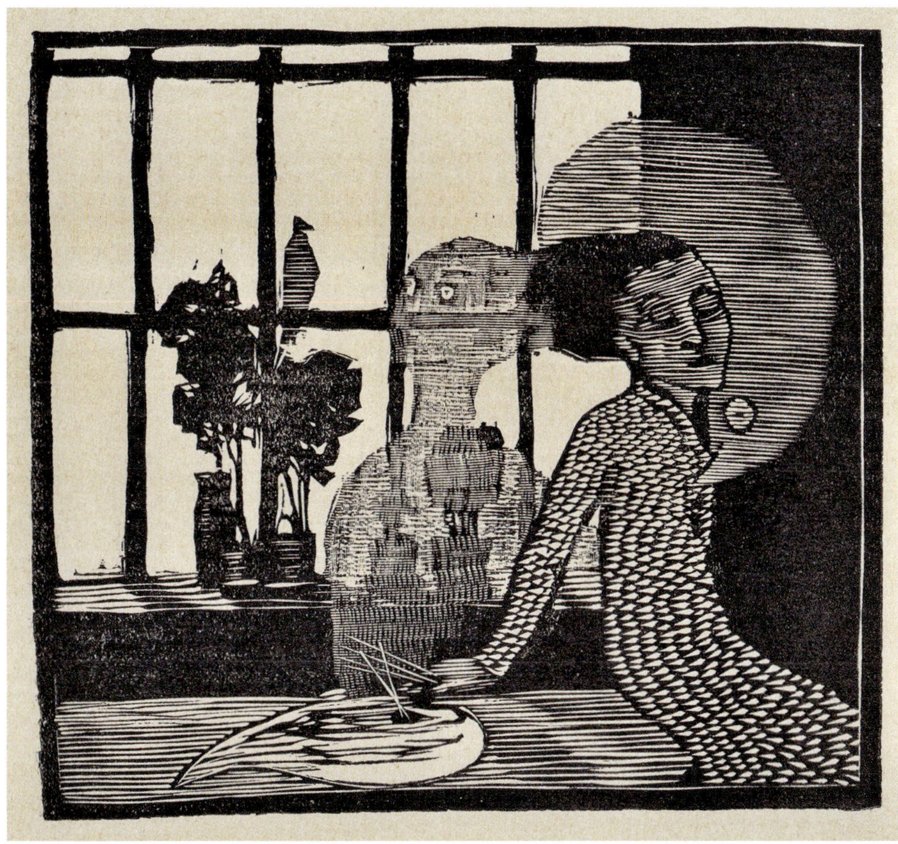

(1909).[191] The painting's carved frame is a reminder that Váchal was also a remarkable sculptor, and it prompts comparisons with Bílek's cartoon *Mother!* from 1899, which is in fact the antithesis of Váchal's painting. For Bílek, the cosmic theme expressed his metaphysical and mystical leanings, while for Váchal, Satan was a manifestation of the deep forces of the earth. In Váchal's painting, the cycle of birth and death is not related to some ethereal light but has returned to the earth, as expressed by the skulls in the trees. This is also suggested by the intense colours of the worshippers and the gleaming golden aura of this dark celebration.

Váchal's woodcut *Fantasy* (1912) illustrates his concept of art. A mysterious bird sits on the bars of a studio window; for years it had apparently always sung to Váchal at midnight, "loudly, beautifully and long," but none of his neighbours had ever heard it. In the studio, a meditating woman has put aside her palette. She symbolises Art, and she is connected to her phantasmic astral double, who can understand the bird's song. The shapeless cloud of this spiritual materialisation curves down to the woman's heart. This was Váchal's primitivist reference to old Renaissance Neoplatonic ideas about the imagination as the supreme state of the artistic conception of the world in its totality, and he also included here other themes relating to spiritual communication. With Váchal, as with Konůpek, there was a fundamental ambivalence between the corporeal and the incorporeal, and related to this was the problem of unity. It seems

309 Josef Váchal, *Fantasy*, 1912, woodcut, 9 × 9.7 cm

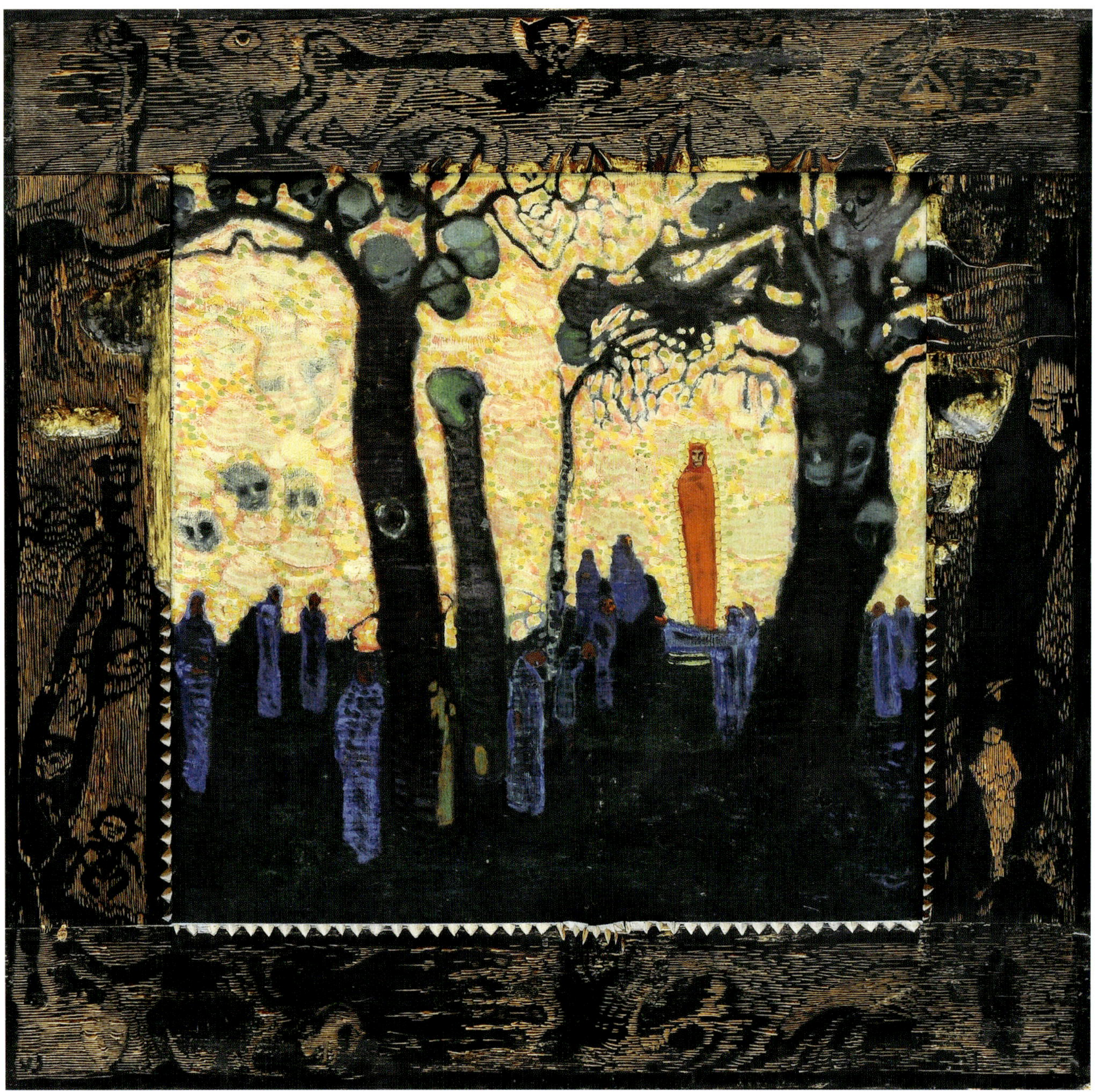

310 Josef Váchal, *Devil Worshippers*, 1909, oil, 100 × 100 cm

very characteristic of the younger generation's position on this key question that there was no truly complete interpermeation of all elements, as was the case with the Secession's supreme monism (whether Symbolist or Impressionist). Instead, it was more a matter of the expressive will intervening in an emotional unity. In Váchal's woodcut, an immaterial yet imperious substance intervenes between the mysterious voice of nature and its enraptured listener, Painting, and it is only the presence of this substance that leads from the passivity of dreaming to active creation. In this context, Váchal would later write in *The Perfect Magic of the Future* (where he critically evaluated his work to date) that, unlike all forms of religion, which enforce a passive tranquillity, art alone allows one to confront the lure of death, over and over again.

Sursum's artists were all influenced by the first generation of Symbolists, and their contribution was to restructure this common foundation in an attempt to align Symbolism with more realistic psychological, philosophical, and aesthetic problems. However, this evidently gave rise to a diversity of opinions for which no clear-cut common programme could then be formulated. The high point for Sursum's art department, and also its swansong, was an exhibition held in 1912 at a new exhibition venue, the Municipal House in Prague. Besides Kobliha, it included all of Sursum's founding members, as well as Rudolf Adámek and Miroslav Sylla, with Jaroslav Horejc, who was a member of SVU Mánes, as a special guest.

Horejc had from the start been inspired by ancient Greek sculpture and Mycenaean art, whose stylisation had once vividly illustrated great myths. Horejc's oeuvre, his response to the origins of the European conception of the world, reflected the contemporary interest in tradition following the crisis of naturalism. This appeal for order and regularity suited a structural treatment of sculptural form that combined the principles of decorative ornament with a plastic monumentality. In Horejc's work there was also a certain fundamental dualism in the artistic structure. This gave rise to an unusual effect, with a figure that at first sight seemed to be almost impersonally respecting the whole rather than the detail also having a very sensitive psychological characterisation. Just as ancient Greek drama interwove impersonal fate with the entirely human aspect of personality, Horejc's sculptures contained the same polarity of perfection and imperfection on the basis of tragic necessity.

The sculpture in which these two aspects were perhaps most present was *Perseus* (1915), a portrayal of the Medusa's mythical vanquisher. The resulting form evidences a peculiar tension between the massively modelled basic volumes and the nervous sharpness of the facial features and ornamental details. In comparison with other sculptors working in this vein, whether Czech or from other countries, Horejc's archaism was unique not in the overall structuring of his sculptures but in their psychological modelling, which can be considered his response to the specific aesthetic shared by Sursum's members. In the contemporary wave of primitivism that young artists favoured over naturalistic illusion and classical eclectic traditionalism, Horejc, together with Váchal and his Expressionist art, was unquestionably closest to what French theorists had offered as a strategic objective for modern art under the label of synthetic classicism. However, when compared with other Czech representatives of this movement, such as Jan Štursa – who based his work on vitalism and sought through the creative will to grasp the physical reality of the living model – Horejc's affinity with the imaginary world of Sursum's artists is immediately apparent.

Horejc's sculptures were an embodiment of a continuity that was held together through all the mutations of form by a more general world view manifested in a sense of the tragedy of life. Although its source lay outside art, it found in art its fullest expression of the problem of individuality confronting great and impersonal pressures. The Secession mentality was familiar with gestures of revolt against society's reality, but it sought harmony and surrendered to what it revered as the eternal order, through which it challenged the injustices and chaos of the prevailing social structure. It saw this surrender as an identifying with natural and metaphysical forces, but also as the sacrificing of the individual. To express this position, it sought mythological models

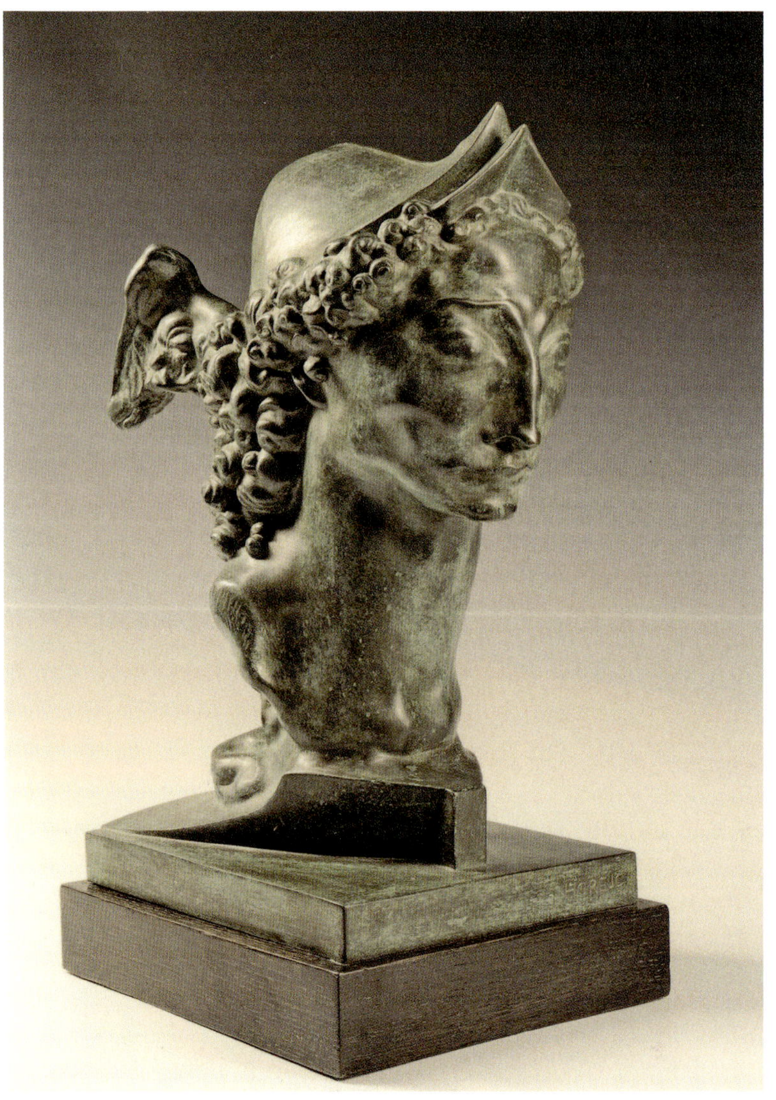

311 Jaroslav Horejc, *Perseus*, 1915, polychrome plaster, 42.5 cm

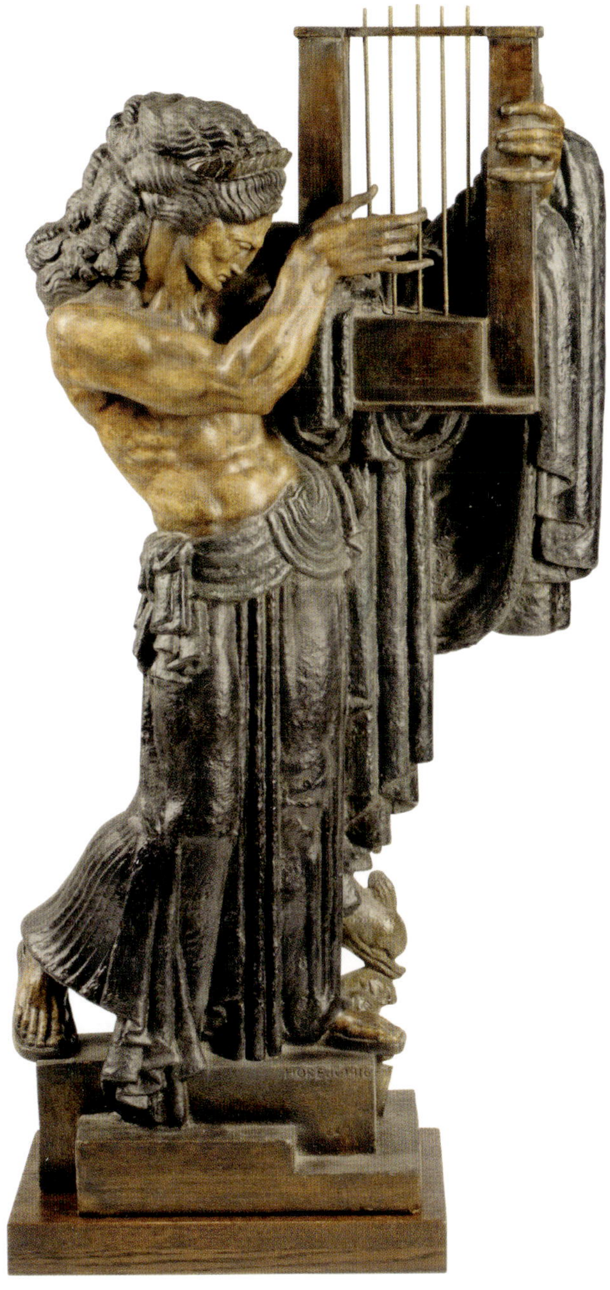

that combined the personal and impersonal in a tragic harmony. One such symbolic figure was Orpheus, who was understood as an archetype of the artist. Horejc's *Orpheus* (1908 and 1916) is an example of late Symbolist typification crystallised from older beliefs, and it concluded the Symbolist cycle, in the sense of a retrospective of its content.

Yet this cycle was also revised and updated. This was mainly the path taken by artists who were much influenced by Munch's painting, in which reality was mythologised

312 Jaroslav Horejc, *Orpheus*, 1916, polychrome plaster, 75 cm

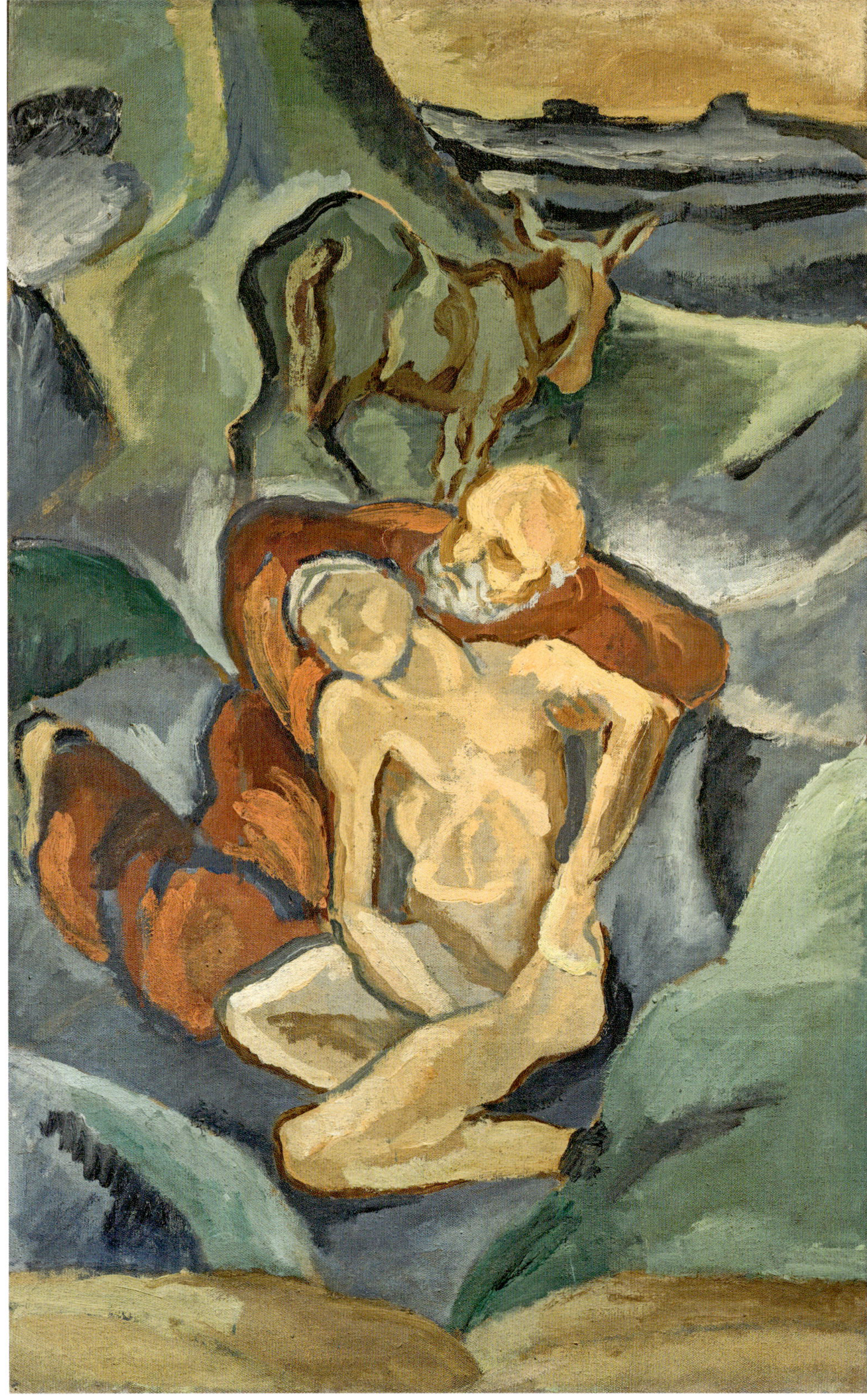

313 Emil Filla, *The Good Samaritan*, 1910, oil, 96.5 × 59.5 cm

not through static examples but by regressing to the very foundation of the life energy, to the idea of life as a constantly circulating instinctual force. Here too, however, it was a matter of finding equivalents in art for an idea that was in itself abstract, a question of the symbolism of expressive lines and pure colours that interpreted the world in terms of its dynamic inner essence.

In 1909 most of the young painters who had introduced this programme at Osma's exhibitions became members of SVU Mánes, thanks primarily to Miloš Jiránek and Jan Preisler, who were keen to attract new blood. These new members immediately became very involved in the association's activities. It was thanks to them that an exhibition was held in 1910 for French painters who exhibited at the Salon des Indépendants. In the catalogue, Antonín Matějček, the young painters' theorist and spokesman, proclaimed the merits of Expressionism, by which he meant the supremacy of colour in a painting and a stylising of form that served for self-expression. He asserted that a painting's form could not be evaluated by comparing it with reality, for in the picture plane the subject became part of a new whole and a new unity. This unity also required deformations to maintain its expansive force and generate a driving rhythm animating the subject's lifeless forms. Modern painting's goal was to create a perfect accord between emotional expression and decorative composition. This could be achieved with a new concept of colour, through which artists could express their sentiments and develop the picture space and its form.

French Fauvist painting should also have been a source of support for primitivism in Czech painting, but Czech painters had reservations over its Romanesque harmoniousness. In an article published in Šalda's *Novina*, Bohumil Kubišta criticised Matisse for his "otiose decorativism."[192] The Czech painters were guided not by hedonistic delight but by a kind of wounded exaltation as they sought to unravel the mystery of life. Young Czech art's intentions were apparent in Kubišta's sombre and severe paintings from the city's outskirts, and in Emil Filla's *The Good Samaritan* (1910). Unlike Impressionism's picturesque fortuitousness, these paintings were intended as an expression of necessity. Their very subjects were no mere academic pretext, for they contained a message. Filla's *The Good Samaritan* was in this respect evidently a call for solidarity and an expression of his conviction that the new painting would rescue art from its helplessness. The muted colours, characteristic of developments in art at this time, facilitated seeing the entire picture plane as a single whole. The arrangement of the figures also promoted this wholeness, whose chief innovation was that it was no longer decorative. The painting's forms were not two-dimensional but plastic, although this plasticity was a consequence not of clear-cut volumes in the Neoclassical style but rather of a pulsing line, saturated with colour, that ran throughout the entire painting, deforming the figures and the landscape to produce a uniform effect.

Filla's *The Good Samaritan* was a typical example of the reworking of the older Secession foundation with an expressive dynamism that connected its two-dimensional linearity to the new plasticity, resulting in a deeper internalisation. In the same year that Filla painted it, Kubišta wrote to Vincenc Beneš from Paris that colour would have to

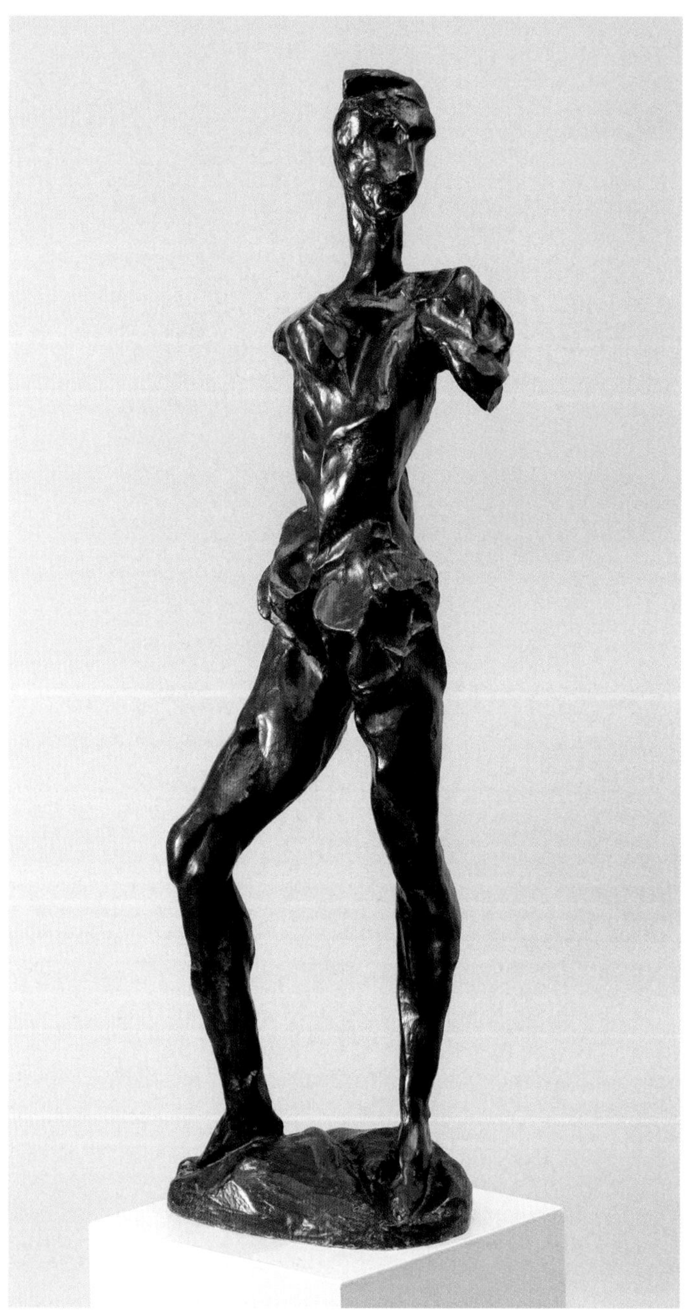

be abandoned, and that developments favoured a line based on the Gothic tradition and primitive art. The plasticity that appears in Filla's painting was an issue in the development of art, as is also evident from how it was being worked on intensively by the sculptor Otto Gutfreund, who had joined these painters after briefly studying under Antoine Bourdelle. Gutfreund's *Hamlet* from 1911 likewise took a traditional theme and tried to answer Hamlet's question through its plastic rendition. In Gutfreund's "Gothi-

314 Otto Gutfreund, *Hamlet*, 1911, bronze, 69.5 cm

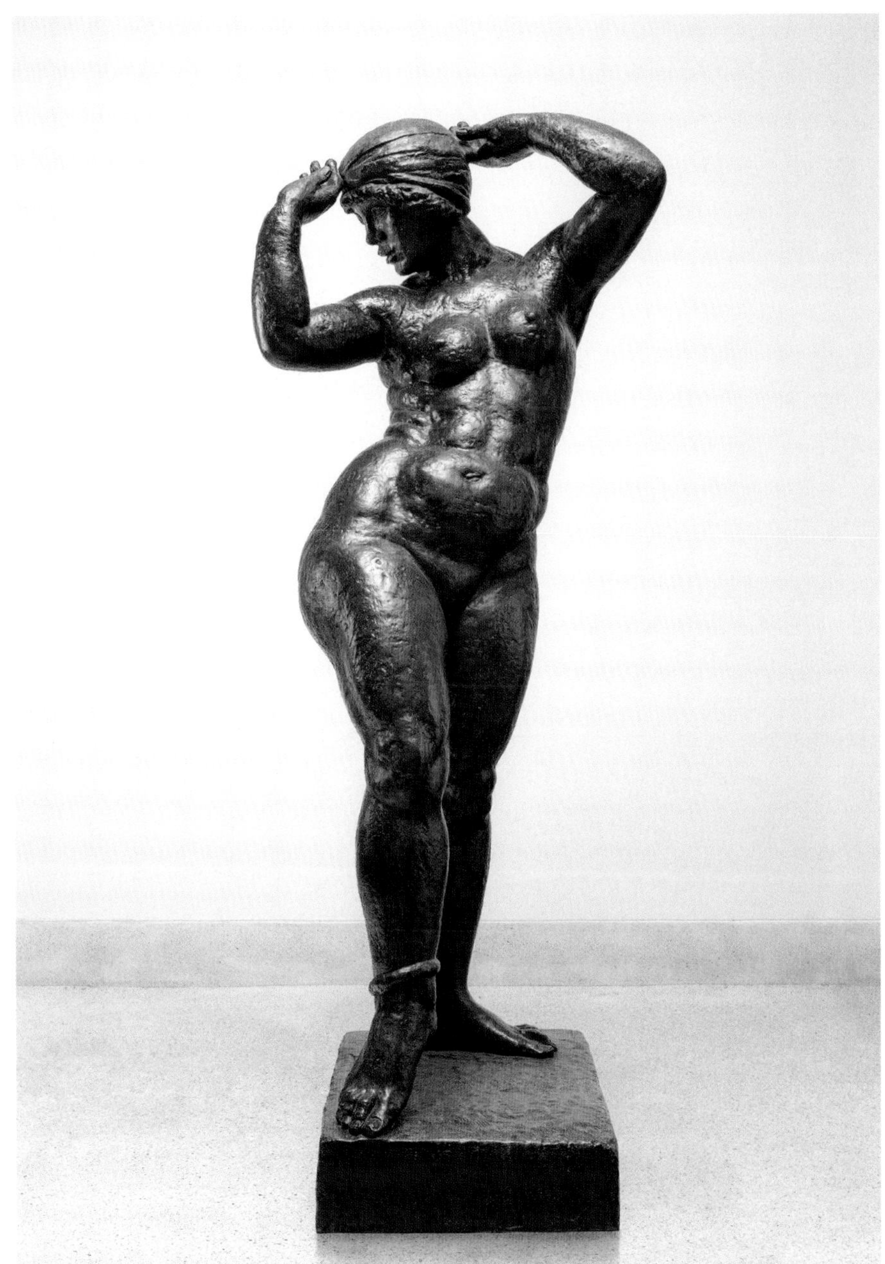

cally" elongated figure, it is even more apparent how the basic dynamic linear outline is beginning to crystallise into Expressionist spatial planes that disregard decorativism's abstract projections, creating instead an unusual three-dimensional structure as a quite specific extension of the sculpture. This approach had nothing in common with contemporary ornamental schematism, nor with the popular maxim that Émile Bernard had taken from Cézanne's pronouncement that everything in nature was formed by the sphere, the cone, and the cylinder. This doctrine of archetypal forms was helpful

315 Jan Štursa, *Sulamit Rahu*, 1910–11, bronze, 198 cm

in contemporary endeavours to see the inner structure of the world, but often it was merely a formula that masked a lack of content.[193] Gutfreund's *Hamlet* belonged more to the young artists' rediscovery of the work of El Greco, in whose tension between emotionality and its rendition in art they found a direct parallel to their own situation.

Art that understood visual form as a symbol of inner emotion led, of necessity, to striking deformations of the normal, natural, appearance.[194] While the young artists considered their creations the logical outcome of a broadly based concept, older artists viewed them with incomprehension. Understandably irritated by the younger generation, they began to consider such artworks a wilful violation. This increasing animosity came to a head at the SVU Mánes members' exhibition at the beginning of 1911. F. X. Šalda added fuel to the fire with his essay on the exhibition, "The Old and the New Mánes," in which he criticised the older generation for their indolence and inertia, and for the poor standard of their work.[195] He praised the young artists for their efforts to overcome this stagnation, although he did not entirely agree with them on the question of artistic quality. Open conflict between the SVU Mánes leadership – represented chiefly by Jan Kotěra, Stanislav Sucharda, and Jan Štenc – and its young members broke out when Emil Filla and Antonín Matějček published an issue of *Volné směry* with reproductions of Picasso's paintings and an article with the title "On the Virtues of Neo-Primitivism," which was a manifesto for the new movement. In his account of the situation, Filla, the manifesto's author, went so far as to declare naturalism a symptom of helplessness and a negation of progress. According to him, naturalism emerged whenever a particular cultural cycle had been exhausted, and naturalists wasted their energy in tearing down old dogmas and customs without offering any substitute or any prospect of a new form and style. The Impressionists' greatest sin as modern naturalists was their indifference to an artwork's constructive and compositional essence, their insufficient sense of its style and rhythmic pathos, its monumentality and unity of form. Filla saw the ideal of art in classicism as the perfect mastering of reality in a form that preserved in full both poles of the painter's interest: a love of nature and an admiration for abstract and purely formal beauty. However, Filla also pointed to the dangers of premature classicism, which would only be a replacement. He saw the only true hope in the strength of the contemporary primitivist movement, which would prepare the ground for the classic art of the future insofar as it quite deliberately and almost ascetically confined itself to the fundamentals, to the straightforward construction of a painting, in order to achieve a clear and coherent expression.[196]

This entrenched the positions of the two generations, and the logical outcome was the young generation's departure from SVU Mánes. There was here a fundamental difference of opinion, as is evident by the fact that it was not just painters but also young architects and printmakers who left Mánes. Emil Filla, Vincenc Beneš, Antonín Procházka, Antonín Matějček, Vratislav H. Brunner, František Kysela, Václav Špála, Josef Gočár, Pavel Janák, Vlastislav Hofman, Josef Chochol, and others comprised the core of Skupina výtvarných umělců (the Group of Fine Artists), which was formed shortly afterwards and became the young generation's key collective. In his account of these events, Filla used the word "secession,"[197] which had first appeared in Czech culture thirteen years earlier, in connection with the first Mánes exhibition. This revival of its original meaning also completed the cycle the Secession had initiated. This second secession resulted not just in a definitive break with naturalism, but also in an overall qualitative advance in the history of Czech modern art. It established a foundation on which the richness of the subsequent decades would unfold.

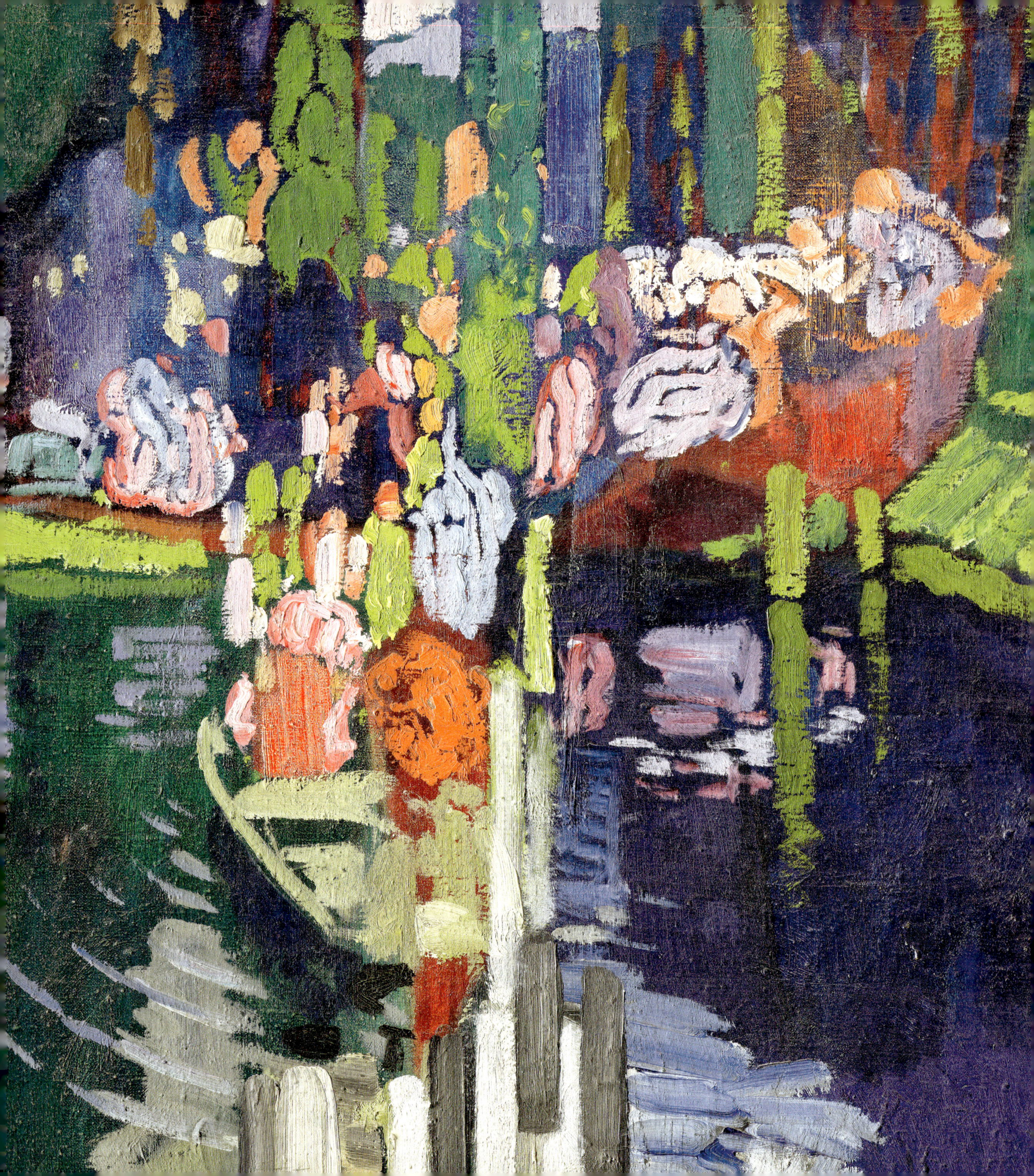

LEGACY

At the heart of the intergenerational dispute that came to a head at the beginning of the 1910s was the conviction among young artists that naturalism was incapable of generating the artistic abstraction required to achieve the Secession's objectives – that is, to fully appropriate and express the world. This signalled a break with what had been the chief criterion for the 1890s' generation, and it was one of the fundamental agendas guiding the subsequent development of Czech art. In reality, of course, the groundwork for this dramatic turnabout had been laid long in advance in artistic practice itself, and when it came to pass, it was more an escalation of what the Secession had learned from naturalism. For Secession art, naturalism – the principal target of the hostility of critics from the younger generation – was not merely a matter of the illusionistic imitating of nature's outward appearance, for it occupied a deeper and more central position. The Secession's cult of nature was the cornerstone of contemporary art, which essentially only developed out of a single fundamental inner polarity: between a sense of wonder at the natural world's multifaceted richness, and an attempt to penetrate below the surface, to master nature's exuberant chaos by examining its internal relationships. These would be revealed not through logical reasoning, but by cultivating the capacity for visual perception in order to highlight and structure this theme. This rigorous initial naturalism was essential for the Secession's reduction of eclecticism in art, which had been exhausted, and it allowed art to reconnect with a vital source of reality. However, naturalism could not remain an eternally valid norm. The revolt against naturalism declared by the younger generation of Czech artists was in fact a protest against the persistence of forms that had fulfilled their purpose and now threatened to stifle the vigorous and ambitious demands placed on art, just as historicism had once done.

However, there was an opportunity here to dynamically develop and revise naturalism, for where attention turned to the unique, there logically also arose a need to capture the general. The study and developing of these relationships had been the foundation for the practice and genesis of Secession ornament. In organic botanical nature there is a direct connection between the unique and the general, where each individual is firmly tied to the regular template for its group, and this same regularity could also be applied to ornament. This was also why such connections had been the foundation of the Secession's attempts at style. In fine art, the imagination and emotional affect played a greater role, and this resulted in the typical contemporary "experiencing" of nature. Emotional euphoria would often turn naturalism into intuitive symbolism, and the study of the surface of things could easily become sheer fantasy. This, the most typical contradiction within the Secession mentality, when naked reality was constantly confronted with the imagination, had perhaps been the greatest catalyst for artistic

316 František Kupka, *Piano Keys. Lake*, 1909, oil, 79 × 72 cm, detail

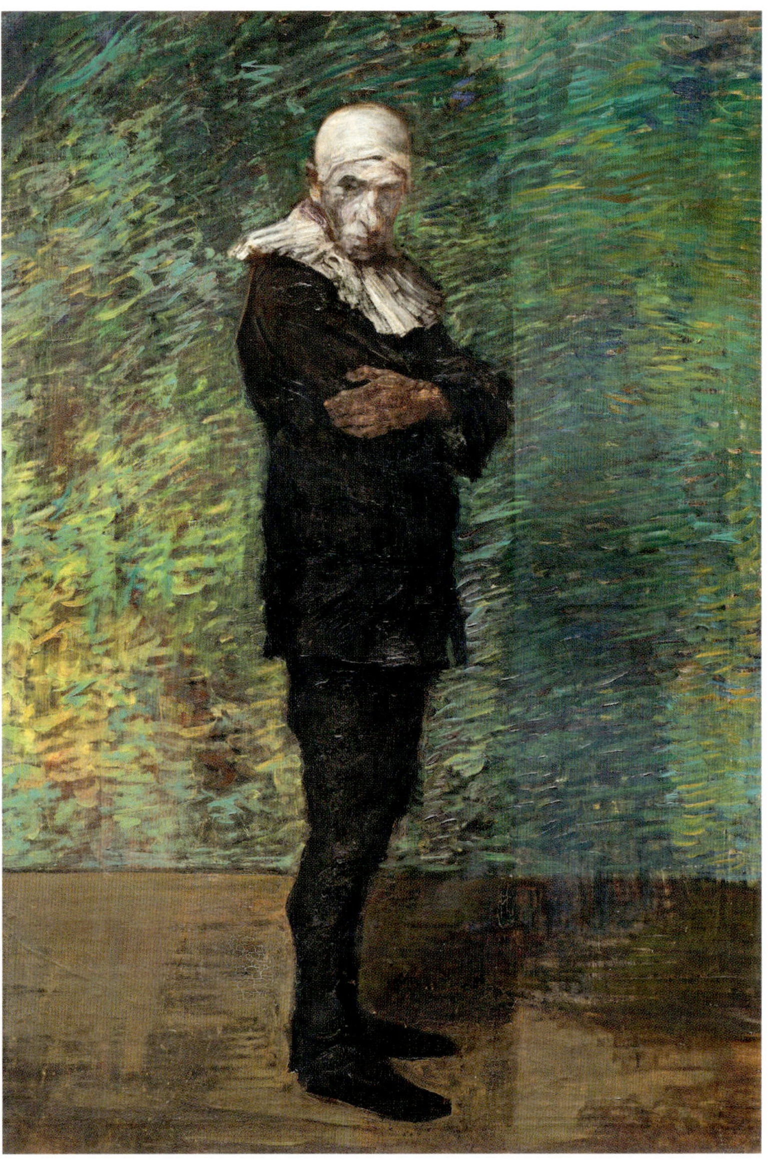

development. The imagination's strained oscillation between real and unreal produced a desire for a new synthesis, a need to combine these contradictory elements in a new unity of artistic form, which would also be crucial as a stylistic symbol expressing the superseding of this vexing dualism by means of a new fullness of expression.

The significance of the individual types and genres of painting had also changed in response to these strategic objectives. Mood landscape painting, which until recently had been a sensitive reflection of the traumatic perceiving and intuiting of these relationships, had been overtaken by the greater voluntaristic element in the new world view that was emerging in art. Painters now focused less on general scenery and more on the human aspect. However, while Secession figure painting had typically been split

317 Karel Myslbek, *Black Pierrot*, 1907, oil, 139 × 93 cm

between portraits of individuals and allegorical paintings that sought within their decorativism more of a mythological archetype, younger painters began to see the figure as a symbol of the individual's struggle with the forces of destiny. In this, they were unquestionably influenced by Edvard Munch. Instead of a landscape, the setting for this vision was now a modern metropolis, which was seen as a labyrinth of existential relationships. In *Reader of Dostoevsky*, Emil Filla depicted through the window not a landscape, as an older artist would have done, but a city with a Gothic spire that was perhaps a symbol of hope. Young painters understood the new synthesis that had organically arisen from the contradiction within the Secession much more dramatically than artists from the older generation, who associated it with the ideals of natural beauty or moral truth. However, Karel Myslbek's paintings suggest that naturalism had already put in place the preconditions for this new elaborating of fateful determinism.

Karel Myslbek had studied under Pirner and Hynais in the late 1890s, and he had therefore been initiated into painting by a certain conflict between the ideoplastic and the physioplastic. His friendship with Miloš Jiránek had steered him towards Impressionism, but for Myslbek this was never a matter of carefree sketching. He was interested in old Spanish realism, and something of its earthiness found its way into his *Bullfighting* (1904), where his use of light gives this realistic scene a dramatic subtext. In this painting the seriousness of Myslbek's view of the theatre of life was already apparent. Having a famous sculptor for a father was more of a hindrance than a help, and Myslbek was increasingly drawn to the world of the marginalised and downtrodden. *Black Pierrot* from 1907 encapsulated his fascination with the cruelty of life. In his treatment of this theme, there remained nothing of the Secession's fairy-tale decorativism. *Black Pierrot* could be compared with Quido Kocián's *The Artist's Lot* from the beginning of the century, but unlike that sculpture's Neo-Baroque exaggeration, Myslbek's painting is devoid of pathos, and this makes it all the more oppressive.

In its content, Bohumil Kubišta's *Circus* from 1911 is closer to *Black Pierrot*, but here instead of individualistic naturalism the individual's performance is measured against the spectators' reactions, and this is also reflected in Kubišta's structuring of form. Myslbek too sought a more collective basis for the blind alley of individualism, which he found in social criticism. In the monumentality of their conception, his paintings *Exiles* (1908), *Accident on a Building Site* (1909), and *In Hospital* (1910) were important in the development of social art. They surpassed the generic aspect of Schikaneder's *Murder in the House* and anticipated the later revival of this theme in the 1920s. However, what characteristically separates Myslbek from later social realism is his great pessimism. His vision of social themes still fell within a category that was dominated by the idea of compassion, whereas the social realists might understand the world of labour and poverty quite differently, as undermining any optimistic collective values, and in their generation's initial primitivism they had already created the conditions to express this in their art.

With Karel Myslbek, the Secession's theme of defiance became modern socially critical painting. His indictment of society found an effective means of communication in the naturalistic basis of his form. However, this also meant that Myslbek could not

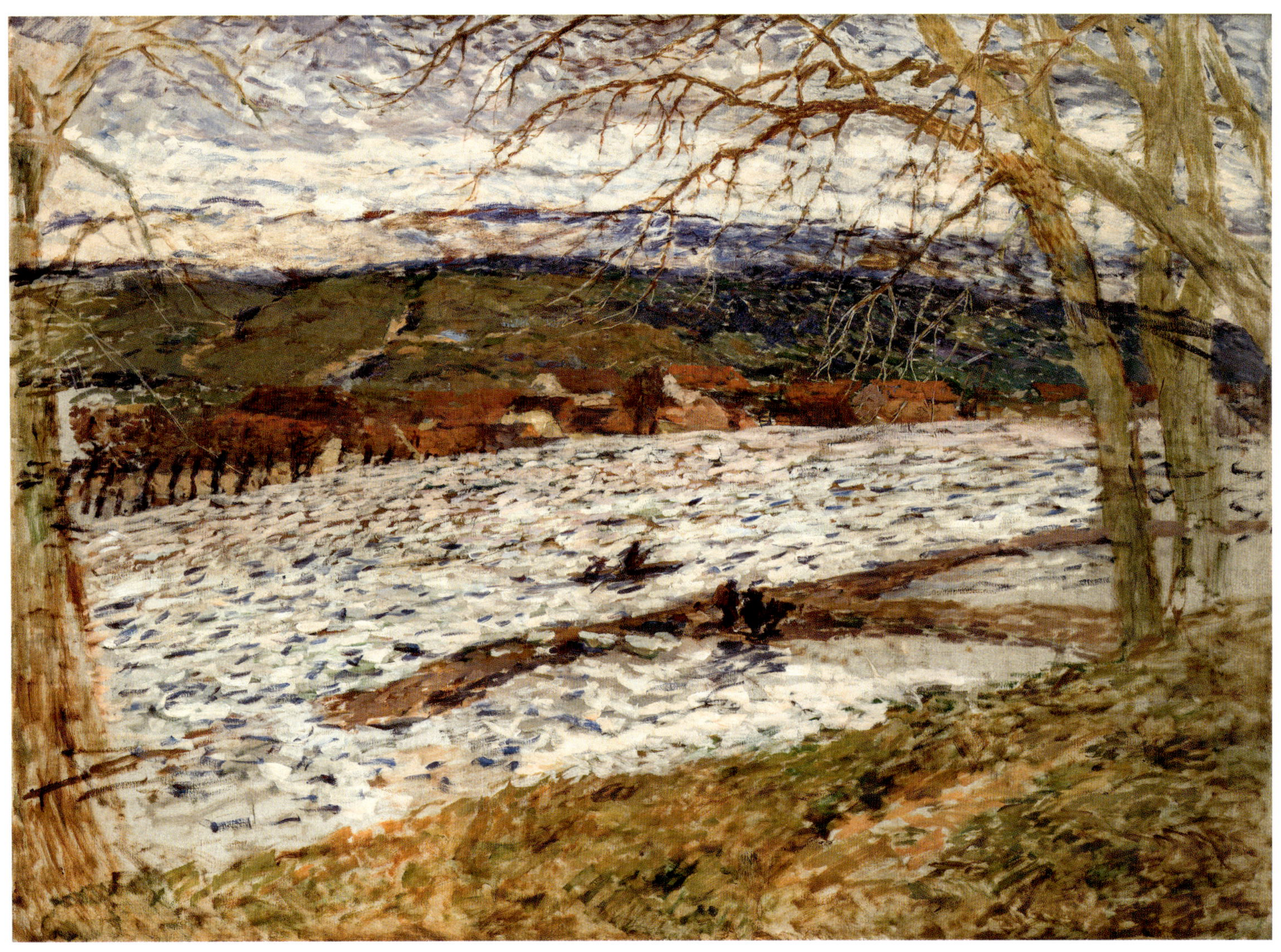

318 Antonín Slavíček, *View of Troja*, 1908, oil, 144 × 193 cm

escape the more general determinations that this form brought with it. His pessimism was partly shaped by contemporary literature and poetry exploring social themes, and partly by Schopenhauer, whose philosophy had powerfully influenced the contemporary world view. However, it was also a consequence of the fundamental ideoplastic ideas that permeated all contemporary art, sentiment, and thought.

One of these ideas concerned an intense sense of temporality. This did not only apply to the Impressionist passion for capturing the real moment as the sole factual existence in a flood of critically examined conventionality, for it also became a living basis for building new myths. Temporality also led through a zone of death and nothingness, but in artistic concentration this was breached by an inner emotion that brought forth a new wholeness. Rather than the symbolism of the Secession's endless ornamental curves, paintings that captured the very inception and transformation of this idea's inner dynamics offered greater evidence of the subtlety of variations on this idea and the process of how it was internalised and charged with a positive artistic content. Such paintings include one of Antonín Slavíček's finest works, *View of Troja* (1908), depicting ice flowing downstream in an early spring landscape. It was the product of numerous Secession ideas associated with the concept of time. There was the idea of the line's energetic progress as a manifestation of the elementary force behind life and growth. The mental energy the artist had taken from his enthusiastic contemplation of nature's theatre was applied to the canvas, where it could permeate all parts of the painting in order to convey its message. A landscape scene composed of many individual objects thereby became a new and greater whole that included a specific human activity. This is all manifested in Slavíček's painting, in which it occurs as a living process. The passage of time is thus transformed from the passing of an individual life into the greater life of the whole, which transcends the individual's finiteness. In *View of Troja*, Slavíček revised what was formerly a sense of futility to create a new value. This painting was the triumphant culmination of the struggle for the meaning of life and art that had led him from decadence, to melancholy longing, and ultimately to ecstasy at the possibility of embracing the world through the power of his painting.

The desire for an outcome of this kind was deeply rooted in the whole generation, and it also shaped the criteria placed on art as a whole. On 6 April 1909 Miloš Jiránek gave a lecture at SVU Mánes "On Czech Modern Painting," which was significant in that it substantially influenced opinions on a broad sweep of Czech art since the early 19th century. In his appraisal of the results of all specifically Czech art to date, Jiránek's principal yardstick was the idea of artistic development, which he saw as the fulfilment of some deeper meaning over time. His account, however, was sceptical:

> Our art is characterised by incompleteness, artistic irresponsibility, a failure to think through and fully enunciate. We have had many talented people, but few artists, i.e., responsible people who would execute work that was desired and intentional … they are more or less happy accidents, where the motif and the positive aspects of the artist's talent were in accord such that his shortcomings did not come to light and remained hidden. You will not find here the strongly integrated and logical development that distinguishes French art. What reaches us here are delayed

> waves and faint echoes of great currents and events abroad, and then there are several personalities, several individuals so strong that they achieved certain results on their own merit, but whose growth and influence suffered from the isolation in which they lived, where their efforts found neither support nor resonance.[198]

Jiránek's concept was not entirely consistent, for it combined a requirement for strict developmental logic with a romantic notion of the artistic personality. It did, however, encapsulate many of the weaknesses of the Czech artistic tradition, and there is no question that it profoundly affected all those present, and later readers too. It is no exaggeration to say that Miloš Jiránek's scepticism unleashed an avalanche of theoretical thinking and critical demands that would ultimately overwhelm him. In the wake of his lecture, the young generation's response was unusually forceful, directed at catching up with what was happening internationally, and also at theoretical argumentation. This all contributed to creating a hectic situation on the art scene, in the shadow of which Jiránek suffered a nervous breakdown and died a year later of tuberculosis.

Among the melancholy artists of the older generation, the initial response to this crisis was a greater sense of futility. In the same year, Jan Preisler wrote pessimistically to Sucharda, "somehow it seems to me that we have achieved very little of what we wanted, and that we are not much closer to the aspirations we talked about, for which we burned so ardently."[199] Writing to Otakar Nejedlý, who followed Gauguin's example by seeking in Ceylon (Sri Lanka) a virgin land for painters, Preisler was more pessimistic still:

> There is nothing but sadness here. Perhaps it is only old age speaking, but that is how it is (at least for me). This is a strange country, a little one, where there is nothing to spur you on, nothing driving you forward. Life is sleepy here and the air is heavy. Everything is petty. I feel this very keenly, but I cannot remedy it. I make the best of it, I accept things as they are. I'm going grey and falling asleep.[200]

However, resignation would not be Preisler's final word. Perhaps in response to Filla's theme of human solidarity, he painted his unusually expressive *The Good Samaritan*, in which he interpreted Kubišta's lessons on the geometrical essence of composition created with the aid of golden sections. Preisler refused to exhibit further and retreated to his studio to concentrate on scenes of bathing, which in Cézanne's late work had been key to the subsequent development of figure painting.[201]

From 1910 to 1912 Preisler worked on this theme with unusual intensity, sketching dozens of variations on several basic motifs, and today it is very difficult to order them chronologically.[202] It is interesting that he created these works almost in parallel with his large wall paintings for the Municipal House's Palacký Salon, although with quite different results. Preisler's overall intention at this time was unquestionably to add to the "regularity" of his painting, to shift artistic intuition into the compass of a conscious and deliberate plan. His canvases for the Municipal House were large two-dimensional wall decorations that marked the culmination of the inspiration he had taken from Puvis de Chavannes, but his *Bathing* paintings focused on the monumentality of the female nudes themselves, which he achieved by means of the greater plasticity of their volumes. These figures, for which landscape is merely a backdrop and whose colours are reduced to a basic harmony of yellow and blue, are indeed often almost sculptural; in this respect, there was evidently mutual understanding between Preisler and the sculptor Jan Štursa. Preisler's painting only again became softer and richer when the contrast between decorative two-dimensionality and the new plasticity had become sufficiently pronounced – which was also reflected in a not entirely related form in his definitive paintings for the Municipal House, and was the reason for their somewhat hesitant reception (Preisler himself would ultimately speak of these paintings, on which he had laboured for three years, merely as a "job"). In the *Bathing*

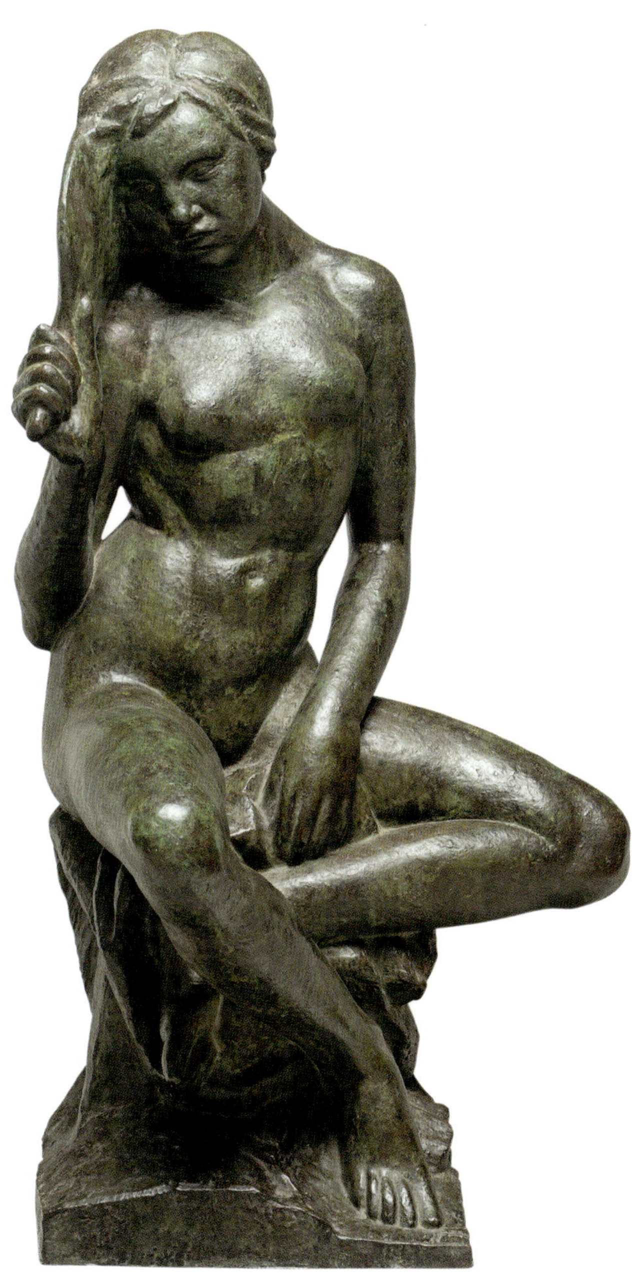

319 Jan Štursa, *Dancer Resting*, 1913, bronze, 118.5 cm

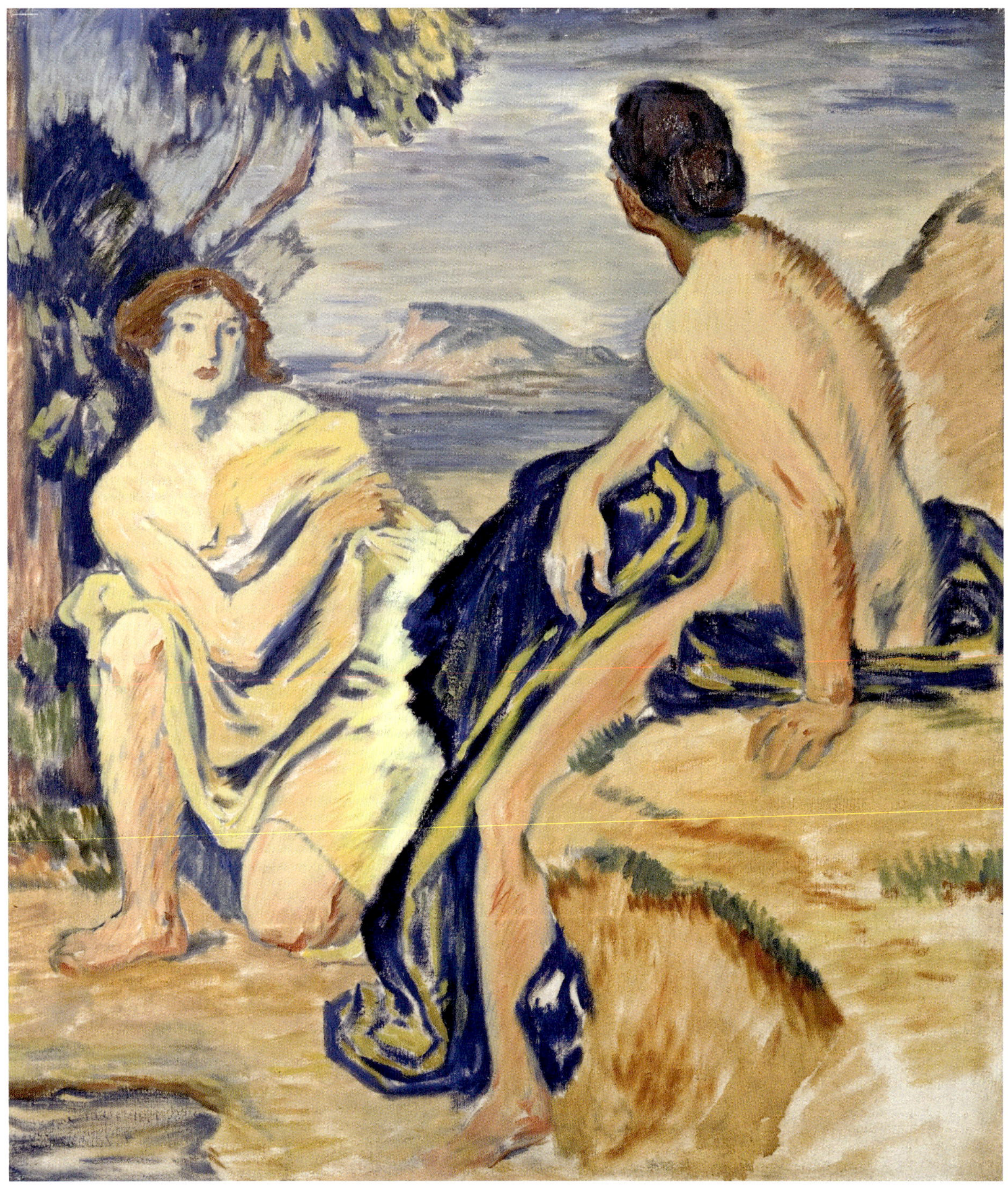

320 Jan Preisler, *Bathing*, 1912, oil, 90 × 76.5 cm

paintings, the landscape entered into a new harmony with the figures, and now on an entirely different basis, in which nature no longer dominated as a general emotional state. Instead, there was a true equilibrium between the natural and human elements, and the aspect of capturing nature in art was predominant, giving these oil paintings a Neoclassical accent.

What Preisler gained from this fraught struggle was new work that took him well beyond what decorative stylisation could offer. He had always gravitated towards a synthesis, and now he began to accomplish this in the depth of a painting. It was as if he had heard Cézanne's words: "These artists had not yet discovered that nature has more to do with depth than with surfaces. I can tell you, you can do things to the surface … but by going deep you automatically go to the truth. You feel a healthy need to be truthful."[203] However, here too the psychological barriers that Preisler shared with all of his generation began to make themselves felt. As was noted by Emil Filla, a keen observer from the younger generation, all the best artists from the beginning of the 20th century had a deep-rooted sense of inferiority, and they all questioned the value of their work.[204] This was not only a consequence of the adversity and limitations they faced in Czech society, for their doubts were amplified by their exaggerated esteem for the standard of art elsewhere in Europe. The explosion of information in the Czech art world in the first decade of the new century had stimulated the extraordinary advances they had made, but it also meant they had rashly adopted criteria that frequently resulted in undue diffidence about their own and other artists' abilities and achievements. The extraordinary sacrifices that all these innovators had made only magnified the seriousness with which they viewed the question of enduring or supreme artistic value.

In a situation in which artists had to muster the courage for their daily existential and creative struggle, and the idea of temporality was an entirely realistic symbol of the creative individual's status in the world, ideas about the timelessness of a supreme artwork and its eternal values could be very appealing; such ideas were also promoted by the contemporary wave of neo-idealist aesthetics and philosophy. However, in practice this made the notion of ideal value even less attainable. This was compounded by the younger generation's harsh criticism of naturalism, and the bitterness of these intergenerational conflicts can best be understood from this perspective.

Today, it is possible to distinguish a more objectively based evolutionary continuity, even where there was pronounced divergence. Although Stanislav Sucharda was greatly opposed to the abstract tendencies promoted by the young artists, his late works displayed a number of new formal characteristics that aligned him with them. Some of his portrait plaquettes from the end of the first decade already indicated a marked interest in converting Impressionistic modelling into expressive surfaces, and in *Portrait of Kamila Heverochová* (1910) he achieved the same quality in a three-dimensional work. Similarly, the figure of František Palacký, which was produced as the final part of his monument in Prague and whose head was sculpted by Sucharda himself, had a conspicuously simplified form compared with the other parts of the monument. In this respect, Sucharda was in fact living (if unacknowledged) proof

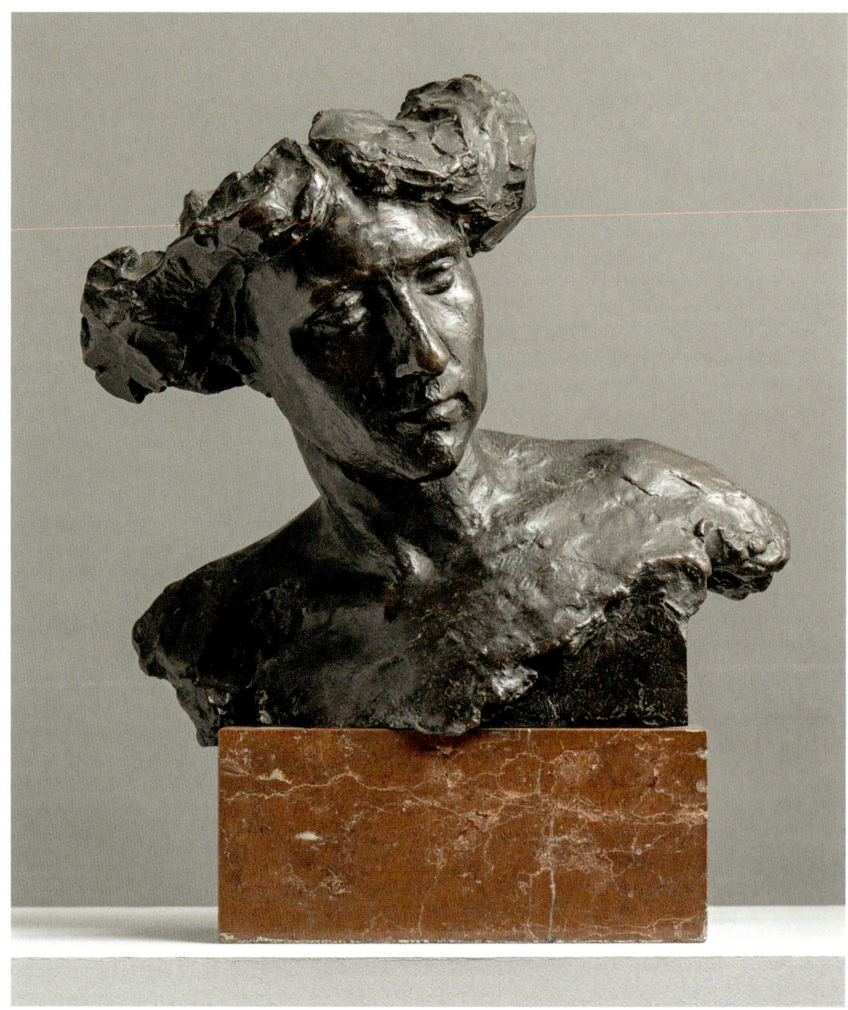

of Wilhelm Worringer's complicated theories of evolutionary change, which young architects reprinted in *Styl*.[205] Worringer wrote about the significance of the relief, and about the changes in artistic volition between antiquity and the early Middle Ages, when light was no longer used to enhance the illusion of vitality, and the alternation of light and shadow became instead a compositional device.

However, objective evolutionary connections of this kind could evidently not be discerned by the contemporary mind, for what was required was programmatic differentiation. The older generation's response to the calls for a generalising stylistic abstraction – which had been raised by practice itself, and which were ideologically underpinned by Worringer as the basis of all artistic endeavour in the great historical evolutionary cycle – was an attempt to revive the classical ideal. In this respect, Šalda's 1912 essay on Neoclassicism was typical, seeking to establish a fundamental distinction between the fruitless academic classical formula and the healthy classical foundation of living art.[206] Its counterparts in art at this time were Preisler's paintings and Jan

321 Stanislav Sucharda, Portrait of Kamila Heverochová, 1910, bronze, 37 cm

Štursa's sculptures. In architecture, Jan Kotěra superseded late Secession decorativism by amplifying the tectonic aspect of his work, as in the simple yet tectonically and rhythmically pure façade of his Hotel Grand in Hradec Králové (1911). When sketching, Kotěra exchanged his pencil for a geometry set, and in its complexity his triangulation of the design for the façade of a university building (1913–14) could rival the young artists' geometrical speculations. There was, however, an important difference: Kotěra's compositions were strictly symmetrical, based on a circle, with a careful balancing of the masses, whereas the young artists' geometry was of a fundamentally different character.

Kotěra's geometrical triangulation could in essence be compared with classic designs from the High Renaissance, and in this respect it was an example of the new sense of tradition and rationality that characterised the end of the Secession's synthetic period. At the same time, however, the dynamic component that was the very backbone of the new art began to be lost. It is almost paradoxical, but nevertheless quite logical,

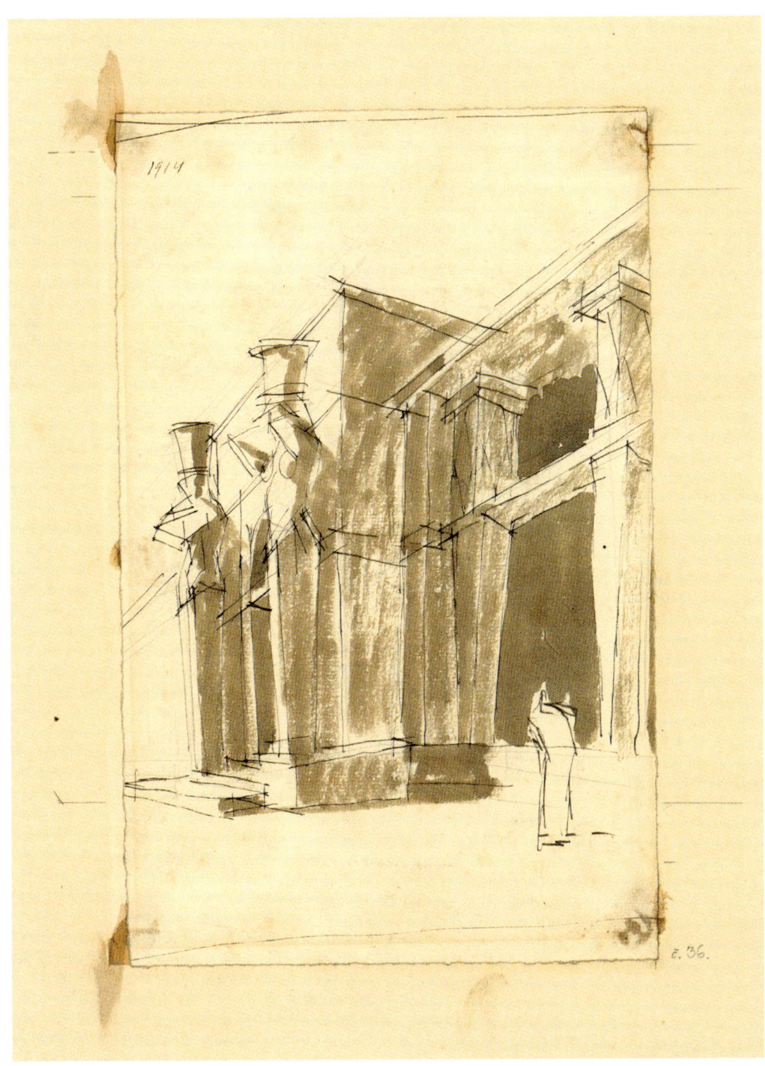

322 Jan Kotěra, Sketch of a portal (not built) for the Lehnerger-Olbrich villa in Vienna, 1914, ink wash, 27.5 × 17 cm

that ultimately it was leading figures from the younger generation who had a greater sense of this legacy, and they can therefore be considered the true bearers of evolutionary continuity. In his 1911 essay "On the Prerequisites of Style," Bohumil Kubišta set out the philosophical foundation for their position.[207] In the interests of the application of the new abstract tendency, he made a fundamental distinction between internal and external artistic form. External form is empirical and sensory, whereas internal form, which includes the fundamental geometrical figures that organise a painting's structure, has a "transcendental" aspect: this is where the artist's relationship to the infinite, the very essence of his work, is decided. Kubišta's understanding of a painting's fundamental geometrical infrastructure, which is created as the priority, is therefore the opposite of Kotěra's classical concept. This infrastructure does not consist in the immanence of a beautiful artistic form, but in its expressive aspect, opening an artwork to deeper meanings.

This idea also lay behind Kubišta's move away from the simple structuring of his paintings with the aid of traditional golden sections and equilateral triangles in favour of a much more dynamic concept. In her analysis of *Saint Sebastian*, which Kubišta painted at the turn of 1911 and 1912, Mahulena Nešlehová has demonstrated how the complicated composition of triangular forms and spirally inclined ellipses is developed from a basic motif of two triangles descending about a circle.[208] This kind of dynamic projection does not serve to express a sense of tranquillity or celebrate the beauty of life, but acts as the basis of a theme that illustrates, in an allegorical self-portrait, the suffering and anguish of the artist's sacrifice. If the older generation had preferred to retreat from the cataclysms of real life into idealised utopias, reflecting their tendency towards a fundamental monism of one kind or another, Kubišta decided to let these contradictions do battle in the painting itself, even though his desire for some ultimate synthesis never waned.

This geometrically based dynamic expressiveness was the first truly evolutionary reappraisal of the Secession's key idea of temporality. The passage of time was to be halted by "immortalisation," which in the language of art meant replacing naturalistic randomness with archetypal geometrical forms. Young artists' self-confidence was greatly boosted in this respect by the emergence of Cubism in Paris, but their principal motifs were deeply rooted in the evolutionary needs of Czech art. With Otto Gutfreund, for instance, this is evident both in his sculptures (the *Head of My Father* series from 1911) and in his theorising. In his 1913 essay "Surface and Space," Gutfreund presented a Symbolist and Secessionist definition of a sculpture, as

> an incessant undulation of the surfaces, of the illusions of volumes, an undulation whose current breaks down the banks that confine space and carries them away, an undulation with whirlpools that indicate depth through the surface, an undulation whose currents reflect fragments of reality without ever stopping.[209]

It is as though the pantheistic vision of Slavíček's *View of Troja* has simply been converted into a vocabulary revealing the influence of vitalist writings, but, behind all this, there was also the new Cubo-Expressionist interpretation of an object, changing its ordinary extension into a symbol of new plastic and mental energies.

The importance of the Secession's dynamic element for the new Cubist position is also evident in an article that Vlastislav Hofman published in *Styl* in 1913. "On the Secession" recapitulated the development of Czech modern architecture to date, as viewed by the younger generation.[210] Hofman wrote about the Secession as "an idea of one period that is now in the past," but in reality he updated it for the current situation. His article, one of the most perceptive to be written on this subject in Bohemia, pointed to the Secession's fundamental opposition to tradition, manifested chiefly in architecture, applied art, and decorative art. The Secession had entailed "the spontaneous application of the potency of form in the present day," and through nature and its world of free, mobile forms, always serving some function, it had revitalised form. In botanical forms it had found a way to express its intuition of a constructively binding purpose that differed from Wagner's technical construction of his material. Ornamental elements had thereby acquired a curious and mysterious appearance, and this was something that was sensed collectively. The Secession did not come out of the aesthetics of taste. Instead, it was an expression of its environment; it was democratic, and it also took account of folk art and the ahistorical qualities of prehistoric and primitive art. Its character was the result of a particular mode of synthesis, a mutual connection in the manner of a coalescing of masses as if impregnated with vegetable sap, and the adopting of the great form of a unifying line as the principal factor in representation. It was also quite different from the ancient Greek systems, based as they were on the right-angled intersecting of horizontals and verticals.

In addition to the original "pure" organic Secession represented by Henry van de Velde, Hofman also wrote about Viennese "modernity," which had been partly inspired by the English movement and had swiftly abandoned its original naturalness in favour of an interest in its materials. This also characterised the Secession's second stylistic aspect, which had become more prominent in Czech architecture during the latter half of the 1900s, in the late Secession phase. Hofman's distinction between the naturalistic, organic "pure Secession" and the right-angled stylisation of decorative "modernity" was later adopted in the Czech literature as a way of expressing these two stylistically different phases in early 20th-century Czech architecture, but this would often obscure their common starting point and dualistic connectedness. It is symptomatic of Hofman's position, which reflected the views of young Cubist architects, that, while he appreciated that "modernity" had introduced a greater interest in the three-dimensionality of masses and their cubic surfaces, for the most part he criticised it as a return to the traditions of the Empire and the bourgeois Biedermeier styles. He believed that the new thinking on architecture "can return more to an acknowledgement of the pure Secession, for it contains the more significant capacity for sculpture and the developing of space, whereas Viennese modernity is inert and composed."

For similar reasons, Hofman also defended the Secession against Neoclassicism. Here he differentiated between two types of contemporary artist. "Classics" were distinguished by their desire for traditional beauty, which was calm and serious, and by their sense of harmony. This made the present day intolerable for them, such that

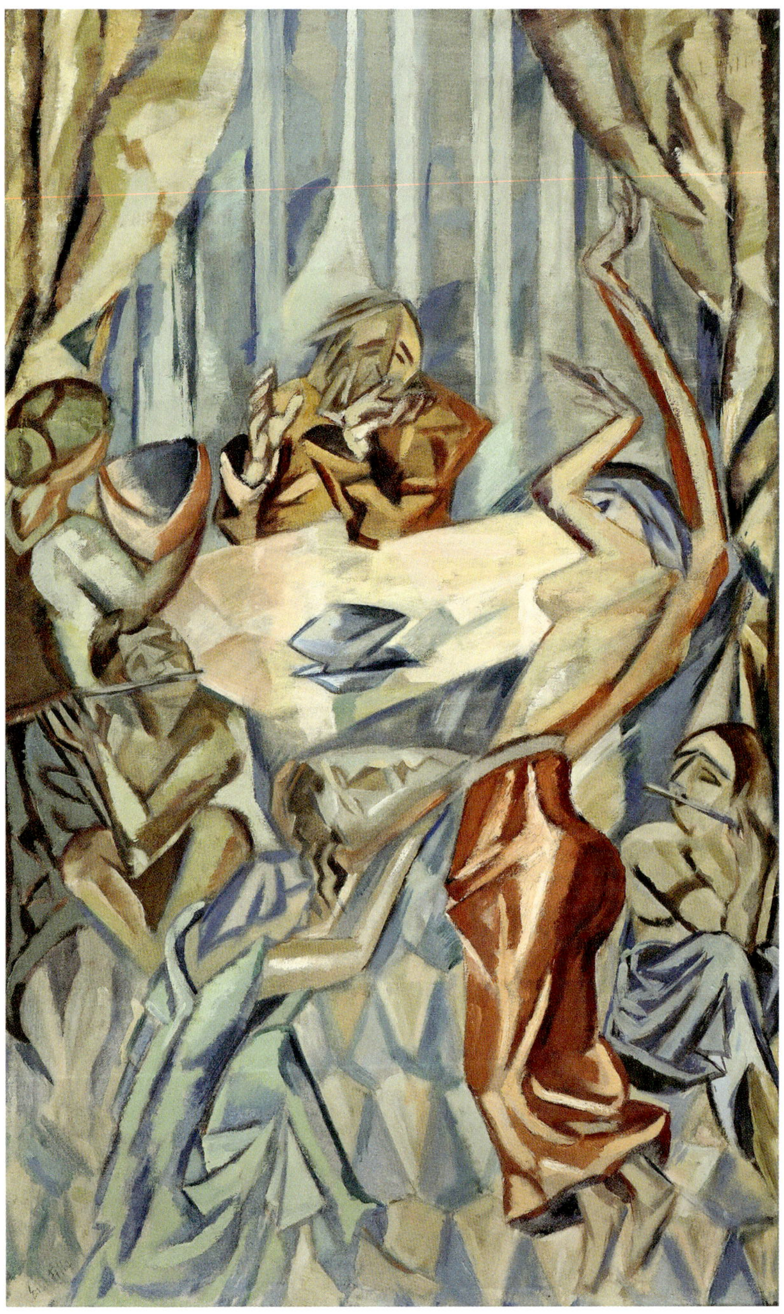

they sought to retreat into the supposedly eternal forms of tradition. In contrast, modern "progressive artists" were entirely at one with the tempo of contemporary life, finding fulfilment in its sensitivity and intensity, and this led them to invent new forms. The new architecture they devised corresponded more to "ideas resulting from their opinion of the motion of matter and its internal organisation. Antiquity mastered matter very gradually, stacking it up like boxes and panels; for the modern sentiment,

323 Emil Filla, *The Dance of Salome*, 1912, oil, 137 × 82 cm

this method is something dead." Classical surfaces were like elevations, seemingly lacking perspective, and the modern architectural emotion wanted to break them down,

> into planes that are inclined, dislocated, seemingly non-static, mobile in their form, austere and acute-angled rather than calm (for matter is most logically fixed in a triangular arrangement), by which means matter is organised and mastered as a natural phenomenon and extended sculpture. The Secession also attempted something similar in its principle of form; the present day, of course, requires an alternative exposition and an alternative structure of architecture.

Hofman's demands for an internal dynamism of architectural form were his response to criticisms of the conspicuous primacy of geometrical formulas in the art of these young innovators. F. X. Šalda had taken their side in his 1911 essay "The Old and the New Mánes," but he had also found fault with them for so far only coming up with formulas when what was expected was some great artistic achievement, and he remarked that an artwork arose from layers of the artist's psyche that were deeper than mere conscious intention. By 1912, in response to an exhibition by Skupina výtvarných umělců, he was even more critical, writing that "abstraction applied so radically holds no appeal for me other than a cold and indifferent marvel at the bizarre hypothesis"; Šalda required "a warm undercurrent of creative intuition" for true artistic expression. Yet ultimately this criticism was still defined by the older individualism, something that was generally secondary to the young artists' ideas on style:

> However, the sources of art are deeper and darker than our youngest artists want to admit: they spring from the mysteries of a great personality, and all interest in art is an interest in the struggle between an ardent personality and the objective external conditions that seize and bind it. Dogmatic orthodoxy will never replace this unique, I would say cosmic, theatre.[211]

Šalda made similar criticisms of the Neoclassicists, despite evidently finding their programme more to his liking.

The young Cubists were concerned with a psychological deepening of their geometrism. This was also apparent in their interest in the themes explored by the other, Symbolist, offshoot of their generation, represented by Sursum. More or less by chance, in 1912 both Sursum and Skupina výtvarných umělců had exhibitions at Prague's new Municipal House. On this occasion, Skupina's theorist, V. V. Štech, accused Sursum's members of a preoccupation more with literature than with art, although *The Dance of Salome* by Emil Filla from the same year was a typical Symbolist literary theme. Filla's concept was not directed towards an individual psychological symbol; instead, he used the theme to express the total dynamism of the picture plane by means of an Expressionistic faceting of forms. This in turn influenced some of Sursum's members. In the following year, when Sursum had practically broken up, Jan Konůpek took a similar approach in a series of prints. Konůpek had already executed *The Good Samaritan* in this style in 1912, but unlike Filla he had presented the story in three episodes, following the medieval custom. However, Filla would henceforward consistently follow the example of Picasso's Analytical Cubism. There was much more intensive cooperation and discussion between Jan Zrzavý and Bohumil Kubišta; the latter had not joined Skupina výtvarných umělců and was thereby spared polemical orthodoxy. This continued from the autumn of 1911 to the spring of 1913, when Kubišta's straitened circumstances prompted him to volunteer for military service in Pula. In the context of contemporary developments, their friendship was a remarkable aligning of the young generation's rationally volitive and intuitively expressive elements. Central to their conversations was the question of the idea comprising the content of a painting, and how it could be expressed.[212] In his 1912 essay "On the Spiritual Basis of the Modern Age," Kubišta wrote about the need for more profound content in the new form, which he sought in its "active force," something that had a magical effect on the viewer and allowed the vital cosmic forces that sustained life to be transformed by the artist's creative will into a symbol with a real character.

In paintings from 1911 such as *Resurrection of Lazarus* and *Epileptic Woman*, Kubišta was already using pentagons, hexagons, and other geometrical figures in the infrastructure of his paintings, seeking to underline the principal idea behind individual works

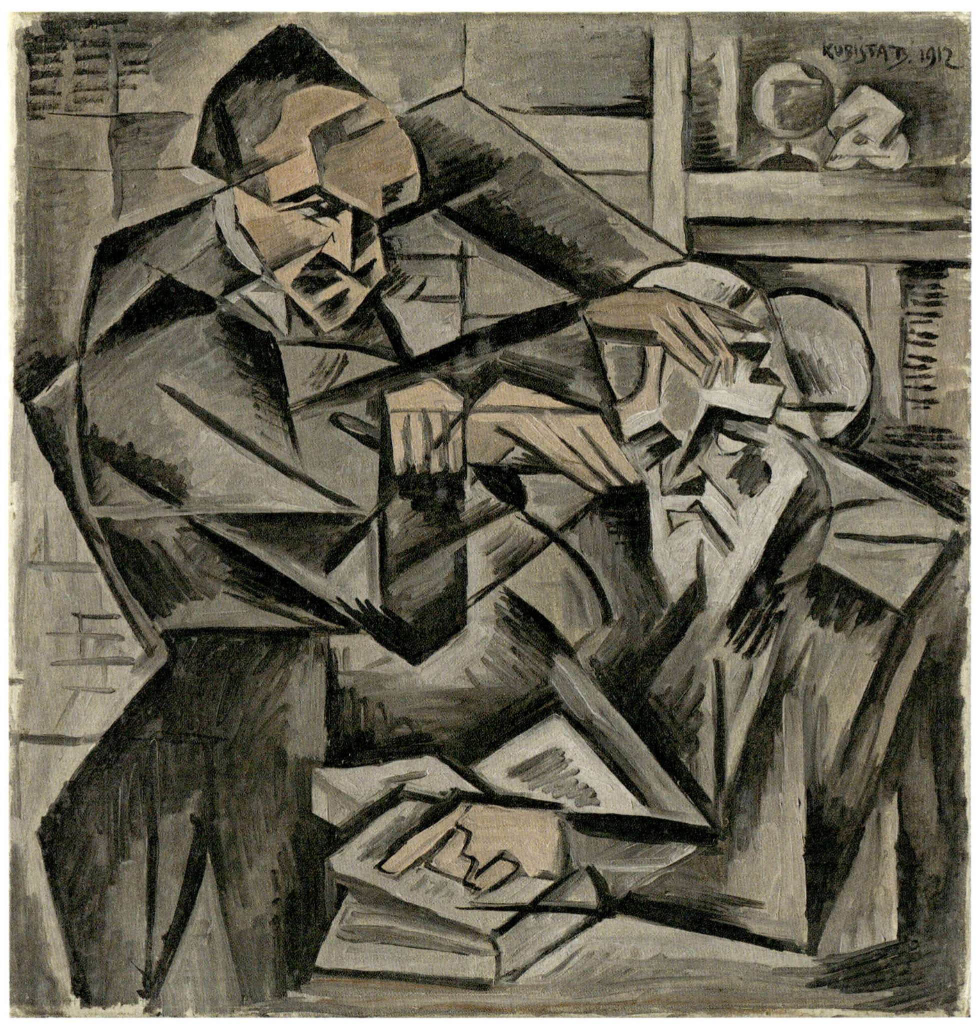

324 Bohumil Kubišta, *The Hypnotist*, 1912, oil, 60.5 × 58 cm

through reference to the ancient meanings of these figures.[213] There was also the symbolic significance of colour, which extended the idea to encompass its psychological and emotional effects.[214] Kubišta's move away from his earlier interest in artistic form is evident in the entirely non-Cubist iconography of his new work, which was concerned with explicitly Symbolist themes. However, unlike Symbolism's surrender to the mysterious forces of fate, Kubišta always reinterpreted these themes to emphasise the human appropriation and use of psychological energies (*The Hypnotist*, 1912).

What Jan Zrzavý gained above all from this acquaintance was a greater ability to articulate in his art the images that arose from his poetic unconscious. However, the geometrical quality of *The Sermon on the Mount* (1911–12), with its complicated system of triangles, or the brush with Cubism that is most apparent in *Still Life with Lilies of the Valley* (1913), were merely devices that Zrzavý used to magnify a work's psychological impact. The Symbolist core of Zrzavý's images remained intact in *Sleeping Boy* (1912), which was typical of his oneiric internalisation of the world, or in *Moon with Lilies of the Valley* (1913), which used a familiar poetic metaphor to convey the mysterious influence of the cosmos on humanity and the earth, in line with modern primitivism.

However, Zrzavý's chief significance in this context was that his work again focused attention on colour. While geometrical tendencies, which primarily sought new compositional methods, had tended to suppress the role of colour in painting, with Zrzavý it returned in an unusual fullness and purity. It was thanks to him that colour again became the main element in painting. This was no longer the natural colour of Impressionism's local tones, but the impulsively applied emotional colour from the time of young artists' initial response to Munch. Primitivism had been subjected to internal discipline, and its passion and robustness were now muted and ethereal, as if in a dream. Zrzavý's mature paintings introduced the remarkable phenomenon of a colourful luminosity emanating from the paintings themselves. The plasticity that Kubišta had thought a distinct quality of Zrzavý's work on first encountering it was created by colour rather than the illusion of volume, reappraising the objects depicted while losing nothing of their legibility. *Meditation* from 1915, which seemed to conclude this period of Zrzavý's direct inspiration from turn-of-the-century Symbolism, was an exemplary summation of his new ability to use colour to present the inner idea. It was only later, in 1921, that Zrzavý wrote down his thoughts on colour and outlined his colour system.[215] For him, colour was an intangible quality that was purely visual. It was an aspect of matter through which the painter could paradoxically express the materiality of the world with immaterial means. However, the light and shadow of real objects had to be replaced with the painter's own colour qualities: the polarity of black and white, between which lay a contrastingly ordered band of all the other colours. By using them sensitively, the painter could express all situations and states of mind in human life, for everything in life and nature was related, everything emerged from the tension between the two fundamental poles of activity and passivity.

Zrzavý's oeuvre can be considered a key part of the culmination of the great evolutionary process that had preoccupied Czech art since the middle of the first decade and had mainly been manifested as a process of superseding Impressionistic naturalism.

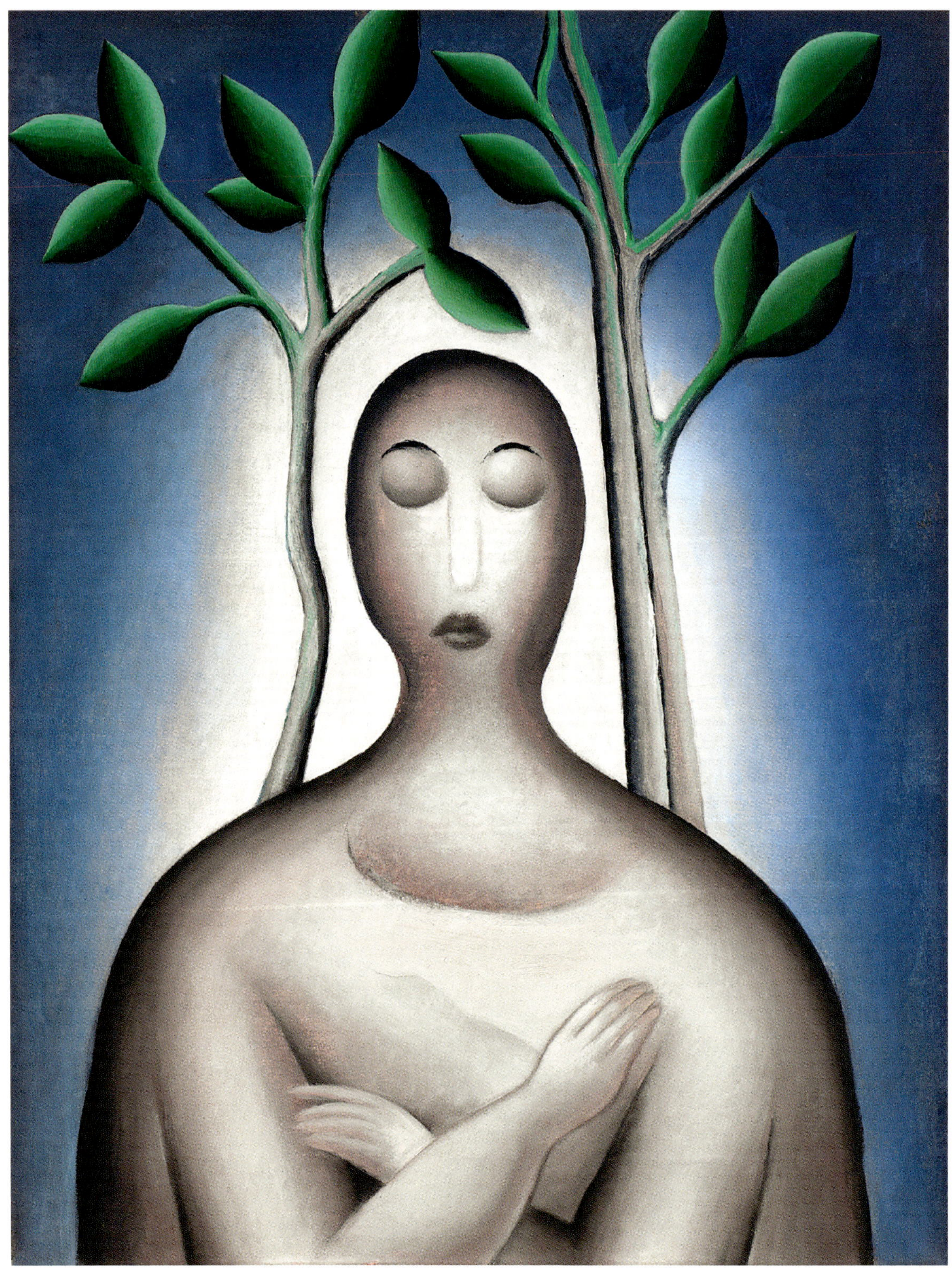

325 Jan Zrzavý, *Meditation*, 1915, oil, 50.2 × 37.5 cm

The significance of this process is principally evident in that it became the starting point for the entire subsequent development of Czech modern art, in all its various aspects and tendencies. That such a quality was able to come to the fore was essentially due to the artists' striving for synthesis. Symbolism, which the Czech Secession's naturalistic aesthetics had initially driven out of fine art and into literature, now returned by way of new formal qualities, and this unquestionably changed it: Symbolism now shed its Decadent characteristics and became a positive creative value. In 1915 Zrzavý painted two versions of *The Good Samaritan*, on the theme of his love for humanity and art, that he considered among his finest paintings. The synthetism of the beginning of the second decade had incorporated decorative ornamental elements in an original way by accentuating their abstract capacity, and at a certain point in its development it had transposed them from surface to space – not by means of their external plasticisation, which had proved fatal to naturalistic decor, but through a new concept of two-dimensionality that was related to the requirements of a specific world view. In its desire to "encompass the absolute," this process also entailed an immobilising of inner events, their "fixing in eternity,"[216] which was another consequence of Symbolist aesthetics and the influence of neo-idealism in the humanities. It was also an attempt to escape from the flow of unquiet being and use the subject depicted in its material individuality and integrity. This aspect was increasingly expressed as a desire to depict a subject as static and complete, and later it gave rise to variously motivated forms of Neoclassicism.

In this situation, naturalism became synonymous with conservatism in art, and although it did not lack militant defenders, the fact that these were second-rate artists only compounded its rejection. Slavíček and Jiránek, the true pillars of Czech Impressionism, who had been able to develop it in response to new demands, had both died around the end of the first decade of the 20th century, but the deficit this created in Czech art bizarrely brought forth their replacements, one of whom was Jindřich Prucha.

Prucha already stood somewhat apart from his generation, having not attended the same schools as his peers in Prague. Nevertheless, in 1909 he became a member of SVU Mánes, and in its own way his art was no less concerned with contemporary issues. Prucha's starting point was naturalism and Impressionism, but at the time of the generational crisis he modernised this to create a form that can best be described as a combination of Fauvism and Expressionism (*In a Beech Wood*, 1911). In 1912 he painted a remarkable copy of El Greco's *Laocoön*, where he was most closely aligned with Skupina výtvarných umělců, but Prucha had evidently studied El Greco from a rather different perspective than the Cubists. Other aspects of Prucha's art revived Symbolism, especially his treatment of the figure in landscape. However, these attempts at combining allegory with an Impressionist take on reality were never very convincing. In 1914 Prucha produced a series of paintings in which he clearly distanced himself from the avant-garde and returned to the legacy of Antonín Slavíček, although in his paintings he now accentuated the nervous intensity of the colours. In variations of *In a Beech Wood*, a motif that ran throughout his oeuvre, Prucha tried to achieve a maximal orchestration of the sensual qualities of colour by again measuring his paintings against reality.

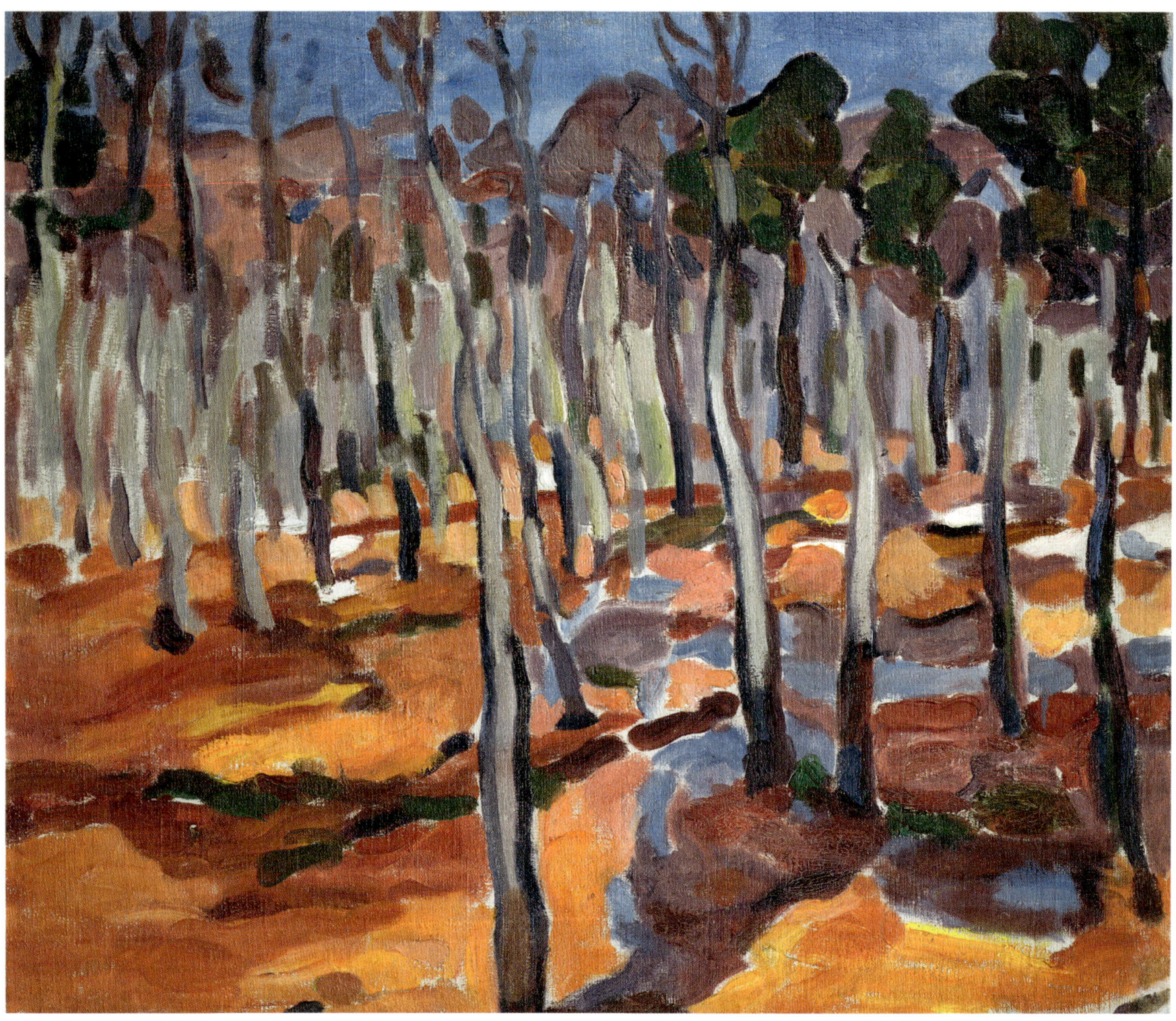

Prucha's "desertion" shows how generational affiliation was not an impassable barrier. It was primarily a matter of internal differentiation, which was related more to artists' creative potential and their overall intuition of actuality than to any theoretical concepts. Prucha's paintings from 1914 can be considered an extreme that sought to express in painting that which Slavíček had indicated in his sketches, although Slavíček himself had countered this with his interest in monumentality. What Prucha painted was pure sensory ecstasy, almost a religion of nature, in which he escalated naturalism and Impressionism to the point where they became a symbol. As with the emphasis on intellectuality in the work of the Cubists, for Prucha this was a consequence of

326 Jindřich Prucha, *In a Beech Wood*, 1911, oil, 84 × 95.5 cm contemporary radicalism. His aims of course were quite different, for against the "purity of construction" he held up the purity of emotion. Like Karel Myslbek, Jindřich Prucha would eventually die in the First World War.

The four harsh years of the Great War were a watershed for Czech art, definitively bringing the Secession epoch to a close. It left society greatly changed, and several artists had passed away. Jan Preisler died not long after he was appointed a professor at the academy in Prague. He left behind a series of works in progress called *Temptation*, a nostalgic return to the theme of an adolescent surrounded by the voices of life, now painted in more saturated tones. There was also a final, unfinished *Bathing*, in which Preisler abandoned the monumentality of his earlier versions. With its layout divided evenly between the landscape and the figures, it was more reminiscent of Cézanne. Stanislav Sucharda had died two years before Preisler, after briefly teaching in the academy's new medal studio. Max Švabinský became a professor at the academy in 1910, where he taught printmaking, and Jan Kotěra was appointed professor of architecture. Kotěra died in 1923; he had been dissatisfied with his post-war projects. Of the old SVU Mánes members, Švabinský still remained, and he now mostly depicted fairy-tale scenes of earthly paradises, in which he celebrated the inexhaustible bounty of nature and the beauty of woman.

The war had transformed the criteria placed on art, shifting attention to social problems, and also to technicism, which was universally promoted by a society fascinated with the performance and reliability of the machine.[217] For the post-war mentality, the Secession belonged to the past. Everything was to be done anew, and differently. The Secession's decorative nature cult did survive, but it had become synonymous with petit bourgeois bad taste. The word *secession* now designated an ephemeral and

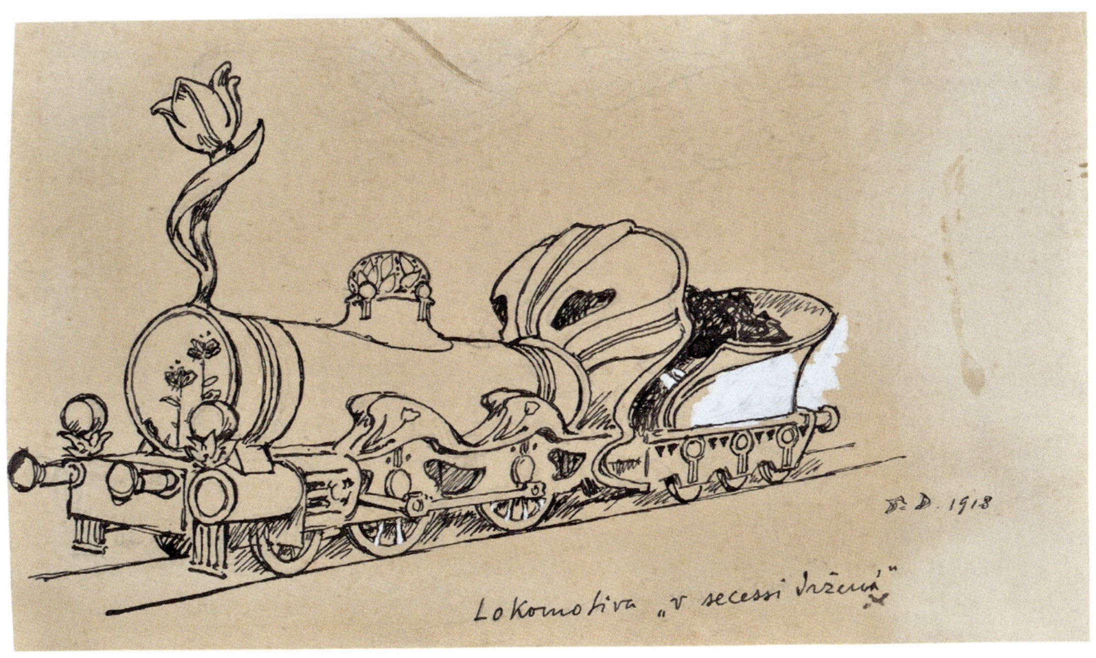

327 Hugo Böttinger, "Secession-style" locomotive, 1918, Indian ink and white, 14 × 23 cm

bizarre fashion that was only fit for caricature, as in the "Secession-style" locomotive from a series of humorous drawings by Hugo Böttinger, who evidently thought that a modern means of transport would best parody the Secession's botanical ornamentation. Yet had he looked at the locomotives that were actually constructed during the Secession era, he would have seen that this period had been able to give a purely utilitarian product a form that accurately reflected its function.[218] The Cubist locomotive fared equally poorly in Böttinger's series. Confronted with the machine, all artistic styles and schools collapsed, and the Secession was consigned to historicism's cabinet of curiosities.

The humour with which Böttinger, himself a member of the Secession generation, viewed this situation was far from the worst of it. Much weightier were the new norms in theory and criticism, which confirmed the verdict passed on the Secession for the next few decades. In 1923, when Václav Nebeský wrote about the foundations of modern sculpture for *Volné směry*, he sought its essence in monumentality, which he contrasted with picturesqueness and decorativeness, in which form "had only ornamented an old theme," culminating in "the Secession's stylised naturalism, where its role in an artwork was complete when it was uncoupled from the subject and freely developed into self-sufficient ornament."[219] All awareness of the Secession's role in the development in art was swept away in the interests of a programmatic escalation, and the Secession would henceforward be considered a mistake, a blind alley for modern art. Just ten years after Vlastislav Hofman's article in *Styl*, the evaluation of the Secession in relation to the avant-garde had been turned upside down. In this climate, the work of the surviving members of the Secession generation was deliberately sidelined. Many of them no longer had sufficient strength to understand what was required of them, and they found themselves becoming conservative. Even the best of them did little better. Just after the war there had been some interest in František Bílek, but he would soon be dismissed as "unartistic." At the beginning of the 1940s a monograph on the artist had to argue at length that Bílek's ideas on sculpture were a valid alternative to those of Myslbek.[220] Bílek's "literariness" was seen as problematic, but even when the emphasis was solely on the artistic qualities of his work, there was a tangible distance. František Kupka was recognised more as an expert on French art than as a painter. When Vojtěch Preissig returned to his homeland at the beginning of the 1930s, his exhibition was ignored. However, the memorable *Poetry 32* exhibition, held the following year, marked Czech modern art's turn to the imagination, and it also helped to create the conditions for a more generous appraisal of turn-of-the-century art. During the 1940s retrospectives of the lives and work of members of the 1890s' generation brought recognition for individual artists, but the Secession would have to wait another dozen years before it was understood and appreciated in its entirety. *The Czech Secession – The Art of 1900*, a comprehensive exhibition presented in 1966 by Jiří Kotalík and his colleagues in Hluboká nad Vltavou and Brno, finally heralded a positive and definitive change in the Secession's broader cultural appreciation.

The Secession's reinstatement was chiefly due to a greater requirement for profundity in art. This meant seeing the Secession not simply as one of many attempts at

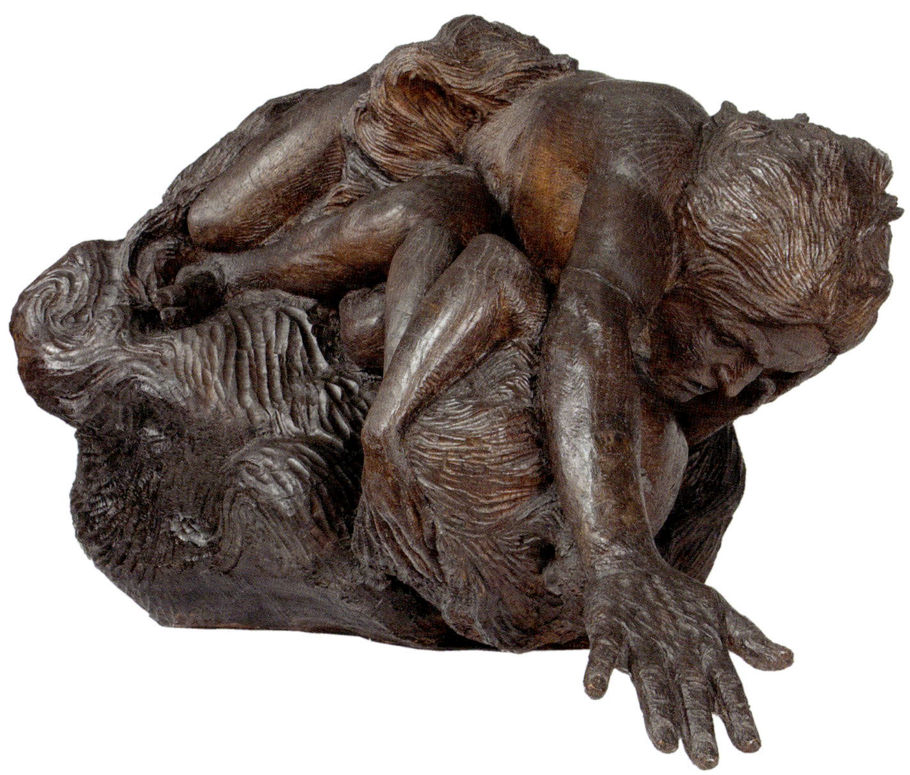

a decorative "style," a mere reflection of the turbulent moods at the end of the 19th century, and a fixation with a bizarrely stylised language of flowers. Instead, it should be seen as a rebuilding of the entire internal structure of the system of depiction in art, conducted with an unusual sensitivity to the world view and influence conveyed by artistic communication.

Fears over the so-called literariness of an artwork had been part of the Secession's original programme, but this did not mean the same thing as formalism. The Secession had on the contrary succeeded in developing a type of artwork in which a sensually full form was organically charged with emotional and intellectual content on the basis of the evocative principle of the universal correlations between the processes of nature, life, and thought. Behind this synthesis lay a dynamic concept of the world, an understanding of the inner unity of its metamorphoses, and an extraordinary sense of how the particular related to the whole. Of course, it was impossible for the Secession's output to be entirely homogeneous, and it too had its formalists. Within the Secession there was a conflict between creation and imitation, a word that František Bílek, for instance, used disparagingly when describing Vienna's influence on Czech art. He himself was an ardent admirer of William Blake, whom art historians would later recognise as one of the forefathers of the entire Secession movement.[221] However, the strained dynamics of Czech Secession art were reflected in this relationship too.

In 1921 Bílek carved *Adam and Eve* from the trunk of an oak felled by a gale. It was the second work in his *Journey* cycle, which he would never complete. In the dynamic

328 František Bílek, *Adam and Eve*, 1921, wood, 95 cm

curves of the bodies, he returned to the linear problem that was so important for the Secession, and for the expressive qualities of his own work. He had evidently worked on the theme of Adam and Eve since the mid-1890s,[222] but he only succeeded in expressing it in this sculpture, which represented the Secession curve's ideoplastic consummation. It was as if Bílek had gone back to Blake's prints for Dante's *Divine Comedy* (*The Circle of the Lustful*, 1827), which in their turn drew on Michelangelo. Bílek thereby overcame the by now definitively somnambulistic stylism of the Secession curve with a dramatic impetus inspired by the fundamental antithesis at work in the world and our resulting desire for a new unity. However, Bílek's tendency to preach meant that this inspiration subsequently led him to produce moralistic symbols that were essentially static (*Future Conquerors*, 1931–37).

The same idea was also the starting point for František Kupka's reappraisal of the Secession. In *The Rhythm of History* from around 1905, one of his illustrations for

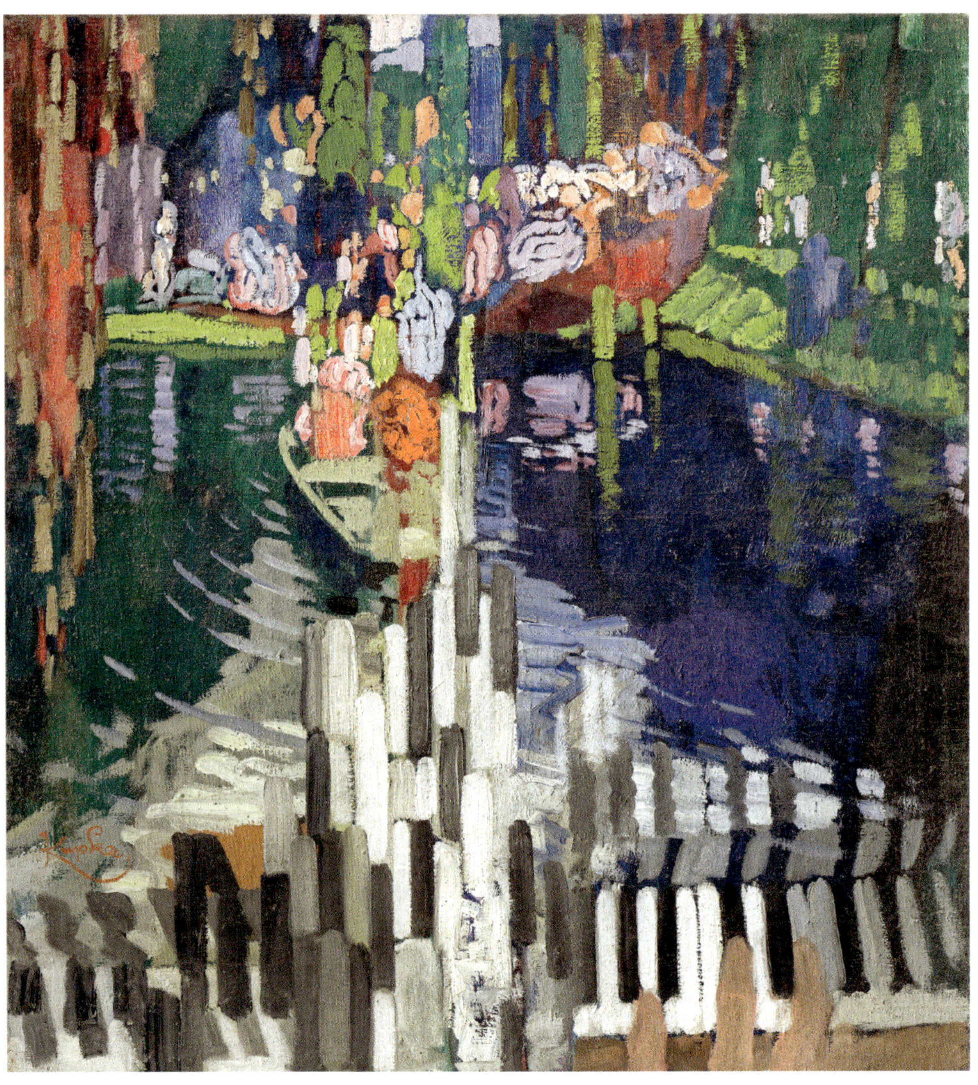

329 František Kupka, *Piano Keys. Lake*, 1909, oil, 79 × 72 cm

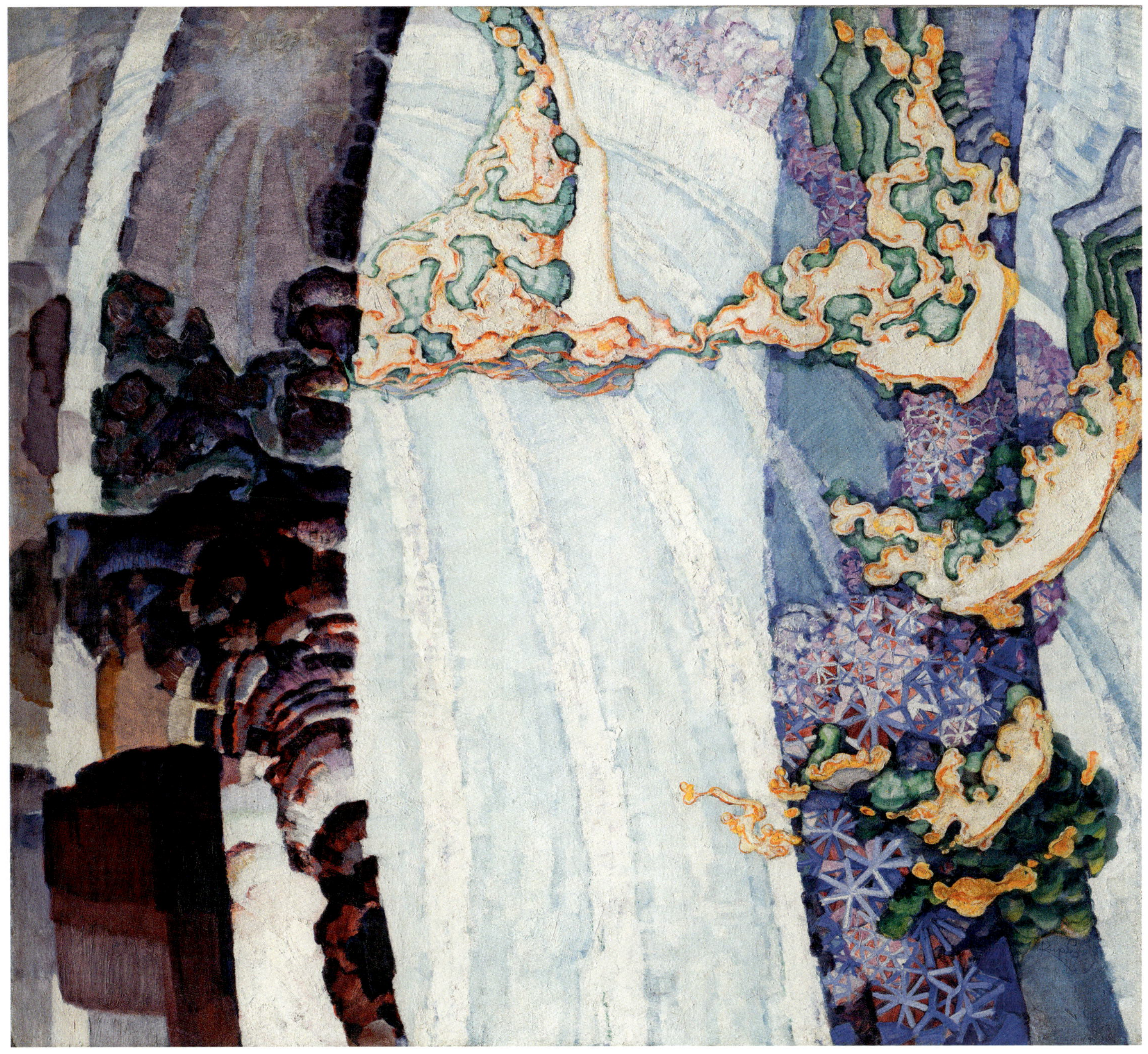

330 František Kupka, *Cosmic Spring II*, 1911–20, oil, 115 × 125 cm

Élisée Reclus's *Man and Earth*, he visualised this idea (influenced by Rodin) as a stylised wave of light carrying humanity through cosmic space. While this image may have still contained a sense of fateful determinism, over the next few years Kupka developed a complicated creative process of re-evaluating the expressive and geometrical possibilities for depicting motion, ultimately resulting in his famous *Amorpha, Fugue in Two Colours*, the painting with which he surprised Paris in 1912.[223] One of the first abstract paintings, it could not be straightforwardly categorised under any of the contemporary currents on the Paris art scene, for Kupka's abstraction was not directed towards a pure, immanent artwork, but was instead an extraordinarily intensified symbol of the transcendentalism that was the essence of the Secession. This is also why the paintings in which Kupka converted into a pure form the theme he had heralded in *The Rhythm of History* – as in his *Moving Blues* series from the 1920s – were ornamental in their appearance. In their composition, there was ultimately also a distinct dualism between two fundamental forms, male and female, between which an equilibrium was sought through art. It is interesting that the female form in these paintings, despite the ornamental complexity of how it is combined with the water element, recalls with its pulsing curve Jan Zrzavý's *Cleopatra* paintings from 1908–9. Kupka's and Zrzavý's paintings also share an erotic subtext that stems from general ideas within the Secession world view, about how the life force fundamentally operates in the universe.

Fin de siècle artists were fascinated by dramatic contrasts, be they social, ideological, or artistic. Their diligent attempts to bridge the most antithetical tendencies produced shocking new forms that nevertheless gave art a new universality. In the 1910s Kupka painted several versions of *Cosmic Spring*, with colours resonating in a celebration of the miracle of the life-giving whirl of cosmic energies as they crystallise in a fantastical aggregate of organic and inorganic forms. Here he developed the Secession's comparing of a flower to the cosmos into a rich orchestration of the essential questions in painting – above all, the possibility of directly combining the greatest sensory and emotional fullness with a fundamental and universal concept. This was the central concern that the naturalistic Secession had only been able to suggest in ornament, and it had gradually lost its original emotional charge and become a convention that ultimately served only to obscure the contradictions that had first given rise to the Secession as a way of finding a synthesis. Despite their enthusiasm and vitality, Kupka's *Cosmic Spring* paintings could not halt this process of mortification, but they did offer an alternative to the cult of the machine, which, after the trauma of the First World War, was the psyche's natural response to waning pseudo-Secession sentimentality. In the 1920s Kupka too was unable to resist the lure of the machine, at least for a brief period, but ultimately this only stimulated him to apply the universalistic content of his earlier ornamentalism to a new foundation (*Another Construction*, 1951–53).[224]

Kupka was not the only one to revisit the turn of the century. Vojtěch Preissig was inspired to do the same as early as 1920, and his late work was far more significant than his original prints. After returning to Czechoslovakia, from 1935 onwards Preissig created a series of paintings that summarised his extensive technical experiments and

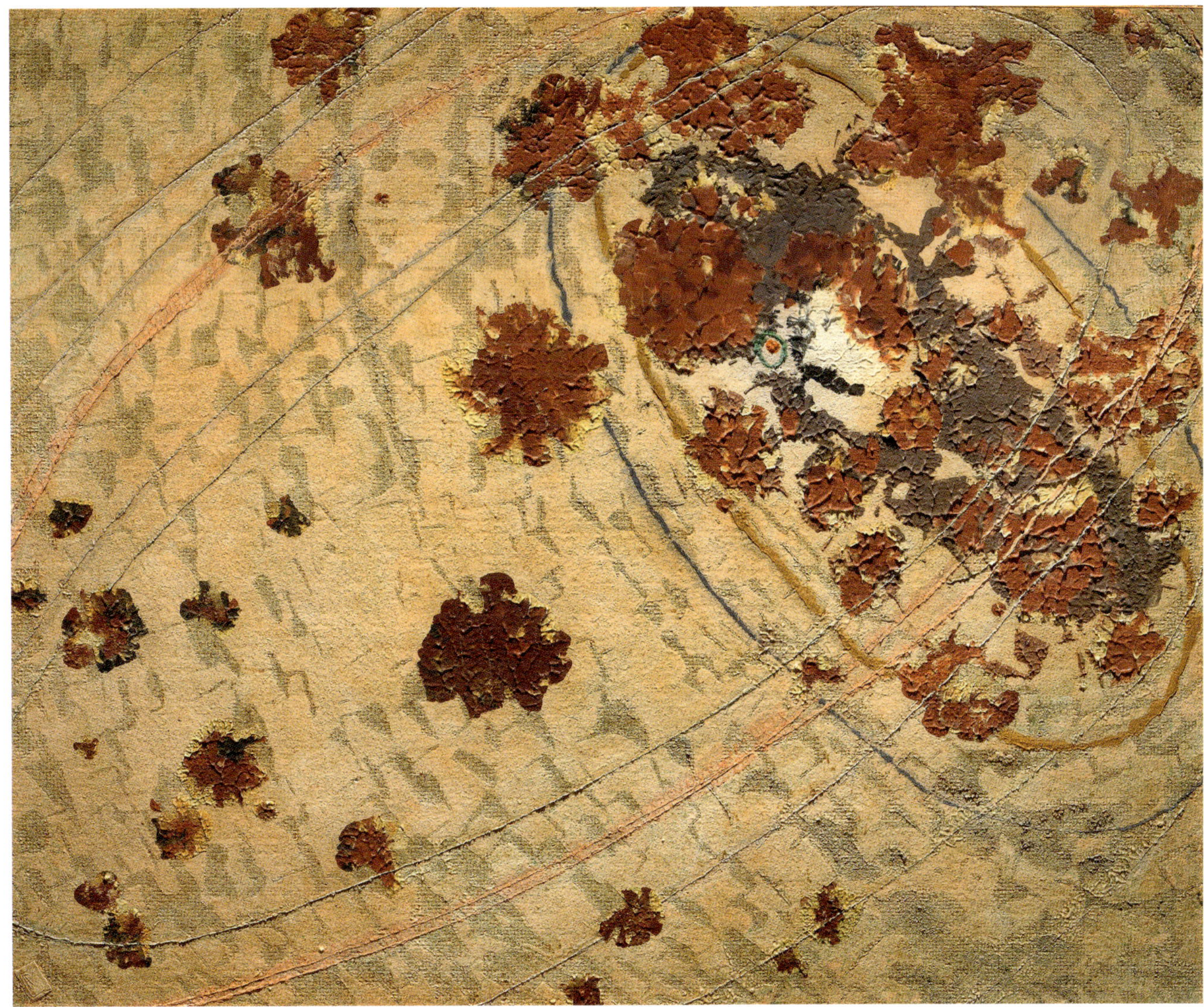

marked the philosophical high point of his oeuvre. This group of works seems at first sight to be considerably diverse, lacking any stylistic unity, and its morphology freely blends linear and geometrical elements with free painting. Preissig's abstraction is not based on elevating an artistic element to a stylistic morphological constant – as the spherical triangle was in Cubism, for instance – but instead displays an almost kaleidoscopic vision that blends organic and geometrical principles. Yet the series does not lack a certain, if unusual, integrity. In fact, an entirely new style emerges from it, one that does not appeal to a single set of principles but respects the natural world's structural multiplicity and inner contradictions. This concept of style reflected the Secession's original intentions,[225] and it marked the true culmination of the Secession's synthetic tendencies in the sense of an extraordinary extending of art's syntactical

331 Vojtěch Preissig, *The Origin of the Earth*, 1936, mixed media, 60.5 × 72 cm foundations. Preissig retained reality's diversity while expressing its unity at the level of its imaginative rendition. Here the appropriating of reality was accomplished not by imitating its phenomena, but by presenting the correlations between natural processes, capturing them in art through variable symbols. Compared with Kupka's monumentality, Preissig is far more intimate and lyrical, but he is no less penetrating. While Kupka tried to find a common language with the international groups who comprised the interwar avant-garde, Preissig, who remained isolated, was more consistent in his efforts to develop the Secession's original propositions.

Like Kupka's *Cosmic Spring* paintings, Preissig's *The Origin of the Earth* (1936) was the end result of the Secession's quest for an image as a universal symbol. From the first depictions of a human figure in landscape, the process of internalising this motif had now brought about a unity of both elements in their pictorial counterpart. The resulting symbol, however, was to retain the dynamism of their encounter and express the authentic existence of this process, playing out for eternity. Preissig embodied this in a pastose layer of radiant splashes of paint, through which runs a formation of two ellipses, poured from the artist's hand. In terms of the development of art, this painting could be described as an attempt to combine Impressionism's painterliness with the cosmological ideas of Symbolism and a spontaneously applied ornamental geometrism. This would encapsulate the sum of the individual Secession tendencies here, but it does not capture this painting's new integrative quality, which is the true legacy of this synthesis. Kupka's and Preissig's work demonstrates that, even in non-objective abstraction, the foundation was still nature as the general framework for externalisation. Unlike the younger generation, influenced as they were by Worringer's theory, members of the 1890s' generation did not see abstraction and empathy as opposites but looked instead for a fundamental organic whole. For this reason too, their sense of the tragedy of life did not lead only to decadence, and the theme of our submission to the forces of fate and the cosmos could become true wisdom. This, however, required sustained hard work on oneself.

The Road to Žamberk (1909), Antonín Slavíček's last, unfinished painting before his crippling stroke and subsequent suicide, remains a permanent symbol of the Secession generation's heroic stance on life and art. The motif of this road in the Orlické Mountains is a symbolic summons to life's pilgrimage through the world. The trees along the roadside, growing from the earth to the sky, are a vivid representation of the symbolism of the tree of life, which is viewed as singularly as the individual trees and people on the road. There is also here the motif of variations, the individual and the whole, and ultimately man the creator is in harmony with the world through the process of painting. An image is created as a symbol that is open to reality, and an artwork is a means for developing art and culture as an open system for the exchange of expressive content between man and his environment. At its core, the Secession was a struggle for such meaning in an artwork. Its artists were well aware of the profound impact of their mission, and they developed it to the point at which an artist's work could address both humanity and the universe.

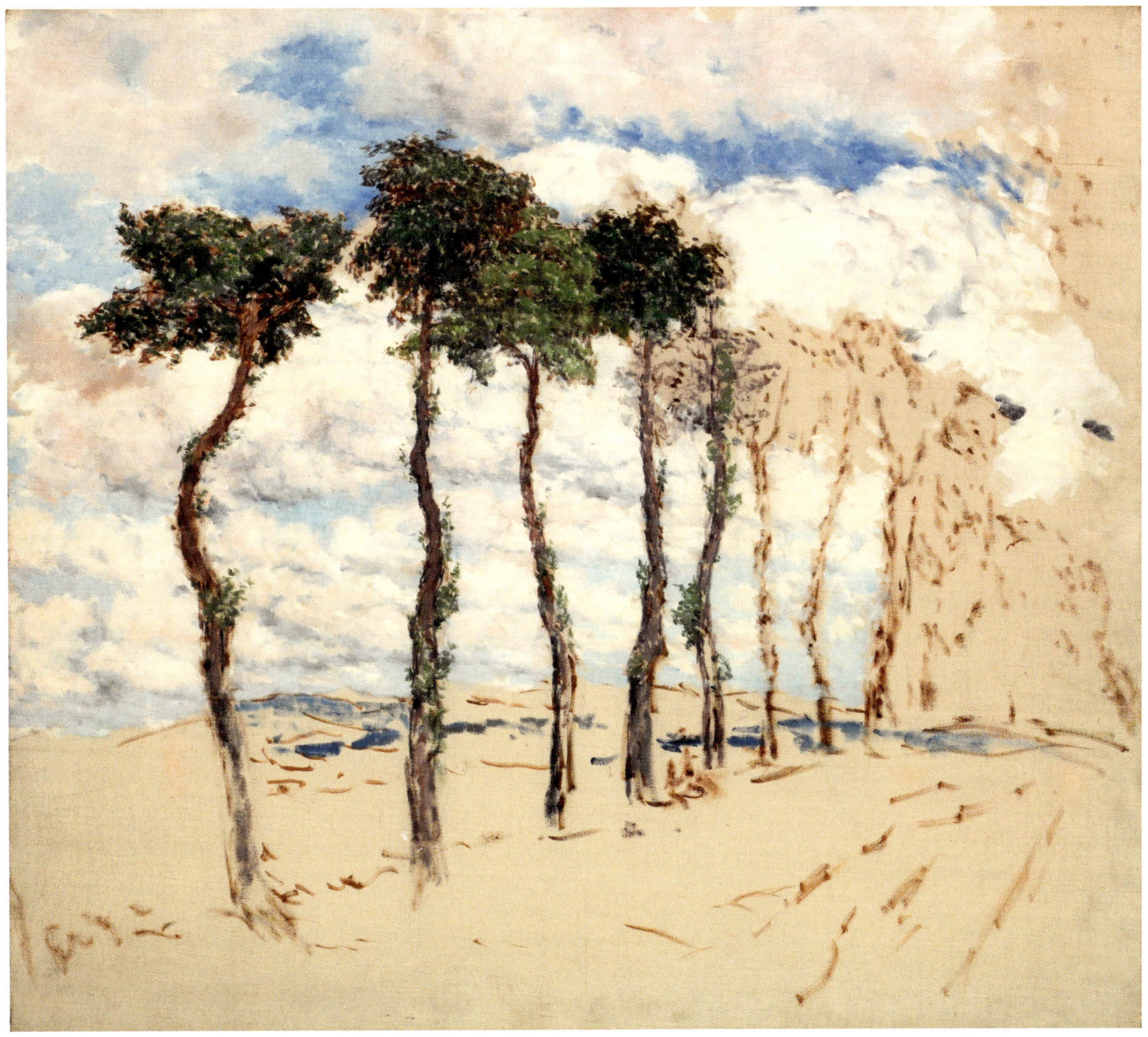

332 Antonín Slavíček, *The Road to Žamberk*, 1909, oil, 90.5 × 99 cm

NOTES

Secession

1 *Volné směry* 2 (1898): 231ff.
2 Miloš Jiránek, "Druhá výstava spolku Mánes," *Radikální listy*, no. 89 (5 November 1898): 582. Reprinted in Miloš Jiránek, *Literární dílo*, vol. 2, *O českém malířství moderním a jiné práce* (Prague: 1962), 29.
3 The early years of SVU Mánes, especially with regard to the publishing of *Volné směry*, are covered in Karel Mašek, *Tři léta s „Mánesem"* (Prague: n.d.).
4 The façade of the Secession Building in Vienna from 1898 bears the motto "To every age its art, to every art its freedom."
5 Miloš Jiránek, "Výstava Jednoty umělců výtvarných," *Radikální listy*, no. 126 (4 November 1899): 806; and *Radikální listy*, no. 127 (7 November 1899): 814. Reprinted in Jiránek, *O českém malířství moderním*, 51.
6 Ibid.
7 Especially in his reviews of Vojtěch Preissig's exhibition in 1907, and earlier too, when he wrote how sad Županský's frieze and Dryák's arch looked as remnants from the SVU Mánes exhibition at the Topič Salon, among the detritus of the Christmas Exhibition in 1898.
8 *Volné směry* 4 (1900): 23. Here Neumann criticises the ornamentation of an exhibition by Jednota umělců výtvarných as "compromising every serious thing, and a callously brazen sin against the new decorative endeavours."
9 K. B. Mádl, *Umění včera a dnes*, vol. 2, *Pětadvacet výstav „Mánesa," kronika deseti let 1898–1908* (Prague: n. d.), 124.
10 Alphonse Mucha was also involved in this, designing the cover for the catalogue for the Austro-Hungarian section at the Exposition Universelle in Paris in 1900.
11 Karel Vítězslav Mašek, "Studium ornamentiky," *Dílo* 1 (1903): 121ff.
12 Miloš Jiránek, "Třetí německá uměleckoprůmyslová výstava v Drážďanech," *Volné směry* 10 (1906): 370ff. Reprinted in Jiránek, *O českém malířství moderním*, 227ff.
13 F. X. Šalda, "Nová krása: její geneze a charakter," *Volné směry* 7 (1903): 169ff., 181ff. Reprinted in F. X. Šalda, *Boje o zítřek* (Prague: 1905, 1915, 1918, 1922, 1948).
14 F. X. Šalda, "Etika dnešní obrody aplikovaného umění," *Volné směry* 7 (1903): 137ff. Reprinted in ibid.
15 Mašek, *Tři léta s „Mánesem"*, 56–57, recalls the controversy between SVU Mánes and *Moderní revue* concerning an exhibition of Anna Costenoble's cycle of paintings *The Tragedy of Woman*, at the end of 1896. Mánes's orientation at this time was markedly naturalistic.
16 "To name the thing means forsaking three quarters of a poem's enjoyment – which is derived from unravelling it gradually, by happy guesswork: to suggest the thing creates the dream. Symbols are formed when this secret is used to perfection: to evoke little by little the image of an object in order to demonstrate a mood; or, conversely, to choose an object and to extract from it a mood." Stéphane Mallarmé, "Réponse à une enquête," *L'Art Moderne* (9 August 1891). Quoted in Arthur Koestler, *The Act of Creation* (London: 1976), 337.
17 Preissig's *Meditation* was preceded by an etching depicting a woman sitting and reading by a wall ornamented in the Secession style. It demonstrates the continuity of a motif originally taken from the Romanticist repertoire (Caspar David Friedrich's *The Garden Terrace*). However, the Secession and Symbolist aspects of *Meditation* principally concern the way the figure is connected to the cosmic theatre.
18 Tomáš Vlček, "Preissigovy fotografie krajin," *Výtvarné umění* 20 (1970): 269ff. Here Vlček points out the link between this drawing and the photographs of the coast that Preissig took in the United States. Vlček remarks that the intention in these drawings was not to create a rigorous system, but to capture a universal sense of life based on our identification with nature and its processes.

Signals

19 Miloš Jiránek, *Hanuš Schwaiger* (Prague: 1912), 30.
20 *Jubilejní výstava zemská království Českého v Praze 1891* (Prague: 1894), 147.
21 Ibid., 154.
22 Ibid.
23 The main sources for this account of Bílek's early years are his handwritten biographical notes, of which there are several versions, and also writings by Zdenka Braunerová, who accompanied Bílek in Paris for a time.
24 To understand the genesis of Bílek's art, it would be

useful to ascertain whether he visited an exhibition by the Salon de la Rose + Croix, the radical wing of the French Symbolists, in the spring of 1892.

25 Zdenka Braunerová, "Úvod k Bílkovým ‚Modlitbám'," in *Básník a sochař. Dopisy Julia Zeyera a Františka Bílka z let 1896–1901*, edited by Josef Richard Marek (Prague: 1948), 200ff.

26 Myslbek held that Bílek had squandered the opportunity the grant had offered, and that he was unworthy of comparison even with Myslbek's last pupil. Three years later, however, he changed his mind, praising Bílek's *Tilling with the Cross*.

The End of the Century

27 Jiří Kotalík, in his introduction to the catalogue of Slavíček's exhibition at the Prague Castle Riding School, September–November 1961.

28 Josef Václav Myslbek and Alois Lodr, eds., *Korespondence* (Prague: 1960), 128.

29 This echoes a well-known episode from Myslbek's visit to Paris, when, upon seeing Paul Delaroche's *Hémicycle* at Beaux-Arts de Paris, he greeted the artist's depiction of a muse wearing a laurel wreath with the words "I'll wrest it from you!"

30 Myslbek and Lodr, *Korespondence*, 187.

31 Hegel's idea of "peaceful ideality" as the achieving of a sensitive equilibrium between corporeality and spirituality, when a beauty is created that is not an expression of anything, but free, independent expression for its own sake, was very influential in 19th-century aesthetics. While Hegel himself saw beauty exemplified by classical Greek sculpture, late 19th-century artistic practice tried to crystallise the proportions of the basic components somewhat differently. See G. W. F. Hegel, *Aesthetics: Lectures on Fine Art* (Oxford: 1975), 2:741.

32 Vojtěch Volavka commented on Myslbek's friendship with Zeyer in his analysis of Myslbek's self-portrait from 1902–3. See Vojtěch Volavka, *J. V. Myslbek* (Prague: 1942), 80.

33 František Bílek's remark that Czech art used a pyramid composition was reported by Zdenka Braunerová, in "Úvod k Bílkovým ‚Modlitbám'."

34 In 1898, Heinrich Wölfflin completed his *Die klassische Kunst: Eine Einführung in die italienische Renaissance*, which was later published in Czech translation.

35 Zdeněk Wirth and Antonín Matějček, *Česká architektura XIX. století* (Prague: 1922), 67.

36 "Moderna či směr národní? (Z kruhů architektů)," *Volné směry* 2 (1898): 281–91, 327–36.

37 *Volné směry* 6 (1902): 89.

38 *Volné směry* 2 (1898): 231ff.

39 Ibid., 523.

40 Jindřich Vybíral and Friedrich Ohmann, *Objev baroku a počátky moderní architektury v Čechách* (Prague: 2013), 265–69.

Go to the People

41 See the Uprka issue from March 1897: *Volné směry* 1 (1897): 227ff.

42 Ibid., 195.

43 A significant part of Miloš Jiránek's oeuvre was devoted to Moravian Slovakia. When Auguste Rodin came to Prague, a visit to Uprka in Hroznová Lhota was arranged, where Rodin was greeted by a band of musicians on horseback; he later remarked that he had felt as if he were in ancient Greece.

44 In 1884 Kuba began publishing the first volumes of his monumental *Slovanstvo ve svých zpěvech* (Slavism in Its Songs), which he only completed in the 1920s.

45 In 1894 František Bílek had also taken Božetěch as his subject, in a large cartoon in which the abbot's appearance somewhat resembled the artist himself.

46 *Volné směry* 1 (1897): 243, 335.

47 Jan Koula published *Památky uměleckého průmyslu v Čechách*, vol. 1 (1883–86) and vol. 2 (1888), at his own expense.

48 Exhibitions held in Darmstadt by Joseph Maria Olbrich, Jan Kotěra's fellow student from Otto Wagner's architecture school at the Academy of Fine Arts in Vienna, were inspirational for Czech modernism.

49 The village from Moravian Wallachia at the Ethnographic Exhibition is described in František Žákavec, *Dílo Dušana Jurkoviče* (Prague: 1929), 25ff.

50 Ibid., 37ff.

51 Secession motifs featured in Jurkovičov's dining hall in the shape of the staircase and in some of the ornamental details that combined a folk-art dove with a Secession peacock. See ibid., 39ff.

52 Alois Mrštík wrote in an article for *Moravská Orlice* in 1903, "Anyone who still doubts what is art and what is crude craftsmanship can have no better opportunity than here to compare this delightful 'toy' with its commonplace neighbourhood, as offensive as an abhorrent piece of factory furniture."

53 Žákavec, *Dílo Dušana Jurkoviče*, 128.

54 Jan Kotěra had fulsome praise for Jurkovič's work in Luhačovice. See *Volné směry* 8 (1904): 59ff.

55 See Petr Wittlich, "Secesní Orfeus: Symbolika formy v českém secesním sochařství," *Umění* 16 (1968): 26ff.
56 Anna Masaryková, *Josef Mařatka* (Prague: 1958), 18. Mařatka based his sculpture on natural models whom he brought into the studio.
57 S. K. Neumann described *Icemen* as an example of "lifeless, false realism." See *Volné směry* 4 (1900): 205.

Into the Wider World

58 Miloš Jiránek, "O mrtvém materiálu," *Styl* 1 (1909): 81ff. Reprinted in Jiránek, "Druhá výstava spolku Mánes," 174ff.
59 K. B. Mádl, "Luděk Marold," *Volné směry* 3 (1899): 180ff.
60 Symbolism's relationship to the Neoplatonic tradition was developed in practice (for instance, Rodin worked with Michelangelo's legacy) and in theory. See Philippe Jullian, *The Symbolists* (London: 1973); Arnold Hauser, *Mannerism: The Crisis of the Renaissance and the Origin of Modern Art* (London: 1965); E. H. Gombrich, *Symbolic Images* (London: 1972).
61 See Jiří Mucha, *Kankán se svatozáří* (Prague: 1969), 168ff.
62 Jiránek, "Druhá výstava spolku Mánes," 55.
63 Karolína Fabelová, *Karel Vítězslav Mašek* (Prague: 2002), 127–32.

Defiance

64 Tomáš Vlček presented a new appreciation of Hlaváček's art and an analysis of how it relates to his poetry, in Tomáš Vlček, "Velká lyra českého symbolistního básníka, proletáře Karla Hlaváčka," *Umění* 23 (1975): 299ff.
65 See Ingrid Schuster-Schirmer, *Traumbilder von 1770 bis 1900* (Bremen: 1975), 34ff.
66 Josef Richard Marek, ed., *Básník a sochař. Dopisy Julia Zeyera a Františka Bílka z let 1896–1901* (Prague: 1948).
67 Ibid., 208.
68 Zdenka Braunerová, "František Bílek," *Volné směry* 4 (1900): 113ff.
69 The concept for Sucharda and Kotěra's designs for the Hus Memorial was probably based on a pen drawing by Mikoláš Aleš from 1880, showing the gigantic figure of Josef Mánes holding a burning candle as he walks across Prague's Old Town Square, oblivious to the townspeople around him.
70 Mádl, *Pětadvacet výstav „Mánesa"*, 151.
71 Arnošt Procházka, *Rozhovory s knihami, obrazy i lidmi* (Prague: 1916), 40.
72 Jiránek, "Druhá výstava spolku Mánes," 55.
73 František Kupka's Viennese period is covered in Werner Hofmann, "Kupka a Vídeň," *Výtvarné umění* 18, no. 7 (1968): 340ff.; Meda Mládková, *František Kupka, 1871–1957: A Retrospective* (New York: Solomon R. Guggenheim Museum, 1975).

Painters of the Soul

74 K. B. Mádl, "Příchozí umění," *Volné směry* 3 (1899): 117ff.
75 "The animation of his creations, the ambiguity, the gentle melancholy of his art and its overall independence of sentiment rank his oeuvre among the foremost of our age." *Volné směry* 2 (1898): 475.
76 The first example of this idea in Czech art was Vojtěch Hynais's 1894 design for the cover of the magazine *Die Kunst für alle*.
77 *Volné směry* 1 (1896–97): 3.
78 Alois Riegl, "Die Stimmung als Inhalt der modernen Kunst," *Die Graphischen Künste* 12 (1899): 47ff.
79 It appears in the work of Gustav Klimt, for instance, where its use was also programmatic.
80 For Symbolism in Kaván's paintings, see Karel Vancl, *František Kaván* (Liberec: 1962), 32ff.
81 Olga Macková, *Otakar Lebeda* (Prague: 1957), 16.
82 In the Middle Ages, triptych and diptych altarpieces had different functions. Triptychs addressed the broader congregation, and the central image usually featured a religious scene from the dogma, while diptychs were typical of individual devotion, and their subject matter was usually composed as contrasting opposites that invited religious contemplation.
83 In *The Symbolists*, Philippe Jullian covers the periodisation of Symbolism as a movement in painting, and he offers examples of how Symbolist aesthetics were starting to wane in Paris at this time.
84 *Soubor díla F. X. Šaldy*, vol. 12, *Kritické projevy 3, 1896–1897* (Prague: 1950), 389.
85 Mašek, *Tři léta s „Mánesem"*, 76.
86 Mádl, *Umění včera a dnes*, 48.

Spring

87 Ibid., 3.
88 Jiří Kotalík, *Antonín Slavíček 1870–1910* [exh. cat.] (Prague: Jízdárna Pražského hradu, September–November 1961), 13.
89 Water was a frequent symbol in contemporary poetry and popular non-fiction, and Élisée Reclus's *Histoire d'un ruisseau* was translated into Czech (his principal

anthropological work, *L'Homme et la terre*, was illustrated by František Kupka).

90 *Volné směry* 2 (1898): 191.

91 Mádl, *Umění včera a dnes*, 26.

92 Riegl's university lectures from the end of the 1890s included his theory of "artistic volition." See Alois Riegl, *Historische Grammatik der bildenden Künste* (Graz and Cologne: 1966).

93 John Ruskin, *The Two Paths* (London: 1906), 31.

94 The contemporary painting vocabulary is explained in Mašek, *Tři léta s „Mánesem"*, 83, 93. He presents an interesting example of how Antonín Slavíček's ideas on art, although seemingly derived from direct observation, were in fact influenced by contemporary critical thinking.

95 Christian von Ehrenfels had published "Über Gestaltqualitäten," his key essay on Gestalt psychology, in 1890.

96 Oil, 235 × 375 cm, Musée d'Orsay, Paris.

97 As related in Aleksa Celebonovic, *Peinture kitsch ou réalisme bourgeois* (Paris: 1974), 39.

98 Antonín Matějček, "Preislerovo mládí. Kritická studie," *Umění* 16 (1944–45): 116.

99 Aimée Brown Price explained the character and significance of the decorative concept of painting in the work of Puvis de Chavannes in *Puvis de Chavannes 1824–1898* [exh. cat.] (Paris: Grand Palais, Novembre 1976 – Février 1977), 21ff. The frequent critical attention that Gauguin paid to Puvis's work indicates its great genetic significance for Post-Impressionist synthetism.

100 *Volné směry* 4 (1900): 189ff.

101 Otakar Novotný's monograph *Jan Kotěra a jeho doba* (Prague: 1958) tried to defend Kotěra against later criticism, but Novotný was as yet unable to fully clarify these relationships in the context of art history.

102 The interior by the School of Decorative Arts was published in the monographic 4th edition of *Volné směry* 5 (1901), while the Prague Chamber of Trade and Commerce's interior was featured in *Dílo* 1 (1903). In 1900 the Museum of Decorative Arts in Prague acquired the principal exhibits from both installations.

103 The model for these ideas was a ceramic vase by Gauguin, featuring his self-portrait with closed eyes. Edvard Munch also developed this concept as a fatally alluring erotic symbol in his lithograph *The Urn* (1896).

104 Karel Mašek, "Studium ornamentiky," *Dílo* 1 (1903): 121ff.

105 C. G. Jung, "Traumsymbole des Individuationsprozesses," *Eranos Jahrbuch* 3 (1935): 13ff.

106 It was mainly artists associated with the magazine *Dílo* who protested.

Fairy Tales

107 Mádl, *Umění včera a dnes*, 134.

108 Sculptors especially carved puppets (Ladislav Šaloun and, later, principally Vojtěch Sucharda).

109 F. X. Šalda, "Géniova mateřština," in *Sochař A. Rodin* (Prague: 1902).

110 *Volné směry* 9 (1905): 185.

111 From a letter by Preisler to Stanislav Sucharda, in Jan Preisler, *Výbor z jeho díla* (Prague: 1919).

112 Ibid.

113 Mádl, *Umění včera a dnes*, 269.

114 Jarmila Kubíčková, "Arnošt Hofbauer," *Umění* 16 (1944–45): 197. Kubíčková describes *Pilgrim* as "a strange and unusual painting," probably prompted by Hofbauer's "desire to stand alongside his peers at the members' exhibition with a single painting that could rival theirs."

Senses

115 This and the following quotation from Kupka's correspondence with Machar are from Ludmila Vachtová, *František Kupka* (Prague: 1968), 39.

116 Although these psychological typologies were only published later, their dualistic orientation was unquestionably based on approaches from the turn of the century.

117 Vachtová, *František Kupka*, 144.

118 Quoted in Jaromír Pečírka, *Josef Mařatka* (Prague: 1942).

119 Jiránek, "Druhá výstava spolku Mánes," 147.

120 F. X. Šalda, "Nová krása: její geneze i charakter," *Volné směry* 7 (1903): 169ff., 181ff. Reprinted in Šalda, *Boje o zítřek.*

121 Ibid.

122 Letter to Jaroslav Goll, in Antonín Slavíček, *Vybrané listy Antonína Slavíčka* (Prague: 1930), 73.

123 One example of a reaction to an experience of this sort is the prose piece "Slovácké noci" (Nights in Moravian Slovakia) in Miloš Jiránek, *Dojmy a potulky: 1901–1908* (Prague: 1908).

124 On the question of Rodin and Impressionism, see Petr Wittlich, "Secesní Orfeus: Symbolika formy v českém secesním sochařství," *Umění* 16 (1968): 26ff., esp. n19.

Epoch

125 Mádl, *Umění včera a dnes*, 185.

126 Ibid.

127 Quoted in Karel Vancl, *František Kaván* (Liberec: 1962), 40.

128 Letter to Jaroslav Goll, in Slavíček, *Vybrané listy Antonína Slavíčka*, 74.
129 Ibid., 67.
130 Ibid., 95.
131 *Styl* 1 (1908–9): 13.
132 Letter to August Švagrovský, in Slavíček, *Vybrané listy Antonína Slavíčka*, 129.
133 Letter to Ladislav Janík, in ibid., 57.
134 Letter to Jan Herben, in ibid., 151.
135 *Volné směry* 5 (1901): 143.
136 Stanislav Sucharda, *Historie pomníku Františka Palackého v Praze* (Prague: 1912).
137 The crisis was reflected in "Saint Wenceslas," a short story that Jakub Arbes published in *Volné směry* 3. Arbes's sculptor bitterly lists all the constraints on his work: "The first, and usually the sternest diktat is the client's. Whatever someone orders has to be done exactly as the order says. Remonstrate all you like – protest, refuse, advise, interpret, implore – it won't do any good. They might give you some leeway, but basically it'll only be tacked onto a work that is essentially highly traditional. … Next, there are ordinarily, as you know, our esteemed art committees with their usual elected members, who have often acquired the appropriate qualifications to serve the judiciary simply by virtue of being elected. … In short, compared with you pen-pushers and other artists, we clay-diggers are without contest the most wretched, precisely because we cannot do our work as cheaply as the other varieties of art. We are slaves to all sorts of elements that we cannot defend ourselves against – that's right, there's no point even trying to defy them. And yet it's high time something was done about it. Our young and our youngest generation must emancipate themselves from the shackles of this dreary tradition."
138 "His petty art, assembled by robbing assorted cultural tombs, was always very minor, and of late it has become staler than the cheapest fragrance." F. X. Šalda, "Mistr Mucha v Praze," *Novina* 3 (1909): 63. Reprinted in *Soubor díla F. X. Šaldy*, vol. 16, *Kritické projevy 7, 1908–1909* (Prague: 1953), 432.

Synthesis

139 Mádl, *Pětadvacet výstav „Mánesa"*, 255ff.
140 Miloš Jiránek, "E. Munch," *Nová česká revue* 2 (1905): 336ff. Reprinted in Jiránek, *O českém malířství moderním*, 175ff.
141 F. X. Šalda, "Edvard Munch a tzv. česká kritika," *Volné směry* 9 (1905): 131. Reprinted in *Soubor díla F. X. Šaldy*, vol. 15, *Kritické projevy 6, 1906–1907* (Prague: 1951), 60.
142 F. X. Šalda, "Násilník snu. Několik glos k dílu E. Munchovu," *Volné směry* 9 (1905): 103. Reprinted in Šalda, *Boje o zítřek*.
143 Letter to Ladislav Janík, in Slavíček, *Vybrané listy Antonína Slavíčka*, 33.
144 Jiránek, *O českém malířství moderním*, 178.
145 Miloš Jiránek, "O mrtvém materiálu," *Styl* 1 (1908–9): 81ff.
146 See Žákavec, *Dílo Dušana Jurkoviče*, 87.
147 See the report on Böcklin's death, accompanied by a poem by Turgenev, in *Volné směry* 5 (1901): 49.
148 F. X. Šalda, "Boj o uměleckou kulturu," *Volné směry* 9 (1905): 291–306.
149 F. X. Šalda himself, in a polemic with K. B. Mádl, wrote that Meier-Graefe's criticism was "probably rather narrow in places, and wrong about some details," but he saw its relevance "in its diagnosis of German artistic non-culture." *Volné směry* 10 (1906): 80.
150 Šalda published his essay "Impresionism: jeho rozvoj, rezultáty i dědicové" after he had left *Volné směry*, in *Pokroková revue* 4 (1907): 70ff., 159ff. Reprinted in F. X. Šalda, *Hájemství zraku* (Prague: 1940), and in *Soubor díla F. X. Šaldy*, 15:198ff.
151 Recorded by Zdeněk Kratochvíl in his memoir of Jan Preisler in *Kmen*. Quoted in Jan Preisler, *Výbor z jeho díla* (Prague: 1919), 47.
152 From a letter by Preisler to Stanislav Sucharda, in ibid.
153 Jiří Kotalík examines Fauvist elements in Preisler's painting at this time in *Jan Preisler* (Prague: 1968), 57.

Expression

154 The design was published in *Styl* 1 (1908–9): 4ff.
155 Ladislav Šaloun, "Husův pomník," *Dílo* 13 (1918): 19ff.; Ladislav Šaloun, "Moje Husovy pomníky," *Dílo* 18 (1924–25): 57ff.
156 *Volné směry* 11 (1907): 177.
157 Ladislav Šaloun, "Dílo," *Dílo* 15 (1920): 10ff.; Ladislav Šaloun, "Z duševní dílny umělcovy," *Dílo* 15 (1920): 83ff.; Ladislav Šaloun, "Jak hledím na umění," *Dílo* 25 (1933–34): 117.
158 *Volné směry* 9 (1905): 31.
159 *Volné směry* 35 (1938–40): 16.
160 Ibid.
161 Miloš Šejn examined the genesis of Váchal's world view and ideas on art in his doctoral thesis "Ideové problémy českého symbolismu" (PhD thesis, Charles University, 1976).
162 For a better understanding of this context, see Mikhail Bakhtin, *Rabelais and His World* (Bloomington: 1984).
163 *L. Šalouna Husův pomník v Hořicích* (Hořice: 1914).

Geometrisation

164 *Dílo* 8 (1910): 51.
165 Karl Kerényi, *Labyrinth Studien* (Amsterdam and Leipzig: 1941).
166 *Dílo* 7 (1909): 151ff.
167 *Volné směry* 11 (1907): 367–68.
168 *Volné směry* 10 (1906): 338.
169 *Styl* 4 (1912): 93.
170 František Šmejkal has pointed out the "hierarchical" value of the figure in Konůpek's early work, distinguishing his ornamental system from that of Mucha, in *Sursum* (Hradec Králové: 1976), 25.
171 *Styl* 2 (1909–10): 89.
172 *Styl* 3 (1911): 189ff.
173 *Styl* 2 (1909–10): 105ff.
174 Ibid., 67ff.
175 "Charakter zahrady," ibid., 188ff.
176 Ibid., 115.
177 Arnošt Hofbauer published a long essay on Japanese art in *Volné směry* in 1908, including examples of woodblock prints that had an interesting combination of curvilinear and geometrical forms.

The Second Secession

178 Jan Zrzavý, *Jan Zrzavý vzpomíná* (Prague: 1971), 50.
179 Miroslav Lamač, "Symbol v obrazech Jana Zrzavého," *Výtvarné umění* 13 (1963): 137ff.
180 Zrzavý, *Jan Zrzavý vzpomíná*, 66.
181 For an analysis of Miloš Marten's criticism, especially his later opinions, see Mireia Ryšková, "Miloš Marten jako výtvarný kritik," in "Příspěvky k dějinám umění II," special issue, *Acta Universitatis Carolinae Philosophica et Historica* 4 (1978): 67ff.
182 Ibid.
183 František Šmejkal, "Básník noci. K rané tvorbě Františka Koblihy," *Umění* 22 (1974): 340ff.
184 František Kobliha, "Odilon Redon," *Hollar* 4 (1927–28): 86.
185 For the history of Sursum, its members, and their art, see Šmejkal, *Sursum*.
186 Láďa Novák, "Bílkův náhrobek V. B. Třebízskému," *Dílo* 7 (1909): 231.
187 *Novina* 2 (1909): 640, 671.
188 During the Second World War the occupying German forces ordered the destruction of Bílek's Jan Hus monument in Kolín.
189 This situation prompted František Kobliha to leave Sursum.
190 "Dva listy Františka Bílka," *Okénko do dílny umělcovy* 5 (1949): 9.
191 This painting was formerly dated 1920, but a photograph from Váchal's studio indicates that he painted it in 1909, which also corresponds to the painting's style.
192 Bohumil Kubišta, "Henri Matisse," *Novina* 3 (1910): 464, 497, 534.
193 For Cézanne's opinion on the doctrine of archetypal forms, see Petr Wittlich, "Povaha inovace v moderním umění," pt. 1, in "Příspěvky k dějinám umění II," 39ff.
194 Gutfreund's critical thinking was compiled and published in *Volné směry* 25 (1927): 147ff. See also Petr Wittlich, "Gutfreundův kubismus," *Umění* 14 (1966): 247ff.
195 F. X. Šalda, "Starý a nový Mánes – dojmy a reflexe," *Novina* 4 (1911): 161, 202ff. Reprinted in F. X. Šalda, *Hájemství zraku* (Prague: 1940), 40ff.
196 Emil Filla, "O ctnosti novoprimitivismu," *Volné směry* 15 (1911): 62. Reprinted in Emil Filla, *Otázky a úvahy* (Prague: 1930), 13ff.
197 Emil Filla, *Rozpravy Aventina* 7, no. 30 (14 March 1932).

Legacy

198 Miloš Jiránek, "O českém malířství moderním," *Volné směry* 13 (1909): 199, 251. Reprinted separately (Prague: 1934) and in Jiránek, "Druhá výstava spolku Mánes," 3ff.
199 From a letter by Preisler to Stanislav Sucharda, in Preisler, *Výbor z jeho díla*.
200 From Otakar Nejedlý's essay on the painter, in ibid., 37ff.
201 Preisler's choice of this theme may have been prompted by the Salon des Indépendants exhibition in Prague, whose centrepiece was André Derain's *Bathing*, influenced by Cézanne. Artists who were members of SVU Mánes raised the money to buy Derain's painting for the association.
202 This was last attempted by Jiří Kotalík, in *Jan Preisler* (Prague: 1968), 68.
203 Joachim Gasquet, *Cézanne: A Memoir with Conversations* (London: 1991), 157.
204 Emil Filla, "Naše generace impresionistů," in *O výtvarném umění* (Prague: 1948), 57.
205 Wilhelm Worringer, "Architektura a plastika z hlediska abstrakce a vcítění," *Styl* 4 (1912): 77ff.
206 F. X. Šalda, "Novoklasicism," *Národní listy* (5 January 1912; 12 January 1912; 19 January 1912). Reprinted in *Soubor díla F. X. Šaldy*, vol. 18, *Kritické projevy 9, 1912–1915* (Prague: 1954), 15ff.
207 Bohumil Kubišta, "O předpokladech slohu," *Přehled* 10 (1911): 37ff. Reprinted in Kubišta, *Předpoklady slohu* (Prague: 1947).

208 Mahulena Nešlehová, "K vrcholnému dílu Bohumila Kubišty," *Umění* 23 (1975): 325ff.
209 Otto Gutfreund, "Plocha a prostor," *Volné směry* 25 (1927–28): 147ff.
210 Vlastislav Hofman, "O secesi," *Styl* 5 (1913): 118ff.
211 F. X. Šalda, "Umělecká výstava v Obecním domě u Prašné brány," *Novina* 5 (1912): 247. Reprinted in *Soubor díla F. X. Šaldy*, 18:85.
212 Zrzavý, *Jan Zrzavý vzpomíná*, 77.
213 See Nešlehová, "Bohumila Kubišty."
214 See Šmejkal, *Sursum*, 43.
215 Jan Zrzavý, "Barva," *Volné směry* 21 (1921–22): 15–24.
216 Jan Zrzavý, "Z úvodu k první samostatné výstavě 1918," in ibid.
217 Josef Čapek parodied the technicist euphoria of the 1920s in his illustrated essay *Umělý člověk* (The Artificial Man), published by Aventinum in 1924, where he compared Secession and mechanical motifs.
218 Such locomotives can be seen at the National Technical Museum in Prague.
219 Václav Nebeský, "Základy moderního sochařství," *Volné směry* 22 (1923–24): 37.
220 František Kovárna, *František Bílek* (Prague: 1941).
221 Robert Schmutzler, *Art Nouveau – Jugendstil* (Stuttgart: 1962).
222 See *František Bílek. Výbor z díla* [exh. cat.] (Prague: 1966), 19.
223 Vachtová, *František Kupka*, 63ff.
224 Kupka's late work of this kind demonstrates that even minimalist art can seek its pedigree in the application of ornamentalism.
225 Preissig's heterogeneous concept of style reflected the standpoint adopted by authentic Secessionists elsewhere. Georg Hirth, the publisher of the Munich-based magazine *Jugend* (which also influenced the Czech Secession), wrote: "The Jugendstil differs from everything that came before, inasmuch as it is not really a style at all in the strict sense of the word, but rather the principle of liberation and the supremacy of functionality and artistic sentiment." Quoted in Gerd-Dieter Stein, "Die ‚Jugend' und der Jugendstil – ‚Vereinigung von Kunst und Leben'," *Alte und Moderne Kunst* 22, no. 150 (1977): 32.

KEY FIGURES IN THE CZECH SECESSION

Mikoláš Aleš (1852–1913), painter and illustrator
1869–76 Academy of Fine Arts in Prague (Josef Matyáš Trenkwald, Jan Sweerts). 1879–1880 Aleš and František Ženíšek enter a competition for the ornamentation of the National Theatre. 1870s begins illustrating Czech magazines and painting pictures with historical subject matter. 1880s begins drawing cartoons to apply to townhouses as ornament. 1895–96 ornamentation for a church in Vodňany. 1895 works on the Czech-Slav Ethnographic Exhibition in Prague. Exhibitions: 1896, 1902, 1908, 1912, 1932, 1976, 2007 in Prague.

Bedřich Bendelmayer (1872–1932), architect
Studies at the School of Decorative Arts in Prague (Friedrich Ohmann). Bendelmayer and Alois Dryák finish Ohmann's Hotel Central on Hybernská ulice in Prague (1889–1900). 1902–04 designs his key buildings: the Archduke Stephen Hotel on Wenceslas Square and an apartment building by the Powder Gate in Prague. 1905–13 designs numerous apartment buildings in Prague, especially in the Old Town, Josefov, and Vinohrady.

František Bílek (1872–1941), sculptor and printmaker
1887 Academy of Fine Arts in Prague (Maxmilián Pirner), subsequently sculpture (Josef Mauder). 1890–92 scholarship to Paris. 1894 begins working in Chýnov, where he builds himself a house with a studio. 1895–1901 friendship with Julius Zeyer. 1900 *Volné směry* devotes an issue to Bílek, with an essay by Zdenka Braunerová. 1904 exhibition in Bílek's apartment in Prague. 1908 retrospective exhibition at the Church of St. Martin in the Wall in Prague. Member of Umělecká beseda, SVU Mánes, and SČUG Hollar. 1909 publishes his book *Journey*. 1911 builds himself a villa with a studio in Hradčany in Prague. Exhibitions: 1922, 1926, 1933, 2000 in Prague. 2010 the reconstruction of Bílek's villa and studio in Prague is completed and a permanent exhibition is opened.

Zdenka Braunerová (1858–1934), painter and printmaker
Private painting studies (Soběslav Pinkas, Amalie Mánesová, Antonín Chittussi). 1880s–90s frequent visits to France. Friendships with František Bílek, Julius Zeyer, F. X. Šalda, and Miloš Marten. 1899 begins making prints. 1906 begins illustrating books; works on eight volumes of *Moderní revue*. Member of SVU Mánes and SČUG Hollar. Exhibitions: 1932 in Prague; 1983 in Roztoky.

Josef Fanta (1856–1954), architect, designer, and conservationist
Studies at the Czech Technical University in Prague, where in 1881 he becomes Josef Schulz's assistant and in 1909 a professor. Involved in designing interiors for exhibitions and apartments (the Czech exhibition at the 1900 Exposition Universelle in Paris is awarded a gold medal). He completes his patron Josef Hlávka's buildings on Vodičkova ulice in Prague and designs Hlávka's hall of residence on Jenštejnská ulice in Prague (1903–04). His work culminates in 1901–09 with the Main Railway Station (originally the Franz Joseph Railway Station) in Prague. He also works on historicist reconstructions, as well as designing furniture, liturgical implements, and textiles.

Emil Filla (1882–1953), painter and critic
1903–06 Academy of Fine Arts in Prague (František Thiele, Vlaho Bukovac). 1907–08 exhibits with Osma. 1909–11 member of SVU Mánes, co-editor of *Volné směry*. 1911–14 member of Skupina výtvarných umělců. Exhibitions: 1908, 1925 in Brno; 1932, 1968, 1987 in Prague.

Karel Hlaváček (1874–1898), art critic, poet, and draughtsman
Initially enthused by the ideals of the Sokol movement. 1895–98 writes exhibition reviews and longer articles for *Moderní revue*, as well as drawing for this monthly periodical. Illustrates his own and his contemporaries' poems (Otokar Březina, Arnošt Procházka), designs covers for *Volné směry* (not used) and for Stanisław Przybyszewski's magazine *Życie*.

Arnošt Hofbauer (1869–1944), painter and printmaker
1885–89 School of Decorative Arts in Prague (František Ženíšek). 1889–97 Academy of Fine Arts in Prague (Maxmilián Pirner, Vojtěch Hynais). 1895 works on the Czech-Slav Ethnographic Exhibition in Prague under Mikoláš Aleš's guidance. As a member of SVU Mánes, in 1898 he designs the posters for its first two exhibitions. 1899 travels to Venice. Co-editor of *Volné směry*. 1909 publishes a book

on Japanese art. Exhibitions: 1935, 1944 in Prague; 2013 posthumous exhibition in Prague.

Vlastislav Hofman (1884–1964), architect and set designer
Studies at the Czech Technical University in Prague. 1908 starts contributing to *Styl* magazine. 1910–11 designs furniture and applied art for the Artěl cooperative. Member of SVU Mánes, Skupina výtvarných umělců, and Tvrdošíjní. Exhibitions: 1922, 1935, 1948, 1960 in Prague; 2017 in Ostrava.

Jaroslav Horejc (1886–1983), sculptor and engraver
1906–1910 School of Decorative Arts in Prague (Stanislav Sucharda). 1911 joins SVU Mánes. 1912 takes part in an exhibition by Sursum. 1919 appointed a professor at the School of Decorative Arts in Prague. Exhibitions: 1971, 1976, 2016 in Prague.

Antonín Hudeček (1872–1941), painter
1887–91 Academy of Fine Arts in Prague (Maxmilián Pirner). 1891–93 Academy of Fine Arts in Munich (Anton Ažbe, Otto Seitz); after returning to Prague he continues his studies at the Academy (Václav Brožík, Julius Mařák). Member of SVU Mánes. In summer 1897 begins visiting Okoř with the Academy's landscape painting school. 1905 begins travelling abroad, especially to Southern Italy. 1909–15 paints in the countryside around Police nad Metují, and from 1925 onwards mostly in Častolovice. Exhibitions: 1902, 1907, 1922, 1925, 1932, 1942 in Prague; 1982 in Pardubice.

Vojtěch Hynais (1854–1925), painter
1870–74 Academy of Fine Arts in Vienna (Anselm Feuerbach). 1874 scholarship to Rome. 1878–80 École des Beaux-Arts in Paris (Paul Baudry, Jean-Léon Gérôme). Member of Jednota umělců výtvarných. 1880 enters a competition for the ornamentation of the National Theatre. 1881 produces a new curtain after the National Theatre is destroyed by fire. In the 1880s he becomes well-known as a portrait painter. 1894 finishes *The Judgement of Paris*. 1893 appointed a professor at the Academy in Prague. Exhibitions: 1924 retrospective in Prague; 1925 in Brno; 2000 in Prague.

Miloš Jiránek (1875–1911), painter and writer
1894–99 Charles University Faculty of Arts and Academy of Fine Arts in Prague (Vojtěch Hynais). Member of SVU Mánes. Writes reviews for *Radikální listy* and essays for *Volné směry*. 1900 Exposition Universelle in Paris. Promotes an orientation towards French Impressionism. Co-editor of *Volné směry*. 1908 publishes his book *Impressions and Wanderings*. Exhibitions: 1910 retrospective in Prague; 1912 posthumous exhibition in Prague; 2012 exhibition in Cheb.

Dušan Jurkovič (1868–1947), architect and ethnographer
Studies at the Staatsgewerbeschule in Vienna. 1890 begins working in Brno. In 1895 his work on the Czech-Slav Ethnographic Exhibition in Prague (village from Moravian Wallachia), with its romantic ethnographic vision, prefigures his life's work, which is then fully realised in his buildings for Pustevny on Radhošť (1899) and for the spa in Luhačovice (1902 onwards). After 1918 he also designs several military cemeteries and memorials. Publishes his ethnographic photographs in a volume with the title *Práce lidu našeho. Slowakische Voksarbeiten. Les ouvrages populaires des slovaques* (1905–14). 1993 exhibition in Bratislava.

Bohumil Kafka (1878–1942), sculptor
1891–95 Sculpture and Stonemasonry School in Hořice. 1896–98 School of Decorative Arts in Prague (Stanislav Sucharda). 1898–1901 Academy of Fine Arts in Prague (Josef Václav Myslbek). Member of SVU Mánes. 1902 travels to Paris and visits Rodin's studio. 1904–08 lives in Paris. 1916 appointed a professor at the School of Decorative Arts in Prague. 1925 appointed a professor at the Academy of Fine Arts in Prague. Exhibitions: 1949 posthumous exhibition in Prague; 1962 exhibition in Prague.

František Kaván (1866–1941), painter
1890–96 Academy of Fine Arts in Prague (Julius Mařák). Member of Umělecká beseda, SVU Mánes and Jednota umělců výtvarných. 1895 paints in the Iron Mountains, 1896 in Southern Bohemia with Otakar Lebeda. Influenced by *Moderní revue* and Symbolist poetry. 1898–1900 at Vranov Castle, near Malá Skála. 1900–04 in Železnice, near Jičín. 1939 receives the National Award for Fine Art. Exhibitions: 1923 retrospective exhibition in Hlinsko; 1941 exhibitions in Prague and Hlinsko; 1980 in Pardubice; 2012, 2016 in Prague.

Celda Klouček (1855–1935), sculptor and designer
1878–81 Arts and Crafts School in Vienna (Otto König). 1881–87 professor at the Arts and Crafts School in Frankfurt. 1888–1916 professor at the School of Decorative Arts in Prague. 1895 begins using naturalistic Secession ornament in ceramics and architecture. 1900 exhibits with the School of Decorative Arts at the Exposition Universelle in Paris, and in 1908 at the International Architecture Exhibition in Vienna. 1906 *Celda Klouček and His Pupils* is published in Vienna. 2010 exhibition in Pilsen.

František Kobliha (1877–1962), printmaker
1896–99 School of Decorative Arts in Prague. 1901–05 Academy of Fine Arts in Prague (František Ženíšek). 1911 begins working with *Moderní revue*. Founding member of

Sursum and SČUG Hollar. Exhibitions: 1942 in Prague; 1973 in Hradec Králové; 1990 in Roudnice nad Labem.

Quido Kocián (1874–1928), sculptor
1889–93 Sculpture and Stonemasonry School in Hořice, 1893–96 School of Decorative Arts in Prague (Celda Klouček), 1896–99 Academy of Fine Arts (Josef Václav Myslbek). 1901 in Munich, 1902 in Italy, 1904 in Paris. 1906 appointed a professor at the Sculpture and Stonemasonry School in Hořice. Exhibitions: 1932, 2004 in Hořice.

Jan Konůpek (1883–1950), printmaker and painter
1906 graduates from the Czech Technical University in Prague. 1906–08 Academy of Fine Arts in Prague (Maxmilián Pirner). 1905 begins working on printmaking. 1910 founding member of Sursum. Member of SČUG Hollar. Exhibitions: 1934, 1969, 1998 in Prague; 1980 in Bochum.

Jan Kotěra (1871–1923), architect
1894–97 Academy of Fine Arts in Vienna (Otto Wagner). 1897–98 travels to Italy and exhibits his work in Prague. 1898 appointed a professor at the School of Decorative Arts in Prague. Active member of SVU Mánes. 1902 *My Own and My Pupils' Work* is published. 1904 designs the exhibition space for the School of Decorative Arts at the Louisiana Purchase Exposition. 1910 appointed professor of the architecture studio at the Academy in Prague. 1910 appointed an expert on the Czech Committee for Regulatory Affairs. Exhibitions: 1926 posthumous exhibition in Prague; 2001 retrospective in Prague.

Jan Koula (1855–1919), architect
1872–77 studies at the Polytechnic in Prague and 1877–78 at the Academy of Fine Arts in Vienna. 1878 becomes Josef Schulz's assistant at the Czech Technical University in Prague, 1897–1919 appointed a professor. Works on the General Land Centennial Exhibition (the Czech Cottage) and the Czech-Slav Ethnographic Exhibition in Prague (the Magistrate's House) in 1895. Enters competitions for public construction projects in Prague (Čech Bridge 1906–08, proposal for the Letná cutting 1897–1911). 1896 builds himself a house in Bubeneč in Prague. Active in conservation (the reconstruction of the Old Town Hall in Prague). 1955 exhibition in Prague.

Ludvík Kuba (1863–1956), painter
1890–92 Academy of Fine Arts in Prague (Maxmilián Pirner). 1893 Académie Julian in Paris. 1895–1904 Anton Ažbe's school in Munich. 1904 moves to Vienna, exhibits with the Hagenbund. 1911 returns to Prague. 1950 named a national artist. Exhibitions: 1904 in Poděbrady; 1909 in Kolín; 1929, 1935, 1954, 2013 in Prague.

Bohumil Kubišta (1884–1918), painter and critic
1903–04 School of Decorative Arts in Prague. 1904–05 Academy of Fine Arts in Prague (Vlaho Bukovac). 1906–07 Royal Institute of Fine Arts in Florence. 1907–08 group exhibitions with Osma. 1909–10 discovers Cubism in Paris. Writes essays on theory for *Volné směry* and other journals. 1910 joins SVU Mánes. 1911–12 member of Die Brücke. 1913 straitened circumstances prompt him to volunteer for military service in Pula. Exhibitions: 1910 in Kouřim; 1920, 1929, 1960, 1993 in Prague; 2014 in Ostrava.

František Kupka (1871–1957), painter and printmaker
1887–91 Academy of Fine Arts in Prague (František Sequens). Becomes a Spiritist medium. 1891–92 Academy of Fine Arts in Vienna (August Eisenmenger). Exhibits at the Kunstverein. 1895 moves to Paris. 1902 visits Vienna. 1904 visits London. 1904 moves to Puteaux. 1905 travelling exhibition in Bohemia. 1907–11 publishes *Creation in the Plastic Arts*. 1912 exhibits his abstract paintings in Paris. 1914 joins the Czech Resistance. 1919 appointed a professor at the Academy of Fine Arts in Prague. 1931 becomes honorary president of Abstraction-Création. Retrospective exhibitions: 1924, 1936, 1958, 1990, 2018 in Paris; 1946, 1968, 2018 in Prague; 1951, 1975 in New York.

František Kysela (1881–1941), painter, printmaker, and designer
1900–04 School of Decorative Arts in Prague. 1904–05 Academy of Fine Arts in Prague (Hanuš Schwaiger). 1906–08 School of Decorative Arts in Prague again. Member of SVU Mánes. 1913 becomes a teacher at the School of Decorative Arts in Prague, where he is appointed a professor in 1917.

Otakar Lebeda (1877–1901), painter
1892–97 Academy of Fine Arts in Prague (Julius Mařák). Paints in Okoř and Zákolany, 1895 paints in Southern Bohemia, 1896 in Krkonoše, 1898 in Karlovy Vary. 1898 Académie Colarossi in Paris. 1899 paints in Bechyně, 1900 in the Chodsko region. Exhibits with SVU Mánes and Umělecká beseda. Exhibitions: 1901 posthumous exhibition in Prague; 1977 in Roudnice nad Labem; 2009 in Prague.

Karel Boromejský Mádl (1859–1932), art historian and critic
1880–83 history of art (private studies) at the University of Vienna and the city's Museum of Art and Industry. 1894–1916 professor at the School of Decorative Arts in Prague. Very active in cultural life, writes for many periodicals, including *Volné směry*, where in 1900 he publishes a key essay "The Style of Our Time." His art criticism is collected in *Art Yesterday and Today I* and *II* (Prague: 1904, 1908).

Luděk Marold (1865–1898), painter and illustrator
1881–82 Academy of Fine Arts in Prague (expelled). 1881–87 Academy of Fine Arts in Munich (Nikolaus Gysis, Ludwig von Löfftz). 1887–89 Academy of Fine Arts in Prague (Maxmilián Pirner) and School of Decorative Arts in Prague. 1889 leaves for Paris, where he works on illustration, something he began in Munich. 1892 awarded a Gold Medal for his illustrations at an international exhibition in Munich. 1897 returns to Prague. 1898 works on the Architecture and Engineering Exhibition (a panorama of the Battle of Lipany). Exhibitions: 1899 posthumous exhibition in Prague; 1935, 1998 retrospectives in Prague.

Josef Mařatka (1874–1937), sculptor
1889–96 School of Decorative Arts in Prague (Josef Václav Myslbek). 1896–99 Academy of Fine Arts in Prague (Josef Václav Myslbek). 1900 scholarship to Paris, works in Rodin's studio. 1902 organises the Rodin exhibition in Prague. 1904 returns to Prague. 1908–09 lives in Paris. 1909 organises Antoine Bourdelle's exhibition in Prague. Member of SVU Mánes. 1920 appointed professor at the School of Decorative Arts in Prague. Exhibitions: 1938 posthumous exhibition in Prague; 1944, 1969 exhibitions in Prague; 1975 in Genoa.

Karel Vítězslav Mašek (1865–1927), painter and architect
Studies at the Academy of Fine Arts in Prague. 1884–86 Academy of Fine Arts in Munich, 1887 Académie Julian in Paris. 1898 appointed professor of decorative painting and ornamental drawing at the School of Decorative Arts in Prague. Member of Krasoumná jednota. 1901 builds his own house in Bubeneč in Prague. 1897 exhibition in Prague.

Alphonse Mucha (1860–1939), painter, printmaker, and designer
1879–81 paints theatre scenery for the company Kautsky-Brioschi-Burghard in Vienna. 1884–88 Academy of Fine Arts in Munich. Chairman of the Czech students' society Škréta. 1888 moves to Paris. 1895 contract with Sarah Bernhardt. 1897 exhibitions in Paris, Munich, Brussels, London, and Prague. 1898 starts teaching his own course at Académie Carmen. 1898–1900 works on the Exposition Universelle in Paris. 1902 publishes *Documents décoratifs*, a style book. 1905 travels to the United States. 1910 returns to Bohemia. 1928 *Slav Epic* exhibition in Prague. 1936 exhibition at the Jeu de Paume in Paris. 1980–2011 numerous major and minor exhibitions held by the National Gallery in Prague, Prague City Gallery, and the Mucha Foundation. Other exhibitions: 1980 in Paris, Darmstadt, Prague; 1983, 1991 in Tokyo; 1994 in Krems; 1995 in Hokkaido; 1997 in Lisbon; 2002, 2005, 2011 Prague; 2009 in Vienna.

Josef Václav Myslbek (1848–1922), sculptor
Trains in Tomáš Seidan's and Václav Levý's studios. 1868–72 Academy of Fine Arts in Prague (Josef Matyáš Trenkwald). 1878 discovers French sculpture at the Exposition Universelle in Paris. 1881 wins a competition for the ornamentation of Palacký Bridge. 1885 appointed a professor at the School of Decorative Arts in Prague. 1894 wins a competition for a statue of Saint Wenceslas in Prague. 1896 appointed a professor at the Academy of Fine Arts in Prague. Exhibitions: 1929–30 retrospective in Prague; 1973 exhibition in Pilsen.

Karel Myslbek (1874–1915), painter
1896–99 Academy of Fine Arts in Prague (Maxmilián Pirner, Vojtěch Hynais). 1903 joins SVU Mánes. Member of the Hagenbund in Vienna. 1914 mobilised. Exhibitions: 1908, 1925, 1974 in Prague.

Friedrich Ohmann (1858–1927), architect
1878–83 studies in Vienna at the Technical University (Heinrich von Ferstel and Karl König) and the Academy of Fine Arts (Friedrich von Schmidt). 1889–98 professor of decorative architecture at the School of Decorative Arts in Prague. 1897 designs the Café Corso in Prague. 1898 appointed a professor at the Academy of Fine Arts in Vienna. Exhibitions: 1928 retrospective in Vienna; 2013 exhibition in Prague.

Jaroslav Panuška (1872–1958), painter
1889–90 Academy of Fine Arts in Prague (Maxmilián Pirner). 1892–96 and 1897–98 Academy of Fine Arts in Prague (Julius Mařák). 1893 travels to the Balkans and Venice. Illustration work for the magazines *Zlatá Praha* and *Švanda dudák*. Member of SVU Mánes and Jednota umělců výtvarných. 1907 begins concentrating on landscape painting. 1922 moves to Kochanov, a village not far from Světlá nad Sázavou. Exhibitions: 1919, 1935, 1994 in Prague; 1933, 2011 in Hradec Králové; 1978 in Pardubice.

Maxmilián Pirner (1854–1924), painter
1875–79 Academy of Fine Arts in Vienna (Josef Matyáš Trenkwald). 1883 travels to Italy. 1885 awarded the Reichel Prize for his *Demon Love* cycle. 1887 appointed a professor at the Academy in Prague. 1890 joins Krasoumná jednota. 1898 exhibits at the Vienna Secession's first exhibition. 1899 *Ver Sacrum* devotes an issue to Pirner. 1911–12 Rector of the Academy in Prague. Exhibitions: 1887 exhibition (at the Ruch gallery), 1987 in Prague; 1924 retrospective in Prague; 1979 in Pilsen.

Osvald Polívka (1859–1931), architect
Studies at the Czech Technical University; Josef Zítek's assistant until 1889. His work in the 1890s includes large financial institutions in Prague – e.g., the Provincial Bank on Na Příkopě and the Prague City Insurance Company on the Old Town Square. 1900 begins working with noted artists on the ornamentation of his buildings in Prague: with Jan Preisler for the Novák Department Store on Vodičkova ulice (1901–04), and with Ladislav Šaloun for the Prague Insurance Company on Národní třída (1906–07). Co-author of the Municipal House in Prague (1905–11).

Jan Preisler (1872–1918), painter
1887–95 School of Decorative Arts in Prague (František Ženíšek). 1896 awarded a prize by *Světozor* magazine for *Easter*. 1900 shows the *Spring* triptych at the third SVU Mánes exhibition. Co-editor of *Volné směry*. 1902 travels to Italy. 1903 becomes an external teacher at the School of Decorative Arts in Prague. 1906 travels to Paris, Belgium, and Holland. 1908–12 teaches life drawing at the School of Decorative Arts in Prague. Member of SVU Mánes. 1917 appointed a professor at the Academy of Fine Arts in Prague. Exhibitions: 1913 in Munich. 1919 posthumous exhibition in Prague; 1935 exhibition in Brno; 1955, 1964, 1994, 2003 in Prague.

Vojtěch Preissig (1873–1944), printmaker and painter
1892–96 School of Decorative Arts in Prague (Friedrich Ohmann). 1897 travels to Paris via Vienna and Munich. Employed in Alphonse Mucha's studio. 1903 returns to Prague. 1905 opens a printmaking studio in Prague. 1906 publishes an album called *Coloured Etchings*. 1910 travels to the United States, where he teaches. 1931 returns to Czechoslovakia. 1935 receives an award from the Academy. Series of abstract paintings. 1941 arrested for his involvement with the Resistance. 1943 taken to Dachau concentration camp. Exhibitions: 1907 in Prague and Vienna; 1945 posthumous exhibition in Prague; 1907, 1931, 1968, 2004 exhibitions in Prague.

Jindřich Prucha (1886–1914), painter
1907–08 Ludvík Vacátko's private painting school in Prague. 1911–12 Ludwig Herterich's painting school in Munich. 1909 joins SVU Mánes. 1914 mobilised. Exhibitions: 1926, 1959, 1999 in Prague; 2003 in Litoměřice.

Jakub Schikaneder (1855–1924), painter
1870–78 Academy of Fine Arts in Prague (Josef Matyáš Trenkwald, Antonín Lhota, Jan Sweerts). 1878–80 in Munich, where he probably has private lessons from Gabriel Max at the Academy. 1880 enters a competition for the ornamentation of the National Theatre. 1885 becomes František Ženíšek's assistant at the School of Decorative Arts in Prague, where in 1890 he is appointed professor of decorative painting and in 1894 is given a chair. 1891 exhibits *Murder in the House* at the Centennial Exhibition in Prague. 1899 joins Jednota umělců výtvarných. Exhibitions: 1926 posthumous exhibition in Prague; 2012 retrospective in Prague.

Hanuš Schwaiger (1854–1912), painter
1874–81 Academy of Fine Arts in Vienna (Josef Matyáš Trenkwald and Hans Makart). 1888 first trip to Holland. 1892 paints a fresco of Saint George in Průhonice. 1896 second trip to Holland. 1899 moves to Moravia; appointed professor of drawing at the Brno University of Technology. 1901 appointed a professor at the Academy in Prague. 1906 third trip to Holland. Exhibitions: 1887 exhibition (at the Ruch gallery), 1912, 1937, 1954 in Prague.

Antonín Slavíček (1870–1910), painter
1886–87 lives in Munich. 1887–99 studies intermittently at the Academy of Fine Arts (Julius Mařák). Paints in Okoř, Veltrusy, and Bechyně. Member of SVU Mánes, exhibiting with the group from 1898 onwards. 1899 his hopes of a professorship at the Academy of Fine Arts are dashed. 1900 awarded a bronze medal at the Exposition Universelle in Paris. 1902 paints in Hostišov, 1903–06 in Kameničky in the Bohemian-Moravian Highlands, 1905 in Kraskovo. 1906 visits Paris. 1908 paints panoramic views of Prague. 1909 suffers a stroke. Exhibitions: 1926 posthumous exhibition in Prague; 1910, 1932, 1961, 2004 exhibitions in Prague.

Stanislav Sucharda (1866–1916), sculptor
1884 studies at the State Industrial School in Prague (Josef Mauder), 1886–92 at the School of Decorative Arts in Prague (Josef Václav Myslbek). 1892 awarded the Reichel Prize in Vienna for *Lullaby*. 1892 teaches modelling, 1899 appointed a professor at the School of Decorative Arts in Prague. 1896–99 president of SVU Mánes. 1902 commissioned to produce the František Palacký Monument in Prague. 1915 appointed professor of the medal studio at the Academy in Prague. Exhibitions: 1916 posthumous exhibition in his Prague studio; 1978, 2006 exhibitions in Nová Paka; 2019 in Prague.

František Xaver Šalda (1867–1937), literary and art historian and critic, poet, and writer
Law graduate. 1919 appointed professor of the history of modern literature at Charles University's Faculty of Arts. 1892 begins writing for journals, some of which he founds

and/or edits. 1903–07 editor at *Volné směry*. Noted essays in *Volné směry*: "The Mother Tongue of Genius" prologue to Rodin's exhibition, 1902; "The New Beauty: Its Genesis and Character," 1903; "The Question of Nationality in Art," 1904; "The Dream Violator: Several Remarks on the Work of Edvard Munch," 1905; collected in *Boje o zítřek*, Praha 1905. 1908–12 editor of *Novina* magazine. 1928–37 publishes the journal *Šaldův zápisník*.

Ladislav Šaloun (1870–1946), sculptor
1885–91 attends the Reynier drawing school in Prague, trains in Tomáš Seidan's and Bohuslav Schnirch's studios. 1896 wins a competition for the ornamentation of the City of Prague Museum; joins SVU Mánes. 1901 first prize in a competition for the Jan Hus Memorial in Prague. Co-editor of *Volné směry*. 1903–06 teaches at a private school with Antonín Slavíček and Vladimír Županský. 1906 leaves SVU Mánes. 1906–14 external teacher at the School of Decorative Arts in Prague. 1912 member of the Czech Academy. 1914 exhibition in Hořice to mark the unveiling of a second Jan Hus Memorial. 1921–22 co-editor of *Dílo* magazine. 1927 appointed artistic advisor to the City of Prague. 1946 named a national artist. Exhibitions: 1914 in Hořice; 1980 in Hradec Králové; 2000 in Prague.

Jan Štursa (1880–1925), sculptor
1894–98 Sculpture and Stonemasonry School in Hořice. 1899–1903 Academy of Fine Arts in Prague (Josef Václav Myslbek). 1904 member of SVU Mánes. Trip to Paris. 1906 *Melancholy Girl*. 1907 travels to Italy. 1914 mobilised. 1916 appointed a professor at the Academy of Fine Arts in Prague. Exhibitions: 1926, 1980 in Prague.

Maxmilián Švabinský (1873–1962), painter and printmaker
1891–98 Academy of Fine Arts in Prague (Maxmilián Pirner). 1891 joins SVU Mánes. 1898–99 studies in Paris. 1901 first prize from the Czech Academy, for which he becomes a correspondent. 1904 gold medal at the Louisiana Purchase Exposition. 1910 appointed a professor at the Academy in Prague, where he sets up a printmaking school. 1918 founding member of SČUG Hollar. 1945 named a national artist. Exhibitions: 1923, 1932, 1948, 1953, 1958, 2001 in Prague.

Joža Uprka (1861–1940), painter
1881–83 Academy of Fine Arts in Prague (František Čermák, Antonín Lhota). 1884–87 Academy of Fine Arts in Munich (Nikolaus Gysis, Otto Seitz). Member of Škréta. 1887 Academy of Fine Arts in Prague (Maxmilián Pirner). Moves to Moravian Slovakia. Member of SVU Mánes. 1900 founding member of Klub přátel výtvarného umění in Brno. 1907 founding member of Sdružení výtvarných umělců moravských. Exhibitions: 1897 in Brno and Prague; 1900 in Vienna; 1904, 1931–32, 2011 in Prague.

Josef Váchal (1884–1969), printmaker and painter
1902 bookbinding apprenticeship. 1904–05 studies at Alois Kalvoda and Rudolf Bém's private painting school. 1906 studies at Antonín Hervert's private printmaking school. 1910 founding member of Sursum. 1916 mobilised. Exhibitions: 1926 in Brno; 1934, 1966, 1994, 2014 in Prague; 2014 in Pilsen.

Jan Zrzavý (1890–1977), painter
1907–09 School of Decorative Arts in Prague (Emanuel Dítě). 1910 founding member of Sursum. Friendship with Bohumil Kubišta. 1912–17 member of SVU Mánes. 1966 named a national artist. Exhibitions: 1918, 1923, 1931, 1940, 1990 in Prague; 2012 in Ostrava.

Vladimír Županský (1869–1928), painter and printmaker
1887–88 studies at the Academy of Fine Arts in Vienna. 1896–97 Academy of Fine Arts in Prague (Maxmilián Pirner, Vojtěch Hynais). 1889 joins SVU Mánes. 1929 posthumous exhibition in Prague.

BIBLIOGRAPHY

A) Books and articles (selection)

Adlerová, A. – Ploil, E. – Ricke, H. – Vlček, T.: *Löetz Böhmisches Glas 1880–1940. Band I: Werkmonographie, Band II: Katalog der Musterschnitte.* München 1989.

Alexandre, A. – Mauclair, C. – Hofbauer, A. – Jiránek, M. – Sucharda, S. (et al.): 'A. Rodin', *Volné směry* V, 1901, special Rodin issue, pp. 97–145.

Anonym: 'I. výstava spolku Mánes', *Volné směry* II, 1898, cols. 231–236.

Anonym: 'Jos. Lad. Němec', *Dílo* IV, 1906, p. 98.

Benda, J. – Beneš, V. – Žákavec, F. (eds.): *Jan Preisler – Výbor z díla.* Praha 1919.

Bendelmayer, B. – Dryák, A.: 'Hotel Central v Praze', *Volné směry* VI, 1902, pp. 163–166, 173–176.

Beneš, V.: 'Jan Preisler', *Volné směry* XX, 1919–1920, pp. 1–24.

Beneš, V.: *Antonín Slavíček.* Praha 1938.

Benešová, M. – Pošva R.: *Pražské ghetto – asanace.* Praha 1993.

Berka, C.: 'Problém impresionismu', *Výtvarné umění* VI, 1956, pp. 366, 411, 463.

Bílek, F.: *Cesta.* Praha 1909.

Bílek, F.: *Jak mi dřeva povídala.* Praha 1946.

Birnbaumová, A. – Černá, V.: *Opuštěná paleta.* Praha 1942.

Blümlová, D. – Gilarová, Z. et al.: *Čas secese: Kapitoly z kulturních dějin přelomu 19. a 20. století.* České Budějovice 2007.

Brabcová, J.: *Luděk Marold.* Praha 1988.

Bráf, A.: 'Máme-li napodobovati nebo tvořiti', *Dílo* I, 1903, pp. 98–108.

Braunerová, Z.: 'František Bílek', *Volné směry* IV, 1900, pp. 113–134.

Braunerová, Z.: 'Vzpomínky na první desítiletí moderní české grafiky', *Hollar* I, 1924, pp. 175–188.

Březina, O.: 'Meditace o kráse a umění', *Volné směry* VI, 1902, pp. 115–117.

Březina, O.: 'Nebezpečí sklizně', *Volné směry* VII, 1903, pp. 3–5.

Březina, O.: 'Jediné dílo', *Volné směry* IX, 1905, pp. 67–70.

Březina, O.: 'Smysl boje', *Volné směry* XI, 1907, pp. 3–5.

Bridges, A. (ed.).: *Alphonse Mucha: The Complete Graphic Works.* London 1980.

Brynychová, M. A. (Masaryková, A.): *Antonín Hudeček.* Praha 1942.

Čadík, J. (et al.): *Výtvarníci S. V. U. M. – B. Jaroněk, A. Kalvoda, F. Ondrušek, Fr. Úprka,* Hodonín 1935.

Čadík, J.: *Viktor Stretti.* Praha 1938.

Chalupný, E.: *František Bílek – Tvůrce a člověk.* České Budějovice 1970.

Chytil, K.: Vojtěch Preissig, *Hollar* II, 1924–1925, pp. 20–34.

Císařovský, J.: *Portrétní umění Maxe Švabinského.* Praha 1954.

Čižinská, H.: *Beuronská umělecká škola v opatství svatého Gabriela v Praze. / Die Beuroner Kunstschule in der Abtei Sankt Gabriel in Prag.* Praha 1999.

Clegg, E.: *Art, Design & Architecture in Central Europe 1890–1920.* New Haven, London 2006.

Deml, J.: 'Slovo o díle F. Bílka. K padesátinám sochařovým', *Volné směry* XXI, 1921–1922, pp. 225–248.

Denis, M.: 'Vliv Paula Gauguina', *Volné směry* X, 1906, pp. 47– 51.

Dolenský, A.: *Moderní česká grafika.* Praha 1912.

Drahoňovský, J.: 'Profesor Celda Klouček', *Dílo* XIX, 1926, pp. 5–7, 13–15, 19–22.

Dvořák, V.: 'Výstava Fr. Bílka', *Volné směry* XIX, 1918, pp. 38–39.

Engel, A.: 'Dům nájemný', *Styl* III, 1911, pp. 189–196.

Engel, A.: 'Veřejné budovy pražské', *Styl* IV, 1912, pp. 30–37.

Fabelová, K.: *Karel Vítězslav Mašek.* Praha 2002.

Fabelová, K.: 'Bourdelle à Prague en 1909 et son rapport aux artistes tchéques et à Auguste Rodin', *Umění* 57, 2009, pp. 364–384.

Fahr-Becker, G.: *Art Nouveau.* Köln 1997.

Fanta, J.: 'Stavby pražské a směry umělecké', *Volné směry* III, 1899, cols. 239–243.

Fanta, J.: 'Interiér na výstavě 1900 v Paříži', *Dílo* I, 1903, pp. 91–97.

Filla, E.: 'O ctnosti novoprimitivismu', *Volné směry* XV, 1911, pp. 62–70.

Filla, E.: *Otázky a úvahy.* Praha 1930.

Filla, E.: *O výtvarném umění.* Praha 1948.

Friedl, A.: 'Jan Konůpek', *Umění* XV, 1944, pp. 385–390.

Graul, R.: 'Hans Schwaiger', *Die graphischen Künste* XVI, 1893, pp. 65–77.
Grémilly, L. A.: *Frank Kupka*, Paris 1922.
Harlas, F. X.: *Malířství.* Praha 1908.
Hellmuth-Brauner, V.: 'Povahový dualismus Zd. Braunerové', *Hollar* XIV, 1938, pp. 73–85.
Herain, K.: 'František Bílek a chýnovští hrnčíři', *Umění* XIV, 1943, pp. 321–326.
Hevesi, L.: 'Hans Schwaiger', *Ver Sacrum* I, 1898, pp. 247–253.
Hlaváček, L.: 'Kresby Antonína Slavíčka', *Umění* 8, 1960, pp. 493–514.
Hlaváček, L.: 'Kresba Jana Preislera', *Hollar* XXXI, 1960, pp. 49–58.
Hlaváček, L.: 'Začátky moderní české knihy', *Výtvarné umění* XX, 1970, pp. 350–376.
Hlaváček, L.: 'Miloš Marten a výtvarné umění', *Umění* 28, 1980, pp. 505–514.
Hnídková, V. (ed.): *Pavel Janák: Obrys doby.* Praha 2009.
Hofbauer, A.: 'Něco z moderního dekorativního umění', *Volné směry* V, 1901, pp. 43–47.
Hofman, V.: 'Nový princip v architektuře', *Styl* V, 1913, pp. 13–24.
Hofman, V.: 'O secesi', *Styl* V, 1913, pp. 118–119.
Hofmann, W.: 'Kupka a Vídeň', *Výtvarné umění* XVIII, 1968, pp. 340–346.
Hojda, Z. – Pokorný, J.: *Pomníky a zapomníky.* Litomyšl 1996.
Holý, P.: *Český sochař Quido Kocián.* Hradec Králové 2013.
Hubatová-Vacková, L.: *Tiché revoluce uvnitř ornamentu. Studie z dějin uměleckého průmyslu a dekorativního umění 1880–1930.* Praha 2011.
Hubatová-Vacková, L. – Pachmanová, M. – Pečinková, P. (eds.): *Věci a slova: Umělecký průmysl, užité umění a design v české teorii a kritice 1870–1970.* Praha 2014.
Hylmar, T. – Pujmanová-Stretti, O. (eds.): *Viktor Stretti, z Mnichova do Paříže: korespondence a skicáře z let 1898–1902.* Praha 2015.

Jan Kotěra: jeho učitelé, doba a žáci. Sborník textů Mezinárodní konference k výstavě Kotěra: po stopách moderny. Hradec Králové, Muzeum východních Čech 2013.
Jan Štursa – Dílo. Praha 1926.
Janák, P.: 'Otto Wagner', *Styl* I, 1909, pp. 41– 49.
Janoušek, F.: 'Otakar Lebeda', *Volné směry* XXV, 1928, pp. 261–263.
Jež, Š.: *Joža Uprka.* Praha 1944.
Jiránek, M. (-en-): 'II. výstava spolku Mánes', *Volné směry* III, 1899, cols. 60–61.
Jiránek, M.: 'Výstava Jednoty umělců výtvarných', *Radikální listy* 1899, pp. 806, 814.
Jiránek, M.: *Hanuš Schwaiger.* Praha 1908, 1912.
Jiránek, M.: 'Francouzští impresionisté', *Volné směry* XII, 1909, pp. 7–10.
Jiránek, M. – Hodačová-Gollová, A. – Herben, J.: *Antonín Slavíček – Výbor z jeho díla.* Praha 1910.
Jiránek, M.: *O českém malířství moderním.* Praha 1934.
Jiránek, M.: *Literární dílo.* Praha 1936.
Jiránek, M.: *Literární dílo I – Dojmy a potulky a jiné práce.* Foreword by J. Kotalík. Praha 1959.
Jiránek, M.: *Literární dílo II – O českém malířství moderním a jiné práce.* Foreword by J. Kotalík. Praha 1962.
Jiřík, F. X.: 'Moderní interiér', *Dílo* II, 1904, pp. 30–40, 132–143.

'K výstavě Alf. Muchy', *Volné směry* II, 1898, cols. 127–134.
Kalvoda, A.: 'Luděk Marold, Ladislav Šaloun, Stanislav Lolek', *Dílo* IX, 1911, pp. 129–136, 149–150, 253–260.
Karásek ze Lvovic, J.: 'Grafika Františka Bílka', *Hollar* III, 1926, pp. 49–58.
Karlíková, L.: 'K obsahovosti díla Jana Preislera', *Výtvarné umění* XV, 1965, pp. 64–73.
Karlíková, L.: *Antonín Hudeček.* Praha 1983.
Karlíková, L.: *František Kaván.* Praha 1992.
Kaván, F.: 'Julius Mařák ve vzpomínce žákově', *Volné směry* III, 1899, cols. 413–424.
Kiesling, N.: *Pavel Janák.* Řevnice 2011.
Klouček, C.: 'Moje škola', *Dílo* IV, 1906, pp. 221–252.
Klvaňa, J.: *Joža Uprka*, s.l. 1896.
Kobliha, F.: 'Jaromír Stretti-Zamponi', *Hollar* V, 1928, pp. 59–68.
Kobliha, F.: *Sedm statí o výtvarném umění.* Praha 1929.
Kobliha, F.: 'Karel Hlaváček', *Hollar* XV, 1939, pp. 25–29.
Kobliha, F.: 'Konůpkův svět myšlenek a snů', *Hollar* XIX, 1943, no. 3, annex.
Konůpek, J.: 'O Františku Koblihoví', *Marginalie* XV, 1943, pp. 39–44.
Konůpek, J.: *Život v umění.* Praha 1947.
Kopa, J.: *Čeští malíři impresionisté.* Brno 1934.
Kotalík, J.: 'Moderní československé malířství'. *Československo* 2, 1947, pp. 125–207.
Kotalík, J. – Hovorková, M. – Karlíková, L.: *Antonín Slavíček 1870–1910. Soupis díla.* Praha 1965
Kotalík, J.: 'O třech umělcích secese (Bílek – Mucha – Kupka)', *Výtvarné umění* XVII, 1967, pp. 173–188.
Kotalík, J.: *Jan Preisler.* Praha 1968.
Kotěra, J.: 'O novém umění. Několik thesí o architektuře a uměleckém průmyslu', *Volné směry* IV, 1900, pp. 189–195.
Kotěra, J.: 'Joža Plečnik', *Volné směry* VI, 1902, pp. 59–76.
Kotěra, J.: *Meine und meiner Schüler Arbeiten 1898–1901*, Wien s.d. (1902).
Kotěra, J.: 'Luhačovice', *Volné směry* VIII, 1904, pp. 59–60.

Kotěra, J.: 'Interiér c. k. Uměleckoprůmyslové školy pražské pro Světovou výstavu v St. Louis 1904', *Volné směry* VIII, 1904, pp. 119–141.
Kovárna, F.: *Antonín Slavíček*. Praha 1930.
Kovárna, F.: *Malířství ornamentální a obrazové*. Praha 1934.
Kovárna, F.: *Ludvík Kuba*. Praha 1935.
Kovárna, F.: *České malířství let devadesátých*. Praha 1940.
Kovárna, F.: *František Bílek*. Praha 1941.
Kovárna, F.: *František Kaván*. Praha 1941.
Kovárna, F.: 'Pokolení devadesátých let', *Dílo* XXXV, 1947, pp. 154–158.
Kratochvíl, Z.: 'Jan Preisler a V. H. Brunner', *Volné směry* XXVI, 1929, pp. 265–285.
Krecar, J.: 'Moderní knižní umění', *Dílo* XXIII, 1931, pp. 212–220, 252–258.
Krecar, J.: 'Jiránkova účast v grafice', *Hollar* X, 1934, pp. 147–153.
Kříž, J.: 'František Kupka a pojem českého umění', *Výtvarné umění* XVIII, 1968, pp. 354–356.
Kroutvor, J.: 'Fenomén ornamentu a secese', *Umění a řemesla* 1973, no. 3, pp. 22–26.
Kroutvor, J.: *Pražský chodec. Dějiny českého plakátu 1890–1945*. Praha 1985.
Kuba, L.: 'Od Bucka k Pirnerovi', *Výtvarné umění* IV, 1954, pp. 423–426.
Kuba, L.: *Zaschlá paleta. Paměti*. Praha 1955.
Kubíčková, J.: *Malíř předjaří a jara. Jindřich Prucha, život a dílo*. Praha 1941.
Kubíčková, J.: 'Arnošt Hofbauer. Poznámky k malířskému dílu', *Umění* XVI, 1945, pp. 197–212.
Kubišta, B.: *Předpoklady slohu*. Praha 1947.
Květ, J.: *Má vlast – Česká krajina v díle našich malířů*. Praha 1943.
Květ, J.: *Max Švabinský krajinář*. Praha 1948.

La Plume, M. M.: *Alphonse Mucha et son Oeuvre*. Paris 1897.
Lahoda, V.: *Český kubismus*. Praha 1996.
Lahoda, V.: *Emil Filla*. Praha 2007.
Lahoda, V. – Nešlehová, M. – Platovská, M. – Švácha, R. – Bydžovská, L. (eds.): *Dějiny českého výtvarného umění 1890–1938*, IV/1. Praha 1998.
Lamač, M.: *Hanuš Schwaiger*. Praha 1957.
Lamač, M.: 'Symbol v obrazech Jana Zrzavého', *Výtvarné umění* XIII, 1963, pp. 137–50.
Lamač, M.: *František Kupka*. Praha 1984.
Lamač, M.: *Osma a Skupina výtvarných umělců: 1907–1917*. Praha 1988.
Lamač, M. – Padrta, J.: *Osma a Skupina výtvarných umělců: 1907–1917. Teorie, kritika, polemika*. Praha 1992.
Lekeš, V. – Husslein-Arco, A. – Lekeš, L. – Zlatohlávková, E.: *František Kupka: catalogue raisonné des huiles / catalogue raisonné of oil paintings*. London 2016.
Lenderová, M.: *Zdenka Braunerová*. Praha 2000.
Loriš, J.: 'Bohumil Kafka' *Umění* XIV, 1943, pp. 381–395.
Lukeš, Z. – Svoboda, J. E.: 'Architekt Emil Králíček – zapomenutý zjev české secese a kubismu', *Umění* 32, 1984, pp. 441–449.
Lukeš, Z. – Svoboda, J. E.: 'Josef Zasche', *Umění* 38, 1990, pp. 534–543.

Macková, O.: *Otakar Lebeda*. Praha 1957.
Mádl, K. B.: 'Mánesu', *Volné směry* III, 1899, cols. 1–6.
Mádl, K. B.: 'Příchozí umění', *Volné směry* III, 1899, cols. 117–142.
Mádl, K. B.: 'Luděk Marold', *Volné směry* III, 1899, special Marold issue, February – March, cols. 173–238.
Mádl, K. B.: 'Václav Radimský', *Volné směry* III, 1899, cols. 278–289.
Mádl, K. B.: 'Hanuš Schwaiger', *Volné směry* IV, 1900, pp. 30–47.
Mádl, K. B.: 'Sloh naší doby', *Volné směry* IV, 1900, pp. 157–180.
Mádl, K. B.: 'F. Ohmann', *Volné směry* IV, 1900, pp. 181–186.
Mádl, K. B.: 'Husův pomník', *Volné směry* V, 1901, pp. 51–69.
Mádl, K. B.: *Joža Uprka*. Praha 1901.
Mádl, K. B.: *Umění včera a dnes* I. Praha s.d. (1904).
Mádl, K. B.: *Umění včera a dnes II – Pětadvacet výstav „Mánesa". Kronika deseti let 1898–1908*. Praha s.d. (1908).
Mádl, K. B.: 'Stanislav Sucharda', *Volné směry* XIX, 1918, pp. 1–5.
Mádl, K. B.: *Bohumil Kafka. Jeho dílo od r. 1900 do r. 1918*. Praha 1919.
Mádl, K. B., Pohribný, A. (ed.): *Výbor z kritických projevů a drobných spisů*. Praha 1959.
Mařatka, J.: *Vzpomínky a záznamy*. Praha 1987.
Marek, Jos. Richard (ed.): *Básník a sochař. Dopisy Julia Zeyera a Františka Bílka z let 1896–1901*. Praha 1948.
Marten, M.: 'Krize umění', *Dílo* XII, 1914, pp. 153–167.
Marten, M., Macek E. (ed.): *Imprese a řád*. Praha 1983.
Masaryková, A.: *Josef Mařatka*. Praha 1958.
Masaryková, A.: *České sochařství XIX. a XX. století*. Praha 1963.
Mašek, K.: *Tři léta s „Mánesem"*. Praha s.d. (1921).
Mašek, K. V.: 'Studium ornamentiky', *Dílo* I, 1903, p. 121.
Mašín, J.: 'Auguste Rodin', *Volné směry* IL, 1948, p. 198.
Matějček, A.: 'Úvod k výstavě Nezávislých', *Volné směry* XIV, 1910, pp. 136–151.
Matějček, A.: 'Miloš Jiránek', *Volné směry* XVI, 1912, pp. 141–148.
Matějček, A.: *Antonín Slavíček*. Praha 1921.

Matějček, A.: 'Maxmilián Pirner 1854–1924', *Volné směry* XXIII, 1925, pp. 23–24.
Matějček, A.: 'Slavíčkova mladá léta', *Umění* III, 1930, pp. 19–28.
Matějček, A.: 'Kupkův Prométheus', *Umění* III, 1930, pp. 125–135.
Matějček, A.: *Hlasy světa a domova.* Praha 1931.
Matějček, A.: *T. F. Šimon.* Praha 1934
Matějček, A.: *Max Švabinský.* Praha 1937, 1948.
Matějček, A.: 'Hudečkova léta okořská', *Umění* XIV, 1943, pp. 167–202.
Matějček, A.: 'Preislerovo mládí. Kritická studie', *Umění* XVI, 1944–45, pp. 3–33, 85–116.
Matějček, A.: 'Preislerovo mládí. Léta závěrná', *Umění* XVII, 1945–49, pp. 13–45.
Matějček, A.: *Antonín Hudeček.* Praha 1947.
Matějček, A.: *Jan Preisler.* Praha 1950.
Matějček, A.: *Jan Štursa.* Praha 1950.
Míčko, M. – Štech, V. V. – Seifert, J. – Nezval, V.: *Ludvík Kuba – malíř.* Praha 1946.
Míčko, M. – Svoboda, E.: *Mikoláš Aleš – Nástěnné malby.* Praha 1955.
Mráz, B. – Mrázová, M.: *Secese.* Praha 1971.
Mrázová-Schusterová, M.: 'Duchovní umění Františka Bílka', *Výtvarné umění* XVI, 1966, pp. 63–73.
Mrázová-Schusterová, M.: *Josef Váchal a kniha.* Praha 1968.
Mucha, J.: *Alphonse Mucha, the Master of Art Nouveau.* Prague 1966.
Mucha, J.: *Kankán se svatozáří.* Praha 1969.
Mucha, J. – Henderson I.: *The Graphic Work of Alphonse Mucha.* London 1973.
Mucha, J.: *Alphonse Maria Mucha. His Life and Art.* London 1989.
Mukařovský, J.: 'Mezi poezií a výtvarnictvím', *Slovo a slovesnost* VII, 1941.
Mžyková, M.: *Vojtěch Hynais.* Praha 1989.

Nebeský, V.: 'Kol padesátin Fr. Bílka', *Volné směry* XXII, 1923–1924, pp. 74–76.
Nechvátalová, M.: *Viktor Oliva: dekoratér všednosti: život a dílo umělce z přelomu 19. a 20. století.* Praha 2016.
Nešlehová, M.: 'K vrcholnému dílu Bohumila Kubišty', *Umění* 23, 1975, pp. 325–346.
Nešlehová, M.: *Bohumil Kubišta.* Praha 1984.
Nešlehová, M. – Hilmera, J. – Švácha, R.: *Vlastislav Hofman.* Praha 2004.
Neumann, S. K.: 'Aubrey Beardsley', *Volné směry* IX, 1905, pp. 97–98.
Nezval, V.: *Antonín Slavíček.* Praha 1952.
Novotný, K.: *Miloš Jiránek.* Praha 1936.
Novotný, K.: *Jan Štursa.* Praha 1940.
Novotný, K.: 'Arnošt Hofbauer', *Volné směry* XXXVIII, 1942–1944, pp. 245–251.
Novotný, O.: 'Interiér, architekt a obecenstvo', *Styl* II, 1910, pp. 67–70.
Novotný, O.: 'Tvoření formy v architektuře', *Styl* IV, 1912, pp. 3–10.
Novotný, O.: 'Architektonický impresionismus', *Styl* IV, 1912, pp. 105–37.
Novotný, O.: *Jan Kotěra a jeho doba.* Praha 1958.
Novotný, V.: 'Slavíčkův impresionismus', *Volné směry* XXIX, 1932, pp. 121–125.
Novotný, V.: 'Kresby Jindřicha Pruchy', *Umění* XVI, 1944–45, pp. 217–222.
Novotný, V.: *Národní galerie* IV. Praha 1957.

Opolský, J.: 'Dílo F. Koblihy', *Hollar* XIII, 1937, pp. 153–176.

Padesát let státní Uměleckoprůmyslové školy v Praze, 1885–1935. Praha 1935.
Páleníček, L.: *Mladý Švabinský.* Gottwaldov (Zlín) 1958.
Palkovský, B.: *Max Švabinský – Popisný seznam grafického díla 1897–1923.* Praha 1923.
Pavelka, J.: 'Umělecký profil Vojtěcha Preissiga', *Hollar* XX, 1947, pp. 1–8.
Pečírka, J.: *Jan Preisler.* Praha 1940.
Pečírka, J.: *Josef Mařatka.* Praha 1942.
Pešina, J.: *Česká moderní grafika.* Praha 1940.
Petrasová, T. – Prahl, R. (eds.).: *Mnichov – Praha: Výtvarné umění mezi tradicí a modernou / München – Prag: Kunst zwischen Tradition und Moderne.* Praha 2012.
Petříček, M.: 'Krajiny duše', *Umění* 44, 1996, pp. 9–15.
Poche, E.: *František Kysela.* Praha 1956.
Prahl, R.: 'Příroda a ornament 1850–1900', *Umění a řemesla* 1973, no. 3, pp. 20–22.
Prahl, R. – Bydžovská, L. (eds.): *Volné směry: časopis secese a moderny.* Praha 1993.
Prahl, R.: 'Die tschechischen Secessionisten und ihre Aufnahme in Wien um 1900', *Umění* 41, 1993, pp. 3–25.
Prahl, R.: 'Hagenbund a Mánes: mezi Vídní a Prahou', *Umění* 45, 1997, pp. 445–466.
Prahl, R.: 'The "Pre-history" of Czech Art Modernism in Munich', *Umění* 54, 2006, pp. 57–68.
Prahl, R. – Šámal, P.: *Umění jako dekorace a symbol: výzdoba representačních staveb Prahy v éře historismu, secese a moderny.* Praha 2012.
Preisler, J., 'Dopis Jana Preislera Stanislavu Suchardovi', *Výtvarné umění* VI, 1956, pp. 228–229.

Rakušanová, M.: *Sabat nucených prací ve věznici vůle. Vlivy filozofie Arthura Schopenhauera na české umění a uměleckou teorii.* České Budějovice 2005.
Rakušanová, M.: 'Josef Váchal. Podvratník, technolog a magik o umění', *Umění* 60, 2012, pp. 478–508.
Rambousek, J.: 'Grafika Joži Uprky', *Hollar* VIII, 1931, pp. 1–8.
Rennert, J. – Weil, A.: *Alphonse Mucha, toutes les Affiches et Panneaux,* Uppsala 1984.
Ritter, W.: 'Bohumír Jaroněk', *Dílo* VII, 1909, pp. 151–167.
Rodin, A.: *O umění.* Praha 1961.
Rouček, R.: 'Dílo Josefa Mařatky', *Výtvarné umění* V, 1955, pp. 252–257.
Ruskin, J.: *Dvě stezky.* Praha 1909.

Šalda, F. X.: 'Nová krása: její geneze a charakter', *Volné směry* VII, 1903, pp. 169–178, 181–190.
Šalda, F. X.: 'Násilník snu', *Volné směry* IX, 1905, pp. 103–107.
Šalda, F. X.: *Boje o zítřek.* Praha 1905.
Šalda, F. X.: 'Prokletý malíř (Cézanne)', *Volné směry* XI, 1907, pp. 11–13.
Šaloun, L.: 'Z duševní dílny umělcovy', *Dílo* XV, 1920, pp. 83–90.
Savický, N.: *Francouzské moderní umění a česká politika v letech 1900–1939.* Praha 2011.
Sawicki, N.: *Na cestě k modernosti. Umělecké sdružení Osma a jeho okruh v letech 1900–1910.* Praha 2014.
Schneiderová, M.: 'Prehistorie v díle Jaroslava Panušky', *Umění* 58, 2010, pp. 123–135.
Šebek, J. (ed.) : *Jan Štursa. Svědectví současníků a dopisy.* Praha 1962.
Sedlář, J.: 'Secesní grafika Bohumíra Jaroňka', in: *Památková péče a ochrana přírody v Jihomoravském kraji.* Brno 1989, pp. 130–153.
Siblík, E.: 'František Kupka', *Hollar* VII, 1931, pp. 45–56.
Siblík, E.: *Josef Mařatka.* Praha 1935.
Silverman, L.: *Art Nouveau in Fin-de-Siécle France. Politics, Psychology and Style,* Berkeley – Los Angeles – London 1992.
Šindelář, D.: 'Korespondence Antonína Slavíčka z hlediska teorie umění', *Výtvarné umění* IV, 1954, pp. 128–134.
Slavíček, A.: *Malíře Antonína Slavíčka vybraná korespondence.* Edice Volných směrů Dráhy a cíle. Vol. 8. Praha 1910.
Slavíček, A.: *Vybrané listy Antonína Slavíčka.* Foreword by O. Nejedlý. Praha 1930.
Slavíček, A.: *Antonín Slavíček – Dopisy.* Foreword by V. Nezval. Praha 1954.
Šmejkal, F.: 'Nové hodnocení secese', *Výtvarná práce* IX, 1961, no. 4, pp. 4–5.
Šmejkal, F.: 'Povaha a význam secese', *Výtvarné umění* XII, 1962, pp. 20–32.
Šmejkal, F.: 'Česká symbolistní grafika', *Umění* 16, 1968, pp. 1–25.
Šmejkal, F.: 'Básník noci – K rané tvorbě Fr. Koblihy', *Umění* 22, 1974, pp. 340–354.
Šmejkal, F.: *Sursum 1910–1912.* Hradec Králové 1976.
Šmejkal, F.: 'Symbolika sfingy v umění přelomu století', *Umění* 27, 1979, pp. 401–426.
Šmejkal, F.: 'Secesně-symbolistní tvorba Ladislava Šalouna. Drobná plastika a kresba', *Umění* 28, 1980, pp. 469–479.
de Solier, R.: 'Prostor a barva u Kupky', *Výtvarné umění* XVIII, 1968, pp. 348–349.
Sombart, W.: *Umělecký průmysl a kultura.* Praha 1912.
Šourek, K. (ed.): *Dílo Jana Zrzavého.* Praha 1941.
Srp, K. – Orlíková, J.: *Jan Zrzavý.* Praha 2003.
Srp, K.: *František Kupka – geometrie myšlenek,* Řevnice 2012.
Šťastný, J. (Konůpek, J.): 'Kresebné dílo Felixe Jeneweina', *Hollar* III, 1926, pp. 26–36.
Šťastný, J. (Konůpek, J.).: 'Bohumír Jaroněk', *Hollar* VII, 1931, pp. 1–10.
Šťastný, J. (Konůpek, J.): 'O Josefu Váchalovi', *Hollar* XI, 1935, pp. 1–14.
Štech, V. V.: 'B. Ohmann', *Styl* I, 1909, pp. 120–121.
Štech, V. V.: 'Výstava uměleckého sdružení Sursum', *Umělecký měsíčník* I, 1912, pp. 338.
Štech, V. V.: *Včera a dnes.* Praha 1921
Štech, V. V.: 'Vzpomínka na A. Bourdella', *Volné směry* XXVII, 1929–1930, pp. 170–176.
Štech, V. V.: 'Úloha Joži Uprky', *Umění* V, 1932, pp. 276–282.
Štech, V. V.: 'O Zdence Braunerové', *Hollar* VIII, 1931–1932, pp. 49–56.
Štech, V. V.: 'Dílo a život – Poznámky o Antonínu Slavíčkovi', *Umění* VI, 1933, pp. 3–18, 119–134.
Štech, V. V.: *Moderní český dřevoryt.* Praha 1933.
Štech, V. V.: 'Miloš Jiránek', *Umění* X, 1937, pp. 3–8.
Štech, V. V.: *Pod povrchem tvarů.* Praha 1941.
Štech, V. V.: *Čtení o Antonínu Slavíčkovi.* Praha 1947.
Štech, V. V.: *Otakar Španiel.* Praha 1954.
Štech, V. V.: *Ludvík Kuba.* Praha 1949.
Stibral, J.: 'Dekorativní umění na Světové výstavě ve St. Louis', *Dílo* III, 1905, pp. 109–118, 122–130, 154–166.
Sucharda, S.: 'K soutěži na pomník Palackého', *Volné směry* II, 1898, cols. 426–436.
Sucharda, S.: 'Sochař Rodin', *Volné směry* V, 1901, pp. 143–146.
Sucharda, S.: *Historie pomníku Palackého v Praze.* Praha 1912.
Sůva, J.: *Soupis celoživotního díla Quido Kociána.* Hradec Králové 1975.
Švabinská, E.: *Vzpomínky z mládí.* Afterword by Z. Švabinská-Vejrychová. Praha 1960, 1962.
Švabinská, Z. – Ševčík, V. – Kuna, M.: *Max Švabinský: soupis kreslířského a malířského díla 1879–1916.* Kroměříž 2014.

Švácha, R.: *Od moderny k funkcionalismu. Proměny pražské architektury první poloviny dvacátého století.* Praha 1985.
Švácha, R.: 'Josef Chochol. Pokus o intimnější portrét', *Umění* 42, 1994, pp. 21–49.
Svrček, J. B.: *Miloš Jiránek.* Praha 1932.
Svrček, J. B.: *F. X. Šaldy boje a zápasy o výtvarné umění.* Praha 1947.

Táborský, F.: *Hanuš Schwaiger.* Praha 1904.
Teige, K.: *Jan Zrzavý.* Praha 1923.
Toman, P.: *Nový slovník čsl. výtvarných umělců,* 3rd edition, volume I Praha 1947, volume II Praha 1950.
Toman, P. H.: *Zdenka Braunerová.* Praha 1963.
Tomeš, J.: *Antonín Slavíček.* Praha 1966.

Uhlíř, L.: *Ladislav Šaloun a jeho dílo.* Praha 1930.
Urban, B. S.: 'Plakáty Arnošta Hofbauera', *Hollar* XII, 1936, pp. 23–29, 119–125.
Urban, O. M.: 'Kritik duše. Výtvarný kritik Karel Hlaváček', *Umění* 40, 1992, pp. 17–22.
Urban, O. M.: 'Procházkovo *prostibolo* a Hlaváčkova *duše*', *Umění* 45, 1997, pp. 430–444.
Urban, O. M.: *Karel Hlaváček: Výtvarné a kritické dílo.* Řevnice 2002.
Urban, O. M. – Vrbová, J. – Vrba, T.: *Edvard Munch. Být sám. Obrazy – deníky – ohlasy.* Řevnice 2006.

Vachtová, L.: *František Kupka.* Praha 1968.
Vancl, K.: *František Kaván.* Liberec 1962.
Vlček, T.: 'Der Baum im Schaffen Vojtěch Preissigs', *Jahrbuch der Hamburger Kunstsammlungen* XXI, 1976, p. 165n.
Vlček, T.: 'Vojtěch Preissig', *Výtvarné umění* XVIII, 1968, p. 306.
Vlček, T.: 'Preissigovy fotografie krajin', *Výtvarné umění* XX, 1970, p. 269.
Vlček, T.: 'Velká lyra českého symbolistního básníka, proletáře Karla Hlaváčka', *Umění* 23, 1975, pp. 299–325.
Vlček, T.: 'Ornament a styl. K problematice českého umění přelomu století', *Umění* 28, 1980, pp. 425–435.
Vlček, T., Sekalová, H. (eds.): *České secesní sklo: sborník mezinár. uměnovědného symposia pořádaného ÚTDU ČSAV v Srní 9.-12. 10.1985.* Praha 1985.
Vlček, T.: *Jakub Schikaneder.* Praha 1986.
Vlček, T.: *Praha 1900. Studie k dějinám kultury a umění Prahy v letech 1890–1914.* Praha 1986.
Vlčková, L.: *Vojtěch Preissig.* Praha 2012.
Volavka, V.: *J. V. Myslbek.* Praha 1942.
Volavková, H.: *Max Švabinský.* Praha 1977, 1982.
Vybíral, J.: *Česká architektura na prahu nové doby.* Praha 2002.
Vybíral, J.: *Mladí mistři. Architekti ze školy Otto Wagnera na Moravě a ve Slezsku.* Praha 2002.
Vybíral, J.: 'Německá architektura v Praze v letech 1900–1918. Tvůrci a záměry', *Umění* 51, 2003, pp. 306–324.
Vybíral, J.: *Friedrich Ohmann. Objev baroku a počátky moderní architektury v Čechách. / Die Entdeckung des Barocks und die Anfänge der modernen Architektur in Böhmen.* Praha 2013.
'Výstava Joži Uprky', *Volné směry* I, 1897, cols. 227–234.

Wagner, O.: *Moderní architektura.* Praha 1910.
Wenig, J.: *Malíř chodského lidu Jaroslav Špillar.* Plzeň 1960.
Winter, T.: 'Vodník a nevědomí', *Umění* 56, 2008, pp. 206–220.
Wirth, Z.: 'Okresní dům v Hradci Králové', *Volné směry* X, 1906, pp. 297–299.
Wirth, Z.: 'Nové budovy české univerzity', *Volné směry* XI, 1907, pp. 47–48.
Wirth, Z.: 'Jubilejní výstava v Praze', *Styl* I, 1909, pp. 183–193.
Wirth, Z.: 'Vila v Čechách', *Styl* II, 1910, pp. III.–VI.
Wirth, Z.: 'Životní dílo J. M. Olbricha', *Styl* II, 1910, pp. 93–95.
Wirth, Z. – Matějček, A.: *Česká architektura XIX. století (1800–1920).* Praha 1922.
Wirth, Z.: 'Jan Kotěra kreslíř', *Umění* XV, 1944, pp. 253– 270.
Wittlich, P.: 'E. A. Bourdelle a jeho výstava r. 1909 v Praze', *Umění* 9, 1961, pp. 476–484.
Wittlich, P.: 'Mladý Bohumil Kafka', *Výtvarné umění* XII, 1962, pp. 353–359.
Wittlich, P.: 'Gutfreundův kubismus', *Umění* 14, 1966, pp. 247–256.
Wittlich, P.: 'Secesní Orfeus. Symbolika formy v českém secesním sochařství', *Umění* 16, 1968, pp. 26–49.
Wittlich, P.: 'Kupka a dealegorizace pohybu', *Umění* 17, 1969, no. 2, pp. 168–172.
Wittlich, P.: 'Poznámky k významu secesního ornamentu v díle Alfonse Muchy', *Umění a řemesla* 1973, no. 3, pp. 28–29.
Wittlich, P.: *Zeichnungen aus der Epoche des Jugendstils* (also published in English, French and Japanese editions). Praha 1974.
Wittlich, P.: *České sochařství ve XX. století.* Praha 1978.
Wittlich, P.: 'Preislerovo Jaro. Slohová syntéza a vývojové tendence českého umění kolem 1900', *Umění* 28, 1980, pp. 401–424.
Wittlich, P.: *Česká secese.* Praha 1982.
Wittlich, P.: 'Edvard Munch a české umění', *Umění* 30, 1982, pp. 422–447.
Wittlich, P.: *Umění a život. Doba secese.* Praha 1987.
Wittlich, P.: *Jan Preisler: Kresby.* Praha 1988.
Wittlich, P.: *Prague. Fin de Siécle,* Paris 1992.
Wittlich, P.: *Sochařství české secese.* Praha 2000.
Wittlich, P.: *Jan Štursa.* Praha 2008.
Wittlich, P.: *Horizonty umění.* Praha 2010.
Wittlich, P.: *Malíři české secese.* Praha 2012.

Wittlich, P.: 'Pod velkým stromem. Pařížský pobyt sochaře Bohumila Kafky 1904–1908', *Umění* 60, 2012, pp. 470–477.
Wittlich, P.: *Bohumil Kafka 1878–1942. Příběh sochaře*. Praha 2014.

Zachař, M.: *František Kaván*. Praha 2009.
Žákavec, F.: *O českých výtvarnících*. Praha 1920.
Žákavec, F.: *Dílo Dušana Jurkoviče*. Praha 1929.
Žákavec, F.: 'Raný Švabinský (Skizza z monografie)', *Umění* V, 1932, pp. 441–497.
Žákavec, F.: *Max Švabinský* I. Praha 1933.
Žákavec, F.: 'Artuš Scheiner sedmdesátníkem', *Umění* VII, 1934, pp. 397–401.
Žákavec, F.: *Max Švabinský* II. Praha 1936
Žákavec, F.: 'Posmrtný soubor díla Aloise Kalvody', *Umění* IX, 1936, pp. 365–371.
Žákavec, F.: 'O spolupráci F. X. Šaldy s „Mánesem"', *Umění* X, 1937, pp. 379, 429.
Žákavec, F.: 'František Kaván', *Umění* XI, 1938, pp. 109–124.
Zemina, J. (ed.): *Svět Jana Zrzavého*. Praha 1963.

B) Exhibition catalogues and publications (selection). Monographic (by artist)

Mikoláš Aleš. Antonín Hudeček. Francouzská grafika. Praha, pavilon SVU Mánes v Kinského zahradě 1902.
Mikoláš Aleš. J. Brabcová. Praha, Národní galerie 1976.
Mikoláš Aleš 1852–2007. O. Chrobák. Praha, Národní galerie and Správa Pražského hradu 2007.

Výstava prací Františka Bílka. Praha, kostel sv. Martina ve zdi 1908.
František Bílek – výbor z díla. M. Mrázová-Schusterová. Praha, Galerie hl. města Prahy 1966.
František Bílek a kniha. J. Kudláček. Praha, Galerie D 1966.
František Bílek – výběr z kreseb. M. Mrázová. Praha, Galerie hl. města Prahy and Národní galerie 1978.
František Bílek (1872–1941). P. Wittlich, O. M. Urban, A. Filip – R. Musil, H. Larvová (ed.), D. Mikulejská, J. Med, J. Vojvodík, X. Galmiche, M. Kreuzzieger, J. Rous, J. Vybíral, D. Koudelková, M. Růžička, M. Mrázová. Praha, Galerie hlavního města Prahy 2000.
František Bílek (1872–1941). P. Wittlich, O. M. Urban, H. Larvová, M. Kreuzzieger, J. Rous, M. Růžička, D. Koudelková, J. Vybíral, Paris, Musée Bourdelle 2002.
František Bílek a jeho pražský ateliér. S. Baborovská, K. Srp (eds.). P. Wittlich, J. Vybíral, Z. Lukeš, M. Krummholz, F. Bílek, H. Larvová. Praha, Galerie hlavního města Prahy 2010.
Zdenka Braunerová. M. Nováková. Roztoky u Prahy, Středočeské muzeum 1983.

Posmrtná výstava V. H. Brunnera a vzpomínková výstava Jana Preislera. J. Pečírka. Praha, SVU Mánes, Obecní dům 1928.

Architekt Alois Dryák. V. Šuman. Praha, F. Topič 1930
Bohuslav Dvořák – souborná výstava. A. Matějček. Praha, SVU Mánes 1949.

Josef Gočár – výstava architektonických návrhů. M. Benešová. Praha, Galerie Jaroslava Fragnera 1971.

Arnošt Hofbauer – posmrtná výstava. K. Novotný. Praha, SVU Mánes 1944.
Vlastislav Hofman. M. Nešlehová (ed.), P. Gába, J. Fronek, G. Pelikánová, M. Svobodová, J. Trtíková, V. Velemanová, L. Vlčková, A. Dean. Ostrava, Galerie výtvarného umění 2017.
Jan Honsa 1876–1937: výběr z malířského díla. P. Chalupa, A. Rezler. Kutná Hora, Galerie Felixe Jeneweina 2007.
Jaroslav Horejc – souborné dílo. M. Krejčí. Praha, Galerie hl. města Prahy 1976
Jaroslav Horejc 1886–1983: Mistr českého art deca. O. Malá (ed.), V. Hnídková, M. Lehmannová, E. Neumannová. Praha, Galerie hlavního města Prahy 2016.
Václav Hradecký, 1867–1940. J. Kohoutek. Praha, Památník národního písemnictví 1972.
Antonín Hudeček – posmrtná výstava. A. Brynychová (A. Masaryková). Praha, SVU Mánes 1942.
Antonín Hudeček – souborná výstava. K. Wellner. Štramberk 1912.
Antonín Hudeček – souborná výstava. F. Žákavec. Praha, SVU Mánes, Obecní dům 1922.
Antonín Hudeček – souborná výstava. A. Matějček. Praha, SVU Mánes 1932.
Antonín Hudeček – posmrtná výstava. A. Brynychová (A. Masaryková). Praha, SVU Mánes 1942.
Antonín Hudeček – obrazy. M. Chaloupková, Hradec Králové, Krajská galerie výtvarného umění 1972.
Antonín Hudeček. J. Boučková. Pardubice, Východočeská galerie 1982.

Bohumír Jaroněk (1866–1933). V. Jůza. Ostrava, Galerie výtvarného umění 1990.
Felix Jenewein 1857–1905. R. Musil. Praha, Národní galerie 1996.
Posmrtná souborná výstava Miloše Jiránka. Praha, pavilon SVU Mánes v Kinského zahradě 1912.
Souborná výstava Miloše Jiránka. Praha, SVU Mánes 1936.
Miloš Jiránek. Zápas o moderní malbu. 1875–1911. T. Winter. Cheb, Galerie výtvarného umění 2012.
Dušan Jurkovič: architekt a jeho dům. D. Bořutová, M. Lehmannová. Brno, Moravská galerie 2010.

Bohumil Kafka – životní dílo. V. Procházka. Praha, Národní galerie 1962.

Alois Kalvoda. Život a dílo. J. Zemanová. Jihlava, Oblastní galerie Vysočiny 1998.

František Kaván: krajiny. M. Zachař. Praha, SVU Mánes 2016.

František Kaván: symbolistní, dekadentní. Z. Novotná. Praha, Národní galerie 2012.

Celda Klouček, sochař, návrhář a paleontolog. J. Mergl, M. Mergl. Plzeň, Západočeské muzeum 2010.

Beneš Knüpfer 1844–1910. J. Fialová. Praha, Národní galerie 1984.

František Kobliha – výběr z životního díla. F. Šmejkal. Hradec Králové, Krajská galerie výtvarného umění 1973.

Katalog výstavy Quido Kociána. F. K. Hořice v Podkrkonoší, Městské muzeum 1932.

Quido Kocián 1874–1928. Výběr z díla. J. Sůva. Hradec Králové, Krajská galerie výtvarného umění 1975.

Český sochař Quido Kocián (1874–1928). Výběr z díla. P. Holý. Hořice v Podkrkonoší, Galerie plastik 2004.

Ladislav Jan Kofránek (1880–1954). Výbor z díla. M. Halířová. Praha, Galerie hl. města Prahy 1973.

Ladislav Jan Kofránek (1880–1954): sochař mezi tradicí a modernou. S. Baborovská (ed.), P. Wittlich, M. Pencák, V. Hnídková, J. Cermanová. Praha, Vysoká škola uměleckoprůmyslová 2008.

Jan Konůpek. Poutník v nekonečnu. / A Pilgrim to Infinity. H. Larvová (ed.), J. Rous, V. Šusová, J. Horneková. Praha, Galerie hlavního města Prahy and Památník národního písemnictví 1998.

Jan Kotěra. M. Benešová. Praha, Mánes 1972.

Jan Kotěra 1871–1923, zakladatel moderní české architektury. V. Šlapeta (ed.), J. Vybíral, D. Prelovšek, Z. Lukeš, R. Švácha, P. Krajči, R. Kreuzziegerová, A. Pomajzlová, D. Karasová, V. Skálová, L. Losos, V. Valchářová, P. Šopák. Praha, Obecní dům 2001.

Kotěra. Po stopách moderny. J. Potůček. Hradec Králové, Muzeum východních Čech 2013.

Jan Koula. J. E. Koula. Praha, Národní technické muzeum 1955.

Emil Králíček: zapomenutý mistr secese a kubismu. Z. Lukeš, V. Hnídková. Praha, Galerie Jaroslava Fragnera 2005.

Ludvík Kuba (1863–1956), poslední impresionista. V. Hulíková (ed.), P. Kaleta, J. Langhammerová, P. Štembera. Praha, Národní galerie 2013.

Bohumil Kubišta – grafika. M. Nešlehová, Praha, Galerie Zdeňka Sklenáře 2014.

Bohumil Kubišta. Zářivý krystal. K. Srp (ed.), G. Pelikánová, Z. Novotná. Ostrava, Galerie výtvarného umění 2014.

Kupka. J. Cassou. Paris, Musée national d'art moderne 1958.

Kupka. Malby, kresby, grafika z let 1899–1946. L. Vachtová. Písek, Vlastivědné museum, České Budějovice, Dům umění 1962.

František Kupka, 1871–1957. J. Kotalík, B. Dorival, L. Vachtová. Praha, Národní galerie 1968.

František Kupka. L. Vachtová. Hradec Králové, Krajská galerie výtvarného umění 1971.

František Kupka 1871–1957: A Retrospective. M. Mladek, M. Rowell. New York, The Solomon R. Guggenheim Museum 1975.

František Kupka (1871–1957) ou l'invention d'une abstraction. S. Pagé, J. Kotalík, L. Vachtová, M. Lamač. Paris, Musée d'art moderne de la Ville de Paris 1989.

František Kupka ze sbírky Jana a Medy Mládkových ve Washingtonu. J. Sekera, M. Mládková. Praha, České muzeum výtvarných umění 1996.

František Kupka. Průkopník abstrakce, malíř kosmu. J. Anděl, B. B. Mandelbrot, D. Kosinská (ed.), P. Brullé, M. Theinhardtová. Praha, Národní galerie 1998.

Vers des temps nouveaux: Kupka, oeuvres graphiques 1894–1912. P. Brullé, M.-P. Salé, M. Theinhardt. Paris, Musée d'Orsay 2002.

František Kupka: la collection du Centre Georges Pompidou. P. Brullé, B. Leal, F. Malsch. Paris, Musée national d'art moderne, Centre Georges Pompidou 2003.

František Kupka: Cesta k Amorfě. Kupkovy salony 1899–1913. H. Musilová, M. Theinhardtová, P. Brullé (eds.), V. Lahoda, B. Leal, T. Pospiszyl, K. Srp. Praha, Národní galerie 2012.

Orbis pictus Františka Kupky. Mezi symbolismem a reportáží. P. Brullé, M. Theinhardtová (eds.), M. Dixmier. Plzeň, Západočeská galerie 2014.

Posmrtná výstava obrazů Otakara Lebedy. K. D. Mráz (K. Domorázek). Praha 1901.

Otakar Lebeda. J. Kotalík. Roudnice n. L., Galerie výtvarného umění 1977. Praha, Středočeská galerie 1978.

Otakar Lebeda (1877–1901). V. Hulíková. Praha, Národní galerie 2009.

Josef Mařatka – kresby a plastiky. M. Halířová-Muchová. Praha, Galerie hl. města Prahy 1969.

Výstava Maroldova. W. Ritter, K. M. Čapek. Praha, Jednota umělců výtvarných 1899.

Luděk Marold 1865–1898. J. Orlíková, P. Štembera. Praha, Národní galerie and Obecní dům 1998.

Alfons Mucha 1860–1939. M. Laclotte, J. Kotalík, J. Brabcová, G. Lacambre, M. Bascou. Paris, Grand Palais, Darmstadt, Mathildenhöhe, Praha, Národní galerie 1980.

Alfons Mucha. Tjeckisk Art Nouveau. J. Kotalík, J. Brabcová, E. Högestätt (et al.). Malmö, Konsthall 1981.

Alphonse Mucha. The Spirit of Art Nouveau. J. Kotalík, J. Brabcová, N. Shimada. Tokyo 1983

The 50th year anniversary exhibition of Alphonse Mucha. J. Brabcová, V. Čiháková, J. Kotalík, J. Mucha, I. Saito, N. Shimada. Hokkaido, Museum of Modern Art 1991

Alfons Mucha: pastely, plakáty, kresby a fotografie. P. Wittlich, S. Mucha, G. Mucha. Praha, Mucha Foundation, Správa Pražského hradu 1994.

Alfons Mucha: das slawische Epos. K. Srp, L. Bydžovská (eds.), W. Denk, Z. Hojda, A. Mucha, M. Petříček, J. Šetřilová, Z. Váňa, E. Vyslonzil. Krems, Kunstalle 1994.

Alphonse Mucha: His Life and Art. P. Wittlich (ed.), L. Bydžovská, K. Srp, N. Shimada, V. Čiháková. Tokyo, Mucha Foundation, The Bunkamura Museum of Art 1995.

Alphonse Mucha and the Spirit of Art Nouveau. Y. K. Centeno, P. Wittlich. Lisbon, Calouste Gulbenkian Museum 1997.

Alfons Mucha – Paříž 1900: Le Pater / Otčenáš. Alphonse Mucha – Paris 1900: Le Pater / The Lord's Prayer. A. Dvořák, H. Bieri Thomson, B. de Boysson. Praha, Obecní dům 2002.

Alfons Mucha – Paříž 1900: Pavilon Bosny a Hercegoviny na Světové výstavě. Alphonse Mucha – Paris 1900: The Pavilion of Bosnia and Herzegovina at the World Exhibition. M. Hlavačka, J. Orlíková, P. Štembera. Praha, Obecní dům 2002.

Alfons Mucha: Slovanstvo bratrské – Fraternal Slavdom – Brüderliches Slawentum – les Slaves fraternels. L. Bydžovská, K. Srp (eds.), F. S. Procházka. Praha, Galerie hlavního města Prahy 2005.

Alfons Mucha. J.-L. Gaillemin, K. Srp, L. Bydžovská, A. Husslein-Arco, M. Hilaire, Ch. Lange. Wien, Oesterreichische Galerie Belvedere 2009.

Alfons Mucha. Tváře / Faces. P. Wittlich. Kutná Hora, Galerie Středočeského kraje 2010.

Alfons Mucha. Slovanská epopej. L. Bydžovská, K. Srp (eds.), D. Lobstein, M. Petříček, M. Theinhardtová, T. Berger. Praha, Galerie hlavního města Prahy 2011.

Almanach Slovanské epopeje. J. Orlíková, H. Larvová, P. Nosek, J. Mucha-Plocková, T. Berger, H. Svatošová, R. Sedláková, V. Králíček, V. Čiháková-Noshiro (ed.). Praha, AICA, Galerie kritiků 2011.

Edvard Munch. K. Svoboda. Praha, pavilon SVU Mánes v Kinského zahradě 1905.

Edvard Munch og den tsjekkiske Kunst. B. Torjusen, J. Kotalík. Oslo, Munch Museet 1971.

Karel Myslbek. M. Mrázová. Praha, Špálova galerie 1974.

Willy Nowak (1886–1977): výběr z malířského díla. J. Orlíková. Cheb, Galerie výtvarného umění 2007.

Jaroslav Panuška. J. Boučková. Pardubice, Východočeská galerie 1978.

Jaroslav Panuška (1872–1958). O. Hanel. Praha, České muzeum výtvarných umění 1994.

Soubor díla Maxe Pirnera (1854–1924). A. Matějček. Praha, SVU Mánes 1924.

Maxmilian Pirner (1854–1924): výbor z malířského díla. R. Prahl. Plzeň, Západočeská galerie 1979.

Maxmilian Pirner 1854–1924. R. Prahl. Praha, Národní galerie 1987.

Jan Preisler. V. Beneš. Praha, SVU Mánes, Rudolfinum 1919.

Souborná výstava Jana Preislera, 1872–1918. J. Zamazal. Brno, Klub výtvarných umělců Aleš 1935.

Jan Preisler. V. Rada. Praha, Alšova síň Umělecké besedy 1955.

Jan Preisler, 1872–1918. J. Kotalík. Praha, Národní galerie 1964.

Jan Preisler. Putování krajinami duše. P. Wittlich. Plzeň, Západočeská galerie 1994.

Jan Preisler 1872–1918. L. Bydžovská, K. Srp, P. Wittlich (ed.). Praha, Obecní dům 2003.

Výstava grafických prací a kreseb Vojtěcha Preissiga. K. D. Mráz (K. Domorázek). Praha, Topičův salon 1907.

Vojtěch Preissig 1873–1944. Výběr z grafické tvorby. F. Dvořák. Praha, Hollar 1963.

Vojtěch Preissig. T. Vlček. Praha, Galerie V. Špály and Nová síň 1968.

Vojtěch Preissig 1873–1944. J. Boučková. Pardubice, Východočeská galerie 1973.

Vojtěch Preissig 1873–1944. Průvodce výstavou životního díla Vojtěcha Preissiga. T. Vlček. Praha, Národní galerie 2004.

Jindřich Prucha. V. V. Štech. Praha, SVU Mánes 1926.

Jindřich Prucha – Lomy. T. Pospiszyl. Praha, Národní galerie 1999.

Jindřich Prucha: malby a kresby z let 1907–1914. J. Zemina, Z. Sejček. Litoměřice, Severočeská galerie výtvarného umění 2003.

Václav Radimský 1867–1946. N. Blažíčková-Horová (ed.), M. Theinhardtová. Praha, Galerie hlavního města Prahy 2011.

Katalog výstavy děl sochaře Aust. Rodina v Praze. F. X. Šalda, S. Sucharda. Praha SVU Mánes 1902.

Pocta Rodinovi: 1902–1992. M. Halířová, P. Wittlich, M. Juříková. Praha, Galerie hlavního města Prahy, Národní galerie and Uměleckoprůmyslové muzeum 1992.

L. Šaloun. Drobná plastika a kresby. F. Šmejkal. Hradec Králové, Krajská galerie výtvarného umění 1980.

Tvorba sochaře Ladislava Šalouna (1870–1946). P. Wittlich, D. Došková. Praha, Národní muzeum 2000.

Jakub Schikaneder 1855–1924. J. Kotalík. Praha, Středočeská galerie 1977.

Jakub Schikaneder 1855–1924. Malíř Prahy přelomu století. Tematický průvodce retrospektivní výstavou. T. Vlček. Praha, Národní galerie 1998.
Jakub Schikaneder (1855–1924). V. Hulíková (ed.), T. Vlček, T. Sekyrka, Z. Grohmanová, V. Cedlová, R. Šefců. Praha, Národní galerie 2012.
Hanuš Schwaiger – souborná výstava. Praha, galerie Ruch, leden 1887.
Hanuš. Schwaiger – posmrtná výstava. Praha, pavilon SVU Mánes v Kinského zahradě 1912.
Hanuš Schwaiger – souborná výstava. V. V. Štech. Praha, Jednota umělců výtvarných 1937.
Hanuš Schwaiger – souborná výstava. M. Lamač. Praha, Mánes 1954. Brno, Dům umění 1955.
Hanuš Schwaiger (1854–1912). T. Mikuláštík. Zlín, Oblastní galerie výtvarného umění 1982.
Malíř a grafik T. F. Šimon 1877–1942. E. Bužgová. Praha, Národní galerie 1994.
T. F. Šimon – cesta kolem světa v 80 obrazech. V. Háje, P. Šimon, J. Třeštík. Praha, Galerie U Křižovníků 2004.
Antonín Slavíček. Anon. Praha, pavilon SVU Mánes v Kinského zahradě 1910.
Jubilejní výstava díla Antonína Slavíčka. V. Beneš. Praha, SVU Mánes 1932.
Antonín Slavíček 1870–1910. J. Kotalík. Praha, Národní galerie 1961.
Antonín Slavíček 1870–1910. P. Wittlich, R. Prahl, M. Rakušanová, K. Srp. Praha, Galerie hlavního města Prahy and Gallery 2004.
Otakar Španiel 1881–1955, životní dílo. V. V. Štech. Praha, Mánes 1956.
Karel Špillar 1871–1939. N. Řeháková, P. Štembera. Praha, Obecní dům 2000.
Jan Štursa 1880–1925. V. V. Štech. Praha, SVU Mánes, refektář Klementina 1926.
Jan Štursa 1880–1925. J. Kotalík. Praha, Národní galerie 1980.
Stanislav Sucharda 1866–1916. M. Krummholz. Nová Paka, Městské muzeum 2006.
Vojta Sucharda – český sochař. J. A. Novotný. Praha, Galerie hl. města Prahy 1978. Nová Paka, Suchardovský dům 1978.
Max Švabinský – soubor prací. V. V. Štech. Praha, SVU Mánes, Obecní dům 1923.
Max Švabinský – souborná výstava díla. A. Matějček. Praha, SVU Mánes 1932.
Památník Maxe Švabinského. L. Páleníček, J. Kotalík. Kroměříž, Uměleckohistorické muzeum 1965.
Max Švabinský, 1873–1962. J. Kotalík, L. Páleníček, V. Silovský, M. Holý. Kroměříž, Okresní muzeum – Památník Maxe Švabinského. Praha 1973.
Max Švabinský. Ráj a mýtus. J. Orlíková (ed.), J. Wittlichová, E. Růžička – K. Urbánek. Praha, Gallery, Valdštejnská jízdárna 2001.

Franta Uprka 1868–1929. J. Kačer, Hodonín, Galerie výtvarného umění 2008.
Joža Uprka. Z. Braunerová. Brno, Pavilon v Lužánkách 1897. Praha, Topičův salon 1897.
Joža Uprka 1861–1940. Evropan slováckého venkova. H. Musilová (ed.), E. Bendová. Praha, Národní galerie 2011.

Josef Váchal – dřevorytec. A. Sáňka. Brno, pavilon KVU Aleš 1926.
Josef Váchal, výbor z celoživotního díla 1906–1954. M. Mrázová-Schusterová. Praha, Galerie hl. města Prahy 1966.
Josef Váchal. J. Pellarová. Hradec Králové, Krajská galerie výtvarného umění 1970.
Josef Váchal. Dílo. M. Šejn, J. Čeliš. Roudnice nad Labem, Oblastní galerie výtvarného umění 1984.
Josef Váchal. M. Ajvaz, P. Hruška, J. Kroutvor, J. Pelánek. Praha, Galerie Rudolfinum 1994.
Josef Váchal – magie hledání. M. Rakušanová. Praha, Galerie hl. města Prahy 2014.
Josef Váchal: napsal, vyryl, vytiskl a svázal. M. Rakušanová. Praha, Galerie hlavního města Prahy 2014.

Souborná výstava prací Jana Zrzavého. Jan Zrzavý. Praha, Topičův salon 1918.
Souborná výstava prací Jana Zrzavého 1918–1923. Praha, Umělecká beseda 1923.
Katalog výstavy prací Jana Zrzavého. J. Šíma. Praha, Umělecká beseda 1931.
Jan Zrzavý. J. A. Brabcová, J. Zemina, J. Zrzavý. Praha, Národní galerie 1990.
Jan Zrzavý – Božská hra. K. Srp (ed.), L. Bydžovská, V. Lahoda, Z. Novotná. Ostrava, Dům umění 2012.

Group and thematic (chronological)

Jubilejní výstava zemská království Českého v Praze 1891. Praha 1894.
Národopisná výstava českoslovanská. Hlavní katalog a průvodce. J. Kafka (ed.), Praha 1895.
Výstava architektury a inženýrství. Hlavní katalog a průvodce. J. Kafka (ed.), Praha 1898.
Moderní francouzské umění. F. X. Šalda. Praha, pavilon SVU Mánes v Kinského zahradě 1902.
Worpswede. R. Muther. Praha, pavilon SVU Mánes v Kinského zahradě 1902.

Umění 1900: obrazy, plastiky, plakáty, knihy. V. Volavka, Praha, Topičův salon 1940.
Zakladatelé moderního českého umění. M. Lamač. Brno, Dům umění 1957.
Sbírka českého sochařství. V. Procházka. Zámek Zbraslav, Národní galerie 1961.
Česká secese – Umění 1900. J. Kotalík (ed.), J. Mašín, E. Poche. Hluboká n. V., AJG 1966. Brno, Dům umění 1966.
Na rozhraní století – výstava ze sbírek Karáskovy galerie. E. Štiková. Praha, Památník národního písemnictví 1967.
F. X. Šalda a výtvarné umění. J. Kotalík, P. Spielmann. Liberec, Galerie výtvarného umění 1967. Praha, Národní galerie 1968.
Symbolismus v českém výtvarném umění. J. Rous. Cheb, Galerie výtvarného umění 1970. Praha, Galerie U Řečických 1970.
České malířství XX. století ze sbírek Národní galerie v Praze, díl I. – generace let devadesátých. J. Kotalík. Praha, Národní galerie 1971.
České malířství 1850–1918. M. Mrázová-Schusterová. Praha, Galerie hl. města Prahy 1971.
Český plakát 1890–1914. T. Vlček. Praha, Uměleckoprůmyslové muzeum, 1971.
České malířství XX. století ze sbírek Národní galerie v Praze, díl II. – generace Osmy, Tvrdošíjných, Umělecké besedy. J. Kotalík. Praha, Národní galerie 1973.
Česká kresba z přelomu století I – Symbolismus. F. Šmejkal. Hradec Králové, Krajská galerie výtvarného umění 1974.
Osma. L. Nosková. Roudnice, Galerie výtvarného umění 1977.
Česká secese. Užité umění. A. Adlerová, G. Urbánek, J. Svoboda. Praha, Uměleckoprůmyslové muzeum 1981.
Světlo v českém malířství – generace osmdesátých a devadesátých let 19. století. T. Vlček. Praha, Galerie hlavního města Prahy 1982.
Česká kniha z přelomu 19. a 20. století. J. Rous. Praha, Uměleckoprůmyslové muzeum 1983.
Tschechische Kunst 1878–1914. Auf dem Weg in die Moderne. J. Kotalík (et al.), Darmstadt, Mathildenhöhe 1984.
Secesní cín 1894–1914 ze sbírek Uměleckoprůmyslového muzea v Praze a Krajského vlastivědného muzea v Olomouci. H. Koenigsmarková. Olomouc, Krajské vlastivědné muzeum 1984.
Secesní sklo z Klášterského Mlýna 1895–1914. A. Adlerová. Kašperské Hory, Muzeum Šumavy, Praha, Uměleckoprůmyslové muzeum 1984–1985.
Czech Modernism 1900–1945. J. Anděl, A. W. Tucker. Houston, Museum of Fine Arts 1989.
Umění na Jubilejní výstavě před sto lety. R. Prahl, J. Vybíral, V. Erben, J. Noll, Z. Hojda. Plzeň, Západočeská galerie v Plzni 1991.
Moderní galerie tenkrát: 1902–1942. A. Pomajzlová, T. Sekyrka, R. Prahl, V. Vlnas, J. Vybíral, R. Musil (ed.), N. Savický, M. Nejezchlebová. Praha, Národní galerie 1992.
Vergangene Zukunft. Tschechische Moderne 1890 bis 1918. L. Bydžovská, T. Vlček (ed.), P. Wittlich, V. Lahoda, K. Srp. Vídeň, Künstlerhaus 1993.
Expresionismus a české umění 1905–1927. R. Grebeníčková, P. Liška, V. Lahoda, K. Srp, A. Pomajzlová (ed.), V. Erben, J. Doubravová, I. Janáková, R. Vondráček, R. Švácha, J. Vybíral, Z. Lukeš, V. Ptáčková, M. Bregant. Praha, Národní galerie 1994.
Mezery v historii 1890–1938: polemický duch střední Evropy – Němci, Židé, Češi. H. Rousová (ed.), O. Urban, A. Pařík, A. Janištinová, N. Řeháková, J. Sedlářová, J. Kroutvor, I. Tomaschke, J. Vybíral, Z. Lukeš. Praha, Galerie hlavního města Prahy 1994.
Moderní revue 1894–1925. O. M. Urban, L. Merhaut (eds.), J. Zizler, J. Med, Z. Pešat, Z. Hrbata, P. Wittlich, R. Prahl, V. Lahoda, H. Kadečková, C. Servant, D. Chirico, I. Slavík, R. B. Pynsent, F. Wittlich, I. Janáková, A. Zach. Praha, Národní galerie 1995.
Umělecké sdružení Sursum 1910–1912. H. Larvová (ed.), K. Srp, R. Dačeva, J. Dejmková, O. Malá, L. Bydžovská. Praha, Galerie hlavního města Prahy and Památník národního písemnictví 1996.
Důvěrný prostor – nová dálka: umění pražské secese. P. Wittlich (ed.), O. M. Urban, L. Bydžovská, K. Srp, Z. Lukeš, D. Stehlíková, I. Janáková, D. Karasová, V. Vokáčová, S. Petrová, J. Horneková, K. Hlaváčková, E. Uchalová. Praha, Obecní dům 1997.
Od valčíku po tango. Česká móda 1890–1918. E. Uchalová. Praha, Uměleckoprůmyslové muzeum 1997.
Prague Art Nouveau: Métamorphoses d'un style. P. Wittlich (ed.), J. Vybíral, V. Vokáčová, E. Uchalová, O. M. Urban, R. Švácha, J. Mlčoch, Z. Lukeš, V. Lahoda. Bruxelles, Palais des Beaux-Arts 1998
Prague 1900. Poetry and Ecstasy. M. Huig, L. Merhaut, M. Ottlová, R. Prahl (ed.), P. Wittlich, I. Janáková, S. Petrová, A. Pomajzlová. Amsterdam, Van Gogh Museum 1999.
Křídla slávy. Vojtěch Hynais, čeští Pařížané a Francie. M. Mžyková, P. Vaisse, T. Burollet, G.-G. Lemaire, M. Theinhardtová, P. Štembera, S. Le Men. Praha, Galerie Rudolfinum 2000.
Zajatci hvězd a snů. Katolická moderna a její časopis Nový život (1896–1907). R. Musil, A. Filip (eds.), J. Rak, J. Hanuš, P. Marek, E. Burget, A. K. K. Kudláč, H. Klínková, M. C. Putna, V. Skalická, P. Holman, J. Gabrielová, I. Janáková, F. Suchomel. Brno, Moravská galerie 2000.
Sen o říši krásy. Sbírka Jiřího Karáska ze Lvovic. R. Dačeva (ed.), J. Med, L. Slavíček, P. Preiss, T. Vlček, J. Assmann, J. Orlíková.

Praha, Obecní dům and Památník národního písemnictví 2001.
Vídeňská secese a moderna 1900–1925: užité umění a fotografie v českých zemích. M. Ambroz (et al.). Brno, Moravská galerie 2005.
V barvách chorobných. Idea dekadence a umění v českých zemích 1880–1914. O. M. Urban (ed.), D. Vojtěch, L. Merhaut. Praha, Obecní dům 2006.
Neklidem k bohu. Náboženské výtvarné umění v Čechách a na Moravě v letech 1870–1914. A. Filip, R. Musil (eds.), T. Petráček, R. Prahl, J. Vojvodík, L. Jirásko, J. T. Kotalík, T. Sekyrka, V. Birgus, T. Petrasová, Z. Hojda. Olomouc, Muzeum umění 2007.
Křičte ústa. Předpoklady expresionismu. M. Rakušanová, P. Wittlich, V. Lahoda, J. Vomáčka, K. Ocovská, J. Esser, M. Rauschmeyer. Praha, Galerie hlavního města Prahy 2007.
Sváry zření. Fazety modernity na přelomu 19. a 20. století 1890–1918. P. Wittlich, V. Lahoda, M. Rakušanová, K. Srp. Ostrava, Galerie výtvarného umění 2008.
Artěl: umění pro všední den: 1908–1935. J. Fronek, H. Brožková, K. Hlaváčková. Praha, Uměleckoprůmyslové muzeum 2009.
Metamorfózy politiky. Pražské pomníky 19. století. K. Kuthanová (ed.), J. Pokorný, Z. Hojda, A. Hnojil, M. Krummholz, P. Šámal, V. Vlnas, D. Stehlíková. Praha, Archiv hlavního města Prahy and Národní galerie 2013.
Secese – vitální umění 1900. L. Vlčková, R. Vondráček (eds.), H. Koenigsmarková, P. Wittlich, O. M. Urban, I. Knobloch. Praha, Uměleckoprůmyslové muzeum 2013.
Japonismus v českém umění. M. Hánová. Praha, Národní galerie v 2014.
Na okraji davu. Umění a sociální otázka v 19. století. E. Bendová, I. Jonáková, R. Prahl. Plzeň, Západočeská galerie 2014.
Tajemné dálky. Symbolismus v českých zemích 1880–1914. O. M. Urban (ed.), L. Merhaut, P. Ježková. Olomouc, Muzeum umění 2014.
Mnichov: zářící metropole umění 1870–1918 / München: leuchtende Kunstmetropole 1870–1918. A. Filip, R. Musil (eds.), E. Bendová, V. Hulíková, I. Jonáková, G. Leistner (et al.). Plzeň, Západočeská galerie 2015.
Topičův salon 1894–1899. K. Brožová, A. Hekrdlová, I. Lehkoživová, T. Novotná, P. Šámal, P. Štembera. Praha, Společnost Topičova salonu 2015.
Syntonos a plenérová krajinomalba přelomu 19. a 20. století. M. Fišer, M. Zachař, H. Bilavčíková. Cheb, Galerie výtvarného umění 2016.
Neklidná figura: exprese v českém sochařství 1880–1914. S. Baborovská, P. Wittlich (eds.), M. Rakušanová, T. Hylmar. Praha, Galerie hlavního města Prahy 2016.

LIST OF ILLUSTRATIONS

35 František Bílek, *An Allegory of the Great Fall of the Czechs*, 1898, wood, 52 cm. Národní galerie Praha.
36 Bedřich Ohmann, Hotel Central in Prague, 1898–1902, detail of the façade. Photograph: Věroslav Škrabánek.

Go to the People

37 Jan Koula, House in Prague (Koula Villa), 1896. Photograph: Věroslav Škrabánek.
38 Hanuš Schwaiger, *Pluhař the Rag-and-Bone Man*, 1891, pencil and watercolour, 18.8 × 8.5 cm. Národní galerie Praha.
39 Joža Uprka, *Shawls from Velká*, 1896, oil, 80 × 130 cm. Národní galerie Praha.
40 Joža Uprka, *All Souls' Day*, 1897, oil, 79.5 × 102 cm. Národní galerie Praha.
41 Vojtěch Hynais, Poster for the Czech-Slav Ethnographic Exhibition in Prague, 1894, colour lithograph, 104 × 134 cm. Uměleckoprůmyslové museum v Praze.
42 Jan Koula, Stein and plate, 1900, glazed earthenware, 19.8 cm and 26 cm. Uměleckoprůmyslové museum v Praze.
43 Mikoláš Aleš, *Jan Kozina Sladký*, 1894, watercolour, 124 × 100 cm. Národní galerie Praha.
44 Dušan Jurkovič, Villa in Rezek, 1900. Photograph: Martin Micka.
45–46 Dušan Jurkovič, Jan Building in Luhačovice, 1902. Photograph: Martin Micka.
47 Stanislav Sucharda, *Willow*, 1897, bronze, 60.5 × 16.5 cm. Národní galerie Praha.
48 František Hošek, *Farewell*, 1895, bronze, 120 × 68 cm. Národní galerie Praha.
49 Josef Mařatka, *Icemen*, 1900, bronze, 40 cm. Národní galerie Praha.

Into the Wider World

50 Alphonse Mucha, Second design for the Pavilion of Man at the Exposition Universelle in Paris, 1897, pencil and watercolour, 50.1 × 64.9 cm. Národní galerie Praha.
51 Luděk Marold, *The Painter Viktor Oliva*, c. 1890, charcoal, pencil, and gouache, 49.5 × 31.6 cm. Národní galerie Praha.
52 Luděk Marold, *A Poor Excuse*, after 1890, watercolour and gouache, 43.8 × 28.5 cm. Národní galerie Praha.
53 Luděk Marold, *Lady with a Little Dog*, after 1890, Indian ink and watercolour, 37 × 28.5 cm. Národní galerie Praha.
54 Luděk Marold, Study for a portrait of Anna Červená, 1897, oil, 52.8 × 46.5 cm. Národní galerie Praha.
55 Luděk Marold, Poster for *Our Apartment is Under Renovation* at the Exhibition Theatre, 1898, colour lithograph, 124 × 92 cm. Uměleckoprůmyslové museum v Praze.
56 Luděk Marold, Poster design, after 1895, gouache, 23.7 × 46.5 cm. Národní galerie Praha.
57 Luděk Marold, *The Battle of Lipany*, 1898, detail. ČTK – René Volfík.
58 Alphonse Mucha, Poster design for *Gismonda*, 1894, tempera, 198 × 67 cm. Národní galerie Praha.
59 Alphonse Mucha, Poster for *Médée*, 1898, colour lithograph, 205 × 74 cm. Uměleckoprůmyslové museum v Praze.
60 Alphonse Mucha, Poster for *La Dame aux camélias*, 1896, colour lithograph, 210 × 77 cm. Uměleckoprůmyslové museum v Praze.
61 Alphonse Mucha, Poster design for the Architecture and Engineering Exhibition, 1897, charcoal and watercolour, 108.5 × 85 cm. Národní galerie Praha.
62 Karel Vítězslav Mašek, Poster for the Architecture and Engineering Exhibition, 1898, colour lithograph, 128 × 68 cm. Uměleckoprůmyslové museum v Praze.
63 Alphonse Mucha, *Salon des Cent*, 1896, colour lithograph, 63.6 × 43.2 cm. Private collection.
64 Alphonse Mucha, *Woman Sitting in an Armchair*, before 1900, pencil and watercolour, 49.5 × 44 cm. Národní galerie Praha.
65 Alphonse Mucha, *Absinthe*, after 1900, charcoal and coloured chalks, 48 × 62 cm. Národní galerie Praha.

Defiance

66 Quido Kocián, *The Artist's Lot*, 1900, patinated plaster, 64 cm. Galerie v Hořicích.
67 Karel Hlaváček, *Head of a Demon*, 1897, Indian ink, 7.3 × 16 cm. Památník národního písemnictví v Praze. Photograph: Wikimedia Commons.
68 Karel Hlaváček, *Expellee*, 1897, charcoal, 26.3 × 24.3 cm. Památník národního písemnictví v Praze.
69 Karel Hlaváček, *Apparition*, 1897, pastel, 32.6 × 48 cm. Památník národního písemnictví v Praze.
70 František Bílek, *The Crucified*, 1896, charcoal, 200 × 142 cm. Galerie hlavního města Prahy. Photograph: Martin Micka.
71 František Bílek, *The Meaning of the Word Madonna*, 1897, wood, 153 × 93.5 cm. Národní galerie Praha.
72 František Bílek, *Mother!*, 1899, charcoal, 139 × 83 cm. Národní galerie Praha.
73 František Bílek, Page from the tract *The Reckoning and Reading in Letters of the Body of Man*, 1899, pencil, ink,

Indian ink, and white chalk, 34.1 × 45.6 cm. Národní galerie Praha.

74 František Bílek, *Jan Hus*, 1901, plaster, 89 cm. Galerie hlavního města Prahy.

75 František Bílek, Sketch for a monument to Julius Zeyer, 1901, terracotta, 50 cm. Galerie hlavního města Prahy. Photograph: Martin Micka.

76 František Bílek's house ("The Cottage") in Chýnov. Photograph: Martin Micka.

77 Felix Jenewein, *Judas*, 1896, gouache, 36.4 × 51.3 cm. Moravská galerie v Brně.

78 Felix Jenewein, Final image in the cycle *The Plague*, 1900, Indian ink, charcoal, and watercolour, 46 × 62 cm. Národní galerie Praha.

79 Maxmilián Pirner, *Homo Homini Lupus*, 1901, watercolour, 96 × 47.4 cm. Národní galerie Praha.

80 Quido Kocián, *Sick Soul*, 1903, patinated plaster, 52 cm. Galerie v Hořicích. Photograph: Martin Micka.

81 Quido Kocián, *Life Is Struggle!*, 1902, patinated plaster, 38 cm. Galerie v Hořicích.

82 František Kupka, *Money*, 1899, oil, 81 × 81 cm. Národní galerie Praha.

83 František Kupka, *Defiance – The Black Idol*, 1900–1903, coloured aquatint, 34.7 × 34.7 cm. Národní galerie Praha.

84 František Kupka, *The Way of Silence*, 1900–1903, aquatint coloured with gouache and watercolour, 34.8 × 34.5 cm. Collection of Patrik Šimon.

85 František Kupka, *Meditation*, 1899, charcoal and chalk, 60 × 24.3 cm. Galerie výtvarného umění v Ostravě.

Painters of the Soul

86 Maxmilián Švabinský, *Communion of Souls*, 1896, oil, 65.5 × 45.5 cm, detail. Národní galerie Praha.

87 Jan Preisler, *The Kiss*, 1895–96, oil, 32 × 35 cm. Národní galerie Praha.

88 Maxmilián Švabinský, *Communion of Souls*, 1896, oil, 65.5 × 45.5 cm. Národní galerie Praha.

89 Jan Kotěra, *The Temple of Amor and Psyche – A Roman Fantasy*, 1898, reproduced in *Volné směry* 3 (1899): 124.

90 Stanislav Sucharda, *Nameplate*, 1896, bronze, 6.2 × 9.4 cm. Národní galerie Praha.

91 Jan Preisler, *Autumn*, 1897, oil, 31 × 22 cm. Západočeská galerie v Plzni.

92 Maxmilián Švabinský, *Circular Portrait*, 1897, oil, 105.5 cm. Národní galerie Praha.

93 Václav Radimský, *Meadow with Trees*, 1895, oil, 65 × 81 cm. Národní galerie Praha.

94 František Kaván, *Flowing*, 1896, oil, 102 × 132 cm. Národní galerie Praha.

95 Antonín Slavíček, *Birch Mood*, 1897, oil, 91.5 × 114.5 cm. Národní galerie Praha.

96 Otakar Lebeda, *Above the River Lužnice*, 1899, oil, 50.5 × 66 cm. Národní galerie Praha.

97 Otakar Lebeda, *Tarn*, 1896, oil, 78 × 98 cm. Národní galerie Praha.

98 Jan Preisler, *Easter*, centre of the triptych, 1897, charcoal, 55 × 43 cm. Muzeum umění Olomouc. Photograph: Markéta Ondrušková.

99 Antonín Slavíček, *Autumn in the Mist*, 1897, Syntonos paint, 68 × 101.5 cm. Národní galerie Praha.

100 Jan Preisler, Study for the cycle *The Adventurous Knight*, 1898, oil, 87.5 × 46 cm. Národní galerie Praha.

101 František Kupka, *The Lotus Soul*, 1898, watercolour, 38.5 × 57.7 cm. Národní galerie Praha.

102 Jan Preisler, *Remembrance*, 1898, charcoal, 60 × 45 cm. Private collection.

103 Maxmilián Švabinský, *Maurice Maeterlinck*, 1899, Indian ink, 25.8 × 22.7 cm. Private collection.

104 Maxmilián Švabinský, *Old Pavlína Stripping Feathers*, 1896, Indian ink, 57.6 × 45.5 cm. Národní galerie Praha.

105 Antonín Hudeček, *Stillness at Dusk*, 1900, oil, 120 × 180.5 cm. Národní galerie Praha.

106 Maxmilián Švabinský, *A Poor Land*, 1900, oil, 179 × 246 cm. Národní galerie Praha.

Spring

107 Antonín Hudeček, *Stream*, 1898, Syntonos paint, 70 × 104 cm, detail. Národní galerie Praha.

108 Antonín Slavíček, *June Day*, 1898, tempera, 71 × 105.5 cm. Národní galerie Praha.

109 Antonín Hudeček, *Stream*, 1898, Syntonos paint, 70 × 104 cm. Národní galerie Praha.

110 Maxmilián Švabinský, *Youth*, 1897, Indian ink, 43 × 31.5 cm. Private collection.

111 Josef Schusser, *Lady with a Red Parasol*, 1898, oil, 95 × 82.5 cm. Národní galerie Praha.

112 Arnošt Hofbauer, Poster for the second SVU Mánes exhibition, 1898, colour lithograph, 110 × 84 cm. Uměleckoprůmyslové museum v Praze.

113 Arnošt Hofbauer, Poster for a recital by Hana Kvapilová, 1899, colour lithograph, 110 × 81 cm. Uměleckoprůmyslové museum v Praze.

114 Jan Preisler, *The Adventurous Knight*, 1898, oil, 87 × 115 cm. Západočeská galerie v Plzni.

115 Georges Antoine Rochegrosse, *The Knight of Flowers*, 1894, oil, 235 × 375 cm. Musée d'Orsay, Paris. Petr Wittlich, *Česká secese*, Praha, Odeon 1982.

116 Jan Preisler, Drawing for *Spring*, 1900, charcoal and white chalk, 43.3 × 28 cm. Národní galerie Praha.
117 Jan Preisler, *Spring*, 1900, oil, 112 × 70 cm, 112 × 186 cm, 112 × 70 cm. Západočeská galerie v Plzni.
118 Jan Kotěra, Peterka House in Prague, 1899–1900. Photograph: Collection of the author.
119 Jan Kotěra, Peterka House in Prague, 1899–1900, detail. Photograph: Martin Micka.
120 Jan Kotěra, Drawing for the Peterka House in Prague, 1899, watercolour, 41 × 18 cm. Národní technické muzeum, Muzeum architektury a stavitelství, 20070603/01, LHB-A 14.02.08.
121 Maxmilián Švabinský, *Jan Kotěra*, 1900, Indian ink, 33 × 25.5 cm. Private collection.
122 Jan Kotěra, Robitschko Tomb in the New Jewish Cemetery in Prague, 1901–2. Photograph: Věroslav Škrabánek.
123 Jan Kotěra, Elbogen Tomb in the New Jewish Cemetery in Prague, 1901–2. Photograph: Věroslav Škrabánek.
124 Josef Fanta, Chair, 1899, wood and metal, 68 cm. Uměleckoprůmyslové museum v Praze.
125 Josef Fanta, Interior for the Chamber of Trade and Commerce at the Exposition Universelle in Paris, 1900. Collection of the author.
126 Josef Kastner, Folding chair, 1899, wood, mother-of-pearl, and metal, 92 cm. Uměleckoprůmyslové museum v Praze.
127 Celda Klouček, Bowl decorated with leaves and fruit, 1895 (made 1899), glazed chamotte, 31 cm. Uměleckoprůmyslové museum v Praze.
128 Václav Mařan, Vase, 1899, glazed earthenware, 22.5 cm. Uměleckoprůmyslové museum v Praze.
129–130 Anna Boudová-Suchardová, Two vases, c. 1900, glazed earthenware, 23 cm, 38.5 cm. Uměleckoprůmyslové museum v Praze.
131–132 Rudolf Hameršmíd and Celda Klouček, Two vases, 1904, 1899, glazed earthenware, 22.5 cm, 27 cm. Uměleckoprůmyslové museum v Praze.
133 František Soukup, Vase, 1904, glazed earthenware, 18 cm. Uměleckoprůmyslové museum v Praze.
134 Karel Vítězslav Mašek, Study of plants, c. 1900, watercolour, 30.3 × 21.5 cm. Národní galerie Praha.
135 Celda Klouček and Josef Škorpil, Staircase of the Museum of Decorative Arts in Pilsen, 1900. Photograph: Martin Micka.
136 Emanuel Novák, Clasp, 1900, silver, 8 cm. Uměleckoprůmyslové museum v Praze.
137–139 Emanuel Novák, Three brooches, 1900, silver and brass, 3.5 cm. Uměleckoprůmyslové museum v Praze.
140–142 Josef Ladislav Němec, Three brooches, after 1900, metal. Muzeum v Jablonci nad Nisou.
143 Vojtěch Preissig, Wallpaper design, after 1900, gouache, 49 × 32 cm. Uměleckoprůmyslové museum v Praze.
144 Vojtěch Preissig, Wallpaper design, after 1900, gouache, 49 × 32 cm. Uměleckoprůmyslové museum v Praze.
145 Jan Kotěra, Divan, 1899, textiles, 49 cm. Uměleckoprůmyslové museum v Praze.
146 Jan Kotěra, Bowl, 1903 (1910 version), lead glass, 41 cm. Uměleckoprůmyslové museum v Praze.
147 Jan Kotěra, Interior for the School of Decorative Arts at the Louisiana Purchase Exposition, 1904, detail with chandelier. Collection of the author.

Fairy Tales

148 Jan Kotěra, SVU Mánes exhibition pavilion in Prague, 1902. *Jan Kotěra 1871–1923: Zakladatel moderní české architektury*, Praha, Obecní dům/Kant 2001, p. 122.
149 Jan Kotěra, Illustration for "The Tale of the Red Knight," published in *Volné směry* 7 (1903): 81.
150 Jan Kotěra, Drawing of the SVU Mánes exhibition pavilion, 1902, coloured Indian inks, 32 × 47 cm. Národní technické muzeum, Muzeum architektury a stavitelství, 2007603/05, LBH-A 14.02.07.
151 Jan Preisler, *Knight-Errant*, 1901, charcoal and white chalk, 36.3 × 40.6 cm. Collection of the author.
152 Jan Preisler, *Fairy Tale*, 1902, oil, 101.5 × 79 cm. Galerie výtvarného umění v Ostravě.
153 Vojtěch Preissig, *Bluebird*, 1900, coloured etching, 49.5 × 37.5 cm. Východočeská galerie v Pardubicích.
154 Maxmilián Švabinský, *Paradisaea Apoda*, 1901, charcoal, coloured chalks, and watercolour, 72 × 50 cm. Východočeská galerie v Pardubicích.
155 Stanislav Sucharda, Plaquette from a series for "The Tale of the Beautiful Maiden Liliana," 1902–9, bronze, 9.9 × 10.4 cm. Národní galerie Praha.
156 Bohumil Kafka, *Grave Relief*, 1903, bronze, 172 × 96 cm. Národní galerie Praha.
157 Maxmilián Pirner, Epilogue from the series *Hans Heiling*, after 1900, pastel, 51 × 71 cm. Národní galerie Praha.
158 Hanuš Schwaiger, *Long, Broad and Quickeye*, 1900, Indian ink and watercolour, 105 × 70 cm. Národní galerie Praha.
159 Ladislav Šaloun, *Krakonoš*, 1902–6, sandstone, Smetanovy sady in Hořice. Photograph: Martin Micka.
160 Jaroslav Panuška, *Ghost of a Mother*, c. 1900, oil, 68 × 48 cm. Východočeská galerie v Pardubicích.
161 Jaroslav Panuška, *Revenant Pursued by Ravens*, 1898, charcoal, 65 × 72 cm. Východočeská galerie v Pardubicích.
162 Vojtěch Preissig, Drawing for the cover of Jan Karafiát's *Fireflies*, 1901–3, Indian ink, 57 × 42 cm. Uměleckoprůmyslové museum v Praze.

163 František Bílek, *The Poet's Vision*, 1902–3, linocut, 29 × 14.2 cm. Národní galerie Praha.
164 František Bílek, *The Blind*, 1902 (made 1926), wood, 216 cm. Národní galerie Praha.
165 Vladimír Županský, Poster for the Rodin exhibition in Prague, 1902, colour lithograph, 158 × 84 cm. Uměleckoprůmyslové museum v Praze.
166 Jan Preisler, *Black Lake*, 1904, oil, 111 × 153 cm. Národní galerie Praha.
167 Jan Preisler, *Adolescent by a Lake*, 1903, oil, 44 × 53 cm. Západočeská galerie v Plzni.
168 Arnošt Hofbauer, *Pilgrim*, 1904, oil, 111 × 114.5 cm. Národní galerie Praha.

Senses

169 Jan Štursa, *Puberty*, 1905, patinated plaster, 86 cm. Galerie v Hořicích.
170 František Kupka, Study of a nude for *Ballad-Joys*, 1901–2, coloured pencils, 44.1 × 28.3 cm. Collection of Patrik Šimon.
171 František Kupka, *Ballad-Joys*, 1902, oil, 83.5 × 126.5 cm. Národní galerie Praha.
172 Josef Mařatka, Sketch of a nude, 1902, pencil, 31 × 20 cm. Národní galerie Praha.
173 Josef Mařatka, *Fat Woman*, 1903, bronze, 34.2 cm. Petr Wittlich, *Sochařství české secese*, Praha, Karolinum 2000, p. 308.
174 Josef Mařatka, *Ariadne Abandoned*, 1903, bronze, 30.5 cm. Národní galerie Praha.
175 Josef Mařatka, Study of a hand, 1903, bronze, 19.5 cm. Národní galerie Praha.
176 Otakar Lebeda, *Horní Sadová třída in Karlovy Vary*, 1898, tempera, 67 × 50 cm. Národní galerie Praha.
177 Antonín Slavíček, *Větrný Jeníkov*, 1904, oil, 111.5 × 135 cm. Západočeská galerie v Plzni.
178 Antonín Slavíček, *Mountain Village*, 1902, oil, 114 × 135 cm. Národní galerie Praha.
179 Antonín Slavíček, *Garden Wall*, c. 1902, tempera, 88.5 × 100 cm. Národní galerie Praha.
180 Stanislav Sucharda, *Portrait of Mrs. Grohová*, 1905, marble, 8 cm. Galerie v Hořicích.
181 Miloš Jiránek, *Showers at a Prague Sokol*, 1903, oil, 140 × 169 cm. Národní galerie Praha.
182 Otakar Španiel, *Discobolus*, 1907, bronze, 28 × 27.5 cm. Národní galerie Praha.
183 Bohumil Kafka, *Moulting Camel*, 1905, plaster, 42 cm. Petr Wittlich, *Bohumil Kafka (1878–1942): Příběh sochaře*. Praha, Karolinum 2014, illus. no. 30.

Epoch

184 Antonín Balšánek and Osvald Polívka, Municipal House in Prague, 1905–11, façade. Photograph: Věroslav Škrabánek.
185 Jan Preisler, Poster for the Provincial Economic, Industrial and Trade Exhibition in Beroun, 1899, colour lithograph, 95 × 130 cm. Uměleckoprůmyslové museum v Praze.
186 Joža Uprka, *Girls in Flowers*, after 1900, oil, 150 × 100 cm. Galerie výtvarného umění v Ostravě.
187 Alois Kalvoda, *Birch Wood*, after 1900, colour lithograph, 32.5 × 39 cm. Galerie moderního umění v Hradci Králové.
188 František Kaván, *Showers from Tábor*, 1903, oil, 76 × 100 cm. Galerie v Hořicích.
189 Antonín Slavíček, *Road in Kameničky*, 1904, oil, 116 × 136 cm. Západočeská galerie v Plzni.
190 Antonín Slavíček, *Funeral in Kameničky*, 1905, oil, 26.5 × 35.5 cm. Galerie moderního umění v Roudnici nad Labem.
191 Karel Špillar, *In a Café*, 1904, oil, 58 × 47.5 cm. Národní galerie Praha.
192 Alois Dryák and Bedřich Bendelmayer, Main hall of the Hotel Central in Prague, 1898–1902. Collection of the author.
193 Karel Vítězslav Mašek, House in Prague, 1902. Photograph: Věroslav Škrabánek.
194 Alois Dryák and Bedřich Bendelmayer, Hotel Evropa in Prague, 1903–4. Photograph: Věroslav Škrabánek.
195 Jan Kotěra, District House in Hradec Králové, 1903–4. Photograph: Martin Micka.
196 Bedřich Bendelmayer, Apartment building by the Powder Gate in Prague, 1904. Photograph: Věroslav Škrabánek.
197 Josef Fanta, Prague Main Railway Station, 1900–1909. Photograph: Věroslav Škrabánek.
198 Stanislav Sucharda, *Prague and the Vltava*, 1902, bronze, 7.5 × 5.7 cm. Národní galerie Praha.
199 Mikoláš Aleš, *Old Bard*, 1900, watercolour, 36 × 13.5 cm. Uměleckoprůmyslové museum v Praze.
200 Vojtěch Hynais, Study for *Winter*, 1901, oil, 29 × 35 cm. Národní galerie Praha.
201 Osvald Polívka, Prague Insurance Company, 1906–7. Photograph: Věroslav Škrabánek.
202 Osvald Polívka, Topič Building in Prague, 1905–6. Photograph: Martin Micka.
203 Josef Václav Myslbek, Study of the head of Saint Wenceslas, 1902–3, bronze, 42 cm. Národní galerie Praha.
204 Ladislav Kofránek, *Dreaming*, 1904, marble, 31 cm. Galerie v Hořicích.

205 Tavík František Šimon, *The Sea*, 1904, coloured etching, 24.6 × 27.4 cm. Národní galerie Praha.
206 Jakub Schikaneder, *Street in the Evening*, 1906, oil, 110 × 95 cm. Národní galerie Praha.
207 Miloš Jiránek, *White Study I*, 1910, oil, 75 × 63 cm. Galerie výtvarného umění v Liberci.
208 Maxmilián Švabinský, *Large Family Portrait*, 1905, Indian ink and watercolour, 182 × 206 cm. Národní galerie Praha.
209 Antonín Slavíček, *Prague from Letná*, 1908, tempera, 188 × 390 cm. Národní galerie Praha.
210 Antonín Slavíček, *In Stromovka*, 1907, oil, 18.7 × 24 cm. Galerie moderního umění v Roudnici nad Labem.
211 Bohumil Kafka, Sketch for *The Embrace of Love and Death*, 1906, bronze, 32.5 cm. Národní galerie Praha.
212 Bohumil Kafka, *The Embrace of Love and Death*, 1906–7, bronze, 176 cm. Photograph: Collection of the author.
213–215 Stanislav Sucharda, František Palacký Monument in Prague, 1898–1912. Photograph: Oto Palán.
216 Antonín Balšánek and Osvald Polívka, Grand Restaurant of the Municipal House in Prague, 1905–11. Photograph: Věroslav Škrabánek.
217 Antonín Balšánek and Osvald Polívka, Smetana Hall of the Municipal House in Prague, 1905–11. Photograph: Věroslav Škrabánek.
218 Antonín Balšánek and Osvald Polívka, Mayor's Salon of the Municipal House in Prague, 1905–11. Photograph: Věroslav Škrabánek.
219 Antonín Balšánek and Osvald Polívka, Municipal House in Prague, 1905–11, detail of the dome. Photograph: Věroslav Škrabánek.
220 Alphonse Mucha, *Slavia*, 1908, oil and tempera, 154 × 92.5 cm. Národní galerie Praha.

Synthesis

221 Jan Kotěra, National House and theatre in Prostějov, 1905–7, detail of the theatre façade. Photograph: Martin Micka.
222 Jan Preisler, Poster for the Edvard Munch exhibition in Prague, 1905, colour lithograph, 157.5 × 101 cm. Uměleckoprůmyslové museum v Praze.
223 Jan Preisler, *Lovers*, 1905, oil, 120 × 150 cm. Národní galerie Praha.
224 Jan Kotěra, National House and theatre in Prostějov, 1905–7. Photograph: Martin Micka.
225 Jan Kotěra, Fountain with a sculpture by Stanislav Sucharda at the National House and theatre in Prostějov, 1905–7. Photograph: Martin Micka.
226 Jan Štursa, *Eve*, 1908–9, bronze, 190 cm. Národní galerie Praha.
227 Jan Štursa, *Melancholy Girl*, 1906, French limestone, 90 cm. Národní galerie Praha.
228 Josef Ladislav Němec, Necklace, 1907, gold, garnets, and translucent enamel. Uměleckoprůmyslové museum v Praze.
229 Vojtěch Preissig, Exhibition poster, 1907, coloured linocut, 141 × 100 cm. Uměleckoprůmyslové museum v Praze.
230 Vojtěch Preissig, *Evening*, 1906, coloured etching, 63.5 × 44.5 cm. Národní galerie Praha.
231 Dušan Jurkovič, House in Žabovřesky in Brno, 1906. Photograph: Martin Micka.
232 Dušan Jurkovič, Hall / Living room in Žabovřesky in Brno, 1906. Photograph: Martin Micka.
233 Jan Preisler, *Green Landscape*, 1908, oil, 95.5 × 76 cm. Národní galerie Praha.
234 Jan Preisler, Study for *Adam and Eve*, 1908, oil, 40 × 30 cm. Západočeská galerie v Plzni.
235 Antonín Hudeček, *Evening in Machov*, 1910, oil, 118 × 132 cm. Galerie výtvarného umění v Ostravě.
236 Jan Kotěra, Reception room in Kotěra's house in Prague, 1909. Photograph: Collection of the author.
237 Jan Kotěra, History sculpture by Stanislav Sucharda at the City Museum in Hradec Králové, 1909–13. Photograph: Martin Micka.
238 Jan Kotěra, City Museum in Hradec Králové, 1909–13. Photograph: Martin Micka.
239 Jan Kotěra, Interior of the City Museum in Hradec Králové, 1909–13. Photograph: Martin Micka.
240–241 Jan Kotěra, Façade and interior of the Laichter House in Prague, 1908–9. Photograph: Věroslav Škrabánek.
242 Otakar Novotný, Štenc House in Prague, 1909. Photograph: Věroslav Škrabánek..

Expression

243 František Bílek, *Moses*, 1905, bronze, larger than life-size, Prague. Photograph: Věroslav Škrabánek.
244 František Bílek, *Prayer over the Graves*, 1905, cement, larger than life-size, Chýnov. Photograph: Martin Micka.
245 František Bílek, *Wonder*, 1907, wood, 307 cm. Národní galerie Praha. Petr Wittlich, *Sochařství české secese*, Praha, Karolinum 2000, p. 179.
246 František Bílek, Design for the National Monument for White Mountain, 1908, chalk, 45 × 90 cm. Galerie hlavního města Prahy. Photograph: Martin Micka.
247 Quido Kocián, *Žalov*, 1905, patinated plaster, 171 cm. Galerie v Hořicích.
248 Quido Kocián, *Idiot*, 1907, patinated plaster, 37 cm. Private collection.

249 Ladislav Šaloun, Jan Hus Memorial in Prague, 1900–1915. Photograph: Martin Micka.
250 Josef Mařatka, Study for *Bust of Antonín Dvořák*, 1906, bronze, 53 cm. Národní galerie Praha.
251 Stanislav Sucharda, *Tomb Sculpture*, c. 1909, bronze, 40 cm. Národní galerie Praha.
252–253 Bohumil Kafka, *Sleepwalker*, 1906, bronze, 81.5 cm. Národní galerie Praha. Petr Wittlich, *Bohumil Kafka. (1878–1942): Příběh sochaře*, Praha, Karolinum 2014, illus. no. 41.
254 Bohumil Kafka, *The Eternal Drama*, 1906, bronze, 59 cm. Národní galerie Praha. Petr Wittlich, *Bohumil Kafka. (1878–1942): Příběh sochaře*, Praha, Karolinum 2014, illus. no. 52.
255 Ladislav Šaloun, *Concentration*, after 1905, bronze, 29.5 cm. Národní galerie Praha.
256 Emil Filla, *Night of Love*, 1907, oil, 73 × 110 cm. Národní galerie Praha.
257 Emil Filla, *Child by a Forest*, 1907, oil, 96 × 138 cm. Národní galerie Praha.
258 Emil Filla, *Reader of Dostoevsky*, 1907, oil, 98.5 × 80 cm. Národní galerie Praha.
259 Emil Filla, *Portrait of Josef Uher*, 1908, oil, 68.8 × 54.5 cm. Moravská galerie v Brně.
260 Bohumil Kubišta, *Landscape with Tree Alley*, 1908, oil, 62 × 60 cm. Galerie moderního umění v Hradci Králové.
261 Bohumil Kubišta, *Promenade in a Florence Park*, 1907, oil, 84 × 90 cm. Západočeská galerie v Plzni.
262 Bohumil Kubišta, *On the Train (Third-Class Passengers)*, 1908, oil, 64 × 76 cm. Moravská galerie v Brně.
263 Antonín Procházka, *Circus*, 1907, oil, 47.5 × 65 cm. Národní galerie Praha.
264 Josef Váchal, *Women*, 1906–8, etching, 17.2 × 15.5 cm. Národní galerie Praha.
265 Josef Váchal, *Magic*, 1909, coloured woodcut, 52.5 × 38.5 cm. Regionální muzeum a galerie v Jičíně.
266 Josef Váchal, *The Astral Plane – Spiritist Séance*, 1906, Indian ink and watercolour, 35.7 × 52 cm. Památník národního písemnictví v Praze.
267 Josef Váchal, *The Elemental Plane – The Plane of Passions and Instincts*, 1907, Indian ink and watercolour, 30.6 × 52.5 cm. Památník národního písemnictví v Praze.
268–270 Ladislav Šaloun, Jan Hus Memorial in Hořice, 1911–13. Photograph: Martin Micka.
271 Ladislav Šaloun, *Scribe*, 1920, serpentinite, 63 cm. Galerie v Hořicích.

Geometrisation

272 Dušan Jurkovič, Garden Room at the castle in Nové Město nad Metují, 1909, detail. Photograph: Martin Micka.
273 Zdenka Braunerová, Title page of Miloš Marten's *The Cycle of Pleasure and Death*, 1907. Uměleckoprůmyslové museum v Praze.
274 Vratislav H. Brunner, Cover of Jiří Mahen's poetry collection *Little Flames*, 1907. Uměleckoprůmyslové museum v Praze.
275–276 Vladimír Županský, Title page and cover of George Moore's *Modern Painting*, 1909. Uměleckoprůmyslové museum v Praze.
277 Karel Ebner, Box with fish motif, 1909, silver, stones, and pearls, 6 cm. Uměleckoprůmyslové museum v Praze.
278 Jan Štursa, *Primavera*, 1907, marble, 102 cm. Národní galerie Praha.
279 Bohumír Jaroněk, Motif from Štramberk, c. 1907, coloured woodcut, 44 × 51 cm. Národní galerie Praha.
280 František Kupka, *Red and Blue Prometheus*, 1908, watercolour, 32.1 × 29.3 cm. Národní galerie Praha.
281 Jan Kotěra and Jan Štursa, Trade and Industry Pavilion at the Anniversary Exhibition of the Chamber of Trade and Commerce in Prague, 1908. Collection of the author.
282 Jan Konůpek, *Vanitas*, 1908, Indian ink and watercolour, 59 × 38.5 cm. Private collection. Photograph: Martin Micka.
283 Jan Kotěra, Ornamental section on the staircase at the City Museum in Hradec Králové, 1909–13. Photograph: Martin Micka.
284 Jan Kotěra, Staircase at the City Museum in Hradec Králové, 1909–13. Photograph: Martin Micka.
285 Jan Konůpek, Title page and frontispiece of Johannes Jörgensen's *Pilgrim Book*, 1910. Photograph: Collection of the author.
286 Jan Konůpek, Design for the cover of *Meditace*, 1909, Indian ink, 49.4 × 37.4 cm. Národní galerie Praha.
287 Dušan Jurkovič, Garden Room at the castle in Nové Město nad Metují, 1909. Photograph: Martin Micka.
288 František Kysela, Poster for the Second Czech Horticultural and Fruit Exhibition, 1910, colour lithograph, 82 × 120 cm. Uměleckoprůmyslové museum v Praze.
289 Antonín Engel, Apartment building in Prague, Břehová 1, 1911. Photograph: Věroslav Škrabánek.
290 Josef Gočár, Interior of the Wenke Department Store in Jaroměř, 1909–10. Collection of the author.
291 Pavel Janák, Box, 1911, glazed earthenware, 12 cm. Uměleckoprůmyslové museum v Praze.
292 Pavel Janák, Box, 1911, glazed earthenware, 11.5 cm. Uměleckoprůmyslové museum v Praze.
293 Jaroslav Benda, Poster for Hanuš Schwaiger's posthumous exhibition, 1912, colour linotype, 62 × 95 cm. Uměleckoprůmyslové museum v Praze.

The Second Secession

294 Jaroslav Horejc, *Orpheus*, 1908, polychrome plaster and glass, 89.5 cm. Arthouse Hejtmánek.
295 Jan Zrzavý, *Persian Garden*, 1907, oil, 23 × 24.5 cm. Národní galerie Praha.
296 Jan Zrzavý, *Nocturne*, 1908, oil, 20 × 25.5 cm. Národní galerie Praha.
297 Jan Zrzavý, *The Head of John the Baptist*, 1910, charcoal, 22.4 × 26.8 cm. Památník národního písemnictví v Praze.
298 František Kobliha, *Sphinx*, 1908, woodcut, 20 × 14.2 cm. Private collection.
299 František Kobliha, *Reverie*, 1909, charcoal, 32 × 24 cm. Národní galerie Praha.
300 František Kobliha, *Vampire*, 1909, woodcut, 20.7 × 15.2 cm, illustration for Karel Hlaváček's poetry collection *Late before Morning*. Národní galerie Praha.
301 František Kobliha, *Undersea Forests*, 1909, woodcut, 20.8 × 15 cm. Private collection.
302 František Bílek, *The Beauty of Youth in Its Struggle*, 1910, wood, 80 cm. Galerie hlavního města Prahy.
303 František Bílek, *The Hall of Dread*, 1912, woodcut, 29.5 × 22.7 cm. Národní galerie Praha.
304 Jan Konůpek, *Renunciation*, 1909, varnished ink, 59.5 × 41.1 cm. Národní galerie Praha.
305 Jan Konůpek, *Resignation – Dream*, 1910, etching, 12 × 9 cm. Private collection.
306 Jan Konůpek, *Evocation*, 1911, etching, 24.4 × 19.4 cm. Moravská galerie Brno.
307 Jan Konůpek, *Beheading*, 1910, etching, 27.2 × 23.5 cm. Private collection.
308 Jan Konůpek, *Egypt*, 1911, etching, 9.5 × 6.7 cm. Private collection.
309 Josef Váchal, *Fantasy*, 1912, woodcut, 9 × 9.7 cm. Galerie moderního umění v Hradci Králové.
310 Josef Váchal, *Devil Worshippers*, 1909, oil, 100 × 100 cm. Galerie moderního umění v Hradci Králové.
311 Jaroslav Horejc, *Perseus*, 1915, polychrome plaster, 42.5 cm. Arthouse Hejtmánek.
312 Jaroslav Horejc, *Orpheus*, 1916, polychrome plaster, 75 cm. Arthouse Hejtmánek.
313 Emil Filla, *The Good Samaritan*, 1910, oil, 96.5 × 59.5 cm. Národní galerie Praha.
314 Otto Gutfreund, *Hamlet*, 1911, bronze, 69.5 cm. Národní galerie Praha.
315 Jan Štursa, *Sulamit Rahu*, 1910–11, bronze, 198 cm. Národní galerie Praha.

Legacy

316 František Kupka, *Piano Keys. Lake*, 1909, oil, 79 × 72 cm, detail. Národní galerie Praha.
317 Karel Myslbek, *Black Pierrot*, 1907, oil, 139 × 93 cm. Národní galerie Praha.
318 Antonín Slavíček, *View of Troja*, 1908, oil, 144 × 193 cm. Národní galerie Praha.
319 Jan Štursa, *Dancer Resting*, 1913, bronze, 118.5 cm. Národní galerie Praha.
320 Jan Preisler, *Bathing*, 1912, oil, 90 × 76.5 cm. Západočeská galerie v Plzni.
321 Stanislav Sucharda, *Portrait of Kamila Heverochová*, 1910, bronze, 37 cm. Národní galerie Praha.
322 Jan Kotěra, Sketch of a portal (not built) for the Lehnerger-Olbrich villa in Vienna, 1914, ink wash, 27.5 × 17 cm. Národní technické muzeum, Muzeum architektury a stavitelství, 2007603/04, LHB-A 14.02.07.
323 Emil Filla, *The Dance of Salome*, 1912, oil, 137 × 82 cm. Galerie moderního umění v Hradci Králové.
324 Bohumil Kubišta, *The Hypnotist*, 1912, oil, 60.5 × 58 cm. Galerie výtvarného umění v Ostravě.
325 Jan Zrzavý, *Meditation*, 1915, oil, 50.2 × 37.5 cm. Národní galerie Praha.
326 Jindřich Prucha, *In a Beech Wood*, 1911, oil, 84 × 95.5 cm. Národní galerie Praha.
327 Hugo Böttinger, "Secession-style" locomotive, 1918, Indian ink and white, 14 × 23 cm. Galerie moderního umění v Hradci Králové.
328 František Bílek, *Adam and Eve*, 1921, wood, 95 cm. Galerie hlavního města Prahy.
329 František Kupka, *Piano Keys. Lake*, 1909, oil, 79 × 72 cm. Národní galerie Praha.
330 František Kupka, *Cosmic Spring II*, 1911–20, oil, 115 × 125 cm. Národní galerie Praha.
331 Vojtěch Preissig, *The Origin of the Earth*, 1936, mixed media, 60.5 × 72 cm. Národní galerie Praha.
332 Antonín Slavíček, *The Road to Žamberk*, 1909, oil, 90.5 × 99 cm. Národní galerie Praha.

ACKNOWLEDGEMENTS

Karolinum Press would like to thank the galleries, museums, owners, and curators of collections for kindly providing images for this book and permitting their reproduction.

INDEX

ABOUT THE AUTHOR

Petr Wittlich, Ph.D. (1932) studied history of art at Charles University's Faculty of Arts, where he was subsequently appointed assistant professor (1959), reader (1990), and professor (1992). From 1992 to 2000 he headed the Faculty's Department of Art History. In the 1990s he was president of the Czech and Slovak section of the International Association of Art Critics (AICA) and president of the Czech Association of Art Historians. He has greatly contributed to our understanding of Czech art from the turn of the 20th century and the interwar years, which is his main field of interest, and he is recognised throughout Europe as an expert on the Czech Secession. He has written for scholarly journals in this country and abroad, as well as working on numerous exhibitions. His monographs have been translated into several languages. He holds the František Palacký Honorary Medal for Merit in the Historical Sciences, the Charles University Faculty of Arts Silver Medal, and the Charles University Gold Medal. In 2012 he was awarded the Ministry of Culture Award for Merit in Visual Arts and the Czech Republic Medal of Merit in art and culture.

Exhibitions

Situace 92. Prague, Mánes 1992 | *Vergangene Zukunft. Tschechische Moderne 1890 bis 1918*. Vienna, Künstlerhaus 1994 | *Alfons Mucha*. Prague, Prague Castle 1994 | *Jan Preisler. Putování krajinami duše*. Pilsen, Západočeská galerie 1994 | *Alfons Mucha. Triumph des Jugendstils*. Hamburg, Museum für Kunst und Gewerbe 1997 | *Alphonse Mucha and the Spirit of Art Nouveau*. Lisbon, Calouste Gulbenkian Museum 1997 | *Důvěrný prostor – nová dálka. Umění pražské secese*. Prague, Obecní dům 1997 | *Prague Art Nouveau. Métamorphoses d'un style*. Brussels, Palais des Beaux-Arts 1998 | *Prague 1900. Poetry and Ecstasy*. Amsterdam, Van Gogh Museum 1999 | *Sochař Ladislav Šaloun*. Prague, Lobkovický palác 2000 | *František Bílek*. Paris, Musée Bourdelle 2002 | *Josef Mařatka a August Rodin v Praze*. Prague, VŠUP 2002 | *Jan Preisler. 1872–1918*. Prague, Obecní dům 2003 | *Bílkova vila*. Prague and Chýnov, Galerie hlavního města Prahy 2010 | *Alfons Mucha – tváře*. Kutná Hora, Galerie Středočeského kraje 2010 | *Neklidná figura. Exprese v českém sochařství 1880–1914*. Prague, Galerie hlavního města Prahy 2016

Monographs

Kresby Jana Štursy. Prague, Nakladatelství čs. výtvarných umělců 1959 | *Art Nouveau 1900*. Paris, Gründ 1975 | *Art Nouveau Drawings*. London, Octopus Books 1974, 1975; Prague, Artia 1976 | *České sochařství ve XX. století. 1890–1945*. Prague, SPN 1978 | *Česká secese*. Prague, Odeon 1982, 1985 | *Edvard Munch*. Prague, Odeon 1985; Stockholm, Bokförlaget Prisma 1987 | *Umění a život – doba secese*. Prague, Artia 1987 | *Jan Preisler. Kresby. Prague*, Odeon 1988 | *Art Nouveau. Pintura, grabado, escultura, arquitectura, artes aplicadas*. Madrid, Editorial Libsa 1990 | *Art Nouveau. Pittura – oreficeria – soprammobili – scultura – architettura*. La Spezia, Fratelli Neplita 1990 | *Prague Fin de siècle*. Paris, Flammarion 1992; New York, Abbeville 1992; Cologne, Taschen Verlag 1999 | *Sochařství české secese*. Prague, Karolinum 2000; *Die Bildhauerkunst der Tschechischen Sezession* 2001; *Sculpture of the Czech Art Nouveau* 2001 | *Secesní Prahou – Podoby stylu*. Prague, Karolinum 2005; *Prag im Jugendstil – Ein Stil in seinen Formen* 2007; *Art Nouveau Prague – Forms of the Style* 2007, 2009, 2011 | *Jan Štursa*. Prague, Academia 2008 | *Horizonty umění*. Prague, Karolinum 2010 | *Malířství české secese*. Prague, Karolinum 2012; *Czech Modern Painters* 2012 | *Bohumil Kafka (1878–1942). Příběh sochaře*. Prague, Karolinum 2014 | *Praha secesní*. Prague, Karolinum 2017; *Art Nouveau Prague*, 2020

CZECH SECESSION
ART AND ARCHITECTURE 1890–1914
PETR WITTLICH

Translation by Adrian Dean

Originally published in Czech as *Česká secese*,
Prague: Odeon 1982. This first English translation
follows the third, updated Czech edition,
Prague: Karolinum Press, 2020.

Published by Charles University
Karolinum Press
Ovocný trh 560/5, 116 36 Prague 1, Czech Republic
www.karolinum.cz
Prague 2022
Edited by Milada Motlová, Martin Janeček
Copyediting by Julia Tatiana Bailey
Cover and layout by Jan Šerých
Typeset by DTP Karolinum Press
Printed by PBtisk a.s.
First English edition

ISBN 978-80-246-5133-0

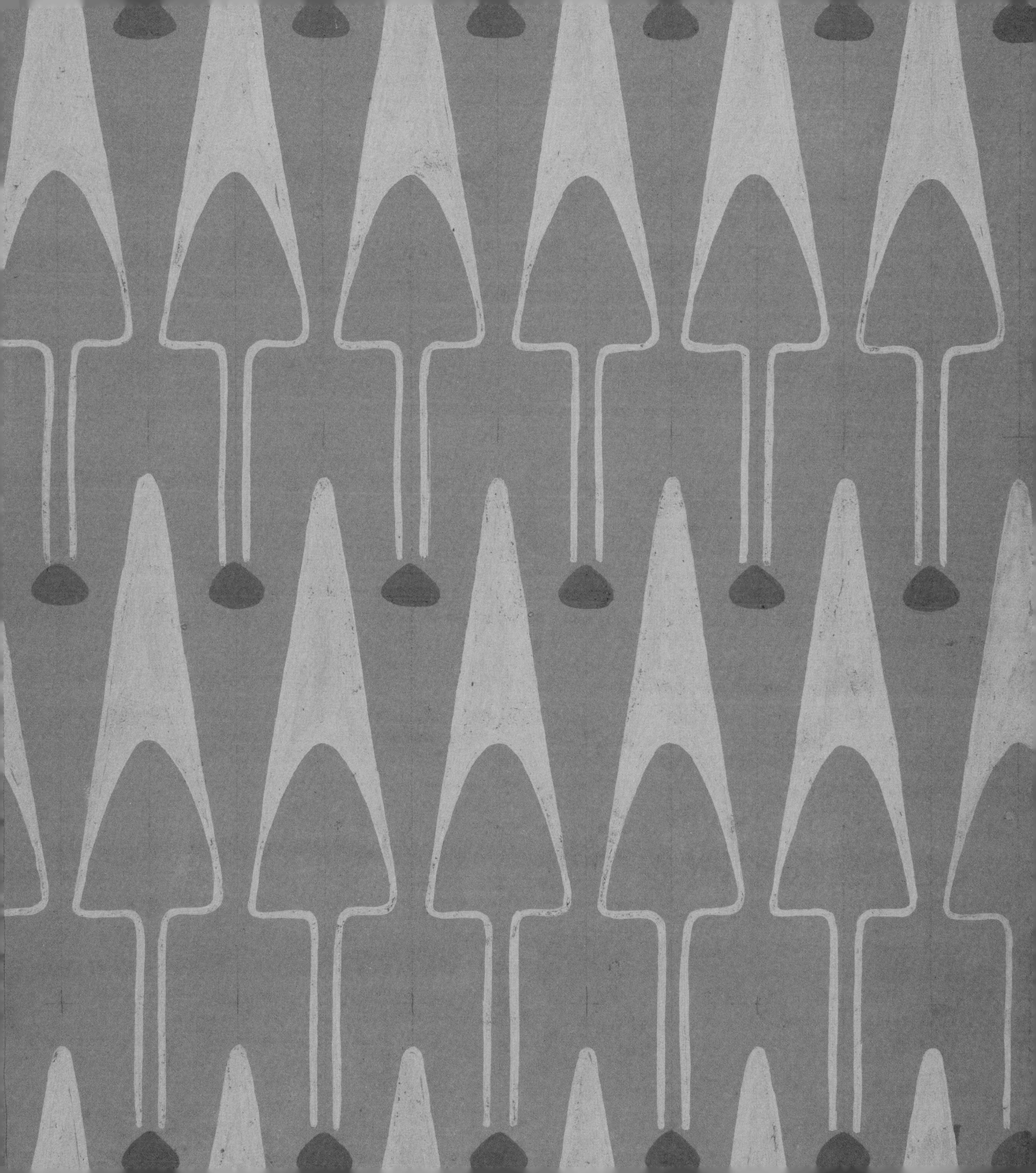

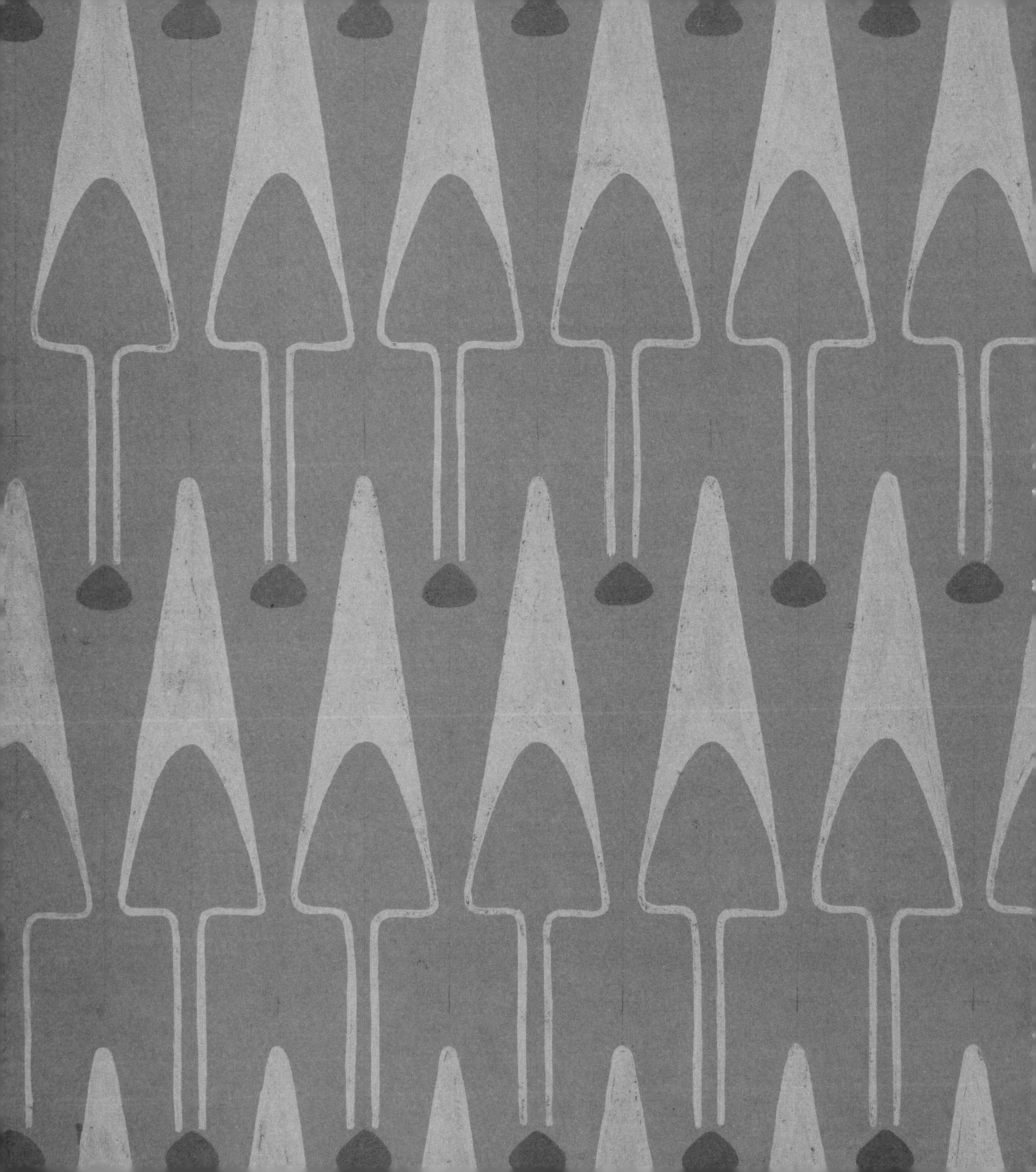